*The Professional's Companion to Windows 95*

**W9-BGR-962**

**The Technical Guide**

**to Planning for,**

**Installing, Configuring,**

**and Supporting**

**Windows 95 in**

**Your Organization**

# Microsoft® Windows®95 Resource Kit

PUBLISHED BY
Microsoft Press
A Division of Microsoft Corporation
One Microsoft Way
Redmond, Washington 98052-6399

Library of Congress Cataloging-in-Publication Data pending.

Printed and bound in the United States of America.

4 5 6 7 8 9   RMRM   0 9 8 7 6 5

Distributed to the book trade in Canada by Macmillan of Canada, a division of Canada Publishing Corporation.

A CIP catalogue record for this book is available from the British Library.

Microsoft Press books are available through booksellers and distributors worldwide. For further information about international editions, contact your local Microsoft Corporation office. Or contact Microsoft Press International directly at fax (206) 936-7329.

**Project Team:** Annie Pearson, Emily Warn, Doralee Moynihan, Jane Dow, Audrey Wehba, and Yong Ok Chung

**Project Managers:** Steven Guggenheimer and Yusuf Mehdi

**Editorial Support and Production:** Tony Nahra, Susie Hunter, David Thornbrugh, Bob Bristow, Dianne Parkin, Brad Matter, and Daniel Tyler

**Graphic Design and Production:** Sue Wyble, Gwen Gray, Elizabeth Read, Kathy Hall, and Shane Gonzalez

**Technical Contributors:** Doug Sheresh, Matthew Bookspan, Kristen Crupi, Joseph Davies, Pete Delaney, Brent Ethington, Brad Hastings, Jeff Howard, Kris Iverson, Jean Kaiser, Keith Laepple, Mike Laverty, Phyllis Levy, Rob MacKaughan, Dave Pollon, Adam Taylor, Christopher Vaughan, and Autumn Womack

**Technical Consultants:** George Allen, Craig Beilinson, Robert Bennett, Eric Bidstrup, Brian Boston, Jane Dailey, Harold Daniels, Alec Dun, Micheal Dunn, Tod Edwards, Metin Elyazar, Brian Emanuels, Wassef Haroun, Ross Heise, Petra Hoffmann, Phil Holden, David Jaffe, Margaret Jasso, Michael Kammer, Nadine Kano, Steven Lambert, Rhonda Landy, Denise La Rue, Sarah Lefko, Joo Shian Shirley Leong, Greg Lowney, Roman Lutz, Trang Luyen, Scott McArthur, Joe Mendel, Brita Meng, George Moore, Gary Natividad, Gale Nelson, Doug Ota, Kevin Otnes, Ted Padua, Irene Pasternack, Renee Prukop, Jim Reitz, Brian Reynolds, Stephen Shay, Mark Sundt, Stan Takemoto, Viroon Touranachun, Michael Tuchen, Marianne VanDeVrede, Keith White, and Robert J. Williams

We are particularly grateful to our most important contributors and reviewers, the Microsoft Windows 95 product development and product support services teams.

*continued on page 1349*

# Contents

**Welcome to Windows 95** . . . . . . . . . . . . . . . . . . . . . . . . . . . . . . . . . . . . . . **xv**

How to Use the Windows 95 Resource Kit. . . . . . . . . . . . . . . . . . . . . . . . . . xv

Windows 95 Resource Kit Utilities . . . . . . . . . . . . . . . . . . . . . . . . . . . . . . xvii

Conventions. . . . . . . . . . . . . . . . . . . . . . . . . . . . . . . . . . . . . . . . . . . . . xvii

**Guided Tour for Administrators** . . . . . . . . . . . . . . . . . . . . . . . . . . . . . . . . **1**

## Part 1   Deployment Planning Guide

**Chapter 1   Deployment Planning Basics** . . . . . . . . . . . . . . . . . . . . . . . . . **19**

Overview of the Deployment Process . . . . . . . . . . . . . . . . . . . . . . . . . . . . 20

Reviewing Windows 95 Features: An Overview . . . . . . . . . . . . . . . . . . . . . 21

Preparing the Teams: An Overview . . . . . . . . . . . . . . . . . . . . . . . . . . . . . 22

Deciding on the Preferred Client Configuration: An Overview . . . . . . . . . . . . 23

Performing the Lab Test: An Overview . . . . . . . . . . . . . . . . . . . . . . . . . . . 29

Planning the Pilot Rollout: An Overview . . . . . . . . . . . . . . . . . . . . . . . . . . 31

Conducting the Pilot Rollout: An Overview . . . . . . . . . . . . . . . . . . . . . . . . 32

Finalizing the Rollout Plan: An Overview . . . . . . . . . . . . . . . . . . . . . . . . . 34

Rolling Out Windows 95: An Overview. . . . . . . . . . . . . . . . . . . . . . . . . . . 35

**Chapter 2   Deployment Strategy and Details** . . . . . . . . . . . . . . . . . . . . . . **37**

Reviewing Windows 95 Features: The Details . . . . . . . . . . . . . . . . . . . . . . 39

Preparing the Teams: The Details . . . . . . . . . . . . . . . . . . . . . . . . . . . . . . 41

Deciding on the Preferred Client Configuration: The Details . . . . . . . . . . . . . 43

Performing the Lab Test: The Details. . . . . . . . . . . . . . . . . . . . . . . . . . . . 49

Planning the Pilot Rollout: The Details. . . . . . . . . . . . . . . . . . . . . . . . . . . 52

Conducting the Pilot Rollout: The Details. . . . . . . . . . . . . . . . . . . . . . . . . 56

Finalizing the Rollout Plan: The Details. . . . . . . . . . . . . . . . . . . . . . . . . . 57

Rolling Out Windows 95: The Details . . . . . . . . . . . . . . . . . . . . . . . . . . . 59

# Part 2    Installation

**Chapter 3    Introduction to Windows 95 Setup . . . . . . . . . . . . . . . . . . . . . . . 63**

Windows 95 Setup Overview . . . . . . . . . . . . . . . . . . . . . . . . . . . . . . . . . . 65

Installation Requirements . . . . . . . . . . . . . . . . . . . . . . . . . . . . . . . . . . . . 67

Options for Windows 95 Installations . . . . . . . . . . . . . . . . . . . . . . . . . . . . 72

Before Starting Windows 95 Setup . . . . . . . . . . . . . . . . . . . . . . . . . . . . . 77

Starting Windows 95 Setup . . . . . . . . . . . . . . . . . . . . . . . . . . . . . . . . . . 79

Running Windows 95 Setup . . . . . . . . . . . . . . . . . . . . . . . . . . . . . . . . . . 85

**Chapter 4    Server-Based Setup for Windows 95 . . . . . . . . . . . . . . . . . . . . . 105**

Server-Based Setup: The Basics . . . . . . . . . . . . . . . . . . . . . . . . . . . . . . 106

Server-Based Setup: The Issues . . . . . . . . . . . . . . . . . . . . . . . . . . . . . . 107

Server-Based Setup: An Overview . . . . . . . . . . . . . . . . . . . . . . . . . . . . . 113

Task 1: Copying Windows 95 Files to a Server . . . . . . . . . . . . . . . . . . . . . 114

Task 2: Creating Machine Directories . . . . . . . . . . . . . . . . . . . . . . . . . . . 122

Installing Windows 95 for Shared Installations . . . . . . . . . . . . . . . . . . . . . 124

Configuring Shared Installations . . . . . . . . . . . . . . . . . . . . . . . . . . . . . . 126

Technical Notes for Shared Installations . . . . . . . . . . . . . . . . . . . . . . . . . 139

**Chapter 5    Custom, Automated, and Push Installations . . . . . . . . . . . . . . . . 143**

Custom Installations for Windows 95: The Basics . . . . . . . . . . . . . . . . . . . 144

Custom Installations of Windows 95: The Issues . . . . . . . . . . . . . . . . . . . . 145

Customizing Windows 95 with Setup Scripts . . . . . . . . . . . . . . . . . . . . . . 146

Customizing Detection for NetWare Networks . . . . . . . . . . . . . . . . . . . . . 159

Running Custom Setup Scripts . . . . . . . . . . . . . . . . . . . . . . . . . . . . . . . 162

Customizing Windows 95 with WRKGRP.INI Files . . . . . . . . . . . . . . . . . . . 164

Customizing Windows 95 with Profiles and Policy Files . . . . . . . . . . . . . . . 166

Overview of Push Installations . . . . . . . . . . . . . . . . . . . . . . . . . . . . . . . 167

Using Login Scripts for Push Installation . . . . . . . . . . . . . . . . . . . . . . . . . 169

**Chapter 6    Setup Technical Discussion . . . . . . . . . . . . . . . . . . . . . . . . . . . 177**

Phases of the Setup Process . . . . . . . . . . . . . . . . . . . . . . . . . . . . . . . . 179

Safe Detection, Safe Recovery, and Verification . . . . . . . . . . . . . . . . . . . . 184

Windows 95 Startup Process . . . . . . . . . . . . . . . . . . . . . . . . . . . . . . . . 195

System Startup Files . . . . . . . . . . . . . . . . . . . . . . . . . . . . . . . . . . . . . 200

Windows 95 Setup with Other Operating Systems . . . . . . . . . . . . . . . . . . . 219

Removing Windows 95 from a Computer . . . . . . . . . . . . . . . . . . . . . . . . . 227

Troubleshooting Setup and System Startup . . . . . . . . . . . . . . . . . . . . . . . 233

# Part 3    Networking

### Chapter 7    Introduction to Windows 95 Networking . . . . . . . . . . . . . . . . . . . . **249**
Windows 95 Networking: The Basics . . . . . . . . . . . . . . . . . . . . 250
Windows 95 Networking: The Issues . . . . . . . . . . . . . . . . . . . . . 253
Network Configuration Overview . . . . . . . . . . . . . . . . . . . . . 254
Plug and Play Networking Overview . . . . . . . . . . . . . . . . . . . . 258
Basic Troubleshooting for Networking . . . . . . . . . . . . . . . . . . . 259

### Chapter 8    Windows 95 on Microsoft Networks . . . . . . . . . . . . . . . . . . . . **263**
Windows 95 and Microsoft Networking: The Basics . . . . . . . . . . . . . 264
Windows 95 and Microsoft Networking: The Issues . . . . . . . . . . . . . 265
Installing Client for Microsoft Networks . . . . . . . . . . . . . . . . . . 268
Configuring Client for Microsoft Networks . . . . . . . . . . . . . . . . . 268
Running Windows 95 in a Mixed Microsoft Environment . . . . . . . . . . . 271
PROTOCOL.INI: Real-Mode Network Initialization File . . . . . . . . . . . 277

### Chapter 9    Windows 95 on NetWare Networks . . . . . . . . . . . . . . . . . . . . **281**
Windows 95 on NetWare Networks: The Basics . . . . . . . . . . . . . . . 283
Windows 95 on NetWare Networks: The Issues . . . . . . . . . . . . . . . 287
Setting Up Windows 95 for NetWare Networks: An Overview . . . . . . . . . 293
Using Microsoft Client for NetWare Networks . . . . . . . . . . . . . . . . 295
Using a Novell NetWare Client . . . . . . . . . . . . . . . . . . . . . . . 306
Technical Notes for Windows 95 on NetWare Networks . . . . . . . . . . . . 325
Troubleshooting Windows 95 on NetWare Networks . . . . . . . . . . . . . 329

### Chapter 10    Windows 95 on Other Networks . . . . . . . . . . . . . . . . . . . . **333**
Windows 95 on Other Networks: The Basics . . . . . . . . . . . . . . . . . 334
Windows 95 on Other Networks: The Issues . . . . . . . . . . . . . . . . . 335
Installing Support for Other Networks: An Overview . . . . . . . . . . . . . 336
Using Real-Mode WinNet16 Drivers . . . . . . . . . . . . . . . . . . . . 338
Artisoft LANtastic . . . . . . . . . . . . . . . . . . . . . . . . . . . . . 339
Banyan VINES . . . . . . . . . . . . . . . . . . . . . . . . . . . . . . . 341
DEC PATHWORKS . . . . . . . . . . . . . . . . . . . . . . . . . . . . . 344
IBM OS/2 LAN Server . . . . . . . . . . . . . . . . . . . . . . . . . . . 346
SunSoft PC-NFS . . . . . . . . . . . . . . . . . . . . . . . . . . . . . . 347
Host Connectivity and Windows 95 . . . . . . . . . . . . . . . . . . . . . 349

**Chapter 11   Logon, Browsing, and Resource Sharing** . . . . . . . . . . . . . . . . . . . . **361**

Logon, Browsing, and Resource Sharing: The Basics . . . . . . . . . . . . . . . . . 363

Logon, Browsing, and Resource Sharing: The Issues . . . . . . . . . . . . . . . . . 366

Overview of Logging on to Windows 95 . . . . . . . . . . . . . . . . . . . . . . . . . . . 367

Configuring Network Logon. . . . . . . . . . . . . . . . . . . . . . . . . . . . . . . . . . . . 369

Using Login Scripts. . . . . . . . . . . . . . . . . . . . . . . . . . . . . . . . . . . . . . . . . . 374

Technical Notes for the Logon Process . . . . . . . . . . . . . . . . . . . . . . . . . . . 379

Browsing Overview. . . . . . . . . . . . . . . . . . . . . . . . . . . . . . . . . . . . . . . . . . 380

Browsing on Microsoft Networks . . . . . . . . . . . . . . . . . . . . . . . . . . . . . . . 384

Browsing on NetWare Networks . . . . . . . . . . . . . . . . . . . . . . . . . . . . . . . . 388

Overview of Peer Resource Sharing . . . . . . . . . . . . . . . . . . . . . . . . . . . . . 396

Using File and Printer Sharing for Microsoft Networks. . . . . . . . . . . . . . . . 398

Using File and Printer Sharing for NetWare Networks . . . . . . . . . . . . . . . . 401

Troubleshooting for Logon, Browsing, and Peer Resource Sharing. . . . . . . . 408

**Chapter 12   Network Technical Discussion.** . . . . . . . . . . . . . . . . . . . . . . . . . **413**

Network Adapter Drivers and Protocols: The Basics . . . . . . . . . . . . . . . . . 414

Network Adapters and Protocols: The Issues . . . . . . . . . . . . . . . . . . . . . . . 417

Network Adapters and Windows 95 . . . . . . . . . . . . . . . . . . . . . . . . . . . . . . 419

IPX/SPX-Compatible Protocol . . . . . . . . . . . . . . . . . . . . . . . . . . . . . . . . . 427

TCP/IP Protocol . . . . . . . . . . . . . . . . . . . . . . . . . . . . . . . . . . . . . . . . . . . 431

Microsoft NetBEUI Protocol . . . . . . . . . . . . . . . . . . . . . . . . . . . . . . . . . . 444

Using WinPopup to Broadcast a Pop-Up Message . . . . . . . . . . . . . . . . . . . 445

Troubleshooting Protocol Problems. . . . . . . . . . . . . . . . . . . . . . . . . . . . . . 447

**Part 4   System Management**

**Chapter 13   Introduction to System Management** . . . . . . . . . . . . . . . . . . . . . . **455**

System Management with Windows 95 . . . . . . . . . . . . . . . . . . . . . . . . . . . . 456

Sources for Windows 95 System Management Tools . . . . . . . . . . . . . . . . . . 457

**Chapter 14   Security** . . . . . . . . . . . . . . . . . . . . . . . . . . . . . . . . . . . . . . . . . . **459**

Windows 95 Security: The Basics. . . . . . . . . . . . . . . . . . . . . . . . . . . . . . . . 460

Windows 95 Security: The Issues . . . . . . . . . . . . . . . . . . . . . . . . . . . . . . . 461

Windows 95 Network Security Overview . . . . . . . . . . . . . . . . . . . . . . . . . . 462

Setting Up Security for Shared Resources . . . . . . . . . . . . . . . . . . . . . . . . . 464

Using Share-Level Security . . . . . . . . . . . . . . . . . . . . . . . . . . . . . . . . . . . . 466

Using User-Level Security . . . . . . . . . . . . . . . . . . . . . . . . . . . . . . . . . . . . . 467

Using the Windows 95 Password Cache . . . . . . . . . . . . . . . . . . . . . . . . . . . 470

Using Password List Editor . . . . . . . . . . . . . . . . . . . . . . . . . . . . . . . . . . . . 471

Using the Windows 95 Logon Password. . . . . . . . . . . . . . . . . . . . . . . . . 472
Using Windows 95 with NetWare Passwords. . . . . . . . . . . . . . . . . . . . 474
Using System Policies to Enforce Password Security. . . . . . . . . . . . . . . 475
Guidelines for Setting Password Policy . . . . . . . . . . . . . . . . . . . . . . . 476

**Chapter 15    User Profiles and System Policies** . . . . . . . . . . . . . . . . . . . . **477**
User Profiles and System Policies: The Basics . . . . . . . . . . . . . . . . . . . 479
User Profiles and System Policies: The Issues. . . . . . . . . . . . . . . . . . . 480
User Profiles Overview . . . . . . . . . . . . . . . . . . . . . . . . . . . . . . . . . 482
Enabling User Profiles . . . . . . . . . . . . . . . . . . . . . . . . . . . . . . . . . 485
System Policies Overview. . . . . . . . . . . . . . . . . . . . . . . . . . . . . . . . 490
System Policy Editor . . . . . . . . . . . . . . . . . . . . . . . . . . . . . . . . . . 493
Preparing to Use System Policies on the Network . . . . . . . . . . . . . . . . 498
Creating System Policies . . . . . . . . . . . . . . . . . . . . . . . . . . . . . . . 501
System Policy Examples. . . . . . . . . . . . . . . . . . . . . . . . . . . . . . . . . 506
System Policy Settings Summary. . . . . . . . . . . . . . . . . . . . . . . . . . . 508
System Policy Templates . . . . . . . . . . . . . . . . . . . . . . . . . . . . . . . 518
Troubleshooting with System Policy Editor . . . . . . . . . . . . . . . . . . . . 525

**Chapter 16    Remote Administration** . . . . . . . . . . . . . . . . . . . . . . . . . . . **529**
Remote Administration: The Basics. . . . . . . . . . . . . . . . . . . . . . . . . 530
Remote Administration: The Issues . . . . . . . . . . . . . . . . . . . . . . . . . 531
Setting Up for Remote Administration . . . . . . . . . . . . . . . . . . . . . . . 532
Accessing Remote Registries by Using System Policy Editor . . . . . . . . . . . 535
Accessing Remote Registries by Using Registry Editor . . . . . . . . . . . . . . 536
Viewing a Remote Computer by Using System Monitor. . . . . . . . . . . . . . 537
Using Net Watcher for Remote Administration. . . . . . . . . . . . . . . . . . 537
Using Network Neighborhood for Remote Administration . . . . . . . . . . . . 539
Using Network Backup Agents . . . . . . . . . . . . . . . . . . . . . . . . . . . . 540
Preparing for Microsoft Network Monitor . . . . . . . . . . . . . . . . . . . . . 544
Using Remote Administration Tools from Other Vendors. . . . . . . . . . . . . 547
Removing Remote Agents and Services . . . . . . . . . . . . . . . . . . . . . . . 551

**Chapter 17    Performance Tuning** . . . . . . . . . . . . . . . . . . . . . . . . . . . . **553**
Windows 95 Performance Tuning: The Basics . . . . . . . . . . . . . . . . . . . 554
Windows 95 Performance Tuning: The Issues. . . . . . . . . . . . . . . . . . . 556
System Performance Overview . . . . . . . . . . . . . . . . . . . . . . . . . . . . 558
Optimizing the Swap File . . . . . . . . . . . . . . . . . . . . . . . . . . . . . . . 562
Optimizing File System Performance . . . . . . . . . . . . . . . . . . . . . . . . 564
Setting Graphics Compatibility Options . . . . . . . . . . . . . . . . . . . . . . 570
Optimizing Printing . . . . . . . . . . . . . . . . . . . . . . . . . . . . . . . . . . 572

Optimizing Network Performance. . . . . . . . . . . . . . . . . . . . . . . . . . . . . . . 573
Optimizing Conventional Memory . . . . . . . . . . . . . . . . . . . . . . . . . . . . . . 575
Tracking Performance with System Monitor . . . . . . . . . . . . . . . . . . . . . . . 576

## Part 5   System Configuration

### Chapter 18    Introduction to System Configuration . . . . . . . . . . . . . . . . . . . . . . 587
System Configuration Overview . . . . . . . . . . . . . . . . . . . . . . . . . . . . . . . . 588
Improved Device Support in Windows 95 . . . . . . . . . . . . . . . . . . . . . . . . . 589
Windows 95 Device Classes . . . . . . . . . . . . . . . . . . . . . . . . . . . . . . . . . . 591
Plug and Play Support in Windows 95. . . . . . . . . . . . . . . . . . . . . . . . . . . . 592
Plug and Play Device Types . . . . . . . . . . . . . . . . . . . . . . . . . . . . . . . . . . . 594

### Chapter 19    Devices . . . . . . . . . . . . . . . . . . . . . . . . . . . . . . . . . . . . . . . . . . . . 599
Devices: The Basics . . . . . . . . . . . . . . . . . . . . . . . . . . . . . . . . . . . . . . . . 600
Devices: The Issues. . . . . . . . . . . . . . . . . . . . . . . . . . . . . . . . . . . . . . . . . 603
Devices Overview. . . . . . . . . . . . . . . . . . . . . . . . . . . . . . . . . . . . . . . . . . 604
Installing New Devices . . . . . . . . . . . . . . . . . . . . . . . . . . . . . . . . . . . . . . 606
Changing Settings with Device Manager . . . . . . . . . . . . . . . . . . . . . . . . . . 608
Enabling PCMCIA Cards. . . . . . . . . . . . . . . . . . . . . . . . . . . . . . . . . . . . . 614
Using Hardware Profiles for Alternate Configurations . . . . . . . . . . . . . . . . 617
Configuring the Display. . . . . . . . . . . . . . . . . . . . . . . . . . . . . . . . . . . . . . 619
Configuring the Mouse . . . . . . . . . . . . . . . . . . . . . . . . . . . . . . . . . . . . . . 626
Configuring Communications Ports and Printer Ports . . . . . . . . . . . . . . . . 628
Real-Mode Drivers and the IOS.INI Safe Driver List . . . . . . . . . . . . . . . . . 630
Troubleshooting Device Configuration . . . . . . . . . . . . . . . . . . . . . . . . . . . 634

### Chapter 20    Disks and File Systems. . . . . . . . . . . . . . . . . . . . . . . . . . . . . . . . . 643
Disks and File Systems: The Basics . . . . . . . . . . . . . . . . . . . . . . . . . . . . . 645
Disks and File Systems: The Issues. . . . . . . . . . . . . . . . . . . . . . . . . . . . . . 646
Partitioning Hard Disks . . . . . . . . . . . . . . . . . . . . . . . . . . . . . . . . . . . . . . 647
Disk Management Overview . . . . . . . . . . . . . . . . . . . . . . . . . . . . . . . . . . . 653
Managing the Recycle Bin to Free Disk Space. . . . . . . . . . . . . . . . . . . . . . 655
Using Microsoft Backup . . . . . . . . . . . . . . . . . . . . . . . . . . . . . . . . . . . . . 656
Defragmenting Disks. . . . . . . . . . . . . . . . . . . . . . . . . . . . . . . . . . . . . . . . 656
Using ScanDisk . . . . . . . . . . . . . . . . . . . . . . . . . . . . . . . . . . . . . . . . . . . 658
Using Disk Compression with Windows 95 . . . . . . . . . . . . . . . . . . . . . . . . 661
Microsoft Plus! Utilities for Disk Management . . . . . . . . . . . . . . . . . . . . . 670
File Systems Overview . . . . . . . . . . . . . . . . . . . . . . . . . . . . . . . . . . . . . . . 678

Using Long Filenames . . . . . . . . . . . . . . . . . . . . . . . . . . . . 679
Technical Notes on Disk Device Support . . . . . . . . . . . . . . . . . . . . 690
Troubleshooting File and Disk Problems . . . . . . . . . . . . . . . . . . . . 696

**Chapter 21   Multimedia** . . . . . . . . . . . . . . . . . . . . . . . . . . **699**
Multimedia: The Basics . . . . . . . . . . . . . . . . . . . . . . . . . . . . 700
Multimedia: The Issues. . . . . . . . . . . . . . . . . . . . . . . . . . . . . 700
Multimedia Overview. . . . . . . . . . . . . . . . . . . . . . . . . . . . . . 701
Recording, Editing, and Playing Audio. . . . . . . . . . . . . . . . . . . . . 703
Playing and Recording Digital Video. . . . . . . . . . . . . . . . . . . . . . 705
Buying a Multimedia Computer. . . . . . . . . . . . . . . . . . . . . . . . . 706
Troubleshooting Multimedia Software . . . . . . . . . . . . . . . . . . . . . 709

**Chapter 22   Application Support** . . . . . . . . . . . . . . . . . . . . . **713**
Application Support: The Basics . . . . . . . . . . . . . . . . . . . . . . . . 714
Application Support: The Issues . . . . . . . . . . . . . . . . . . . . . . . . 716
Installing Applications . . . . . . . . . . . . . . . . . . . . . . . . . . . . . 717
Removing Applications. . . . . . . . . . . . . . . . . . . . . . . . . . . . . 720
Running Applications. . . . . . . . . . . . . . . . . . . . . . . . . . . . . . 720
Configuring MS-DOS – Based Applications. . . . . . . . . . . . . . . . . . . 726
Using OLE to Share Data Between Applications. . . . . . . . . . . . . . . . . 739
Technical Notes on Application Support. . . . . . . . . . . . . . . . . . . . . 741
Troubleshooting Applications . . . . . . . . . . . . . . . . . . . . . . . . . 749

**Chapter 23   Printing and Fonts.** . . . . . . . . . . . . . . . . . . . . . **753**
Windows 95 Printing and Fonts: The Basics. . . . . . . . . . . . . . . . . . 755
Printing and Fonts: The Issues. . . . . . . . . . . . . . . . . . . . . . . . . 756
Windows 95 Printing Support Overview . . . . . . . . . . . . . . . . . . . . 757
Installing a Printer . . . . . . . . . . . . . . . . . . . . . . . . . . . . . . . 758
Using Microsoft Print Services for NetWare. . . . . . . . . . . . . . . . . . . 763
Using DEC PrintServer Software for Windows 95 . . . . . . . . . . . . . . . 766
Using the Hewlett-Packard JetAdmin Utility . . . . . . . . . . . . . . . . . . 766
Using the Microsoft RPC Print Provider. . . . . . . . . . . . . . . . . . . . . 767
Technical Notes on Windows 95 Printing. . . . . . . . . . . . . . . . . . . . 767
Windows 95 Fonts Overview . . . . . . . . . . . . . . . . . . . . . . . . . . 774
Font Matching Table . . . . . . . . . . . . . . . . . . . . . . . . . . . . . . 775
How Fonts Are Matched in Windows 95 . . . . . . . . . . . . . . . . . . . . 776
Loading Fonts in Windows 95. . . . . . . . . . . . . . . . . . . . . . . . . . 777
Installing Additional Fonts . . . . . . . . . . . . . . . . . . . . . . . . . . . 778
Troubleshooting Printing Problems . . . . . . . . . . . . . . . . . . . . . . . 779
Troubleshooting Font Errors . . . . . . . . . . . . . . . . . . . . . . . . . . 785

# Part 6   Communications

**Chapter 24   Introduction to Windows 95 Communications** . . . . . . . . . . . . . . . . **791**
Overview of Communications in Windows 95 . . . . . . . . . . . . . . . . . . . . . . . 792
Improved Communications in Windows 95 . . . . . . . . . . . . . . . . . . . . . . . . 794
Communications Architecture. . . . . . . . . . . . . . . . . . . . . . . . . . . . . . . . . 795

**Chapter 25   Modems and Communications Tools** . . . . . . . . . . . . . . . . . . . . . . **799**
Modems and Communications Tools: The Basics . . . . . . . . . . . . . . . . . . . 800
Modems and Communications Tools: The Issues . . . . . . . . . . . . . . . . . . . 801
Setting Up a Modem . . . . . . . . . . . . . . . . . . . . . . . . . . . . . . . . . . . . . . . 801
Modem Registry Keys . . . . . . . . . . . . . . . . . . . . . . . . . . . . . . . . . . . . . . 810
Using HyperTerminal . . . . . . . . . . . . . . . . . . . . . . . . . . . . . . . . . . . . . . 813
Using Phone Dialer . . . . . . . . . . . . . . . . . . . . . . . . . . . . . . . . . . . . . . . . 815
Using Dialing Properties . . . . . . . . . . . . . . . . . . . . . . . . . . . . . . . . . . . . 817
Using Microsoft File Transfer . . . . . . . . . . . . . . . . . . . . . . . . . . . . . . . . 821
Telephony Drivers from Other Vendors. . . . . . . . . . . . . . . . . . . . . . . . . . 822
Troubleshooting Communications Problems. . . . . . . . . . . . . . . . . . . . . . . 822

**Chapter 26   Electronic Mail and Microsoft Exchange.** . . . . . . . . . . . . . . . . . . **831**
Microsoft Exchange: The Basics. . . . . . . . . . . . . . . . . . . . . . . . . . . . . . . 832
Microsoft Exchange: The Issues . . . . . . . . . . . . . . . . . . . . . . . . . . . . . . . 832
Overview of Microsoft Exchange and Windows 95 Messaging . . . . . . . . . . 834
Setting Up the Microsoft Exchange Client . . . . . . . . . . . . . . . . . . . . . . . . 836
Using the Microsoft Exchange Client . . . . . . . . . . . . . . . . . . . . . . . . . . . 838
Working with Documents. . . . . . . . . . . . . . . . . . . . . . . . . . . . . . . . . . . . 845
Using Multiple Microsoft Exchange Profiles . . . . . . . . . . . . . . . . . . . . . . 846
Using the Microsoft Exchange Client with Microsoft Mail . . . . . . . . . . . . . 848
Accessing a Microsoft Mail Workgroup Postoffice Remotely . . . . . . . . . . . 853
Technical Notes on the Microsoft Exchange Client and MAPI. . . . . . . . . . . 858
Upgrading to Microsoft Mail Server . . . . . . . . . . . . . . . . . . . . . . . . . . . . 860
Upgrading to Microsoft Exchange Server . . . . . . . . . . . . . . . . . . . . . . . . 861
Microsoft Mail Gateways . . . . . . . . . . . . . . . . . . . . . . . . . . . . . . . . . . . 862

**Chapter 27   Microsoft Fax** . . . . . . . . . . . . . . . . . . . . . . . . . . . . . . . . . . . . . **865**
Microsoft Fax: The Basics . . . . . . . . . . . . . . . . . . . . . . . . . . . . . . . . . . . 866
Microsoft Fax: The Issues . . . . . . . . . . . . . . . . . . . . . . . . . . . . . . . . . . . 868
Overview of Microsoft Fax . . . . . . . . . . . . . . . . . . . . . . . . . . . . . . . . . . 869
Setting Up Microsoft Fax for the User. . . . . . . . . . . . . . . . . . . . . . . . . . . 870

Sending Faxes . . . . . . . . . . . . . . . . . . . . . . . . . . . . . . . . . . . . . . . . . . 872
Retrieving Faxes . . . . . . . . . . . . . . . . . . . . . . . . . . . . . . . . . . . . . . . . 874
Network Fax Service . . . . . . . . . . . . . . . . . . . . . . . . . . . . . . . . . . . . 874
Security for Microsoft Fax . . . . . . . . . . . . . . . . . . . . . . . . . . . . . . . . 877
Technical Notes for Microsoft Fax . . . . . . . . . . . . . . . . . . . . . . . . . . 880

**Chapter 28   Dial-Up Networking and Mobile Computing. . . . . . . . . . . . . . . . . 883**
Dial-Up Networking and Mobile Computing: The Basics. . . . . . . . . . . . . 885
Dial-Up Networking and Mobile Computing: The Issues . . . . . . . . . . . . . 886
Overview of Dial-Up Networking . . . . . . . . . . . . . . . . . . . . . . . . . . . . 888
Installing Dial-Up Networking . . . . . . . . . . . . . . . . . . . . . . . . . . . . . 892
Configuring Dial-Up Networking Clients and Servers . . . . . . . . . . . . . . . 893
Connecting to a Novell NetWare Connect Server . . . . . . . . . . . . . . . . . 907
Connecting to Shiva Remote Access Servers. . . . . . . . . . . . . . . . . . . . . 908
Overview of Windows 95 Mobile Computing Features . . . . . . . . . . . . . 915
Direct Cable Connection. . . . . . . . . . . . . . . . . . . . . . . . . . . . . . . . . . 916
Using Briefcase for File Synchronization . . . . . . . . . . . . . . . . . . . . . . . 918
Troubleshooting Dial-Up Networking . . . . . . . . . . . . . . . . . . . . . . . . . 920

**Chapter 29   The Microsoft Network . . . . . . . . . . . . . . . . . . . . . . . . . . . . . 923**
The Microsoft Network: The Basics. . . . . . . . . . . . . . . . . . . . . . . . . . . 924
The Microsoft Network: The Issues . . . . . . . . . . . . . . . . . . . . . . . . . . 926
Becoming a Member of The Microsoft Network . . . . . . . . . . . . . . . . . . 927
Security for The Microsoft Network . . . . . . . . . . . . . . . . . . . . . . . . . . 927
Navigating The Microsoft Network . . . . . . . . . . . . . . . . . . . . . . . . . . 928
Using Bulletin Boards . . . . . . . . . . . . . . . . . . . . . . . . . . . . . . . . . . . 931
Using Microsoft Exchange with The Microsoft Network . . . . . . . . . . . . . 935
Billing. . . . . . . . . . . . . . . . . . . . . . . . . . . . . . . . . . . . . . . . . . . . . . 937
Becoming an Independent Content Provider (ICP). . . . . . . . . . . . . . . . . 937

**Chapter 30   Internet Access. . . . . . . . . . . . . . . . . . . . . . . . . . . . . . . . . . 939**
Internet Access: The Basics . . . . . . . . . . . . . . . . . . . . . . . . . . . . . . . 940
Connecting to the Internet . . . . . . . . . . . . . . . . . . . . . . . . . . . . . . . . 944
Navigating the Internet . . . . . . . . . . . . . . . . . . . . . . . . . . . . . . . . . . 955
Troubleshooting Internet Connections . . . . . . . . . . . . . . . . . . . . . . . . 961

# Part 7   Windows 95 Reference

**Chapter 31    Windows 95 Architecture** ............................... **965**
Windows 95 Architecture Components ............................. 966
Windows 95 Registry ........................................ 967
Device Drivers ............................................ 969
Configuration Manager ...................................... 970
Virtual Machine Manager .................................... 973
Installable File Systems ..................................... 977
Core System Components...................................... 984
User Interface ............................................ 990
Application Support......................................... 990

**Chapter 32    Windows 95 Network Architecture** ....................... **991**
Windows 95 Network Architecture Overview ....................... 992
Multiple Network Support .................................... 995
NDIS Overview ........................................... 1002
Architecture for Network Protocols............................. 1004
Architecture for Clients, Peer Servers, and IPC .................... 1006

**Chapter 33    Windows 95 Registry** ................................ **1017**
Windows 95 Registry Overview ................................ 1018
Getting Started with Registry Editor ............................ 1019
How Windows 95 Components Use the Registry .................... 1020
Registry Structure ......................................... 1021
Hkey_Local_Machine ....................................... 1026
Hkey_Current_User and Hkey_Users ........................... 1032
Hkey_Current_Config and Hkey_Dyn_Data ...................... 1033
Initialization Files and the Registry............................. 1034

**Chapter 34    International Windows 95** ............................. **1039**
Overview of Windows 95 Local Editions.......................... 1040
Overview of International Language Support ....................... 1041
Specifying International Settings................................ 1042
Using Multiple Languages in Windows 95......................... 1048

**Chapter 35    General Troubleshooting.** ............................. **1057**
Troubleshooting Strategy ..................................... 1059
Windows 95 Troubleshooting Aids for Startup...................... 1061
Troubleshooting Procedures ................................... 1069

# Part 8    Appendixes

**Glossary** . . . . . . . . . . . . . . . . . . . . . . . . . . . . . . . . . . . . . . . . . . . . . . **1081**

**Appendix A    Command-Line Commands Summary** . . . . . . . . . . . . . . . . . . . . **1095**
Command Syntax . . . . . . . . . . . . . . . . . . . . . . . . . . . . . . . . . . . . . . . . 1097
Using the Command Prompt . . . . . . . . . . . . . . . . . . . . . . . . . . . . . . . . 1099
Native Windows 95 Commands . . . . . . . . . . . . . . . . . . . . . . . . . . . . . . 1102
Command-Line Switches for Specific Commands . . . . . . . . . . . . . . . . . . 1111
Command-Line Switches for Disk Utilities . . . . . . . . . . . . . . . . . . . . . . 1123
TCP/IP Utilities . . . . . . . . . . . . . . . . . . . . . . . . . . . . . . . . . . . . . . . . . 1136

**Appendix B    Windows 95 System Files** . . . . . . . . . . . . . . . . . . . . . . . . . . . **1149**
Windows 95 Distribution Disk Storage Overview . . . . . . . . . . . . . . . . . . 1150
Using the Extract Program to Extract Files . . . . . . . . . . . . . . . . . . . . . . 1150
Setup Files Overview . . . . . . . . . . . . . . . . . . . . . . . . . . . . . . . . . . . . . 1152
Directory File Structure and File Locations . . . . . . . . . . . . . . . . . . . . . . 1153

**Appendix C    Windows 95 INF Files** . . . . . . . . . . . . . . . . . . . . . . . . . . . . . . **1157**
Windows 95 Device Information Files Overview . . . . . . . . . . . . . . . . . . . 1158
General INF File Format . . . . . . . . . . . . . . . . . . . . . . . . . . . . . . . . . . . 1158
[Version] Section . . . . . . . . . . . . . . . . . . . . . . . . . . . . . . . . . . . . . . . . 1159
[Manufacturer] Section . . . . . . . . . . . . . . . . . . . . . . . . . . . . . . . . . . . . 1160
[Manufacturer Name] Section . . . . . . . . . . . . . . . . . . . . . . . . . . . . . . . 1160
[Install] Section . . . . . . . . . . . . . . . . . . . . . . . . . . . . . . . . . . . . . . . . . 1161
[ClassInstall] Section . . . . . . . . . . . . . . . . . . . . . . . . . . . . . . . . . . . . . 1170
[Strings] Section . . . . . . . . . . . . . . . . . . . . . . . . . . . . . . . . . . . . . . . . 1171
Sample INF File . . . . . . . . . . . . . . . . . . . . . . . . . . . . . . . . . . . . . . . . . 1172

**Appendix D    MSBATCH.INF Parameters** . . . . . . . . . . . . . . . . . . . . . . . . . . **1175**
Setup Script Parameters . . . . . . . . . . . . . . . . . . . . . . . . . . . . . . . . . . . 1176
MSBATCH.INF Sample File . . . . . . . . . . . . . . . . . . . . . . . . . . . . . . . . 1204
Windows 95 Network Adapter INF Summary . . . . . . . . . . . . . . . . . . . . . 1207

**Appendix E    Microsoft Systems Management Server** . . . . . . . . . . . . . . . . . . **1213**
Microsoft Systems Management Server Overview . . . . . . . . . . . . . . . . . . 1214
Systems Management Server Requirements . . . . . . . . . . . . . . . . . . . . . . 1215
Systems Management Server Services . . . . . . . . . . . . . . . . . . . . . . . . . . 1217
Using Systems Management Server to Deploy Windows 95 . . . . . . . . . . . . 1219

**Appendix F    Macintosh and Windows 95** . . . . . . . . . . . . . . . . . . . . . . . . . **1221**

Windows NT Services for Macintosh . . . . . . . . . . . . . . . . . . . . . . . . . . . . . 1222

Exchanging Mail Between Windows 95 and Macintosh . . . . . . . . . . . . . . 1222

Switching from Macintosh to Windows 95. . . . . . . . . . . . . . . . . . . . . . . . . 1223

**Appendix G    HOSTS and LMHOSTS Files for Windows 95** . . . . . . . . . . . . . . **1225**

Setting Up HOSTS Files . . . . . . . . . . . . . . . . . . . . . . . . . . . . . . . . . . . . . . 1226

Setting Up LMHOSTS Files. . . . . . . . . . . . . . . . . . . . . . . . . . . . . . . . . . . . 1227

**Appendix H    Shortcuts for Windows 95** . . . . . . . . . . . . . . . . . . . . . . . . . . . **1231**

Shortcuts for Objects, Folders, and Windows Explorer . . . . . . . . . . . . . . 1232

General Keyboard-Only Commands . . . . . . . . . . . . . . . . . . . . . . . . . . . . . 1234

Accessibility Shortcuts. . . . . . . . . . . . . . . . . . . . . . . . . . . . . . . . . . . . . . . . 1234

Microsoft Natural Keyboard Keys . . . . . . . . . . . . . . . . . . . . . . . . . . . . . . . 1235

**Appendix I    Accessibility.** . . . . . . . . . . . . . . . . . . . . . . . . . . . . . . . . . . . . . . **1237**

Accessibility in Windows 95: Overview . . . . . . . . . . . . . . . . . . . . . . . . . . 1238

Windows 95 Accessibility Features. . . . . . . . . . . . . . . . . . . . . . . . . . . . . . 1239

Microsoft Services for People Who Are Deaf or Hard-of-Hearing . . . . . . . . . 1251

Keyboard Layouts for Single-Handed Users . . . . . . . . . . . . . . . . . . . . . . 1251

Microsoft Documentation on Audio Cassettes and Floppy Disks . . . . . . . . . 1252

Accessibility-Enhancing Utilities from Other Vendors . . . . . . . . . . . . . . 1252

Getting More Information on Accessibility . . . . . . . . . . . . . . . . . . . . . . . . 1253

**Appendix J    Windows 95 Resource Directory** . . . . . . . . . . . . . . . . . . . . . . . **1255**

Online Information About Windows 95. . . . . . . . . . . . . . . . . . . . . . . . . . . 1256

Getting Answers to Your Technical Questions . . . . . . . . . . . . . . . . . . . . . 1256

Hardware Compatibility Information. . . . . . . . . . . . . . . . . . . . . . . . . . . . . 1258

Windows 95 SDK Information . . . . . . . . . . . . . . . . . . . . . . . . . . . . . . . . . 1258

Microsoft TechNet . . . . . . . . . . . . . . . . . . . . . . . . . . . . . . . . . . . . . . . . . . 1258

Microsoft Developer Network . . . . . . . . . . . . . . . . . . . . . . . . . . . . . . . . . 1258

Microsoft Solution Providers . . . . . . . . . . . . . . . . . . . . . . . . . . . . . . . . . . 1259

Microsoft Technical Education. . . . . . . . . . . . . . . . . . . . . . . . . . . . . . . . . . 1259

Microsoft Consulting Services . . . . . . . . . . . . . . . . . . . . . . . . . . . . . . . . . 1259

Microsoft Knowledge Base . . . . . . . . . . . . . . . . . . . . . . . . . . . . . . . . . . . . 1260

Microsoft Software Library . . . . . . . . . . . . . . . . . . . . . . . . . . . . . . . . . . . . 1260

Microsoft Download Service . . . . . . . . . . . . . . . . . . . . . . . . . . . . . . . . . . . 1260

Microsoft CompuServe Forums . . . . . . . . . . . . . . . . . . . . . . . . . . . . . . . . 1261

Obtaining Drivers Electronically . . . . . . . . . . . . . . . . . . . . . . . . . . . . . . . 1261

Resources for ICM . . . . . . . . . . . . . . . . . . . . . . . . . . . . . . . . . . . . . . . . . . 1262

**Index** . . . . . . . . . . . . . . . . . . . . . . . . . . . . . . . . . . . . . . . . . . . . . . . . . . . . . . . **1263**

# Welcome to Windows 95

The Microsoft® Windows® 95 operating system is the newest version of the Microsoft Windows operating system. It is the successor to MS-DOS®, Windows version 3.1, and Windows for Workgroups version 3.x.

Windows 95 was designed to provide network administrators and systems-support professionals with a variety of powerful tools and capabilities to better manage personal computers and reduce company support costs. In addition, Windows 95 offers new features and an improved user interface to help users be more productive.

This *Windows 95 Resource Kit,* written for administrators and MIS professionals, provides the information required for rolling out, supporting, and understanding Windows 95. This Resource Kit is a technical resource that supplements the documentation included with the Windows 95 product. For information about how to use Windows 95 features and utilities, see the product documentation and online Help information supplied with Windows 95.

# How to Use the Windows 95 Resource Kit

This chapter describes the contents of the Resource Kit and lists conventions used throughout the document. The Guided Tour for Administrators, which follows, explores the benefits of implementing Windows 95 on corporate networks including cost reduction, system management, and user productivity. The remainder of the kit describes major topics related to installing and implementing Windows 95:

**Part 1, Deployment Planning Guide.**  Provides an overview for MIS managers and technical support personnel of the process for testing and deploying Windows 95 on the corporate network, plus details about how to make decisions and how to plan, test, and prepare for a major rollout of Windows 95.

---

**Note**  Be sure to read Chapter 1, "Deployment Planning Basics" and Chapter 2, "Deployment Strategy and Details" before attempting to deploy Windows 95 in your organization. These chapters provide essential information for developing, testing, and carrying out a deployment plan that will result in a successful company-wide installation of Windows 95.

---

**Part 2, Installation.**  Presents technical details for installing Windows 95 on multiple computers, including information about creating custom installations and installing Windows 95 from setup scripts. This part also presents technical details about internal processes for Windows 95 Setup and operating system startup.

**Part 3, Networking.**  Describes how to install and configure Windows 95 on different kinds of networks (such as Windows NT™ and Novell® NetWare®) plus information about installing Windows 95 to run with a real-mode network client from other network vendors. This part also presents technical details about configuring peer resource sharing services with Windows 95, plus details about configuring network adapters and protocols.

**Part 4, System Management.**  Describes the system-management features provided with Windows 95, including system policies, management tools, and remote administration capabilities. This part also describes how to take advantage of user profiles, and how to install and use various agent software provided for backup and other system-management tasks. Finally, this part also discusses how to monitor and change parameters affecting Windows 95 performance.

**Part 5, System Configuration.**  Describes how to install and troubleshoot devices, configure and run applications, and set up and manage printers.

**Part 6, Communications.**  Provides details about the built-in communications features in Windows 95, including configuring and using modems and related software, and setting up and using Microsoft Exchange and Microsoft Fax. This part also includes information about Dial-Up Networking (also known as remote network access), The Microsoft Network online service, and Internet access.

**Part 7, Windows 95 Reference.**  Provides technical details about the Windows 95 architecture and the Registry (which stores system configuration, networking, and software settings). This part also summarizes the Windows 95 features that make it easy to use among multiple languages and locales. Finally, this part provides a summary of how to troubleshoot problems in Windows 95 and how you can use the built-in tools to solve problems.

**Part 8, Appendixes.**  Provides a glossary and a summary of commands that can be used at the command prompt or in batch files. In addition, separate appendixes provide supporting details for creating custom setup scripts, configuring the network, using shortcuts and accessibility features, and finding more information about Microsoft resources supporting Windows 95 users and software developers.

Each part begins with a brief table of contents that summarizes the chapters contained in that part. In general, the first chapter is an introduction, providing background information related to the part topic and identifying the specific Windows 95 features or capabilities discussed in the remaining chapters. Each of the remaining chapters discusses benefits of a particular feature or functionality, covers implementation issues, and provides specific procedures that will help administrators take advantage of that feature or functionality.

# Windows 95 Resource Kit Utilities

In addition to the printed book, the *Windows 95 Resource Kit* provides a compact disc containing utilities for use with Windows 95. For a list of the available tools and information about how to use them, see the online Help and README files provided.

Microsoft also provides Windows 95 utilities in these other ways:

- Microsoft Plus! for Windows 95. This product contains advanced utilities for drive compression and maintenance, in addition to new font features, animated cursors, and a dial-up networking server.

- The Microsoft Network and other online services. For information about what's available from Microsoft using online sources, see Chapter 29, "The Microsoft Network," and Appendix J, "Windows 95 Resource Directory."

# Conventions

The following conventional terms, text formats, and symbols are used throughout the printed documentation for Windows 95.

| Convention | Meaning |
|---|---|
| [brackets] | In syntax statements, indicates an optional item. For example, [*password*] indicates that you can choose to type a password with the command. Type only the information within the brackets, not the brackets themselves. |
| ... (ellipsis) | In syntax statements, indicates that you can repeat the previous items. For example, **/route:***devicename*[**,**...] indicates that you can specify more than one device, separating each device with a comma. |
| | | Stands for "or" and separates items within braces or brackets. For example, {**/hold** | **/release** | **/delete**} indicates that you must type **/hold** or **/release** or **/delete**. |
| %...% | Used at the beginning and at the end of an item to indicate that it is a string identifier. |
| **Bold** | Indicates the actual commands, words, or characters that you type in a dialog box or at the command prompt. |
| *Italic* | Indicates a placeholder for information or parameters that you must provide. For example, if the procedure asks you to type *filename*, you must type the actual name of a file. |

| Convention | Meaning |
|---|---|
| ALL UPPERCASE | Indicates a directory, filename, or acronym. You can use lowercase letters when you type directory names or filenames in a dialog box or at the command prompt, unless otherwise indicated for a specific application or utility. |
| Monospace | Represents examples of screen text or entries that you might type at the command line or in initialization files. |
| right-click | Refers to clicking the secondary mouse button, which is usually the right mouse button. |
| Windows NT | Refers to operating system and networking functionality that is available in the Windows NT operating system. |
| Windows directory | Refers to the Windows 95 system directory tree. This can be C:\WINDOWS or whatever other directory name you specified when installing Windows 95. |
| x86 | Refers to computers based on 32-bit, x86-based microprocessors (such as Intel® 80386 or higher) or based on Intel Pentium™ microprocessors. |

The following are standard abbreviations or acronyms used throughout this Resource Kit, with their meanings.

| Acronym | Meaning | Acronym | Meaning |
|---|---|---|---|
| API | Application programming interface | ISV | Independent software vendor |
| BIOS | Basic input/output system | K | Kilobyte or kilobytes |
| CPU | Central processing unit | LAN | Local area network |
| DLL | Dynamic-link library | MB | Megabyte or megabytes |
| DMA | Direct memory access | MIS | Management information system |
| FAT | File allocation table | OEM | Original equipment manufacturer |
| GB | Gigabyte or gigabytes | SMB | Server message block |
| HPFS | The file system provided with OS/2 | TSR | Terminate-and-stay-resident |
| I/O | Input/output | UNC | Universal naming convention |
| IHV | Independent hardware vendor | VM | Virtual machine |
| IRQ | Interrupt request lines | WAN | Wide area network |

# Guided Tour for Administrators

This chapter of the *Windows 95 Resource Kit* explains how Windows 95 can help you—network administrators and systems-support professionals—to realize benefits such as reducing support costs, increasing control of user desktops, improving user productivity, and achieving a smooth and easy migration within your organization.

Each page of the Guided Tour covers a Windows 95 feature that yields a specific benefit for managing and supporting corporate networks. For each feature described, the tour provides an illustrated summary plus tips for the administrator. Use this Guided Tour to learn how Windows 95 can reduce the total cost of ownership for personal computers in your organization.

# A Better User Interface

*Easier to use, reduces support calls*

Windows 95 introduces a new user interface that makes using the personal computer easier and more efficient for users, regardless of their expertise.

## Start Button

By clicking this button, novice users have access to nearly everything they need—from starting programs and documents to changing computer settings and getting Help. The Start button provides users with an obvious starting point for the functions they perform on their computers every day—a more intuitive approach than Program Manager.

## Desktop

The desktop makes it easy to start tasks and find connections to resources. The Network Neighborhood icon provides a single location for viewing network servers and making connections —just point and click to connect to the server you want.

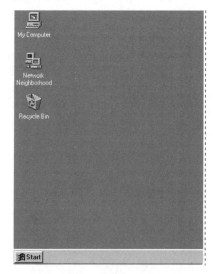

For information about customizing the user interface, see Chapter 5, "Custom, Automated, and Push Installations," and Chapter 15, "User Profiles and System Policies."

---

**Tips for the administrator**

- You can centrally control and customize the desktop with system policies and user profiles. Also for the rare cases in which users are more comfortable with the Program Manager and File Manager, you can install these applications through Custom Setup.

# Plug and Play

*Easier to set up, add, and remove hardware*

Plug and Play technology provides a logical and consistent way for devices to identify themselves and for their settings to be configured on the computer. With Plug and Play, Windows 95 makes it easier to set up new hardware and software.

## Plug and Play Hardware

Windows 95 enables many new hardware devices to automatically configure themselves on the computer. Plug and Play devices choose settings, such as IRQs or DMA channels, without requiring you to set them. And, under Windows 95, Plug and Play devices can be added to a computer that doesn't have a Plug and Play BIOS.

## Legacy Devices

Windows 95 simplifies setup and configuration of devices that aren't Plug and Play-compliant. The Add New Hardware wizard detects legacy devices and migrates hardware settings to the Registry during installation. This ensures that legacy device settings are not overwritten when Plug and Play devices are added.

## On-the-Fly Configuration for PCMCIA

Support for PCMCIA and portable "hot" docking and undocking means that users can add or remove a device such as a PCMCIA card while the computer is running. The computer automatically detects that the state of the hardware has changed and adjusts the system settings accordingly.

For more information about Plug and Play and hardware detection, see Chapter 6, "Setup Technical Discussion," and Chapter 19, "Devices." Also see Chapter 31, "Windows 95 Architecture."

---

**Tips for the administrator**

- Whenever you can, choose Plug and Play-compliant devices and components for your computers, whether or not they are legacy computers. Look for the "Designed for Microsoft Windows 95" logo.

- Plug and Play means the system selects and assigns values to hardware devices. To override these values manually, use Device Manager.

- Check for any known hardware issues in the README file for Windows 95 and modify your installation accordingly.

# 32-Bit Operating System Architecture

*Greater system reliability and performance*

The 32-bit architecture and superior resource handling in Windows 95 reduce downtime and support calls by providing a more stable operating system environment.

## 32-bit, Protected-Mode Subsystems

With 32-bit support for networking and all other subsystems under Windows 95, computers continue to run, even if the server goes down. Similarly, an errant application is less likely to stop the system because 32-bit applications run in their own address space. And, for 16-bit applications, closing an errant process will not affect other programs.

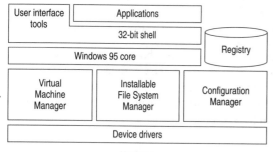

## Expanded System Resources

Out-of-memory errors are not a practical issue in Windows 95 because the system resource constraints have been virtually eliminated. This lets your users run numerous applications without running out of memory.

## Better Application Cleanup

Compared with Windows 3.1, Windows 95 does a better job of tracking program resources and cleaning up after an errant application stops. The freeing of system resources after an application is closed means system performance is less likely to degrade over time.

For more information, see Part 1, "Deployment Planning Guide," Chapter 20, "Disks and File Systems," Chapter 22, "Application Support," and Chapter 31, "Windows 95 Architecture."

---

**Tips for the administrator**

- Although system components are predominantly 32-bit, for compatibility reasons Windows 95 also offers support for a variety of 16-bit component options. For example, Windows 95 supports the existing 16-bit network redirector for Novell NetWare. Read the Deployment Planning Guide to understand choices and trade-offs in detail.

# Built-in Networking

*Easy, powerful, and stable connectivity*

Windows 95 comes complete with 32-bit networking components to allow it to work seamlessly with all major networks—including Novell® NetWare® and Windows NT™ Server—and other Windows 95 peer servers.

## 32-bit Networking Components

Windows 95 support for 32-bit components includes the redirector, the protocol, the network adapter, and File and Printer Sharing services. Written to run in a multitasking environment, these components take up no real-mode memory and offer fast and stable networking.

Windows 95 comes with 32-bit versions of an IPX/SPX-compatible protocol and TCP/IP (with a DHCP client). A variety of other protocols and 16-bit network clients are also supported.

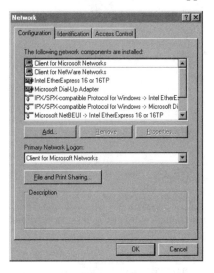

## Network Neighborhood

With Network Neighborhood, users can browse network servers—even those from different network vendors—all from a single location. And, with support for universal naming convention (UNC) pathnames, it's as easy to access resources on the network as it is those on the local hard disk.

For more information, see Part 3, "Networking," and Chapter 32, "Windows 95 Network Architecture."

---

**Tips for the administrator**

- Use 32-bit protected-mode networking software components instead of the real-mode equivalents to ensure speed and stability. You need to evaluate whether to upgrade your NetWare protocols and client software to 32-bit. Compatibility problems with certain programs might cause you to choose not to upgrade your real-mode components.

- You need to use Windows NT Server to take advantage of DHCP autoconfiguring options and WINS name-resolution capabilities if you are moving to TCP/IP as your strategic protocol.

# Centralized Security

*Increased system security and control*

Windows 95 supports pass-through, server-based security for NetWare and Windows NT networks, allowing each client computer to leverage the existing security scheme. This makes implementing network security easy and efficient using your existing user accounts.

## Validated Logon

Windows 95 supports requiring a validated logon to the server before the user can use Windows 95 in a network environment. This means users cannot get past the logon screen until they provide a correct user name and password combination. Although Windows 95 is not as secure as a Windows NT workstation on the local computer, it provides you with dependable network security through the use of validated logon and other methods of system customization.

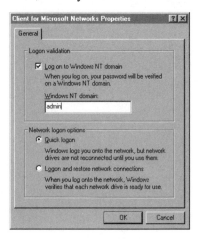

## User-Level Security

Using the NetWare bindery information or the user accounts on the Windows NT Server domain controller, you can enable security on a user-specific basis for all resources on the network, including the optional File and Printer Sharing services in Windows 95.

## Additional Security

Windows 95 provides added security for tasks such as Dial-Up Networking. Windows 95 supports encrypted dial-in passwords and callback options, plus hardware devices from other vendors. For more information, see Chapter 14, "Security," and Chapter 28, "Dial-Up Networking and Mobile Computing."

---

**Tips for the administrator**

As you plan your network:

- Define password requirements and access rights before installing Windows 95.

- Enable user-level security and set up a validated logon process if you are connecting computers running Windows 95 to a Windows NT or a NetWare network. Users can also synchronize the Windows password with the network password.

- Define the security needed for Dial-Up Networking.

# System Policies

*Powerful system administration and configuration*

System policies allow you to centrally define and control user access to the network and desktop functionality, such as the ability to share data and edit system settings. You can set these restrictions for the user, the computer, or the group.

## System Policy Editor

System Policy Editor is on administration tool you can use to set rights and restrictions for specific users and computers and to create policies that define general default settings. You can use system policies to control access to the network, specify desktop configuration settings, and prevent users from modifying applications or desktop settings. You can also limit users to running only a defined list of applications. System Policy Editor can be used remotely to modify Registry settings on individual computers. Policy files can be automatically downloaded when the user logs on to NetWare or Windows NT Server networks.

## Systems Management Agents

In addition to System Policy Editor, Windows 95 provides support for SNMP agents to query and manage the Registry on the client computer. As a result, you can write in-house system-management software or use software from other vendors for more powerful network management.

For more information, see Chapter 15, "User Profiles and System Policies," and Chapter 16, "Remote Administration."

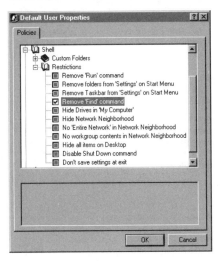

---

**Tips for the administrator**

- System policies are a must for any network administrator who wants to manage access rights and permissions for system configuration. System policies are easily enabled and modified at any time. To add support for group policies, or change the default of the central policy file, enable them manually. System Policy Editor is located in the ADMIN\APPTOOLS directory on the Windows 95 compact disc.

# User and Hardware Profiles

*Easy user-specific and hardware-specific configuration*

User profiles describe user-specific or computer-specific information, such as software preferences and settings. Hardware profiles define current hardware settings for the computer. With profiles, users can work in a consistent and customized environment, which makes it easier to use and manage computers.

## User Profiles

User profiles define user-specific settings, such as the icons on the desktop or the choice of screen saver.

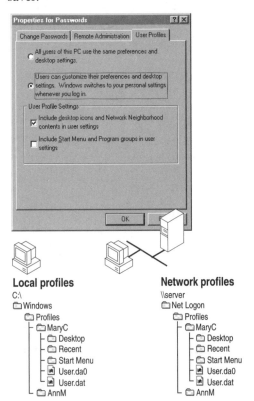

**Local profiles**
C:\
☐ Windows
  ☐ Profiles
    ├ ☐ MaryC
    │ ├ ☐ Desktop
    │ ├ ☐ Recent
    │ ├ ☐ Start Menu
    │ ├ ▨ User.da0
    │ └ ▨ User.dat
    └ ☐ AnnM

**Network profiles**
\\server
☐ Net Logon
  ☐ Profiles
    ├ ☐ MaryC
    │ ├ ☐ Desktop
    │ ├ ☐ Recent
    │ ├ ☐ Start Menu
    │ ├ ▨ User.da0
    │ └ ▨ User.dat
    └ ☐ AnnM

For "roving" users who log on to different computers at different times, user profiles stored on the network server ensure that the user has the same work environment at every logon location.

For multiple users of the same computer, user profiles determine the desktop environment and the associated privileges for each user to maintain a secure and consistent environment.

## Hardware Profiles

Hardware profiles are known configuration states for a specific computer—such as docked or undocked, in the case of a portable computer. Hardware profiles enable Windows 95 to adjust system capabilities to match the current state of the hardware. For example, when a portable computer is undocked, Windows 95 removes the system's printing and networking capabilities.

For more information, see Chapter 15, "User Profiles and System Policies," and Chapter 19, "Devices."

---

**Tips for the administrator**

- User profiles are an option that you can enable at any time. They are not installed by default. A 32-bit network client is required to support user profiles.

- You can also define mandatory user profiles in a file called USER.MAN for all users who log on to a specific home directory of a network server. This mandatory user profile protects novice users from inadvertently making changes to their environment.

# Remote Administration and Backup

*Control over remote computers*

Windows 95 includes remote administration tools —System Monitor, Registry Editor, and Net Watcher—and backup agents for popular server-based backup programs. Windows 95 also provides agents for other system-management tools.

## System Monitor

System Monitor provides graphical measurements of network traffic, file system performance, and other activity on remote computers. With these measurements, you can identify and troubleshoot problems on remote computers.

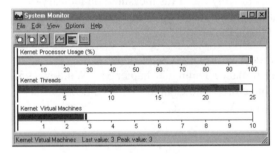

## Registry Editor

With Registry Editor, you can remotely edit the Registry for a particular computer. When used in combination with System Monitor and Net Watcher, Registry Editor enables you to correct computer problems for remote users without traveling to the remote site.

## Net Watcher

Net Watcher allows you to remotely view and disconnect network connections, and to control the File and Printer Sharing services for any computer running Windows 95 with the Remote Registry service.

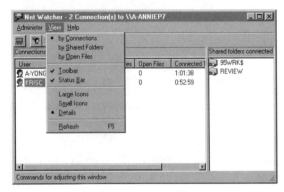

## Backup Agents

Windows 95 includes backup agents for the Cheyenne® and Arcada® server-based backup systems. With the appropriate server software, Windows 95 can be easily backed up to a NetWare server with these agents.

For more information, see Chapter 16, "Remote Administration."

---

**Tips for the administrator**

- To manage network computers remotely, enable the Remote Registry and Network Monitor agent, and assign remote administration privilege for each computer when installing Windows 95.

# Faster Computing

*More efficient for users*

New 32-bit printing, graphics, and other subsystems speed up operations for common tasks.

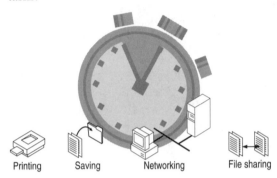

Printing        Saving        Networking        File sharing

## Faster Printing

Printing is faster in Windows 95, both in terms of the return-to-application time, and in terms of the speed of printing output.

## Faster File Saving and Copying

With a new 32-bit file system and caching algorithms, operations that access the hard disk, such as sorting a database and saving or copying a file, are completed more quickly than under Windows 3.1.

## Faster Networking

Networking is also faster in Windows 95 because the new 32-bit networking components provide raw speed improvements. In addition, new browsing and data-caching algorithms improve network responsiveness.

## Overall Performance

In general, Windows 95 is as fast or faster than Windows 3.1 on a 4-MB 386DX or better computer. In addition, as RAM is added, a computer running Windows 95 becomes comparatively faster (as measured on industry-standard benchmarks), scaling to handle the additional memory.

For more information, see Chapter 17, "Performance Tuning," Chapter 31, "Windows 95 Architecture," and Chapter 32, "Windows 95 Network Architecture."

---

**Tips for the administrator**

- Wherever possible, the 32-bit subsystems are enabled by default during installation, so no additional work is required for setup. In rare cases, you can disable or use a 16-bit component alternative, such as a real-mode networking client, to maintain compatibility with certain programs.

# Preemptive Multitasking and Multithreading for 32-bit Applications

*More responsive and stable for users*

Windows 95 supports and enables a whole new class of 32-bit applications with preemptive multitasking, allowing the computer to do more than one task at a time.

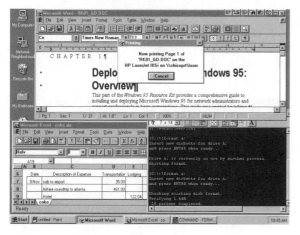

## Preemptive Multitasking

With 32-bit applications, users do not need to wait for completion of a particular task, such as downloading a large file from the network, before they can begin work on another task.

## 32-bit Applications

Similar to Windows NT, Windows 95 supports the Win32® API, which enables software vendors to write preemptive multitasking applications. This means more productive and more stable applications for users.

Because these applications are based on the same API as Windows NT, applications are binary-compatible between the two operating systems.

## Long Filenames and UNC Names

Under Windows 95, 32-bit applications also support new capabilities such as long filenames and UNC paths in common dialog boxes. This makes it easier and more efficient for users to name files what they want and to find and open files without mapping drives.

## MS-DOS and Windows 16-bit Applications

Because of its 32-bit system components, Windows 95 provides a more stable environment than Windows 3.1 for running your Windows-based and MS-DOS–based applications.

For more information, see Chapter 22, "Application Support," and Chapter 20, "Disks and File Systems."

---

**Tips for the administrator**

- Even though Windows 95 provides a more stable and functional environment for your existing applications, to take advantage of multitasking and long filenames, you'll want to upgrade to the latest 32-bit applications.

# Dial-Up Networking

*Easy access to remote information*

Windows 95 makes computing more efficient for remote and mobile users by supporting several capabilities such as dial-up network access and file synchronization.

## Dial-Up Networking

Dial-Up Networking in Windows 95 allows the user to connect to network resources, such as files and electronic mail, using Point-to-Point Protocol or server-based dial-in packages such as NetWare Connect, Windows NT RAS, or Shiva® NetModem.

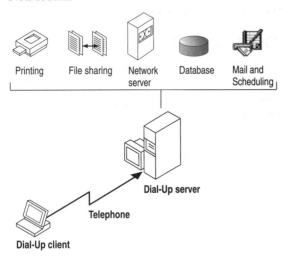

## Briefcase

Briefcase is a tool that allows mobile users to easily track and update copies of files stored on two or more computers—usually an office computer and a portable computer. Users put the files that need to stay in sync into Briefcase before going on the road. When users return, connect to the network, and open Briefcase, Windows 95 prompts them to synchronize the files. Briefcase then updates the file on the network to match the file on the portable computer.

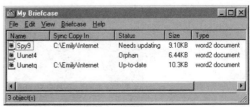

---

**Tips for the administrator**

- Although Dial-Up Networking is a powerful productivity feature for users, it might present security and control concerns. To disable Dial-Up Networking, use system policies to centrally configure Windows 95. Also, you can use additional security, such as callback or hardware signature devices.

# Built-in Messaging

*Easy to stay in touch*

Windows 95 includes support for a variety of messaging services including electronic mail and fax, plus access to the Internet and online services. These services enable users to communicate more easily with others.

## Universal Inbox

The Windows 95 Microsoft Exchange feature provides a single inbox for all messaging services that support MAPI, so that users go to only one location to retrieve their electronic mail and fax information.

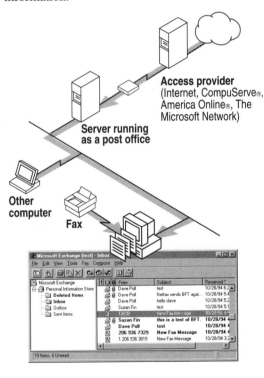

**Access provider**
(Internet, CompuServe®,
America Online®, The
Microsoft Network)

**Server running
as a post office**

**Other
computer**

**Fax**

## Electronic Mail

Windows 95 supports a wide variety of electronic mail systems and includes a simple workgroup mail system for messaging, based on MS® Mail for Windows version 3.2.

## Fax Capability

Microsoft Fax provides built-in fax capability to Windows 95 and supports client and server fax software from other vendors.

## Internet Access

Windows 95 includes all the necessary protocols and modem software for access to the Internet. Support for basic FTP and Telnet TCP/IP utilities and for advanced software such as Mosaic makes Windows 95 Internet-ready.

## Online Services

Similar to Windows 3.1, Windows 95 supports a wide variety of online services. For those unfamiliar with online services, The Microsoft Network introduces users to online features such as product information and chat forums.

For more information about messaging services in Windows 95, see Part 6, "Communications."

---

**Tips for the administrator**

- Many of the messaging services in Windows 95 (including Microsoft Exchange, Microsoft Fox, and The Microsoft Network) are optional during installation, so you'll need to select them if you want them installed. You also need to set up the appropriate protocols and dial-up connections for access to the Internet.

# Server-Based Setup

*Easier customization and setup for multiple computers*

Windows 95 includes a setup program that automates installation and provides easy customization when installing Windows 95 from source files on the network.

## Server-Based Setup

This setup program automatically copies Windows 95 files to the selected server path, so that Windows 95 can be installed on individual computers directly from the network without accessing disk or CD-ROM drives. You can manually adjust the source files on the shared directory, adding or removing files as necessary to specify those to be copied for local computer setup.

## Home Directories

During Server-based Setup, you can view or add home directories on the server for particular computers on the server. This enables you to configure and store the user-specific or computer-specific information in these directories for use in installing Windows 95 in custom configurations.

## Remote-Boot Installations

For greater network security and manageability, Windows 95 can be set up to run from a server, either partially or completely (as in the case of remote booting (RIPL) from a ROM card).

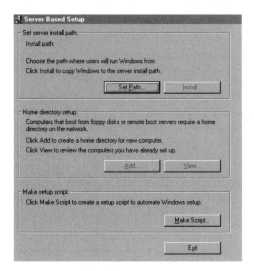

For more information, see Chapter 4, "Server-Based Setup for Windows 95," and Chapter 5, "Custom, Automated, and Push Installations."

---

**Tips for the administrator**

- Although Server-based Setup automates the copying of files to the server, you might want to customize the shared directory by adding or removing files that are specific to your network.

# Custom Setup Scripts

*Automate the installation process*

Windows 95 supports scripting of the installation process so that predetermined settings and responses to setup prompts can be automatically read from a single file, significantly reducing the installation time.

## Graphical Script Creation

Server-based Setup has an option for creating setup scripts. By choosing this option, you can easily create scripts by clicking check boxes and typing in text strings as prompted by the program. There's no need to edit a text file for the correct syntax of every option.

## Support for Systems Management Server

With Microsoft Systems Management Server commands and a Windows 95 setup script, you can install Windows 95 on a computer without having to physically visit the site. As soon as the user logs on to the network, the installation runs by itself.

For more information, see Chapter 5, "Custom, Automated, and Push Installations," Appendix D, "MSBATCH.INF Parameters," and Appendix E, "Microsoft Systems Management Server."

---

**Tips for the administrator**

- To ensure that the batch file installs all the software correctly, define a default computer configuration and test setup from a setup script in the lab before rolling it out to the network.

- To automate the user and computer name entries in the setup script, either copy them from your current server or create a text file with the predefined names.

# New Tutorial and Help

*Easy to learn and use*

Windows 95 includes new task-based Help and a tutorial that assists users in getting up to speed.

## Online Help

Windows 95 Help is designed to make it easier for users to get the information they need to perform a specific task. Most procedures have moved out of documentation and into online Help, where they're easier to access while you're working.

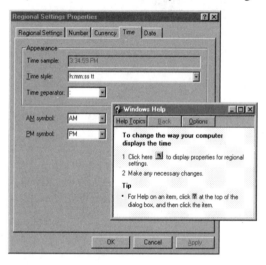

Also, Help is streamlined and task-oriented, so it is easier to remember and to use.

Whenever a user wants Help for a task, a Help window appears beside the window where the task is running, or, if no task is running, Help provides a single-click shortcut to the dialog box or feature that the user needs to use to complete the task.

## New Tutorial

Windows 95 also introduces a new tutorial that makes it easier for users to get "up and running" on common tasks. Its graphical approach illustrates the steps for tasks, such as opening files by using the Start button. Also, to help with migration, the Introducing Windows Tutorial includes tips and examples of how common Windows 3.1 are now performed under Windows 95.

For more information, click Help on the Start menu.

## Context Help

To get specific help information in a dialog box, right-click an item, and then click What Is This? Or click the question mark button in the title bar, and then click the item in the dialog box that you want to read about.

---

**Tips for the administrator**

- To speed up user training in Windows 95, use system policies to modify the computer's startup so that the Tutorial runs in full-screen mode in the Startup group. After training is complete, change the system policies to remove the Tutorial from the startup.

---

# Deployment Planning Guide

This part of the *Windows 95 Resource Kit* provides network administrators and systems-support professionals with a comprehensive guide to installing and deploying (or rolling out) Microsoft Windows 95 in corporations. In this guide, based on interviews with administrators of corporate networks about their testing and rollout plans for Windows 95, you can find important information about how to develop and implement a plan for company-wide deployment of Windows 95.

### Chapter 1    Deployment Planning Basics

Provides an overview of major deployment steps and a timeline for the deployment process.

### Chapter 2    Deployment Strategy and Details

Provides detailed explanations of steps in the deployment process and the key decisions or actions related to performing them.

A Microsoft Project (.MPP) file is available with the *Windows 95 Resource Kit* utilities to use as a template for the overview and details of deployment planning described in Chapter 1, "Deployment Planning Basics" and Chapter 2, "Deployment Strategy and Details."

Notice that these chapters serve as a guide for creating and carrying out a rollout plan in an organization. Your company's specific rollout plan may be different, due to existing policies and processes.

CHAPTER 1

# Deployment Planning Basics

This chapter is for administrators who are responsible for corporate implementation of Windows 95. It provides an overview of the major steps in the deployment process. Chapter 2, "Deployment Strategy and Details," contains the details about how to make decisions and perform actions listed in the overview.

Notice that some tasks may not be necessary for your organization.

For step-by-step instructions on conducting the installation, see Chapter 3, "Introduction to Windows 95 Setup" and Chapter 5, "Custom, Automated, and Push Installations," in the *Windows 95 Resource Kit*.

**In This Chapter**

Overview of the Deployment Process    20
Reviewing Windows 95 Features: An Overview    21
Preparing the Teams: An Overview    22
Deciding on the Preferred Client Configuration: An Overview    23
Performing the Lab Test: An Overview    29
Planning the Pilot Rollout: An Overview    31
Conducting the Pilot Rollout: An Overview    32
Finalizing the Rollout Plan: An Overview    34
Rolling Out Windows 95: An Overview    35

# Overview of the Deployment Process

The deployment process for Windows 95 consists of several distinct phases, including the following:

- Reviewing Windows 95
- Preparing the Planning and Support teams
- Identifying the preferred network-client configuration
- Performing lab tests of the client configuration
- Planning the pilot rollout
- Conducting the pilot rollout
- Finalizing the rollout plan
- Rolling out Windows 95

For each phase, this chapter contains a section outlining in checklist form the required tasks for that deployment phase. Chapter 2, "Deployment Strategy and Details" provides details for performing each task according to the deployment phase.

The *Windows 95 Resource Kit* utilities include document templates containing the deployment checklist plus a Microsoft Project file for planning the deployment process at your site.

The following sample shows how to read a deployment checklist for any phase.

**Description of the Deployment Phase**

| Task | Team | Start week | Duration |
|------|------|------------|----------|
| 1: Summary of the task. | Who will perform this task? | When does the team begin this task? | How long will it take to complete? |

The following teams, made up of employees from your organization, are responsible for performing the tasks described in deployment checklists:

- The Executive team includes the deployment project manager (usually the head of the Information Systems department) and members of the executive committee of the corporation. This team must include one or more individuals with decision-making authority over company policies and procedures.
- The Planning team includes the deployment project manager, key Installation team members, and a representative from the Support and Training teams.

- The Installation team includes technicians and individuals who will be conducting the installation. This team must include a specialist in 32-bit applications who can evaluate the proposed Windows 95 configuration for compatibility.

- The Support team includes staff of the help desk or Support department, and select individuals from the Planning team. This team develops a plan for supporting Windows 95 during and after deployment, integrating new methods and processes as needed into the existing support scheme.

- The Training team includes individuals responsible for user training.

At certain phases, you may choose to vary the makeup of the teams by adding or omitting individuals.

# Reviewing Windows 95 Features: An Overview

When implemented, Windows 95 can yield significant benefits to your organization in terms of reduced costs and increased system control. Because many decisions—starting with the decision to acquire Windows 95—depend on these and other anticipated benefits, becoming familiar with the features and benefits of Windows 95 is the first step in deployment planning.

The following checklist lists sources of information on Windows 95 features and benefits.

**Reviewing Windows 95 Features**

| Task | Team | Start week | Duration |
|------|------|-----------|----------|
| **1:** Read *Introducing Microsoft Windows 95*, available from Microsoft Press (ISBN 1-55615-860-2) or the *Windows 95 Reviewer's Guide* (available from WinNews forums on the Internet and other online services). | Executive, Planning | Week 1 | 7 days |
| **2:** Review total cost of ownership, migration, and productivity studies published by analysts such as Gartner Group, Inc. if appropriate. Use these studies to assess the impact of Windows 95 on your business's bottom line. | Executive, Planning | Week 1 | 14 days |
| **3:** Acquire additional copies of the *Windows 95 Resource Kit* for review during the deployment process. | Planning | Week 2 | 1 day |

# Preparing the Teams: An Overview

After the review of Windows 95 features and benefits, the next step is to prepare the Planning, Installation, and Support teams for the deployment process. If you did not fully staff the Planning team for the review phase, assemble the people you need for both the Planning and Installation teams at this time. Then gather the equipment and tools to be used in planning the Windows 95 implementation and arrange for Support team training. The following checklist outlines the processes of assembling the Planning and Installation teams and its resources and coordinating Support team training.

**Preparing the Teams**

| Task | Team | Start week | Duration |
|---|---|---|---|
| **1:** Assign the project manager, if appropriate (usually this is the head of the Information Systems department). | Planning | Week 2 | — |
| **2:** Select key Planning and Installation team members, if appropriate. Make sure to include an applications specialist, for evaluating 32-bit applications. | Planning, Installation | Week 2 | 5 days |
| **3:** Acquire Windows 95 (the compact disc version is preferred because it contains system administration tools). | Planning | Week 2 | 1 day |
| **4:** Identify your client and server hardware and software configurations on the network. | Planning | Week 3 | 5 days |
| **5:** Set up a testing lab. | Planning | Week 2 | 1 day |
| **6:** Acquire test computers for use as the network server and clients. Choose computer models that are typical of those used in your organization. | Planning | Week 2 | 5 days |
| **7:** Install the applications software and line-of-business tools in the lab to simulate the network environment. Also identify the mission-critical and noncritical business and other applications typically used in your organization. Create a checklist for evaluating the compatibility and performance of these applications during testing. | Planning | Week 3 | 3 days |
| **8:** Review detailed discussions of product features in the "Guided Tour for Administrators" in the *Windows 95 Resource Kit*; study Part 2, "Installation," of the Resource Kit to prepare for configuration planning. | Planning, Installation | Week 3 | 3 days |

**Preparing the Teams** (*continued*)

| Task | Team | Start week | Duration |
|---|---|---|---|
| **9:** Study the entire *Windows 95 Resource Kit*. As an option, obtain Windows 95 TrainCast instructional videotapes from Microsoft. As another option, arrange for the team and other individuals, as appropriate, to attend training at a Microsoft Authorized Technical Education Center and participate in the Microsoft Certified Professional program to prepare for supporting Windows 95. | Support | Week 3 | 10 days |
| **10:** As an option, read *Inside Windows 95* from Microsoft Press, for technical details on the internal operation of Windows 95. | Planning, Installation, Support | Week 2 | 10 days |

# Deciding on the Preferred Client Configuration: An Overview

With the Planning and Installation teams assembled and educated about Windows 95 capabilities, the next task for these teams is to determine the preferred configuration for client computers on the network. (For the purposes of this discussion, "client computer" refers to any computer running Windows 95, including computers that act as peer servers by running File and Printer Sharing services.) The teams will use this configuration for evaluation and testing, prior to full implementation of Windows 95 in your organization.

The tables in this section summarize options to consider in planning your preferred configuration. Using the information in these tables, evaluate the available features and the related alternatives before making a decision. Microsoft recommends that you begin your evaluation with the "ideal" configuration, that is, a configuration that uses all of the most powerful features of Windows 95. Then gradually modify this configuration, adding or removing features, until you achieve a configuration that more closely fits your company's needs. When you have identified the preferred configuration, document the configuration layout and the selected features to make sure you install and test the correct configuration.

To learn more about product features as they relate to your system configuration, see Chapter 2, "Deployment Strategy and Details," or the related chapters of the Resource Kit.

The following table presents an overview of configuration layout decisions and feature options for the ideal network client. An additional table lists features which Microsoft recommends for implementation by all organizations; these features define how Windows 95 will be installed and administered in your organization. The final table shows optional features that may be useful in some organizations.

**Configuration Layout Decisions**

| Configuration option | Decisions and issues |
|---|---|
| Location of Windows files<br><br>*To maximize performance, security, or hard disk space on the client computer* | Depends on your need to maximize central security and administration versus performance on the client computer. Also depends on the hardware platform of the client computer.<br><br>Options:<br><br>• Run Windows 95 on the client computer for best performance and reduced network traffic.<br><br>• Run Windows 95 from the server to save hard disk space on client computers and make it easier to upgrade components or drivers later, especially for multiple computers.<br><br>• Run completely from the server for the highest degree of security or for diskless workstations.<br><br>For information, see Chapter 4, "Server-Based Setup for Windows 95." |

**Key Features of the Ideal Network Client**

| Preferred feature | Decisions and issues |
|---|---|
| Use 32-bit, protected-mode network client software<br><br>*To provide the best network performance and functionality* | Depends on the compatibility of your required applications. Options vary based on your network. For example, for Novell® NetWare® networks:<br><br>• Protected-mode Client for NetWare Networks is the preferred client, because of the performance and increased functionality, and because it's easy to install and configure.<br><br>• Real-mode Novell NETX or VLM clients may offer slightly better compatibility with some network utilities.<br><br>• A real-mode network client for another network can also be used with Client for NetWare Networks.<br><br>For information, see Part 3, "Networking." |

**Key Features of the Ideal Network Client** (*continued*)

| Preferred feature | Decisions and issues |
|---|---|
| Use 32-bit, protected-mode protocols<br><br>*To provide the best network performance and functionality* | Depends on compatibility with your choice of client. Options depend on your choice of protocol. For example, for IPX/SPX:<br><br>■ Microsoft IPX/SPX-compatible protocol is preferred (with or without IPX over NetBIOS).<br><br>■ Keep real-mode IPXODI for use with a real-mode Novell-supplied client.<br><br>■ Both the real-mode and Microsoft protected-mode implementations can be used if some of your applications (such as TSRs) require the real-mode protocol.<br><br>For information, see Chapter 12, "Network Technical Discussion." |
| Use the latest network adapter drivers<br><br>*To provide improved performance and the ability to both load and unload the network and notify the rest of the system, use NDIS 3.1 drivers, which support Plug and Play* | Depends on the availability and compatibility of the new driver. The 32-bit, protected mode drivers offer vastly improved performance and reliability over older versions. For PCMCIA cards, the 32-bit drivers are extremely easy to manage.<br><br>Options:<br><br>■ Always use the newest drivers available; implemented by default.<br><br>■ Manually choose to keep using an older driver, including ODI drivers, if new drivers are not available.<br><br>For information, see Chapter 12, "Network Technical Discussion." |
| Use the new Windows 95 user interface<br><br>*To provide ease of use and maximum functionality in accessing Windows 95 features* | Depends on timing or preference rather than functionality because the new user interface is significantly more functional and efficient. But, if a rapid migration is required, and training is not immediately available, the Windows 3.1 user interface can be used temporarily.<br><br>Options:<br><br>■ Use the new user interface; this is preferred and installed by default.<br><br>■ Install the Windows 3.x File Manager and Program Manager.<br><br>For information, see Chapter 22, "Application Support." |

**Recommended Windows 95 Features for Client Configurations**

| Windows 95 feature | Decisions and issues |
|---|---|
| Use system policies<br><br>*To enable centralized administration capabilities of Windows 95 or add control of the user's desktop* | Choose this feature to enable centralized administration or add control.<br><br>Options:<br><br>▪ Use System Policy Editor to define policies at any time.<br><br>▪ For computers running a shared copy of Windows 95 from a server, configure the shared installation directory with a limited set of components for Windows 95. This is not a recommended choice.<br><br>For information, see Chapter 15, "User Profiles and System Policies." |
| Use user profiles<br><br>*To allow multiple users to use a single computer with their own settings or, conversely, to allow personalized settings per user on multiple computers* | Choose this feature to maintain consistent desktop and environment settings on a user-specific basis. Enabling user profiles causes a slight delay during logon.<br><br>Options:<br><br>▪ Users can control changes to their user profiles and update them as they want.<br><br>▪ Administrators can predefine a mandatory profile for specific users, that can only be changed by the administrator.<br><br>For information, see Chapter 15, "User Profiles and System Policies." |
| Enable remote administration<br><br>*To allow an administrator to remotely manage the file system, network sharing, or Registry of the individual computers* | Install this service to allow remote administration. To use it, you must use a 32-bit network client and also enable user-level access.<br><br>For information, see Chapter 16, "Remote Administration." |
| Use setup scripts (batch files) for installation<br><br>*To allow automated installation on client computers* | Choose this feature if you must install Windows 95 on more than five computers.<br><br>Server-based Setup offers an easy to use, graphical tool for creating setup scripts. You can also manually create a script with additional options by creating a text file with the appropriate entries.<br><br>For information, see Chapter 5, "Custom, Automated, and Push Installations," and Appendix D, "MSBATCH.INF Parameters." |

**Recommended Windows 95 Features for Client Configurations** (*continued*)

| Windows 95 feature | Decisions and issues |
|---|---|
| Set up for push installation<br><br>*To allow the administrator to push the installation from the server without touching the client computer* | Choose to use a push installation, based on the location and number of computers you must upgrade.<br><br>Options:<br><br>■ Edit the login script to run a setup script.<br><br>■ Use a tool such as the Microsoft Systems Management Server to facilitate the setup.<br><br>For information, see Chapter 5, "Custom, Automated, and Push Installations," and Appendix E, "Microsoft Systems Management Server." |
| Use peer resource sharing services<br><br>*To allow a client computer to share files and resources such as printers and CD-ROM drives with other computers* | Choose this feature based on your site's security needs. If users are allowed to share local resources on their computers, then peer resource sharing can save network traffic and hard disk space on the server. For central control or to prevent users from turning on this feature, use system policies.<br><br>This feature can only be installed on computers that use a 32-bit, protected-mode network client.<br><br>For information, see Chapter 11, "Logon, Browsing, and Resource Sharing." |
| Use user-level security<br><br>*To implement control for a variety of services beyond network resource access, including File and Printer Sharing, Remote Registry, backup agents, and other network and system management functions* | Choose this feature to enable users to specify the users and groups who have access to local shared resources (including the Registry). Validation by a Windows NT Server or a NetWare server can also be required before access to any resources is possible under Windows 95.<br><br>Options:<br><br>■ Users can specify access rights for individuals and groups to shared resources.<br><br>■ User access is validated based on user accounts on a Windows NT domain or a Novell NetWare bindery.<br><br>■ User-level security is required for remote administration of the Registry and for network access to full user profiles.<br><br>■ Optionally, share-level security can be used to protect files on Windows NT networks or Windows 95 peer networks.<br><br>For information, see Chapter 14, "Security." |

**Other Optional Windows 95 Features**

| Windows 95 feature | Decisions and issues |
| --- | --- |
| Use Microsoft Exchange Mail<br><br>*To have a unified inbox for messages, faxes, and so on* | Depends on whether you have an existing mail system and whether you want the added integration of messaging services offered by Microsoft Exchange.<br><br>Options:<br><br>■ Install all or part of Microsoft Exchange during the installation.<br><br>■ Run your existing mail client as usual.<br><br>For information, see Chapter 26, "Electronic Mail and Microsoft Exchange." |
| Use Windows 95 mobile computing features<br><br>*To enable Windows 95 features that support mobile computing or switching between portable and docking-station configurations* | Depends on the particular hardware and the working needs of mobile-computing users. Some of these features are not installed by default but can be specified during Setup or installed later:<br><br>■ Dial-Up Networking client software for dial-up connection to popular servers<br><br>■ Windows 95 Briefcase for synchronizing files between computers, and Direct Cable Connection for directly linking two computers, plus other built-in communications applications<br><br>■ Remote mail and deferred printing, for working away from the main office<br><br>■ Automatic configuration for PCMCIA cards, and for all components with Plug and Play-compliant hardware<br><br>■ User profiles to provide a custom desktop for each user, no matter where users log on to the network<br><br>For information, see Chapter 19, "Devices," and Chapter 28, "Dial-Up Networking and Mobile Computing." |

**Other Optional Windows 95 Features** (*continued*)

| Windows 95 feature | Decisions and issues |
|---|---|
| Use other Windows 95 value-added features<br><br>*To enable other Windows 95 ease-of-use innovations and capabilities such as The Microsoft Network and Microsoft Fax* | Depends on your existing services and needs. In general, if client computers have the hard disk space and use a utility or an application with the same capabilities from another vendor, you should install the new features and test their value.<br><br>These features are not installed by default but can be specified during Setup or installed later:<br><br>■   Microsoft Fax for fax receipt and transmission<br><br>■   The Microsoft Network for online services<br><br>For information, see Chapter 26, "Electronic Mail and Microsoft Exchange," Chapter 27, "Microsoft Fax," and Chapter 29, "The Microsoft Network." |

# Performing the Lab Test: An Overview

Using the preferred client configuration specified in the previous phase, proceed with installing the configuration in the lab for testing and evaluation. Because only the client-computer configuration is being installed (server installation is described in the following section), this test only determines whether the preferred configuration performs as expected, and whether it is compatible with your current applications and processes.

Depending on how the test installation proceeds, it may be necessary to modify the configuration, by either adding or removing selected features. If more than one configuration is being considered, side-by-side evaluations of different configurations can be performed to help determine which one works best.

The following checklist outlines the tasks in performing the lab test of the client configuration. These tasks apply for each computer used to install a client configuration. For step-by-step instructions on installing and selecting features, see Chapter 3, "Introduction to Windows 95 Setup."

## Performing the Lab Test

| Task | Team | Start week | Duration |
|---|---|---|---|
| **1:** Make sure that the computer meets your company's standards and the Windows 95 minimum standards for operation—at least a 4-MB 386DX or better. If not, perform the hardware upgrades now. | Installation | Week 4 | 0.1 day |
| **2:** Defragment the hard disk and scan it for viruses. | Installation | Week 4 | 0.1 day |
| **3:** Back up and verify key data and configuration files, such as INI, AUTOEXEC.BAT, and CONFIG.SYS files. Also back up the Windows and DOS directories, and all files in the root directory. Make a system startup disk containing COMMAND.COM, SYS.COM, and FDISK.EXE. | Installation | Week 4 | 0.1 day |
| **4:** Make sure that the current network client software is functioning properly and, referring to the checklist of inventoried applications, make sure that all important applications operate correctly. | Installation | Week 4 | 1 day |
| **5:** Install Windows 95 on the test computer in the lab, using the preferred client configuration identified in the previous phase. | Planning, Installation | Week 4 | 1 day |
| **6:** Test the installation:<br><br>• Can you connect to and browse the network?<br><br>• Can you print both locally and across the network?<br><br>• Can you perform the core operations of each application locally and on the network (including opening, closing, and printing)?<br><br>• Can you shut down successfully? | Planning, Installation | Week 4 | 2 days |
| **7:** Optionally, if you have several test computers, compare your old client configuration under Windows 3.x and your new preferred configuration. How do the two compare in terms of the following:<br><br>• Functionality for administering the computer?<br><br>• Performance for local disk and network actions?<br><br>• Ease of use for performing common tasks?<br><br>• Stability of the computer under stress?<br><br>• Compatibility with applications and hardware? | Installation, Planning | Week 5 | 2 days |
| **8:** If the specified client configuration did not work as expected, modify and document the differences until a working preferred client configuration is installed. | Planning, Installation | Week 5 | As required |
| **9:** Perform a complete restoration of operating system files and system capabilities for your old client configuration on the computer running Windows 95. | Installation | Week 5 | 1 day |

**Performing the Lab Test** (*continued*)

| Task | Team | Start week | Duration |
|---|---|---|---|
| **10:** Evaluate the restoration process for problems. Document the process and the modifications made. | Installation, Planning | Week 5 | 0.5 day |
| **11:** Have all team members participate in installing the preferred configuration on a variety of hardware. | Installation, Planning | Week 5 | 3 days |

# Planning the Pilot Rollout: An Overview

In this phase, appointed teams determine the best methods for automatically installing the specified configuration for a pilot or trial rollout. Planning for this pilot program involves creating the automated installation process, determining the logistics of testing, and preparing a training plan for users. The following checklist outlines the tasks in planning the pilot rollout.

**Planning the Pilot Rollout**

| Task | Team | Start week | Duration |
|---|---|---|---|
| **1:** Use Server-based Setup to install Windows 95 source files on a server. Make setup choices based on your client configuration, including whether you will run a shared copy of Windows 95 from the server, or run Windows 95 locally on the client computer. Perform the following steps:<br><br>■ Set up the distribution server<br><br>■ Set up the client from the network<br><br>See Chapter 4, "Server-Based Setup for Windows 95," for step-by-step instructions. Document any changes to this process. | Planning, Installation | Week 6 | 1 day |
| **2:** Create and test an automated installation by creating a setup script to predefine settings for Setup. Document the key parts of the setup script that vary by installation. | Planning, Installation | Week 6 | 2 days |
| **3:** Determine and test how you will push the installation from the server without having to touch the client computers. (See Chapter 5, "Custom, Automated, and Push Installations") Options:<br><br>■ Modify login scripts on the server.<br><br>■ Use management software such as Microsoft Systems Management Server.<br><br>■ Send a setup script (batch file) that runs Windows 95 Setup as an embedded link in an electronic mail message.<br><br>Document the process for the rest of the Installation team. | Planning, Installation | Week 6 | 3 days |

**Planning the Pilot Rollout** (*continued*)

| Task | Team | Start week | Duration |
|---|---|---|---|
| **4:** Evaluate the Windows 95 installation process for opportunities to upgrade or improve your organization's existing technology infrastructure. For example, a system management software tool can help you administer computers on the network more easily, and it can help with the push installation process. | Planning, Executive | Week 7 | 2 days |
| **5:** Document in checklist form the logistics of the pilot installation, such as the total time for installation, the new software or tools to be purchased, the group selected as the pilot users, and the scheduling of specific installations. Use this prior to the rollout to make sure you are completely prepared.<br><br>Also, document goals for the pilot rollout to be used as evaluation criteria for rating the success of the rollout. | Installation, Planning | Week 7 | 3 days |
| **6:** Send a memo to your users to clearly explain how the installation process will affect their daily work schedule and describe the differences they will see after the installation is completed. | Planning | Week 7 | 1 day |
| **7:** Develop a user training course (or hire a training vendor to prepare one). Use the Windows 95 Help and *Introducing Microsoft Windows 95* (supplied with the Windows 95 distribution disks) to "jump start" your training efforts. | Planning, Support, Training | Week 6 | 5 days |
| **8:** Establish a support plan for the pilot user group. This includes the names and phone numbers of persons to contact for assistance, a short list of the top questions and answers, and troubleshooting tips. | Planning, Support | Week 7 | 5 days |
| **9:** Set up the lab or classroom with computers for training. | Training | Week 7 | 2 days |
| **10:** Edit the Windows 95 Help file (if appropriate) to include any company-specific information. Repeat this after the pilot rollout is completed. | Planning, Support | Week 8 | 4 days |

# Conducting the Pilot Rollout: An Overview

The goal of the pilot program is to test your automated installation in everyday use among a limited group of users (for example, between 15 and 50). This process helps to identify problems that may impede or delay the deployment process, and helps to determine what resources you'll require for the final, company-wide rollout. It's important to make the pilot rollout as successful as possible because it sets the tone for the rest of the deployment process. If pilot users are satisfied, their enthusiasm can influence others to cooperate, which in turn helps the rest of the process to move smoothly.

The following checklist outlines the tasks in conducting the pilot rollout. Use the same pilot user group and follow the same tasks when rolling out 32-bit applications.

**Conducting the Pilot Rollout**

| Task | Team | Start week | Duration |
|---|---|---|---|
| **1:** Select a pilot user group that is willing and able (particularly in terms of their workload) to handle the installation process. | Planning | Week 8 | 2 days |
| **2:** Train the users. | Training | Week 8 | 5 days |
| **3:** Back up the Windows and DOS directories and the files on the root directory of the test computers. | Installation | Week 9 | 5 days |
| **4:** Following the logistics checklist prepared in the previous phase, perform the installation in the same manner that you expect to install Windows 95 throughout the company. Compare your results against goals and evaluation criteria (developed in the previous task) for this process. | Installation | Week 9 | 10 days |
| **5:** Have your technicians on-site for the initial installations to document the process and problems and to support the users. Have other technicians monitor time and all measurable factors in the installation process. Record these measurements for later evaluation. | Support | Week 9 | 15 days |
| **6:** Make sure that all computers are "up and running" as expected. Make note of possible improvements to the installation, training, or support, where appropriate. | Planning, Installation, Support | Week 11 | 3 days |
| **7:** Survey members of the pilot user group about their satisfaction with the installation process and take feedback on what could have been done better. | Planning | Week 12 | 3 days |
| **8:** Continue to monitor the pilot installation for a week to make sure that everything continues to run smoothly. | Support, Planning | Week 11 | 5 days |
| **9:** Prepare a checklist of issues to resolve for the final rollout. Include in this checklist the areas identified in step 6 as needing improvement, comments from the user survey, and the results of comparing your rollout goals and evaluation criteria against actual performance. | Support, Planning | Week 11 | 5 days |
| **10:** If the pilot program did not run smoothly or user feedback was poor, conduct additional pilot installations until the process works well. | Planning, Installation | Week 12 | See "Planning the Pilot Rollout: An Overview" |

# Finalizing the Rollout Plan: An Overview

The results of the pilot installation provide the basis for developing a final plan for rollout. Using the actual time and resource requirements from the smaller-scale pilot rollout, teams make projections for time and resources, corresponding to the company-wide scope of the final rollout. If additional resources are required, identify these and acquire them at this time. In addition, update company policies and standards regarding computer and network use to accommodate the Windows 95 implementation.

**Finalize the Rollout Plan**

| Task | Team | Start week | Duration |
|---|---|---|---|
| **1:** Determine your rollout goals—specifically the number of computers on which you will install Windows 95 and the time expected for completion. During preparation for final rollout, check off items on this list as they are resolved. | Planning, Executive | Week 12 | 5 days |
| **2:** Budget the resources, in terms of personnel and tools, required to meet your goals. | Planning | Week 12 | 3 days |
| **3:** If necessary, present the budget and obtain approval for the resources and the rollout process. | Executive, Planning | Week 13 | 2 days |
| **4:** Hire and train the extended Installation team and purchase the additional software or tools needed. | Training, Installation | Week 13 | 10 days |
| **5:** Update the company's hardware and software standards lists. | Planning | Week 13 | 2 days |
| **6:** Update the company's policies and practices manuals or guidelines for use of computers and the network. | Planning | Week 13 | 2 days |
| **7:** Notify your users that company standards and policies for computer use will be enforced prior to the installation and that they must bring their computers into compliance. | Planning | Week 13 | 1 day |
| **8:** If appropriate, edit the Windows 95 Help file to add company-specific Help for line-of-business applications. | Planning, Support | Week 14 | 3 days |
| **9:** For each computer, create a template as a database for documenting and tracking any system problems or deficiencies that require further attention. | Installation | Week 13 | 2 days |
| **10:** Post the updated template to a central network location. | Installation | Week 13 | 2 days |

# Rolling Out Windows 95: An Overview

After the extensive research, planning, testing, and analysis performed in the previous phases, the deployment teams arrive at the final phase—rolling out the Windows 95 installation to the entire company. Although each prior phase was critical to the overall success of the deployment process, only this phase can fulfill the purpose of the entire planning process, by delivering the substantial new benefits of Windows 95 to your broadest base of users. At this phase, weeks of preparation pay off in a smooth migration of all your users to an operating system that is more powerful, more robust, and easier to use.

The following checklist outlines the tasks required for the final rollout of Windows 95.

**Rolling Out Windows 95**

| Task | Team | Start week | Duration |
|---|---|---|---|
| **1:** Set up the distribution servers by using the Server-based Setup and configuring the system policy files. | Installation | Week 15 | 1 day |
| **2:** Customize the server installation by adding or removing the appropriate files, including the MSBATCH.INF file. | Installation | Week 15 | 2 days |
| **3:** Notify the users of the upcoming installation. | Planning | Week 15 | 1 day |
| **4:** Train the users on Windows 95. | Training | Week 16 | As required |
| **5:** If needed, upgrade the hardware on the client computers and remove any software not complying with company policy. | Installation | Week 16 | As required |
| **6:** If needed, back up critical data and configuration files on the client computers. | Installation | Week 16 | As required |
| **7:** If needed, defragment the client hard disks. | Installation | Week 16 | As required |
| **8:** Optionally, you can temporarily reset the user password and ID for each computer, to allow your technicians easy access to the client computer and make sure that the login scripts and environment operate correctly. | Planning | Week 17 | As required |
| **9:** Make sure that the client computers are fully operational and the real-mode network, if present, is running. | Installation | Week 17 | As required |
| **10:** Prepare the client computers for the push installation process: edit the login scripts; run the management software; or send the setup script, by electronic mail, to the user. | Installation | Week 18 | As required |
| **11:** Initiate the installation by having the user log on, double-click the setup script file, and so on. | Installation | Week 18 | As required |

For details of each task in the deployment checklists, see Chapter 2, "Deployment Strategy and Details." For step-by-step instructions on how to set up, maintain, and use Windows 95 in a corporate environment, see the appropriate chapters of the *Resource Kit*.

C H A P T E R   2

# Deployment Strategy and Details

This chapter contains details on the phases and tasks for rolling out Windows 95 that are summarized in Chapter 1, "Deployment Planning Basics." If you are comfortable with the early planning phases of deployment, you can skip ahead to "Deciding on the Preferred Client Configuration: The Details" later in this chapter.

Notice that some tasks may not be necessary for your organization.

**In This Chapter**     Reviewing Windows 95 Features: The Details   39
   Publications from Microsoft Press   39
   Reports from Industry Experts   40
  Preparing the Teams: The Details   41
   Acquiring Staff and Software   41
   Conducting a Sample Inventory   42
   Testing Lab Setup and Equipment   42
   Training the Teams   43
  Deciding on the Preferred Client Configuration: The Details   43
   Configuration Layout   44
   Key Features of the Ideal Configuration   44
   Recommended Features for Network Clients (Optional)   45
   Other Optional Features   48
  Performing the Lab Test: The Details   49
   Preparing the Test Site and Equipment   49
   Installing Windows 95 on Test Computers   50
   Testing the Installation   50
   Testing the Restoration Process   52

*(continued)*

Planning the Pilot Rollout: The Details    52
    Installing the Source Files for Setup    52
    Automating the Installation    52
    Documenting Rollout Logistics    53
    Notifying Users of the Rollout    54
    Developing User Training    55
    Developing the Support Plan    56
Conducting the Pilot Rollout: The Details    56
    Simulating the Installation Process    56
    Testing Windows 95 Performance and Capabilities    57
    Surveying Users for Feedback    57
Finalizing the Rollout Plan: The Details    57
    Completing the Rollout Logistics and Budget    58
    Updating the Policies and Practices Guidelines    58
    Creating a Template for the Rollout Database    58
Rolling Out Windows 95: The Details    59

# Reviewing Windows 95 Features: The Details

This is the first phase of the deployment process in which the Executive and Planning teams learn about Windows 95 features and benefits. In this phase, those responsible for planning and conducting the rollout learn how Windows 95 helps reduce support costs and increase business profitability. Publications are available from Microsoft Press and from independent industry analysts to provide the information you need.

## Publications from Microsoft Press

The Executive and Planning teams need to acquire and review *Introducing Microsoft Windows 95* and the *Microsoft Windows 95 Resource Kit* during this phase:

*Introducing Microsoft Windows 95* (ISBN 1-55615-860-2), available from Microsoft Press, provides information about Windows 95 features and functionality. This book discusses the changes and enhancements made to the Microsoft Windows operating system to provide easier management and support in a network environment. To order this or other Microsoft Press® titles, call (800) MSPRESS (or (800) 677-7377).

The information contained in *Introducing Microsoft Windows 95* is also available online as the *Windows 95 Reviewer's Guide*. For online access to the Reviewer's Guide or other current information on Windows 95, connect to the Microsoft WinNews forum at any of the following electronic locations.

| Online service | How to access |
|---|---|
| The Microsoft Network | From the Windows 95 desktop, click the icon for The Microsoft Network. Then click Microsoft and, in the Microsoft menu, select Windows 95. Click WinNews. |
| America Online® | Use the keyword **winnews** |
| CompuServe® | Type **go winnews** |
| FTP on the Internet | Type **ftp://ftp.microsoft.com/PerOpSys/Win_News** |
| GEnie™ | Download files from the WinNews area under the Windows 95 RTC. |
| Prodigy™ | Type **jump winnews** |
| World Wide Web on the Internet | Type **http://www.microsoft.com** |

The *Windows 95 Resource Kit* is important equipment for your deployment teams. Written to assist administrators in installing, supporting, and managing Windows 95 on corporate networks, the Resource Kit is a technical supplement to the Windows 95 product documentation. Each Planning and Installation team member should obtain a copy of the Resource Kit for review as they prepare for deployment planning.

# Reports from Industry Experts

Many leading industry analysts have developed independent assessments of the impact of Windows 95 on corporate operations. The reports of two firms, Gartner Group, Inc. and Usability Sciences Corporation, discussed in this section, can assist rollout planners in understanding specifically how Windows 95 reduces the total cost of ownership for a personal computer in your organization.

## Gartner Group, Inc. Reports

Two published reports are available that describe the cost of migrating to Windows 95 from Windows 3.x and the effect of Windows 95 on the total cost of ownership of a personal computer. This section summarizes key findings of the reports. To receive the complete report, contact Gartner Group, Inc. at (203) 967-6700 and ask for the Total Cost of Ownership study (reference Personal Computing Service K-820-1094) and the report titled "GUI Operating System Migration: How Sticky Will It Be?" (August 22, 1994).

Highlights of these reports include the following.

**Payback period is short.**  Gartner Group projects that a typical organization will earn back the cost of migrating to Windows 95 within three to six months, based on support cost savings alone. Assuming that, on an annual basis, Windows 95 costs $1180 less per user to run than Windows 3.1, over five years, Gartner Group estimates that organizations will save nearly $6000 per user. Notice that, even if organizations do not realize this precise reduction in costs, the support-cost savings should substantially exceed the cost of migration.

**Migration is justified even when only using 16-bit applications.**  Gartner Group recommends that organizations migrate to Windows 95 "if only to run 16-bit Windows applications on a more stable, easier to use platform."

**Planning Windows 95 deployment increases potential savings.**  In its "Cost of Migration" study, Gartner Group demonstrates that organizations benefit substantially through decreased costs by planning their deployment of Windows 95. In fact, by planning the traditional labor-intensive operations (for example, the installation process) and automating the process, an organization could realize costs of migrating to Windows 95 that are less than the average upgrade cost from Windows 3.0 to Windows 3.1.

Although not cited in these reports, additional payback should result from increased user productivity due to features such as Dial-Up Networking, multitasking, multithreading, and so on.

### Usability Sciences Corporation Report

Usability Sciences Corporation, an independent usability testing group, performed a study on how users are affected by moving to Windows 95. Their study included 75 existing Windows 3.1 users with varied levels of skill in performing common tasks. Details of the study and its findings are available from the WinNews electronic forum.

Highlights of the study's results include the following.

**Users get started quickly.**   After testing users as they performed specified tasks in Windows 3.1, and then allowing them a 20-minute "play" period with Windows 95, the study found that the same users were almost as fast under Windows 95 in performing comparable tasks as they were in Windows 3.1.

**Users perform faster.**   Usability Sciences reported that, within 1.5 hours of first using Windows 95, users performed operations nearly twice as fast as they did on Windows 3.1.

**Extensive user training is not needed.**   Because all tests in the study were performed using the online Help that comes with Windows 95, the results demonstrate that lengthy training sessions are not necessary.

As additional reports and studies are published, they'll be placed on the WinNews online forums. Check these forums for periodic updates.

# Preparing the Teams: The Details

This phase involves gathering the resources, including equipment, software, and staff, to properly plan for testing and evaluating Windows 95. Members of the Support team should receive training during this phase.

# Acquiring Staff and Software

The deployment project manager participates in the Executive team and leads the Planning team. This individual is usually the head of the Information Systems department; however, the executive committee may find another individual to be more appropriate, depending on the organization.

When setting up the Planning team, it is important to include a set of individuals representing the groups involved in the deployment process. This includes people from the Corporate Support and Employee Training departments, the Corporate Standards Committee, and key Installation team members. Individuals from the Finance and Accounting group will need to take part in planning and evaluation later on, but need not be assigned to the team for the full duration of the deployment process.

Your Installation team should include an applications expert, who can evaluate 32-bit applications run with Windows 95.

Obtain Windows 95 during this phase. Microsoft recommends that you purchase the compact-disc version, so that you can use Server-based Setup and administrative software tools not provided on the floppy disks.

# Conducting a Sample Inventory

You'll need to survey a representative sample of your network to identify the hardware and software typically used on client and server computers. By doing this sample inventory of your company's active equipment, you can accurately simulate the organizational environment in the lab. Such a simulation helps you make broad decisions about your company's computing infrastructure, such as the choice of protocol or the default desktop configuration as it pertains to applications.

Software management tools are available to query computers on the network for hardware and software configurations. For detailed information about a large number of computers on a network, use a system management program such as the Microsoft Systems Management Server to conduct the inventory.

# Testing Lab Setup and Equipment

To effectively evaluate and test the Windows 95 installation process, you need to set aside enough physical space and assemble a sufficient number of computers to test everything from Server-based Setup to hand-tuning options for the local computer. In addition, if your network environment includes the use of portable computers that dial in to the company, or if you use additional servers or mainframe computers for business data, you need to make sure that the lab computers have full access to the network and an analog phone line.

It is important that you test and implement all of the Windows 95 features comprehensively in the lab with all of your mission-critical and noncritical business applications before moving to the pilot installation.

Installation of Windows 95 on a server requires 90 MB of disk space.

# Training the Teams

By reviewing specific portions of the *Windows 95 Resource Kit*, the Installation and Planning teams can gain an extensive understanding of Windows 95 features and functionality. A review of the "Guided Tour for Administrators" and of the chapters contained in Part 2, "Installation," can provide the teams with the information necessary to evaluate product features for system configuration.

Support team members must become familiar with all information in the Resource Kit to prepare for their role in the deployment process. Windows 95 TrainCast instructional videotapes are also available from Microsoft (to obtain these, call (800) 597-3200). For more extensive training, team members can receive instruction at a Microsoft Authorized Technical Education Center and participate the Certified Professional program. Call (800) SOLPROV (or (800) 765-7768) for information about authorized training offered for Windows 95 and the Certified Professional program, and for referral to a local Microsoft Solution Provider Authorized Technical Education Center (ATEC).

For additional information about Windows 95, particularly the background of its design and the history of its development, team members can read *Inside Windows 95* from Microsoft Press. This book contains guidelines and tips for applications developers working with Windows 95.

For other training information, see Appendix J, "Windows 95 Resource Directory."

# Deciding on the Preferred Client Configuration: The Details

Detailed analysis is required to determine your preferred client-computer configuration. Starting with the ideal configuration, which uses the most functional and best-performing client software, evaluate each feature against your organization's needs and environment to determine whether the feature is appropriate and compatible. If you are considering different configuration alternatives, repeat this evaluation for each configuration.

The following sections describe feature options and decisions to evaluate in specifying the network client configuration.

# Configuration Layout

When deciding where to place Windows 95 files, consider how the computer will be used and evaluate the benefits of each placement option. If the computers are personal workstations, or portable computers that occasionally connect to the network, or are used in workgroups that only share data and applications such as word processors (not operating system software), then you might want to install Windows 95 executable files and applications on the local hard disk and run these locally. Swap files and TEMP files are also located on the local hard disk. The network is used only to store commonly used data.

On the other hand, if you want to run a shared copy of Windows 95 on computers that do not have hard disks or to provide a central location for managing users' system configurations, then you would install Windows 95 files so that all Windows 95 executable files and applications run from the network. All data is saved on the network. Swap files and TEMP directories are placed on network drives.

Support for diskless workstations is available for NetWare networks with the initial release of Windows 95. For information about support under Windows NT, contact your Microsoft sales support representative.

# Key Features of the Ideal Configuration

This section provides detailed discussions of the features which might be included in an ideal network client configuration.

## Using a 32-bit, Protected-Mode Network Client

For best performance, select a network client that uses a 32-bit redirector for network access. Windows 95 includes the 32-bit Microsoft Client for NetWare Networks and the Client for Microsoft Networks; each of these has a 32-bit redirector. The benefits of using a 32-bit, protected-mode client include the following:

- Provides for easy installation and configuration using built-in Windows 95 tools
- Uses no real-mode memory
- Provides faster data I/O across the network
- Offers greater stability than real-mode redirectors
- Allows more than one redirector to be run at one time, and thereby enables access to servers for multiple networks without having to reload the operating system for a new network client
- Makes networking seamless in the Windows 95 user interface; users can browse the server for multiple networks in Network Neighborhood, all within the same name space—users don't need to know which type of network they are browsing

If you are using another type of network, contact your network vendor regarding the availability of a 32-bit, protected-mode network client. If a protected-mode client is unavailable, you can run a protected-mode Windows 95 client such as Client for Microsoft Networks in conjunction with a real-mode network client.

## Using a 32-bit, Protected-Mode Protocol

If you select a 32-bit, protected-mode network client, then by default Windows 95 also sets up a 32-bit, protected-mode protocol. Even if you are running a real-mode client such as the Novell® 3.x workstation shell (NETX) with a real-mode implementation of IPX/SPX to access NetWare® servers, you can still load the 32-bit version of the Microsoft IPX/SPX-compatible protocol. The benefits of adding the protected-mode protocol are better performance and better stability for network communications to servers that are not running NetWare (for example, computers running Windows 95 or Windows NT).

In addition, for protocols such as TCP/IP, the Microsoft 32-bit version enables additional functionality such as the ability to use DHCP and WINS servers that dynamically set the IP addresses and resolve computer names for client computers on the network. Each protocol has a number of benefits, as discussed in Chapter 12, "Network Technical Discussion."

## Using the Latest Network Adapter Drivers

For best performance, use the latest network adapter drivers available. These should be NDIS 3.1-compatible drivers which provide Plug and Play capabilities. Such drivers take up no real-mode memory and can be loaded or unloaded dynamically as required.

The only instances in which you wouldn't use the latest drivers are:

- The newest driver isn't available for your network adapter.
- Your site requires ODI cards and drivers.

# Recommended Features for Network Clients (Optional)

The following optional features are recommended for your preferred configuration. These features define how Windows 95 will be installed and administered in your organization.

## Using System Policies

For centralized administration of client computers, you must enable system policies. System policies allow you to centrally edit and control individual user and computer configurations. For example, if you want to place a custom Start menu on user desktops or limit access to Control Panel options, system policies make it easy to do this from a central location for a large number of users.

Enabling policies creates a single file that resides on the server, and thus does not involve physically touching the client computer. In general, the policy file can be modified on the server after Windows 95 is installed; however, some types of changes, such as adding group support or a nonstandard server path for product updates, require configuration on the client computer. For information on the types of restrictions available and for details on how to implement system policies, see Chapter 15, "User Profiles and System Policies."

## Using User Profiles

With user profiles, users can use personalized desktop settings each time they log on to a computer. This is especially useful for multiple users sharing a single computer who want to customize their desktops and have those custom settings loaded at logon. Conversely, a single user can move between computers using the same profile if the administrator stores that profile on the server. An administrator can also take advantage of profiles to require that a mandatory desktop configuration be loaded each time a user logs on. The ability to change profile settings can be controlled by the administrator. For information on how to use user profiles, see Chapter 15, "User Profiles and System Policies."

User profiles are not needed when only one person uses the computer or when a custom desktop adds no value. By not enabling user profiles, the logon process is shortened slightly, because the system does not need to locate and load the profile.

## Enabling Remote Administration

To remotely administer a computer's Registry, you must first install the network service called Microsoft Remote Registry service, enable user-level security, and enable the Remote Administration feature. Remote administration capabilities allow you to conduct a variety of tasks remotely over the network such as administering the file system, sharing or restricting directories, or querying and making changes to the Registry. If you plan to do any of these tasks, be sure to enable this feature during Windows 95 installation.

You should not enable remote administration if you don't need these services, because doing so causes unnecessary, extra processes to run on the client computer and on the network. These extra remote services could then *theoretically* be used by individuals on the network—provided they knew the appropriate password—to access information on client computers. However, Windows 95 comes with security capabilities to protect against unauthorized use of the Remote Registry service. For more information, see Chapter 16, "Remote Administration."

## Using Setup Scripts for Windows 95 Setup

Setup scripts (which are batch files) allow you to predefine responses to prompts that appear during Windows 95 Setup. Setup scripts go hand-in-hand with push installations to completely automate the installation process. The choice to use a setup script is very straightforward. If you need to conduct a similar installation more than five times, you should use a setup script. Begin planning for setup scripts and push installations during this phase, as you are specifying the preferred client configuration. Make sure that you document each feature needed, so that you can automate the selection of these features. For more information, see Chapter 5, "Custom, Automated, and Push Installations."

## Using Push Installations for Windows 95 Setup

You need to understand and plan in advance how the push installation process will work for a given computer. There are several alternatives for remotely initiating the installation, ranging from editing the client's login script, to sending by electronic mail a link that contains a setup script. You will want to consider how to push the installation for each computer and make sure that the client computers are configured to support this process.

For organizations with 50 or more computers, being physically present to install each client computer is not a viable option because of the cost. In that case, you may need to turn to an administrative software solution such as Microsoft Systems Management Server. When using administrative software tools, additional client-side software may be needed. Be sure to include this software in the installation plan.

For more information about using push installations, see Chapter 5, "Custom, Automated, and Push Installations."

## Using Peer Resource Sharing Services

The peer resource sharing capability in Windows 95 allows your client computers to share files and printers directly from a local personal computer, instead of on a central server. Peer resource sharing may reduce the traffic and disk space required on central servers, because you are leveraging the power of individual computers.

Security for peer resource sharing services may take the form of user-level security based on the user accounts on a Windows NT or NetWare network. Notice that a Microsoft Windows NT Client Access License is required if the computer will be connecting to servers running Windows NT Server. For information, see Chapter 8, "Windows 95 on Microsoft Networks," or contact your Microsoft reseller.

If you don't have servers to provide security validation or don't want to use user-level security, you can use share-level security, with each individual implementing security and a password scheme on the local computer. Share-level security is set on a directory-by-directory basis.

If you do not want to use peer resource sharing services and want to disable the capability on each client computer, you can do so by selecting the appropriate option in system policies.

## Using User-Level Security

User-level security is based on user account lists stored on Windows NT or Novell NetWare servers. The user accounts specify which users have access rights on the network. Windows 95 passes on a user's request for access to the servers for validation. Pass-through user-level security protects shared network resources by requiring that a security provider authenticate a user's request to access resources.

User-level security is required for remote administration of the Registry and for network access to full user profiles. For information on implementing security in Windows 95, see Chapter 14, "Security."

# Other Optional Features

The following features may be useful in your organization. Review the related discussion before making a decision.

## Using Microsoft Exchange Mail

The new Microsoft Exchange feature in Windows 95 manages all messaging information in one place, with a single inbox for electronic mail, faxes, and other messages. In addition, Windows 95 comes with a complete small-business mail system—that is, a mail client and a postoffice—that allows users to exchange electronic mail through a single postoffice. This mail client integrates well with Microsoft Mail servers, and the postoffice can be upgraded to provide an enterprise mail system.

You can also use a variety of other mail or messaging systems through Microsoft Exchange as long as they use a MAPI 1.0 driver. If you have an existing mail system that doesn't use a MAPI 1.0 driver, you can continue to use that mail system without running the Microsoft Exchange Mail capability. In this case, you would install Microsoft Exchange only if you wanted to use the Microsoft Fax capability so that incoming faxes are collected by Microsoft Exchange. For more information, see Chapter 26, "Electronic Mail and Microsoft Exchange" and Chapter 27, "Microsoft Fax."

## Using Microsoft Fax

Microsoft Fax provides a built-in fax capability that allows a computer running Windows 95 to send and receive faxes as bitmap and binary files without any additional software. It also allows users within a Windows 95 workgroup to share a fax modem, but if you have an existing fax server in your organization, you should probably to continue to use that server for computers on the network. In that case, Microsoft Fax features would still be useful for portable computer users who travel. For more information, see Chapter 27, "Microsoft Fax."

## Using Dial-Up Networking

This client software allows the computer to use popular, server-based dial-in packages such as Windows NT RAS, Novell NetWare Connect, and Shiva NetModem. Dial-Up Networking provides additional security for remote dial-up connections and requires some additional configuration of procotols and software. For more information, see Chapter 28, "Dial-Up Networking and Mobile Computing."

## Using The Microsoft Network

The Microsoft Network is an online service that offers chat capability, information bulletin boards, and electronic mail. It is the best place to obtain Microsoft product information and technical support. For more information, see Chapter 29, "The Microsoft Network."

## Using Disk Management Tools

Windows 95 ships with useful disk tools such as disk compression and defragmenting utilities that run from within Windows 95. The disk compression utility upgrades DoubleSpace® and DriveSpace™ programs from MS-DOS 6.2x. For details, see Chapter 20, "Disks and File Systems."

# Performing the Lab Test: The Details

This phase in the deployment process involves four significant efforts: preparing the site, conducting the installation, testing the installation, and restoring the system.

# Preparing the Test Site and Equipment

Preparing the site involves ensuring that the location of each computer, the computer itself, and the hard disk in particular are all ready for Windows 95 to be installed. In terms of the physical site, make sure that you have the appropriate jacks for connecting to the network.

For the computer itself, make sure that it has the appropriate hard disk space, RAM (at least 4 MB, but 8 MB is recommended), and processor (386DX or better is recommended) to run Windows 95. To review the requirements for running a shared copy of Windows 95 from a server, see Chapter 4, "Server-Based Setup for Windows 95."

In addition, run virus detection, disk scanning, and defragmentation programs on the computer to correct any problems prior to installation. Although the computer may appear to be operating properly, software upgrades often uncover hardware or software problems, because of the way they read and write data to the hard disk. Correct any such problems before installing Windows 95.

Lastly, when preparing the site, be sure to back up critical data and configuration files for the system, in case the installation fails or you need to revert to the previous operating system for some reason. This includes backing up INI files (such as WIN.INI and SYSTEM.INI), GRP files, AUTOEXEC.BAT, CONFIG.SYS, and all key data files. As an added precaution, create a system startup disk and back up the Windows and DOS directories and all the files in the root directory.

If you need to automate the restoration, consider using a commercial backup program, instead of copying the files by hand.

# Installing Windows 95 on Test Computers

Before setting up Windows 95 for the first time, verify that the computer's existing network is working properly. Then use Part 2, "Installation," in the *Windows 95 Resource Kit* to help you install and configure Windows 95 correctly. Chapter 5, "Custom, Automated, and Push Installations," includes instructions on how to automate the installation process using setup scripts. Take note of which options you want to predefine as entries for the MSBATCH.INF file used for the setup script.

# Testing the Installation

After you've set up a computer with Windows 95, you'll need to run a variety of tests to make sure that it runs correctly on your network and that you can still perform all of your usual tasks. Use your own testing methodology or test the following to verify correct system operation:

- Connect to and browse the network
- Set up a printer and test printing to local and network printers
- Open, run, and close applications on both the client computer and on the server
- Shut down completely

Make sure to test all mission-critical applications for proper function. If you encounter problems, try removing related features from the proposed configuration as a solution. Document any changes made to the original configuration.

If the preferred client configuration works as expected, you may also want to conduct additional testing of the optional software features and components in Windows 95. This can help you determine whether you are running Windows 95 optimally. For this kind of testing, conduct side-by-side evaluations on two computers, changing individual features on each one, to determine the following:

- Performance in terms of responsiveness and throughput
- Ease of use
- Stability
- Compatibility
- Functionality

To evaluate network client software for Novell NetWare, run your network performance tests in the following configurations:

- Windows 95 installed with an existing 16-bit, Novell-supplied workstation client (NETX), using ODI drivers
- Windows 95 added to an existing installation of Windows 3.x and NetWare, using Client for NetWare Networks and protected-mode networking support components (NDIS adapter drivers)
- Windows 95 as a new installation using all protected-mode components, including both Client for NetWare Networks and Client for Microsoft Networks, plus peer resource sharing support

Perform several common tasks such as connecting to the network, administering a remote NetWare server, and so on, to test for ease of use. Similarly, you'll want to run any business-specific NetWare applications under Microsoft Client for NetWare Networks to make sure that they run compatibly. Any stability issues should become apparent during this testing.

When you have identified a configuration that performs well during testing, test the same configuration using other hardware from your company.

See Part 3, "Networking," in the *Windows 95 Resource Kit* to understand the differences in functionality between network clients.

## Testing the Restoration Process

After thorough testing of the preferred client configuration, completely restore one of the test computers to the previous client configuration and document the process. The degree to which you need to test and restore the computer depends on the tools available. Chapter 6, "Setup Technical Discussion" documents how to remove Windows 95 and restore the previous operating system manually.

# Planning the Pilot Rollout: The Details

This phase involves three major efforts: automating the installation, documenting the logistics of the pilot installation, and preparing the user training plan. These efforts are a combination of planning and lab-testing work.

## Installing the Source Files for Setup

You need to designate a network server that will be used as the source file installing Windows 95 over the network using custom setup scripts. Then use Server-based Setup to install Windows 95 source files on a server. This program is available only on the Windows 95 compact disc (in the ADMIN\NETTOOLS\NETSETUP directory).

You must make choices based on your client configuration, including whether client computers will run a shared copy of Windows 95 from the server, or run Windows 95 locally from the hard disk.

See Chapter 4, "Server-Based Setup for Windows 95," for step-by-step instructions. Document any changes to this process.

## Automating the Installation

Automating the installation is a key step in reducing the cost of migration. By creating a setup script with predetermined answers for installation questions, the installation process can run from start to finish without user intervention. It is also possible to "push" the installation from the server, so that you can install Windows 95 on an individual personal computer without ever touching the computer. This automation work is done in the lab, prior to conducting the pilot rollout.

Automating the installation consists of creating a setup script, setting up Windows 95 on the server, and creating a push installation process. With a setup script you can perform a "hands free" installation, so that the user need not respond to any prompts or even touch the computer during Windows 95 Setup.

Setting up Windows 95 on the server requires the Server-based Setup program (NETSETUP.EXE) from the Windows 95 compact disc. Installing Windows 95 source files on the server is a separate and distinct process from the Windows 95 Setup program (SETUP.EXE) that you ran in the initial lab installation.

When you run Server-based Setup to install source files on the server, you can also create a default setup script, and you can specify whether the Windows 95 source files on the server will be used to set up Windows 95 to run locally from a single computer or to run a shared copy from the server for client computers that require a shared installation.

Depending on the common network configuration at your site, you may determine that you need to remove a line from one or more configuration files as a global procedure before starting Windows 95 Setup. For example, you may want to use a protected-mode protocol such as Microsoft TCP/IP during Setup instead of the real-mode version of TCP/IP currently used on the target computers. In addition, users may be running certain TSRs or applications that should be closed before running Windows 95 Setup. In these cases, you can modify NETDET.INI on NetWare networks as described in Chapter 9, "Windows 95 on NetWare Networks." On other networks, including Microsoft networks, modify the [Install] section of MSBATCH.INF to automate these changes. (For more information, see Appendix D, "MSBATCH.INF Parameters.")

In addition, you may want to manually add other files to the shared directory on the server, such as custom bitmaps for screens or a predefined WKGRP.INI file for workgroup organization, so that client computers are fully configured when Windows 95 is installed.

Creating a push installation process involves doing some final work on the server, such as editing the login script for the user, or sending a link in electronic mail to a batch file that runs Windows 95 Setup, so that the user only needs to log on or double-click an icon to start the installation. System management software such as Microsoft Systems Management Server can also be used to start the installation centrally. If you plan to use system management software in automating the installation, make sure this has been acquired and tested.

For more information, see Chapter 5, "Custom, Automated, and Push Installations."

# Documenting Rollout Logistics

This task involves determining the timing and the process for pilot installation and choosing the pilot user group.

Although it is a test, the first pilot rollout sets the tone for and presents an example of the final rollout, so it is important to be completely prepared with all aspects of the rollout. This requires that you determine the time it will take for installation, the personnel and tools needed to facilitate the process, and the overall schedule.

Start by identifying the target computers and their location. Then use the following list as the basis of your checklist for rollout logistics:

- Has a verified backup been performed for each of the target computers?

- Have passwords been reset for CMOS, the network, and applications?

- Have virus checking and disk defragmentation been performed?

- How many systems will be installed per day? Start with a conservative estimate and then increase or decrease the number, based on your experiences with the initial installations.

- At what time of day should the installations occur? You may want to schedule installations to occur on weekdays after normal business hours or on weekends.

- Who are the pilot users? Choose a pilot user group or department that is willing and able to accommodate the rollout. This group, ranging from 15 to 50 persons, should be representative of your overall user base. Try not to select a department that is attempting to meet a schedule deadline during the rollout, or a group that is traditionally slow in adopting new technology.

- What is the schedule for pilot installations? When determining the installation time for the pilot rollout, base the projections on how long it takes for installation of an individual computer; remember to schedule the downtime for each user.

- Who will participate in the installations? In addition to the Installation team members, be sure to assign a system administrator with full rights on the server, including the right to administer mail or database server passwords.

- Is the deployment methodology as automated as possible?

As you develop the checklist of logistics, consider your goals for the pilot rollout and the factors that define its success. For example, you might set a percentage for successful upgrades or for automated installations that, if achieved, would indicate that the rollout had been successful. Document these goals and criteria, so that teams can monitor performance against them during the rollout.

# Notifying Users of the Rollout

Another step at this stage is informing users about the pilot rollout plan. You can use a videotape presentation, an interoffice memo, or a company meeting as the means for communicating with users about the rollout. But, regardless of the form used, the message must explain to users the benefits of moving to Windows 95, and describe the overall plan and process by which each group or department will make the move. This makes it easier for your users to plan for and accept the migration to Windows 95 as part of their schedules.

# Developing User Training

The first steps in developing a training plan are to acquire a training lab, set up computers in the lab, and appoint a team member as instructor. (If in-house resources are not available, use a vendor to develop and conduct the training.) The instructor will be responsible for creating and testing the training program.

There are a number of training approaches and a variety of tools you can use. A recommended approach is to divide the training into sessions corresponding to three distinct topics: The Basics, Corporate-Specific Applications, and Customization.

The session entitled "The Basics" includes the top 10 functions any user needs to know to accomplish daily work, such as the following:

| Function | To do the function, use this |
| --- | --- |
| Run programs, load documents, find a file | Start button |
| Change settings | Control Panel |
| Get help on a specific topic | F1 or Help command |
| Switch between applications | Taskbar |
| Minimize, maximize, and close windows | Window buttons |
| Browse your hard disk | My Computer and Windows Explorer |
| Connect to a network drive | Network Neighborhood |
| Print a document | Point and Print |

The Windows 95 online Help and *Introducing Microsoft Windows 95* supplied with the product disks provide the information you need to train users in the basics. Schedule training sessions of no more than 30 minutes each; in each session, users receive information that is *just enough* to be productive using Windows 95.

The "Corporate-Specific Applications" session varies by the environment and the types of applications run on the network. This session should focus on the top 5 to 10 functions that will change because of the upgrade to Windows 95.

The "Customization" session is intended for more experienced users. The purpose of this session is to provide information and guidance that will help these users learn on their own after the training, and teach them how to work more productively with Windows 95. Some of these topics could include:

- Adding items to the Start button
- Adding items to the desktop (move, copy, shortcut)
- Using options controlled by the right mouse button
- Adding a new device (for example, a printer)
- Changing the desktop (for example, screen saver settings)

After creating and testing the program, schedule training sessions to occur immediately before the rollout so that the instruction is *just in time,* ensuring that users retain most of what they learn by putting it to use right away.

## Developing the Support Plan

Similar to the training plan, the support plan must be ready to go online the first day you begin performing Windows 95 installations. Because the quality of support that's available during the pilot rollout will be seen as an indicator of the quality of the rollout as a whole, it is important that you plan carefully to make sure effective support is available.

Staff the Support team for your pilot rollout with some of your best technicians dedicated solely to the pilot group for the first few weeks. The assigned technicians should carry pagers or be available by phone at all times, to give immediate assistance to users.

And, to help users help themselves, edit Windows 95 Help with company-specific information on applications or features. Doing so requires placing an OEM.CNT file and your custom help file in the user's Windows directory. For information about OEM.CNT and the format of Windows 95 help files, see the *Win32 Software Development Kit for Windows 95 and Windows NT*.

# Conducting the Pilot Rollout: The Details

This phase consists of simulating the final installation process, testing the capabilities and performance of the system, surveying user feedback, and making adjustments as needed.

Repeat this pilot rollout process for 32-bit applications.

## Simulating the Installation Process

The schedule for the pilot rollout should simulate—on a smaller scale—the schedule of the final rollout. As you conduct the pilot rollout, you may find that certain tasks take more or less time than expected, that some tasks need to be added, or that some tasks can be left out. Modify the pilot rollout schedule to account for such changes, and use the pilot schedule for projecting the final rollout timetable.

# Testing Windows 95 Performance and Capabilities

In addition to the technicians responsible for conducting the pilot installation, extra technicians should be assigned to measure, observe, and test the installation. By tracking the time per installation, handling problems that arise, and identifying areas for improvement or automation, these individuals help make sure the success of both the pilot and final rollouts by making the installation more efficient.

In addition, after Windows 95 is installed, these technicians test system capabilities, such as remote administration, for proper operation and monitor the client computers for performance, stability, and functionality, highlighting any inconsistencies with the lab configuration.

# Surveying Users for Feedback

The final part of the pilot rollout involves surveying the users to gauge their satisfaction and proficiency with the new installation and to evaluate the level of training and support provided. Test users' proficiency by having them perform a few common tasks or use several of the new features in Windows 95—for example, have these users register their survey results on the server.

When collected, combine the survey results with the ideas for improvements identified during the pilot rollout. Use this information to prepare a checklist of open issues which must be resolved prior to the final rollout. Then assign team members to take the actions necessary for solving problems or making improvements. Indicate on the checklist how and when each item was resolved, adjusting the deployment plan if appropriate.

# Finalizing the Rollout Plan: The Details

The final rollout plan is an extension of the pilot planning process, with the added steps of documenting, budgeting for, and carrying out the final logistics. As you perform these steps, you should also update the policies and practices guidelines governing network and computer use in your company, and create a template for a central database that tracks specific configurations and uses of each network computer.

# Completing the Rollout Logistics and Budget

As you prepare for final rollout, estimate the length and scope of the overall installation process. Also plan for all tools needed to complete the process within the stated timeframe. If necessary, propose a formal budget for the company-wide implementation and present it to management for approval. Your budget should include the costs for personnel and resources such as system management software.

After obtaining any necessary approval, purchase the resources required to facilitate the installation. If you need additional staff, be sure to hire experienced and qualified individuals for the team, and train them extensively before getting started.

Complete your training, communication, and staffing plans for the final rollout at this time.

# Updating the Policies and Practices Guidelines

Prior to final rollout, update all company policies regarding the use of the network and computers by employees. Make sure to cover items such as password length and expiration requirements, and the level of approval needed to obtain remote dial-up privileges.

In addition, update the corporate standards lists for hardware and software usage; use this is a reference for bringing all computers into compliance during the rollout process.

Because Windows 95 enables the use of many new 32-bit applications and of Plug and Play-compliant hardware, these new products should be added to the list, and their older counterparts should be deleted.

# Creating a Template for the Rollout Database

A template is used to create a central database for monitoring the progress of the rollout and to document any areas requiring further action. During preparations for the final rollout, create the template, using appropriate database management software. Complete the template with configuration information for every computer and user in the company, and place the template on the server. Then, during company-wide installation, the Installation team fills in the template for each computer and user, indicating whether any additional upgrading is needed. The team can then use the template to track open items following the rollout and to measure actual progress against original objectives.

# Rolling Out Windows 95: The Details

Following weeks of planning, organization, testing, communication, and training, the deployment teams and your organization as a whole should be ready for full-scale rollout of Windows 95. The extensive preparation for this event may make deployment seem almost routine for the teams involved; however, that's exactly the kind of uncomplicated rollout a systems administrator dreams of. And, soon after the installations, users may not know how they got their work done without Windows 95. If this happens in your company, then you know your rollout has been a success!

The information in this chapter has been provided to assist organizations in achieving a smooth migration with Windows 95. The remainder of this Resource Kit contains information intended to illustrate other benefits and capabilities of your Windows 95 implementation. Following this Planning Guide, information is presented in these parts:

- Part 2, "Installation"
- Part 3, "Networking"
- Part 4, "System Management"
- Part 5, "System Configuration"
- Part 6, "Communications"
- Part 7, "Windows 95 Reference"
- Part 8, "Appendixes"

P A R T  2

# Installation

This part of the *Windows 95 Resource Kit* contains the following chapters which describe how to set up Windows 95.

### Chapter 3    Introduction to Windows 95 Setup

Describes installation requirements for installing Windows 95, provides an overview of the types of Windows 95 installations available, and presents a step-by-step description of how Windows 95 Setup installs Windows 95 to run on the local hard disk of a single computer.

### Chapter 4    Server-Based Setup for Windows 95

Describes how to prepare the server for running Windows 95 Setup from a shared directory, and provides the procedures for installing Windows 95 to run from a shared copy of source files on the network, including setup for remote-boot and floppy disk-based workstations.

### Chapter 5    Custom, Automated, and Push Installations

Describes how to customize Windows 95 using setup scripts, policy files, and other options. This chapter also provides procedures for automating Windows 95 Setup so that users do not have to make choices and administrators can ensure installation results.

### Chapter 6    Setup Technical Discussion

Describes the internal setup and system startup processes, and provides procedures for installing Windows 95 on computers that have operating systems other than MS-DOS. This chapter also describes how to remove Windows 95 from a computer.

CHAPTER 3

# Introduction to Windows 95 Setup

This chapter presents requirements for installing Windows 95, provides an overview of the types of Windows 95 installations available, and presents a step-by-step description of running Windows 95 Setup to install Windows 95 on the local hard disk of a single computer.

**Important** Before running Windows 95 Setup, read the SETUP.TXT file on Disk 1 of the Windows 95 floppy disks or on the compact disc for information about hardware and software that might already be installed on your computer.

**In This Chapter**

Windows 95 Setup Overview   65
    Quick Start for Windows 95 Setup   65
    New Windows 95 Setup Features   66
Installation Requirements   67
    Operating System Requirements   67
    Requirements for Windows 95 Setup   68
    System Requirements for Windows 95   69
    Partition Requirements   71
Options for Windows 95 Installations   72
    Deciding to Run Setup from MS-DOS or Windows   72
    Deciding to Use Typical, Portable, Compact, or Custom Setup   73
    Deciding Between Local and Shared Installation   75
    Deciding to Use Customized or Automated Setup   76
    Deciding to Use Maintenance or Repair Setup   76
Before Starting Windows 95 Setup   77
Starting Windows 95 Setup   79
    Using Setup Command-Line Switches   80
    Beginning Windows 95 Setup and Safe Recovery   82

*(continued)*

Running Windows 95 Setup    85
    Gathering Information    85
    Analyzing the Computer    88
    Selecting Software Components    91
    Selecting Network Components in Custom Setup    93
    Specifying Computer Identification    98
    Changing Computer Settings in Custom Setup    99
    Creating a Startup Disk    101
    Copying Files and Completing Setup    102

# Windows 95 Setup Overview

This section provides a brief summary of the installation steps in Windows 95 Setup, plus an overview of the new features in Windows 95 Setup.

This information is designed to provide a fundamental description of Setup for administrators who are responsible for installing Windows 95 on many computers. However, the information provided here will also help individuals who are installing Windows 95 on the local hard disk of their personal computers.

---

**Note**  In the *Windows 95 Resource Kit*, "local computer" refers to a personal computer with Windows 95 system files installed on the local hard disk; a local computer running Windows 95 can also include networking software.

The term "shared installation" is used to refer to a computer that runs a shared copy of Windows 95 from a network server, with few or no Windows 95 files installed on the local workstation.

---

# Quick Start for Windows 95 Setup

The following are the basic tasks you perform when installing Windows 95 on a computer for the first time:

1. Check that the computer's hardware is supported and meets the minimum requirements for Windows 95. Close all applications and disable unnecessary TSRs. Check and defragment the hard drive, and back up key files. These tasks are described in "Before Starting Windows 95 Setup" later in this chapter.

2. Start Windows 95 Setup.

   How you start Setup depends on whether you are running Setup from floppy disks, a CD-ROM compact disc, or a shared network directory. For information, see "Starting Windows 95 Setup" later in this chapter.

3. Choose the directory where you want the Windows 95 system files to be installed on the computer. If you want to preserve your existing Windows and MS-DOS operating system, you must install Windows 95 in a new directory, as described in "Gathering Information" later in this chapter.

4. Choose the type of setup: Typical, Compact, Portable, or Custom. For most users, Microsoft recommends the Typical Setup, which installs standard options with default settings. For information, see "Deciding to Use Typical, Portable, Compact, or Custom Setup" later in this chapter.

5. Provide identification information about your user name, computer name, and other identifiers. For information, see "Providing User Information" later in this chapter and "Specifying Computer Identification" later in this chapter.

6. If you choose Custom Setup, you must specify the options you want to install and make other choices about the system components, including networking. For information, see "Selecting Software Components" later in this chapter, "Selecting Network Components in Custom Setup" later in this chapter, and "Changing Computer Settings in Custom Setup" later in this chapter.

7. Create a startup disk for emergency recovery, as prompted by Windows 95 Setup. This is a highly recommended step. For information, see "Creating a Startup Disk" later in this chapter.

8. Restart the computer after Setup copies the required files. Then, depending on the type of installation, select the local time zone and complete other tasks for configuring certain devices and software. For information, see "Copying Files and Completing Setup" later in this chapter.

Windows 95 Setup automatically guides you through each of these tasks and provides Help for any step if you need it before proceeding.

# New Windows 95 Setup Features

Windows 95 Setup ensures easier installation and also offers greater flexibility and better customization options than earlier versions of Windows. The following list summarizes these improvements.

**A complete Windows-based setup process.**  Windows 95 Setup provides better visual feedback and greater flexibility for navigating through the setup process than was available for Windows 3.x. Windows 95 Setup runs entirely from within the Windows environment, even if an earlier version of Windows 3.x is not already on the computer. The Windows 95 Setup wizard leads users through the process of choosing all configuration options. After all choices have been made, Windows 95 Setup proceeds without further user actions.

**Modular architecture for Setup.**  To make installation easier and more flexible, the Windows 95 development team completely rewrote the installation code. Windows 95 Setup also incorporates the use of safe defaults and mechanisms for automatically configuring or installing all components with minimal user intervention.

**Improved hardware device detection and configuration support.**  Windows 95 Setup detects the hardware devices and components already configured on the computer and uses this information to install drivers and set Registry entries. Windows 95 provides more versatile detection and configuration for a wider range of devices than was available for Windows 3.x. For information, see Chapter 6, "Setup Technical Discussion."

**Safe Recovery for Setup failures.**  Windows 95 Setup provides a recovery mechanism in the case of Setup failure. Safe Recovery uses a log that is maintained throughout the setup process. If Setup fails—for example, due to problems during hardware detection—the last entry in the Setup log identifies where the process was interrupted. When you rerun Windows 95 Setup, it uses the log to bypass the module where the problem occurred. During Setup (and during subsequent maintenance of Windows 95), Windows 95 also creates and maintains a log of installed components. For information, see Chapter 6, "Setup Technical Discussion."

**Network installation integrated with Windows 95 Setup.**  These elements are summarized in "Selecting Network Components in Custom Setup" later in this chapter. For more information, see Part 3, "Networking."

**Improved customization of installation.**  Windows 95 provides easier, more flexible customization of Setup than was available for Windows 3.x, giving you better control for configuring desktop settings, network components, and hardware devices. System administrators can simplify installation for users by using setup scripts that define required settings. Installation of Windows 95 using setup scripts is more flexible and full-featured than for Windows 3.x, and it includes the option for hands-free "push" installation with no user intervention. For information, see Chapter 5, "Custom, Automated, and Push Installations."

# Installation Requirements

There are requirements for running Windows 95 Setup in addition to the requirements for installing and running Windows 95 on a computer. This section lists the following kinds of requirements:

- Operating system requirements
- Windows 95 Setup memory, disk space, and user information requirements
- Windows 95 hardware, disk space, partition, and other requirements

# Operating System Requirements

You must install the retail version of Windows 95 as an upgrade over an existing operating system. You can install Windows 95 over a number of different operating systems, including MS-DOS, Windows, and Windows for Workgroups. Windows 95 can also be installed over Novell® DR DOS® (or Novell DOS™), PC-DOS, and OS/2, and as a dual-boot operating system with Windows NT.

The minimum operating system software required to install Windows 95 is any of the following:

- MS-DOS version 3.2 or higher, or an equivalent version from the hardware manufacturer that supports partitions greater than 32 MB
- Windows 3.x
- Windows for Workgroups 3.1x
- Dual-boot OS/2 (with MS-DOS)
- Dual-boot Windows NT (with MS-DOS)

### Tip for MS-DOS Versions and Windows 95 Setup

Windows 95 Setup attempts to install Windows 95 on a computer with an operating system version equivalent to MS-DOS 3.2 only if that version can exceed the 32-MB partition limit (such as COMPAQ® version 3.31) because the operational disk space requirements for Windows 95 can exceed the 32-MB partition limitation.

The computer must have MS-DOS version 3.2 or later. Because there are many variations of MS-DOS 3.2, Microsoft recommends that you upgrade to Windows 95 from MS-DOS version 5.0 or later.

To check the MS-DOS version, type **ver** at the command prompt.

For information about how Windows 95 Setup treats disk partitions created under other operating systems, see "Partition Requirements" later in this chapter. For information about how Windows 95 Setup deals with the boot sector and installs files for dual-boot operation with other operating systems, see Chapter 6, "Setup Technical Discussion."

# Requirements for Windows 95 Setup

Usually, you need to supply very little information during Windows 95 Setup for a successful Windows 95 installation. The unique information required for a typical installation consists only of the following (which can be predefined in a custom setup script):

- User name
- Computer and workgroup names, if the computer is connected to the network

Windows 95 Setup needs at least 417K of conventional memory to run. The amount of disk space required for Windows 95 Setup varies, due to the types of hardware on the computer, the required drivers, and the optional components installed.

**Approximate Disk Space Requirements for Windows 95**

| Installation option | Compact[1] | Typical |
|---|---|---|
| New installation | 30 MB | 40 MB |
| Windows 3.1 upgrade | 20 MB | 30 MB |
| Windows for Workgroups upgrade | 10 MB | 20 MB |

[1]  You might not get typical functionality for all Windows 95 features (including networking) with a compact configuration, as described in "Deciding to Use Typical, Portable, Compact, or Custom Setup" later in this chapter

# System Requirements for Windows 95

The following table describes the basic hardware requirements for running Windows 95 from the hard disk of a local computer. Windows 95 is designed for computers that use Intel x86-based processors; it cannot be installed on any other processor. Windows 95 does not have symmetric multiple processor (SMP) support and, therefore, cannot take advantage of multiple processors (as Windows NT does). For information about requirements for shared installations, see Chapter 4, "Server-Based Setup for Windows 95."

| Component | Windows 95 requirement |
|---|---|
| Computer | 80386DX, 20 MHz (or higher) processor |
| | For installing Windows 95 to run from a local hard disk, a high-density floppy disk drive and hard disk drive are required. |
| | For installing Windows 95 as a shared installation, the computer does not need a hard disk or floppy disk drive. |
| | You cannot install Windows 95 on a 80386 computer that has a B-step processor (that is, with ID 0303). |
| Peripheral | Mouse or equivalent pointing device |
| Memory | 4 MB of RAM (minimum); 8 MB (recommended) |
| | 8 MB are required for using Microsoft Exchange and The Microsoft Network, or for running multiple Win32®-based applications. |
| Video display | VGA (minimum); Super VGA (recommended) |

| Component | Windows 95 requirement |
|-----------|------------------------|
| Disk space | 20 MB of free hard-disk space is required for a local installation. For information about requirements for a shared installation, see Chapter 4, "Server-Based Setup for Windows 95." |
| | A custom installation requires a minimum of 19 MB. A compact installation requires 10 MB of disk space. |
| | You also need a certain amount free disk space for a swap file, depending on how much RAM the computer has. As a guideline, you need at least 14 MB of memory, which can be divided between RAM and hard disk space. For example, if the computer has 4 MB of RAM, you need at least 10 MB of free disk space for a swap file. If the computer has 16 MB of memory, you will need very little disk space for a swap file. |
| Optional | Modem (for The Microsoft Network and other components)<br>CD-ROM drive<br>Network adapter (required for networking)<br>Sound card<br>Other multimedia hardware components |

### Tips for Required Disk Space with Compressed Disks

If you have disk compression software installed, the required amount of uncompressed disk space on the host drive before installing Windows 95 depends on several factors:

- The type of compression used (Microsoft DriveSpace™ or DoubleSpace®, STAC Electronics Stacker®, and so on)
- The available free space on other drives
- The existence of a permanent swap file (if any), and its location
- The amount of available free space on other drives

If the computer does not have a swap file already, you might have to resize the host drive to accommodate the swap file requirements. For more information, consult your compression software documentation; see also Chapter 20, "Disks and File Systems."

# Partition Requirements

Windows 95 Setup cannot install Windows 95 unless a FAT partition exists on the hard disk. It cannot install Windows 95 on a computer that has only HPFS or Windows NT file system (NTFS) partitions. Windows 95 Setup reads most partitioning schemes and writes to the master boot record, unless disk partitioning schemes from other vendors are used.

The following table describes how Windows 95 Setup handles different types of disk partitions. For more information, consult the documentation for the related operating system.

| Partition type | How Windows 95 Setup handles such partitions |
| --- | --- |
| MS-DOS (Fdisk and other vendors' partitioning software) | Windows 95 Setup recognizes and begins installation over existing MS-DOS FAT partitions, if the partition is large enough to accommodate Windows 95 files (including swap files). |
| | Windows 95 supports MS-DOS Fdisk partitions on removable media drives such as the Iomega® Bernoulli Box™ drives. |
| | Windows 95 recognizes and translates disk partitioning schemes created by other vendors' partitioning software, including Disk Manager DMDRVR.BIN and Storage Dimensions SpeedStor® SSTOR.SYS. |
| Windows NT | Windows 95 cannot recognize information on an NTFS partition on the local computer. Windows 95 can be installed on Windows NT multiple-boot systems if enough disk space is available on a FAT partition. On a Windows NT multiple-boot system, Windows 95 Setup can either install Windows 95 on an existing FAT partition with MS-DOS and, optionally, Windows 3.x, or you must partition and format free space on the hard disk in a FAT partition, then perform a new installation onto this new FAT partition. |
| OS/2 | You must run Windows 95 Setup from MS-DOS. If it is not already present on the computer, you must first install MS-DOS and configure the computer for dual-booting with OS/2. |

Windows 95 works with disk compression drivers, including those in the following list. For more information, see Chapter 20, "Disks and File Systems."

- Microsoft DriveSpace and DoubleSpace
- Stacker versions 3.0 and 4.x
- AddStor® SuperStor™

If you use other disk compression software, see the Windows README file, or contact your product support representative to determine compatibility.

# Options for Windows 95 Installations

As either an individual user or a network administrator, you can choose from various options for Windows 95 installations:

- Run Windows 95 Setup from MS-DOS or Windows 3.x
- Install a typical, compact, or custom version on a desktop computer, or install Windows 95 for a portable computer
- Install Windows 95 system files locally or run a shared copy from a server
- Create customized and automated installations
- Use Windows 95 features to maintain or update an installation

These options are described in the following sections.

# Deciding to Run Setup from MS-DOS or Windows

Windows 95 Setup is a protected-mode, 16-bit, Windows-based application. There are two different scenarios in which Windows 95 Setup can be run:

- From within Windows 3.1 or Windows for Workgroups 3.1x
- From MS-DOS at the command prompt (not from the MS-DOS Prompt under Windows)

The preferred method for running Windows 95 Setup is from within Windows 3.1 or Windows for Workgroups. Run Windows 95 Setup from MS-DOS when neither Windows 3.1 nor Windows for Workgroups is installed on the computer, but MS-DOS, OS/2, Windows NT, or Windows 3.0 is installed.

Setup detects whether Windows 3.1 or any version of Windows for Workgroups is installed on the computer, and, if it finds one of them, it offers to install Windows 95 in the same directory in order to upgrade the existing installation. If you choose to install in the same directory, Windows 95 Setup moves the configuration settings in SYSTEM.INI, WIN.INI, and PROTOCOL.INI, plus file associations from the Windows 3.x Registry into the Windows 95 Registry, so all applications and networking settings will work automatically in the new Windows 95 environment. Also, Windows 3.x Program Manager groups are converted to directories in the PROGRAMS directory, so that they can be displayed on the Windows 95 Start menu.

**Note**  You must choose to install Windows 95 in a new directory if you want to preserve the existing MS-DOS or Windows installation. In this case, you might have to reinstall most Windows-based applications before they can function properly in the new environment.

Dual-boot capabilities are not enabled by default. For information about installing Windows 95 on computers with other operating systems and for information about configuring dual-boot options, see Chapter 6, "Setup Technical Discussion."

# Deciding to Use Typical, Portable, Compact, or Custom Setup

In Windows 95 Setup, you can choose from several types of installation option. The choice you make dictates the size of the Windows 95 installation on the computer (and, of course, the number of features installed) and the amount of control the user has in customizing the installation.

| Setup type | Description |
| --- | --- |
| Typical | The default option, recommended for most users with desktop computers. Performs most installation steps automatically for a standard Windows 95 installation with minimal user action. You need to confirm only the directory where Windows 95 files are to be installed, provide user and computer identification information, and specify whether to create a startup disk. |
| Portable | The recommended option for mobile users with portable computers. Installs the appropriate set of files for a portable computer. This includes installing Briefcase for file synchronization and the supporting software for direct cable connections to exchange files. |
| Compact | The option for users who have extremely limited disk space. Installs the minimum files required to run Windows 95. |
| Custom | The option for users who want to select application and network components to be installed, and confirm the configuration settings for devices. Installs the appropriate files based on user selections. This type of Setup is recommended for experienced users who want to control various elements of Windows 95 Setup. |

The following table compares many of the differences in components installed for Typical and Portable installations. For Custom Setup, the options selected by default are the same as for a Typical installation. For Compact Setup, no optional components are installed.

**Components Installed for Typical and Portable Installations**

| Optional component | Typical | Portable |
| --- | --- | --- |
| Accessibility Options | X | – |
| Audio Compression | – | – |
| Backup | – | – |
| Briefcase | – | X |
| Calculator | X | X |
| CD Player | – | – |
| Character Map | – | – |
| Clipboard Viewer | – | – |
| Defrag | X | X |
| Desktop Wallpaper | – | – |
| Dial-Up Networking | – | X |
| Direct Cable Connection | – | X |
| Disk Compression Tools | – | X |
| Document Templates | X | – |
| Games | – | – |
| HyperTerminal | X | X |
| Media Player | X | – |
| Microsoft Exchange | – | – |
| Microsoft Fax | – | – |
| Microsoft Mail Services | – | – |
| Mouse Pointers | – | – |
| Net Watcher | – | – |
| Object Packager | X | – |
| Online User's Guide | – | – |
| Paint | X | – |
| Phone Dialer | X | X |
| Quick View | X | X |
| Screen Savers | X | X |
| Sound and Video Clips | – | – |
| Sound Recorder | – | – |
| System Monitor | – | – |
| The Microsoft Network | – | – |
| Video Compression | X | X |

**Components Installed for Typical and Portable Installations** (*continued*)

| Optional component | Typical | Portable |
|---|---|---|
| Volume Control | – | – |
| Windows 95 Tour | X | – |
| WordPad | X | – |

# Deciding Between Local and Shared Installation

Windows 95 can run on the local hard disk of a computer or as a shared copy on the server for network workstations.

Windows 95 files are distributed in the following three forms for installation on computers that already have other operating systems in place:

- Windows 3.0 (or higher) upgrade on CD-ROM
- Windows 3.0 (or higher) upgrade on 3.5-inch high-density disks
- MS-DOS upgrade on 3.5-inch high-density disks

Depending on the license agreement at your site, you can also copy the Windows 95 source files to a shared network directory. Users can connect to this directory and run Windows 95 Setup.

You can also configure servers to support installing and running shared installations of Windows 95 in one of the following three ways:

- On a computer with a local hard disk, with system files stored on and running from the server
- On a computer with only a floppy disk drive, with system files stored on and running from the server
- From a Novell NetWare® server to support diskless workstations that remote boot from a startup disk image on the server

In these cases, most or all of the Windows 95 program files reside on the server instead of the workstation. For information, see Chapter 4, "Server-Based Setup for Windows 95."

# Deciding to Use Customized or Automated Setup

You can choose any combination of methods for configuring custom versions of Windows 95:

- Create custom setup scripts based on the MSBATCH.INF format. Custom setup scripts contain predefined settings for all Setup options, and they can contain instructions for installing additional software.

- Define WRKGRP.INI files to control users' choices for workgroups to join on the network.

- Enable user profiles and create system policies to specify and maintain the system configuration.

You can use setup scripts to create an automated mandatory installation scheme for installing Windows 95 on multiple computers from Windows 95 source files on servers. The following methods are possible:

- Use a login script to run Setup from a custom setup script, automatically installing Windows 95 when each user logs on.

- Use Microsoft Systems Management Server to run Windows 95 Setup with a custom setup script as a mandatory action.

- Use network management software from another vendor to install Windows 95 automatically based on custom setup scripts.

In this chapter, notations in the margin indicate the MSBATCH.INF section name and option that you can specify to customize a particular part of Setup in a script. For more information, Chapter 5, "Custom, Automated, and Push Installations."

# Deciding to Use Maintenance or Repair Setup

If Setup encounters an error or stops during hardware detection so that you have to run Windows 95 Setup again, the Safe Recovery option in Setup automatically skips previous problems so that Setup can be completed. You can also use Safe Recovery to repair damaged or corrupt installations. For more information, see "Beginning Windows 95 Setup and Safe Recovery" later in this chapter and Chapter 6, "Setup Technical Discussion."

If you run Windows 95 Setup after the operating system is installed, Setup asks if you want to verify the existing installation. You can use this feature to verify or repair the files that make up the Windows 95 operating system. You might be able to restore damaged files without completely reinstalling Windows.

Also, you can create an emergency startup disk during Windows 95 Setup, which you can use to start the computer in case of configuration problems. For information, see "Creating a Startup Disk" later in this chapter.

Windows 95 provides a variety of maintenance applications for adding, removing, and configuring Windows 95 components. Many of these applications are summarized in the following table.

| Icon | Application | Description |
|------|-------------|-------------|
|  | Add/Remove Programs | Installs or removes applications created for Windows 95; runs Windows 95 Setup to add or remove components; or creates a startup disk. To run this wizard, click the Add/Remove Programs icon in Control Panel. |
|  | Add New Hardware | Installs hardware device drivers. To run this wizard, click the Add New Hardware icon in Control Panel. |
|  | Display | Installs and configures display drivers. To run this option, click the Display icon in Control Panel. |
|  | Printer | Installs and configures printers. To run this wizard, click the New Printer icon in the Printers folder. |
|  | Modems | Installs and configures modems. To run this wizard, click the Modems icon in Control Panel. |
|  | Network | Installs and configures network components. To run this option, click the Network icon in Control Panel. |

# Before Starting Windows 95 Setup

You should consider the following questions before proceeding with Windows 95 Setup on an individual computer:

**Is the hardware supported?**  Check the Windows 95 README file and SETUP.TXT on the installation disks for any notes related to your computer hardware. If any specific computer component is not supported, Windows 95 selects a generic driver or uses the existing driver installed on the computer. If you install support manually for a hardware component that doesn't appear in the installation dialog boxes, select the model that your hardware can emulate or that is of the closest type. (All supported hardware components are listed when you run the Add New Hardware wizard, as described in Chapter 19, "Devices.")

**Do the computer components meet the minimum requirements?**  Read "Installation Requirements" earlier in this chapter, and check your computer hardware and software components. Verify that all components meet the minimum requirements.

**Are all unnecessary TSRs and time-out features disabled?**  Disable all TSRs and device drivers loaded in CONFIG.SYS or AUTOEXEC.BAT (or in any batch files called from AUTOEXEC.BAT), except those required for partition or hard disk control, network drivers, or any driver required for operation of a device such as video, CD-ROM, and so on.

Some portable computers (such as the IBM ThinkPad®) automatically suspend operation after a specified time-out interval, or when the cover is closed. You should disable this feature while Windows 95 Setup is running.

**Is the installation drive checked and defragmented?**  Windows 95 Setup automatically runs ScanDisk to check the integrity of the drive where Windows 95 is to be installed. However, you might want to check and defragment the hard disk drive thoroughly before beginning Setup, using your usual defragmentation software.

Also, be sure to defragment all compressed drives, because a highly fragmented compressed drive reports more available disk space than is available. If you use disk compression software other than DriveSpace or DoubleSpace, be sure to run the disk-checking utility provided with your compression software. For information, see the documentation provided with the compression software.

---

**Tip**  When you run Windows 95 Setup, ScanDisk performs a quick check of the hard disk. You can skip this quick check (for example, if the computer uses disk compression software from another vendor) by using the **/iq** or **/is** switch with the **setup** command, as described in "Using Setup Command-Line Switches" later in this chapter. If you choose to skip automatically running ScanDisk, be sure to use another utility to check the integrity of the hard disk before running Setup.

---

**Are all key system files backed up?**  Any time you upgrade an operating system, backing up critical business or personal data is a prudent precaution. The files you should back up before installing Windows 95 include the following:

- All initialization (.INI) files in the Windows directory
- All Registry data (.DAT) files in the Windows directory
- All password (.PWL) files in the Windows directory
- All Program Manager group (.GRP) files in the Windows directory
- All critical real-mode drivers specified in CONFIG.SYS and AUTOEXEC.BAT
- CONFIG.SYS and AUTOEXEC.BAT in the root directory
- Proprietary network configuration files and login scripts

**Does the networking software work correctly?**  Make sure that the network software is running correctly before you start Windows 95 Setup. Windows 95 uses the settings from the existing network configuration to set up the new configuration. Check the Windows 95 README file for additional notes related to your networking software.

# Starting Windows 95 Setup

The Windows 95 Setup program (SETUP.EXE) is found on the Windows 95 installation disks, or it can be stored on a shared network resource. For information about the installation media, see "Options for Windows 95 Installations" earlier in this chapter.

This section describes methods for starting Windows 95 Setup on computers that will run Windows 95 from the local hard disk after installation. For information about setting up a computer to run a shared copy of Windows 95, see Chapter 4, "Server-Based Setup for Windows 95."

Caution  Except for TSRs required for partition or hard disk control, network drivers, or device drivers such as CD-ROM, no TSRs or Windows-based applications should be running when you start Windows 95 Setup. Close any such applications before continuing with Setup.

▶ **To start Windows 95 Setup from Windows 3.1 or Windows for Workgroups**

1. Start your computer in the usual way, and run Windows.

2. If you are installing Windows 95 from floppy disks, insert Disk 1 in the drive and make that the active drive in File Manager.

   –Or–

   If you are installing Windows 95 from CD-ROM, put the compact disc in the drive and make that the active drive.

   –Or–

   If you are installing Windows 95 from source files on a network server, connect to that server and switch to the shared network directory that contains the Windows 95 source files.

3. Double-click SETUP.EXE in the directory of the Windows 95 installation files.

   –Or–

   From the File menu, choose Run, and then type **setup** and press ENTER.

4. Follow the instructions on-screen, as described in the following sections of this chapter.

▶ **To start Windows 95 Setup from MS-DOS**

1. Start your computer in the usual way.

2. If you are installing Windows 95 from floppy disks, insert Disk 1 in the drive and make that the active drive. For example, type **a:** if the disk is in the A drive.

   –Or–

   If you are installing Windows 95 from CD-ROM, put the compact disc in the drive and make that the active drive.

   –Or–

   If you are installing Windows 95 from source files on a network server, connect to that server and switch to the shared network directory that contains the Windows 95 source files.

3. At the command prompt, type **setup**, and then press ENTER.

4. Follow the instructions on-screen, as described in the following sections of this chapter.

▶ **To start Windows 95 Setup from a network computer using a setup script**

1. Log on to the network, running the existing network client.

2. Connect to the server that contains the Windows 95 distribution files.

3. At the command prompt, run Windows 95 Setup by specifying the batch file that contains the setup script, using this syntax:

   **setup** *msbatch.inf*

   For example, type **setup \\ntserver\win95\mybatch.inf** to run Setup using a setup script named MYBATCH.INF that is stored in the WIN95 directory on a server named NTSERVER. For more information, see Chapter 5, "Custom, Automated, and Push Installations."

---

**Note** If Windows 95 is installed from a server, the location of that network directory is stored in the Registry. When you add a device or require additional support files to run Windows 95, Setup automatically attempts to retrieve the files from that same location on the server. This eliminates the need to maintain a permanent network connection on the computer and makes it easier to modify the configuration of a computer in a networked environment.

---

# Using Setup Command-Line Switches

Windows 95 Setup provides options to control the installation process. These options, or switches, are specified on the command line as arguments for the **setup** command (such as **setup /d**). Similar to MS-DOS command arguments, the specific option is preceded by a forward slash (/) character (not the backslash used to specify directory arguments).

Windows 95 Setup can be run with the **setup** command with the following switches.

| Switch | Meaning |
| --- | --- |
| /? | Provides help for syntax and use of **setup** command-line switches. |
| /C | Instructs Windows 95 Setup not to load the SmartDrive disk cache. |
| /d | Instructs Windows 95 Setup not to use the existing version of Windows for the early phases of Setup. Use this switch if you have problems starting Setup that might be due to missing or damaged supporting files for Windows. |
| /id | Instructs Windows 95 Setup not to check for the minimum disk space required to install Windows 95. |
| /ih | Runs ScanDisk in the foreground so that you can see the results. Use this switch if the system stalls during the ScanDisk check or if an error results. |
| /iL | Loads the Logitech mouse driver. Use this option if you have a Logitech Series C mouse. |
| /iq | Instructs Windows 95 Setup not to perform the ScanDisk quick check when running Setup from MS-DOS. You probably want to use this switch if you use compression software other than DriveSpace or DoubleSpace. |
| /is | Instructs Windows 95 Setup not to run the ScanDisk quick check when starting Setup from Windows. You probably want to use this switch if you use compression software other than DriveSpace or DoubleSpace. |
| **/nostart** | Instructs Windows 95 Setup to copy a minimal installation of the required Windows 3.x DLLs used by Windows 95 Setup, and then to exit to MS-DOS without installing Windows 95. |
| *script_filename* | Instructs Windows 95 Setup to use settings in the specified script to install Windows 95 automatically; for example, **setup msbatch.inf** specifies that Setup should use the settings in MSBATCH.INF. For more information, see Chapter 5, "Custom, Automated, and Push Installations." |
| **/t:***tempdir* | Specifies the directory where Setup is to copy its temporary files. This directory must already exist, but any existing files in the directory will be deleted. |

**Tip for Accessibility Needs and Windows 95 Setup**

Users who require accessibility aids with Windows might find it difficult to install Windows 95 in the usual way because accessibility aids cannot run with Windows 95 Setup.

To solve this problem, users (or their system administrator) can provide setup answers in a setup script, which is a text file that is created before running Setup. Then the user can run Setup from the command prompt using this setup script. Windows 95 Setup will run without requiring additional user input. For more information, see Chapter 5, "Custom, Automated, and Push Installations."

# Beginning Windows 95 Setup and Safe Recovery

As soon as you start Windows 95 Setup, the screen indicates that Setup is being initialized. During this earliest phase, several files needed to run Setup are copied to the local computer, and Setup runs ScanDisk to check the integrity of the hard disk. After Windows 95 Setup completes these activities, the Welcome message shows the estimated time that it will take to complete the process, plus the basic phases of Windows 95 installation.

MSBATCH.INF
[setup]
express=1
bypasses this screen

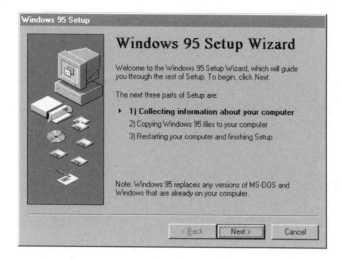

### ▶ To navigate in Windows 95 Setup

- Click the Next or Back buttons on the Setup screens to navigate through choosing installation options.

  Click the Next button to accept the choices you made on the current screen and to continue to the next screen; click the Back button to return to the previous screen to make changes.

If a previous attempt to install Windows 95 has failed, Windows 95 Setup provides an option to use the Safe Recovery feature or to run a full new Setup process. If the Safe Recovery dialog box appears when you start Windows 95 Setup, you should select the Use Safe Recovery option. When you select this option, Windows 95 Setup can use built-in methods to avoid problems that occurred previously.

After you start Safe Recovery, the standard Windows 95 Setup wizard screen appears. For more information about Safe Recovery, see Chapter 6, "Setup Technical Discussion."

MSBATCH.INF
[setup]
express=1
bypasses this screen

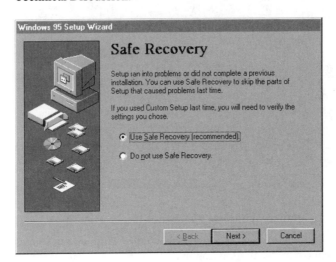

### Technical Note on ScanDisk for Windows 95 Setup

When you run Windows 95 Setup from MS-DOS (rather than Windows), ScanDisk runs in interactive mode. If you choose not to fix errors that ScanDisk finds or if you try to exit before ScanDisk is finished, Setup will not continue. By default, ScanDisk checks all drives, except the A drive if you run Setup from floppy disks.

When you run Windows 95 Setup from Windows 3.x or Windows for Workgroups, Setup runs ScanDisk in a non-interactive mode. If ScanDisk finds errors, Setup asks you to exit Windows and run ScanDisk as a standalone program. If ScanDisk finds only long filenames, Setup allows you to continue. Lost clusters are not detected, nor are mismatched FAT file systems or certain other file system problems.

When you run Windows 95 Setup on a computer with MS-DOS DoubleSpace or DriveSpace compressed drives, ScanDisk treats these as regular compressed volumes and also checks your host volumes. If SSTOR (or any other compression software from another vendor) is in memory, then ScanDisk acts as if it doesn't see any compressed drives and treat all drives as normal FAT drives.

# Running Windows 95 Setup

This section describes the procedures for installing Windows 95 on the hard disk of a computer that is not running a shared copy from a network server. The following series of tasks are described:

- Gathering information
- Analyzing the computer (hardware detection)
- Selecting software components in Custom Setup
- Selecting network components in Custom Setup
- Specifying computer identification
- Changing computer settings in Custom Setup
- Creating a startup disk
- Copying files and completing Setup

# Gathering Information

Most information needed to install Windows 95 is gathered automatically by Windows 95 Setup before you are asked to do anything. The following series of tasks are presented by Windows 95 Setup to guide you through providing the information needed to install and configure the new operating system:

- Choosing the Windows directory
- Selecting the setup type
- Checking disk space for Windows 95

## Choosing the Windows Directory

This option is available for all setup types

If a previous installation of Windows 3.1 or Windows for Workgroups 3.x exists, Windows 95 asks you to confirm the directory where Windows 95 is to be installed. By default, the directory containing the existing Windows installation is selected.

For information about deciding whether to install Windows 95 in a new directory, see "Deciding to Run Setup from MS-DOS or Windows" earlier in this chapter.

> ► **To install Windows 95 in a new directory**

1. Click the Other Directory option, and then click the Next button.

MSBATCH.INF
[setup]
InstallDir=*dirname*
sets this value and
bypasses confirmation

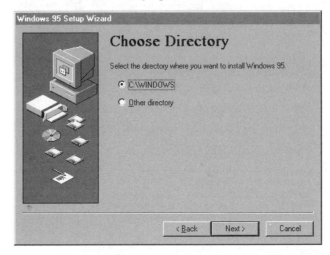

2. Type a new directory name, and then click the Next button.

MSBATCH.INF
[setup]
InstallDir=*dirname*
bypasses this screen

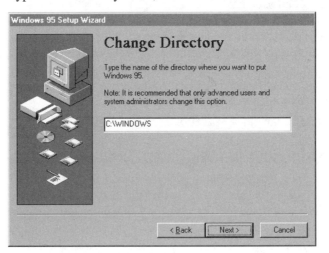

If you choose to install Windows 95 in a new directory, you might need to reinstall Windows-based applications because Windows 95 uses a different method from Windows 3.x for storing configuration information, and because application support files such as DLLs will be missing from the Windows 95 directory. Windows 95 Setup cannot transfer this information automatically.

**Note**   You cannot migrate system settings and groups under Windows 3.1 and Windows for Workgroups 3.x by copying all the .GRP and .INI files into the new installation directory. This does not work with Windows 95, because .GRP files and .INI file entries cannot be used by Windows 95 unless Windows 95 Setup migrates this information to the Registry. You must run Windows 95 Setup and install Windows 95 in the existing Windows directory to migrate .GRP and .INI file information from Windows 3.x.

## Selecting the Type of Setup

Windows 95 Setup asks you to select the type of setup you want. For a description of these options, see "Deciding to Use Typical, Portable, Compact, or Custom Setup" earlier in this chapter. By default, the Typical Setup option is selected.

MSBATCH.INF
[setup]
express=1
bypasses this screen;

InstallType=0, 1, 2, or 3 selects Compact, Typical, Portable, or Custom, respectively

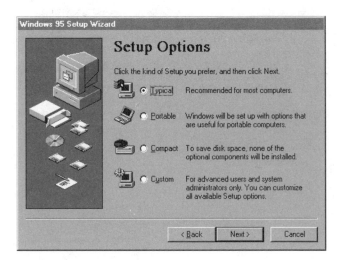

▶   **To specify Custom Setup**

- In the Setup Options screen, click Custom, and then click the Next button.

## Checking Disk Space for Windows 95

After you select the directory for Windows 95, Setup checks the hard disk, prepares the directory, and verifies that there is enough free disk space for Windows 95. If there is insufficient space on the destination drive, Windows 95 Setup warns you about the lack of space, and displays the minimum and complete installation space requirements.

If Windows 95 Setup detects that there is insufficient disk space for a normal upgrade of an existing version of Windows, you can choose to install a compact configuration of Windows 95. If you continue even though there is insufficient disk space, the installation might be incomplete. If Setup runs out of disk space, it stops and displays an error message; you must free additional disk space and then run Setup again.

## Providing User Information

This option is available for all setup types

The information requested during this part of Setup is required, no matter what setup type you specified.

After completing the disk-space check, Windows 95 Setup asks you to type your name and company name, which Windows 95 uses to identify you for various operations. You must type and verify a response for Setup to continue.

MSBATCH.INF
[NameAndOrg]
name=value
org=company
sets these values;
display=0
bypasses displaying
this screen

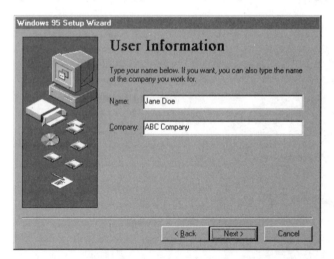

Windows 95 Setup next requests a product identification number. You must type and verify a response for Setup to continue. The Product ID dialog box might not appear if you are installing Windows 95 from the network, depending on the requirements at your site. The product ID number can be found on your Windows 95 disks or your Certificate of Authenticity.

# Analyzing the Computer

This option is available for all setup types

After you complete the user information, Windows 95 Setup prepares for the hardware detection phase. Setup can search automatically for all basic system components such as disk drives and controllers, display devices, pointing devices, and keyboards.

For Typical Setup, you can choose to skip detection for certain hardware, such as CD-ROM or multimedia devices, depending on what Setup finds during its safe-detection examination of the hardware. If Setup proposes to skip detection of certain hardware, but you know that these types of devices are attached to the computer, you can override the suggestion and have Setup detect the devices. Otherwise, skipping detection for the devices as suggested by Setup saves time during installation.

For Custom Setup, you can specify whether you want Setup to skip detecting any specific devices attached to your computer. Usually, you should let Setup detect the hardware unless you know that the computer contains devices that cause problems during hardware detection. For example, you should skip detection of a particular device if Setup failed previously while detecting that device and if Safe Recovery does not automatically skip detecting that device when you run Setup again.

For information about specific device types supported in Windows 95, see the Manufacturers and Models lists in the Add New Hardware wizard, and see the Windows 95 README.TXT and SETUP.TXT files.

MSBATCH.INF
express=1
bypasses this
screen

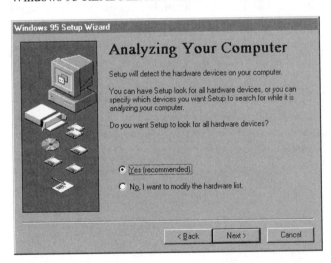

▶ **To have Windows 95 Setup attempt to detect all system hardware**

- On the first Analyzing Your Computer screen, click the Yes option, and then click the Next button.

▶ **To modify the list of hardware to be detected in Custom Setup**

1. On the first Analyzing Your Computer screen, click the option named No, I Want To Modify The Hardware List, and then click the Next button.

   The second Analyzing Your Computer screen appears, containing lists of the components that Windows 95 Setup proposes to detect.

2. To avoid detecting a specific class of hardware, make sure the hardware class is not checked in the Hardware Types list.

   –Or–

   To avoid detecting a specific manufacturer and model of a hardware device (while detecting other devices in that class), make sure the related hardware type is checked, and then make sure the item you want to skip in the Manufacturer And Model list is not checked.

   If a Hardware Type is dimmed (but not checked), then you cannot change how Windows 95 Setup detects that class of hardware.

   ---

   **Note** The list of CD-ROM drives shows only proprietary drives that require special installation consideration. All other CD-ROM drives are detected automatically.

   ---

3. To begin hardware detection, click the Next button, and then click it again.

MSBATCH.INF does not allow you to skip parts of detection

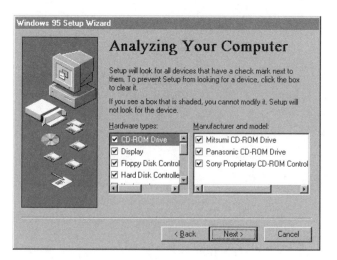

The hardware detection process can take several minutes. The progress indicator shows what portion of hardware detection has been completed. Notice that this is also the point at which Windows 95 Setup can stall if hardware detection fails for a particular system component.

▶ **To continue if Windows 95 Setup stops during hardware detection**

1. Press F3 or click the Cancel button to quit Setup.

   If the computer does not respond to the Cancel button, restart the computer by turning it off and then back on again.

2. Run Setup again.

   Setup prompts you to use Safe Recovery to recover the failed installation.

3. Click Use Safe Recovery, and then click the Next button.

4. Repeat your installation choices.

   Hardware detection runs again, but Setup skips the portion that caused the initial failure.

5. If the computer stops again during the hardware detection process, repeat this procedure until the hardware detection portion of Setup completes successfully.

# Selecting Software Components

If you are running Typical Setup, the following screen appears so that you can specify whether you want to choose the accessories and other software to be installed with Windows 95:

This screen appears
for Typical Setup

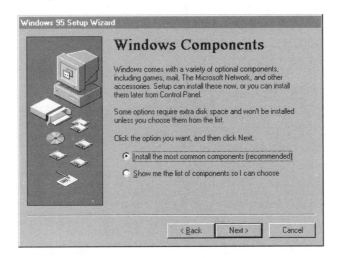

If you choose the option for customizing the list of components to be installed, the Select Components dialog box appears. (For Custom Setup, the Select Components screen appears automatically.) Notice that the Components list includes information about the disk space required for that component.

MSBATCH.INF
[OptionalComponents]
can define the
components to be
installed

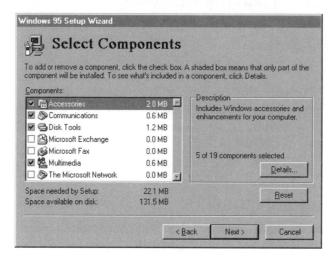

▶ **To change whether any component is installed**

1. In the Components list, select a component category, and then click the Details button.

   A dialog box appears, listing the components in the category.

2. Select the component you want to install, and then click OK.

   ▪ To add a component, make sure the component is checked.

   ▪ To prevent a component from being installed, make sure the component is not checked.

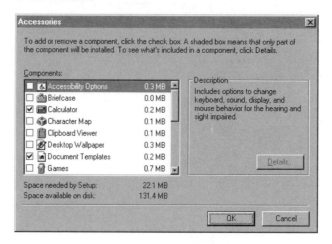

3. Repeat this procedure for each category in the Components list on the Select Component screen.

4. When you are satisfied with your selections, click the Next button.

**Note**  You can install or remove any of these components after Windows 95 is installed by using the Add/Remove Programs option in Control Panel, as described in Chapter 22, "Application Support."

# Selecting Network Components in Custom Setup

This option is available only for Custom Setup

Windows 95 Setup allows you to specify network components and settings. This section summarizes the options for modifying network settings during setup. For information about network support, see Chapter 7, "Introduction to Windows 95 Networking."

**Note**  Windows 95 Setup provides appropriate settings based on hardware and software detection for the network components running when you start Setup. You should accept the default settings unless you know that particular settings need to be changed.

▶ **To remove a network component from the list of components to be installed**

- In the Network Configuration screen, select the component you do not want to install, and then click the Remove button.

MSBATCH.INF
[setup]
network=0
bypasses installing
networking
components;

[network] settings can
define networking
components to be
installed;
display=0
bypasses
this screen

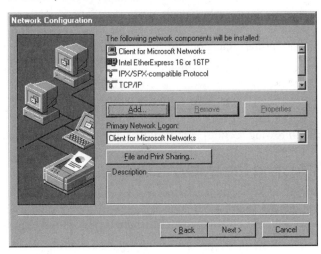

▶  **To add a network component to the list of components to be installed**

1. In the Network Configuration screen, click the Add button.

2. In the Select Network Component Type dialog box, select the type of component you want to add, and then click the Add button.

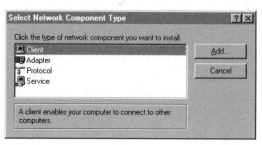

**Note**  If you are installing a real-mode (16-bit) network client from another vendor, the Adapter, Protocol, and Service component types are not available.

3. In the dialog box for the selected component type, select the manufacturer of the component in the Manufacturers list, and then click the appropriate version in the list of models. Click OK.

4. To configure settings for the component you just added, click the component, and then click the Properties button.

**Important**  If your computer is connected to a Windows NT domain, be sure to configure Client for Microsoft Networks to specify the correct domain for logon validation. This ensures that you can log on to your preferred domain and your network printer selections are available automatically.

If you do not specify a domain name when you are installing Windows 95 from source files on the network, Setup might not be able to access required files for completing the final stages of installation.

The following sections summarize each type of network option.

## Selecting the Network Client

If you choose to add a network client, Windows 95 Setup displays a list of supported networks. Windows 95 supports the following network types, although in most cases you also need to use supporting software from the network vendor:

- Microsoft networks, such as Windows NT, Windows for Workgroups, LAN Manager 2.x, or LAN Manager-compatible networks such as IBM LAN Server, or DEC™ PATHWORKS™

- Artisoft® LANtastic® version 5.0 and later
- Banyan® VINES® version 5.52 and later
- Novell NetWare version 3.11 and later
- SunSoft™ PC-NFS® version 5.0 and later

---

**Note**   Artisoft LANtastic cannot be used with a 32-bit, protected-mode networking client such as Client for Microsoft Networks. This client must be installed as the sole network client on the computer.

---

MSBATCH.INF
[network]
clients=*value*
defines this option,
where the value is a
device ID defined in
NETCLI.INF or
NETCLI3.INF

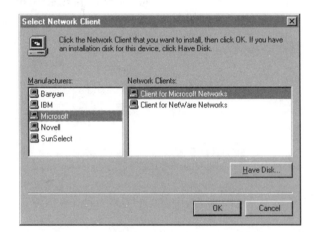

To use Microsoft networking features, you must install Client for Microsoft Networks. For information about configuring this client, see Chapter 8, "Windows 95 on Microsoft Networks." For information about installing and configuring network clients for other kinds of networks, see Chapter 10, "Windows 95 on Other Networks."

To use Windows 95 on a NetWare network, you must install supporting client software, as described in Chapter 9, "Windows 95 on NetWare Networks." If you let Setup automatically install the Microsoft 32-bit, protected-mode Client for NetWare Networks, you can take advantage of automatic reconnection to servers and client-side caching for network information, in addition to the improved performance of the protected-mode networking components.

## Selecting and Configuring a Network Adapter

Windows 95 supports multiple network adapters (also called network interface cards, or NICs) in a manner similar to Windows for Workgroups 3.11—that is, up to four network adapters can be supported in a single computer.

Network detection automatically determines the type of network adapter and its required resource settings. This is always the recommended method for configuring network adapters.

If you choose to add a network adapter, Windows 95 displays a list of supported network adapters. For information about technical issues for network adapters, see Chapter 12, "Network Technical Discussion."

MSBATCH.INF
[network]
netcards=*value*
defines this option,
where the value is a
device ID defined in
the related INF file

In most cases,
network detection is
the best method for
installing network
adapters

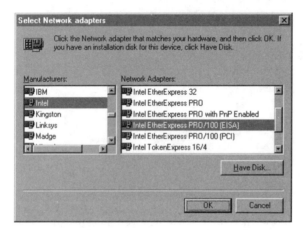

## Selecting and Configuring the Network Protocols

Windows 95 Setup automatically installs the appropriate protocol for the network client you select. Microsoft provides 32-bit, protected-mode versions of these protocols:

- IPX/SPX-compatible protocol
- Microsoft NetBEUI
- Microsoft TCP/IP

Protocols to support other network clients are also provided with Windows 95. For information about the three principal network protocols, see Chapter 12, "Network Technical Discussion."

MSBATCH.INF
[network]
protocols=*value*
defines this option,
where the value is a
device ID defined in
NETTRANS.INF

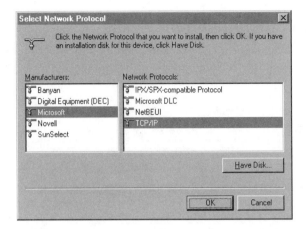

## Selecting and Configuring a Network Service

Network services provide additional networking support. Microsoft provides several supporting network services for Windows 95. Services included on the Windows 95 installation disks include peer resource sharing services (File and Printer Sharing for NetWare Networks or File and Printer Sharing for Microsoft Networks). These services allow other computers on the network to share file, printer, and CD-ROM resources on this computer. For more information about installing, configuring, and using these services, see Chapter 11, "Logon, Browsing, and Resource Sharing."

MSBATCH.INF
[network]
services=*value*
defines this option,
where the value is a
device ID defined in
the related INF file

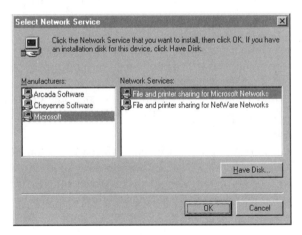

Additional network services, such as backup agents, a Simple Network Management Protocol (SNMP) agent, the Microsoft Remote Registry agent, are also provided on the Windows 95 compact disc in the ADMIN directory, as described in Chapter 16, "Remote Administration."

# Specifying Computer Identification

The Identification screen allows you to specify how the computer is identified on the network. This option is available for all setup option types on networked computers.

MSBATCH.INF
[network]
computername=*value*
workgroup=*value*
description=*value*
define these options

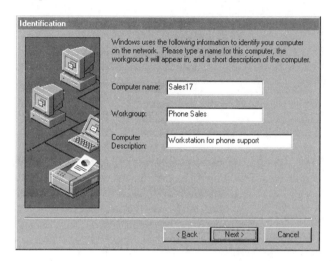

- The computer name must be unique on the network, and can be up to 15 characters long with no spaces (no blank characters). The name can contain only alphanumeric characters and the following special characters:

  ! @ # $ % ^ & ( ) - _ ' { } . ~

- The workgroup name can be up to 15 characters long and uses the same naming convention as the computer name. The workgroup is used to associate groups of computers together for more efficient browsing. The network administrator can provide guidelines for workgroup selection by using WRKGRP.INI, as described in Chapter 5, "Custom, Automated, and Push Installations."

- The computer description can be up to 48 characters long, but it cannot contain any commas (,). This text appears as a comment next to the computer name when users are browsing the network, so you can use it to describe the department or location of the computer, or the type of shared information.

# Changing Computer Settings in Custom Setup

This option is
available only for
Custom Setup

Windows 95 Setup detects the hardware in the computer and determines
appropriate default values for configuring the hardware. Usually, you should
accept the values determined through hardware detection, unless you know
that a manual setting must be supplied.

---

**Note**   You can select options in the Computer Settings screen for Advanced Power
Management (an option on some portable computers), Regional Settings (the local
language preference), and Windows User Interface (Windows 95 versus Program
Manager). You can also add multilanguage support for Eastern European, Greek,
or Cyrillic languages if you are installing an English or Western European version
of Windows 95.

---

▶   **To configure system hardware options**

1.  In the Computer Settings screen, click the item in the list you want to change,
    and then click the Change button.

MSBATCH.INF
[system] entries
define these options;
display=0
bypasses this screen

[setup]
express=1 also
bypasses this screen

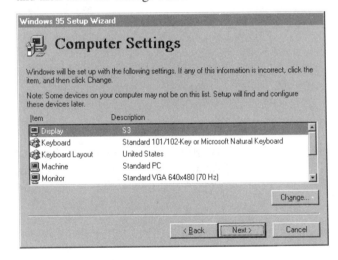

The Select Device dialog box appears. A list displays the models that are identified as compatible for the hardware detected in your computer.

MSBATCH.INF
[system]
display=*value*
defines this option;
the value is a section
name in that device's
INF file

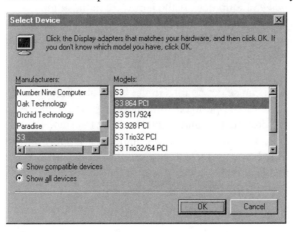

2. In the Select Device dialog box, select the model name that matches your device.

   –Or–

   If you want to display all possible entries for the selected device category, click the Show All Devices option, and then select the model that matches your device.

3. Click OK. For information about configuring a device, see Chapter 19, "Devices."

The following chapters provide information about changing specific hardware settings. You use the same procedures during Custom Setup to change settings as are used after Windows 95 is installed.

| To change this device setting | See this chapter |
| --- | --- |
| Display, mouse, and COM ports | Chapter 19, "Devices" |
| Network adapter | Chapter 12, "Network Technical Discussion" |
| Keyboard | Chapter 34, "International Windows 95" |

If Windows 95 does not have a new driver for your display adapter when upgrading over a previous version of Windows, it reports it as Standard Display Adapter (VGA) in the Computer Settings list. Later, Windows 95 displays a message stating that your display driver is invalid; however, you can select your Windows 3.1 driver from the list and continue. Although you can install Windows 3.1 display drivers , Microsoft recommends that you upgrade to Windows 95 drivers wherever possible for improved performance and reliability. For information, see Chapter 19, "Devices."

# Creating a Startup Disk

This option is
available for all
setup types

In the Startup Disk screen, Windows 95 Setup offers to create an emergency
startup disk that contains basic system files. You can use this disk to start
Windows 95 when you cannot start the operating system from the hard disk.
Creating the startup disk is the default option, but you can choose to bypass
this step.

**Important**  It is strongly recommended that you create a startup disk during
Windows 95 Setup. If you want to create a startup disk later, you can use the
Add/Remove Programs option in Control Panel to create one.

MSBATCH.INF
[setup]
EBD=1
forces creation of a
startup disk

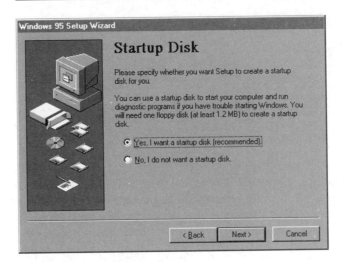

▶ **To create a startup disk**

- Click the option named Yes, I Want A Startup Disk, and then click the Next
  button.

# Copying Files and Completing Setup

After hardware detection is complete and Windows 95 Setup has obtained all required information, the next phase of Windows 95 Setup begins. During this phase, the Windows 95 files are copied to the destination drive and directory.

MSBATCH.INF
[setup]
express=1
bypasses this screen

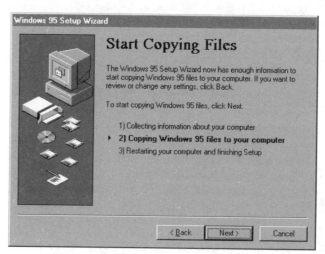

If you chose to have Windows 95 Setup create a startup disk, Setup asks you to insert a floppy disk into drive A. The disk does not need to be formatted or empty, but any information you have stored on the disk will be permanently deleted. After you insert the disk, click OK to create the startup disk. Windows 95 Setup formats the disk and copies the appropriate files.

When the basic installation steps are completed, Windows 95 Setup asks you to remove any disks from the floppy disk drives. After you click OK, the computer is restarted, and the final phase of the installation process begins, which includes converting Windows Program Manager groups and migrating various system configuration settings to the Registry.

Near the end of the installation process, Windows 95 Setup asks you to complete several configuration options. These configuration options are referred to as Run-Once options, because after you have completed the installation steps for these options, that particular set of activities is not repeated again when you choose the related option in Control Panel. Some Run-Once installation procedures are described in the following sections.

For more information about this phase, see Chapter 6, "Setup Technical Discussion."

## Setting the Local Time Zone

Setup prompts you to set the time zone for your location. This is an important step for network computers that need to keep time stamps synchronized.

▶ **To configure the local time zone**

- Click your location on the map.

  –Or–

  Select your time zone from the list.

MSBATCH.INF
[install]
timezone=*string*
defines this option

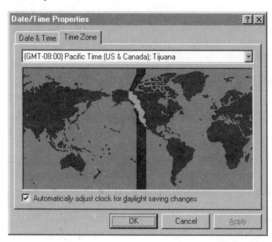

## Installing and Configuring a Printer

If you are installing Windows 95 in a new directory or on a computer that did not have a previous version of Windows, Windows 95 Setup automatically runs the Add Printer wizard the first time that Windows 95 is started after the basic installation is complete.

MSBATCH.INF
[Printers]
*printer=driver,port*
defines this option

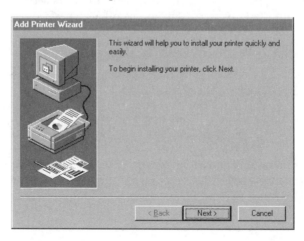

▶ **To configure a printer during Windows 95 Setup**

- In the Add Printers wizard, click Next and follow the instructions on the screen.

  –Or–

  Click Cancel if you do not want to install a printer.

If you want to install or change a printer after Windows 95 is installed, double-click the Printers folder in My Computer. For information about installing and managing printers in Windows 95, see Chapter 23, "Printing and Fonts."

If you are installing Windows 95 in the same directory as an earlier version of Windows, then your previous printer configuration is incorporated into Windows 95 and the wizard for installing printers does not run during Setup.

## Configuring Microsoft Exchange

During the final stages of Windows 95 Setup, the Inbox Setup wizard runs automatically if you selected Microsoft Exchange in the Select Components screen.

If the administrator has already created a postoffice, added users to it, and shared it with all users on the network, the postoffice name and location appear in the dialog box automatically without requiring you to type this information. This makes setting up the Microsoft Exchange client with the Microsoft Mail workgroup postoffice easy for all users in the workgroup. For information about setting up a Microsoft Mail workgroup postoffice, see Chapter 26, "Electronic Mail and Microsoft Exchange."

▶ **To configure the Microsoft Exchange client**

1. When the Inbox Setup wizard appears, follow the instructions on the screen for configuring the Microsoft Exchange client on your computer.

2. If you also selected Microsoft Mail Services in addition to Microsoft Exchange, the wizard prompts you for the path name for the postoffice location, your Microsoft Mail user name, and Microsoft Mail password.

## Completing Windows 95 Setup

Depending on the options you selected during Setup, the hardware devices you have, or the computer you have, additional Run-Once options might need to be completed, such as the wizard for configuring MIDI devices. After all the Run-Once options are completed, all of the files are installed, and the computer is configured to run your applications.

For technical information about initializing the operating system at the completion of Setup and for a detailed description of the system startup process, see Chapter 6, "Setup Technical Discussion."

C H A P T E R   4

# Server-Based Setup for
# Windows 95

This chapter provides information about the Server-based Setup program, which is used to install Windows 95 source files on a server, and to prepare for installing Windows 95 to run as a shared copy on client computers.

**In This Chapter**

Server-Based Setup: The Basics   106
Server-Based Setup: The Issues   107
   Planning for Machine Directories   108
   Planning for Shared Installations   110
Server-Based Setup: An Overview   113
Task 1: Copying Windows 95 Files to a Server   114
   Selecting the Server   116
   Setting the Destination Path and Installation Policy   117
   Creating a Default Setup Script   119
   Installing Files on the Server   120
Task 2: Creating Machine Directories   122
Installing Windows 95 for Shared Installations   124
Configuring Shared Installations   126
   Configuring Shared Installations for Protected-Mode Clients   126
   Configuring Shared Installations for Real-Mode Clients   134
   Creating the Disk Image for RIPL   135
Technical Notes for Shared Installations   139
   System Startup and Networking for Shared Installations   139
   Technical Notes on MACHINES.INI and SETMDIR   140
   Other Notes on Shared Installations   142

# Server-Based Setup: The Basics

Server-based Setup (NETSETUP.EXE) is used to prepare the server to run Windows 95 Setup (SETUP.EXE) on network client computers. Windows 95 provides improved support over Windows 3.x for installing and running a shared copy of Windows 95 (that is, "shared installations"). After installing Windows 95 source files on a server, Server-based Setup can be used to create and manage machine directories, which contain the specific configuration information for each computer on a shared installation. You can also use Server-based Setup to create setup scripts (which are batch files for automated setup), as described in Chapter 5, "Custom, Automated, and Push Installations." Windows 95 supports the following kinds of shared installations:

- Computers that start from the local hard disk and then run a shared copy of Windows 95 from the server.

- Computers that start locally from a floppy disk and then run a shared copy of Windows 95 from the server.

- Diskless workstations that remote boot (sometimes called RIPL or remote IPL) from servers and run a shared copy of Windows 95.

    At the time of the release of Windows 95, the remote-boot option can be used only for diskless workstations on Novell® NetWare® version 3.x and 4.0 networks. Support for remote boot of Windows 95 workstations will be available in upcoming releases of Windows NT. For information about Windows NT support, contact your sales support representative.

Server-based Setup replaces the Administrative Setup process used for Windows 3.x and Windows for Workgroups. The following table compares the actions required on older versions of Windows to the Windows 95 methods.

**Methods for Creating Network-based Setup and Shared Installations**

| Windows for Workgroups | Windows 95 |
|---|---|
| Run **setup /a** to create a Windows distribution directory on the network | Run Server-based Setup under Windows 95 (**netsetup**) |
| Customize INF files for system, desktop, applications, and Program Manager | Create a setup script in MSBATCH.INF format |
| For shared installations, create network directories and configure shared files | Included automatically as part of Server-based Setup |
| For shared installations, create correct configuration files and startup disks for each workstation to define settings for MS-DOS, Windows, and networking software | Included automatically as part of the setup script and Windows 95 Setup |
| Run **setup /n** on each workstation | Run Windows 95 Setup with setup script (**setup** *msbatch.inf*) |

When you use Server-based Setup to create shared installations for computers that start from a floppy disk or for remote-boot workstations that use a disk image on a server, you need to run Setup only once for each type of computer. Server-based Setup can create machine directories for the other similar computers. So you only have to make copies of the startup disk (either the floppy disk or the boot image).

Therefore, for example, for shared installations of Windows for Workgroups on remote-boot workstations, users simply restart their workstations to upgrade to Windows 95. For upgrading shared installations that start from floppy disks, users can upgrade by simply restarting their computers with the new startup disk.

# Server-Based Setup: The Issues

The Server-based Setup program is available only on the Windows 95 compact disc in the ADMIN\NETTOOLS\NETSETUP directory. Server-based Setup is not provided on the Windows 95 floppy distribution disks.

---

**Important**   Server-based Setup can be run only from a computer running Windows 95.

You cannot run Server-based Setup from Windows 3.1, Windows for Workgroups, Windows NT, or MS-DOS.

---

Typically, shared installations are used where there might be users who need to access various computers for tasks such as point-of-sale data entry. Shared installations are also typically used on enterprise networks with many thousands of similar computers.

The most important consideration in deciding how to run Windows 95 in the corporate environment is the current configuration for workstations running Windows 3.x. If the largest portion of workstations currently run shared Windows, then the upgrade process is straightforward if you continue to use a shared configuration. If you decide to change a workstation to run Windows 95 from the local hard disk, applications must be reinstalled and desktop settings reconfigured in addition to installing the new operating system.

The basic benefits of installing Windows 95 on the local hard disk of a computer include the following:

- Performance is superior

- Less network traffic is generated

- The system can start and continue running if the server is not available

- The user has more freedom to customize the system, if system policies don't restrict this

The benefits of a shared installation include the following:

- Little or no hard disk space is required on the local computer
- Updating drivers for multiple computers is easier
- The workstation is more secure and operation is safer for novice users, because network logon is required and access to system files is limited (although you can use system policies to enforce the same restrictions for local installations)

Although an entirely shared configuration makes it easy to maintain the system, a shared configuration also means more network traffic and requires larger servers.

The following sections provide some guidelines and summary information for planning the installation process for computers that will run a shared copy of Windows 95. This information supplements that planning and implementation information presented in Part 1, "Deployment Planning Guide."

# Planning for Machine Directories

For a shared installation on each computer that starts from a floppy disk or a remote-boot disk image, the machine directory is a required network directory that contains the particular files required for that specific configuration. The machine directory contains WIN.COM, the full Registry, and startup configuration files such as SYSTEM.INI.

Both Windows 95 Setup and Server-based Setup can create machine directories automatically, as described in "Task 2: Creating Machine Directories" later in this chapter. For shared installations for floppy disk-based and remote-boot workstations, you need to run Windows 95 Setup only once for each type of computer configuration. Then you can use Server-based Setup to create machine directories for other computers. You can replicate the startup disks (or boot images) for other computers of the same type.

For computers that start from the hard disk, machine directories are optional; however, you must run Windows 95 Setup on each computer that has a hard disk, even if the computer will use a machine directory on the network.

The machine directory is for computer-specific settings. This is different from the individual user directories on Windows NT networks or the individual Mail directories on NetWare networks, which contain user-specific files such as login scripts or user profiles for individual users. Using machine directories offers several benefits:

- Computer-specific settings are saved in a central location, rather than with user-specific settings. So the correct configuration is available for the particular computer, no matter which user logs on.
- A single boot image on the network (or single version of the floppy startup disk) can be used to start several computers.
- The administrator can easily create and replicate shared Windows 95 installations for new computers from a central location, often without having to run Windows 95 Setup repeatedly.

Windows 95 files for a shared installation are stored in the locations described in the following table.

| File location | Description |
| --- | --- |
| Startup disk | Contains the real-mode software necessary to start the computer and connect to the shared Windows directory, including the mini Registry used to start the computer. The startup disk for a shared installation can be a local hard disk, a floppy disk, or a remote-boot disk image stored on a server. |
| Machine directory | Contains files specific to a particular computer (not a particular user), including the full Registry. This also includes the default USER.DAT file, which is updated with the user's personal USER.DAT if user profiles are enabled on the network. The machine directory can exist on any shared network resource. Machine directories must exist on the network for computers that start from a floppy disk or for remote-boot workstations, and are created locally by default for shared installations on computers that have hard disks. |
| Shared Windows 95 directory on a server | Contains all the shared Windows 95 files. This directory is marked read-only automatically during installation of the source files. |

# Planning for Shared Installations

This section summarizes some technical issues related to shared installations of Windows 95.

**Technical issues for all network clients on shared installations.** Network logon is required before running Windows 95 on shared installations, because network connectivity is required before Windows 95 can run across the network. This can be a generic logon, rather than specific user logon. For more information, see "Configuring Shared Installations" later in this chapter.

- One Windows 95 software license is required for each computer that will run Windows 95.

- Because most or all of the Windows 95 files are located on the server for shared installations, loading the shared Windows 95 components increases network traffic.

- Each client computer must use all 32-bit, protected-mode networking components or all 16-bit, real-mode components, not a combination of real-mode and protected-mode components.

---

**Important** After Windows 95 installation is complete, all path statements in login scripts must specify Windows 95 locations, and not Windows 3.x or MS-DOS. Make sure that **path** variables are set correctly in login scripts to avoid unexpected behavior.

---

**Technical issues for Microsoft protected-mode clients.** These issues are important in your planning for shared installations that use Microsoft Client for NetWare Networks or Client for Microsoft Networks:

- Each client computer must use all 32-bit, protected-mode networking components. For example, a computer running a shared installation cannot run a network client such as Microsoft Client for NetWare Networks using ODI network adapter drivers.

- Real-mode components are required for the first connection to the network during system startup. Microsoft TCP/IP in Windows 95 runs only in protected mode, so the computer must load an IPX/SPX or NetBEUI protocol to make the real-mode connection to the network. After the system loads and switches to protected mode, then Microsoft TCP/IP can be used. Real-mode versions of NetBEUI and IPX/SPX-compatible protocols are built into the real-mode software that is used to make the first connection to the server before Windows 95 starts.

- You cannot use existing NDIS 2.x or ODI drivers to support protected-mode networking clients. For either Client for NetWare Networks or Client for Microsoft Networks, the network adapter must have an NDIS 3.1 driver (although an NDIS 2 driver is used for the first connection to the server during system startup).

- For protected-mode network clients, you cannot use a PCI or EISA network adapter for system startup over the network. This is because PCI and EISA network adapters do not start until the second booting of Windows 95. For shared installations, the adapter must start on the first boot.

---

**Note**  If a computer has an IBM 16/4 token-ring adapter and has been using ODI drivers, Windows 95 Setup uses the existing ODI driver by default. To use this adapter with a 32-bit, protected-mode network client, you must remove the existing ODI driver and replace it with the Windows 95 NDIS 3.1 driver for the IBM 16/4 token-ring adapter. For information about the specific statements for installing the NDIS 3.1 driver for this adapter as part of a setup script, see Appendix D, "MSBATCH.INF Parameters."

---

**Technical issues for other network clients.**  Client computers can run a shared copy of Windows 95 from a server using real-mode network software other than the Microsoft real-mode networking software used for system startup. However, computers that don't use the Microsoft real-mode network software for system startup cannot use protected-mode network clients (such as Client for Microsoft Networks or Client for NetWare Networks).

**Shared installation requirements.**  Server-based Setup operates on one server at a time. You specify a particular server where Windows 95 files are to be installed and where related machine directories will be created for shared installations.

However, the machine directories do not need to be created on the same server where the Windows 95 files are installed. In fact, to balance the network load, you might prefer to designate specific servers to maintain the Windows 95 source files, and other servers to contain the machine directories and login scripts. Typically, you need to make Windows 95 source files available from multiple servers, both to provide fault tolerance and to reduce network traffic.

On the server, 90 MB of hard disk space is required for the Windows 95 source files. The following summarizes the disk space required for each machine directory on a shared installation, not including the swap file space requirements.

**Disk Space Requirements for Server and Local Hard Disks**

| Startup type | Local disk space | Server disk space |
|---|---|---|
| Local hard-disk startup, local Windows 95 | 20 MB | 0 |
| Local hard-disk startup, Windows 95 on a server[1] | 2 MB (1 MB) | 1.5 MB (optional) |
| Floppy-disk startup, Windows 95 on a server | 1.2 MB floppy drive | 2 MB |
| Remote-boot startup, Windows 95 on a server | 0 | 2 MB |

[1] If this configuration uses a machine directory on a server, only the Registry and basic files are local.

The following table summarizes the memory requirements for client computers running Windows 95.

**Recommended Client System Configuration for Windows 95**

| Startup type | Protected-mode[1] RAM | Real-mode[2] RAM |
|---|---|---|
| Local hard-disk startup, local Windows 95 | 8 MB (4 MB)[3] | 8 MB (4 MB) |
| Local hard-disk startup, Windows 95 on a server | 8 MB (4 MB) | 8 MB (4 MB) |
| Floppy-disk startup, Windows 95 on a server | 8 MB (4 MB) | 8 MB (4 MB) |
| Remote-boot startup, Windows 95 on a server | 8 MB (6 MB) | 8 MB (4 MB) |

[1] Microsoft Client for NetWare Networks or Client for Microsoft Networks.

[2] For example, Novell NetWare NETX real-mode client.

[3] The first number indicates recommended memory; the second value is the minimum requirement.

**Swap file requirements for shared installations.**  By default, the swap file for a shared installation is stored in the machine directory. For floppy-disk and remote-boot computers, this means that all paging occurs across the network. If computers configured for floppy-disk or remote-boot startup have hard disks, you will see noticeable performance improvements as the swap file is placed on the hard disk.

To change the location for the swap file, add the entry **pagingfile=c:\win386.swp** in the [386Enh] section of the SYSTEM.INI file stored in the machine directory. You can add this setting automatically using an [Install] section in the setup script, as described in Appendix D, "MSBATCH.INF Parameters."

The swap file size requirements vary, depending on the amount of RAM in the client computer, the number and kinds of applications that are run, and other factors. For guidelines on swap file size, see Chapter 17, "Performance Tuning."

# Server-Based Setup: An Overview

To install Windows 95 source files on the network and create setup scripts, you must run Server-based Setup under Windows 95, and follow the instructions to do the following:

- Copy the Windows 95 source files onto the server, as described in "Task 1: Copying Windows 95 Files to a Server" later in this chapter.

  This is the only step required to make Windows 95 source files available for running Windows 95 Setup from a network source.

- For shared installations, create a machine directory for each computer, as described in "Task 2: Creating Machine Directories" later in this chapter. This step is required for floppy disk-based and remote-boot installations. For computers that start from the hard disk, you must run Windows 95 Setup on each computer, even if the computer will use a machine directory on the network.

- Create setup scripts for automated installation of Windows 95 on client computers, as described in Chapter 5, "Custom, Automated, and Push Installations."

The following illustration summarizes the main tasks that are performed using Server-based Setup.

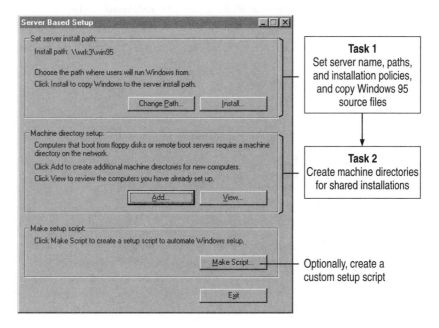

After you have completed these preliminary tasks, you can run Windows 95 Setup to complete the installation, as described in "Installing Windows 95 for Shared Installations" later in this chapter.

---

**Note**  Run Windows 95 Setup from the directory where SETUP.EXE is stored.

In Windows 3.x, you had to switch to the directory you were setting up before running **setup /n**. This is no longer necessary in Windows 95.

---

The files that make up Server-based Setup are uncompressed files in the ADMIN\NETTOOLS\NETSETUP directory on the Windows 95 compact disc. The program can be run directly from the compact disc, which is the recommended method.

# Task 1: Copying Windows 95 Files to a Server

To place the Windows 95 source files on a server, you must run the Server-based Setup program. Using **netsetup** replaces the **setup /a** method used for Windows 3.x and Windows for Workgroups.

---

**Note**  The procedures for Task 1 are the only steps you need to complete if you want to place Windows 95 source files on a server for installation on computers that will run Windows 95 from their local hard disks.

---

You can install the source files for shared Windows 95 installation on one of the following networks:

- Banyan® VINES® 5.52
- Microsoft Windows NT Server
- Novell NetWare 3.x and 4.x

You can also place the Windows 95 source files on servers for installing Windows 95 locally on the following kinds of networks:

- Artisoft® LANtastic® 5.x
- DEC™ PATHWORKS™
- IBM® OS/2® LAN Server 1.2 or greater
- Microsoft LAN Manager 2.x
- Microsoft Windows 95 peer server (for Microsoft or NetWare networks)
- SunSoft™ PC-NFS® 5.0

▶ **To get ready to copy Windows 95 source files on to a server**

- From the network administrator's computer, log on to the network file server where you will place the Windows 95 source files.

  Make sure you log on with security privileges that allow you to create directories and copy files on the network file server.

▶ **To run Server-based Setup**

1. Run Windows 95.

2. Insert the Windows 95 compact disc in the CD-ROM drive, and make sure that it is the active drive. Then switch to the ADMIN\NETTOOLS\NETSETUP directory.

3. In Windows Explorer, double-click NETSETUP.EXE.

   The Server-Based Setup dialog box appears so that you can begin installing source files and other tasks.

The Server-Based Setup dialog box shows the currently selected server where source files are to be installed.

The following procedure summarizes the steps for installing source files using Server-based Setup. The following sections provide details about the steps required to set up the server.

▶ **To install Windows 95 source files on a server**

1. In the Server-Based Setup dialog box, click the Set Path button, and then specify the server path. Then click OK.

   The button name becomes Change Path if a server path was defined previously.

2. Click Install. Server-based Setup presents a series of dialog boxes so that you can complete these actions:

   - Set the server path where the source files are to be installed

   - Specify how users can install Windows 95 from the server—on a local hard disk, as a shared copy, or as the user chooses

   - Install Windows 95 source files in the shared directory you specify

   - Specify whether you want to create a default setup script, and then define the settings in the script, if you choose to create one

   - Provide a CD Key number for product identification

---

**Tip**  After installing the Windows 95 source files in a network directory, make sure to copy any required VxDs or DLLs from other vendors into the appropriate Windows 95 subdirectory on the server. For information, see Chapter 5, "Custom, Automated, and Push Installations."

---

# Selecting the Server

In the Server-Based Setup dialog box, the Set Server Install Path box shows the mapped drive or the UNC path for the selected server.

▶ **To define the path where source files will be installed**

1. In the Server-Based Setup dialog box, click Set Path (or Change Path, if a path has already been set).

2. In the Server Path dialog box, type the drive letter for a mapped drive or the UNC path to the server where you want to install Windows 95 source files. Then click OK.

   For example, if the server where you want to install the files is named NWSVR1 and the share is WIN95SRC, type:

   ```
   \\nwsvr1\win95src
   ```

   Notice that you can specify a UNC path for a NetWare server if you are already attached to that server.

If you specify a subdirectory on the server and that directory does not already exist, Server-based Setup asks if you want to create the directory, and then completes this action if you confirm the message.

If you have insufficient privileges for connecting to or creating a directory on the specified server, a message warns you. You can specify another server, or quit Server-based Setup and log on using an account that has sufficient privileges on the specified server.

When Server-based Setup is set to a new path, it looks for the Registry file (NETSETUP.POL) that it uses to track which computers have been set up. Each time you use Server-based Setup to create a machine directory, an entry is added to this file. No entry is added when a user runs Windows 95 Setup from that shared directory.

---

**Note**  NETSETUP.POL is read only by Server-based Setup to create MSBATCH.INF. You cannot run System Policy Editor to read or modify NETSETUP.POL. Also, you cannot edit MSBATCH.INF using Server-based Setup; you must edit setup scripts using a text editor.

---

# Setting the Destination Path and Installation Policy

After you set the server name, you can install the Windows 95 source files on that server. You must specify the source and destination paths for copying the source files, and set the installation policy that specifies whether users running Windows 95 Setup from this server are installing Windows 95 to run from their local hard disk or are preparing to run a shared copy from the server.

▶  **To set the destination path and installation policy for a server**

1.  In the first Server-Based Setup dialog box, click the Install button to display the Source Path dialog box.

    Server-based Setup stores the settings made in this dialog box in the default MSBATCH.INF file created as part of the Server-based Setup process.

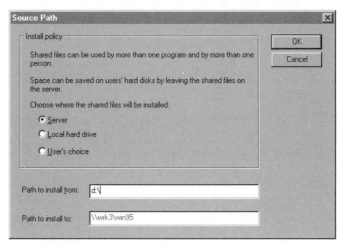

2. Select an installation policy option as described in the following table.

| Installation policy | Resulting installation capability |
|---|---|
| Server | Allows only shared installation of Windows 95. Select this option if the source files on this server are to be used by client computers to run a shared copy of Windows 95. |
| Local Hard Disk | Allows installation only on a local hard disk. Select this option if all Windows 95 files are to be stored on each computer's local hard disk. |
| User's Choice | Prompts the user to specify either shared or local installation. Select this option if you are allowing users to choose whether to run a shared installation, or if you are using setup scripts to install different types of installations using the same source files. |

If you select either User's Choice or Local Hard disk, you will not be prompted to specify machine directories. If you do not define machine directories, Setup will use a default machine directory. For information about creating machine directories, see "Task 2: Creating Machine Directories" later in this chapter.

3. In the Path To Install From box, type the path for the source of the Windows 95 distribution files.

The first time you install the source files, this is the path to the CD-ROM drive and directory that contains the source files on the Windows 95 compact disc.

If you subsequently install source files on other servers, you can specify the path to a network directory that contains the Windows 95 source files.

4. In the Path To Install To box, type the path to the directory where the Windows 95 source files are to be installed.

This must be a directory on the selected server where you want to copy the source files. (Server-based Setup will create the directory if it does not already exist on the server.)

For both Path boxes, you can either type a drive and directory path or specify a UNC path name.

5. Click OK to continue to the next part of Server-based Setup.

# Creating a Default Setup Script

Server-based Setup can create a default setup script automatically by storing the setup options you specify in an MSBATCH.INF file that is placed with the Windows 95 source files on the server. This default setup script can be used to install Windows 95 on individual computers, or it can be used as a template to create other versions of the setup script.

This section summarizes the procedural steps related to creating a default script while installing Windows 95 source files on a server. For information about making a script based on choosing the Make Script button in the Server-Based Setup dialog box, see Chapter 5, "Custom, Automated, and Push Installations." For information about the specific settings in MSBATCH.INF, see Appendix D, "MSBATCH.INF Parameters."

When you click OK in the Source Path dialog box after specifying the destination path and installation policy option, Server-based Setup automatically prompts you to specify whether a default setup script should be created. If you choose to create a default script, it will be saved as MSBATCH.INF on the server.

The decision about whether to create a default setup script depends on the following:

- Principally, whether you want to control installation settings for users who install Windows 95 from this server

- Whether you want to use the default settings to create custom scripts

- Whether you previously created a setup script and do not require a new default script

▶ **To continue with Server-based Setup without creating a default script**

- In the Source Path dialog box, click OK. Then, in the Create Default dialog box, click the Don't Create Default button to begin installing Windows 95 source files on the server.

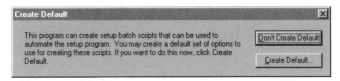

▶ **To create a default script for automating Windows 95 Setup**

1. In the Create Default dialog box, click the Create Default button.

   Server-based Setup displays the SBS Default Policies page for creating an MSBATCH.INF file that contains the specific configuration settings.

2. Click options to check all the components you want to define in the setup script and, where required, type values in the Settings box. After you have defined all components for the script, click OK.

   For information about the values defined in the setup script, see Appendix D, "MSBATCH.INF Parameters."

Some options require that you select or type additional information in the Settings box at the bottom of this dialog box.

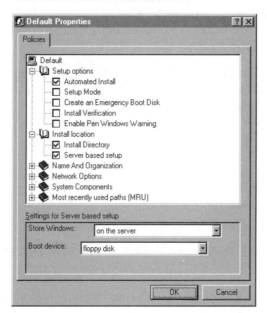

Notice that although Server-based Setup uses the System Policy Editor user interface, this procedure does not create system policies. Only a setup script is created.

# Installing Files on the Server

After you complete all choices for a default setup script, Server-based Setup prompts you to supply the CD Key identification number. You can find the 10-digit CD Key number on the yellow sticker on the Windows 95 compact disc case.

When Server-based Setup has all the information it needs, it installs Windows 95 source files on the selected server, performing the following tasks:

- Windows 95 source files are copied to the server, using the same hierarchical directory structure used when files are copied to the hard disk.

- An MSBATCH.INF file is created on the server, based on the default computer settings. This setup script is used whenever users run Windows 95 Setup from the shared directory on the server without specifying the filename for another setup script.

When Server-based Setup is finished, the server should have the following directory structure (rather than the flat directory structure created by the Windows 3.x **setup /a** command):

```
destination directory
    Command
    Config
    Cursors
    Fonts
    Inf
    Media
    Progra~1
        Access~1
        Themic~1
        Micros~1
    Shellnew
    System
        Color
        Iosubsys
        Viewers
        Vmm32
```

**Note**  Windows 95 source files and other shared system files are marked read-only automatically during installation of the source files. You do not need to use the NetWare FLAG command or any other procedure to set sharable attributes.

# Task 2: Creating Machine Directories

When you run Windows 95 Setup to create a shared installation for a client computer, information is stored in the client computer's machine directory (not in individual users' home directories). The machine directory contains the following kinds of configuration information:

- Appropriate initialization and configuration files (including WIN.INI and SYSTEM.INI)
- SYSTEM.DAT and USER.DAT files, which make up the Registry for the shared installation
- Files that define the Desktop, Start menu directories, and other programs
- The spool directory for printing

For floppy disk-based and remote-boot computers, the swap file and TEMP directory are also placed in the machine directory. You must create machine directories on a server for floppy disk-based and remote-boot shared installations. Using machine directories is optional for computers with hard disks that are running a shared version of Windows 95.

You can set up the machine directory for a single computer or specify the filename of a text file that defines machine directories for multiple computer names.

▶ **To specify machine directories for multiple computers**

1. Create a text file that contains a list of computer names with the related location of machine directories that are to contain Windows 95 computer-specific files.

   In this text file, the entry for each machine directory must appear on a separate line, in the following format:

   *computername,\\UNC_server_name\directory\machine_directory*

   For example:

   ```
   machine1,\\nwsvr1\netsetup\machine1
   machine2,\\nwsvr1\netsetup\machine2
   ```

2. Save the file in text-only (ASCII) format, using any filename and storing it in any shared directory.

▶ **To create machine directories using Server-based Setup**

1. In the Server-Based Setup dialog box, click Set Path (or Change Path), and specify the path for the server that contains the Windows 95 source files. Then click OK.

2. Click the Add button.

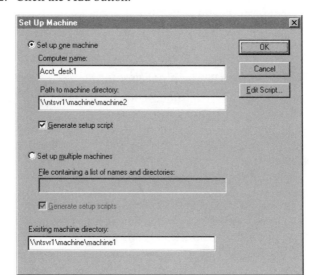

3. In the Set Up Machine dialog box, click an option to specify whether you are adding a single machine directory or multiple directories:

   - If you want to add a machine directory for a single computer, click Set Up One Machine. Then specify the name of the computer and the path to its machine directory.

   - If you want to add multiple machine directories using a batch file, click Set Up Multiple Machines. Then type the path and filename of the batch file that contains the list of computer names and machine directories. (This is the file created in the previous procedure.)

   If the file is stored on another server, type the UNC path to the directory.

4. If you want Server-based Setup to create setup scripts based on the values set in this dialog box and the default script created in Task 1, make sure the related Generate Setup Script option is checked.

5. If you want to create a shared installation based on the configuration in an existing machine directory, specify that directory in the box named Existing Machine Directory.

   You can see a list of the machine directories created in the currently selected server by clicking the View button in the Server-based Setup dialog box.

6. After you have specified all the options you want, click OK.

Server-based Setup creates the specified machine directories and, if you specified that a setup script should be created, it stores a setup script in each machine directory.

### Tip for Setting Up Machine Directories

The best way to take advantage of Server-based Setup for setting up multiple computers is to specify options and run Windows 95 Setup to create a shared installation for one computer. Then, for each group of computers that have the same network adapter and that will start a shared copy of Windows 95, you can use the Set Up Machine dialog box to automatically create machine directories for all computers of the same type.

By using Server-based Setup in this way, you only need to run Windows 95 Setup once for each type of computer configuration. Setup will automatically create machine directories and copy the main Windows 95 files, such as the Registry files, INI files, program groups, and so on, to each new machine directory. For each machine directory, Setup also updates the Registry to set the correct path to the machine directory and to prepare the Run-Once actions to convert program groups and complete other actions.

# Installing Windows 95 for Shared Installations

Each computer that starts from a hard disk must run Windows 95 Setup. For remote-boot workstations or floppy disk-based computers, run Windows 95 Setup once for each class of computers—that is, workstations that have identical network adapter configurations. Similar computers can then use their own machine directories with the startup floppy disk or boot image to run Windows 95.

The setup script tells Windows 95 Setup what kind of installation is allowed, based on the installation policy specified in Server-based Setup. The script can force a local hard-disk installation or a shared installation, or allow either. If the script is set to allow either, Setup asks the user to specify a shared or local installation.

Notice, however, that Windows 95 can be installed for remote-boot workstations only by specifying **RPLSetup=1** in the [Network] section of a setup script.

For shared installations, you can use the default version of MSBATCH.INF stored on the server plus a list of computer names and machine directories to generate a setup script for each client computer. You can also create custom setup scripts using the MSBATCH.INF format. Also, you can archive setup scripts, in case you need to run Setup again for a particular computer (for example, if the Registry becomes corrupted and cannot be restored).

The appropriate setup script is specified as a command-line parameter when running Windows 95 Setup. As described in Chapter 5, "Custom, Automated, and Push Installations," you can use the following basic approaches for installing Windows 95 with setup scripts:

- Run Windows 95 Setup with a setup script from the command line; for example:

```
setup n:\bob\bob.inf
```

- Use a login script that includes a command line to run Setup with a setup script, automatically installing Windows 95 when the user logs on
- Use Microsoft Systems Management Server or network management software from other vendors to run Windows 95 Setup with a setup script

When Windows 95 Setup runs with a setup script, Setup performs the following for both local hard-disk and shared installations:

- Detects and configures the hardware, storing the configuration in the computer's machine directory
- Prompts the user to specify or change any settings that are not defined in the setup script

For shared installations, the following additional installation tasks are performed:

- If **DisplayWorkstationSetup=1** is specified in the setup script, Setup prompts the user for the path to the machine directory, if a path isn't specified in the setup script
- Setup creates the startup disk (or boot image), as described in "Configuring Shared Installations" later in this chapter
- If a protected-mode network client is to be used, Setup configures the system for making the transition from real-mode networking

# Configuring Shared Installations

The following sections present information about the specific configuration files for each type of shared installation.

The default settings defined in MSDOS.SYS will also affect system startup on shared installations. For information about these defaults and how to change settings, see Chapter 6, "Setup Technical Discussion."

---

**Important**   After Windows 95 is installed, make sure that all path statements in login scripts specify Windows 95 locations, and not Windows 3.x or MS-DOS. Unexpected behavior or system instability can occur when erroneous **path** variables are set in login scripts.

---

## Configuring Shared Installations for Protected-Mode Clients

For shared installations, Windows 95 Setup adds the following basic kinds of entries in AUTOEXEC.BAT for computers that will run a shared copy of Windows 95 and use basic Microsoft networking for the first connection to the server:

```
snapshot
net start redir
net use drive: \\server\shared_source
net use drive: \\server\share\machine_dir
setmdir
```

If AUTOEXEC.BAT previously included **net start** or **net init** statements, Windows 95 Setup adds the commands for a shared installation at the same location. If AUTOEXEC.BAT included command lines for MS-DOS–based utilities before the **net start** entry, you must place these after **net start** for an AUTOEXEC.BAT file to be used with Windows 95.

For example, the earlier version of AUTOEXEC.BAT might contain these statements:

```
doskey
net start
```

Windows 95 Setup would change this AUTOEXEC.BAT to contain these statements:

```
drive:\sharreddir\doskey
net start basic
net logon /y
```

You must then manually edit AUTOEXEC.BAT to move the **doskey** statement after the **net** statements.

The SNAPSHOT.EXE utility called in AUTOEXEC.BAT is a real-mode program that prepares for the transition to protected-mode networking. A protected-mode counterpart (SNAPSHOT.VXD, stored in the shared Windows SYSTEM directory) uses this information to load the protected-mode network client. The following list shows command-line parameters that Setup might add in AUTOEXEC.BAT.

**Parameters for SNAPSHOT.EXE**

| Parameter | Description |
| --- | --- |
| **/B:**_n_ | Sets _n_ as the boot drive, where _n_ is a drive letter A through Z. Usually this is set to **/b:c**. |
| **/M:**_n_ | Sets the amount of memory to reserve for the real-mode network, where _n_ is a number in kilobytes. The default is 160K. |
| **/S** | Enables shutdown trapping, which causes Snapshot to intercept the Windows shutdown process and restart the workstation as soon as it is disconnected from the network. This parameter is used for floppy disk-based and remote-boot computers that use swap files on the network. |
| **/R** | Indicates that this is a diskless workstation that has no floppy disk drives. (On some remote-boot computers, the BIOS reports drives A and B when these drives don't exist; this parameter solves that problem.) |
| **/V** | Sets verbose mode. |

The **net start** command includes either the **basic** or **nwredir** parameter to start real-mode Microsoft networking. For either parameter (and any type of network), the **net use** command is then used to connect to make the initial network connection. The user is prompted for a user name and password for this real-mode connection. Otherwise, you can modify AUTOEXEC.BAT to use a generic logon for this first connection.

---

**Note**  If the computer uses more than one network client, the first client specified in the **clients=** entry in the setup script will be used to run Windows 95. If the first client specified in **clients=** is a Windows 95 protected-mode client, then that client is used with the **net start** command.

---

The **net use** entries in AUTOEXEC.BAT map drives for the shared Windows 95 files and the machine directory for the computer. The **setmdir** command (that is, Set Machine Directory) searches for MACHINES.INI in the shared Windows 95 directory to locate an entry that specifies the path to the machine directory that contains the full Registry for this computer. For more information, see "Technical Notes on MACHINES.INI and SETMDIR" later in this chapter.

The startup disk for a shared installation contains all the software required to connect to the network and start Windows 95. One startup disk can be used for computers with the same kinds of network adapters and settings. The same configuration can be used to run a shared copy of Windows 95 on remote-boot workstations with similar hardware configurations.

For computers that start from floppy disks, the contents of the startup disk fit on a 1.2 MB floppy disk. After Setup, you should make sure that the startup disk is write-protected. The software on the disk does not require writing information to the startup disk.

## Configuring a Computer that Starts from a Hard Disk

If you want to run a shared copy of Windows 95 on a computer that starts from its local hard disk, the setup script should contain the following entries:

```
[network]
WorkstationSetup=1
HDBoot=1
```

In this case, if there is a hard disk present on the computer with sufficient space for the required files, Windows 95 Setup creates the configuration required to start the computer from the Windows directory on the local hard disk and run a shared copy from the network.

Optionally, if the entry **DisplayWorkstationSetup=1** is specified in the setup script, the user can choose to create a local installation or a shared installation of Windows 95. For a shared installation, the user must specify the path for the machine directory.

For a computer that starts from a hard disk and uses Client for Microsoft Networks, AUTOEXEC.BAT is set up as follows for a shared installation:

```
snapshot.exe
net start basic
net logon /savepw:no /y
net use x: \\server\share
```

For computers running a NetWare-compatible client as the default network client, AUTOEXEC.BAT is as follows:

```
snapshot.exe
net start nwredir
net use drive: \\server\directory
```

The following shows an example of AUTOEXEC.BAT for a computer that starts from its local hard disk:

```
snapshot
c:\windows\net start nwredir
c:\windows\net use * /d
c:\windows\net use r: \\nwsvr\sys
path c:\windows;r:\sbsdist;r:\sbsdist\command
set tmp=c:\windows
set temp=c:\windows
```

Setup creates a machine directory and copies the following files to the machine directory:

- WIN.COM

- All initialization files, including WIN.INI and SYSTEM.INI

- USER.DAT

  Notice that the USER.DAT portion of the Registry must be in the machine directory for user profiles to work. During network logon, Windows 95 copies the correct USER.DAT to use if user profiles are enabled.

  Setup places SYSTEM.DAT on the local hard disk.

Because all Windows 95 source files are on the server, Setup does not need to copy Windows 95 locally as it does for installation on a local hard disk. The File Copy step in Setup should only copy about 2 MB of files.

For shared installations on computers with hard disks, Setup modifies the Windows 95 startup disk by changing the boot sector and copying new IO.SYS, COMMAND.COM, and MSDOS.SYS files. The files in the following list are copied to the startup disk.

**Files on Startup Disk for Shared Installations on Hard-Disk Computers**

| | | |
|---|---|---|
| autoexec.bat | msdos.sys | protman.exe |
| command.com | ndishlp.sys | protocol.ini |
| config.sys | net.exe | snapshot.exe |
| himem.sys | net.msg | system.dat |
| ifshlp.sys | neth.msg | NDIS 2 adapter driver |
| io.sys | protman.dos | |

For a client computer that contains a hard disk, the swap file and TEMP directory are stored on the local hard disk. To change the location for the swap file in this configuration, add a **pagingfile=***path* entry in the [386Enh] section of the SYSTEM.INI file that is stored in the machine directory.

## Configuring a Computer that Starts from a Floppy Disk

If you want to run a shared copy of Windows 95 on a computer that starts from a floppy disk, the setup script should contain the following entries:

```
[network]
WorkstationSetup=1
HDBoot=0
RPLSetup=0
```

Windows 95 Setup creates the configuration required to start the computer from a floppy-based startup disk and run a shared copy from the network. Setup also creates this configuration if **HDBoot=1** is specified but there is no hard disk present or there is insufficient space on the hard disk to install the required files.

---

**Note**  You must add an entry for the client computer in MACHINES.INI before that computer can start Windows 95.

---

For shared installations on floppy disk-based computers, Setup creates a mini Registry in a machine directory on the startup floppy disk. This reduced version of the computer's SYSTEM.DAT file contains only the information needed by IO.SYS and the real-mode network that makes the initial connection to the server. After connecting to the machine directory on the network, Windows 95 uses the full Registry stored there.

The swap file and TEMP directory are also stored in the machine directory for a client computer that starts from a floppy disk. To change the location for the swap file in this configuration, add a **pagingfile=***path* entry in the [386Enh] section of the SYSTEM.INI file that is stored in the machine directory.

The following shows an example of AUTOEXEC.BAT for a computer that starts from a floppy disk to run Windows 95 from a NetWare server:

```
snapshot
net start nwredir
net use * /d
net use r: \\server\share
setmdir
path=sbsdist;r:\sbsdist\command
```

---

**Note**  Do not include the machine directory in the path. The **setmdir** command manages this requirement automatically.

---

Windows 95 Setup creates the startup floppy disk by modifying the boot sector and copying IO.SYS. After Setup, make sure that the startup disk for this configuration is write-protected. The following table lists the files on the startup disk for this configuration.

**Files on the Startup Disk for a Shared Installation on a Floppy-Disk Computer**

| | | |
|---|---|---|
| autoexec.bat | msdos.sys | protman.exe |
| config.sys | ndishlp.sys | protocol.ini |
| command.com | net.exe | snapshot.exe |
| himem.sys | net.msg | system.dat (mini version) |
| ifshlp.sys | neth.msg | NDIS 2 adapter driver |
| io.sys | protman.dos | |

# Configuring a Remote-Boot Workstation for Client for NetWare Networks

Windows 95 can be installed on remote-boot workstations that start from Novell NetWare 3.x and 4.x servers. Remote-boot workstations contain a Remote Boot PROM that queries the network for instructions. Before installing Windows 95 to run on a remote-boot workstation, you should first make sure that the workstation successfully starts and runs with ODI drivers over RIPL.

If you want to run a shared copy of Windows 95 on a remote-boot workstation, the setup script should contain the following entries:

```
[network]
WorkstationSetup=1
HDBoot=0
RPLSetup=1
```

Windows 95 Setup creates the configuration required for starting and running a shared copy wholly from the network. Setup also creates this configuration on computers with NetWare-compatible clients if **HDBoot=1** is specified but there is no hard disk or floppy drive present or there is insufficient space on the hard disk to install the required files.

At system startup for a remote-boot workstation that will run Microsoft Client for NetWare Networks, the network provides instructions to create a RAM drive and then copies a disk image from the server to the workstation's RAM drive. Then the workstation continues booting from the RAM drive. The RAM drive is removed from memory after the operating system switches to protected mode. Windows 95 Setup creates the disk image that is copied from the server to the workstation's RAM drive. For information about customizing boot images, see "Creating the Disk Image for RIPL" later in this chapter.

To accomplish these actions for remote-boot workstations, Setup adds the following line to the workstation's CONFIG.SYS to create the RAM drive:

```
device=a:\ramdrive.sys 1440
```

The following lines are added to AUTOEXEC.BAT:

```
@mkdir ramdrv:\
@copy a:\ ramdrv:\
```

When you run Windows 95 Setup on a remote-boot workstation, a mini Registry is created and copied to the RAM drive. Windows 95 Setup also copies other supporting startup files to the RAM drive. When Setup is finished, it creates a file containing a disk image of the workstation's RAM drive on the server. The startup disk image contains a reduced version of the computer's SYSTEM.DAT file, which contains the Registry information needed by IO.SYS and the real-mode network. After connecting to the workstation's machine directory, Windows 95 uses the full Registry stored there.

The following shows an example of AUTOEXEC.BAT created for a remote-boot workstation:

```
@copy a:\ c:\
c:
```

The following shows an example of WIN.BAT, which runs automatically after AUTOEXEC.BAT is run:

```
set comspec=c:\command.com
nwrpltrm
snapshot /R /S /B:C
net start nwredir
net use * /d
net use N: \\nwserverbasedsetup\sbsdist
path=n:\netsetup\rpl;n:\netsetup\rpl\command
setmdir
win.com
```

The machine directory is created on the server. Windows 95 Setup copies the files listed in the following table.

**Startup Files for Remote-Boot Installations**

| | | |
|---|---|---|
| autoexec.bat | msdos.sys | protman.exe |
| bootdrv.com | ndishlp.sys | protocol.ini |
| config.sys | net.exe | ramdrive.sys |
| command.com | net.msg | rplboot.sys |
| himem.sys | neth.msg | snapshot.exe |
| ifshlp.sys | nwrpltrm.com | system.dat |
| io.sys | protman.dos | NDIS 2 adapter driver |

On remote-boot workstations, the NWRPLTRM.COM file runs during system startup to terminate the connection to the disk image. Users looking at the boot image on remote-boot workstations cannot see the RPLBOOT.SYS file

For remote-boot workstations, the network adapter is considered the boot device, and the real-mode operating system files are stored with the disk image in the machine directory. The swap file and TEMP directory are also stored in the machine directory. To change the location for the swap file in this configuration, add a **pagingfile=***path* entry in the [386Enh] section of the SYSTEM.INI file that is stored in the machine directory.

# Configuring Shared Installations for Real-Mode Clients

All three types of shared installations can be used on computers that run real-mode network clients such as the Novell-supplied NETX or VLM workstation shells.

When a shared installation is created for a real-mode network, the system startup does not include a transition to 32-bit networking. After the initial connection to the network server, the networking software continues to run in real mode. This means that many performance and feature enhancements for Windows 95 are not available, but it also ensures that you can create shared installations on networks where 32-bit, protected-mode networking solutions are not yet available.

As for local installation of Windows 95, you should make sure that the real-mode networking software is installed and running correctly when you start Windows 95 Setup. Then run Windows 95 Setup, specifying the machine directory and other information required to create a shared installation.

The configuration settings created for shared installations using real-mode network clients does not include **snapshot** or **net** commands. Other configuration issues are described in the following notes.

**Hard-disk computers with real-mode networking.**  For computers that start from the hard disk, the configuration and system startup process are similar to that for computers that use protected-mode clients, except there is no transition to protected mode.

**Floppy-disk computers with real-mode networking.**  For computers that start from the floppy disk, Setup first asks for the old boot disk for the network, and then copies the information from the root directory on this disk to a temporary directory. Then Setup copies the required Windows 95 components to that directory. Finally, Setup copies the directory contents to the new startup disk for Windows 95. The startup disk still contains the original real-mode network software. This configuration uses **setmdir** (in the same way as configurations for protected-mode networking) in AUTOEXEC.BAT to find the correct machine directory, but the path is specified on the command line rather than in a MACHINES.INI file.

**Remote-boot computers with real-mode networking.**  This configuration uses setmdir (in the same way as configurations for protected-mode networking) in AUTOEXEC.BAT to find the correct machine directory, but the path is specified on the command line rather than in a MACHINES.INI file.

To prepare for running a remote-boot workstation using a NETX or VLM client with Windows 95, you must complete the following additional tasks:

- You must include the entry **SaveSuBoot=1** in the [Setup] section of the setup script.
- You must manually copy the Novell-supplied files to the *machine_dir*\SUBOOT directory and then run RPLIMAGE again, as described in "Creating the Disk Image for RIPL" later in this chapter. For information about the required files, see your Novell documentation.

# Creating the Disk Image for RIPL

Novell NetWare does not provide RIPL support with its basic networking software. To obtain the latest versions of RIPL software, you can contact your Novell dealer or download the self-extracting file RPLKT1.EXE from the NOVLIB forum on CompuServe®. Configuring a remote-boot workstation is governed by the terms of your Novell license agreement.

As with all NetWare software used with Windows 95, you should make sure that you have the latest MS-DOS and Windows supporting files, including ODI drivers, network shell, LSL, and other required DLLs.

To prepare for RIPL support on the server, you must load and bind the Novell-supplied RPL.NLM file in AUTOEXEC.NCF and copy all .RPL files to the SYS:LOGIN directory.

To use RIPL to support a diskless workstation, the workstation must have an RPL ROM Module (PROM) installed on the network adapter that can send the correct RPL frame sequence. You must also create a disk image file in the server's SYS:LOGIN directory, as described later in this section.

For more information, see your Novell documentation; see also the Novell-supplied document, RPLNLM.DOC, and *IBM Remote Program Load User's Guide* from the NOVLIB forum on CompuServe.

Notice that some older PROMs (such as NE2000 boot PROMs) use only 802.3 Ethernet frame types; RIPL.NLM cannot run with this frame type and usually binds to the 802.2 frame type. Such older PROMs also cannot use BOOTCONF.SYS. For information about determining whether your site is using such older PROMs, and to find the software solutions, see the Novell-supplied document RIPLODI.DOC, available from the NOVLIB forum on CompuServe.

To allow a remote-boot workstation to start from a Novell NetWare server, the following actions must be completed:

1. Create a boot disk, and then create a disk image file using the boot disk.

   Windows 95 Setup installs a new disk image file, as described later in this section.

2. Copy the remote-boot files to the server.

3. Create a BOOTCONF.SYS file on the server.

4. Install the Enhanced Remote Boot PROM on the network adapter.

5. Install the network adapter in the remote-boot workstation.

6. Add an entry for the workstation in MACHINES.INI, as described in "Technical Notes on MACHINES.INI and SETMDIR" later in this chapter.

7. Connect the remote-boot workstation to the network.

---

**Note** Do not run RPLFIX.EXE or DOSGEN.EXE under Windows 95. These utilities are included with the Novell RIPL software. DOSGEN is used to create IMAGE.SYS (the disk image for startup) and NET$DOS.SYS to support RIPL on MS-DOS–based computers.

---

If you want to customize the disk images further using the Microsoft RPLIMAGE utility, first you must set **SaveSUBoot=1** in the [Setup] section of MSBATCH.INF. The files to be included in the boot image will be saved in the SUBOOT subdirectory under the machine directory. Then, use the RPLIMAGE utility that is included in the ADMIN\NETTOOLS\NETSETUP directory on the Windows 95 compact disc.

---

**Important** The RPLIMAGE utility creates a file name NET$DOS.SYS that consists of all the files in the current directory. You must then move NET$DOS.SYS from the machine directory to the server's SYS:\LOGIN directory.

---

You can use the following command-line parameters with RPLIMAGE.EXE to make a disk image of files and directories, including lower level directories:

**rplimage** [*pathname1*] [*pathname2*] [**/t:***n*] [**/n:***n*] [**/sc:***n*] [**/nf:***n*] [**/fs:***n*] [**/h:***n*] [**/f:***n*] [**/ss:***n*] [**/e:***n*] [**label:***string*] [**/date:***yyyy.mm.dd*] [**/time:***hh.mm.ss*] [**/sort**]

**Parameters for Microsoft RPLIMAGE.EXE**

| Parameter | Description |
|-----------|-------------|
| **/t** | Specifies the number of tracks |
| **/n** | Specifies the number of sectors per track |
| **/sc** | Specifies the number of sectors per cluster |
| **/nf** | Specifies the number of FATs in the image |
| **/fs** | Specifies the size of FATs in sectors |
| **/h** | Specifies the number of heads |
| **/f** | Specifies one of the standard formats |
| **/ss** | Specifies the sector size in bytes |
| **/e** | Specifies the FAT type (12-bit or 16-bit) |
| **/label** | Specifies a volume label for the image |
| **/date** | Specifies the date to touch all files and directories |
| **/time** | Specifies the time to touch all files and directories |
| **/sort** | Sorts the image by *filename.ext* in ascending order |

The following information describes how Windows 95 Setup installs a new disk image file. It also provides information to help you create a BOOTCONF.SYS file to support remote-boot workstations running a shared copy of Windows 95 from a NetWare server. For more information, see the Novell publication *Installing Enhanced Remote Boot PROMs on Novell Ethernet Network Interface Cards*. To obtain this document, contact your NetWare vendor.

When Windows 95 Setup is finished, it automatically creates a disk image on the server. This file contains a disk image of the RAM drive for the remote-boot workstation.

You can include the boot image filename plus the workstation's network address and node address in the BOOTCONF.SYS file on the NetWare server that is the repository for boot image files. BOOTCONF.SYS is stored in the SYS:LOGIN directory of the server, and is a text file that contains one record for each remote-boot workstation or group of workstations. Multiple workstations can be specified by using wildcards or question marks within the network address.

The following shows the format for each record in BOOTCONF.SYS. The parameters are defined later in this section.

**0x**[*network_address,*]*node_address* = *image_filename*.**sys** [**ack**] [**frame=***ff*] [**gns**] [**noack**] [**nogns**] [**noprotect**] [**notro**] [**protect**] [**ps=***server*] [**tro**] [**wait time=***sss*]

Each record ends in a carriage return or linefeed character.

The NetWare server that contains the boot image files should have Novell RIPL.NLM loaded and bound to the appropriate network adapter. The following procedures summarize this process.

▶ **To load RPL on a NetWare 3.x or 4.x server**

1. At the command prompt, type **load rpl**

2. Then type the following:

   **bind rpl to** *board* [**ack**] [**frame=***ff*] [**gns**], [**nodefault**], [**protect**], [**ps=***server*], [**tro**], [**wait time=***sss*]

The parameters for BOOTCONF.SYS records and for binding RPL are not case-sensitive. The parameters can be entered in any order, and can be separated by either commas or blank spaces. The following table briefly defines these parameters. For more information, see your Novell-supplied documentation on BOOTCONF.SYS.

**Novell NetWare Parameters for BOOTCONF.SYS and BIND Commands**

| Parameter | Description |
|---|---|
| **ack** | Requires a per-frame acknowledgment so slower workstations can pace RPL when it sends frames in burst mode. |
| **bind** *board* | Binds RPL to a board configured for 802.2 frames. The board can be specified by the name of the network adapter board number. |
| **frame=***ff* | Configures RBOOT to use the following frame types: **802.2** (default), **EII** (Ethernet_II), or **snap**. |
| **gns** | Causes the workstation to use a Get Nearest Server request after RBOOT is downloaded. Use this parameter when the workstation should find a server other than the one containing RPL. |
| **nodefault** | Causes RPL to ignore remote-boot requests when the node address is not in BOOTCONF.SYS. |
| **nogns** | Overrides **gns**. |
| **noprotect** | Overrides **protect** specified with BIND. |
| **notro** | Overrides **tro** with BIND. |
| **protect** | Adjusts memory size in BIOS data area to reflect the amount of memory used by RBOOT, reducing available memory by 12K. Do not use unless absolutely necessary. |

**Novell NetWare Parameters for BOOTCONF.SYS and BIND Commands** (*continued*)

| Parameter | Description |
|---|---|
| **ps=**_server_ | Specifies that RBOOT attach to a preferred server other than the server where RPL is located. |
| **tro** | Causes the bootstrap program to perform This Ring Only Count Of 3 on all broadcast frames. Used in source routing environments. |
| **wait time=**_sss_ | Specifies how many seconds (0000 to 665535) the workstation waits before selecting a Disk Image Name automatically, when multiple names are specified in BOOTCONF.SYS. |

# Technical Notes for Shared Installations

This section presents some technical notes related to running a shared copy of Windows 95.

## System Startup and Networking for Shared Installations

For shared installations, the first access to the network must occur in real mode. For shared installations that use a Windows 95 protected-mode network client, Microsoft real-mode networking (NET.EXE) is used for the first network connection, even for connecting to a NetWare network. After Windows 95 is loaded, the protected-mode drivers take over if the computer is configured to use a Microsoft protected-mode client such as Client for NetWare Networks.

Real-mode versions of NetBEUI and the IPX/SPX-compatible protocols are built into NET.EXE. Real-mode networking includes only the basic redirector; there is no support for mailslots or named pipes. Microsoft TCP/IP cannot be used until after the system loads and switches to protected mode.

The following briefly summarizes the software portion of the startup process for a computer that starts from a floppy or hard disk to run a shared copy of Windows 95 from a server. For a general description of the Windows 95 startup process, see Chapter 6, "Setup Technical Discussion."

- IO.SYS starts and reads the Registry to determine whether the computer is running Windows 95 over the network.

- COMMAND.COM runs AUTOEXEC.BAT and NETSTART.BAT (if present), which starts the network.

- During the first real-mode network connection, the system asks for a user name and password, and then logs on the user. If the administrator configures AUTOEXEC.BAT for logon using a generic user name, the user is not prompted to type a name and password.

- The network connects to the shared Windows directory. For computers running Windows 95 protected-mode network clients with machine directories on the network, the network also connects to MACHINES.INI.

- IO.SYS starts Windows.

- If the computer is configured to run a Windows 95 protected-mode network client, the system completes the transition to protected-mode networking.

Because there is both a real-mode and protected-mode network logon, it is possible that the user will be prompted for logon information twice. To avoid this, you can configure the **net logon** statement in AUTOEXEC.BAT to use a generic user name, so that the user isn't prompted to enter information for the real-mode logon. To do this, use a statement in this format:

```
net logon generic_name password /y
```

Notice, however, that the network connection made during the original real-mode network logon remains throughout the work session, even when the system switches to protected-mode network components after the first connection. For example, if a generic login is used to make the first connection to \\NWSVR1\SYS, and in protected mode you subsequently log on under your own user name with a different logon server, the generic connection to \\NWSVR1\SYS still remains.

The following describes some configuration issues and hints related to the real-mode and protected-mode network logon:

- For Windows NT networks, you can make sure that the generic logon in real mode uses the same domain as the user's actual logon in protected mode. This avoids the connection problem altogether.

- For NetWare networks, if Client for NetWare Networks is configured to use the same preferred server as specified in the real-mode logon, Windows 95 automatically tries the same user name and password for protected-mode logon. If this is successful, the user will not see a second prompt for protected-mode logon.

Notice in all cases that for shared installations, if you make the user name and password the same for real-mode and protected-mode network logon and for Windows logon, the real-mode logon prompt always appears.

# Technical Notes on MACHINES.INI and SETMDIR

MACHINES.INI is a file that lists, for each client, the location of the machine directory and other drive letters to connect. This file is stored on the server containing the shared Windows 95 files. The following shows the format of each entry in MACHINES.INI:

```
[Node_address]
sysdatpath=drive:\path
drive=\\server\share specified in sysdatpath
```

The *Node_address* section name is the 12-character address of the network adapter for a particular computer. You can find this address on NetWare networks by using the **userlist/a** command. On computers running Windows for Workgroups or Microsoft Workgroup Add-on for MS-DOS, you can find this address using the **net diag /s** command. If the node address you find is less than 12 characters long, you must add 0 (zero) characters at the front of the address. For example, if the node address is AA00578902, then the section name must be [00AA00578902].

The path defined in **sysdatpath=** must be a drive that is mapped to a drive letter in the same MACHINE.INI section.

In the following example, the machine directory is set to E:\DIR1\DIR2, and drives C, D, and E are set to network locations:

```
[00AA0051E4FB]
SysDatPath=e:\dir1\dir2
c=\\server1\share1
d=\\server2\share2
e=\\server3\share3
```

---

**Note** A section entry must be included in MACHINES.INI for each remote-boot workstation or floppy-disk computer in order for the computer to be started.

---

The **setmdir** command is used to set the machine directory for the computer and load the full Registry.

The floppy startup disk or disk image for shared installations contains only a mini Registry large enough to start the real-mode network. The startup disk for shared installations does not contain the information to find the machine directory, so that a single boot image on the network (or floppy startup disk) can be used to start several computers. The **setmdir** command solves this problem.

For computers running Client for Microsoft Networks and Microsoft Client for NetWare Networks, the **setmdir** command connects to the directory that contains the shared Windows 95 files and looks for MACHINES.INI. When the **setmdir** command finds the computer entry in MACHINES.INI, it switches the Registry APIs to point to the full Registry.

For computers that use real-mode networking clients, the **setmdir** command-line includes the path to the machine directory, rather than using MACHINES.INI. This is because the system has no guaranteed way of finding node addresses on other networks.

**Parameters for SETMDIR**

| Parameter | Description |
| --- | --- |
| /V | Sets verbose mode, so information is displayed while the program is running. |
| /R:*path* | Sets the current Registry and environment variables to the specified path. For example, **setmdir /R:d:\users\anniep** does the following: |

- Sets the Registry to D:\USERS\ANNIEP\SYSTEM.DATA
- Adds D:\USERS\ANNIEP to the path
- Sets the following environment variables:

```
comspec=d:\users\anniep\command.com
temp=d:\users\anniep
tmp=d:\users\anniep
```

# Other Notes on Shared Installations

**MS-DOS Mode is disabled.** When the user starts a program that runs in MS-DOS Mode, Windows 95 shuts down and uses real-mode MS-DOS to run the program. When the program quits, Windows 95 starts again. This mode is available as a last resort mode for compatibility with existing software. Computers that run a shared version of Windows 95 lose their network when Windows 95 shuts down. Because of the related problems, MS-DOS Mode is not available for computers running Windows 95 over the network. When a user tries to run a program in this mode, Windows 95 warns that the mode has been disabled.

**Hot docking for network adapters is not supported.** When Windows 95 starts over the network, real-mode drivers control the network adapter. If the network adapter is a Plug and Play card, the driver is responsible for setting the card to the active state. (You can use the setup program provided with the card to do this.) Computers that run over the network do not support hot Plug and Play disconnects, because the operating system is on the network.

**Users cannot log off and log on as a different user.** For another user to log on to a shared installation, the computer must be shut down and restarted.

**Safe Mode startup always runs configuration files.** To perform a Safe Mode system startup for a shared installation, the network must be started, so IO.SYS always runs AUTOEXEC.BAT, CONFIG.SYS, and NETSTART.BAT. Information in the machine directory controls how and when to perform a Safe Mode startup.

C H A P T E R   5

# Custom, Automated, and Push Installations

This chapter provides information about customizing Windows 95 and using login scripts for automated installation of Windows 95.

**In This Chapter**

Custom Installations for Windows 95: The Basics   144
Custom Installations of Windows 95: The Issues   145
Customizing Windows 95 with Setup Scripts   146
    Using Server-Based Setup to Create Custom Scripts   147
    Using BATCH.EXE to Create Setup Scripts   153
    Editing MSBATCH.INF for Custom Settings   154
    Customizing Setup for Accessibility Requirements   155
    Installing Other Software Using Custom Scripts   157
Customizing Detection for NetWare Networks   159
Running Custom Setup Scripts   162
Customizing Windows 95 with WRKGRP.INI Files   164
Customizing Windows 95 with Profiles and Policy Files   166
Overview of Push Installations   167
Using Login Scripts for Push Installation   169
    Preparing a STARTUP.GRP File   170
    Preparing Login Scripts for Push Installations   172
    Setting Up a Windows NT Server for Push Installations   174
    Setting Up a NetWare Server for Push Installations   175
    Running Login Scripts for Push Installations   176

# Custom Installations for Windows 95: The Basics

You can use the Server-based Setup program, as described in Chapter 4, "Server-Based Setup for Windows 95," to install source files and create setup scripts to automate all kinds of Window 95 installations. After using Server-based Setup to create a basic setup script, you can use a text editor to customize setup scripts for your site.

You have several options for customizing Windows 95 when users install Windows 95 using source files on a server. The most basic options include the following:

- Create custom MSBATCH.INF files. The custom setup scripts contain predefined settings for all the options that can be specified during Setup, and can contain instructions for installing additional software.

- Create user profiles and system policies to customize the desktop and system settings, or to restrict users' abilities to change the configuration.

The following table compares the customization methods formerly used for Windows for Workgroups versus the methods prescribed for Windows 95.

**Comparison of Customization Methods**

| Windows for Workgroups | Windows 95 |
|---|---|
| SETUP.SHH to customize system settings | MSBATCH.INF settings |
| SETUP.INF to copy additional files or to force Setup options | MSBATCH.INF settings |
| CONTROL.INF to list incompatible TSRs or force selection of devices or network clients | NETDET.INI for NetWare TSRs; built into Setup for all others |
| APPS.INF to create PIFs for applications | APPS.INF (same format) |
| WRKGRP.INI to control workgroup membership | WRKGRP.INI (similar format, with a new entry for Windows 95 features) |
| [New.Groups] in SETUP.INF for custom program groups | System policies to customize the desktop contents |
| **setup /p** to restore program groups; manually copying .GRP files to restore desktop contents | GRPCONV.EXE to convert program groups or restore default menus, as described in Chapter 6, "Setup Technical Discussion" |
| SYSTEM.INI, WIN.INI, or CONTROL.INI to modify system or desktop settings | For upgrades from Windows 3.x, custom settings are migrated; for the rare cases in which there is no equivalent in the user interface or in system policies, you can still modify INI files |

After a setup script and other customization files are created, Windows 95 can be installed automatically by running Setup at each client computer, using the name of the setup script as a command-line parameter. Setup can be run from any of the following:

- A login script

- From server-based system management software

- From a batch file that contains the appropriate setup command line, distributed on floppy disk or by electronic mail

# Custom Installations of Windows 95: The Issues

In Windows 95, you cannot modify the default INF files to customize the setup process or the final Windows 95 installation. Instead, Windows 95 provides more flexible, easier to use methods that rely principally on MSBATCH.INF and system policies to control installation options or manage the final configuration.

To take advantage of user profiles, the client computers must be running a 32-bit, protected-mode network client, such as Microsoft Client for NetWare Networks or Client for Microsoft Networks. Additional issues for using user profiles and system policies are described in Chapter 15, "User Profiles and System Policies."

To take advantage of WRKGRP.INI for restricting workgroup choices, the file should be stored in the shared directory that contains the Windows 95 source files. For shared installations, WRKGRP.INI should be stored in the shared Windows directory on the server.

The following list summarizes the items that cannot be customized or the screens that cannot be skipped during Windows 95 Setup.

**Setup Components That Cannot Be Skipped or Customized**

| Dialog box or message | Comment |
| --- | --- |
| MS-DOS Uninstall | This message appears if Setup detects MS-DOS Uninstall information on the computer. You cannot turn off this display or automate a response. |
| OS/2 Detected | This message appears if Setup detects that a version of OS/2 is installed on the system. You cannot turn off this display or automate a response. |
| Quit All Windows Programs | This message appears if Setup detects that other programs are running. You cannot turn off this display or automate a response. This message always appears if Setup is run using a Windows-based network management tool such as Microsoft Systems Management Server. |

**Setup Components That Cannot Be Skipped or Customized** (*continued*)

| Dialog box or message | Comment |
|---|---|
| Not Enough Disk Space | This message appears if there is not enough hard disk space to support the specified installation type. You cannot turn off this display from a setup script. However, to avoid this message, start Windows 95 Setup using the **setup /id** switch. |
| | Caution  Setup will fail during installation if it runs out of disk space. |
| Checking Your Hard Disk | This information message always appears. You cannot turn off this display, but no response is required. |
| Preparing Directory | This information message always appears. You cannot turn off this display, but no response is required. |
| Analyzing Your Computer | This information message always appears. You cannot turn off this display, but no response is required. |

# Customizing Windows 95 with Setup Scripts

You can specify custom settings for Windows 95 installations by creating a custom file in MSBATCH.INF format and using this setup script for installation. The default setup script is stored with the source files on the server. Custom setup scripts can be stored in users' home directories or in other central locations.

There are several ways to create a custom setup script:

- Use Server-based Setup (NETSETUP.EXE) to specify many custom settings
- Use Batch Setup (BATCH.EXE in the *Windows 95 Resource Kit* utilities) to specify most settings
- Create or edit a file in MSBATCH.INF format to specify all possible custom settings

These methods are described in the following sections.

**Tip**  The *Windows 95 Resource Kit* utilities include generic setup scripts for a variety of cases. These scripts can be used as is or modified to automate Windows 95 Setup.

# Using Server-Based Setup to Create Custom Scripts

You can use the Make Script button in Server-based Setup to create a default setup script. This option can only be used to create a setup script, not to edit an existing script. To edit an existing script, you must use a text editor, as described in "Editing MSBATCH.INF for Custom Settings" later in this chapter.

▶ **To create a custom setup script using the Server-based Setup program**

1. In Server-Based Setup, click the Make Script button.

2. In the Save As dialog box, specify the filename for this setup script, then specify the path where the script is to be stored, and click OK.

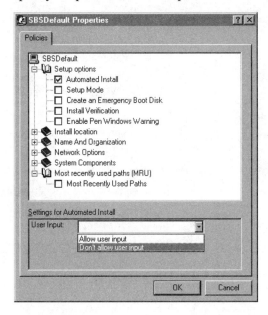

3. Use the SBS Default Properties dialog box to specify custom settings.

The following table summarizes what is set when a particular option is checked in the SBS Default Properties dialog box. For more information about each of these options when specified in a setup script, see Appendix D, "MSBATCH.INF Parameters."

**Server-Based Setup Options for Custom Scripts**

| Option | Description and related script setting |
|---|---|
| **Setup Options [Setup]:** | |
| Automated Install | Specifies whether to allow user input during Setup; sets **Express=1**. |
| Setup Mode | Selects Compact or Custom as the Setup type; sets the **InstallType=** value. |
| Create an Emergency Boot Disk | Ensures that Setup will create a startup disk; sets **EBD=1**. The user will be prompted to insert a floppy disk when Setup is ready to create this disk. |
| Install Verification | Specifies full installation or verification only; sets the **Verify=** value: <ul><li>Do a full installation</li><li>Verify install but don't copy files</li></ul> |
| Enable Pen Windows Warning | Ensures that a warning appears if Setup finds an unknown version of Pen Windows; sets **PenWinWarning=1**. |
| **Install Location [Setup]:** | |
| Install Directory | Specifies the path for where Windows 95 is to be installed; sets the **InstallDir=** value. |
| Server based Setup | Specifies where to install and how to start Windows 95. |
| | The Store Windows item offers two options: <ul><li>On the server (for shared installations)</li><li>On the user's hard disk (for local installations)</li></ul> |
| | The Boot Device item offers three options that apply only for shared installations: <ul><li>Floppy disk</li><li>Hard disk</li><li>Remote-boot server</li></ul> |
| | For information about shared installations of Windows 95, see Chapter 4, "Server-Based Setup for Windows 95." |
| **Name and Organization [NameAndOrg]:** | |
| Display name and organization page | Prevents the User Information dialog box from appearing during Setup; sets **Display=0**. |
| Name | Specifies a user name; sets the **Name=** value. |
| Organization | Specifies a company name; sets the **Organization=** value. |

**Server-Based Setup Options for Custom Scripts** (*continued*)

| Option | Description and related script setting |
| --- | --- |

**Network Options [Network]:**

| | |
| --- | --- |
| Display network pages during custom setup | Prevents the Network Configuration dialog box from appearing during Setup; sets **Display=0**. |
| Clients to Install | Specifies a comma-separated list of network clients to be installed; sets the **Clients=** value. |

- VREDIR installs Client for Microsoft Networks
- NWREDIR installs Client for NetWare Networks
- NETX or VLM retains existing Novell-supplied clients

The first client in the list becomes the default client, which loads first when the computer is started.

**Client for Windows Networks [VRedir]:**

| | |
| --- | --- |
| Validated Logon | Permits network logon only if the user has a valid account on the domain; sets **ValidatedLogon=1**. |
| Logon Domain | Specifies a Microsoft network domain name; sets the **LogonDomain=** value. |

**Client for NetWare Networks [NWRedir]:**

| | |
| --- | --- |
| Preferred Server | Specifies a NetWare server name; sets the **PreferredServer=** value. |
| First Network Drive | Specifies a drive letter; sets the **FirstNetDrive=** value. |

**Protocols [Network]:**

| | |
| --- | --- |
| Protocols to Install | Specifies a comma-separated list to set the **Protocols=** value. The following values install the standard protocols provided with Windows 95: |

- NWLINK indicates IPX/SPX-compatible protocol
- NETBEUI indicates Microsoft NetBEUI
- MSTCP indicates Microsoft TCP/IP

The first protocol in the list becomes the default protocol, which also sets LANA 0.

**IPX/SPX-compatible protocol [NWLink]:**

| | |
| --- | --- |
| Frame Type | Selects a frame type; sets the **FrameType=** value. The recommended setting for this is **Auto** unless you are absolutely certain of the frame type. |
| NetBIOS support | Installs support for NetBIOS over IPX; sets **NetBIOS=1**. |

**Server-Based Setup Options for Custom Scripts** (*continued*)

| Option | Description and related script setting |
|---|---|
| **Microsoft TCP/IP [MSTCP]:** | |
| DHCP | Enables DHCP for configuring TCP/IP; sets **DHCP=1**. |
| IP Address | Specifies an IP address for the computer in the form ###.###.###.###; sets the **IPAddress=** value. |
| Subnet Mask | Specifies a subnet mask in the form ###.###.###.###; sets the **SubnetMask=** value. |
| WINS | Specifies whether WINS servers are used for name resolution and how WINS is configured; sets the **WINS=** value. The following are the possible choices:<br><br>• Disable WINS<br>• Enable WINS; get parameters from DHCP<br>• Enable WINS resolution (you must type WINS addresses) |
| Primary WINS | Specifies an IP address for a WINS server in the form ###.###.###.###; sets the **PrimaryWINS=** value. |
| Secondary WINS | Specifies an IP address for a WINS server in the form ###.###.###.###; sets the **SecondaryWINS=** value. |
| Scope ID | Specifies a scope ID string; sets the **ScopeID=** value. |
| Enable DNS | Enables the use of DNS servers or LMHOSTS files for name resolution; sets **DNS=1**. |
| Hostname | Specifies a host name for the computer (usually the same as the value of **ComputerName=**); sets the **Hostname=** value. |
| Domain | Specifies the DNS domain name for this computer; sets the **Domain=** value. |
| DNS Server search order | Specifies a comma-separated list of DNS servers in the order to be searched, each in the form ###.###.###.###; sets the **DNSServers=** value. |
| Domain search order | Specifies a comma-separated list of DNS domain suffixes; sets the **DomainOrder=** value. |
| LMHOST Path | Specifies the path where the LMHOST file is stored; sets the **LMHostPath=** value. Notice that you must also check the Enable DNS option to use LMHOSTS. |
| Gateways | Specifies a comma-separated list of gateways to be used, each in the form ###.###.###.###; sets the **Gateways=** value. |

**Server-Based Setup Options for Custom Scripts** (*continued*)

| Option | Description and related script setting |
| --- | --- |
| **Net cards [*netcard*]:** | |
| Net cards to install | Specifies a comma-separated list of network adapter driver names, which sets the **Netcards=** value. |
| | **Note**  In general, this value should not be defined in a setup script; you should let Windows 95 Setup use detection to identify and configure network adapters. |
| **Services [Network]:** | |
| Services to install | Specifies a comma-separated list of network services to be installed; sets the **Services=** value. For File and Printer Sharing services, specify one of the following values: |
| | ▪ VSERVER installs support for Microsoft networks |
| | ▪ NWSERVER installs support for NetWare networks |
| **File and Printer Sharing for NetWare Networks [NWServer]:** | |
| SAP Browsing | Enables SAP Advertising for this computer; sets **Use_SAP=1**. |
| Browse Master | Enables Workgroup Advertising for this computer, and specifies the browser master role for this computer; sets the **BrowseMaster=** value. The following choices are possible: |
| | ▪ This machine can be a browse master |
| | ▪ This machine cannot be a browse master |
| | ▪ This machine is the preferred browse master |
| **File and Printer Sharing for Microsoft Networks [VServer]:** | |
| LMAnnounce | Allows computers running Microsoft LAN Manager to see this computer; sets **LMAnnounce=1**. |
| Browse Master | Specifies the computer's browser master role; sets the **MaintainServerList=** value. The following choices are possible: |
| | ▪ Auto (the computer can be a browse master if required) |
| | ▪ Enabled (this computer is the browse master) |
| | ▪ Disabled (this computer cannot be a browse master) |

**Server-Based Setup Options for Custom Scripts** (*continued*)

| Option | Description and related script setting |
|---|---|
| **Identification [Network]:** | |
| Computer Name | Specifies a unique name on the network; sets the **ComputerName=** value. |
| Workgroup | Specifies a unique name on the network; sets the **Workgroup=** value. |
| Description | Specifies any string, with no commas; sets the **Description=** value. |
| **Access Control [Network]:** | |
| Security Type | Defines the type of security to be used to protect shared resources, and the type of pass-through security agent, if user-level security is specified; sets the **Security=** value. The following choices are possible:<br><br>■ Share (for share-level security)<br>■ User-level—Windows NT domain<br>■ User-level—Windows NT computer<br>■ User-level—NetWare server |
| Pass-through Agent | Specifies the server or domain that is to provide pass-through validation for user-level security; sets the **PassThroughAgent=** value. |
| **System Components [System]:** | |
| Various device types | Specifies the related INF section name for installing and configuring a specific device. This includes Advanced Power Management, locale, machine, pen windows, tablet, keyboard, monitor, display, and mouse devices.<br><br>**Note** The recommended method for installing and configuring all these devices is for Windows 95 Setup to use detection. |
| **Most Recently Used Paths [InstallLocationsMRU]:** | |
| Most Recently Used Path | Specifies UNC names for up to four paths that can be displayed in dialog boxes that request the location of files during Setup. |

**Tip for Ensuring User Logon Capabilities in Setup Scripts**

By default, Windows 95 Setup preserves the network identification information from the user's previous networking configuration, including the logon domain or preferred server. However, in cases where this configuration information is not already defined, you must specify settings in the setup script.

If users are installing Windows 95 from a server that requires logon validation, make sure the custom setup script defines the correct logon server. For a computer that will run Client for Microsoft Networks and use the Windows NT network for network logon validation, you should define values for **LogonDomain=** and **ValidatedLogon=** in the [VRedir] section. For a computer that will run Client for NetWare Networks, define a correct value for **PreferredServer=** in the [NWRedir] section.

If the appropriate values aren't defined in a setup script, the user might not have the validated access required to complete the final Setup steps for installing printers and other actions.

# Using BATCH.EXE to Create Setup Scripts

Batch Setup (BATCH.EXE) is a Windows-based program that makes it easy to create setup scripts that can be used to automate Windows 95 installation. By running Batch Setup and completing the options, you create a file in MSBATCH.INF format that can be used to run Windows 95 Setup with minimal user intervention.

This tool is especially useful when you are testing alternate configurations and need to run Setup repeatedly. Batch Setup can be used to define all options in a setup script; however, unlike Server-based Setup, it cannot be used to install source files or create machine directories for a shared installation.

The following summarizes the suggested method for running and using Batch Setup.

▶ **To use Batch Setup (recommended method)**

- From the Start menu, click Run. Type **batch.exe** and then complete all the options to create a customized setup script.

  For assistance in completing any options, see the online Help for Batch Setup.

After you create the setup script, you can run Windows 95 Setup by specifying the name of the script as a command-line parameter, as described in "Running Custom Setup Scripts" later in this chapter. Depending on how many options you completed in Batch Setup, you might not have to provide any additional input while installing Windows 95.

For more information, see the BATCH.HLP and README.TXT files in the BATCH directory. For a description of the parameters in the file created by Batch Setup, see Appendix D, "MSBATCH.INF Parameters." If you want to modify the file that is created, follow the guidelines for editing setup scripts, as described in "Editing MSBATCH.INF for Custom Settings" later in this chapter.

# Editing MSBATCH.INF for Custom Settings

After you have used Server-based Setup or BATCH.EXE to create a setup script in MSBATCH.INF format, you can edit and save this file with a text editor to create alternate or more detailed setup scripts.

▶ **To edit MSBATCH.INF**

1. Use a text editor such as Notepad to open the MSBATCH.INF file.

2. Edit the file, and save it in text-only format.

The following are the editing guidelines for MSBATCH.INF:

- Each section starts with a unique section name enclosed in brackets ([ ]).

- Only sections and key words defined in Appendix D, "MSBATCH.INF Parameters," are evaluated by Windows 95 Setup.

- Each section can contain one or more entries. The typical entry consists of a key word and a value separated by an equal sign.

- Key words within a section do not have to be unique, but each key word and its value should follow the guidelines for that key word.

- A comment can be included anywhere on a line by starting the comment with a semicolon.

**Tip for Defining Custom Entries in Setup Scripts**

Use the Custom Setup option to install Windows 95 on a single computer. You can define all the optional components and other items you want installed for other similar computers at your site.

After Windows 95 is completely installed on this single computer, you can use any text editor to copy the [OptionalComponents], [Setup], [NameAndOrg], and [System] sections from SETUPLOG.TXT in the computer's root directory. Add this information to define settings for the same sections in the custom setup script.

This is especially useful for defining entries for [OptionalComponents] or when many computers require the same [System] settings. Some settings for the [Network] section can also be copied from SETUPLOG.TXT.

# Customizing Setup for Accessibility Requirements

Users who require accessibility aids to work with Windows can experience problems with Windows 95 Setup, because their accessibility aids are not available while Setup is running.

As the system administrator, you can assist users in such cases by creating setup scripts that define all options so that Setup can run without user intervention. In such cases, be sure to include the Windows 95 Accessibility Options among the optional components to be installed with Windows 95.

The following suggestions can help individuals who require accessibility aids but do not have a system administrator to create a setup script. In such cases, you have two options, depending on whether you want to create the script while running Windows 3.x or MS-DOS:

- If you are running Windows 3.1 or Windows for Workgroups, use BATCH.EXE to create a setup script

- If you are running MS-DOS, create or edit the AUTOMATE.INF setup script provided with the *Windows 95 Resource Kit* utilities

When you install Windows 95 over an earlier version of Windows, Setup automatically moves your Startup group and other Program Manager groups for use under Windows 95. So any accessibility options in your previous Startup group will start automatically under Windows 95 after Setup is completed.

Whichever method you choose for creating the script, you can use it to control Windows 95 installation automatically, by using it with the **setup** command, as described in "Running Custom Setup Scripts" later in this chapter. For information about the accessibility options that can be installed automatically with Windows 95, see Appendix I, "Accessibility."

▶ **To use Batch Setup to create a hands-free setup script**

1. Run Batch Setup, as described in "Using BATCH.EXE to Create Setup Scripts" earlier in this chapter.

2. In the Windows 95 Batch Setup window, type the Setup Identification information.

3. Click the Installation Options button.

4. In the Windows 95 Installation Options dialog box, click the Type Of Installation list and select Custom.

   You can make any other changes you want. However, the recommended method is to accept all the default settings and let Windows 95 Setup complete the actions automatically.

5. Click the Set button.

6. In the Batch Setup Administrative Options dialog box, make sure the option named Don't Stop During Setup is selected. Then click OK.

7. In the Windows 95 Batch Setup window, click the Optional Components button.

8. In the Available Areas list in the Windows 95 Optional Components dialog box, click Accessories. Then in the Available Components list, click Accessibility Options so that it is checked.

   You can use the same method to add any additional components to be installed with Windows 95. Then click OK.

9. When you finish setting all the options you want, click the Done button. In the Save As dialog box, specify the path and filename for saving this script.

   For networking components, the recommended method is to allow Windows 95 Setup to install and configure components automatically.

▶ **To edit AUTOMATE.INF to create a hands-free setup script**

1. Use any text editor to edit a copy of the AUTOMATE.INF sample script provided in the SAMPLES directory with the *Windows 95 Resource Kit* utilities. You can also create this script by typing the entries in the sample script following this procedure.

2. Change entries to specify your correct time zone, product identification number, and user name. To make these changes, delete the semicolon at the start of the line, and type the correct text between quotation marks.

   For a list of correct values for time zones, see Appendix D, "MSBATCH.INF Parameters."

   Your product identification number is the CD Key number on the Windows 95 compact disc case or the number provided on your Certificate of Authenticity.

3. Under the [Optional Components] section, include this entry:

   ```
   "Accessibility Options"=1
   ```

The following shows an example of the entries defined in AUTOMATE.INF:

```
[Setup]
Express=1
InstallType=1
EBD=0
;TimeZone=""        ;remove semicolon and add correct zone in quotes
;productid=""       ;remove semicolon and type the product ID
vrc=1               ;saves old files without warning you

[NameandOrg]
Display=0
Name=""             ;type your username between the quotes

[Network]
Display=0

[OptionalComponents]
"Accessibility Options"=1
; add any other components to be installed in this section
```

# Installing Other Software Using Custom Scripts

This section describes how to use INF Installer to prepare for installing other software with Windows 95 and how to add Run-Once actions that occur at the end of Setup.

Server-based Setup cannot be used to add extra components, such as *Windows 95 Resource Kit* utilities or applications and services from the ADMIN directory on the Windows 95 compact disc. To add such components or to add any other software that uses Windows 95 INF files, you must make sure that the source files are installed correctly, the INF files used by Windows 95 Setup are modified properly, and correct entries are added to MSBATCH.INF.

The INF Installer utility (INFINST.EXE) accomplishes these actions automatically for any software that has a Windows 95 INF file. INF Installer is part of the *Windows 95 Resource Kit* utilities. Before you can use INF Installer, you must use Server-based Setup to install the Windows 95 source files in a network directory, as described in Chapter 4, "Server-Based Setup for Windows 95."

▶ **To use INF Installer to add components in MSBATCH.INF**

1. Copy INFINST.EXE to the Windows directory on your computer.

2. From the Start menu, click Run, and then type **infinst**

3. In the INF Installer window, click the Set Path button and type the UNC path name for the Windows 95 source files on the network.

4. To add a component's INF and other files to the Windows 95 source files, click the Install INF button, and then browse for the path name for the current location of the component's INF, executable, and supporting files.

INF Installer copies the files listed in the component's INF file and makes the following modifications in the MSBATCH.INF file that's in the Windows directory on the server that contains the Windows 95 source files:

- If the component is a network service, then the device ID as specified in the INF file is added to the **services=** entry in the [Network] section.

- If the component is an application, the components listed in the INF file are added as comments in the [OptionalComponents] section.

---

**Note**   For any component to be installed using this setup script, you must manually remove the semicolon before the entry for the component name.

---

If you want to add to the Run-Once operations that occur the first time Windows 95 starts, you can define entries for these actions in MSBATCH.INF. In addition, you must make sure that the required files are available with the Windows 95 source files, or are otherwise available on a shared resource that users installing Windows 95 have access to. For software components that have Windows 95 INF files, you can use INF Installer to prepare files to be included with Windows 95 Setup. You must also add these entries in the setup script:

- Create an **AddReg=** entry in the [Install] section for each software component that you want to run during the Run-Once part of Setup. For example:

```
[install]
AddReg=myprogram.addreg
```

For more examples of [Install] section entries, see Appendix D, "MSBATCH.INF Parameters."

- In the related [*software*] section, add the following kind of entry for the operation:

```
[myprogram.addreg]
HKLM,Software\Microsoft\Windows\CurrentVersion\RunOnce\reg_values
```

The following shows the Run-Once entry from MSMAIL.INF that causes the setup routine for Microsoft Mail to run after Windows 95 is installed:

```
[MSMailAddReg]
HKLM,Software\Microsoft\Windows\CurrentVersion
    \RunOnce\Setup,"%EmailRunOnce%",,"%25%\mlset32.exe"
```

**Important**  To create definitions in MSBATCH.INF for Run-Once statements or other actions, you must provide the precise Registry settings that the program uses to read or write to the Registry. This requires programmatic understanding of the software, or you must use values provided by the software manufacturer.

For information about how to install custom software by using the CUSTOM.INF script provided with the *Windows 95 Resource Kit* utilities, see WIN95RK.HLP.

If you want to add other software as part of Windows 95 installation, but that software does not have a Windows 95 INF file, you must use a system management tool for software distribution, such as Microsoft Systems Management Server.

**Tip**  Avoid using relative path names in setup scripts so that you can make sure the commands are run from the correct directory.

# Customizing Detection for NetWare Networks

This section describes the format of NETDET.INI, which is used to detect NetWare components and TSRs during Windows 95 Setup. You can use this information to add custom entries for detecting components on NetWare networks and defining actions to be taken during Setup based on detection results.

**Note**  If you do not need to modify the default detection behavior for setting up Windows 95 on NetWare networks, you can skip this section.

The NETDET.INI and related NETOS.DLL files are stored in the PRECOPY2.CAB file on the Windows 95 floppy disks or compact disc. The version used by Windows 95 Setup is stored in the Windows directory on the local computer. If you modify this file, you can place the revised version of NETDET.INI in the Windows directory on the server that contains the Windows 95 source files.

Each component section in NETDET.INI consists of one or more *detection* entries, and one or more *event* entries. A detection entry has the following format:

*detectionN=method1*[,*method2*...]

Alternate *detection* entries can be used to define different actions to be taken, depending on how a component is detected. For example, a TSR detected in memory but not in a batch file might require different actions from the actions required when an entry for the TSR is found in AUTOEXEC.BAT. For example:

```
detection0=mcb
detection1=autoexec.bat
full_install0=migrate
full_install1=prevent
```

Each *method#* parameter in the *detection* statement defines a detection method, as listed in the following table. Setup assumes that the component has been detected if one method detects it.

| Detection method | Meaning |
| --- | --- |
| assumed | Always detected; used to force an action unconditionally |
| autoexec.bat | Detected in an uncommented line in AUTOEXEC.BAT |
| config.sys | Detected in an uncommented line in CONFIG.SYS |
| custom_dll | Detected by calling external DLL detection code |
| mcb | Detected by checking the list of TSRs maintained by MS-DOS in the memory control blocks (MCB) |
| mcb_nobat | Detected in the MCB chain but not in AUTOEXEC.BAT |
| system.ini | Detected in an uncommented line in SYSTEM.INI |

The special detection method **custom_dll** requires two additional entries: **detection_dll**, which contains the filename of the DLL to be loaded, and **detection_call**, which contains the name of the entry point consistent with the following **typedef**:

```
typedef BOOL (WINAPI *LPDCALL)(LPSTR)
```

Adding custom entries based on this detection method requires that you have sufficient programmatic understanding of the calls made in the relevant DLLs. For an example of required entries for **custom_dll**, see the example entry for VLM later in this section.

The NETDET.INI file includes one or more *event* entries grouped by numerical suffixes that match the suffixes in *detection* entries (that is, *N* must be 0 or 1). Each *event* entry contains a list of actions to be performed if the associated *detection* action was successful. The following shows the form of *event* entries:

*eventN=action1*[(*parameter*)][,*action2*[(*parameter*)]...]

The *event* name is the name of the Setup code for handling installation of components related to the detected TSR or NetWare component. The following list shows the defined events.

| Event | Meaning |
| --- | --- |
| protstack_install*N* | The protected-mode protocol will be installed |
| nwredir_install*N* | The protected-mode network client will be installed |
| full_install*N* | The protected-mode protocol and network client will be installed |

The following table lists the defined action codes related to events in NETDET.INI.

| Action code | Meaning |
| --- | --- |
| none | Do not do anything (NOP) |
| prevent | Recommend against using during recommendation phase |
| remove | Comment out using REM in AUTOEXEC.BAT or a batch file called from AUTOEXEC.BAT |
| unremove | Remove REM comment from AUTOEXEC.BAT or a batch file called from AUTOEXEC.BAT |
| migrate | Comment out using REM in AUTOEXEC.BAT, and add to WINSTART.BAT |
| unmigrate | Remove REM comment in AUTOEXEC.BAT, and remove from WINSTART.BAT |
| install_devnode(*devnode*) | Cause specified device node to be installed |
| uninstall_devnode(*devnode*) | Cause specified device node to be removed |
| gen_install(*section*) | Cause action in an *install* section to run (see the example for Source Routing for NetWare later in this section) |

Notice that the event named **prevent** is a special case that is used during the recommendation phase when Setup is determining which new Windows 95 components can be installed without interfering with TSR dependencies defined in NETDET.INI. If a component is detected by the defined method and the **prevent** action is associated with the related event, then Setup will recommend against the usual Setup action for the event.

The following shows some examples of entries in NETDET.INI:

```
;;;;;; VLM 4.x ;;;;;;;;
; prevents installation of Client for NetWare Networks
; if Novell NDS is used
[VLM]
detection0=custom_dll
detection_dll=NETOS.DLL
detection_call=NW_IsNDSinUsefull_install0=prevent

;;;;;; Btrieve ;;;;;;;;;;;
[Brequest.exe]
detection0=mcb; installs all protected-mode components
full_install0=migrate; if Btrieve is present

;;;;;; NOVELL NETBIOS ;;;;;;;;;;;;;;;;;;;
; installs NETBIOS over IPX if Novell NETBIOS is present
[NETBIOS]
detection0=mcb
full_install0=remove,install_devnode(NWNBLINK)

;;;;;;;;;; SOURCE ROUTING FOR NETWARE ;;;;;;;;;
; adds cache size for Source Routing
[ROUTE]
detection0=mcb
full_install0=remove,gen_install(NWSRCR)

[NWSRCR]
AddReg=NWSRCR.reg

[NWSRCR.reg]
HKLM,System\CurrentControlSet\Services\VxD\NWLINK,cachesize,,"16"
HKLM,System\CurrentControlSet\Services\VxD\NWLINK\Ndi\params
    \cachesize,"",,"16"
```

# Running Custom Setup Scripts

The following procedure describes how to run Windows 95 Setup from a setup script.

▶  **To run Windows 95 Setup using a setup script with minimal user action**

1. Start the computer running the existing network client software.

2. Connect to the server or drive that contains the Windows 95 source files.

   The network administrator can include this step in the login script to avoid user action.

3. Change to the directory where the Windows 95 Setup files are located.

4. At the command line, run Windows 95 Setup by specifying the batch file that contains the setup script, using this syntax:

   `setup msbatch.inf`

   If MSBATCH.INF exists in the Windows directory on the server containing the Windows 95 source files, Setup uses it by default. Otherwise, for example, you would type **setup e:\mybatch.inf** to run Setup using a setup script named MYSCRIPT.INF on drive E. To use a script in the SCRIPTS directory on a server named NTSVR1, you would type **setup \\ntsvr1\scripts\mybatch.inf** (provided, of course, that your operating system software can interpret UNC path names).

   –Or–

   Include the entire statement for running Windows 95 Setup in the login script, so that the user does not have to type anything at the command prompt.

When you run Windows 95 Setup in this way, Setup takes all settings from the custom script. For information not defined in the setup script, Windows 95 Setup migrates settings from an earlier version of Windows 3.x on the computer, uses built-in defaults, or prompts the user to provide information.

After copying files, Windows 95 Setup restarts the computer and begins the Run-Once setup operations (printer setup, program group conversions, and so on). When these operations are finished, Windows 95 is completely installed.

When the user quits Windows 95 Setup at this point, Setup writes all changes to the Registry. The user can restart the computer and log on with the usual logon name and password.

The network administrator can automate this process by providing each user with a floppy disk that contains the necessary files for starting the computer, connecting to the network, and running Windows 95 Setup with a custom setup script.

# Customizing Windows 95 with WRKGRP.INI Files

You can use a file named WRKGRP.INI to specify a list of workgroups that users can choose to join. You can use WRKGRP.INI in these ways:

- To help reduce the proliferation of workgroup names on the network
- To control the workgroup choices that users can make
- To specify defaults for the NetWare preferred server or Windows NT domain on a per-workgroup basis

The WRKGRP.INI file is stored in the Windows directory on the server that contains the Windows 95 source files.

Windows 95 Setup uses the values defined in WRKGRP.INI to set Registry values in the workgroup, logon domain, preferred server, and other values. The same values are used to control options available for users to select in the Network option in Control Panel. The WRKGRP.INI file contains the following sections:

- [Options] specifies the recognized options for workgroups
- [Workgroups] contains a list of workgroups from which the user can choose

In Windows 95, for each workgroup, you can specify the domain, preferred server, and so on, that everyone in a workgroup will use, depending on the network providers used.

The following table describes the format of the Windows 95 WRKGRP.INI file.

**WRKGRP.INI Settings**

| Section or entry | Description |
| --- | --- |
| **[Options] section:** | |
| **ANSI=true \| false** | Specifies whether the workgroups need to be converted from an OEM character set to ANSI. Default is **false**. |
| **Required=true \| false** | Specifies whether users can type their own workgroup name or forces them to choose from those listed. |
| **ForceMapping=true \| false** | Specifies whether users can change the workgroup, logon domain, or preferred server that are set by a mapping. |

**WRKGRP.INI Settings** (*continued*)

| Section or entry | Description |
|---|---|
| **Mapping=***NP1, NP2, NP3,...* (comma-separated list of network providers) | Specifies a comma-separated list of the network providers to which workgroups can be mapped. Also specifies the order in which values will be listed in the [Workgroups] section. Implicitly, this specifies where in the Registry to store settings. This parameter is optional. By default, workgroups map to *domain, preferred server.* |
| **Default=***NP1 default,NP2 default, NP3 default,...* | Specifies the default mapping for workgroups listed in the [Workgroups] section that don't have a mapping defined. This allows you to add a single entry to an existing Windows for Workgroups WRKGRP.INI file to get minimal mapping functionality. The format is the same as for specifying a mapping in [Workgroups]. |
| **[Workgroups] section:** | |
| *workgroup=**optional_mapping** | Specifies a workgroup that users can choose and its mappings will automatically be defined in the order specified in **Mapping=**. There can be a *workgroup=* entry in the file for every workgroup that users can choose. Each name of a workgroup must be followed by an equal sign (=) for the workgroup name to be interpreted correctly. |

The entry that defines the network providers for each workgroup has the following format in the [Workgroups] section:

*workgroup_name=mapping1,mapping2,mapping3,...*

By default in Windows 95, workgroups can be mapped to both Windows NT domains and NetWare preferred servers. (This is because Windows 95 includes network providers for these two networks.) For example:

```
MktMain=MktDom1,master1
```

This example specifies that the workgroup named MktMain has these two mappings: MktDom1 is the logon domain for the Windows NT network, and Master1 is the preferred server for the NetWare network.

Administrators can specify the 32-bit, protected-mode network providers that can be mapped for a workgroup by setting the **Mapping=** parameter in the [Options] section of WRKGRP.INI. For example, if the network uses two network providers (MSNP32 for Microsoft networks and NWNP32 for NetWare networks), the following is defined in WRKGRP.INI:

```
[options]
mapping=msnp32,nwnp32
```

The order specified in the **Mapping=** entry also specifies the order of items in the [Workgroups] section.

You can also use the **Default=** entry to specify a default mapping for workgroups that do not have an explicit mapping. This allows you to use an existing WRKGRP.INI created for Windows for Workgroups 3.11, and add one entry to take advantage of Windows 95 functionality. For example, add the entry **Default=MktDom1,Master1** to use the servers described in the previous example as the default mapping.

If a WRKGRP.INI exists, the Workgroup field in Windows 95 Setup and the Network option in Control Panel both show all the workgroups listed in WRKGRP.INI. Users can choose a workgroup from the list or type a workgroup name. If **Required=true** in WRKGRP.INI, the user must choose from the list.

In WRKGRP.INI, **ForceMapping=** controls whether mapped values can be changed in the Windows 95 user interface. For example, if **ForceMapping=true** and the user selects a workgroup that is mapped to a domain, the user cannot change the value in the Logon Domain box in the Network option in Control Panel and in the logon dialog box.

---

**Note** If Windows 95 Setup finds the WRKGRP.INI file in the Windows 95 source files, it copies the file to the shared Windows directory.

---

# Customizing Windows 95 with Profiles and Policy Files

You can predefine settings in user profiles and system policy files to control user actions. For example:

- You can enforce a mandatory desktop configuration by installing a mandatory user profile (USER.MAN) in users' home directories. (On NetWare networks, this is the MAIL subdirectory for each user.)

- You can control the user's security privileges, network access, and desktop configuration if you install system policy files on the logon server. This is the PUBLIC directory on a NetWare server or the NETLOGON directory on the primary domain controller for a Windows NT domain.

To take advantage of these features in Windows 95, you must define the user profile and system policy settings to be used. Then place these files in the appropriate directories before users run Windows 95 Setup. When users log on to Windows 95, the profiles and policies will be used automatically.

For information about creating and using user profiles and system policy files, see Chapter 15, "User Profiles and System Policies." For an example of setup script statements that enable user profiles, group policies, and remote administration, see Appendix D, "MSBATCH.INF Parameters."

# Overview of Push Installations

A push installation uses Windows 95 Setup with a setup script, plus login scripts and user accounts on a NetWare or Windows NT network, to create an automated, mandatory installation scheme for installing Windows 95 on multiple computers. This allows you to install Windows 95 remotely, without actually going to the computer being upgraded.

You will probably want to create an automated push installation scheme if you are responsible for installing Windows 95 on more than 50 computers.

After you use Server-based Setup to set up the source files on one or more servers and create setup scripts, you can perform push installations in these ways:

- Use a login script that includes a statement to run Setup with a setup script, automatically installing Windows 95 when each user logs on. Details are provided in the following sections.

- Insert an object in an electronic mail message that will start Windows 95 Setup with a setup script when the user clicks the object.

- Use Microsoft Systems Management Server to run Windows 95 Setup with a setup script as a mandatory job, as described in Appendix E, "Microsoft Systems Management Server."

- Use network management software from other vendors to install Windows 95 based on the setup scripts you create. Refer to the documentation for your network management software for information about performing remote installation of software.

**Push installation example for migration of shared Windows 3.x.**  Because Windows 95 installation and management methods differ significantly from Windows 3.x, it might be helpful to look at an example of how one type of corporate installation can make the move to Windows 95. The following example focuses on migrating shared installations to Windows 95.

In the corporation in this example, Windows 3.x was installed in shared directories on the network (using **setup /a**). Workstations each contain a hard disk, where the swap file, TEMP directory, and hardware-specific SYSTEM.INI file are stored. Windows 3.x components were installed in each user's home directory. All workstations run NetWare real-mode networking with ODI drivers. When users log on to the network, the login script runs WINSTART.BAT, which copies the workstation's SYSTEM.INI to the user's home directory and starts Windows. All applications are also stored on and run from servers.

To migrate to Windows 95 using push installations that maintain similar functionality for users on shared installations, the administrator does the following:

1.  Install Windows 95 source files and create machine directories for each computer. This step includes using INF Installer to prepare any supporting software that uses Windows 95 INF files, and manually copying any additional networking or applications software to the shared Windows 95 directory on the network.

2.  Create the setup script that specifies any custom settings. This should include installing all protected-mode networking components, so that both the administrator and user can take advantage of Windows 95 protected-mode networking features.

3.  Create system policies, including setting policies that enable user profiles.

    Alternately, you can enable user profiles using setup script statements, as defined in Appendix D, "MSBATCH.INF Parameters." This is the only method for enabling group policies.

4.  At each client computer, run a login script with statements to do the following:

    - Copy the contents of the user's home directory to C:\WINDOWS.

      This should include copying the Windows 3.x .GRP, .INI, and REG.DAT files that define the user's personal preferences and working environment. In this case, make sure that the Windows 3.x REG.DAT file includes registration settings for all the shared applications that users run at your site.

---

**Note**  This process is related to the particular configuration used in the example; this is not a required process for creating shared installations or using push installation methods to install Windows 95.

---

    - Run Windows 95 Setup with a custom setup script.

      You can set **installdir=c:\windows** to define the machine directory in the setup script.

In this example, Windows 95 Setup installs the shared Windows 95 files on the local hard disk and in the machine directory for the client computer. The settings in the Windows 3.x .GRP, .INI, and REG.DAT files are migrated automatically to the Registry. Notice that in this case, where user profiles are enabled, the current version of USER.DAT file is also stored automatically in the user's home directory when the user logs off. This copy of USER.DAT is the user profile that is then copied to the current machine directory wherever the user logs on.

To install Windows 95 on the local hard disk of client computers, the steps for the administrator are similar to those in the preceding example. However, no machine directories are created for the computers. The following section discusses specific issues related to login scripts for local installations of Windows 95.

# Using Login Scripts for Push Installation

Push installation from login scripts can be used on computers running MS-DOS or Windows 3.x with the following real-mode network clients:

- Microsoft Workgroup Add-on for MS-DOS
- LAN Manager 2.x real-mode network client
- Novell® NetWare® real-mode network client (NETX or VLM)
- Windows for Workgroups real-mode and protected-mode network clients

The following sections describe how to use a common Upgrade account rather than changing every user's login script to install Windows 95. This method avoids activating the Setup process again after Windows 95 has been installed. However, using a common Upgrade account might not work in some corporate environments, where INI files are copied to users' directories based on the user name specified at logon. In such cases, if Windows 95 is installed using an Upgrade account, each user's application settings will not be migrated to Windows 95. In such cases, you can add statements to setup scripts to copy the related INI files to C:\WINDOWS as part of the installation process.

Another method you can use with login scripts to avoid the problem of running Setup a second time is to add a statement to the login scripts to check the MS-DOS version with alternate actions defined when the version is Windows 95.

To use the method described in this section for push installations (for either protected-mode or real-mode network clients), you must do the following in addition to installing the Windows 95 source files and creating setup scripts:

- For Windows for Workgroups computers, create a STARTUP.GRP file that contains the command line for starting Windows 95 Setup, as described in "Preparing a STARTUP.GRP File" later in this chapter.
- Create the login scripts that will be used to start the installation process.
- Create the special user accounts that will be used to run the login scripts.

A push installation actually begins when the user logs on to the client computer.

---

**Important**  If the login script processor stays in memory after starting Windows 95, and if the computer is not correctly configured to use extended memory, then there might not be sufficient memory available to run Setup. However, the method presented here for using a STARTUP.GRP file with Windows for Workgroups avoids memory problems in push installations. For login scripts on NetWare networks, you can use an exit command that runs Windows 95 Setup after the login script is complete.

You can also remove unnecessary TSRs and device drivers to increase the available memory before Setup begins. For information about how to define statements in a setup script for changing the system configuration as part of installation, see Appendix D, "MSBATCH.INF Parameters."

---

# Preparing a STARTUP.GRP File

If you are upgrading computers that run Windows for Workgroups, you can create a special Startup group that is used just once to run the login script.

The use of the Startup group is only mandatory when the user is running Windows for Workgroups 3.11 with logon validated performed by Windows NT Server. In this case, the user starts Windows for Workgroups, which loads the protected-mode protocols and processes the login script. The login script runs in a VM; although Windows 95 Setup cannot be run in a VM, the login script can be used to create a modified STARTUP.GRP file that causes Setup to run as a Windows-based application after the login script finishes running.

**Note**  For computers that use a real-mode network client, login scripts can run Windows 95 Setup directly, without using a special STARTUP.GRP.

Only computers that use a protected-mode network client need to use the STARTUP.GRP method to run Setup from within Windows for Workgroups.

▶ **To prepare for push installations to upgrade earlier versions of Windows**

1. Run Windows for Workgroups on a computer.

2. If the Startup group is not present, use the File New command in Program Manager to create a Startup group.

3. In the Startup group, use the File New command to create an Upgrade icon that contains the following command line:

   *source_drive*: setup [*source_drive:msbatch_format.inf*]

   If the setup script is named MSBATCH.INF and is in the Windows directory in the source files, you do not need to specify the script name on the command line. Otherwise, specify the drive and script name. For example:

   ```
   k:\setup k:\myscript.inf
   ```

   Specify the same source drive used in the login script statements, as described in the following sections on preparing the server for push installations.

4. Copy the STARTUP.GRP file to the shared directory on the server that contains the Windows 95 source files.

5. Delete the group or icon that you just created, so that it is no longer stored on the computer where you are working.

6. In the MSBATCH.INF file, add the following statements to make sure that STARTUP.GRP is replaced after Setup:

   ```
   [install]
   renfiles=replace.startup.grp

   [replace.startup.grp]
   startup.grp, startup.sav

   [destinationdirs]
   replace.startup.grp=10
   ```

# Preparing Login Scripts for Push Installations

This section presents some information about creating login scripts that use an Upgrade account for installing Windows 95 on client computers. Some of the login script statements described in this section are related to using the STARTUP.GRP file for Windows for Workgroups, as described in "Preparing a STARTUP.GRP File" earlier in this chapter.

---

**Tip**  Avoid using relative path names in login scripts and setup scripts so that you can ensure the commands are run from the correct directory.

Also, for shared installations, after Windows 95 Setup is complete, make sure that all path statements in users' login scripts point to Windows 95, and not Windows 3.x or MS-DOS directories.

---

**Login scripts for Microsoft real-mode network clients.**  For a computer running MS-DOS or Windows 3.1 with a Microsoft real-mode network client, the login script should be similar to the following:

```
net start full
net use drive_letter: \\server\distshare
drive_letter:setup drive_letter:msbatch.inf
```

If the client computer is running on a LAN Manager or Windows for Workgroups network, the login script must contain a **net start full** statement. On a Windows for Workgroups network, the real-mode network client for Windows for Workgroups or Windows 3.1 also requires the entry **lmlogon=1** in the [Network] section of SYSTEM.INI. This ensures that the full network redirector is loaded and the user is validated for network logon. Other login script issues are discussed in the following section.

**Login scripts for Windows NT networks.**  For client computers running MS-DOS or Windows 3.1 on a Windows NT network where an Upgrade account is to be used to install Windows 95, the login script must contain the following kinds of entries:

```
net use source_drive \\ntserver\distshare
source_drive:setup source_drive:msbatch.inf
```

If this login script will be used to upgrade computers that are currently running Windows for Workgroups, the login script must contain the following kinds of entries to use a STARTUP.GRP:

```
net use source_drive \\ntserver\distshare
rename windowsdir\startup.grp *.sav
copy path\startup.grp windowsdir\startup.grp
```

| Value | Description |
|-------|-------------|
| *Source_Drive* | Maps a drive letter for the server containing the source files. This must be the same drive letter as specified in the STARTUP.GRP file. Check the **lastdrive=** setting in CONFIG.SYS to make sure that the drive letter specified on the preceding command line is a valid logical drive letter. If it is not, the network connection will not be made, and the Setup process will fail. |
| *\\NTServer\DistShare* | Specifies the Windows NT computer that contains the Windows 95 source files. |
| *WindowsDir* | Specifies the relative path to the user's Windows directory. |
| *Path* | Specifies the path to the Startup group file. |
| *User_Windows* | Specifies the relative path to the user's Windows directory that will contain STARTUP.GRP. Use the relative drive and directory designation ( . ) instead of the actual path to the Windows directory (for example, C:\WINDOWS). Do not use the **WinDir** environment variable, because **WinDir** is not an accessible environment variable in the script. |

For example, for a computer running Windows for Workgroups, the login script could be similar to the following:

```
net use k: \\ntserver\distshare
rename .\startup.grp *.sav
copy \winnt\system32\repl\import\scripts\startup.grp .\startup.grp
exit
```

**Login scripts for NetWare networks.**  The login script for client computers running MS-DOS or Windows 3.1 must contain the following kinds of entries:

```
attach nwserver/ DistShare:
map source_drive: nwserver/DistShare
source_drive: setup source_drive: msbatch.inf
```

| Value | Description |
|---|---|
| *Source_Drive* | Specifies the same drive letter as specified in the Startup group |
| *NWServer/DistShare* | Specifies the NetWare server that contains the Windows 95 source files |

For example, for a computer running MS-DOS or Windows 3.1 with a real-mode network client, the login script could be similar to the following:

```
attach nwserver1/win95
map k:nwserver1/win95
k:setup k:msbatch.inf
```

# Setting Up a Windows NT Server for Push Installations

This section summarizes the procedures for running login scripts from a Windows NT server for push installations.

▶ **To prepare the server for push installations on a Windows NT network**

1. Run Server-based Setup, and install the Windows 95 source files in the shared directory on the Windows NT Server, as described in Chapter 4, "Server-Based Setup for Windows 95."

2. Create an MSBATCH.INF file to meet your installation requirements, and copy this file into the Windows 95 source directory on the server.

3. Using User Manager for Domains on a computer running Windows NT Server, create a user account named Upgrade, and specify **upgrade** as the password. Also, make sure the following options are selected for the Upgrade user account:

   - User Cannot Change Password

   - Password Never Expires

   By default, the user account is created in the domain where you logged on to the network. To create the user account in another domain, you must select that domain before creating the account. If your users log on to multiple domains, create the Upgrade user account in each domain.

4. Create the login scripts that run Windows 95 Setup. For examples that use the Upgrade user account, see "Preparing Login Scripts for Push Installations" earlier in this chapter.

5. Assign the login script to the Upgrade user account. The login script must be placed in the *winnt*\SYSTEM32\REPL\EXPORT\SCRIPTS directory on the computer running Windows NT Server.

   The replication service replicates this from the export server to the import server, so the file is copied to *winnt*\SYSTEM32\REPL\IMPORT\SCRIPTS on the server.

# Setting Up a NetWare Server for Push Installations

This section summarizes the procedures for running login scripts from a NetWare server for push installations.

▶ **To prepare the server for push installations on a NetWare network**

1. Run Server-based Setup, and install the Windows 95 source files in the shared directory on the NetWare server, as described in Chapter 4, "Server-Based Setup for Windows 95."

2. Create an MSBATCH.INF file to meet your installation requirements, and copy this file into the directory that contains the Windows 95 source files on the network.

3. On the NetWare server, create a user account named Upgrade and specify **upgrade1** as the password. Also, set the types of options for this account as described in the following list.

   - Allow User To Change Password = No
   - Force Periodic Password Changes = No

4. Assign the Upgrade user account to the preferred server to which users have access.

5. Create a login script and assign it to the Upgrade user. The login script must be placed in the appropriate directory on the server where users will log on. For examples of login scripts that use the Upgrade user account, see "Preparing Login Scripts for Push Installations" earlier in this chapter.

# Running Login Scripts for Push Installations

Push installations from login scripts are the same whether you are running a network client with MS-DOS, Windows 3.1, or Windows for Workgroups. If you are using an Upgrade account, as described earlier, these are the requirements:

- For computers running Windows for Workgruops, the Upgrade account has been created on the Windows NT domain or NetWare server, with a corresponding Upgrade login script, as described in the previous section.

- The Upgrade login script contains these principal entries:

  - The **net use** statements to connect to the appropriate shared directory for the Windows 95 source files (or similar statement for starting the network and connecting to the server on a NetWare network).

  - Statements to start Windows 95 Setup. These statements might involve renaming the user's Startup group and copying the alternate Startup group from the server, as described in "Preparing a STARTUP.GRP File" earlier in this chapter.

  - An **exit** statement that closes the login script so that Setup can continue.

▶ **To run a login script for a push installation**

- Tell users to log on to the network using the Upgrade user account and the **upgrade** password.

  When a user logs on, the Windows 95 installation process begins automatically, using the settings in the MSBATCH.INF file specified in the login script.

After copying files, Windows 95 restarts the computer and begins the Run-Once operations (group conversions, and so on). When the Run-Once operations are finished, Windows 95 is completely installed. Notice that this stage requires the user to log on to the network, so all configuration values must be specified in the setup script to support correct logon and to allow Windows 95 Setup to connect to shared resources containing Windows 95 source files.

When the user quits Windows 95 at this point, Setup writes all changes to the Registry. The user can restart the computer and log on using the usual logon name and password.

C H A P T E R  6

# Setup Technical Discussion

This chapter provides technical information about Windows 95 Setup, including background information about Safe Recovery and detailed descriptions of the Setup and system startup processes. You will find this technical information helpful if you are responsible for troubleshooting Windows 95.

**In This Chapter**

Phases of the Setup Process  179
   Startup and Information Gathering Phase for Windows 95 Setup  179
   Hardware Detection Phase  180
   File Copy Phase  181
   Final System Configuration Phase  183
Safe Detection, Safe Recovery, and Verification  184
   Safe Detection in Windows 95 Setup  185
   Safe Recovery with Setup Log Files  187
Windows 95 Startup Process  195
   Bootstrapping in the BIOS Phase  196
   Loading Hardware Profiles and Real-Mode Drivers  197
   Initializing Static VxDs at Startup  197
   Loading the Protected-Mode Operating System at Startup  199
System Startup Files  200
   IO.SYS: The Real-Mode Operating System  201
   MSDOS.SYS: Special Startup Values  203
   CONFIG.SYS and AUTOEXEC.BAT  205
   SYSTEM.INI and WIN.INI  213
   BOOTLOG.TXT: The Startup Process Log  216

(*continued*)

Windows 95 Setup with Other Operating Systems    219
    Installing Windows 95 over Windows 3.x    219
    Installing Windows 95 for Dual Booting with Windows 3.x    221
    Installing Windows 95 over MS-DOS    222
    Installing Windows 95 for Dual Booting with Windows NT    225
    Installing Windows 95 over DR DOS    226
    Installing Windows 95 over OS/2    226
Removing Windows 95 from a Computer    227
    Removing Windows 95 with Command-Line Startup    227
    Removing Windows 95 with Your Previous Operating System    230
Troubleshooting Setup and System Startup    233
    Troubleshooting Specific Setup Errors    233
    Troubleshooting Specific Startup Errors    241
    Converting Windows 3.x Program Groups    245

# Phases of the Setup Process

Windows 95 Setup is divided into the following logical phases:

- Startup and information gathering
- Hardware detection
- File copy
- Final system configuration

The following sections provide technical details about what happens in each of these phases.

# Startup and Information Gathering Phase for Windows 95 Setup

When you start Windows 95 Setup, the following steps occur:

1. If you started Windows 95 Setup from MS-DOS, Setup searches the local hard disks for previous versions of Windows. If a version of Windows is found, the program prompts you to quit and run Setup from Windows. You can, however, bypass this warning.

2. Setup runs ScanDisk and performs system checks to confirm that the computer is capable of running Windows 95 (enough CPU, memory, and disk space; the correct version of MS-DOS; and so on). If there are insufficient resources, Setup informs you of the problem. For a description of system requirements, see Chapter 3, "Introduction to Windows 95 Setup."

3. If you started Windows 95 Setup from MS-DOS, Setup checks for an extended memory specification (XMS) provider and installs one if one is not present. Windows 95 Setup looks for existing disk caching and automatically loads SMARTDrive if no other caching is found. The cache size varies, depending on available XMS memory.

4. Setup checks for the existence of certain TSR applications and device drivers that are known to cause problems. If any of these applications are running, Setup warns you before proceeding.

5. If you started Windows 95 Setup from MS-DOS, your Setup installs the minimal Windows 3.1 components and starts these components by using the **shell=setup.exe** command.

   The Windows graphical user interface appears. In a normal installation, this is the first thing you see. Up to this point, the processor is operating in real mode.

6. If you started Windows 95 Setup from MS-DOS, Setup switches the processor to standard mode and makes extended memory available.

Windows 95 Setup begins gathering installation information to determine the components to be installed, including the directory for Windows 95 files, user information, and specifics about the devices and software to be installed. For more information, see Chapter 3, "Introduction to Windows 95 Setup."

# Hardware Detection Phase

During the hardware detection phase, Windows 95 Setup analyzes installed computer components, and detects installed hardware devices and connected peripherals. Windows 95 Setup also identifies the hardware resources that are available (for example, IRQs, I/O addresses, and DMAs), identifies the configuration of installed hardware components (for example, IRQs in use), and builds the hardware tree in the Registry.

Windows 95 Setup uses several mechanisms to detect installed hardware devices:

- For a non-Plug and Play-compliant computer (called a legacy computer), Windows 95 checks for known hardware devices by checking I/O ports and specific memory addresses to attempt to identify whether they are being used by known devices. Windows 95 also checks for Plug and Play peripherals connected to legacy computers, which return their own device identification codes.

- For a computer with a Plug and Play BIOS, Windows 95 queries the computer for installed components and their configuration. Windows 95 also checks the computer for connected Plug and Play peripheral devices.

During this phase, Windows 95 Setup tries to identify and resolve hardware conflicts.

Setup uses the Windows 95 hardware detection module to detect hardware components. If a Plug and Play device is detected, its configuration information is added to the Registry. Device drivers are installed based on the Registry settings. Plug and Play ensures that the correct files are installed and that the configuration options are set properly each time Windows 95 is started. For information about Plug and Play, see Chapter 18, "Introduction to System Configuration" and Chapter 31, "Windows 95 Architecture."

Windows 95 uses the same hardware detection procedures when you run the Add New Hardware option in Control Panel, when you use the PCMCIA wizard to enable protected-mode support, and the first time you start a computer using a new docking state.

For more information about how detection works, see "Safe Detection, Safe Recovery, and Verification" later in this chapter.

# File Copy Phase

After you identify and confirm the components to install, Windows 95 Setup begins copying files from the Windows 95 installation disks, compact disc, or network server (whichever was specified). If you selected the option to create a startup disk, this disk is created before the files are copied.

After the necessary files are copied to the computer, Windows 95 Setup prompts you to remove any disks in floppy disk drives and restart the computer to proceed with the final phase of Setup. The following topics describe what happens during the file copy phase.

## Creating the Startup Disk

A startup disk is a bootable floppy disk contains utilities that you can use to troubleshoot a malfunctioning system. The startup disk loads the operating system and presents an MS-DOS command line. It is strongly recommended that you create a startup disk for every computer you install Windows 95 on. You can create a Windows 95 startup disk during the file copy phase of Windows 95 Setup, or you can create or update a disk after Windows 95 has been installed by using the Add/Remove Programs option in Control Panel. For information about using the startup disk, see Chapter 35, "General Troubleshooting."

In general, the startup disk does not provide the following:

- Real-mode support for disk-management software such as ATDOSXL.SYS or Stacker® 4.0
- Access to the network
- Access to CD-ROM drives
- Access to compressed drives from other vendors

To create a startup disk, Windows 95 formats the floppy disk in drive A, and then copies files to the disk in drive A. The files that are copied are described in the following table.

| Filename | Description |
| --- | --- |
| attrib.exe | File attribute utility |
| command.com | Core operating system file |
| drvspace.bin | Disk compression utility |
| ebd.sys | Utility for the startup disk |
| edit.com | Text editor |
| fdisk.exe | Disk partition utility |
| format.com | Disk format utility |
| io.sys | Core operating system file |
| msdos.sys | Core operating system file |
| regedit.exe | Real-mode Registry Editor |
| scandisk.exe | Disk status and repair utility |
| scandisk.ini | Disk status utility configuration file |
| sys.com | System transfer utility |

For recovery purposes, you might want to copy the following files into a subdirectory on the startup disk: SYSTEM.DAT, CONFIG.SYS, AUTOEXEC.BAT, WIN.INI, and SYSTEM.INI, plus any CD-ROM or other device drivers. (If you do not place these files into a subdirectory, you'll have to rename them to prevent problems with the startup disk.)

## Creating Directories and Copying Files

Windows 95 Setup creates a list of files to copy, depending on the components selected during the information gathering phase. Then various Setup DLLs run to install the network and other components. These DLLs determine exactly which files should be copied from the installation source and which additional directories should be created.

## Creating Registry Entries

The Setup DLLs for installing various system components also create appropriate entries in the Registry and change INI file settings as required. (The Registry is created during the hardware detection phase.)

The SYSTEM.1ST file in the root directory is a copy of the Registry created when Setup is complete. To restore a damaged Registry, you can change the file attributes on this file and copy it to SYSTEM.DAT.

# Final System Configuration Phase

During the final system configuration phase, Windows 95 Setup upgrades the existing configuration of Windows and replaces the existing version of MS-DOS with the new Windows 95 operating system (if you are upgrading an existing version of Windows). During this process, Setup restarts the computer running Windows 95.

When Windows 95 Setup completes this phase, it displays a message to indicate that the installation was successful and it prompts you to restart the computer. After you click OK but before Windows 95 Setup restarts the computer, Setup modifies the boot sector of the boot drive by adding a new system file (IO.SYS) that takes the place of the MS-DOS files IO.SYS and MSDOS.SYS. The old files are renamed to IO.DOS and MSDOS.DOS.

After the files are updated and the operating system is configured, Windows 95 Setup uses wizards to guide you through a process to configure peripheral devices (such as printers) connected to the computer. More files might also be copied here, and you might be asked to restart the computer again.

## Initializing the System after Setup

After first restarting the computer during the final system configuration phase, Windows 95 Setup updates configuration files by performing the following steps:

- WININIT.EXE processes three sections in WININIT.INI to combine all the virtual devices (VxDs) into VMM32.VXD and to rename files initially used by Setup, including ARIAL.WIN, USER32.TMP, and LOGO.SYS.

- SYSTEM.DAT is renamed to SYSTEM.DA0, and SYSTEM.NEW is renamed to SYSTEM.DAT.

- A flag is set in the Registry that indicates this is the first time Windows 95 is being run after a new installation. Hardware manufacturers can also add specific entries to the Run-Once Registry key.

- The Run-Once module is run to complete the initial configuration of PCMCIA and MIDI devices, to set up printers (if you are not installing in an existing Windows directory), and to run custom hardware manufacturers' setup programs.

---

**Important**  If the system fails when running these first-time programs, restart Windows 95 rather than rerunning Windows 95 Setup.

---

- The Program Group converter (GRPCONV) adds existing Windows 3.x .GRP files to the PROGRAMS directory and renames the files using long filenames.

Windows 95 installation is now complete.

## Modifying the Boot Drive after Setup

Windows 95 places the real-mode operating system files named IO.SYS, MSDOS.SYS, and COMMAND.COM in the root directory of the computer's boot drive. The real-mode files needed to connect to the network are also placed on the computer's boot drive or device. (These filenames vary, depending on the network you use.)

Windows 95 detects boot drives and compression drivers, and writes certain startup files to the boot device.

## Verifying the Installation

Setup has an option for verifying the installation, as described in "Introduction: Safe Detection, Safe Recovery, and Verification" later in this chapter. So, Windows 95 Setup can install files on your disk without actually having to transfer all of the file data from the floppy disk drive, network, or other source. As a part of this process, Windows 95 rebuilds VMM32.VXD or recopies any files it finds to be damaged.

For Safe Recovery, Windows 95 Setup places the following two lines in AUTOEXEC.BAT during installation:

```
@if exist c:\wininst0.400\suwarn.bat call C:\wininst0.400\suwarn.bat
@if exist c:\wininst0.400\suwarn.bat del C:\wininst0.400\suwarn.bat
```

The SUWARN.BAT file is run only once after a failed installation. These lines are removed when Windows 95 Setup is complete.

# Safe Detection, Safe Recovery, and Verification

This section provides technical details about the features that ensure safe hardware detection, recovery from Setup problems, and configuration verification in Windows 95 Setup.

# Safe Detection in Windows 95 Setup

Devices and buses are grouped as classes in Windows 95 for purposes of detecting and installing device drivers and managing system resources. Windows 95 differentiates between devices and drivers that comply with the Plug and Play specification and earlier versions of devices and drivers (which are referred to in the *Windows 95 Resource Kit* as legacy devices). Because of this differentiation, Windows 95 Setup detects hardware components and devices in two ways:

- Using an interactive query detection process for legacy devices and peripherals
- Using Plug and Play detection to identify Plug and Play-compliant devices and peripherals

After Setup detects a device, it adds configuration information to the Registry and installs the appropriate device drivers. The same procedures used during Setup for detecting Plug and Play or legacy hardware devices are also used to detect or configure new devices after Windows 95 is installed.

Windows 95 supports detection for base computer components such as communications ports and processor type, and provides more robust detection of computer devices, such as display adapters, pointing devices, hard-disk controllers, floppy-disk controllers, and network adapters.

Windows 95 Setup also tries to detect any hardware resource conflicts early in the installation process. This helps to avoid the problems that occur when hardware resources such as IRQs, I/O addresses, or DMAs are used by more than one device.

To avoid computer failure during the detection process, Windows 95 uses a safe detection method to search for hints from configuration files, read-only memory (ROM) strings, or drivers loaded in memory to determine whether the computer contains each class of hardware. If no such hints are found, the detection process skips detecting the entire class. If hints are found, then the detection process seeks information from specific I/O ports.

Windows 95 automatically reads the command lines in CONFIG.SYS to find hints for device class detection. Then Windows 95 loads detection modules based on information in the MSDET.INF file, which lists the hardware to be detected and points to specific INF files for each device class (for example, SCSI.INF for SCSI host adapters). Device information from the INF files is written to the Registry. For more information about the format of these files, see Appendix C, "Windows 95 INF Files."

Windows 95 can also read a particular CONFIG.SYS **device=** line for resource information to be avoided (that is, protected) during the detection process. This is useful if Windows 95 Setup cannot detect or support a certain device when it's known that the detection process can cause such a device to fail. For example, the detection process could render a fax modem inoperative because scanning the I/O port might confuse the device driver. Windows 95 can read the **device=** line in CONFIG.SYS for this model and protect the associated I/O region from other detection modules.

Windows 95 Setup asks you to confirm which classes should be skipped in the detection process. If you know that the computer has a device in one of those classes, Setup can be forced to detect that device class.

Safe detection exists for four classes of devices:

- Network adapters
- SCSI controllers
- Proprietary adapters for CD-ROM
- Sound cards

## Safe Detection for Network Adapters

Windows 95 Setup performs the following kinds of steps for safe detection of network adapters:

- Find LSL.COM in memory and, if present, inquire for network adapter settings.
- Find IPX.COM in memory and, if present, inquire for network adapter settings.
- Search the Windows, Windows for Workgroups, and LAN Manager directories for PROTOCOL.INI; if present, read the file to find network adapter settings.

## Safe Detection for SCSI Controllers

When trying to detect SCSI adapters, Windows 95 Setup checks for device drivers in CONFIG.SYS, and then scans ROM strings from the SCSI adapter for manufacturer names. If known drivers or known strings are found, then the corresponding detection procedure for that class is used; otherwise, the entire class is skipped. A list of the known strings and drivers that Windows 95 Setup checks is stored internally in a detection DLL. (For more information about the SCSI devices and drivers that Windows 95 supports, see the Manufacturers and Models lists in the Add New Hardware option in Control Panel.)

Different SCSI devices require different methods for safe detection. For example, a SCSI card typically is used with a combination of hard disks, CD-ROM drives, tape backup drives, scanners, and similar devices. For everything to work (except the hard disk), some sort of device driver must be loaded in CONFIG.SYS.

For hard disk drives, however, the driver usually is not loaded in CONFIG.SYS, but INT 13 ROM are enabled. Therefore, safe detection for SCSI class devices looks for a ROM string with a manufacturer's name.

## Safe Detection for Proprietary Adapters for CD-ROM

Windows 95 supports Mitsumi, SONY, and Panasonic proprietary adapters for CD-ROM. Because drivers for these devices are loaded in CONFIG.SYS, safe detection first scans CONFIG.SYS for the drivers that are present. If a **device=** line for such a driver is found, the corresponding detection module is loaded for that type of device.

## Safe Detection for Sound Cards

Safe detection scans CONFIG.SYS and reads SYSTEM.INI for hints about sound cards. If known drivers are not found, the entire class is skipped.

If Windows 95 doesn't have detection code for certain hardware, the equipment manufacturer can force a device to be detected by adding information about it in the MSDET.INF file. Windows 95 detection behaves as if it has detected the device and installs the device according to the INF information provided by the equipment manufacturer.

Windows 95 Setup does not detect sound cards by scanning I/O ports; instead, it checks only CONFIG.SYS and SYSTEM.INI and performs detection prescribed in MSDET.INF. Detection of sound cards by scanning I/O ports can cause the computer to stall. This is because detection calls a driver specific to a device class to send a signal to an I/O port. The driver expects a predetermined response, such as a signature from the adapter's ROM. If the wrong driver sends a signal to an I/O port address occupied by a different device class, the computer can stall.

# Safe Recovery with Setup Log Files

Windows 95 Setup creates several log files: BOOTLOG.TXT, DETLOG.TXT, NETLOG.TXT, and SETUPLOG.TXT, plus DETCRASH.LOG if Setup fails. The following sections describe these files.

Basically, there are three points at which the computer might stop or stall during Windows 95 Setup: before, during, or after hardware detection.

- If Setup fails before hardware detection, Windows 95 Setup recovers by reading SETUPLOG.TXT to determine where the system stalled, what to redo, and what to skip.

- If Setup fails during hardware detection, the DETCRASH.LOG file is created, containing information about the detection module that was running and the I/O port or memory resources it was accessing when the failure occurred.

  When the detection process finds this file, it automatically runs in Safe Recovery mode to verify all the devices already in the Registry and then skips all detection modules up to the failed module. Safe Recovery then skips detection and any attempts to configure the failed module, in effect skipping the action that caused the failure. Then, Safe Recovery continues the detection process, starting with the next module. If the detection process is completed successfully, DETCRASH.LOG is deleted.

  DETCRASH.LOG can be read only by Setup. For information about the text equivalent of this information, see "DETLOG.TXT: The Hardware Detection Log File" later in this chapter.

- Sometimes the detection process causes some devices to quit working (such as a CD-ROM drive or a network connection). If you rerun Setup, Safe Recovery recognizes that the detection process has already been completed successfully and assumes that all the necessary hardware information is in the Registry. Therefore, it skips the detection process completely at this point and continues the installation process.

## SETUPLOG.TXT: The Setup Log File

The SETUPLOG.TXT file is an ASCII text file that contains Windows 95 Setup information created during the installation process. While Windows 95 is being installed, corresponding entries are written to SETUPLOG.TXT, listing information about the specific steps, their sequence, and the error conditions encountered. This file is used by Setup for recovery in case of setup failure, and it can also be used for troubleshooting errors that occur during the installation process.

Setup uses the information in SETUPLOG.TXT to ensure that the installation does not fail twice because of the same problem. If you restart Windows 95 Setup after a setup process fails, Setup reviews the contents of SETUPLOG.TXT to determine which steps completed successfully. If SETUPLOG.TXT indicates that a process started but does not indicate that the process completed, then that part of the installation process is skipped and the next part is processed. Even if Setup encounters devices that cause several installation attempts, the installation process will always progress and skip the modules that failed.

SETUPLOG.TXT is stored on the computer's root directory. Information is added to the file according to the order of the steps of the installation process. If an error occurs during installation, you can determine the probable cause of the error by examining the entries at the end of SETUPLOG.TXT.

Information in SETUPLOG.TXT is divided into the following basic categories:

- Selected Setup sections, including [OptionalComponents], [System], [NameAndOrg], and [*batch_settings*]
- Setting up of system startup parameters
- Selecting the directory
- Beginning of installation process
- Queuing of needed files
- Copying of needed files
- Preparing for restarting the system

---

**Tip**  The [OptionalComponents], [System], and [NameAndOrg] sections can be copied from SETUPLOG.TXT on a computer with a complete installation of Windows 95 and then added to equivalent sections in MSBATCH.INF, as described in Chapter 5, "Custom, Automated, and Push Installations." Notice, however, that these sections in SETUPLOG.TXT do not include networking information.

---

The following table shows entries in SETUPLOG.TXT file to check for information about the Setup process. Because entries are added to SETUPLOG.TXT in the order that the related actions occur during Setup, you might be able to find a probable cause of any error by examining the entries at the end of the file.

| SETUPLOG.TXT entry | Description |
| --- | --- |
| InstallType | Type of installation |
| InstallDir | Directory where Windows 95 is installed |
| detection | Detection status |
| RunningApp | Applications running during installation |
| RootFilesRenamed | Files renamed in the root directory |
| error | Errors logged during installation |
| failed | Failures that occurred during installation |
| [OptionalComponents] | Optional components installed |
| [System] | System hardware configuration |
| batch settings | Installation parameters (that is, MSBATCH.INF settings) |
| Registry | Registry initialization status |
| *filename* | Verification that a specific file was loaded during Setup |
| [Choose Directory] | Location and type of Windows files |
| [FileCopy] | Files copied during Setup |
| [Restart] | Issues to be completed after the computer is restarted |

**Tip for Verifying System Files**

With Windows 3.x, it was not easy to recover files, such as a component file that was accidentally deleted or a system file that was corrupted. You either had to use the Expand utility to copy the file, or you had to reinstall Windows 3.x to restore the lost file. SETUPLOG.TXT is part of the Windows 95 solution to verifying the integrity of installed components.

If you run Windows 95 Setup after Windows 95 is already installed, Setup prompts you either to reinstall Windows 95 or simply to verify installed components. If you want to verify installed components, Setup examines SETUPLOG.TXT and reruns the installation process without completely copying all operating system components. Windows 95 verifies the integrity of files installed during Setup with the files on the Windows 95 installation disks. If the integrity check fails due to a missing or corrupted file on the computer, Setup automatically reinstalls that file.

# DETLOG.TXT: The Hardware Detection Log File

The DETLOG.TXT file contains a record of whether a specific hardware device was detected and identifies the parameters for the detected device.

During Windows 95 Setup, after the information gathering phase, Setup begins hardware detection, which can also occur when you use the Add New Hardware option in Control Panel to add a new device. Both Windows 95 Setup and Device Manager use SYSDETMG.DLL, which contains all the detection modules for each device class and specific devices.

Windows 95 loads detection modules based on information in MSDET.INF that points to specific INF files for each device class, from which information is retrieved and written to the Registry. The device class installers are DLLs that work with Device Manager to install, configure, and remove devices or classes of devices in the system. Device Manager generates a list of compatible drivers for the device from the appropriate INF file. For information about using Device Manager to configure device drivers, and for information about the device classes used to identify logical device types, such as display, keyboard, and network adapters, see Chapter 19, "Devices."

By creating an updated DETLOG.TXT file every time the detection process runs, the detection module tracks the detected devices and the I/O port addresses used. Any existing DETLOG.TXT is renamed DETLOG.OLD. If the detection process causes Setup to stall or the computer to lock up, then a binary file named

DETCRASH.LOG is created. DETLOG.TXT is an ASCII text file created only for users to read; Windows 95 Setup reads the binary information in DETCRASH.LOG. Any changes made to DETLOG.TXT are not passed to DETCRASH.LOG.

The DETLOG.TXT file can be found in the root directory of the startup drive after Windows 95 is installed. The entries in DETLOG.TXT are placed in the order of the hardware information discovered as each step of the detection process is carried out. The following table briefly describes entries that appear in DETLOG.TXT.

**Summary of DETLOG.TXT Entries**

| Entry | Description |
| --- | --- |
| **Beginning of DETLOG.TXT:** | |
| `Parameters="xxxxxx"` | Shows the switches specified in the Setup command line (that is, **setup** /p *xxxxxx*). For example:<br><br>`Parameters "", Flags=01002233` |
| `WinVer = ########` | Shows that environment detection is run. The MS-DOS version is in the high word and the Windows version is in the low word. For example:<br><br>`WinVer=0614030b,` |
| `AvoidMem=`<br>`#####h-#####h` | If present, indicates the address range specified as upper memory blocks (UMB), which detection avoids. For example:<br><br>`AvoidMem=cd4a0-cd50f` |
| `DetectClass: Skip`<br>`Class Media` | Indicates that detection found no hints that the computer might have a particular device, so it skipped that class. For example, **DetectClass: Skip Class Media** indicates that no sound entries appear in the configuration files, so detection skips all the sound card detection modules. For **DetectClass: Skip Class Adapter**, detection skips searching for proprietary CD-ROM adapters such as SONY, Mitsumi, and Panasonic. **DetectClass: Skip Class Net** indicates that detection was skipped for network adapters. |
| `DetectClass Override:` | If one or more **skip class** entries appear in DETLOG.TXT, the Analyzing Your Computer screen appears in Setup to confirm skipping those classes, so you can override the decision. Related **DetectClass Override** lines appear in DETLOG.TXT for the classes checked. |

**Summary of DETLOG.TXT Entries** (*continued*)

| Entry | Description |
|-------|-------------|
| `Custom Mode:` | Describes your selection for the devices you tell Windows 95 not to detect. For example:<br><br>`CustomMode: resetting class ADAPTER`<br>`; Don't detect EtherLinkIII`<br>`CustomMode: DETECTELNK3=0` |
| `Devices verified =` | Indicates the number of devices verified from the Registry. If the number is 0, it usually means there was no existing Registry or the Registry was empty. |

**Detecting system devices:**

| | |
|-------|-------------|
| `Checking for:` | Specifies that detection began looking for that device. The entry is followed by description of the device or class being sought. When detection is checking for a device such as the Programmable Interrupt Controller, the **Checking for:** entry is followed by a **QueryIOMem:** entry specifying the Caller, rcQuery, and I/O range checked. If a device is detected, then a **Detected:** entry is added, specifying the device resource information. For example:<br><br>`Checking for: Programmable Interrupt Controller`<br>`QueryIOMem: Caller=DETECTPIC, rcQuery=0`<br>`     IO=20-21,a0-a1`<br>`Detected: *PNP0000\0000 =`<br>`          [1] Programmable Interrupt Controller`<br>`     IO=20-21,a0-a1`<br>`     IRQ=2` |

**Detecting network adapters:**

| | |
|-------|-------------|
| `Checking for:` | This section lists the attempts to detect network adapters. For example:<br><br>`Checking for: Network Cards using Novell`<br>`          ODI Driver`<br>`Checking for: EISA Network Cards` |
| `PROTOCOL.INI Section` | If detection finds PROTOCOL.INI, it saves the [*net_card*] section in DETLOG.TXT. For example:<br><br>`Checking for: Network Cards using`<br>`          Microsoft Windows For Workgroups`<br>`; path to WFW protocol.INI`<br>`WFW: path=d:\w311\protocol.ini`<br>`; protocol.ini mac driver section`<br>`Protocol.ini: [MS$EE16]`<br>`Protocol.ini: DriverName=EXP16$` |

**Summary of DETLOG.TXT Entries** (*continued*)

| Entry | Description |
|---|---|
| NCD: detecting network adapter | Indicates that detection has found a network adapter using safe detection (usually PROTOCOL.INI), but the system has information for verifying this adapter. If this adapter is verified, a **Detected** line follows. For example:<br><br>`NCD: detecting network adapter *pnp812d`<br>`QueryIOMem: Caller=DETECTWFW, rcQuery=0`<br>`IO=300-30f` |

The hardware detection process continues examining computer hardware. The "|" symbol in the **IO=** line (for example, **IO=200-201 | 3e0-3e1**) indicates a range of I/O entries that are checked during the detection process. In the DETLOG.TXT file, you will find a **QueryIOMem:** and an **IO=** line for each I/O address checked.

For most devices, multiple I/O addresses are checked, which can result in a detailed and redundant device detection list. The I/O address ranges checked during detection are grouped on one I/O line. Multiple addresses on an **IO=** line are separated by commas. For example:

```
Checking for: ATI Ultra Pro/Plus (Mach 32) Display Adapter
QueryIOMem: Caller=DETECTMACH32, rcQuery=0
    IO=3b0-3bb,3c0-3df
QueryIOMem: Caller=DETECTMACH32, rcQuery=0
    Mem=a0000-affff
```

If the system stalls during hardware detection, you can determine the probable cause of the error by examining the last entries in DETLOG.TXT. You can use the information in this file to determine specific error conditions occurring in the hardware detection, and reconfigure or replace the specific adapter or device. The following table shows specific kinds of entries to check in DETLOG.TXT for information about the results of the hardware detection process.

**DETLOG.TXT Entries to Check for Troubleshooting**

| Entry | Description |
|---|---|
| detected | Detected devices |
| AvoidMem | Address ranges of UMBs avoided during detection |
| error | Errors logged during system detection |
| WinFlags | Setup mode used |
| PROTOCOL.INI | PROTOCOL.INI information that was saved during system upgrade |
| CustomMode | Hardware that was removed from detection in the custom Analyzing Your Computer dialog box |
| Devices verified | Devices found in Registry; if the value is 0, then there was no existing Registry or the Registry was empty |

Some additional notes on DETLOG.TXT and hardware detection:

- Detection does not detect enumerated devices such as ISA Plug and Play devices, PCI devices, and PCMCIA devices. For information about these devices, see Chapter 18, "Introduction to System Configuration."

- If the computer stalls during detection, and you rerun Windows 95 Setup and choose Safe Recovery, new detection information is appended to the previous DETLOG.TXT file. The previous version of DETLOG.TXT is saved as DETLOG.OLD, overwriting any previous DETLOG.OLD files.

The hardware that has been tested and shown to be compatible with Windows 95 appears in the Manufacturers and Models lists in the Add New Hardware option in Control Panel.

## NETLOG.TXT: The Network Setup Log File

This file describes the detection results for network components during Windows 95 Setup. For information about NETDET.INI, the file that Setup uses to determine how to install networking components on computers running NetWare clients, see Chapter 9, "Windows 95 on NetWare Networks."

The following table describes typical entries in a NETLOG.TXT file after you run Windows 95 Setup for the first time. In this example, Client for Microsoft Networks is installed with the IPX/SPX-compatible protocol, and both are bound to an Intel® EtherExpress™ network adapter.

| NETLOG.TXT entry | Description |
| --- | --- |
| ClassInstall (0x6) on Intel EtherExpress 16 or 16TP at Enum\Root\*PNP812D\0000 | Network installation begins. |
| Examining class NET | Network detection is searching for network software of four class types: NET (network adapters), NETTRANS (protocols), NETCLIENT (clients), and NETSERVICES (services such as File and Printer Sharing). |
| Upgrade 2.00025000=VREDIR | A network client was found on the computer. |
| Upgrade to: VREDIR | The version of the network client was upgraded to the version included in Windows 95. |
| NdiCreate (Client for Microsoft Networks) OK | Setup successfully created an internal object representing the network client. |
| NdiCreate (Intel EtherExpress 16 or 16TP) | Setup successfully created an internal object representing the network adapter. |

| NETLOG.TXT entry | Description |
|---|---|
| `CreateNetwork, Batch=0` | Setup referenced a batch file. |
| `NdiCreate (IPX/SPX-compatible Protocol)` | Setup successfully created an internal object representing the IPX/SPX-compatible protocol. |
| `ClassInstall (0x6) end` | |
| `ClassInstall (0x9) on Intel EtherExpress 16 or 16TP at Enum\Root\*PNP812D\0000` | Protocols are about to be bound to the network adapter. |
| `Validating  IPX/SPX-compatible Protocol at Enum\Network\NWLINK\0000, rc=0x0` | The IPX/SPX-compatible protocol is added to the Registry and bound to the network adapter. |
| `ClassInstall (0x9) on Intel EtherExpress 16 or 16TP at Enum\Root\*PNP812D\0000` | Clients are about to be bound to the network adapter. |
| `Validating  Client for Microsoft Networks at Enum\Network\VREDIR \0000, rc=0x0` | Client for Microsoft Networks is added to the Registry and bound to the network adapter. |
| `ClassInstall (0x9) end` | Setup has finished binding the protocol to the network adapter. |
| `ClassInstall (0xa) on Intel EtherExpress 16 or 16TP at Enum\Root\*PNP812D\0000` | The network setup process is concluded. |
| `ClassInstall (0xa) end` | |
| `ClassInstall (0xc) on Intel EtherExpress 16 or 16TP at Enum\Root\*PNP812D\0000` | |
| `ClassInstall (0xc) end` | |

# Windows 95 Startup Process

Windows 95 includes new system files, Plug and Play mechanisms, and various options for starting the operating system. This section describes the Windows 95 system startup sequence.

During the real-mode startup process, devices use only static configurations; that is, no dynamic resource allocation or arbitration is provided. When the system startup process switches to protected mode, Configuration Manager ensures all devices are configured properly, as described in Chapter 31, "Windows 95 Architecture."

The system startup includes four phases:

- Bootstrapping the system with BIOS in control
- Loading MS-DOS drivers and TSRs for compatibility
- Initializing static VxDs in real mode
- Putting the protected-mode operating system in control and loading the remaining VxDs

# Bootstrapping in the BIOS Phase

Microsoft worked with several hardware manufacturers to define a new Plug and Play BIOS specification, which defines the interactions among a Plug and Play BIOS, Plug and Play devices, and option ROMs (sometimes called adapter ROMs). The Plug and Play BIOS enables and configures Plug and Play boot devices. The Plug and Play BIOS also passes configuration information to Configuration Manager in Windows 95 for configuring the remaining adapters and devices.

## Booting with a Legacy BIOS

For legacy computers that do not have Plug and Play BIOS, the BIOS enables all devices on the ISA bus. A Plug and Play ISA card that has an option ROM must start up when the computer is turned on with the option ROM enabled.

## Booting with a Plug and Play BIOS

A Plug and Play BIOS accesses nonvolatile RAM to determine which Plug and Play ISA cards should be enabled, where their option ROMs should be mapped, and what I/O, DMA, and other assignments are to be given to the cards.

The BIOS then programs the Plug and Play cards before the power-on self-test (POST). All cards that do not have configurations stored in the BIOS are disabled completely, reducing the chance of a conflict.

The Plug and Play BIOS also configures all devices on the motherboard. Some devices might have been disabled or assigned to different I/O addresses, IRQ settings, and so on, by Configuration Manager.

# Loading Hardware Profiles and Real-Mode Drivers

After BIOS initialization, the operating system attempts to determine the current configuration, including whether the computer is a docking station. This is done by using a hardware profile that Windows 95 selects before CONFIG.SYS is processed. The hardware profile is built by a detection process that collects information about interrupt usage, BIOS serial and parallel ports, BIOS computer identification, Plug and Play BIOS docking-station data, and, if possible, docking-station data that is unique to each OEM. Then the detection process builds a 2-byte value known as the current hardware profile (or the current configuration).

Each hardware profile has a name that matches a top-level menu item in a multiconfigured CONFIG.SYS file (that is, the long text in the menu, not the section name enclosed in square brackets). Windows 95 automatically selects that multiconfiguration menu item and processes the corresponding section of CONFIG.SYS.

CONFIG.SYS and AUTOEXEC.BAT are processed at this point. Although these files are not required for Windows 95, they are used for backward compatibility with applications created for MS-DOS or Windows 3.x. In Windows 95, CONFIG.SYS and AUTOEXEC.BAT are processed much like they are processed under MS-DOS 6.x. Drivers and TSRs specified in these files are loaded in real mode.

For more information, see "System Startup Files" later in this chapter.

---

**Note**  The real-mode MS-DOS errors are standard, as documented in the *MS-DOS 6.0 Programmer's Reference.*

---

# Initializing Static VxDs at Startup

Windows 95 supports static VxDs that load during system startup in the same way as Windows 3.x VxDs, and it also supports dynamically loaded VxDs. VMM32.VXD includes the real-mode loader, the executable Virtual Machine Manager, and common static VxDs. Notice, however, that if a VxD file is in the Windows SYSTEM\VMM32 directory, Windows 95 loads it in addition to the combined VxDs in MRCI2.VXD.

---

**Note**  If you want to update a VxD that has been bound into the monolithic VMM32.VXD, place the VxD file in the SYSTEM\VMM32 directory. Windows 95 always checks that directory and uses any individual VxDs it finds instead of loading those bound in VMM32.VXD.

---

The following list shows the VxDs typically combined to create VMM32.VXD. (A custom list is built for each computer.) These drivers used to be specified in the [386enh] section of SYSTEM.INI.

**Typical VxDs Combined to Create VMM32.VXD**

| | | | |
|---|---|---|---|
| *biosxlat | *ios | *vdd | *vmouse |
| *configmg | *parity | *vdef | *vmpoll |
| *dynapage | *reboot | *vfat | *vsd |
| *ebios | *vcache | *vfbackup | *vtdapi |
| *ifsmgr | *vcomm | *vkd | *vwin32 |
| *int13 | *vcond | *vmcpd | *vxdldr |

VMM32 loads VxDs in three steps:

- VMM32 loads base drivers specified in the Registry, which contains entries for every VxD not directly associated with any hardware. VxDs are located in this branch of the Registry:

  ```
  Hkey_Local_Machine\System\CurrentControlSet\Services\VxD
  ```

- If VMM32 finds a value **StaticVxD=** in any Registry key, it loads that VxD and runs its real-mode initialization. For example, the following entry loads *V86MMGR:

  ```
  SYSTEM\CurrentControlSet\Services\VxD\V86MemoryManger
      Description=MS-DOS Virtual 8086 Memory Manager
      Manufacturer=Microsoft
      StaticVxD=*V86MMGR
      EMMEXCLUDE=E000-EFFF
  ```

- VMM32 loads the static VxDs specified in the **device=**\*VxD lines in the [386enh] section of SYSTEM.INI. These VxDs are actually loaded from VMM32, and appear in SYSTEM.INI only for backward compatibility.

If a specific device conflicts with a device loaded from the Registry, the device specified in SYSTEM.INI takes precedence. However, if the device specified in SYSTEM.INI cannot be found, an error will occur.

Many Windows 95 driver models, such as IOS (for disk drivers) and the network, support dynamically loaded device drivers. These VxDs are not loaded by the VMM32 real-mode loader, but are loaded by a device loader that is responsible for loading and initializing the drivers at the correct time and in the correct order.

For example, for SCSI adapter miniport drivers, the device loader is *IOS. The entries for a SCSI adapter are found in this Registry key:

```
Hkey_Local_Machine\System\CurrentControlSet\Services\Class
```

Because there is no **StaticVxD=***xxx* line in this Registry entry, the VMM32 real-mode loader does nothing when Windows 95 identifies this device.

Configuration Manager attempts to find any device node that has a **DevLoader=** entry in the Registry. The device loader (in the previous example, *IOS) examines the Registry, finds the **PortDriver=** entry, loads the driver and any associated support drivers, and initializes the adapter.

# Loading the Protected-Mode Operating System at Startup

In the previous phase, these elements of the operating system were loaded:

- WIN.COM, which controls the initial checks and loading of the core Windows 95 components
- VMM32.VXD, which creates virtual machines and initiates VxD loading
- SYSTEM.INI, which is read for entries that differ from Registry entries

After all static VxDs are loaded, VMM32.VXD switches the processor to operate in protected mode, and the last phase of the boot process begins. This phase involves loading the protected-mode components of the operating system.

## Loading Protected-Mode VxDs at Startup

The protected-mode Configuration Manager is initialized for importing configuration information from a Plug and Play BIOS (if available); otherwise, it develops the Plug and Play hardware tree by enumerating devices and loading dynamically loadable device drivers. These device drivers are identified by loading drivers from a specific directory.

The next phase resolves device resource conflicts for every device in the tree and then informs the devices of their configuration. When all devices have been enumerated, all conflicts have been resolved, and all devices have been initialized, Windows 95 is ready to be used.

## Loading the Final System Components at Startup

The remaining Windows 95 system components are loaded in the following sequence:

- KERNEL32.DLL provides the main Windows components, and KRNL386.EXE loads the Windows device drivers

- GDI.EXE and GDI32.EXE provide the graphic device interface code

- USER.EXE and USER32.EXE provide the user interface code

- Associated resources, such as fonts, are loaded

- WIN.INI values are checked

- The shell and desktop components are loaded

At this point, a prompt appears so that you can log on by typing a user name and a password. After you log on, Windows 95 can process user-specific configuration information. If you do not log on, default settings are used. If Windows 95 is configured for network logon, the unified Windows 95 logon can be used to log on to the network during this process.

After Windows 95 is loaded and you log on, the STARTUP directory is processed.

# System Startup Files

This section describes the following files involved in Windows 95 system startup:

- IO.SYS, which is the real-mode operating system that replaces the MS-DOS version; VMM32 and Windows 95 device drivers take control from IO.SYS

- MSDOS.SYS, which contains special information for Windows 95 and is also created for compatibility with applications that require this file to be present before they can be installed

- CONFIG.SYS and AUTOEXEC.BAT

- SYSTEM.INI and WIN.INI

- BOOTLOG.TXT, the log file that describes the system startup processes

The following table summarizes how Setup renames the system files for the previous operating system when Windows 95 is installed. (The Windows 95 files are renamed with .W40 filename extensions when you start the computer with the other operating system.)

| Original MS-DOS filename | Renamed file under Windows 95 |
| --- | --- |
| autoexec.bat | autoexec.dos |
| command.com | command.dos |
| config.sys | config.dos |
| io.sys (or ibmbio.com) | io.dos |
| mode.com | mode_dos.com |
| msdos.sys (or ibmdos.com) | msdos.dos |

# IO.SYS: The Real-Mode Operating System

Windows 95 uses a new system file, IO.SYS, which replaces the MS-DOS system files (IO.SYS and MSDOS.SYS). This real-mode operating system file contains the information needed to start the computer. Your computer no longer needs CONFIG.SYS and AUTOEXEC.BAT to start the Windows 95 operating system (although these files are preserved for backward compatibility with certain applications and drivers).

**Note**  The Windows 95 IO.SYS file is automatically renamed to WINBOOT.SYS if you start the computer using your previous operating system.

The drivers loaded by default in IO.SYS include the following, if these files are found on the hard disk:

- HIMEM.SYS
- IFSHLP.SYS
- SETVER.EXE
- DBLSPACE.BIN or DRVSPACE.BIN

Most of the common functionality provided by the various CONFIG.SYS file entries are now provided by default in IO.SYS. The following table lists the common entries in CONFIG.SYS that are now incorporated into IO.SYS for Windows 95.

**CONFIG.SYS Settings Incorporated in Windows 95 IO.SYS**

| Setting | Description |
| --- | --- |
| dos=high | Specifies that MS-DOS should be loaded in the high memory area (HMA). Also, the **umb** value is included if EMM386 is loaded from CONFIG.SYS. (IO.SYS does not load EMM386.) |
| himem.sys | Enables access to the HMA. This line loads and runs the real-mode Memory Manager. HIMEM.SYS is loaded by default in Windows 95. |
| ifshlp.sys | Installable File System Helper, which loads device drivers. This allows the system to make file system calls. Until this is loaded, only the minimal file system from IO.SYS is used. After this point, the full file system is available. |
| setver.exe | Optional TSR-type device. It is included for compatibility reasons. Some MS-DOS–based applications require a specific version of MS-DOS to be running. This file responds to applications that query for the version number and sets the version number required. |
| files= | Specifies the number of file handle buffers to create. This is specifically for files opened using MS-DOS calls and is not required by Windows 95. It is included for compatibility with older applications. The default value is 60. |
| lastdrive= | Specifies the last drive letter available for assignment. This is not required for Windows 95 but is included for compatibility with older applications. If Windows 95 Setup finds this entry, it is moved to the Registry. The default value is z. |
| buffers= | Specifies the number of file buffers to create. This is specifically for applications using IO.SYS calls and is not required by Windows 95. The default value is 30. |
| stacks= | Specifies the number and size of stack frames. This is not required for Windows 95 but is included for compatibility with older applications. The default value is 9,256. |

**CONFIG.SYS Settings Incorporated in Windows 95 IO.SYS** (*continued*)

| Setting | Description |
|---------|-------------|
| `shell=command.com` | Indicates what command process to use. By default, the **/p** switch is included to indicate that the command process is permanent and should not be unloaded. If the **/p** switch is not specified, AUTOEXEC.BAT is not processed and the command process can be unloaded when quitting the operating system. |
| `fcbs=` | Specifies the number of file control blocks that can be open at the same time. You should use a **fcbs=** line in CONFIG.SYS only if you have an older program that requires such a setting. The default value is 4. |

▶ **To override default values in Windows 95 IO.SYS**

- Place an entry in CONFIG.SYS with the value you want.

The values in IO.SYS cannot be edited. If CONFIG.SYS contains switches or other parameters for any of the drivers or settings created by IO.SYS, the CONFIG.SYS entries override the IO.SYS defaults. Entries for **files=**, **buffers=**, and **stacks=** must be set in CONFIG.SYS to at least the default values in IO.SYS.

**Note**  IO.SYS does not load EMM386.EXE. If any of your applications requires expanded memory or loads data into the high memory area, EMM386 must be loaded in CONFIG.SYS. For details about using EMM386, see Appendix A, "Command-Line Commands Summary."

# MSDOS.SYS: Special Startup Values

Windows 95 Setup creates a hidden, read-only system file named MSDOS.SYS in the root of the computer's boot drive. This file contains important paths used to locate other Windows files, including the Registry. MSDOS.SYS also supports an [Options] section, which you can add to tailor the startup process.

The following example shows a typical file with default values:

```
[Options]
BootGUI=1

[Paths]
WinDir=C:\WINDOWS
WinBootDir=C:\WINDOWS
HostWinBootDrv=C
```

Most values in the [Options] section are Boolean—that is, the value can be 1 (enabled) or 0 (disabled). The following table describes entries in MSDOS.SYS, using the typical default values.

**MSDOS.SYS Values**

| Entry | Description |
|---|---|
| **[Paths] section:** | |
| `HostWinBootDrv=c` | Defines the location of the boot drive root directory. |
| `WinBootDir=` | Defines the location of the necessary startup files. The default is the directory specified during Setup; for example, C:\WINDOWS. |
| `WinDir=` | Defines the location of the Windows 95 directory as specified during Setup. |
| **[Options] section:** | |
| `BootDelay=n` | Sets the initial startup delay to *n* seconds. The default is 2. **BootKeys=0** disables the delay. The only purpose of the delay is to give the user sufficient time to press F8 after the Starting Windows message appears. |
| `BootFailSafe=` | Enables Safe Mode for system startup. The default is 0. (This setting is enabled typically by equipment manufacturers for installation.) |
| `BootGUI=` | Enables automatic graphical startup into Windows 95. The default is 1. |
| `BootKeys=` | Enables the startup option keys (that is, F5, F6, and F8). The default is 1. Setting this value to 0 overrides the value of **BootDelay=n** and prevents any startup keys from functioning. This setting allows system administrators to configure more secure systems. (These startup keys are described in Chapter 35, "General Troubleshooting.") |
| `BootMenu=` | Enables automatic display of the Windows 95 Startup menu, so that the user must press F8 to see the menu. The default is 0. Setting this value to 1 eliminates the need to press F8 to see the menu. |
| `BootMenuDefault=#` | Sets the default menu item on the Windows Startup menu; the default is 3 for a computer with no networking components, and 4 for a networked computer. |
| `BootMenuDelay=#` | Sets the number of seconds to display the Windows Startup menu before running the default menu item. The default is 30. |
| `BootMulti=` | Enables dual-boot capabilities. The default is 0. Setting this value to 1 enables the ability to start MS-DOS by pressing F4 or by pressing F8 to use the Windows Startup menu. |

**MSDOS.SYS Values** (*continued*)

| Entry | Description |
|---|---|
| `BootWarn=` | Enables the Safe Mode startup warning. The default is 1. |
| `BootWin=` | Enables Windows 95 as the default operating system. Setting this value to 0 disables Windows 95 as the default; this is useful only with MS-DOS version 5 or 6.x on the computer. The default is 1. |
| `DblSpace=` | Enables automatic loading of DBLSPACE.BIN. The default is 1. |
| `DoubleBuffer=` | Enables loading of a double-buffering driver for a SCSI controller. The default is 0. Setting this value to 1 enables double-buffering, if required by the SCSI controller. |
| `DrvSpace=` | Enables automatic loading of DRVSPACE.BIN. The default is 1. |
| `LoadTop=` | Enables loading of COMMAND.COM or DRVSPACE.BIN at the top of 640K memory. The default is 1. Set this value to 0 with Novell® NetWare® or any software that makes assumptions about what is used in specific memory areas. |
| `Logo=` | Enables display of the animated logo. The default is 1. Setting this value to 0 also avoids hooking a variety of interrupts that can create incompatibilities with certain memory managers from other vendors. |
| `Network=` | Enables Safe Mode With Networking as a menu option. The default is 1 for computers with networking installed. This value should be 0 if network software components are not installed. |

### Tip for Starting an Earlier Version of MS-DOS

If you installed Windows 95 in its own directory, the earlier version of MS-DOS is preserved on your hard disk. If you set **BootMulti=1** in the [Options] section in the Windows 95 version of MSDOS.SYS, you can start the earlier version of MS-DOS by pressing F4 when the Starting Windows message appears during system startup.

# CONFIG.SYS and AUTOEXEC.BAT

For Windows 95, both the content and method have changed for handling CONFIG.SYS and AUTOEXEC.BAT during system startup. Windows 95 automatically loads drivers and sets defaults by using IO.SYS, the Registry, and other mechanisms, rather than CONFIG.SYS and AUTOEXEC.BAT.

However, computers that require certain real-mode drivers or TSRs will continue to require that software be loaded from these configuration files. Also, CONFIG.SYS and AUTOEXEC.BAT might be required to enable certain software options. However, some options, such as long command lines, can also be enabled by using the COMMAND.COM program properties, as shown in the following illustration.

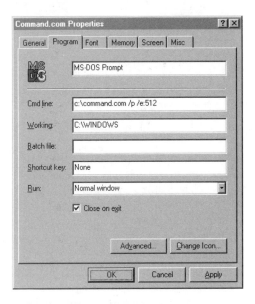

## CONFIG.SYS Processing

CONFIG.SYS defaults are implemented by IO.SYS, as described in the previous section. However, CONFIG.SYS can contain application-specific entries in addition to information stored in IO.SYS. These are processed in the sequence they are listed. After the base CONFIG.SYS file has been read, all devices are loaded, and COMMAND.COM is running.

Windows 95 loads memory managers supplied by other vendors if they are present in CONFIG.SYS; however, some might cause errors. Similarly, Windows 95 allows the use of command shells from other vendors, but, for example, long filenames are disabled, which might also indicate that other problems can occur using these command shells.

## CONFIG.SYS Changes for Windows 95

Windows 95 has predefined settings built in for most common CONFIG.SYS settings, so Windows 95 Setup removes many of these lines (such as settings for **files**, **buffers**, and **stacks**) if they are equivalent to the default values, by using REM to comment out the line.

### Tips for Editing CONFIG.SYS

If you edit CONFIG.SYS in Windows 95, observe the following basic guidelines:

- Do not include the **smartdrv** command. Windows 95 includes built-in disk-caching, and double-buffering is now provided by DBLBUFF.SYS.

- Remove any **device=mouse.sys** lines or similar lines. Windows 95 includes built-in mouse support.

The following tables describe the changes that Setup makes to CONFIG.SYS.

### Device Entries Deleted from CONFIG.SYS if Found

| | | | |
|---|---|---|---|
| cmd640x.sys | fastopen.exe | share.com | smartdrv.exe |
| ifshlp.sys | rambios.sys | share | |
| fastopen | share.exe | smartdrv.sys | |

### Lines Removed from CONFIG.SYS for Non–MS-DOS Operating Systems

| | | | |
|---|---|---|---|
| delwatch.exe | hidos.sys | pckwik.sys | touch.exe |
| delpurge.exe | lock.exe | rendir.exe | vdisk.sys |
| diskmap.exe | login.exe | script.exe | xdel.exe |
| diskopt.exe | memmax.exe | superpck.exe | xdir.exe |
| dpms.exe | nwcache.exe | taskmax.exe | |
| emmxma.sys | password.exe | taskmgr.exe | |

### Miscellaneous Lines Removed from CONFIG.SYS

| | | | |
|---|---|---|---|
| biling.sys | island.sys | nav_.sys | tcpdrv.dos |
| country | jdisp.sys | navtsr.exe | ubxps.dos |
| cpqcm.sys | jfont.sys | nemm.dos | undelete.exe |
| display.sys | jkeyb.sys | nfs-ndis.sys | vaccine.exe |
| dos-up.sys | kkcfunc.sys | pcnfs.sys | vdefend.com |
| dosdata.sys | kkfunc.sys | pcshel.exe | vdefend.sys |
| doshost.exe | memdrv.exe | pcshell | virstop.exe |
| driver.sys | mirror | protman.sys | vsafe.com |
| dwcfgmg.sys | mirror.com | rambios.sys | vsafe.sys |
| ega.sys | mirror.exe | redirect.sys | vwatch.com |
| extrados.max | msime.sys | sockdrv.sys | wbide |
| isl850.sys | msimek.sys | st-dbl.sys | workgrp.sys |
| isl861.sys | nav.drv | st-dspc.sys | |

**Lines Removed from CONFIG.SYS That Start Disk Caches**

| | |
|---|---|
| cache-at.sys | Golden Bow Systems software |
| cacheclk.exe | |
| cache-em.sys | Golden Bow Systems software |
| cache.exe | Disk cache utility |
| faste.exe | |
| fastx.exe | |
| fast512.sys | |
| flash.exe | Flash disk cache utility |
| hyper286.exe | Hyper disk cache utility |
| hyper386.exe | Shareware disk cache |
| hyperdkc.exe | Hyper disk cache utility |
| hyperdke.exe | Hyper disk cache utility |
| hyperdkx.exe | Hyper disk cache utility |
| ibmcache.sys | |
| icache.sys | |
| l.com | Lightning disk cache |
| mcache.sys | Paul Mace utilities |
| ncache.exe | Norton Utilities® disk cache utility |
| pc-cache.com | PC Tools™ disk cache utility |
| pckkey.exe | Multisoft Super PC-Kwik Windows driver |
| pckscrn.exe | Multisoft Super PC-Kwik Windows driver |
| pc-kwik.exe | PC-Kwik disk cache utility |
| pckwin.sys | Multisoft Super PC-Kwik Windows driver |
| poweron.bat | Batch file that turns on Super PC-Kwik |
| qcache.exe | 386MAX® disk cache utility |
| qcache.win | 386MAX/BlueMAX™ disk cache utility |
| scpcdext.exe | Norton CD-ROM Cache |
| scplus.exe | SpeedCache for disks and CD-ROM |
| sdcdext.exe | Norton CD-ROM Cache |
| speedrv.exe | Norton Speed Drive |
| super.exe | Super PC-Kwik |
| superon.bat | Batch file that turns on Super PC-Kwik |
| superpck.exe | Multisoft Super PC-Kwik disk cache |
| zcache.sys | Zenith Data Systems OEM disk cache from DOS 3.3 and 4.01 |

**Lines Removed from CONFIG.SYS for Previous Versions of OEM-DOS**

| | |
|---|---|
| astcache.sys | AST® 3.30 |
| cache.sys | COMPAQ® 3.20, Dell® 3.30 |
| cacher.sys | AST 3.30, Olivetti® 3.30 |
| cemm.exe | MS-DOS 3.20, 3.21, 3.30, 3.31, 4.00 |
| cemmp.exe | MS-DOS 3.20, 3.21, 3.30, 3.31, 4.00, COMPAQ 5.00 |
| enhdisk.sys | COMPAQ 3.20, 3.31, 4.00 |
| emmdrv.sys | NCR® 3.30 |
| fastdisk.sys | AST 3.30 |
| hardrive.sys | HP® 3.20, 3.30, 4.00 |
| hpdcache.sys | HP 4.0 |
| kboard.sys | Toshiba® 3.20 |
| mlpart.sys | Tandy® 3.20, 3.30 |
| olicache.sys | Olivetti 3.30 |
| ramboost.exe | IBM 6.3 |
| shelldrv.sys | NCR 3.30 |
| spooler.sys | Tandy 3.20, 3.30 |
| xdisk.sys | Unisys® 3.20 |
| xma2ems.sys | MS-DOS 4.00 |
| xmaem.sys | MS-DOS 4.00 |
| zspool.sys | Zenith Data Systems 3.20, 3.21 |

## AUTOEXEC.BAT Processing

AUTOEXEC.BAT is not required for Windows 95, but it is included for compatibility purposes. If the computer has an AUTOEXEC.BAT file, each line is processed in sequence during system startup. AUTOEXEC.BAT can contain additional application-specific entries that are run in the sequence they are listed.

Windows 95 passes the initial environment to COMMAND.COM with the correct Windows and Windows COMMAND directories already in the path and with the environment variables PROMPT, TMP, and TEMP already set. (**TEMP=** and **TMP=** indicate locations for temporary directories; both are specified for compatibility reasons.)

The following AUTOEXEC.BAT commands have equivalent default settings created in IO.SYS for Windows 95.

**AUTOEXEC.BAT Equivalents for Windows 95 IO.SYS Default Settings**

| Command | Meaning |
| --- | --- |
| **net start** | Loads the real-mode network components and validates the binding. Any errors received are placed in the NDISLOG.TXT file. (SYSINIT or COMMAND.COM performs the necessary **net start** command.) |
| **set path** | Sets the path as specified. |

The default Windows 95 environment includes the following:

```
tmp=c:\windows\temp
temp=c:\windows\temp
prompt=$p$g
path=c:\windows;c:\windows\command
comspec=c:\windows\command\command.com
```

## AUTOEXEC.BAT Changes for Windows 95

Windows 95 Setup makes the following basic changes to AUTOEXEC.BAT:

- Updates the **path=** line statement
- Uses **rem** to comment out incompatible TSRs
- Deletes any **win** statement (or equivalent) and SHARE.EXE
- Copies the original AUTOEXEC.BAT to AUTOEXEC.DOS
- Sets the TEMP directory

For diskless workstations, if the TEMP and TMP environment variables are not set, Windows 95 Setup creates a TEMP directory in the home directory (which can be on the local hard disk or on the network), and adds **set tmp=** and **set temp=** entries in AUTOEXEC.BAT that point to the new directory.

## Tips for Editing AUTOEXEC.BAT in Windows 95

If you edit AUTOEXEC.BAT, observe the following basic guidelines:

- Do not include other versions of Windows in your path.

- Start the path with C:\WINDOWS;C:\WINDOWS\COMMAND (using the name for the Windows 95 directory on your hard disk if it is not WINDOWS).

- Windows 95 Setup leaves your previous MS-DOS directory in the path. Do not change this.

- Do not add SMARTDrive or other disk caches. Windows 95 includes built-in caching.

- Do not include any statements for loading mouse support software. Windows 95 includes built-in mouse support.

- If it is necessary to connect to a network server when you start Windows 95, create a batch file, and run it from the STARTUP directory, rather than placing an entry in AUTOEXEC.BAT.

The following tables describe changes that Setup makes to AUTOEXEC.BAT. For entries that are removed, Setup uses **rem** to comment out the line.

**Commands Removed from AUTOEXEC.BAT**

| | | | |
|---|---|---|---|
| dosshell | setcfg | UnSet=comspec | =ascsi |
| fastopen | share | win | |

**Commands Removed from AUTOEXEC.BAT for Non–MS-DOS Operating Systems**

| | | | |
|---|---|---|---|
| delpurge | dpms | nwcache | taskmax |
| delq | eraq | password | taskmgr |
| delwatch | lock | ramboost | touch |
| diskmap | login | rendir | xdel |
| diskopt | memmax | script | xdir |

## Miscellaneous Lines Removed from AUTOEXEC.BAT

| | | | |
|---|---|---|---|
| 3C503ban | diagintr | irmban | rinAsync |
| 3C507ban | diagipa | isoban | script |
| 3C523ban | diagiso | mirror | snban |
| 3C603ban | diagomni | navtsr.exe | sockets |
| 6510ban | diagpcnt | ndarcban | tcptsr |
| 8023ban | diagpro4 | nddgban | tinyrfc |
| acinfo | diagtokn | neban | tokbanmc |
| arcban | diagungr | net | toknban |
| arcmcban | diagvlan | netbind | tokuiban |
| asyncban | diagwd | netbind | trban |
| attstban | dnr | nicmcban | ubniuban |
| call | doshost | nmtsr | umb |
| csiban | drvspace,1 | oliban | undelete,1 |
| dblspace,1 | emsbfr | omniban | ungerban |
| dellmenu,1 | etherban | pcnetban | vaccine |
| diag5210 | expban | pcshell | vdefend |
| diag9210 | hughsban | pro16ban | virstop.exe |
| diagarc | i92ban | pro4ban | vlanban |
| diage503 | intelban | proban | vsafe.com |
| diage523 | interban | probanmc | vwatch.com |
| diage603 | intr2ban | redirect | wbide |
| diagethr | ipaban | rin | wdban |

## Lines Removed from AUTOEXEC.BAT That Start Disk Caches

| Command line | Disk cache |
|---|---|
| cache-at | Golden Bow Systems software |
| cacheclk | Helix Multimedia Cloaking version 1.0 |
| cache-em | Golden Bow Systems software |
| cache | |
| fast | |
| faste | |
| fastx | |
| fast512 | |
| flash | Flash disk cache utility |
| hyper286 | Hyper disk cache utility |
| hyper386 | Shareware disk cache |
| hyperdkc | Hyper disk cache utility |
| hyperdke | Hyper disk cache utility |
| hyperdkx | Hyper disk cache utility |

**Lines Removed from AUTOEXEC.BAT That Start Disk Caches** (*continued*)

| Command line | Disk cache |
| --- | --- |
| ibmcache | |
| icache | |
| l | Lightning disk cache |
| mcache | Paul Mace utilities |
| ncache | Norton Utilities disk cache utility |
| ncache2 | Norton Utilities disk cache utility |
| pc-cache | PC Tools disk cache utility |
| pckkey | Multisoft Super PC-Kwik Windows driver |
| pckscrn | Multisoft Super PC-Kwik Windows driver |
| pc-kwik | PC-Kwik disk cache utility |
| pckwin | Multisoft Super PC-Kwik Windows driver |
| poweron.bat,1 | Super PC-Kwik |
| qcache | 386MAX disk cache utility |
| scpcdext | Norton CD-ROM cache |
| scplus | SpeedCache for disks and CD-ROM |
| sdcdext | Norton CD-ROM cache |
| smartdrv | Microsoft SMARTDrive disk utility |
| speedrv | Norton Speed Drive |
| super | Super PC-Kwik |
| superon | Batch file that turns on Super PC-Kwik |
| superpck | Multisoft Super PC-Kwik disk cache |
| zcache | Zenith Data Systems OEM from DOS 3.3 and 4.01 |

# SYSTEM.INI and WIN.INI

This section describes changes related to system startup made by Windows 95 Setup to SYSTEM.INI and WIN.INI. Mappings for other changes between Windows 3.x and Windows 95 are described in Chapter 33, "Windows 95 Registry."

# Changes to SYSTEM.INI

Most configuration options for Windows 95 are now stored in the Registry and are no longer required in SYSTEM.INI. The following options have been moved to the Registry or are no longer valid in Windows 95:

- All parameters are moved from the [Network drivers] section of SYSTEM.INI to the Registry.

- The **lanabase=** parameter is moved from the [nwnblink] section of SYSTEM.INI to the Registry.

The following tables describe other changes made in SYSTEM.INI.

### Entries Added to the [Boot] Section of SYSTEM.INI

| | | |
|---|---|---|
| comm.drv=comm.drv | gdi.exe=gdi.exe | user.exe=user.exe |
| dibeng.drv=dibeng.dll | sound.drv=sound.drv | |

### Entries Added to the [386Enh] Section of SYSTEM.INI

| | |
|---|---|
| device=*vshare | device=*int13 |
| device=*vcd | device=*dynapage |

### Entries Deleted in the [386Enh] Section of SYSTEM.INI

| | | |
|---|---|---|
| device=*vfd | device=lpt.386 | device=isapnp.386 |
| device=*configmg | device=pagefile.386 | device=wshell.386 |
| device=serial.386 | timercriticalsection= | maxbps= |

### Entries Moved from the [386Enh] Section of SYSTEM.INI to the Registry

| | | |
|---|---|---|
| Network= | SecondNet= | V86ModeLANAs= |
| Network3= | Transport= | |

### Entries Moved from the [Network] Section of SYSTEM.INI to the Registry

| | | |
|---|---|---|
| AuditEnabled= | FileSharing= | PasswordCaching= |
| AuditEvents= | LANAs= | PrintSharing= |
| AuditLogSize= | LMAnnounce= | Reshare= |
| AutoLogon= | LMLogon= | SlowLanas= |
| Comment= | LogonDisconnected= | Winnet= |
| ComputerName= | LogonDomain= | Workgroup= |
| DirectHost= | LogonValidated= | |
| EnableSharing= | Multinet= | |

The following list summarizes where you should set the related parameters using Windows 95 tools:

- Set all memory-related parameters by using the System option in Control Panel. For information, see Chapter 17, "Performance Tuning."

- Set parameters for hardware devices by using Device Manager in the System option in Control Panel. For information, see Chapter 19, "Devices."

- Set all networking and resource sharing parameters by using the Network option in Control Panel. For information, see Part 3, "Networking."

## Changes to WIN.INI

The font and desktop information in WIN.INI is transferred to the Registry, as described in the following lists.

**Entries Moved from the [Windows] Section of WIN.INI to the Registry**

| | | |
|---|---|---|
| Beep | KeyboardDelay | MouseSpeed |
| BorderWidth | KeyboardSpeed | ScreenSaveActive |
| CursorBlinkRate | MouseThreshold1 | ScreenSaveTimeOut |
| DoubleClickSpeed | MouseThreshold2 | SwapMouseButtons |

**Entries Moved from the [WindowMetrics] Section of WIN.INI to the Registry**

| | | |
|---|---|---|
| BorderWidth | MinArrange | ScrollHeight |
| CaptionHeight | MinHorzGap | ScrollWidth |
| CaptionWidth | MinVertGap | SmCaptionHeight |
| MenuHeight | MinWidth | SmCaptionWidth |
| MenuWidth | | |

In addition, Setup always adds **ATMWorkaround=1** to the [Pscript.Drv] section in WIN.INI.

The following list summarizes where you should set the related parameters using Windows 95 tools:

- Set all mouse parameters by using the Mouse option in Control Panel. For information, see Chapter 19, "Devices."

- Set parameters for the keyboard by using the Keyboard option in Control Panel. For information, see online Help.

- Set all screen and window display parameters by using the Display option in Control Panel. For information, see Chapter 19, "Devices."

# BOOTLOG.TXT: The Startup Process Log

The BOOTLOG.TXT file contains a record of the current startup process for starting Windows 95. This file is created during Setup when the Windows 95 operating system is first started from Windows 95 Setup. This file shows the Windows 95 components and drivers loaded and initialized, and the status of each.

When you use the F8 option for interactive system startup, you can choose to create a boot log during system startup. You can also use the **/b** switch to create a boot log when running WIN.COM from the command line to isolate configuration problems. For information, see Chapter 35, "General Troubleshooting."

The information in BOOTLOG.TXT is written in sequence during startup, in roughly five major sections. Depending upon a specific error condition, you might need to examine multiple sections. Notice, however, that a **loadfailed=** entry means only that the related VxD refused to load. For example, **loadfailed=ebios** indicates that the EBIOS driver did not detect EBIOS in the computer and so reported that it should not be loaded. The following table shows the sections to examine, and describes the possible errors and methods for correcting those errors.

**BOOTLOG.TXT Sections for Determining Errors**

| Section and errors | Corrective action |
| --- | --- |
| **Loading real-mode drivers:** | |
| No XMS memory | Verify that the section contains this entry:<br><br>`loadsuccess=c:\windows\himem.sys`<br><br>If not, verify the file and entry in CONFIG.SYS |
| Incorrect MS-DOS version (message appears when driver loads) | If this error appears when loading drivers or programs that worked before, verify that the section contains this entry:<br><br>`loadsuccess=c:\windows\setver.exe.` |
| Windows 95 doesn't start on a SCSI hard drive | Verify that the section contains this entry:<br><br>`loadsuccess=c:\windows\dblbuff.sys` |
| IFSHLP.SYS message occurs | Verify that the section contains this entry:<br><br>`loadsuccess=c:\windows\ifshlp.sys` |

**BOOTLOG.TXT Sections for Determining Errors** (*continued*)

| Section and errors | Corrective action |
| --- | --- |
| **Loading VxDs:** | |
| | Verify the loading, system, and device initialization of all VxDs by checking the section for these entries:<br><br>`loading vxd = ios`<br>`loadsuccess = ios` |
| Cannot access D??SPACE drives | Verify that the section contains this entry:<br><br>`loadsuccess = c:\dblspace.bin` |
| Sharing violations occur | Might be due to failure of the Vshare VxD to load. The section might contain an entry such as:<br><br>`loadfailed  = vshare` |
| **System-critical initialization of VxDs:** | |
| System-critical initialization error occurs | Verify that this section contains entries such as:<br><br>`syscritinit=ios`<br>`syscritinitsuccess=ios` |
| **Device initialization of VxDs:** | |
| | Verify that the section contains entries such as:<br><br>`deviceinit=ios`<br>`deviceinitsuccess=ios` |
| **Successful VxD initialization:** | |
| | Verify that the section contains entries such as:<br><br>`initcomplete=ios`<br>`initcompletesuccess=ios` |

The following table shows the kinds of entries in BOOTLOG.TXT to examine for information about the system startup process.

| BOOTLOG.TXT entry | Description |
| --- | --- |
| `Error` | Errors that were logged during startup |
| `Fail` | Failures that occurred during startup |
| `Dynamic load success` | Dynamically loaded VxDs |
| `INITCOMPLETESUCCESS` | Loaded VxDs |
| `LoadStart, LoadSuccess, Loading Device, Loading Vxd` | Indication of loading processes |
| `LoadFailed` | Indication that component failed to load |
| `SYSCRITINIT, SYSCRITINITSUCCESS` | System initialization actions |
| `DEVICEINIT, DEVICEINITSUCCESS` | Device initialization actions |
| `Dynamic load device, Dynamic init device` | Dynamic loading and initialization of devices |
| `Initing, Init Success, INITCOMPLETE, Init, InitDone` | Initialization actions |
| `Status` | Current status indicator |

For example, if you see an entry such as **DynamicInitDevice=PPPMAC** but there is no matching entry such as **DynamicInitSuccess=PPPMAC**, then that VxD failed to load. If a driver in the Windows SYSTEM\IOSUBSYS directory stalls when it is being initialized, you can sometimes successfully start the system by renaming that file.

The following shows a sample BOOTLOG.TXT file:

```
Loading Device = C:\WINDOWS\HIMEM.SYS
LoadSuccess    = C:\WINDOWS\HIMEM.SYS
Loading Device = C:\WINDOWS\EMM386.EXE
LoadSuccess    = C:\WINDOWS\EMM386.EXE
Loading Device = C:\WINDOWS\SETVER.EXE
LoadSuccess    = C:\WINDOWS\SETVER.EXE
Loading Device = C:\WINDOWS\COMMAND\ANSI.SYS
LoadSuccess    = C:\WINDOWS\COMMAND\ANSI.SYS
Loading Device = C:\WINDOWS\IFSHLP.SYS
LoadSuccess    = C:\WINDOWS\IFSHLP.SYS
Loading Vxd = VMM
LoadSuccess = VMM
Loading Vxd = nwlink.vxd
LoadSuccess = nwlink.vxd
Loading Vxd = vnetsup.vxd
LoadSuccess = vnetsup.vxd
```

# Windows 95 Setup with Other Operating Systems

This section presents technical details related to installing Windows 95 over an existing operating system, including changes made to system files by Windows 95 Setup and configuring for dual-booting with the previous operating system.

The following table summarizes some of the available options for upgrading with Windows 3.x, MS-DOS, and Windows NT, and how you should install Windows 95 to take advantage of these options.

**Upgrade versus New Installation Options**

| Feature | Install Windows 95 in a new directory | Upgrade existing Windows 3.x installation with Windows 95 |
|---|---|---|
| Migrate existing Windows application settings and files | – | X |
| Dual boot Windows 95 and MS-DOS | X | – |
| Dual boot Windows 95 and Windows NT[1] | X | – |

[1]  Windows 95 and Windows NT can work together properly if the computer is configured for dual booting between MS-DOS and Windows NT. However, you must install Windows 95 in a new directory.

The issues discussed in this section include the following:

- Installing Windows 95 over Windows 3.x, plus installing for dual booting with Windows 3.x
- Installing Windows 95 over MS-DOS, including running on multiple-configuration computers
- Installing Windows 95 for dual-booting with Windows NT
- Installing Windows 95 over Novell® DR DOS®
- Installing Windows 95 over IBM® OS/2®

# Installing Windows 95 over Windows 3.x

If you have Windows 3.x or Windows for Workgroups 3.x, you can either upgrade the current installation to Windows 95 (the preferred method) or install this version of Windows 95 in a new directory.

If you choose to upgrade your existing Windows installation, Windows 95 Setup uses existing configuration information to set installation defaults and to set other configuration options. Windows 95 Setup converts all Windows 3.x Program Manager groups to folders inside the Programs directory, so they appear on the Windows 95 Start menu. These folders can be opened or explored to find the applications previously contained in them. Windows 95 automatically creates a shortcut for each original icon you had under the previous version of Windows.

Windows 95 Setup checks for the following files to determine whether the current installation is an upgrade to Windows 3.x: WINVER.EXE, USER.EXE, WIN.COM, SYSTEM.INI, and WINI.INI, plus PROTOCOL.INI for Windows for Workgroups 3.x. When searching for these files, Windows 95 Setup also checks the files for version information. (False files with the same name won't work.)

▶ **To upgrade from Windows 3.1 or Windows for Workgroups to Windows 95**

1. Start Windows 3.1 or Windows for Workgroups on your computer.

2. Insert the first Windows 95 Setup floppy disk or the compact disc in the appropriate disk drive.

   –Or–

   Connect to the shared network resource that contains the Windows 95 source files.

3. In File Manager, select the disk drive you used in step 2.

4. Click the File menu, click Run, and then type **setup**

All of your current system settings (such as program groups and desktop preferences) are moved automatically to Windows 95. Windows 95 Setup also saves settings so that you can continue to use the network configuration that you had previously.

▶ **To upgrade from Windows 3.0**

1. Start your computer with MS-DOS. Do not run Windows 3.0.

2. Insert the first Windows 95 Setup floppy disk or the compact disc in the appropriate disk drive.

   –Or–

   Connect to the shared network resource that contains the Windows 95 source files.

3. Switch to the directory that contains the Windows 95 source files. At the command prompt, type **setup** and follow the directions on screen.

# Installing Windows 95 for Dual Booting with Windows 3.x

To install Windows 95 with dual-boot capabilities for MS-DOS, the computer must already be running version 5.x or 6.x of MS-DOS or PC-DOS.

**Important**  In order to take advantage of the Windows 95 dual-boot capabilities, the entry **BootMulti=1** must be set in the Windows 95 MSDOS.SYS file in the root directory. For more information, see "MSDOS.SYS: Special Startup Values" earlier in this chapter.

▶ **To set up dual-boot capabilities for a new installation of Windows 95**

- During Windows 95 Setup, when you are installing Windows 95 for the first time, make sure you specify a new directory that does not already have another version of Windows in it.

Windows 95 Setup makes all of the necessary changes to preserve your existing version of MS-DOS, Windows 3.x, or Windows for Workgroups 3.x, and your current AUTOEXEC.BAT and CONFIG.SYS files.

If you have already installed Windows 95 without dual-boot capabilities, you can follow these steps to allow MS-DOS to dual boot with Windows 95. However, you will not be able to dual boot with your previous version of Windows.

▶ **To set up dual-boot capabilities after Windows 95 has been installed**

1. On a bootable floppy disk that starts MS-DOS 5.0 or greater, rename the IO.SYS and MSDOS.SYS files on the disk to IO.DOS and MSDOS.DOS. Then copy these files to the root directory of your boot drive (usually drive C).

   These files must be placed in the root directory. Usually these files are marked with the hidden, system, and read-only attributes, so you might need to use the MS-DOS **attrib** command on these files while they are on the floppy disk, to view and copy them (for example, type **attrib -h -s -r io.sys**).

   **Caution**  You must rename the MS-DOS versions of these files before copying them to the root directory. Otherwise, you will destroy your Windows 95 installation.

2. On a bootable floppy disk that starts MS-DOS 5.0 or greater, rename the COMMAND.COM file on the disk to COMMAND.DOS. Then copy this file to the root directory of your boot drive.

   **Note**  If you are using disk compression software, you need to copy IO.DOS, MSDOS.DOS, COMMAND.DOS, CONFIG.DOS, and AUTOEXEC.BAT to your host drive also.

3. Use a text editor to create CONFIG.DOS and AUTOEXEC.DOS files that are appropriate for the MS-DOS version that you are using and store them in the root directory.

4. To use Windows 95 or the earlier version of MS-DOS in the usual way, restart the computer.

# Installing Windows 95 over MS-DOS

The versions of MS-DOS supported for installing Windows 95 are versions 3.2 or greater (for partitions that are greater than 32 MB), 4.x, 5.x, and 6.x.

### Tip for Running MS-DOS After Windows 95 Is Installed

If you install Windows 95 in a different directory from the one containing your previous Windows 3.x version, you can start the computer by using the previous version of MS-DOS. To do this, make sure the entry **BootMulti=1** is in the Windows 95 MSDOS.SYS file, and then press F8 during system startup and choose the related option.

### Files Deleted by Windows 95 Setup

This section lists MS-DOS and other files that are deleted by Windows 95 Setup. Notice, however, that these files are deleted from the old MS-DOS directory only if you install Windows 95 in the existing Windows 3.x directory. Otherwise, the old MS-DOS files are all preserved so that you can start the computer using the older version of MS-DOS.

The Windows 95 command-line commands are stored in the COMMAND subdirectory of the Windows directory. Deleting the related MS-DOS command file will not affect your ability to use the command under Windows 95. The versions that are deleted by Setup are known to be incompatible with Windows 95; for example, many of these MS-DOS commands do not support long filenames.

### MS-DOS and Windows 3.x Files Deleted by Windows 95 Setup

| | | | |
|---|---|---|---|
| ansi.sys | d??space.exe[1] | keyb.com | ramdrive.sys |
| attrib.exe | d??space.sys[1] | keyboard.sys | readme.txt |
| chkdsk.exe | edit.com | label.exe | scandisk.exe |
| choice.exe | edit.hlp | mem.exe | scandisk.ini |
| country.sys | ega.cpi | mode.exe | setver.exe |
| debug.exe | emm386.exe | more.com | share.exe |
| defrag.exe | fc.exe | move.com | smartdrv.exe |
| deltree.exe | fdisk.exe | mscdex.exe | sort.exe |
| diskcopy.exe | find.exe | msd.exe | start.exe |
| display.sys | format.com | networks.txt | subst.exe |
| doskey.com | help.com | nlsfunc.exe | sys.com |
| d??space.bin[1] | help.hlp | os2.txt | xcopy.exe |

[1] DRVSPACE.* or DBLSPACE.*

### COMPAQ DOS 5.0 Files Deleted by Windows 95 Setup

| | | | |
|---|---|---|---|
| cache.exe | dos5help.chd | fsedit.exe | tu.exe |
| cemm.exe | fastart.exe | help.exe | upcu.exe |
| cemmp.exe | | | |

### Non–MS-DOS Operating System Files Deleted by Windows 95 Setup

| | | | |
|---|---|---|---|
| delpurge.exe | hidos.sys | rendir.exe | touch.exe |
| delwatch.exe | lock.exe | setup.exe | uninstal.exe |
| diskmap.exe | login.exe | sys.com | xdel.exe |
| diskopt.exe | memmax.exe | taskmax.exe | xdir.exe |
| dosbook.exe | password.exe | taskmax.ini | |

**Pre–MS-DOS 5.0 Files Deleted by Windows 95 Setup**

| | | | |
|---|---|---|---|
| append.com | enhdisk.sys | keybfr.exe | print.exe |
| asgnpart.com | fastopen.exe | keybgk.com | recover.exe |
| backup.exe | fastart.exe | keybgr.com | restore.exe |
| bootf.com | fdisk.com | keybgr.exe | select.com |
| cache.sys | filesys.exe | keybit.com | select.dat |
| cemm.exe | for150.exe | keybit.exe | select.exe |
| cemmp.exe | format.exe | keybno.com | select.hlp |
| chkdsk.exe | gdu.exe | keybsp.com | select.prt |
| cmpqadap.com | graftabl.exe | keybsv.exe | select1.dat |
| compact.exe | graphics.exe | keybsw.com | select2.dat |
| configur.com | hardrive.sys | keybuk.com | setup.exe |
| debug.exe | hpcache.com | keybuk.exe | shell.clr |
| detect.com | hpdcache.com | keybus.com | shell.hlp |
| diskcomp.exe | ifsfunc.exe | label.exe | shell.meu |
| diskcopy.exe | indskbio.sys | mode.exe | shellb.com |
| diskinit.com | install.exe | mvbuild.exe | shellc.exe |
| diskinit.exe | keyb32.com | pamcode.com | tree.exe |
| dosutil.meu | keybchf.com | paminstl.com | vdisk.sys |
| dskscan.exe | keybchg.com | part.exe | xmaem.sys |
| dsksetup.com | keybda.com | password.exe | zcache.sys |
| edlin.exe | keybfr.com | prep.exe | zspool.com |
| emm386.sys | | | |

# System Startup with MS-DOS Multiple Configurations

Windows 95 supports multiple configurations for the same computer, and it
dynamically determines which configuration is being used. If Windows 95 cannot
determine the specific configuration used during system startup before processing
CONFIG.SYS, then it presents a menu of available configurations as listed in the
Registry, and it prompts you to select the configuration you want.

If you have a multiple configuration established in CONFIG.SYS, that menu is
presented next. However, if you use a multiple configuration to switch between
different versions of Windows, you must edit CONFIG.SYS manually to repair
this configuration after Windows 95 is installed. For information about how to
create multiple configurations for the same computer under Windows 95, see
Chapter 19, "Devices."

# Installing Windows 95 for Dual Booting with Windows NT

You can install Windows 95 to dual boot with Windows NT on a computer. This section provides some notes for installing Windows 95 with Windows NT.

---

**Important**  In order to take advantage of the Windows 95 dual-boot capabilities, the entry **BootMulti=1** must be set in the Windows 95 version of MSDOS.SYS file in the root directory of your startup drive. For more information, see "MSDOS.SYS: Special Startup Values" earlier in this chapter.

---

▶ **To install Windows 95 to dual boot with Windows NT**

1. Ensure that the computer is configured to dual boot between Windows NT and MS-DOS. Check your Windows NT documentation for details.

2. Start the computer by using the MS-DOS operating system.

3. Run Windows 95 Setup as described in Chapter 3, "Introduction to Windows 95 Setup."

Remember that if your computer has any Windows NT file system (NTFS) partitions, they are not available locally from within Windows 95.

If you run MS-DOS from a floppy disk in order to install Windows 95, you will not be able to start Windows NT afterward. You can restore the multiboot configuration by starting the computer with your Windows NT emergency repair disk and selecting the Repair option.

To run MS-DOS after Windows 95 has been installed, you must select the MS-DOS option from the Windows NT multiboot menu. Then, from the Windows 95 Startup menu, select the Previous Version of MS-DOS option.

▶ **To install Windows NT on a computer where Windows 95 is installed**

- At the command prompt, switch to the directory that contains the Windows NT source files, and then type **winnt /w**

The WINNT program is an MS-DOS–based application that creates the Windows NT Setup startup files and copies the system files to the hard disk from the source files. The **/w** switch allows WINNT to run under Windows. Using this switch also causes Windows NT Setup to skip the CPU detection process and the automatic restart at the end of Setup. You can also include the **/b** switch to copy the required startup files for Setup so that you do not have to create floppy disks for Setup.

For more information about the Windows NT operating system and about running computers with Windows 95 on a Windows NT network, see Chapter 8, "Windows 95 on Microsoft Networks."

# Installing Windows 95 over DR DOS

DR DOS is a disk operating system manufactured by Novell. The latest version of Novell DOS™ available at the release of Windows 95 was version 7.

You cannot configure dual-boot capabilities for Windows 95 and DR DOS.

Windows 95 Setup checks for the following DR DOS files that could cause conflicts.

**DR DOS Files That Cause Conflicts**

| | | | |
|---|---|---|---|
| delwatch.exe | fastopen.exe | rendir.exe | taskmax.exe |
| delpurge.exe | lock.exe | script.exe | touch.exe |
| diskmap.exe | memmax.exe | superpck.exe | xdel.exe |
| diskopt.exe | password.exe | | |

DR DOS is upgraded in the same way as versions of MS-DOS (as described earlier in this section). However, these additional changes are made during Windows 95 Setup:

- Some DR DOS utilities can cause compatibility problems with the Windows 95 real-mode kernel; Windows 95 Setup uses **rem** to comment out any command lines in the configuration files that start such utilities.

- If you use DR DOS password protection, Windows 95 Setup warns that this should be removed; otherwise, Windows 95 Setup cannot use the protected volume.

# Installing Windows 95 over OS/2

You can install Windows 95 on a computer running any version of OS/2 as long as a FAT partition is available. If the computer has any HPFS partitions, these partitions are not available from within Windows 95. Setup reminds you of this when it detects an HPFS partition.

The following notes apply to installing Windows 95 on a computer running OS/2:

- You must install Windows 95 in a new directory.

- Windows 95 Setup cannot migrate desktop or other settings from OS/2.

- You might have to reinstall any Windows-based applications to run under Windows 95.

Windows 95 Setup cannot run from within either OS/2 or OS/2 for Windows. You must start the computer by using MS-DOS and then run Windows 95 Setup from an MS-DOS command prompt. If your OS/2 system is not configured to dual boot with MS-DOS, install MS-DOS first, and then start Windows 95 Setup from MS-DOS.

If your computer has OS/2 Boot Manager, a message warns you that continuing with Windows 95 Setup will disable Boot Manager. If you choose to continue, Windows 95 Setup removes the OS/2 Boot Manager partition information because Windows 95 Setup cannot determine which operating system or configuration Boot Manager will use to restart the computer. This ensures that Windows 95 starts during the installation process.

Windows 95 Setup leaves all other OS/2 files intact and does not remove any files from the OS/2 directory.

### Tip for Restoring Boot Manager After Windows 95 Is Installed

Windows 95 runs normally with Boot Manager after installation is complete. After Windows 95 is installed, you can make Boot Manager active again by using the OS/2 boot disk to run the OS/2 Fdisk utility.

# Removing Windows 95 from a Computer

Windows 95 can be removed from a computer by using the procedures described in the following section. If the computer is configured for dual booting, you will be left with the previous versions of MS-DOS and Windows 3.x intact. If you upgraded Windows 3.x, then you will need to reinstall Windows 3.x after Windows 95 is removed.

The recommended method for removing Windows 95 is to start the computer and use the F8 key to get to a command line, as described in the following procedure. When this is done, real-mode Windows 95 operating system files start the computer. If you encounter problems starting Windows 95 in this way, start your computer from the previous operating system (which might require using a floppy disk).

## Removing Windows 95 with Command-Line Startup

Before you begin this process, make sure you have a system startup disk that contains an earlier version of MS-DOS and the SYS.COM file. You need this startup disk because the Windows 95 startup files (real-mode operating system files) must be deleted, so the process for removing Windows 95 makes your hard disk temporarily unbootable.

**Note**  The MS-DOS 6.x disk #1 is bootable, but the retail MS-DOS 5.0 disk #1 is not, and OEM versions might vary. To make a startup disk with MS-DOS 6.x, run **setup /f** from disk #1.

▶ **To remove Windows 95 when the computer is started to the command line**

1. Start the computer and press F8 when the Starting Windows message appears.

   If you have problems starting the computer in this way, you can use the procedure entitled "Removing Windows 95 with Your Previous Operating System" later in this chapter.

2. Select the Command Prompt Only option.

3. To make it easier to delete files and directories, copy the Windows 95 version of DELTREE.EXE to the boot drive. At the command prompt, type:

   **copy \windows\command\deltree.exe c:\**

4. To use the Windows 95 version of ScanDisk to clear invalid entries and long filenames, copy the ScanDisk files from the Windows COMMAND directory to the root directory. At the command prompt, type:

   **copy \windows\command\scandisk.\* c:\**

5. Use Notepad or a similar text editor to edit SCANDISK.INI in the Windows directory. Change the entries controlling whether ScanDisk looks for invalid characters in filenames and volume labels:

   - Set **labelcheck=on** to specify that ScanDisk should check volume labels for invalid characters.

   - Set **spacecheck= on** to specify that ScanDisk should check for invalid spaces in filenames.

   For information about the entries in SCANDISK.INI, see that file in the Windows directory.

6. To remove all entries that your earlier version of MS-DOS might see as invalid, at the command prompt, type **scandisk** followed by the letter identifying the drive containing the Windows 95 installation. For example:

   **scandisk c:**

   If you receive error messages during the ScanDisk process, refer to the online Help for information to help you resolve the error.

7. To delete the Windows 95 directory, in the root directory of the drive containing the Windows 95 installation, type:

   **deltree** *windows*

   In this command, *windows* is the name of the directory containing the Windows 95 files.

   ---

   Caution    All subdirectories of the Windows 95 directory will be deleted by this command. Before performing this step, make sure that the Windows 95 directory tree does not contain any critical data that has not been backed up.

   This step will also require that you reinstall all Windows-based programs at the end of this procedure, so that the correct drivers and settings will be available in the restored Windows directory.

   ---

8. To delete the Windows 95 CONFIG.SYS and AUTOEXEC.BAT files, in the root directory of the boot drive, type:

   **deltree config.sys**
   **deltree autoexec.bat**

9. To delete the WINBOOT.INI file and the WINBOOT directory, if present, type:

   **deltree winboot.***

10. To delete the setup, boot, and detection log files, type:

    **deltree setuplog.***
    **deltree bootlog.***
    **deltree detlog.***

11. To delete the real-mode operating system files IO.SYS and MSDOS.SYS, in the root directory of the boot drive (or from the root directory of the host drive, if the boot drive is compressed), type:

    **deltree io.sys**

    **deltree msdos.sys**

12. If you are using STAC Electronics Stacker® version 3.1, either skip this step or back up the STAC DBLSPACE.BIN file before completing this step.

    To delete the Windows 95 compression drivers (DBLSPACE.BIN and DRVSPACE.BIN), if present, in the root directory of the boot drive (or from the root directory of the host drive, if the boot drive is compressed), type:

    **deltree d??space.bin**

13. To delete the Windows 95 command processor (COMMAND.COM), in the root directory of the boot drive (or both from the C drive and from the root of the host drive, if the boot drive is compressed), type:

    **deltree command.com**

14. Put a bootable floppy disk with your earlier version of MS-DOS into drive A, and then restart the computer. After the computer starts from the floppy disk, put your earlier version of MS-DOS back on the boot drive (or the host drive, if the C drive is compressed) by typing **sys** followed by the letter identifying the boot or host drive and a colon. For example:

    **sys c:**

15. If you have MS-DOS version 6.0 and are using compression, copy DBLSPACE.BIN from the DOS directory to the root directory of the boot drive. Also, for all versions of MS-DOS, if you have a **shell=** statement referencing COMMAND.COM from a different directory, copy COMMAND.COM to the root directory. Then remove the floppy disk, and restart the computer from the hard disk.

To start the system with previous configuration files, copy CONFIG.DOS to CONFIG.SYS and AUTOEXEC.DOS to AUTOEXEC.BAT.

If you remove Windows 95 from a dual-boot installation, Windows 95 will be removed completely, and the computer will start the same way it did before installing Windows 95.

If you removed Windows 95 from an upgraded Windows 3.x installation, drivers that were located in the Windows directory (such as HIMEM.SYS, IFSLHLP.SYS, and EMM386.EXE) will be missing until you reinstall Windows 3.x. Then the computer will start the same way it did before Windows 95 was installed.

You might need to reinstall the previous version of MS-DOS, if needed files were removed by Windows 95 Setup.

# Removing Windows 95 with Your Previous Operating System

Use this procedure if you cannot start a computer in Windows 95 real mode, as described in the preceding section.

Before you begin this process, make sure you have a bootable floppy disk that contains an earlier version of MS-DOS and the SYS.COM file. The process for removing Windows 95 makes your hard disk temporarily unbootable, and the Windows 95 startup files (real-mode operating system files) must also be deleted.

**Note**  The MS-DOS 6.x disk #1 is bootable, but the retail MS-DOS 5.0 disk #1 is not, and OEM versions might vary. To make a startup disk with MS-DOS 6.x, run **setup /f** from disk #1.

▶ **To remove Windows 95 when the computer is started with the previous operating system**

1. Start the computer and press the F8 key when the Starting Windows message appears.

2. Select the Previous Version Of MS-DOS option.

3. To make it easier to delete files and directories, copy the Windows 95 version of DELTREE.EXE to the boot drive. At the command prompt, type:

   **copy \windows\command\deltree.exe c:\**

4. To copy the Windows 95 version of ScanDisk files from the Windows COMMAND directory to the root directory, type:

   **copy \windows\command\scandisk.* c:\**

5. Use Notepad or a similar text editor to edit SCANDISK.INI. Change the entries controlling whether ScanDisk looks for invalid characters in filenames and volume labels:

   - Set **labelcheck=on** to specify that ScanDisk should check volume labels for invalid characters.

   - Set **spacecheck=on** to specify that ScanDisk should check for invalid spaces in filenames.

6. To remove all entries that your earlier version of MS-DOS might see as invalid, at the command prompt, type **scandisk** followed by the letter identifying the drive containing the Windows 95 installation. For example:

   **scandisk c:**

   If you receive error messages during the ScanDisk process, refer to the online Help for information to help you resolve the error.

7. To delete the Windows 95 directory, in the root directory of the drive containing the Windows 95 installation, type:

   **deltree** *windows*

   In this command, *windows* is the name of the directory containing the Windows 95 files.

**Caution**  All subdirectories of the Windows 95 directory will be deleted by this command. Before performing this step, make sure that the Windows 95 directory tree does not contain any critical data that has not been backed up.

8. To delete the Windows 95 real-mode operating system file named WINBOOT.SYS, which was renamed from IO.SYS when you started the computer with your previous operating system, type the following command from the boot drive (or from the root directory of the host drive, if the boot drive is compressed):

   **deltree winboot.***

9. Delete the Windows 95 files MSDOS.W40, COMMAND.W40, CONFIG.W40, and AUTOEXEC.W40 files. (The renaming of these operating system files occurred when you used F8 to start the previous operating system.) To do this, type the following command at the command prompt (if the boot drive is not compressed):

   **deltree *.w40**

   If the boot drive is compressed, you must delete MSDOS.W40 from the root directory of the host drive and COMMAND.W40 from the root directories of both the host drive and the boot drive.

10. To delete the setup, boot, and detection log files, type:

    **deltree setuplog.***
    **deltree bootlog.***
    **deltree detlog.***

11. If you are using Stacker version 3.1, either skip this step or back up the STAC DBLSPACE.BIN file before completing this step. To delete the Windows 95 compression drivers (DBLSPACE.BIN and DRVSPACE.BIN), in the root directory of the boot drive (or from the root directory of the host drive, if the boot drive is compressed), type:

    **deltree d??space.bin**

12. Put a bootable floppy disk with the earlier version of MS-DOS into drive A, and then restart the computer. After the computer starts from the floppy disk, put the earlier version of MS-DOS back on the boot drive (or the host drive, if the C drive is compressed) by typing **sys** followed by the letter identifying the drive and a colon. For example:

    **sys c:**

13. If you have MS-DOS version 6.0 and are using compression, copy DBLSPACE.BIN to the root directory of the boot drive. Also, for all versions of MS-DOS, if you have a **shell=** statement referencing COMMAND.COM from a different directory, copy COMMAND.COM to the root directory. Then remove the floppy disk, and restart the computer from the hard disk.

If you remove Windows 95 from a dual-boot installation, Windows 95 will be removed completely, and the computer will start the same way it did before installing Windows 95.

If you removed Windows 95 from an upgraded Windows 3.x installation, you might need to reinstall your previous version of MS-DOS if some of the necessary files were removed by Windows 95 Setup. Drivers that were located in the Windows directory (such as HIMEM.SYS, IFSLHLP.SYS, and EMM386.EXE) will be missing until you reinstall Windows 3.x into the Windows directory. After you have reinstalled Windows 3.x, the computer will start the same way it did before Windows 95 was installed.

▶ **To remove Windows 95 from a computer with Windows NT installed**

1. Follow the steps in the procedure named "To remove Windows 95 when the computer is started with the previous operating system" earlier in this section.

2. Use the Windows NT Setup disk #1 to restart your computer.

3. When prompted, choose Repair. Then insert the Windows NT Emergency Repair Disk and choose the option to repair the boot files.

4. Restore your original MS-DOS and Windows 3.x configuration.

# Troubleshooting Setup and System Startup

This section provides information about solving problems that might occur during Setup or system startup. For specific information about troubleshooting procedures and the tools provided with Windows 95 (including details about using the Startup menu and Safe Mode for troubleshooting), see Chapter 35, "General Troubleshooting."

---

**Note**  If you have MS-DOS−based applications that require complete access to system resources, see the information about using MS-DOS Mode in Chapter 22, "Application Support."

---

# Troubleshooting Specific Setup Errors

This section describes Setup problems and how to diagnose and correct them.

You can also get useful troubleshooting information from the SETUPLOG.TXT log file that Setup creates in the root directory of your startup drive, as described in "SETUPLOG.TXT: The Setup Log File" earlier in this chapter.

If Setup fails, attempt to restart it by using the following procedure.

▶ **To restart Setup after a failure**

1. Press F3 or click the Exit button.

   If the system does not respond, restart the computer by pressing CTRL+ALT+DEL. If this fails, turn off the computer, wait 10 seconds, and then turn it on again.

2. Start Setup again. Setup prompts you to use Safe Recovery to recover the failed installation. Choose the Safe Recovery option and click the Continue button. Setup will skip the portion that caused the initial failure.

3. If the computer stops again during the hardware detection process, restart Setup again, and repeat the process until the hardware detection portion of Setup is completed.

You can use the information in SETUPLOG.TXT and DETLOG.TXT to check for the device or devices that caused the problems. Also review any messages added by Setup in the AUTOEXEC.BAT file for instructions on correcting setup problems.

The following sections describe specific setup problems and how to resolve them.

### Setup fails to start.

If Setup fails to start, you should check memory, check for hardware detection conflicts, and check the access to the source for the Windows 95 installation files. Use the following checklist and procedures to find a solution.

- Check the computer for viruses.
- Check for sufficient conventional memory.

   Windows 95 requires 420K. If this is not available, check for unnecessary drivers or TSRs, remove them and then try again. You can also run the MS-DOS MEMMAKER utility to optimize conventional memory.

- Check the RAM configuration in CONFIG.SYS.

  For MS-DOS 4.x or earlier, settings should contain the following:

  ```
  device=himem.sys
  ```

  For MS-DOS 5 or later, settings should contain the following:

  ```
  device=himem.sys
  device=emm386.exe noems
  dos=high,umb
  ```

  ---

  **Note**   The path to these drivers is not specified in the preceding example. If you don't specify the path, you need to copy the drivers to the root of the startup drive. Using **emm386** and **dos=high,umb** enables UMBs, but it is optional.

  ---

- Check for adequate XMS memory. Windows 95 requires at least 3 MB of XMS. If you are using MS-DOS 6.xx, press F4 when you start the computer and the Starting MS-DOS message appears. Choose Step-by-Step Confirmation to verify that HIMEM.SYS is loading. If not, make sure that verify the startup file syntax.

- At the command prompt, use **mem /c /p** to check for free conventional and XMS memory.

- If installing from a floppy disk or compact disc, check access to the drive.

- Remove all extra entries in CONFIG.SYS and AUTOEXEC.BAT, except those required to start the system and, for a networked computer, to start the network. It is especially helpful to remove any entries related to non-Microsoft disk caching software.

**Setup starts but an error is reported during the installation process.**

- Restart Windows 95 Setup and use Safe Recovery.

- Check the SETUPLOG.TXT or DETLOG.TXT files.

- Check the computer for viruses. This is an especially important step if Setup fails on disk 2 with floppy disk source files, or if it fails when the Windows 95 Startup wizard is preparing to run.

- Verify that all system and networking components function normally. Run virus detection software and **scandisk** (specifying a Thorough Type of Test) to identify system problems that might cause errors.

- Check the content of the error message. Windows 95 Setup errors contain additional information about the condition causing Setup to fail. Examine the device or condition that the error describes.

- Verify that system hardware is compatible. If Setup repeatedly fails, or if you suspect hardware conflicts with the Setup process, verify that the system components are supported. You might want to skip hardware detection. To do this, see "Troubleshooting Specific Setup Errors" earlier in this chapter.

- Check for a missing or damaged file. If a driver or system component file is referenced in the error, check to see if the file exists, if it is in the expected location, and if it has the correct file size, date, and version. For more information, see Chapter 35, "General Troubleshooting."

**Setup fails when run from floppy disks.**

When Setup fails when it is being run from floppy disks, you might see a message asking you to insert a disk in the floppy drive when a disk is already in the drive. Or, you might use the **dir** command to examine a Setup floppy disk and find that it fails or that garbled characters appear on the screen.

To solve this problem, first disable any BIOS-enable virus checking routine. Then check your computer hardware documentation or check with the manufacturer to ensure that the computer's CMOS settings are correct. If changing settings as advised by the manufacturer does not solve the problem, you can use the DRIVPARM utility.

▶ **To use DRIVPARM to solve floppy-disk hardware problems**

1. Start the computer using the most basic configuration files possible, loading no additional hardware drivers or other software in CONFIG.SYS and AUTOEXEC.BAT.

2. Insert a standard disk in drive A or drive B. At the command prompt, switch to that drive and type **dir**

3. If this works, insert a disk from the Windows 95 floppy disks in the same drive, and type **dir**

4. If this fails, garbled characters appear on the screen, or subsequent attempts to read the floppy disk fail, insert one of the following statements at the end of CONFIG.SYS.

For a 1.44-MB A drive, add:

```
drivparm=/d:0 /f:7
```

For a 1.44-MB B drive, add:

```
drivparm=/d:1 /f:7
```

5. If CONFIG.SYS contains an entry for DRIVER.SYS, disable it by adding **rem** before the related command line.

6. Save the CONFIG.SYS file, and restart the computer. Then repeat steps 2 and 3. If these steps are successful, leave the **drivparm** statement in CONFIG.SYS so that you can run Windows 95 Setup.

If this procedure is not successful, the problem is related to the CMOS settings on the computer. For information and assistance, contact your computer manufacturer.

### You cannot access the server when installing from the network.

- Verify that the network domain is validating the user account.
- Check the user name, password, and access rights.
- Check basic network functionality.
- Check conventional and XMS memory.
- Check for and remove unnecessary drivers and TSRs.
- If using a login script, check that the login script runs properly.

For more information, see Chapter 7, "Introduction to Windows 95 Networking."

### The network connection fails when you are installing from the network.

- Try to reconnect to the network share.
- If you cannot reconnect, restart the computer, and try again.
- Use another computer on the network to verify the installation server is working.
- Check the basic network connection.

### Setup stops during hardware detection.

When Setup stalls during hardware detection, you might need to disable hardware detection for a device or class of devices. Before you do this, wait until at least three minutes have passed with neither disk nor screen activity (that is, the mouse pointer cannot be moved). Some detection routines take long enough that the computer might appear to stop temporarily.

▶ **To skip hardware detection in order to avoid problems**

1. Run Windows 95 Setup from MS-DOS and, if this is not the first attempt to install, select Safe Recovery.

2. To disable the specific device detection during Setup, in the Hardware Detection dialog box, select the option to specify the hardware devices to detect. Then make sure the check box next to the device is not checked.

### Setup cannot communicate with a device.

If Setup cannot communicate with a specific hardware device on the system during the installation of Windows 95, a message states that Setup has found a hardware device on your computer that is not responding and prompts you to try this device again. For persistent problems, the message provides instructions on how to exit Setup and restart the computer.

This error message can be caused by one of the following:

- The network has stopped responding

- A CD-ROM drive has stopped responding

- A floppy disk drive has stopped responding

- Setup can no longer access the hard drive to complete the installation process

Follow the recommendation in the message to turn off the computer, turn it back on, and then rerun Setup with Safe Recovery. If the problem persists, identify the problem from the preceding list and correct it.

### Setup fails with error B1.

A B1 error message indicates that Setup has detected an older 80386 processor that is not supported and instructs you to upgrade your processor. Intel 80386 microprocessors dated before April 1987 are known as B1 stepping chips. These chips introduce random math errors when performing 32-bit operations, thus making them incompatible with Windows 95. If your 80386 chip was manufactured before April 1987 or has a label on it that reads "For 16-bit operations only," contact your hardware manufacturer about an upgrade.

### Problems occur during the file-copying phase of Setup.

If this occurs, exit Setup, restart your computer, and then rerun Setup. When prompted, select the Safe Recovery option and click Continue. The installation process should complete successfully.

If your computer stalls after all files have been copied, or if you receive an error at this point, it might be due to virus-protection software. Some computers have virus protection built into the ROM BIOS. You should disable the virus protection software or run your computer's configuration program to disable virus checking and then restart Setup. Select the Safe Recovery option, and the installation process should complete successfully.

### An "Incorrect MS-DOS version" error message appears.

When starting Setup from MS-DOS, you might receive an error stating that
MS-DOS 3.1 or greater is required. MS-DOS versions earlier than 3.1 are not
compatible with Windows 95.

This error can also occur when starting Setup from MS-DOS if you are using the
386MAX software utility. If this error occurs, temporarily disable the 386MAX
commands from the startup files, and then run Setup again.

### A "Standard Mode: Fault in MS-DOS Extender" error message appears.

When running Windows 95 Setup from MS-DOS you might receive this error,
indicating there might be a conflict in the upper memory region. To resolve this,
either disable UMBs or remove EMM386 statements from CONFIG.SYS and
rerun Setup. Or run Setup from Windows 3.x.

### A "Cannot open file *.INF" error message appears.

If you receive an error that states that an *.INF file cannot be opened, you might
need to free memory by disabling SMARTDrive in AUTOEXEC.BAT, or by
closing any applications running in Windows.

### Setup requests a new source path.

If this occurs, check the file source (the floppy disk drive or the CD-ROM drive).

- In Windows File Manager, click the floppy disk drive, and verify that the drive
  and files are accessible by viewing directories and loading readable text files.

  –Or–

  At the MS-DOS command prompt, use the **dir** and **type** commands to verify
  that the drive and files are accessible by viewing directories and loading
  readable text files.

- If the floppy disk drive is inaccessible, try reading a different disk. If that
  doesn't work, shut down and restart the computer. Check CMOS settings for
  the floppy disk drive using the hardware manufacturer's diagnostic routine
  (consult your hardware documentation).

- If installing from a compact disc, verify that MSCDEX and the CD-ROM
  drivers are loaded and configured properly.

### Setup is unable to find a valid boot partition.

A valid MS-DOS partition must exist in order for Setup to install Windows 95.
If Windows 95 Setup is unable to find a valid boot partition during installation,
it displays an error message. If you receive an error message, there might be
an actual partition error, but it is more likely that disk compression software or
network components are mapping over the boot drive. This might occur if you
are mapping a network drive to E, but E is the hidden host drive for your disk
compression software, or you are using a LANtastic network and drive C is being
mapped or shared.

To resolve the invalid partition error:

- Verify the drive is not mapped over (or logically remapped).

- Verify a valid, active partition using Fdisk. If no valid partition exists, take appropriate drive or data recovery efforts. If no active partition exists, use Fdisk to mark an appropriate partition as active.

- Remove interfering drivers from the startup configuration files, and run Setup again.

- If you are using disk compression software, ensure that none of your mapped network drive letters conflict with the host drive for disk compression.

### Setup finds insufficient disk space.

If Setup does not find sufficient space to install Windows 95, check for space on the destination and boot drives, and if you are using compression, check actual free space.

### Setup error occurs on a system with OS/2.

Setup disables OS/2 Boot Manager to ensure that Windows 95 can restart the computer and complete its installation. Therefore, if you are using OS/2 Boot Manager to choose operating systems at startup, OS/2 Boot Manager must be reset after Windows 95 is installed. Boot Manager can be reactivated by starting the computer with an OS/2 boot disk and by using the OS/2 Fdisk utility.

If you are not using Boot Manager, you should configure the computer to use Boot Manager, and then follow the preceding instructions. If you start MS-DOS from a floppy disk and run Setup, you will no longer be able to start OS/2 after Windows 95 has been installed. To avoid this, rename or delete the AUTOEXEC.BAT and CONFIG.SYS files that OS/2 uses before running Windows 95 Setup.

### Setup fails automated installation from MSBATCH.INF.

If the automated installation fails, check the following:

- Verify the network connection if source files are on the network

- Check errors messages, if any

- Check the MSBATCH.INF file contents and syntax

- Check the network validation of user logon

- Check for enough memory

- Check for and remove unnecessary drivers and TSRs

- If using a login script, verify that the script ran properly

# Troubleshooting Specific Startup Errors

This section describes specific conditions that might interfere with starting a Windows 95 computer and how to fix them.

In general, for system startup problems, the first problem-solving method is to start Windows 95 in Safe Mode. For information about how to start in Safe Mode and use BOOTLOG.TXT for troubleshooting, see Chapter 35, "General Troubleshooting."

### Windows 95 stalls during the first restart after installation.

Usually this occurs because of legacy hardware that was configured incorrectly before Windows 95 was installed. Remove settings for hardware services in CONFIG.SYS and AUTOEXEC.BAT. Also, ensure that any SCSI devices are terminated correctly. You might also need to disable the ISA enumerator. This software detects a new type of adapter that can be configured from the operating system. The detection sequence requires the ISA enumerator for I/O processes on some ports. Although every effort has been made to avoid ports commonly in use, you might have hardware that is also trying to use these I/O ports.

▶ **To disable the ISA enumerator**

- Remove the following line from the [386Enh] section of SYSTEM.INI:

  ```
  device = ISAPNP.386
  ```

### Bad or missing file error occurs on startup.

If you receive a "Bad or missing *filename*" message when the system is starting (where *filename* might contain HIMEM.SYS, IFSHLP.SYS, and so on), do the following:

- Check the syntax of the entry in CONFIG.SYS or other startup file.
- Verify the existence, location, version, and integrity of the file.

If the filename to which the message refers is a device driver the computer needs for accessing the drive where Windows 95 is installed, you need to move the **device=** line that contains the device driver to the beginning of CONFIG.SYS to allow access to the drive when CONFIG.SYS tries to load files from the Windows directory.

### Windows 95 has damaged or missing core files.

When Windows 95 loads, it counts on key files being available and undamaged. If a system file is damaged or missing, it might prevent loading or normal operation. If VMM32.VXD or other core files are missing or damaged, you might need to run Windows 95 Setup and select the Verify option in Safe Recovery to replace the files.

### System Registry file is missing.

The Windows 95 Registry file is required for operation. This is contained in SYSTEM.DAT and USER.DAT, which are backed up as .DA0 files. If only the SYSTEM.DAT Registry file is missing, Windows 95 does one of the following:

- Windows 95 automatically replaces SYSTEM.DAT from the backup Registry .DA0 file.

  –Or–

- Windows 95 automatically uses Safe Mode to start Windows 95 and displays the Registry Problem dialog box. Click the Restore From Backup And Restart button to restore the Registry, which copies SYSTEM.DA0 and USER.DA0 to .DAT files.

If both SYSTEM.DAT and SYSTEM.DA0 files are missing (or if the **WinDir=** entry in MSDOS.SYS is not set), a message informs you that the Registry file is missing and that Registry services are not available for this session. (This means that most operations in Windows 95 will fail.) After this message appears, Windows 95 automatically starts in Safe Mode and displays another message offering an option to restore the Registry. However, if there is no .DA0 file, the Registry cannot be restored. To resolve this problem, either restore SYSTEM.DAT from backup or run Windows 95 Setup.

For information about backing up and restoring the Registry, see Chapter 33, "Windows 95 Registry."

### BIOS or a BIOS setting is incompatible.

A ROM BIOS setting might prevent Windows 95 from installing or loading, because some computers have a feature that prevents applications from writing to the boot sector. This is usually in the form of anti-virus protection set through your computer's CMOS. If this is enabled, Windows 95 cannot complete the installation or cannot start properly.

If boot sector protection is enabled in the computer's BIOS, one of the following symptoms occurs:

- Windows 95 Setup stalls.
- Windows 95 stalls while starting.
- The anti-virus software prompts you to overwrite the boot sector. Choosing Yes might allow you to complete the Setup procedure, but Windows 95 stalls when it attempts to load.

To correct this problem, disable the Boot Sector protection feature through your computer's CMOS, then reinstall Windows 95. For information about disabling this feature, consult your hardware documentation or service center.

### VxD error returns you to the command prompt.

If a VxD is missing or damaged, Windows 95 displays an error message that indicates which VxD is involved. If the VxD is critical to the operation of Windows 95, then Windows 95 does not start and the screen displays the command prompt. You might need to run Windows 95 Setup and select Verify or Safe Recovery to replace the missing VxD.

You can selectively override a VxD that is included within VMM32.VxD. If the same VxD is loaded twice, the second instance intercepts all the calls to that particular VxD. There are two ways to override this:

- Copy the related .VXD file into the Windows SYSTEM\VMM32 directory.
- Edit SYSTEM.INI to add the entry **device=** *filename*.**vxd** in the [386enh] section.

### You cannot use dual boot to run a previous operating system.

To take advantage of the dual-boot support in Windows 95, you cannot install Windows 95 into an existing Windows 3.x directory, and the value **BootMulti=1** must be defined in the Windows 95 version of MSDOS.SYS.

DR DOS and versions of MS-DOS earlier than 5.0 do not support Windows 95 dual-boot functionality. To return to your previous operating system, you have to remove Windows 95 and reinstall your previous operating system, as described earlier in this chapter.

### "Previous MS-DOS files not found" message appears.

When trying to dual-boot to the previous version of MS-DOS, you might receive an error message stating that your previous MS-DOS files were not found. It is probable that either the files are missing, or that your previous version of MS-DOS was not version 5.0 or higher.

You must have MS-DOS 5.0 or higher in order to start to a previous version of MS-DOS. Any version of MS-DOS earlier than 5.0 looks for the first three sectors of the IO.SYS file in the first three sectors of the data area of the drive. In MS-DOS 5.0 or higher, IO.SYS is designed to allow itself to be located outside the first three sectors of a drive's data area. In this situation, the only way to start to a version of MS-DOS prior to 5.0 is from a startup floppy disk.

Drivers, such as DBLSPACE.SYS, that are loaded when you start the computer using the earlier version of MS-DOS might not be available.

### Required real-mode drivers are missing or damaged.

The previous operating system might have required certain real-mode drivers (compression, partitioning, hard disk drivers, and so on), and does not start correctly without them.

- At system startup, press F8 and select Step-By-Step Confirmation to verify the correct loading of all specified drivers.

- Verify that any drivers required to support your hardware are all specified in the appropriate startup file.

### Windows 95 doesn't recognize a device.

In some cases, Windows 95 is unable to recognize an installed device, and the device resources are unavailable to Windows 95. If Windows 95 doesn't recognize an installed device, remove it in Device Manager, and reinstall it by using the Add New Hardware option in Control Panel. You can also use Device Manager to check resource conflicts. For information, see Chapter 19, "Devices." Or see the hardware conflict troubleshooting information in online Help.

### Installing drivers causes Windows 95 system startup to fail.

If you try to install drivers for Windows 3.x from other vendors over Windows 95 (such as sound or video drivers), running the provided installation program can cause Windows 95 to fail to start or operate correctly.

▶ **To recover, when using a device that is supported by Windows 95**

1. Remove all entries in SYSTEM.INI that were added by the installation software from another vendor.

2. Delete the device in Device Manager in the System properties, as described in Chapter 19, "Devices."

3. Shut down and restart Windows 95.

4. Use the Add New Hardware option in Control Panel to reinstall the device by using the Windows 95 drivers.

### The wrong applications run after Windows 95 starts.

- In Windows Explorer, double-click the Windows Start Menu\Programs\Startup directory, and then delete any items that you do not want to run when Windows 95 starts.

- If the programs that are running do not appear in the Start Menu folder in Windows Explorer, run Registry Editor and find this key:

```
HKey_Current_User\Software\Microsoft\Windows\CurrentVersion
\Explorer\Shell Folders
```

The value of **Startup=** should be *Windows***\Start Menu\Program\Startup**, where *Windows* is the drive and directory containing the Windows 95 files.

# Converting Windows 3.x Program Groups

Windows 95 uses folders and links to provide the same functionality as groups and items in previous versions of Windows. As part of the upgrade from Windows to Windows 95, the GRPCONV.EXE utility provides the translation of groups and group items to folders and links.

GRPCONV runs automatically after Setup has copied most of the files needed for a complete installation and restarted the computer. It searches through all .GRP files listed in the PROGMAN.INI file, and then creates shortcuts for those entries in the Applications folder. GRPCONV also searches the SETUP.INI file and creates shortcuts in the Programs folder for all the items currently specified on the Windows Setup tab in Add/Remove Programs.

GRPCONV uses information from the Registry to track changes in group files that have occurred since the last time GRPCONV.EXE was run. There are no entries in either the SYSTEM.INI or WIN.INI file that take precedence over these Registry entries. The last modified date and time of the PROGMAN.INI file and all group files are stored in the following Registry key:

```
Hkey_Current_User\Software\Microsoft\Windows\CurrentVersion\GrpConv
```

You can also run GRPCONV manually to recreate default folders or to convert other Windows 3.x program groups. Notice that .GRP files are unique to earlier versions of Windows. If you install an application after Windows 95 is installed, no .GRP file is created in the PROGMAN.INI file. Therefore, running GRPCONV after Windows 95 is installed recreates only those groups that existed before you installed Windows 95.

▶ **To recreate the default folders provided with Windows 95**

1. In the Windows directory, change the filename of SETUP.OLD to SETUP.INI.

2. From the Start button, click Run and then type **grpconv /s**

   This command rebuilds the default Windows 95 folders. A status dialog box titled Start Menu Shortcuts appears during the rebuilding process. When it is complete, you are returned to the desktop.

You can manually convert one group at a time using GRPCONV.

▶ **To manually convert existing Windows groups to Windows 95 format**

1. From the Start button, click Run and then type **grpconv /m**

2. Click the group you want to convert, then do one of the following:

   ▪ Click Open, then click Yes in the Program Manager Group Converter dialog box, and complete entries in the Start Menu Shortcuts dialog box.

     –Or–

   ▪ Convert the group by double-clicking the group name. For example, if you have a group called MYGROUP.GRP, you can double-click MYGROUP.GRP to convert it to the Windows 95 folder format.

The following presents some additional notes on GRPCONV:

▪ The first time GRPCONV runs, the search path criteria for finding existing groups is based on the contents of the PROGMAN.INI file in the current Windows directory (if it exists).

▪ All data in a .GRP file except icon location ($x,y$ coordinates in a group) is used during conversion and migrated to folders in the Windows 95 Programs folder.

▪ GRPCONV migrates the [Restrictions] section of the PROGMAN.INI file from previous versions of Windows into the Policies key in the Registry.

P A R T   3

# Networking

This part of the *Windows 95 Resource Kit* contains the following chapters, describing how to run Windows 95 on Microsoft networks, Novell® NetWare®, and other networks.

### Chapter 7    Introduction to Windows 95 Networking

Provides an overview of Windows 95 networking, including a discussion of compatibility and operational improvements introduced with Windows 95, streamlined steps for network configuration, and a summary of Plug and Play networking support.

### Chapter 8    Windows 95 on Microsoft Networks

Presents procedures and technical information for using Windows 95 on Microsoft networks. Computers running Windows 95 can communicate with other computers running Windows 95, Windows for Workgroups, Windows NT, and LAN Manager on Microsoft networks.

### Chapter 9    Windows 95 on NetWare Networks

Presents information for configuring and integrating Windows 95 on Novell NetWare networks.

### Chapter 10    Windows 95 on Other Networks

Provides details about installing and running Windows 95 on other networks. This chapter also discusses mainframe connectivity for computers running Windows 95.

### Chapter 11    Logon, Browsing, and Resource Sharing

Describes how to configure and use the Windows 95 logon process, browse network resources, and use the peer resource sharing capabilities.

### Chapter 12    Network Technical Discussion

Describes technical issues related to network adapters and protocols for Windows 95, and also presents some technical notes and troubleshooting tips for networking.

C H A P T E R  7

# Introduction to Windows 95 Networking

This chapter provides an overview of Windows 95 networking, including a discussion of compatibility and operational improvements introduced with Windows 95, streamlined steps for network configuration, and a summary of Plug and Play networking support.

**In This Chapter**

Windows 95 Networking: The Basics   250
Windows 95 Networking: The Issues   253
Network Configuration Overview   254
   Installing Networking Components   254
   Setting Computer Name and Workgroup   257
   Starting the Network During System Startup   258
Plug and Play Networking Overview   258
Basic Troubleshooting for Networking   259

# Windows 95 Networking: The Basics

The Windows 95 operating system includes built-in networking support with a wide range of improvements over earlier versions of Windows. This includes built-in support for popular networks, plus an open, extensible networking architecture.

For supported networks other than Microsoft networking, the computer must already have the networking software from another vendor installed. Windows 95 Setup adds only the client or protocols required to work with Windows 95. The following networks are supported:

- Artisoft® LANtastic® version 5.0 and greater
- Banyan® VINES® version 5.52 and greater
- DEC™ PATHWORKS™ (installed as a protocol)
- Microsoft networking—Microsoft LAN Manager, Windows for Workgroups 3.x, and Windows NT
- Novell® NetWare® version 3.11 and greater
- SunSoft™ PC-NFS® version 5.0 and greater

The built-in networking components include support for a wide range of network transports (such as TCP/IP and IPX/SPX), industry-wide communications protocols (such as RPC, NetBIOS, and named pipes), and existing network device standards (such as NDIS and ODI). Because of the extensible architecture, other network vendors can add network connectivity enhancements and application support, and you can mix and match components at every layer. For information, see Chapter 32, "Windows 95 Network Architecture."

The following list summarizes the benefits of networking features in Windows 95.

**Robust networking components using no conventional memory.**  The protected-mode clients provided with Windows 95—Microsoft Client for NetWare Networks and Client for Microsoft Networks—use only 32-bit, protected-mode protocols, drivers, and supporting files. On large block transfers over the network, these protected-mode clients are up to twice as fast as real-mode clients under Windows 3.x. Windows 95 includes new 32-bit drivers for network protocols and adapters, plus a new implementation of TCP/IP.

**Easy, graphical configuration for all networking components.**  All network clients, adapter drivers, protocols, and services are installed and configured by using the Network option in Control Panel rather than by editing configuration files manually. All configuration values for protected-mode components are stored in the Registry.

**Automatic setup of Windows 95 on network workstations.**  For both Windows-based and MS-DOS–based computers, Setup upgrades the network software whenever possible to a Windows 95 protected-mode client and supporting protected-mode components, based on information detected about existing networking components. Setup also supports automated installation and customization during installation from setup scripts, plus installing Windows 95 to run from a local hard disk or from a shared network copy. For information, see Chapter 4, "Server-Based Setup for Windows 95," and Chapter 5, "Custom, Automated, and Push Installations."

**Peer resource sharing with protected-mode network clients.**  Any computer running the protected-mode Microsoft Client for NetWare Networks or Client for Microsoft Networks can be set up to serve as a file and print server for other computers on the network. Resources can be protected with user-level security on NetWare or Windows NT networks using existing user account databases. On Microsoft networks, resources can also be protected with share-level security.

**Simultaneous connection to multiple networks on a computer.**  The number of network connections allowed on a computer running Windows 95 depends only on the limits of your networking software. (Windows 3.x supported connection to only one network. Windows for Workgroups 3.11 allowed simultaneous connection to only two networks.) For information, see Chapter 32, "Windows 95 Network Architecture."

**Plug and Play networking support.**  You can insert or remove a PCMCIA network adapter while the computer is running, and Windows 95 assigns the required resources automatically and makes or removes the network connection. For any network adapter that uses an NDIS 3.1 driver, you can remove a docking unit without turning off the computer. If you disconnect the network cable from a computer running Windows 95 with Plug and Play components, the system continues to function. With most real-mode network clients, this causes the system to stall. For more information, see "Plug and Play Networking Overview" later in this chapter.

**Unified logon, login script processing, and resource browsing.**  You can use the Windows 95 unified user logon and password caching to log on to Windows NT, Novell NetWare, and other networks. Automatic login script processing is provided for Microsoft and NetWare networks. Users can access network resources by using Network Neighborhood or common dialog boxes, such as the Open or Save As dialog boxes. For more information, see Chapter 11, "Logon, Browsing, and Resource Sharing."

**Automatic reconnection for lost server connections.** When servers are available again after the loss of a network connection, Windows 95 reconnects automatically and rebuilds the user's environment, including connection status, drive mappings, and printer connections.

**Client-side caching of network data with protected-mode clients.** A protected-mode network client is a file system driver that uses the same 32-bit cache (VCACHE) used by all Windows 95 file system drivers, so it can cache network data for quick access. Files read across the network are copied to the RAM cache and made available to applications much faster than they would by rereading the file across the network. For a given file request, the cache is checked for the needed data before checking the network. This feature is available when running Client for NetWare Networks or Client for Microsoft Networks. For more information, see Chapter 20, "Disks and File Systems."

**Long filenames for network resources.** Computers running Windows 95 can recognize and use long filenames on other computers running Windows 95, on Windows NT servers, and on NetWare 3.x and 4.x volumes that have been configured to use the OS/2® name space. For more information, see Chapter 20, "Disks and File Systems."

**Support for the Win32 WinNet interface.** This is an API that allows developers to create applications that run unmodified on different networks. The Win32 WinNet interface in Windows 95 supports 16-bit and 32-bit applications (as opposed to the WinNet interface in Windows 3.x, which supports only 16-bit applications). For information, see Chapter 32, "Windows 95 Network Architecture."

**User profiles and system policies for automatic configuration.** To take advantage of system policies, the computer must be running a protected-mode network client such as Microsoft Client for NetWare Networks or Client for Microsoft Networks. For information, see Chapter 15, "User Profiles and System Policies."

**Agents for network backup and remote management.** Windows 95 includes backup agents for Cheyenne® ARCserve and Arcada® Backup Exec. Agents for Simple Network Management Protocols (SNMP) and Microsoft Network Monitor are available in the ADMIN\NETTOOLS directory of the Windows 95 compact disc. When the correct system management agent is installed on client computers, you can use a service such as HP® Open View or Microsoft Systems Management Server to manage workstations remotely. For information about remote administration, see Chapter 16, "Remote Administration."

**Dial-up networking for remote access.** Windows 95 supports multiple protocols for remote access, including TCP/IP, IPX/SPX and the industry standard, Point-to-Point Protocol (PPP). For information about remote access protocols and connection types, see Chapter 28, "Dial-Up Networking and Mobile Computing."

# Windows 95 Networking: The Issues

If the real-mode network is running when you start Windows 95 Setup, the appropriate network client is installed automatically. This is the recommended method for installing networking support in all cases. When Setup detects existing network components, it installs the appropriate supporting software automatically and moves the configuration settings to the Registry, wherever possible.

If Windows 95 Setup detects that NetWare networking components are present, it installs the new protected-mode client, Microsoft Client for NetWare Networks, plus the supporting protected-mode protocol and adapter drivers. Client for NetWare Networks is not installed automatically, however, if Setup detects VLM running with NDS support. To maintain the existing real-mode client and support configuration, you must run Setup in Custom mode and manually select the NetWare client. For more information, see Chapter 9, "Windows 95 on NetWare Networks."

Microsoft recommends using the 32-bit, protected-mode networking components wherever possible. With protected-mode networking components, all configuration settings are stored in the Registry, so you do not have to maintain configuration files such as AUTOEXEC.BAT, PROTOCOL.INI, or NET.CFG. The protected-mode networking components also allow you to take advantage of the many related benefits such as:

- Performance and reliability
- Peer resource sharing capabilities
- Use of system policies for administrative control, remote administration of the Registry, and use of the network agents, such as Network Monitor and Remote Registry service, available in the ADMIN\NETTOOLS directory on the Windows 95 compact disc

If you must run a real-mode client, networking settings are required in AUTOEXEC.BAT, plus a NETSTART.BAT file might be required to start the network during system startup. Configuration settings are maintained in PROTOCOL.INI or a similar file, depending on the particular network.

# Network Configuration Overview

You can install and configure all networking options for Windows 95 automatically or manually during Windows 95 Setup. You can also install and configure networking support after installing Windows 95 by using the Network option in Control Panel. In the Network option, you can set properties for the following:

- Configuration of network clients, adapters, protocols, and services
- Identification of the computer on the network
- Access control, to specify the security used when other users access this computer over the network

In the procedures presented in the following sections, it is assumed that Windows 95 and the appropriate networking hardware have already been installed on your computer. You might also need to install or configure various supporting components, such as security, mobile networking components, agents for backup and remote administration software, and support for user profiles and system policies.

---

**Tip**  To quickly display the Network option in Control Panel, right-click the Network Neighborhood icon on the desktop, and then click Properties on the context menu.

---

# Installing Networking Components

The recommended method for installing networking components for Windows 95 is to ensure that the existing real-mode networking components are running when you start Windows 95 Setup. In this case, Setup detects the existing components and installs corresponding support for Windows 95 automatically and, wherever possible, migrates configuration settings to the Registry. For more information about how to do this, see Chapter 3, "Introduction to Windows 95 Setup."

This section summarizes how to install networking support by using the Network option in Control Panel after Windows 95 is installed. Specific issues for installing various network components are discussed in the other chapters in this part of *Windows 95 Resource Kit*. The following procedures describe the general steps that are required for installing networking components.

▶ **To install a driver for a new network adapter after Windows 95 is installed**

- Run the Add New Hardware option in Control Panel, and be sure to answer Yes when asked whether Windows 95 should search for new hardware.

▶ **To install networking components after Windows 95 is installed**

1. In the Network option in Control Panel, click the Configuration tab, and then click Add.

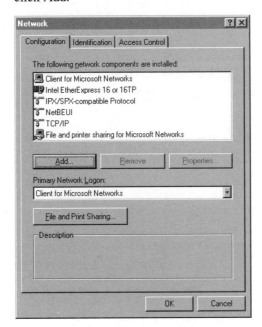

2. In the Select Network Component Type dialog box, double-click the type of component to install, as described in the following list.

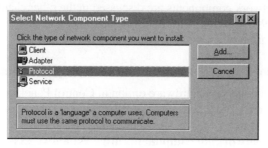

| Component | Description |
|---|---|
| Client | Installs client software for the types of networks the computer is connected to. You can use either a 32-bit network client (which needs no real-mode components) or older real-mode networking clients. There is no limit to the number of 32-bit network clients you can install, but you can have only one real-mode network client installed at a time. Some networks are supported only as primary networks. For information, see Chapter 10, "Windows 95 on Other Networks." |
| Adapter | Installs drivers for the network adapters in the computer. However, the recommended method for installing a new adapter is to use the Add New Hardware option in Control Panel. You can configure the type of driver to use (such as enhanced-mode NDIS, real-mode NDIS, or ODI), specify the resources for the adapters you are using (such as I/O, IRQ, and transceiver type), and define other options for the adapter. For information, see Chapter 12, "Network Technical Discussion." |
| Protocol | Installs network protocols and sets related options. For information, see Chapter 12, "Network Technical Discussion." |
| Service | Installs peer file and printer sharing services and other types of network services, such as backup agents, additional print services, Microsoft Remote Registry, and Network Monitor. For information, see Chapter 16, "Remote Administration." |

3. In the Select dialog box, select the name of the component manufacturer in the Manufacturers list, and then select the specific component in the Models list. Then click OK.

---

**Note**  Some components require that you shut down and restart the computer after installing them.

---

You can also install and configure networking components by using custom setup scripts or system policies. For information, see Chapter 5, "Custom, Automated, and Push Installations," and Chapter 15, "User Profiles and System Policies."

# Setting Computer Name and Workgroup

Windows 95 requires that you define a workgroup and computer name for each networked computer, independent of the type of networking software you use. This information is required if you install networking software during Windows 95 Setup. You can also change the computer name or workgroup after Setup is complete.

▶ **To specify the computer name, workgroup, and description for a computer**

1. In the Network option in Control Panel, click the Identification tab.

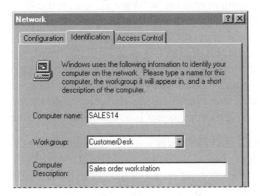

2. Type the values for the computer identification settings as described in the following list.

| Setting | Description |
| --- | --- |
| Computer Name | The computer name must be unique on the network. It can be up to 15 characters long, with no blank spaces. The computer name can contain only alphanumeric characters, plus the following special characters:<br><br>! @ # $ % ^ & ( ) - _ ' { } . ~ |
| Workgroup | The workgroup name does not need to be unique, but it uses the same naming conventions as the computer name. For information about using WRKGRP.INI to set administrative guidelines for specifying the workgroup that can be selected, see Chapter 5, "Custom, Automated, and Push Installations." |
| Computer Description | This information is displayed as a comment next to the computer name when users are browsing the network. |

## Starting the Network During System Startup

If your computer uses 32-bit, protected-mode networking components exclusively, you do not need statements in AUTOEXEC.BAT or other startup batch files to start the network when you start the computer. The installation of the correct protected-mode network client, protocol, and network adapter driver, as shown in the Network option in Control Panel, is all you need to ensure that networking is available whenever you start Windows 95.

If your computer uses any real-mode components for the client, protocol, or network adapter driver, then you must include commands to start the network in AUTOEXEC.BAT or a batch file that is called from AUTOEXEC.BAT. This is because real-mode components must be inserted properly in the startup sequence to be available to other parts of the system.

For real-mode components on NetWare networks, the NET.CFG or similar file is used to start and configure networking during system startup. The user or network administrator must maintain this file. For Microsoft networks, the **net start** statement in AUTOEXEC.BAT is used to start any real-mode networking components. If this statement is required for any components, the operating system automatically places the **net start** statement at the beginning of AUTOEXEC.BAT. If you (or another user) removes this statement, the system replaces it so that the real-mode networking component is available the next time the computer is started.

The PROTOCOL.INI file stores settings for real-mode networking components. The only sections that might be read are [PROTMAN$], [*netcard*], and [NDISHLP$]. For information about the content of PROTOCOL.INI, see Chapter 8, "Windows 95 on Microsoft Networks."

# Plug and Play Networking Overview

The networking components in Windows 95 are designed for dynamic Plug and Play operation with most ISA, EISA, PCI, IBM Micro Channel®, and PCMCIA network adapters. To take advantage of these features, the computer must be running all protected-mode networking components, including client, protocols, and network adapter drivers.

NDIS 3.1 supports adding and removing Plug and Play network adapters dynamically while the computer is running. If an event occurs such as undocking a portable computer, the Windows 95 protocols can remove themselves from memory automatically. However, the Windows 95 protocols must load information during system startup to be available. So when an event occurs such as the dynamic addition of a PCI network adapter, the operating system prompts you to restart the computer. If you are certain that the required protocol is already loaded, you can ignore this message.

Additional Plug and Play networking benefits are available when you use 32-bit sockets with PCMCIA cards. You can click the PCMCIA icon on the taskbar to remove the card without shutting down Windows 95 or turning off the computer. Using the PCMCIA icon causes the operating system to perform an orderly shutdown. Windows 95 notifies applications that the network is no longer available and automatically unloads any related drivers or protocols.

To help mobile users who might need to change adapters in their hardware, Windows 95 uses 32-bit Card and Socket Services to support hot removal and insertion of PCMCIA cards, including network adapters. Support for hot docking means that users do not have to restart their computers each time they make a change to the configuration. For information about using and configuring PCMCIA cards, including how to enable 32-bit Card and Socket Services, see Chapter 19, "Devices."

Network Plug and Play support in Windows 95 includes application-level support. An application created for Windows 95 might be designed with the ability to determine whether the network is available. Therefore, if a network adapter is removed, for example, the application automatically puts itself into "offline" mode to allow the user to continue to work, or it shuts down.

# Basic Troubleshooting for Networking

This section provides basic troubleshooting information for installing network components with Windows 95. For additional information about troubleshooting for particular networks, see the chapters in Part 3, "Networking." For information about general troubleshooting procedures and the supporting tools provided with Windows 95, see Chapter 35, "General Troubleshooting"; for information about troubleshooting network problems, see online Help.

When troubleshooting network problems, start by verifying the network operations status prior to and during the error condition. To evaluate the network problem, check these factors:

- Did the network work before? If so, what has changed? If any hardware or software has been added or removed, reset the original network hardware or software, and try again.

- If the network was provided by another vendor, was it installed previously and working? If not, reinstall the other vendor's network. Verify that the network operates correctly. Reinstall Windows 95.

- Has any network cable been moved or added? Check cables, connections, and terminators.

- Have any protocols been added or removed? Check protocol settings, protocol bindings, and the compatibility of the protocol with the network.

- Are the network adapter settings correct? Check network adapter settings. Consult the documentation for the correct settings. Reset the adapter settings to the correct values if necessary. Restart the computer and try again.

- Has any network adapter been moved or added? Check the adapter connection, and check any other working adapter.

- Are the network connections live? Look at the status lights on the back of the network adapter or on the media attachment unit. If the status lights show activity, the connection is live. If the status lights show no activity, disconnect and reconnect the network cable and check for activity. If the lights on the adapter are off, try a different network outlet.

### Check domain or server validation.

Verify that the network domain or server is validating the user account. If the logon isn't validated, connections to required servers cannot be made, login scripts won't run, and so on. If the network domain or server doesn't validate the account, perform each of the following procedures.

▶ **To check the logon setting**

1. In the Network option in Control Panel, double-click the network client (for example, Client for NetWare Networks or Client for Microsoft Networks).

2. In General properties, do the following:

   - For Client for Microsoft Networks, verify that logon validation is enabled and that the correct domain name or preferred server is shown.

   - For Client for NetWare Networks, verify that the correct server is specified as the Preferred Server.

▶ **To check the user and workgroup names**

- In the Network option in Control Panel, click the Identification tab. Check the computer name and workgroup name.

Also check basic logon requirements. For example, verify that the user password and the domain or preferred server account are correct, and test basic network functionality, such as viewing or connecting to other servers.

### Check connections to network resources.

Determine whether domains, workgroups, and workstations appear in Network Neighborhood. If they appear, try connecting to a server or workstation. If they do not appear, then verify that at least one server exists on the local network and that client services and protocols are installed. Also, check cable termination.

If you cannot connect to the server or workstation you want, review the error messages. At the command prompt, use the **net use** command (as described in Chapter 11, "Logon, Browsing, and Resource Sharing") to verify that you can connect to at least one server and workstation. If you cannot connect to any server or workstation, then check workgroup assignment, domain assignment, domain logon, and basic network operations.

If you still cannot connect, determine whether you can connect to a server from another computer. If this doesn't work, it probably indicates a problem with the server you are trying to connect to, or with the cabling or routing to that server.

Verify that the File and Printer Sharing service appears in the list of installed network components to ensure that peer resource sharing is enabled. Also verify that the correct settings for the browsing method are configured in the properties for the File and Printer Sharing service. For information, see Chapter 11, "Logon, Browsing, and Resource Sharing."

### Check network adapter and protocol configuration.

The following procedure summarizes how to check settings for network adapters. For more information about configuring network adapters, or for detailed troubleshooting steps for protocols, see Chapter 12, "Network Technical Discussion."

---

**Note**  If the network adapter is not terminated, Windows 95 stalls during system startup (similar to Windows for Workgroups 3.11). To test whether this is causing a computer to stall, try terminating the network adapter directly.

---

▶ **To check network adapter settings**

1. In the Network option in Control Panel, double-click the entry for the network adapter in the list of installed components.

2. Click the Advanced tab, and verify that each entry in the Property area has an appropriate value specified in the Value area. For information, see your hardware documentation.

3. Click the Resources tab, and then verify that the configuration type, I/O address range, and IRQ are correct. Again, for information, see your hardware documentation.

4. Click the Driver Type tab, and then verify that the appropriate driver type is selected. (If you are using a protected-mode network client, the default is an Enhanced Mode NDIS Driver.)

5. Click the Bindings tab, and verify that each protocol is checked. If a protocol is not checked, that protocol is not providing network functionality using that adapter.

### Check real-mode network components.

To check basic network communications, you can use the **net diag** command with a second computer connected to the same local network. As a diagnostic tool, **net diag** can assist you in troubleshooting network connectivity problems by establishing a diagnostic server and then verifying that the local computer can connect to this server.

▶ **To establish a diagnostic server on a second local computer**

1. At the command prompt, type:

   **net diag**

2. When a message appears showing you the protocols in use, press one of the numbers indicated in the message to specify the protocol to test.

3. When a message appears prompting you to specify whether a diagnostic server exists, press N.

▶ **To verify that the diagnostic server is detected in a Windows 95 VM**

1. On the computer that is not the diagnostic server, at the command prompt, type:

   **net diag**

   A message appears showing the protocols in use.

2. To specify the protocol to test, type one of the numbers in the message for the protocol used on the diagnostic server.

   A message appears stating that the diagnostic server has been detected.

▶ **To reinstall the protected-mode drivers in Windows 95**

1. In the Network option in Control Panel, make note of each installed component.

2. For each component, click the component, and then click the Remove button.

3. Install the components by following the procedure named "To install networking components after Windows 95 is installed" in "Installing Networking Components" earlier in this chapter.

C H A P T E R   8

# Windows 95 on Microsoft Networks

Computers running Windows 95 can communicate and share resources with other computers running Windows 95, Windows for Workgroups, Windows NT Server and Windows NT Workstation, and LAN Manager on Microsoft networks. This chapter presents procedures and technical information about using Windows 95 on Microsoft networks.

**Important**  Each computer running Windows 95 must have a client access license if it will access Window NT Server 3.5 servers on a network. For more information, see "Client Access Licenses for Windows NT Server" later in this chapter.

**In This Chapter**

Windows 95 and Microsoft Networking: The Basics  264

Windows 95 and Microsoft Networking: The Issues  265

    Issues for Server-Based Microsoft Networks  265

    Issues for Peer-to-Peer Networks  266

Installing Client for Microsoft Networks  268

Configuring Client for Microsoft Networks  268

    Configuring the Primary Client for Network Logon  269

    Configuring Logon and Reconnection Options  269

Running Windows 95 in a Mixed Microsoft Environment  271

    Running Windows 95 with Windows NT  272

    Running Windows 95 with LAN Manager  275

    Running Windows 95 with Windows for Workgroups  276

    Running Windows 95 with Workgroup Add-on for MS-DOS  277

PROTOCOL.INI: Real-Mode Network Initialization File  277

# Windows 95 and Microsoft Networking: The Basics

Client for Microsoft Networks is the 32-bit, protected-mode network client for Windows 95 that provides the redirector and other software components for Microsoft networking. Client for Microsoft Networks also supports limited interoperability with other Microsoft-compatible server message block-based (SMB) servers such as IBM® LAN Server, DEC™ PATHWORKS™, AT&T® StarLAN, and LAN Manager for UNIX® Systems local area network software.

You can install Client for Microsoft Networks to serve as the sole network support for Windows 95 or to coexist with Client for NetWare Networks or clients from other network vendors, as described in Chapter 10, "Windows 95 on Other Networks." For technical information about these optional configurations, see Chapter 32, "Windows 95 Network Architecture."

Support for computers running Client for Microsoft Networks includes all the robust networking features built into Windows 95:

- Automatic setup, user profiles, and system policies for configuring computers
- Dial-Up Networking, share-level and pass-through user-level security, and remote administration capabilities
- Unified logon and automatic reconnection to network resources

The following list summarizes the additional key benefits of using Client for Microsoft Networks.

**A high-performance system using no conventional memory.**   Client for Microsoft Networks uses only 32-bit, protected-mode supporting networking components and, as a file system driver, uses Windows 95 caching (VCACHE). Client for Microsoft Networks uses 32-bit versions of NetBEUI, Microsoft TCP/IP, and the Microsoft IPX/SPX-compatible protocol and NDIS 3.1-compliant network adapter drivers. This protected-mode client is designed to be used in a multitasking environment, providing robust performance and using no MS-DOS conventional memory space. For information about supporting protocols and network adapter drivers, see Chapter 12, "Network Technical Discussion."

**Protected-mode peer resource sharing services.**   You can configure computers running Client for Microsoft Networks to provide peer server capabilities using File and Printer Sharing for Microsoft Networks. For information, see Chapter 11, "Logon, Browsing, and Resource Sharing."

**Security and other support on Windows NT networks.** You can use Windows NT servers to validate user logon and to provide pass-through security for shared resources on computers running Windows 95. Computers running Windows 95 can recognize and use long filenames on Windows NT servers because the two operating systems use the same algorithm for long filenames and aliases. For information, see Chapter 14, "Security."

In addition, a computer running Windows 95 can start from a floppy disk or local hard disk and run a shared copy of Windows 95 stored on a Windows NT server. Support for booting diskless workstations will be available in Windows NT Server update releases. For information about shared installations, see Chapter 4, "Server-Based Setup for Windows 95." For information about installing Windows 95 from login scripts using Windows NT Server, see Chapter 5, "Custom, Automated, and Push Installations."

# Windows 95 and Microsoft Networking: The Issues

This section summarizes some issues you should consider when using Windows 95 with Client for Microsoft Networks, whether your site uses server-based or peer-to-peer networking.

## Issues for Server-Based Microsoft Networks

On server-based networks, central servers running Windows NT Server or Microsoft LAN Manager 2.x act as file and print servers and provide support for managing network logon and security. For information about the benefits of server-based networks using Windows NT Server, see "Running Windows 95 with Windows NT" later in this chapter.

- You must configure Client for Microsoft Networks as the Primary Network Logon client if you want to take advantage of user profiles for configuring or managing custom desktops on a Microsoft network, or if you want users to use system policies stored on a Windows NT server.

- To share resources with computers running other Microsoft networking products, the computers must be running a common protocol.

- Client for Microsoft Networks can use a LAN Manager domain controller for logon validation. However, File and Printer Sharing Services for Microsoft Networks cannot use a LAN Manager domain controller for pass-through validation. To take advantage of the user-level security support on Microsoft networks, the user must have an account on a Windows NT domain.

# Issues for Peer-to-Peer Networks

In the peer-to-peer networking model, at least one computer must—but each computer can—act as both a client and a server. As a client in a peer network, the computer can access the network resources shared on another computer. A peer network can be an appropriate networking solution for small offices with only five to ten users.

Any computer running Windows 95 can act as both a client and a server on peer networks. If you have the technical expertise, you can establish the wiring for a small peer network using Windows 95 yourself; otherwise, use the services of a system integrator. The following sections summarize issues either you or the system integrator need to consider for peer networking with Windows 95. For technical information about configuring and using File and Printer Sharing for Microsoft Networks, see Chapter 11, "Logon, Browsing, and Resource Sharing."

## Choosing Thinnet or Twisted Pair for Cabling

Thinnet (also called thin-Ethernet or Thin Coax) is the simplest method of cabling 10 or fewer connections on a network. Thinnet cabling uses coaxial cable with a BNC connector at each end. The cable attaches to each computer with a BNC T-connector. The major disadvantage in using thinnet cabling is that if there is a fault in the cabling at any computer, it affects all computers on the network. Thinnet cabling is only appropriate for Ethernet topologies.

Unshielded Twisted Pair cabling (called VTP or twisted pair) cabling is based on common telephone wiring technology, using connectors similar to those inserted in telephone jacks. Twisted-pair cabling is appropriate if your network has or will have more than 10 computers, and if computers are located in low-noise environments such as an office—it's not appropriate for manufacturing or warehousing environments. You can use twisted-pair cabling for Ethernet or token-ring networks.

When cabling the network, make sure not to use twisted-pair wiring that was previously used for telephone systems or that is more than five years old. To make the network active, you need additional components such as hubs and concentrators. These components help to isolate cabling failures.

# Choosing the Peer Network Components

This section summarizes issues for networking components and organization.

**Choosing protocols and other networking components.**  Microsoft NetBEUI is a fast protocol, requiring no additional configuration settings; it is a good choice for peer-to-peer networks. The IPX/SPX-compatible protocol is another alternative for small peer-to-peer networks. You also need an NDIS 3.1 network adapter driver. For information about these components, see Chapter 12, "Network Technical Discussion."

**Setting up security and automated backup.**  Share-level security is the only security option available on peer-to-peer networks. With share-level security, you create passwords to control access to shared resources on a peer server. For information about managing passwords for Windows 95, see Chapter 14, "Security." If you need to control access to files or to particular computers based on user identity, create a server-based network.

You can use any backup software that is compatible with Windows 95 to back up files on peer servers and other computers. To make sure data on the network is backed up automatically, use a server-based network.

**Setting up peer servers.**  Each computer that is running File and Printer Sharing for Microsoft Networks can act as a server, so that other computers can connect to it to use files or printers created on that peer server. Because work on a peer server can slow down if many users are using services on the peer server, you might want to dedicate one computer as a print server. In this configuration, users can return to work immediately after printing, and the dedicated computer can manage the print queue.

For optimal performance on each computer that is extensively used as a file or print server, use the System option in Control Panel to optimize the performance of the file system for supporting network server activities. For information, see Chapter 17, "Performance Tuning."

**Managing a peer network.**  Most of the remote administration features in Windows 95 rely on user-level security, which requires a server running Windows NT or NetWare to provide pass-through authentication of users for access to resources on remote computers. Therefore, on peer-to-peer networks, you cannot use Microsoft Remote Registry services, or any administrative features that require remote access to the Registry. However, you can use Net Watcher to manage the file system on remote computers, as described in Chapter 16, "Remote Administration."

If you want to take advantage of remote administrative features or user-level security, consider a small server-based network using Windows NT.

# Installing Client for Microsoft Networks

In Windows 95, Client for Microsoft Networks provides the redirector (VREDIR.VXD) to support all Microsoft networking products that use the SMB protocol. This includes support for connecting computers running Windows 95, LAN Manager, Windows NT, Windows for Workgroups, and Workgroup Add-on for MS-DOS networking software for personal computers running MS-DOS.

Because Windows 95 network redirectors are implemented as file system drivers, Client for Microsoft Networks provides mechanisms for locating, opening, reading, writing, and deleting files, submitting print jobs, and making available application services (such as named pipes and mailslots).

If a previous Microsoft network client is running when Windows 95 Setup is started, then Client for Microsoft Networks is installed automatically. You can also add Client for Microsoft Networks after you add network hardware to the computer.

▶ **To install Client for Microsoft Networks**

1. In the Network option in Control Panel, click the Add button.
2. In the Select Network Component Type dialog box, double-click Client.
3. In the Select Network Client dialog box, click Microsoft in the Manufacturers list, and then click Client for Microsoft Networks in the Network Clients list. Click OK.

# Configuring Client for Microsoft Networks

To configure Client for Microsoft Networks, you need to consider the following:

- Will Client for Microsoft Networks be the Primary Network Logon client?
- Will users log on to a Windows NT domain for logon a single Windows NT computer, or a LAN Manager domain validation?
- Will persistent connections to network drives be restored when the user logs on to Windows 95 or only when the resource is used?

This section describes these options and how to configure the network client.

# Configuring the Primary Client for Network Logon

If you set Client for Microsoft Networks as the Primary Network Logon, the Microsoft network is used to download system policies and user profiles, and the first logon prompt that appears will be for the Windows NT network. Also, if more than one network client is installed, the last login script will be run from Windows NT (or LAN Manager, depending on your network).

▶ **To make Client for Microsoft Networks the Primary Network Logon client**

1. In the Network option in Control Panel, click the Configuration tab.

2. In the Primary Network Logon list, click Client for Microsoft Networks.

# Configuring Logon and Reconnection Options

In the Network option in Control Panel, you can specify network validation and resource connection options. If you enable logon validation, Windows 95 automatically attempts to validate the user by checking the specified domain. You must enable this option if you want to access user profiles and system policies on a Windows NT domain. If logon validation is required on your network and this option is not configured, you might not be able to access most network resources. If this option is configured and you (or another user) do not provide a correct password, you might not have access to network resources.

---

**Note**  The user's user name and password must be specified in a user account on the specified Windows NT domain, LAN Manager domain, or Windows NT computer for logon validation to work.

---

You can also set logon validation by using system policies. With system policies, you can prevent the user from accessing resources on the local computer if the correct logon password is not provided. For more information, see Chapter 15, "User Profiles and System Policies."

---

**Note**  Windows 95 does not support using a LAN Manager domain controller as a pass-through security provider, but LAN Manager can provide logon validation.

---

▶ **To enable logon validation for Client for Microsoft Networks**

1. In the Network option in Control Panel, double-click Client for Microsoft Networks in the list of network components.

2. In General properties, check the Log On To Windows NT Domain option if you want to log on to a Windows NT or LAN Manager domain automatically when starting Windows 95.

   If you do not want to log on to a domain when starting Windows 95, make sure this option is cleared.

3. If you select logon validation, you must also specify the domain to be used for validation by typing or selecting a name in the Windows NT Domain box.

   You can specify a Windows NT or LAN Manager domain name or the name of a Windows NT computer (version 3.1 or 3.5) where you have a user account.

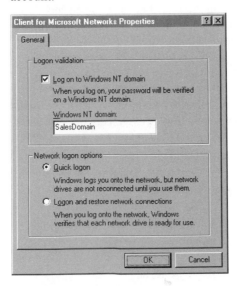

You can also specify whether Windows 95 should use "ghosted connections" or reestablish and verify each persistent connection at system startup.

▶ **To configure how persistent connections are restored**

1. In the Network Option in Control Panel, double-click Client for Microsoft Networks in the list of installed components.

2. To map the drive letters when you log on without actually establishing a session for each persistent network connection, in the Network Logon Options area, click Quick Logon.

   –Or–

   To have Windows 95 verify each persistent network connection at startup by establishing a session for each persistent connection, click Logon And Restore Network Connections.

Quick Logon works in essentially the same way that Ghosted Connections worked under Windows for Workgroups 3.11. That is, Windows 95 initializes data structures for mapping local drives and local printer ports to network resources, but it does not physically attach to the network resource until the user tries to access it.

When you use Quick Logon (which is the default), Windows 95 can start u return control of the user interface faster than if the physical connections Because your computer might not be attached to the resource when you drive icon for the first time (for example, in My Computer), you migh delay before the contents of that network drive are displayed. This d against a possibly long startup time, depending on the number of pe connections you maintain.

---

**Note**  Quick Logon requires password caching to function pro policies are used to disable password caching, users cannot r successfully with peer servers configured with share-level

---

# Running Windows 95 in a Mixed Micros

This section presents some technical information fr network includes computers running Windows N Microsoft networking products in addition to co

# Running Windows 95 with Windows NT

Microsoft Windows NT Server networks provide both client-server and peer networking with user-level security using a domain structure. You can run Windows 95 on a Windows NT network, and you can install Windows 95 for dual-booting on computers running Windows NT 3.1 or Windows NT 3.5.

The following notes summarize important issues for this configuration:

- Windows 95 and Windows NT versions 3.1 or 3.5 can be installed on the same computer, but not in the same directory.

- You cannot run Windows 95 Setup from within Windows NT. You must run Setup from MS-DOS, Windows 3.1, or Windows for Workgroups.

- If your computer has any Windows NT file system (NTFS) partitions, they will not be available locally while the computer is running Windows 95.

For a description of the support for running login scripts from Windows NT Server, see Chapter 11, "Logon, Browsing, and Resource Sharing." For information about installing Windows 95 as a dual-boot operating system with Windows NT, see Chapter 6, "Setup Technical Discussion."

## Running Windows 95 in a Mixed Environment with Windows NT

In Windows 95, computers are grouped logically in workgroups, where each computer in the workgroup maintains its own security system for validating local user logon and access to resources. Computers in workgroups do not share security with other computers, and they do not rely on other computers to provide security. On Windows NT networks, computers can be grouped in domains, which allow multiple servers and workstations to be grouped for unified administration. With Windows NT domains, centralized user accounts are used to validate user logon and access to resources.

Windows 95 and Windows NT use the same workgroup model for browsing network resources, so computers running File and Printer Sharing for Microsoft Networks can appear in the same workgroup as computers running Windows NT. Computers running Windows NT will be favored in Browse Master elections because of the higher version number of the browser software.

Users running Client for Microsoft Networks can access the shared resources on a computer running Windows NT if both computers are using a common protocol. For resources protected with user-level security, the user running Windows 95 must have been granted access to those resources. Conversely, a user running Windows NT can connect to the shared resources on a computer running Windows 95 if the same conditions are met.

# Notes on Windows NT Server Benefits

The Microsoft Windows NT Server operating system is the high-end member of the family of Microsoft Windows operating systems, providing a powerful, reliable, and scalable operating system to support the demands of client-server computing.

Windows NT Server provides the ideal platform for the server backbone in a mixed-network environment. It is especially versatile and powerful for enterprise networks made up of LANs that use a variety of network types and require dial-in support for network access. Also, on a peer-to-peer network where the computers are running Client for Microsoft Networks, you can add Windows NT to the network without changing the networking software on the existing computers.

Windows NT Server is designed to support complex business applications and administrative requirements. The following list summarizes important features.

**Networking and workgroup support.** Windows NT Server provides built-in file and printer sharing capabilities for workgroup computing, and an open network system interface that includes built-in support for IPX/SPX, TCP/IP, NetBEUI, and other protocols. Windows NT Server provides administrative tools for controlling network services, auditing system events, changing hardware configuration and system performance, managing and backing up disks, and more. Windows NT also provides robust support for server-based and client-server applications.

**Interoperability.** Windows NT Server is compatible with networks such as Windows 95, Banyan® VINES®, Novell® NetWare®, UNIX®, LAN Manager 2.x, and Microsoft Windows for Workgroups. Windows NT Server can add value to your current network environment without disruption. Even though networks and interoperability are complicated, a Windows NT network is easy to use and reliable, with automatic configuration provided wherever possible, and remote administration available for most administration tasks.

**A single network logon.** Users can access network resources, including client-server applications, using one user account and one password per user.

**Centralized management of user accounts.** The administrator can work from a single computer across divisions, departments, and workgroups.

**Advanced data-protection features.** These include disk mirroring, disk striping with parity (RAID 5), and uninterruptible power supply support.

**Remote Access Service (RAS).** Users can access network resources even when they are off-site, traveling, or working at home. Users can dial in over asynchronous telephone lines or Integrated Services Digital Network (ISDN) lines to access the network from computers running Windows 95, MS-DOS, Windows for Workgroups, or Windows NT operating systems. Windows NT RAS also supports X.25 networks.

**Access to Apple® Macintosh® resources.** When Services for Apple Macintosh is installed on a Windows NT Server, Macintoshes and computers running Windows 95 can work together to share files, printers, and client-server applications. Macintosh users can access resources on a computer running Windows NT Server, similar to any other AppleShare® server.

## Client Access Licenses for Windows NT Server

Windows NT Server and Windows NT Workstation are licensed separately from Microsoft, allowing you to purchase only the components you need to build a network solution for your organization. For Windows NT Server, you must have a *Server License for Microsoft Windows NT Server* for each server on the network. In addition to a Server License, a *Client Access License for Windows NT Server* is required for computers that will access or otherwise use the following basic network services:

- File services (sharing and managing files and disk storage)
- Printing services (sharing and managing printers)
- Remote access services (accessing the server from a remote location through a communications link)

Microsoft offers two licensing options for Windows NT Server:

- "Per Seat" licensing. In this case, the Client Access License applies to a specific workstation ("seat"). Using this alternative, an unlimited number of computers or workstations can access Windows NT Server, provided each one is licensed with a Client Access License. After a workstation has been licensed, it has permission to access all Windows NT Server products installed throughout your organization.

  A Client Access License is required whether you use client software supplied by Microsoft or software from another vendor. In particular, for each computer running Windows 95, Windows for Workgroups, Windows NT Workstation, or any client software Windows NT Server supports, a separate Client Access License is required.

- "Per Server" licensing. In this case, each Client Access License is assigned to a particular server and allows one connection to that server for basic network services. Under this option, you designate during setup the number of licenses that apply to this server.

You can convert a Per Server license to a Per Seat license at no cost and without notifying Microsoft. You cannot, however, switch from a Per Seat option to a Per Server option. Also, all the servers in your environment are not required to be licensed using the same option—some servers can be licensed on a Per Server basis and others on a Per Seat basis.

You do not need a separate Client Access License if you access or run server applications only from Microsoft or other vendors on Windows NT Server. Examples of such server applications include Microsoft SQL Server, Microsoft SNA Server, Microsoft Systems Management Server, Lotus® Notes®, Btrieve® for Windows NT and ORACLE® Server. A Client Access License is required, however, when using utilities such as Windows NT File and Print Services for NetWare that use the basic networking services of Windows NT Server.

---

**Note**  It is a violation of the terms of the Server License to access Windows NT Server without an appropriate number of Client Access Licenses. For more information, see your Server License.

---

Client Access Licenses are available in single-client and 20-client configurations and in volume quantities through the Microsoft Select licensing program. For more information, contact your Microsoft reseller. If you have questions, in the United States, contact the Microsoft Sales Information Center at (800) 426-9400. In Canada, contact the Microsoft Canada Customer Support Centre at (800) 563-9048. For other locations, contact your local Microsoft subsidiary.

# Running Windows 95 with LAN Manager

Either Windows 95 or Windows NT Server can be installed as upgrades for all versions of LAN Manager and IBM OS/2® LAN Server, depending on the role you want that computer to serve on the network. Microsoft recommends that you upgrade these servers, rather than maintain these legacy systems on your network.

A workgroup in Windows 95 is analogous to a LAN Manager domain in that it's a logical grouping of workstations. However, a workgroup in Windows 95 does not share any of the advanced security features offered as part of a LAN Manager domain. Windows 95 does not support using a LAN Manager domain controller as a security provider, so only share-level security can be used for computers running Windows 95 on LAN Manager networks. (User-level security requires a Windows NT domain.)

To ensure computers running Windows 95 can browse for LAN Manager servers, make sure that at least one computer running Client for Microsoft Networks sets its workgroup name to the LAN Manager domain name. After a computer running Windows 95 becomes a member of the LAN Manager domain, it can distribute the names of LAN Manager servers in that domain to other computers running Windows 95 on the network. The configuration must be duplicated for each LAN Manager domain.

▶ **To ensure LAN Manager workstations can see and access resources on computers running File and Printer Sharing Services for Microsoft Networks**

1. Make sure that all the computers are using a common protocol.

2. Make sure that users running LAN Manager clients have been granted access to the resources on the computers running Windows 95.

3. Set the value of the LM Announce property to Yes on each computer running Windows 95 with File and Printer Sharing services, as described in "Configuring File and Printer Sharing for Microsoft Networks" in Chapter 11, "Logon, Browsing, and Resource Sharing."

The LM Announce setting ensures that the computer running Windows 95 peer resource sharing services announces its presence to LAN Manager workstations and servers. By default, the LM Announce property is set to No to reduce broadcast traffic on the network.

### Tips for LAN Manager Variations

IBM OS/2 LAN Server supports a domain model and is equivalent to LAN Manager for interoperating with Windows 95. Just as with Windows for Workgroups, the Client for Microsoft Networks in Windows 95 does not support LAN Server aliases.

DEC PATHWORKS is a LAN Manager-compatible network, but it does not support a domain model for browsing servers and shared resources. DEC PATHWORKS servers will appear in Network Neighborhood.

For more information about both of these networks, see Chapter 10, "Windows 95 on Other Networks."

# Running Windows 95 with Windows for Workgroups

Windows 95 uses the same workgroup model as Windows for Workgroups. Because of this, computers running File and Printer Sharing for Microsoft Networks can be seen by computers running Windows for Workgroups. The Windows 95 computers will be favored in Browse Master elections because of the higher version number of the browser software.

A user running Client for Microsoft Networks can access the shared resources on a computer running Windows for Workgroups if both computers are using a common protocol. A user running Windows for Workgroups can connect to the shared resources on a computer running File and Printer Sharing for Microsoft Networks, if both computers are using a common protocol and the user has been granted access to the resources on the computer running Windows 95.

## Running Windows 95 with Workgroup Add-on for MS-DOS

Computers running File and Printer Sharing for Microsoft Networks can appear in the same workgroup as a computer running the peer server supported in Workgroup Add-on for MS-DOS. For a list of peer servers to be available in the workgroup, there must be at least one computer in the workgroup configured as Browse Master that is running Windows 95, Windows for Workgroups, or Windows NT. A computer running Workgroup Add-on for MS-DOS cannot be a Browse master.

A user running Client for Microsoft Networks can access the shared resources on a computer running Workgroup Add-on for MS-DOS if both computers are using a common protocol. A user on a computer running Workgroup Add-on for MS-DOS can access resources on a computer running File and Printer Sharing for Microsoft Networks if both computers are using a common protocol, and if the user has been granted access to the shared resources.

# PROTOCOL.INI: Real-Mode Network Initialization File

For real-mode networking, Windows 95 uses a file called PROTOCOL.INI in the Windows directory to determine the parameters for the protocol and network adapter drivers. Setup creates and modifies PROTOCOL.INI from information in INF files if any real-mode networking components are installed, such as NDIS 2 adapter drivers.

If you typically run Client for Microsoft Networks, the PROTOCOL.INI file on your computer is used to support Safe Mode Command Prompt Only with networking for system startup.

Caution   Never edit PROTOCOL.INI manually. Actual settings are stored in the Registry, and changes in PROTOCOL.INI will be overwritten automatically. Instead, always use the Network option in Control Panel and the setup software for your network hardware to configure network settings.

The information presented in this section is for troubleshooting purposes only.

PROTOCOL.INI also contains network adapter configuration information, such as the I/O address, DMA, and IRQs. The PROTOCOL.INI file contains sections for [Protman] plus separate sections for each network adapter and network protocol.

### Tip for Configuring Adapters with Real-Mode Networking

When multiple hardware adapters are used on a computer, some entries in PROTOCOL.INI, such as interrupt settings and shared memory addresses, might need adjustments to avoid hardware conflicts. Because Windows 95 Setup cannot anticipate every possible conflict, watch for error messages when you start the computer in the real-mode networking.

For example, if a network adapter and a video controller adapter both try to use the same memory address, you must adjust one of the adapters to a different address by using either the setup software for the adapter or the switches on the adapter (or both, which is the typical case). Also, the PROTOCOL.INI entries must agree with the jumper setting on each adapter.

**[Protman] section.**  This section provides the settings for the system component that manages protocols. The following list shows the format for this section.

| [protman] entry | Description |
| --- | --- |
| **drivername=** | Entry defines the driver name for the component that manages protocols. |
| **priority=** | Entry determines the order in which incoming frames are processed. |

The following shows an example of entries in this section for a computer configured with multiple NDIS protocols:

```
[protman$]
priority=ndishlp$
DriverName=protman$
```

**[*Netcard*] section.**   This section lists the set of parameters for an NDIS network adapter. A [*netcard*] section is present for each network adapter configured in the computer, and the specific entries present in this section will vary depending on the network adapter installed. The following is an example of entries in this section for an Intel® EtherExpress™ 16 or 16TP adapter:

```
[EXP16$]
DriverName=EXP16$
transceiver=Twisted-Pair (TPE)
iochrdy=Late
irq=5
ioaddress=0x300
```

**[*Protocol*] section.**   This section defines the settings used by a network protocol. A [*protocol*] section is present for each network transport protocol installed on the computer, and the specific entries present in this section will vary depending on the protocol installed. The following list shows the format for entries common to each configured protocol.

| [*protocol*] entry | Description |
| --- | --- |
| **bindings=** | Indicates the network adapter drivers to which each transport protocol binds. The *netcard* name for the network adapter driver and protocol must appear in the **bindings=** entry for at least one of the protocol drivers. The entry can specify one or more [*netcard*] sections (separated by commas). |
| **lanabase=** | For NetBIOS protocols only, defines the first LANA number the protocol is to accept. |

The following is an example of entries in this section for IPX/SPX-compatible protocol and Microsoft NetBEUI:

```
[nwlink$]
DriverName=nwlink$
Frame_Type=4
cachesize=0
Bindings=EXP16$

[NETBEUI$]
DriverName=NETBEUI$
Lanabase=0
sessions=10
ncbs=12
Bindings=EXP16$
```

C H A P T E R   9

# Windows 95 on NetWare Networks

This chapter presents information for installing and configuring Windows 95 on Novell® NetWare® networks.

---

**Note** For computers that use Microsoft Client for NetWare, all the files required for networking are included with Windows 95. However, Windows 95 does not include any Novell-supplied components required for real-mode NETX and VLM. For information about obtaining updates for Novell-supplied files, see "Obtaining Current Novell-Supplied Files" later in this chapter.

For information about configuring Novell-supplied components and running NetWare utilities, consult your Novell documentation. For information about licensing requirements, see your Novell NetWare license agreement.

---

**In This Chapter**   Windows 95 on NetWare Networks: The Basics    283
    Microsoft Client for NetWare Networks: The Benefits    284
    Novell-Supplied NetWare Clients: The Benefits    286
Windows 95 on NetWare Networks: The Issues    287
    Choosing the Network Client    287
    Choosing Protocols on NetWare Networks    288
    Configuring NetWare Servers to Support Windows 95    289
Setting Up Windows 95 for NetWare Networks: An Overview    293
Using Microsoft Client for NetWare Networks    295
    Setting Up Microsoft Client for NetWare Networks    296
    Configuring Microsoft Client for NetWare Networks    297
    Client for NetWare Networks Technical Notes    299

(*continued*)

Using a Novell NetWare Client    306
    Setting Up Windows 95 with a Novell-Supplied NetWare Client    306
    Configuring Network Adapter Drivers for Novell NetWare Clients    309
    NETX Technical Notes    314
    VLM Technical Notes    319
Technical Notes for Windows 95 on NetWare Networks    325
    Obtaining Current Novell-Supplied Files    325
    Search Mode with Windows 95 on NetWare Networks    327
Troubleshooting Windows 95 on NetWare Networks    329
    Troubleshooting Client for NetWare Networks    329
    Troubleshooting Windows 95 Using Novell NetWare Clients    331

# Windows 95 on NetWare Networks: The Basics

Windows 95 runs on NetWare workstations that use Novell NetWare versions 2.15, 2.2, 3.x, and 4.x servers. You can use several different networking clients:

- The new 32-bit, protected-mode Microsoft Client for NetWare Networks
- Novell NetWare 3.x real-mode networking client (NETX)
- Novell NetWare 4.x real-mode networking client (VLM)

---

**Note**   In the *Windows 95 Resource Kit*, NETX is used to refer to the Novell NetWare workstation shell for NetWare version 3.x; VLM (Virtual Loadable Module) is used to refer to the workstation shell for version 4.x.

---

Whichever client you choose, you can use the built-in features and commands in Windows 95 to perform most common network operation and administration tasks. Microsoft Client for NetWare Networks can process login scripts, and also supports all 16-bit NetWare 3.x and most 4.x command-line utilities for both users and administrators, so that you can use these utilities in the same way as with NETX or VLM clients running under MS-DOS or an earlier version of Windows.

Windows 95 provides complete 32-bit, protected-mode software for running on NetWare networks, including a network client (sometimes called the redirector or requestor), an IPX/SPX-compatible protocol, network adapter drivers, and administrative tools. With Microsoft Client for NetWare Networks in Windows 95, users can access NetWare server services, browse and connect to NetWare servers, and queue print jobs by using either the Windows 95 network user interface or NetWare utilities.

Whichever network client you use, the following networking features are available in Windows 95 to support computers running on NetWare networks:

- Automatic setup and customization of Windows 95 on NetWare workstations, as described in Chapter 5, "Custom, Automated, and Push Installations."
- Running a shared network copy of Windows 95 for remote-boot workstations and other shared installations, as described in Chapter 4, "Server-Based Setup for Windows 95."
- System policies to enforce desktop and system settings for individual or multiple computers, as described in Chapter 15, "User Profiles and System Policies."

- Backup agents for Cheyenne® ARCserve and Arcada® Backup Exec, plus an agent for Simple Network Management Protocols (SNMP), as described in Chapter 16, "Remote Administration."

- Complete integration of network resources in Network Neighborhood, and common controls such as the Open or Save As dialog boxes, as described in Chapter 11, "Logon, Browsing, and Resource Sharing."

- Password caching for network connections and user-level security with pass-through validation to NetWare servers, as described in Chapter 14, "Security."

- Printing to NetWare print queues using Point and Print. Also, the Win32-based Microsoft Print Services for NetWare Networks, available on the Windows 95 compact disc, can be used to despool print jobs from NetWare print queues to printers connected to computers running Client for NetWare Networks. For information, see Chapter 23, "Printing and Fonts."

The following sections describe the different features available, depending on whether you choose to run Windows 95 using the Microsoft Client for NetWare Networks or using a Novell-supplied NETX or VLM client.

# Microsoft Client for NetWare Networks: The Benefits

Architecture for Client for NetWare Network

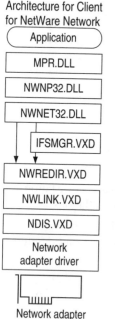

If you are installing Windows 95 to run on a NetWare network, Microsoft recommends that you use the Microsoft Client for NetWare Networks, which provides a 32-bit, protected-mode redirector. Client for NetWare Networks can be installed to coexist with Client for Microsoft Networks or a 16-bit network client, or it can be used as the sole network support for Windows 95. For technical information about these optional configurations, see Chapter 32, "Windows 95 Network Architecture."

Using Client for NetWare Networks provides the following benefits.

**A high-performance system using no conventional memory.** Client for NetWare Networks uses only 32-bit protocols, drivers, and supporting files. This client is designed to be used in a multitasking environment and provides the robust performance available for all protected-mode components in Windows 95, using no conventional memory space. On large block transfers over the network, Client for NetWare Networks is up to 200 percent faster than Windows 3.x with the VLM client. For most network operations that are a mix of reading and writing, Client for NetWare Networks is 50 to 200 percent faster, depending upon the mix of I/O operations.

**Protected-mode peer resource sharing services.**  This includes the ability to share resources such as a CD-ROM drive as a network resource. To use Microsoft File and Printer Sharing for NetWare Networks, the computer must be running Client for NetWare Networks. For more information, see Chapter 11, "Logon, Browsing, and Resource Sharing."

**Interoperation and logon with NetWare 2.15, 3.x, and 4.x servers.**  This includes support for running NetWare login scripts. Client for NetWare Networks can access servers running NetWare 2.15 and above, NetWare 3.x servers (which are bindery-based), and NetWare 4.x servers using bindery emulation. Windows 95 provides a script processor for running login scripts.

**Support for packet-burst protocol for faster data transfer.**  Client for NetWare Networks with peer resource sharing supports burst-mode NCPs, a sliding window implementation. This feature can also be disabled, as described in Chapter 11, "Logon, Browsing, and Resource Sharing."

**Automatic reconnection for lost server connection.**  When servers are available again after the loss of a NetWare Core Protocol (NCP) connection, Windows 95 reconnects automatically and rebuilds the user's environment, including connection status, drive mappings, and printer connections. (Novell-supplied AUTO.VLM only reconnects servers.) This also means that the client is not affected if the server is down or the network cable is not working.

**Large Internetwork Packet (LIP) protocol support.**  LIP works to increase the speed of data transmission when communication occurs over a router. Previously, if a server identified a router between itself and the client, the packet size was set to 576 bytes (including 64 bytes of header information). Using LIP, the client and server can negotiate the packet size used when communication occurs through a router. With LIP, the packets can be set to a maximum of 4202 bytes, based on the maximum physical packet size of the server. LIP is enabled between computers running Client for NetWare Networks and NetWare 3.12–4.x servers or any computer running Microsoft File and Printer Sharing for NetWare Networks.

**Support for all documented MS-DOS and NetWare APIs defined by Novell.**
This includes support for all NetWare 3.x APIs defined in *Novell NetWare Client SDK*. NetWare-aware applications that use only these documented APIs are compatible with Client for NetWare Networks. For more information, see "Client for NetWare Networks Technical Notes" later in this chapter.

**Enhanced performance and new networking features.** These features, which are made available when using protected-mode networking components, are described in detail elsewhere in the *Windows 95 Resource Kit*:

- Client-side caching for network information and complete Plug and Play support, as described in Chapter 7, "Introduction to Windows 95 Networking."

- Remote network access to NetWare networks, as described in Chapter 28, "Dial-Up Networking and Mobile Computing."

- User profiles for system configuration, as described in Chapter 15, "User Profiles and System Policies."

- Long filenames on the local computer, on computers running File and Printer Sharing Services for NetWare Networks, and on NetWare 3.x and 4.x volumes configured to use the OS/2 name space. For information, see "Configuring NetWare Servers to Support Windows 95" later in this chapter.

# Novell-Supplied NetWare Clients: The Benefits

Architecture for Novell real-mode clients

Novell-supplied components appear in bold

( Application )

| MPR.DLL |

| NWNP32.DLL |

| NWNET32.DLL |

| **NETWARE.DRV** | NW16.DLL |

| **VNETWARE.386** |

| **NETX.EXE** |

| **IPXODI.COM** |

| **LSL.COM** |

| **Network adapter driver** |

Network adapter

Windows 95 can be installed to use Client for Microsoft Networks in conjunction with a NETX or VLM client, or a Novell-supplied real-mode network client can be used as the sole network support in Windows 95. For technical information about these optional configurations, see "Using a Novell NetWare Client" later in this chapter.

Windows 95 provides new and improved support over Windows 3.x for computers that use NetWare clients supplied by Novell, including the following.

**Improved network adapter driver support.** Windows 95 networking components can be installed to work with Open Datalink Interface (ODI) network adapter drivers. This is the preferred configuration with a Novell-supplied NetWare client, and is also supported with Client for NetWare Networks. You can install Windows 95 to run with the IPX monolithic protocol stack (IPX.COM), although it is strongly recommended that you upgrade to a newer NetWare version using ODI drivers. Windows 95 can also run on NetWare networks using Datapoint Corporation ArcNet® network adapters.

**Protected-mode IPX/SPX-compatible protocol.** You can use the Microsoft implementation of this protocol for network connectivity with other computers running the IPX/SPX protocol with Windows 95, Windows NT, or MS-DOS operating systems. Windows 95 also provides protected-mode NetBIOS over IPX to support NetBIOS-compliant applications, providing better performance and reduced network traffic. Alternatively, you can use the real-mode Novell-supplied driver, NETBIOS.EXE, in conjunction with the Novell-supplied real-mode client.

**Compatibility with native NetWare services and commands.**   Users can run native NetWare services and commands without special configuration changes in Windows 95. This includes support for NDS, NetWare IP, NCP packet signatures, 3270 emulators, TSRs, and NetWare login scripts. (Microsoft Client for NetWare Networks does not support NDS, NetWare IP, or NCP packet signatures.)

# Windows 95 on NetWare Networks: The Issues

In most cases, Windows 95 Setup automatically installs Microsoft Client for NetWare Networks if it detects NetWare networking components on the computer. To install Windows 95 with Novell-supplied networking support, you must use a custom setup script that specifies the network client you want, or choose Custom and then select a Novell-supplied network client. For instructions on how to install Windows 95 with a Novell-supplied client, see "Introduction: Using a Novell NetWare Client" later in this chapter.

## Choosing the Network Client

Microsoft Client for NetWare does not support the use of NetWare domains or the distributed name server called NetWare Naming Service (NNS). NNS is installed as an add-on product that is supported by NetWare 3.x servers. NNS uses a domain model for NetWare servers by grouping them and distributing the domain's account list to all servers in the domain. Users running NETX or VLM can log on to servers that run NNS, but cannot use NNS tools while running Windows 95.

You might choose not to use Client for NetWare Networks in these cases:

- If you want to take advantage of NetWare NCP Packet Signature for enhanced protection of servers and client computers using NCP, then you must use VLM, because Client for NetWare Networks does not support this feature.

- If your site needs to use NetWare IP, you should use NETX or VLM. Client for NetWare Networks does not support NetWare IP, and you cannot use Microsoft TCP/IP to communicate with NetWare servers using NetWare IP.

- If you use 3270 emulators that rely on DOS-helper TSRs or need 3270 emulation for applications in MS-DOS sessions, you should use NETX or VLM.

- If you are using custom VLM components such as PNW or Novell utilities such as NWADMIN or NETADMIN, you should use VLM.

- If your site needs to use NetWare Directory Services (NDS), you should use VLM. Microsoft Client for NetWare Networks does not support this feature in the release of Windows 95.

Conversely, you might choose not to use the Novell-supplied client and instead use Client for NetWare Networks in these cases:

- If you want the performance advantages of 32-bit, protected-mode network clients and network adapter drivers, including complete Plug and Play support

- If you want to take advantage of the Windows 95 unified logon and user interface for navigating the network, plus the Windows 95 network management tools

- If you want to take advantage of long filenames, client-side caching, automatic reconnections, and other performance enhancements provided in Client for NetWare Networks

- If you want to take advantage of user profiles to manage desktop configurations

- If you want to take advantage of Windows 95 peer resource sharing without running another network client

## Choosing Protocols on NetWare Networks

The Microsoft 32-bit IPX/SPX-compatible protocol is an NDIS 3.1-compliant, routable protocol that conforms to the IPX specification, which requires routable datagram packets. This protocol can use Novell NetWare servers configured as routers (and other IPX routers) to transfer packets across LANs to access resources on other computers running any IPX/SPX protocol. With the Microsoft IPX/SPX-compatible protocol, it is not necessary to load the Novell-supplied VIPX.386 driver.

- The Microsoft IPX/SPX-compatible protocol is installed automatically if you install Client for NetWare Networks. However, if you configure Windows 95 to maintain the existing NetWare client and protocol software, you can later try using the protected-mode protocol provided with Windows 95. For details about installing and configuring the IPX/SPX-compatible protocol and NetBIOS over IPX, see Chapter 12, "Network Technical Discussion."

- You can install both protected-mode and real-mode IPX drivers on the same adapter with ODI drivers. Notice, however, that you cannot install or use the IPX/SPX-compatible protocol to run over an IPX monolithic configuration or over ArcNet.

Client for NetWare Networks does not support NetWare IP. Microsoft TCP/IP, which is fully compliant with the standard RFCs specifying TCP/IP, cannot be used to provide TCP/IP support on NetWare networks. NetWare IP uses other protocol implementations for IP functionality, so that the two protocol suites cannot communicate with each other.

Although Microsoft TCP/IP cannot be used as the supporting protocol for Client for NetWare Networks or for Novell-supplied networking clients, Microsoft TCP/IP can be installed to support other networking clients on the same computer. Use this configuration when TCP/IP-based communications are used on the internetwork. To connect to the Internet using Microsoft TCP/IP, you do not have to install another network client in addition to Client for NetWare Networks.

# Configuring NetWare Servers to Support Windows 95

This section presents information about installing Windows 95 source files on NetWare servers, automating Setup for NetWare workstations, support for long filenames on NetWare servers, and where to place user profiles and system policy files on NetWare servers.

## Installing Windows 95 Source Files on NetWare Servers

The Windows 95 master files can be placed on a NetWare server to be used as source files for installing Windows 95 locally on NetWare workstations, or to be used as a shared copy for running Windows 95 across the network. To create a directory structure and place the Windows 95 source files on a server, you must run Server-based Setup (NETSETUP.EXE), the administrative setup program provided on the Windows 95 compact disc. (This is roughly equivalent to **setup /a** in Windows 3.x and Windows for Workgroups.)

▶ **To set up Windows 95 source files on a NetWare server**

1. On the network administrator's computer, log on to the NetWare file server where you want to place the Windows 95 source files.

   This should be a network computer that is running a local copy of Windows 95 and that is used only by support personnel for network maintenance. Make sure you log on with security privileges that allow you to create directories and copy files to the file server.

2. On the administrator's computer, run **castoff all** to ensure that server-to-workstation or workstation-to-workstation messages do not affect Setup.

3. Follow the procedures for copying Windows 95 source files to a server in Chapter 4, "Server-Based Setup for Windows 95."

## Automating Setup for NetWare Workstations

You can create automatic installation procedures for installing Windows 95 on multiple workstations. The steps include the following:

- Creating setup scripts for installing Windows 95 on computers connected to NetWare networks, specifying the network client and supporting components, plus defining other software components to be installed

- Defining user and computer settings to be used in setup scripts for specific NetWare workstation configurations

- Creating login scripts to set up Windows 95 automatically on NetWare workstations when users log on

For a complete description of the procedures for preparing and managing automatic installation of Windows 95 on multiple computers, see Chapter 5, "Custom, Automated, and Push Installations."

# Supporting Long Filenames on NetWare Servers

Computers running Windows 95 can use long filenames on NetWare 3.x and 4.x volumes configured to use the OS/2 name space, which emulates an HPFS volume. Filenames on such NetWare volumes have a maximum length of 254 characters and use an 8.3 truncation on the first instance of the filename. For example:

```
longfilenameold.tst --> LONGFILE.TST
longfilenamenew.tst --> LONGFIL0.TST
```

▶ **To enable long filenames on a NetWare volume**

1. At the NetWare server console prompt, type the following lines:

   ```
   load os2
   add name space os2 to volume sys
   ```

2. Then add the following line to the STARTUP.CNF file:

   ```
   load os2
   ```

3. Shut down the file server. Then copy the file OS2.NAM from the NetWare distribution disks or compact disc to the same disk and directory that contains SERVER.EXE on the NetWare file server.

4. Restart the NetWare file server.

If you have problems with this procedure, contact Novell for more information.

When you use long filenames for files on a NetWare volume while running Windows 95, the following exceptions occur:

- You cannot use a combination of short names and long names for a path used in an MS-DOS Prompt window

- You cannot use **cd** in an MS-DOS Prompt window to switch directories using first a long filename, then using a truncated name, or vice versa

- You cannot use **dir** in an MS-DOS Prompt window to check a directory on a NetWare server if you used a truncated name to switch to that directory

To avoid these problems, use Windows Explorer. Otherwise, avoid long directory names if you do a lot of work at the command prompt.

NetWare 3.11 servers experience problems with applications that open a large number of files. Error messages report these problems as sharing or lock violations, or report a "file not found" error when you know the file exists, or report other errors in opening files. Novell supplies a patch for this problem, which you can obtain from the Novell forum on CompuServe®.

However, if you have not applied the patch, this problem affects how NetWare 3.11 servers handle long filenames, even if the OS/2 name space is enabled. To avoid such problems, Windows 95 Setup only enables long-filename support with NetWare servers version 3.12 or higher.

If the NetWare patch has been applied at your site, you can ensure support for long filenames with all NetWare servers by setting **SupportLFN=2** in the following Registry key:

```
Hkey_Local_Machine\System\CurrentControlSet\Services\VxD\Nwredir
```

The possible values for this Registry key are the following:

- 0, which indicates that long filenames are not supported on NetWare servers.

- 1 (the default), which indicates that long filenames are supported on NetWare servers version 3.12 and greater.

- 2, which indicates that long filenames are supported if the NetWare server supports long filenames. This can include NetWare 3.11 servers where the patch has been applied.

These values can also be set globally using system policies. The related policy name is Support Long Filenames under the policies for Client for NetWare Networks.

## Supporting Pass-Through Security for Peer Resource Sharing

If computers running Windows 95 will be providing File and Printer Sharing Services for NetWare Networks, then the NetWare server providing access validation must be configured with a special WINDOWS_PASSTHRU account. This special account is used to support pass-through validation for user-level security.

For more information about configuring and managing pass-through and user-level security for Windows 95 on NetWare networks, see Chapter 14, "Security."

## Placing Profile and Policy Files on NetWare Servers

User profiles, which consist of the user-specific information in the Registry, can be used to ensure a consistent desktop for individual users who log on to multiple computers, or for multiple users logging on to the same computer. User profiles can be used on a NetWare network with computers configured to use Microsoft Client for NetWare Network. When a user account is created on a NetWare server, a subdirectory of the MAIL directory is created automatically for that user. Because a Mail directory is always available for each user, Windows 95 uses these individual directories to store user profiles. If you want to use user profiles to enforce a mandatory desktop, place the related USER.MAN file in the users' MAIL directories.

If you are using system policies to enforce specific desktop or system settings, the appropriate CONFIG.POL file must be stored in the SYS:PUBLIC directory on each NetWare server that users use as a preferred server. Windows 95 automatically downloads policies from this file.

For more information about using user profiles or creating system policies, see Chapter 15, "User Profiles and System Policies."

# Setting Up Windows 95 for NetWare Networks: An Overview

If you are administering a NetWare network, the move to Windows 95 will involve incremental planning, testing, and gradual implementation of Windows 95 on many computers on the network. Typically, the administrator will take awhile to complete the following tasks:

1. Install Windows 95 on a single workstation, and experiment with various configuration alternatives, including the following:

   - Windows 95 protected-mode network client vs. Novell real-mode client

   - Protected-mode NDIS 3.1-compliant network adapter drivers vs. real-mode Open Datalink Interface (ODI) drivers

   - Protected-mode IPX/SPX-compatible protocol vs. existing IPX

   - Using a sole client vs. adding Client for Microsoft Networks

   This task includes experimenting with the typical applications used at your site and working over the network to assess the performance, reliability, and robustness available under Windows 95.

2. Prepare an implementation strategy, as summarized in Chapter 1, "Deployment Planning Basics."

3. Test the selected configuration of network clients, protocols, and drivers on a small network. This could include any combinations of the following:

   - Windows 95 installed over an existing 16-bit, Novell-supplied workstation client, using ODI drivers

   - Windows 95 added to an existing Windows 3.x-and-NetWare installation, using Client for NetWare Networks and protected-mode network components

   - Windows 95 as a new installation using all protected-mode components, including both Client for NetWare Networks and Client for Microsoft Networks, plus peer resource sharing support

4. Create default user profiles, system policies, and setup scripts, and perform other customization tasks for automatic installation and configuration, based on the inventory and implementation strategy.

5. Test automatic installation on a small network.

6. Prepare and implement the strategy for rollout on the larger network.

To support Novell NetWare integration with Windows 95, any computer on which you are installing Windows 95 should be connected to a NetWare server when you start Windows 95 Setup. This requires that the computer be configured with either an ODI driver (recommended) or the monolithic IPX driver, in addition to either NETX or VLM to access resources on a NetWare server.

Windows 95 Setup detects whether a Novell NetWare workstation shell is running on the computer. If Setup finds at least version 3.26 of NET*.COM, it automatically configures networking for NetWare networks. During the detection phase, Windows 95 Setup also tries to determine whether the computer is using real-mode TSRs that cannot be replaced (such as DOSNP.COM, TCP/IP client software, or 3720 emulators).

After detection is complete, Windows 95 Setup prepares to install protected-mode networking support based on Client for NetWare Networks, unless detection has found incompatible software components or the user specifies that network support should be based on Novell-supplied components. The new Windows 95 protected-mode components are not installed automatically if detection finds the following:

- The computer is using VLM with NetWare 4.x NDS. In this case, Setup leaves all existing networking components in place.

- Certain TSRs are present that require ODI. In this case, Setup installs Client for NetWare Networks, but configures it to run over ODI.

- Certain TSRs are present that are not compatible with the protected-mode client, but can use the new implementation of the IPX/SPX-compatible protocol. In this case, the real-mode network client and adapter drivers are left in place, but Setup installs the new protocol.

- Certain TSRs are present that are not compatible with Client for NetWare Networks or other protected-mode components. In this case, Setup leaves all existing real-mode networking components in place.

To install Client for NetWare Networks and other protected-mode networking components, Setup might perform the following actions:

- Comment out NetWare-related TSRs in AUTOEXEC.BAT that are not required with Client for NetWare Networks or other Windows 95 components

- Move certain TSRs from AUTOEXEC.BAT to WINSTART.BAT so that this software can be loaded at the appropriate time during system startup

- Install new 32-bit, protected-mode versions of networking components such as protocols and network adapter drivers

- Comment out entries from SYSTEM.INI that are not required when using protected-mode networking components

- Configure settings in the Registry related to support for NetWare networks

The actions for software detection and installation of new networking components are defined in a file named NETDET.INI in the Windows directory. Installation actions are defined in NETDET.INI for the software listed in the following table. For a complete and current list, see NETDET.INI in your Windows directory.

| Software detected | Windows 95 Setup default action |
|---|---|
| Btrieve® (BREQUEST.EXE) | Installs Client for NetWare Networks, with all protected-mode components |
| DOSNP.EXE | Keeps the real-mode IPX protocol in place |
| LAN Workplace® | Installs Client for NetWare Networks, but keeps the real-mode ODI network adapter and IPX protocol in place |
| Novell NetBIOS TSR | Installs the Microsoft IPX/SPX-compatible protocol and enables NetBIOS support |
| NACS/NASI (NASI.EXE) | Retains all existing Novell-supplied networking components |

For information about the format of entries in NETDET.INI and how to customize this file, see Chapter 5, "Custom, Automated, and Push Installations."

Windows 95 Setup automatically configures settings for network adapters and protocols. The specific issues for configuring drivers and protocols depend on whether the computer is using Client for NetWare Networks or a Novell-supplied workstation shell.

# Using Microsoft Client for NetWare Networks

The redirector provided by Client for NetWare Networks (NWREDIR.VXD) is a file system driver that supports the NCP file sharing protocol for NetWare 2.15 and above, NetWare 3.x, and NetWare 4.x. Client for NetWare Networks also supports Microsoft File and Printer Sharing for NetWare Networks (NWSERVER.VXD, the NCP peer server provided with Windows 95).

This section describes how to set up and configure Client for NetWare Networks, and provides some supporting technical notes on supporting files.

For the architectural details of this configuration, see Chapter 32, "Windows 95 Network Architecture." For information about logging on to a NetWare server, browsing NetWare resources, and using File and Printer Sharing for NetWare Networks, see Chapter 11, "Logon, Browsing, and Resource Sharing."

# Setting Up Microsoft Client for NetWare Networks

When using Client for NetWare Networks, you do not need to load any Novell-supplied drivers or components. This client runs with the Microsoft IPX/SPX-compatible protocol and NDIS-compliant, protected-mode drivers, which Windows 95 Setup installs automatically when you select this client.

When Windows 95 is installed with Client for NetWare Networks, Windows 95 Setup automatically moves any relevant NET.CFG settings to the Windows 95 Registry. You can configure the related settings using the Network option in Control Panel. You can also configure the network adapter driver and the IPX/SPX-compatible protocol, as described in Chapter 12, "Network Technical Discussion."

If you did not install Client for NetWare Networks during Windows 95 Setup, you can switch to this client any time after Windows 95 is installed, as described in the following procedure. You can also install Client for NetWare Networks and configure related options when installing Windows 95 using custom setup scripts, as described in Chapter 5, "Custom, Automated, and Push Installations."

---

**Tip**  To display the Network option without opening Control Panel, right-click the Network Neighborhood icon on the desktop. Then click Properties on the context menu.

---

▶ **To add Client for NetWare Networks after Windows 95 is installed**

1. In the Network option in Control Panel, examine the list of installed components.

   If the computer currently has NETX or VLM installed, then select that NetWare Workstation Shell client in the list of installed components, and click Remove. Also, select and remove the IPXODI protocol if it appears in the list.

2. Click Add, and then double-click Client in the Select Network Component dialog box.

3. In the Select Network Client dialog box, click Microsoft in the Manufacturers list, and then click Client for NetWare Networks in the Network Clients list. Then click OK.

You must shut down and restart the computer for the changes to take effect.

Setup automatically installs and configures all related components. Windows 95 Setup also adds the value **lastdrive=32** to the parameters for the network client in the Registry. This value makes room for entries in a table to store drive information. For Microsoft networking, the last drive would be set to Z (or 26), but NetWare allows six additional entries in its drive table. The extra drives are used only by NetWare-aware applications; these drives are not available to users.

# Configuring Microsoft Client for NetWare Networks

This section presents information for configuring and using Microsoft Client for NetWare Networks, including the following topics:

- Configuring protected-mode NDIS network adapter drivers for Client for NetWare Networks
- Configuring Client for NetWare Networks with ODI network adapter drivers
- Running NetWare utilities with Client for NetWare Networks

For information about configuring logon options for Client for NetWare Networks, see Chapter 11, "Logon, Browsing, and Resource Sharing."

## Configuring Protected-Mode Network Adapter Drivers for Client for NetWare Networks

When you install Client for NetWare Networks, a 32-bit, protected-mode, NDIS 3.1-compliant network adapter driver is installed automatically, unless the computer is running software cited in the table in "Setting Up Windows 95 for NetWare Networks: An Overview" earlier in this chapter. If you configure Client for NetWare Networks to use ODI drivers instead, you can switch to the protected-mode drivers at any time.

Although it is possible to run Client for NetWare Networks over ODI drivers, Microsoft recommends that you install a 32-bit, protected-mode network adapter driver to take advantage of the performance improvements offered by these drivers, as described in Chapter 12, "Network Technical Discussion."

For a shared installation, you must use protected-mode drivers if the computers will run Client for NetWare Networks.

Depending on when you install Client for NetWare Networks, you might have to install the 32-bit, protected-mode network adapter driver before you can install the network client. Setup prompts you to do this if it is necessary.

▶ **To switch to a 32-bit, protected-mode network adapter driver**

1. In the Network option in Control Panel, double-click the network adapter in the list of installed network components.

2. In the properties for the adapter, click the Driver Type tab.

3. Click the option named Enhanced Mode (32 Bit And 16 Bit) NDIS Driver, and then click OK. Then shut down and restart the computer.

## Configuring Client for NetWare Networks with ODI Network Adapter Drivers

Architecture for protected-mode client with ODI drivers

Novell-supplied components appear in bold

| NWREDIR.VXD |
| IPX/SPX compatible protocol |
| MSODISUP.VXD |
| ODIHLP.EXE |
| **LSL.COM** |
| **ODI adapter driver** |

Network adapter

You might choose to keep existing ODI drivers when using Client for NetWare Networks. The best reason for doing this is if your users need to run a TSR that requires IPX/SPX support and that is used by applications created for both Windows and MS-DOS. In this case, the TSR should be loaded by placing an entry just after the IPXODI statement in either AUTOEXEC.BAT or in WINSTART.BAT (which is the batch file used to start TSRs to be used by Windows-based applications).

Using an ODI driver instead of an NDIS 3.1 driver with Client for NetWare Networks has the following drawbacks:

- There is some use of conventional memory, and overall performance on the network is not as good as can be realized with NDIS 3.1 drivers.

- There are no Plug and Play capabilities for the networking components.

- You cannot use this configuration to run a shared installation of Windows 95.

However, you do retain the following benefits from using an ODI driver with Client for NetWare Networks instead of a real-mode network client:

- Support for long filenames

- Automatic reconnection for lost server connections

- Dial-up networking for remote access

- Client-side caching for network information

If you want to use the current ODI driver instead of a Windows 95 NDIS network adapter driver, you can select that driver using the Network option in Control Panel. For more information about using ODI drivers, see "Configuring Windows 95 with ODI Drivers" later in this chapter. For information about the related files, see "Obtaining Current Novell-Supplied Files" later in this chapter.

▶ **To use ODI drivers with Client for NetWare Networks**

1. In the properties for the network adapter, click the Driver Type tab.

2. Click the option named Real Mode (16-bit) ODI Driver, and then click OK. Then shut down and restart the computer.

**Note**  Shared installations that use Client for NetWare Networks cannot use real-mode ODI drivers. In this case, protected-mode networking components can be used.

# Client for NetWare Networks Technical Notes

This section presents some technical issues you should be aware of when using Client for NetWare Networks, including a summary of configuration settings and required support files, and configuration notes, plus notes about NetWare API support and running NetWare utilities with Client for NetWare Networks.

## Summary of Settings for Client for NetWare Networks

The following table lists the required and possible settings for CONFIG.SYS and AUTOEXEC.BAT files if you install Client for NetWare Networks.

**Configuration File Settings for Client for NetWare Networks**

| Filename | Required settings |
| --- | --- |
| autoexec.bat | None |
| startnet.bat[1] | None |
| config.sys | None |

[1] The STARTNET.BAT file is a startup batch file created when VLM is installed, and is called from AUTOEXEC.BAT. This file is not required with Microsoft Client for NetWare Networks.

Notice that LOGIN.EXE is not loaded from any configuration file. Windows 95 Setup removes this entry automatically. Also, if either NETX or VLM is initialized from AUTOEXEC.BAT or another batch file, then Client for NetWare Networks will not be loaded. No real-mode drivers are needed if a network adapter driver appears in the list of installed components in the Network option in Control Panel.

The following table summarizes the minimum settings that you should see in the Network option in Control Panel if you install Client for NetWare Networks.

**Required Network Settings for Client for NetWare Networks[1]**

| Network component | Configuration options |
| --- | --- |
| Client for NetWare Networks | If the computer will be downloading system policies or user profiles from NetWare servers, Client for NetWare Networks should be selected in the Primary Network Logon box. |
| | In the General properties for Client for NetWare Networks, Preferred Server should show the name of the NetWare server to be used for initial logon. If login scripts are used, the option that enables login scripts should be checked. |

**Required Network Settings for Client for NetWare Networks**[1] (*continued*)

| Network component | Configuration options |
|---|---|
| Network adapter | In the General properties for the adapter, the driver type should be Enhanced Mode (32-Bit and 16-Bit) NDIS.[1] |
| IPX/SPX-compatible protocol | In its Advanced properties, the Frame Type should be Auto. If any network applications at your site require support for NetBIOS over IPX, that option should be checked in the NetBIOS properties. |

[1] You can also specify 16-bit ODI drivers. You do not need to load such drivers from CONFIG.SYS or another configuration file.

# Required Support Files for Client for NetWare Networks

The following table summarizes the support files required for Client for NetWare Networks. All of these files are found in the Windows SYSTEM directory and are provided with Windows 95; no Novell-supplied components are required. For more information about these components, see Chapter 32, "Windows 95 Network Architecture."

**Required Files for Client for NetWare Networks**[1]

| File | Description |
|---|---|
| netware.drv | Emulates a WinNet driver required by some NetWare-aware applications that check for this file, such as Lotus Notes®. Notice that this file is supplied with Windows 95, and is not the same as the similarly-named Novell-supplied file. (The Windows 95 version is approximately 2K in size.) |
| nwlink.vxd | Provides the IPX/SPX-compatible protocol. |
| nwlsproc.exe, nwlscon.exe | Optionally, provides the 32-bit login script processor and console used by Client for NetWare Networks. |
| nwnet32.dll | Provides common NetWare networking functions for the 32-bit network provider and print provider. |
| nwnp32.dll | Provides access to NetWare network resources using Windows Explorer, Network Neighborhood, and so on. This 32-bit network provider for NetWare networks is the service provider interface to the Multiple Provider Router. |
| nwpp32.dll | Provides the print provider interface to the print router in SPOOLSS.DLL. This 32-bit print provider supports the ability to print to NetWare printing resources. |
| nwredir.vxd | Provides a 32-bit file system driver (redirector) to support applications that use the NCP file sharing protocol. |

[1] These files are all supplied on the Windows 95 product disks. The NETWARE.DRV file in this configuration is a replacement for an identically named Novell-supplied file.

The following tables summarize entries that are changed automatically in configuration files when Client for NetWare Networks is installed with Windows 95.

**AUTOEXEC.BAT Additions for Client for NetWare Networks**

| | |
|---|---|
| dosagent | winagent |

**AUTOEXEC.BAT Deletions for Client for NetWare Networks**

| | | |
|---|---|---|
| bnetx | ipx | odihlp |
| brequest | lsl | odinsup |
| emsnetx | msipx | startnet |
| emsnet5 | netbios | vlm |
| emsnet4 | net3 | xmsnet3 |
| emsnet3 | net4 | xmsnet4 |
| int2f | net5 | xmsnet5 |
| ipxodi | netx | xmsnetxp |

**SYSTEM.INI Additions for Client for NetWare Networks**

[Boot]
networks32=nwnp32

**SYSTEM.INI Deletions for Client for NetWare Networks**

| [386enh] | [Boot] | [boot.description] |
|---|---|---|
| network= | network.drv= | network.drv= |
| uniquedospsp= | | |
| pspincrements= | | |
| timercriticalsection= | | |
| reflectdosint2a= | | |

**NET.CFG Deletions for Client for NetWare Networks**

msipx

**Files Renamed in Windows or SYSTEM Directories[1]**

| | | |
|---|---|---|
| nwuser.exe | nwgdi.dll | vnetware.386 |
| netware.drv | nwpopup.exe | vipx.386 |
| netware.hlp | | |

[1] Files are renamed *filename.ex~*.

## Client for NetWare Networks Configuration Notes

This section presents some configuration notes for Client for NetWare Networks.

- When Windows 95 attempts to connect to a NetWare server, it first silently tries to use the user's logon name and password to make the connection. If you use system policies, you can set a policy that turns off this behavior for Client for NetWare Networks. For information, see Chapter 15, "User Profiles and System Policies."

- Client for NetWare Networks is always bound only to the IPX/SPX-compatible protocol. This is the only protocol this network client can use. If you require an additional protocol for your network, such as TCP/IP, you must install an additional network client, such as Client for Microsoft Networks.

  Notice, however, that you can install Microsoft TCP/IP to connect to the Internet without installing an additional network client.

- Windows 95 automatically provides a real-mode NetWare-compatible network client for use in emergency startup and recovery situations. It is not a full-featured, robust network client and, therefore, does not support features such as long filenames, automatic reconnection to servers, and the packet-burst (burst-mode) protocol. For more information about Safe Mode with Networking, see Chapter 35, "General Troubleshooting."

- With Client for NetWare Networks, you cannot map drives for individual VM sessions; drive mappings are always global. This is the equivalent of the behavior specified in earlier versions of Windows by the SYSTEM.INI setting **NWShareHandles=True** (when using NETX or VLM). Notice, however, that with Client for NetWare Networks, each VM can have a different current directory on network drives, unlike earlier versions of Windows.

- If you are using File and Printer Sharing for NetWare Networks, then CONFIG.SYS should not have a **LastDrive=** statement.

- The NWPopUp messaging utility is not supported with Client for NetWare Networks. You can use WinPopup to broadcast pop-up messages, as described in Chapter 12, "Network Technical Discussion."

## Additional Settings for Client for NetWare Networks

This section describes some additional settings that can be added to the Registry for Client for NetWare Networks or for File and Printer Sharing for NetWare Networks. For information about how to add Registry values, see Chapter 33, "Windows 95 Registry."

**Setting maximum IPX packet size for the LIP protocol.**   You can set a global value for the maximum IPX packet size for the LIP protocol. To do this, add a Registry entry named **MaxLIP** and specify a binary or DWORD value that is the greatest value allowed on any one network segment. This global setting is also used on the local network. For example, if a client on a token-ring segment (which allows 4K packet sizes) communicates over an Ethernet segment (which allows 1.5K packets) to a server on another token-ring segment, the size specified for **MaxLIP** should be limited to the lowest packet size allowed.

Add **MaxLIP** as an entry under the following Registry key:

```
Hkey_Local_Machine\System\CurrentControlSet\Services\VxD\Nwredir
```

To continue the earlier example, you would specify a value for 1.5K (0x000005DC in hexadecimal). The actual optimal value depends on the frame-header size, which is the IPX portion of the packet. You might want to experiment to get the right size but, in general, specifying a size that is too small is better than too large, because you want to make sure that the echo packet goes through on the first try.

**Turning off support for packet-burst protocol.**   If you want to turn off support for the packet-burst protocol (which is enabled by default for File and Printer Sharing for NetWare Networks), set **SupportBurst=0** in the following Registry key:

```
Hkey_Local_Machine\System\CurrentControlSet\Services\VxD\Nwserver
```

**Setting the shell version for .OVL files.**   The versions of NetWare available for the United States that run on x86-based computers use Novell-supplied IBM*.OVL (overlay) files to present the NetWare shell. This is the default assumed by Windows 95. However, other locales use other versions of .OVL files to account for different architecture. For example, NetWare 3.x J (for Japan) uses the following overlay files for various computer types.

| Overlay file | Computer architecture |
| --- | --- |
| pc98$run.ovl | NEC® PC9800 |
| dosv$run.ovl | IBM® PC-compatible |
| j31$run.ovl | Toshiba® J3100 |
| fmr$run.ovl | Fujitsu® FMR |
| ps55$run.ovl | IBM Japan |

For real-mode clients, alternate .OVL files are specified in NET.CFG as the SHORT MACHINE TYPE. For Microsoft Client for NetWare Networks, alternate .OVL files can be specified as the **ShellVersion** value in the following Registry key:

```
Hkey_Local_Machine\System\CurrentControlSet\Services\VxD\Nwredir
```

The default value is **MDOS\0V7.00\0IBM_PC\0IBM\0**, where \0 indicates a binary zero (null value). This value represents the four concatenated strings returned by the INT 21 function 0xEA. You must replace the last string (0IBM) with the one used to generate the *$RUN.OVL name. The value in the Registry must have a binary type; however, you can enter the required combination of raw ASCII and binary data in the Enter Binary Data dialog box.

## NetWare API Support in Client for NetWare Networks

Client for NetWare Networks includes built-in support for MS-DOS–based APIs defined by Novell for NetWare 3.x, as summarized in the following table.

| API for MS-DOS | Description |
| --- | --- |
| INT21H | Used by applications for NetWare information, bindery services, and so on |
| INT64 and INT7A | Used by applications to submit IPX/SPX requests |

Client for NetWare Networks supports MS-DOS–based API calls documented in *Novell NetWare Client SDK*. If problems occur with applications that make proprietary or undocumented API calls, then you should use a real-mode Novell-supplied client. Also, please report this problem to both Microsoft and the application vendor.

The Windows 3.x APIs for NetWare consist of a series of DLLs provided by Novell with the version 3.x WinNet16 driver for the VLM client. The 16-bit Novell-supplied DLLs for Windows can run with Client for NetWare Networks. This ensures that Windows-based applications and utilities that are NetWare-aware will run with Microsoft Client for NetWare Networks.

If any of your applications requires one or more of these DLLs when running on a Novell-supplied client (NETX or VLM), then you must also run the same DLLs when using that application under Client for NetWare Networks.

The NetWare DLLs are described in the following list.

| API for Windows | Description |
| --- | --- |
| nwcalls.dll | APIs for NCP communication between the file server and the client computer |
| nwgdi.dll | NetWare Graphical Device Interface |
| nwipxspx.dll | APIs for IPX/SPX communication |
| nwlocale.dll | APIs for localization of applications |
| nwnetapi.dll | Network API support for NDS |
| nwpsrv.dll | Print server services APIs |

These Novell-supplied DLLs are not provided with Windows 95. They are provided by Novell with NetWare versions 3.12 and 4.x, and are updated on CompuServe and other electronic forums. Also, you must follow the directions provided in your Novell documentation to install these files. For information about obtaining the most recent files, see "Obtaining Current Novell-Supplied Files" later in this chapter.

## Running NetWare Utilities with Client for NetWare Networks

In addition to the 32-bit, protected-mode graphical tools built into Windows 95, you can use the 16-bit command-line utilities provided with NetWare for managing and sharing resources.

With Microsoft Client for NetWare Networks, you can run all NetWare 3.x utilities that reside on the NetWare server, such as SYSCON. You can run most NetWare 4.x utilities when you are using Client for NetWare Networks, except those that require NDS, such as NWADMIN, CX, and NETADMIN. You can also run NetWare 2.x file and printer utilities. However, you cannot use the VLM NWUSER utility with Client for NetWare Networks.

---

**Tip**  To use Novell-supplied utilities such as SYSCON, map the SYS:PUBLIC directory in the login script.

---

▶ **To run NetWare 3.x utilities in Windows 95**

1. Map a drive to the volume containing the NetWare utilities by using statements in a login script or by using the Map Network Drive dialog box.

   When you use Map Network Drive, you can make this a persistent connection by clicking the Reconnect At Logon box.

2. From the Start button, point to Programs, and then click MS-DOS Prompt to start an MS-DOS session.

3. Switch to the mapped network drive, and then run the utilities in the usual way.

# Using a Novell NetWare Client

Windows 95 can run with the NetWare NETX and VLM client software. Before installing Windows 95, make sure that you have the necessary Novell-supplied files for Windows support, which can be obtained from Novell.

---

Caution  Novell-supplied components for using the NetWare client with Windows 95 require that you log on to the appropriate NetWare server before starting Windows 95. As with earlier versions of Windows, you should not log on to a NetWare server from within Windows 95.

Instead, log on to the server from AUTOEXEC.BAT or from a batch file that is called from AUTOEXEC.BAT. You should also continue to load the necessary MS-DOS–based TSR programs using AUTOEXEC.BAT or STARTNET.BAT.

For information about where a logon command should be placed in system startup files, see Chapter 11, "Logon, Browsing, and Resource Sharing."

---

The following section describes how to set up and configure Windows 95 with a Novell-supplied client.

## Setting Up Windows 95 with a Novell-Supplied NetWare Client

To help you ensure successful installation of Windows 95, make sure that the Novell-supplied NetWare client software is running before you start Windows 95 Setup. To verify that the Novell-supplied software is running, make sure you can successfully connect to and use resources on a NetWare server. Running the Novell-supplied software helps to ensure that Setup can detect the network configuration for successful installation of Windows 95.

Also, if you currently use IPX.COM, you should upgrade to the latest versions of NetWare client software that use ODI drivers before installing Windows 95. For information about using ODI drivers versus monolithic IPX.COM, see "Configuring Network Adapter Drivers for Novell NetWare Clients" later in this chapter.

### Installing Windows 95 with a Novell NetWare Client

This section presents the procedures for installing Windows 95 to run with a Novell-supplied client, depending on various installation situations:

- Installing Novell-supplied NetWare client support during Windows 95 Setup
- Installing Client for Microsoft Networks in addition to a Novell-supplied NetWare client
- Installing a Novell-supplied NetWare client after installing Windows 95 with no network support

**Note**  The method for installing VLM support is different if VLM support was not installed previously under Windows 3.x, as described in "VLM Technical Notes" later in this chapter.

Also notice that, if the NetWare client software is not running at the time Windows 95 is installed, you must configure Windows 95 manually after Setup to work in conjunction with the NetWare client software.

By default, Windows 95 Setup automatically installs Microsoft Client for NetWare Networks if it detects NetWare software, except in the cases described in "Setting Up Windows 95 for NetWare Networks: An Overview" earlier in this chapter. You can select the Custom setup type and specify that the Novell-supplied software be retained during Setup. In this case, Windows 95 will use the existing networking configuration specified in NET.CFG for protocols, adapter drivers, and other values.

▶ **To select the Novell-supplied NETX client support during Windows 95 Setup**

1. Start the computer as usual, making sure that the Novell-supplied network software is running. Then run Windows 95 Setup, and select Custom as the Setup type.

2. When the Network Configuration dialog box appears, select Client for NetWare Networks in the list of components, and then click Remove.

3. Click Add, and then double-click Client in the Select Network Component Type dialog box.

4. In the Select Network Client dialog box, click Novell in the Manufacturers list, and click Workstation Shell 3.X [NETX] in the Network Clients list. Then click OK.

   If you also want to use Client for Microsoft Networks, follow the steps in the next procedure.

5. Click the Next button in the Network Configuration dialog box.

   If you want to use only the NETX client, you do not need to specify settings for your network adapter driver or protocols. Setup automatically adds support for the ODI adapter and IPXODI (or for IPX.COM) by reading NET.CFG.

6. Continue with Windows 95 Setup.

**Note**  You cannot install Client for Microsoft Networks as an additional network client if you are installing Windows 95 to run with an IPX monolithic configuration.

▶ **To install Client for Microsoft Networks with a Novell NetWare client**

1. In the Network Configuration dialog box, click Add, and then double-click Client.

2. In the Select Network Client dialog box, click Microsoft in the Manufacturers list, and click Client for Microsoft Networks in the Network Clients list. Then click OK.

▶ **To determine whether the correct adapter driver is installed**

1. In the Network option in Control Panel, double-click the network adapter (or IPX Monolithic) in the list of components.

2. In the properties for the network adapter, click the Driver Type tab.

3. Make sure the Real Mode (16 bit) ODI driver is selected.

▶ **To install a Novell NetWare client with no previous networking**

1. Run the Novell-supplied installation program to install a NetWare client.

2. In the Network option in Control Panel, click Add, and then double-click Client in the Select Network Component Type dialog box.

3. In the Select Network Client dialog box, click Novell in the Manufacturers list, and click the workstation shell that you want (NETX or VLM) in the Network Clients list. Then click OK.

## Switching Back to NETX from Client for NetWare Networks

If you install the protected-mode Client for NetWare Networks and later decide to return to your original Novell NetWare NETX configuration, follow these steps.

---

**Important**  Be sure to use the Network option in Control Panel to remove Client for NetWare Networks, and then to configure Windows 95 to use NETX or VLM.

---

For details about adding or returning to VLM, see "VLM Technical Notes" later in this chapter.

▶ **To return to NETX after installing Client for NetWare Networks**

1. In the Network option in Control Panel, select Client for NetWare Networks, and then click Remove.

2. Click Add, and then double-click Client.

3. In the Select Network Client dialog box, click Novell in the Manufacturers list, and click Workstation Shell 3.X [NETX] in the Network Clients list. Then click OK.

   Windows 95 automatically installs IPXODI support.

4. Click OK in Network properties, and provide a disk or a location for any files that Windows 95 requests to complete the installation. Then shut down and restart the computer.

Usually, you will have to reinstall Novell-supplied files at this stage, because Windows 95 Setup previously replaced these files with versions required by Client for NetWare Networks. You must also make sure that NET.CFG is present and contains correct settings, and that the required settings are present in CONFIG.SYS and AUTOEXEC.BAT. See your Novell documentation for information about these required settings.

# Configuring Network Adapter Drivers for Novell NetWare Clients

This section presents some technical information related to the network adapter drivers used when configuring Windows 95 to run with Novell-supplied network clients. The topics include configuring Windows 95 with ODI drivers, monolithic IPX, or ArcNet network adapters, and setting options in NET.CFG.

NET.CFG, the Novell NetWare configuration file, is an ASCII text file that specifies various settings for the adapter, protocol, and client. For information about the format and contents of NET.CFG, consult your Novell documentation.

## Configuring Windows 95 with ODI Drivers

The Open Datalink Interface (ODI) specification was defined by Novell and Apple® Computer to provide a protocol and a consistent API for communicating with a network adapter driver and to support the use of multiple protocols by a network adapter driver.

---

**Note**  Microsoft recommends that you use ODI drivers when running Windows 95 with a Novell-supplied network client. Novell also recommends using ODI-based client software rather than monolithic IPX drivers.

---

Architecture for ODI drivers

| Network client |
| --- |

| Protocol driver |
| --- |

| Link Support Layer |
| --- |

| ODI driver (MLID) |
| --- |

Network adapter

ODI consists of the following components.

**An ODI-compliant version of the IPX/SPX protocol.** This component provides the network protocol for communicating between NetWare clients and servers. With NETX or VLM clients, this must be the Novell-supplied IPXODI.COM (you can also use the Microsoft IPX/SPX-compatible protocol for other network clients).

**The Link Support Layer (LSL).** This component, provided in the Novell-supplied LSL.COM file, sets the foundation for network adapter drivers to communicate with multiple protocol drivers, and vice versa.

**The ODI driver.** Also called the Multiple Link Interface Driver (MLID), the ODI-compliant network adapter driver is created by the adapter manufacturer. This component usually identifies the name of the supported adapter in the filename, such as NE2000.COM for the Novell NE-2000 adapter, 3c5x9.COM for the 3Com® EtherLink® III adapter, and EXP16ODI.COM for the Intel® EtherExpress™ 16 adapter. Windows 95 supports using such drivers, but these drivers are not included with Windows 95.

For information about required files, see "Obtaining Current Novell-Supplied Files" later in this chapter.

### Tips for Installing Windows 95 with ODI Drivers

Before you install Windows 95 on a computer, the real-mode IPXODI network should be configured and working properly using your Novell-supplied installation program. Test to confirm that there are no errors when loading the Novell-supplied files LSL.COM, IPXODI.COM, the ODI driver, and NETX.EXE, or when accessing resources on NetWare servers. If these components are running on the computer when Windows 95 is installed, Windows 95 Setup detects the drivers, identifies the network adapter, and automatically configures Windows 95 to run with the ODI drivers.

If Windows 95 Setup cannot identify the ODI driver being used, you might have to configure the network adapter driver manually. In this case, click Have Disk in the Select Network Adapter dialog box in the Network option in Control Panel. You must provide a file for the correct IPXODI support driver to match the type of network adapter used, using a file supplied by Novell or the adapter manufacturer.

# Setting Network Adapter Options in NET.CFG

Because a computer using ODI drivers can have multiple ODI drivers and multiple protocols loaded and bound, the networking software uses NET.CFG to identify the network adapters, protocol configuration, and binding information. NET.CFG is responsible for configuring the network environment for a Novell-supplied client, and is used to configure custom parameters for NETX, IPX, NetBIOS, or the general NetWare environment. To configure any options, edit NET.CFG as described in your Novell documentation.

Monolithic IPX (IPX.COM) does not require a settings file because there is only one protocol and one network adapter driver bound together in a specific way. The IPX.COM file contains all network adapter configuration information.

NetWare began using SHELL.CFG as the configuration filename with monolithic IPX and is now using NET.CFG for ODI. NET.CFG is the preferred file to use and has some specific uses for ODI. Neither SHELL.CFG nor NET.CFG is required for a NetWare client computer. If these files do not exist, default settings are used. If both SHELL.CFG and NET.CFG exist, both are processed (first SHELL.CFG, then NET.CFG).

If you are using ODI drivers, the Novell-supplied LSL.COM file uses information from NET.CFG to configure the ODI driver before the NETX workstation shell does. For the LSL driver to load and initialize information from NET.CFG, the proper NET.CFG file should reside in the same directory as LSL.COM and the Novell-supplied NETX.EXE network client. To verify that there is not more than one NET.CFG file present on a computer, type **dir /s net.cfg** at the command prompt (or from the Start button, click Find and search for NET.CFG).

Network adapter configuration information is contained in a **Link Driver** section in NET.CFG, where you can specify the network adapter's interrupt, I/O address, memory address, frame types, and protocols. For example, the following example shows NET.CFG entries for an SMC® Ethercard Plus Elite 16 adapter:

```
show dots=on
file handles=60
preferred server=nw_311
link driver smc8000
    int 5
    port 240
    mem d000
    frame ethernet_802.3
```

The following table describes selected information commonly found in NET.CFG under the **Link Driver** section. For information not found in NET.CFG, default settings for the network adapter are assumed. For more information, consult your Novell documentation.

**Network Adapter Driver Settings in NET.CFG**

| NET.CFG setting | Description |
|---|---|
| DMA | DMA channel number. Can assign up to two DMA channels by designating them DMA #1 x and DMA #2 y. |
| FRAME | Alternate Media Access Control (MAC) layer frame encapsulations for the network adapter. The default is ETHERNET_802.3 if not specified. Frame types are the following:<br><br>ETHERNET_802.3   ETHERNET_SNAP<br>ETHERNET_802.2   TOKEN_RING<br>ETHERNET_II      TOKEN_RING_SNAP |
| INT | IRQ number. Can assign up to two IRQs by designating them IRQ #1 x and IRQ #2 y. |
| MEM | Memory address in upper memory area (UMA). Can assign up to two UMA addresses by designating them MEM #1 x and MEM # y. |
| NODE ADDRESS | New 12-digit MAC address assigned to the network adapter. |
| PORT | I/O port address. Can assign up to two I/O port addresses by designating them PORT #1 x and PORT #2 y. |
| PROTOCOL | Protocols to be used with ODI drivers. You do not need to specify this in NET.CFG if NETX is running only IPX and no other protocol. If other protocols are running, you must specify the protocol, protocol ID, and the frame type. |
| SLOT | Network adapter slot number (MCA, EISA). |

# Configuring Windows 95 for Monolithic IPX

Although the monolithic IPX legacy configuration is supported in Windows 95, Novell recommends that the ODI client software be used instead of dedicated IPX drivers. Notice particularly the following exceptions for monolithic IPX:

- If you want to install Windows 95 with monolithic support, all networking components must be installed and working before you install Windows 95.

Architecture for
monolithic IPX

| Network client |
| --- |

| Monolithic
protocol driver |
| --- |

| IPX.COM |
| --- |

| IPX.OBJ and
*netcard*.OBJ |
| --- |

Network adapter

- If you want to use Client for NetWare Networks with ODI drivers, you should first upgrade your Novell-supplied networking software to a recent version of the ODI client software.

- You cannot install any Windows 95 protected-mode networking components if you are using the IPX monolithic configuration.

- You cannot install monolithic support under Windows 95 if the workstation has Novell-supplied VLM software installed.

**Caution**  Microsoft strongly recommends upgrading to 32-bit, protected-mode software for a computer running Windows 95 on NetWare networks.

If you must use Windows 95 on monolithic IPX, then configure the real-mode monolithic IPX network and verify that it is working properly before installing Windows 95. Test to confirm that there are no errors when loading IPX.COM and NETX.EXE or when accessing resources on NetWare servers.

The monolithic implementation of the IPX protocol, IPX.COM, includes a single driver file that contains both the IPX/SPX protocol stack and the network adapter driver for communicating with the network adapter. IPX.COM must be configured for each computer based on the network adapter and its hardware configuration (IRQ, I/O address, RAM address in the upper memory area, and DMA channel). IPX.COM is generated from the IPX.OBJ file and a particular network adapter driver file (*netcard*.OBJ) using the NetWare SHGEN or WSGEN programs.

▶ **To add monolithic IPX after Windows 95 is installed**

1. In the Network option in Control Panel, select all installed networking components, and then click Remove.

2. Click Add, and then double-click Adapter in the Select Network Component Type dialog box.

3. From the Manufacturers list in the Select Network Adapters dialog box, click Novell. From the Network Adapters list, click Novell IPX Monolithic Driver. Then click OK.

4. Shut down and restart the computer for the changes to take effect.

An entry will appear for Novell IPX Monolithic Driver in the list of installed components in the Network option in Control Panel. For information about required files, see "Obtaining Current Novell-Supplied Files" later in this chapter.

## Configuring Windows 95 with ArcNet Network Adapters

Windows 95 supports connectivity to Novell NetWare servers and other computers running Windows 95 over an ArcNet network. To configure Windows 95 to support NetWare over ArcNet, you must use NETX or VLM with real-mode IPX drivers on ArcNet network adapters, with NetBIOS support. This is true whether you are using a monolithic IPX driver or an ODI ArcNet driver.

You cannot use the Windows 95 IPX/SPX-compatible protocol or Client for Microsoft Networks with ODI drivers. If you are running Client for Microsoft Networks to connect to other Microsoft networking computers on an ArcNet network, you must also install NDIS 2 network adapter drivers and another protocol used in the network, such as NetBEUI. (Notice that in this configuration, you cannot also access a NetWare network.)

If the ArcNet driver and NetWare workstation shell are running when Windows 95 is installed, Windows 95 Setup detects the configuration and automatically installs the proper components. However, if the computer is using a generic ArcNet driver or if Windows 95 is unable to detect an ArcNet driver, you might have to configure Windows 95 manually to run on an ArcNet configuration. You will also need to install the ODI ArcNet Support transport with NetBIOS. If Windows 95 Setup can detect the configuration properly, this network protocol is installed automatically for an ODI ArcNet driver.

# NETX Technical Notes

This section describes specific notes related to using the Novell-supplied NetWare 3.x client software with Windows 95.

## Using NETX with Client for Microsoft Networks

When running NETX with Windows 95, you keep all the same functionality that you had when running with MS-DOS or Windows 3.x. You also gain the features described in "Windows 95 on NetWare Networks: The Basics" earlier in this chapter.

If you are using NETX as the network client, you might also choose to install the 32-bit, protected-mode Client for Microsoft Networks if you want to connect to other Microsoft network computers, such as computers running Windows for Workgroups 3.x, LAN Manager, or Windows NT.

When you run the NetWare NETX client with Windows 95 in this configuration, you should continue to load the necessary Novell-supplied client components and MS-DOS–based TSR programs (LSL, ODI driver, IPXODI, and NETX) in AUTOEXEC.BAT or STARTNET.BAT, just as you did with MS-DOS or Windows 3.1. Windows 95 Setup automatically adds the configuration settings if they are not present. For information about required configuration settings, see your Novell documentation.

Notice that this configuration requires a Microsoft Windows NT Client Access license if the computer will be connecting to servers running Windows NT Server. For information, see Chapter 8, "Windows 95 on Microsoft Networks."

Architecture for Novell-supplied NETX with Client for Microsoft Networks

Novell-supplied components appear in bold

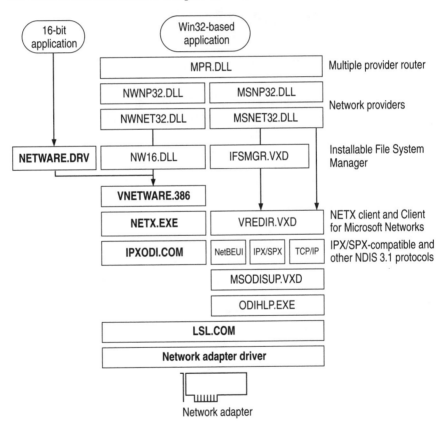

Network adapter

In this configuration, the Novell-supplied version of NETWARE.DRV is installed and loaded only for applications that call it directly. Because this driver is not used by Windows 95, all access to NetWare resources occurs by using the Windows 95 user interface, not the NETWARE.DRV dialog boxes provided by Novell. The NW16.DLL component translates 32-bit network calls to 16-bit network calls that can be passed to VNETWARE.386.

**Note** You cannot install Client for Microsoft Networks as an additional networking client if you are using the IPX monolithic configuration.

## Using NETX as the Sole Client

This configuration is for use in either of these cases:

- The IPX monolithic configuration is used.

- You do not need to connect to other computers running Windows for Workgroups 3.x, LAN Manager, or Windows NT. Of course, you can connect to computers running Microsoft File and Printer Sharing Services for NetWare.

To use only NETX client support, use the Network option in Control Panel to remove Client for NetWare Networks and Client for Microsoft Networks, if either of these clients is installed. Then add the Novell NetWare (Workstation Shell 3.X [NETX]) client, as described in "Installing Windows 95 with a Novell NetWare Client" earlier in this chapter.

Architecture for
Novell-supplied NETX
as the sole client

Novell-supplied
components appear in
bold

The following table lists the required settings for CONFIG.SYS and
AUTOEXEC.BAT files if you use NETX as the sole network client.

**Configuration File Settings for NETX as the Sole Client**

| Filename | Required settings |
|---|---|
| config.sys | `lastdrive=`*drive letter* |
| autoexec.bat[1] | `lsl.com` <br> *odi_driver* <br> `ipxodi.com` <br> `netx.exe` <br> `q:           ; that is, lastdrive+1` <br> `login` <br> `c:` |

[1] Or this could be the name of a batch file called from AUTOEXEC.BAT.

The following table summarizes the minimum settings that you should see in the Network option in Control Panel if you use NETX as the sole client.

**Network Settings for NETX as the Sole Network Client**

| Component | Options |
| --- | --- |
| NetWare (Workstation Shell 3.X [NETX]) | Novell NetWare (Workstation Shell 3.X [NETX]) should appear in the list of installed components. All other settings are configured in NET.CFG. |
| Network adapter | In the General properties for the adapter, the option named Real Mode (16-Bit) ODI Driver should be checked. |
| Novell IPXODI | Settings are configured in NET.CFG. |

## Setting the LastDrive Parameter for NETX

Windows 95 uses the value of the **LastDrive=** entry in the Registry (or CONFIG.SYS) to allocate enough storage space in the internal memory structures to recognize drive letters for devices. For example, a setting of **LastDrive=Z** tells Windows 95 to recognize drive letters from A to Z.

Windows 95 uses all drive letters up to the letter assigned as the last drive. NetWare servers use all the drive letters following the last drive. For example, if **LastDrive=P** is specified, you can assign drive letters D through P for networks other than NetWare (assuming drive C is the only physical hard disk drive in the system). In this same example, NetWare begins mapping NetWare volumes with Q.

Unlike Windows 95 for Workgroups, Windows 95 does not update the value of the **LastDrive=** if a value is already set. If no value is specified in CONFIG.SYS, Windows 95 adds **LastDrive=E** to the Registry.

## Setting Show Dots and File Access Limits

A NetWare file server does not include the directory entries dot (.) and double dot (..) as MS-DOS and Windows 95 do. However, the NetWare workstation shell version 3.01 or later can emulate these entries when applications attempt to list the files in a directory.

▶ **To turn on the Show Dots feature**

- If you have problems listing files or deleting directories, add the following line to the beginning of NET.CFG:

```
show dots=on
```

By default, NetWare client software allows you access to only 40 files at a time. When you are running many applications under Windows 95, it is possible to exceed this limit, so you will want to increase the settings for file limits.

▶ **To increase the file access limit**

1. Add the following line to the beginning of NET.CFG:

```
file handles=60
```

2. Add the following to CONFIG.SYS for the local computer:

```
files=60
```

# VLM Technical Notes

VLM, the network client provided with Novell NetWare version 4.x, provides the same support and behavior under Windows 95 as it does under MS-DOS or Windows 3.1. In addition, you gain the benefits described in "Microsoft Client for NetWare Networks: The Benefits" earlier in this chapter.

If the computer is using VLM, you should still load the Novell-supplied client components and TSR programs, and log on from either AUTOEXEC.BAT or STARTNET.BAT. Login scripts also work in the same way they do with MS-DOS and Windows 3.x. After Windows 95 starts, you can use the Windows 95 user interface to make drive and printer connections, or you can run NetWare utilities by running NWUSER or other commands at the command prompt. Notice, however, that you cannot use NDS names in Windows 95 dialog boxes.

Installing Windows 95 with the VLM client requires special steps if an earlier version of Windows is not installed, as described in this section. This section also presents specific notes related to using the Novell-supplied NetWare 4.x client software with Windows 95.

# Setting Up Windows 95 with VLM

If you install Windows 95 into the existing Windows directory on a computer where VLM is already configured to run with an earlier version of Windows, then to install VLM support, follow the steps described in "Installing Windows 95 with a Novell NetWare Client" earlier in this chapter.

However, if you are installing Windows 95 into a new directory, or if you are installing it on a computer that has only the MS-DOS operating system (but no earlier version of Windows), you must follow special steps to set up the computer properly. This is because Windows support for VLM requires software supplied only through the Novell-supplied VLM installation program. Follow the instructions under the procedure in this section that most closely describes your configuration.

Windows 95 Setup tries to detect VLM by looking for an NLS directory. If NLS is present, it begins installing Windows 95 for VLM. If the NLS directory is not present but you select the VLM client to install in Setup, Windows 95 Setup asks you to first install VLM using the Novell installation program. Then you can continue with Windows 95 Setup.

---

**Important**  Automatic logon for the NetWare network from AUTOEXEC.BAT needs to be configured before running Windows 95 Setup; otherwise, your login script will not be run under Windows 95 (and therefore any mapped drives will not be available).

---

▶ **If you already run VLM with Windows 3.x and install Windows 95 over Windows 3.x**

- Start the computer as usual, and make sure that the Novell software is running. Then run Windows 95 Setup and choose support for Novell NetWare 4.0, as described in "Installing Windows 95 with a Novell NetWare Client" earlier in this chapter.

   –Or–

1. After Setup is complete, in the Network option in Control Panel, select Client for NetWare Networks (if this has been installed), and then click Remove.

2. Click Add, and then double-click Client.

3. In the Select Network Client dialog box, click Novell in the Manufacturers list, and click the option named Novell NetWare (Workstation Shell 4.0 and above [VLM]) in the Network Clients list. Then click OK.

4. If you want to install Client for Microsoft Networks at this time, you can repeat the steps in the Select Network Client dialog box to install it. Then shut down and restart the computer.

▶ **If you already run VLM with Windows 3.1 and install Windows 95 in a new directory, or if you are running VLM with MS-DOS**

1. Start the computer as usual, making sure that the Novell-supplied network software is running. Then run Windows 95 Setup, and select Custom as the setup type.

2. When the Network Configuration dialog box appears, select Client for NetWare Networks in the list of components (if this has been installed), and then click Remove.

---

**Note**  If you were logged into NDS when Setup was started, then VLM appears in this list and you can skip the following steps.

---

3. Click Add, and then double-click Client in the Select Network Component Type dialog box.

4. In the Select Network Client dialog box, click Novell in the Manufacturers list, and click Novell NetWare (Workstation Shell 4.0 And Above [VLM]) in the Network Clients list. Then click OK.

   Setup partially configures Windows 95, and then prompts you to run the Novell Workstation Shell Install program after Windows 95 has been installed.

5. Setup places information in AUTOEXEC.BAT that instructs you to run the Novell Workstation Shell Install program, after the Copying Files phase is complete. Complete this step to install the Novell-supplied support for Windows.

---

**Note**  Setup also places the entry **device=vnetbios** in SYSTEM.INI, which causes a blue screen to appear when you restart the computer. You can ignore this screen.

---

6. Restart the computer again, and let Windows 95 start normally.

In the Network option in Control Panel, you will see that Setup has added Novell NetWare (Workstation Shell 4.0 And Above [VLM]) as a network client. Information in NET.CFG is used to configure the other network components.

For information about required files, see "Obtaining Current Novell-Supplied Files" later in this chapter.

## Using VLM with Client for Microsoft Networks

If you are using VLM as the network client, you might also choose to install the 32-bit, protected-mode Client for Microsoft Networks if you want to connect to other Microsoft networking computers, such as computers running Windows for Workgroups 3.x, LAN Manager, or Windows NT. The following illustration describes this configuration.

Architecture for Novell-supplied VLM with Client for NetWare Networks

Novell-supplied components appear in bold

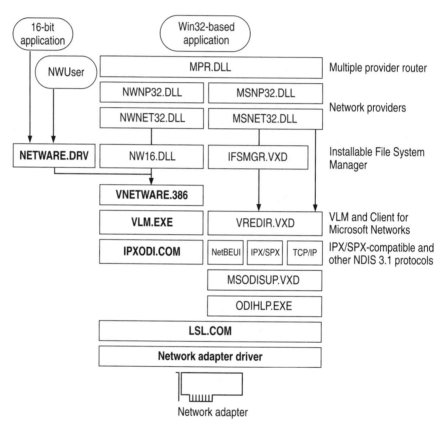

In this configuration, the Novell-supplied version of NETWARE.DRV is not used by Windows 95. It is installed and loaded only for applications that call it directly. All access to NetWare resources is through the Windows 95 user interface, not the NETWARE.DRV dialog boxes. The NWUSER utility calls NETWARE.DRV directly to bring up the central NetWare Version 3.0 WinNet16 dialog box.

Notice that this configuration requires a Microsoft Windows NT Client Access License if this computer will be connecting to servers running Windows NT Server. For more information, see Chapter 8, "Windows 95 on Microsoft Networks."

## Using VLM as the Sole Client

This configuration can be used if you do not need to connect to other computers that are running Windows for Workgroups 3.x, LAN Manager, or Windows NT. (Of course, you can connect to a Windows 95 computer running Microsoft File and Printer Sharing for NetWare.)

The following illustration summarizes this configuration.

Architecture for Novell-supplied VLM as the sole client

Novell-supplied components appear in bold

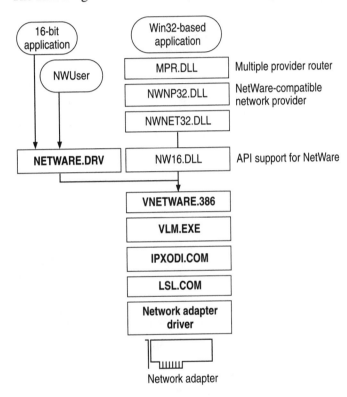

The following table lists the required settings for CONFIG.SYS and AUTOEXEC.BAT files if you use VLM as the sole network client.

**Configuration File Settings for VLM as the Sole Client**

| Filename | Required settings |
|---|---|
| config.sys | `lastdrive=`*drive_letter* |
| autoexec.bat | `startnet.bat` |
| startnet.bat | `lsl.com`<br>`odi driver`<br>`ipxodi.com`<br>`vlm.exe`<br>`f:      ; that is, first network drive in net.cfg`<br>`login`<br>`c:` |

The following table summarizes the minimum settings that you should see in the Network option in Control Panel if you install Windows 95 with VLM as the sole client.

**Network Settings for VLM as the Sole Client**

| Component | Options |
|---|---|
| NetWare (Workstation Shell 4.X [VLM]) | Novell NetWare (Workstation Shell 4.X [VLM]) appears in the list of installed components. All other settings are configured in NET.CFG. |
| Network adapter | In the General properties for the adapter, the Real Mode (16 Bit) ODI Driver option should be checked. |
| Novell IPX ODI | Settings are configured in NET.CFG. |

# Setting the LastDrive Parameter for VLM

Windows 95 uses the value of the **LastDrive=** entry in the Registry to allocate enough storage space in the internal memory structures to recognize drive letters for devices. For example, a setting of **LastDrive=Z** tells Windows 95 to recognize drive letters from A to Z.

The Novell-supplied NetWare 4.x redirector handles the **LastDrive=** entry the same way that Windows 95 does. That is, both the NetWare 4.x redirector and Windows 95 allow drive letters to be used to connect to redirected network drives up through the drive letter specified by the **LastDrive=** entry.

The NetWare 4.x redirector uses the **First Network Drive=** entry in the NET.CFG file to identify the first network drive that can be mapped. For more information about this setting, consult your Novell documentation.

# Technical Notes for Windows 95 on NetWare Networks

This section contains information about obtaining current Novell-supplied files and technical notes on the IPX/SPX-compatible protocol and Microsoft TCP/IP.

## Obtaining Current Novell-Supplied Files

If your computer is not configured with the necessary NetWare software, or if you don't have the support files that Windows 95 Setup requires to configure your computer, several sources are available for these files.

---

**Important**  Use the latest available version of Novell-supplied driver files. At the release of Windows 95, the following were some of the current files posted on the Novell forum on CompuServe: DOSUP9, WINDR2; WINUP9, and VLMUP9.

---

▶ **To obtain current NetWare software files**

- Check with your NetWare network administrator or your local Novell representative to see if the latest client files are available locally.

    –Or–

    Over the Internet, obtain files from ftp.novell.com.

    –Or–

    Check the Novell Files forum on CompuServe by typing **go novlib** at a system prompt. Novell posts revisions of NetWare client software and drivers on this forum.

### Required Support Files for Novell-Supplied Clients

In addition to the base Novell-supplied NetWare client software required to communicate with a NetWare server, some additional NetWare support files are necessary for the Novell-supplied components to work properly in the Windows 95 environment. When Windows 95 is configured to support a Novell NetWare client, Setup checks to see if the required supporting files for Windows are in the Windows directory. If the files are not in the Windows directory, Setup asks for a disk or network drive location for these files.

The required Novell-supplied supporting files for NetWare connectivity under Windows are shown in the following list.

**Novell-Supplied Files for Windows Support**

| File | Description |
|------|-------------|
| netware.drv, netware.hlp | Windows-compatible network driver and associated help file to provide access to network redirector functionality from 16-bit applications. Notice that this must be the version 2.x WinNet16 driver for the NETX client. Also, the Novell-supplied version of NETWARE.DRV for NETX is approximately 124K in size; for VLM, the size is approximately 144K or 162K, depending on the version. |
| nwpopup.exe | NetWare messaging utility. Used to receive messages and alerts from a NetWare server. |
| vnetware.386 | Virtual device driver providing virtualization services for the NetWare redirector in the Windows environment and across VMs. |
| vipx.386 | Virtual device driver providing virtualization services for the NetWare IPX protocol for the Windows environment and across VMs. |
| nw16.dll[1] | A thunk layer for passing 32-bit calls to 16-bit NETX APIs. |

[1] Required for VLM, but not for NETX.

# Required Support Files for ODI Drivers

A computer using Novell-supplied ODI and the IPX/SPX protocol requires certain files, depending on whether you choose to keep the Novell-supplied client when installing Windows 95 on a NetWare network.

**Required Files for ODI Drivers with Novell-Supplied Client**

**Windows 95 drivers:**

vnetbios.386

**Novell-supplied NETX drivers:**

| | | |
|---|---|---|
| ipxodi.com | netware.hlp | vipx.386 |
| lsl.com | netx.exe | nnetware.386 |
| netware.drv | nwpopup.exe | |

A network adapter driver such as ne2000.com

**Novell-supplied VLM drivers:**

netx.vlm, version 4.0 or later
VLM client supporting files, version 1.02 or later

**Required Files for ODI Drivers with Microsoft Client for NetWare Networks**

**Windows 95 drivers:**

| | | |
|---|---|---|
| msodisup.vxd[1] | nwnblink.vxd | nwredir.vxd |
| ndis.vxd | nwnet32.dll | odihlp.exe |
| nwlink.vxd | nwnp32.dll | vnetbios.386 |

**Novell-supplied drivers:**

lsl.com
A network adapter driver such as ne2000.com

[1] MSODISUP.VXD is the ODI support layer that maps NDIS 3.1 protocols to an ODI driver, and ODIHLP.EXE is the real-mode stub that allows LSL to complete its binding process in real mode.

# Required Support Files for Monolithic IPX

After Windows 95 is installed on a monolithic IPX configuration, the required drivers include the following files, which must all be supplied by Novell:

| | | |
|---|---|---|
| ipx.com | netware.hlp | vnetware.386 |
| netware.drv | netx.exe | vipx.386. |

# Required Support Files for ArcNet Drivers

This configuration is similar to configuring Windows 95 to run with a monolithic IPX driver, except that Novell-supplied ODI drivers are used. The drivers used in this configuration include the following files, which must all be supplied by Novell:

| | | |
|---|---|---|
| smc8000.com (ODI driver) | netware.drv | vnetware.386 |
| lsl.com | netx.exe | vipx.386 |
| ipxodi.com | | |

# Search Mode with Windows 95 on NetWare Networks

Many applications, when started, also open a number of other files (such as overlay files and data files) that are used as application resources. To find these files, older NetWare-aware applications, such as the FILER version 3.x NetWare utility, look for files in NetWare search drives in these ways:

- Using the PATH environment to search for executable files
- Using a NetWare search path to find supporting files, such as required data files

Under Windows 95, the search mode defines how files are found, depending on the network client you use, as described in the following table.

| Client | Search mode |
|---|---|
| Client for NetWare Networks | Search from a drive mapped to the server where the utility is stored |
| Novell-supplied NETX | Search from any local drive or any network drive |
| Novell-supplied VLM | Search from any network drive. Cannot search from a local drive |

If you see an error message that a supporting file could not be found, the search mode is not set properly, or you are not opening the application from the correct place. For example, in FILER, the message might be: "System message library file SYS$MSG.DAT could not be opened." In such a case, you will have to set the search mode.

---

**Note**  Most newer NetWare-aware applications and utilities, such as SYSCON, do not use search mode to find auxiliary files.

---

▶ **To set the search mode in Windows 95**

1. From the File menu in System Policy Editor, click Open Registry. Then click the icon for Local Computer.

   For more information about using System Policy Editor in Registry mode, see Chapter 15, "User Profiles and System Policies."

2. Click Network, click Microsoft Client for NetWare Networks, and then click Search Mode.

3. Specify a setting based on the table following this procedure. Then shut down and restart the computer.

You can also use system policies to define the search mode for multiple computers.

Search Mode has five settings: Modes 1 (also shown as 0), 2, 3, 5, and 7. (Modes 4 and 6 are not used currently.) Check your application documentation to determine whether the application only reads its supporting files, or reads and writes to them. The search mode applies to all applications that use it, so select the mode that works for most programs.

| Search mode | Meaning |
| --- | --- |
| 0 or 1 | Uses the default search mode. Client for NetWare Networks will look in the search drives only when no path is specified in the application and after the default directory has been searched. |
| 2 | Causes Client for NetWare Networks not to look in any search drives to find supporting files. The application will behave as if you were running it without networking. If the application has a defined directory path for searching and opening files, the application searches for the files in that path. NetWare calls this mode "Do not search." |
| 3 | The same as Mode 1, except that if the application has no defined directory path to search and open files, Client for NetWare Networks looks in the search drives only if the open request is a read-only request. NetWare calls this mode "Search on Read-Only opens with no path." |
| 5 | Causes Client for NetWare Networks to always look in the search drives, even if the application specifies a path. NetWare calls to this mode "Search on all opens." |
| 7 | The same as Mode 5, except that Client for NetWare Networks looks in the search drives only if the open request is a read-only request. NetWare calls this mode "Search on all Read-Only opens." |

# Troubleshooting Windows 95 on NetWare Networks

This section presents troubleshooting tips for some common problems that might occur, depending on whether you are running Microsoft Client for NetWare Networks or a Novell-supplied network client.

For more troubleshooting tips related to system logon and browsing on NetWare networks, and for File and Printer Services for NetWare Networks, see Chapter 11, "Logon, Browsing, and Resource Sharing."

## Troubleshooting Client for NetWare Networks

This section discusses some common problems that might occur while installing, configuring, or using Microsoft Client for NetWare Networks.

As a general troubleshooting step, make sure that the version of NETWARE.DRV is a size of about 2K. If it is much larger, remove Client for NetWare Networks in the Network option in Control Panel, and then reinstall it.

### No network is available after Windows 95 starts.

Verify that Client for NetWare Networks is installed. Use the Network option in Control Panel to view a list of installed clients, protocols, and services. Verify that the IPX/SPX-compatible protocol is in the list of installed components.

### The login script does not run.

Make sure the correct preferred server is set and that Enable Login Script Processing is checked in the properties for Client for NetWare Networks.

### NetWare servers can't be found.

You might not be able to see NetWare servers if you are using an incorrect frame type for the servers. To ensure that you are using the correct frame type for the server, verify the frame type set in the Advanced properties for the IPX/SPX-compatible protocol in the Network option in Control Panel. You can switch the setting from Auto to the specific frame type used on the server.

Client for NetWare Networks supports NetWare 4.x bindery emulation. Be sure that the bindery context you set for your NetWare server directory includes the Windows 95 users who should have access to the servers. To view and set your bindery context on NetWare 4.x servers, load the SERVMAN NetWare loadable module (NLM) and then view and set the SET BINDERY CONTEXT parameter. Or, you can type **set** at the command prompt to view the miscellaneous SET parameters. For more information, see your NetWare 4.x server documentation.

### You are asked for a Windows 95 password and a NetWare password at each logon.

Client for NetWare Networks asks for a Windows 95 password after you log on to the network because the user name and password for your NetWare preferred server differs from your Windows 95 password. If you don't want to be prompted for a second password, make the passwords the same for both the NetWare preferred server and Windows 95.

### Access to NetWare servers is denied.

By default, Client for NetWare Networks uses the credentials provided for preferred server authentication to access other NetWare servers. To see files on NetWare servers for which you have access, synchronize your credentials on all the NetWare servers, using the Novell SETPASS command at the command prompt.

# Troubleshooting Windows 95 Using Novell NetWare Clients

This section describes some common problems that might occur when running a Novell-supplied client with Windows 95.

As a general troubleshooting step, make sure that the NETWARE.DRV file version 3.03.94.280 or later for VLM is present, plus version 2.02 or later for NETX. If necessary, restore this file from the Novell-supplied installation source.

- Check the version numbers of all Novell-supplied NetWare workstation shell components, including IPX, NETX, VLM, LSL, IPXODI, and the ODI driver files. Make sure the latest versions are being used.

  To get the version number for the Novell-supplied software you are using, run *driver_name* **i** or *driver_name* **?** at the command prompt. For example, type **netx i** to get the version number for the Novell-supplied NET*.COM or NET*.EXE file.

  If you are not using the latest software, upgrade as described in "Obtaining Current Novell-Supplied Files" earlier in this chapter.

- Check for multiple instances of the NetWare files, specifically the ODI driver and NET.CFG. If there are multiple instances, remove all but the most recent version.

- Verify that IPXODI is binding to the network adapter by running the NetWare NVER utility, using the same settings as NET.CFG and the same [**link driver** *ODI_driver*] name. If IPXODI is not bound to the network adapter, change the entries in NET.CFG to correct this problem.

- For a monolithic configuration, verify that the configuration does not use the **/o#** switch on IPX.COM or the **config option=** statement in SHELL.CFG.

- If the user is running a shared copy of Windows 95, verify that the home directory and shared Windows directory are the first two items in the path.

### Setup requires Novell Workstation Shell Installation Program.

If, during installation, Setup fails to load Novell drivers and displays a message that it requires the Novell Workstation Shell Install Program for installing the VLM network client with Windows 95, follow the instructions presented in "VLM Technical Notes" earlier in this chapter.

### You cannot attach to the NetWare file server after installing Windows 95.

Verify the frame type being used by the NetWare server. If the NetWare server is using a different frame type from the one configured for the computer running Windows 95, the user cannot see the server. The Novell-supplied IPXODI protocol binds only to the first logical board, which is the first frame type in the **link driver** *ODI_driver* section in NET.CFG.

To correct this problem, manually edit NET.CFG so that the correct frame type is first in the **link driver** *ODI_driver* section.

### You cannot see other computers running Windows 95 or NetWare server.

- Determine which frame type is used at your site, and then verify that the correct frame type you want to use on the network are listed in NET.CFG. The frame type that IPXODI will use must be first or must be set explicitly.

- Verify that the correct NET.CFG is being processed by LSL.COM. To do this, check the local drive for other NET.CFG files. There should be only one, and it should be in the same directory as the NetWare driver files. If you are loading these files from AUTOEXEC.BAT or another batch file, modify the batch file to change to this directory, run the necessary ODI drivers, and change back to the directory you want. This ensures that the current directory is the same as the location of the LSL.COM file when it is being loaded.

- Verify that NET.CFG contains the correct settings for the network adapter. If necessary, restore this file from a correct backup version, or edit it to include correct settings.

- Verify that you are running the latest version of the Novell-supplied ODI drivers and support files. Check with your network adapter manufacturer to determine whether a newer ODI driver is available.

- Verify that both client computers are running the same protocols. If the client computers are on different sides of a router, make sure that an IPX/SPX-compatible protocol is being used on both computers.

### You cannot access the login drive after installing Windows 95.

A common misconception is that users must log on to their NetWare server using the drive letter F. However, this is not true. For a client computer using the NETX workstation shell, the NetWare login drive is the next drive letter available after the **LastDrive=** statement in the Registry.

You can alter the **LastDrive=** statement to change the login drive, but you must leave enough drives before the **LastDrive=** that Windows 95 can use for its own connections.

### Computer doesn't run after installing VLM support under Windows 95.

If a message says that the system cannot find a device file needed to run Windows, make sure that the VLM client has been installed using the Network option in Control Panel. This step ensures that the correct VLM information is placed in SYSTEM.INI. (The Novell-supplied installation program for VLM sets the path in SYSTEM.INI to the Windows SYSTEM directory rather than to VMM32.)

### The Windows directory contains NWSYSVOL\LOGIN\LOGIN.EXE.

This stub file is installed with File and Printer Sharing for NetWare Networks to prevent the computer from incorrectly responding as the preferred server for other NetWare clients. For information, see WIN95RK.HLP.

CHAPTER 10

# Windows 95 on Other Networks

This chapter provides details about installing and running Windows 95 on other networks. This chapter also includes information about host (that is, mainframe) connectivity for Windows 95.

---

**Note** Be sure to read the Windows 95 README.TXT and SETUP.TXT notes on networking. Also check the Microsoft WinNews forums on online services for specific information about your network and about particular network adapters.

---

**In This Chapter**

Windows 95 on Other Networks: The Basics    334

Windows 95 on Other Networks: The Issues    335

Installing Support for Other Networks: An Overview    336

Installing Network Support During Windows 95 Setup    336

Installing Client for Microsoft Networks with Other Networks    337

Using Real-Mode WinNet16 Drivers    338

Artisoft LANtastic    339

Banyan VINES    341

DEC PATHWORKS    344

IBM OS/2 LAN Server    346

SunSoft PC-NFS    347

Host Connectivity and Windows 95    349

Using DLC for Connectivity    350

Using Gateways for Connectivity    358

Using TCP/IP for Host Connectivity    358

Using Terminal Emulation Applications    359

Troubleshooting Connection Problems with Microsoft DLC    360

# Windows 95 on Other Networks: The Basics

Integrated networking support is a key feature of Windows 95. The new architecture that supports multiple network providers means that it's easier to install and manage support for a single network or multiple networks simultaneously using Windows 95 than in earlier versions of Windows. Windows 95 can support configuration on a single computer of as many 32-bit, protected-mode network clients as you want and one 16-bit, real-mode client using the network provider interface of Windows 95.

Windows 95 includes two protected-mode network clients (Client for Microsoft Networks and Client for NetWare Networks), plus built-in support for several types of 16-bit, real-mode network clients. In most cases, you also need to use supporting software from the network vendors in the following list:

- Artisoft® LANtastic® version 5.0 and later
- Banyan® VINES® version 5.52 and later
- DEC™ PATHWORKS™ version 5.0 and later
- IBM® OS/2® LAN Server
- Novell® NetWare® version 3.11 and later
- SunSoft™ PC-NFS® version 5.0 and later

### Tip for Using Protected-Mode Network Clients from Other Vendors

The network provider interface defines a set of APIs used by Windows 95 to access the network for actions such as logging on to the server, browsing and connecting to servers, and so on. Microsoft has made this set of APIs widely available to network vendors so that they can develop new protected-mode network providers that are compatible with Windows 95.

For example, when a Banyan VINES 32-bit network provider becomes available, then Windows 95 can support Microsoft networks, Novell NetWare, and Banyan VINES connectivity at the same time through the Network Neighborhood.

Contact your network vendor to determine when protected-mode software for Windows 95 will be available for your network.

Multiple network support in Windows 95 consists of these components:

- Win32 WinNet API
- Multiple provider router and service provider interface
- Network providers, including the WinNet16 interface, as described in "Using Real-Mode WinNet16 Drivers" later in this chapter

For information about the system components that provide multiple network support, see Chapter 32, "Windows 95 Network Architecture." For information about networking printing and support for printing when using a 16-bit network client, see Chapter 23, "Printing and Fonts."

# Windows 95 on Other Networks: The Issues

Although you can run any number of 32-bit network clients simultaneously, you can only run a single 16-bit, real-mode network client.

The network software should be installed and running on the workstation when you start Windows 95 Setup to install Windows 95, so that Setup can detect the network and install support for it automatically.

If your network vendor does not provide a 32-bit, protected-mode client that is compatible with Windows 95, and if you don't (or can't) run Client for Microsoft Networks in addition to your other network client, you cannot take advantage of the protected-mode networking features of Windows 95. For example:

- You won't gain the performance advantages of 32-bit, protected-mode network components, including Plug and Play networking support, long filenames, client-side caching, automatic reconnections, and other performance enhancements.
- You can't use the Windows 95 unified logon and user interface for navigating the network, or use the Windows 95 network management tools.
- You can't use user profiles for management of desktop configurations.

Specific issues for particular 16-bit network clients—including whether support for a particular network includes browsing in Network Neighborhood and whether you can also use a 32-bit, protected-mode client such as Client for Microsoft Networks simultaneously with that network—are presented in the section describing that network.

If support for your network's 16-bit client is not included with Windows 95, contact your network vendor to obtain a Windows 95 INF file.

Support for FTP NFS protocols can be installed by using the Network option in Control Panel. The required components (client, network provider, and so on) must be obtained from FTP.

# Installing Support for Other Networks: An Overview

This section describes how to install Windows 95 with network support from another vendor. For installation details related to your specific network, see the section for that network.

## Installing Network Support During Windows 95 Setup

If you want to install Windows 95 on a computer that already has networking support from a network vendor other than Microsoft or Novell NetWare, you should be sure the network client from that vendor is installed correctly under MS-DOS, Windows version 3.1, or Windows for Workgroups.

The network software should be running when you start Windows 95 Setup. If Setup detects a network adapter but the computer is not running network software when you install Windows 95, then Setup installs Client for Microsoft Networks by default. Although in most cases the Network option in Control Panel provides the same controls for adding and removing networking components after Windows 95 Setup is complete, Microsoft recommends that you install networking support during Windows 95 Setup.

**Note**  For computers running multiple network clients, Windows 95 Setup can install but cannot remove support for networks from other vendors.

▶ **To add a network client while running Windows 95 Setup**

1. Make sure that the network client from your vendor is already installed under MS-DOS, Windows 3.1, or Windows for Workgroups. The network software should be running when you start Windows 95 Setup.

2. Start Windows 95 Setup as described in Chapter 3, "Introduction to Windows 95 Setup," and choose the Custom setup type.

3. When the Network Configuration screen appears during Setup, your network client should appear in this list automatically, because Setup should detect the network you are running. If the list is correct, click OK to continue with Setup.

   If you need to add the network client manually, click the Add button. Then double-click Client in the Select Network Component Type dialog box. In the Select Network Client dialog box, click the appropriate network vendor in the Manufacturers list, and click the name of the client in the Network Clients list. Then click OK.

   **Note**  Support for DEC PATHWORKS 5.x is installed as a protocol together with Client for Microsoft Networks, so DEC PATHWORKS does not appear in the Select Network Client dialog box. For information about installing support for this product, see "DEC PATHWORKS" later in this chapter.

4.  Because the network client keeps track of the network adapter and protocols, no protocols or adapters should be listed in the Network Configuration dialog box.

    If you want to install Client for Microsoft Networks in addition to the network client from your vendor, follow the steps described in "Installing Client for Microsoft Networks with Other Networks" later in this chapter. Otherwise, click the Next button and continue with Windows 95 Setup.

5.  After Windows 95 is installed, check AUTOEXEC.BAT to make sure that all commands point to the correct directory for your network software.

On computers running multiple clients, Windows 95 Setup stores all real-mode networking components, including PROTOCOL.INI, in the Windows directory. On computers running a real-mode client as the primary network, the networking components are left in place. The settings in PROTOCOL.INI affect only real-mode NDIS drivers. Changing these values has no effect on protected-mode NDIS drivers. If you need to change settings in PROTOCOL.INI, use the Network option in Control Panel whenever possible. For information about PROTOCOL.INI entries, see Chapter 8, "Windows 95 on Microsoft Networks."

All the Setup options for installing and configuring network support described in this chapter can be defined in custom setup scripts for automatic installation. To install Windows 95 using setup scripts, the Windows 95 source files must be placed on a server using Server-based Setup, and custom setup scripts must be created, as described in Chapter 4, "Server-Based Setup for Windows 95." For information about installing support for another network client in custom setup scripts, see Appendix D, "MSBATCH.INF Parameters."

# Installing Client for Microsoft Networks with Other Networks

If you want to install the 32-bit, protected-mode Client for Microsoft Networks in addition to a network client from another vendor, follow these steps. For information about configuring and using this network client, see Chapter 8, "Windows 95 on Microsoft Networks."

---

**Note**  Artisoft LANtastic cannot be used together with a 32-bit, protected-mode networking client such as Client for Microsoft Networks. This client can only be installed as the sole network client on the computer.

---

▶ **To install Client for Microsoft Networks after another network has been installed**

1. Start Windows 95 Setup as described in Chapter 3, "Introduction to Windows 95 Setup," and choose the Custom setup type.

   –Or–

   After Setup, double-click the Network option in Control Panel.

2. In the Network Configuration dialog box, click the Add button. In the Select Network Component Type dialog box, double-click Client.

3. In the Select Network Client dialog box, click Microsoft in the Manufacturers list, and click Client for Microsoft Networks in the Network Clients list. Click OK.

4. Usually hardware detection detects the correct network adapter and selects the corresponding driver. If you must add a network adapter, follow the steps in Chapter 7, "Introduction to Windows 95 Networking."

5. In the Network Configuration dialog box, double-click the network adapter in the list of components. Verify the settings in the properties for the network adapter. Then click OK. For information, see Chapter 12, "Network Technical Discussion." See also the documentation for your network adapter to verify its software settings.

   Setup automatically installs a protected-mode version of any protocol that the installed network clients are using. If you need to install another protocol, follow the steps in Chapter 7, "Introduction to Windows 95 Networking."

6. Click Next to continue with Setup.

   –Or–

   If you are adding support after Windows 95 has been installed, you must shut down and restart the computer.

# Using Real-Mode WinNet16 Drivers

| Application |
| --- |
| MPR.DLL |
| WINNET16.DLL |
| *WinNet16*.DRV |
| Network adapter driver |
| Real-mode networking software |

Network adapter

In addition to multiple 32-bit Windows 95 network providers, Windows 95 can also support a single 16-bit WinNet driver. This is the basic configuration that must be used for a network product that does not offer a 32-bit network provider.

If the 16-bit network provider from another network vendor does not provide a browsing scheme, Network Neighborhood will be empty in Windows 95, indicating that this is not a browsable network. You must use the Map Network Drive dialog box for network access. Also, notice that a drive connected through the Windows 95 user interface is accessible in all VMs. A connection made at a command prompt, however, will be available in that VM only and will not be available throughout the Windows 95 user interface.

The following list summarizes the components for the 16-bit, real-mode network drivers.

| Component | Description |
|---|---|
| WINNET16.DLL | Provides a 32-bit to 16-bit thunk and translation between the 32-bit Windows 95 network provider interface and the 16-bit WinNet API. |
| *winnet16*.DRV | A 16-bit Windows 3.x network driver that provides a basic Map Network Drive dialog box. |
| *network*.VXD (or .386) | A Windows 3.x virtual device driver that allows virtualized access to the real-mode network software for all virtual machines (including the *winnet16*.DRV). |
| Real-mode network software | This can include proprietary network adapter drivers, protocol drivers, client (redirector), and network utilities loaded through CONFIG.SYS and AUTOEXEC.BAT (or other batch file). |

# Artisoft LANtastic

Application

MPR.DLL

WINNET16.DLL

LANTNET.DRV

LANTASI.386

LANtastic
real-mode client

Network adapter

Windows 95 can be installed to run with Artisoft LANtastic version 5.x. or later client software. You must install Artisoft LANtastic by letting Windows 95 Setup detect this client while installing Windows 95. You cannot install support for this client after installation is complete.

LANtastic servers will not appear in Network Neighborhood. You can connect to servers at the command prompt.

Artisoft LANtastic can be configured only as the primary network. Additional 32-bit network providers, such as Client for Microsoft Networks or Client for NetWare Networks, are not possible in this case.

▶ **To set up Windows 95 with an Artisoft LANtastic real-mode network client**

1. Make sure that the LANtastic server is not running. The LANtastic server cannot be run during Windows 95 Setup.

2. Make sure that the LANtastic client is already installed under MS-DOS, Windows 3.1, or Windows for Workgroups. The network software should be running when you start Windows 95 Setup. Then follow the steps in "Installing Support for Other Networks: An Overview" earlier in this chapter. No other steps are required.

▶ **To connect to a LANtastic server when running Windows 95**

- You must type the complete server name and share name in a Map Network Drive dialog box or at the MS-DOS Prompt.

The following table shows the entries required in configuration files when Artisoft LANtastic real-mode network support is installed with Windows 95.

| Configuration file | Entries |
|---|---|
| autoexec.bat | `@echo off`<br>`path c:\windows;c:\windows\command;c:\dos;`<br>`prompt $p$g`<br>`rem lh c:\dos\share.exe`<br>`call c:\lantasti\startnet.bat` |
| config.sys | `dos=high,umb`<br>`device=c:\windows\himem.sys`<br>`device=c:\windows\emm386.exe noems`<br>`devicehigh=c:\windows\setver.exe`<br>`rem - By Windows 95 Setup - stacks=9,256`<br>`files=100`<br>`rem - by Windows 95 Setup - buffers=30`<br>`fcbs =16,8` |
| protocol.ini | `[NDISHLP$]`<br>`drivername=ndishlp$`<br>`bindings=`<br><br>`[PROTMAN$]`<br>`drivername=protman$`<br><br>`[DATA]`<br>`version=v4.00.166`<br>`netcards=` |
| system.ini | `[LANTASTIC]`<br>`network_irq=15` |

# Banyan VINES

Application

MPR.DLL

WINNET16.DLL

VINES.DRV

VVINESD.386

Banyan
real-mode client

Network adapter

Windows 95 can be installed and run with Banyan VINES version 5.52(5) or later. Banyan VINES servers do not show up in Network Neighborhood. You can use the Map Network Drive dialog box in Windows 95 to connect to servers.

**Banyan VINES as the primary network.**  If real-mode support for Banyan is installed using a Banyan LAN driver, Windows 95 can support Banyan as the primary network. Banyan is also providing a 32-bit network client to be available after the release of Windows 95. Contact your vendor's sales support representative for information about the availability and features provided with this new client.

**Banyan VINES as an additional 16-bit Windows 95 client.**  If Banyan is installed with an NDIS 2 network adapter driver, then Banyan can be installed as an additional 16-bit network client, and you can install 32-bit, protected-mode clients such as Client for Microsoft Networks or Client for NetWare Networks.

▶ **To set up Windows 95 with Banyan VINES real-mode network client support**

- If you are running on an Ethernet network, make sure that the Banyan VINES client is already installed under MS-DOS, Windows 3.1, or Windows for Workgroups. The network should be running when you start Windows 95 Setup. Then follow the steps in "Installing Support for Other Networks: An Overview" earlier in this chapter. No other steps are required.

  –Or–

- If you are running on a token-ring network, run Windows 95 Setup and choose the Custom setup type. In the Network Configuration dialog box, add Banyan Token Ring as the network client. Setup cannot detect Banyan as a token-ring network client.

---

**Note**  If you are running Banyan VINES with monolithic drivers, you must use the PCCONFIG utility provided by Banyan to change Banyan drivers to NDIS drivers. Make sure that the section name matches the driver name.

---

The following table shows the entries required in configuration files when Banyan VINES real-mode network support is installed with Windows 95, depending on whether Banyan VINES is installed as the primary network only (connecting to a Banyan server) or is installed with Client for Microsoft Networks. These entries are for NDIS drivers.

**Banyan VINES as Primary Network**

| Configuration file | Entries |
|---|---|
| autoexec.bat | ```cd \banfiles```<br>```ban```<br>```ndisban ; ndtokban for token ring```<br>```redirall```<br>```netbind```<br>```arswait```<br>```z:login```<br>```c:```<br>```cd\``` |
| config.sys | ```device=c:\banfiles\protman.dos /i:c:\banfiles```<br>```device=c:\banfiles\ndis2driver    eg: exp16.dos``` |
| protocol.ini | ```[PROTOCOL MANAGER]```<br>```drivername=protman$```<br><br>```[VINES_XIF]```<br>```drivername=ndisban$ ; ndtokban$ for token ring```<br>```bindings=MS$EE16```<br><br>```[MS$EE16]```<br>```drivername=EXP16$```<br>```interrupt=5```<br>```ioaddress=0x300```<br>```iochrdy=late``` |

**Banyan VINES with Client for Microsoft Networks**

| Configuration file | Entries |
|---|---|
| autoexec.bat | `c:\windows\net initialize`<br>`cd \banfiles`<br>`ban`<br>`ndisban ; ndtokban for token ring`<br>`redirall`<br>`c:\windows\net start`<br>`arswait`<br>`z:login`<br>`c:`<br>`cd\` |
| config.sys | `rem device=c:\banfiles\protman.dos /i:c:\banfiles`<br>`rem device=c:\banfiles\ndis2driver    eg: elnkii.dos` |
| protocol.ini | `[NDISBAN$] ; NDTOKBAN$ for token ring`<br>`drivername=NDISBAN$ ; NDTOKBAN$ for token ring`<br>`bindings=ELNKII$`<br><br>`[NWLINK$]`<br>`drivername=NWLINK$`<br>`frame_type=4`<br>`cachesize=0`<br>`bindings=ELNKII$`<br><br>`[NETBEUI$]`<br>`drivername=NETBEUI$`<br>`lanabase=0`<br>`sessions=10`<br>`ncbs=12`<br>`bindings=ELNKII$`<br><br>`[ELNKII$]`<br>`drivername=ELNKII$`<br>`transceiver=external`<br>`interrupt=2`<br>`ioaddress=0x280`<br>`maxtransmits=12`<br>`datatransfer=pio_word`<br>`xmitbufs=2`<br><br>`[PROTMAN$]`<br>`priority=ndishlp$`<br>`drivername=protman$`<br><br>`[NDISHLP$]`<br>`drivername=ndishlp$`<br>`bindings=ELNKII$` |

# DEC PATHWORKS

Windows 95 can be installed and run with DEC PATHWORKS version 5.x. You must install Client for Microsoft Networks plus the DEC PATHWORKS protocol (there is no DEC PATHWORKS real-mode client). DEC PATHWORKS uses NDIS 2 network adapter drivers. Also, the Windows 95 AUTOEXEC.BAT file must contain a **startnet.bat** line to refer to the batch file used to start DEC PATHWORKS.

To install support for DEC PATHWORKS 4.1, you must install support for Windows for Workgroups 3.11 before running Windows 95 Setup. This software is available from the DECPI forum on CompuServe®. This is not necessary for installing support for DEC PATHWORKS 5.x.

If you are running DEC PATHWORKS 5.x, Windows 95 Setup detects the network. And, if you are using an NDIS, DLC, ODI, built-in DEPCA or Etherworks™ 3 data-link layer, Windows 95 Setup converts the configuration to NDIS drivers; Setup does not support X.25 or asynchronous data-link layers.

DEC is providing a 32-bit network client to be available after the release of Windows 95. Contact your vendor's sales support representative for information about the availability and features provided with this new client.

After Windows 95 is installed, you can use Network Neighborhood to browse DEC PATHWORKS servers running version 5.x. You can also use the standard Windows 95 methods for connecting to printers. Long filename support is possible only if you are connecting to a DEC PATHWORKS server version 5.0 or greater.

Also, if you are upgrading from Windows 3.1, you must install additional network components supplied by DEC; these are provided on the Windows 95 compact disc and installed automatically by Windows 95 Setup.

▶ **To set up Windows 95 with DEC PATHWORKS real-mode support**

1. In Windows 95 Setup, choose the Custom setup type.

2. Install Client for Microsoft Networks, as described in "Installing Client for Microsoft Networks with Other Networks" earlier in this chapter.

3. In the Network Configuration dialog box, click Add, and then double-click Protocol in the Select Network Component Type dialog box.

4. In the Select Network Protocol dialog box, click Digital Equipment (DEC) in the Manufacturers list, and click a DEC PATHWORKS protocol in the Network Protocols list, depending on the server version number and whether you are running on a token-ring or Ethernet network. Click OK. Then click the Next button to continue with Setup.

---

**Note**  For DEC PATHWORKS 5.x, you can use a DECnet™ protocol, or you can use NetBEUI or Microsoft TCP/IP.

---

The following table shows the entries required in configuration files when DEC PATHWORKS real-mode network support is installed with Windows 95.

| Configuration file | Entries |
| --- | --- |
| autoexec.bat | `c:\windows\net start`<br>`@echo off`<br>`prompt $p$g`<br>`path c:\windows;c:\windows\command;c:\dos;c:\`<br>`set temp=c:\dos`<br>`c:\pw\startnet.bat` |
| config.sys | `dos=high,umb`<br>`device=c:\windows\himem.sys`<br>`device=c:\windows\emm386.exe noems`<br>`devicehigh=c:\windows\setver.exe`<br>`rem - By Windows 95 Setup - stacks=9,256`<br>`files=100`<br>`rem - by Windows 95 Setup - buffers=30`<br>`fcbs =16,8` |

| Configuration file | Entries |
|---|---|
| protocol.ini | `[DLL$MAC]`<br>`drivername=DLL$MAC`<br>`lanabase=0`<br>`bindings=DEPCA$`<br><br>`[NWLINK$]`<br>`drivername=NWLINK$`<br>`frame_type=4`<br>`cachesize=0`<br>`bindings=DEPCA$`<br><br>`[NETBEUI$]`<br>`drivername=NETBEUI$`<br>`lanabase=1`<br>`sessions=10`<br>`ncbs=12`<br>`bindings=DEPCA$`<br><br>`[DEPCA$]`<br>`drivername=DEPCA$`<br>`maxmulticast=8`<br>`maxtransmits=16`<br>`adaptername=DE100`<br>`interrupt=5`<br>`ioaddress=0x200`<br>`ramaddress=0xd000`<br><br>`[PROTMAN$]`<br>`priority=ndishlp$`<br>`drivername=protman$`<br><br>`[NDISHLP$]`<br>`drivername=ndishlp$` |

# IBM OS/2 LAN Server

Application

MPR.DLL

WINNET16.DLL

LANSRV.DRV

*netcard*.386

OS/2 LAN Server
real-mode client

Network adapter

Windows 95 can be installed and run with these versions:

- IBM OS/2 LAN Server version 1.3 CSD
- IBM OS/2 LAN Server versions 1.2, 1.3, 2.0, and 4.0

**Note**  If OS/2 LAN Server is installed using an OS/2 LAN Server LAN driver, Windows 95 can support OS/2 LAN Server as a primary network only. In this case, you cannot also install Client for Microsoft Networks as an additional network client.

Users can connect to servers using the Map Network Drive dialog box or command prompt. For OS/2 LAN Server servers to appear in Network Neighborhood for browsing, at least one computer in the LAN Server domain must be running File and Printer Sharing for Microsoft Networks and acting as the Browse Master (as described in Chapter 11, "Logon, Browsing, and Resource Sharing"). Also, the workgroup name for the computer running File and Printer Sharing for Microsoft Networks must match the LAN Server domain name.

When support for OS/2 LAN Server is installed for use with Client for Microsoft Networks, aliasing is not supported.

If you are using custom setup scripts to install Windows 95 on multiple computers, make sure that at least one computer running Windows 95 in the LAN Server domain is already configured as the Browse Master. Also, make sure that the [Network] section of the custom setup script includes a correct value for **workgroup=**_LANServer_domain_.

▶ **To set up Windows 95 with IBM OS/2 LAN Server real-mode network client support**

- Make sure that the OS/2 LAN Server client is already installed. The network should be running when you follow the steps in "Installing Support for Other Networks: An Overview" earlier in this chapter. No other steps are required. However, you probably want to specify the LAN Server domain name as the workgroup name under Windows 95.

# SunSoft PC-NFS

| Application |
| :---: |
| MPR.DLL |
| WINNET16.DLL |
| PCNFS.DRV |
| PCNFS.386 |
| PC-NFS<br>real-mode client |

Network adapter

Windows 95 can be installed and run with SunSoft PC-NFS version 5.0. SunSoft servers will not appear in Network Neighborhood. You can use the Map Network Drive dialog box to connect to servers.

**SunSoft PC-NFS as the primary network.**  If SunSoft PC-NFS is installed using a SunSoft PC-NFS LAN driver, Windows 95 can support SunSoft PC-NFS as the primary network. Additional 32-bit network providers are not possible in this case.

**SunSoft PC-NFS as an additional 16-bit Windows 95 client.**  If SunSoft PC-NFS is installed with an NDIS 2 network adapter driver or with an ODI driver, then SunSoft PC-NFS can be installed as an additional 16-bit network client, and you can install 32-bit, protected-mode clients such as Client for Microsoft Networks or Client for NetWare Networks.

If you obtain supporting SunSoft PRO NFS components from the network vendor, you can use Microsoft TCP/IP with this client.

▶ **To set up Windows 95 with SunSoft PC-NFS real-mode network client support**

- Make sure that the SunSoft PC-NFS client is already installed under MS-DOS, Windows 3.1, or Windows for Workgroups. The network should be running when you follow the steps in "Installing Support for Other Networks: An Overview" earlier in this chapter. No other steps are required.

The following table shows the entries required in configuration files when SunSoft PC-NFS real-mode network support is installed with Windows 95, depending on whether PC-NFS is installed as the primary network only, or installed with Client for Microsoft Networks.

**SunSoft PC-NFS as Primary Network**

| Configuration file | Entries |
|---|---|
| autoexec.bat | `set tz=pst8pdt`<br>`set path=c:\nfs;c:\dos;c:\net`<br>`rem c:\net\net start`<br>`c:\lanman\netbind`<br>`set nfsdrive=c`<br>`set nfspath=c:\nfs`<br>`set tn_dir=c:\nfs\telnet`<br>`c:\nfs\prt *`<br>`c:\nfs\net init.`<br>`c:\nfs\rtm` |
| config.sys | `rem device=c:\net\ifshlp.sys`<br>`lastdrive=z`<br>`device=c:\nfs\pcnfs.sys`<br>`device=c:\nfs\sockdrv.sys`<br>`device=c:\lanman\protman.sys /i:c:\lanman`<br>`device=c:\lanman\nfs-ndis.sys`<br>`device=c:\lanman\exp16.dos` |

**SunSoft PC-NFS with Client for Microsoft Networks**

| Configuration file | Entries |
|---|---|
| autoexec.bat | `c:\windows\net start`<br>`set tz=pst8pdt`<br>`set path=c:\nfs;c:\dos;c:\net`<br>`set nfsdrive=c`<br>`set nfspath=c:\nfs`<br>`set tn_dir=c:\nfs\telnet`<br>`c:\nfs\prt *`<br>`c:\nfs\net init.`<br>`c:\nfs\rtm` |
| config.sys | `rem device=c:\net\ifshlp.sys`<br>`lastdrive=z` |

# Host Connectivity and Windows 95

Host connectivity in this section refers to connecting to legacy IBM mainframe computers, the mid-range IBM AS/400® computers, DEC VAX®/VMS, UNIX, and HP® 3000 computers. Host terminal emulation applications running in Windows 95 require network protocols to connect to their respective hosts.

The common network protocols used to support host connectivity include the following:

- IPX/SPX. The IPX/SPX-compatible transport provided with Windows 95 is compatible with Novell NetWare IPX/SPX, and can be installed to support host connectivity using terminal emulation programs and gateways supporting an IPX/SPX interface.

- NetBEUI. The NetBEUI protocol provided with Windows 95 supports a NetBIOS programming interface and conforms to the IBM NetBEUI specifications. It also includes performance enhancements related to NetBIOS 3.0. Microsoft NetBEUI can be installed on computers running Windows 95 to provide NetBIOS support for host connectivity using terminal emulation programs and gateways supporting a NetBIOS interface.

- TCP/IP. The TCP/IP protocol provided with Windows 95 is a complete implementation of the most common and accepted protocol available. It allows connectivity between interconnected networks with different operating systems and hardware architectures such as UNIX, IBM mainframes, and Microsoft networks. Usually, host connectivity with the TCP/IP protocol is provided using Telnet services such as TN3270 connecting to legacy mainframes, TN5250 connecting to an IBM AS/400, and using gateways supporting a TCP/IP interface. Microsoft TCP/IP supports the Windows Sockets 1.1 interface.

- DLC. Data Link Control (DLC) protocol is used primarily to access IBM mainframe computers. This protocol is not used for general networking with Windows 95. Host terminal emulation programs use this protocol directly to communicate with IBM mainframe computers.

For information about using Microsoft NetBEUI, the IPX/SPX-compatible protocol, and TCP/IP, see Chapter 12, "Network Technical Discussion."

Windows 95 includes a real-mode version of the DLC protocol. This section discusses how to install the Microsoft DLC protocol for host connectivity, and how Windows 95 upgrades over existing DLC configurations. This section also provides tips for using terminal emulation applications and connectivity through gateways.

# Using DLC for Connectivity

For direct connection and communication with a mainframe computer that uses DLC, the DLC protocol must be installed on the client computer that is running Windows 95. The Microsoft DLC protocol works with either token-ring or Ethernet network adapter drivers.

Microsoft DLC is also used to provide connectivity to local area printers connected directly to the network. For example, DLC can be used for printing to a printer such as a Hewlett-Packard HP® LaserJet® 4Si that uses an HP JetDirect® network adapter to connect directly to the network (rather than to a port on a print server). The DLC protocol must be installed and running on the print server for the printer. Computers sending print jobs to a print server for a DLC network printer do not need the DLC protocol—only the print server requires DLC. To take advantage of the DLC protocol device driver, you must create a network printer in the Printers folder.

The following sections describe how to install the Microsoft DLC protocol and how to configure it with Novell NetWare ODI drivers and IBM LanSupport.

---

**Note**  Windows 95 contains the most up-to-date Microsoft DLC protocol. Make sure you are running the latest version, which is also available from Microsoft Download Service (MSDL) and CompuServe. For more information about MSDL, see Appendix J, "Windows 95 Resource Directory."

---

## Installing and Configuring Real-Mode Microsoft DLC

Architecture for real-mode DLC with NDIS 2 network adapter drivers

| VREDIR or NWREDIR |
| :---: |
| NDIS3.1 protocols |
| NDIS.VXD |
| NDIS2SUP.VXD |
| MSDLC.EXE |
| NDISHLP.SYS |
| PROTMAN.DOS |

Network adapter

This section describes how to install the real-mode NDIS 2 Microsoft DLC protocol to bind with an NDIS 2 network adapter driver. This is an NDIS 2 protocol that, when installed, is bound to an NDIS 2 network adapter driver. The Windows 95 protected-mode protocols use the NDIS2SUP.VXD module to coexist with and run over the real-mode NDIS 2 network adapter drivers.

When you install Windows 95, Windows 95 Setup detects whether the computer already has the Microsoft DLC protocol installed; if so, Setup migrates the protocol and its settings to Windows 95. Otherwise, you can add Microsoft DLC as a protocol after Windows 95 is installed.

---

**Note**  You must install the version of Microsoft DLC provided with Windows 95. You cannot use the Microsoft DLC INF file from Windows for Workgroups 3.x to install this protocol; Windows 95 uses a new INF file format.

You can also install Microsoft DLC using setup scripts, as described in Appendix D, "MSBATCH.INF Parameters."

---

▶ **To install the Microsoft DLC protocol on a computer running Windows 95**

1. In the Network option in Control Panel, click Add.

2. In the Select Network Component Type dialog box, double-click Protocol.

3. In the Select Network Protocol dialog box, click Microsoft in the Manufacturers list, and then click Microsoft DLC in the Network Protocols list. Then click OK.

4. Shut down and restart the computer for the changes to take effect.

5. Make sure that there is only one **net start** entry in AUTOEXEC.BAT, because Setup automatically adds an entry to support DLC, even if such an entry already exists.

The properties in the following table are set by default for real-mode Microsoft DLC. You can use the Network option in Control Panel to change these default values, or to set values for other parameters that you might use, in the Advanced properties for Microsoft DLC protocol.

| Value | Description |
|-------|-------------|
| Saps | Indicates the number of SAPs that can be opened simultaneously. The range for SAPs is 1 to 255 inclusive. The default is 3. |
| | For a description of SAPs, see the *IBM Local Area Network Technical Reference*. For more information about adjusting the SAPs value, see the entry for Stations. |
| Stations | Indicates the number of link stations that can be opened simultaneously. The range for stations is 1 to 255 inclusive. The default is 20. |
| | Each application requires a certain number of SAPs and stations. Because each SAP or station takes up memory, you should provide only enough for your application to run. |
| Swap | Turns on address bit-swapping when it is enabled and Microsoft DLC is bound to an Ethernet driver. The default is 1 (enabled). |
| Usedix | Sets the frame format. By default, this value is 0 (disabled), which is the correct value for 802.3 Ethernet format. Set this value to 1 for Ethernet DIX 2.0 (Ethertype 0x80D5) format. Ethernet DIX frames have an extra type-field. |

The default values for Swap and Usedix are appropriate for most token-ring LAN environments. If the computer has an Ethernet adapter, then you should set the correct values for these parameters in the Advanced properties for Microsoft DLC. If you previously used the IBM DXME0MOD.SYS driver, use the following table to map the XMIT_SWAP parameter to set values for the two Microsoft DLC parameters.

| DXME0MOD.SYS xmit_swap | Microsoft DLC parameters |
|------------------------|--------------------------|
| 0 | swap=1<br>usedix=0 |
| 1 | swap=1<br>usedix=1 |
| 2 | swap=0<br>usedix=0 |
| 3 | swap=0<br>usedix=1 |

The following example shows some typical settings in AUTOEXEC.BAT and
PROTOCOL.INI for Microsoft DLC with an Intel EtherExpress PRO LAN
NDIS 2 network adapter driver on an Ethernet network. Notice that the [Msdlc$]
section is added automatically by Windows 95 when the protocol is installed.

**Sample Configuration File Settings for Microsoft DLC with NDIS 2 Adapters**

| Filename | Required settings |
|---|---|
| autoexec.bat | ```net init```<br>```msdlc.exe```<br>```net start``` |
| protocol.ini | ```[netbeui$]```<br>```DriverName=NETBEUI$```<br>```Lanabase=0```<br>```sessions=10```<br>```ncbs=12```<br>```Bindings=EPRO$```<br><br>```[nwlink$]```<br>```DriverName=nwlink$```<br>```Frame_Type=4```<br>```cachesize=0```<br>```Bindings=EPRO$```<br><br>```[epro$]```<br>```DriverName=EPRO$```<br>```INTERRUPT=10```<br>```ioaddress=0x300```<br><br>```[protman$]```<br>```priority=ndishlp$```<br>```DriverName=protman$```<br><br>```[ndishlp$]```<br>```DriverName=ndishlp$```<br>```Bindings=EPRO$```<br><br>```[data]```<br>```version=v4.00.000```<br>```netcards=EPRO$,*PNP8132```<br><br>```[msdlc$]```<br>```DriverName=msdlc$```<br>```stations=20```<br>```saps=3```<br>```swap=0```<br>```usedix=1```<br><br>```Bindings=EPRO$``` |

# Configuring Microsoft DLC with ODI Drivers

Architecture for real-mode DLC with ODI network adapter drivers

| NDIS.VXD |
| :---: |
| NDIS2SUP.VXD |
| MSDLC.EXE |
| ODINSUP.EXE |
| LSL.COM |
| ODI network adapter driver |

For computers that are running Microsoft DLC with ODI drivers using the Novell-supplied ODINSUP.EXE file, Windows 95 Setup installs over this configuration and leaves entries for ODINSUP and MSDLC in AUTOEXEC.BAT. Microsoft does not provide direct support for Microsoft DLC used with ODINSUP.EXE.

If you must run a real-mode network redirector or TSR (NETX.EXE, VLM.EXE, and so on), you need to configure Microsoft DLC by binding the Microsoft DLC protocol to an ODI network adapter driver, as shown in the illustration. Otherwise, install Microsoft DLC over NDIS 2 with the protected-mode Microsoft Client for NetWare Networks.

The following table shows settings used to configure Microsoft DLC with ODI drivers.

**Configuration File Settings for Real-Mode Microsoft DLC over ODI Drivers**

| Filename | Required settings | |
| :--- | :--- | :--- |
| autoexec.bat | `lsl` | `;Novell-supplied component` |
| | `mlid_driver.com` | `;Novell-supplied component` |
| | `odinhlp.exe` | `;Windows 95 component` |
| | `odinsup.exe` | `;Novell-supplied component` |
| | `msdlc.exe` | `;Windows 95 component` |
| | `net start netbind` | `;Windows 95 component` |
| net.cfg | `Protocol ODINSUP` | |
| | `    Bind EPROODI` | |
| | `    BUFFERED` | |
| | `Link Driver EPROODI` | |
| | `    Port 300` | |
| | `    Frame Ethernet_802.2` | |
| | `    Frame Ethernet_802.3` | |
| | `    Frame Ethernet_II` | |
| | `    Frame Ethernet_Snap` | |

**Configuration File Settings for Real-Mode Microsoft DLC over ODI Drivers**
(*continued*)

| Filename | Required settings |
|----------|-------------------|
| protocol.ini | ```[protman$]```<br>```priority=ndishlp$```<br>```DriverName=protman$``` |
|  | ```[ndishlp$]```<br>```DriverName=ndishlp$```<br>```Bindings=``` |
|  | ```[data]```<br>```version=v4.00.000```<br>```netcards=``` |
|  | ```[nwlink$]```<br>```Frame_Type=4```<br>```cachesize=0```<br>```DriverName=nwlink$``` |
|  | ```[msdlc$]```<br>```DriverName=msdlc$```<br>```xstations0=0```<br>```xstations1=0```<br>```stations=20```<br>```saps=3```<br>```xsaps0=1```<br>```xsaps1=1```<br>```swap=0```<br>```usedix=1```<br>```Bindings=EPROODI``` |
|  | ```[EPROODI]```<br>```Drivername=EPROODI```<br>```INTERRUPT=10```<br>```ioaddress=0x300``` |

# Upgrading Existing IBM LanSupport Installations

If you are using DLC support supplied by IBM to connect to host computers,
Windows 95 Setup can detect IBM DLC; it leaves the installation intact and
configures Windows 95 to run over that configuration. Although support for IBM
DLC can be installed using the Network option in Control Panel, the required
components must be provided by your network vendor.

This section describes two typical IBM LanSupport configurations, using
DXMC0MOD.SYS and DXME0MOD.SYS.

**DXMC0MOD.SYS, the monolithic IBM DLC driver.** For this configuration, Windows 95 Setup does one of two things:

- If the computer is running NetWare, Setup keeps the DXMC0MOD.SYS driver and related settings, and installs the Generic ODI driver plus Microsoft Client for NetWare Networks, or keeps the real-mode client, as described in Chapter 9, "Windows 95 on NetWare Networks."

- If the computer is running DXMC0MOD.SYS and no other networking components, Setups keeps the DXMC0MOD.SYS driver and does not install any Windows 95 networking components.

The following shows a sample configuration for IBM DXMC0MOD.SYS with Microsoft Client for NetWare Networks.

**Example of Configuration Settings for DXMC0MOD.SYS with ODI Drivers**

| Filename | Required settings |
|----------|-------------------|
| autoexec.bat | `lsl          ; Novell-supplied component`<br>`lansup       ; Novell-supplied component`<br>`odihlp.exe   ; Microsoft component` |
| config.sys | `device=path\dxmaood.sys   ;IBM-supplied component`<br>`device=path\dxmcomod.sys   ;IBM-supplied component` |

**DXME0MOD.SYS, the NDIS driver for IBM DLC.**

For this configuration, Windows 95 Setup does one of three things:

- If the computer is running DXME0MOD.SYS and no other networking components, Setup keeps the DXME0MOD.SYS driver and does not install any Windows 95 networking components.

- If the computer is running DXME0MOD.SYS and Novell NetWare, Setup installs an NDIS network adapter driver plus Microsoft Client for NetWare Networks, and leaves the DXME0MOD.SYS driver intact.

- If the computer is running DXME0MOD.SYS with the IBM DOS LAN Requestor, Setup installs an NDIS 2 adapter driver, keeps the DXME0MOD.SYS driver, installs Client for Microsoft Networks, and removes the IBM DOS LAN Requestor redirector components.

The following shows a sample configuration for IBM DXME0MOD.SYS with Client for Microsoft Networks using an NDIS 2 adapter driver. The same basic kinds of settings are used for a computer running Microsoft Client for NetWare Networks with an NDIS 2 adapter driver.

Architecture for real-mode DLC with NDIS 2 network adapter and IBM LanSupport

| NWREDIR.VXD |
|---|
| NWLINK.VXD |
| NDIS.VXD |
| MSODISUP.VXD |
| ODIHELP.EXE |
| LANSUP |
| LSL.COM |
| DXMAOMOD.SYS<br>DXMCOMOD.SYS |

**Example of Settings for DXMCE0MOD.SYS with Client for Microsoft Networks**

| Filename | Required settings |
|----------|-------------------|
| autoexec.bat | `net start netbind` |
| config.sys | `device=c:\windows\protman.dos /i:c:\windows`<br>`device=c:\windows\epro.dos        ;ndis2 driver`<br>`device=c:\lsp\dxma0mod.sys         ;IBM-supplied`<br>`device=c:\lsp\dxme0mod.sys ,,3     ;IBM-supplied`<br>`device=c:\windows\ndishlp.sys      ;Windows 95` |
| protocol.ini | `[protman$]`<br>`priority=ndishlp$`<br>`DriverName=protman$`<br><br>`[ndishlp$]`<br>`DriverName=ndishlp$`<br>`Bindings=EPRO$`<br><br>`[data]`<br>`version=v4.00.000`<br>`netcards=EPRO$,*pnp8132`<br><br>`[netbeui$]`<br>`DriverName=NETBEUI$`<br>`Lanabase=0`<br>`sessions=10`<br>`ncbs=12`<br>`Bindings=EPRO$`<br><br>`[nwlink$]`<br>`DriverName=nwlink$`<br>`Frame_Type=4`<br>`cachesize=0`<br>`Bindings=EPRO$`<br><br>`[EPRO$]`<br>`DriverName=EPRO$`<br>`INTERRUPT=10`<br>`ioaddress=0x300`<br><br>`[DXMAIDXCFG]`<br>`dxme0_nif=dxme0.nif`<br>`dxmj0mod_nif=dxmj0mod.nif`<br>`smcdosjp_nif=smcdosjp.nif`<br>`smcdosjp2_nif=smcdosjp.nif`<br>`smcdosat_nif=smcdosat.nif`<br>`smcdosat2_nif=smcdosat.nif`<br>`smcdosmc_nif=smcdosmc.nif`<br>`smcdosmc2_nif=smcdosmc.nif`<br><br>`[ETHERAND]`<br><br>`DriverName=DXME0$`<br>`Bindings=EPRO$` |

# Using Gateways for Connectivity

When your network uses a gateway to communicate with a host computer, the client computer running Windows 95 communicates with the gateway computer just as it does with any other computer on the network. The gateway computer translates requests from the client into a form that can be understood by the host, then communicates with the host, and returns the information to the client. In this configuration, the client computer can connect to the gateway using any protocol that the gateway supports. The gateway uses some form of the DLC protocol to communicate with the host.

The following table shows commonly used gateways and the supported operating systems.

| Gateway | Operating system |
| --- | --- |
| Microsoft SNA Server 2.0 and 2.1 | Microsoft Windows NT 3.x |
| NetWare for SAA | Novell NetWare 3.x and 4.x |
| Wall Data Rumba Gateway | Microsoft Windows 3.x |
| Attachmate® Gateway 4.0 or higher | MS-DOS |
| DCA™ IRMALAN Gateway | MS-DOS |
| EICON | MS-DOS and Windows 3.x |

Many of the gateways in the preceding table have MS-DOS versions, which run only under MS-DOS, not under Windows. Windows 95 does not support running the MS-DOS–based gateways in a VM. For information about support for a particular gateway under Windows 95, contact your gateway vendor.

# Using TCP/IP for Host Connectivity

Many utilities and terminal emulation programs from other vendors allow direct communication with a mainframe or host computer using a TCP/IP protocol stack. The protected-mode version of Microsoft TCP/IP included with Windows 95 relies on the Windows Sockets version 1.1 interface. Any terminal emulation program or utility that you use to connect to a mainframe or host computer over Microsoft TCP/IP must support Windows Sockets 1.1.

If you want to connect to a host computer using Telnet or TCP/IP and you are running an application that emulates an IBM 3270 or 5250, or a DEC VT xx computer terminal, you can use Microsoft TCP/IP. Before configuring Windows 95 for Microsoft TCP/IP, make sure that the emulation application supports Windows Sockets 1.1 as a TCP/IP interface option.

If your emulation software requires a TSR to communicate with another vendor's TCP/IP protocol stack, you must remove the TSR and reconfigure the emulation software for Windows Sockets in order to communicate using Microsoft TCP/IP in Windows 95. To determine the proper configuration with Windows Sockets, see the documentation for the emulation software. If the application does not support Windows Sockets 1.1, contact the application vendor to obtain a version that does; otherwise, do not use Microsoft TCP/IP.

# Using Terminal Emulation Applications

Terminal emulation applications offer several different connectivity options for connecting to a host IBM AS/400, or DEC VAX computer. This section describes configuration and other issues related to using terminal emulation programs.

**Connecting to a NetWare for SAA gateway.**   For most emulation applications, configuring Windows 95 with the Microsoft IPX/SPX-compatible protocol enables connectivity to a NetWare for SAA gateway or to any gateway supporting IPX/SPX connectivity. If you are using a token-ring network with source routing, use the Network option in Control Panel to make sure that Microsoft IPX/SPX-compatible protocol appears in the list of network components. In Advanced properties for the protocol, set the Source Routing property to a 16-entry cache size.

If this configuration does not work well, configure Windows 95 to use a Novell-supplied real-mode NetWare client.

**Connecting to a Windows NT SNA 2.0 or 2.1 server.**   Windows 3.x client software supports connectivity to a Windows NT SNA 2.0 or 2.1 server. The Windows NT 32-bit client for SNA should not be used; it was designed to work only with client computers running Windows NT Workstation.

**Connecting to an AS/400 with IBM PC Support software.**   You can use Windows 95 to connect to an AS/400 using the IBM PC Support software. To do so, configure the PC Support application for Basic Mode; do not use Extended Mode. If the PC Support application was configured to connect using DLC, make sure that Microsoft DLC or IBM LanSupport is already installed on the computer.

You can also use Windows 95 to connect to an AS/400 using the NetWare for SAA gateway and the IBM PC Support application. Configure the PC Support application for Basic Mode; do not use Extended Mode. The IBM-supplied DOS16M.386 file is not compatible with Windows 95.

If Windows 95 is configured to use the IPX/SPX-compatible protocol, then you must create a WINSTART.BAT batch file in the Windows directory and add entries in this file to run PCSWIN.COM and STRNRTR.EXE (the Novell-compatible router). If you encounter problems using the protected-mode IPX/SPX-compatible transport with the Novell-compatible PC Support router, then configure Windows 95 to use the Novell-supplied NETX or VLM client with IPXODI, as described in Chapter 9, "Windows 95 on NetWare Networks."

**Connecting to host computer using a coaxial adapter.** If you are using a coaxial connection with a coaxial adapter (CUT/DFT) supplied by IBM or another vendor, use the real-mode drivers provided with the adapter or emulation software for setting up hardware. No 32-bit drivers are available for connectivity with this type of adapter.

For information about using TCP/IP with IBM 3270 terminal emulation, see "Using TCP/IP for Host Connectivity" earlier in this chapter.

# Troubleshooting Connection Problems with Microsoft DLC

If you encounter problems using the real-mode Microsoft DLC protocol, check the following items:

- When adding the Microsoft DLC protocol, make sure that there is only one **net start** entry in AUTOEXEC.BAT. Setup adds an entry for Microsoft DLC, even if an entry already exists. Also, make sure that AUTOEXEC.BAT is configured properly, as described in "Installing and Configuring Real-Mode Microsoft DLC" earlier in this chapter.

- Do not make direct entries or changes in PROTOCOL.INI for Microsoft DLC. Instead, make all changes in the Advanced properties for Microsoft DLC by using the Network option in Control Panel. If you make changes directly in PROTOCOL.INI, then the next time you change any values by using the Network option in Control Panel, all settings in PROTOCOL.INI for Microsoft DLC will be overwritten.

- Some terminal emulation applications use TSRs to communicate with the Microsoft DLC protocol. If your emulation application uses a TSR that runs from AUTOEXEC.BAT, then make sure that the entry for the TSR still exists (usually, the TSR entry occurs after the **msdlc** and **net start** lines). Windows 95 Setup removes or comments out many TSRs.

- The option named Set This Protocol To Be The Default Protocol in the Advanced properties for Microsoft DLC does not provide any functionality. This option should not be checked, because Microsoft DLC does not use LANA settings.

- Real-mode Microsoft DLC is an NDIS 2 protocol, so the network adapter must have an NDIS 2-compatible network adapter driver for use with Windows 95. Windows 95 includes many compatible drivers, but some Windows 95 drivers for certain PCI and PCMCIA cards do not have a corresponding NDIS 2 driver to allow loading real-mode Microsoft DLC.

CHAPTER 1 1

# Logon, Browsing, and Resource Sharing

This chapter describes how to configure and use the Windows 95 logon process, network browsing, and peer resource sharing capabilities.

**In This Chapter**

Logon, Browsing, and Resource Sharing: The Basics    363
    Unified System Logon Basics    363
    Network Browsing Basics    364
    Peer Resource Sharing Basics    364
Logon, Browsing, and Resource Sharing: The Issues    366
Overview of Logging on to Windows 95    367
Configuring Network Logon    369
    Configuring Logon for Client for Microsoft Networks    370
    Configuring Logon for NetWare Networks    371
    Setting Network Logon Options with System Policies    373
Using Login Scripts    374
    Using Login Scripts with Microsoft Networking    374
    Using Login Scripts on NetWare Networks    375
Technical Notes for the Logon Process    379
Browsing Overview    380
    Using Network Neighborhood    380
    Browsing in Common Dialog Boxes    382
    Connecting to Drive and Printer Resources    383
    Browsing with the Net View Command    384
Browsing on Microsoft Networks    384
    Designating a Browse Master for Microsoft Networks    384
    Building the Browse List for Microsoft Networks    386
    Technical Notes on Browsing on Microsoft Networks    387

*(continued)*

Browsing on NetWare Networks    388
    Using Network Neighborhood on NetWare Networks    388
    Managing Connections with Client for NetWare Networks    391
    Using Commands to Connect to NetWare Servers    391
    Using Windows NT to Connect to NetWare Servers    394
Overview of Peer Resource Sharing    396
    Installing Peer Resource Sharing    396
    Overview of Security for Peer Resource Sharing    397
Using File and Printer Sharing for Microsoft Networks    398
Using File and Printer Sharing for NetWare Networks    401
    Sharing Resources on a NetWare Network    403
    Using Bindery Emulation for Pass-Through Security    408
Troubleshooting for Logon, Browsing, and Peer Resource Sharing    408

# Logon, Browsing, and Resource Sharing: The Basics

This section summarizes key Windows 95 features that you can use to make network logon, resource browsing, and peer resource sharing easier and more secure for computers running Windows 95 on your network.

## Unified System Logon Basics

Windows 95 offers a consistent user interface for logging on to and validating access to network resources. The first time the user logs on to Windows 95, logon dialog boxes appear for each network client on that computer and for Windows 95. If the user's password for Windows 95 or for another network is made the same as the password for the primary logon client, Windows 95 automatically logs the user on to Windows 95 and all networks using that password every time the user logs on. This means that, for users, network logon is simplified in that a single logon dialog box is presented each time the operating system starts. For network administrators, it means they can use existing user accounts to validate access to the network for users running Windows 95.

---

**Note**  The Passwords option in Control Panel provides a way to synchronize logon passwords for different networks so they can be made the same if one is changed. For more information, see Chapter 14, "Security."

---

When a user logs on to other networks with different passwords and chooses to save them, the passwords are stored in a password cache. The Windows 95 password unlocks this password cache. Thereafter, Windows 95 uses the passwords stored in the password cache to log a user on to other networks so no additional passwords need to be typed.

For NetWare networks, Windows 95 provides graphical logon to Novell NetWare versions 3.x, or 4.x if the network is configured for bindery emulation, plus a NetWare-compatible login script processor. This means that if you are using Microsoft Client for NetWare Networks, Windows 95 can process NetWare login scripts. If drive mappings and search drives are specified in a login script, then under Windows 95 the same user configuration is used for network connections as was specified under the previous operating system, with no administrative changes necessary.

For Microsoft networks, Windows 95 supports network logon using domain user accounts and login script processing (as supported by LAN Manager version 2.x and Windows NT).

# Network Browsing Basics

Network Neighborhood is the central point for browsing in Windows 95. It offers the following benefits:

- Users can browse the network as easily as browsing the local hard disk.

- Users can create shortcuts to network resources on the desktop.

- Users can easily connect to network resources by clicking the Map Network Drive button that appears on most toolbars.

- Users can open files and complete other actions by using new common dialog boxes in applications. This new standard provides a consistent way to open or save files on both network and local drives.

- The network administrator can customize Network Neighborhood by using system policies, as described in Chapter 15, "User Profiles and System Policies." A custom Network Neighborhood can include shortcuts to commonly used resources, including Dial-Up Networking resources.

In any situation in which you can type a path name for connecting to a server— such as in the Map Network Drive dialog box or at the command prompt—you can specify the server name with two backslashes (\\) if your network uses UNC path names. For example, to connect to the server CORP, volume DOCS, directory WORD, and subdirectory Q1, type the UNC name **\\corp\docs\word\q1**.

On NetWare networks, you can use the UNC name or standard NetWare syntax. For the previous example, you would type **corp/docs:word\q1**. (Notice that, in the NetWare environment, "/" and "\" are interchangeable.) However, Windows 95 does not support the NetWare 4.0 naming convention of \\\\*nwserver_sys\directory_path\filename.ext* where \\\\*nwserver_sys* is the name of the NetWare Directory Services (NDS) server volume object.

# Peer Resource Sharing Basics

The two peer resource sharing services in Windows 95—Microsoft File and Printer Sharing for NetWare Networks and File and Printer Sharing for Microsoft Networks—are 32-bit, protected-mode networking components that allow users to share directories, printers, and CD-ROM drives on computers running Windows 95. File and Printer Sharing services work with existing servers to add complementary peer resource sharing services.

For example, a NetWare network and its users will realize the following benefits by using File and Printer Sharing for NetWare Networks:

- Users can share files, printers, and CD-ROM drives without running two network clients. This saves memory, improves performance, and reduces the number of protocols running on your network. (Under Windows for Workgroups, Novell users had to also run a Microsoft network client to take advantage of peer resource sharing.)

- Security is user-based, not share-based. You can administer user accounts, passwords, and group lists in one place (on the NetWare server) because File and Printer Sharing for NetWare Networks uses the NetWare server's authentication database.

- Users running VLM or NETX clients can access shared resources on computers running Windows 95. The computer running Windows 95 looks as if it is just another NetWare server if it uses SAP Advertising, as "Using File and Printer Sharing for NetWare Networks" later in this chapter. The computer providing File and Printer Sharing services can handle up to 250 concurrent connections.

- You can add secure storage space and printing to the network inexpensively, while using familiar NetWare tools to manage these resources. You can reduce the load and improve the performance of NetWare servers by moving selected shared resources to one or more computers running File and Printer Sharing services. This allows you to manage load balancing for users without adding a new NetWare server.

- You get a scalable, high-performance 32-bit peer server that uses multiple 32-bit threads, the new Windows 95 VFAT 32-bit file system, 32-bit NDIS drivers, 32-bit IPX/SPX-compatible protocol, and the burst-mode protocol.

Similar benefits are available when you use File and Printer Sharing for Microsoft Networks. You can also use either share-level security or, on a Windows NT network, user-level security to protect access to peer resources.

# Logon, Browsing, and Resource Sharing: The Issues

This section summarizes the issues you need to consider when planning to use logon, browsing, and resource sharing features in Windows 95.

The network logon issues include the following:

- To use unified logon, a logon server (such as a Windows NT domain controller or a NetWare preferred server) must be available on the network and contain user account information for the user (unless, of course, the user is logging on as a guest).

- The Windows 95 logon processor can parse most statements in the NetWare login scripts. However, any statements loading TSRs must be removed from the scripts and loaded from AUTOEXEC.BAT. Because the Windows 95 logon processor operates in protected mode, it is not possible to load TSRs for global use from the login script. These TSRs should be loaded from AUTOEXEC.BAT before protected-mode operation begins, or using other methods described in "Using Login Scripts" later in this chapter.

  In some cases, login scripts load backup agents as TSRs. In such cases, protected-mode equivalents built into Windows 95 can be used, making it unnecessary to load these TSRs.

The network browsing issues include the following:

- You can plan ahead to configure workgroups for effective browsing by using WRKGRP.INI to control the workgroups that people can choose. For information about configuring WRKGRP.INI, see Chapter 5, "Custom, Automated, and Push Installations."

- If your enterprise network based on Microsoft networking is connected by a slow-link WAN and includes satellite offices with only Windows 95, then workstations in the satellites cannot browse the central corporate network. Consequently, they can connect to computers outside of their workgroups only by typing the computer name in a Map Network Drive dialog box. To provide full browsing capabilities, the satellite office must have a Windows NT server.

- You can use system policies, such as Hide Drives In My Computer or Hide Network Neighborhood, to limit or prevent browsing by users. For information, see Chapter 15, "User Profiles and System Policies."

The resource sharing issues include the following:

- If you want to configure a computer to share its files or printers, the choice of which File and Printer Sharing service you install depends on whether users who will be browsing for shared resources are running Microsoft or NetWare network clients.

- If you want to use File and Printer Sharing for NetWare Networks, there must be a NetWare server available on the network. This peer resource sharing service uses only user-level security, not share-level security, so a NetWare server must be available to validate user accounts. Also, the NetWare server must include a Windows_Passthru account (with no password) in its user accounts database.

- If you plan to use File and Printer Sharing for Microsoft Networks with user-level security, then a Windows NT server or domain must be available to validate user accounts.

- If you plan to use Net Watcher to remotely monitor connections on a computer running File and Printer Sharing services, that computer must have the Microsoft Remote Registry service installed. This is also true if you want to use Registry Editor or System Policy Editor to change settings on a remote computer. For information, see Chapter 16, "Remote Administration."

- If you are configuring a user's workstation to act as a peer server, you might also want to specify that this computer cannot run MS-DOS–based applications (which take exclusive control of the operating system, shutting down File and Printer Sharing services). To do this, you can set the system policy named Disable Single-Mode MS-DOS Applications.

# Overview of Logging on to Windows 95

There can be two levels of system logon on Microsoft or NetWare networks:

- Log on to Windows 95 by using a user name and a password that is cached locally

- Log on to a NetWare network or a Windows NT domain for validation, "Overview of Logging on to Windows 95" earlier in this chapter

When other network vendors make 32-bit, protected-mode networking clients available, network logon will be automatically available for those networks because of the Windows 95 network provider interface, as described in Chapter 32, "Windows 95 Network Architecture."

Windows 95 provides a single unified logon prompt. This prompt allows the user to log on to all networks and Windows 95 at the same time. The first time a user starts Windows 95, there are separate logon prompts for each network, plus one for Windows 95. If these passwords are made identical, the logon prompt for Windows 95 is not displayed again.

Logging on to Windows 95 unlocks the password cache file (.PWL) that caches encrypted passwords. This is the only logon prompt that appears if no other network clients are configured on that computer.

▶ **To log on to Windows 95 when no other network logon is configured**

- When the Welcome to Windows dialog box appears after starting Windows 95 for the first time, specify the user name and password.

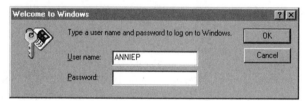

Windows 95 uses this logon information to identify the user and to find any user profile information. User profiles define user preferences, such as the fonts and colors used on the desktop, and access information for the user. (For more information, see Chapter 15, "User Profiles and System Policies.")

▶ **To log on to Windows 95 on a Microsoft network**

1. When the Enter Network Password dialog box appears after starting Windows 95 for the first time, specify the user name and password.

   For network logon on a Microsoft network, type the name of the Windows NT domain, LAN Manager domain, or Windows NT computer that contains the related user account.

This dialog box appears for logging on to Windows NT networks

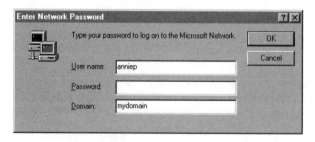

After the user name and password pair are validated by the network server, the user is allowed to use resources on the network. If the user is not validated, the user cannot gain access to network resources.

2. The first time Windows 95 starts, the Welcome to Windows dialog box appears, prompting you to type the user name and password defined for Windows 95.

### ▶ To log on to Windows 95 on a NetWare network

1. To log on to a NetWare network, type the name of the NetWare server, which is the preferred server where the related user account is stored.

This dialog box appears for logging on to NetWare networks

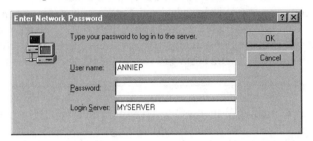

After the user name and password pair are validated by the NetWare server, the user is allowed to use resources on the network. If the user is not validated, the user will be prompted to type a password when connecting to a NetWare server during this work session.

2. The first time Windows 95 starts, the Welcome to Windows dialog box appears, prompting you to type the user name and password defined for Windows 95. Type this information and click OK.

The next time this computer is started, Windows 95 displays the name of the last user who logged on and the name of the domain or preferred server used for validation. If the same user is logging on again, only the password for the network server or domain needs to be entered. If another user is logging on, that user's unique user name and password must be entered. If the passwords are the same for the network and Windows 95, the second dialog box for logging on to Windows 95 does not appear again.

# Configuring Network Logon

If you install either Client for Microsoft Networks or Client for NetWare Networks, you can configure a computer running Windows 95 to participate on a Windows NT or NetWare network.

Before you can use network logon on a computer running Windows 95, however, you must have a Windows NT domain controller or NetWare server on the network that contains user account information for the Windows 95 user. For more information about setting up permissions on a Windows NT or NetWare server, see the administrator's documentation for the server. For related information, see Chapter 8, "Windows 95 on Microsoft Networks" and Chapter 9, "Windows 95 on NetWare Networks."

The validation of a user's network password at system startup might not be required for accessing network resources later during that work session. However, system startup is the only time the login script can run, and it is the only time at which user profiles and system policies can be downloaded on the local computer. Therefore, proper network logon can be extremely important.

The following sections provide information about configuring network logon for computers on Windows NT and NetWare networks when using a 32-bit, protected-mode network client. You can also use system policies to control network logon options, as summarized at the end of this section. For information about enforcing logon password requirements, see Chapter 14, "Security."

---

**Tip**  Logon validation will control only user access to network resources, not access to running Windows 95. To require validation by a network logon server before allowing access to Windows 95, you must use system policies. For information, see "Setting Network Logon Options with System Policies" later in this chapter.

Notice, however, that Windows 95 security cannot prevent a user from starting the computer by using Safe Mode or a floppy disk. If you require complete user validation before starting the computer in any way, use Windows NT as the sole operating system.

---

# Configuring Logon for Client for Microsoft Networks

When the computer is configured to use Client for Microsoft Networks as the Primary Network Logon client, you can specify Microsoft Windows NT logon options in the Network option in Control Panel. This section describes how to configure these options.

Network logon automatically validates the user on the specified Windows NT domain during the process of logging on to Windows 95. If this option is not configured, the user cannot access most network resources. If this option is configured and the user does not provide a correct password, Windows 95 operation might seem normal, but the user will not have access to most network resources.

When you configure network logon options, you can specify whether you want to automatically establish a connection for each persistent connection to a network resource or verify whether to reestablish connections at system startup. You can also specify basic network logon options in custom setup scripts used to install Windows 95.

For complete procedures for configuring network logon and persistent connections for Client for Microsoft Networks, see Chapter 8, "Windows 95 on Microsoft Networks." For information about defining network logon options in custom setup scripts, see Chapter 5, "Custom, Automated, and Push Installations." For information about controlling network logon by using system policies, see Chapter 15, "User Profiles and System Policies."

# Configuring Logon for NetWare Networks

Each Windows 95 user must have an account on the NetWare server before being able to use its files, applications, or print queues. The NetWare server account contains user credentials (user names and passwords).

With Client for NetWare Networks, there is no real-mode logon before Windows 95 starts, just the single, unified logon prompt for Windows 95 that allows users to log on to the system and to all networks at the same time. The first time a user starts Windows 95, there are two separate logon prompts: one for Windows 95 and one for the NetWare preferred server. As long as the two passwords are the same, the second logon prompt for Windows 95 is not displayed again.

If the computer uses a Novell-supplied real-mode network client, network logon occurs in real mode, and uses all the NetWare configuration settings that were in place before Windows 95 was installed. There are no required changes.

To configure Client for NetWare Networks for network logon, you need to specify whether Client for NetWare Networks is the Primary Network Logon client, which means the following:

- System policies and user profiles are downloaded from NetWare servers, if you use these features.

- Users are prompted first to log on to a NetWare server for validation when Windows 95 starts (before being prompted to log on to any other networks).

- For this computer, the last login script runs from a NetWare server.

---

**Tip**  When you start Windows 95 with Client for NetWare Networks configured as the Primary Network Logon client, Windows 95 automatically prompts you to provide logon information such as your password on the NetWare server.

You should never run the Novell-supplied LOGIN.EXE utility from a batch file or at the command prompt when you are using Client for NetWare Networks.

---

When you designate Client for NetWare Networks as the Primary Network Logon client, you must also specify a preferred NetWare server. Windows 95 uses the preferred server to validate user logon credentials and to find user profiles and system policy files. You can change the preferred NetWare server at any time.

The following procedure describes how to configure Client for NetWare Networks to log on to a NetWare network. If you use a NETX or VLM client, you can configure the setting for the preferred server using NET.CFG or using the **/ps** option in STARTNET.BAT, AUTOEXEC.BAT, or wherever you start NETX or VLM. For more information, consult your Novell-supplied documentation.

▶ **To use a NetWare server for network logon**

1. In the Network option in Control Panel, select Client for NetWare Networks in the Primary Network Logon box.

2. Double-click Client for NetWare Networks in the list of installed components.

3. In the Client for NetWare Networks properties, set values for the configuration options, as described in the following table.

| Property | Meaning |
|---|---|
| Preferred Server | Designates the name of the NetWare server that appears automatically in the network logon dialog box. Windows 95 obtains the NetWare login script from this server, unless you specify a different NetWare server in the Enter Network Password dialog box. This is also the server used to store user profiles and system policies, if these are used on your network. The Preferred Server setting is for the computer, not for individual users. |
| First Network Drive | Specifies the first drive letter that you want assigned to the first network connection. |
| Enable Logon Script Processing | Specifies that this computer will process NetWare login scripts when a user logs on to the network. |

Client for NetWare Networks attempts to connect to the preferred server rather than the first server that responds to the Get Nearest Server broadcast. Client for NetWare Networks also attempts a number of server connections in case the client computer can't establish a connection with the preferred server.

### Tip for Passwords on Windows 95 and NetWare Servers

After you log on to the network and you are validated by a NetWare server, Windows 95 automatically supplies the same user name and password for logging on to Windows 95. You are asked to supply your user name and password to log on to Windows 95 only if the user name or password is different from your NetWare user account. Therefore, you might want to keep your user name and password the same for both the Windows 95 and the NetWare networks.

Maintaining the same user name and password for both networks also makes it easier for network administrators to coordinate user accounts. For more information about passwords, including brief information on changing passwords on a NetWare server, see Chapter 14, "Security."

With NETX and VLM clients, network logon occurs in real mode during system startup. Therefore, the logon prompt for Windows 95 always appears when these clients are used because the unified logon process is not available.

# Setting Network Logon Options with System Policies

The network administrator can define system policies to enforce requirements for network logon. For example, you may want to make sure that users cannot access the local computer without network validation, or you may want to disable password caching.

For network logon in general, use these policies:

- Logon Banner, to specify a caption and other text, such as a legal notice, to be displayed before the logon dialog box appears.
- Require Validation By Network For Windows Access, to specify that each logon must be validated by a server before access to Windows is allowed.

For Microsoft Client for NetWare Networks, use this policy:

- Disable Automatic NetWare Login, to specify that when Windows 95 attempts to connect to a NetWare server, it does not automatically try to use the user's network logon name and password and the Windows logon password to make the connection.

For Client for Microsoft Networks, use these policies:

- Log On To Windows NT, to specify that this computer can participate in a Windows NT domain.

- Display Domain Logon Validation, to display a message when the domain controller has validated user logon.

- Disable Caching Of Domain Password, to specify that no caching is used for the network password. However, do not enable the Quick Logon feature when password caching has been disabled using system policies. The Quick Logon feature requires password caching to function properly.

For information about these policies and others that enforce password requirements, see Chapter 15, "User Profiles and System Policies."

If a computer has the Microsoft Remote Registry agent installed, you can use System Policy Editor to remotely set network logon options on individual computers without using system policies. This is useful in cases in which you have not previously enforced logon requirements using system policies but you want to make sure that network logon is configured properly on a specific computer.

# Using Login Scripts

This section summarizes some information about using login scripts on Windows NT and NetWare networks. For details about using login scripts for push installation of Windows 95, see Chapter 5, "Custom, Automated, and Push Installations."

## Using Login Scripts with Microsoft Networking

This section summarizes how to use login scripts for Windows 95 on Windows NT networks.

Login scripts are batch files or executable files that run automatically when a user logs on to a computer running either Windows NT, Windows 95, or MS-DOS. Login scripts are often used to configure users' working environments by making network connections and starting applications.

There are several reasons that you might want to use login scripts:

- You want to manage part of the user environment (such as network connections) without managing or dictating the entire environment.

- You want to create common network connections for multiple users.

- You already have LAN Manager 2.x running on your network, and you want to continue to use login scripts you have created for that system.

To assign a user a login script, designate the path name of the login script file in the user's account on the server. Then, whenever that user logs on, the login script is downloaded and run. You can assign a different login script to each user or create login scripts for use by multiple users.

To create a batch-file login script, create an MS-DOS batch file. (For more information about creating batch files, see the *Windows NT Server System Guide* or your MS-DOS documentation.)

A login script is always downloaded from the server that validates a user's logon request. For users with accounts on Windows NT server domains that have one or more backup domain controllers and a primary domain controller, any one of the domain controllers can authorize a user's logon attempt. To ensure that login scripts always work for users, you should be sure that login scripts for all user accounts in a domain exist on every primary and backup domain controller in the domain. You can do this by using the Windows NT Replicator service, as described in the *Windows NT Server System Guide*.

Home directories on Windows NT networks are used to store user profiles and can also serve as private storage spaces for users. Typically, users also control access to their home directories and can restrict or grant access to other users.

To ensure access to user profiles, you should assign each user a home directory on a server. You can also assign users home directories on their own workstations (although this means that users won't have access to their user profiles from other computers); you might want to do this if you don't want the user to be able to access files and directories on the rest of the workstation.

# Using Login Scripts on NetWare Networks

On NetWare networks (version 3.x or using the bindery), the system login script named NET$LOG.DAT is stored in the PUBLIC directory on the server. Individual user scripts are stored in their MAIL subdirectories. The network administrator can use SYSCON (or NWADMIN for VLM) to edit login scripts for any NetWare-compatible client running under Windows 95.

Login scripts are stored differently on NetWare 3.x servers (using bindery services) versus NetWare 4.x servers (using NDS). On a bindery server, the System login script is stored in the NET$LOG.DAT file in the PUBLIC directory, and User login scripts are stored in the LOGIN file in MAIL subdirectories that correspond to the users' internal IDs. On an NDS server, the Container, Profile, and User login scripts are stored in the NDS database as properties of those objects.

The issues related to running login scripts depend on whether the computer is configured with Client for NetWare Networks or uses a Novell-supplied network client.

## Running Login Scripts with Client for NetWare Networks

If the computer is running Client for NetWare Networks, the special Windows 95 login script processor runs the login script after the user completes entries in the network logon dialog box during system startup. Microsoft Client for NetWare Networks makes only bindery connections. When it connects to a NetWare 4.x server, the server must be running bindery emulation, so that the login scripts can be accessed in the same way as on a bindery server. If bindery-type login script files aren't available, you must use SYSCON from a NetWare 3.x server to connect to the NetWare 4.x server and create bindery-type System and User login scripts.

The Windows 95 login script processor runs NetWare 3.x system and user login scripts, using commands in these scripts, such as MAP and CAPTURE, to make global changes to the system environment. For example, a script might include SET statements or PATH statements to specify search drives.

The login script appears in a window if the user's login script contains the WRITE, DISPLAY, FDISPLAY, PAUSE, or WAIT commands.

The Login Script
Processor window

```
▀ Login Script Processor for NetWare                    _ □ ✕
Welcome to <<< TRIKE >>>
Drive F: = TRIKE\SYS:       \
SEARCH1: Z:\PUBLIC [TRIKE\SYS:     \PUBLIC]
Attempt to map drive to invalid path in map command "G:
Drive G: = TRIKE\PUBLIC:    \
Thank you for using Windows 95 this afternoon, ANNIEP

Drive A: maps to a local disk.
Drive B: maps to a local disk.
Drive C: maps to a local disk.
Drive D: maps to a local disk.
Drive E: maps to a local disk.
Drive F: = TRIKE\SYS:       \
Drive G: = TRIKE\PUBLIC:    \
Drive P: maps to a local disk.
───────────
SEARCH1: = Y:\PUBLIC [TRIKE\SYS:     \PUBLIC]
SEARCH2: = X:\ [TRIKE\SYS:  \]
SEARCH3: = Z:\PUBLIC [TRIKE\SYS:     \PUBLIC]
SEARCH4: = C:\WINDOWS
SEARCH5: = C:\WINDOWS\COMMAND
SEARCH6: = C:\DOS
```

Any NetWare or MS-DOS command (in conjunction with NetWare login script commands) can be used in a login script except those that load TSRs. The Windows 95 login script processor operates in protected-mode, so loading real-mode TSRs from a login script is not possible because login scripts are run after all real-mode actions are completed at system startup. Any TSR that is run from a login script is loaded in a single VM, which is subsequently shut down when login script processing is completed. In these cases, the login script processor displays an error message.

For loading components such as backup agents, protected-mode equivalents in Windows 95 can be used instead of running TSRs. If you need to run a TSR to support an application, use one of the options described in the following table.

**Loading TSRs with Client for NetWare Networks**

| What the TSR must support | Where to load the TSR |
|---|---|
| **With NDIS 3.1 drivers:** | |
| All applications created for MS-DOS or Windows, without IPX/SPX support | AUTOEXEC.BAT |
| All Windows-based applications that require IPX/SPX support[1] | WINSTART.BAT in the Windows directory |
| Any MS-DOS–based application that requires IPX/SPX support[2] | At the command prompt before running the application |
| **With ODI drivers:** | |
| All applications created for MS-DOS or Windows with IPX/SPX support | After the entry that loads IPXODI in AUTOEXEC.BAT |

[1] The IPX/SPX-compatible protocol (NWLINK) is loaded after real mode is complete but before login scripts are processed, so this protocol is available for TSRs loaded from WINSTART.BAT.

[2] The TSR must be loaded in each separate VM for each application that requires that TSR before the application is loaded. This can be done in a batch file used to run the application.

The network administrator might want to warn users that, in the following circumstances, the login script processor can display special windows and messages, and that this is not an error condition:

- When the login script runs, a message announces that the operating system is processing login scripts. The user can click a button to see details. However, if any statement in the script writes to the screen or if there is a PAUSE statement, the Logon Script Processor window appears and displays all subsequent statements as they run.

- If any *#DOS_command* statement is included in the script, a special VM is used to process the command. An MS-DOS Prompt window appears while the command is running and then closes automatically when the command is complete.

The following list presents some tips for testing and running login scripts with Client for NetWare Networks:

- In your testing laboratory, run the login script on a NETX computer and check the drive mappings and printer capture statements. Then run the script under Client for NetWare Networks and make sure the results are the same.

- Insert PAUSE statements frequently in the scripts you are testing so that you can study each screenful of information as it appears in the Logon Script Processor window.

- While testing scripts, check carefully for script errors that appear in the Logon Script Processor window.

- Insert PAUSE statements following any text that you want the user to read during system logon.

---

**Note**  The Windows 95 login script processor can handle any documented NetWare login script commands. Any undocumented variations on NetWare commands might not be processed as legal statements.

---

You can make persistent connections (using the same drive letter each time) to NetWare volumes and directories by using the Windows 95 user interface. Using persistent connections eliminates the need for some NetWare MAP commands in login scripts. However, if persistent connections are made to a server, you should avoid using the ATTACH command in login scripts. For information about making persistent connections, see "Connecting to the Internet" in Chapter 30, "Internet Access."

Client for NetWare Networks also differs from NETX and VLM in that it does not map the first network drive to the logon directory of the preferred server. All subsequent connections to NetWare servers must be made by using Windows 95 tools.

## Running Login Scripts with Novell-Supplied Clients

If a computer is running the Novell-supplied NETX or VLM networking client, login scripts are processed as they were before Windows 95 was installed.

With NETX or VLM, login scripts are run during system startup after real mode at the command prompt before Windows 95 switches to protected mode. Therefore, all statements and TSRs will run as expected and be available globally for all applications created for Windows or MS-DOS.

**Important**   Users running a Novell-supplied client should always log on to the NetWare server before running Windows 95. Otherwise, many operational problems will occur. For example, if a user instead logs on at command prompt while already running Windows 95, then all the drive mappings created by the login scripts will be local only to that VM.

# Technical Notes for the Logon Process

The notes in this section provide a brief overview of the logon process in Windows 95.

If user profiles are enabled (using the Passwords option in Control Panel or by setting the related system policy), then a logon dialog box will always appear at system startup (even if the user's password is blank) because the user must be identified so the operating system can load the correct profile.

If user profiles are not enabled, then what happens in the logon process depends on the setting specified in the Primary Network Logon box in the Network option in Control Panel. If the Primary Network Logon setting is for a network provider such as Client for NetWare Networks or Client for Microsoft Networks, then an Enter Network Password dialog box will always appear at system startup if the network is active. These network providers cannot allow automatic logon without the user entering a password because the provider does not know which network password the user wants to use.

On a portable computer that has a network adapter that can be changed (for example, using the adapter on a docking station versus using a PCMCIA card), the logon dialog box appears when there is an active network. Only the Windows 95 system logon dialog box appears when the network is not active.

If the user selects Windows Logon as the value in the Primary Network Logon box in the Network option in Control Panel, then the Windows logon dialog box will appear first, followed by logon dialog boxes for any other network providers. In this case, if the Windows password and the passwords for any other network providers are all blank, then Windows 95 can attempt an automatic or "silent" logon (opening the user's password file with a blank password).

You might choose this configuration, for example, for peer servers that are physically secure from user access when you want such servers to be able to automatically recover from power outages or other failures without user intervention.

---

**Note**  The administrator can use system policies to restrict users' access to the Passwords option in Control Panel or to require a minimum password length to prevent automatic logon using blank passwords.

---

# Browsing Overview

Browsing in Windows 95 is the same for all network providers, whether the network is based on Windows NT Server, Novell NetWare, another network, or Windows 95 itself.

Users can browse network resources to connect to them. For example, users on NetWare networks can see NetWare servers and printers, plus computers running File and Printer Sharing for NetWare Networks. Users on Microsoft networks can find network resources by scrolling through a list of available workgroups, a list of available computers in a given workgroup, and a list of available resources on a given computer.

For technical details about network computing with Windows 95 on Microsoft and NetWare networks, see "Browsing on Microsoft Networks" later in this chapter and "Browsing on NetWare Networks" later in this chapter.

# Using Network Neighborhood

When you use Network Neighborhood, you can access shared resources on a server without having to map a network drive. Browsing and connecting to the resource consists of a single step: clicking an icon.

For information about what happens internally when Network Neighborhood is used to browse multiple networks, see the description of the Multiple Provider Router in Chapter 32, "Windows 95 Network Architecture."

## Using Workgroups in Windows 95

On Microsoft networks, computers are logically grouped in workgroups for convenient browsing of network resources. If share-level security is used, each computer in the workgroup maintains its own security system for validating local user logon and access to local resources.

NetWare networks do not use the workgroup concept, so computers running Windows 95 with VLM or NETX clients cannot be members of workgroups. However, computers running File and Printer Sharing for NetWare Networks with Workgroup Advertising enabled can appear in workgroups.

To set the workgroup for a computer, click the Identification tab in the Network option in Control Panel and type a name.

For more information about using Network Neighborhood, see online Help.

▶ **To browse a server quickly without mapping a drive**

1. From the Start menu, click Run, and then type the server name. For example:

   `\\nwsrv1`

2. To browse any shared directory in the window that appears, double-click its icon.

3. To browse this server's workgroup, press BACKSPACE. This is the equivalent of clicking the Up One Level button on the toolbar.

▶ **To create a shortcut on the desktop to a network resource**

1. In Network Neighborhood, find the network resource for which you want to create a shortcut.

2. Using the right mouse button, drag the icon for that resource onto the desktop.

3. In the context menu, click Create Shortcut Here.

4. Double-click the shortcut icon to view the contents of the network directory in a new window. This shortcut is available every time you start Windows 95.

As the network administrator, you can use system policies to create a custom Network Neighborhood for individuals or multiple users. You can create shortcuts using UNC names for any network connections, including Dial-Up Networking connections, as part of the custom Network Neighborhood provided when using system policies. However, do not place directories in the custom Network Neighborhood. Windows 95 does not support this feature, and unpredictable results can occur. In System Policy Editor, enable the policy named Custom Network Neighborhood:

- Use Registry mode to enable this option on a local or a remote computer
- Use Policy mode to create or modify a policy file for one or more users

You can also set the following system policies to control users' access to built-in Windows 95 browsing features:

- Hide Network Neighborhood, to prevent access to Network Neighborhood
- No Entire Network In Network Neighborhood, to prevent access to the Entire Network icon in Network Neighborhood
- No Workgroup Contents In Network Neighborhood, to prevent workgroup contents from being displayed in Network Neighborhood

For more information about specific policies and about using System Policy Editor, see Chapter 15, "User Profiles and System Policies."

# Browsing in Common Dialog Boxes

The new common dialog boxes (such as File Open and File Save) are standard in programs that use the Windows 95 user interface. They provide a consistent way to open or save files on network resources and local drives. Also, you can browse Network Neighborhood and you can perform most basic file management tasks by using a common dialog box.

---

**Note**  Windows-based applications created for earlier versions of Windows do not use the new common dialog boxes.

---

In Windows 95, you can create new directories (also called folders) when you are saving a document (unlike Windows 3.1 in which you had to start File Manager or exit to the MS-DOS command prompt). This means that you can also create a new directory on a shared network resource when saving documents, as shown in the following procedure. This procedure can be used in any application that uses the Window 95 common dialog boxes.

▶ **To create a new directory on the network while saving a file**

1. In the File menu, click Save As.

2. In the Save In list, select a network location. If you need to, you can click Network Neighborhood in this list to browse for the computer on which you want to save the file.

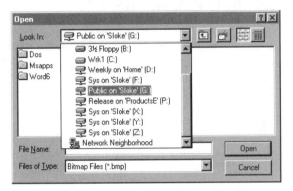

3. Click the Create New Folder icon, and type text for the new directory label.

4. In the File Name box, type a name for the file, and then click Save.

# Connecting to Drive and Printer Resources

The toolbar is available in every window and includes the Map Network Drive button. If you click this button, the Map Network Drive dialog box appears. In this dialog box, you can type the name of a network server and shared directory using the UNC name. For example, the UNC name for the server CORP and the shared directory DOCS is \\CORP\DOCS. On NetWare networks, you can also type any remote computer name understood by the network (for example, TRIKE/SYS:public).

You can make a persistent connection to any drive (that is, you can store its name and automatically reconnect to it at startup) by clicking the Reconnect At Logon check box in the Map Network Drive dialog box. Persistent connections are restored to the same drive letters each time Windows 95 is started.

You can display this dialog box by right-clicking the Network Neighborhood icon.

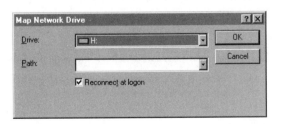

When installing a new printer, you can specify a shared printer resource by using the UNC name or the Point and Print method. For example, for the shared printer named HP_III on the server CORP, the name UNC is \\CORP\HP_III. For more information about Point and Print, see Chapter 23, "Printing and Fonts."

## Browsing with the Net View Command

Browsing network resources at the command prompt is handled by the real-mode networking components. You can use the **net view** command to perform most of the same browsing actions as Network Neighborhood or Windows Explorer, except that it cannot provide a list of workgroups.

For specific notes about using the **net** commands on NetWare networks, see "Browsing on NetWare Networks" later in this chapter.

▶ **To display a list of computers with shared resources in a workgroup**

- At the command prompt, type the following and then press ENTER.

  **net view** [\\\\*computername*]

  –Or–

  **net view** [**/workgroup:***workgroupname*]

  Where *computername* is the name of the computer with shared resources you want to view; **/workgroup** specifies that you want to view the names of the computers that share resources in another workgroup; and *workgroupname* is the name of the workgroup that has computer names you want to view.

# Browsing on Microsoft Networks

The Windows 95 browsing scheme for Microsoft networks is based on the scheme currently used for Windows NT and Windows for Workgroups. The Windows 95 browse service attempts to minimize the network traffic related to browsing activity, while also providing an implementation that scales well to support both small and large networks.

This section describes how the browse service designates browse servers and maintains the browse list.

## Designating a Browse Master for Microsoft Networks

The Windows 95 browse service uses the concept of a master browse server and a backup browse server to maintain the browse list. There is only one master browse server for a given Windows 95 workgroup for each protocol used in the workgroup; however, there can be one or more backup browse servers for each protocol for a given workgroup.

The master browse server is responsible for maintaining the master list of workgroups, domains, and computers in a given workgroup. To minimize the network traffic that the master browse server can be subjected to when handling browsing services, backup browse servers can be designated in a workgroup to help off-load some query requests. Usually, there is one browse server for every 15 computers assigned to a given workgroup.

When Windows 95 is started on a computer, the computer first checks to see if a master browse server is already present for the given workgroup. If a master browse server does not exist, an election creates a master browse server for the workgroup.

If a master browse server already exists, Windows 95 checks the number of computers in the workgroup, and the number of browse servers present. If the number of computers in the workgroup exceeds the defined ratio of browse servers to computers in a workgroup, an additional computer in the workgroup might become a backup browse server.

The Browse Master parameter in the Advanced properties for File and Printer Sharing for Microsoft Networks provides a mechanism for controlling which computers can become browse servers in a workgroup. If this parameter is set to Automatic, the master browse server can designate that computer as a backup browse server when needed, or that computer can be elected as master browse server. For information about configuring this parameter, see "Using File and Printer Sharing for Microsoft Networks" later in this chapter.

### Tip for Using the Net View Command to Check the Browse Server

The **net view** command is a valuable troubleshooting tool if you suspect the browse list maintained by a browse server is incomplete or inaccurate. You can use **net view /workgroup**: *workgroupname* at the command prompt to get the list of known computers directly from the master browse server. The request is not handled by a backup browse server.

If the list of computers returned by a master browse server is inaccurate, you could reset this computer by quitting Windows 95. Another computer will then be promoted to master browse server for the workgroup.

# Building the Browse List for Microsoft Networks

In Windows 95, the browse service maintains an up-to-date list of domains, workgroups, and computers, and provides this list to applications when requested. The user sees the list in the following types of circumstances:

- If a user requests a list of computers in a workgroup, the browse service on the local computer randomly chooses one of the browse servers it is aware of and sends the request.

- If a user selects a workgroup to which the computer does not belong, Windows 95 requests a list of computers defined in the selected workgroup from a browse server in the selected workgroup.

The selected browse server also sends a list of the other workgroups it knows about that are defined on the network, along with a list of computers in the workgroup to which the user belongs.

The browse list is displayed in the Map Network Drive and Connect Network Printer dialog boxes, or anywhere that Windows 95 presents lists of resources that can be browsed. The browse list can also be displayed by using the **net view** command. The list can contain the names of domains, workgroups, and computers running the File and Printer Sharing service, including the following:

- Computers running Windows 95, Windows for Workgroups, and Windows NT Workstation

- Windows NT Server domains and servers

- Workgroups defined in Windows 95, Windows for Workgroups, and Windows NT

- Workgroup Add-on for MS-DOS peer servers

- LAN Manager 2.x domains and servers

## Adding New Computers to the Browse List

When a computer running Windows 95 is started on the network, it announces itself to the master browse server for its workgroup, and the master browse server adds that computer to the list of available computers in the workgroup. The master browse server then notifies backup browse servers that a change to the browse list is available. The backup browse servers then request the new information to update their local browse lists. It might take as long as 15 minutes before a backup browse server receives an updated browse list, and new computers on the network do not show up in a user's request for a browse list until then.

## Removing Computers from the Browse List

When a user shuts down a computer properly, the operating system informs the master browse server that it is shutting down. The master browse server then notifies backup browse servers that a change to the browse list is available. The backup browse servers then request the changes to the browse list.

If a user turns off the computer without shutting down, the computer does not get a chance to send the message to the master browse server. In this case, the computer name might continue to appear in the browse list until the name entry times out, which can take up to 45 minutes.

# Technical Notes on Browsing on Microsoft Networks

This section presents some brief notes related to browsing on Microsoft networks.

- The Windows 95 browser has been updated to support browsing across TCP/IP subnetworks. To take advantage of this, the network must use a WINS server or you must use #DOM entries in LMHOSTS files for name resolution.

- Microsoft LAN Manager-compatible networks such as Microsoft LAN Manager for UNIX® and IBM® LAN Server support browsing of servers and shared directories using the Windows 95 user interface or **net view**.

- DEC™ PATHWORKS™ is an example of a Microsoft LAN Manager-compatible network that does not support browsing. AT&T® StarLAN is an example of a Microsoft Network-compatible network that is not based on Microsoft LAN Manager and that does not support remote browsing of servers and shared directories. These servers do not appear in Network Neighborhood; with Windows 95, however, users can still access the servers and shared directories through a network connection dialog box.

- When a known slow network connection is used (for example, the remote access driver), Windows 95 is automatically configured not to designate that computer to be a browse server for the network connection. The **SlowLanas** parameter in the Registry identifies the network LANA numbers for which the local computer will not serve as a master browse server. However, the user can still request a list of available workgroups and computers on the network across the slow network connection.

# Browsing on NetWare Networks

The Windows 95 user interface includes support for browsing and connecting to network resources on Novell NetWare and other networks. Except for workgroups, this support is the same whether you use Client for NetWare Networks or the Novell-supplied NETX or VLM client. After you connect to a NetWare volume or a computer running File and Printer Sharing for NetWare Networks, you can drag and drop directories and files to move and copy them between your computer and the NetWare server.

For information about printer connections, see Chapter 23, "Printing and Fonts."

# Using Network Neighborhood on NetWare Networks

Network Neighborhood is the primary way you can browse the network. When you open Network Neighborhood on a computer running a NetWare-compatible networking client, all the NetWare bindery-based servers your computer is connected to are displayed. All computers running File and Printer Sharing for NetWare Networks that use Workgroup Advertising also appear in Network Neighborhood.

Clicking the Entire Network icon displays a list of all NetWare servers on the network. This list also contains a list of workgroups that include computers running File and Printer Sharing for NetWare Networks. You can view the contents of any server without having to map a network drive.

If your computer has both Client for Microsoft Networks and Client for NetWare Networks installed, then you will also see a list of computers running Windows for Workgroups, Windows 95, and Windows NT. The list of NetWare servers is at the beginning of the list of workgroups or domains in the Entire Network window.

In both the Network Neighborhood and Entire Network views, you can open a server to access its contents without having to map a network drive. You will be asked for security information, if necessary, and you can choose to save your password in the password cache so that you will not have to type it again.

If the computer is running Client for NetWare Networks, drive mappings are limited to the available drive letters. However, Windows 95 supports unlimited UNC connections. (If the computer is running NETX or VLM, it is limited to only eight server connections.)

▶ **To connect to a NetWare server in Network Neighborhood**

1. In Network Neighborhood, right-click a NetWare server.

2. In the context menu, click Attach As. Then type a user name and password, and click OK.

3. If you want to map a directory on this server, double-click the server icon. Right-click the directory you want to map, and click Map Network Drive in the context menu. Fill in the Map Network Drive dialog box, and click OK.

---

**Tip**   You can also create a shortcut to frequently used resources. For information, see "Using Network Neighborhood" earlier in this chapter. When you double-click a shortcut, you have to supply only a password to connect to it.

---

The toolbar on every window includes the Map Network Drive button, which you can use to specify the name of a NetWare server and volume (or directory) that you want to map to a drive letter.

▶ **To connect to a directory as the root of the drive**

1. In Network Neighborhood, right-click a directory on a NetWare server. In the context menu, click Map Network Drive.

2. In the Map Network Drive dialog box, make sure Connect As Root Of The Drive is checked, and then click OK.

With this option enabled, if you switch to this mapped directory in a VM window, you will see the prompt as *drive*:\> not *drive*:\*directory*>). You cannot go further up the directory tree from the command prompt.

The context menu for a NetWare server shows everything you can do with the related server, volume, or directory. To view the context menu, in Network Neighborhood, right-click a NetWare server.

The following table describes the commands available on the context menu.

| Command | Description |
| --- | --- |
| Open | Connects to that server. |
| Explore | Shows the resources available on that server without making a connection. |
| Who Am I | Specifies whether the user is logged on or attached to the server; if a user is logged on and the computer is attached, specifies that user's name. |
| Log Out | Logs the user off the server. |
| Attach As | Presents a dialog box for typing a password to log on to the server. This dialog box allows the user to connect to the server by using a different user name from the one used to log on to the network. |
| Map Network Drive | Presents a dialog box for mapping a network drive to a drive letter. |
| Create Shortcut | Creates a shortcut on the desktop for the selected server. |
| Properties | Shows the properties for the server. Notice that listing the properties of a NetWare server creates an attachment without logging on, thereby using up one of the allowable connections. |

If a computer running File and Printer Sharing for NetWare Networks has been configured to allow remote administration, and if you have the authority to administer that server, you can use the administration options in the computer's properties. To do this, in Network Neighborhood, right-click the computer's icon. In the context menu, click Properties, and then click the Tools tab. Use the buttons to run Net Watcher or System Monitor, or to administer the file system.

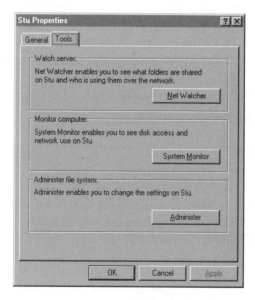

For more information about preparing computers for remote administration under Windows 95, and about using Net Watcher and other tools, see Chapter 16, "Remote Administration."

# Managing Connections with Client for NetWare Networks

Client for NetWare Networks is different from NETX and VLM in that it does not map the first network drive to the logon directory of the preferred server. All subsequent connections to NetWare servers must be made in the Windows 95 user interface.

With Client for NetWare Networks, you can manage connections to the NetWare network by using Network Neighborhood and common network-connection dialog boxes such as the Open and Save dialog boxes. (These are the same techniques used for Microsoft networks.)

With Client for NetWare Networks, you can define persistent connections (which use the same drive letter each time the computer starts) to NetWare volumes and directories. Using persistent connections eliminates the need for NetWare MAP commands in login scripts; however, you can still use MAP, ATTACH, and other commands at the command prompt or in login scripts, as described in the following section.

# Using Commands to Connect to NetWare Servers

If you are running Client for NetWare Networks, all NetWare commands run in the same way as they do for a Novell-supplied networking client. The ATTACH and SLIST commands provided with Windows 95 use the same syntax and work in exactly the same way as the counterparts provided by Novell.

The following should be noted about certain Novell-supplied commands:

- For the ATTACH command, configure the networking client to use SAP Browsing.

- It is recommended that you do not use the LOGIN utility to create an attachment to a computer running File and Printer Sharing for NetWare Networks. Use the ATTACH command instead.

- For the MAP command, drive mappings in Windows 95 are global to all sessions.

You can also use the Microsoft networking **net** commands at the command prompt or in login scripts to manage connections on NetWare networks. For example, the **net use** command can be used to do the following:

- Perform the same functions as the NetWare ATTACH and MAP commands.
- Supply similar functionality to the CAPTURE utility for printing when programs require printing to a specific port.

You can use the Windows 95 **net view** command to perform the same function as the NETX SLIST or VLM NLIST SERVER commands.

The following brief procedures show built-in Windows 95 commands that can be used at the command prompt or in scripts to manage resource connections.

▶ **To view NetWare servers**

- At the command prompt or in a login script, type **net view**

For example:

```
D:\WIN\COMMAND>net view
NetWare Servers
-----------------------------
\\386
\\TRIKE
\\WRK
```

▶ **To view volumes on a server**

- At the command prompt or in a login script, type **net view \\**_servername_

For example:

```
D:\WIN\COMMAND>net view \\trike

Shared resources at \\trike
Sharename    Type        Comment
-----------------------------------
SYS          Disk
PUBLIC       Disk
```

The **net view** command creates an attachment without logging on. Viewing a NetWare server or a computer running File and Printer Sharing for NetWare Networks does not show print queues. However, viewing a computer running File and Printer Sharing for Microsoft Networks shows both shared directories and shared printers.

Use the **/network** parameter to specify the volumes on the particular network you want to view. For example:

**net view \\**_nwserver_name_ **/network:nw**

▶ **To create a drive connection**

- At the command prompt or in a login script, type **net use** *drive*:
  \\*servername*\*volume*

  For example:

  ```
  D:\WIN\COMMAND>net use l: \\trike\sys
  The password is invalid for \\TRIKE\SYS.
  Enter user name for server TRIKE:joed
  Enter the password for user JoeD on server TRIKE:
  ```

The **net use** command is equivalent to MAP *drive*:=*servername\volume*: and it maps only to the root of the volume.

---

**Tip**  To use the next available drive letter when connecting to the volume, replace the drive letter with an asterisk (*).

---

By typing the **net use** command without parameters, you can list the current network connections. For example:

```
Status   Local   Remote                   Network
------   -----   ------                   -------
  −       E:      \\NW4\SYS                 NetWare
 OK       F:      \\WINDOWS\DROOT           Microsoft
  −       H:      \\NETWARE40\THOR\APPS     NetWare
```

▶ **To delete a drive connection**

- At the command prompt or in a login script, type **net use** *drive*: **/d**

  For example:

  ```
  D:\WIN\COMMAND>net use l: /d
  ```

The **/d** switch and the NetWare command MAP DEL *drive* are equivalent.

▶ **To create a print connection**

- At the command prompt or in a login script, type **net use** *port:*
  \\*servername*\*queuename*

  For example:

  ```
  D:\WIN\COMMAND>net use lpt3: \\trike\pscript1
  ```

This is equivalent to CAPTURE l=*port* S=*servername* Q=*queuename*.

▶ **To delete a print connection**

- At the command prompt or in a login script, type **net use** *port*: **/d**

  For example:

  ```
  D:\WIN\COMMAND>net use lpt3: /d
  ```

This is equivalent to ENDCAP L=*port#*.

The **net** command in Windows 95 does not support the following:

- The functionality of the NetWare MAP ROOT command or search drive mappings.

- Any of the command-line options of the CAPTURE command, except the equivalents for specifying port, server name, and queue name. To use specific CAPTURE options, use the Novell CAPTURE command.

- The functionality of the Novell NetWare print job designations (the J=*jobname* parameter for the CAPTURE command).

**Note**  You can still use the NetWare commands SLIST instead of **net view**, MAP instead of **net use**, or CAPTURE instead of **net use** to connect to a printer.

# Using Windows NT to Connect to NetWare Servers

If your site includes both a Novell NetWare network and a Windows NT Server network, computers using Microsoft networking will need to communicate and share resources with the NetWare network. This section summarizes several options using Windows NT.

**Windows NT Gateway Service for NetWare.**  For Microsoft networking clients that cannot use multiple protocols, you can configure a computer running Windows NT Server 3.5 as a file or print gateway using Windows NT Gateway Service for NetWare to connect to and share NetWare resources. Notice that a Microsoft Windows NT Client Access License is required if the computer will be connecting to servers running Windows NT Server. For information, contact your Microsoft reseller.

As shown in the following illustration, Windows NT Gateway Service for NetWare acts as a translator between the SMB protocol used by Microsoft networks and the NCP protocol used on NetWare networks.

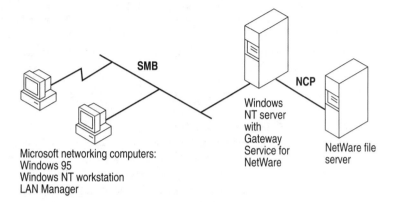

The file gateway uses a NetWare account on the Windows NT Server computer to create a validated connection to the NetWare server, which then appears on the Windows NT Server computer as a redirected drive. When the administrator shares the redirected drive, it looks similar to any other shared resource on the Windows NT Server computer. A print gateway functions in much the same way as the file gateway: the NetWare printer appears on the Windows NT network as if it were any other shared printer.

Because access over the gateway is slower than direct access from the client for computers running Windows 95 that require frequent access to NetWare resources, Client for NetWare Networks is a better solution. For information about setting up a Windows NT Server computer with Gateway Service for NetWare, see *Windows NT Server Services for NetWare Networks* in the Windows NT Server 3.5 documentation set.

**Microsoft File and Print Services for NetWare.**  This utility for Windows NT Server provides users running a NetWare-compatible client with access to basic NetWare file and print services and to powerful server applications on the same Windows NT Server-based computer. You can use Microsoft File and Print Services for NetWare to add a multipurpose file, print, and application server to your NetWare network without changing users' network client software.

**Microsoft Directory Service Manager for NetWare.**  This utility for Windows NT Server allows you to maintain a single directory for managing mixed Windows NT Server and NetWare 2.x and 3.x server networks.

For more information about these features or how to obtain Microsoft File and Print Services for NetWare, or the Microsoft Directory Service Manager for NetWare, contact your Microsoft sales representative.

# Overview of Peer Resource Sharing

When a computer is running File and Printer Sharing services, other users running a compatible network client can connect to shared printers, volumes, CD-ROM drives, and directories on that computer by using the standard techniques for connecting the network resources, as described in "Browsing on NetWare Networks" earlier in this chapter and "Browsing on Microsoft Networks" earlier in this chapter.

Using computers running Windows 95 as peer servers allows you to add secure storage space and printing to the network at a low cost. The peer service is based on a 32-bit, protected-mode architecture, which means all the Windows 95 benefits for robust, high performance are available. In addition, administrators can take advantage of features provided with Windows 95, such as Net Watcher and system policies, to centrally administer peer servers. In addition, user-level security is available as an additional enhancement beyond the peer server capabilities built into Windows for Workgroups.

---

**Tip**  Using Net Watcher, a network administrator can remotely monitor and manage files on any computer running File and Printer Sharing services if remote administration has been enabled for that computer. Net Watcher allows an administrator to disconnect users, change access rights, and administer the file system on remote computers. For more information, see Chapter 16, "Remote Administration."

---

# Installing Peer Resource Sharing

If you use custom setup scripts or choose the Custom option as the setup type in Windows 95 Setup, you can specify that File and Printer Sharing services be installed with Windows 95. Otherwise, you can add the service later by using the Network option in Control Panel.

---

**Tip**  For a computer that will share resources with other users on the networks, choose which File and Printer Sharing service to install based on what other users require:

- If most users who need to share these resources are running NETX, VLM, or Client for NetWare Networks, then install File and Printer Sharing for NetWare Networks.

- If most users who need to share these resources are running Client for Microsoft Networks, Windows NT, Windows for Workgroups, or Workgroup Add-on for MS-DOS, then install File and Printer Sharing for Microsoft Networks.

---

▶ **To install File and Printer Sharing after Setup**

1. In the Network option in Control Panel, click Add.

2. In the Select Network Component Type dialog box, double-click Service.

3. In the Select Network Service dialog box, click Microsoft in the Manufacturers list. Then, in the Network Service list, click the File and Printer Sharing service you want to install.

For information about enabling File and Printer Sharing in custom setup scripts, see Chapter 5, "Custom, Automated, and Push Installations." For information about controlling peer resource sharing capabilities using system policies, see Chapter 15, "User Profiles and System Policies."

# Overview of Security for Peer Resource Sharing

For File and Printer Sharing for Microsoft Networks (but not NetWare), Windows 95 supports share-level security similar to the security provided with Windows for Workgroups. This level of security associates a password with a shared disk directory or printer. Share-level security for peer resource sharing can be implemented in a Windows 95-only peer-to-peer network or on a network supported by Windows NT or other Microsoft Windows network-compatible servers.

For File and Printer Sharing services on both Windows NT and NetWare networks, Windows 95 supports user-level security by linking a peer server directly to another server for user account validation. For network administrators, the user account list is centrally controlled at the Windows NT domain controller or NetWare server; on a Windows NT network, the user account list on a single server can also be used for validation. The resources on the Windows 95 peer server can be accessed only by users with accounts in the central database. Users can also be assigned specified access rights in Windows 95 for particular resources. For information about using and managing security, see Chapter 14, "Security."

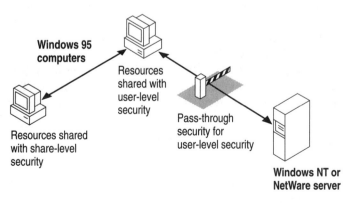

The 32-bit, protected mode network client and the File and Printer Sharing service are separate network processes, but they share connection information and pass requests to each other when validating a user-level security request.

For user-level security on a computer running either version of File and Printer Sharing service, you specify the server that contains the database of user accounts that are allowed to connect to this peer resource sharing server. You can do the following to customize access to a shared resource:

- You can use the Windows 95 user interface to specify which users can access the shared resources, and which rights they have. For details, see "Controlling Access to Peer Server Resources on NetWare Networks" later in this chapter.

- For File and Printer Sharing on NetWare Networks, you can set up user rights remotely on the computer running Windows 95 by using NetWare utilities such as FILER.

- For File and Printer Sharing on Microsoft Networks, you can set up user rights remotely by using User Manager for Windows NT.

- You can use Net Watcher to monitor, add, and remove shared resources, as described in Chapter 16, "Remote Administration."

When a user requests access to a shared resource under user-level security, Windows 95 checks for the user's logon name against the list of user accounts maintained on the server. If this is a valid user logon name, Windows 95 then checks whether this user has access privileges for this resource. If the user has access privileges, then the requested operation is allowed.

For an example of how pass-through validation works with peer resource sharing, see Chapter 14, "Security."

# Using File and Printer Sharing for Microsoft Networks

File and Printer Sharing for Microsoft Networks is the 32-bit, protected-mode Windows 95 SMB server (VSERVER.VXD) that supports all Microsoft networking products that use the SMB file-sharing protocol, including Windows for Workgroups, Windows NT, LAN Manager, LAN Manager for UNIX, AT&T StarLAN, IBM LAN Server, 3Com® 3+Open® and 3+Share®, and DEC PATHWORKS. Windows 95 enhances the features of Windows for Workgroups peer services by providing administrative control over whether peer sharing services are enabled, by adding user-based security capabilities, and by supporting long filenames.

The following summarizes some requirements for File and Printer Sharing for Microsoft Networks:

- The computer must use Client for Microsoft Networks.
- File and Printer Sharing for Microsoft Networks cannot run at the same time as NCP-based File and Printer Sharing for NetWare Networks.
- If user-level security is used, a Windows NT domain controller must be used for authentication.

The default settings for File and Printer Sharing are correct for most installations. You should need to change these settings in the following circumstances only:

- If you need to set Browse Master properties, as described in "Browsing on Microsoft Networks" earlier in this chapter.
- If you want LAN Manager 2.x clients on your network to use resources on a computer running File and Printer Sharing for Microsoft Networks.

Use the Network option in Control Panel to configure the Browse Master and LM Announce parameters for the File and Printer Sharing service. For information about configuring security in Access Control properties, see Chapter 14, "Security."

▶ **To specify Browse Master settings**

1. In the Network option in Control Panel, double-click File and Printer Sharing for Microsoft Networks in the list of installed components.

2. In Advanced properties for File and Printer Sharing for Microsoft Networks, select Browse Master in the Property list.

3. Select an option in the Value list, as described in the following table.

| Option | Description |
|---|---|
| Automatic | Specifies that this computer will maintain the browse list if Windows 95 determines that it is necessary. This is the default. |
| Yes | Specifies that this computer is to be used to maintain the browse list for computers in this workgroup. |
| No | Specifies that this computer is never used to maintain the browse list. Use this setting if the computer has little free memory or is connected by a slow link (such as a dial-up connection), or if other conditions create special performance problems. |

At least one computer in the workgroup must have the value of Automatic or Yes for this parameter to ensure the browse list is available to network computers. This parameter is equivalent to the **MaintainServerList=** entry in the [network] section of SYSTEM.INI in Windows for Workgroups 3.11.

The LM Announce property controls whether a computer running File and Printer Sharing for Microsoft Networks can be seen by LAN Manager 2.x clients.

▶ **To specify LM Announce settings**

1. In Advanced properties for File and Printer Sharing for Microsoft Networks, select LM Announce in the Properties list.

2. Select an option in the Value list, as described in the following table.

| Option | Meaning |
| --- | --- |
| Yes | Specifies that you want this computer to announce its presence to other Microsoft networking computers in the workgroup, because there is a LAN Manager 2.x domain on the network. This value must be set to Yes if other computers in your workgroup need to see this computer when browsing the network. |
| No | Specifies that you do not want this computer to broadcast its presence to other computers. Setting this value to No minimizes the level of network traffic. Other users can still connect to this computer by specifying its UNC name in a Map Network Drive dialog box, but the computer will not appear in browse lists. |

This parameter is the equivalent of the **LMAnnounce=** entry in the [Network] section of SYSTEM.INI in Windows for Workgroups 3.11. This value should be No unless there is a LAN Manager 2.x domain on your network.

A LAN Manager 2.x domain is known by browse servers in a workgroup only if at least one computer running Windows 95 (or Windows NT in the domain) is a member of that LAN Manager 2.x domain.

▶ **To make a computer running Windows 95 a member of a LAN Manager 2.x domain**

- Set the workgroup name for the computer to be the same as the LAN Manager 2.x domain name.

You can share a directory (or other resource) by selecting it in Windows Explorer or in My Computer and then configuring the related options. The following procedure describes how to share a directory on a computer where user-level security has been specified in the Network option in Control Panel. The steps for sharing resources with share-level security are similar to those for user-level security except that you do not select specific users. Rather, specify the type of access and define a password for the shared resource.

▶ **To share a directory (folder) with user-level security**

1. In Windows Explorer, right-click the icon for the directory you want to share. In the context menu that appears, click Sharing.

2. Click the Sharing tab, and then type a share name for the directory.

---

**Tip**  If you add a dollar sign ($) to the end of the share name, the resource will not appear in Network Neighborhood or elsewhere when people browse network resources.

---

3. Click the Add button, and use the Add Users dialog box to specify which users can access the directory.

For more information about sharing folders on a Microsoft network, see online Help.

# Using File and Printer Sharing for NetWare Networks

If you want to use File and Printer Sharing for NetWare Networks:

- The computer must use Client for NetWare Networks, rather than Novell-supplied client software.

- Only user-level security (not share-level security) is available.

- The service cannot run on the same computer as SMB-based File and Printer Sharing for Microsoft Networks.

- For pass-through validation when user-level security is enabled, there must be a Windows_Passthru account (with no password) on the NetWare server that is used as the security provider.

A computer configured with File and Printer Sharing for NetWare Networks uses the NCP file-sharing protocol to share resources with MS-DOS–based Novell NetWare computers, computers running Windows NT, and computers that have Client for NetWare Networks installed.

File and Printer Sharing for NetWare Networks supports long filenames and is Plug and Play-aware. This new implementation differs from peer resource sharing in Windows for Workgroups in two fundamental ways:

- File and Printer Sharing for NetWare Networks uses the NCP protocol instead of the SMB protocol. This means that any NetWare-compatible client (Client for NetWare Networks, NETX, or VLM) can connect to a computer running File and Printer Sharing for NetWare Networks.

- File and Printer Sharing for NetWare Networks uses user-level security. Access to a shared resource is based on the user's identity instead of on a password associated with that resource. The user database for verifying user identity is the bindery on a specified NetWare server.

This feature means that hundreds of NetWare users can, for example, access a shared CD-ROM using a single NetWare server connection. Also, trustee or other access rights can be defined per-directory for a shared CD-ROM.

When File and Printer Sharing for NetWare Networks is running on a computer, how that peer server appears to users browsing the network depends on how the peer server advertises itself:

- For another computer running Microsoft Client for NetWare Networks, the resources on the peer server appear exactly as any shared resources on the network. If the peer server is using Workgroup Advertising, it appears in a workgroup. A peer server using Service Advertising Protocol (SAP, the NetWare broadcasting protocol) Advertising will not appear in a workgroup, but it will appear in the Entire Network list.

- For a computer running NETX or VLM, any shared directories on a peer server that uses SAP advertising appear the same as volumes on any server. Any shared printers will appear as print queues. Most NetWare administrative commands work as expected, including RIGHTS, FILER, SYSCON, MAP, SLIST, VOLINFO, PCONSOLE, and CAPTURE. If the peer server is not using SAP Advertising, then users running NETX or VLM cannot see or connect to the peer server when browsing the network.

### Sharing Resources on a NetWare Network: An Example

During the beta test phase for Windows 95, one NetWare system administrator found the peer resource sharing service to be an administrative lifesaver. A vice president at the company had CD-ROM hardware problems just when he needed immediate access to a tax program that was available only on compact disc.

The quick-thinking administrator installed File and Printer Sharing for NetWare Networks on a computer that had a CD-ROM drive. After making sure the vice president was assigned access rights, the administrator mapped a drive on the vice president's computer to access the shared CD-ROM.

The Windows 95 peer resource sharing service allowed the administrator to provide an immediate software solution to a hardware problem that would have taken much longer to solve.

# Sharing Resources on a NetWare Network

To allow NETX and VLM clients on the network to access resources on the peer server, you must enable SAP Browsing in the properties for File and Print Sharing for NetWare Networks. The computer then appears as a server in SLIST listings, and users can map drives to connect to this computer. To see a list of volumes, users can use the VOLINFO command.

---

**Note**  Administrative control over File and Printer Sharing for NetWare Networks is coupled with the printer sharing control—the option controlling the user's ability to share a local printer. If these sharing options are not selected in the Network option in Control Panel, then the File and Printer Sharing service is not loaded. However, if the administrator disables printer sharing or file sharing by setting the related option in a system policy file, then the File and Printer Sharing service still runs on the computer, but the related sharing options are not available.

---

## Configuring Browsing for Resource Sharing on NetWare Networks

After you install File and Printer Sharing for NetWare Networks, you need to choose the method that computers browsing on the network will use to find this computer. You can browse by using two options:

- Workgroup Advertising, which uses the same broadcast method as used by workgroups on Microsoft networks.
- SAP Advertising, which is used by Novell NetWare 2.15 and above, 3.x, and 4.x servers to advertise their presence on the network. You must enable this option if you want the shared resources to be available to computers running NETX or VLM.

---

**Note**  SAP browsing has a theoretical limit of 7000 systems for browsing, and a practical limit of about 1500 systems. For a large peer network, use Workgroup Advertising.

---

For a general discussion of browsing when using NetWare-compatible clients, see "Browsing on NetWare Networks" earlier in this chapter.

▶ **To specify the browsing preference**

1. In the Network option in Control Panel, double-click File and Printer Sharing for NetWare Networks in the list of installed components.

2. In Advanced properties, select Workgroup Advertising to define how you want computers running Client for NetWare Networks to see and connect to this peer server.

   –Or–

   Select SAP Advertising if you want NETX and VLM clients to be able to connect to this peer server.

   If you select Workgroup Advertising, you can set the following values.

| Value | Description |
|---|---|
| Disabled | This computer will not be added to the browse list, and it cannot be seen by other members of the workgroup by using any method for browsing network resources. |
| Enabled: May Be Master | This computer is added to the browse list and can be promoted to master browse server if the preferred master is not available. |
| Enabled: Preferred Master | This computer is the master browse server for the workgroup. |
| Enabled: Will Not Be Master | This computer is added to the browse list by the master browse server, but it cannot be promoted to master browse server. |

For more information about master browse server options, see "Building the Browse List for Microsoft Networks" earlier in this chapter.

---

**Note**  If Workgroup Advertising is used, each workgroup must have a master browse server at all times to track names and addresses for computers in the workgroup.

---

If you select SAP Advertising, you can set the following values.

| Value | Description |
|---|---|
| Disabled | This computer will not advertise its presence, and NETX or VLM clients cannot see it by using SLIST or other browsing options, and cannot connect to it. Users running Client for NetWare Networks can see it if Workgroup Advertising is enabled on the peer server. |
| Enabled | This computer will advertise its presence. It will appear in the Entire Network list. Users running VLM, NETX, and Client for NetWare Networks can see it by using any browsing methods, and they can connect to it as they do for any server. |

By default, computers running File and Printer Sharing for NetWare Networks are placed in and browsed by workgroups. You can use the Identification properties in the Network option in Control Panel to specify the workgroup and computer name for the computer.

Although computers that use SAP advertising appear in the list of NetWare servers, you cannot use them in all the same ways that you use NetWare servers.

- When using NETX, you cannot log on to a computer running Windows 95 at the command line, although you can attach to one and map drives to its directories.

- When using VLM, you cannot log on to a computer running Windows 95 at the command line, but you can run a **login /ns** command and use the Login button in the NWUSER utility.

- If you run SYSCON on a NetWare server, you can change the server to one of the computers running Windows 95. However, the computer running Windows 95 does not have a bindery, so when you display all the users (or groups) in SYSCON, you will see the user list (or group list) from the NetWare server that was selected as the user-level security provider.

- If you run VOLINFO on a NetWare server, you can select one of the computers running Windows 95 and display its volume information (if you are attached to it). This shows all the available shared disk resources for the computer running Windows 95.

In Windows 95, you can do the same things to resources on computers running File and Printer Sharing for NetWare Networks as you can to any other network resource. If you have appropriate rights to connect to the shared resources, you can also create a link to the computer or map a drive to its shared directories, and so on.

---

**Note**   Each computer configured with File and Printer Sharing for NetWare Networks logs on to the NetWare server that provides security, to get access to the bindery, using the Windows_Passthru account. This logon process takes place in the background, without user intervention. One connection to that NetWare server is used as needed for each computer running File and Printer Sharing for NetWare Networks, and it is disconnected if it is not needed for 30 seconds.

If a connection already exists, Windows 95 uses that connection and makes a new connection only when required.

---

# Controlling Access to Peer Server Resources on NetWare Networks

You can add to the list of users who can access the resources on the peer server. To do this, add the users to the NetWare pass-through server that provides security. These users can then be given access to the peer server by adding them to the Sharing properties associated with the shared resource.

Passwords for users' resources on the peer server are the same as those for the NetWare pass-through server. Passwords must be changed at that server, as described in "Unified System Logon Basics" earlier in this chapter.

▶ **To make sure all users have the required server access**

- Make sure that one NetWare server on the network has the accounts for all users or all servers, and then set that server as the security provider for every computer configured with File and Printer Sharing for NetWare Networks.

  If server access is not set properly, each time the computer running Windows 95 is started a message warns that the pass-through server has not been specified.

▶ **To share a directory and specify users on a NetWare network**

1. In Windows Explorer, right-click the directory you want to share. In the context menu, click Sharing.

2. In the Sharing dialog box, type a share name for the directory.

3. Click the Add button. In the Add Users dialog box, select the user name in the list on the left, and then click the related button to specify the kind of access that user is allowed.

   For more information about using the Add Users dialog box, see online Help. For more information about specifying directory access rights, see Chapter 14, "Security."

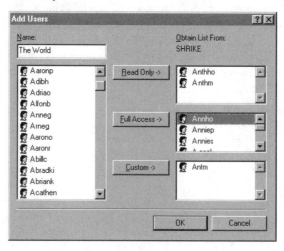

Notice in the illustration that the list of users shown in the Add Users dialog box is from the TRIKE server's bindery. This means two things:

- All user management is done in the name space of the existing NetWare server. The NetWare server is administered by using all the same tools that are currently in place; Windows 95 has not added another name space to administer.
- Only valid user accounts and groups on TRIKE can be specified for shared resources on the peer server.

When the computer running Windows 95 receives a request from a user attempting to access a shared device, Windows 95 uses the NetWare server to validate the user name or group membership. If the name or group membership is validated, then Windows 95 checks to see if this validated name or group has been granted access rights to the shared resource, and then it grants or denies the connection request.

## Share Names vs. NetWare Volume Names

When you share resources on a local hard disk drive using File and Printer Sharing for NetWare Networks, the share name associated with the shared directory structure becomes a volume name in the Novell designation *server/volume:* or the UNC designation \\\\*server*\\*volume*.

You can use the UNC designation with **net** commands to connect to and disconnect from either Microsoft networking \\\\*server*\\*sharename* shares or NetWare *server/volume* shares.

Windows 95 does not make this distinction between shares and volumes because all shares and volumes appear as directories (also called folders). This distinction becomes important when you use NETX or VLM and NetWare utilities. NetWare does not use or understand the concept of share names. NetWare uses volumes for drive resources and print queue names for print resources.

Therefore, for a shared drive or printer resource to be available to all the different types of clients, when a computer configured with File and Printer Sharing for NetWare Networks shares a drive resource, the share name becomes equivalent to a NetWare volume. When this same computer shares a printer resource, the share name becomes equivalent to the NetWare print queue.

```
DIRECTORY SHARE NAME ---->   VOLUME
PRINTER SHARE NAME ------>   PRINT QUEUE
```

# Using Bindery Emulation for Pass-Through Security

File and Printer Sharing for NetWare Networks grants access to printers and directories on a per-user basis, which requires the name of the server to retrieve the names of users on a network. For NetWare versions 2.15 and 3.x servers, all the information for users, groups, passwords, and rights is stored in a database on the server called the bindery. NetWare version 4.x servers can appear to have a bindery using bindery emulation, which is enabled by default. Windows 95 can use the bindery of one NetWare server.

Usually, companies have multiple NetWare servers for different departments, and individual users log on to a different server by department. Problems can occur when the list of accounts differs between NetWare servers. For example, assume that AnnieP and YusufM log on to the SALES server, and KrisI is on the R&D server. AnnieP can select only one server for pass-through validation, so she must select the SALES server, because that's where this account is located for logon. She can grant access to YusufM, but not to KrisI.

# Troubleshooting for Logon, Browsing, and Peer Resource Sharing

This section provides some general methods for troubleshooting.

### Setup doesn't run the login script.

If the network logon server or domain controller is not validating the user account, the login script will not run. Check the following:

- The network connection
- The user name
- The user password
- The basic network functionality
- The domain or server logon validation

If the network logon server or domain controller is validating the user account, do the following:

- Check the network connection.
- Verify that the login script is present in the home directory (on a Windows NT network) or in the user's mail directory (on a NetWare network).
- Check for enough memory on the client computer.
- Check for and remove unnecessary drivers and TSRs, and then try to log on again.

**You cannot browse to find SMB-based servers in the workgroup while using Client for Microsoft Networks.**

There might be no SMB-based servers in the workgroup (computers running Windows NT, LAN Manager, or File and Printer Sharing for Microsoft Networks). Windows 95 does not support browsing in a workgroup that does not contain an SMB-based server if the computer is running Client for Microsoft Networks. The following presents a solution.

▶ **To make sure there is an SMB-based server in the workgroup**

- On a computer running File and Printer Sharing for Microsoft Networks, make sure the service is configured as the master browser server.

  –Or–

  Make sure that a Windows NT server computer is a member of the workgroup (or domain).

**Access to an NCP-based server changes if SAP Advertising is defined.**

Where you access an NCP-based peer resource server in Network Neighborhood can change, depending on whether the server is configured for Workgroup Advertising or SAP Advertising.

- If the computer running File and Printer Sharing for NetWare Networks is configured for Workgroup Advertising, that peer server appears as a computer in its workgroup.

- If the File and Printer Sharing server is configured for SAP Advertising, it appears with the other Novell NetWare servers at the beginning of the list of workgroups in the Entire Network window of Network Neighborhood.

To set SAP Advertising or Workgroup Advertising, follow the procedures in "Configuring Browsing for Resource Sharing on NetWare Networks" earlier in this chapter.

**User cannot connect to any network resource.**

- Check the workgroup assignment.

- Check the domain or preferred server assignment for the protected-mode network client.

- Check the rights for the user as defined on the domain or preferred server.

- Check the basic network operations.

- Use **net view** \\*computer name* to view shared resources.

- Check for the termination of the local network cable.

### Others cannot connect to my shared resources.

- In the Network option in Control Panel, verify that the File and Print Sharing service appears in the list of installed components.

- Make sure other users are running a common protocol.

### Network Neighborhood doesn't show servers.

- Verify that at least one active server is on the local network.

- Verify that the proper network clients are installed and, if necessary, reinstall them.

- Verify that the user is logged on to the particular network.

- Check the network protocol settings.

- Check that the IPX Frame Type is set to Auto or to the same type as the server.

- Check the network cable termination.

### You can't connect to a specific server.

- Check error message details, if available.

- Verify that you can connect to any server.

- Verify that you can connect to a specific server from other computers. If you cannot connect to the specific server from other systems, it probably indicates a problem with that server or the cabling or routing to it. Also verify termination of the local network cable.

### The network redirector or server is not responding.

If the computer running Windows 95 is not responding properly as a client or server, use System Monitor to view statistics about the activity of the installed network servers and redirectors. If there is no activity, remove the client or server on the Network option in Control Panel, and then reinstall and try again.

### You cannot see computers running Windows 95 on the other side of a router on a NetWare network.

This might be related to the IPX network number. An IPX client (such as a computer running Client for NetWare Networks) determines its network number by sending Routing Information Protocol (RIP) requests to the nearest IPX router. If the router is configured incorrectly, all IPX clients on that network can be adversely affected. Network numbers are assigned in the server's AUTOEXEC.NCF file when the network adapter drivers are loaded and IPX is bound to the logical adapter.

**Access is denied for Windows for Workgroups users trying to connect to shared resources on a computer running File and Printer Sharing for Microsoft Networks.**

If the user with the Windows for Workgroups client computer is logging on to a different domain from the computer running File and Printer Sharing services (the peer server), then Windows 95 cannot confirm logon validation for access to shared resources. To solve this problem, do one of the following:

- Upgrade the Windows for Workgroups clients to Windows 95 (recommended).
- Set the LM Announce option to Yes in the Advanced properties for File and Printer Sharing for Microsoft Networks on the peer server.
- Switch to share-level security on the peer server.
- Change the logon domain for the Windows for Workgroups clients.

This problem will not occur in these cases: if the client computers are running Windows 95 or Windows NT; if the peer server uses share-level security; or if the same domains are used for the client computer's logon domain and the domain specified for pass-through validation in the peer server's Access Control properties.

**A user is incorrectly denied access to resources on a peer server on a Windows NT network.**

If a user is denied access to resources on a computer running File and Printer Sharing for Microsoft Networks with user-level security, you should first determine which security provider is specified for the peer server. Then, see if the client can be validated by that security provider directly without going through the peer server.

If this is successful, verify that the user is on the access control list for the shared resource on the peer server. Remove that user from the list of users and then add the name back. If this is unsuccessful, reconfigure the peer server to use another security provider that you know can validate the user.

**You need to manage SAP Advertising on computers running File and Printer Sharing for NetWare Networks.**

The SAP Advertising option is disabled by default for File and Printer Sharing on NetWare Networks. If you need to enforce the configuration of the File and Printer Sharing service, you can set the Disable SAP Advertising policy under the Default Computer policies.

In general, you will want to enable SAP Advertising only on computers with resources such as CD-ROM drives that you want to share with NETX and VLM clients. SAP Advertising is not required for sharing resources only among computers running Windows 95. Notice the following:

- SAP Advertising is not required if you want to use Net Watcher to administer the file system on a computer running File and Printer Sharing for NetWare Networks.

- Neither SAP Advertising nor File and Printer Sharing for NetWare Networks is required for remote Registry administration. The only requirement is user-level security with a pass-through server specified.

Windows 95 peer servers with SAP Advertising enabled will respond to **GetNearestServer** broadcasts. If this causes a NETX or VLM client to attempt to log in to a peer server, Windows 95 makes sure these NETX and VLM clients connect to a real NetWare server by using a stub file named LOGIN.EXE in the Windows NWSYSVOL\LOGIN directory. This directory is created automatically when File and Printer Sharing for NetWare Networks is installed, and it is automatically shared with read-only privileges whenever SAP Advertising is enabled on the peer server.

For more information, see WIN95RK.HLP.

CHAPTER 12

# Network Technical Discussion

This chapter describes technical issues related to network adapters and protocols for Windows 95, and also presents some technical notes and tips for networking.

**In This Chapter**

Network Adapter Drivers and Protocols: The Basics   414
  NDIS Driver Basics   414
  Network Protocol Basics   415
Network Adapters and Protocols: The Issues   417
Network Adapters and Windows 95   419
  Configuring Network Adapters   420
  Setting LAN Adapter Numbers   426
  Technical Notes on Network Adapters   427
IPX/SPX-Compatible Protocol   427
  Configuring IPX/SPX-Compatible Protocol   428
  Using NetBIOS over IPX   430
  IPX/SPX Technical Notes on NetWare Networks   431
TCP/IP Protocol   431
  Configuring TCP/IP with DHCP   432
  Configuring TCP/IP Settings Manually   433
  Name Resolution for Windows Networking   436
  Using WINS for Name Resolution   437
  Using DNS for Name Resolution   440
Microsoft NetBEUI Protocol   444
Using WinPopup to Broadcast a Pop-Up Message   445
Troubleshooting Protocol Problems   447

# Network Adapter Drivers and Protocols: The Basics

A network adapter (sometimes called a network interface card, or NIC) is a hardware card installed in a computer so it can communicate on a network. The network adapter provides one or more ports for the network cable to connect to, and it transmits and receives data onto the network cable.

Every networked computer must also have a network adapter driver, which controls the network adapter. Each network adapter driver is configured to run with a certain type of network adapter.

A networked computer must also have one or more protocol drivers (sometimes called a transport protocol or just a protocol). The protocol driver works between the upper-level network software and the network adapter to package data to be sent on the network.

For two computers to communicate on a network, they must use identical protocols. Sometimes, a computer is configured to use multiple protocols. In this case, two computers need only one protocol in common to communicate. For example, a computer running File and Printer Sharing for Microsoft Networks that uses both NetBEUI and TCP/IP can communicate with computers using only NetBEUI or only TCP/IP.

In Windows 95, all network adapter drivers and protocols supporting protected-mode clients are configured by using the Network option in Control Panel rather than by manually editing configuration files. Configuration values are stored in the Registry.

## NDIS Driver Basics

Windows 95 supports the Network Device Interface Specification (NDIS) versions 2.x and 3.1 protocol and adapter drivers, and provides an NDIS 3.1 replacement for version 3.0 drivers, which are incompatible with Windows 95.

By using NDIS 3.1 drivers, Windows 95 can support a wide range of network media, including Ethernet, token ring, and ArcNet®. The NDIS 3.1 specification accommodates Plug and Play features, so that in many cases network adapters can be added and removed dynamically while the computer is running. The related features and benefits are summarized in the following discussion.

**Plug and Play support for network protocols and adapters.**  Because of Plug and Play enhancements, the operating system can determine automatically the adapters to which each protocol should bind. If a Plug and Play event occurs, such as removing a PCMCIA network adapter from a portable computer, the NDIS 3.1 protocols and network adapter drivers remove themselves from memory automatically. (This Plug and Play capability is supported for most PCMCIA adapters, but not for most ISA adapters, which have power considerations.)

**New NDIS mini-driver model.**  The mini-driver provided by the adapter manufacturer implements only the half of the Media Access Control (MAC) layer functionality that is specific to the network adapter, which includes establishing communications with the adapter, turning on and off electrical isolation for Plug and Play, providing media detection, and enabling any value-added features the network adapter may contain.

The Windows 95 NDIS wrapper implements the half of the MAC functionality that is common to all NDIS drivers. The new mini-drivers are faster and roughly 40 percent smaller than earlier versions of NDIS 3.x network adapter drivers. The Windows 95 mini-drivers are also binary-compatible with Windows NT 3.5 mini-drivers, which means they can be used without recompiling. (You can recognize a mini-driver by its .SYS filename extension; other drivers have .VXD extensions.)

**Real-mode NDIS 2 support.**  An NDIS 2.x protocol under Windows 95 must use an NDIS 2.x network adapter driver. Both the protocol and network adapter drivers must load and bind in real mode before running for Windows 95. Values in PROTOCOL.INI are used to load the real-mode NDIS drivers, as described in Chapter 8, "Windows 95 on Microsoft Networks." However, you still use the Network option in Control Panel to configure NDIS 2 adapters.

When you run a real-mode network (for example, when using Safe Mode with Networking for system startup), Windows 95 uses NDIS 2 versions of NetBEUI and IPX/SPX protocols. These protocols are not intended for everyday use, since Windows 95 supplies faster protected-mode versions of these protocols. These real-mode protocols are also provided for client computers that start from a floppy disk and run a shared copy of Windows 95 from a server.

Windows 95 also supports existing ODI drivers with Novell® NetWare®-compatible network clients. For information, see Chapter 9, "Windows 95 on NetWare Networks."

# Network Protocol Basics

Windows 95 network protocols are implemented as 32-bit, protected-mode VxDs that offer high performance and use no conventional memory. Windows 95 can support multiple protocols simultaneously, and protocol stacks can be shared among the installed network clients. For example, the IPX/SPX-compatible protocol can support both Client for NetWare Networks and Client for Microsoft Networks. The following protocols are included with Windows 95.

**Microsoft IPX/SPX-compatible protocol.** This protocol is compatible with the Novell NetWare Internetwork Packet Exchange/Sequential Packet Exchange (IPX/SPX) implementation. Windows 95 includes both 32-bit, protected-mode and real-mode support for this protocol. This protected-mode protocol provides the following benefits:

- Supports any Novell NetWare-compatible network client

- Supports packet-burst mode to offer improved network performance

- Supports the Windows Sockets, NetBIOS, and ECB programming interfaces

- Support for automatic detection of frame type, network address, and other configuration settings

- Connectivity with servers and workstations on NetWare or Windows NT Server 3.5 networks, and mixed networks

- Routable connectivity across all network bridges and routers configured for IPX/SPX routing

**Microsoft TCP/IP.** This is a complete implementation of the standard, routable Transmission Control Protocol/Internet Protocol (TCP/IP) protocol. Windows 95 includes only protected-mode support for this protocol. Microsoft TCP/IP provides the following benefits:

- Support for Internet connectivity and the Point-to-Point Protocol (PPP) used for asynchronous communication

- Connectivity across interconnected networks with different operating systems and hardware platforms, including communication with many non-Microsoft systems, such as Internet hosts, Apple® Macintosh® systems, IBM® mainframes, UNIX® systems, and Open VMS™ systems

- Support for automatic TCP/IP configuration using Windows NT Dynamic Host Configuration Protocol (DHCP) servers

- Support for automatic IP-address-to-NetBIOS computer name resolution using Windows NT Windows Internet Naming Service (WINS) servers

- Support for the Windows Sockets 1.1 interface, which is used by many client-server applications and many public-domain Internet tools

- Support for the NetBIOS interface, commonly known as NetBIOS over TCP/IP

- Support for many commonly used utilities, which are installed with the protocol

**Microsoft NetBEUI.** This protocol is compatible with existing networks that use the NetBIOS extended user interface (NetBEUI), including Windows for Workgroups peer networks, Windows NT Server, LAN Manager, and other networks, and includes support for a NetBIOS programming interface. Windows 95 provides both protected-mode and real-mode support for this protocol.

NetBEUI was first introduced by IBM in 1985, when it was assumed that LANs would be segmented into workgroups of 20 to 200 computers and that gateways would be used to connect one LAN segment to other LAN segments or to a mainframe. NetBEUI is optimized for high performance when used in departmental LANs or LAN segments. Microsoft NetBEUI under Windows 95 is completely self-tuning and provides much better performance over slow links than did earlier versions of NetBEUI.

All three protocols are Plug and Play-compliant, so they can be loaded and unloaded automatically. For example, if a PCMCIA network adapter is removed from the computer so that the network is no longer available, the protocols are unloaded automatically after any dependent applications have been notified.

# Network Adapters and Protocols: The Issues

Windows 95 Setup automatically configures a computer to use protocols and drivers to match network components that are running when Setup is started.

If you are setting up Windows 95 for a new networking option, you must choose which types of network adapter drivers and protocols to use. Because Windows 95 has an open architecture, you have a lot of flexibility in this decision. Windows 95 supports both NDIS and Transport Driver Interface (TDI) standards, allowing Windows 95 to communicate with many other networking products and making it possible to choose from a variety of network adapters and protocols.

This section describes basic issues for choosing network adapter drivers and protocols to support your networking needs.

**Choosing adapters and drivers for best performance.**   Network adapters have become exceptionally reliable and inexpensive. The low cost of Ethernet adapters, including new Plug and Play hardware, means that usually the cost-effective way to improve network performance is to replace an older network adapter with a new model. The cost for the new hardware is offset almost immediately by savings in support time and improved performance. In choosing a new network adapter, you should also consider buying an adapter that matches the computer bus. For example, PCI network adapters are available for use in PCI computers.

**Choosing separate protocol and adapter drivers.**   With some networks, each computer's network adapter driver and protocol are separate pieces of software. With other networks, a single piece of software called a monolithic protocol stack acts as both adapter driver and protocol. Microsoft recommends that you choose separate 32-bit, protected-mode protocols and drivers rather than monolithic stacks, which run only in real mode. However, Windows 95 includes mapping technology for users who must continue to use real-mode NDIS 2 or ODI drivers.

**Choosing NDIS versus ODI drivers.** Windows 95 supports NDIS versions 2.x and 3.1. All network adapter drivers and protocols provided with Windows 95 conform to NDIS. You can use any combination of protocol and network adapter drivers that conforms to NDIS. Microsoft recommends that you use NDIS 3.1 drivers whenever possible with Windows 95.

The Open Datalink Interface (ODI) specification was defined by Novell and Apple Computer to provide a protocol and API for communicating with network adapter drivers, and to support the use of multiple protocols by a network adapter driver. To ensure the most flexibility in Windows 95, Microsoft recommends that you use NDIS 3.1 drivers whenever possible if you are running Windows 95 with Microsoft Client for NetWare Networks. If you are using a Novell-supplied network client, Novell recommends using ODI-based client software rather than monolithic IPX drivers.

**Choosing a protocol.** Windows 95 can support multiple network protocols, and can share a protocol among the network providers that are installed. You might choose more than one protocol to ensure communication compatibility with all systems in the enterprise. However, choosing multiple protocols can cause more network traffic, more memory used on the local workstations, and more network delays. You probably want to choose a single protocol wherever possible. The following briefly presents some issues for each Windows 95 protocol.

For the IPX/SPX-compatible protocol:

- This protocol is required and installed automatically with Microsoft Client for NetWare. When Windows 95 Setup determines that it cannot install Client for NetWare Networks on a computer running a Novell-supplied network client, Setup still tries to install this protected-mode protocol. For information about how Setup determines whether to install this protocol automatically, see Chapter 9, "Windows 95 on NetWare Networks."

- This protocol cannot be used to configure Windows 95 to support NetWare over ArcNet. Instead, you must use real-mode IPX drivers with NetBIOS support on ArcNet network adapters.

- With this protocol, it is not necessary to load the Novell-supplied VIPX.386 driver, because the Microsoft protocol provides virtualized services to all VMs and applications.

For Microsoft TCP/IP:

- TCP/IP in general has been known to require careful planning and management of the IP address space. However, this problem is vastly reduced when DHCP servers are used to manage assignment of IP addresses for computers running Microsoft TCP/IP.

- If you want to take advantage of DHCP for automatic IP addressing or use WINS for name resolution on computers running Windows 95, the appropriate Windows NT servers must be in place on the network.

- This protocol cannot be used on NetWare networks that require NetWare/IP.

For Microsoft NetBEUI:

- NetBEUI is a nonroutable protocol that cannot cross routers, although it can cross bridges and source routing bridges.

- NetBEUI is optimized for high performance only for use in departmental LANs or LAN segments.

One common method for setting up a network is to use NetBEUI plus a protocol such as TCP/IP on each computer that needs to access computers across a router. If you set NetBEUI as the default protocol, Windows 95 uses NetBEUI for communication within the LAN segment and uses TCP/IP for communication across routers to other parts of the WAN.

# Network Adapters and Windows 95

Windows 95 supports up to four network adapters in a single computer. Windows 95 Setup automatically detects most network adapters, installs the appropriate driver for the adapter, and provides appropriate default settings to configure the adapter. If you add a new network adapter, its driver is bound automatically to all NDIS protocols currently running on the computer; if any protocols are added later, they will also be bound automatically to the network adapter driver.

This section provides technical details for configuring network adapters, setting LAN adapter numbers, and other technical notes. For specific information about PCMCIA adapters, see Chapter 19, "Devices."

**Note**  For information about specific network adapters, see the SETUP.TXT and README.TXT files in the Windows 95 distribution disks.

# Configuring Network Adapters

This section discusses how to configure properties for network adapter drivers.

---

**Important**  If you add a new network adapter after Windows 95 is installed, you should use the Add New Hardware option in Control Panel to install the correct driver for the adapter.

When you use the Add New Hardware option, be sure to choose Detection for determining the correct driver and resource assignment. You should configure network adapter drivers manually only after you have tried all detection and automatic configuration methods.

If you experience problems with settings for a network adapter, you should begin troubleshooting by removing the network adapter driver in the Network option in Control Panel. Then use the Add New Hardware option to reinstall support for the network adapter, using detection to ensure that Windows 95 determines the correct adapter driver and standard settings for that network adapter.

---

▶ **To configure properties manually for network adapter drivers**

- In the Network option in Control Panel, click the Configuration tab. Select the driver in the list, and then click Properties.

▶ **To specify the driver type for a selected network adapter**

1. In the properties for the network adapter, click the Driver Type tab.

2. Click one of three options (if available for the specific adapter), as described in the following table.

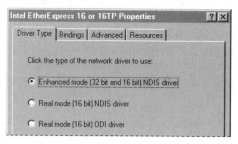

| Network adapter driver type | Description |
| --- | --- |
| Enhanced mode (32-bit and 16-bit) NDIS driver | Installs an NDIS 3.1-compliant driver. This is the preferred driver type for use with 32-bit, protected-mode network clients. |
| Real-mode NDIS driver | Installs an NDIS 2.x-compliant driver. |
| Real-mode (16-bit) ODI driver | Installs a real-mode driver created to support ODI for Windows 3.1 on NetWare networks. |

## Binding Network Adapter Drivers to Protocols

For a protocol to communicate with each network adapter on your computer, the network adapter driver must be bound to the protocol. The bindings define the relationships between networking software components. Windows 95 automatically binds the appropriate protocols to the network adapter.

You can change the bindings, for example, if you do not want to use a specific protocol with a particular network adapter. Or, as another example, if the computer is on a local area network and is also connected to the enterprise internetwork, you might not want the computer's shared resources to be seen on the internetwork. In that case, you can disable the binding between the related protocol and the adapter that connects the computer to the internetwork.

▶ **To configure bindings between a network adapter and installed protocols**

1. In the properties for the selected network adapter, click the Bindings tab.

   In the list, the protocols that are bound to the selected adapter are checked. If a particular protocol does not appear in the list, check that it is installed correctly by returning to the Configuration properties dialog box and reinstalling it.

2. If you do not want this network adapter to be bound to a particular protocol, click the check box beside the protocol to clear the check.

## Configuring Network Adapter Resource Settings

Windows 95 can determine hardware settings for most network adapters. For this reason, the recommended method for installing or configuring network adapter drivers is to use the Add New Hardware option in Control Panel, using detection to determine the correct driver and resource settings. You should accept the proposed settings unless you are absolutely sure they are incorrect.

Most devices cannot share IRQ settings, memory buffer addresses, or ROM addresses. Where possible, Windows 95 identifies and resolves conflicts. However, if one of the supported devices does not seem to work, the problem may be the particular hardware configuration. To make sure there are no conflicts among network adapters or other peripherals, or between the system board and adapters, check the settings in Device Manager, as described in Chapter 19, "Devices."

Sometimes settings for network adapters are set with software, sometimes with jumpers or switches on the hardware (refer to your hardware documentation for specific details). If settings for a network adapter can be configured through software, you can configure settings using the Network option in Control Panel.

▶ **To configure resources in a network adapter's properties**

1. In the properties for the network adapter, click the Resources tab.

2. Click the option named Use These Hardware Settings, and confirm values for the listed settings by comparing the proposed settings with the values recommended in the documentation for the adapter.

3. To select from the available values for a setting, click the arrow beside the setting's current value.

   - A hash (#) character appears by current settings.

   - An asterisk (*) appears beside settings that conflict with another device in the system. You should avoid this setting or reconfigure the other devices to use different settings.

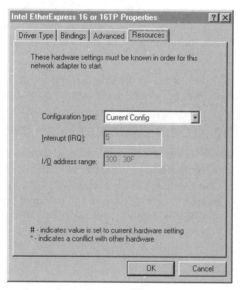

The settings available depend on the type of network adapter. For example, for Intel adapters, you cannot set the IRQ using the adapter's properties. The following table describes a few typical settings.

**Examples of Hardware Resource Settings for a Network Adapter**

| Setting type | Description |
|---|---|
| I/O Address Range | Specifies the reserved memory address range (as a hexa-decimal value) that the adapter can use for temporary storage of I/O data. |
| Interrupt (IRQ) | Specifies the hardware line over which the device can send interrupts (requests for service) to the computer's CPU. |
| Memory Address | Specifies the base memory address (as a hexadecimal value) used by this network adapter. This number must match the adapter's memory address settings, as specified in the documentation for the adapter. |

Each alternate Configuration Type that might be listed in the Resources properties for a network adapter refers to a possible hardware configuration for the adapter (rather than software settings for the driver) as defined by the manufacturer.

▶ **To configure a network adapter that has alternate Configuration Types**

- Run the Add New Hardware option in Control Panel, and let Windows 95 detect the hardware.

  If you must set the configuration manually, use the settings prescribed in the documentation provided by the manufacturer to set Resources and Advanced properties using the Network option in Control Panel.

The following table describes the network adapters that have alternate Configuration Types under Windows 95. For more information about these configurations, see the documentation from the hardware manufacturer.

| Network adapter | Alternate Configuration Types |
|---|---|
| 3Com® EtherLink II®-16 | Memory Mapped (RAM), Programmed I/O (PIO) |
| DEC™ Etherworks™ 3 | 2K (option 0), 32K (option 1), 64K (option 2) |
| HP® ISA | Memory Mapped (RAM), Programmed I/O (PIO) |
| NE2000+ | Can use shared RAM (memory-mapped), but this mode is not supported under Windows 95 |
| Proteon 1390, 1392, 1392+ | Memory Mapped (RAM), Programmed I/O (PIO) |

For legacy network adapters, the settings that appear in the Resources properties are only some possible settings for the adapter driver, but many adapters have additional settings that can be programmed by running a configuration utility from the adapter manufacturer or by setting jumpers on the adapter itself. Although some of these settings do not appear in the adapter's properties, the resources used could cause conflicts with other system components.

This also means that configuring most legacy network adapters in Windows 95 consists only of specifying the preprogrammed values for the adapter hardware. Changing values for most network adapters by setting properties in Windows 95 does not reprogram the adapter itself. You can verify hardware settings for network adapters only by running the hardware configuration program to view settings, or by checking how the jumpers are set on the adapter itself.

▶ **To reprogram adapter settings**

1. Use the configuration disk that came with the adapter to reprogram it.

2. Write down the settings made so that you can refer to them in the following step.

3. In the Network option in Control Panel, change the settings to the ones you noted. Then shut down and restart the computer.

For some legacy adapters, it is possible that the adapter uses resources not listed with the Resource properties. For these adapters, the NDIS driver determines the resource settings directly from the adapter itself. Even though these resources do not appear in the list, they can still conflict with other devices. For example, the resource list for the IBM Token Ring adapter shows only the I/O settings, but this adapter also uses IRQ and Memory resources.

## Configuring Advanced Properties for Network Adapters

The options available in the Advanced properties vary, depending on the type of network adapter. For information about specific settings that appear for a selected network adapter, see the documentation provided by the manufacturer for the adapter and driver. The manufacturer can also provide guidelines for when to change the default values for advanced configuration options.

▶ **To specify advanced settings for the network adapter**

1. In the properties for the selected network adapter, click the Advanced tab.

2. To change these values, select an item in the Property list, and then select a setting in the Value box.

3. Click the OK button. Then restart the computer for the changes to take effect.

This example shows the advanced options for an Intel EtherExpress network adapter.

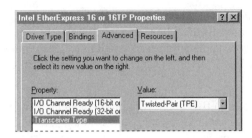

The following examples show some typical settings for general types of network adapters. Network adapters that use the new, fast Ethernet technology might have many more settings. Examples of such adapters include SMC EtherPower 10/100 (9332) PCI Ethernet Adapter, DEC Etherworks 435, and Intel EtherExpress PRO/100. For an explanation of specific settings for a network adapter, see the documentation provided by the adapter manufacturer.

| Example setting | Description |
|---|---|
| **For Ethernet adapters:** | |
| Transceiver Type (cable connector) | The transceiver is the device that connects a computer to the network, defined as one of the following values: |
| | ▪ Thick Net, for an AUI or DEC/Intel/Xerox (DIX) connection. |
| | ▪ Thin Net, for a BNC or coaxial (COAX) connection. |
| | ▪ Twisted Pair, for a TPE connection. |
| **For token-ring adapters:** | |
| I/O Port Base Address | This value specifies the base memory address used by the adapter. To set the I/O address of an IBM 4/16 token-ring adapter, select either Primary (A20) or Secondary (A24) for this value. In this case, the driver ignores the I/O settings in the Resource properties. |
| Network Address | By default, Windows 95 hardware detection uses the address burned into the adapter. To use another network address, type the network address in hexadecimal form, in the format *XX-XX-XX-XX-XX-XX*; for example, 01-02-03-4E-2D-1F. |
| Ring Speed | The ring speed is 4 or 16 megabits per second (MBS), and is set by changing a jumper on the adapter or by running the adapter's configuration utility. For example, for an Intel TokenExpress 16/4 adapter, this is set on the adapter itself. The value in Windows 95 should match the physical or software setting. |

# Setting LAN Adapter Numbers

NetBIOS defines the interface between the network client and the protocol layers using a set of function calls that allow an application to use the protocol services. Because many network applications use NetBIOS to send commands to the protocol driver, the NetBIOS interface is supported by all protocols provided with Windows 95.

Each combination of a NetBIOS network protocol and a network adapter forms a logical network over which computers can communicate with each other. For example, a computer can have a token-ring adapter and an Ethernet adapter, and might use NetBEUI on the token-ring network and both NetBEUI and TCP/IP on the Ethernet network. In this case, the computer is connected to three logical networks, each of which is assigned a NetBIOS LAN adapter (LANA) number that Windows 95 uses for communication.

When Windows 95 uses multiple protocols, it transmits data first using one protocol, then again using the next protocol, and so on. When multiple protocols are installed on a computer, the first protocol to be used is called the primary protocol.

On a computer running Windows 95, each binding of a protocol to a network adapter has a LAN adapter number assigned to it. (For example, one protocol bound to two network adapters requires two LAN adapter numbers; two protocols each bound to two adapters requires four LAN adapter numbers.)

In Windows 95, LANA numbers are assigned dynamically in sequence of binding order for the protocols, beginning with 7 and then 0, 1, and so on. This accommodates dynamic Plug and Play events such as removing a network adapter while the computer is running. If you are running Windows 95 in such a dynamic environment, Windows 95 cannot guarantee that a given protocol will receive the same LANA number each time the system is started. Although if the computer's network hardware never changes, the LANA numbers may not change at each startup. However, the default protocol is always LANA 0.

You need to change a LAN adapter number only if you have a NetBIOS application that needs to know the LANA number. For example, Lotus Notes® requires that you enter the LANA number that Lotus Notes will use. To configure Windows 95 to use Lotus Notes, set the default protocol to be the NetBIOS-based protocol on which you want to run Lotus Notes. (Setting the default protocol makes it LANA 0.) This protocol can be NetBEUI, IPX/SPX-compatible with NetBIOS support, or TCP/IP.

▶ **To select a default protocol for LANA settings**

1. In the Network option in Control Panel, click the Configuration tab.

2. Double-click the protocol you want to be the default.

3. In the protocol's properties, click the Advanced tab.

4. Click the option named Set This Protocol To Be The Default Protocol so that the check box is checked. Then click OK, and shut down and restart the computer for the changes to take effect.

## Technical Notes on Network Adapters

This section provides some technical notes for specific network adapters and briefly describes changes to network adapter driver support as compared to Windows for Workgroups 3.11.

NDIS 3.0 network adapter drivers that worked with Windows for Workgroups 3.11 do not work under Windows 95. You must use an NDIS 2.x real-mode driver, an ODI driver, or an updated NDIS 3.1 protected-mode driver for the network adapter. The driver must have a Windows 95 INF file. Many real-mode drivers, updated protected-mode drivers, and supporting INF files are included with Windows 95.

If the network adapter does not appear in the list of adapters in the Network option in Control Panel, you can use information for a Windows 3.x adapter to install it under Windows 95. If you have an OEMSETUP.INF file created for an earlier version of Windows, you can use that INF file by clicking Have Disk in the Select Network Adapter dialog box to install that older network adapter driver.

The major reason that the INF file format has changed for all types of Windows 95 network adapter drivers is that INF files are now used to add information to the Windows 95 Registry. The INF files created for earlier versions of Windows do not contain this kind of information.

# IPX/SPX-Compatible Protocol

The Microsoft IPX/SPX-compatible protocol (NWLINK.VXD) supports the 32-bit Windows Sockets programming interface, so that any Win32-based Windows Socket application can run on IPX/SPX with Windows 95. (There are no 16-bit Windows Sockets applications using IPX/SPX.)

The IPX/SPX-compatible protocol can be used by Client for NetWare Networks to communicate with NetWare servers or computers running File and Printer Sharing for NetWare Networks.

This protocol can also be used by Client for Microsoft Networks to communicate with computers running Windows for Workgroups 3.11 or Windows NT that are running the same protocol.

The IPX/SPX-compatible protocol uses the NWNBLINK.VXD module to support computers that use NetBIOS over IPX and to support the NetBIOS programming interface. This protocol can also use NetWare servers configured as routers (and other IPX routers) to transfer packets across LANs.

# Configuring IPX/SPX-Compatible Protocol

The Microsoft IPX/SPX-compatible protocol is installed automatically when Client for NetWare Networks is installed. You can also install this protocol to support other network clients, including Client for Microsoft Networks.

When you install the IPX/SPX-compatible protocol, Windows 95 automatically detects and sets appropriate values for the frame type, network address, and other settings. However, in some cases you might need to configure settings for this protocol manually.

▶ **To configure the IPX/SPX-compatible protocol**

1. In the Network option in Control Panel, double-click IPX/SPX Compatible Protocol.

   If the computer has multiple network adapters, the list will contain an instance of the IPX/SPX-compatible protocol for each network adapter. You must configure each adapter with its own settings.

2. Click the Advanced tab.

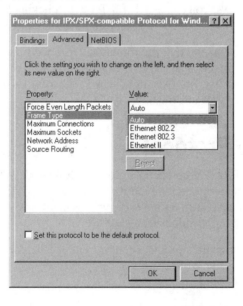

3. Most values have correct defaults in typical installations. If you need to change a value for a particular purpose, select the item in the Property list and specify a setting in the Value list based on the information in the following table.

| Property | Value |
| --- | --- |
| Force even-length IPX packets | Enabled only for Ethernet 802.3 on monolithic implementations that cannot handle odd-length packets. |
| Frame type[1] | Specifies the frame type based on detection. This value is used for network adapters that support multiple frame types. The possible values are:<br><br>▪ Auto-detect (recommended)<br>▪ Ethernet 802.2 (default for NetWare 3.12 and later)<br>▪ Ethernet 802.3<br>▪ Ethernet II<br>▪ Token ring<br>▪ Token ring SNAP |
| Maximum connections | Specifies the maximum number of connections that IPX will allow. Configured dynamically. |
| Maximum sockets | Specifies the maximum number of IPX sockets that IPX assigns. Configured dynamically. |
| Network address | Specifies the IPX network address as a four-byte value. Configured dynamically. |
| Source routing[2] | Specifies the cache size to use with source routing. This parameter is used only on token-ring networks, where it is used to turn on source routing.<br><br>**Important** Cache size is specified by entry count, not byte count. The recommended value of 16 entries is the most efficient and best setting for most installations. |

[1] Each time the computer starts, Windows 95 detects the frame type by sending a general RIP request in each frame format. Based on the responses received from routers, Windows 95 determines the most prevalent frame type used and sets that as the default frame type.

[2] Source routing is a method of routing data across bridges. For NetWare networks, this means forwarding NetWare frames across an IBM token-ring bridge. With NDIS protocols, source routing is done by the protocol. With ODI-based protocols, source routing is configured with the network adapter driver or using the NetWare ROUTE.COM utility.

You should not need to change bindings in most circumstances. However, you can disable the bindings for a protocol if you do not want other computers using that protocol to see this computer. At least one protocol, however, must be bound to the network client for the computer to communicate with the network.

▶ **To change bindings for the IPX/SPX-compatible protocol**

1. In the properties for the IPX/SPX-compatible protocol, click the Bindings tab.

2. Click any network component to change its bindings.

   If the option is checked, it is bound to the protocol. If it is not checked, that network component is not using the IPX/SPX-compatible protocol. For more information, see "Configuring Network Adapters" earlier in this chapter.

---

**Note**  Microsoft Client for NetWare Networks is always bound only to the IPX/SPX-Compatible Protocol. This network client cannot use another protocol.

---

# Using NetBIOS over IPX

NetBIOS is an interface used by network applications to communicate with other NetBIOS-compliant applications. The NetBIOS interface is responsible for the following:

- Establishing logical names on the network

- Establishing connections (called sessions) between two computers by use of their logical names on the network

- Transmitting data between networked computers

Windows 95 provides a 32-bit, protected-mode driver to support NetBIOS services over IPX (VNETBIOS.386). This implementation is compatible with the Novell NetBIOS support driver. Performance enhancements include acknowledgment of previous frames in response frames (called PiggyBackAck), plus a "sliding window" acknowledgment mechanism.

These NetBIOS enhancements are used only when the computer is communicating with other computers using IPX over NetBIOS, such as other computers running Windows 95, Windows NT, or NetWare when running Lotus Notes or other NetBIOS applications. NetBIOS over IPX is not necessary for computers running Windows 95 to be able to communicate with each other. The redirector and server networking components in Windows 95 communicate with the IPX protocol directly without NetBIOS.

Novell provides a TSR NetBIOS driver named NETBIOS.EXE, which is a Level 1 NetBIOS provider that consumes about 40K of conventional memory. This driver acknowledges each frame received, thus increasing the amount of traffic generated when NetBIOS is used. With the Microsoft implementation of NetBIOS over IPX, you can remove the real-mode NETBIOS.EXE TSR.

**Note**   A computer running Windows 95 that uses IPX without NetBIOS can connect to a Windows NT 3.5 server that uses IPX without NetBIOS. However, the Windows NT 3.5 workstation service (not Windows NT Workstation) can only connect to a computer running File and Printer Sharing for Microsoft Networks when the computer running Windows 95 is using NetBIOS over IPX.

▶   **To use the IPX/SPX-compatible protocol with NetBIOS on a computer**

- In the properties for the IPX/SPX-compatible protocol, click the NetBIOS tab, and then click I Want To Enable NetBIOS Over IPX/SPX.

## IPX/SPX Technical Notes on NetWare Networks

- There is no need to enable Source Routing on token-ring networks if the communication is on the same ring, even if one computer has it enabled.

- SPX-II is a protocol definition for windowing and transmitting large packets over SPX. You can run any SPX-II application under Windows 95 using the IPX/SPX-compatible protocol. The related Novell-supplied file TLI.DLL must be available on the computer to support SPX-II.

- The IPX/SPX-compatible protocol in Windows 95 uses NET.CFG parameters for NetBIOS over IPX on NetWare networks. However, it should not be necessary for you to configure these parameters, because most parameters are dynamic and self-adjusting. (When you install Windows 95 with protected-mode networking components, NET.CFG and SHELL.CFG parameters are moved to the Registry.)

- To determine the network address in IPX packets, Windows 95 checks the wire for RIP packets and chooses the most likely address. The network address is dynamic and changes when a new network address becomes more prevalent.

- All Transport Layer Interface (TLI) libraries can run on the IPX/SPX-compatible protocol in Windows 95. TLI is similar to TDI in Microsoft networking as a layer between the protocol and network adapter driver; this implementation is similar to STREAMS and provides a STREAMS environment for NetWare, but Windows 95 uses Windows Sockets instead.

# TCP/IP Protocol

Microsoft TCP/IP provides communication across interconnected networks that use diverse hardware architectures and various operating systems. TCP/IP can be used to communicate with computers running Windows 95, with devices using other Microsoft networking products, or with non-Microsoft systems such as UNIX.

Microsoft TCP/IP provides all the following elements necessary for networking:

- Core TCP/IP protocols, including the Transmission Control Protocol (TCP), Internet Protocol (IP), User Datagram Protocol (UDP), Address Resolution Protocol (ARP), Internet Control Message Protocol (ICMP), and Domain Name Protocol (DNS). This suite of Internet protocols provides a set of standards for how computers communicate and how networks are interconnected.

- Support for application programming interfaces, including Windows Sockets and NetBIOS.

- TCP/IP diagnostic tools to detect and resolve TCP/IP networking problems, including **arp**, **ftp**, **nbtstat**, **netstat**, **ping**, **route**, and **tracert**, plus Windows-based Telnet and IP Configuration (WINIPCFG) utilities.

In addition, when you install Microsoft TCP/IP under Windows 95, the following enhancements are included:

- Client for DHCP, for automatic configuration of computers running TCP/IP on networks that have DHCP servers

- Client for WINS, for dynamic resolution of IP addresses to computer names on networks that have WINS servers

- Point-to-Point Protocol for asynchronous communication, as described in Chapter 28, "Dial-Up Networking and Mobile Computing."

For a summary of the command-line options for TCP/IP utilities, see Appendix A, "Command-Line Commands Summary."

# Configuring TCP/IP with DHCP

In an effort to make implementing the TCP/IP protocol more manageable, Microsoft worked with other industry leaders to create an Internet standard called Dynamic Host Configuration Protocol (DHCP) for the automatic allocation of IP addresses. DHCP is not a Microsoft standard, but a public Request for Comments (RFC 1541) that Microsoft has implemented.

DHCP allows you to establish a range of valid IP addresses to be used per subnetwork. An individual IP address from the range is assigned dynamically to any DHCP client requesting an address. DHCP also allows you to establish a lease time that defines how long an IP address is to remain valid. Other configuration parameters can also be assigned using DHCP, such as subnet mask, DNS and WINS server identification, and so on.

A computer running Windows 95 cannot be a DHCP server. A DHCP server runs as a service on a Windows NT 3.5 Server computer. If DHCP is available company-wide, users can move from subnet to subnet and always have a valid IP address. The IP Configuration utility (WINIPCFG) allows users or administrators to examine the current IP address assigned to the computer, the IP address lease time, and other useful data about the TCP/IP configuration.

When TCP/IP is installed, Windows 95 automatically enables the option to obtain an IP address from a DHCP server. This option can be disabled using the Network option in Control Panel if you want to enter an IP address manually.

If Microsoft TCP/IP is configured to obtain an IP address from a DHCP server when a DHCP server is not available on the network, the next time Windows 95 starts, an error message announces that the DHCP client could not obtain an IP address. To solve this problem, use the procedure described in the following section to configure TCP/IP manually.

# Configuring TCP/IP Settings Manually

If you cannot use DHCP for automatic configuration, the network administrator must provide values so that individual users can configure TCP/IP manually. Or, if custom setup scripts are used to install Windows 95, the correct values can be defined in the setup script. The required values include the following:

- The IP address and subnet mask for each network adapter installed on the computer.
- The IP address for the default gateways (IP routers).
- Whether the computer will use Domain Name System (DNS) and, if so, the IP addresses of the DNS servers on the internetwork.
- WINS server addresses, if WINS servers are available on the network.

The following procedure describes the basic configuration options for TCP/IP. If you want to configure the computer to use WINS or DNS for name resolution, see the procedures in "Using WINS for Name Resolution" later in this chapter and "Using DNS for Name Resolution" later in this chapter.

▶ **To configure the TCP/IP protocol manually**

1. In the Network option in Control Panel, double-click Microsoft TCP/IP in the list of installed components.

---

**Note** If your computer has multiple network adapters, the list includes an instance of TCP/IP for each network adapter. You must configure each adapter with its own IP address, subnet mask, and gateway. All other settings apply system-wide.

---

2. In Microsoft TCP/IP properties, click the IP Address tab.

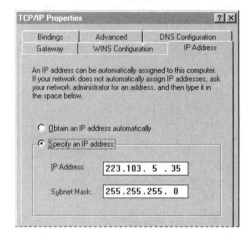

3. Click the option named Specify An IP Address.

4. Type an IP address and subnet mask in the respective boxes.

   The network administrator must provide these values for individual users, based on the network ID and the host ID plan for your site.

   - The value in the IP Address box identifies the IP address for the local computer or, if more than one network adapter is installed, for the network adapter selected in the Configuration dialog box.

   - The value in the Subnet Mask box identifies the network membership and its host ID for the selected network adapter. The subnet mask defaults to an appropriate value, as shown in the following list.

| Address class | Range of first octet in the IP address | Subnet mask |
|---|---|---|
| Class A | 1–126 | 255.0.0.0 |
| Class B | 128–191 | 255.255.0.0 |
| Class C | 192–223 | 255.255.255.0 |

5. To view or specify which network clients are bound to the TCP/IP protocol, click the Bindings tab.

   - To keep a network client from using the TCP/IP protocol, make sure the checkmark beside the client name is cleared.

   - If the network client for which you want to use TCP/IP does not appear in this list, that client might not be installed properly. Return to the Configuration dialog box and reinstall that network client.

---

**Note**   The only network client provided with Windows 95 that can use Microsoft TCP/IP is Client for Microsoft Networks. Client for NetWare Networks does not use Microsoft TCP/IP.

NetWare/IP from Novell allows the NCP request to be sent over an IP header. You can use NetWare/IP only with a Novell-provided, real-mode client.

---

6. Click the Gateway tab. Type at least one IP address for the default gateway (IP router) on the network, and then click Add.

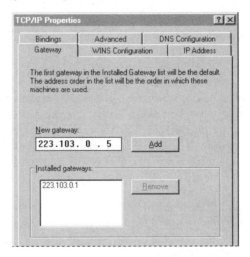

7. To specify an IP address for an additional gateway, type the IP address in the New Gateway box, and then click the Add button.

   The first gateway in the list is the default gateway. Gateway addresses can be prioritized by dragging the IP address in the list of installed gateways. Windows 95 attempts to connect to other gateways only if the primary gateway is unavailable.

8. Click OK, and then restart the computer for changes to take effect.

If you are using Dial-Up Networking to connect to the Internet, you can manually configure DNS and IP addresses for each connection that you define. For more information about defining IP addresses for each connection and about IP addresses on TCP/IP networks, see Chapter 30, "Internet Access." For more information about TCP/IP Registry entries, see WIN95RK.HLP in the *Windows 95 Resource Kit* utilities.

# Name Resolution for Windows Networking

For TCP/IP and the Internet, the globally known system name is the computer's host name, appended with a DNS domain name (for example, rhit.microsoft.com). This defaults to the computer name (NetBIOS name) defined during Windows 95 Setup. The default name can be changed in the DNS dialog box when you are configuring TCP/IP properties.

Computers use IP addresses to identify each other, but users usually find it easier to work with computer names. A mechanism must be available on a TCP/IP network to resolve names to IP addresses. To ensure that both the name and the address are unique, the computer using Microsoft TCP/IP registers its name and IP address on the network during system startup. Computers running Microsoft TCP/IP on the network can use one or more methods for name resolution in TCP/IP internetworks, as summarized in this section.

**Broadcast name resolution.**  Computers running Microsoft TCP/IP can use broadcast name resolution, which is a NetBIOS-over-TCP/IP mode of operation defined in RFC 1001/1002 as b-node. This method relies on a computer making IP-level broadcasts to register its name by announcing it on the network. Each computer in the broadcast area is responsible for challenging attempts to register a duplicate name and for responding to name queries for its registered name.

**LMHOSTS or HOSTS files.**  An LMHOSTS file specifies the NetBIOS computer name and IP address mappings; a HOSTS file specifies the DNS name and IP address. On a local computer, the HOSTS file (used by Windows Sockets applications to find TCP/IP host names) and LMHOSTS file (used by NetBIOS over TCP/IP to find NetBIOS computer names) can be used to list known IP addresses mapped with corresponding computer names. LMHOSTS is used for name resolution in Windows 95 for internetworks where WINS is not available.

- The HOSTS file is used as a local DNS equivalent to resolve host names to IP addresses.

- The LMHOSTS file is used as a local WINS equivalent to resolve NetBIOS computer names to IP addresses.

Each of these files is also known as a *host table*. Sample versions of LMHOSTS (called LMHOSTS.SAM) and HOSTS files are added to the Windows directory when you install Windows 95 with TCP/IP support. These files can be edited using any ASCII editor, such as WordPad or Edit. To take advantage of HOSTS or LMHOSTS, DNS must be enabled on the computer. For information about setting up and using HOSTS and LMHOSTS files, see Appendix G, "HOSTS and LMHOSTS Files for Windows 95."

**Windows Internet Naming Service.**  Computers running Microsoft TCP/IP can use WINS if one or more Windows NT Server computers configured as WINS servers are available, containing a dynamic database for mapping computer names to IP addresses. WINS can be used in conjunction with broadcast name resolution for an internetwork, where other name resolution methods are inadequate. WINS is a NetBIOS-over-TCP/IP mode of operation defined in RFC 1001/1002 as h-node or m-node; WINS clients default to h-node. Notice that WINS is a dynamic replacement for the LMHOSTS file. For more information, see "Using WINS for Name Resolution" later in this chapter.

**Domain Name System name resolution.**  DNS provides a way to look up name mappings when connecting a computer to foreign hosts using NetBIOS over TCP/IP or Windows Sockets applications such as FTP. DNS is a distributed database designed to relieve the traffic problems that arose with the first growth explosion on the Internet in the early 1980s. A DNS name server must be configured and available on the network. Notice that DNS replaces the functionality of the HOSTS file by providing a dynamic mapping of IP addresses to host names used by TCP/IP applications and utilities. For more information, see "Using DNS for Name Resolution" later in this chapter.

Windows 95 provides support for multiple DNS servers and up to two WINS servers. Support for either service can be configured automatically from a DHCP server, manually in Windows 95 Setup, or after Setup by using the Network option in Control Panel.

# Using WINS for Name Resolution

WINS provides a distributed database for registering and querying dynamic computer name-to-IP address mappings in a routed network environment. If you are administering a routed network that includes computers running Windows NT Server, WINS is your best choice for name resolution, because it is designed to solve the problems that occur with name resolution in more complex internetworks.

WINS reduces the use of local broadcasts for name resolution and allows users to locate computers on remote networks automatically. Furthermore, when dynamic addressing through DHCP results in new IP addresses for computers that move between subnetworks, the changes are updated automatically in the WINS database. Neither the user nor the network administrator needs to make manual accommodations for name resolution in such a case.

The WINS protocol is based on and is compatible with the protocol defined for WINS server in Requests for Comments (RFCs) 1001 and 1002, so it is interoperable with any other implementations of these RFCs. WINS consists of two components: the WINS server, which handles name queries and registrations, and the client software (NetBIOS over TCP/IP), which queries for computer name resolution. A WINS server is a Windows NT Server 3.5 computer with WINS server software installed. When Microsoft TCP/IP is installed under Windows 95, WINS client software is installed automatically.

Windows networking clients that are WINS-enabled can use WINS directly. Non-WINS computers on the internetwork that are b-node–compatible, as described in RFCs 1001 and 1002, can access WINS through proxies, which are WINS-enabled computers that listen to name query broadcasts and then respond for names that are not on the local subnet or are h-nodes.

On a Windows network, users can browse transparently across routers. To allow browsing without WINS, you must ensure that the users' primary domain has Windows NT Server computers on both sides of the router to act as master browsers. These computers need to contain correctly configured LMHOSTS files with entries for the domain controllers across the subnet.

With WINS, such strategies are not necessary, because the WINS servers and proxies provide the support necessary for browsing Windows NT domains across routers. For a technical discussion of how WINS works and how it can be set up on the network, see *Windows NT Server 3.5 TCP/IP* in the Windows NT Server 3.5 documentation set.

If there are WINS servers installed on your network, you can use WINS in combination with broadcast name queries to resolve NetBIOS computer names to IP addresses. If you do not use this option, Windows 95 can use name query broadcasts (b-node mode of NetBIOS over TCP/IP) plus the local LMHOSTS file to resolve computer names to IP addresses. Broadcast resolution is limited to the local network, as described earlier in this section.

If DHCP is used for automatic configuration, these parameters can be provided by the DHCP server. Otherwise, you must configure information about WINS servers manually. WINS configuration is global for all network adapters on a computer.

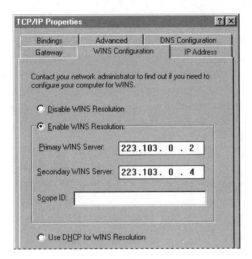

▶ **To configure a computer to use WINS for name resolution**

1. In the Microsoft TCP/IP properties, click the WINS Configuration tab.

2. If a DHCP server is available that is configured to provide information on available WINS servers, select Use DHCP For WINS Resolution.

   –Or–

   If a WINS server is available but not a DHCP server, select Enable WINS Resolution and type the IP addresses of the Primary and Secondary WINS servers. These values should be provided by the network administrator, based on the IP addresses assigned to these Windows NT Server computers.

3. If WINS is enabled, in the Scope ID box, type the computer's scope identifier, if required on an internetwork that uses NetBIOS over TCP/IP.

   Usually this value is left blank. Scope IDs are used only for communication based on NetBIOS over TCP/IP. In such a case, all computers on a TCP/IP internetwork must have the same scope ID. A scope ID can be assigned to a group of computers if those computers communicate only with each other and not with computers outside the group. Such computers can find each other if their scope IDs are identical.

# Using DNS for Name Resolution

DNS provides a distributed database that contains a hierarchical naming system for identifying hosts on the Internet. The specifications for DNS are defined in Requests for Comments (RFCs) 1034 and 1035.

Although DNS may seem similar to WINS, there is one major difference: DNS requires static configuration of IP addresses for name-to-address mapping. WINS can provide name-to-address mapping dynamically and requires far less administration.

The DNS database is a tree structure called the domain name space, where each node or domain is named and can contain subdomains. The domain name identifies the domain's position in the database in relation to its parent domain, with a period (.) separating each part of the name for the network nodes of the DNS domain.

The root of the DNS database is managed by the Internet Network Information Center. The top-level domains were assigned organizationally and by country. These domain names follow the International Standard 3166. Two-letter and three-letter abbreviations are used for countries, and various abbreviations are reserved for use by organizations, as shown in the following example.

| DNS domain name | Type of organization |
| --- | --- |
| com | Commercial (for example, microsoft.com) |
| edu | Educational (for example, mit.edu for Massachusetts Institute of Technology) |
| gov | Government (for example, nsf.gov for the National Science Foundation) |
| org | Noncommercial organizations (for example, fidonet.org for FidoNet) |
| net | Networking organizations (for example, nsf.net for NSFNET) |

DNS uses a client-server model, where the DNS servers contain information about a portion of the DNS database and make this information available to clients, called *resolvers*, that query the name server across the network. DNS *name servers* are programs that store information about parts of the domain name space called *zones*. The administrator for a domain sets up name servers that contain the database files with all the resource records describing all hosts in their zones. DNS resolvers are clients that are trying to use name servers to gain information about the domain name space.

All the resolver software necessary for using DNS on the Internet is installed with Microsoft TCP/IP. Microsoft TCP/IP includes the DNS resolver functionality used by NetBIOS over TCP/IP and Windows Sockets connectivity applications such as FTP and Telnet to query the name server and interpret the responses.

The key task for DNS is to present friendly names for users and then resolve those names to IP addresses, as required by the internetwork. If a local name server doesn't contain the data requested in a query, it sends back names and addresses of other name servers that could contain the information. The resolver then queries the other name servers until it finds the specific name and address it needs. This process is made faster because name servers continuously cache the information learned about the domain name space as the result of queries.

Although TCP/IP uses IP addresses to identify and reach computers, users typically prefer to use host names. DNS is a naming service generally used in the UNIX networking community to provide standard naming conventions for IP workstations. TCP/IP utilities, such as FTP and Telnet, can also use DNS in addition to the HOSTS file to find computers, when connecting to foreign hosts or computers on your network.

You need to determine whether users should configure their computers to use DNS. Usually you will use DNS if you are using TCP/IP to communicate over the Internet or if your private internetwork uses DNS to distribute host information.

Microsoft TCP/IP provides a DNS client for resolving Internet or UNIX system names. Windows networking provides dynamic name resolution for NetBIOS computer names using WINS servers and NetBIOS over TCP/IP, as described in the previous section.

If you choose to use DNS, you must configure how the computer will use DNS and the HOSTS file. DNS configuration is global for all network adapters installed on a computer. If DHCP is used for automatic configuration, these parameters can be provided by the DHCP server.

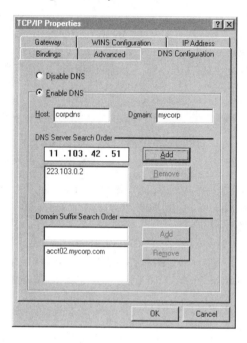

▶ **To configure a computer to use DNS for name resolution**

1. In the Microsoft TCP/IP properties, click the DNS Configuration tab.

2. If a DNS server is available, click Enable DNS. Then specify a host name and complete the other configuration information as described in the following procedure.

---

**Tip**  You must enable DNS on each computer that needs to use LMHOSTS for name resolution.

---

The host name is used to identify the local computer for authentication by some utilities. Other TCP/IP-based utilities can use this value to learn the name of the local computer. Host names are stored on DNS servers in a table that maps names to IP addresses for use by DNS.

▶  **To set the host name for DNS**

- Type a name in the Host Name box.

  The name can be any combination of the letters A through Z, the numerals 0 through 9, and the hyphen (-), plus the period (.) character used as a separator. By default, this value is the Microsoft networking computer name, but the network administrator can assign another host name without affecting the computer name.

---

**Note**  Some characters that can be used in computer names, especially the underscore, cannot be used in host names.

---

The TCP Domain Name is used with the host name to create a fully qualified domain name (FQDN) for the computer. The FQDN is the host name followed by a period (.), followed by the domain name. For example, this could be **johndoe.microsoft.com**, where **johndoe** is the host name and **microsoft.com** is the domain name.

During DNS queries, the local domain name is appended to short names. A short name consists of only a host name, such as **janedoe**. When querying the DNS server for the IP address of **janedoe**, the domain name is appended to the short name, and the DNS server is actually asked to resolve the FQDN of **janedoe.microsoft.com**. Notice that the FQDN of Jane Doe at Microsoft (janedoe.microsoft.com) is not the same as her Internet electronic mail address of janedoe@microsoft.com.

▶  **To set the DNS domain name**

- Optionally, type a name in the Domain Name box.

  This is usually an organization name followed by a period and an extension that indicates the type of organization, such as microsoft.com. The name can be any combination of the letters A through Z, the numerals 0 through 9, and the hyphen (-), plus the period (.) character used as a separator.

---

**Note**  A DNS domain is not the same as a Windows NT or LAN Manager domain. A DNS domain is a hierarchical structure for organizing TCP/IP hosts and provides a naming scheme used in UNIX environments. A Windows NT or LAN Manager domain is a grouping of computers for security and administrative purposes.

---

You can add up to three IP addresses for DNS servers. For a given DNS query, Windows 95 attempts to get DNS information from the first IP address in the list. If no response is received, Windows 95 goes to the second server in the list, and so on. To change the order of the IP addresses, you must remove them and retype them in the order that you want the servers to be searched.

▶ **To set the DNS server search order**

1. In the Domain Name System (DNS) Search Order box, type the IP address of a DNS server that will provide name resolution. Then click the Add button to add the IP address to the list.

   The network administrator should provide the correct values for this parameter, based on the IP address assigned to the DNS server used at your site.

2. To remove an IP address from the list, select it, and then click the Remove button.

---

**Note** If you have two servers listed in this dialog box, Windows 95 checks the second server only if no response is received from the first server. If Windows 95 attempts to check a host name with the first server and receives a message that the host name is not recognized, the system does not try the second DNS server.

---

The Domain Suffix Search Order specifies the DNS domain suffixes to be appended to host names during name resolution. You can add up to five domain suffixes. Domain suffixes are placed in the list in alphabetic order.

▶ **To set the domain suffix search order**

1. In the Domain Suffix Search Order box, type the domain suffixes to add to your domain suffix search list, and then click the Add button.

2. To remove a domain name from the list, select it, and then click the Remove button.

When attempting to resolve a fully qualified domain name (FQDN) from a short name, Windows 95 will first append the local domain name. If this is not successful, Windows 95 will use the Domain Suffix list to create additional FQDNs and query DNS servers in the order listed.

# Microsoft NetBEUI Protocol

Windows 95 provides the NetBIOS extended user interface (NetBEUI) protocol for compatibility with existing networks that use NetBEUI. Because NetBEUI is nonroutable and was designed for smaller LANs, you should use the TCP/IP or IPX/SPX-compatible protocol for enterprise-wide networks that require a routable protocol.

NetBEUI in Windows 95 supports a NetBIOS programming interface that conforms to the IBM NetBEUI specifications and includes several performance enhancements. The NetBEUI module, NETBEUI.VXD, is accessible through the NetBIOS interface.

If Windows 95 Setup detects NetBEUI during installation, it installs support for Microsoft NetBEUI automatically. You can add this protocol at any time. The Advanced properties for NetBEUI affect onloy real-mode NetBEUI. These values are set dynamically for protected-mode NetBEUI.

▶ **To configure real-mode NetBEUI manually**

1. In the Network option in Control Panel, click the Configuration tab. Then double-click Microsoft NetBEUI.

   If your computer has multiple network adapters, an instance of NetBEUI appears for each network adapter. You must configure each adapter with its own settings.

   The Bindings tab shows which clients and services are currently using the NetBEUI protocol. For information about configuring bindings, see "Configuring Network Adapters" earlier in this chapter.

2. Click the Advanced tab to modify settings for Maximum Sessions and NCBs for the real-mode NetBEUI.

| Option | Description |
|---|---|
| Maximum Sessions | Used to identify the maximum number of connections to remote computers that can be supported from the redirector. This is equivalent to the **sessions=** parameter formerly specified in PROTOCOL.INI. |
| NCBS (network control blocks) | Used to identify the maximum number of NetBIOS commands that can be used. This is equivalent to the **ncbs=** parameter formerly specified in PROTOCOL.INI. |

3. Click OK. Then shut down and restart the computer.

# Using WinPopup to Broadcast a Pop-Up Message

You can use WinPopup to send a message to one person or to a whole workgroup. WinPopup can also display a message from someone else on your network or from a printer when your print job is done. With WinPopup, you can send and receive messages and alerts from LAN Manager, Windows for Workgroups, Windows NT, and Windows 95 servers and clients.

On a NetWare network, you can also use WinPopup to send messages in the following cases:

- If you are running a NetWare-compatible client, you can receive pop-up messages from the server you are attached to. You can also receive messages from other users running Novell-supplied network clients if the message is sent to you on the server using NetWare utilities.

- You can use WinPopup to send a message to a user on a computer running Client for NetWare Networks or a Novell-supplied client if that user is attached to your preferred server.

- If you are running both Client for NetWare Networks and Client for Microsoft Networks, and if the message reaches the specified computer or user through Windows 95 networking, the message is not also sent through the NetWare server.

WinPopup is installed automatically with either Microsoft Client for NetWare Networks or Client for Microsoft Networks.

▶ **To configure WinPopup on a client computer**

1. Place WINPOPUP.EXE in the Startup folder on each computer that you want to receive messages.

2. On each computer, click the Messages Menu, and then click Options to specify choices for how WinPopup will present messages.

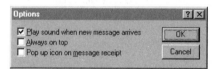

▶ **To send a message using WinPopup**

1. Click the Send button on the toolbar. Or, from the Messages menu, click Send.

2. Click an option to specify whether to send the message to a specific user or computer or to a workgroup. Then type the name for where the message is to be sent.

3.  Type a message, and then click OK.

As an example of how this might be used in a workgroup, you might want to run WinPopup on a computer running File and Printer Sharing services. Every computer in the workgroup that uses shared resources on this computer can also run WinPopup. On each client computer, WinPopup can report messages from the printer (such as notification that a print job has been completed). Or administrators can send messages to users and computers in the workgroup with pop-up notification.

To remove WinPopup from a computer, use the Add/Remove Programs option in Control Panel.

# Troubleshooting Protocol Problems

This section contains information about troubleshooting problems related to network protocols. For general information about troubleshooting the network installation, including how to use **net diag**, see Chapter 7, "Introduction to Windows 95 Networking." For information about troubleshooting procedures and tools provided with Windows 95, see Chapter 35, "General Troubleshooting."

### You cannot connect using NetBEUI.

- Use **net diag** to test for NetBIOS connectivity over the LANA that NetBEUI is using. If it fails, check the transceiver type, cabling, and adapter.

- Check the NetBEUI protocol bindings.

- Verify that routing is not involved.

### A NetBIOS application fails to start.

This might be because the application is hard-coded to use the protocol on LANA 0 (such as Lotus Notes). You can force a particular protocol to always occupy LANA 0 by selecting it as the default protocol, as described in "Setting LAN Adapter Numbers" earlier in this chapter.

### You cannot connect using the IPX/SPX-compatible protocol.

Verify that both computers trying to connect are using the same frame type and that other settings are correct for this protocol.

- Verify the following in the Advanced properties for this protocol, as described in "Configuring IPX/SPX-Compatible Protocol" earlier in this chapter:

  - The correct Frame Type is set. The recommended setting is Auto, but this frame type only checks SAP broadcast traffic on the network and might be selecting an incorrect frame type in a mixed frame-type environment.

  - Source Routing is enabled and a cache size is set if needed.

  - The option named Force Even Length Packets is set properly. NetWare servers with older NetWare Ethernet drivers or older IPX routers may require even-sized packets. If required, change this setting to make sure the computer transmits only even-length IPX frames.

- On the IPX routers, check the setting for Type 20 Packets (NetBIOS packets). When using NetBIOS over IPX, the IPX packet type is set to 14h (decimal 20). Manufacturers of routers might consider all NetBIOS traffic as being nonroutable LAN traffic even when carried over the routable IPX protocol, and so, by default, will not pass Type 20 NetBIOS IPX packets. To use NetBIOS over IPX connectivity, Type 20 packet passing must be enabled on the router.

- Use **net diag** to test for IPX connectivity over the related LANA number used by NetBIOS over IPX.

- Use System Monitor to view statistics for the IPX/SPX-compatible protocol. Then retry network operation and check the activity. If there is none, remove and reinstall the protocol, and then retry and retest the operation.

### You cannot connect using TCP/IP.

Use the TCP/IP diagnostic utilities included with Microsoft TCP/IP to isolate network hardware problems and incompatible configurations. The following list describes which utility helps to identify various problems.

| Use this utility | To accomplish this action |
| --- | --- |
| **ping** | Check host name, host IP address, and TCP/IP configuration; verify physical connection and remote TCP/IP computer |
| **arp** | Detect invalid entries in the ARP table on the local computer |
| **nbtstat** | Check the state of NetBIOS over TCP/IP connections, update LMHOSTS cache, and determine registered name and scope ID |
| **netstat** | Display statistics and state of current TCP/IP connections |
| **tracert** | Check the route to a remote computer |

You can also use the IP Configuration utility (WINIPCFG) to display, update, or release TCP/IP configuration values.

▶ **To test TCP/IP using ping**

- Check the loopback address by typing **ping 127.0.0.1** and pressing ENTER at the command prompt. The computer should respond immediately. (If you are using DHCP, use the IP Configuration utility to find the IP address.) To determine whether you configured IP properly, use **ping** with the IP address of your computer, your default gateway, and a remote host.

If you cannot use **ping** successfully at any point, verify the following:

- The computer was restarted after TCP/IP was installed and configured.
- The local computer's IP address is valid and appears correctly in the TCP/IP Properties dialog box.
- The IP address of the default gateway and remote host are correct.
- IP routing is enabled on the router, and the link between routers is operational.
- The local computer's Registry includes an entry for **lmhosts=c:\\***directory* that correctly indicates the location of LMHOSTS.

If you can use **ping** to connect to other computers running Windows 95 on a different subnetwork but cannot connect using Windows Explorer or **net use** \\\\*server*\\*share*, verify the following:

- The correct host computer name was used.

- The target host uses NetBIOS. If not, you must use FTP or Telnet to make a connection, and the target host must be configured with the FTP server daemon or Telnet daemon, and you must have correct permissions on the target host.

- The scope ID on the target host is the same as the local computer.

- A router path exists between your computer and the target computer.

- LMHOSTS contains correct entries, so the computer name can be resolved.

- The computer is configured to use WINS, the WINS server addresses are correct, and WINS servers are functioning.

### The "Unable to connect to a server" message appears.

This message appears if name resolution fails for a particular computer name. If the computer is on the local subnetwork, confirm that the target server name is spelled correctly and that the target server is running TCP/IP. If the computer is not on the local subnetwork, be sure that its name and IP address mapping are available in the LMHOSTS file or the WINS database. If all TCP/IP elements appear to be installed properly, use **ping** with the remote computer to be sure that its TCP/IP software is working.

Use the **nbtstat -n** command to determine what name (or names) the server registered on the network. The **nbtstat** command can also display the cached entries for remote computers from either #PRE entries in LMHOSTS or recently resolved names. If the remote computers are using the same name for the server, and the other computers are on a remote subnetwork, be sure that they have the computer's mapping in their LMHOSTS files.

### IP address connects but host names do not.

Verify that the HOSTS file and DNS settings have been configured for the computer by checking settings on the DNS Configuration tab.

- If you are using a HOSTS file, verify that the DNS host name of the remote computer is identical—especially in terms of spelling and capitalization—to the name in the file and the application using it.

- If you are using DNS, verify that the IP addresses of the DNS servers are correct and in proper order. Use **ping** with the remote computer, and type both the host name and IP address to determine if the host name is resolved properly.

Use the **netstat -a** command to show the status of all activity on TCP and UDP ports on the local computer. A good TCP connection is usually established with 0 bytes in the send and receive queues. If data is blocked in either queue or if the state is irregular, there might be a problem with the connection. If not, you are probably experiencing network or application delays.

## Connect times are long after adding to LMHOSTS.

You might experience long connect times with a large LMHOSTS file if there is an entry at the end of the file. If so, mark the entry in LMHOSTS as a preloaded entry by following the mapping with the #PRE tag, or place the mapping higher in the LMHOSTS file. Then use the **nbtstat -R** command to update the local name cache immediately. The LMHOSTS file is parsed sequentially to locate entries without the #PRE keyword. You should place frequently used entries near the top of the file, and place the #PRE entries near the bottom.

P A R T   4

# System Management

This part of the *Windows 95 Resource Kit* contains the following chapters, describing system management of individual and network computers running Windows 95.

### Chapter 13   Introduction to System Management

Describes how user profiles, system policies, remote administration, and network backup functionality make it easier for administrators to manage corporate networks. This chapter also describes where to find system management tools to use with Windows 95.

### Chapter 14   Security

Describes the security features of Windows 95, including security for network and system logon, and security for shared resources on computers running Windows 95. It also describes options for using password caching, and describes Windows 95 security for remote administration.

### Chapter 15   User Profiles and System Policies

Describes how to use user profiles to define desktop preferences and application settings for individuals. This chapter also describes how to use system policies to control what users can and cannot do on the desktop and the network.

### Chapter 16   Remote Administration

Describes the Windows 95 management features that allow you to manage network computers from your own computer. This chapter also includes information about administration applications and network backup agents from other vendors to support network administrators in the corporate enterprise.

### Chapter 17   Performance Tuning

Describes how the built-in features for Windows 95 manage memory and ensure peak performance from hardware, software, and the network. This chapter describes how to use tools for configuring swap files and the file system, and how to use System Monitor to monitor performance in Windows 95.

C H A P T E R   1 3

# Introduction to System Management

The Windows 95 system architecture supports security and centralized system management for configuring remote computers on the network. This chapter summarizes the features that support system management in Windows 95.

**In This Chapter**

System Management with Windows 95   456
Sources for Windows 95 System Management Tools   457

# System Management with Windows 95

The system management tools and agents provided with Windows 95 support system management for three management areas:

- Operating system software, including drivers, system services, and user interface components. These require system software distribution, system and user configuration management, security, and data backup.

- Hardware, including the computer's motherboard, add-in cards, hard disk and CD-ROM drives, monitors, tape drives, pointing devices, and keyboards.

- Application software that must be licensed and installed.

Windows 95 provides Registry-based support for remote management of configuration settings for hardware and software settings—either on individual computers or (through system policies) on multiple computers on the network. In addition, the Windows 95 compact disc includes agents for remote system administration using other management software.

The following summarizes the important features in Windows 95 that support system management on corporate networks.

**Security for system logon and resource access.**  The administrator can take advantage of centralized user accounts on Windows NT or Novell® NetWare® networks to restrict network logon and access to shared resources on computers running Windows 95. Windows 95 provides password caching to make it easier for users to manage connections to password-protected resources, yet also allows network administrators to restrict users' capabilities and, consequently, enforce strict security policies. For information, see Chapter 14, "Security."

**User profiles.**  When user profiles are enabled, individual users, desktop configurations are available wherever they log on to the network. This solution permits multiple users to share one computer and "roving" users to log on to other networked computers while maintaining their personal settings. Administrators can also enforce a "mandatory" user profile, which can be useful for managing a common desktop for novice users. For information, see Chapter 15, "User Profiles and System Policies."

**System policies.**  The administrator can use system policies to specify required system settings and to restrict network access, security privileges, and system settings from a convenient central source. Policies can be specified for groups, for specific users, and for multiple computers, providing administrators significant control over users' ability to configure computer and desktop settings. For information, see Chapter 15, "User Profiles and System Policies."

**Remote administration.**  Built-in capabilities for remote administration assist administrators in managing networking computers from a central location, reducing the burden of supporting system configuration and troubleshooting on the corporate network. For information, see Chapter 16, "Remote Administration."

**Backup capabilities.**  Backup agents used with Windows 95 support network-based data backup without requiring user intervention. Windows 95 includes network backup agents from Arcada and Cheyenne. For information, see Chapter 16, "Remote Administration."

**System administration agents.**  The Windows 95 compact disc includes agents that run as services for use with system management products from various vendors, including Microsoft Systems Management Server, HP® Openview, Intel® LANDesk™, IBM® LAN NetView®, Sun® NetManager, and Novell NMS. For information, see Chapter 16, "Remote Administration."

**Windows 95 Registry.**  In Windows 95, the operating system collects information about the hardware, system configuration settings, and applications and stores it in the Registry. The Windows 95 Registry is a structured database that consolidates configuration and status information for hardware and software components. As a result, this information is available to system management applications ensuring flexible system management capabilities.

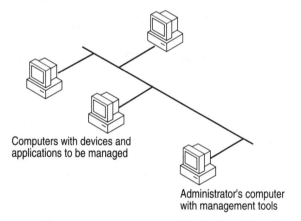

Computers with devices and
applications to be managed

Administrator's computer
with management tools

# Sources for Windows 95 System Management Tools

The tools and agents that network administrators can use for system management are available from various installation sources. System management software can be installed during Setup or from Control Panel after Windows 95 is installed.

When you install Windows 95 from the installation floppy disks, System Policy Editor is installed automatically with the operational system files. This tool can be used to modify INI files, CONFIG.SYS, and AUTOEXEC.BAT. When you install Windows 95 from the compact disc, Setup installs Registry Editor, the utility used to modify the Registry. The following tools can be installed optionally from the Windows 95 installation disks (either floppy disks or compact disc):

- Disk Defragmenter, DriveSpace, ScanDisk, and Microsoft Backup, as described in Chapter 20, "Disks and File Systems."
- Net Watcher, as described in Chapter 16, "Remote Administration."

Some agents and tools are provided only on the Windows 95 compact disc (in the directories shown in the illustration), and not the Windows 95 floppy disks. This software can be installed directly from the compact disc, or the administrator can copy the software to the shared network directory that contains the Windows 95 source files. This software can be installed from custom setup scripts during Windows 95 installation, or by using Control Panel after Windows 95 is installed.

The following administrative tools can be installed from the Windows 95 compact disc by using the Network option in Control Panel:

- Arcada® Backup Exec agent
- Cheyenne® ARCserve agent

The following tools are available only in the ADMIN\APPTOOLS directory on the Windows 95 compact disc. You can run these tools directly from the compact disc or install them locally by using the Add/Remove Programs option in Control Panel:

- Password List Editor (in the PWLEDIT subdirectory), as described in Chapter 14, "Security."
- System Policy Editor (in the POLEDIT subdirectory), as described in Chapter 15, "User Profiles and System Policies."

The following agents and services are available only in the ADMIN\NETTOOLS directory on the Windows 95 compact disc. You can install them on a local computer by using the Network option in Control Panel.

- For remote administration:
  - Microsoft Remote Registry service (in the REMOTREG subdirectory)
  - Microsoft SNMP agent (in the SNMP subdirectory)
  - Microsoft Network Monitor agent (in the NETMON subdirectory)

For information about including options from the ADMIN directory on the Windows 95 compact disc—such as the Microsoft Network Monitor agent, SNMP, or SLIP—when installing Windows 95 from a network source, see Chapter 5, "Custom, Automated, and Push Installations."

C H A P T E R    1 4

# Security

This chapter presents an overview of the security features provided with Windows 95 and describes how to use them in a networking environment.

**In This Chapter**

Windows 95 Security: The Basics    460

Windows 95 Security: The Issues    461

Windows 95 Network Security Overview    462

Setting Up Security for Shared Resources    464

Using Share-Level Security    466

Using User-Level Security    467

   Specifying Directory Access Rights in User-Level Security    468

   Managing User Lists    469

   Security for Windows 95 in NetWare Bindery Environments    469

Using the Windows 95 Password Cache    470

Using Password List Editor    471

Using the Windows 95 Logon Password    472

Using Windows 95 with NetWare Passwords    474

Using System Policies to Enforce Password Security    475

Guidelines for Setting Password Policy    476

# Windows 95 Security: The Basics

You can use Windows 95 security to prevent unauthorized access to the network and to shared resources on computers in a network. The following security features are built into Windows 95.

**Unified logon prompt.**  With Windows 95, users can log on to all networks and Windows 95 at the same time. If a user's password for Windows 95 or for another network is the same as the password for the primary logon client, Windows 95 automatically logs the user on to Windows 95 and all networks using that password. For more information, see "Using the Windows 95 Logon Password" later in this chapter.

**Windows 95 logon security.**  With system policies, you can prevent users from logging on to Windows 95 if their Windows NT or Novell® NetWare® network logon is not validated. To require validation by a Windows NT domain controller or NetWare server before allowing access to Windows 95, you must use system policies to enable Require Validation By Network For Windows Access. For more information, see Chapter 15, "User Profiles and System Policies."

**User-level or share-level security for peer resource sharing.**  When a computer is running Windows 95 with File and Printer Sharing services, other users can connect to shared printers, volumes, directories, and CD-ROM drives on that computer. To protect these shared resources, Windows 95 provides user-level and share-level security. With user-level security, a user's request to access a shared resource is passed through to a security provider, a Windows NT or NetWare server, which grants or denies the request. With shared-level security, users assign passwords to their shared resources, and any user who can provide the correct password can access the shared resource.

---

**Note**  You can use user-level security without installing File and Printer Sharing services, such as when using the Remote Registry service.

---

**Password caching.**  When a user first types and saves a password when connecting to a password-protected resource, Windows 95 caches the password in the password list file. Logging on with a Windows 95 password unlocks the password list file and associates those passwords with the Windows 95 password. To the user, it seems as if the passwords for Windows 95 and for password-protected resources are the same. If password caching is disabled, users must type the password each time they connect to a password-protected resource.

**Password List Editor.**  This tool allows you to view and delete the contents of users' password list files.

**Password controls in system policies.**   You can use system policies to enforce a password policy with greater restrictions, including the following:

- Disable password caching
- Require alphanumeric Windows 95 logon password
- Require minimum Windows 95 logon password length

**Other system policies.**   You can define policies to prevent users from enabling peer resource sharing services and to enforce other security components, such as preventing users from configuring system components. For more information, see Chapter 15, "User Profiles and System Policies." See also "Using System Policies to Enforce Password Security" later in this chapter.

# Windows 95 Security: The Issues

Before you integrate Windows 95 security into your network security model, you should consider the following issues:

- What kind of logon security do you need? Do you want to require that users log on to Windows 95 and the network with the same password? Do you want to require alphanumeric or minimum-length passwords for the Windows 95 logon password? Do you want to require that users be validated by the network security provider before being able to log on to Windows 95?

  For both Windows NT and NetWare networks, you can use system policies to require validation by a Windows NT or NetWare server before allowing access to Windows 95 and to specify other Windows 95 password restrictions.

- What kind of resource protection do you need on Microsoft networks? If you allow users to enable peer resource sharing, then you must decide whether users can protect those resources with share-level or user-level security. User-level security provides greater security because the network security provider must authenticate the user name and password before access to the resource is granted. (Share-level security is not available for File and Printer Sharing for NetWare Networks.)

- What kinds of access rights will users have to resources protected by user-level security? You can specify the types of rights users or groups of users have to resources by setting Access Control properties in the Network option in Control Panel. For example, you can restrict other users to read-only access to files or give them read and write access to files.

- How do you want to enable user-level security? You can enable security in a setup script, in the Network option in Control Panel, or in system policies. If you enable user-level security in either a setup script or in the Control Panel, then Remote Administration is enabled by default for domain administrators on a Windows NT network and for supervisors on a NetWare network.

- Do you want to disable password caching for password-protected resources? You can use system policies to disable password caching and require users to type a password each time they access a password-protected resource.

- Do you want users to be able to configure system components, their desktops, applications, or network connections in Control Panel? You can use system policies to restrict users' ability to configure components.

- Do you need to control access to a computer's hard disk drive? Because Windows 95 uses network-based security instead of workstation security, an individual computer running Windows 95 is vulnerable to someone accessing data stored on the hard disk by starting the computer using Safe Mode or a floppy disk. If specific data requires greater levels of security, you should store critical files on a secure server. If computers require greater levels of security, Windows NT Workstation is recommended because it provides a means to protect resources on a hard disk based on a user's identity.

- Do you need to prevent users from modifying computer settings or from running certain applications? To implement this type of security, you should use system policies as described in Chapter 15, "User Profiles and System Policies."

# Windows 95 Network Security Overview

Windows 95 provides shared-level and user-level security for protecting shared resources on computers running Windows 95 with File and Printer Sharing services.

- Share-level security protects shared network resources on the computer running Windows 95 with individually assigned passwords. For example, you can assign a password to a directory or a locally attached printer. If other users want to access it, they need to type in the appropriate password. If you do not assign a password to a shared resource, every user with access to the network can access that resource. (This option is not supported with File and Printer Sharing for NetWare Networks.)

- Pass-through user-level security protects shared network resources by requiring that a security provider authenticate a user's request to access resources. The security provider, such as a Windows NT domain control or NetWare server, grants access to the shared resource by verifying that the user name and password are the same as those on the user account list stored on the network security provider. Because the security provider maintains a network-wide list of user accounts and passwords, each computer running Windows 95 does not have to store a list of accounts.

> **Note**  If you are running File and Printer Sharing for Microsoft Networks, the security provider must be the name of a Windows NT domain or Windows NT workstation. If you are running Microsoft File and Printer Sharing for NetWare Networks, the security provider must be either a NetWare server or a NetWare 4.x server running bindery emulation.

The following illustration shows how user-level security works on a computer running File and Printer Sharing service and Client for Microsoft Networks. The numbers are explained following the illustration.

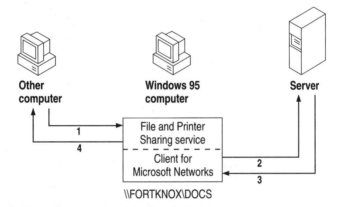

1. A user tries to access a shared resource protected by pass-through user-level security.

2. A request is passed to the security provider to verify the user's identity.

3. The security provider sends a verification to the computer running Windows 95 if the user name and password combination is valid.

4. Windows 95 grants access to the shared resource, and gives permission to use the resource according to rights assigned to the user in Sharing properties for that Windows 95 resource. The user's rights are stored on the computer running Windows 95.

Planning and implementing security in a Windows 95 networking environment requires the following basic kinds of steps:

- Defining user accounts on a network server or domain controller for user-level security. For more information, see the documentation for the software on the network security provider.

- Installing File and Printer Sharing services and enabling user-level or share-level security. For more information, see Chapter 11, "Logon, Browsing, and Resource Sharing."

- Defining access rights for resources protected by user-level security.

- Making the Windows 95 logon password and network logon password the same, disabling password caching if you do not want this feature. For more information, see "Using the Windows 95 Password Cache" later in this chapter and "Using the Windows 95 Logon Password" later in this chapter.

- Defining system policies to restrict users' ability to configure the system or shared resources, and to enforce password policies. For information, see Chapter 15, "User Profiles and System Policies."

# Setting Up Security for Shared Resources

Before a user can share a resource on a computer running Windows 95, the computer must be configured for share-level or user-level security, and File and Printer Sharing services must be installed by using the Network option in Control Panel. Configuring share-level or user-level security is described briefly in the following sections, and in Chapter 11, "Logon, Browsing, and Resource Sharing."

---

**Note**  Share-level security is not available on computers running Microsoft File and Printer Sharing for NetWare.

---

▶ **To set up share-level security for a single computer**

1. Install File and Printer Sharing for Microsoft Networks, as described in Chapter 11, "Logon, Browsing, and Resource Sharing."

2. In the Network option in Control Panel, click the Access Control tab, and then click Share-Level Access Control.

▶ **To set up user-level security on a computer on a NetWare network**

1. Install File and Printer Sharing services for NetWare Networks, as described in Chapter 11, "Logon, Browsing, and Resource Sharing."

2. In the Network option in Control Panel, click the Access Control tab, and then click User-level Access Control.

3. In the User-level Access Control box, type the name of the NetWare server, and then click OK.

▶ **To set up user-level security on a computer on a Microsoft network**

1. In the Network option in Control Panel, click the Access Control tab, and then click User-level Access Control.

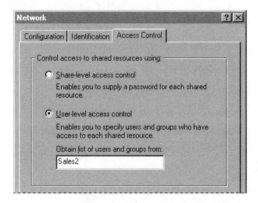

2. Type the name of the Windows NT domain or Windows NT workstation where the user accounts reside, and then click OK.

For information about specifying values for security in custom setup scripts, see Appendix D, "MSBATCH.INF Parameters." For information about using System Policy Editor to set user-level security and other security options, see Chapter 15, "User Profiles and System Policies."

# Using Share-Level Security

You can restrict access to a shared directory or printer by either defining it as read-only or assigning a password to it.

▶ **To share a directory or printer with share-level security**

1. In Windows Explorer or My Computer, right-click the icon for the directory or printer you want to share and, in the context menu, click Sharing.

2. Click the Sharing tab. Then click Share As, and type the resource's share name.

   The shared resource name will be the computer name plus the share name. For example, in the following illustration, if the computer name is mycomputer, then this shared resource in \\mycomputer\adamt.

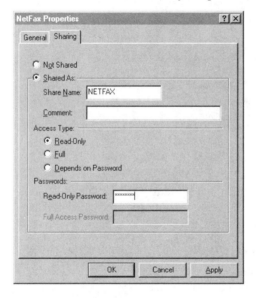

3. Specify whether you want users to have read-only or full access to this resource.

4. Optionally, type the password (or passwords) for read-only or full access, and click OK.

---

**Tip**  You can share a directory but hide it from the Network Neighborhood browsing list by adding a dollar-sign character ($) to the end of its share name (for example, PRIVATE$).

---

# Using User-Level Security

For each network resource or service governed by user-level security, there is a list of users and groups that can access that resource.

▶ **To share a directory or printer with user-level security**

1. In Windows Explorer or My Computer, right-click a resource and, in the context menu, click Sharing.

2. In the resource's properties, click Add.

3. In the Add Users dialog box, click a user or group, and then assign access rights as described in the following section.

For each user, there is a set of rights assigned for a resource. The kinds of rights that you assign depend on the kind of resource you are securing:

- For shared directories, you can allow a user to have read-only access, full access, or custom access. Within custom access, you can grant the user any or all of the following rights: read, write, create, list, delete, change file attributes, and change access rights.

- For shared printers, a user either has the right to access the printer or not.

- For remote administration, a user either has the right to be an administrator or not as defined in the Passwords option in Control Panel.

Permissions are enforced for a resource as follows:

- If the user has explicit rights to the resource, then those rights are enforced.

- If the user does not have explicit rights to the resource, then the permissions are determined by taking all of the rights of each group to which the user belongs.

- If none of the groups to which the user belongs has any rights to that resource, then the user is not granted access to the resource.

When you do not explicitly assign access rights to a file or directory, Windows 95 uses implied rights. Implied rights are those assigned to a file or directory's nearest parent directory. If none of the parent directories (up to and including the root directory of the drive) have explicit rights, no access is allowed.

**Note**   Implied rights are displayed automatically in the properties dialog boxes of the shared file or directory.

# Specifying Directory Access Rights in User-Level Security

Access rights specify what a user can do in a directory protected by user-level security. The access rights you define for a directory apply to all of its subdirectories. You cannot, however, assign permissions to individual files in Windows 95. (Both Windows NT and NetWare allow you to assign permissions to files.)

For each directory, you can assign read-only, full, or custom access. (Read-only and full access are equivalent to the same values used by Windows for Workgroups with share-level security.) Custom access allows you to further specify exactly what each user or group can do in the directory, as specified in the following list.

| File operation | Required permissions |
|---|---|
| Read from a closed file | Read files |
| See a filename | List files |
| Search a directory for files | List files |
| Write to a closed file | Write, create, delete, change file attributes |
| Run an executable file | Read, list files |
| Create and write to a file | Create files |
| Copy files from a directory | Read, list files |
| Copy files to a directory | Write, create, list files |
| Make a new directory | Create files |
| Delete a file | Delete files |
| Remove a directory | Delete files |
| Change directory or file attributes | Change file attributes |
| Rename a file or directory | Change file attributes |
| Change access rights | Change access control |

▶ **To define custom access**

1. Open the Add Users dialog box in a shared resource's properties as described in the preceding procedure.

2. In the Add Users dialog box, click a user or group, click Custom, and then click OK.

3. In the Add Users dialog box, click a user or group from the Name list, and then click Custom.

4. In the Change Access Rights dialog box, click the type of rights the user or group of users can have in the directory, and then click OK.

5. To remove a user or group of users, click the user or group of users, and then click Remove.

6. To edit the access rights for a user or group of users, click the user or group of users, and then click Edit.

# Managing User Lists

Windows 95 user-level security depends on a list of accounts and groups located on a security provider. You cannot add or remove users and groups from the security provider list by using Windows 95 tools. However, you can do this by running User Manager for a Windows NT domain, SYSCON for NetWare 3.x, and NETADMIN for NetWare 4.x. in a NetWare bindery environment. You can use these tools on a computer running Windows 95. These tools are provided by the respective vendors and not by Windows 95.

Under Windows 95, you specify what rights users have to specific resources on the local computer as described in the preceding section. For more information about changing a user's access rights, see "Specifying Directory Access Rights in User-Level Security" earlier in this chapter.

---

**Note**  Although Windows NT networks allow multiple domains, a computer running Windows 95 can specify only one domain for user-level security. To use a trust relationship to access multiple domains, you should consult the *Windows NT Server 3.5 Concepts and Planning Guide* that is part of the Windows NT Server documentation set.

---

# Security for Windows 95 in NetWare Bindery Environments

NetWare 3.x servers store all the information about users, groups, passwords, and rights in a database stored on the server called the bindery. NetWare 4.x servers can appear to have a bindery through bindery emulation, a feature which is enabled by default. There is a separate bindery for each NetWare server. Windows 95 can use the bindery of only one NetWare server as the security provider.

It is common for a company to have one or more NetWare servers per department, where users log on to the server for their department. This scenario can pose a problem when the list of accounts differs from one NetWare server to another.

For example, Sue and Bob log on to the Sales server and Fred logs on to the R&D server. Because Sue is running Windows 95 and can specify only one server for pass-through validation, she specifies Sales (the server she uses for logon). She can now grant access to shared resources on her computer to Bob but cannot grant access to Fred.

The only way to solve this problem is to include all user accounts for all servers on one NetWare server. This server should be specified as the security provider for every computer running Windows 95 with File and Printer Sharing for NetWare Networks.

**Note**  User-level security in Windows 95 does not support the use of NetWare domains and the NetWare Name Service (NNS), an Add-On service for NetWare 4.x servers to obtain user lists. Windows 95 does support NetWare 4.x with bindery emulation to obtain user lists.

# Using the Windows 95 Password Cache

Keeping track of multiple passwords can be a problem for users. Often, they either forget the passwords or write them down and post lists of passwords near their computers. When this happens, the security policy is no longer doing the job it was meant to do—to allow access to those who should have it and to deny access to those who shouldn't.

Windows 95 solves this problem by storing passwords for resources in a password list file (.PWL). This file stores passwords for the following network resources:

- Resources on a computer running Windows 95 protected by share-level security

- Applications that are password-protected: these applications must be specifically written to the Master Password API

- Windows NT computers that don't participate in a domain, or the Windows NT logon password if it isn't the Primary Network Logon

- NetWare servers

The password list file is stored in the Windows directory on the local computer. Each resource typically has its own password. The password file is encrypted by using an algorithm. An unencrypted password is never sent across the network.

**Caution**  If you delete .PWL files, you will lose all previously stored passwords. You will need to retype each password.

Password caching is enabled by default when you install Windows 95. When you access a password-protected resource for the first time, make sure the Save This Password In Your Password List option is checked to save the password to the password list file.

**Note**  If, during logon, you click the Cancel button to bypass the logon screen, the cache will not be opened and you will be prompted for a password each time you attempt to use a protected resource.

You can disable password caching by using System Policy Editor.

▶ **To disable password caching by using system policies**

1.  In System Policy Editor, double-click the Local Computer icon.

2.  In the Local Computer Properties, click Network, and then click Passwords.

3.  Click the policy named Disable Password Caching.

For more information, see Chapter 15, "User Profiles and System Policies."

**Note**  If you have any share-level security servers and you disable password caching and are running Client for Microsoft Networks, you should not use the Quick Logon feature in the Network option in Control Panel.

# Using Password List Editor

If password caching is enabled, Windows 95 caches passwords in the password list file when you connect to a password-protected network resource. Password List Editor (PWLEDIT) allows you to view the resources listed in a user's password list file (.PWL). It does not allow you to view the actual passwords, but it allows you to remove specific password entries if problems are encountered using a cached password.

Password List Editor works only if the password list file is unlocked, that is, if the user is logged on. It can be used to view only the contents of the logged-on user's password list file, so you should run it on the user's computer.

Password List Editor can be found in the ADMIN\APPTOOLS\PWLEDIT directory on the Windows 95 compact disc.

▶ **To install Password List Editor**

1. In the Add/Remove Programs option in Control Panel, click the Windows Setup tab, and then click Have Disk button.

2. In the Install From Disk dialog box, click Browse. Type the path name to ADMIN\APPTOOLS\PWLEDIT\PWLEDIT.INF, and then click OK.

3. In the Have Disk dialog box, click Password List Editor, and then click Install.

▶ **To run Password List Editor**

• From the Start menu, click Run, and type **pwledit**

# Using the Windows 95 Logon Password

With Windows 95, users can log on to all networks and Windows 95 at the same time. The first time a user starts Windows 95, logon dialog boxes appear for Windows 95 and for each network client on that computer. This is useful for you as a network administrator because you can use existing user accounts on a network security provider to validate access to the network for users running Windows 95. For more information, see Chapter 11, "Logon, Browsing, and Resource Sharing."

If a user's password for Windows 95 or for another network is the same as the password for the primary logon client, Windows 95 logs the user on to Windows 95 and the network automatically using that password. When a user logs on to other networks with different passwords and chooses to save them, the passwords are stored in the password list file. The Windows 95 password unlocks this password list file. Thereafter, Windows 95 uses the passwords stored in the password list file to log a user on to other networks so no additional passwords need to be typed.

The Passwords option in Control Panel provides a way to synchronize logon passwords for different networks. This allows users to use the password for whatever logon dialog box appears first (the primary network logon client or Windows 95 logon) for logging on to all the other network clients.

You can also use the Passwords option to change individual passwords to other network resources to be different than the Windows 95 logon password.

▶ **To change a password for a network resource to be the same as the Windows 95 logon password**

1. In the Passwords icon option in Control Panel, click Change Windows Password.

2. In the Change Windows Password dialog box, check the other passwords you would like to change to use the same password as the Windows 95 password, and then click OK.

   To appear in this list, the related software must include a function that allows its password to be changed.

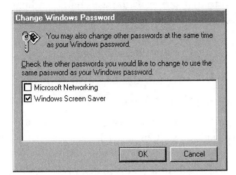

3. In the second Change Windows Password dialog box, type the current (old) Windows 95 password, type a new password, and then, in the Confirm New Password box, type the new password again.

---

**Note** The Windows Screen Saver passwords option will show up here only if the Windows screen saver has been turned on and the password-protected option has been selected.

---

You can maintain separate passwords for a network resource and require users to type a password each time they access it.

▶ **To change a password for a network resource**

1. In the Passwords option in Control Panel, click Change Other Passwords.

2. In the Select Password dialog box, click the password you want to change, and then click Change.

3. In the Change Password dialog box, type the current (old) password, type a new password, and then in the Confirm New Password box, type the new password again. Click OK.

   You now must type a separate password to access the resource.

# Using Windows 95 with NetWare Passwords

To log on to a NetWare network, you must type the name of the preferred server on which the related user account is stored. After the user name and password are validated by the network server, you can use resources shared on that server. If you are not validated, you will be prompted to enter a password whenever connecting to a NetWare server during this work session.

The first time you attempt to connect to a NetWare server other than the preferred server, the NetWare server searches the Windows 95 password list file for a user name and password to that server. If the user name and password pair are not valid, NetWare displays a dialog box and asks you to type a user name and password. If there is no NetWare user name and password in the password list file, NetWare tries using the Windows 95 logon password. You can disable this automatic attempt to log on to NetWare resources.

▶ **To avoid use of automatic NetWare logon**

- Use system policies to enable the policy named Disable Automatic NetWare Login. For information, see Chapter 15, "User Profiles and System Policies."

▶ **To change your password on a NetWare server**

1. At the command prompt, use the **net use** command to connect to the NetWare server's SYS volume. For example, for a server name NWSVR2, you would type:

```
net use * \\nwsvr2\sys
```

2. At the command prompt, change to the drive for the NetWare server, and then make the PUBLIC directory the current directory. For example, if the drive is mapped to drive N, type:

```
n:
```

Then type:

```
mdcd \public
```

---

**Note**  If you want to change your password on more than one server, connect to all affected servers before running the **setpass** command. Setpass is a utility provided by Novell and is not part of Windows 95.

---

3. At the command prompt, type **setpass**

   If the server on which you want to change your password is different from the one on the current drive, type **setpass** and the server name.

   For example, to change your password on the server named NWSERVE1, type:

   ```
   setpass nwserve1
   ```

4. When you are prompted, type your old password, then type and confirm the new password.

5. If you are connected to other NetWare servers that also use your old password, these servers are listed, and you are asked if you want to change your password on these servers also.

# Using System Policies to Enforce Password Security

You can use system policies to increase security by forcing users to follow specific password guidelines. Using system policies, you can enforce the following password policies:

- Require Validation By Network For Windows Access, to specify that each logon be validated by a server before access to Windows is allowed. This applies to Windows NT and NetWare networks.

- Disable Automatic NetWare Login, to specify that when Windows 95 attempts to connect to a NetWare server, it does not automatically use the user's logon name and password or the password list file.

- Minimum Windows Logon Password Length, to control the minimum number of characters accepted for a Windows 95 logon password.

- Require Alphanumeric Windows Logon Password, to force a Windows 95 logon password to be a combination of numbers and letters.

- Hide Share Passwords With Asterisks, to cause asterisks to replace characters that users type when accessing a shared resource. This setting applies only to share-level security and is enabled by default.

- Disable Passwords Control Panel, to prevent access to the Passwords option in Control Panel.

- Hide Change Passwords Page, to hide this properties dialog box in the Passwords option in Control Panel.

- Disable Password Caching, to prevent saving of passwords for share-level resources, applications, and for NetWare passwords.

- Disable Caching Of Domain Password, to prevent the caching of the network password.

For information about restricting settings with system policies, see Chapter 15, "User Profiles and System Policies."

# Guidelines for Setting Password Policy

A good password policy helps users protect their passwords from other individuals. This helps to reduce the probability of someone logging on with another user's password and gaining unauthorized access to data.

The following guidelines should help you create a basic security policy:

- Tell users not to write down their passwords.
- Tell users not to use obvious passwords, such as their name, their spouse's name, the names of their children, and so on.
- Do not distribute user accounts and passwords in the same communication. For example, if you are sending a new user's account name and password in writing, send the user name and the password at different times.

You can use the following Windows NT and NetWare security features to enhance Windows 95 security:

- Enforce a reasonable minimum password length, which increases the number of permutations needed to randomly or programmatically guess someone's password. Additionally, you can enforce an alphanumeric password combination to achieve the same security.
- Enforce maximum and minimum password age. A maximum password age forces the user to change the password, preventing someone else from discovering it as a result of the password being in use for a long time. A minimum password age prevents a user from immediately reverting back to a previous password after a change.
- Enforce password uniqueness and maintain password history. This prevents users from toggling between their favorite passwords. You can specify the number of unique passwords that a user must have before that user can use a password that has previously been used.

C H A P T E R   1 5

# User Profiles and System Policies

This chapter describes how user profiles can help users maintain their own preferences, network settings, and application settings when logging on to a workstation. This chapter also describes how you can use system policies to control what users can and cannot do on the desktop and on the network. These features can help decrease the cost of managing numerous computers by allowing you to manage configurations remotely.

**In This Chapter**

User Profiles and System Policies: The Basics   479
User Profiles and System Policies: The Issues   480
User Profiles Overview   482
Enabling User Profiles   485
    Setting Up User Profiles on a Windows NT Network   486
    Setting Up User Profiles on a NetWare Network   487
    Disabling Standard Roving Profiles   487
    Maintaining Roving User Profiles on Other Networks   488
    Defining Mandatory User Profiles   489
System Policies Overview   490
    Overview of System Policies for Users   492
    Overview of System Policies for Computers   493
System Policy Editor   493
    Installing System Policy Editor   494
    Using System Policy Editor   495
Preparing to Use System Policies on the Network   498
    Setting Up for Automatic Downloading of System Policies   499
    Setting Up for Manual Downloading of System Policies   499

*(continued)*

Creating System Policies   501
Creating Policies for Individual Users or Computers   502
Creating Policies for Groups   502
Managing Custom Folders for Use with System Policies   504
System Policy Examples   506
Recommended Standard Desktop Configuration   506
Recommended Maximum Control Desktop Configuration   507
System Policy Settings Summary   508
Restricting Access to User-Specific Settings   509
Restricting Access to Computer-Specific Settings   514
System Policy Templates   518
Troubleshooting with System Policy Editor   525

# User Profiles and System Policies: The Basics

A user profile consists of user-specific information contained in the file USER.DAT, which is one of the two files in the Windows 95 Registry. Optionally, a user profile can also contain special Windows 95 directories. The benefits of using user profiles are summarized in this section.

**Multiple users on a computer can retain their personal settings.** "Roving" users can log on to the network from any computer and work with the same desktop settings as long as the computer is running a Windows 95 32-bit, protected-mode network client.

**Windows 95 automatically maintains each user's profile.** Whether profiles are stored locally or on the network, you need to enable user profiles only for the computers where they will be used.

**Mandatory profiles can be used to enforce consistent desktops.** This is useful for novice users who cannot manage their own desktop settings. Mandatory profiles increase user productivity and ease the burden of training and support for system managers.

System policies allow you to override local Registry values for user or computer settings. Policies are defined in a policy (.POL) file, usually called CONFIG.POL. When a user logs on, system policy settings overwrite default settings in the Registry. You can also set system policies to contain additional custom settings specific to the network.

Unlike SYSTEM.DAT and USER.DAT (the two files that make up the Registry), CONFIG.POL is not a required component of Windows 95 Setup and, when implemented, is stored on the logon server, not the local computer. The following list summarizes the benefits of system policies.

**System policies can be used to enforce system configuration.** You can restrict what users are allowed to do from the desktop and what they are allowed to configure using Control Panel. Also, you can use system policies to centrally configure network settings, such as the network client configuration options and the ability to install or configure File and Printer Sharing services. Finally, policies can be used to customize certain parts of the desktop, such as Network Neighborhood or the Programs folder.

**Registry settings can be changed by using System Policy Editor.** You can use System Policy Editor to change many common Registry settings, either for an individual local or remote computer. You can use these settings in a system policy file to change Registry values on multiple computers.

**System policies can be applied individually or per group.**  You can use group policies to define a set of policies to be applied on the basis of membership in the groups already defined on a NetWare or Windows NT network. Group policies make computer management on the corporate network easier by leveraging the current administrative organization of users.

Windows 95 provides a set of policies that you can use to specify settings for users. You can also add new Registry settings to this set of policies or you can modify policy templates to create new custom policies for any applications that use the Windows 95 Registry.

# User Profiles and System Policies: The Issues

You can use system policies or mandatory user profiles to enforce user settings. You should choose to use one method or the other, but not both. The two features differ in the following ways:

- System policies let you mandate user-specific and computer-specific settings. Mandatory user profiles let you mandate only user-specific settings.

- System policies let you selectively determine a subset of user settings to control, and each user controls the remaining settings. Mandatory user profiles always control every user-specific setting.

Before implementing user profiles, you should consider the following issues:

- Do you want to use system policies for user settings? If so, you must enable user profiles on the computer.

- What do you want to include in user profiles? For example, you might choose to include the desktop, Start menu, or Network Neighborhood in the user profile.

- Do you want user profiles to work across the network so that they are available to roving users? If so, the computers must be running a 32-bit, protected-mode network client. Also, you must make sure that each user has a home directory on the network.

- Should mandatory user profiles be used? If so, you must copy the necessary files to each user's home directory.

If you want to make user profiles available on the network (rather than on individual computers), you must perform the following preliminary steps:

- Install and run a 32-bit, protected mode networking client (such as Client for NetWare Networks or Client for Microsoft Networks) on the computers.

- Make sure that the server supports long filenames for full user profile functionality. If the server doesn't support long filenames, only USER.DAT will follow a user around the network. Users will not be able to download other folders (such as those that support the Start menu and Network Neighborhood configuration).

- For Microsoft networks, make sure that a network home directory exists for each user because this is where user profiles are placed. (On Novell® NetWare® networks, profiles are placed in the MAIL/*user_ID* directory, which always exists.)

- For each computer, use the same names for the directory and the hard disk drive in which Windows 95 is installed. If Windows 95 is installed in C:\WINDOWS on one computer and in C:\WIN95 on another computer, some components of the user profile will not be transferred between the two computers. This is also true if Windows 95 is installed on different hard disks on different computers (for example, C:\WINDOWS on one computer, and D:\WINDOWS on another).

Before implementing system policies, you should consider the following issues:

- What types of restrictions and settings would you like to define and manage centrally? For example, do you want to limit access to the MS-DOS prompt and other applications or to Control Panel options, or do you want to implement a standard desktop for all users?

- Do you want to use one set of standard settings for all users and computers, or do you want to customize settings by groups of users? Also, do you want to maintain individual settings for users and computers? Typically, you customize settings by groups, where the majority of users are in groups such as Accounting, Marketing, and so on, and a small group of individuals (such as administrators) have special privileges. If so, you must install special files to support group policies.

- Will you be using user system policies (as opposed to defining only computer policies)? If so, user profiles must be enabled on the computers running Windows 95, which in turn requires that the computers use 32-bit, protected-mode network clients.

- Do system policies in Windows 95 meet your system administration needs, or do you need a more sophisticated system? If you need a high level of administrative control, you might want to consider using a more sophisticated management software tool, such as Microsoft Systems Management Server, rather than System Policy Editor. For information, see Appendix E, "Microsoft Systems Management Server."

If you want to use system policies, you must perform the following preliminary steps:

- On the administrator's computer, install System Policy Editor from the ADMIN\APPTOOLS\POLEDIT directory on the Windows 95 compact disc. Decide which users can install and have access to this tool for modifying policies. For most client computers, you probably will not install System Policy Editor.

- On the client computers, enable user profiles to ensure full support for system policies. If user profiles are not enabled, only the computer settings in any system policy will be written to the Registry.

- Install support for group policies on the client computers if your site will use these. For information, see "System Policy Editor" later in this chapter.

---

**Tip**  You can enable user profiles and related settings automatically when installing Windows 95 by using custom setup scripts. For information, see Appendix D, "MSBATCH.INF Parameters."

---

# User Profiles Overview

In Windows 95, user profiles contain configuration preferences and options for each user. They are particularly useful when users are encouraged to customize their computing environment, yet are forced to share computers with others who are also customizing their environments. User profiles are also beneficial to network administrators or help desk personnel who typically roam around, accessing the network from a variety of locations. Such users can work anywhere as if they were sitting at their own desks.

User profile settings include everything in the Hkey_Current_User section of the Windows 95 Registry, such as the following:

- Control Panel settings and preferences for the Windows 95 user interface, including settings for desktop layout, background, font selection, colors, shortcuts on the desktop, the Start menu, and so on.

- Settings for persistent network connections, plus information for recently used resources, including documents, Find Computer results, installation locations for setup, and printer ports.

- Application settings (for applications that can write directly to the Windows 95 Registry), including settings for the accessories and applications installed with Windows 95, menu and toolbar configurations, fonts, and so on.

Each user profile includes several parts: a USER.DAT file, a backup USER.DA0 file, a Desktop folder, a Recent folder, and a Start Menu folder, plus the Programs folder under Start Menu. These folders are in the directories for each user, which are in the Windows Profiles directory, as shown in the following illustration.

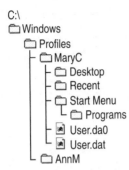

When user profiles are enabled, users get their own configuration when they log on to a computer. Users can define their own preferences by customizing their desktops. Alternatively, you can define a standard user profile for use across the network or for a set of specific users.

Each user's preferences are saved to a user profile that Windows 95 uses to configure the desktop each time that user logs on. When a second user logs on to the same computer with a different user name, Windows 95 creates a separate user profile for that user. A roving user's profile is stored on a network server and downloaded to any computer on the network to which the user logs on. This occurs automatically on a NetWare and a Windows NT network. However, although Windows 95 offers the ability for roving users to move from one computer running Windows 95 to another, it does not offer the ability to move between a computer running Windows NT and one running Windows 95.

---

**Important**   Although a user profile is based on the USER.DAT file that makes up part of the Windows 95 Registry, this file cannot be edited with a text editor. To define and manage user profiles, you must use the Windows 95 tools such as Control Panel for setting configuration options, and perform the procedures described in the following sections.

---

In the PROFILES subdirectory of the Windows directory, a folder is created for each user who has a profile on that computer. Each of these folders contains the following:

- A USER.DAT file that contains the user portion of the Registry
- A USER.DA0 file that contains the backup for USER.DAT
- A Desktop folder that contains the contents of Desktop
- A Recent folder that contains the contents of the Documents option on the Start menu
- A Start Menu folder that contains the contents of the Start menu, and includes the Programs folder

## How Do User Profiles Work?

Each time the user logs on to a computer, Windows 95 searches the Registry under the following key to determine whether the user has a local profile:

```
Hkey_Local_Machine\Software\Microsoft\Windows\Current Version
    \Profile List
```

Windows 95 also checks for the user profile in the user's home directory on the server. If the user profile on the server is the most current, Windows 95 copies it to the local computer for use during the current session, and then it loads the settings in this local copy into the Registry. If no local user profile exists, Windows 95 copies the server version to the local computer. If no profile is found, Windows 95 creates a new user profile on the local computer using default settings. If the user doesn't log on, then Windows 95 automatically uses the default user profile.

Both the local and network copies of the user profile are automatically updated with current settings when the user logs off.

If the user is logged on at more than one computer at the same time, any changes made to the profile on the computer where the user first logs off will be overwritten when the user logs off the other computer. In other words, the last logoff is saved, and no merging of changes occurs.

# Enabling User Profiles

You can enable user profiles after Windows 95 is installed, either locally on a single computer or for multiple computers. You can avoid having to go to each computer to enable user profiles by creating a system policy that can be downloaded automatically when the initial Windows 95 installation is complete. For information about enabling user profiles centrally on multiple computers, see "System Policies Overview" later in this chapter.

▶ **To enable user profiles on a local computer after setup**

1. In the Passwords option in Control Panel, click the User Profiles tab.

2. Click to select the option named Users Can Customize Their Preferences And Desktop Settings.

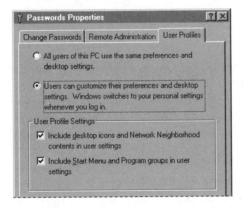

3. Click the options you want under User Profile Settings. These options describe what should be included as part of the user profile.

4. Shut down and restart the computer.

---

**Tip**   If you include desktop icons in your user profile, only the shortcuts (icons that represent links) will be available when you log on to the network from another computer. Actual files on your desktop are part of your local user profile only.

---

▶ **To disable user profiles on a local computer**

- In the Passwords option in Control Panel, click the User Profiles tab. Make sure the option named All Users Of This PC Use The Same Preferences And Desktop Settings is selected.

---

**Note** If an application is installed after user profiles are enabled with the option to include the Start menu and Programs in the profile, only the user who was logged on when the application was installed will have an entry for that application on the Programs menu. Other users will have to create shortcuts to the application on their Programs menus.

---

# Setting Up User Profiles on a Windows NT Network

You can use user profiles with Windows 95 on a Windows NT network if the computer is configured to use Client for Microsoft Networks.

---

**Note** Windows 95 does not use the PROFILES directory on a Windows NT server; that directory is used only for Windows NT profiles.

---

▶ **To set up user profiles on a Windows NT network**

1. For each computer, make sure that user profiles are enabled, as described in "Enabling User Profiles" earlier in this chapter.

2. In the Network option in Control Panel, make sure Client for Microsoft Networks is selected as the Primary Network Logon client.

3. On the Windows NT server, make sure each user is properly set up and has an assigned home directory on a Windows NT network server. (You can use the Windows NT User Manager tool to create this directory.)

When the user logs off, Windows 95 automatically places an updated copy of the user profile in the user's assigned home directory on the Windows NT network, in the following path.

\\ *logon_server*\ *user's home directory*

For information about User Manager and home directories, see *Microsoft Windows NT Server 3.5 User Guide*.

# Setting Up User Profiles on a NetWare Network

You can use user profiles with Windows 95 on a NetWare network if the computer is configured to use Microsoft Client for NetWare Networks.

When a user account is created on a NetWare server, a subdirectory of the MAIL directory is automatically created for that user. Windows 95 uses this directory to store user profiles.

▶ **To set up user profiles for a Novell NetWare network**

1. For each computer, make sure that user profiles are enabled, as described in "Enabling User Profiles" earlier in this chapter.

2. In the Network option in Control Panel, make sure Client for NetWare Networks is selected as the Primary Network Logon client.

3. Make sure each user has an established MAIL directory.

When the user logs off, Windows 95 automatically places an updated copy of the user profile in the user's assigned MAIL directory on the NetWare network, as indicated in the following. (The user's 8-digit ID can be determined by using the NetWare SYSCON utility.)

\\*preferred_server*\sys\mail\*user_id*

# Disabling Standard Roving Profiles

You might want to have user profiles enabled on a computer, but not allow the profiles to move between that computer and others. For example, if a user simultaneously uses a main computer running File and Printer Sharing services and other auxiliary computers, the roving profile for the auxiliary computers might include persistent connections to shared directories on the user's main computer. This profile would not work well on the main computer itself, since a computer cannot connect to itself.

▶ **To disable roving profiles on a particular computer**

1. In Registry Editor, expand the Hkey_Local_Machine\Network key, and select the Logon subkey.

2. On the Edit menu, point to New, and then click DWORD Value.

3. Type **UseHomeDirectory** and press ENTER.

# Maintaining Roving User Profiles on Other Networks

Windows 95 has limited support for user profiles if the network does not have support for a 32-bit, protected-mode client or centralized network logon. This includes networks that provide only 16-bit network clients and peer networks such as Windows for Workgroups or Windows 95 without a Windows NT domain.

To enable roving user profiles on such a network, you must first establish a network directory that can be accessed by all users. For security reasons, you should make sure that this directory has read-only permissions so that users cannot modify it. You must create a text file in that directory that lists the home directories for all users who can use roving user profiles. For example, such a file might be named PROFILES.INI on \\BIGSERVER\PROFILES, and have the following contents:

```
[Profiles]
Mary=\\bigserver\homedirs\mary
John=\\bigserver\homedirs\john
Pat=\\bigserver\homedirs\pat
```

After you have created this file, you must configure each computer running Windows 95 to use it. First, disable roving profiles. For more information about disabling roving profiles, see "Enabling User Profiles" earlier in this chapter. Then do the following:

▶ **To configure a computer for roving user profiles on other networks**

1. In Registry Editor, select the Hkey_Local_Machine\Network\Logon subkey.

2. On the Edit menu, point to New, and then click String Value.

3. Type **SharedProfileList** and press ENTER. Then press ENTER again.

4. In the Edit String dialog box, type the UNC path and filename for the home directory list (for example, \\BIGSERVER\PROFILES\PROFILES.INI). Click OK.

Thereafter, when a user logs on at this computer, Windows 95 will look in the specified text file to determine the user's home directory. The user's profile will be loaded from that home directory as it is from other networks. If the user is not listed in the text file, the user profile will be local only.

# Defining Mandatory User Profiles

In Windows 95, you can create mandatory user profiles for use on Windows NT or NetWare networks. You can use this feature to create a standard user profile for each computer and make sure it is implemented at every logon. To do this, create a USER.DAT file with the settings you want, save it as USER.MAN, and place it in the network directory for each user you want to use that profile. The network directory is either the user's home directory (on a Windows NT network) or MAIL directory (on a NetWare network).

If USER.MAN is present when the user logs on, Windows 95 uses this mandatory copy to load settings into the Registry rather than any previous local user profile. If the user manually makes changes to the desktop configuration during the work session, these changes are not saved to the master copy in the user's network directory when the user logs off.

▶ **To create a mandatory user profile**

1. Enable user profiles. For information about enabling user profiles, see "Enabling User Profiles" earlier in this chapter.

2. On any computer running Windows 95, customize the desktop as you want it to be for the mandatory user profile.

3. Copy the required files for the user profile to the home directory for Windows NT networks or to the MAIL directory for NetWare networks, as described in "Setting Up User Profiles on a NetWare Network" earlier in this chapter.

---

**Note**  Windows 95 copies these files automatically for normal user profiles, but not for mandatory user profiles.

---

4. Rename USER.DAT to USER.MAN in the user's home directory.

# System Policies Overview

System policies offer you a powerful mechanism for increasing control and manageability of computers across the network. You do not need to use a 32-bit, protected-mode client to use system policies. (If you want to define user settings, however, you must enable user profiles.) With system policies, you can do the following:

- Restrict access to Control Panel options
- Restrict what users can do from the desktop
- Customize parts of the desktop
- Configure network settings

For example, you can preset a user's environment so that the MS-DOS prompt or unapproved applications are not available. You can choose from the set of system policies offered by Windows 95 or create custom system policies.

---

**Note**  You should make some decisions about the default set of system policies before installing Windows 95. For information, see Part 1, "Deployment Planning Guide."

---

The system policy entries you set through System Policy Editor are reflected in the policy file (CONFIG.POL), which overwrites default USER.DAT and SYSTEM.DAT settings in the Registry when the user logs on. Policy entries change Registry settings in the following way:

- Desktop settings modify the Hkey_Current_User key in the Registry, which defines the contents of USER.DAT. All policy settings affecting USER.DAT are defined for a specific user or for the default user.
- Logon and network access settings modify the Hkey_Local_Machine key in the Registry, which defines the contents of SYSTEM.DAT. All policy settings affecting SYSTEM.DAT are defined for a specific computer or for the default computer.

The following figure shows how these settings are interrelated.

To use System Policy Editor, you must install the following files from ADMIN\APPTOOLS\POLEDIT: ADMIN.ADM, POLEDIT.EXE, and POLEDIT.INF. ADMIN.ADM is placed in the INF subdirectory of the Windows directory, and it provides the template to use with System Policy Editor for creating a CONFIG.POL file. CONFIG.POL must be placed in a secure network location. Any custom templates that you create will use the .ADM filename extension.

If you want to use group policies, GROUPPOL.DLL must be placed in the SYSTEM subdirectory of the Windows directory on each client computer. In addition, you must make some changes to the Registry on each computer to use GROUPPOL.DLL. For more information, see "System Policy Editor" later in this chapter.

---

**Important** System policies are based on the content of the Registry and cannot be edited with a text editor. To define and manage system policies, you must use System Policy Editor and other supporting tools.

You can, however, use a text editor to edit the template files used by System Policy Editor, as described in "System Policy Templates" later in this chapter.

---

### How Do System Policies Work?

When the user logs on, Windows 95 checks the user's configuration information for the location of the policy file. Windows 95 then downloads the policies and copies the information into the Registry by using the following process:

1. If user profiles are enabled, Windows 95 checks for a user policy file that matches the user name. If it finds one, Windows 95 applies the user-specific policy. If Windows 95 does not find a user policy file, it applies the Default User policy file.

   If support for group policies is installed on the computer, then Windows 95 checks whether the user is registered as a member of any groups. If so, group policies are downloaded starting with the lowest priority group and ending with the highest priority group. Group policies are processed for all groups the user belongs to. The group with the highest priority is processed last so that the settings in that group's policy file supersede those in lower priority groups. Group policies are not applied if there is a policy file for a specific user.

   Then, all settings are copied into the USER.DAT portion of the Registry.

2. Windows 95 checks for a computer policy file to match the computer name. If one exists, Windows 95 applies the computer-specific policies to the user's desktop environment. If a policy file for that computer name doesn't exist, Windows 95 applies the default computer policies. This data is then copied into the SYSTEM.DAT portion of the Registry.

By default, Windows 95 automatically attempts to download computer and user policies from the NETLOGON directory on a Windows NT server or the PUBLIC directory on a NetWare server. This default location can be overridden in a policy file setting. If no server is present, Windows 95 uses the settings currently on the computer.

# Overview of System Policies for Users

You can manage user settings in system policies only if user profiles are enabled on the target computer. System Policy Editor uses the properties for Default User to define the default policies in the following areas:

**Control Panel.**  Set policies to prevent the user from accessing Control Panel features, such as network, password, or system settings.

**Desktop.**  Set policies to use standard wallpaper and color schemes.

**Network.**  Set policies to restrict peer resource sharing or to specify networking components and settings.

**Shell.**  Set policies to customize folders on the desktop and to restrict changes to the user interface.

**System.**  Set policies to restrict the use of Registry editing tools, applications, and MS-DOS–based applications.

You can apply these policies to the default user, to specific named users, or to groups of users. For more information about the settings for each of these categories, see "System Policy Settings Summary" later in this chapter.

# Overview of System Policies for Computers

You can use System Policy Editor to define settings for a default computer or for specific named computers. The default computer settings are used when a new user logs on to a computer that does not have individual policies assigned.

Computer settings in system policies prevent users from modifying the hardware and environment settings for the operating system, ensuring that Windows 95 starts up in a predictable way. You can set options to restrict access to computer-specific system and network features, as described in "System Policy Settings Summary" later in this chapter.

# System Policy Editor

You can use System Policy Editor to create system policies. More specifically, you can do the following with System Policy Editor:

- Set entries for the default computer and user policy entries. This creates a default policy file for all users and computers, which is downloaded when the user logs on.

- Create entries for individual users, individual computers, or groups of users. By default, these include the policy entries you defined for Default User and default computer.

- Specify whether and in what manner you want policies downloaded from a centralized server or specify whether you want to have policies downloaded from other specific locations for all or some users.

Caution   System Policy Editor is a powerful tool; you should restrict its use to network administrators only. To avoid unauthorized use, do not install this tool on users' computers, and restrict access to the source files so that users cannot install it themselves.

# Installing System Policy Editor

You can install and use System Policy Editor from the ADMIN directory on the Windows 95 compact disc.

▶ **To install System Policy Editor**

1. In the Add/Remove Programs option in Control Panel, click the Windows Setup tab, and then click Have Disk.

2. In the Install From Disk dialog box, click Browse and specify the ADMIN\APPTOOLS\POLEDIT directory on the Windows 95 compact disc. Click OK, and then click OK again.

3. In the Have Disk dialog box, make sure System Policy Editor is checked, and then click the Install button.

▶ **To run System Policy Editor**

- On the Start menu, click Run. Type **poledit** and then click OK.

If you want to use group policies, you must install that capability on each computer running Windows 95, either when you install Windows 95 using a custom setup script, or by using the Add/Remove Programs option in Control Panel.

▶ **To set up capabilities for group policies using Add/Remove Programs**

1. In the Add/Remove Programs option in Control Panel, click the Windows Setup tab, and then click Have Disk button.

2. In the Install From Disk dialog box, click Browse and specify the ADMIN\APPTOOLS\POLEDIT directory on the Windows 95 compact disc. Click OK, and then click OK again.

3. In the Have Disk dialog box, make sure Group Policies is checked, and then click the Install button.

Windows 95 Setup places GROUPPOL.DLL in the Windows SYSTEM directory on the client computer and makes the required Registry changes.

For information about adding the ability to use group policies when installing Windows 95 using custom setup scripts, see Chapter 5, "Custom, Automated, and Push Installations."

# Using System Policy Editor

You can use System Policy Editor in two different modes: Registry mode and Policy File mode:

- In Registry mode, you can directly edit the Registry of the local or remote computer, and changes are reflected immediately. For more information about editing the Registry for a remote computer, see Chapter 16, "Remote Administration."

- In Policy File mode, you can create and modify system policy files (.POL) for use on other computers. In this mode, the Registry is edited indirectly. Changes are reflected only after the policy is downloaded when the user logs on.

▶ **To use System Policy Editor in Registry mode**

- In System Policy Editor, click the File menu, and then click Open Registry. Then, double-click the appropriate User or Computer icon, depending on what part of the Registry you want to edit. After you make changes, you must shut down and restart the computer for the changes to take effect.

System Policy Editor in Registry mode

Notice that the title bar shows "Local Registry."

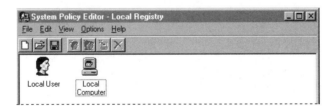

**Important**  Use Registry mode only when you want to make direct changes to the Registry. You should typically change system settings by using the Control Panel options and other tools provided with Windows 95.

▶ **To use System Policy Editor in Policy File mode**

- In System Policy Editor, click the File menu, and then click New or Open to open a policy file.

System Policy Editor
in Policy File mode

The title bar shows
the policy filename.

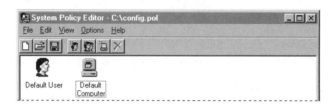

When you edit settings in Policy File mode, clicking a Registry option sets one of three possible states: checked, cleared, or grayed. Each time you click an option, the display cycles to show the next possible state. This is different from clicking a standard check box, which only sets an option to on or off. The following summarizes the three possible states for options in a policy file.

| Option state | Meaning |
| --- | --- |
| ☑ | Checked—this policy will be implemented, changing the state of the user's computer to conform to the policy when the user logs on. If the option was previously checked the last time the user logged on, Windows 95 makes no changes. |
| ☐ | Cleared—the policy will not be implemented. If it was implemented previously (either through a policy setting or the user's configuration settings), the previously specified settings are removed from the Registry. |
| ▓ | Grayed—the setting is unchanged from the last time the user logged on, and Windows 95 will make no related modifications to the system configuration. |
| | The grayed state ensures that Windows 95 provides quick processing at system startup because it does not need to process each entry each time a user logs on. |

Caution   When you define policy options, make sure you have set the proper state for the option. If you set an option by checking it, and then change your mind and clear the option, you can inadvertently destroy the user's previous configuration. If you decide not to set a particular policy option, make sure that option is grayed, so that the user's previous configuration for that setting will be used.

For example, you might check the option to specify Microsoft Client for NetWare Networks, and then click again to clear that option. When the user logs on and the policy is downloaded, this setting would wipe out the user's current configuration that specifies Client for NetWare Networks.

If a setting requires additional information, then an edit control appears at the bottom of the properties dialog box. For example, if Wallpaper is checked in the Desktop settings, the following dialog box appears.

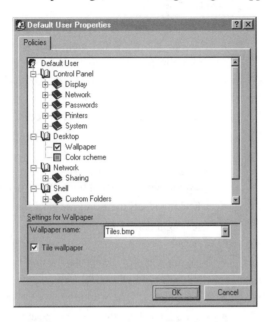

Usually, if a policy has been checked, and you no longer want to enforce it, you should clear the box to cancel the policy. However, in the following cases, a few policies might behave differently from how you might expect if the check box is cleared:

- The policy setting contains an edit box that must be completed (as opposed to a simple check box)
- The policy setting can also be set by users by using Control Panel

In these cases, you should consider making sure the check box is grayed when you no longer want to enforce the policies.

The following list describes the results of different settings for such policies and how they behave.

| Policy | Behavior |
|--------|----------|
| Settings for Wallpaper | ■ Checking it forces the specified wallpaper to be used. |
| | ■ Clearing it removes the wallpaper (the user will not have any wallpaper). |
| | ■ Leaving it grayed means that the user can choose wallpaper in the Display option in Control Panel. |
| Client for NetWare Networks: Preferred Server | ■ Checking it sets the preferred server. |
| | ■ Clearing it deletes the preferred server from the computer's Registry. |
| | ■ Leaving it grayed means that the user can specify the preferred server in the Network option in Control Panel. |
| Microsoft Client for Windows Networks: Domain | ■ Checking it sets the Windows NT Logon domain. |
| | ■ Clearing it deletes the domain setting from the computer's Registry. |
| | ■ Leaving it grayed means that the user can specify the domain in the Network option in Control Panel. |
| Microsoft Client for Windows Networks: Workgroup | ■ Checking it sets the workgroup for that computer. |
| | ■ Clearing it deletes the workgroup setting from the computer's Registry. |
| | ■ Leaving it grayed means that the user can specify the workgroup in the Network option in Control Panel. |

# Preparing to Use System Policies on the Network

You can copy system policies from the network either manually or automatically. If you want to copy system policies automatically, Windows 95 locates the system policy file (CONFIG.POL) in the proper directory on the network and downloads its policy settings into the Registry of the local computer when the user logs on. If you want to copy system policies manually, Windows 95 copies the system policy file from a location you specify. Automatic downloading works only if the filename for the system policy file is CONFIG.POL.

**Note**  Windows 95 supports automatic downloading for Windows NT and NetWare networks. The 32-bit, protected-mode network clients subsequently made available for other networks might also provide support for automatic downloading.

# Setting Up for Automatic Downloading of System Policies

By default, Windows 95 downloads system policies automatically. However, if you switch to manual downloading, the following procedures describe how to return to automatic downloading.

If you created a .POL file, Windows 95 automatically downloads this file from the NETLOGON directory on a Windows NT network or from the PUBLIC directory on a NetWare network.

▶ **To set up for automatic downloading on Windows NT networks**

1. In the Network option in Control Panel, make sure that Client for Microsoft Networks is specified as the Primary Network Logon client, and that the domain is defined. For more information, see Chapter 11, "Logon, Browsing, and Resource Sharing."

2. Create the policy file to be downloaded and save it in the following location:

   \\*primary domain controller*\netlogon\config.pol

▶ **To set up for automatic downloading on NetWare networks**

1. In the Network option in Control Panel, make sure that Microsoft Client for NetWare Networks is specified as the Primary Network Logon client, and that a preferred server is specified in properties for the network client. For more information, see Chapter 9, "Windows 95 on NetWare Networks."

2. Create the policy file to be downloaded and save it in the following location:

   \\*preferred server*\sys\public\config.pol

For NetWare networks, the client computers must be running Microsoft Client for NetWare Networks. If the client computers are using NETX or VLM, then policies must be downloaded manually.

---

**Important**  Make sure you place system policy files on the user's preferred server. Policy files are not available if they are stored on other NetWare servers or on computers running File and Printer Sharing for NetWare Networks.

---

# Setting Up for Manual Downloading of System Policies

If you use the Remote Update policy, you can configure Windows 95 to manually download policy files (even when they are stored locally) by indicating a separate network or local computer location. Manual downloading overrides automatic downloading and allows you to choose where a user's policies should be stored.

It's possible to set up each computer for manual downloading individually, but this can be time-consuming. If possible (that is, when the client computers use 32-bit, protected-mode network clients), you should set up each computer for automatic downloading, and then use the Remote Update policy to point specific computers to other servers as appropriate for your environment and users.

However, for real-mode network clients such as Novell NETX or VLM, you must enable manual downloading on each computer. After you configure the client computer, the system policy file will be downloaded the next time the user logs on.

▶ **To configure a computer for manual downloading of system policies**

1. In System Policy Editor, click the File menu, and then click Open Registry. Click Local Computer.

   –Or–

   In the File menu, click Connect. Type the name of the computer you want to configure remotely, and then click OK. Double-click the icon for that computer.

   **Note** The remote computer must be running the Microsoft Remote Registry service, Remote Administration must be enabled, and user-level security must be enabled.

2. Double-click Network, double-click Update, and click Remote Update so that this policy is checked.

   **Note** If the client computer uses NETX or VLM, the policy file must be placed on a mapped drive.

   Make sure to type the UNC path and the filename in the Path For Manual Update box.

On Windows NT or NetWare networks where you are using automatic downloading of policies, you can set a system policy to allow manual downloading. This option works only after system policies have been downloaded automatically the first time after Windows 95 is installed. The first automatic downloading includes information in the system policies that defines the location to be used subsequently for manual downloading.

▶ **To define the location of policies for manual downloading**

1. In System Policy Editor, open CONFIG.POL, and then double-click the Default Computer icon.

2. Double-click Network, then double-click Update, and then click Remote Update so that this policy is checked.

3. In the Update Mode box, click Manual. In the Path For Manual Update box, type the UNC path and filename for the system policy file you want to download. Make sure this file exists in the location you specify. (Otherwise, an error will result.)

On large networks, when thousands of users log on at the same time, all accessing the same policy file, you might experience slow network performance. To avoid a bottleneck, Windows 95 offers load balancing on Windows NT networks. With load balancing enabled, policies are taken from the logon server (which can be a domain controller or a backup domain controller) rather than the primary domain controller. This spreads the load over a number of servers, but it does require that you replicate the policy file on each server.

▶  **To enable load balancing**

1. Perform the previous procedure, "To define the location of policies for manual downloading."

2. In the Settings For Remote Update box, make sure Load-Balance is checked.

If you want to use load balancing, make sure it is enabled on each client computer. Also, make sure you have a current policy file on each server that will participate in load balancing, including all Windows NT domain controllers and servers. One convenient way to implement load balancing is to set this policy in the CONFIG.POL file that is on the primary domain controller. As each client computer downloads this policy, it will then subsequently look for CONFIG.POL on the logon server.

# Creating System Policies

This section describes procedures for creating system policies.

To take advantage of automatic downloading discussed earlier, you should create a policy file that contains user, computer, and group entries to reside in the NETLOGON directory of a Windows NT server or the PUBLIC directory of a NetWare server. Based on the client selected, Windows 95 automatically looks in one of these locations to download your newly created system policy.

▶  **To view or edit default system policies**

1. In System Policy Editor, click the File menu, and then click New File.

2. Double-click the Default User icon to define the default settings for user-specific policies.

–Or–

Double-click the Default Computer icon to define the settings for computer-specific policies.

3. Click the policies you want to put in place.

# Creating Policies for Individual Users or Computers

This section describes how to create a system policy for a user or computer.

---

**Tip**  To reduce the management load, minimize the number of user and computer entries in system policy files. Consider first creating one standard system policy for all users by editing default settings, and then create settings for individuals on an exception basis. For more information, see the STANDARD.POL example in "System Policy Examples" later in this chapter.

---

▶ **To create system policies for a new user or computer**

1. In System Policy Editor, click the Edit menu, and then click Add User or Add Computer.

2. Type the name of the user or computer you want to add.

   System Policy Editor adds an icon for each user or computer that you add.

▶ **To edit existing system policies**

1. In System Policy Editor, double-click the icon for the user or computer policies you want to edit.

2. Check or clear policies by clicking the policy name.

# Creating Policies for Groups

Group policies are supported for both Windows NT and NetWare networks. Creating policies for groups is similar to the process for creating policies for users or computers.

You must first make sure that GROUPPOL.DLL, which supports group policies, has been successfully installed on each client computer. For more information, see "System Policy Editor" earlier in this chapter.

You cannot create new groups by using System Policy Editor; you can use only existing groups on the NetWare or Windows NT network. To create a new group, use the tools provided with your network administrative software.

▶ **To create system policies for groups**

1. In System Policy Editor, click the Edit menu, and then click Add Group.

2. Type the name of the group you want to add, and click OK.

   –Or–

   If user-level security is enabled, click Browse and find the name of the group. Then click OK.

3. Click or clear policies by clicking the policy name.

Group policies are downloaded starting with the lowest priority group and ending with the highest priority group. All groups are processed. The group with the highest priority is processed last so that any the settings in that group's policy file supersede those in lower priority groups. You can use one policy file for each group, even if some of the client computers in the group don't have support installed for group policies. Client computers that aren't configured for using group policies will ignore group policy files.

---

**Important**  If a policy exists for a specific named user, then group policies are not applied for that user.

---

▶ **To set priority levels for groups**

1. In System Policy Editor, click the File Menu, and then click Open File.

2. Locate the CONFIG.POL file, and then click Open.

3. Click the Options menu, and then click Group Priority.

4. In the Group Priority dialog box, click a group, and then use the Move Up and Move Down buttons to move it into its relative priority.

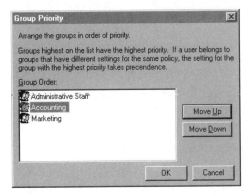

# Managing Custom Folders for Use with System Policies

The administrator can define five system policies to create a custom desktop. These policies use custom folders, created by the administrator, which contain the specific settings for the customized desktop. The following list summarizes the policies used to create a custom desktop.

| Policy | Description |
| --- | --- |
| Custom Programs Folder | Shortcuts that appear in the Programs group on the Start menu |
| Custom Network Neighborhood | Shortcuts to resources that appear in Network Neighborhood, including shortcuts to shared printers and files and to Dial-Up Networking connections |
| Custom Desktop Icons | Shortcuts that appear on the desktop |
| Custom Start Menu | Shortcuts and other options that appear on the Start menu, as defined by using the Taskbar Properties dialog box |
| Custom Startup Folder | Programs or batch files that appear in the Startup group on the Start menu |

Before you create a custom desktop by using system policies, you must define custom folders.

▶ **To define custom folders for use with policy files**

1. Create and place the custom folders in a central location where users have access. You can use any valid folder names for the folders you create. Windows 95 uses the path defined for the related policy to find the folder.

   **Note**  To prevent accidental removal or unauthorized changes, you should place custom folders in directories where users are restricted to read-only access.

2. Place the custom set of files and shortcuts you want in each folder.

   - You can place any kind of files in the custom folders.

   - For shortcuts, make sure that the path specified in the Target box in Shortcut properties is a UNC name, rather than a mapped directory. Otherwise, the users who will access resources using these shortcuts will have to have the same drives mapped in their login scripts.

   **Caution**  Do not place folders in the custom Network Neighborhood. Windows 95 does not support this feature, and unpredictable results can occur.

▶ **To create a custom desktop by using system policies**

1. In System Policy Editor, open the system policy file.

2. In the system policy file, set the related policies.

3. In the Path To Get Program Items From box, type the path to the folder's location.

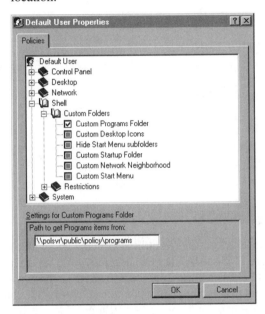

4. If you checked the Custom Programs Folder policy, also check the Hide Start Menu Subfolders policy to enable it.

   Otherwise, multiple Programs entries will appear on the user's Start menu— one for the location of the Custom Program Folder and one for the default location.

If the custom folders will not be stored in the directories where Windows 95 automatically looks for them, then you must specify another location when you specify the Custom Folder policies. For example, you might want to create these folders where the system policy files are located on the server.

The following list shows the default locations for custom folders.

- Custom Program folders:

  ```
  c:\windows\profiles\username\start menu\programs
  ```

- Custom desktop icons:

  ```
  c:\windows\profiles\username\desktop
  ```

- Custom Startup folder:

  ```
  c:\windows\profiles\username\start menu\programs\startup
  ```

- Custom Network Neighborhood:

  ```
  c:\windows\profiles\username\nethood
  ```

- Custom Start menu:

  ```
  c:\windows\profiles\username\start menu
  ```

# System Policy Examples

The *Windows 95 Resource Kit* utilities provide you with two examples of system policies. STANDARD.POL is a policy file for defining a standard desktop. MAXIMUM.POL is a policy file for maximum security and control. These example policy files are ready for you to use after minor changes such as specifying paths and file locations for custom folders at your site.

## Recommended Standard Desktop Configuration

The STANDARD.POL system policy file is an example of settings that allow you to implement a level of control over users' desktop functionality while allowing specific corporate customization. STANDARD.POL includes the following additions.

**STANDARD.POL Settings**

| Category | Policy setting |
|---|---|
| **Computer settings:** | |
| Network Logon | Logon Banner (modify banner text as needed) |
| | Require Validation by Network for Windows Access |
| Network Passwords | Hide Share Passwords with Asterisks |
| | Minimum Windows Password Length (6) |
| System | Enable User Profiles |
| **User settings:** | |
| Control Panel | Disable Deletion of Printer (printer restrictions) |
| System | Disable Registry Editing Tools[1] |
| | Disable MS-DOS Prompt |
| Custom Folders[2] | Custom Desktop Icons |
| | Custom Programs Folder |
| | Custom Startup Folder |
| | Custom Network Neighborhood |
| | Custom Start Menu |
| | Hide Start menu Subfolders (custom folders are defined) |

[1] This setting disables only Registry Editor, not System Policy Editor.

[2] These options provide an opportunity for corporate customization, such as defining a program group containing corporate applications, applications that run at system startup, a custom Network Neighborhood, or a custom Start menu with standard choices.

To implement the custom settings specified in the STANDARD.POL policy file, make sure you define the UNC path names for the custom settings. Also make sure to place the customized folders for Programs, Startup, Network Neighborhood, and Start Menu in a secure network location, as described in "Managing Custom Folders for Use with System Policies" earlier in this chapter.

# Recommended Maximum Control Desktop Configuration

The system policy defined in MAXIMUM.POL is useful if you need to have as much control as possible over the users' computing environments. The following sample policy file will assist you in establishing the highest possible level of control.

MAXIMUM.POL is based on the STANDARD.POL file, as described in the previous section, with the following additional restrictions.

**Additional MAXIMUM.POL Settings**

| Category | Policy setting |
|---|---|
| **Computer settings:** | |
| Network Dial-Up | Disable Dial-In |
| **User settings:** | |
| Control Panel | Disable Display Control Panel (display restrictions) |
| Restrict System Control Panel | Hide Device Manager Page |
| | Hide Hardware Profiles Page |
| | Hide File System Button |
| | Hide Virtual Memory Button |
| Network Sharing | Disable File Sharing Controls |
| | Disable Print Sharing Controls |
| Shell Restrictions | Remove Run Command |
| | Remove Folders from Settings on Start Menu |
| | Remove Taskbar from Settings on Start Menu |
| | No Entire Network in Network Neighborhood |
| | No Workgroup Contents in Network Neighborhood |
| | Don't Save Settings at Exit |

# System Policy Settings Summary

This section summarizes the policy options that you can set by default in Windows 95. These options are determined by a template (ADMIN.ADM), which can be modified as discussed in "System Policy Templates" later in this chapter. You might find it helpful to run System Policy Editor while you study these options.

These policies are described in the order that they appear in System Policy Editor. For each category, you must click the option that appears in bold type to display the related policies that you can define for that category.

# Restricting Access to User-Specific Settings

When you double-click the Default User icon in System Policy Editor, a list of Control Panel, desktop, network, shell (user interface), and system settings appears so that you can predefine or restrict access to settings that will apply when the user logs on to the system. These system policy settings are stored in USER.DAT.

## Restricting Access to Control Panels

The following table describes the system policies you can apply to restrict access to settings in the Display, Network, Printers, System, and Passwords options of Control Panel.

**User Policies for Restricting Access to Control Panel Options**

| Option | Description |
| --- | --- |
| **Restrict Display Control Panel** | |
| Disable Display Control Panel | Prevents access to the Display option in Control Panel. |
| Hide Background Page | Hides the Background properties of the Display option in Control Panel. |
| Hide Screen Saver Page | Hides the Screen Saver properties of the Display option in Control Panel. |
| Hide Appearance Page | Hides the Appearance properties of the Display option in Control Panel. |
| Hide Settings Page | Hides the Settings properties of the Display option in Control Panel. |
| **Restrict Network Control Panel** | |
| Disable Network Control Panel | Prevents access to the Network option in Control Panel. |
| Hide Identification Page | Hides the Identification properties of the Network option in Control Panel. |
| Hide Access Control Page | Hides the Access Control (user level vs. share level) properties of the Network option in Control Panel. |

**User Policies for Restricting Access to Control Panel Options** (*continued*)

| Option | Description |
|---|---|
| **Restrict Passwords Control Panel** | |
| Disable Passwords Control Panel | Prevents access to the Passwords option in Control Panel. |
| Hide Change Passwords Page | Hides the Change Passwords properties of the Passwords option in Control Panel. |
| Hide Remote Administration Page | Hides the Remote Administration properties of the Passwords option in Control Panel. |
| Hide User Profiles Page | Hides the Profiles properties of the Passwords option in Control Panel. |
| **Restrict Printers Settings** | |
| Hide General And Details Pages | Hides the General and Details properties for the Printer option in Control Panel. |
| Disable Deletion Of Printers | Prevents the deletion of installed printers. |
| Disable Addition Of Printers | Prevents the installation of printers. |
| **Restrict System Control Panel** | |
| Hide Device Manager Page | Hides the Device Manager properties from the System option in Control Panel. |
| Hide Hardware Profiles Page | Hides the Hardware Profiles properties from the System option in Control Panel. |
| Hide File System Button | Hides the File System button from the Performance properties in the System option in Control Panel. |
| Hide Virtual Memory Button | Hides the Virtual Memory button from the Performance properties in the System option in Control Panel. |

# Defining User Policies for Desktop Settings

Within this category of options, you can predefine settings or restrict users from defining wallpaper and color scheme settings, as listed in the following table.

**User Policies for Wallpaper and Color Scheme Settings**

| Option | Description |
| --- | --- |
| Wallpaper Name | When checked, the specified bitmap will be used as the wallpaper. |
| Tile Wallpaper | When checked, the wallpaper file will be tiled in the background of the desktop. |
| Color Scheme | When checked, the user will automatically see the specified color scheme. |

# Restricting Access to Network Settings

Within this category of options, you can restrict the user's ability to share files and printers. Typically, you might want to set these policies to apply when File and Printer Sharing services are installed, but when you do not want users to change which resources are shared on their computers.

**User Policies for Restricting Access to File and Printer Sharing**

| Option | Description |
| --- | --- |
| **Sharing** | |
| Disable File Sharing Controls | Removes the Sharing properties from directories in Windows Explorer. |
| Disable Print Sharing Controls | Removes the Sharing properties from the Printer directory. |

## Restricting Access to Shell Settings

The following table describes the system policies you can apply to directories and user interface options.

**User Policies for Restricting Access to Shell Settings**

| Option | Description |
|---|---|
| **Custom Folders** | |
| Custom Programs Folder | Customizes the contents of the Programs directory. You must also type a path for the directory containing complete files or .LNK files that define the Programs directory items. |
| Custom Desktop Icons | Customizes desktop icons. You must also type a path for the directory containing complete files or .LNK files that define the desktop shortcuts. |
| Hide Start Menu Subfolders | Check this when you use a custom Programs folder. Otherwise, two Programs entries will appear on the user's Start menu. |
| Custom Startup Folder | Customizes the contents of the Startup directory. You must also type a path for the directory containing complete files or .LNK files that define the Startup directory items. |
| Custom Network Neighborhood | Customizes the contents of Network Neighborhood. You must also type a path for the directory containing complete files or .LNK files that define the Network Neighborhood items. |
| Custom Start Menu | Customizes what is listed on the Start menu. You must also type a path for the directory containing complete files or .LNK files that define the Start menu items. |
| **Restrictions** | |
| Remove Run command | Prevents access to the Run command on the Start menu. |
| Remove Folders From Settings On Start Menu | Prevents access to any item listed under Settings on the Start menu. |
| Remove Taskbar From Settings On Start Menu | Prevents access to the Taskbar item listed under Settings on the Start menu. |
| Remove Find Command | Prevents access to any of the items listed under Find on the Start menu. |

**User Policies for Restricting Access to Shell Settings** (*continued*)

| Option | Description |
| --- | --- |
| Hide Drives In My Computer | Prevents access to My Computer. |
| Hide Network Neighborhood | Prevents access to Network Neighborhood. |
| No Entire Network In Network Neighborhood | Prevents access to the Entire Network icon in Network Neighborhood. |
| No Workgroup Contents In Network Neighborhood | Prevents workgroup contents from being displayed in Network Neighborhood. |
| Hide All Items On Desktop | Prevents access to all items on the desktop. |
| Disable Shut Down Command | Prevents access to the Shut Down command on the Start menu; displays explanation in a dialog box. |
| Don't Save Settings At Exit | Prevents settings from being written to the file system. |

## Restricting Access to System Settings

The system policies in this category restrict the use of Registry editing tools, applications, and MS-DOS–based applications. The following table describes the policies you can set within this category.

**User Policies Restricting Access to System Settings**

| Option | Description |
| --- | --- |
| **Restrictions** | |
| Disable Registry Editing Tools | Prevents access to Registry Editor. It does not prevent access to the Registry mode in System Policy Editor. |
| Only Run Allowed Windows Applications | Prevents users from running any Windows-based applications except those that are listed. Click Show to define the allowed applications. |
| Disable MS-DOS Prompt | Prevents access to the MS-DOS prompt. |
| Disable Single-Mode MS-DOS Applications | Prevents users from running MS-DOS–based applications in MS-DOS Mode. |

# Restricting Access to Computer-Specific Settings

When you double-click the Default Computer icon in System Policy Editor, a list of system policy options for settings that apply to the computer appears. This section describes these options.

## Restricting Access to Computer-Specific Network Settings

This category of options includes system policy settings for the following:

- Enabling user-level security
- Logon dialog box settings
- Client for Microsoft Networks settings
- Microsoft Client for NetWare Networks settings
- Password settings
- Dial-Up Networking settings
- Sharing settings
- Simple Network Management Protocol (SNMP) settings
- Update settings for policy downloading

These system policies are applied for the computer and are stored in SYSTEM.DAT. The following table describes the system policies you can set within this category.

**Computer Policies Restricting Access to Network Settings**

| Option | Description |
|---|---|
| **Access Control** | |
| User-Level Access Control | When checked, enables user-level security on the local computer using pass-through logon validation by a Windows NT or a NetWare server. You must specify the server and the type of authenticator for validation. |
| **Logon** | |
| Logon Banner | When checked, allows you to specify text for a caption and other text to be displayed in a logon banner. |
| Require Validation By Network For Windows Access | When you check this option, each logon must be validated by a server before access to Windows is allowed. This policy has no effect on a portable computer after it is undocked. |

**Computer Policies Restricting Access to Network Settings** (*continued*)

| Option | Description |
|---|---|
| **Microsoft Client for NetWare Networks** | |
| Preferred Server | When checked, allows you to specify the name of the NetWare network server used by this computer as the first server logged on to. |
| Support Long Filenames | When checked, allows support for long filenames. The values are 0 (no support for long filenames on NetWare servers), 1 (support on NetWare servers version 3.12 and greater), and 2 (support if the NetWare server supports long filenames). |
| Search Mode | Sets NetWare search mode (the value is 0–7). |
| Disable Automatic NetWare Login | Specifies that Windows 95 should not first silently use the user's name and password to attempt to connect to a NetWare server, which is the default behavior. |
| **Microsoft Client for Windows Networks** | |
| Log On To Windows NT | When checked, specifies that this computer can participate in a Windows NT domain. Type the name of the domain. If this option is checked, the next two options are also available. |
| Display Domain Logon Validation | When checked, displays a message when the domain controller has validated user logon. |
| Disable Caching Of Domain Password | When checked, specifies that no caching is used for the network password. |
| Workgroup | When checked, specifies that this computer can participate in a workgroup. Type the name of the workgroup. |
| Alternative Workgroup | Specifies that an alternate workgroup must be defined to see Microsoft peer servers in other workgroups if your workgroup does not have any computers running File and Printer Sharing for Microsoft Networks (that is, they all run File and Printer Sharing for NetWare), but the computer runs a Microsoft network client. The workgroup specified should include at least one computer running File and Printer Sharing for Microsoft Networks. |

**Computer Policies Restricting Access to Network Settings** (*continued*)

| Option | Description |
|---|---|
| **Passwords** | |
| Hide Share Passwords With Asterisks | Replaces characters with asterisks when users type passwords to access a shared resource. Applies to share-level security only; this setting is on by default. |
| Disable Password Caching | Prevents saving passwords. (Notice that the user cannot successfully use the Quick Logon feature for Microsoft networks if password caching is disabled.) |
| Require Alphanumeric Windows Password | Requires that the Windows password contain a combination of letters and numbers. |
| Minimum Windows Password Length | Requires that the Windows logon password has at least the specified number of characters. |
| **Dial-Up Networking** | |
| Disable Dial-In | Prevents dial-in connections to the computer. |
| **Sharing** | |
| Disable File Sharing | Prevents file sharing over a network. |
| Disable Print Sharing | Prevents printer sharing over a network. |
| **SNMP** | |
| Communities | Specifies one or more groups of hosts to which this computer belongs for purposes of SNMP administration. These are the communities that are allowed to query the SNMP agent. |
| Permitted Managers | Specifies IP or IPX addresses allowed to obtain information from an SNMP agent. If this policy is not checked, any SNMP console can query the agent. |
| Traps For Public Community | Specifies *trap destinations*, or IP or IPX addresses of hosts in the public community to which you want the SNMP service to send traps. |
| | For information about sending traps to other communities, see Chapter 16, "Remote Administration." |
| Internet MIB (RFC 1156) | Allows you to specify the contact name and location if you are using Internet MIB. |

**Computer Policies Restricting Access to Network Settings** (*continued*)

| Option | Description |
|---|---|
| **Update** | |
| Remote Update | Defines how system policies will be updated. When checked, the following options appear. |
| Update Mode | Determines whether system policies are downloaded automatically (the default) or manually. |
| Path For Manual Update | Specifies the UNC path and filename for manual downloading of system policies. |
| Display Error Message | When a user logs on, if the system policy file is not available, displays an error message. |
| Load-Balance | For Windows NT networks, allows Windows 95 to look for policy files on that server. |

# Restricting Access to Computer-Specific System Settings

This category of options includes system policy settings for the network path for setup and user profiles. The following table describes the system policies you can set within this category.

**Computer Policies for System Settings**

| Option | Description |
|---|---|
| Enable User Profiles | When checked, this setting enables user profiles. |
| Network Path For Windows Setup | Defines the network location of the Windows 95 Setup program and files. You must also type a UNC path for the setup directory. |
| Run | Defines applications and utilities to run when the user logs on. Click Show to specify items to run. |
| Run Once | Defines applications and utilities to run once when the user logs on. Click Show to specify items to run. (See comment below.) |
| Run Services | Defines services to run at system startup. Click Show to specify items to run. |

You can set the Run Once system policy to set values in the Run Once Registry key, which allows any executable file to be run just once after a user logs on to the computer. After the related program is started, its name is removed automatically from the Registry so that it does not run again. However, if you leave this option checked in the policy file, then each time the user logs on, that executable name will be placed in the Run Once Registry key to be run again. To ensure that the executable runs only once, the policy must be checked only long enough to be downloaded once into the user's Registry. Then the policy must be cleared or changed so that the same Run Once entry will not run the next time the user logs on.

# System Policy Templates

When you run System Policy Editor, Windows 95 opens the default policy template, which contains existing policies that you can enable or modify. A template is a listing of the possible policies that you can use. By default, this template file is named ADMIN.ADM and is stored in the Windows INF directory.

This section describes how you can create custom system policy templates (.ADM files) and switch between multiple templates in System Policy Editor.

For example, it might be helpful to have system policy settings for corporate-specific applications, such as an in-house database, custom front end, or electronic mail package. After a template has been customized, you can then load the template and use it to set values in the Registry.

---

**Note**  If you want to define system policies for applications, the applications must be able to read the Windows 95 Registry.

---

Creating your own template is helpful when you want to define a specific set of Registry settings in your system policies, including settings not definable by default through System Policy Editor. As shown in the following illustration, the template defines the policies you can set through System Policy Editor. Changes you make there are reflected in the policy file (shown in the example as CONFIG.POL), which in turn updates the Registry when the user logs on.

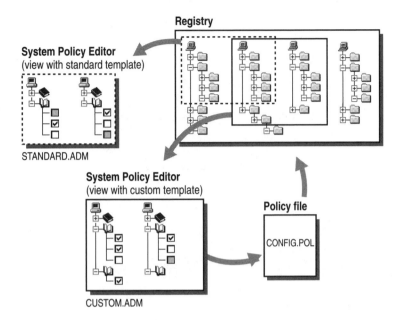

▶  **To use a template other than the default template**

1. In System Policy Editor, make sure all policy files are closed.

2. On the Options menu, click Template.

3. Click Open Template, and select an .ADM file to be your template to begin setting system policies. Click Open.

4. Click Close to return to System Policy Editor.

You can create your own templates that can be read by System Policy Editor. Users can then load the template and use it to set values in the Registry. To create a template, use a text editor such as WordPad to edit or write an .ADM file. You can open the default template named ADMIN.ADM in the Windows INF directory to use as an example.

A template uses several key words, syntaxes, and symbols, as summarized in the following list.

- Class:

  CLASS *category_type*

- Category:

  CATEGORY *name*
      [KEYNAME *key_name*]
      [... *policy definition statements* ...]
  END CATEGORY

- Policy:

  POLICY *name*
      [KEYNAME *key_name*]
      [... *part definition statements* ...]
  END POLICY

- Part:

  PART *name part_type*
      *type-dependent data*
      [KEYNAME *key_name* ]
      VALUENAME *value_name*
  END PART

The following table describes the keywords in system policy templates. Following this table are lists of the controls and values that can be defined in templates.

**System Policy Template Key Words**

| Template key word | Description |
|---|---|
| CLASS | Defines the Registry key that can be edited; the value must be USER or MACHINE, corresponding to Hkey_Current_User or Hkey_Local_Machine, respectively. |
| CATEGORY *name* | Defines a category in System Policy Editor. If a *name* contains spaces, it must be enclosed in quotes. A category statement can appear only once for each category name. |
| END CATEGORY | Defines the end of a category and all of its policies. |
| POLICY *name* | Defines a policy within a category. Policy names that contain spaces must be enclosed in quotes. |
| END POLICY | Defines the end of a policy and all its parts. |
| PART *name* | Defines one or more controls that can be used to set the values of a policy. Part names that contain spaces must be enclosed in quotes. Policy part types and type-dependent data are described in the following tables. |

**System Policy Template Key Words** (*continued*)

| Template key word | Description |
| --- | --- |
| END PART | Defines the end of the control list. |
| VALUEON | Specifies the setting to assign to the value when the policy is checked. |
| VALUEOFF | Specifies the setting to assign to the value when it is not checked. |
| *KEYNAME* | Specifies the full path of the Registry key. This is an optional Registry key name to use for the category or policy. If there is a key name specified, it is used by all child categories, policies, and parts, unless they define a key name of their own. |
| *VALUENAME* | Defines the Registry value entry name. |
| *VALUE* | Specifies the Registry value to set to a *VALUENAME*. |
| !! | Indicates a string value. |
| [strings] | Defines a section containing string values. |

A system policy template uses the following part control indicators.

**System Policy Template Part Control Indicators**

| Part Control Indicator | Description |
| --- | --- |
| CHECKBOX | Displays a check box. The value is nonzero if checked by the user, and its value entry is deleted if it is unchecked. |
| NUMERIC | Displays an edit field with an optional spin control that accepts a numeric value. |
| EDITTEXT | Displays an edit field that accepts alphanumeric text. |
| COMBOBOX | Displays a combo box, which is an edit field plus a drop-down list for suggested values. |
| TEXT | Displays a line of static (label) text. There is no Registry value associated with this part type. |
| DROPDOWNLIST | Displays a drop-down list. The user can choose from only one of the entries supplied. The main advantage of a drop-down list is that, based on the user's selection, a number of extra Registry edits can be performed. |
| LISTBOX | Displays a list box with Add and Remove buttons. This is the only part type that can be used to manage multiple values under one key. |

A system policy template uses the following type-specific information.

**System Policy Template Type-Specific Information**

| Type-specific modifier | Description |
| --- | --- |
| **CHECKBOX:** | |
| DEFCHECKED | Causes the check box initially to be checked. |
| VALUEON | If specified, overrides the default "on" behavior of the check box. For example: **VALUEON "On"** writes "On" to the Registry. |
| VALUEOFF | If specified, overrides the default "off" behavior of the check box. For example: **VALUEOFF "Off"** writes "Off" to the Registry. |
| ACTIONLISTON | Specifies optional action list to be taken if check box is "on." |
| ACTIONLISTOFF | Specifies optional action list to be taken if check box is "off." |
| **NUMERIC:** | |
| DEFAULT *value* | Specifies initial numeric value for the edit field. If this statement is not specified, the edit field is initially empty. |
| MIN *value* | Specifies minimum value for number. Default value is 0. |
| MAX *value* | Specifies maximum value for number. Default value is 9999. |
| SPIN *value* | Specifies increments to use for a spin control. Specifying **SPIN 0** removes the spin control; **SPIN 1** is the default. |
| REQUIRED | If specified, System Policy Editor will not allow a policy containing this part to be enabled unless a value has been entered. |
| TXTCONVERT | Writes values as strings rather than binary values. |
| **EDITTEXT:** | |
| DEFAULT *value* | Specifies the initial string to place in the edit field. If this is not specified, the field is empty initially. |
| MAXLEN *value* | Specifies the maximum length of the string in the edit field. |
| REQUIRED | If specified, System Policy Editor will not allow a policy containing this part to be enabled unless a value has been entered. |

**System Policy Template Type-Specific Information** (*continued*)

| Type-specific modifier | Description |
| --- | --- |
| **COMBOBOX:** | |
| | Accepts all the key words that EDITTEXT does, plus SUGGESTIONS. |
| SUGGESTIONS | Begins a list of suggestions to be placed in the drop-down list. Suggestions are separated with spaces and can be enclosed by quotes. The list is terminated with END SUGGESTIONS. For example: |

```
SUGGESTIONS
Alaska   Alabama   Mississippi   "New York"
END SUGGESTIONS
```

| | |
| --- | --- |
| **TEXT:** | Contains no type-specific data. |
| **DROPDOWNLIST:** | |
| REQUIRED | If specified, System Policy Editor will not allow a policy containing this part to be enabled unless a value has been entered. |
| ITEMLIST | Begins a list of the items in the drop-down list. The end of the list must be terminated by END ITEMLIST. Each item in the list is specified as follows: |

```
NAME name VALUE value
[ACTIONLIST actionlist]
. . .
```

*name* is the text to be displayed in the related drop-down list.

*value* is the value to be written for the part's value if this item is selected. Values are assumed to be strings, unless they are preceded by the key word NUMERIC. For example:

```
VALUE "Some value"
VALUE NUMERIC 1
```

If the VALUE key word is followed by the DELETE key word (that is, VALUE DELETE), then this Registry name/value pair will be deleted.

*actionlist* is an optional list to be used if this value is selected.

**System Policy Template Type-Specific Information** (*continued*)

| Type-specific modifier | Description |
| --- | --- |
| **LISTBOX:** | |
| VALUENAME | Cannot be used with the list box type, because there is no single value name associated with this type. By default, only one column appears in the list box, and for each entry a value is created with an identical value name and value data. For instance, the **List Entry** value in the list box would create a value named "List Entry" containing "List Entry" as data. |
| VALUEPREFIX *prefix* | Defines the prefix to be used in determining value names. If a prefix is specified, then this prefix plus "1," "2," and so on will be used instead of the default value naming scheme listed earlier in this table. The prefix can be empty (" "), which will cause the value names to be "1," "2," and so on. A prefix of **SomeName** will generate value names "SomeName1," "SomeName2," and so on. |
| EXPLICITVALUE | Causes the user to specify the value data and the value name. The list box shows two columns for each item, one for the name and one for the data. This key word cannot be used with the VALUEPREFIX key word. |
| ADDITIVE | If specified, values set in the list box are added to whatever values exist in the target Registry. Existing values are not deleted; by default, the content of list boxes will "override" whatever values are set in the target Registry. Specifically, a control value is inserted in the policy file which causes existing values to be deleted before the values set in the policy file are merged. |
| **Strings:** | |
| !! | Indicates a string value. For example:<br><br>`!!StrConst` |
| [*strings*] | Defines a section of string values; the values are defined in the following format:<br><br>*var_name=string value*<br><br>For example:<br><br>`StrConst="Control Name"` |
| Comments | Can be added by preceding the line with a semicolon (;). |

# Troubleshooting with System Policy Editor

This section contains some common problems that you might encounter when implementing system policies and some suggestions for fixing those problems.

In general, when troubleshooting problems with system policies, verify the following:

- The related Registry key is correct in the policy template (.ADM) file.
- The related policy is set properly in the policy (.POL) file.
- The related application actually uses the Registry key being changed.
- The policy file is located in the correct network location, and the network location is accessible from the computer running Windows 95.
- For group policies, the user name, group name, and computer name are correct, and the user is a member of the specified group.

When troubleshooting system policies, you should turn on error messages. You can do this from the Remote Update policy, as explained in "Setting Up for Manual Downloading of System Policies" earlier in this chapter. This setting displays error messages when policies cannot be downloaded correctly; the error messages might help identify the problem.

### The computer seems to be picking up some of the policies, but not all of them.

In this case, the computer might not be picking up any policies for Default User or for a particular user; it might be picking up only policies set for Default Computer or for a particular computer. In this case, make sure that user profiles are enabled on that computer. In the Passwords option in Control Panel, click the User Profile tab and set the desired options.

### The computer does not seem to be picking up policies from a CONFIG.POL file on the Windows NT domain.

- Make sure that there is a CONFIG.POL file in the NETLOGON directory on the primary domain controller on the Windows NT network.
- Make sure that the client computer has its domain set properly in the properties for Client for Microsoft Networks in the Network option in Control Panel.
- Make sure that the client computer is successfully logging on to that domain.
- Make sure that the client computer is configured for automatic policy downloading. You can set this by using the Remote Update policy, as described in "Setting Up for Manual Downloading of System Policies" earlier in this chapter. Windows 95 is configured for automatic policy downloading by default.
- Enable error messages on the client computer and see if an error message is displayed.

**The computer running Microsoft Client for NetWare Networks does not seem to be picking up the policies from a CONFIG.POL file on the NetWare server.**

- Make sure that there is a CONFIG.POL in the PUBLIC directory on the SYS: volume of a NetWare 3.x or 4.x server. You cannot put the CONFIG.POL file on a computer running Windows 95 with File and Print Sharing for NetWare Networks.

- Make sure that the client computer has its Preferred Server set to the NetWare server that contains CONFIG.POL. This setting is located in the properties for Client for NetWare Networks in the Network option in Control Panel.

- Make sure that the client computer is successfully logging on to that preferred server.

- Make sure that the client computer is configured for automatic policy downloading. You can set this by using the Remote Update policy, as described in "Setting Up for Manual Downloading of System Policies" earlier in this chapter.

- Enable error messages on the client computer and see if an error message is displayed.

**The computer running a Novell-supplied VLM or NETX client does not seem to be picking up the policies from the CONFIG.POL on the NetWare server, even though the file is in SYS:PUBLIC.**

Automatic downloading of system policies on a NetWare server works only when the client computer is running Microsoft Client for NetWare Networks. If the computer is running the Novell-supplied VLM or NETX client, then you must use manual downloading from a mapped drive. For information, see "Setting Up for Manual Downloading of System Policies" earlier in this chapter.

**The client computer is set for manual downloading, but it is not picking up the policies.**

- Make sure that the path specified for manual downloading includes the name of the policy file itself.

- Make sure that the directory in which you placed the policy file can be accessed by the user that is logging on to the computer running Windows 95.

**You have implemented a policy and then cleared it, but it appears to still be in effect, or it does not do what you thought it would do.**

Does the policy have an edit box that needs to be completed? For example, do you need to specify the wallpaper or workgroup name? If so, then by clearing the policy, you are actually deleting the Registry setting for that value. For example, by clearing the wallpaper policy, the wallpaper Registry setting is made to be blank, and thus the user will have no wallpaper.

For all policies that involve settings that users can manipulate by using an option in Control Panel, the best way to stop enforcing that policy is to make sure that policy setting is grayed, in order to allow the users to make their own choices. These policies are listed in "System Policy Editor" earlier in this chapter.

### You set up group policies, but one or more of the users do not get these group policies when they log on.

- Is there a policy for that particular user? If so, then group policies are ignored by design. This allows you to make exceptions to group policies for particular users.

- Make sure that the client computer is set up for group support.

- Make sure that the user or users are really members of that group.

- Make sure that user profiles are enabled on the client computer.

### You used the policy named Only Run Allowed Windows Applications, but then you could not turn off this policy because you forgot to include POLEDIT.EXE in the list.

- Did you set this policy for all users? If not, then log on as another user, and run System Policy Editor to cancel this policy.

- If you can run Registry Editor, go to the following key and delete the RestrictRun entry:

```
Hkey_Current_User\Software\Microsoft\Windows\CurrentVersion\Policies
    \Explore
```

- If you previously set this policy for the Default User and, as a result, no user can run System Policy Editor or Registry Editor, then try the following:

    - If possible, disable user profiles in the Passwords option in Control Panel. Then you should be able to log on and run System Policy Editor. Then undo the policy and re-enable user profiles.

    - If you cannot disable user profiles because the Passwords option in Control Panel has been disabled, you must either reinstall Windows 95 (so that user profiles will not be enabled). Or use the Windows 95 startup disk and run the real-mode Registry Editor to disable user profiles.

**You need to prevent users from modifying their computer configuration, including even more restrictions than are available through standard system policies.**

Use one or more of the following methods for ensuring administrative control of the computer's configuration.

- In MSDOS.SYS for the user's computer, set **BootKeys=1** so the user cannot press F8 to avoid starting Windows 95. In addition, make sure that floppy-disk startup is not enabled in the computer's CMOS settings, and use password protection to prevent CMOS modifications. For information about making these changes, see the documentation from your computer's manufacturer.

- For the Registry on the user's computer, use System Policy Editor to enable the Registry setting named Require Validation By Network For Windows Access.

- In the system policies that are downloaded when the user logs on, set the policy named Disable Registry Editing Tools.

- Set the policy named Only Run Allowed Windows Applications, and make sure that System Policy Editor and Registry Editor are not on the list of allowed applications.

- Set up the user's computer to run Windows 95 as a shared installation, as described in Chapter 4, "Server-Based Setup for Windows 95."

CHAPTER 16

# Remote Administration

This chapter describes the Windows 95 management features that allow you to manage network computers from your own computer. This chapter also includes information about system management applications and agents, plus network backup agents from other vendors.

**In This Chapter**

Remote Administration: The Basics   530
Remote Administration: The Issues   531
Setting Up for Remote Administration   532
Accessing Remote Registries by Using System Policy Editor   535
Accessing Remote Registries by Using Registry Editor   536
Viewing a Remote Computer by Using System Monitor   537
Using Net Watcher for Remote Administration   537
Using Network Neighborhood for Remote Administration   539
Using Network Backup Agents   540
    Setting Up Network-Based Backup with the Arcada Agent   541
    Setting Up Network-Based Backup with the Cheyenne Agent   542
Preparing for Microsoft Network Monitor   544
    Installing the Network Monitor Agent and Driver   544
    Running Network Monitor Agent   545
    Configuring Network Monitor Driver   546
Using Remote Administration Tools from Other Vendors   547
Removing Remote Agents and Services   551

# Remote Administration: The Basics

The remote management tools provided with Windows 95 are designed to make it easier for you to identify and solve problems encountered by users without dispatching support personnel to make changes at the users' work site. The following list describes the benefits of using these remote administration tools.

**System Policy Editor.**  You can use System Policy Editor to edit Registry entries in real time for remote computers. You can also create, edit, and manage system policies to control system settings for multiple computers on the network. For information, see Chapter 15, "User Profiles and System Policies."

**Registry Editor.**  You can use Registry Editor to read and write values directly in the Registry. You can read settings, create new keys and entries, or delete existing keys. Registry Editor should be used only by those who have appropriate access rights to identify and correct problems.

**System Monitor.**  You can use System Monitor to troubleshoot performance problems by monitoring virtual device drivers across the network. System Monitor can provide you with performance information from many system components, including the file system and network clients.

**Net Watcher.**  If you use File and Printer Sharing services, you can use Net Watcher to create, add, and delete shared resources on remote computers, and to monitor and manage connections to shared resources. This is especially useful when you need to know who is connected to a computer and which files are open.

You can manage file systems remotely by browsing specific computers in Network Neighborhood, as described in "Using Network Neighborhood for Remote Administration" later in this chapter.

Windows 95 also provides agents for remote administration, including an agent for Microsoft Network Monitor and an SNMP agent for administration with Simple Network Management Protocol (SNMP) system management products, as described in "Using Remote Administration Tools from Other Vendors" later in this chapter.

# Remote Administration: The Issues

Before you use the remote administration features, you should understand the following aspects of your networking and administrative needs.

To take advantage of the remote administration capabilities of Windows 95, you should do the following:

- Enable remote administration and user-level security on every computer that you will administer remotely. If you want to administer a remote computer using Registry Editor, System Monitor, or System Policy Editor, then the Microsoft Remote Registry service must be installed on your computer and the remote computer. Notice, however, that although the remote computer requires user-level security, it does not also require File and Printer Sharing services.

  Optionally, the SNMP agent or the Microsoft Network Monitor agent should be installed if required for your administrative tools. For information, see "Setting Up for Remote Administration" later in this chapter.

- Run a common network protocol, such as the Microsoft versions of the IPX/SPX-compatible protocol, TCP/IP, or NetBEUI.

- Train help desk personnel on System Monitor if they will use it. They should understand what each measurement provided by System Monitor means and what course of action is required in response to these measurements. For information, see Chapter 17, "Performance Tuning."

- Train help desk personnel on what problems can be identified and repaired by using System Policy Editor or Registry Editor.

Both Registry Editor and System Policy Editor allow you to access a remote computer's Registry. However, System Policy Editor allows you to access only a subset of keys, while Registry Editor allows you to access the entire Registry. As a result, Registry Editor requires significantly more training. Also, it's important to remember that some changes made to the Registry on a remote computer require the user to shut down and restart the computer, while other changes take effect immediately. As a rule, if you must restart the computer when changing a setting by using Control Panel or other tools, then you must restart it when changing that setting in the Registry directly.

You can enable remote administration capabilities on a computer as part of the process for installing Windows 95 from custom scripts. For more information, see Appendix D, "MSBATCH.INF Parameters."

# Setting Up for Remote Administration

This section provides details about how to set up remote administration after Windows 95 is installed.

The following table describes what you need to set up on the remote computer to complete an administrative task.

| Remote administration task | Requirement on the remote computer |
|---|---|
| Browse and manage shared resources on a remote computer by using Net Watcher | Enable user-level security, remote administration, and File and Printer Sharing services; grant remote administration privilege to the network administrator |
| Manage the file system of a remote computer by using Net Watcher | Enable user-level security and remote administration; grant remote administration privilege to the network administrator |
| Edit a remote computer's Registry by using Registry Editor or System Policy Editor | Enable user-level security and remote administration, and install Microsoft Remote Registry services |
| Monitor performance of a remote computer by using System Monitor | Enable user-level security and remote administration, and install Microsoft Remote Registry services |

Granting remote administration privilege gives that person full access to all shared resources on the system (including the ability to add and remove other remote administrators). Granting or removing access to remote administration capabilities for a user does not take effect until the next time the user connects to the computer running Windows 95.

When remote administration is enabled on a computer, two special shared directories are created:

- ADMIN$ gives administrators access to the file system on the remote computer.

- IPC$ provides an interprocess communication (IPC) channel between the two computers.

---

**Important**  If you enable user-level security by using the Network option in Control Panel or in a setup script, remote administration is enabled automatically for the Domain Administrator group on a Windows NT domain. On a Novell® NetWare® network, the Supervisor account (for version 3.x) or the Admin account (for version 4.0) is enabled automatically. For more information, see Chapter 14, "Security."

If you want to enable user-level security without automatically enabling remote administration, you can use system policies to enable the User-Level Access Control option. In this case, you must enable remote administration manually by using the Password option in Control Panel on each individual computer.

---

▶ **To enable remote administration manually**

1. In the Passwords option in Control Panel, click the Remote Administration tab.

2. Make sure Enable Remote Administration Of This Server is checked.

3. If the computer is configured for share-level access control, specify the password for remote administration.

This dialog box is available only when share-level security is enabled.

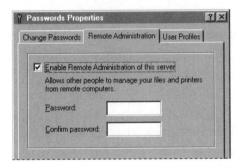

If the computer is configured for user-level access control, click the Add button, and add the appropriate administrators. Click OK.

This dialog box is available only when user-level security is enabled.

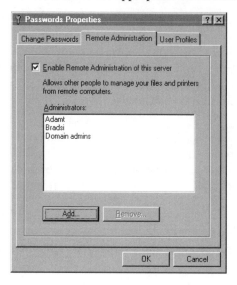

▶ **To install Microsoft Remote Registry services**

1. In the Network option in Control Panel, click Add.

2. In the Select Network Component Type dialog box, double-click Service.

3. In the Select Network Service dialog box, click the Have Disk button.

4. In the Install From Disk dialog box, type the path to the ADMIN\NETTOOLS\REMOTREG directory on the Windows 95 compact disc, and then click OK.

5. In the Install From Disk dialog box, click OK.

6. In the Select Network Service dialog box, click Microsoft Remote Registry, and then click OK.

   If you are prompted to specify the location of additional files, specify the path to the Windows 95 source files on a shared network directory or on the Windows 95 compact disc.

For information about installing the Microsoft Remote Registry service and enabling remote administration by using setup scripts, see Appendix D, "MSBATCH.INF Parameters."

**Technical Notes on the Microsoft Remote Registry Service**

- You must also install the Remote Registry service on the administrator's computer to ensure that the WINREG.DLL file is in the Windows SYSTEM directory on that computer.

- Make sure that both the administrator's and user's computers have at least one protocol in common. That can be either Microsoft NetBEUI, Microsoft TCP/IP, or the IPX/SPX-compatible protocol (with or without NetBIOS).

# Accessing Remote Registries by Using System Policy Editor

When you run System Policy Editor in Registry mode, you have direct access to the Registry for a local or remote computer. This section discusses how to access the Registry on a remote computer by using System Policy Editor. For information about installing and using System Policy Editor, see Chapter 15, "User Profiles and System Policies."

As with Registry Editor, most of the changes you make with System Policy Editor in Registry mode modify the remote Registry as soon as you save the changes. These Registry changes apply to the user or to the computer. Some of these changes require the user to log off and then log back on.

▶ **To edit a remote computer's Registry by using System Policy Editor**

1. In System Policy Editor, click the File menu, and then click Connect.

2. In the Connect dialog box, type the name of the computer you want to remotely administer, using the computer name for that computer as it appears in the Network option in Control Panel. Windows 95 connects to the Registry on the computer specified (assuming you have appropriate permissions).

   The title bar of System Policy Editor shows whether you are viewing a local or a remote Registry.

3. Make changes by using the methods described in Chapter 15, "User Profiles and System Policies."

After you have made a connection to the remote computer, you can use System Policy Editor for modifying user and computer properties just as you would on a local computer.

# Accessing Remote Registries by Using Registry Editor

To solve a problem on a remote computer running Windows 95, you might need to access the entire Registry for the computer. In this case, you should use Registry Editor because System Policy Editor allows access to only a subset of Registry settings.

**Note**  To use Registry Editor to edit the Registry on a remote computer, the Microsoft Remote Registry service must be installed on the remote computer, as described in "Setting Up for Remote Administration" earlier in this chapter.

▶ **To edit the Registry on a remote computer by using Registry Editor**

1. In Registry Editor, click the Registry menu, and then click Connect Network Registry.

2. In the Connect Network Registry dialog box, type the name of the computer you want to remotely administer.

   Windows 95 adds the contents of the remote Registry below the contents of the local Registry.

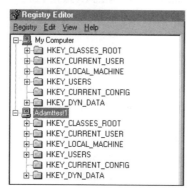

3. Make changes by using the methods described in Chapter 33, "Windows 95 Registry."

# Viewing a Remote Computer by Using System Monitor

System Monitor is a tracking tool that monitors the real-time performance of various computer components, functions, and behaviors and displays the results in graphs or charts. This information is useful in locating bottlenecks and solving other performance problems.

With the appropriate administrative privileges, you can use System Monitor over the network to track the performance of remote computers. To monitor more than one computer simultaneously, you can start multiple instances of System Monitor and connect to the appropriate computers.

For more information about installing and using System Monitor, see Chapter 17, "Performance Tuning."

**Note**  To use System Monitor to connect to a remote computer, the Microsoft Remote Registry service must be installed on the remote computer.

▶ **To view performance data on a remote computer by using System Monitor**

1. In System Monitor, click the File menu, and then click Connect.
2. Type the name of the computer, and click OK.

# Using Net Watcher for Remote Administration

Net Watcher is a Windows 95 tool for creating, controlling, and monitoring remote shared resources. This is a useful way to manage peer sharing services in Windows 95.

**Note**  If you are not using File and Printer Sharing services, you can skip this section.

Net Watcher includes a set of icons that make it easy to do the following:

- Add a shared resource or stop sharing a resource
- Show all shared resources, connected users, and open files
- Close files users have opened
- Disconnect a user

▶ **To connect to a remote computer by using Net Watcher**

1. From the Start button, click Run, and then type **netwatch**

2. From the Administer menu, click Select Server, and then type the name of the computer you want to connect to.

3. Type the password for remote administration on the computer you are connecting to.

   The password depends on the type of security used on the remote computer:

   - For share-level security, the password is the Remote Administration password specified in the Passwords option in Control Panel.

   - For user-level security, the password is the one for an Administrator account specified in the Passwords option in Control Panel.

When using Net Watcher to view a remote computer, you should understand the following constraints:

- The remote computer must be running File and Printer Sharing services.

- If your computer uses share-level security, you can use Net Watcher to connect only to other computers that use share-level security. However, if the computer uses user-level security, you can use Net Watcher to connect to any other remote computers running File and Printer Sharing services. The pass-through server or domain does not have to be the same for the two computers.

- For computers running File and Printer Sharing for NetWare Networks, you can use Net Watcher to connect only to other computers running File and Printer Sharing for NetWare Networks. The pass-through server does not have to be the same for the two computers.

- On a NetWare network, you cannot use Net Watcher to close documents on remote computers. You can, however, use Net Watcher to disconnect users.

---

**Tip** You can prevent a user from sharing files although the user must have File and Printer Sharing services running to allow remote administration. To do this, set the system policies named Disable File Sharing Controls and Disable Print Sharing Controls. Disabling these options by using system policies does not remove the File and Printer Sharing services, while using the Network option in Control Panel does disable the service.

---

The following examples show how to create a shared resource on a remote computer by using Net Watcher.

▶ **To share a resource on a remote computer by using Net Watcher**

1. To connect to a remote computer, follow the procedure named "To connect to a remote computer by using Net Watcher" earlier in this section.

2. Click the View menu, and then click By Shared Folders.

3. Click the Administer menu, and then Click Add Shared Folder.

4. In the Enter Path dialog box, type the drive and complete path of the resource that you want to share, and then click OK.

This example shows the shared directories on a remote computer running File and Printer Sharing for Microsoft Networks.

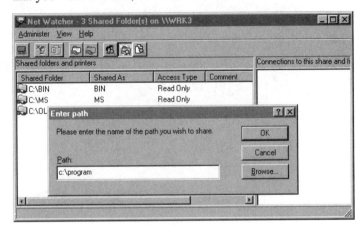

# Using Network Neighborhood for Remote Administration

Another way to use System Policy Editor, Registry Editor, Net Watcher, or System Monitor remotely is to right-click the remote computer from within Network Neighborhood.

▶ **To manage remote computers in the local workgroup by using Network Neighborhood**

1. In Network Neighborhood, right-click the icon of the computer you want to administer, and then click Properties.

2. In the computer's Properties dialog box, click the Tools tab.

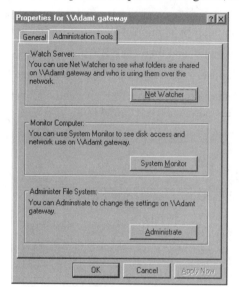

3. Click the button for the remote management task you want to perform, as described in the following list.

| Option | Description |
| --- | --- |
| Net Watcher | Runs the Net Watcher tool and automatically connects to the specified computer. |
| System Monitor | Runs the System Monitor tool and automatically connects to the specified computer. |
| Administrate | Opens a folder on the desktop for the specified remote computer and allows you to access to the remote computer's hard disk drive. |

# Using Network Backup Agents

You can back up user data remotely by using either of the two network-based backup agents included with Windows 95. The Arcada® Backup Exec Agent and Cheyenne® ARCserve Agent allow you to back up computers to a tape drive on a network server. You must have the corresponding server-based network backup software from either Arcada or Cheyenne.

The following sections describe how to install these backup agents on an individual computer, with a summary of the steps for running network-based backup when the agent is installed.

# Setting Up Network-Based Backup with the Arcada Agent

To use the Arcada agent, you must have the following components:

- Arcada Backup Exec Agent (included with Windows 95). The agent includes the following files: BKUPAGNT.EXE, BKUPNET.DLL, and BKUPPROP.DLL.

- Arcada Backup Exec for NetWare, Enterprise Edition or Single Server Edition, version 5.01. To obtain this software, please contact Arcada directly at (800) 327-2232.

To back up a computer running Windows 95 with the Arcada agent, you must first install and enable the Arcada agent. If you didn't already do this during Setup, you can install and enable the Arcada agent by using the Network option in Control Panel. After you install the backup agent, the computer will run the agent automatically in the background when you start Windows 95.

▶ **To install and enable the Arcada Backup Exec Agent**

1. In the Network option in Control Panel, click Add.

2. In the Select Network Component Type dialog box, double-click Service.

3. In the Select Network Service dialog box, click Arcada Software in the Manufacturers list, click Backup Exec Agent in the Network Services list, and then click OK.

To run Arcada network-based backup on a computer running Windows 95, run Arcada Backup Exec Agent (NetWare Enterprise Edition or Single Server Edition). See the product documentation for more information and instructions.

For information about installing the Arcada Backup Exec Agent by using custom setup scripts, see Chapter 5, "Custom, Automated, and Push Installations."

▶ **To configure the Arcada Backup Exec Agent**

1. In the Network option in Control Panel, double-click Backup Exec Agent in the list of network components.

2. Click the General tab, and then click Enable Network Backup.

3. If you want to specify a password to allow backup, make sure Password is checked, and then type the password.

4. If you do not want Registry files to be restored when other files are restored, make sure Allow Registry To Be Restored is not checked.

5. In the Published Folder area, use the Add and Remove buttons to define the list of folders and drives to be backed up.

6. If you want to define access control for selected folders based on password or real-only access, click the Details button.

7. Click the Protocol tab, and then click an option to specify the protocol that Backup Exec Agent should use (SPX/IPX or TCP/IP). For TCP/IP, you must also specify either the host name or IP address for the backup server.

For more information about configuring and using this agent, refer to the documentation provided with your Arcada Backup Exec software.

# Setting Up Network-Based Backup with the Cheyenne Agent

To use the Cheyenne agent, you must have the following components:

- Cheyenne ARCserve Agent (included with Windows 95). The agent includes the following files: ARCSRV32.EXE and CHEYPROP.DLL.

- Cheyenne ARCserve for NetWare (version 5.01).

- New versions of Cheyenne network loadable modules (NLMs), which have been updated specifically for Windows 95. These include the APROCESS.NLM, ARCOPY.NLM, and WSTAPE.NLM files. To obtain these files, contact Cheyenne directly at (800) 243-9832.

To back up a computer running Windows 95 with the Cheyenne agent, you must first install and enable the Cheyenne agent. If you did not already do this during Setup, you can install and enable the Cheyenne agent by using the Network option in Control Panel. After you install the backup agent, the computer will run the agent automatically in the background when you start Windows 95.

▶ **To install and enable the Cheyenne ARCserve Agent**

1. In the Network option in Control Panel, click Add.

2. In the Select Network Component Type dialog box, double-click Service.

3. In the Select Network Service dialog box, click Cheyenne Software in the Manufacturers list, click ARCserve Agent in the Network Services list, and then click OK.

To run Cheyenne network-based backup on a computer running Windows 95, run Cheyenne ARCserve for NetWare. See the product documentation for more information and instructions.

For information about installing the Cheyenne ARCserve Agent by using custom setup scripts, see Chapter 5, "Custom, Automated, and Push Installations."

▶ **To configure the ARCserve agent**

1. In the Network option in Control Panel, double-click ARCserve Agent in the list of network components.

2. Click Enable Network Backup.

3. If you want to specify a password to allow backup, type the password in the Password box, and then type it again in the Confirm Password box.

4. If you do not want Registry to be restored when other files are restored, make sure Do Not Restore Registry is checked.

5. Use the Add and Remove buttons to define the list of folders and drives that should not be backed up.

For more information about configuring and using this agent, see the documentation provided with your Cheyenne ARCserve software.

# Preparing for Microsoft Network Monitor

The Windows 95 compact disc includes a protocol driver and agent for Microsoft Network Monitor. The protocol driver provides performance counters that can be viewed by using System Monitor if you want to assess certain network traffic statistics for NDIS 3.1 protected-mode network adapters. The Network Monitor agent, which runs as a Windows 95 service, works with the protocol driver for use with the Microsoft Network Monitor application. You can use this application to detect and troubleshoot problems on LANs, WANs, and Microsoft Remote Access Service (RAS) connections.

**Note**  The Network Monitor application is provided with Microsoft Systems Management Server, which is a client-server system that allows administrators to perform key management functions for distributed computers from a central location. For more information, see Appendix E, "Microsoft Systems Management Server."

# Installing the Network Monitor Agent and Driver

When you install the Network Monitor agent, the protocol driver is also installed automatically. You must have both the agent and the driver installed if you want to use the agent with Network Monitor to conduct remote captures of network traffic to and from a computer running Windows 95.

However, if you want only to view the performance counters in System Monitor and you want to prevent anyone from accessing the local computer by way of the Network Monitor agent, you can choose to install only the protocol driver.

**Note**  The Network Monitor application uses NetBIOS to control the remote-capture computer. If you are using the IPX/SPX-compatible protocol to connect the agent and manager computers, you must enable NetBIOS support for IPX/SPX, as described in Chapter 12, "Network Technical Discussion."

▶ **To install the Network Monitor agent on a single computer**

1. In the Network option in Control Panel, click Add.

2. In the Select Network Component Type dialog box, double-click Service.

3. In the Select Network Service dialog box, click the Have Disk button.

4. In the Install From Disk dialog box, type the path to the ADMIN\NETTOOLS\NETMON directory on the Windows 95 compact disc, and then click OK.

5. In the Select Network Service dialog box, click Microsoft Network Monitor Agent in the Models list, and then click OK.

▶ **To install only the Microsoft Network Monitor protocol driver**

1. In the Network option in Control Panel, click Add.

2. In the Select Network Component Type dialog box, double-click Protocol.

3. In the Select Network Protocol dialog box, click the Have Disk button.

4. In the Install From Disk dialog box, type the path to the ADMIN\NETTOOLS\NETMON directory on the Windows 95 compact disc, and then click OK.

5. In the Select Network Protocol dialog box, click Microsoft Network Monitor Driver in the Models list, and then click OK.

For information about installing the Microsoft Network Monitor agent and protocol driver by using custom setup scripts, see Chapter 5, "Custom, Automated, and Push Installations." For information about using Network Monitor for performance analysis, see Chapter 17, "Performance Tuning"; for information about using Network Monitor for network protocol analysis, see Appendix E, "Microsoft Systems Management Server."

# Running Network Monitor Agent

You can run the Network Monitor agent as a service, or you can start and stop the agent as an executable application.

▶ **To start Microsoft Network Monitor agent**

• Click the Start button, click Run, and then type **nmagent**

The Network Monitor agent is removed from the system each time you log off, and must be restarted for each user that logs on if the agent is not scheduled to run as a service.

▶ **To run Network Monitor agent as a service**

1. In Registry Editor, select the following Registry key:

   ```
   Hkey_Local_Machine\Software\Microsoft\Windows\CurrentVersion
       \RunServicesOnce
   ```

2. Click the Edit menu, point to New, and then click String Value.

3. Type a label for the value name, such as **nm agent**, and then press ENTER.

4. Click the Edit menu, and then click Modify.

5. In the Value Data box, type:

   **nmagent.exe**

6. Click OK.

The Network Monitor agent will continue to run after a user logs off if it is started as a service. You can, however, type a command to stop running the agent, whether the agent was started as a service or run from the command prompt.

▶ **To stop the Network Monitor agent**

- Click the Start button, click Run, and then type **nmagent -close**

# Configuring Network Monitor Driver

You can configure options for Network Monitor by defining properties for the Network Monitor protocol driver. For information about using the Network Monitor driver to display system performance statistics, see Chapter 17, "Performance Tuning."

▶ **To configure the Microsoft Network Monitor protocol driver**

1. Make sure that the Network Monitor agent is not running and that System Monitor is not monitoring the performance statistics provided by the Network Monitor driver.

2. In the Network option in Control Panel, double-click Microsoft Network Monitor Driver.

3. In the Microsoft Network Monitor Driver Properties dialog box, click the Password tab. You can define the password that users must specify to capture data, view capture files, or access the computer remotely. The following options are available:

   - If you want to change any password that has been previously defined, type a password in the Old Capture Password area.

   - If you want to define a password to restrict users to viewing only previously saved capture files by using the Network Monitor application, type a password in the Display Password area.

   - If you want to define a password to authorize users to connect to the computer and capture files by using the Microsoft Network Monitor application, type a password in the Capture Password area. You can define only one password for all network adapters on a computer with multiple adapters.

   - If you want to allow free access to the computer by anyone running the Network Monitor application, then make sure No Password is checked.

4. If the computer has more than one network adapter, click the Describe tab, and then click the network adapter you want to monitor.

   You can also define a description for each network adapter in this dialog box, so that administrator running the Network Monitor application can determine which adapter to select.

5. Click the Advanced tab. In the Value box, type the user name that will be shown when an administrator running the Network Monitor application selects the Identify Network Monitor Users command.

   This additional information, which is similar to a comment, does not get updated or changed if another user logs on to this computer.

**Note**  The settings on the Bindings tab have no effect.

# Using Remote Administration Tools from Other Vendors

You can also remotely administer computers running Windows 95 by using other system management tools provided by Microsoft or by other vendors. The following list shows some of the system management tools that you can use to manage computers running Windows 95:

- Microsoft Systems Management Server
- Microsoft Windows NT Server
- Novell NMS
- HP® Open View for Windows
- Intel® LANDesk™
- IBM® LAN NetView®
- Sun® NetManager

For networks that use SNMP for system management, Windows 95 includes an SNMP agent which conforms to the SNMP version 1 specification. This agent allows you to monitor, from an SNMP console, remote connections to computers running Windows 95. After this agent is installed, you do not need to make any other modifications to client computers to use SNMP.

The SNMP agent is implemented as a Win32-based service and works using Windows Sockets over both TCP/IP and IPX/SPX. The extension agents are implemented as Win32 DLLs. (For more information about writing SNMP MIBs under Windows 95, see the *Microsoft Win32 Software Development Kit.*)

The configuration information for the RFC 1156 extension agent is placed in the Registry under the following key:

`Hkey_Local_Machine\System\CurrentControlSet\Services\SNMP\Parameters`

▶ **To install the Microsoft SNMP agent**

1. In the Network option in Control Panel, click Add.

2. In the Select Network Component Type dialog box, double-click Service.

3. In the Select Network Service dialog box, click the Have Disk button.

4. In the Install From Disk dialog box, type the path to the ADMIN\NETTOOLS\SNMP directory on the Windows 95 compact disc, and then click OK.

5. In the Select Network Service dialog box, click Microsoft SNMP Agent in the Models list, and then click OK.

   If you are prompted to specify the location of additional files, specify the path to the Windows 95 source files on a shared network directory or on the Windows 95 compact disc.

For information about installing the Microsoft SNMP agent by using custom setup scripts, see Chapter 5, "Custom, Automated, and Push Installations."

When the computer is restarted after the SNMP agent is installed, SNMP automatically starts in an MS-DOS window. You can minimize this window to keep it out of the way while working.

▶ **To configure the SNMP agent**

- Use System Policy Editor to set the following policies for the computer:

| Policy | Description |
|---|---|
| Communities | Specifies one or more groups of hosts to which this computer belongs for purposes of administration using the SNMP service. These are the communities that are allowed to query the SNMP agent. |
| Permitted Managers | Specifies IP or IPX addresses allowed to obtain information from an SNMP agent. If this policy is not checked, any SNMP console can query the agent. |
| Traps for Public Community | Specifies *trap destinations*, or IP or IPX addresses of hosts in the public community to which you want the SNMP service to send traps. |
| Internet MIB (RFC 1156) | Allows you to specify the contact name and location if you are using Internet MIB. |

If you want to configure the Windows 95 SNMP agent to send traps to a community other than the public community, you must either edit the Registry directly or add a new system policy.

▶ **To add SNMP communities by editing the Registry**

1. In Registry Editor, select the following key:

   ```
   Hkey_Local_Machine\System\CurrentControlSet\Services
       \SNMP\Parameters\TrapConfiguration
   ```

2. Click the Edit menu, point to New, and then click Key.

3. Type the name that you want to specify for a new community, and press ENTER.

4. Create a new string value for each console to which the SNMP should send traps:

   - The first value name should be 1, the second value name should be 2, and so on.

   - The value data must be the IP or IPX address of the SNMP console to which traps will be sent.

   To create a string value, click the new key, click the Edit menu, point to New, and then click New String. Type the value name, and then press ENTER.

   To specify the value data, click the value name, click the Edit menu, and then click Modify. In the Value Data box, type the value data, and then click OK.

The following illustration shows an example of what the Registry should look like after adding a new community named Prv1.

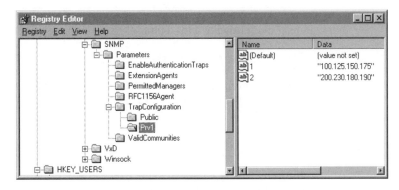

▶ **To add SNMP communities by using system policies**

1. Start a text editor, and open the ADMIN.ADM file in the INF subdirectory of the Windows directory.

2. Add an entry in the section named CATEGORY !!SNMP, specifying the following new values:

   - *Name Of New Policy*, which defines the text that you want to appear in System Policy Editor for this policy. You do not need to include "!!" if you use quotation marks around the name. The "!!" string is used only for Windows 95 localization, and the strings are defined at the bottom of ADMIN.ADM.

   - *Name Of New Community*, which defines the name of the community for which you are adding support.

The following shows the complete syntax for this entry:

```
POLICY  "Name Of New Policy"
    KEYNAME
    System\CurrentControlSet\Services\SNMP\Parameters
            \TrapConfiguration\Name Of New Community
    PART !!Traps_PublicListbox LISTBOX
        VALUEPREFIX ""
    END PART
END POLICY
```

---

**Note**  The Registry key and value names are case-sensitive. Also, the Registry key name (System\...\*Name Of New Community*) must be one continuous line in the ADMIN.ADM file.

---

For example, the following adds a policy for a community named Prv1:

```
POLICY "Traps for Prv1 Community"
    KEYNAME
System\CurrentControlSet\Services\SNMP\Parameters\TrapConfiguration\Prv1
    PART !!Traps_PublicListbox LISTBOX
    VALUEPREFIX ""
    END PART
END POLICY
```

After editing and saving ADMIN.ADM, you can see this new policy by running System Policy Editor and selecting the Computer policy under Network named SNMP. You can use this policy exactly as you would use the policy named Traps For Public Community.

# Removing Remote Agents and Services

Any agent that runs as a network service and that appears in the Network option in Control Panel can be removed by selecting it and clicking the Remove button.

You can use System Policy Editor to turn off services by setting system policies, or by using Registry mode to modify a computer's Registry. To do this, in the computer properties, click System. Then delete the services that you no longer want under the Run and Run Services policies.

Some agents, such as the SNMP agent, can be removed only by modifying the Registry. For a single computer, you can do this by using either Registry Editor or System Policy Editor. The following Registry keys list the services running on the computer:

```
Hkey_Local_Machine\Software\Microsoft\Windows\CurrentVersion\RunServices
Hkey_Local_Machine\Software\Microsoft\Windows\CurrentVersion\Run
```

C H A P T E R   1 7

# Performance Tuning

Windows 95 provides the easiest methods and best defaults ever offered for configuring system memory and ensuring good performance on an x86-based computer. This chapter summarizes system features related to performance and describes tools for monitoring and managing system performance.

**In This Chapter**

Windows 95 Performance Tuning: The Basics   554

Windows 95 Performance Tuning: The Issues   556

System Performance Overview   558

    System Resource Capacity in Windows 95   559

    Technical Notes on MS-DOS Components in Windows 95   560

Optimizing the Swap File   562

Optimizing File System Performance   564

    Optimizing File System Performance with Profiles   565

    Optimizing CD-ROM File System Performance   567

    Using File-System Troubleshooting Options   569

Setting Graphics Compatibility Options   570

Optimizing Printing   572

Optimizing Network Performance   573

Optimizing Conventional Memory   575

Tracking Performance with System Monitor   576

    Configuring Performance Charts in System Monitor   576

    Identifying Performance Problems with System Monitor   578

    Summary of System Monitor Categories   579

# Windows 95 Performance Tuning: The Basics

The Windows 95 architecture includes several improvements over earlier versions of Windows. These changes, which strongly impact most areas of system performance, include the following:

- Fully integrated 32-bit, protected-mode operating system, eliminating the need to run MS-DOS separately

- Complete 32-bit kernel, providing improved memory management and process scheduling, plus improved system-wide robustness and improved cleanup after an application closes or fails, delivering a more stable and reliable operating environment

- Preemptive multitasking and multithreading support, providing improved system responsiveness, smooth background processing, and improved system capacity, allowing multiple applications and system tasks to run well concurrently

- 32-bit installable file systems to support better performance and long filenames

- 32-bit device drivers for all system components, ensuring better performance and better resource management

Many Windows 95 features provide dynamic configuration, reducing or eliminating the need for users to adjust their system settings. The following self-tuning features in Windows 95 are designed to improve performance and reduce support costs.

**Dynamic swap file and dynamic caching using VCACHE.**  Windows 95 uses dynamic sizes for the virtual-memory swap file, the cache for file and network access, and the CD-ROM cache. Both the swap file and cache sizes can grow or shrink, depending on the computer's memory configuration and the demand for memory from applications. This relieves users or administrators from having to change the cache parameters as new memory or new applications are added. Windows 95 can take advantage of new memory automatically and expand or reduce the file and cache sizes automatically based on demands when applications are loaded or unloaded. Also, the networking, disk, CD-ROM, and paging caches are integrated and will scale as more memory is added to the computer. For more information, see "Optimizing the Swap File" later in this chapter and "Optimizing File System Performance" later in this chapter.

**32-bit disk and file access for fast hard-disk access.**  These mechanisms allow Windows 95 to access the hard disk or file system directly, bypassing the computer's BIOS. Using 32-bit file and disk access improves performance and allows Windows 95 to handle BIOS requests in protected mode, rather than in real mode. For more information, see Chapter 20, "Disks and File Systems."

**Background print rendering.**  For a computer that has sufficient memory to take advantage of it, background print rendering is available automatically to reduce the return-to-application time for printing. With this feature, Windows 95 first writes an enhanced metafile (EMF) format file, which is a device-independent rendering of the print job that is much faster to produce than a device-specific rendering. In the background, Windows 95 uses the EMF file to create the device-dependent rendering while the user continues to work in the application. For more information, see "Optimizing Printing" later in this chapter.

**Automatic system adjustments during Windows 95 Setup.**  During installation, Windows 95 Setup makes decisions about certain operating system features based on the hardware configuration. For example, in a computer with low memory, Windows 95 turns off background print rendering, because this feature increases the operating system working set that is loaded into memory and cannot be paged out to the swap file.

**Built-in tools for monitoring and adjusting system performance.**  The following tools in Windows 95 are available for managing performance-related settings:

- System option in Control Panel provides settings for tuning and troubleshooting. For information, see "Optimizing the Swap File" later in this chapter, "Optimizing File System Performance" later in this chapter, and "Setting Graphics Compatibility Options" later in this chapter.

- System Monitor can be used to track the performance of key system components, as described in "Tracking Performance with System Monitor" later in this chapter.

- DriveSpace includes a protected-mode driver that is installed by default, providing faster performance than the earlier real-mode compression driver and using only an additional 10 or 15 percent overhead. If you are using any real-mode disk-compression utilities other than DriveSpace or DoubleSpace, plan to switch to a protected-mode version. Contact the manufacturer to determine availability of protected-mode drivers that are compatible with Windows 95.

- Disk Defragmenter can improve file access time by defragmenting uncompressed FAT drives and compressed DriveSpace or DoubleSpace drives. Fragmentation occurs over time, as programs read from and write to the hard disk. Eventually, files must be stored in noncontiguous sectors on a disk. Fragmentation doesn't affect the validity of the information, but it takes much longer for the computer to read and write fragmented files.

For more information about DriveSpace and Disk Defragmenter, see Chapter 20, "Disks and File Systems."

# Windows 95 Performance Tuning: The Issues

This section summarizes performance issues, which are related principally to computer hardware.

**486 versus 386 processors.** Windows 95 uses more 32-bit code than Windows 3.1, so it benefits more than Windows 3.1 did from a 486-based processor. This is because the 486-class chip is better optimized for 32-bit code than the 386-class chip. For a given clock rate, if you run a 16-bit performance benchmark on a 386-based versus a 486-based computer, the 486-based computer will outperform the other computer. If you run the same benchmark using 32-bit code, the 486-based computer will outperform the 386-based computer by an even greater margin. Overall, Windows 95 provides significant performance improvements on a 486-based (or higher) processor.

**DX versus SX processors.** Although the minimum requirement to run Windows 95 is a 386SX-based processor, the SX processor is not a full 32-bit CPU. The SX-based processor accesses memory using 32-bit addressing, but it accesses data in 16-bit increments. Although Windows 95 will run on an SX-based processor, you will most likely not be satisfied with the perceived performance when compared to a 16-bit operating system such as Windows 3.1.

**Hard disk speed.** Hard disk speed affects Windows 95 more than Windows 3.1. To support many applications running at once, applications are paged out to the swap file when there is more demand for memory than what is available physically. This is a very efficient mechanism for running many applications in a constrained memory environment. Windows 95 performance can be enhanced greatly by installing a faster hard disk. Hard disk speed will also have a great effect on performance when running File and Printer Sharing services.

**Processor and bus speed.** In Windows 95, processor and bus speed have a greater impact on display performance than under Windows 3.1. Display performance under Windows 3.1 was affected by inefficiencies in the monolithic display drivers and typically poor bus throughput (mostly ISA), so the CPU would typically encounter bottlenecks in either the bus or monolithic driver when writing to the display. With PCI and the miniport driver model under Windows 95, a CPU can send data as fast as possible down the PCI bus and through the miniport driver without encountering a bottleneck. This means that CPU performance can greatly affect display performance in Windows 95.

**Miniport drivers for display adapters.**  The new display drivers in Windows 95 have been optimized for enhanced display speed and improved graphics performance. Microsoft created a new universal driver with a better mechanism for manipulating memory bitmaps, which provides fast, reliable graphics support. Microsoft provides miniport drivers for most current display adapters, and these new drivers should be used whenever possible. Contact the hardware manufacturer to obtain new drivers if the correct driver is not provided with Windows 95.

**Protected-mode drivers for increased performance and reliability.**  Windows 95 provides protected-mode drivers for most devices, including display, network, disk, and so on. These drivers have been developed and tested to ensure better performance and increased reliability over real-mode drivers. After Windows 95 switches into protected mode during system startup, any time an I/O operation uses a device controlled by a real-mode driver, the computer has to switch from protected mode to virtual 8088 mode. This is a very expensive operation in terms of CPU cycles and typically has to be done several times during a single I/O operation, adversely impacting performance. Relying on a real-mode driver for I/O operations also reduces the degree of multitasking that Windows 95 can provide because real-mode drivers were not designed for a preemptively multitasking environment. Therefore, wherever possible, use protected-mode device drivers.

**Added memory.**  Unlike Windows 3.1, caching in Windows 95 is dynamic, which means that Windows 95 performs better than Windows 3.1 when you increase the amount of system memory. Also, under Windows 95 you do not have to reconfigure the operating system when you change the memory configuration; Windows 95 reconfigures itself automatically.

**Low memory (4-MB) computers.**  Most of the tuning necessary for a computer with low memory happens automatically, but to reduce the size of the Windows 95 working set and give the maximum amount of memory to applications, run only one network client; if possible, run a single network protocol; and run the fewest possible network services.

**Extended Capabilities Port (ECP) for printers.**  For locally attached printers, or for computers acting as print servers, it's helpful to use a computer that supports the ECP specification. This ensures better print throughput and bidirectional communications.

For information about performance related to network adapters, see "Optimizing Network Performance" later in this chapter.

# System Performance Overview

Windows 95 greatly reduces the system resource limitations that many users experienced with Windows 3.1. Windows 95 also cleans up resources that have not been freed to help reduce system resource limitations. When Windows 95 determines that an application that owned certain resources no longer needs those resources in memory, it deallocates remaining data structures, freeing the resources for use elsewhere in the system.

Wherever possible, Windows 95 is self-tuning, adjusting cache sizes or other elements of the system environment to provide the best performance for the current configuration. Windows 95 can also detect when the drivers loaded or other performance-related components are not providing the optimal performance.

▶ **To see a report of performance problems**

- In the System option in Control Panel, click the Performance tab.

  Windows 95 reports the current performance status, including whether 32-bit, protected-mode components are being used.

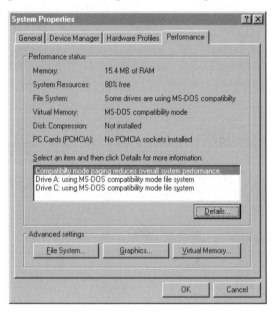

If the performance status shows that real-mode components are being used for any device—and especially for disk drivers—you need to solve all the problems that prevent protected-mode drivers from loading. For information, see Chapter 19, "Devices." This chapter describes methods for optimizing or solving problems related to virtual memory, file system, or graphics performance.

# System Resource Capacity in Windows 95

Windows 95 provides a significant increase in the system resources available to Windows-based and MS-DOS–based applications over what was available under earlier versions of Windows. The net result for users is that they can count on more system resources being available for creating windows, using fonts, running five or more applications simultaneously, and so on.

Windows 3.1 maintained 64K regions of memory *heaps* for use by the graphics device interface (GDI) and USER system components. These heaps stored GDI or memory object information allocated when an application called a Windows API function. The amount of space available in the combination of these two heaps is identified as a percentage of system resources that are free (that percentage appears in the Help About dialog box in My Computer and other Windows-based applications). Under Windows 3.1, when the calculated amount of free space dropped to a low number, the system often reported that it was out of memory even though the amount of free memory shown in the About dialog box was still quite high. This was often due to low memory in either the GDI or USER heap, or both.

In Windows 95, to help reduce the system resource limitation, many data structures formerly stored in the 16-bit GDI and USER heaps are now stored in 32-bit heaps. This provides more room for the remaining data elements to be created.

The following table shows the system limits in Windows 95, as compared to the constraining limits under Windows 3.1. For information about how to assess performance of key system resources, see "Identifying Performance Problems with System Monitor" later in this chapter. For information about the supporting architecture, see Chapter 31, "Windows 95 Architecture."

**Windows 95 System Limits**

| Resource | Windows 3.1[1] | Windows 95[2] |
|---|---|---|
| Windows Menu handles | ~299 | 32K |
| Timers | 32 | Unlimited |
| COM and LPT ports | 4 per type | Unlimited |
| Items per listbox | 8K | 32K |
| Data per listbox | 64K | Unlimited |
| Data per edit control | 64K | Unlimited |
| Regions | All in 64K segment | Unlimited |
| Physical pens and brushes | All in 64K segment | Unlimited |
| Logical pens and brushes | All in 64K segment | All in 64K segment |
| Logical fonts | All in 64K segment | 750–800 |
| Installed fonts | 250–300 (best case) | 1000 |
| Device contexts | 200 (best case) | 16K |

[1] Limits for GDI objects in Windows 3.1 are not exact because all regions, physical objects, logical objects, device contexts (DCs), and installed fonts had to fit in a single 64K segment. Because many of these have been moved to the 32-bit heap, Windows 95 provides much more room for those remaining items, such as logical pens, brushes, and so on. The remaining items in the Windows 95 local heap are all less than 10–20 bytes each.

[2] System-wide resources, unless noted otherwise.

# Technical Notes on MS-DOS Components in Windows 95

Many users have wondered whether Windows 95 contains MS-DOS code, and if so, whether that means that Windows 95 is somehow built on top of MS-DOS. Many of these questions relate to how Windows 95 achieves the highest possible degree of compatibility with existing devices and the myriad applications created for MS-DOS and Windows 3.x. Three key questions are answered here:

- How does Windows 95 support internal processes and certain application services?

- How does Windows 95 reclaim memory from real-mode drivers?

- Why does IO.SYS load WIN.COM rather than directly loading VMM32.VXD?

The following services are based on entirely new code created for Windows 95, not revisions to MS-DOS code:

- Process and thread memory management
- Interprocess communications and synchronization
- Preemptive Win32 subsystem
- CD-ROM, hard disk, and network I/O services
- High-level graphics operations and window management
- Printing services

Some functions, however, are handled by MS-DOS code, although the code itself is running in virtual 8086 mode, not real mode. Functions implemented in this manner ensure backwards compatibility with existing real-mode software, such as the Novell® NetWare® client. The following list shows such functions:

| | |
|---|---|
| Create Program Segment Prefix (function 55h) | Get DOS Version (function 30h) |
| | International (function 65h) |
| Create Temp File (function 5Ah) | Set/Get Drive (functions 0Eh and 19h) |
| Dup File Handle (function 45h) | Set/Get Program Segment Prefix (functions 50h and 51h) |
| Exit (function 4Ch) | |
| Get Date/Time (functions 2Ah and 2Ch) | NetWare Get Station Num (function DCh) |

An important example of how Windows 95 reclaims memory from real-mode device drivers is MSCDEX, the CD-ROM driver. After Windows 95 Setup is completed and Windows 95 starts from the hard disk for the first time, special code runs to determine whether the protected-mode CDFS drivers have taken over the CD-ROM drive completely. If so, the real-mode MSCDEX driver in memory is matched to the related lines in AUTOEXEC.BAT, and the MSCDEX entries are then commented out. This provides a trail in AUTOEXEC.BAT to show what has happened. Similar methods are used for other device drivers that Windows 95 knows to be safe to remove, such as other vendors' real-mode disk cache utilities and redundant protected-mode VxDs.

As a final example, some users have wondered whether the fact that IO.SYS loads WIN.COM (rather than loading VMM32.VXD directly) is an indication that Windows 95 is built on Windows 3.x code, with the addition of new virtual device drivers. However, IO.SYS is used to load WIN.COM only for purposes of backward compatibility. Certain real-mode drivers and TSRs insert themselves at various places in the Windows 3.1 startup process. If Windows 95 were to bypass the loading of WIN.COM and instead load virtual device drivers directly, any driver that needs to insert itself when WIN.COM is loaded would never be called. Instead, Windows 95 starts in precisely the same way as Windows 3.1 and loads the same components in the same order, ensuring compatibility with earlier versions of applications and device drivers.

# Optimizing the Swap File

Windows 95 uses a special file on your hard disk called a virtual-memory swap file (or paging file). With virtual memory under Windows 95, some of the program code and other information are kept in RAM while other information is swapped temporarily to virtual memory. When that information is required again, Windows 95 pulls it back into RAM and, if necessary, swaps other information to virtual memory. This activity is invisible, although you might notice that your hard disk is working. The resulting benefit is that you can run more programs at one time than the computer's RAM would usually allow.

On Windows 3.x, users could enhance performance by changing virtual memory settings. The Windows 95 swap file is dynamic, so it can shrink or grow based on the operations performed on the system and based on available disk space. A dynamic swap file is usually the most efficient use of resources. The swap file can also occupy a fragmented region of the hard disk with no substantial performance penalty.

### Tip for Swap File Performance

The single best way you can ensure high swap file performance is to make sure that the disk containing the swap file has ample free space so that the swap file size can shrink and grow as needed.

The Windows 95 swap file (WIN386.SWP) is not a permanent file. However, Windows 95 can also use a permanent Windows 3.1 swap file. In this case, the file cannot shrink below the permanent size set for it in Windows 3.1, although the file can grow bigger if required.

Under Windows 95, the swap file can reside on a compressed drive if a protected-mode driver (that is, DRVSPACE.VXD) controls the compressed drive. DriveSpace marks the swap file as uncompressible and, to reduce the risk of fragmentation, places the swap file as the last file in the sector heap, which allows room for the swap file to grow.

For a computer that runs a shared version of Windows 95 from a server, the swap file is placed in the computer's machine directory. If the computer is started from a floppy disk or uses remote booting, the swap file is in the machine directory on the network. If the computer is started from the local hard disk, the swap file can be stored in the machine directory on the local computer.

Although the system defaults usually provide the best performance, you can adjust the parameters used to define the swap file. For example, to optimize swap file performance on a computer with multiple hard disk drives, you might want to override the default location of the Windows 95 swap file. The swap file should be placed on the drive with the fastest performance (unless that disk is overused). If a user usually loads all software from the same drive in a computer that has multiple drives, performance might be boosted by placing the swap file on one of the drives that is not as busy.

---

**Caution**   Completely disabling virtual memory might cause the computer to stop operating properly. You might not be able to restart the computer, or system performance might be degraded. Do not disable virtual memory unless instructed to do so by a technical support representative.

---

▶ **To adjust the virtual memory swap file**

1. In the System option in Control Panel, click the Performance tab.

2. Click the Virtual Memory button.

3. To specify a different hard disk, click the option named Let Me Specify My Own Virtual Memory Settings. Then specify the new disk in the Hard Disk box. Or, type values (in kilobytes) in the Minimum or Maximum boxes. Then click OK.

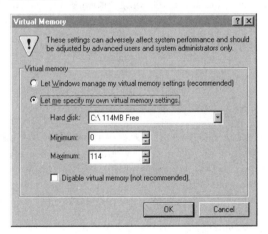

If you set the maximum swap file size in the Virtual Memory dialog box to the amount of free space currently on a drive, Windows 95 assumes that it can increase the swap file beyond that size if more free disk space becomes available. If you want to impose a fixed limit on the swap file size, make sure that the limit you choose is less than the current maximum.

# Optimizing File System Performance

In Windows 95, the disk cache is dynamic. You do not need to configure its size as part of system configuration. Because of this, the following types of settings used for Windows 3.x are not required in Windows 95 and should be removed from the configuration files.

| Configuration file | Configuration setting to remove |
|---|---|
| autoexec.bat | SHARE |
| | SMARTDRV settings |
| | Any entries for other disk cache software[1] |
| config.sys | SMARTDRV settings (double-buffer driver) |
| | Any entries for other disk cache software |

[1] For a list of the disk caching software that is removed by Windows 95 Setup, see Chapter 6, "Setup Technical Discussion."

The overall performance, for example, of a computer with 8 MB of memory is better under Windows 95 than under Windows 3.1. However, the amount of paging might be more under Windows 95 for several reasons:

- Windows 95 aggressively writes the contents of dirty memory pages (pages that contain changes) during system idle time, even if it doesn't need the memory at that time. This causes more idle-time disk activity but speeds up future memory allocations by doing some of the work when the system is idle.

- Much more of Windows 95 can be paged out to disk than Windows 3.1. That's why it's even possible to still run applications on low-memory computers when Windows 95 requires a working set of 4 MB. However, the working set isn't the amount of memory you need to hold all code and data; it's just the amount of memory you need to avoid an unacceptable amount of paging.

Changing the cache size (even if you could) probably wouldn't have much effect on paging. Paging through the cache would quickly overwhelm it and make it useless for other file I/O. Although swap file I/O operations don't go through the cache, memory-mapped files and executable files do. The cache, however, is designed to make sure it can't be overwhelmed by such I/O operations.

The cache grows and shrinks as needed. If the system begins to page a lot, the cache shrinks automatically. However, people often think they are seeing a lot of paging, but they are really seeing other disk activity, such as Windows 95 building its icon cache or the cache lazy writing.

If the amount of paging is extreme, to the point where system performance is poor, then you probably have a hard disk that requires a real-mode device driver. If Windows 95 needs to use real-mode for its disk I/O operations, then a lot of code has to be locked down that would otherwise be pageable, and your working set increases significantly. Paging through a real-mode driver does increase paging, but on a computer with 8 MB of memory, it shouldn't cause unacceptable performance.

### Tip for 32-bit Disk Access in Windows 95

The 32-bit disk access feature is always turned on in Windows 95 unless Windows 95 detects a real-mode disk driver that doesn't have a protected-mode replacement. This could be, for example, an older Stacker® driver or a hard-disk security or encryption driver for a disk drive.

To prevent the performance loss that occurs when Windows 95 is forced to use a real-mode disk driver, upgrade to a protected-mode replacement for that driver. If you need to determine why a Windows 95 real-mode disk driver was installed, check the IOS.LOG file. For more information, see Chapter 19, "Devices."

# Optimizing File System Performance with Profiles

In Windows 95, file system and disk performance can be controlled based on how the computer is used in most situations. The option for configuring file system performance is controlled only by the user. None of these settings are affected by other configuration changes that might be made in Windows 95, such as installing File and Printer Sharing services, or choosing the Portable option as the setup type when installing Windows 95.

▶ **To optimize file system performance**

1. In the System option in Control Panel, click the Performance tab, and then click the File System.

2. In the list named Typical Role Of This Machine, select the most common role for this computer, and then click OK. The following table describes each role in the list.

| Role | Description |
| --- | --- |
| Desktop Computer | A normal computer acting primarily as a network client, or an individual computer with no networking. This configuration assumes there is more than the minimum required RAM, and that the computer is running on power (rather than battery). |
| Mobile Or Docking System | Any computer with limited memory. This configuration assumes limited RAM and that the computer is running on battery, so the disk cache should be flushed frequently. |
| Network Server | A computer used primarily as a peer server for file or printer sharing. This configuration assumes that the computer has adequate RAM and frequent disk activity, so the system is optimized for a high amount of disk access. |

Each disk performance profile adjusts the values of the following file-system settings in the Registry:

- **PathCache**, which specifies the size of the cache that VFAT can use to save the locations of the most recently accessed directory paths. This cache improves performance by reducing the number of times the file system must seek paths by searching the file allocation table. The number of paths is 32 for the Desktop computer profile, 16 for Mobile Or Docking System, and 64 for Network Server.

- **NameCache**, which stores the locations of the most recently accessed filenames. The combined use of PathCache and NameCache means that VFAT never searches the disk for the location of cached filenames. Both PathCache and NameCache use memory out of the general system heap. The number of filenames is about 677 names (8 KB) for the Desktop computer profile, 337 names (4 KB) for Mobile Or Docking System, and 2729 names (16 KB) for Network Server.

- **BufferIdleTimeout**, **BufferAgeTimeout**, and **VolumeIdleTimeout**, which control the time between when changes are placed in the buffer to when they are written to the hard disk.

The values to be assigned to each disk performance profile are stored in the following Registry key:

```
Hkey_Local_Machine\Software\Microsoft\Windows\CurrentVersion
    \FS Templates
```

The following subkey contains the actual settings for the profile currently used:

```
Hkey_Local_Machine\System\CurrentControlSet\Control\FileSystem
```

An additional performance setting in the FileSystem subkey, **ContigFileAllocSize**, can be used to change the size of the contiguous space that VFAT searches for when allocating disk space. Under MS-DOS, the file system began allocating the first available space found on the disk, which ensured a great deal of disk fragmentation and related performance problems. By default under Windows 95, VFAT first tries to allocate space in the first contiguous 0.5 MB of free space, then returns to the MS-DOS method if it can't find at least this much contiguous free space. This optimizes performance for both the swap file and multimedia applications.

In some cases, you might choose to set a smaller value in the Registry, such as if you are not running demanding applications on the computer. A smaller value for **ContigFileAllocSize**, however, can lead to more fragmentation on the disk and, consequently, more disk access for the swap file or applications that require larger amounts of disk space.

## Optimizing CD-ROM File System Performance

The CD-ROM cache is separate from the cache used for disk file and network access because the performance characteristics of the CD-ROM are different. This cache can be paged to disk (the file and network cache cannot), which reduces the working set for Windows 95 but still allows for better CD-ROM performance. When Windows 95 is retrieving data from a compact disc, it is still faster to read a record from the cache even if it's been paged to disk because the disk-access time is much faster than the compact-disc access time.

---

**Tip**  A small CD-ROM cache makes a big difference in streaming performance, but a much larger cache does not pay off as significantly, unless the cache is large enough to contain entire multimedia streams.

---

▶ **To set the supplemental cache size for CDFS**

1. In the System option in Control Panel, click the Performance tab, and then click the File System button.

2. In the CD-ROM Optimization area, drag the slider to set the supplemental cache size.

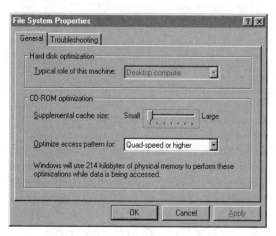

3. In the Optimize Access Pattern For list, select a setting based on the size of your computer's RAM and CD-ROM access speed. The following list shows recommended settings related to RAM size and the size of the cache that's created.

| RAM size | Optimize setting | Cache size |
|---|---|---|
| 8 MB or less | Single-speed drives | 64K |
| 8 MB to 12 MB | Double-speed drives | 626K |
| 12 MB or more | Quad speed or higher | 1238K |

4. Click OK, and then shut down and restart the computer.

For information about how VCACHE and the supplemental CD-ROM cache work, see Chapter 20, "Disks and File Systems."

# Using File-System Troubleshooting Options

The System option in Control Panel presents a set of options for changing file system performance. You can use these options when you experience rare hardware or software compatibility problems.

---

**Important**  Enabling any of the file-system Troubleshooting options will seriously degrade system performance. Typically, you want to enable these options only if instructed to do so by your product support representative.

---

▶ **To display the file-system Troubleshooting options**

1.  In the System option in Control Panel, click the Performance tab.

2.  Click the File System button, and then click the Troubleshooting tab.

The following table summarizes the settings in Troubleshooting properties. Each option sets a value in this Registry key:

```
Hkey_Local_Machine\System\CurrentControlSet\Control\FileSystem
```

| File system option | Description |
| --- | --- |
| Disable New File Sharing And Locking Semantics | This option alters the internal rules for file sharing and locking on hard disks, governing whether certain processes can have access to open files in certain share modes that guarantee a file will not be modified. This option should be checked only in the rare case that an MS-DOS–based application has problems with sharing under Windows 95. This sets **SoftCompatMode=0** in the Registry. |
| Disable Long Name Preservation For Old Programs | This option turns off the tunneling feature, which preserves long filenames when files are opened and saved by applications that do not recognize long filenames. This option should be checked in the rare case that an important legacy application is not compatible with long filenames. This sets **PreserveLongNames=0** in the Registry. |
| Disable Protected-Mode Hard Disk Interrupt Handling | This option prevents Windows 95 from terminating interrupts from the hard disk controller and bypassing the ROM routine that handles these interrupts. Some hard disk drives might require this option to be checked in order for interrupts to be processed correctly. If this option is checked, the ROM routine handles the interrupts, which slows system performance. This sets **VirtualHDIRQ=1** in the Registry. (This setting is off by default for all computers in Windows 95, which is the reverse of Windows 3.x.) |

| File system option | Description |
|---|---|
| Disable All 32-bit, Protected-Mode Disk Drivers | This option ensures that no 32-bit disk drivers are loaded in the system, except the floppy driver. Typically, you would check this option if the computer does not start due to disk peripheral I/O problems. If this option is enabled, all I/O will go through real-mode drivers or the BIOS. Notice that in this case, all disk drives that are visible only in protected mode will no longer be visible. This sets **ForceRMIO=1** in the Registry. |
| Disable Write-Behind Caching For All Drives | This option ensures that all data is flushed continually to the hard disk, removing any performance benefits gained from disk caching. This option should be checked only in the rare cases where you are performing risky operations and must ensure prevention of data loss. For example, a software developer who is debugging data at Ring 0 while creating a virtual device driver would check this option. This sets **DriveWriteBehind=0** in the Registry. |

# Setting Graphics Compatibility Options

In Windows 95, graphics hardware acceleration features can be turned off when system performance indicates incompatibility problems. Specifically, problems can occur when Windows 95 assumes a display adapter can support certain functionality that it cannot. In such cases, the side effects might be anything from small irregularities on the screen to system failure. You can disable hardware acceleration features of the display adapter so that the computer can still be used if there is a problem with the display adapter. If changing these settings fixes otherwise unexplained system crashes or performance problems, then the source of the problem is probably the computer's display adapter.

▶ **To change graphics performance settings**

1. In the System option in Control Panel, click the Performance tab, and then click the Graphics button.

2. Drag the slider to change the hardware acceleration setting, as summarized in the following list. Then click OK.

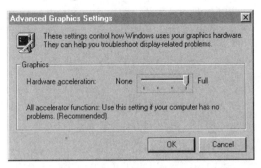

- The default setting is Full, which turns on all graphics hardware acceleration features available in the display driver.

- The first notch from the right can be set to correct mouse pointer display problems. This setting disables hardware cursor support in the display driver by adding **SwCursor=1** to the [Display] section of SYSTEM.INI.

- The second notch from the right can be set to correct certain display errors. This setting prevents some bit block transfers from being performed on the display card and disables memory-mapped I/O for some display drivers. This setting adds **SwCursor=1** and **Mmio=0** to the [Display] section of SYSTEM.INI, and **SafeMode=1** to the [Windows] section of WIN.INI.

- The last notch from the right (None) can be set to correct problems if your computer frequently stops responding to input, or has other severe problems. This setting adds **SafeMode=2** in the [Windows] section of WIN.INI, which removes all driver acceleration support and causes Windows 95 to use only the DIB engine rather than bit block transfers for displaying images.

  For example, if you receive an error message at system startup stating that an application caused "an invalid page fault in module <unknown>," this indicates a problem between the display driver and the Windows 95 DIB engine. In such cases, this setting should correct the problem.

For more information about the built-in graphics performance features in Windows 95, see Chapter 19, "Devices," and Chapter 31, "Windows 95 Architecture."

# Optimizing Printing

Printing to a printer attached to a file or print server occurs differently, depending on the server's operating system. If you print to a server running Windows 95, the rendering from the EMF format to the printer-specific language happens on the server. This means that less work is performed on the client computer, giving the user better performance.

When you print to NetWare or Windows NT servers, the rendering from EMF to the printer-specific format happens on the client computer. Although this happens in the background, it still means more work is performed on the client computer. Printing to a printer attached locally causes both the EMF rendering and the device-specific rendering to happen on the computer. For more information, see Chapter 23, "Printing and Fonts."

You also need to decide on the trade-off between disk use and return-to-application time when configuring printing in Windows 95.

▶ **To define spool settings for print performance**

1. In the Printers option in Control Panel, right-click the printer icon, and then click Properties.

2. Click the Details tab, and then click Spool Settings.

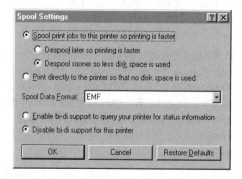

3. Select Spool Print Jobs So Program Finishes Printing Faster, and then click one of the following options:

- Click Start Printing After Last Page Is Spooled if you want the return-to-application time to be faster. This requires more disk space and increases the total print time. The second rendering does not start until the entire file is written to the EMF file, which decreases the amount of work performed on the computer as you print but increases the disk space because the entire file has to be written before the second rendering starts.

- Click Start Printing After Page Is Spooled if you want the second rendering to take place simultaneously with the writing of the EMF file. This reduces the total print time and disk space required, but it increases the return-to-application time.

# Optimizing Network Performance

Windows 95 automatically adjusts system parameters to accommodate user demands and various network configurations. For example, it alters the size of the system paging file and cache buffer as memory requirements change and automatically tunes network time-out values to fit varying LAN topologies.

With a few exceptions, manual tuning of operating system parameters is not required to improve network performance. However, you can take several other measures that can increase file-sharing performance, such as reconfiguring or changing hardware components. This section summarizes these measures.

- Use a 32-bit, protected-mode network client.

  For example, the Microsoft Client for NetWare Networks significantly out-performs the VLM or NETX version of the NetWare client. On large block transfers over the network, Client for NetWare Networks is up to twice as fast as Windows 3.x with the VLM shell, based on benchmarks performed by beta testers. The protected-mode networking client can take advantage of caching and other automatic tuning features. With a real-mode client, you are limited to the same performance tuning capabilities that were available under Windows 3.x.

- Use the new NDIS 3.1 network adapter drivers provided with Windows 95.

- Install a new network adapter. The adapters currently available provide markedly better performance than earlier models. If possible, select an adapter that matches the computer bus. For more information, see Chapter 12, "Network Technical Discussion."

  Network adapters have become exceptionally reliable and inexpensive. The low costs of Ethernet adapters, including new Plug and Play hardware, means that usually the most cost-effective way to improve network performance is to replace an older network adapter with a new model. The cost for the new hardware is offset almost immediately by savings in support time and improved performance.

The following measures can help you obtain the best performance from computers that provide File and Printer Sharing services:

- Let Windows 95 determine the right size for the swap file.

- Make sure the computer has enough memory, depending on the size of your network and the number of users who will be accessing the peer server.

- In the System option in Control Panel, set the typical role of the computer to Network Server, as described in "Optimizing File System Performance with Profiles" earlier in this chapter.

- Install a high-performance network adapter on the peer server. If the computer uses an 8-bit adapter, you can increase performance significantly by replacing it with a high-performance 16-bit or 32-bit adapter.

- Disable rarely used network adapters. This improves overall network performance by decreasing the number of broadcast packets on the network. Each broadcast packet must be processed by every active adapter on the network. High broadcast rates adversely affect LAN performance by increasing network connection time. You can disable a network adapter by disabling its binding to protocols in the Network option in Control Panel.

- Install faster hard disks or disk controllers (or both). Typically, when setting up peer servers, you will want to choose computers configured with the best-performing hardware.

- On a computer running File and Printer Sharing for NetWare Networks, set the read-only attribute on shared files wherever possible. The network client can take better advantage of file caching with read-only files, which will improve network performance and reduce the load on the server.

# Optimizing Conventional Memory

The methods for conventional memory management under Windows 95 are the same as for MS-DOS 6.x:

- In CONFIG.SYS, load **himem** and **emm386** (using either the **ram** or **noems** switches), and load any required real-mode drivers and applications using **devicehigh** or **loadhigh** statements.

- Remove as many real-mode drivers and TSRs from CONFIG.SYS and AUTOEXEC.BAT as possible, and instead use new protected-mode drivers and applications created for Windows 95.

- Use **buffershigh**, **fcbshigh**, **fileshigh**, **lastdrivehigh**, and **stackshigh** to ensure that reserved memory is taken out of the upper memory area. For information about these commands, see Appendix A, "Command-Line Commands Summary."

- Do not load **smartdrv** in your configuration files, except in configuration files for an application that you run in MS-DOS Mode. Windows 95 uses an improved method for disk caching, so loading **smartdrv** typically wastes memory that could be used by MS-DOS–based applications.

You can still run the MEMMAKER utility provided with MS-DOS 6.2x to load real-mode drivers in the upper memory blocks (UMB). This utility is available in the OTHER\OLDDOS directory on the Windows 95 compact disc.

For information about MS-DOS Mode, and other configuration issues related to MS-DOS–based applications, see Chapter 22, "Application Support." For specific information about MS-DOS memory settings, consult the *Microsoft MS-DOS 6.2 Technical Reference* or other books on MS-DOS memory management.

### Tip for MS-DOS Mode

Don't assume that running an MS-DOS–based application in MS-DOS Mode provides better performance. When an application runs in MS-DOS Mode, Windows 95 and all of its protected-mode drivers are unloaded, so the application is running in real mode with exclusive use of the computer's resources.

Although this might help with a few applications that otherwise cannot run under Windows 95, it does not benefit performance overall because the application doesn't get the benefit of protected-mode drivers, VCACHE, 32-bit disk access, and so on. Also, real-mode device drivers must be loaded, reducing the amount of conventional memory available to the application.

# Tracking Performance with System Monitor

System Monitor is a Windows 95 tool you can use to help determine the cause of problems on a local or remote computer by measuring the performance of hardware, software services, and applications. When you make changes to the system configuration, System Monitor shows the effect of your changes on overall system performance. You can also use System Monitor to justify hardware upgrades.

Before making major configuration changes, use System Monitor to evaluate your current configuration; this can help you determine whether a particular system or network component is acting as a performance bottleneck.

▶ **To install and run System Monitor**

1. In the Add/Remove Programs option in Control Panel, click the Windows Setup tab.

2. In the Components list, make sure Accessories is checked, and then click Details.

3. In the Components list, make sure System Monitor is checked, and then click OK.

4. To install System Monitor, click OK.

5. To run System Monitor, click the Start button, click Run, and then type **sysmon**

▶ **To use System Monitor to monitor remote computers**

1. Install the Microsoft Remote Registry service on your computer and on the computer you want to monitor, as described in Chapter 16, "Remote Administration."

2. Click the File menu, and then click Connect.

3. Type the computer name of the computer you want to monitor, and then click OK.

Notice that monitoring a remote computer requires user-level security.

# Configuring Performance Charts in System Monitor

System Monitor uses the dynamic data information in the Registry to report on the state of processes. You can use System Monitor to do the following:

- Monitor real-time system performance and compare it with historical performance to help identify trends over time.

- Determine system capacity and identify bottlenecks.

- Monitor the effects of system configuration changes.

▶ **To use System Monitor to track performance problems**

1. Click the Edit menu, and then click Add Item.

2. In the Category list, click the resource that you want to monitor.

3. In the Item list, select one or more resources that you want to monitor.

   To select more than one item, press CTRL while clicking the items that you want to select. To select several items in a row, click the first item, and then press and hold down SHIFT while clicking the last item.

For more information about a selected resource, click the Explain button, which is dimmed until after step 3.

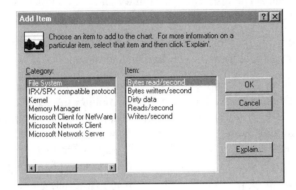

4. Click OK.

To change the view of the data from a line chart to a bar chart or a numeric listing, click the related button on the button bar.

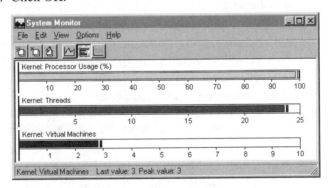

System Monitor offers menu commands for configuring the charts:

- To change the update interval, click the Options menu, and then click Chart.

- To configure the color and scaling for a selected item, click the Edit menu, and then click Edit Item.

- To control the display of the toolbar, status bar, and title bar, click the View menu, and then click Toolbar, Status Bar, or Hide Title Bar, respectively.

# Identifying Performance Problems with System Monitor

If you want to use System Monitor effectively, you need to run it frequently to become familiar with what typical performance looks like for a standard configuration so that you can recognize performance problems when they appear in System Monitor.

To become well-acquainted with System Monitor, run it while you are doing your usual work under Windows 95. To do this, add the System Monitor icon to your desktop. Then run System Monitor and use commands on the View menu to remove the title bar or to force the window to be always on top.

The following presents some general guidelines and key settings for using System Monitor in troubleshooting performance problems:

- If you suspect a application might not be freeing memory when it finishes using it (sometimes called memory leaks), monitor the value of Kernel: Threads over time. This will indicate whether the application is starting threads and not reclaiming them. Windows 95 automatically removes such threads when the application closes, but if you identify a leak while the application is running, you might decide that you should restart the application periodically.

- If the values for Memory Manager: Discards and Memory Manager: Page-outs indicate a great deal of activity, performance problems might be related to system memory stress. These values might indicate a need for more physical memory.

- If a computer seems slow, check the values reported by Kernel: Processor Usage (%) and by Memory Manager: Page Faults and Memory Manager: Locked Memory, as described in the following list:

  - If values for Kernel: Processor Usage are high even when the user is not working, check to see which application might be keeping it busy. To do this, press CTRL+ALT+DEL to see the list of tasks in the Close Program dialog box.

  - If the values for Memory Manager: Page Faults are high, it might indicate that the applications being used have memory needs that are beyond the computer's capabilities.

  - If the Memory Manager: Locked Memory statistics continually are a large portion of the Memory Manager: Allocated Memory value, then inadequate free memory might be affecting performance. Also, you might be running an application that locks memory unnecessarily. (Locked memory indicates the portion of memory used that cannot be paged out.)

The following basic example shows several memory management statistics over a few minutes while Windows-based word processing, spreadsheet, and mail applications were loaded and several files were opened.

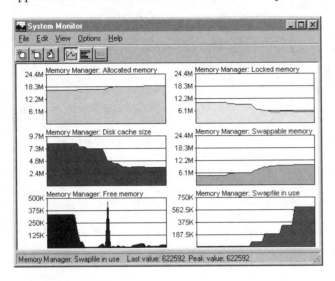

# Summary of System Monitor Categories

System Monitor tracks functionality for the following categories:

- File System
- IPX/SPX Compatible Protocol
- Kernel
- Memory Manager
- Microsoft Client for NetWare Networks and Microsoft Network Client
- Microsoft Network Server (File and Printer Sharing service)
- Microsoft Network Monitor Performance Data

---

**Note**   Because System Monitor uses Registry information, drivers can be written to report additional information in System Monitor. For information about creating such drivers, see the *Windows 95 Device Development Kit.*

---

The following tables describe the settings for the built-in System Monitor categories.

**File System**

| Setting | Description |
| --- | --- |
| Bytes Read/Second | The number of bytes read from the file system each second. |
| Bytes Written/Second | The number of bytes written by the file system each second. |
| Dirty Data | The number of bytes waiting to be written to the disk. Dirty data is stored in cache blocks, so the number reported might be larger than the actual number of bytes waiting. |
| Reads/Second | The number of read operations delivered to the file system each second. |
| Writes/Second | The number of write operations delivered to the file system each second. |

**IPX/SPX Compatible Protocol**

| Setting | Description |
| --- | --- |
| IPX Packets Lost/Second | The number of IPX packets received by the computer from an IPX network that were ignored. |
| IPX Packets Received/Second | The number of packets received by the computer from an IPX network each second. |
| IPX Packets Sent/Second | The number of packets sent by the computer to an IPX network each second. |
| Open Sockets | The number of free sockets. |
| Routing Table Entries | The number of IPX interworking routes known. |
| SAP Table Entries | The number of service advertisements known. |
| SPX Packets Received/Second | The number of packets received by the computer from an SPX network each second. |
| SPX Packets Sent/Second | The number of packets sent by the computer to an SPX network each second. |

**Kernel**

| Setting | Description |
| --- | --- |
| Processor Usage (%)[1] | The approximate percentage of time the processor is busy. |
| Threads | The current number of threads present in the system. |
| Virtual Machines | The current number of virtual machines present in the system. |

[1] Monitoring processor usage will increase processor usage slightly, so don't monitor this setting unless you are investigating a problem.

## Memory Manager (VMM32)

| Setting | Description |
| --- | --- |
| Allocated Memory[1, 2] | The total amount in bytes of Other Memory and Swappable Memory. If this value is changing when there's no activity on the computer, it indicates that the disk cache is resizing itself. |
| Discards | The number of pages discarded from memory each second. (The pages aren't swapped to the disk because the information is already on the disk.) |
| Disk Cache Size | The current size, in bytes, of the disk cache. |
| Free Memory | The total amount of free RAM, in bytes. This number is not related to Allocated Memory. If this value is zero, memory can still be allocated, depending on the free disk space available on the drive that contains the swap file. |
| Instance Faults | The number of instance faults each second. |
| Locked Memory[1] | The amount of allocated memory that is locked. |
| Maximum Disk Cache Size | The largest size possible for a disk cache. This is a fixed value loaded at system startup. |
| Minimum Disk Cache Size | The smallest size possible for a disk cache. This is a fixed value loaded at system startup. |
| Other Memory[1] | The amount of allocated memory not stored in the swap file; for example, code from Win32 DLLs and executable files, memory mapped files, nonpageable memory, and disk cache pages. |
| Page Faults | The number of page faults each second. |
| Page-ins | The number of pages swapped into memory each second, including pages loaded from a Win32-based executable file or memory-mapped files. Consequently, this value does not necessarily indicate low memory. |
| Page-outs | The number of pages swapped out of memory and written to disk each second. |
| Swapfile Defective | The number of bytes in the swap file that are found to be physically defective on the swap medium. Because swap file frames are allocated in 4096-byte blocks, a single damaged sector causes the whole block to be marked as defective. |

**Memory Manager (VMM32)** (*continued*)

| Setting | Description |
|---------|-------------|
| Swapfile In Use | The number of bytes being used in the current swap file. |
| Swapfile Size | The size, in bytes, of the current swap file. |
| Swappable Memory[1] | The number of bytes allocated from the swap file. Locked pages still count for the purpose of this metric. This includes code from 16-bit applications and DLLs, but not code from Win32 DLLs and executable files. |

[1] This number includes the disk cache. To see the actual size, subtract the value of Disk Cache Size.

[2] For any Windows-based application that uses common dialog boxes, the spooler, OLE, and so on, handles are cached for later use, so not all resources will be freed when the application closes.

**Microsoft Client for NetWare Networks**

| Setting | Description |
|---------|-------------|
| Burst Packets Dropped | Number of burst packets from this computer lost in transit. |
| Burst Receive Gap Time | Interpacket gap for incoming traffic, in microseconds. |
| Burst Send Gap Time | Interpacket gap for outgoing traffic, in microseconds. |
| Bytes In Cache | Amount of data, in bytes, currently cached by the redirector. |
| Bytes Read Per Second | Bytes read from the redirector per second. |
| Bytes Written Per Second | Bytes written to the redirector per second. |
| Dirty Bytes In Cache | Amount of dirty data, in bytes, currently cached by the redirector and waiting to be written. |
| NCP Packets Dropped | Number of regular NCP packets lost in transit. |
| Requests Pending | Number of requests waiting to be processed by the server. |

**Microsoft Network Client (Client for Microsoft Networks)**

| Setting | Description |
|---------|-------------|
| Bytes Read/Second | The number of bytes read from the redirector each second. |
| Bytes Written/Second | The number of bytes written to the redirector each second. |
| Number Of Nets | Number of networks currently running. |
| Open Files | Number of open files on the network. |
| Resources | Number of resources. |
| Sessions | Number of sessions. |
| Transactions/ Second | The number of SMB transactions managed by the redirector each second. |

### Microsoft Network Server (File and Printer Sharing for Microsoft or NetWare Networks)

| Setting | Description |
| --- | --- |
| Buffers | The number of buffers used by the server. |
| Bytes Read/Sec | The total number of bytes read from a disk. |
| Bytes Written/Sec | The total number of bytes written to a disk. |
| Bytes/Sec | The total number of bytes read from and written to a disk. |
| Memory | The total memory used by the server. |
| NBs | Server network buffers. |
| Server Threads | The current number of threads used by the server. |

### Microsoft Network Monitor Performance Data[1]

| Setting | Description |
| --- | --- |
| *Mediatype*[2] broadcasts/sec | Broadcast frames transmitted over the network adapter per second. |
| *Mediatype* bytes/sec | Total bytes transmitted over the network adapter per second. |
| *Mediatype* frames/sec | Total frames transmitted over the network adapter per second. |
| *Mediatype* multicasts/sec | Total multicast frames transmitted over the network adapter per second. |

[1] Gathering these statistics on a heavily used, low-performance computer will impact performance.

[2] *Mediatype* can be Ethernet or TokenRing.

P A R T   5

# System Configuration

This part of the *Windows 95 Resource Kit* contains the following chapters, describing how to manage your system configuration under Windows 95.

### Chapter 18 Introduction to System Configuration

Presents some background technical information related to Plug and Play-compliant devices and other device configuration components in Windows 95.

### Chapter 19 Devices

Presents an overview of issues related to both Plug and Play-compliant and legacy devices, and provides specific details for installing and configuring devices, including PCMCIA cards, display adapters, the mouse, and communications ports.

### Chapter 20 Disks and File Systems

Describes how to use Fdisk, Format, DriveSpace, Disk Defragmenter, and ScanDisk to manage disks and data. This chapter also introduces the Windows 95 file system and provides information for using long filenames among many users.

### Chapter 21 Multimedia

Describes the multimedia architecture and features in Windows 95.

### Chapter 22 Application Support

Provides tips for making applications based on Win32, Win16, and MS-DOS run well under Windows 95.

### Chapter 23 Printing and Fonts

Describes the improvements in the printing subsystem and explains how to set up printers with Windows 95. It also describes font support in Windows 95.

CHAPTER 18

# Introduction to System Configuration

This chapter presents overview information about configuring hardware and software for use with Windows 95. It also provides some background information about device support and Plug and Play features within Windows 95.

**In This Chapter**

System Configuration Overview    588

Improved Device Support in Windows 95    589

Windows 95 Device Classes    591

Plug and Play Support in Windows 95    592

Plug and Play Device Types    594

    ISA Devices    594

    EISA Devices    594

    SCSI Devices    595

    PCMCIA Devices    595

    VL and PCI Devices    596

    Other Device Types    597

# System Configuration Overview

Windows 95 includes several tools and built-in features that make it easy to configure the hardware and software on a computer.

**Automatic hardware detection.**  Hardware designed to work with Windows 95 is virtually self-configuring. When you run Windows 95 Setup, an automatic hardware detection routine determines the hardware components that are installed. Whether your system includes Plug and Play-compliant or legacy components, Windows 95 can automatically detect and configure them. Windows 95 Plug and Play features are described in "Plug and Play Support in Windows 95" later in this chapter. For more information about hardware detection during Setup, see Chapter 6, "Setup Technical Discussion."

**Configuration wizards.**  Windows 95 includes wizards for installing new hardware, adding modems and printers, and installing applications. These tools lead you through the steps for configuring the new component on a computer.

**Point and print.**  When you copy a printer icon from the server's window to your own Printers window or desktop, Windows 95 automatically installs the correct printer driver and configures the network connection to a network printer.

**Control Panel options for system configuration.**  The Control Panel includes several tools for configuring various parts of your system. The following table describes some Control Panel tools.

| Icon | Description of tool |
| --- | --- |
| | Accessibility Options. Use this tool to adjust keyboard, sound, display, mouse, and general options to make Windows 95 easier to use for individuals with disabilities. For information, see Appendix I, "Accessibility." |
| | Add New Hardware. Use this wizard to configure newly installed hardware through detection or by selecting the corresponding driver from a list. For information, see Chapter 19, "Devices." |
| | Add/Remove Programs. Use this wizard to install a program from a setup disk. You can also remove any application installed with this tool, add components from the Windows 95 disks, or create a new startup disk. For information, see Chapter 22, "Application Support." |
| | Display. Use this tool to change background and screen saver choices. Modify settings for on-screen fonts, colors, color palette, and so on. For information on configuring the display, see Chapter 19, "Devices." |
| | Fonts. Use this tool to view installed fonts or install new fonts. For more information, see Chapter 23, "Printing and Fonts." |
| | Keyboard. Use this tool to change options for the style of keyboard you use and for the rate at which the characters you type are displayed. For information, see online Help. |

| Icon | Description of tool |
|------|---------------------|
| | Modems. Use this wizard to add a new modem. You can also use this tool to configure or diagnose installed modems. For more information, see Chapter 25, "Modems and Communications Tools." |
| | Mouse. Use this tool to change mouse or pointer options. (The appearance of the icon might be different, depending on the type of mouse used.) For information, see Chapter 19, "Devices." |
| | Multimedia. Use this tool to change options for audio playback and recording, MIDI output and schemes, and CD playback volume. Use the Advanced properties to install or configure multimedia hardware, drivers, and codecs. For information, see Chapter 21, "Multimedia." |
| | Printers. Use this tool to configure existing printers or add a new printer. For more information, see Chapter 23, "Printing and Fonts." |
| | Sound. Use this tool to create or modify sound schemes. (This is available to users who have sound cards on their computers.) For information, see online Help. |
| | System. Use this tool to view general information about your computer. Use Device Manager to list or configure hardware properties. You can also list, copy, or rename hardware profiles and view performance status settings. For information, see Chapter 19, "Devices." |

# Improved Device Support in Windows 95

Windows 95 provides improved support for hardware and peripheral devices, including disk devices, display adapters, pointing devices, modems and other communications devices, and printers.

**Mini-driver architecture for reliable drivers.**  Windows 95 extends the mini-driver architecture for printer drivers used in Windows 3.1 throughout the operating system to the architecture for drivers of other system components, resulting in increased driver stability and forward compatibility. Although it is still possible to write and use monolithic drivers in Windows 95, Microsoft recommends that hardware manufacturers use the mini-driver model.

**Improved support through Plug and Play.**  Plug and Play is designed so that adding a device, either permanently or dynamically, requires nothing more than taking it out of the box and plugging it in. The computer and operating system seamlessly adjust to the new configuration. When using Plug and Play-compliant hardware, users will no longer be required to manually set jumpers and switches to redirect IRQs, DMA channels, or I/O port addresses. This saves time and expense in service calls related to hardware configurations.

Plug and Play is also a benefit to users who install Plug and Play-compliant devices into older, legacy computers. Information about these devices is stored centrally in the Registry, and devices that cannot be reconfigured dynamically receive first priority when resources are allocated.

**The Registry and Device Manager for resource management.**  To properly manage resources such as IRQs, I/O addresses, and DMAs, Windows 95 uses the Registry to track devices and resources allocated for both Plug and Play-compliant devices and legacy devices. The Registry provides a centralized, dynamic data store for all Windows settings, with a "current configuration" branch that stores information on a per-configuration basis. For example, the Display option in Control Panel stores per-configuration information about display resolution changes and Print Manager stores per-configuration information about the default printer.

Device Manager—which is available from the System icon in Control Panel— provides a graphical representation of devices configured in Windows 95, and allows properties used by these devices to be viewed and changed, as appropriate. Device Manager also shows resources allocated for the configured devices. Through the resource configuration information maintained in the Registry, Windows 95 is able to automatically identify and resolve device resource conflicts for Plug and Play-compliant devices. For legacy devices, Device Manager helps users quickly identify and resolve resource conflicts with devices in the system.

**Virtual device drivers.**  Windows 95 uses virtual device drivers (VxDs) where possible to provide improved performance. VxDs replace the real-mode MS-DOS device drivers used in previous versions of Windows for the following:

- MS-DOS FAT file system
- SMARTDrive
- CD-ROM file system
- Network drivers and network transport protocols
- Network client and peer resource sharing server
- Mouse driver
- MS-DOS file sharing and locking support (SHARE.EXE)
- Disk device drivers, including support for SCSI devices
- DriveSpace (and DoubleSpace) disk compression

Windows 95 provides device driver and TSR functionality as protected-mode components that reside in extended memory, avoiding context switches between protected-mode and real-mode when running 32-bit applications. Use of VxDs also improves system stability and reliability over using the MS-DOS device drivers.

**PCMCIA support.** Windows 95 delivers power, compatibility, ease of installation, and dynamic card insertion and removal to PCMCIA users. PCMCIA drivers in Windows 95 are robust, 32-bit, dynamically loadable virtual device drivers that use no conventional memory. Windows 95 includes an updated version of Card and Socket services to support PCMCIA.

To install a PCMCIA device, just insert the card in the computer. For example, when you plug in a PCMCIA network adapter, Windows 95 detects the network adapter, loads the network drivers, and establishes a network connection. Then the user interface is updated to show that the mapped network drives are now active. With earlier versions of Windows or other operating systems, you had to shut down and restart the computer to begin using the device.

**Hot docking support.** Plug and Play allows "hot docking" (that is, docking with the device powered on) and insertion of devices. This means that when a device is inserted, the operating system recognizes the new device, its capabilities, and its requirements, and loads the appropriate driver without requiring the user to restart the system unless the required resources are not available to the new device. Applications are notified about dynamic events, so they can take advantage of the new functionality or stop attempting to use unavailable devices. Instead of changing configuration files and restarting the computer, a user working at a docking station can click Eject PC on the Start menu.

# Windows 95 Device Classes

Devices and buses are grouped as classes in Windows 95, for purposes of installing and managing device drivers and allocating resources. The Registry contains a subkey for every class of device supported, and the hardware tree (as described in the following section) is organized by device class. Windows 95 uses class installers to install drivers for all hardware classes. Device Manager, for example, sends messages to the various class installers to tell them to add, remove, or configure specific hardware.

The following are some examples of class names defined in Windows 95.

| | | | |
|---|---|---|---|
| Adapter | Keyboard | Mouse | PCMCIA |
| Cdrom | MCADevices | MTD | Ports |
| Display | Media | Net | Printer |
| EISAdevices | Modem | NetService | SCSIAdapter |
| FDC | Monitor | Nodriver | System |
| HDC | | | |

The Windows 95 hardware tree is a record of the current system configuration, based on the configuration information for all devices in the hardware branch of the Registry. The hardware tree is created in RAM each time the system is started or whenever a dynamic change occurs to the system configuration.

Each branch in the tree defines a device node with the following requirements for configuration:

- Unique identification code, or device ID
- List of required resources, including the resource type (such as IRQ and memory range) and constraints on specific resources (such as a COM port that requires IRQ3)
- List of allocated resources
- Indication that the device node is a bus, if applicable (each bus device has additional device nodes under it in the tree)

### Tip for Viewing the Hardware Tree

Most information in the Windows 95 hardware tree can be seen by using Device Manager, which you can display by choosing the System option in Control Panel. Device Manager is described in Chapter 19, "Devices."

You can also see the information in the hardware tree in the Hkey_Dyn_Data\Dynamic\Enum section of the Windows 95 Registry.

The configuration process in Windows 95 uses the device nodes to identify the devices and resource requirements for establishing the working system configuration. For information about the components that work together in Windows 95 to configure the system, see Chapter 31, "Windows 95 Architecture."

# Plug and Play Support in Windows 95

Plug and Play is an independent set of computer architecture specifications that hardware manufacturers use to produce computer devices that can be configured with no user intervention.

For Plug and Play-compliant devices, installation consists of plugging in the device and turning on the computer. For example, a user can do the following:

- Insert and remove Plug and Play-compliant devices such as PCMCIA cards with automatic configuration.
- Connect to a docking station or network without restarting the computer or changing configuration parameters.
- Add a new monitor by plugging it in and turning it on.

The Plug and Play capabilities in Windows 95 have been widely described as key benefits to moving to Windows 95, because of the related reduction in hardware and software support costs. When Windows 95 detects the presence of a Plug and Play-compliant device, its device driver can be loaded and configured dynamically, requiring little or no user input. After the device and driver are installed, the driver reacts to system messages when a device is inserted or removed.

Microsoft recommends adding Plug and Play-compliant devices on legacy computers rather than adding non-Plug and Play devices. To use all Plug and Play features, however, your system must include a Plug and Play BIOS (the motherboard), devices (buses), and an operating system (Windows 95).

The following table compares the Plug and Play implementation in the Windows 95 operating system against other implementations.

| Windows 95 Plug and Play | Most other implementations |
| --- | --- |
| Dynamically loads, initializes, and unloads drivers in protected mode. | Run in real mode, with MS-DOS–based drivers loaded in CONFIG.SYS. |
| Supports a wide range of device types (as described in the following section). | Include only basic PCI-based and ISA-based device configuration. |
| Provides robust detection for devices, which is critical for Plug and Play on legacy computers. | Do not provide hardware detection. |
| Notifies other drivers and applications when a new device is available for use. Windows 95 also includes an automatic installation procedure to ensure that appropriate drivers are installed and loaded. | Configure device IRQ settings and so on, but the burden of installation falls on the user. |
| Provides robust, seamless operation through the integration of all subsystems and the startup process. | Might not be as reliable. |
| Provides an architecture with a consistent driver and bus interface for all devices. | In real mode, do not provide a supporting architecture. |

For additional details about the supporting architecture, see Chapter 31, "Windows 95 Architecture."

# Plug and Play Device Types

A variety of devices are compliant with Plug and Play. The following sections describe the types of devices and provide details for Plug and Play versus legacy devices.

## ISA Devices

Industry Standard Architecture (ISA) bus design is the architecture specified for the IBM® PC/AT®. Plug and Play ISA devices can be used on existing computers, because the specification does not require any change to ISA buses. To configure Plug and Play ISA devices, the system performs the following actions:

- Identifies and configures the devices using I/O ports, which enables the Plug and Play logic on the card

- Isolates each card and assigns a unique device ID and serial number

- Reads the resource requirements and capabilities stored on each card

- Allocates resources to each card, which reserves these resources so that other Plug and Play cards in the computer cannot be assigned these resources

- Activates the Plug and Play ISA cards

For legacy devices, standard ISA cards can coexist with Plug and Play ISA cards on the same computer. Windows 95 determines the type of hardware and its configuration during Setup, either by polling the hardware or asking the user to supply values. This configuration information is stored as static values in the Registry, and cannot be changed dynamically, but it is used to determine resource assignments for Plug and Play-compliant devices.

## EISA Devices

Enhanced Industry Standard Architecture (EISA) is a bus design for x86-based computers, specified by an industry consortium. EISA devices use cards that are upwardly compatible from ISA. EISA devices use standard software mechanisms for identification and configuration. As such, they meet most of the Plug and Play requirements. Windows 95 includes a bus enumerator that makes configuration information from these devices accessible to the operating system. This means that Windows 95 does not reconfigure EISA cards, but instead uses the information that hardware detection derives from the EISA nonvolatile RAM storage to determine which resources are used.

# SCSI Devices

Small Computer Standard Interface (SCSI) is a multiple-device chained interface used in many devices such as hard disks and CD-ROM drives. Plug and Play SCSI devices support dynamic changes to the adapter and automatic configuration of device ID and termination.

Configuration of a SCSI device can be separated into two distinct processes:

- Configuring the SCSI bus itself, such as terminating both ends of the SCSI bus and setting device IDs

- Configuring the SCSI host adapter, such as assigning an IRQ channel, DMA channel, and so on

Configuring a SCSI bus that is not Plug and Play-compliant is difficult for most users. The list of issues related to configuring a SCSI bus is long, including:

- SCSI device ID assignment

- Termination

- SCSI parity

- Command sets

- Disk geometry and software

For example, the SCSI-2 specification does not define an automated ID assignment mechanism, so the user is responsible for making sure that no two SCSI devices on the same SCSI bus share the same SCSI ID. Also, you might replace a SCSI host adapter with one from another company and find it doesn't work due to differences in disk geometries or the way devices are mapped to INT 13 parameters.

For more information about support for SCSI devices and drivers, see Chapter 20, "Disks and File Systems."

# PCMCIA Devices

PCMCIA devices meet the Personal Computer Memory Card International Association standard for the credit card-sized interface cards in portable computers and other small computers. PCMCIA technology supports all Plug and Play functionality. Windows 95 provides automatic installation and drivers for Intel-compatible and Databook-compatible PCMCIA sockets. Windows 95 also supports real-mode and protected-mode PCMCIA system software drivers (card services) from other vendors, but some of the Plug and Play capabilities will not be available, such as hot swapping of network adapters and automatic installation.

Windows 95 supports alternate system configurations for PCMCIA devices, depending on whether the PCMCIA device is docked. The alternate configurations are saved under unique identifiers in the hardware tree to be used for dynamic configuration. For more information, see Chapter 19, "Devices."

Depending on how the hardware manufacturer uses the Plug and Play standard, a PCMCIA device driver might be combined with an ISA or an EISA driver for the card, or the system's generic driver can be used.

To take advantage of Plug and Play, a card must contain information that Windows 95 can use to create a unique device ID for the card. Device drivers can be implemented under three possible schemes, depending on how complete the Card Information Structure (CIS) is on the card, whether the driver requires memory services, and whether the drive is bus-sensitive:

- A standard Plug and Play device driver for PCMCIA (the preferred driver) can handle dynamic configuration and removal, and receive configuration information from the operating system without knowledge of the card in the PCMCIA bus. The recommended choices are NDIS 3.x drivers for network adapters and Windows NT miniport drivers for SCSI cards, which do not require PCMCIA-specific services such as memory buffers.

- Generic Windows 95 device drivers are supported automatically for devices such as modems and disk drives. If the card contains complete configuration information, the operating system initializes the device and passes configuration information to the driver.

- Manufacturer-supplied drivers are required for device classes such as network or SCSI adapters that require specific PCMCIA functions, such as memory-mapped I/O or memory window operations. Windows 95 supports these operations through the standard card services API.

# VL and PCI Devices

The Video Electronic Standards Association (VESA) Local (VL) bus standard allows high-speed connections to peripherals. VL bus devices are not totally Plug and Play-compliant, but work similarly to ISA devices. The VL bus is used mostly to support high-performance video cards.

The Peripheral Component Interconnect (PCI) local bus is a standard used in most Pentium™ computers and in the Apple® PowerPC™ Macintosh® and is likely to be the successor to VL. Windows 95 does not reconfigure PCI cards, instead it uses the information that hardware detection derives from the PCI nonvolatile RAM storage to know what resources are used. The PCI bus architecture meets most Plug and Play requirements, and PCI devices use standard mechanisms for identifying themselves and declaring resource requirements.

PCI is usually a secondary bus. If its primary bus is not Plug and Play-compliant, the PCI bus cannot use Plug and Play functions.

# Other Device Types

Other device types can take advantage of Plug and Play if they provide mechanisms for identification and configuration. These include IDE controllers, Extended Capabilities Ports (ECP), and communications ports.

Parallel ports, also known as LPT ports, can also take advantage of Plug and Play. The most common parallel port type is the Centronics® interface. Plug and Play parallel ports meet Compatibility and Nibble mode protocols defined in IEEE P1284. Compatibility mode provides a byte-wide channel from the computer to the peripheral. Nibble mode provides a channel from the peripheral to the host through which data is sent as 4-bit nibbles using the port's status lines. These modes provide two-way communication between the host and the peripheral. Nibble mode is also used to read the device ID from the peripheral for device enumeration.

For computers that are totally Plug and Play-compliant, the BIOS also meets Plug and Play specifications. In this case, the file named BIOS.VXD provides the BIOS Plug and Play enumerator.

C H A P T E R    1 9

# Devices

This chapter presents an overview of issues related to Windows 95 support for both Plug and Play-compliant and legacy devices. It also provides specific details for installing and configuring devices, including PCMCIA cards, display adapters, the mouse, and communications ports.

**In This Chapter**

Devices: The Basics    600

Devices: The Issues    603

Devices Overview    604

Installing New Devices    606

Changing Settings with Device Manager    608

Enabling PCMCIA Cards    614

Using Hardware Profiles for Alternate Configurations    617

Configuring the Display    619

Display Driver Overview    619

Changing the Display Type and Driver    621

Configuring Display Resolution and Color Palette    623

Configuring Display Appearance    625

Configuring the Mouse    626

Mouse and Pointing Device Driver Overview    627

Changing Mouse Drivers    627

Configuring Mouse Behavior    628

Configuring Communications Ports and Printer Ports    628

Real-Mode Drivers and the IOS.INI Safe Driver List    630

Troubleshooting Device Configuration    634

Correcting Problems with Display    634

Correcting Problems with SCSI Devices    637

Correcting Problems with Other Devices    639

# Devices: The Basics

These key features (and related benefits) result from the Windows 95 system design changes (as described in Chapter 18, "Introduction to System Configuration"):

- Automatic installation for new Plug and Play-compliant devices, allowing the user to start working without configuring or, usually, without restarting the computer.

- Centralized places in the Registry and Device Manager to configure legacy devices and set preference for resources.

- Enhanced support for PCMCIA adapters, portable computers, and docking stations.

Windows 95 includes several tools to help install, configure, and manage hardware devices:

- The Add New Hardware option in Control Panel is a wizard that guides you through the steps required to install and configure drivers for legacy devices. For information, see the summary later in this section, plus "Installing New Devices" later in this chapter.

- You can view the hierarchy of devices in the system and print various reports on system settings using Device Manager in the System option in Control Panel. For information, see the summary later in this section, plus "Changing Settings with Device Manager" later in this chapter.

- You can use the Display and Mouse options in Control Panel to install and configure all device driver and user preference settings related to the display and pointing devices. For information, see the summary later in this section, plus "Configuring the Display" later in this chapter and "Configuring the Mouse" later in this chapter.

For other devices, Windows 95 provides installation and configuration wizards. For example, you use wizards to install modems, faxes, printers, multimedia, and sound devices. For information about using these specific tools, see related chapters in the *Windows 95 Resource Kit*.

This section summarizes improvements in support for display adapters, pointing devices, and communications ports.

**Improved display adapter and monitor support.**  Windows 95 Setup automatically detects the display adapter and installs the appropriate display driver. The Windows 95 display drivers are stringently tested to ensure greater reliability and stability than drivers for Windows 3.1.

Also, Windows 95 includes mechanisms to ensure that bad or incompatible display drivers cannot keep you from starting and using the system. If a display driver fails to load or initialize when Windows 95 is started, Windows 95 uses the generic VGA display driver. Benefits of the new display driver support in Windows 95 include the following:

- More stable and reliable display adapter drivers using the mini-driver architecture, with support for many more display adapters

- Support for new features, including the ability to change display resolution without needing to restart Windows 95

- Display driver support for mobile computing, providing functionality to switch automatically between display adapters in a portable computer and a docking station

- Consolidated installation and configuration of display drivers and display properties such as colors, wallpaper patterns, and screen savers in a single Control Panel icon

- Image Color Matching (ICM) support for device-independent color usage (offered through an agreement between Microsoft and Kodak)

- Support for a new generation of hardware and device functionality, such as Energy Star Monitors conforming to the VESA Display Power Management Signaling (DPMS) specification, and detection of monitor properties such as maximum resolution supported when used in conjunction with monitors that support the VESA Display Data Channel (DDC) specification

Windows 95 includes drivers for nearly all popular graphics accelerators, and has been shown to run faster than Windows 3.1 on the following models and chip sets:

| | | |
|---|---|---|
| ATI Technologies Inc. | COMPAQ QVision | Tseng Labs |
| Cirrus Logic | IBM XGA | Western Digital |
| Chips & Technologies | Matrox MGA | |

The graphics accelerators in the preceding list are installed on numerous computers and retail graphics adapters and sold under many different make and model names. Before purchasing a new computer or graphics accelerator card, we recommend that you know what graphics accelerator it uses and whether it is supported by Windows 95 drivers developed by Microsoft or another manufacturer. Other accelerator and adapter manufacturers not included in this list will have drivers available.

**Improved mouse and pointing device support.** As with other device drivers, the mini-driver architecture of Windows 95 simplifies mouse driver development and improves virtualization in a protected-mode mouse driver to better support MS-DOS–based applications in the Windows environment. Windows 95 includes the following improvements to mouse support over Windows 3.1:

- Smooth, reliable input support through the use of protected-mode drivers
- Easy installation for mouse and pointing devices, including Plug and Play support
- A single mouse driver, eliminating the need to use separate mouse drivers for MS-DOS and Windows, which increases robustness and saves conventional memory
- Support for connecting a mouse after Windows 95 has started—to assist mobile computer users who forget to connect a mouse before turning on the computer
- Consolidated mouse configuration and customization support in a single Control Panel option
- Improved device support to allow the use of serial ports COM1 through COM4 for connecting a mouse or other pointing device

**Improved communications hardware support.** Windows 95 provides improved communications device and hardware support over Windows 3.1. A few areas of improvement include the following:

- 16550A UART FIFO support. Windows 95 provides robust, high-quality performance at high speeds for MS-DOS–based and Windows-based communications applications using local serial ports with 16550A compatible UARTs. Communications support in Windows 95 alleviates the need for communications driver replacements to improve performance.
- More ports supported. The Windows 95 communication APIs support the same number of logical ports as MS-DOS: 128 serial ports and 128 parallel ports. This enhanced limit allows use of multiport serial devices. The actual limitation on the number of ports usable is still based on the physical number of ports available to the computer.
- Support for parallel port modems. Additionally, Windows 95 provides support for enhanced capabilities port (ECP) printers and future ECP-based high-speed parallel devices.

**Improved power management support.**  Microsoft worked with Intel to develop an industry standard for Advanced Power Management (APM). Now most major computer manufacturers of both portable and desktop computers widely support the APM specification. Windows 95 includes an APM driver that sends messages to the computer's BIOS to manage such things as conserving power during idle periods, reducing monitor power consumption, and processing suspend and resume requests on computers with such features. For information about enabling APM if it was disabled during Setup, see "Troubleshooting Device Configuration" later in this chapter.

# Devices: The Issues

For information related to the specific devices you are responsible for administering, check the lists of supported hardware in the Add New Hardware wizard and the README.TXT file provided with Windows 95.

If you try to install device drivers that were created to run in 32-bit mode in Windows 3.x, you can damage your Windows 95 configuration, because these particular drivers add VxD information to the SYSTEM.INI file. If the device is supported under Windows 95, the best way to recover and install the device is to do the following.

▶ **To recover from faulty installation of a Windows 3.x driver**

1. Restart the computer. Press F8 when the Starting Windows 95 message appears, and then choose the Safe Mode option.

2. Remove all entries added to SYSTEM.INI by the Windows 3.x driver installation program.

3. Remove the device in Device Manager, as described in "Changing Settings with Device Manager" later in this chapter.

4. Shut down and restart Windows 95.

5. In Control Panel, double-click the Add New Hardware icon to reinstall the device using real-mode drivers. To install real-mode drivers, you must choose to manually select the hardware you want to install, and then provide the path name to the real-mode drivers. The device will function correctly, but will not be operating in 32-bit mode.

   Also, contact the device manufacturer to determine when drivers compatible with Windows 95 will be available.

# Devices Overview

In Windows 95, how you install a device depends on whether the device and the computer are Plug and Play-compliant. To take full advantage of Plug and Play technology, a computer needs the following:

- Plug and Play operating system (Windows 95)
- Plug and Play BIOS
- Plug and Play-compliant hardware devices with drivers

The Plug and Play components perform the following tasks:

- Identify the installed devices
- Determine the device resource requirements
- Create a nonconflicting system configuration
- Program the devices
- Load the device drivers
- Notify the system of a configuration change

Windows 95 handles the installation and configuration of Plug and Play-compliant devices automatically, and it provides a wizard to detect and configure legacy devices. Microsoft recommends that, whenever possible, you choose new Plug and Play-compliant devices, even for a legacy computer which does not have a Plug and Play BIOS.

Windows 95 uses a large number of subsystems to control various classes of devices that identify logical device types such as the display, keyboard, and network. Each subsystem uses a different driver architecture and offers different user options and compatibility constraints, so different installation mechanisms are required for each class. For many devices, you must use Device Manager in the System option in Control Panel for configuration if you need to make manual changes.

The following table lists the default classes and shows where you can find the installation tools for changing the device driver.

| Class and device types | Where to configure this device |
| --- | --- |
| Disk class:<br>Disk drives and adapters | Properties for specific devices displayed under related disk controllers in Device Manager. |
| Display class:<br>Display adapters | Display option in Control Panel. See "Configuring the Display" later in this chapter. |
| Keyboard class:<br>Keyboard devices | Keyboard option in Control Panel. See online Help. |
| Modem class:<br>Data and fax modems | Modem option in Control Panel. See Chapter 25, "Modems and Communications Tools." |
| Mouse class:<br>Mouse devices | Mouse option in Control Panel. See online Help. See also "Configuring the Mouse" later in this chapter. |
| Multimedia class:<br>Multimedia devices | Multimedia option in Control Panel. See the related media devices in Device Manager for game ports; see also Chapter 21, "Multimedia." |
| Network class:<br>Network adapters | Properties for the network adapter under the Network option in Control Panel. See Chapter 12, "Network Technical Discussion." |
| PCMCIA class:<br>PC Card sockets | Specific device's properties in Device Manager. See "Enabling PCMCIA Cards" later in this chapter. |
| Ports class:<br>Ports | Ports properties in Device Manager. See "Configuring Communications Ports and Printer Ports" later in this chapter. |
| Printer class:<br>Printers | Printers Folder (no class installer). See Chapter 23, "Printing and Fonts." |
| System class:<br>System devices | Installation handled by the system. Configure using the device's properties in Device Manager. |
| Unknown class:<br>Detected devices with no driver for Windows 95 | Add New Hardware icon in Control Panel. See "Installing New Devices" later in this chapter. |

### How Windows 95 Installs a New Device: An Overview

Windows 95 Setup performs an inventory of all devices on the computer and records the information about those devices in the Registry. Setup gets configuration information from device INF files. To maintain compatibility, Setup also checks entries in WINI.INI, SYSTEM.INI, and CONFIG.SYS.

When a new device is installed, Windows 95 uses the device ID to search Windows 95 INF files for an entry for that device. Windows 95 uses this information or a default driver to create an entry for the device under the Hkey_Local_Machine branch in the Registry, and it copies the drivers needed. Then the Registry entries are copied from the INF file to the driver's Registry entry, including the **DevLoader=** and **DriverDesc=** values for the Driver entry, and the **Driver=** and **ConfigFlags=** values for the Enum entry.

**Tip**  If you use custom setup scripts to install Windows 95, you can include the setting **devicepath=1** in the [Setup] section to specify that Windows 95 should check a source installation path to find INF files, rather than looking only in the Windows INF directory when installing devices. When you use this parameter in setup scripts, you can later add INF files to a single network source location to ensure that up-to-date drivers are used any time a new device is installed on computers running Windows 95. For information, see Appendix D, "MSBATCH.INF Parameters."

# Installing New Devices

When you need to install a new device, you should first rely on Windows 95 to detect and configure it. For Plug and Play-compliant devices, this means inserting the device into the computer. For legacy devices, this means running the Add New Hardware wizard.

**Note**  Before you install a new device, check the Modems section in the Windows 95 README.TXT file for possible information.

▶ **To install a new Plug and Play-compliant device**

1. Insert the device.

   Whether you need to turn off the power before inserting the device depends on the type of device. Check the documentation for your new device.

2. Windows 95 notifies you that it has identified a new card. If no driver is provided on the system, it asks you to insert a disk that contains a driver that was developed for Windows 95.

3. For PCMCIA cards, after Windows 95 identifies and loads the appropriate driver, the computer emits a beeps when the new device is configured.

   You can begin working with the device immediately. Windows 95 notifies other drivers and applications that the device is available.

If your computer uses PCMCIA cards or other Plug and Play cards and if a driver is not available for the new device, Windows 95 prompts you for a driver file to install. If Windows 95 detects the presence of a new device—either during Setup, device installation, or startup—but does not have a driver, it automatically asks for a disk that can be used to install and configure a driver.

▶ **To install a legacy device**

1. In Control Panel, double-click the Add New Hardware option.

2. In the Add New Hardware wizard, click Next, and then click the option named Automatically Detect Installed Hardware.

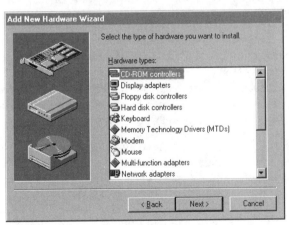

3. Continue to follow the instructions on the screen to install drivers and to configure the device driver.

If Windows 95 does not have a driver for the device, you can install the driver from a disk by using the Add New Hardware wizard.

▶  **To install a legacy device from a disk by using the Add New Hardware wizard**

1. In the Add New Hardware wizard, click Next, and then click Install Specific Hardware.

2. In the list of hardware devices, click a device class, and then click Next.

3. In the next Add New Hardware dialog box, specify the manufacturer and model of the device, and then click Have Disk.

4. In the Install From Disk dialog box, type the path name to the driver files, and then click OK.

# Changing Settings with Device Manager

For Plug and Play-compliant devices, there are no true default settings. Instead, Windows 95 identifies devices and their resource requests, and then arbitrates requests among them. If no other device requests the same resources as another device, its settings should not change. If another device requests its resources, the settings might change to accommodate the request. Consequently, you should never change resource settings for a Plug and Play-compliant device unless absolutely necessary. Doing so will fix its settings, making it impossible for Windows 95 to grant another device's request to use that resource.

All legacy devices have fixed resource settings, which are defined either during Windows Setup from a previous configuration, or afterward in the Add New Hardware wizard in Control Panel.

Certain circumstances might require users to change resource settings after they have been configured. For example, Windows 95 might not be able to configure one device without creating conflicts with another device. In such a case, a message usually appears to explain what is happening and what you can do about the problem—turn off a device to make room for the new device, disable the new device, or reconfigure a legacy device to make room for the new device.

The best place for resolving any conflicts that might occur is the Hardware Conflict troubleshooting aid in Windows 95 online Help. For more information, see "Troubleshooting Device Configuration" later in this chapter.

When you must manually change a device's configuration, you can use Device Manager in the System option in Control Panel. Using Device Manager helps you avoid the errors that can occur if you attempt to edit Registry entries directly.

If you need or want to resolve device conflicts manually, you can use Device Manager and try the following strategies:

- Identify a free resource, and assign the device to use that resource.
- Disable a conflicting Plug and Play-compliant device to free its resources.
- Disable a legacy device by removing the legacy device card and not loading the device drivers.
- Rearrange resources used by another device or other devices to free resources needed by the device with a conflict.
- Change jumpers on your hardware to match the new settings.

Caution   Changing default settings using either Device Manager or Registry Editor can cause conflicts that make one or more devices unavailable on the system.

Device Manager and Registry Editor are provided as configuration tools for advanced users who understand configuration parameters and the ramifications of changing settings.

▶ **To use Device Manager**

1. In the System option in Control Panel, click the Device Manager tab.

   –Or–

   Right-click My Computer, click Properties from the context menu, and then click the Device Manager tab.

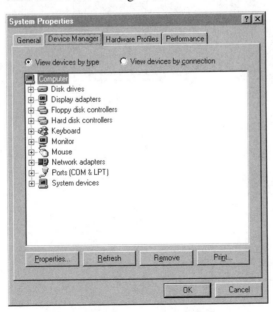

2. Double-click the device type in the list to display the specific devices of that type on your computer.

3. Double-click the device you want to configure. Or select the device, and then click the Properties button to view or change its settings.

▶ **To change the device driver using Device Manager**

1. In Device Manager, double-click the related device type.

2. Double-click your current device to display its properties.

3. Click the Driver tab.

   The Driver properties dialog box shows the driver files and current resource setup for that device.

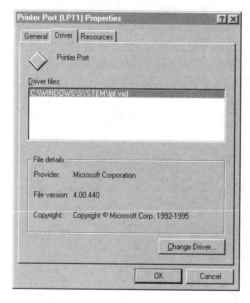

4. Click the Change Driver button.

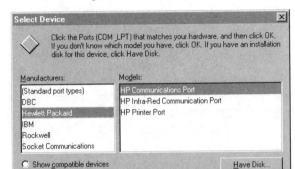

5. In the Select Device dialog box, the Show Compatible Devices option is checked to show you a list of drivers that Windows 95 has identified as compatible for your device.

   –Or–

   Click Show All Devices to see a list of all the drivers available in Windows 95.

---

   **Important**  Be very careful in selecting a driver in the Show All Devices list. You should select a driver from the Show All Devices list only when you know that you are selecting a driver that is compatible with the device.

---

6. In the Models list, select the driver you want to use, and then click OK.
7. If requested, follow the instructions on the screen to provide a disk or a path to a directory that contains the display driver.

In Device Manager, you can print reports about system settings, including reports on the following:

- System summary
- Selected class or device
- All devices and system summary

▶ **To print a report about system settings**

1. In Device Manager, click Print.

2. In the Print dialog box, click the type of report you want.

---

**Caution**   You should quit all MS-DOS–based applications before printing the report named All Devices And System Summary because the device detection code might cause problems for some MS-DOS–based applications. If you do not do this, some applications might report the system is out of memory.

---

▶ **To change a device's resource settings using Device Manager**

1. In Device Manager, double-click a device class.

   The tree expands to show the devices of that class available on the computer.

2. Double-click a device to display its properties.

3. In the device's properties, click the Resources tab.

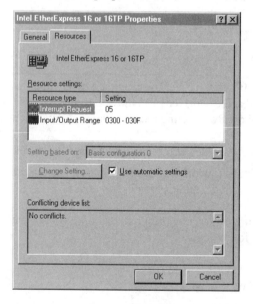

Notice that the Conflicting Devices List shows any conflicting values for resources used by other devices.

4. In the Resource Type list, select the setting you want to change—for example, the Input/Output Range—and then click the Change Setting button.

Notice that you can select and set the IRQ, I/O, and DMA independently, and that if the option named Use Automatic Settings is checked, you cannot change resource settings.

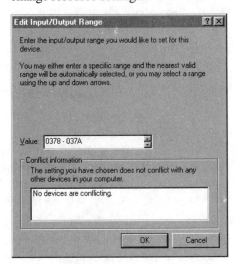

The dialog box shows the various settings that the device supports. Notice that in the Edit Input/Output Range box any interrupt marked with an asterisk (*) will conflict with an existing device. Any interrupt marked with a pound sign (#) indicates that the actual configuration has been tested.

When you clicked the Change Setting button, you might have received an error message saying "This resource setting cannot be modified." If this is the case, you must choose a different basic configuration until you find one that allows you to change resource settings.

5. Choose a setting that does not conflict with any other devices, and then click OK.

6. Shut down and restart Windows 95. Then verify that the settings are correct for the device.

---

**Note**  Most legacy devices have jumpers or switches that set the IRQ, DMA, and I/O addresses. If you change these settings in Device Manager, you must also change the settings on the device to match them.

---

**Tips for Changing Settings with Registry Editor**

You can use Registry Editor to change specific values for devices. Use Registry Editor to change system settings in the following cases:

- When directed to make specific changes by a product support representative.

- When you know the correct Registry key, value settings, and editing restrictions for a specific device.

- When you cannot successfully change the value using Device Manager or other built-in tools.

When you make changes in Registry Editor, always make one change at a time, and then test the system for the results. If you have problems with the system after making a change, restart the computer and press F8 when the Starting Windows 95 message appears, and then choose the Safe Mode option. Then you can change the setting back to its previous value.

You can also use the Connect command in Registry Editor to connect to and view the Registry on a remote computer if that computer has the Microsoft Remote Registry service installed. For information about using Registry Editor, see Chapter 33, "Windows 95 Registry."

# Enabling PCMCIA Cards

To enable Windows 95 Plug and Play support for the PCMCIA socket, you must run the PCMCIA wizard. The PCMCIA wizard comments out the real-mode drivers in the AUTOEXEC.BAT and CONFIG.SYS files and enables the PCMCIA socket. In some cases, Windows 95 disables Plug and Play PCMCIA support if there is a risk of incompatibility.

If you must use old drivers, Windows 95 should work well with your previous PCMCIA drivers, although some Plug and Play capabilities such as automatic installation and friendly device names will not be available.

Windows 95 supports many PCMCIA cards including modems, network adapters, SCSI cards, and others. If Windows 95 includes supporting drivers for the PCMCIA card and for the socket, then installation and configuration should be automatic. This section provides some guidelines for enabling Windows 95 enhanced PCMCIA support when automatic detection and configuration aren't available for your card.

If your PCMCIA card is not shown in the list of manufacturers and models in the Add New Hardware wizard, contact the vendor and request a Windows 95-compatible installation disk before enabling the Windows 95 enhanced PCMCIA support. Also, see these Help topics:

- "Setting Up Other Hardware," if you added a PCMCIA socket after setting up Windows 95
- "If You Have Trouble Using a PCMCIA Card"

---

**Important**  Your PCMCIA socket driver and network driver both must be Plug and Play-compliant drivers (that is, developed for Windows 95 and NDIS 3.1-compliant) or both must be real-mode drivers. If these drivers are of mixed types, the computer might stall or the network might not work.

---

Windows 95 Setup automatically detects the presence of a PCMCIA socket, but to enable it, you must run the PCMCIA wizard.

▶ **To verify that Windows 95 has properly detected your PCMCIA socket**

1. In the System option in Control Panel, click the Device Manager tab.
2. Look for a PCMCIA Socket listing.

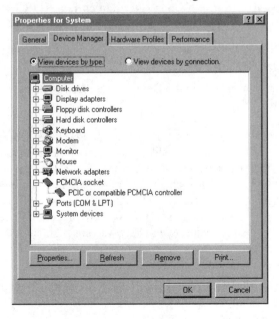

If Windows 95 has not detected a PCMCIA socket, your socket controller might not be supported by Windows 95.

▶ **To find out if a PCMCIA socket is supported**

1. In Control Panel, double-click the Add New Hardware icon.

2. On the first screen in the Add New Hardware wizard, click the Next button, and then click Install Specific Hardware.

3. In the Hardware Types list, select PCMCIA Socket, and then click the Next button.

4. Select the manufacturer for your device, and examine the Models list.

   If your socket does not appear in the list, you should contact the manufacturer to see if new drivers are available.

▶ **To enable support for PCMCIA by running the PCMCIA wizard**

- In Control Panel, double-click the PCMCIA icon.

   –Or–

   Double-click the PCMCIA controller in the Device Manager.

   –Or–

   Look up the topic named "PCMCIA" and then look up "Enable Support For" in the Windows 95 Help Index.

▶ **To find out if Windows 95 has activated enhanced PCMCIA support**

1. In Device Manager, click your PCMCIA controller, and then click the Properties button.

2. Click the General tab.

   If a hardware profile in the Device Usage box is checked, then PCMCIA support is enabled.

If you have the correct drivers and enhanced PCMCIA support is activated, but the device is still not available, your computer is probably using the wrong memory window for the device. Windows 95 selects a default set of commonly supported settings. Your socket might not support certain interrupt settings, so you might be able to get a PCMCIA socket to work by changing the IRQ. Similarly, your socket might not work on certain memory windows, and changing the memory window might solve your problem.

▶ **To change the memory window for a PCMCIA device**

1. In Device Manager, click your PCMCIA socket, and then click the Properties button.

2. In the PCMCIA controller properties, click the Global Settings tab.

3. Make sure that the Automatic Selection check box is not checked.

4. Change the Start address based on information from your hardware manual.

   Typically, selecting a Start value higher than 100000 will work.

5.  Restart Windows 95.

▶  **To change the interrupt for a PCMCIA device**

1.  In Device Manager, click your PCMCIA socket, and then click the Properties button.

2.  Change the IRQ from its default to a value that doesn't conflict with other IRQ settings used on your computer.

3.  Restart Windows 95.

If Windows 95 still doesn't detect your PCMCIA cards, you should disable the Windows 95 enhanced PCMCIA support.

▶  **To disable the enhanced PCMCIA support**

1.  In Device Manager, click your PCMCIA controller, and then click the Properties button.

2.  Click the General tab, and in the Device Usage box, click to clear the check beside the hardware profile.

# Using Hardware Profiles for Alternate Configurations

Windows 95 uses hardware profiles to determine which drivers to load when the system hardware changes. When you start Windows 95, Windows 95 runs detection to see if any hardware on the computer has changed. If the hardware has changed significantly, Windows 95 creates a new hardware profile and prompts you for a name. If you move the computer to a new site and use a different configuration, Windows 95 notices it when you start the computer and loads the appropriate drivers.

The only time Windows 95 prompts you for the name of a hardware profile is when two profiles are so similar that Windows 95 can't differentiate between them. If this happens, Windows 95 displays a Hardware Profile menu from which you can choose the correct one.

Hardware profiles are an especially important feature for portable computers that can be docked. Windows 95 uses one hardware profile to load drivers when the portable is docked, and another profile when the portable is undocked—for example, at a customer site that has a different monitor than at the office.

---

**Note**  It is not necessary to use a different hardware profile for a Plug and Play portable computer, because the computer automatically knows when it is docked or undocked.

---

▶  **To create a hardware profile**

1. In the System option in Control Panel, click the Hardware Profiles tab.

2. Click the name of the hardware profile you want to base the new hardware profile on, and then click Copy.

3. Type a name for the hardware profile you are creating.

4. Change which hardware is enabled or disabled in this profile by using the Device Manager, as described in the following procedure.

---

**Tip**  If you have a hardware profile with the same name as a Windows 95 Startup Menu item, the corresponding menu item will be run automatically when you use that hardware profile for system startup.

---

▶  **To enable or disable hardware in a hardware profile**

1. In Device Manager, click the plus sign next to the hardware type, and then double-click the hardware.

2. In the Device Usage box, click to place a check mark next to each hardware profile in which you want to enable the hardware, or clear the check box to disable the hardware for that hardware profile.

3. If you see a message prompting you to restart your computer, click Yes.

▶  **To delete or rename a hardware profile**

1. In the System option in Control Panel, click the Hardware Profiles tab.

2. Click the name of the hardware profile you want to change.

3. If you want to remove this profile, click Delete.

    –Or–

    If you want to change the name of the profile, click Rename, and then type a new name.

Configurations are created when Windows 95 queries the BIOS for a dock serial ID and then assigns a name for the docked and undocked configuration. Windows 95 then stores the hardware and software associated with this configuration. Applications access and store information for each of the different hardware configurations used by the mobile user. The Registry support enables applications to adapt gracefully to different hardware configurations.

**Tip**  If you are running Multiconfig, you can name a hardware profile the same as a Multiconfig menu option. In this case, Windows 95 detects a hardware profile and automatically runs the corresponding Multiconfig menu option. You can create this by specifying identical names for the Multiconfig menu option and the hardware profile.

# Configuring the Display

Windows 95 consolidates display properties in the Display option in Control Panel, so you can easily customize display adapter settings. You can use the Display option in Control Panel to do the following:

- Change the display type or driver.

- Change screen resolution and color palette (without restarting the computer when using display drivers that support this functionality).

- Change color schemes and text styles in all screen elements, including changing fonts used in dialog boxes, menus, and title bars.

- View changes in colors, text, and other elements of display appearance before the changes are applied.

- Configure display settings for each hardware profile; for example, docked and undocked configurations.

**Tip**  To set display options quickly, right-click the desktop, and then click Properties. Click the Help icon to get Help for setting display properties.

# Display Driver Overview

Windows 95 provides enhanced functionality and easy configuration for display adapters, in addition to resolving many problems inherent in Windows 3.1 display drivers. By using a mini-driver architecture for display drivers, Windows 95 provides better support for a wide range of hardware and provides more stable and reliable drivers.

Windows 95 Setup automatically detects the display adapter in the computer and installs the correct display driver, upgrading to a new driver if a new version is available.

Windows 95 contains a universal display driver called the device independent bitmap (DIB) engine. The DIB engine provides 32-bit graphics code for fast, robust drawing on high-resolution and frame buffer-type display adapters. Windows 95 display mini-drivers use the DIB engine for all in-memory graphics operations and on-screen operations that do not pass to the adapter for hardware acceleration. This architecture makes it easy for hardware developers to write drivers for a new controller type and to add hardware acceleration features incrementally.

To ensure broad support for display adapter devices in Windows 95, Microsoft developed many of the display drivers in cooperation with the major display-controller hardware manufacturers. The Microsoft development team also worked closely with hardware manufacturers to write additional display drivers and assisted in optimizing drivers to enhance display speed for improved graphic performance.

Windows 95 also includes mechanisms to ensure that incompatible display drivers cannot prevent a user from accessing the system. If a display driver fails to load or initialize when Windows 95 is started, Windows 95 automatically uses the generic VGA display driver. This ensures that you can start Windows 95 to fix a display-related problem.

For displays, colors are described in bits per pixel (bpp). The following table lists the bpp-to-colors conversion.

| Bits per pixel | Color conversion |
| --- | --- |
| 1 bpp | Monochrome |
| 4 bpp | 16 colors |
| 8 bpp | 256 colors |
| 15 bpp | 32,768 (32K) colors |
| 16 bpp | 65,536 (64K) colors |
| 24 bpp | 16.7 million (16.7M) colors |
| 32 bpp | 16.7 million colors |

Resolutions are described in horizontal number of pixels multiplied by (x) vertical number of pixels—for example, 640x480.

# Changing the Display Type and Driver

You can change a display driver by using the Display option in Control Panel or by using Device Manager. For more information about adding or changing a device driver, see online Help.

---

Caution   Some monitors can be physically damaged by incorrect display settings. Carefully check the manual for your monitor before choosing a new setting.

---

▶ **To change the display driver by using the Display option in Control Panel**

1. In Control Panel, double-click the Display icon.

   –Or–

   Right-click the desktop, and then click Properties from the context menu.

2. In the Display Properties dialog box, click the Settings tab.

3. In the Display Settings dialog box, click the Change Display Type button, and then click the Change button.

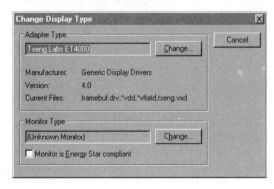

4. In the Select Device dialog box, click the Show Compatible Devices option to see a list of drivers that are compatible with the display adapter.

–Or–

Click Show All Devices to see a list of all the display drivers available in Windows 95.

---

**Important** You can safely select any driver in the Show Compatible Devices list in the Select Driver dialog box. Select the Show All Devices option only if you know that you need to select a driver from the Models list that also supports your display. You must be careful to select a driver that you know to be compatible with your display adapter.

---

5. In the Models list, click the driver you want to use, and then click OK.

If prompted, follow the instructions on your screen to provide a disk or path to a directory that contains the display driver.

---

**Tip** The [boot] section of the SYSTEM.INI file should contain the following line for any Windows 95 version of a display driver:

```
display.drv=pnpdrvr.drv.
```

The actual display driver is loaded from the Registry. This supports docking computers that have different adapters for the portable computer versus the docking station.

---

For display drivers that do not appear in the Select Device dialog box (that is, those that are not provided with Windows 95), the Windows Driver Library (WDL) provides support for drivers from other vendors. For information about the WDL, see Appendix J, "Windows 95 Resource Directory."

You can also install Windows 3.x display drivers, if required. However, Microsoft strongly recommends that you upgrade to Windows 95 display drivers so you can take advantage of the Windows 95-specific display drivers that provide new features and functionality. For example, many display adapters and drivers support Plug and Play detection and "on the fly" resolution changes; these features are not supported by Windows 3.1 drivers.

▶ **To install Windows 3.1 display drivers**

1. In the Display option in Control Panel, click the Settings tab, and then click Change Display Type.

2. Click the Change button next to Adapter Type, and then click the Have Disk button.

3. Specify the path to the disk or directory containing the Windows 3.1 drivers you want to use.

4. Select the correct driver to use from the list that appears, and then click OK to install.

   When Show All Devices is selected in the Select Device dialog box, old drivers appear in the Select Device dialog under the manufacturer type Windows 3.x Drivers.

Notice that some Windows 3.1 drivers require the screen resolution to be specified in the [boot.description] section of SYSTEM.INI. For example:

```
display.drv=Acme Inc. 640x480 256 colors
```

## Configuring Display Resolution and Color Palette

You can configure the display resolution and color palette choices for your display or customize the font size used by using the Display option in Control Panel.

After making these kinds of changes, you must shut down and restart the computer unless you are using a Plug and Play-compliant display adapter and driver that support on-the-fly changes.

▶ **To configure your display resolution**

1. In the Display option in Control Panel, click the Settings tab.

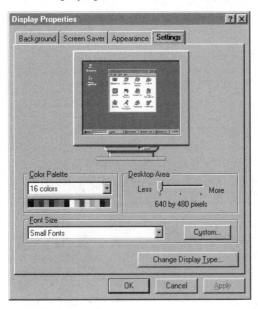

2. In Display properties, use the options described in the following table
   to change your display settings.

| Option | Description |
| --- | --- |
| Color Palette | Select from this list the number of colors you want for your display adapter. The larger the number, the greater the number of colors. |
| Desktop Area | Drag the slider to change the visible screen area used by the display. The larger the desktop area, the smaller everything looks on your screen. |
| Font Size | Select from this list one of the font sizes for your display type. Typically, the selections will be Small Fonts and Large Fonts. To set the font used in dialog boxes, see "Configuring Display Appearance" later in this chapter. |
| Custom | Click to change the size of the text that Windows 95 displays, as described in the following procedure. |
| Change Display Type | Click to display a dialog box for selecting another adapter type or monitor type. Notice that the monitor type setting has no impact on system performance. This setting identifies the characteristics of the monitor in order to define the maximum resolution and power management capabilities that it supports. For information, see "Changing the Display Type and Driver" earlier in this chapter. |

**Note**  Sometimes a larger number of colors requires you to have a smaller
desktop area, and vice versa. This is due to a limitation of the display adapter.
Extra large sizes might adversely affect the display in some applications.

▶  **To customize display of fonts in dialog boxes**

1. In the Display option in Control Panel, click the Settings tab, and then click
   the Custom button.

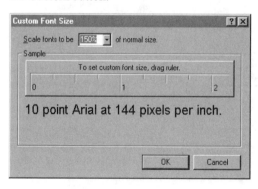

2. Drag the controls until the sample shows the size you want, and then click OK.

For non-Plug and Play devices, you must shut down and restart Windows 95 for the changes to take effect.

Setting the monitor type in the Display properties sheet does not affect the refresh rate output of your display adapter. To change this, you must run a utility supplied by your display adapter manufacturer or computer manufacturer. Some display utilities must be run in the AUTOEXEC.BAT file; however, on other computers, display type is set in BIOS configuration programs. Some examples of such utilities are described in the following list.

| Adapter | Manufacturer's display utility |
|---|---|
| ATI | INSTALL.EXE |
| Cirrus Logic | MONTYPE.EXE, CLMODE.EXE, WINMODE.EXE |
| Diamond Stealth | STLMODE.EXE |
| Diamond Stealth 64 | S64MODE.EXE |
| Matrox | \MGA\SETUP\SETUP.EXE |
| Tseng Labs | VMODE.EXE |
| Western Digital | VGAMODE.EXE |

# Configuring Display Appearance

You can use the Display option in Control Panel to set the screen saver and the background pattern used on the desktop. (These options replace Desktop options in the Windows 3.x Control Panel.)

You can also use settings in Screen Saver properties to take advantage of Energy Star Monitor support in Windows 95 if your hardware supports this feature. This is similar to the standby mode commonly used in portable computers to save power. Windows 95 can support screen saver power management if both of the following conditions are true for your computer:

- In the Change Display Type dialog box, the option named Monitor Is Energy Star Compliant is checked.

  This option is checked automatically if, during Setup, hardware detection determined that the monitor supports the VESA DPMS specification. You can also check this option manually.

- The device driver for this display uses either the Advanced Power Management (APM) 1.1 BIOS interface with support for device "01FF" (which is not supported by every APM 1.1 BIOS), or the VESA BIOS Extensions for Power Management. For information about whether your display adapter supports these BIOS interfaces, see the documentation for your device driver.

The display monitor is typically one of the most "power hungry" components of a computer. Manufacturers of newer display monitors have incorporated energy-saving features into their monitors based on the VESA Display Power Management Signaling (DPMS) specification. Through signals from the display adapter, a software control can place the monitor in standby mode or even turn it off completely, thus reducing the power the monitor uses when inactive. To do this, Windows 95 extends the screen saver capabilities to provide both a time-delay setting that allows the user to put the display monitor in a low-power standby mode, and a delay setting to turn the monitor off completely.

If your computer can use Energy Star power consumption features, additional options appear in Screen Saver properties. To take advantage of these features, both the display adapter and monitor must meet the Energy Star specifications. Also, the display driver must support the extensions needed to control the monitor. Several hardware providers currently manufacture monitors designed to support the Energy Star goals.

▶ **To use Energy Star power consumption features**

- In Display properties, click the Screen Saver tab and specify the time intervals for when to use low-power standby and when to shut off power.

For example, you might want to set these options:

- Display a specific screen saver after 5 minutes of inactivity
- Set the computer to standby after the screen saver has displayed for 10 minutes
- Turn off the monitor after 15 minutes of standby

For information about setting up a screen saver, or changing the appearance of display colors, type styles, background pattern, and wallpaper, see online Help.

# Configuring the Mouse

Mouse drivers based on the Windows 95 mini-driver architecture are protected-mode drivers that provide better support for MS-DOS–based applications in the Windows 95 environment. Windows 95 makes mouse configuration and customization easier by providing a single Control Panel option for mouse settings.

Windows 95 Setup detects Microsoft, Logitech, and Microsoft-compatible mouse device drivers, and then replaces these with new drivers.

# Mouse and Pointing Device Driver Overview

Windows 95 provides the following improvements in mouse and pointing device support:

- Supports Plug and Play for easy installation of pointing devices. For example, the VMOUSE driver interface supports Plug and Play.

- Provides smooth, reliable input when using the new protected-mode drivers.

- Supports multiple simultaneous devices; for example, when using PS/2® and serial devices at the same time.

- Eliminates the need to use separate MS-DOS–based mouse drivers.

  Windows 3.1 required that an MS-DOS–based mouse driver be loaded before starting Windows to use a mouse in an MS-DOS–based application running in a window or running in a full screen.

The protected-mode Windows 95 VxD mouse driver provides mouse support for Windows-based applications, MS-DOS–based applications running in a window, and MS-DOS–based applications running in a full screen. These improvements result in zero use of conventional memory for mouse support in the Windows 95 environment. (However, most legacy real-mode drivers will run in Windows 95.)

In addition to better mouse services, Windows 95 allows the use of serial ports COM1 through COM4 for connecting a mouse or other pointing device.

▶ **To see the improvements in mouse driver support**

1. Be sure the real-mode mouse driver from such entries as MOUSE.COM or MOUSE.SYS has been removed from CONFIG.SYS or AUTOEXEC.BAT.

2. Restart the computer, and start an MS-DOS–based application that supports the use of a mouse.

   For example, use an application such as Edit, and try the MS-DOS–based application both in a window and in a full screen. Notice that the mouse is available in both modes.

# Changing Mouse Drivers

The Mouse option in Control Panel provides customization options, including setting the behavior of the mouse buttons and the mouse pointer. You can use either the Mouse option or Device Manager to change drivers for a pointing device. For information, see online Help.

For pointing device drivers that do not appear in the Select Device dialog box (that is, those that are not provided with Windows 95), the Windows Driver Library (WDL) provides support for additional drivers from other vendors. For information about the WDL, see Appendix J, "Windows 95 Resource Directory."

# Configuring Mouse Behavior

You can use the Mouse option in Control Panel to configure buttons, customize mouse cursor appearance, set mouse speed, and other functions. This section briefly describes these functions. Different functions might be available, depending on the pointing device used with your computer.

▶ **To specify mouse behavior**

- In the Mouse option in Control Panel, click the tab for the behavior you want to set, as described in the following illustrations. After changing the settings to the ones you want, click the Apply Now button.

  For information about the configuration options, see the online Help.

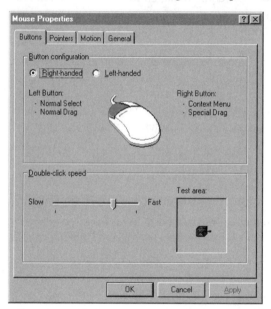

# Configuring Communications Ports and Printer Ports

A communications resource is a physical or logical device that provides a single, asynchronous data stream. Serial ports, parallel ports, and modems are examples of communications resources. In Windows 95, VCOMM is the communications VxD that manages all access to communications devices. Port drivers use VCOMM to register themselves and to manage access to communications devices.

Two types of ports appear in Device Manager:

- Communications ports, also known as COM ports, serial ports, or RS-232 ports, are used to connect RS-232–compatible serial devices such as modems and pointing devices to the computer.

- Printer ports, also known as LPT ports or parallel ports, are used to connect parallel devices such as printers to the computer. For more information about configuring printer ports, see Chapter 23, "Printing and Fonts."

Several types of communications ports might be listed in Device Manager:

- Serial ports, also known as RS-232 COM ports, to which external serial devices can be attached. These usually require a 9-pin or 25-pin plug. Serial ports designed for Windows 95 use the 16550A buffered UART, which has a 16-byte FIFO that gives the CPU more time to serve other processes and that can serve multiple characters in a single interrupt routine.

- An internal modem adapter. In addition to being installed in Device Manager, internal modems should also be installed and configured in the Modems option in Control Panel. For information, see Chapter 25, "Modems and Communications Tools."

- A PCMCIA modem card, if it is using PCMCIA socket drivers designed for Windows 3.1 instead of Windows 95-compatible PCMCIA drivers. In this situation, a PCMCIA modem card is treated as if it were an internal modem adapter; that is, it must be installed as both a COM port and a modem.

When you install a communications device, Windows 95 automatically assigns COM names to communication ports, internal modem adapters, and PCMCIA modem cards according to their base I/O port addresses as shown in the following list:

- COM1 at 3F8 (input/output range)
- COM2 at 2F8
- COM3 at 3E8
- COM4 at 2E8

If a device has a nonstandard base address, or if all four standard ports have been assigned to devices, Windows 95 automatically assigns the modem to COM5 port or higher. Some 16-bit Windows 3.1 applications might not be able to access ports higher than COM4. Consequently, in the System option in Control Panel, you must adjust the base address in Device Manager or delete other devices to free up a lower COM port.

In addition, if some of the devices installed on a computer are not Plug and Play-compliant, you might have to change resource settings for their communications ports. You can change communications port settings by using Device Manager, as described in "Installing New Devices" earlier in this chapter.

**Tip**  For future reference, you might want to record the settings that appear on the Resources sheet for each communications port.

# Real-Mode Drivers and the IOS.INI Safe Driver List

Microsoft strongly recommends that you use 32-bit, protected-mode drivers wherever possible. With protected-mode drivers, configuration information is stored in the Registry rather than in CONFIG.SYS or other files.

The following shows the general guidelines for device entries in CONFIG.SYS, and whether such entries are required or can be removed under Windows 95:

- When you use only protected-mode drivers, the only configuration information the operating system needs to know for system startup is the location of the Windows 95 system files and the directory for the swap file. You do not need to load drivers in CONFIG.SYS or AUTOEXEC.BAT.

- Any boot device in your computer that needs real-mode support does not require an entry in CONFIG.SYS. In the unusual case that the CD-ROM is part of system startup, entries for this device must be included in CONFIG.SYS.

- If your computer requires any real-mode drivers, an entry for loading the driver must be included in CONFIG.SYS and AUTOEXEC.BAT, as was true under earlier versions of MS-DOS.

Windows 95 automatically unloads any real-mode drivers for which it has protected-mode drivers to provide the same functionality. For example, the real-mode DBLSPACE.BIN driver is unloaded and the protected-mode DBLSPACE.VXD driver takes over. However, the protected-mode device driver should take over only when it guarantees similar functionality to the real-mode driver, not merely because it can drive the hardware.

**Tip**  To determine whether a particular driver is running in real mode versus protected mode, click the Performance tab in the System option in Control Panel.

Real-mode drivers that can safely be replaced are identified in the safe driver list, which identifies drivers and TSRs that Windows 95 can replace with corresponding protected-mode drivers. The safe driver list (IOS.INI in the Windows directory) can include the following information:

- Name of the driver or TSR, using the same name as used in CONFIG.SYS or AUTOEXEC.BAT
- Driver requirements
- Whether the driver hooks INT 13
- Whether the driver monitors INT 13 (regardless of whether I/O is controlled by a protected-mode driver)
- Whether the driver accesses hardware directly

Windows 95 does not store the version number of the driver or TSR in the list, so the vendor must change the name of the driver if a future version is enhanced so that the driver is safe or unsafe.

By default, the following drivers are considered safe:

- MS-DOS 5.0-compatible real-mode block device drivers
- INT 13 driver (provides INT 13 functionality and directly accesses hardware)
- INT 13 monitors (hooks INT 13 for monitoring I/O but does not access hardware directly or modify the I/O buffer)
- INT 13 hooker (hooks INT 13 for altering I/O but does not access hardware directly)
- ASPI Manager (implements the Advanced SCSI Programming Interface for MS-DOS specification)
- CAM Manager (implements MS-DOS Common Access Method specification)

A real-mode driver is considered *unsafe* if it implements functionality that is not provided by protected-mode drivers. For example, a real-mode IDE or ESDI driver that uses dynamic encryption is an unsafe driver because Windows 95 does not support encryption. Windows 95 protected-mode drivers do not implement the following functions, so if a real-mode driver uses any of the following functions it is considered unsafe and should not be added to the safe driver list:

- Data compression (other than DriveSpace-compatible compression)

- Data encryption
- Disk mirroring
- Bad sector mapping
- Fault tolerance (maintaining ECC correction on a separate disk)
- IOCTLS defined or extended by the vendor

If Windows 95 provides an appropriate protected-mode driver, you should use only the real-mode driver in these cases:

- If the real-mode driver is used for a boot device.
- If an MS-DOS Mode application uses the driver's device, in which case the protected-mode driver must be unloaded in order to load the real-mode driver.

### Tip for Using Real-Mode versus Safe Protected-Mode Drivers

If a real-mode driver provides better performance or provides some functions not present in the Windows 95 protected-mode driver, you should remove the real-mode driver from the safe driver list, so that Windows 95 uses real mode to access the driver. Similarly, if a real-mode driver can safely be taken over by a protected-mode driver, add the real-mode driver to the safe driver list.

To determine whether you can use a protected-mode driver, you will have to test the equivalent functionality provided from the protected-mode driver versus your existing real-mode driver.

The following is the syntax of the safe driver list in IOS.INI:

*filename, qualifier_string ; comments*

| Qualifier string | Meaning |
|---|---|
| **do_not_care** | Indicates that it is acceptable to load the protected-mode driver and not use the mapper for this real-mode driver because it doesn't matter whether it sees any I/O requests. This is the default. |
| **must_chain** | Implies that the device driver or TSR is safe, but it has an INT 13 hook that needs to see INT 13 requests. In this case, the protected-mode drivers are loaded, but the system routes the logical requests through the real-mode mapper and then switches back to protected-mode at the end of the INT 13 chain. |
| **must_not_chain** | Implies that the driver is safe as long as it does not see any INT 13 requests. In this case, the protected-mode drivers are loaded and the real-mode mapper is not used. |

| Qualifier string | Meaning |
|---|---|
| **non_disk** | Indicates a driver that controls a device that is not a disk, such as Interlnk. IOS issues INT 25 calls to all logical volumes in the system and determines whether the request is mapped to INT 13, ASPI, or CAM. If the request is not mapped, then this is a monolithic driver, as is the case for Interlnk. Adding **non_disk** prevents IOS from considering Interlnk in its safe-driver processing. |
| **monolithic** | Similar to **non_disk**. Any driver that is monolithic and safe must have this qualifier set to indicate to IOS that the protected-mode port drivers can be loaded and the driver's entry point can be handled to prevent contention. |

IOS.INI also contains an Unsafe CD section in IOS.INI. Adding a driver to this section indicates that this CDFS will not be loaded on the CD drives that this driver controls.

The following is an example of some IOS.INI entries.

```
386max.sys       ; Qualitas
4dos.com         ; 4DOS shell program
ad-dos.com       ; Afterdark
ad_wrap.com      ; Afterdark
adi2.com         ; Afterdark
aspi3x90.sys     ; DTC SCSI no PM driver
...
[CDUnsafe]
drd600.sys       ; Acme 60X series CDROM
drd60asp.sys     ; Acme 60X series CDROM
drd60ps.sys      ; Acme 60X series CDROM
```

### Tip for Troubleshooting Protected-Mode Drivers

If you believe that a protected-mode driver should be controlling a device, but the device appears with a real-mode driver in the System option in Control Panel, you can check entries in IOS.LOG. The IOS.LOG file in the Windows directory is created when a protected-mode driver is not available or if the operating system detects that an unknown device driver is controlling a device.

In most cases, the first line in IOS.LOG states why the protected-mode driver was not loaded. If the first line mentions MBRINT13.SYS, then the problem most likely is a virus (except if you are using a driver that replaces the master boot record).

# Troubleshooting Device Configuration

This section describes specific problems in device configuration and how to correct them. For information about general procedures and Windows 95 tools that can be used in troubleshooting, see Chapter 35, "General Troubleshooting."

Your first and best resource for diagnosing problems due to changing device settings is the Hardware Conflict troubleshooting aid in the online Help.

▶ **To use the Hardware Conflict troubleshooting aid**

1. In the Help Topics window, click the Contents tab.

   –Or–

   In any Help window, click the Contents button.

2. Click Troubleshooting, click the option named If You Have A Hardware Conflict, and then follow the instructions on the screen.

# Correcting Problems with Display

**The display doesn't work correctly.**

1. Restart the computer, and then press F8 when the Starting Windows 95 message appears.

2. Choose Safe Mode, which uses the standard VGA (640x480x16-color) driver.

   If this resolves the display problem, then the display driver is probably involved. Try replacing the driver with a newer version, or reinstall the driver from the original disks.

---

**Tip**  Problems can result when Windows 95 incorrectly assumes that a display adapter can support certain functionality. If this occurs, the side effects might be anything from small display irregularities to system lockup.

To determine whether any performance problems might be related to the display adapter, you can progressively disable enhanced display functionality using the System option in Control Panel. On the Performance tab, click the Graphics button, and then use the slider to select new settings. For information, see Chapter 17, "Performance Tuning."

---

**A display error occurs at a specific display resolution.**

If your computer has problems with the display, determine whether the problems persist when you use lower screen resolutions and different color palettes with the display driver.

▶ **To see if the display error changes with resolution**

1. In the Display option in Control Panel, click the Settings tab.

2. In the Color Palette box, click the box that displays available resolutions.

3. If the selection is other than 16-color, select 16-color.

4. Click the Apply button. Then shut down and restart the computer.

5. Retest the condition that was causing the display error. If the error does not recur, you might want to temporarily operate at a lower resolution until you can upgrade the display driver to a version that functions without error.

### A display driver fails to work.

If the display driver fails (and changing resolutions doesn't resolve it), you should check or replace the current display driver.

▶ **To check the display drivers**

1. In Device Manager, click the plus sign next to Display Adapters.

2. Double-click the specific display adapter shown (for example, Cirrus Logic).

3. In the properties dialog box, click the Driver tab.

4. Click each file shown in the Driver Files box. The File Version appears in the File Details box, if available (some vendor's display drivers might not contain version information).

5. Check displayed file versions for compatibility. Windows 95 display driver files have version numbers starting at 4.00 or higher.

6. If you have an incompatible driver, you can reinstall the original driver from the Windows 95 disks, or get new drivers from the Microsoft Download Service (MSDL) as described in Appendix J, "Windows 95 Resource Directory." If Microsoft drivers do not support the display adapter, contact the display-adapter vendor for updated drivers.

▶ **To check where the driver is loading from**

- To ensure that a Windows 95 version of the display driver is installed, check the [boot] section of SYSTEM.INI for this entry:

```
display.drv=pnpdrvr.drv
```

If this entry is specified, the display entries in SYSTEM.INI are ignored, and the display drivers are loaded from the Registry. If the entry specifies any driver other than PNPDRVR.DRV, the display drivers are loaded from SYSTEM.INI.

### The display adapter is not recognized.

If Windows 95 does not recognize the display adapter, try using the basic VGA drivers (a generic 640x480, 16-color driver). If you have a vendor-supplied driver disk for the display adapter, you can install the OEM drivers. If the drivers do not support Windows 95, some advanced display features are disabled.

### Errors occur when initializing the display adapter.

If an error occurs during display adapter initialization, the computer stops responding. To restart the computer, press CTRL+ALT+DEL.

This problem might occur if you are using a video accelerator card and you change the display from the default setting (640x480, 16 colors) to 1024x768, 256 colors in the Display properties dialog box. Although Windows 95 might accept the changes, the error still results. The Super VGA (SVGA) driver (1024x768) included with Windows 95 is designed for nonaccelerated SVGA display adapters only. To correct this problem, change the display driver back to the default VGA setting.

▶ **To change your display driver back to VGA**

1. Restart the computer, press F8 when you see the Starting Windows 95 message, and then choose Safe Mode.

2. In the Display option in Control Panel, click the Settings tab.

3. Click the Change Display Type button, and then click the Change button for the Adapter Type.

4. Click Show all Devices, click Generic Display Drivers, and then click OK. When asked whether to use the current driver or a new driver, click Current.

If you want to use a high-resolution display driver with Windows 95, consult your display adapter manufacturer for the proper driver to use.

### A Windows 3.1 display driver doesn't support advanced features.

Windows 95 cannot support some display features when a Windows 3.1-compatible driver is being used. If you are using a Windows 3.x compatible display driver with Windows 95, some advanced features (such as dynamic resolution changes, font smoothing, and automatic fallback to VGA) will not work.

Some Windows 3.1 drivers require the screen resolution to be specified in the [boot.description] section of the SYSTEM.INI.

### Motion is jerky during multimedia playback.

- Use Add New Hardware in Control Panel to verify that the appropriate display driver is installed for the display adapter you are using.

- Check to see if MSCDEX is installed. If so, remove it and use Windows 95 CD-ROM File System (CDFS) drivers.

- If the problem occurs for MS-DOS–based applications, check and maximize available XMS memory in the VM.

# Correcting Problems with SCSI Devices

### A SCSI device fails to work.

The SCSI and CD-ROM support built into Windows 95 requires that CD-ROM drives provide SCSI parity to function properly. For many drives, this is a configurable option or is active by default. Examples of drives that do not provide or support SCSI parity are the NEC® CDR-36 and CDR-37 drives.

If you have trouble with a SCSI drive, make sure the SCSI bus is set up properly (refer to your hardware documentation for specific details).

In some cases, adding or removing a SCSI adapter might prevent your computer from starting correctly. Check the following:

- The ends of the SCSI bus must have terminating resistor packs (also called terminators) installed.

  If you have only internal or only external SCSI devices, the ends of the bus are probably the SCSI adapter and the last device on the cable. If you have both internal and external SCSI devices, the adapter is probably in the middle of the bus and should not have terminators installed. If you disconnect a device that has terminators installed (such as an external CD-ROM drive), be sure to install terminators on whatever device then becomes the last one on the bus. One of the devices on the SCSI bus (usually the adapter) should be configured to provide termination power to the bus.

  Windows 95 supports up to seven external SCSI devices in a chain, plus internal connections. In addition to the requirement that the last external and last internal SCSI device must be terminated, some hardware has additional requirements for where it must be placed in the SCSI chain.

- Removable media must be mounted on the drive before running Setup.

  If you have a SCSI hard disk drive that uses removable media, such as a cartridge drive, make sure the media is mounted on the drive before running Setup. If no media is mounted on the drive, errors might occur during Setup that prevent installation of Windows 95.

### A SCSI device works with MS-DOS but not Windows 95.

For many SCSI hardware devices, you can specify command-line parameters when the driver is loaded. By default, the Windows 95 miniport driver runs without parameters (in the same way it does for real-mode drivers). If you want to use a command-line parameter, you can add it to the Settings property for the SCSI controller. For real-mode parameters that the controller supports (and if the device has a Windows 95 .MPD file), you can enter parameters in the Adapter Settings box in the controller's properties.

For information about the switches that can be used for a particular SCSI device, see the documentation from the device manufacturer. There are no additional parameters added by Microsoft.

For example, if your SCSI adapter has full functionality under MS-DOS, but not under Windows 95, you can add any device parameters previously specified in CONFIG.SYS to the Adapter Settings box. As another example, for Adaptec™ 7700 SCSI devices, you might specify **removable=off** to disable support for removable media if you want to load another ASPI removable disk.

### Setup does not automatically detect the SCSI CD-ROM drive.

Windows 95 needs exact SCSI ID information for Toshiba® 3201, NEC 3x, and Texel 5201 CD-ROM drives. To make this information available to Windows 95, you must run the Add New Hardware wizard in Control Panel and manually choose to install specific hardware rather than running automatic detection of new hardware.

### When running MSCDEX real-mode drivers, Windows 95 does not load protected-mode drivers from a SCSI CD-ROM drive.

If you are running MSCDEX.EXE and it loads real-mode drivers, you cannot load protected-mode drivers from a CD-ROM. In this case, you should comment out the lines in the AUTOEXEC.BAT and CONFIG.SYS files that MSCDEX.EXE placed there. For example:

```
rem device=c:\sbrpo\drv\sbpcd.sys/d:mscd001 /p:220
rem c:\windows\command\mscdex.exe /s /v /d:mscd001
```

Then you should restart the computer to allow Windows 95 to automatically detect the CD-ROM drive and its protected-mode drivers.

Notice that Windows 95 will automatically comment out these lines if the protected-mode drivers are on the CD-ROM from which you installed the drivers; that is, if you choose automatic detection, Windows 95 detects the hardware and its drivers and automatically comments out the real-mode drivers.

### Setup doesn't recognize the correct SCSI CD-ROM drive.

Windows 95 Setup does recognize multiple CD-ROM drives connected to the same SCSI host adapter. Therefore, if it doesn't recognize one of the CD-ROM drives, it is a hardware problem. For example, it could be caused by a legacy adapter with more than one device with the same SCSI ID.

### A SCSI tape drive or scanner does not show up in Device Manager.

Windows 95 does not assign drive letters to tape drives and scanners because they have no drive to assign a letter to, that is, they have no official class. Therefore, they appear as Unknown Devices in Device Manager. After you start Windows 95, it asks if you have a driver for these devices. If you have Windows 95 drivers, click Yes. To use existing real-mode drivers, click No, and then type the path to where the drivers are located. Windows 95 will continue to recognize and support these devices even though they are listed as Unknown Devices.

**A SCSI drive does not show up in My Computer.**

This probably indicates that there is something wrong with the SCSI drivers in CONFIG.SYS and AUTOEXEC.BAT, or that the protected-mode SCSI drivers fail to load. Look for an IOS.LOG file and check its entries, as described in "Real-Mode Drivers and the IOS.INI Safe Driver List" earlier in this chapter.

**Running the DIR command on the SCSI drive produces strange characters.**

If you type **dir** and strange characters appear on the screen, the hard disk might be a SCSI drive that requires double buffering which is not loaded. Verify that MSDOS.SYS has **DoubleBuffer=1** in the [Options] section. (However, if you start the computer using MS-DOS version 6.0 or higher, double-buffering is provided when SMARTDRV.EXE is loaded in CONFIG.SYS.)

# Correcting Problems with Other Devices

### The system stalls when accessing CD-ROM.

After you press CTRL+ALT+DEL to shut down and restart the computer, Windows 95 might be unable to find the CD-ROM or stall when trying to access the drive; sometimes, pressing CTRL+ALT+DEL will not reset the computer. This might occur if Windows 95 is relying on real-mode drivers for the Sound Blaster® or Media Vision™ Pro Audio proprietary CD-ROM drive. If this is the case, you cannot access anything on the CD-ROM because its drivers cannot load. If this happens, turn off and then restart the computer. Use the Add New Hardware option in Control Panel to install the protected-mode drivers provided with Windows 95 for the specific CD-ROM device.

### CD-ROM performance problems when AutoPlay is enabled.

This problem sometimes occurs with both protected-mode and real-mode (MSCDEX) drivers. To fix it, turn off AutoPlay, which is enabled by default, and then turn it back on again.

### .WAV files cannot be played.

If Windows 95 cannot recognize the sound card, you might not be able to play .WAV files.

▶   **To verify sound card settings**

1.  In Device Manager, click the Sound controller.

2.  Double-click the specific sound card, and then in the card's properties, click the Drivers tab so you can verify the drivers.

3.  Click the Resources tab, and verify IRQ settings.

4.  Check the Conflicting Device List, and verify that no conflicts for the sound card settings appear in the list.

### Ports for sound cards with multiple CD-ROM adapters are not detected.

If a sound card has multiple CD-ROM adapters, they often include a program that activates the port to be used. This program must run before Windows 95 runs. If it doesn't, Windows 95 won't detect the port.

### An input device fails.

- Check the physical connection.
- In Device Manager, check the driver used for the device.
- Check for conflicts with the I/O and IRQ resources used.
- Check for conflicting drivers or applications.

### The mouse moves erratically or keyboard input fails.

- In Device Manager, check the mouse and keyboard drivers, replacing them if necessary.
- In the Mouse option in Control Panel, check Motion configuration for pointer speed.
- Check the port used for the mouse.
- Check the physical connection of the mouse and keyboard.
- Make sure there are no entries for real-mode mouse drivers in CONFIG.SYS, AUTOEXEC.BAT, WIN.INI, and SYSTEM.INI.
- When the Starting Windows 95 message appears, press F8, and then choose the Logged option. Check the BOOTLOG.TXT file and verify that the mouse driver is loading.

### Mouse reports GROWSTUB errors.

If you were using the Microsoft Mouse Manager with Windows 3.1, Windows 95 Setup automatically updates the POINTER.EXE and POINTER.DLL files in the Mouse directory. If these files are not updated correctly, the mouse might stall and report GROWSTUB as a running task in the Close Program dialog box. To fix this problem, remove all references to the mouse in the AUTOEXEC.BAT and CONFIG.SYS files, and make sure the correct POINTER files were copied to the Mouse directory and not just the Windows directory.

### Advanced Power Management 1.0 (APM) is not available.

Windows 95 Setup installs APM support automatically if it was installed on the computer previously. You can enable APM support after Setup by using Device Manager.

▶  **To enable APM under Windows 95 if it was disabled during Setup**

1. In Device Manager, click System Devices, click the APM entry, and then click Properties.

2. In the APM properties, click Settings.

3. In the Settings dialog box, click Enable Power Management Support if this option is not checked.

   If no APM drivers were installed under previous versions of Windows, no check mark appears. Checking this box enables the drivers.

4. Click Force APM 1.0 Mode.

   This option forces Windows 95 to use an APM 1.1 BIOS in APM 1.0 mode. In some cases, a BIOS incorrectly handles the new functions provided by APM 1.1 but functions properly when used in 1.0 mode. On some computers, this is checked automatically during Setup.

5. Click Disable Intel SL Support to disable the SL check.

   In some cases, a BIOS incorrectly handles an unsupported call to the APM interfaces of some SL-type chipsets, causing the computer to stop responding. Disabling this option prevents the system from not responding.

6. Click Disable Power Status Polling to prevent Windows 95 from calling the APM interface to check current battery level.

   Windows 95 calls the APM interface for this purpose with greater frequency than earlier versions of Windows 3.x, causing some computers to shut down. Disabling this feature prevents this, but also disables the battery meter.

# Disks and File Systems

This chapter introduces Windows 95 disk and file system support. It describes how to use Windows 95 utilities to partition and format disks, and how to use DriveSpace, Disk Defragmenter, and ScanDisk to manage disks and data. This chapter also discusses how to manage long filenames.

**In This Chapter**

Disks and File Systems: The Basics  645
Disks and File Systems: The Issues  646
Partitioning Hard Disks  647
    Partitioning Drives  647
    Formatting a Hard Disk  650
    Assigning Drive Letters for Removable Media  652
Disk Management Overview  653
Managing the Recycle Bin to Free Disk Space  655
Using Microsoft Backup  656
Defragmenting Disks  656
Using ScanDisk  658
Using Disk Compression with Windows 95  661
    Overview of Compressed Volume Files and Host Drives  662
    Using DriveSpace for Disk Compression  663
Microsoft Plus! Utilities for Disk Management  670
    DriveSpace 3 Compression: An Overview  671
    Scheduling Programs with System Agent  675
File Systems Overview  678
Using Long Filenames  679
    Long Filename Support in Windows 95  680
    Long Filenames and Network Compatibility  681
    Administrative Considerations for Long Filenames  684

*(continued)*

Technical Notes on Disk Device Support    690
    Supported Disk Devices    690
      VCACHE and CDFS Supplemental Cache    695
Troubleshooting File and Disk Problems    696

# Disks and File Systems: The Basics

The new 32-bit, protected-mode file system support in Windows 95 allows optimal access to hard disks, CD-ROM drives, and network resources. The new file system support means faster, better performance for all file I/O operations than what was available under earlier version of MS-DOS or Windows.

Because of enhancements to the file systems, there is no longer an eight-character limit on filenames that was imposed by the FAT file system under MS-DOS. You can use long filenames and directory names in Windows 95 and in any applications that support long filenames.

The enhanced FAT file system in Windows 95 also permits exclusive access to a disk device for file system utilities. File system utilities, such as ScanDisk, require exclusive access to the file system to ensure data integrity in a multitasking environment. Otherwise, if a file on the disk were to be saved while the utility was writing information to the disk at the same time, data corruption could occur.

Exclusive disk access means you can now run disk management and optimization utilities without quitting Windows. You can even complete tasks such as disk defragmentation without stopping work in other applications. The exclusive access support is used by the disk utilities provided with Windows 95 and can be used in Windows-based disk management utilities from any vendors that take advantage of the related API in their utilities.

The disk utilities provided with Windows 95 include the following.

**Fdisk and Format.**  These utilities, which you can use to partition and format disks, behave exactly as their counterparts in MS-DOS versions 6.x. You can use a graphical form of Format in Windows Explorer.

**Disk Defragmenter.**  This utility (also called a disk optimizer) is used to defragment information on a disk. Using Disk Defragmenter regularly helps to minimize the area on the disk in which Windows 95 needs to look to load information.

**DriveSpace (DBLSPACE).**  The built-in support for DriveSpace disk compression is completely compatible with DoubleSpace and DriveSpace disk compression provided with MS-DOS 6.x. Compression is performed by using a 32-bit virtual device driver that delivers improved performance over previously available real-mode compression drivers, and frees conventional memory for use by MS-DOS–based applications. Existing users of DoubleSpace and DriveSpace do not need to change the compressed volume file (.CVF) that they are using currently, and they do not need to take any special actions when installing Windows 95.

**ScanDisk.**  This graphical disk analysis and repair tool runs under Windows 95 to help users check the integrity of disks and to remedy the problems it detects. Users can choose to scan the computer's files and folders or the disk surface for errors.

# Disks and File Systems: The Issues

You should use disk and file management utilities designed specifically for Windows 95. This way, you can avoid losing long filenames and data. In some cases (as described in "Using the LFNBK Utility for Temporary Compatibility" later in this chapter), you can use the LFNBK utility to remove and later restore long filenames on a disk so that you can run a utility that is not compatible with long filenames.

---

Caution  Stacker® 4.0 from STAC Electronics and similar disk optimization utilities, including DriveSpace 6.x for MS-DOS, are not compatible with long filenames. If you already have such compression software on the computer, you should not experience problems. However, if you install such software under Windows 95, the long filenames already on the computer will be destroyed, and other critical errors could occur.

Contact the software manufacturer for information about Windows 95-compatible upgrades for your disk utilities.

---

You can ensure disk integrity by putting ScanDisk in the STARTUP directory so that it runs each time the operating system starts. Also, back up critical files once a week to ensure data security, and run Disk Defragmenter at regular intervals to optimize disk I/O performance.

Windows 95 automatically provides long filename support. However, Windows 95 file systems and OS/2 HPFS each have slightly different ways of defining 8.3 filename aliases for long filenames. If you are using a mixed network environment, be sure to understand the differences (as described in this chapter). Then to help minimize any naming conflicts, define and publish a file naming policy for users who share files.

# Partitioning Hard Disks

This section describes how to use the Fdisk utility to configure a hard disk. For example, if you want to combine several partitions into one large partition, you must use Fdisk; there is no method for automatically combining partitions.

---

**Caution**   Do not repartition the hard disk by using Fdisk if the computer has certain types of partitions, such as those created by Disk Manager, Storage Dimensions SpeedStor®, Priam®, or Everex™ partitioning programs, which replace the BIOS in interactions between MS-DOS and the hard-disk controller. Instead, use the same disk-partitioning program that was used to partition the disk. For example, if you use SpeedStor on a computer that has more than 1024 cylinders, do not carry out the following procedures.

To determine whether the computer has a partition created by using one of these disk-partitioning programs, search for the following files: DMDRVR.BIN (Disk Manager), SSTOR.SYS (SpeedStor), HARDRIVE.SYS (Priam), and EVDISK.SYS (Everex). Usually, you will find **device=** entries for these files in CONFIG.SYS. If you need help repartitioning the hard disk or are unsure whether the BIOS is being replaced, contact the manufacturer of the original disk-partitioning program.

---

To configure a hard disk, you must perform the following tasks:

- Create a startup disk by using the Add/Remove Programs option in Control Panel
- Back up the files on the hard disk
- Repartition the hard disk by using Fdisk
- Format the hard disk
- Restore the backed-up files

The steps for partitioning and formatting are described in the following section.

# Partitioning Drives

If you want to repartition a hard disk into one drive, you must first use Fdisk to delete all existing partitions and logical drives, and then create a new primary partition and make it active. You can also repartition a hard disk so that it has more than one logical drive. Notice that, although Windows 95 replaces MS-DOS, the partitions that Fdisk creates are still called DOS partitions.

Although Fdisk is an MS-DOS–based application in Windows 95, however, it can run in a window (a VM).

The Windows 95 emergency startup disk contains a copy of Fdisk, which you can use if a hard disk becomes unreadable.

To configure a hard disk by using Fdisk, complete the following tasks:

- Delete DOS partitions, logical drives, the extended DOS partition, and the primary DOS partition

- Create a new primary DOS partition

- Create an extended partition and logical drives, if you want any

**Caution**  If you use Fdisk to repartition a hard disk, all the files on the original partitions will be deleted. Be sure to back up all data files on a partition before using Fdisk.

▶ **To start Fdisk**

- At the command prompt, type **fdisk**

  –Or–

  If you are starting Fdisk from a startup disk, make sure the disk is in drive A, and then restart the computer by pressing CTRL+ALT+DEL. At the command prompt on the A drive, type **fdisk**

When you run Fdisk, the Fdisk Options screen appears, in which you can choose to do the following:

- Create a partition or logical drive

- Set the active partition

- Delete a partition or logical drive

- Display partition information

If the computer has two or more hard disks, Fdisk displays a fifth option on the Fdisk Options screen named Change Current Fixed Disk Drive. You can switch to another disk drive by choosing this option. Changing the current hard disk drive while using Fdisk doesn't change the current drive when you return to the command prompt.

Each Fdisk screen displays a Current Fixed Disk Drive line, followed by a number. If the computer has only one hard disk drive, this number is always 1. If the computer has more than one hard disk drive, the number shows the disk Fdisk is currently working on. The first hard disk drive on the computer is 1, the second is 2, and so on. The Current Fixed Disk Drive line refers only to physical disk drives.

---

**Note**   If you installed a disk-compression program from Microsoft or another vendor, Fdisk displays the uncompressed, not the compressed, size of the drives. Also, Fdisk might not display information about all the drives used by a disk-compression program from another vendor.

---

## Deleting Partitions and Logical Drives

You can use Fdisk to delete partitions before creating a new primary partition. You must delete partitions in the following order:

- Any non-DOS partitions
- Any logical drives in the extended DOS partition
- Any extended DOS partition
- The existing primary DOS partition

---

**Important**   Back up your files before deleting partitions. If the computer has a non-DOS partition on a hard disk, copy the data files from the partition to floppy disks or a network drive to back them up. For more information, see the documentation that came with the non–MS-DOS operating system or the disk-partitioning program from another vendor.

---

▶ **To delete a partition or logical drive**

1. In the Fdisk Options screen, press 3, and then press ENTER. The Delete DOS Partition Or Logical DOS Drive screen appears.

2. Press the number as shown on the screen for the kind of partition you want to delete, and then press ENTER.

3. Follow the directions on the screen, and repeat the steps for deleting any additional logical drives or partitions.

If Fdisk cannot delete a non-DOS partition, quit Fdisk, delete the non-DOS partition by using the software used to create it, and then restart Fdisk.

## Creating a Primary MS-DOS Partition

After you have deleted a primary DOS partition, you can create a new primary DOS partition.

▶ **To create a primary DOS partition**

1. In the Fdisk Options screen, press 1, and then press ENTER. The Create DOS Partition Or Logical DOS Drive screen appears.

2. Press 1, and then press ENTER. The Create Primary DOS Partition screen appears.

3. If you want the partition to be the maximum size, press ENTER. Then insert a startup disk in drive A, and press any key.

   If you do not want the partition to be the maximum size, press N, and then press ENTER. Another Create Primary DOS Partition screen appears.

4. To specify the partition size you want, follow the instructions on-screen, and then press ENTER.

   You can specify the partition size as a percentage of disk space or in megabytes of disk space. If you specify a percentage of disk space, include a percent sign (%) after the number.

5. Press ESC to return to the Fdisk Options screen, and follow the instructions on-screen to make the primary DOS partition active. Then return to the Fdisk Options screen.

   If you have not allocated all the space on a hard disk to the primary DOS partition, you can create an extended DOS partition and logical drives by choosing the Create Extended DOS Partition option in Fdisk. You specify the partition size you want as a percentage or number of megabytes of disk space.

   If you don't want to create an extended partition, press ESC to quit Fdisk. Then insert a startup disk in drive A, and press any key to continue.

# Formatting a Hard Disk

You cannot format a hard disk by using Windows 95 Setup. The hard disk must be formatted before you can run Windows 95 Setup. However, if Windows 95 is already installed, you might need to reformat the hard disk, as described in the following procedure.

---

**Note** If the disk was compressed by using DriveSpace, you must use the Format option in DriveSpace to format the compressed drive.

---

▶ **To format a hard disk drive**

- In Windows Explorer, right-click the drive icon for that disk, and then click Format.

  You cannot use this method on a hard disk containing open files, including the drive where Windows 95 resides.

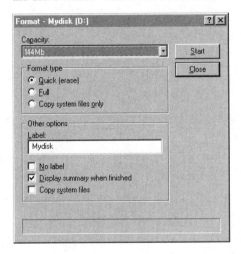

▶ **To format a hard disk by using the Windows 95 startup disk**

1. Make sure a startup disk is in drive A. Then, at the command prompt, type the following:

   **format *drive_letter*:**

   For *drive_letter*, type the letter of the drive you want to format.

   If you are formatting drive C, copy system files to the hard disk by typing the following at the command prompt:

   **format c: /s**

   When the warning message appears, proceed with formatting by pressing Y. Then press ENTER.

2. When formatting is complete, type a volume label (if you want one), and then press ENTER.

3. If you want to format other drives, repeat steps 1 and 2.

4. Remove the floppy disks from all floppy disk drives, and restart the computer by pressing CTRL+ALT+DEL.

# Assigning Drive Letters for Removable Media

Whenever a removable media device is present, the Windows 95 volume tracker ensures that the correct media is in the device and reports improper media removal or insertion.

The volume tracker keeps track of removable media in two ways:

- On non–write-protected floppy disks, the volume tracker writes a unique ID in the disk's FAT header. This ID is different from the volume serial number

- On write-protected floppy disks, the volume tracker caches each disk's label, serial number, and BIOS parameter block

Windows 95 supports existing removable media with MS-DOS–compatible partitions, which usually are created by using Fdisk utilities from other vendors. You can use Fdisk for Windows 95 to create partitions on INT 13-based removable media.

Windows 95 does not perform volume tracking based on the volume serial number because all removable media do not have serial numbers or some might have duplicate serial numbers (as is the case with bulk-formatted floppy disks). Therefore, the file system driver must assign unique serial numbers to removable media the first time there is a request to mount the specific media, unless unique numbers have already been written to the media. These unique numbers identify the media for volume tracking.

---

**Note**  For volume tracking with NEC® floppy-disk change detection, if the system detects a change line on a volume, the change line is used for subsequent I/O requests to the media.

---

You can control the number of drive letters to be reserved during system startup for each removable media drive.

▶ **To reserve drive letters for removable media**

1. In the System option in Control Panel, click the Device Manager tab.

2. In the hardware list, double-click the item that represents the removable device.

3. In the Properties dialog box, click the Settings tab.

4. In the Reserved Drive Letters area, select a letter in the Start Drive Letter list to define the first drive to be assigned to this device. In the End Drive Letter list, select the last drive to be assigned to this device. Click OK.

5. To close the System properties dialog box, click OK.

6. When prompted, restart the computer.

The **MaxRemovableDrivePartition** entry in the Registry allocates the drive letters to be used by partitions on removable media. If this entry is not present in the Registry, the number of drive letters to be assigned is based on the number of partitions present on the media when the system starts. If no media are present at startup, Windows 95 reserves one drive letter for each of the removable media.

To support variable-sized disks and partitions, Windows 95 recalculates the disk geometry every time a media change is detected. If you insert media with more partitions than specified by the **MaxRemovableDrivePartition** entry in the Registry, a message warns you that some partitions on the media are not accessible in the current configuration and prompts you to increase the value of **MaxRemovableDrivePartition**.

# Disk Management Overview

Windows 95 includes several tools for managing disks, protecting data, and ensuring good disk performance. To keep your computer in good working order, use these programs on a regular basis. To determine which tasks are necessary to manage your computer, consider the following.

| To ensure that | Do this |
| --- | --- |
| Files aren't lost if the hard disk fails | Run Microsoft Backup or a network backup agent. For information, see Chapter 16, "Remote Administration." |
| The computer can access files quickly and efficiently | Defragment the hard disk. For information, see "Defragmenting Disks" later in this chapter. |
| Lost clusters don't take up space on a disk, or the hard disk is not damaged | Run ScanDisk. For information, see "Using ScanDisk" later in this chapter. |
| Space is available on the hard disk | Use various tips for freeing disk space, and use disk compression. For information, see "Managing the Recycle Bin to Free Disk Space" later in this chapter and "Using Disk Compression with Windows 95" later in this chapter. |

The routine for managing a computer's hard disks might include automatically running ScanDisk when starting the computer to check the integrity of the hard disk, backing up files once a week, and occasionally using the Disk Defragmenter to defragment the hard disk. No matter what your computer management plan, carry it out at regular intervals.

You can also use a scheduling utility such as System Agent in Microsoft Plus! for automatic disk maintenance. For information, see "Microsoft Plus! Utilities for Disk Management" later in this chapter.

---

**Note**  For best results, do not run other programs while running either Disk Defragmenter or ScanDisk. Although you can use the computer for other tasks while running either of these utilities, each time you write to the disk, the utility automatically reinitiates itself to work with the current view of the disk.

---

### About Volume Locking for Disk Utilities

Windows 95 provides volume-locking APIs that applications such as disk utilities can use to control direct disk access when the computer uses the Windows 95 32-bit file system. (In Windows for Workgroups 3.11, VFAT generated an error whenever a disk utility tried to access the drive in protected mode.)

Disk utilities usually make absolute INT 25 and INT 26 disk calls, which do not require file system drivers. Instead of calling INT 21 and INT 13 to access the disk, the application calls INT 25 for reads and INT 26 for writes.

When an application is going to change the disk structure (such as a disk utility preparing to defragment the disk), it should first use the volume locking APIs to lock that volume or drive, so that no other application can write to that volume and interfere with its operations. When the application has completed its work, it must unlock the volume before the system can resume normal operation.

If a utility does not use volume locking before it attempts to read from or write to the disk, Windows 95 returns an error and causes it to fail. All utilities included with Windows 95, such as the Disk Defragmenter and ScanDisk, use volume locking. Such utilities cannot be used with Windows NT because Windows NT does not allow utilities to make direct calls to the hardware.

# Managing the Recycle Bin to Free Disk Space

When you delete a file or directory, it is moved to the Recycle Bin, but it still takes up space on the hard disk. You can use one of the following methods to ensure disk space is not being used by the contents of the Recycle Bin:

- Avoid moving items to the Recycle Bin by pressing SHIFT when you use the mouse or keyboard to delete items.
- Avoid moving items to the Recycle Bin by specifying that items are removed from the disk immediately when you delete them.
- Empty the Recycle Bin regularly.

You can also configure the Recycle Bin to use only a set amount of space so that you are prompted to empty the bin more often.

▶ **To configure the Recycle Bin**

1. Right-click the Recycle Bin icon, and then click Properties.

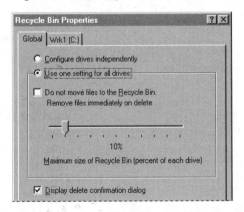

**Note**   You can configure properties separately for each hard disk drive on the computer by clicking the option named Configure Drives Independently.

2. If you want deleted items to be removed from the Recycle Bin immediately, make sure Do Not Move Files To The Recycle Bin is checked.

3. If you want to specify the amount of hard disk space the Recycle Bin can use, drag the slider to the desired percentage.

For more information about the Recycle Bin, see online Help.

# Using Microsoft Backup

Microsoft Backup, a Windows 95 utility for backing up data, provides options for backing up files to floppy disks or tapes, restoring from disks or tapes, and comparing backup file sets to files on the hard disk. Microsoft Backup supports the QIC 113 backup tape specification, which includes support for long filenames.

For users familiar with the Windows 3.1 Backup utility, the following list describes important differences in Backup under Windows 95:

- This version of Microsoft Backup does not support restoring backup sets created by MS-DOS version 6.x backup utilities.

- The recommended method for creating a complete backup file set for the computer is the Full System Backup option. This option automatically selects the files required for a system backup

  If you decide to modify the default selections (by clearing the check boxes for some folders), be sure that you select at least the Windows directory; otherwise, the Registry will not be backed up.

- When using the Backup tab in the Settings Options dialog box, notice that selecting Differential under the Type Of Backup option causes the utility to back up only files that have changed since the last time Backup was run. With this setting, new files will not be added to the file set and deleted files will not be removed.

For information about the Arcada® and Cheyenne® network backup agents, see Chapter 16, "Remote Administration." For information about how to use Backup, see online Help, which includes a list of the tape drives that are supported under Windows 95 and compatible with Windows 95.

# Defragmenting Disks

Over time, as programs read from and write to a hard disk, information stored on the disk can become fragmented—that is, files are stored in noncontiguous sectors. Fragmentation doesn't affect the validity of the information—the files are still complete when they are opened. But it takes much longer for the computer to read and write fragmented files than it does for unfragmented files.

To improve file access time, you can defragment uncompressed drives and compressed DriveSpace or DoubleSpace drives.

---

**Important**  Disk Defragmenter does not work with compressed drives created with most compression software from other vendors (such as those compressed with SuperStor), read-only drives, locked drives, network drives, FFS drives, or drives created with ASSIGN, SUBST, or JOIN.

---

▶ **To defragment a disk drive**

1. Click the Start button, click Run, and then type **defrag**

2. In the Select Drive dialog box, specify the drive that requires defragmentation, and then click OK.

   The Disk Defragmenter displays a dialog box telling you whether defragmentation is recommended for this disk or not. If this disk has low fragmentation, the Disk Defragmenter will not recommend defragmentation.

3. Click the Advanced button if you want to do any of the following:

   - Specify a defragmentation method (all files and free space, files only, or free space only). Depending on how badly the disk is defragmented, you can reduce the amount of time required to defragment a disk by choosing to defragment only files or free space.

   - Specify whether the drive should be checked for errors.

   You can check the option to save these optimization preferences for use each time you run Disk Defragmenter.

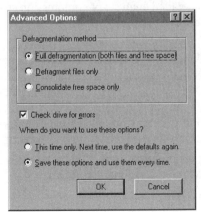

4. In the Disk Defragmenter dialog box, click Start to begin defragmenting the drive.

**Tip**  Showing details while the Disk Defragmenter is running causes it to take longer than it does when showing only summary information or running it minimized. For quickest performance, minimize the Disk Defragmenter window while the utility is running.

▶  **To see defragmentation information for a particular drive**

1. In My Computer, right-click the drive's icon, and then click Properties.

2. Click the Tools tab.

   The Tools properties dialog box shows the number of days since the last complete defragmentation process ran on the drive. You can also run Disk Defragmenter from this dialog box.

You can also use the **defrag** command with switches in a batch file. For more information about this command, see Appendix A, "Command-Line Commands Summary."

# Using ScanDisk

ScanDisk is a full-featured disk analysis and repair program. ScanDisk runs automatically when you start Windows 95 Setup. After Windows 95 is installed, you can use ScanDisk on both uncompressed and compressed drives. ScanDisk checks compressed drives created with compression software from other vendors, but it checks these drives as if they are uncompressed. ScanDisk, however, can provide a detailed analysis of compression structures on DoubleSpace and DriveSpace drives.

**Note**  Windows 95 provides two versions of ScanDisk: a new graphical Windows-based version that you can run from the Start menu or from Windows Explorer, and an MS-DOS–based version that is contained on the Windows 95 startup disk. For information about running ScanDisk from the command line or in batch files, see Appendix A, "Command-Line Commands Summary."

ScanDisk checks and fixes problems in the following areas on hard disk drives, floppy disk drives, RAM drives, and memory cards:

- File allocation table (FAT)
- Long filenames
- File system structure (lost clusters, cross-linked files)

- Directory tree structure
- Physical surface of the drive (bad sectors)
- DriveSpace or DoubleSpace volume header, volume file structure, compression structure, and volume signatures

---

**Note**  ScanDisk cannot find or fix errors on CD-ROM drives, network drives, or drives created by using **assign**, **subst**, **join**, or **interlnk**.

---

ScanDisk can check and repair mounted DriveSpace or DoubleSpace drives. You can run ScanDisk from the command prompt to check and repair unmounted compressed volume files (CVFs). When you run ScanDisk to check a compressed drive, by default, ScanDisk checks the host (physical) drive first. In general, you should allow it to do so because an error on the host drive could cause problems with the compressed drive.

▶ **To run ScanDisk**

1. Click the Start button, click Run, and type **scandisk**

---

**Note**  See the following procedure to run ScanDisk on unmounted CVFs.

---

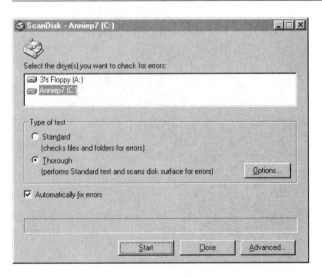

2. Click the drive you want to analyze or repair.

3. In the Type Of Test area, click Standard or Thorough.

   - Standard checks the files and folders on the selected drive for errors.

   - Thorough checks files and folders for errors, but it also checks the physical integrity of the disk's surface.

4. If you do not want ScanDisk to prompt you before repairing each error it finds, make sure Automatically Fix Errors is checked.

5. If you are running a thorough test, click the Options button to specify which areas of the disk to check or which type of processing to perform. Select the options you want to use, and then click OK.

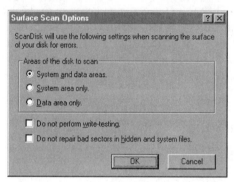

6. Click the Advanced button to set advanced options as needed, and then click OK. For information about each option, see online Help.

7. To begin checking the disk, click the Start button.

▶ **To run ScanDisk on unmounted CVFs**

- Click the Start button, click Run, and then type one of the following commands:

  **scandisk drvspace.*nnn***

  –Or–

  **scandisk dblspace.*nnn***

  where *nnn* is a number. This starts an MS-DOS session and runs ScanDisk on the corresponding DriveSpace or DoubleSpace CVF.

---

### Tips for Running ScanDisk

- Consider putting ScanDisk in the STARTUP directory to run it each time you start your computer.

  Or, if you have installed Microsoft Plus! for Windows 95, keep ScanDisk in the list of scheduled programs run by System Agent. For more information, see "Microsoft Plus! Utilities for Disk Management" later in this chapter.

- You can also run ScanDisk from the Tools properties dialog box for a drive. To do this, right-click that drive's icon, click Properties, and then click the Tools tab. Click the Check Now button to begin running ScanDisk.

- You can use the command-line equivalent command, **scandskw**, in a batch file. For more information about this command, see Appendix A, "Command-Line Commands Summary."

---

# Using Disk Compression with Windows 95

With Windows 95 DriveSpace, you can compress drives and manage drives compressed with DriveSpace or DoubleSpace. (You can even have drives of both compression types on your computer.)

When Windows 95 is installed, Setup replaces the DBLSPACE.BIN or DRVSPACE.BIN file in the root directory of the boot drive with versions that can be unloaded during the system startup process and replaced with DBLSPACX.VXD.

The version of DriveSpace provided with Windows 95 protects long filenames and includes other changes for compatibility with the VFAT file system.

This section presents an overview of CVFs and host drives, plus information about using DriveSpace for disk compression.

# Overview of Compressed Volume Files and Host Drives

A compressed drive is not a real disk drive, although to most programs it appears to be. Instead, a compressed drive exists on the hard disk as a compressed volume file (CVF). A CVF is a file with read-only, hidden, and system attributes, and that contains a compressed drive. Each CVF is located on an uncompressed drive, which is referred to as the CVF's host drive. A CVF is stored in the root directory of its host drive and has a filename such as DRVSPACE.000 or DBLSPACE.000.

Most CVFs can store more data than the space they use on their host drives; for example, a typical CVF might use 100 MB of space on its host drive but contain 200 MB of compressed data. DriveSpace assigns a drive letter to the compressed volume so that you can use it as a disk drive and can access the files it contains. The host drive will have a separate drive letter (although it might be hidden).

---

**Caution**  Do not tamper with a CVF. If you do, you might lose all the files on the compressed drive.

---

This following illustration shows the relationship between a compressed drive and a host drive (drive H), which is uncompressed. The **dir /c** command has been carried out on compressed drive C. This command lists the files in the current directory and displays the compression ratio of each file. The **dir /a** command has been carried out on drive H. This command lists the files in the current directory, including any files that have the hidden attribute. Drive H contains several files, including the compressed volume file for drive C, DBLSPACE.000.

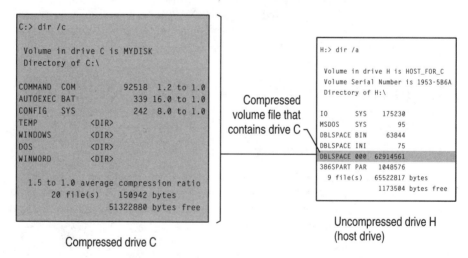

Compressed drive C

Uncompressed drive H
(host drive)

In this example, the CVF for drive C uses a substantial amount of space on drive H. However, drive C provides far more storage capacity than the space it uses on drive H.

# Using DriveSpace for Disk Compression

Using DriveSpace, you can compress and uncompress data on floppy disks, removable media, or hard disk drives. DriveSpace frees space on disks by compressing the data or space the disks contain. The first time you use DriveSpace to compress data or space on a drive, the disk will have 50 to 100 percent more free space than it did before.

You can use a compressed drive just as you did before compressing it. In addition, DriveSpace creates a new uncompressed drive, called the host drive, where it stores the CVF. If the host drive contains any free space in addition to the CVF, you can also use it to store files that must remain uncompressed.

---

**Note**  The version of DriveSpace included with Windows 95 can create a compressed drive of up to 512 MB. If your disk is very large, you might not be able to compress it as a single volume.

The version of DriveSpace available in Microsoft Plus! for Windows 95 can create a compressed drive of up to 2 GB, as described in "Microsoft Plus! Utilities for Disk Management" later in this chapter.

---

You can also create a new compressed drive from the free space on an uncompressed drive that is part of a nonremovable hard disk. After compression, you'll notice that the uncompressed drive contains less free space than it did before. This space is now being used by the new compressed drive, which is stored in a hidden file with a filename such as DBLSPACE.001.

Consider this scenario: suppose you have a 200 MB hard disk with 100 MB of data on it. Uncompressed, this disk has 100 MB of free space. You can increase the amount of disk space in either of two ways:

- You can use DriveSpace to compress both the data and the free space on the disk. Then, because DriveSpace reports file sizes of compressed files as though they were uncompressed, you will see that the disk is now a 400 MB disk with 100 MB of data and 300 MB of free space.

- You create a new compressed drive from the hard disk's free space. DriveSpace will report that you have two drives, one with 200 MB of free space and the other with 100 MB of data and no free space. (You can also create an empty drive using only part of the available free space.)

Although the option to compress a drive provides more usable space, the process takes longer than creating a new compressed drive because DriveSpace has to compress the data on the drive.

### Tip for Registry and Swap Files on Compressed Drives

The Registry can reside on compressed drives that were created by "preload" compression software such as Stacker 4.0, DoubleSpace, DriveSpace, and AddStor® SuperStor™/DS.

The swap file can reside on a compressed drive if a protected-mode driver (that is, DRVSPACE.VXD) controls the compressed drive. DriveSpace marks the swap file as uncompressible and, to reduce the amount of fragmentation, places the swap file as the last file in the CVF. Placing the file there also allows the swap file to expand.

If you want to change the size of the drive and if DriveSpace or a defragmentation utility detects a swap file at the end of the sector heap, you will be prompted to restart the computer.

If your swap file is on a compressed drive created by a real-mode compression drive, you should move the swap file to another drive, such as the host drive. For information about changing the location of your swap file, see Chapter 17, "Performance Tuning."

---

**Important**  Before you use DriveSpace to compress a drive, you should back up the files the drive contains.

---

▶ **To compress a drive**

1. Click the Start button, click Run, and type **drvspace**

2. In DriveSpace, click the drive you want to compress.

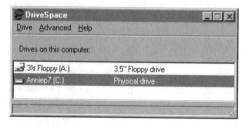

3. Click the Drive menu, and then click Compress.

   The Compress A Drive dialog box appears, listing the drive it is about to compress.

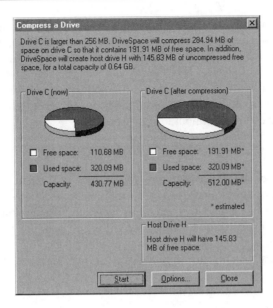

4. If you want to specify the drive letter or free space to leave available for
   the host drive, and whether the host will be hidden, click the Options button.
   Make modifications in the Compression Options dialog box as needed, and
   then click OK.

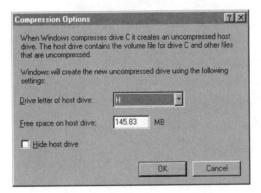

**Note**  By default, DriveSpace hides the host drive if the amount of free space
is less than 2 MB.

5. Click Start to continue.

6. DriveSpace prompts you to back up your files. If you want to back them up
   at this time, click the Back Up Files button.

7. To start compression, click the Compress Now button.

DriveSpace checks the drive for disk errors, and then it compresses the drive. This process can take from several minutes to several hours, depending on the speed of the hard disk and processor and on the amount of data the hard disk contains. Because DriveSpace checks and rechecks the validity of the data as it compresses files, the process is very safe. In fact, if the compression process is interrupted accidentally (for example, by a power outage), DriveSpace will recover and continue without losing any data.

If any files are open on the drive, DriveSpace will prompt you to close them. For drives that always have files opened (such as the drive containing Windows 95 or the drive containing a swap file), DriveSpace will restart the computer and use a limited version of Windows in place of Windows 95 while it compresses the drive. To do this, a directory named FAILSAVE.DRV is created that contains the system files required for this operation. After compression, your computer will restart again, this time with Windows 95. When the compression is completed, DriveSpace shows how much free space is available on the drive.

▶ **To create a new compressed drive**

1. In DriveSpace, click the drive that has free space you want to use to create the new compressed drive.

2. Click the Advanced menu, and then click Create Empty.

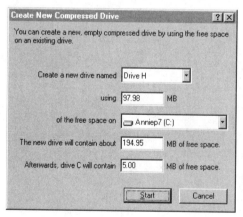

3. If you want to leave some free space on the original drive, decrease the value in the Using box.

4. To start compression, click the Start button.

▶   **To uncompress a drive**

1. In DriveSpace, click a drive to uncompress.

2. Click the Drive menu, and then click Uncompress.

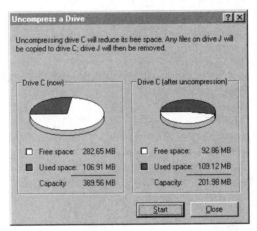

3. To start uncompressing, click the Start button.

   If there isn't enough space on the host drive to contain the uncompressed files, DriveSpace displays a warning. Otherwise, DriveSpace prompts you to back up files and shows the status of the process as it progresses.

---

**Note**  If you try to change the size of a drive that was mounted with a real-mode DriveSpace or DoubleSpace driver, you will be prompted to restart the computer so that the drive can be remounted under Windows 95. This will also occur for other operations using the real-mode DriveSpace driver.

---

## Using DriveSpace with Floppy Disks

You can use DriveSpace to increase the storage capacity of floppy disks. After compressing a floppy disk, you can use it to store data or to transfer data from one computer to another; both computers must be using Windows 95 DriveSpace or MS-DOS 6.x DoubleSpace.

After DriveSpace finishes compressing the floppy disk, the floppy disk contains more free space than it did before. You can use the floppy disk just as you did before compressing it.

Also, the computer has a new drive letter. This new drive letter represents the compressed floppy disk's host drive, which contains the floppy disk's CVF. Although both the new drive letter and the original drive letter refer to the same physical floppy disk drive, you can use only the original to access the disk drive.

In general, you use a compressed removable disk just as you do an uncompressed floppy disk. By default, DriveSpace automatically mounts a compressed floppy disk when you try to use that disk. This makes it possible to use the disk as if it were an uncompressed floppy disk.

▶ **To disable automounting**

1. In DriveSpace, click the Advanced menu, and then click Settings.

2. Make sure the option named Automatically Mount New Compressed Devices is cleared, and then click OK.

---

**Note**  Before it is mounted, a compressed floppy disk appears full. If you have disabled automounting, change to the floppy disk drive, and then type **dir**. The system usually lists only one file: a text file named READTHIS.TXT that briefly explains how to mount the floppy disk. The **dir** command usually reports that the floppy disk contains no free space because all the space is used by the CVF. The CVF is a file, usually named DBLSPACE.000, with hidden, read-only, and system attributes.

---

If automounting is disabled, you can still use compressed floppy disks, but you must mount them yourself.

▶ **To mount a compressed floppy disk in DriveSpace**

1. Insert the compressed floppy disk in a drive.

2. In DriveSpace, click the drive you want to mount.

3. Click the Advanced menu, and then click Mount.

The compressed floppy disk remains mounted and the files on it remain available until you change floppy disks or restart the computer.

## Changing Free Space and the Estimated Compression Ratio of a Compressed Drive

On an uncompressed drive, free space indicates how much additional data you can store on that drive. For example, if a drive has 2 MB of free space, you can expect to fit 2 MB of data on it. However, the free space on a compressed drive is only an estimate of how much data you can fit on that drive.

When you store a file on a compressed drive, DriveSpace compresses the file so that it takes up as little space as possible. Some files can be compressed more than others; for example, a bitmap file can be compressed much more than a program file. DriveSpace cannot detect the compressibility of files you haven't stored yet, so it only estimates a compressed drive's free space.

DriveSpace estimates a drive's free space by using the *estimated compression ratio*, which you can set to specify the compressibility of the files you plan to store. For example, if the estimated compression ratio is 3 to 1, DriveSpace calculates the drive's free space based on the assumption that each file to be stored can be compressed to one-third its original size.

Usually, the best compression estimate to use is the actual compression ratio for the files already stored on the drive. Sometimes you might want to reset the estimated compression ratio of each drive to match that drive's actual compression ratio.

You might want to change the estimated compression ratio if it differs greatly from the actual compressibility of the files to be stored. For example, if you plan to store extremely compressible files, such as bitmap files, you might want to specify a higher estimated compression ratio.

Changing a drive's estimated compression ratio does not affect how much DriveSpace actually compresses the files on that drive; it changes only the way DriveSpace estimates the free space on the compressed drive.

▶  **To change the estimated compression ratio**

1.  In DriveSpace, click the compressed drive you want to change.

2.  Click the Advanced menu, and then click Change Ratio.

3.  In the Compression Ratios area, type a new ratio box or drag the slider to the desired ratio. Click OK.

You can also adjust the amount of free space for a compressed drive or its host drive. This is equivalent to changing the size of the compressed drive and its CVF. When you increase free space on a compressed drive, you decrease it on its host, and vice versa.

▶ **To change the amount of free space on a drive**

1. In DriveSpace, click the drive on which you want to change the amount of free space.

2. Click the Drive menu, and then click Adjust Free Space.

3. In the Adjust Free Space dialog box, type a new value or use the slider to adjust the amount of free space available on the compressed and host drives. Click OK.

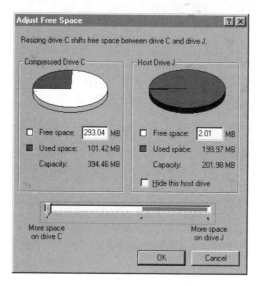

**Tip**  If the free space is highly fragmented, the usable free space might be less than what DriveSpace estimates. In some cases, you might not be able to store files on that drive, even though there appears to be plenty of space. To avoid this problem, run Disk Defragmenter regularly on compressed drives.

# Microsoft Plus! Utilities for Disk Management

Microsoft Plus! for Windows 95 provides the following additional capabilities for managing a computer running Windows 95:

- Enhancements to DriveSpace for higher compression ratios, support for creating compressed drives that are 2 GB in size, and compression information as part of drive and folder properties. To achieve greater performance and compression benefits, the Microsoft Plus! compression manager provides a new CVF format (DriveSpace 3).

- Compression Agent, a recompression utility that can run when your computer is idle to maximize the compression of files. With Compression Agent, the whole drive or designated files can be compressed when no other work is being done on the computer, rather than compressing files as they are saved during a work session. Compression Agent also allows you to designate different compression methods for different files and offers the UltraPack encoding format, a new method for achieving maximum compression.

- System Agent, a general-purpose scheduling program that comes preconfigured to maintain the computer's hard disks by running programs such as ScanDisk or Compression Agent at scheduled times. You can also use System Agent to schedule programs to run at specified intervals.

Microsoft Plus! for Windows 95 also includes features such as font smoothing, animated cursors, a set of themes for personalizing your computer, and more. For information about the dial-up networking server provided with Microsoft Plus!, see Chapter 28, "Dial-Up Networking and Mobile Computing."

Microsoft Plus! for Windows 95 is available as a retail product. Some computer equipment manufacturers might also include these utilities as part of the software provided with the computer. If these utilities were not provided on your computer, contact your software vendor about obtaining this product.

The following sections present some technical details about these additional disk management utilities. For information about installing, configuring, and using the utilities, see the Microsoft Plus! documentation (*Introducing Microsoft Plus!*) and online Help for each program.

# DriveSpace 3 Compression: An Overview

The new compression manager provided with Microsoft Plus! contains several enhancements over Windows 95 DriveSpace. These enhancements include the following:

- Enhanced compression with support for compressed drives up to 2 GB (earlier versions support volumes of up to 512 MB), using a 32K cluster size (earlier versions use 8K clusters)

- Support for storing compressed data for a cluster in multiple fragments when there are not enough continuous sectors on the disk to store the entire cluster

- Compression is up to 20 percent faster than standard Windows 95 compression on Pentium™-based computers. Other x86-based computers should also run faster with DriveSpace 3 when the compression is configured for best performance.

As with earlier CVF versions, a DriveSpace 3 CVF has a name in the form DRVSPACE.*nnn*, where *nnn* is the CVF sequence number in the range 000 through 254.

# DriveSpace and Disk Properties Enhancements

Microsoft Plus! adds the following features to Windows 95 DriveSpace:

- New DriveSpace settings for specifying whether to use compression, what type of compression to use, and how to use it.

- Support for compression enhancements on existing drives. You can upgrade existing DblSpace or DrvSpace drives to the Microsoft Plus! DriveSpace 3 format.

Microsoft Plus! also places drive-specific compression information (and the tools to manipulate it) where you would expect to find it: in the drive's properties. (System-wide compression settings and functions are still available in the DriveSpace programs.) To present this information, a Compression tab is added to the property dialog boxes for all local hard and floppy disk drives, except compressed drives created by software from other vendors. Uncompressed drives that are hosts for one or more compressed volume files also have a Compression tab added to their properties. For hidden host drives, you must use the DriveSpace program to view information about the drive.

# How Compression Works with DriveSpace 3

Microsoft Plus! achieves a higher compression ratio by compressing data in 32K blocks (instead of 8K blocks used for DblSpace or DrvSpace), and by supporting two new levels of compression: HiPack and UltraPack.

HiPack compression uses the same encoding format as standard compression, but searches the entire history buffer for matches instead of being limited to a history window.

UltraPack compression uses a different encoding format. UltraPack format offers better compression than standard or HiPack compression, but files compressed in UltraPack format are also slower to decompress. UltraPack compression is available only by running Compression Agent. You cannot configure DriveSpace to save files in UltraPack format automatically.

Because the new UltraPack encoding format used DriveSpace 3 CVFs, the Microsoft Plus! DRVSPACE.BIN and DRVSPACX.VXD must be installed to read these CVFs.

Microsoft Plus! compression can also store more data on the disk than with standard DriveSpace compression because of improved fragmentation handling. With standard DrvSpace or DblSpace CVFs, the data for a cluster must be stored in contiguous sectors. When the volume is highly fragmented, it is possible to have many free sectors but not enough contiguous sectors to store a cluster (which can require up to 16 sectors on a DblSpace or DrvSpace CVF, and up to 64 sectors on a DriveSpace 3 CVF). Microsoft Plus! compression avoids this problem by storing data for a fragmented cluster in a linked list of sectors when there are not enough continuous sectors to store the entire cluster. Microsoft Plus! compression also stores small directories in a single sector, whereas MS-DOS 6.x or Windows 95 require 16 sectors.

## Using Compression Agent

Compression Agent allows you make the following choices for compression methods:

- Whether specified files should be in UltraPack format, and whether to downgrade a file from UltraPack format

- Whether individual files, folders, or file types should be compressed and, if so, with what method

- Whether to use compression for the rest of your files and, if so, which type

You can start Compression Agent manually or, more commonly, you can have System Agent start it automatically when the computer is idle or at any time you specify. Compression Agent uses the Windows 95 Last Access Date to determine which files have not been used within a defined time (but Compression Agent does not modify the Last Access Date for any files).

The compression policies specified in the Compression Agent Settings dialog box control the standard policy used to compress files. However, you can also force or prevent a particular compression type on a particular file, or set of files, or folders, based on the following exceptions to the standard compression policy:

- Never compress

- Always compress with UltraPack format

- Always compress with HiPack format

The following shows the Compression Agent command line syntax:

**cmpagent** [*drive*: | **/all**] [**/noprompt**]

The following table describes the parameters for this command.

| Parameter | Description |
| --- | --- |
| *drive:* | Specifies drive to be recompressed. |
| **/all** | Specifies all local, fixed drives that are compressed. |
| **/noprompt** | Runs without waiting for the user to click Start, and without displaying a summary at the end. Errors are displayed. This switch can be shortened as **/nop**. |

## Guidelines for Fine-tuning Compression

Typically, you will want to use the default values for Microsoft Plus! compression, which specify using standard or no compression when saving files. You can then set System Agent to run Compression Agent when the computer isn't busy to compress seldom-used files into UltraPack format and all other files into HiPack format.

When you are deciding what methods and formats to use for compression, you must consider whether you want to configure compression to ensure maximum disk space or maximum system performance.

**Maximizing hard disk space.**  If you require that compression provide maximum disk space on a computer, then you might want to specify that UltraPack format be used to compress most files. (UltraPack format is recommended for Pentium-based computers.) In addition, you can specify that files be compressed as they are saved. If your computer is very fast, specify that HiPack format be used.

**Maximizing performance.**  If you require maximum system performance, remember that files compressed in UltraPack format are much slower to decompress, so that if you try to access a document or run an application that is compressed in UltraPack format, you might have to wait before you can begin working again. For slower computers that require maximum performance, you can use System Agent and Compression Agent to specify that all compression is done while the computer is idle instead of compressing the files as they are saved. This provides the benefits of compression without any performance impact related to updating files.

To ensure maximum performance, you might want to define the following when configuring compression:

- Use DriveSpace to specify that compression only occurs offline, not when each file is being saved, or specify that compression occurs only when disk space is low.
- Specify a high threshold for UltraPack, so that, for example, Compression Agent recompresses in UltraPack format only those files that haven't been accessed within 30 or more days.
- Set exceptions for files that should not be compressed in UltraPack format, such as executable files that you do not want to wait to have decompressed, even though you seldom use the files.

Notice that if you configure DriveSpace not to compress files as they are saved, or to compress files only when free space is low (using the Depends On Free Space option), the system reports free space as though files will not be compressed. As a result, the computer appears to have significantly less free space than it does when files are compressed as they are saved. However, if you use Compression Agent regularly, you will be able to store the same amount of data in this space.

# Scheduling Programs with System Agent

System Agent is a Win32-based application for scheduling programs to run at times you specify. After it is installed and configured on a computer, System Agent periodically runs programs according to your preferences. System Agent supports options for specifying when Compression Agent, Disk Defragmenter, ScanDisk, and other programs will run, and it provides notification of exceptional conditions such as low disk space.

Programs can be scheduled to run based on several criteria, such as the exact time and date, or a range of times, or whether the computer is idle or is running on batteries.

## How System Agent Works

System Agent consists of two parts, a scheduling engine (SAGE.EXE) and a separate application (SYSAGENT.EXE) for displaying and modifying the list of scheduled programs. The list of scheduled programs for System Agent is stored in the SAGE.DAT file, which is placed by default on the user's computer in the SYSTEM subdirectory of the folder where Microsoft Plus! is installed. However, this file can also be stored in a network directory. The **ConfigPath** value in the following Registry key defines the location of SAGE.DAT:

```
Hkey_Local_Machine\Software\Microsoft\Plus!\System Agent
```

The System Agent scheduling engine is a system service that runs continuously, monitoring the system and starting programs according to a database that contains the schedule you define for programs to be run. The only way you can interact with SAGE.EXE is by using the System Agent application.

The scheduling service starts automatically when the computer starts because its Setup program adds **sage.exe** as a value under the following Registry key:

```
Hkey_Local_Machine\Software\Microsoft\Windows\CurrentVersion\Run
```

You can quit SAGE.EXE if required—for example, if a setup program such as Windows 95 Setup prompts you to quit all applications before running—by choosing a command in the System Agent application.

▶ **To quit SAGE.EXE (the System Agent scheduling engine)**

- In the System Agent application click the Advanced menu, and then click Stop Using System Agent.

---

**Note** Removing the System Agent scheduling engine in this way completely removes both SAGE.EXE and SYSAGENT.EXE from memory and from the Registry. Consequently, System Agent will not start automatically, and scheduled programs will not be run.

To restore System Agent as an automatic service, run the System Agent application, and answer Yes when prompted to start SAGE.EXE.

---

System Agent also notifies you when the following events occur:

- Disk space falls below a predefined threshold

- System Agent fails to run a program at its scheduled time because the computer was not running, was running on batteries, or was otherwise not idle

- A DblSpace or DrvSpace CVF needs to be upgraded to DriveSpace 3

---

**Note** When Microsoft Plus! is installed, the ScanDisk and Defrag tools are enhanced to support DriveSpace 3 compression.

---

Upgrade notification (UPGRDALM.EXE) is scheduled to run when the computer first starts after Microsoft Plus! Setup. If there are no compressed drives to be upgraded, this notification is removed from the System Agent schedule and never runs again. If you choose to upgrade, the notification runs DriveSpace 3, and then removes itself from the System Agent schedule when it has confirmed that the drives have been upgraded or compressed.

---

**Note** The Upgrade notification runs by default at system startup although it doesn't appear in the list of programs scheduled in System Agent. For the Upgrade notification to appear in System Agent, change the **ShowSystemTasks** string value to **1** in the following Registry key:

`Hkey_Current_User\Software\Microsoft\Plus!\System Agent`

---

# Running Other Programs with System Agent: An Overview

In addition to the disk utilities such as ScanDisk or Compression Agent that can be scheduled to run with System Agent, you can use System Agent to schedule any kind of program that you want to run at a particular time or periodically. For example, you might use System Agent to do the following:

- Dial in to an online service during off-peak hours, look for certain topics, download the results, and hang up.

- Run a spreadsheet application such as Microsoft Excel, and use one or more macros to perform extensive computations on worksheets.

- Run backup software when the computer is not being used.

The methods you use for scheduling and running a program depend on whether the application was designed to work with System Agent.

If the program is designed to run with System Agent, you can use the Settings dialog box in System Agent to choose options to use when running the program. For example, you might designate that ScanDisk run a standard test nightly, but run a thorough test once a month. A System Agent-aware program might offer additional options to choose for running the program.

For all types of programs, you can define a command line for running the program. This command line can be one of the following:

- Any command-line statements that the program accepts. This might include only the program's executable name, the program name and a macro name or target filename, or the program name and any command-line switches.

- A batch file with any allowable actions. If you use a batch file, you can simulate a chained group of commands for running multiple programs or batch files. To do this, use the **start /W** command in the batch file, which starts a program and waits for the results before running the next statement in the batch file.

The general process for scheduling a program to run in System Agent includes the following basic steps:

1. Select the Schedule A New Program command in System Agent, and specify a program to schedule.

   This is where you can specify the command-line switches or a batch file to run (for a program that is not System Agent-aware).

2. Optionally, define a friendly name for the program.

3. Optionally, for System Agent-aware programs such as ScanDisk or Compression Agent, click the Settings button and define the options for running the program.

4. Click the When To Run button and specify the interval at which the program will run, such as daily, weekly, or monthly.

# File Systems Overview

With the Windows 95 installable file system, multiple file systems can coexist on the computer. Windows 95 includes the following file systems.

**VFAT.** In Windows 95, the 32-bit virtual File Allocation Table file system is the primary file system and cannot be disabled. VFAT can use 32-bit, protected-mode drivers or 16-bit real-mode drivers. Actual allocation on disk is still 12-bit or 16-bit (depending on the size of the volume), so FAT on the disk uses the same structure as previous versions of this file system. VFAT handles all hard disk drive requests, using 32-bit code for all file access for hard-disk volumes. VFAT was first introduced in Windows for Workgroups version 3.11 as an optional FAT file system that processed file I/O in protected mode.

**Network redirectors.** A network redirector (such as Microsoft Client for NetWare Networks or Client for Microsoft Networks) is a file system driver that accesses the network file system. Windows 95 supports multiple network redirectors simultaneously, as described in Chapter 32, "Windows 95 Network Architecture."

**CDFS.** The virtual CD-ROM file system has the same responsibilities for a CD-ROM device as VFAT has for a standard hard disk. If a CD-ROM device is detected, the CDFS driver loads dynamically. When CDFS is installed, the standard disk type-specific device and Disk SCSI translator are replaced with CD-ROM versions. The CDFS driver is a protected-mode version of MSCDEX.EXE, providing the interface from the CD-ROM device to the operating system, as described in "VCACHE and CDFS Supplemental Cache" later in this chapter and in Chapter 31, "Windows 95 Architecture."

If the CD-ROM drive and its drivers support the multisession command, CDFS can support multisession capabilities, which provide a method for adding data to a CD-ROM (this is most applicable to CD-Recordable media). The multisession command returns a number that identifies the first sector of the last session on the media so that CDFS can recognize the media.

All these file systems support long filenames and can use the protected-mode cache (VCACHE) for read-ahead. VFAT also supports lazy-write throughput, so applications can write immediately to the cache, and VFAT can write the information to disk later. For more information, see "VCACHE and CDFS Supplemental Cache" later in this chapter.

Other software vendors can also implement file systems. For example, a vendor might provide a file system that allows a computer running Windows 95 to connect to a different operating system (for example, Apple® Macintosh® or UNIX®) to share files.

The Installable File System Manager (IFSMGR) receives all INT 21 calls and determines which file system driver should receive the call to process it. IFSMGR uses a real-mode stub named IFSHLP.SYS to send INT 21 calls back to IFSMGR, as described in Chapter 31, "Windows 95 Architecture."

File system drivers manage the high-level I/O requests from applications. The file system driver processes requests from applications and initiates low-level I/O requests through the I/O Supervisor.

Protected-mode disk compression is not integrated into the file system, but is supported by a layer in the I/O subsystem. Windows 95 supports disk compression software created for earlier versions of MS-DOS, using their real-mode driver loaded from CONFIG.SYS.

# Using Long Filenames

For MS-DOS version 6.22 and earlier, filenames cannot exceed eight characters and filename extensions cannot exceed three characters in length (referred to as "8.3 filenames"). The period character (.) is used only to separate the filename from the filename extension. With long filename support in Windows 95, these 8.3 filename constraints are gone.

For all Windows 95 file systems, users can specify filenames that are up to 255 characters long and that can contain more than one period. These long filenames are any names that exceed 8.3 characters in length or contain any lowercase character or any character that is not valid in the 8.3 name space.

The following sections present information about long-filename support in Windows 95, including information and recommendations for supporting long filenames in a mixed network environment.

# Long Filename Support in Windows 95

For every long filename, an alias entry is generated automatically that complies with the 8.3 filename rules for backward compatibility. Automatically generated aliases are composed of the first six characters of the filename plus ~$n$ (where $n$ is a number) and the first three characters after the last period. So the filename ThisIsALong.File.Name is associated with the automatically generated alias THISIS~1.NAM. If the alias name already exists, the algorithm increments $n$, where $n$ begins with 2 until the system can find a unique filename.

---

**Note**  Neither the user nor an application can control the name created by the automatic alias process. Related issues are discussed in "Long Filenames and Network Compatibility" later in this chapter.

---

For the filename to comply with the 8.3 filename rules, it must use only the valid characters for an alias and it must be all uppercase. Short filenames are converted to uppercase by the IFSMGR before being passed to the file system driver. Valid characters for 8.3 filenames (and aliases) can be any combination of letters and numbers, a blank (ASCII 20H), ASCII characters greater than 127, and the following special characters:

```
$ % ' - _ @ ~ ` ! ( ) ^ # &
```

The following additional characters are valid in long filenames, but are not valid in alias names or 8.3 filenames:

```
+ , ; = [ ]
```

The following rules also apply for Windows 95 file systems:

- Maximum filename component length is 255 characters, including NULL
- Maximum path length is 260 characters, including NULL (compared to 80 characters for a short name)
- The OEM character set can be specified by an application if the application is written for that character set
- The long-filename directory entries use the Unicode character set to store the names

The filename and the alias are the same if the filename meets 8.3-filename rules (that is, if it contains only valid characters for an alias and it is all uppercase). This means that a filename using only valid characters for an alias and following the 8.3-filename format is still not the same as the alias name if it contains lowercase characters. However, in this case the alias is the uppercase version of the filename. For example, if the long filename is Examples.Txt, its alias is EXAMPLES.TXT. The case is preserved in the long filename. (Notice, though, that searches in the Windows 95 file system are not case-sensitive. So a search of the form "examples.txt" or "Examples.Txt" will find the same files.)

**Tip**   To see the alias for a file, right-click the file in any shell program such as Windows Explorer and then select Properties from the context menu. The value for MS-DOS Name in the General properties dialog box shows the alias assigned to this file. Also, the **dir** command at the command prompt shows the long filename.

# Long Filenames and Network Compatibility

By using a process called *tunneling*, Windows 95 preserves long filenames for files that are opened and saved using an application that does not recognize long filenames. Tunneling preserves long filenames on the local computer as well as files accessed across the network.

Tunneling is supported for any file system that IFSMGR recognizes. The file system in turn must "authorize" tunneling to allow its use in that file system. Tunneling is authorized automatically with VFAT.

Correct network tunneling is the responsibility of the server—that is, the server must be configured to support long filenames. A server running any edition of Windows NT 3.5 or Windows 95 file and printer sharing services will preserve long filenames. For example, a user who is running Windows for Workgroups might open and save a file on a peer server that is running file and printer sharing services (for either Microsoft networks or NetWare networks). In this case, the long filename will be preserved by the file system on the peer server, because the peer server uses IFSMGR and VFAT to store the data.

- NTFS, the Windows NT file system, supports long filenames, but includes architecture for security that Windows 95 does not use. Windows NT 3.5 supports long filenames on FAT drives and uses the same algorithm for aliases as used in Windows 95. However, Windows NT 3.1 doesn't recognize long filenames on FAT drives and removes them.

- HPFS file system supports long filenames with aliases similar to the method used in Windows 95.

- CDFS, the CD-ROM file system, also supports long filenames.

The following sections provide details about long filename support on various networks.

## Long Filenames with Windows 95 Protected-Mode Clients

Windows 95 protected-mode network clients (Client for Microsoft Networks and Client for NetWare Networks) support long filenames. If the network server that the computer is connected to supports long filenames, then Windows 95 can read, create, and copy local long-filename files on the network share. On some servers, the length of filenames, restricted characters, and the algorithm for creating 8.3 filenames from long filenames might differ from those under Windows 95.

Client for Microsoft Networks does not authorize tunneling, so tunneling is not used to preserve long filenames on down-level servers connected through the Windows 95 client (for example, a computer running Windows for Workgroups or LAN Manager Services). However, Microsoft Client for NetWare Networks does authorize tunneling, so tunneling can preserve long filenames in connections to older NetWare servers when running Client for NetWare Networks.

Windows 95 can access files on HPFS or NTFS partitions on remote drives. However, there is no built-in support in the release of Windows 95 for adding either of these file systems as another installable file system under Windows 95. Therefore, Windows 95 cannot access either an HPFS or NTFS partition on a local disk drive by using the file system drivers provided with Windows 95. (Other vendors, however, can add HPFS support.)

Please note the following interoperability exceptions for other file systems:

Long filenames can be used on computers running file and printer sharing services and can be viewed on computers using protected-mode Windows 95 network clients. Real-mode network clients running under Windows 95 can see only the 8.3 filename aliases.

If Windows 95 has been configured with File and Printer Sharing for NetWare Networks, any MS-DOS–based NetWare clients using NETX or VLM will see 8.3 filenames when browsing resources on the computer running Windows 95. Computers using Client for NetWare Networks can see long filenames.

Long filenames are supported for NetWare servers if the server is configured to use the OS/2 name space. For information, see Chapter 9, "Windows 95 on NetWare Networks."

---

**Note**   Older Microsoft or Microsoft-compatible clients (for example, LAN Manager, Workgroup Add-on for MS-DOS, Windows for Workgroups, and so on) cannot use shared folders that have long filenames. These older network clients might have problems connecting to and using a shared directory with a long filename as the directory name. Defining a short share name does not correct this problem.

---

## LAN Manager with HPFS and HPFS/386 Volumes

HPFS and HPFS/386 partitions on LAN Manager OS/2-based computers have a maximum filename length of 254 characters and use the 8.3 filename alias on the first instance. For example:

```
longfilenameold.tst --> LONGFILE.TST
longfilenamenew.tst --> LONGFIL0.TST
```

Long filenames on a LAN Manager server with HPFS or HPFS/386 partitions are supported and viewable by Windows 95 protected-mode network clients. Real-mode network clients can see only the 8.3 filename aliases.

LAN Manager workstations with HPFS or HPFS/386 cannot see Windows 95 long filenames. The LAN Manager workstation software has no awareness of the long filename-over-FAT file scheme used by Windows 95.

## Windows NT 3.1 with HPFS or NTFS Volumes

Support for long filenames on FAT volumes is identical in Windows NT 3.5 and Windows 95. Therefore, a computer with dual-boot capabilities for Windows NT 3.5 and Windows 95 can see long filenames on local FAT volumes by using both operating systems.

HPFS partitions exist on Windows NT computers only in the case of an upgrade over OS/2. Filenames on Windows NT 3.1 HPFS partitions have a maximum filename length of 254 characters and use the 8.3 filename alias on the first instance. For example:

```
longfilenameold.tst --> LONGFILE.TST
longfilenamenew.tst --> LONGFIL0.TST
```

Filenames on Windows NT 3.1 NTFS partitions have a maximum filename length of 255 characters and use the 8.3 filename alias on the first instance. For example:

```
longfilenameold.tst --> LONGFI~1.TST
longfilenamenew.tst --> LONGFI~2.TST
```

Long filenames on shared Windows NT 3.1 HPFS and NTFS partitions are supported and viewable by Windows 95 protected-mode network clients. Real-mode network clients can see only the 8.3 filename aliases.

Windows NT 3.1 computers cannot see Windows 95 long filenames. Windows NT 3.1 has no awareness of the long filename-over-FAT file scheme used by Windows 95.

# Administrative Considerations for Long Filenames

If you are supporting long filenames at a site with many users, the following issues must be considered:

- If you back up files to a server that does not support Windows 95 long filenames, use the LFNBK utility to save and restore long filenames. For information, see "Using the LFNBK Utility for Temporary Compatibility" later in this chapter.

- Be aware of utilities that will not work with the new Windows 95 directory entries for long filenames. Some virus scanning programs, disk repair utilities, disk optimizers, and other programs depend on the FAT file system and might not work with long filenames. If you are unsure whether a utility is compatible with the long filename system, check with the manufacturer. If you must use an incompatible program, be sure to turn off long filenames by using the LFNBK utility before proceeding.

- Do not use filenames that are more than 50 to 75 characters long. Although filenames can be up to 255 characters, the full path name cannot be more than 260 characters. To save room for moving a file from one directory to another, use filenames shorter than the limit. Besides, filenames that are too long can make browsing a list difficult.

- Publish a naming convention for your site so that users are aware of naming considerations and can prevent problems with the long filenames they use. For example, your policy could recommend making the first three or four letters significant, so that the 8.3 filename aliases can be distinguished from each other. The following example shows the alias names for some long filenames:

```
Status Report for Oct   ->   STATUS~1.TXT
Status Report for Nov   ->   STATUS~2.TXT
Status Report for Dec   ->   STATUS~3.TXT
```

Using the following alternate filenames, you can distinguish between the 8.3 filenames:

```
Oct Status Report   ->        OCTSTA~1.TXT
Nov Status Report   ->        NOVSTA~1.TXT
Dec Status Report   ->        DECSTA~1.TXT
```

You could also recommend that users give files a short filename as part of the long filename. For example:

```
Mktg_rpt-Marketing Report for our new project  ->  MKTG_R~1.TXT
```

As part of the naming convention, recommend that users check the properties for files to ensure that the alias (the MS-DOS Name in the properties dialog box) is what they expect it to be.

### Tip for Long Filenames in the Root Directory

Usually, it is best to store files in a directory beneath the root directory. This is especially true for files with long filenames. Files with long filenames use more directory entries than files with 8.3 filenames. Because the number of entries in the root is limited to 512, the root directory can fill up with fewer files if long filenames are used.

Notice that typing the command **mkdir Examples** creates a long filename directory entry that contains the name Examples to preserve the case, plus an 8.3 filename alias entry with the name EXAMPLES for compatibility. In this example, two directory entries are used.

## Using the LFNBK Utility for Temporary Compatibility

Most hard disk utility programs released before Windows 95 require updating to work correctly with Windows 95. If you use a hard disk utility that was not created especially for use with Windows 95, you might lose long filenames and you are at risk of losing data. Examples of such programs include the following:

- Norton Utilities® by Peter Norton Computing
- PC Tools™ by Central Point Software, Inc.
- Microsoft Defragmenter for MS-DOS version 6.0, 6.2, 6.21, or 6.22
- Stacker 4.0 by STAC Electronics

In special cases, you might need to run backup or disk management utilities created for older versions of Windows or MS-DOS that are not compatible with the extended file system capabilities of Windows 95. Or you might need occasionally to run an application that is not compatible with long filenames. In such cases, you can use the LFNBK utility to remove (and later restore) long filenames on a disk.

▶ **To install the LFNBK utility**

- From the Windows 95 compact disc, copy LFNBK.EXE to the Windows directory on your computer.

---

Caution  The LFNBK utility is intended for use only by experienced Windows 95 users with special needs for compatibility with older disk utilities. It is not intended for everyday use by average users.

Microsoft recommends that users rely on the disk management utilities included with Windows 95 or use Windows 95-compatible utilities from other vendors, rather than attempting to use older utilities that are not compatible with Windows 95.

Notice also that the DriveSpace utility included with Windows 95 is compatible with long filenames and can be used without LFNBK to manage compressed disks created with older versions of DriveSpace or DoubleSpace.

---

The following shows the syntax for LFNBK:

**lfnbk** [**/v**] [**/b** | **/r** | **/pe**] [**/nt**] [**/force**] [**/p**] [*drive*]

The following table lists and describes the parameters for this command.

| Parameter | Description |
|-----------|-------------|
| **/v** | Reports actions on the screen. |
| **/b** | Backs up and removes long filenames on the disk. |
| **/r** | Restores previously backed-up long filenames. |
| **/pe** | Extracts errors from backup database. |
| **/nt** | Does not restore backup dates and times. |
| **/force** | Forces LFNBK to run, even in unsafe conditions. |
| **/p** | Finds long filenames, but does not convert them to 8.3 filename aliases. This reports the existing long filenames, along with the associated dates for file creation, last access, and last modification of the file. |

▶ **To preserve long filenames with disk utilities that do not recognize them**

1. Turn off tunneling.

   To do this, in the System option in Control Panel, click the Performance tab, and then click File System. In the File System Performance dialog box, click the Troubleshooting tab, and check the option named Disable Long Name Preservation for Old Programs.

2. Close all other applications. LFNBK cannot rename open files.

3. At the command prompt, type **lfnbk /b** [*drive*] to back up and remove long filenames.

4. Restart the computer, and then run the disk utility. If it is an MS-DOS–based utility, run it in MS-DOS Mode. For a Windows-based utility, run it in the usual way.

5. At the command prompt, type **lfnbk /r** [*drive*] to restore long filenames.

6. Turn tunneling on again, and then restart the computer.

The LFNBK utility actually renames each file with a long filename to its associated alias. The filename changes are stored in the LFNBK.DAT file in the root of the drive where you are running LFNBK. This file is used to restore long filenames (when you run LFNBK with the **/r** switch).

The following list provides some brief notes for using the LFNBK utility:

- You cannot use LFNBK to repair long filename problems.

- LFNBK might not be able to rename files with exact matches to long-filename aliases, and the related alias is not guaranteed to be the same as before running LFNBK.

- After you run LFNBK and then restart Windows 95, the default Start menu will appear, rather than your custom Start menu. After you run **lfnbk /r** to restore long filenames, your custom Start menu will also be restored.

- If the directory structure changes after you run **lfnbk /b**, then long filenames cannot be restored with **lfnbk /r**. For example, if you run a disk utility that prunes or removes subdirectories, LFNBK cannot restore the long filenames within those subdirectories.

## Creating Long Filenames at the MS-DOS Prompt

At an MS-DOS prompt or when Windows 95 is started only at the command prompt (from the F8 Startup menu), the keyboard buffer's ability to create long filenames is limited to 127 characters. This is because the default command-line character limitation is 127 characters. In the default configuration, the MS-DOS environment will not allow more than 127 characters in a given command line. (However, in batch files, or for environment variables and other VM elements, the long filename support is 244 characters.)

You can increase the global command-line character limit for the keyboard buffer to its maximum by placing the following line in CONFIG.SYS:

```
shell=c:\windows\command.com /u:255
```

If the **shell** command is already present with the **/u** switch, increase the value to 255.

This command will affect all VMs and the Windows 95 command line.

With the command-line character limit set to its maximum of 255 characters, filenames are limited to 255 characters minus the contents of the command line. For example, the command line might contain the following:

```
copy con "long filename"
```

In this case, the maximum length of the long filename is 244 characters (255 minus the 11 characters of the command).

---

**Note**  It is necessary to put the filename in quotation marks on the command line only if the filename contains special characters such as spaces.

---

Notice, however, MS-DOS–based applications configured to run in MS-DOS Mode use only the real-mode FAT file system. Because of this, long filenames created in a Windows environment are not visible when the system runs in MS-DOS Mode; only the 8.3 filename aliases are visible.

The same is true of files with long filenames that are copied to a floppy disk subsequently used by a down-level FAT file system such as MS-DOS 6.0, Windows 3.1, OS/2 2.11, Windows NT 3.1, and so on.) On down-level file systems, only the 8.3 filename alias is visible on the floppy disk, even if it contains long filenames created in Windows 95.

## Technical Notes on Long Filenames

This section summarizes some technical points with regard to long filenames. This information will be helpful to you if you experience problems with long filenames.

**Long filenames cannot be used on SUBST drives.**  Windows 95 supports SUBST only for backward compatibility with drives created on older systems. Filenames on SUBST drives must comply with the 8.3 filename rule.

**Turning off numeric tails for filename aliases.**  If you do not want to use filename aliases that automatically use a numeric tail (~*n*), you can force the file system to create friendly 8.3 filename aliases, at least for the first instance of the 8.3 filename.

▶   **To use friendly alias names instead of numeric tails**

- Add the value **NameNumericTail = 0** in the following Registry key:

  ```
  Hkey_Local_Machine\System\CurrentControlSet\Control\FileSystem
  ```

**Turning off the extended file system features.**  In extremely rare cases, you might determine that you need to turn off the extended file system features in Windows 95. In this case, you can enable the Windows 3.1 file system by changing the Registry. However, this is not a recommended option.

Using the older Windows 3.1 file system affects many of the features available under Windows 95. Also, the Windows 3.1 file system was not tested extensively under Windows 95 in the same way as the new file system. You can expect the following results if you enable the Windows 3.1 file system:

- No support is provided for long filenames

- No extended file information is available, such as creation date and time, and last access date

- Folders cannot be included with user profiles

▶ **To enable the Windows 3.1 file system**

1. At the command prompt, run **lfnbk /b** to remove long filenames from the hard disk, as described in "Using the LFNBK Utility for Temporary Compatibility" earlier in this chapter.

   –Or–

   At the command prompt, run **scandskw /o** to remove long filenames and all extended file attributes from the disk. To remove long filenames from removable disks, include the drive letter with the command; for example, **scandskw /o a:**

   ───────────────────────────────────────────────────────
   Caution  If you use **scandskw /o** to remove long filenames, ScanDisk will check all fixed disks and will repair disk errors without warning you. Changes made with **scandskw /o** cannot be reversed.
   ───────────────────────────────────────────────────────

2. In Registry Editor, set the value of **Win31FileSystem** to **1** in the following Registry key. Then shut down and restart the computer.

   `Hkey_Local_Machine\System\CurrentControlSet\Control\FileSystem`

# Technical Notes on Disk Device Support

Windows 95 uses layered block device drivers to manage input and output to block devices such as disks and CD-ROM drives. A *block device* is a device such as a disk drive that moves information in groups of bytes (blocks) rather than one byte at a time. Layered block device drivers are 32-bit, flat-model device drivers that run in protected mode. These drivers support conventional and SCSI disk drives, plus partitioned and unpartitioned removable media. Windows 95 also uses layered block device drivers to manage Windows 3.x FastDisk drivers, MS-DOS – based real-mode device drivers, and Windows NT miniport drivers.

Each layered block device driver can be loaded dynamically, so the appropriate driver can be loaded or unloaded as needed without restarting the computer. Although the drivers are virtual device drivers (VxDs), they do not use the standard virtual device services and APIs. Instead, the I/O Supervisor provides the services and functions the device drivers need to complete their tasks.

Specifically, the block I/O subsystem in Windows 95 provides the following:

- Architecture to support all Plug and Play features
- Support for miniport drivers that are compatible with Windows NT
- Compatibility support for Windows 3.1 FastDisk drivers and MS-DOS real-mode disk device drivers
- Protected-mode drivers that take over real-mode MS-DOS device drivers when it is safe to do so

For more information about the block I/O subsystem, see Chapter 31, "Windows 95 Architecture."

## Supported Disk Devices

Windows 95 provides better disk device support than Windows 3.1, but it also ensures compatibility with existing MS-DOS – based and Windows-based disk device drivers. In addition, the disk device drivers in Windows 95 are compatible with Windows NT miniport drivers.

Windows 95 also provides enhanced support for large media using logical block addressing, including hard disks with more than 1024 cylinders. Extensions to the INT 13 disk controller support are provided in the protected-mode disk handler drivers for this support. (Windows 3.1 did not provide this support in its 32-bit disk access drivers.)

The following types of hard disk drives are supported under Windows 95:

| | | |
|---|---|---|
| ESDI | IDE | MFM |
| Hardcards | IDE LBA | |

The following types of bus adapters are supported under Windows 95:

| | | |
|---|---|---|
| EISA | PCMCIA | |
| ISAMCA | RLL | SCSI 2 |
| PCI | SCSI | VL bus |

The following sections describe support in Windows 95 for IDE, SCSI, high-speed floppy disk, and removable media devices. Information about SCSI and non-SCSI port drivers is also included.

## IDE Drives and Controllers

Windows 95 provides improved support for IDE drive configurations, as summarized in this section.

**Support for alternate IDE controllers.**  Windows 95 provides protected-mode support for the use of two IDE controllers in a computer, or the combination of an IDE controller in a portable computer and an alternate controller in a docking station (available, for example, in some COMPAQ docking station products). IDE controllers provide support for multiple disk drives.

**Support for IDE-based CD-ROM drives.**  Currently, most disk devices in personal computers use an IDE-based hard disk controller. Adding a CD-ROM drive typically requires adding an additional controller card to provide either SCSI or a proprietary interface for connecting to the CD-ROM drive. Windows 95 supports new, inexpensive CD-ROM drives that connect to IDE-compatible disk controllers.

Any IDE device that includes mechanisms for identification and declaration of resource requirements can take advantage of Plug and Play.

---

**Note**  To use Syquest removable IDE drives under Windows 95, the entry **RemovableIDE=true** must be added to the [386enh] section of SYSTEM.INI

---

**Support for large IDE disk drives.**  IDE drives are available that support a logical block addressing (LBA) scheme, allowing them to exceed the 0.5 GB (528 MB) size limitation. Windows 95 provides protected-mode support for IDE disk drives larger than 504 MB. The primary partition and the logical drives in an extended partition are each limited to 2 GB, but multiple 2-GB logical drives can be created in an extended partition.

The cluster size for a drive is defined by the Format program, depending on the size of the local drive, as shown in the following table:

**Cluster Sizes for Logical Volumes on Hard Disks**

| Drive size (MB) | Sectors per cluster | Cluster size |
|---|---|---|
| 0–15[1] | 8 | 4K |
| 16–127 | 4 | 2K |
| 128–255 | 8 | 4K |
| 256–511 | 16 | 8K |
| 512–1023 | 32 | 16K |
| 1024–2048 | 64 | 32K |

1  FAT type is 12-bit; all other sizes use 16-bit FAT.

You can also use DriveSpace on 1-GB or 2-GB drives to eliminate the inefficiency of using 32K clusters, but in this case you must create multiple compressed drives. You can also use compression in Microsoft Plus! to create a single compressed drive on disks that are up to 2 GB in size.

## SCSI Devices and Drivers

Windows 95 provides support for SCSI disk devices, which was not available in Windows 3.1. SCSI support in Windows 95 includes disk SCSI translator drivers, the SCSI Port Manager, and SCSI miniport drivers.

- A disk SCSI translator driver (also called a SCSI'izer) are responsible for constructing SCSI command descriptor blocks for a specific device class and carrying out device-level error recovery and logging. There are two of these drivers (one for each class): one for SCSI hard disk devices and one for CD-ROM devices.

- SCSI Port Manager manages the interaction between the SCSI'izer and a SCSI miniport driver, initializes the miniport driver, converts the I/O request format, and provides other services for the miniport driver.

- The SCSI miniport driver is responsible for detecting and initializing a specific set of SCSI adapters. The driver also handles interrupts, transmits I/O requests to the device, and carries out adapter-level error recovery and logging. Windows 95 supports the use of Windows NT miniport SCSI drivers without modification or recompiling. Compatibility with Windows NT-based miniport drivers ensures broad device support for disk devices under Windows 95, while simplifying the driver development efforts for hardware manufacturers.

Windows 95 provides broad support for popular SCSI controllers. Windows 95 includes 32-bit disk device drivers for popular SCSI controllers from Adaptec, Future Domain, and other manufacturers. Windows 95 also provides compatibility support for the Advanced SCSI Programming Interface (ASPI) and Common Access Method (CAM), which allows application and driver developers to submit I/O requests to SCSI devices. This allows existing MS-DOS–based applications and drivers that use the ASPI or CAM specification to work properly under Windows 95. Windows 95 also includes 16-bit and 32-bit drivers to support Windows-based ASPI clients and applications.

Although Windows 95 can use Windows NT miniport drivers, the best choice for a SCSI driver is one that complies with Plug and Play. Most Windows NT miniport drivers ignore configuration information from the SCSI Manager and check I/O ports to identify hardware. Miniport drivers in Windows 95 must honor configuration information without scanning for other adapters if the configuration information is not the default configuration. This is because many adapters supported under Windows 95 have port ranges that conflict with other adapters and are affected adversely by scanning. For example, Artisoft® LANtastic® network adapters occupy a range of port addresses used by Adaptec 154X adapters, and accessing these ports will cause the system to lock up.

Windows 95 provides several .MPD files with Plug and Play capabilities, including the ability to transition from protected mode to real mode (to support MS-DOS–based applications that must run in MS-DOS Mode) and to accept configuration information from the SCSI Manager for dynamically loading and unloading drivers.

For information about troubleshooting SCSI devices, see Chapter 19, "Devices."

## High-Speed Floppy Disk Driver

Windows 95 provides protected-mode support for communicating with floppy disk controllers. Windows 95 provides INT 13 hard disk controller support as 32-bit device drivers, which results in improved performance, stability, and system robustness.

Windows 95 provides floppy disk controller support as a 32-bit device driver, and offers improved performance for file I/O to floppy disk drives, plus improved reliability of the system. You can now format a disk or copy files to and from a disk while performing other tasks.

## Removable Media and Docking Devices

Windows 95 provides protected-mode support for removable media devices with MS-DOS–compatible partitions, including floppy disk drives and controllers, Bernoulli drives, and CD-ROM, plus docking stations for portable computers. Windows 95 allows the system to lock or unlock the device to prevent the media from being removed prematurely.

Windows 95 also supports an eject mechanism for devices that support it, so that users can use software control to eject media from a device (for example, new floppy disk drives that support software-based media ejection).

*Docking* refers to the insertion or removal of a device in the system. Devices that can be docked include almost anything, depending on the hardware—monitors, network access, removable hard disk drives, or any removable resource. A *docking station* is a base unit into which you can insert the portable hardware and which includes drive bays, expansion slots, and additional ports. Port replicators can also be used as docking station substitutes that provide extra functionality not available in the portable docking device.

If a docking change occurs in the computer configuration during operation, such as the insertion of a portable computer into the docking station, the system is notified so that the new device can be configured and applications can be notified of the change.

Windows 95 supports "hot" docking, where the device can be docked or undocked while running at full power, and "cold" docking, where the device must be powered off or restarted before the device can be docked or undocked. Legacy portable computers use cold docking.

In addition, some devices require certain preliminary steps before they can be docked or undocked. For example, if you have a file open and decide to remove the hard disk, the file must be closed. To handle these situations, Windows 95 supports different undocking systems, depending on the type of hardware:

- Auto-ejection, which is a software interface that operates a VCR-type ejection mechanism, allowing Windows 95 to request user action to resolve any open resources. The user can save files and so on before the system ejects the dockable resource.

- Manual ejection, where the user undocks the resource without using any software interface. Because the system cannot be notified when this occurs, any closing of files or other actions must be performed manually to prevent loss of data.

## Non-SCSI Port Drivers

A non-SCSI port driver usually works with a specific adapter, so the driver is retained in memory only if the related adapter is present in the system. Windows 95 includes, for example, port drivers for IDE, ESDI, or NEC floppy disk drives.

A port driver provides the same functionality as the SCSI Manager and miniport driver, but these drivers are monolithic and are not portable to Windows NT. A port driver manages and controls the adapter for a given block device. The port driver detects and initializes the adapter, handles interrupts, transmits I/O requests to the device, and carries out adapter-level error recovery and logging.

---

**Important**  Do not use a **device=** entry in SYSTEM.INI to load a port driver. Windows 95 loads appropriate drivers from the SYSTEM\IOSUBSYS subdirectory in the Windows directory.

---

# VCACHE and CDFS Supplemental Cache

The 32-bit VFAT works in conjunction with a 32-bit, protected-mode cache driver (VCACHE), and replaces and improves on the 16-bit real-mode SMARTDrive disk cache software provided with MS-DOS and Windows 3.1. The VCACHE driver uses an improved caching algorithm over SMARTDrive to cache information read from or written to a disk drive, and results in improved performance for reading information from the cache. Also, the VCACHE driver is responsible for managing the cache pool for CDFS, and the 32-bit network redirectors.

Another big improvement in VCACHE over SMARTDrive is that the memory pool used for the cache is dynamic and is based on the amount of available free system memory. Users no longer need to allocate a block of memory to set aside as a disk cache; the system automatically allocates or deallocates memory used for the cache based on system use. The performance of the system also scales better than earlier versions of Windows, due to the intelligent cache use.

The 32-bit protected-mode CDFS implemented in Windows 95 provides improved CD-ROM access performance over the real-mode MSCDEX driver in Windows 3.1 and is a full 32-bit ISO 9660 CD file system. The CDFS driver replaces the 16-bit real-mode MSCDEX driver, and it features 32-bit protected-mode caching of CD-ROM data. If MSCDEX is specified in the user's AUTOEXEC.BAT when Windows 95 is installed, the 32-bit CDFS driver is used instead.

CDFS has a larger and smarter cache than MSCDEX, optimized just for CD-ROMs and separate from VCACHE. The CDFS driver cache is dynamic and shares the cache memory pool with the 32-bit VFAT driver, requiring no configuration or static allocation on the part of the user.

CDFS reads ahead in parallel with the application so that multimedia presentations play back more smoothly than with earlier versions of Windows. Because CDFS uses a separate cache, the cache memory can be swapped out to the hard disk when CD-ROM activity pauses. This gives applications more room to run and protects the main hard disk cache from being flushed out whenever a very large multimedia stream is played back.

The supplemental cache size for CDFS is used to hold path table, directory, and file information. This particular cache is used to improve CD streaming and to reduce seek latency as effectively as possible with a moderately sized cache. This means that the cache is more complex, using smart priority-based caching schemes to achieve results optimized for CD-ROMs.

For information about configuring the CD-ROM cache to match the characteristics of CD-ROM drive types, see Chapter 17, "Performance Tuning."

# Troubleshooting File and Disk Problems

This section provides information for troubleshooting disk and file system problems, problems with disk utilities, and problems with long filenames.

For information about using the Troubleshooting dialog box for File System Properties in the System option in Control Panel, see Chapter 17, "Performance Tuning."

### There are performance problems with the floppy disk drive.

You can try preventing the floppy disk device driver from attempting to use first-in, first-out (FIFO). To do this, add the value **ForceFIFO=0** to the following Registry key:

```
Hkey_Local_Machine\System\CurrentControlSet\Services\Class\FDC\0000
```

### Windows 95 cannot access the drive or reports 2 GB disk space on a larger drive.

In Windows 95, the network client was designed to maintain compatibility with MS-DOS–based applications that assume a 2-GB drive-size limit. If a network drive, such as an NTFS volume on a Windows NT server, has more than 2 GB of free disk space, Windows 95 reports only that 2 GB are available and 0 bytes are used.

Microsoft does not recommend using Windows 95 with a FAT volume larger than 2 GB created in Windows NT. On a dual-boot computer with both Windows 95 and Windows NT installed, you can read from and write to the drive, but you might experience strange results, such as programs reporting 0 bytes free space on the drive. However, you shouldn't experience data loss when accessing a 4-GB drive.

### Disk utilities fail on a Windows 95 volume.

Disk utilities that were not designed for the Windows 95 VFAT file system can find unexpected values in fields that were once reserved for MS-DOS. Use disk utilities designed for Windows 95 instead. You might be able to use some earlier utilities by first running LFNBK, as described in "Using the LFNBK Utility for Temporary Compatibility" earlier in this chapter.

**Problems occur with shortcuts after compressing the Windows 95 volume with Stacker.**

Stacker does not recognize or accommodate long filenames. If you compress your Windows 95 volume by using the Stacker DOS compression program, your desktop shortcuts will need to be repaired manually. You will also need to move USER.DAT and USER.DA0 from the host volume to your compressed volume. If you are using Stacker, do not run DriveSpace or DoubleSpace.

**A CVF will not mount.**

Check the D??SPACE.INI file in the root directory of the boot drive. If this file is damaged, use the DriveSpace program to rebuild it.

**The d??space /mount command in AUTOEXEC.BAT does not work.**

This occurs because Windows 95 Setup deletes or renames the MS-DOS–based versions of DRVSPACE.EXE and DBLSPACE.EXE. To solve this problem, use **scandisk /mount** as the replacement command live in AUTOEXEC.BAT. The version of ScanDisk provided with Windows 95 has been enhanced for this purpose. For more information, see Appendix A, "Command-Line Commands Summary."

## Long-Filename Troubleshooting Tips

- Long filenames can cause problems for some disk utilities. Be sure to use disk utilities that are long filename-aware. If you are not sure whether your utility is long filename-aware, consult your disk utility documentation. If long filenames are not mentioned, then your utility probably does not support long filenames.

- Using a down-level file system command (such as **copy** or **rename**) rather than the Windows 95 equivalent will destroy a long filename.

- Because the root directory is limited to 512 entries, you can fill the root directory with fewer files by using long filenames because each long filename takes more than one entry in the directory.

- Although you can disable the creation of long filenames, this should be used only if error conditions warrant it and if other troubleshooting efforts have failed. For information about turning off the extended file system features, see "Technical Notes on Long Filenames" earlier in this chapter.

### The 8.3 filename alias was changed.

This can happen when you use options such as Copy, Backup, or Restore. For example, if a file with the name LongFileName is associated with an alias LONGFI~2, and this file is copied to a different directory by using the following:

```
copy LongFileName \TMP\LongFileName
```

Then the alias associated with this file can become LONGFI~1, if such an alias is not already present in the target directory.

### The long filename was destroyed.

This can happen when transferring files to or from file systems that do not support long filenames, when running file searches, or when using certain disk utilities. The long filename cannot be restored.

### A long filename was lost after the file was edited on another computer.

This occurs because down-level file systems are not aware of the long filename extensions to the FAT file system.

### Hard disk device drivers cause the computer to stall.

The I/O Supervisor, which loads hard disk (block) device drivers, requires the driver's files (having filename extensions .PDR, .MPD, .VXD, and .386) to be located in the SYSTEM\IOSUBSYS subdirectory of the Windows directory.

If the computer locks up during startup or hardware detection, try the following:

- Check for Windows NT miniport drivers (.SYS files in the IOSUBSYS directory). These drivers detect the I/O ports and might cause the computer to stop. Replace the Windows NT driver with either a Windows 95 miniport or a real-mode driver.

- Check the IOS.INI file for real-mode drivers not replaced by protected-mode drivers.

- When loading protected-mode drivers, the real-mode driver generally remains loaded in memory even though the protected-mode driver "takes over." If you suspect a conflict, type **rem** at the beginning of the line in CONFIG.SYS that calls the real-mode driver.

- Users might have problems with devices (such as tape backups) that use ASPI drivers. Try using only real-mode drivers, then try using only protected-mode drivers.

### Virus-detection utilities don't remove a virus.

In general, virus-detection utilities created from earlier versions of Windows can detect but not clean viruses from Windows 95. This is because virus-detection utilities use low-level writes to repair the disk. MS-DOS–based utilities can still be run using the **lock** command.

CHAPTER 2 1

# Multimedia

This chapter describes the multimedia architecture and features in Windows 95.

**In This Chapter**

Multimedia: The Basics   700
Multimedia: The Issues   700
Multimedia Overview   701
  Media Control Interface   701
  Multimedia Files   702
  Display Control Interface   702
  Support for Multimedia Devices   703
Recording, Editing, and Playing Audio   703
  Windows 95 Support for MIDI   703
  Recording Sound   704
  Controlling Audio Input Levels   704
Playing and Recording Digital Video   705
Buying a Multimedia Computer   706
Troubleshooting Multimedia Software   709
  Correcting Problems with Playing .WAV Files   709
  Correcting Problems in Playing MIDI Files   710
  Correcting Problems with Playing or Hearing an Audio CD   711
  Correcting Problems with Hearing from Headphones   712

# Multimedia: The Basics

For users of multimedia applications and equipment in your organization, installing Windows 95 provides an immediate multimedia upgrade. Its standard architecture for digital video, digital audio, MIDI, and file handling allow for high-quality multimedia effects. This architecture provides the following benefits:

- You can use the Media Control Interface (MCI) to run multimedia devices independently from each other.

- You have enhanced video support using the new Display Control Interface (DCI). For more information, see Chapter 19, "Devices."

- You can use built-in programs to record, edit, and play digital audio and video.

- You can easily add new multimedia hardware through the Add New Hardware option in Control Panel. The Add New Hardware option is a wizard that guides you through the steps to install and configure drivers for legacy devices. For more information, see Chapter 19, "Devices."

- You can use the new built-in file sharing to share CD-ROM drives across the network. For more information, see Chapter 11, "Logon, Browsing, and Resource Sharing."

The performance benefits from the 32-bit Windows 95 architecture ensures that Windows 95 multimedia titles can include digital video and sound with better quality than ever before.

# Multimedia: The Issues

In the corporate environment, you need to consider what multimedia features your users will be using to determine what extra hardware they'll need. For example, to use the audio capabilities as described in this chapter, computers need a sound card. For more information, see "Buying a Multimedia Computer" later in this chapter.

Windows 95 includes basic audio recording, audio playback, and video playback tools, but your users might need more features than these tools offer. For example, if users will be capturing and compressing digital video, they'll need additional software. Consider which additional multimedia software tools you might need to purchase. For more information, see "Buying a Multimedia Computer" later in this chapter.

If you are planning to play video clips over the network, playback will probably appear somewhat jerky unless your network guarantees a continuous data stream (for example, if you use an isochronous Ethernet network or an asynchronous transfer mode (ATM) network).

# Multimedia Overview

This section describes the Windows 95 components that support multimedia hardware and software.

## Media Control Interface

The Media Control Interface (MCI) provides applications created for Windows 95 with device-independent capabilities for controlling media devices such as audio hardware, videodisc players, and animation players. This interface works with MCI device drivers to interpret and run MCI commands such as **pause**, **play**, and **stop**.

MCI provides a set of core commands for a broad range of media devices. For example, MCI uses the same command to begin playback of a waveform-audio file, a videodisc track, and an animation sequence. MCI also provides extended commands for using particular device types with unique capabilities, such as using a frame-based time format for animation. For more information about MCI drivers and commands, see the *Microsoft Windows 95 Device Development Kit*.

A *device type* identifies a class of MCI devices that respond to a common set of commands. The following table lists the currently defined MCI device types.

| Device type | Description |
|---|---|
| animation | Animation device |
| cdaudio | Compact disc (CD) audio player |
| dat | Digital audiotape player |
| digitalvideo | Digital video in a window (not GDI based) |
| other | Undefined MCI device |
| overlay | Overlay device (analog video in a window) |
| scanner | Image scanner |
| sequencer | MIDI sequencer |
| vcr | Videocassette recorder or player |
| videodisc | Videodisc player |
| waveaudio | Audio device that plays digitized waveform-audio files |

# Multimedia Files

Usually, multimedia files are maintained in one of the formats described in the following table.

| Format | Corresponding filename extension |
| --- | --- |
| Digital-video | .AVI |
| Waveform-audio | .WAV |
| Musical Instrument Digital Interface (MIDI) | .MID |

Multimedia files are stored on a compact disc, a local hard disk drive, a network file server, or another storage medium. The playback quality is constrained by the amount of data that the storage medium can continuously supply to the file system.

A multimedia data stream (such as an .AVI file) generally contains multiple components, such as digital-video data, audio data, text, and perhaps other data (such as hot-spot information, additional audio tracks, and so on). As multimedia information is read from the CD-ROM drive, the multimedia subsystem determines what the data stream contains, and then it separates and routes the data accordingly.

## CD-ROM File System

To get the best possible performance from double-speed and faster CD-ROM drives, Windows 95 includes a new, 32-bit, CD-ROM file system (CDFS) for reading files from CD-ROM drives as quickly and efficiently as possible. For more information about the CDFS, see Chapter 17, "Performance Tuning" and Chapter 31, "Windows 95 Architecture."

CDFS replaces most Windows version 3.1 MSCDEX drivers.

# Display Control Interface

The Display Control Interface (DCI) is a new display driver interface created jointly by Microsoft and Intel Corporation. DCI-compliant drivers provide a fast, direct way for games and digital video in Windows 95 to write to the video frame buffer. It also enables digital-video playback to take advantage of several specific kinds of hardware support included on advanced graphics adapters.

For more information about DCI, see the *DCI Level 2 Specification.* This specification is available through the Microsoft Developer Network (MSDN); to obtain it, call (800) 759-5474, or, from outside the United States and Canada, call (402) 691-0173. For more information about MSDN, see Appendix J, "Windows 95 Resource Directory"

## Support for Multimedia Devices

Windows 95 includes built-in support for common multimedia authoring devices such as laser discs and video-cassette recorders (VCRs). This makes it easy to set up a computer for *step capture*, a process in which a user captures digital-video data one frame at a time; the data is usually compressed later. This is a slow process, but it results in the highest possible quality of digital video.

To play the contents of a videotape on a computer, users must connect the video and audio outputs from the VCR to the video-capture or overlay and to the audio inputs of the computer. Users might also need to install an MCI digital-video device driver.

# Recording, Editing, and Playing Audio

Windows 95 multimedia services provide extensible, device-independent audio support. Windows 95 features services for sound control for computers that have sound cards and for waveform-audio, MIDI, and mixer devices.

With audio support in Windows 95, users can do the following:

- Use the Sound option in Control Panel to assign sound clips to play each time a specific event occurs
- Use CD Player to play audio CDs
- Use Sound Recorder to record sound
- Use built-in Windows 95 OLE support to copy or link audio clips in other documents, as described in Chapter 22, "Application Support"

For more information about recording, editing, and playing multimedia files, see online Help.

## Windows 95 Support for MIDI

Musical Instrument Digital Interface (MIDI) is a serial interface standard that allows for the connection of music synthesizers, musical instruments, and computers. The MIDI standard is based partly on hardware and partly on a description of the way in which music and sounds are encoded and communicated between MIDI devices.

MIDI is used as a development tool for musicians. Virtually all advanced music equipment supports MIDI, and MIDI offers a convenient way to control the equipment very precisely. MIDI is similar to the electronic equivalent of sheet music. For example, if you buy a CD that contains a particular performance of a piece of music, the data on the CD requires no interpretation at all—it's straightforward playback. If you buy the sheet music and have someone play it, it requires very little data, but, depending on the quality of the instruments and the musicians, you can get a good or bad interpretation of that piece of music.

Windows 95 supports the General MIDI Specification to request particular instruments and sounds. This specification is an industry standard that defines how MIDI should be used, and it is supported by Microsoft and most MIDI sound card manufacturers.

Windows 95 supports a new technology called MIDI streams. This technology is used in advanced sound cards to play very complex MIDI sequences with less CPU use. Support for this technology allows Windows 95 to communicate multiple MIDI instructions simultaneously within a single interrupt. As a result, playing MIDI files now requires even less computing power than it did before, and it allows developers to process MIDI instructions, graphics, and other data even more successfully.

For more information about playing a MIDI sound file, see online Help.

# Recording Sound

Users who have microphones connected to their computer can record sound by using Sound Recorder.

When using Sound Recorder, users must use a real-mode compression codec. To turn on voice compression when recording so that the file is compressed in real-time, users must use the GSM 6.10 format in the Sound Selection dialog box in Sound properties.

For more information about recording sound with a microphone, see online Help.

# Controlling Audio Input Levels

Windows 95 includes a Volume Control tool that provides audio line routing services to manage the different audio lines installed on a computer. An audio line consists of one or more channels of waveform-audio data coming from one origin or system resource. For example, a stereo audio line has two data channels, yet it is considered a single audio line. Each audio line also has zero or more mixer controls associated with it. A mixer control can take on a number of different characteristics (such as controlling volume) depending on the characteristics of the associated audio line.

The number of lines users can mix by using Volume Control depends on the number of audio source lines the computer has, and whether they are using Volume Control for input or output.

For more information about mixing sounds, see online Help.

# Playing and Recording Digital Video

Windows 95 video services provide the resources for capturing video clips, compressing the content, and controlling playback.

Displaying digital video involves moving and processing huge streams of data continuously and efficiently. In earlier versions of Windows, the process of displaying digital video relied on a series of 16-bit systems—from reading data from the disk, to decompressing the video data, to displaying it on the screen. With the Windows 95 32-bit architecture, users can display bigger, smoother, and more colorful digital video than ever before, without adding any hardware.

Windows 95 multimedia is fully compatible with 16-bit multimedia titles. Early testing has shown that the 32-bit improvements in file access speed and stream handling result in performance gains for 16-bit multimedia applications and especially for the new generation of 32-bit applications developed for Windows 95.

▶ **To determine the format in which an existing video clip was authored**

- Right-click the icon for the digital-video file, click Properties, and then click the Details tab.

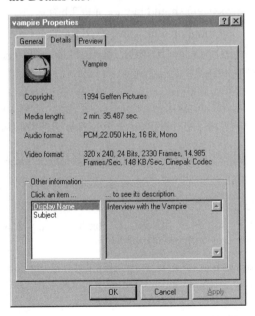

For more information about playing media clips, see online Help.

# Buying a Multimedia Computer

The following list provides guidelines for what to look for in a multimedia system, plus specifics for overall sound components, MIDI components, mixing capabilities, and video components.

### What to look for in basic computing power.

Make sure to select a balanced computer, in which all components work together to meet the demands of supporting multimedia applications. In multimedia systems, balance is more important than speed, because multimedia playback places heavy demands on the CD-ROM (for reading data), on the hard disk (for writing data), on the CPU (for decompressing), and on the video and audio subsystems (for playback). A fast CPU alone does not guarantee a great playback system. For best results, the computer should have the following components:

- Local-bus video. The performance of a computer with a local bus is about 10 times better than one without a local bus, assuming everything else on the computers is equal. Without local-bus video, a computer will not be able to keep up with the amount of video data that consumer multimedia applications and games currently being produced will attempt to display continuously. Preferably, the system should include a PCI bus.

- A 24-bit display monitor. This is required for TrueColor support.

- A double-speed or faster CD-ROM drive. New multimedia applications assume double-speed data rate.

- Super VGA (800x600) resolution or better with 16-bit color. Because multimedia applications display many different colors and they tend to compete for access to the system palette, it's important to have support for more than 8-bit color.

- 16-bit audio and MIDI. Many multimedia applications make use of sound cards with MIDI support.

### What to look for in computer sound support.

The following are some key features to look for when you want to purchase a multimedia computer with great sound support:

- Choose a sound card with a 16-bit digital-to-analog converter (DAC) for playback, and a 16-bit analog-to-digital converter (ADC) for recording (necessary for applications developers).

- Look for a CD-ROM drive with double-speed or faster capabilities and multisession support.

- Look for a system that supports stereo sound and 8, 11, 22, and 44 kilohertz (kHz) waveforms. Compact-disc quality sound uses 44 kHz. The 11 kHz and 22 kHz waveforms are fractions of 44 and are often used for compressed waveforms that are meant to save CPU processing. The 8 kHz waveform is used for Truespeech™ compression.

- Developer systems should also include full-duplex support to record and play sound at the same time.

### What to look for in computer MIDI support.

Microsoft recommends that sound cards for both consumer and developer systems include the following:

- General MIDI support. General MIDI refers to a system of assigning numbers to each kind of instrument, so that, for example, instrument 12 on one computer is the same as instrument 12 on all others.

- Polyphony, which means the ability to play multiple sounds at the same time. Consumer systems should include 16-voice polyphony; developer systems should include at least 20-voice polyphony. Support for more concurrent sounds means a fuller-sounding playback.

- MIDI streams. This is an efficient, new capability in Windows 95 whereby a sound card receives and batch-processes multiple MIDI messages (such as Note On and Note Off). With MIDI-stream sound support in the sound subsystem, the CPU is freed from managing those messages individually. This offers virtually flawless playback, even when the CPU is being heavily taxed by large-frame video playback.

- Sampled sound rather than waveform synthesis. Sampled sound is an actual recording of a sound. Waveform synthesis uses a mathematical approximation of that sound.

- Standard MIDI port. Consumers and developers use this port to plug in MIDI devices, such as piano-style keyboards. It also supports joysticks.

### What to look for in mixing capabilities.

A good multimedia system for either a user or a developer should have mixing capabilities. Look for the following features:

- The mixer should mix input from four sources (WAV, MIDI, Redbook, AUX) and present the output as a stereo, line-level audio signal at the back panel of the computer. Each input should have at least a 3-bit volume control (8 steps) with a logarithmic taper.

- Make sure that all sources are within –10 dB and without attenuation. This will ensure that the mixer will not clip, meaning that if a sound peaks, the audio clicks instead of playing that sound. It also ensures that the mixer will output between 0 dB and +3 dB.

- The preferred system should have individual audio source and master digital volume control registers and extra line-level audio sources.

### What to look for in computer video support.

The following are some key video-support features to look for when purchasing a multimedia computer:

- Look for a balanced system in which each component has sufficient power. This is important because any of several components on the system could adversely affect the playback quality of a multimedia application. The computer might not have enough space on the CD-ROM or hard disk; the hard disk might not be able to retrieve data fast enough to play back well; the CPU might not have enough power to handle the decompression of the video; or the bus on the video display card might not be fast enough to move all of the data to the screen.

- Look for Super VGA resolution. The minimum resolution for a multimedia computer is VGA, which provides a 640x480-pixel image and 256 colors, also expressed as 8 bits per pixel (bpp). Microsoft recommends that a consumer system include at least a Super VGA display, which provides 800x600-pixel resolution with approximately 64,000 colors (16 bpp) for users working with complicated graphics.

  For example, suppose that you are playing a video segment with a shaded maroon background that includes one underwater scene, followed by a skydiving scene, followed by a city street scene. Each scene and its background has very different color qualities. At least one of the scenes or the background will not be displayed well if a full-color clip is translated to a 256-color display.

- Look for a video card with a DCI provider for better performance.

- Look for a computer with a double-speed or faster CD-ROM drive, which reads data from the CD-ROM at a rate of at least 300 kilobytes per second. This is the rate needed to have good-looking 320x240-pixel digital video clips playing at a reasonable frame rate with no undue screen compression. (Screen compression changes resolution, causing a grainy image. At extreme compression, for example, an image of a person might look instead like a bunch of blocks.)

# Troubleshooting Multimedia Software

This section describes how to identify and resolve multimedia software problems.

**Note**  Before you attempt any troubleshooting, shut down and restart the computer to verify that the system functions correctly.

For information about troubleshooting related hardware problems, see Chapter 19, "Devices."

# Correcting Problems with Playing .WAV Files

When a multimedia application is unable to play waveform-audio (.WAV) files, it is usually due to one or more of the following problems:

- The sound card is not installed properly.
- You are using Sound Recorder, and a waveform-audio driver is not installed.
- You are using Media Player, and a waveform-audio MCI driver is not enabled.

### The sound card is not installed properly.

Most sound cards come with MS-DOS–based programs for playing sounds or testing card configurations. Run these test programs; if the sound card does not work with these programs, then it will not work with Windows 95 sound support.

Make sure the sound card settings do not conflict with other hardware. Use the Add New Hardware icon in Control Panel to detect your hardware, which will determine if you have any hardware for which the appropriate driver is not yet installed. Verify port and IRQ settings.

**Note**  If the sound card can play MIDI files, the card is properly installed.

### A waveform-audio driver is not installed.

If you are running Sound Recorder and there is no waveform-audio driver installed, you will receive an error message. In this case, make sure that the waveform-audio driver is listed in the Multimedia Devices list; you can see this list by clicking the Advanced tab in the Multimedia option in Control Panel. If the sound card is compatible with Sound Blaster™, try using the Sound Blaster driver provided with Windows 95. If you cannot find the correct driver for the sound card in the list, try using the Windows 3.1 driver for that card.

### A waveform-audio MCI driver is not enabled.

If you are running Media Player and cannot play .WAV files, perform the following procedure to correct the problem.

▶ **To enable the waveform-audio MCI driver**

1. In the Multimedia option in Control Panel, click the Advanced tab.

2. In the Multimedia Devices list, click the plus (+) sign next to Media Control Devices.

   If Wave Audio Device (Media Control) does not appear in the list, the driver is not installed.

3. Click Wave Audio Device (Media Control), and then click the Properties button.

4. In the properties dialog box, click Use This Media Control Device.

# Correcting Problems in Playing MIDI Files

When a multimedia application is unable to play MIDI files, it is commonly due to one or more of the following problems:

- The sound card is not installed properly.
- You are using Sound Recorder and a MIDI driver is not installed.
- A MIDI MCI driver is not installed.
- The .IDF file is invalid or corrupt.

### The sound card is not installed properly.

Most sound cards come with MS-DOS–based programs for playing sounds or testing card configurations. Run these test programs; if the sound card does not work with these programs, then it will not work with Windows 95 sound support.

Make sure that the sound card settings do not conflict with other hardware. Use the Add New Hardware option in Control Panel to detect your hardware, which will determine whether you have any hardware for which the appropriate driver is not yet installed. Verify port and IRQ settings.

**Note** If the sound card can play .WAV files, the card is properly installed.

### A MIDI driver is not installed.

If you are using Sound Recorder and cannot play a MIDI file, it might be because there is no MIDI driver installed. If the sound card is compatible with AdLib, try using the AdLib driver provided with Windows 95. If you don't find the correct driver for the sound card in the list, try using the Windows 3.1 driver for that card (however, the Windows 3.1 driver might not be compatible with Windows 95).

**A MIDI MCI driver is not installed or enabled.**

In Media Player, make sure that the option named MIDI Sequencer appears in the Device menu. If not, then the MIDI MCI driver is not installed or not enabled.

▶ **To verify that the MIDI MCI driver is enabled**

1. In the Multimedia option in Control Panel, click the Advanced tab.

2. In the Multimedia Devices list, click the plus (+) sign next to Media Control Devices.

   If MIDI Sequencer Device does not appear in the list, the driver is not installed. See the following procedure for instructions.

3. Click MIDI Sequencer Device (Media Control), and then click the Properties button.

4. In the properties dialog box, click Use This Media Control Device.

▶ **To install the MIDI MCI driver**

1. In the Add New Hardware option in Control Panel, click No when prompted to have Windows 95 search for your hardware, and then click the Next button.

2. In the Hardware Types list, click Sound, Video And Game Controllers, and then click the Next button.

3. Click Microsoft MCI in the Manufacturers list, and then click MIDI Sequencer Device (Media Control) in the Models list. Click the Next button.

4. To complete the installation, click the Finish button.

**The .IDF file is corrupt or invalid.**

Copy the appropriate .IDF file for each device installed. For general MIDI devices, obtain a new copy of GENERAL.IDF from the Windows 95 disks. For MIDI devices that come with their own .IDF file, reinstall the file from the device's setup disks.

# Correcting Problems with Playing or Hearing an Audio CD

When a user is unable to hear an audio CD being played, it is commonly due to one or more of the following problems:

- The CD-ROM drive is not installed properly.
- An MCI CD audio driver is not installed.
- The CD-ROM drive and the sound card are not connected.

**The CD-ROM drive is not properly installed.**

Place a data CD in the CD-ROM drive and make sure you can view the files in Windows Explorer or list the files at the command prompt. If you can, then the CD-ROM drive is properly installed. If not, verify your disk drivers (ESDI, SCSI,

Proprietary, MSCDEX) and make the appropriate configuration changes so that you can view the files on a data CD.

### The CD audio MCI driver is not installed.

In Media Player, make sure that the option named CD Audio appears in the Device menu. If not, then the CD audio MCI driver is not installed or not enabled.

▶ **To verify the CD audio MCI driver is enabled**

1. In the Multimedia option in Control Panel, click the Advanced tab.

2. In the Multimedia Devices list, click the plus (+) sign next to Media Control Devices.

   If CD Audio Device (Media Control) does not appear in the list, the driver is not installed. See the following procedure for instructions.

3. Click CD Audio Device (Media Control), and then click the Properties button.

4. In the properties dialog box, click Use This Media Control Device.

▶ **To install the CD audio MCI driver**

1. In the Add New Hardware option in Control Panel, click No when prompted to have Windows 95 search for your hardware, and then click the Next button.

2. In the Hardware Types list, click Sound, Video And Game Controllers, and then click the Next button.

3. Click Microsoft MCI in the Manufacturers list, and then click CD Audio Device (Media Control) in the Models list. Click the Next button.

4. To complete the installation, click the Finish button.

### The CD-ROM is not connected to the sound card.

If the CD-ROM is playing and there is no sound coming from the sound card speakers, try plugging the speakers or headphones into the audio jack on the face of the CD-ROM drive. If you get sound, then check the internal or external audio connection between the CD-ROM drive and the sound card.

# Correcting Problems with Hearing from Headphones

Verify that the sound card is correctly installed by reviewing the card's properties.

▶ **To view your sound card's properties**

1. In the Multimedia option in Control Panel, click the CD Music tab.

2. Make sure that the volume level is set to produce sound from the headphones. If not, use the slider to adjust the volume.

CHAPTER 22

# Application Support

With Windows 95, you can run Win32-based, Win16-based, and MS-DOS–based applications. This chapter offers some tips you can use to ensure that applications run well under Windows 95.

**In This Chapter**

Application Support: The Basics   714
Application Support: The Issues   716
Installing Applications   717
    Installing and Sharing Applications Across the Network   718
    Creating an APPS.INI File   719
Removing Applications   720
Running Applications   720
    Associating a File Type with an Application   721
    Configuring the Start and Programs menus   722
    Using the Windows 3.x Program Manager with Windows 95   723
    Closing Failed Programs   725
Configuring MS-DOS – Based Applications   726
    Changing MS-DOS – Based Application Properties (PIF Files)   726
    Changing Memory Settings for MS-DOS – Based Applications   727
    Setting Properties for MS-DOS – Based Applications   729
    Setting Paths for MS-DOS – Based Applications   736
    Understanding the APPS.INF File   737
Using OLE to Share Data Between Applications   739
Technical Notes on Application Support   741
    System Changes Affecting Application Support   741
    How Windows 95 Accommodates Application Problems   745
Troubleshooting Applications   749

# Application Support: The Basics

Windows 95 optimizes the performance of new Win32-based applications and existing applications created for MS-DOS and earlier versions of Windows. They perform more smoothly because Windows 95 significantly increases system resources available to them and more efficiently manages how they use system memory. Windows 95 also supports new and existing versions of OLE technology, including OLE Controls and OLE Automation for new Windows-based applications.

**Increased system resources.**  Windows 95 increases system resources for all applications by using 32-bit heaps to store applications' data structures, making more resources available for the remaining data elements. In addition, Windows 95 increases the number of timers, COM and LPT ports, Windows menu handles, and other resources available to applications. For more information, see Chapter 17, "Performance Tuning."

**Improved memory management.**  The Virtual Machine Manager, an integral part of Windows 95 architecture, manages the memory that each application needs. A virtual machine (VM) is an environment in memory that seems to function as a separate computer for each application. All Win32-based and Win16-based applications run in the System VM, in which all system processes also run. Each MS-DOS–based application runs in its own VM. For more information, see Chapter 31, "Windows 95 Architecture."

## Win32-Based Applications

Win32-based applications receive the full benefit of the performance enhancement features in Windows 95. Because each Win32-based application runs in a separate memory space, it can take complete advantage of the preemptive multitasking capabilities of Windows 95.

**Requirements for Windows 95 Logo.**  To get the best possible performance, upgrade to versions of applications that were designed for Windows 95 whenever possible. Applications written specifically for Windows 95 carry the "Designed for Windows 95" logo. To qualify for a Windows 95 logo, applications must meet the following requirements:

- Use Win32 APIs executable in the PE (Portable Executable) format

- Support Windows 95 user interface (shell), including the following:
  - Use system metrics for sizing
  - Use system colors (recommended)
  - Use the right mouse button for context menus and not for anything else (recommended)
  - Use Windows 95 Setup guidelines to make the application visible in the shell
- Use long filenames
- Be aware of Plug and Play events (recommended)
- Run successfully on Windows NT 3.5 or later

There are modified requirements for file-based applications, utilities such as virus-checking software, and compilers and other development tools. For more information, contact the Microsoft Developer Network (MSDN). In Canada or the United States, call (800) 759-5474, or in Europe call 31 10 258 88 64.

# Win16-Based and MS-DOS–Based Applications

Win16-based applications designed for Windows 3.1 run under Windows 95 without modification, but these applications run in a shared memory space and cannot take advantage of preemptive multitasking. However, they do benefit from improvements incorporated into the Windows 95 subsystem. For Win16-based and MS-DOS–based applications that are known to need special parameters to run, Windows 95 includes an APPS.INF file that defines parameters for each application.

Because of default settings and other support in Windows 95, you do not need to have CONFIG.SYS, AUTOEXEC.BAT, and INI files to run Win16-based and MS-DOS–based applications, although you can still use settings from existing files. When you upgrade by replacing Windows 3.1 with Windows 95, Windows automatically moves the current settings for your installed applications to the Registry for use with Windows 95.

MS-DOS–based applications can take advantage of the improved memory management and increased system resources that are made possible by the new system architecture. Most applications can now run in a window. MS-DOS–based applications that do not run well under Windows can run the application in exclusive MS-DOS Mode, which makes all system resources available to that application, "Changing Memory Settings for MS-DOS–Based Applications" later in this chapter.

When running under Windows 95, MS-DOS–based applications also benefit from the following:

- Improved robustness, including better virtualization for computer resources, such as support for timers and sound devices.

- Improved support for highly graphical MS-DOS–based applications. This allows you to run video-mode style applications in a window rather than in a full screen.

- Improved memory protection. Windows 95 includes a global memory-protection attribute in the properties dialog box for executable files. This attribute allows the MS-DOS system area to be protected from errant MS-DOS–based applications.

- Improved printing performance and font support, including user-scalable windows with support for TrueType® fonts in virtual machines (VMs).

- Local environmental settings for VMs. You can also customize the VM environment by specifying a batch file in an executable file's properties.

# Application Support: The Issues

Before you install and configure applications for use with Windows 95, consider the following questions:

- How will applications perform in your networking environment? After you set up Windows 95 on the network, you will need to install and test how applications perform. For example, for MS-DOS–based applications that were created for your network, test whether they can run in a window or if you need to run them in MS-DOS Mode. After you test them, disperse information to users about how to run different applications.

- Do the default settings for MS-DOS–based applications work well for each of your applications? You can use the executable file's properties dialog box to modify settings as needed, as described in "Configuring MS-DOS–Based Applications" later in this chapter.

- Do you need to restrict users from running MS-DOS–based applications? Or do you want to allow only certain Windows-based applications to run on a computer? For computers that run File and Printer Sharing services, where access to the shared resources is critical to other users, you may want to restrict the ability to switch to MS-DOS Mode to ensure that shared resources are always available. For information about using system policies to restrict access to MS-DOS Mode or restrict the applications that can run on a computer, see Chapter 15, "User Profiles and System Policies."

- Which applications do you want to share over the network? With Windows 95, most applications can be shared across the network by installing them on a network computer and then creating a shortcut to them. Users can open them from the network location by double-clicking the shortcut. For more information, see "Installing and Sharing Applications Across the Network" later in this chapter.

  To share some large applications, you must run a separate setup on the server and on the workstation. Check the documentation for the application before attempting to share it across the network.

- Which TSRs do you need to run to support applications? If you are running Client for NetWare Networks, you cannot process TSRs in a logon script. For information about how to load a TSR, see "Running Logon Scripts with Client for NetWare Networks" in Chapter 11, "Logon, Browsing, and Resource Sharing."

- Do you want users to have access to the Windows 3.1 Program Manager rather than to the new Windows 95 interface? For information, see "Using the Windows 3.x Program Manager with Windows 95" later in this chapter.

# Installing Applications

How you install and configure an application depends on whether it is created for Windows 95, an earlier version of Windows, or MS-DOS.

**Using Add/Remove Programs with Win32-based applications.**  Windows 95 simplifies installing applications created for Windows 95 by providing an Add/Remove Programs option in Control Panel. When you install an application by using this option, Windows 95 does the following:

- Adds information about the application to the Registry, such as which parameters to use to run the application and which files to delete when removing the application from the computer.

- Searches drives A and B for applications named INSTALL or SETUP. If a setup application uses a name other than INSTALL or SETUP, start the setup application by double-clicking its icon in My Computer.

**Keeping Windows 3.1 settings.**  If you upgrade by placing Windows 95 in the Windows 3.x directory, you do not need to reinstall applications. Setup automatically moves information about currently installed applications to the Registry. Setup also converts existing Program Manager groups and adds them to the Programs menu on the Start menu.

If you install Windows 95 in a separate directory, you must reinstall all Windows-based applications to ensure that they work properly under Windows 95. Copying .GRP and INI files from your previous Windows directory is not sufficient to run applications under Windows 95.

**Creating applications groups and icons.**   When a Windows-based setup application creates an application group and icons, Windows 95 creates folders and icons for the Programs menu on the Start menu. If a setup application fails to create a shortcut correctly, you can do it manually. For information about adding shortcuts to the Start menu, see online Help.

**Running specific applications.**   For information about whether a specific application runs under Windows 95, check the Windows 95 README.TXT file. If you do not find an application listed in the README.TXT file, check with the application's manufacturer or your software vendor. Windows 95 provides a utility that makes an incompatible application compatible with Windows 95. The "make compatible" utility is a file named MKCOMPAT.EXE in the Windows SYSTEM directory. For more information, see "Troubleshooting Applications" later in this chapter.

**Installing MS-DOS–based applications.**   You can install an MS-DOS–based application by running its executable file. Windows 95 copies information about the application from the APPS.INF file to the application's PIF file. If it was installed under an earlier version of Windows 95, Setup automatically moves its settings to the new APPS.INF file. If there is no information about the application in APPS.INF, Windows 95 uses default settings instead, or you can manually set the properties, as described in "Setting Properties for MS-DOS–Based Applications" later in this chapter.

---

**Note**   Windows 95 has no separate PIF Editor. To configure an application, right-click the application's executable file, and then click Properties.

---

For more information about installing applications after you have installed Windows 95, see online Help.

# Installing and Sharing Applications Across the Network

You can share most applications on a network by installing them on a network computer and then creating a shortcut to them. Users can run the application by double-clicking the shortcut or by double-clicking the application's icon in Network Neighborhood.

▶ **To share an application on the network**

1. Install an application on a network server or workstation, as described in the documentation from the vendor.

2. In Network Neighborhood, right-click the icon for the application, and then click Create Shortcut. Windows 95 asks if you want to create a shortcut on the desktop.

For more information about creating shortcuts, see online Help. For information about creating and distributing custom shortcuts using system policies, see Chapter 15, "User Profiles and System Policies."

---

**Tip**  In general, Windows 95 doesn't allow you to specify a working directory in the properties sheet of a Win16-based application. This is because the program file has links assigned to it that rely on unchanging data. However, you can achieve the same effect by creating a shortcut for the application and specifying a working directory in the Start In box in the properties for the shortcut.

---

# Creating an APPS.INI File

If users will be installing applications from source files stored on the network, you can create an APPS.INI file that contains a master list of applications and their network locations. When a user's Registry contains a reference to the APPS.INI file, a new tab named Network Install appears in Add/Remove Programs. The Network Install tab lists all the applications that appear in the APPS.INI file.

▶ **To create an APPS.INI file**

1. Use a text editor to create a file that contains list of applications using the following format:

    *application name* = [*] *UNC path*

    For *application name*, substitute the name that you want users to see on the Network Install tab. For *UNC path*, substitute the network location of the setup application. If a setup application cannot work with UNC names, include an asterisk before it. For example:

    ```
    word for windows=*\\applications\forusers\word60\setup.exe
    ```

2. Save the APPS.INI file on a server to which users have read-only access.

▶ **To display the applications listed in APPS.INI on the Network Install tab**

1. In the Registry, click the following key:

    ```
    Hkey_Local_Machine/Software/Microsoft/Current Version
    ```

2. Right-click a blank area in the right pane, and then click New.

3. Click String Value. Then type **appinstallpath** and press ENTER.

4. Right-click the item you just created. Then click Modify.

5. In the Value Data area, type the UNC path to the APPS.INI file.

For information about adding Registry settings in setup scripts, see Appendix D, "MSBATCH.INF Parameters."

# Removing Applications

If you installed applications designed for Windows 95 by using the Add/Remove Programs option in Control Panel, they can safely be removed in the same way. Because the application's components are tracked through the Registry, Windows 95 deletes all of the application's files unless those files are being used by another installed application. Shared files are retained on the hard disk.

For more information about removing an application that was designed for Windows 95, see online Help. For all other applications, check their documentation to determine which files should be removed.

---

**Note** To appear in the uninstall list in the Add/Remove Programs option, an application must provide an uninstall utility. Only applications designed for Windows 95 include this functionality.

---

Removing a Win16-based or MS-DOS–based application is not always straightforward. You can delete the directory that contains the application but, especially in the case of Win16-based applications, additional files belonging to the application are often located in the Windows or Windows SYSTEM directory. There is no way to determine which applications placed certain files in these directories, so some of the application's files may be left behind on your hard disk.

Conversely, if you try to delete all the files of an application installed in the Windows or Windows SYSTEM directory, you might delete a system file that is used by other applications. If this happens, the other applications will not run properly and must be reinstalled.

To avoid problems when removing Win16-based or MS-DOS–based applications, check their documentation for instructions about removing them, and keep backup copies of DLLs and other essential system files in case you need to restore them.

# Running Applications

There are several ways to start applications in Windows 95:

- Click the Start button, point to Applications, point to the folder that contains the application, and then click the application's name.
- In My Computer or Windows Explorer, double-click the application's icon.
- Click the Start button, click Run, and then type the path and filename for the application's executable file.
- Right-click the desktop, point to New, and then click Shortcut. Use the Create Shortcut wizard to create a shortcut to applications. To start the application, double-click the shortcut icon on the desktop.

- In My Computer or Windows Explorer, click the icon, click the File menu, and then click Open. Or right-click the application's icon, and then click Open.

- Click the Start button, and then click Run. Drag an executable file from My Computer, Windows Explorer, or Network Neighborhood into the Run dialog box. If there is already text in the Run dialog box, the executable file you drag into the dialog box (including the application's path or UNC name) is appended to the existing text.

- Use the Windows 3.1 Program Manager. For more information, see "Using the Windows 3.x Program Manager with Windows 95" later in this chapter.

▶ **To bring a running application to the foreground**

- On the taskbar, click the button for the application.

    –Or–

    Press ALT+TAB until the icon for the application you want is selected.

---

**Tip**  Instead of starting a popular Windows-based application to view a document, you can use Quick View. For example, if you are searching for a particular document, but aren't sure of its name, you can use Quick View to look at individual documents. When you find the document you're looking for, you can click the File menu in Quick View, and then click Open File For Editing. For more information, see online Help.

---

# Associating a File Type with an Application

To open an application when you double-click a related document file, the file's type must be defined in the Registry. If the file type is defined in the Registry, it appears in a list of file types that you can associate with an application.

For information about associating a file type with an application so that the application runs when you double-click a file, see online Help.

If a file type has been associated with an application, you can reassociate the file type to a different application.

▶ **To reassociate a file type**

1. Double-click My Computer, and then click the View menu.
2. Click Options, and then click the File Types tab.
3. Click the type of document you want to reassociate, and then click Edit.
4. In the Actions list, click Open, and then click Edit.
5. In the Application Used To Perform Action area, type the path to the application you want to associate with the file type.

Some applications, such as Microsoft Word, associate multiple extensions with a file type. For example, a Microsoft Word document is associated by default with both a .DOC and an .RTF extension. This can cause problems if a user wants to change which application opens a particular file. To reassociate a file type with an application under these conditions, you must delete all extensions registered to that application, and then re-associate each file type with an application. In addition, you must redefine Open, Print, and DDE commands for each file type. To do this, in My Computer or Windows Explorer, click the View menu, click Options, and then click the File Type tab.

If you click New in the File menu in Windows Explorer or in the context menu, a list of objects appears, such as Folder or Microsoft Excel 5.0 Worksheet. Clicking an object creates a new object in Windows Explorer or on the desktop. You can add an object to this list by adding a key called ShellNew to the corresponding file extension in the Registry for the related filename extension:

`Hkey_Classes_Root\.ext`

After creating the ShellNew key, you need to add a new string value called **FileName** with a data value that equals the path name to a template file in the ShellNew subdirectory. For example:

`filename="c:\windows\shellnew\excel.xls"`

---

**Tip**  In the Open dialog box in a Windows-based application, you can request that multiple file types be displayed by separating the file types with a semicolon. For example, to see .DOC, .TXT, and .RTF files in an Open dialog box you would type **\*.doc**; **\*.txt**; **\*.rtf**.

---

# Configuring the Start and Programs menus

The items that appear on the Start and Programs menus are arranged alphabetically. To specify a different order, rename menu items to include a number as their first character. Renaming menu items in this way also enables users to start an application by pressing the number at the beginning of the application's name.

▶ **To specify the order in which items on the Start or Programs menu appear**

1. Right-click the Start button, and then click Open.

2. To specify the order of items at the top of the Start menu, skip to step 3.

   To specify the order of items on the Programs menu, double-click the Applications folder.

   To specify the order of items on a submenu of the Programs menu, double-click the Applications folder, and then double-click the folder that corresponds to the submenu.

3. Right-click the item that you want to appear first on the menu, and then click Rename.

4. Press HOME, type the number 1 followed by a space, and then press ENTER.

5. Repeat steps 3 and 4 using consecutive numbers until all the menu items that you want to arrange in a different order have been numbered.

For information about the following topics, see online Help:

- Adding an application to the Start or Programs menu

- Adding new submenus (or folders) to the Programs menu

- Rearranging items on the Programs menu

---

**Note**   Windows 95 adds your most recently used documents to the Documents menu or the Start menu. When you open a file in a Win32-based application, Windows 95 adds the data file to the Documents menu. Windows 95 does not add files to this list that were opened in a Win16-based application. However, if you double-click a document in Windows Explorer or My Computer, Windows 95 does add it to the list.

---

# Using the Windows 3.x Program Manager with Windows 95

Some users may not feel comfortable moving to the new Windows 95 interface immediately after you upgrade their computers from Windows 3.x. To ease their transition, you can use the a Windows 3.x Program Manager.

When you replace Windows 3.x with Windows 95, you can choose to include Program Manager on the Windows 95 desktop. Program Manager does not support the following Windows 95 functionality:

- You cannot copy an item from a Program Manager group to the Windows 95 desktop, and you cannot copy My Computer, Network Neighborhood, Control Panel, or the Printers folder to a Program Manager group.

  The folders that were created when you installed Windows 95 are not designed to work with Program Manager. Program Manager recognizes files only.

- When you copy a shortcut to a Program Manager group, the shortcut's name is truncated to eight characters.

  In this case, Program Manager uses the filename (minus the extension) for the shortcut's name. For example, if you copy the MS-DOS Prompt shortcut from My Computer to a Program Manager group, the MS-DOS Prompt description is shortened to MS-DOSPR. This occurs because the MS-DOS Prompt shortcut uses the filename MS-DOSPR.LNK. To rename the shortcut, click it, click the File menu in Program Manager, and then click Properties. In the Description field, type a new name.

- When you copy a shortcut or other item to Program Manager, the item's icon is lost.

  This occurs because the icon created in the Program Manager group references a file with an .LNK extension. Because Program Manager does not recognize this extension, a generic icon appears. To change the icon, click it, click the File menu in Program Manager, and then click Properties. Click Change Icon, and then select a different icon.

- You cannot quit Windows 95 by quitting Program Manager. To quit Windows 95 or restart your computer, click the Start button, and then click Shut Down.

---

**Tip**  For a comparison of Windows 95 and Windows 3.x features, see "If You've Used Windows Before" in online Help.

---

If you want to run Windows 3.1 Program Manager, it must be installed during Windows 95 Setup.

▶  **To install the Windows 3.1 Program Manager during Windows 95 Setup**

1. In Windows 95 Setup, choose Custom as the Setup Option type.

2. In the Computer Settings dialog box, click User Interface, and then click Change.

3. Click Windows 3.1 (Program Manager), and then click OK.

After Setup, a shortcut for Program Manager appears in the StartUp folder. This causes Program Manager to start every time Windows 95 is started.

After users grow familiar with the Windows 95 interface, they will probably prefer to use it to run applications and manage files. At this point, you can remove the shortcut to Program Manager from the StartUp folder.

# Closing Failed Programs

If an application stops responding, or other parts of the computer, such as the keyboard, mouse, or display no longer function correctly, you can end the malfunctioning process or application without quitting other applications or Windows 95. This ability to recover from problems related to a specific application ensures robust performance in Windows 95.

▶ **To end a failed process or quit an application that has stopped responding**

1.  Press CTRL+ALT+DEL.

    The Close Application dialog box appears. If Windows 95 detects that a processor application has failed, the words "not responding" appear beside it.

2.  Click the process or application you want to close, and click End Task.

Some applications may have several processes running simultaneously. For example, a mail application may be running an executable application and a spooler. If a single process fails and you close that process, the rest of the application may continue to run.

Although it is possible to restart your computer by pressing CTRL+ALT+DEL twice, it is not recommended. Correctly restarting or shutting down your computer ensures that all current information is saved in the Registry and that each application is closed correctly before Windows closes. It also ensures that users who are connected to a shared resource do not lose data when a computer running File and Printer Sharing is shut down.

For more information about restarting or shutting down a computer, see online Help.

# Configuring MS-DOS–Based Applications

Windows 95 configures conventional memory in the same way as earlier versions of MS-DOS, allowing MS-DOS–based applications to run smoothly in Windows 95. For more information about how Windows 95 makes system memory available to MS-DOS–based applications, see Chapter 17, "Performance Tuning."

# Changing MS-DOS–Based Application Properties (PIF Files)

You can set unique properties for individual MS-DOS–based applications. You may want to do this to customize the way an application runs or if the default properties that Windows 95 uses do not work correctly.

An application's settings are recorded in its application information file (PIF). Windows 95 has no separate PIF Editor. To configure an application, right-click the application's executable file, and then click Properties. Any settings you change in the Properties dialog box are recorded in the PIF file.

When you replace Windows 3.1 with Windows 95, PIFs are upgraded to the Windows 95 format. All existing settings should be preserved, but you may want to verify that they have been.

Windows 95 first searches for a PIF in the directory that contains the executable file you are starting. If Windows 95 cannot find a PIF there, it searches the Windows PIF directory. If there is no PIF in the Windows PIF directory, Windows 95 searches the path specified in the AUTOEXEC.BAT file. If no PIF is found, Windows 95 searches the APPS.INF file for a match.

If Windows 95 does not find an entry for an application in the APPS.INF file, it uses default settings for the application. If you replace Windows 3.1 with Windows 95, a _DEFAULT.PIF file remains in the directory. In this case, Windows 95 uses information in the _DEFAULT.PIF file to create a PIF for the application.

If you do not have a _DEFAULT.PIF file and want to create one, you can do so by copying the DOSPRMPT.PIF to _DEFAULT.PIF.

Regardless of how the settings for an application are initially established, you can change them by right-clicking the application's executable file, and then clicking Properties. For more information, see the section "Understanding the APPS.INF File" later in this chapter.

---

**Note**  You can run a batch file using that batch file's settings by typing its name directly at the command prompt or in the Run dialog box. To run a batch file using the settings of the command prompt (COMMAND.COM), precede the name of the batch file with **command /c;** for example, **command /c myfile.bat**.

---

# Changing Memory Settings for MS-DOS – Based Applications

Windows 95 provides a flexible environment for running MS-DOS–based applications, even those applications that must have exclusive access to system resources. Almost all MS-DOS–based applications should run under Windows 95. For MS-DOS–based applications that need sole access to computer resources, Windows 95 offers MS-DOS Mode.

When an MS-DOS–based application starts in MS-DOS Mode, Windows 95 removes itself from memory (except for a small stub) and provides the application with full access to all the computer's resources. Before running an application in this mode, Windows 95 ends all running tasks, loads a real-mode copy of MS-DOS, and uses customized versions of the CONFIG.SYS and AUTOEXEC.BAT files to run the application. After you quit the MS-DOS–based application, Windows 95 restarts and returns to the Windows 95 user interface.

---

Caution  Running an MS-DOS–based application in MS-DOS Mode does not necessarily improve its performance, but it does allow you to run it when it might not otherwise run in Windows 95.

---

▶  **To configure an MS-DOS–based application to run in MS-DOS Mode**

1. In My Computer, right-click the application's executable file, and then click Properties.

2. In the application's properties, click the Program tab, and then click Advanced.

3. In the Advanced dialog box, click MS-DOS Mode.

If an MS-DOS–based application, such as a game, performs badly because of insufficient memory or a lack of appropriate drivers, you can try the following:

- Run the application in MS-DOS Mode.
- Adjust the amount of memory available.
- Create a custom startup configuration by modifying the contents of the CONFIG.SYS and AUTOEXEC.BAT files, either at the command prompt or in the application's properties.

▶ **To adjust the amount of memory available to an MS-DOS–based application**

1. In My Computer, right-click the application's executable file, and then click Properties.

2. In the Application's properties, click the Memory tab, and then increase or decrease the amount of memory available to the application. For more information about the types of memory, see "Setting Properties for MS-DOS–Based Applications" later in this chapter.

▶ **To create a custom startup configuration**

1. In My Computer, right-click the application's executable file, and then click Properties.

2. In the application's properties, click the Application tab, and then click Advanced.

3. In the Advanced dialog box, click MS-DOS Mode, click the option named Specify A New MS-DOS Configuration, and then create a custom startup configuration.

---

**Note** Windows 95 automatically provides expanded memory for MS-DOS–based applications that require it to run. Windows cannot provide this memory, however, if you include a statement in CONFIG.SYS that loads EMM386.EXE with the **noems** parameter. When you include EMM386.EXE in CONFIG.SYS, use the **ram** parameter or use the **x=***mmmm-nnnn* statement to allocate enough space in the upper memory area for Windows 95 to create an EMS page frame. For more information, see Appendix A, "Command-Line Commands Summary."

---

### Tip for Running MS-DOS–Based Games

In most cases, MS-DOS–based games run under Windows 95 with no special adjustments. Most popular games are listed in the Windows 95 APPS.INF file. Games that include a Windows 3.1 PIF file should also continue to perform well. Certain PIF settings are now obsolete, however, because Windows 95 manages them automatically. These settings include foreground and background priorities, exclusive priority, video memory usage, and video port monitoring.

If you run a game that uses graphics modes and Windows 95 fails to run it in a full screen, press ALT+ENTER. To run the game in a full screen every time you start it, right-click the game's executable file, and then click Properties. Click the Screen tab, and then click Full Screen. You can also use the Properties dialog box to adjust other settings that improve performance. For more information, see "Setting Properties for MS-DOS–Based Applications" later in this chapter.

# Setting Properties for MS-DOS–Based Applications

In Windows 95, the properties sheets replace PIF Editor, which was used in earlier versions of Windows to optimize settings for MS-DOS–based applications.

▶ **To view or modify the properties settings for an MS-DOS–based program**

1. Right-click the icon for the program, and then click Properties. (If the program's icon is not on the Windows 95 desktop, use Windows Explorer to find the program, then right-click the icon in Windows Explorer.) This displays the properties sheets for the program.

2. Click the tab you want to use and change the options as appropriate. (See the following section for information about all of these options.)

3. Do the same for all other options and tabs, and then click OK.

MS-DOS–based programs have six properties sheets—General, Program, Font, Memory, Screen, and Misc.

Use the General properties to see information about the type, size, and location of the MS-DOS–based application. From this properties sheet, you can turn on and off the Read Only, Archive, Hidden, and System attributes, which have the same meaning as they do in MS-DOS.

**Caution**  Do not change file attributes unless you are absolutely sure of what you are doing.

General properties
for an MS-DOS–
based application

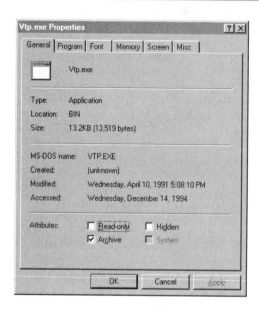

Use the Program properties to identify details about how the program will be run.

Program properties
for an MS-DOS–
based application

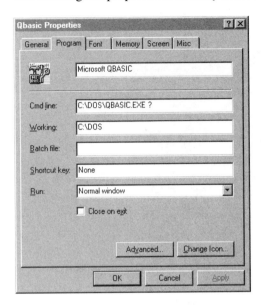

| Option | Comments |
|---|---|
| (Filename) | Include the filename for the application. |
| Command Line | Type the full command line, including the correct drive, path, and options, to run this application. |
| Working | Specify the working directory. |
| Batch File | Type the name of a batch file you want to run before the program starts. |
| Shortcut Key | Specify the key combination (if any) that you want to use to quickly switch to this application. |
| Run | Choose whether to run the program in a normal-sized window, a maximized window, or a minimized window. |
| Close on Exit | Check this box if you want the window to close after the MS-DOS – based program has ended. |

Use the Advanced command button to specify information about the mode in which your program will run.

Advanced properties for an MS-DOS–based application

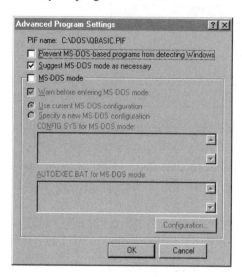

| Option | Comments |
|--------|----------|
| Prevent MS-DOS– based Programs From Detecting Windows | Check this box to hide Windows 95 from MS-DOS–based applications for those applications that cannot run or that perform poorly if they detect the presence of Windows 95. |
| Suggest MS-DOS Mode As Necessary | Check this box to allow Windows 95 to detect whether MS-DOS–based applications run best in MS-DOS Mode. If it detects such an application, Windows 95 runs a wizard to set up a custom command to run the application. |
| MS-DOS Mode | Check this box to run this program in exclusive MS-DOS Mode. No other processes are allowed to run simultaneously if you use this option. |
| Warn Before Entering MS-DOS Mode | Check this box to enable the automatic warning presented when Windows 95 is about to run an application that requires MS-DOS Mode and must shut down all other applications. If this option is checked, Windows 95 will warn the user before beginning the shutdown process. |
| Specify A New MS-DOS Configuration | Check this box to edit the CONFIG.SYS and AUTOEXEC.BAT files in the corresponding text boxes or by clicking the Configuration button. |

| Option | Comments |
|--------|----------|
| CONFIG.SYS For MS-DOS Mode | Type any lines you want to add to CONFIG.SYS to allow this application to run properly. This version of CONFIG.SYS is used only for the MS-DOS Mode session in which this application runs. |
| AUTOEXEC.BAT For MS-DOS Mode | Type any lines you want to add to AUTOEXEC.BAT for this application. This version of AUTOEXEC.BAT is used only for the MS-DOS Mode session in which this application runs. |

As shown in the preceding table, you can set the path for a specific MS-DOS–based application that runs in MS-DOS Mode in the AUTOEXEC.BAT box. For MS-DOS–based applications that don't run in MS-DOS Mode, you can only set a working directory. You can set a global path for all MS-DOS–based applications by adding a path statement in AUTOEXEC.BAT. You can also write a batch file that sets a path for an MS-DOS–based application; for example:

```
path=%path%;c:\utils;c:\norton
```

After you write the batch file, create a shortcut to your MS-DOS–based application, and specify the batch file's path and name in the Batch File field of the Program properties.

From the Font properties, you can specify the font size and type to be used when the MS-DOS–based program runs. From Font properties, you can also preview how the program window and the font will appear.

Font properties for an MS-DOS–based application

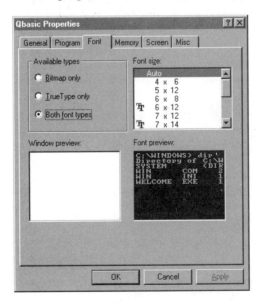

From the Memory properties, you can define the following memory allocation options:

- Conventional memory, which consists of the first 640K of memory available on your computer.

- Expanded memory, which can be installed as an expanded memory card or emulated by an expanded memory manager (EMM). EMM software maps pages of expanded memory onto the system's upper memory area.

- Extended memory, which is essentially a seamless upward extension of the original 1-MB address space available in the memory of 80286 and 80386 computers. Extended memory always starts at exactly 1024K, where the upper memory area ends.

- MS-DOS protected-mode memory, which Windows 95 automatically provides as expanded memory for MS-DOS–based applications that require it to run. It cannot provide this memory, however, if you include a statement in CONFIG.SYS that loads EMM386.EXE with the **noems** parameter. Use the **ram** parameter when loading EMM386.EXE in CONFIG.SYS, or use the **x=**mmmm-nnnn statement to allocate enough space in the upper memory area for Windows 95 to create an EMS page frame.

Using Upper Memory Blocks (UMBs) and High Memory Area (HMA) are two ways to free conventional memory for use by MS-DOS–based applications, and thus improve performance. In conventional memory, UMBs are the unused part of upper memory from 640K to 1 MB, where information can be mapped to free memory below 640K. HMA is the first 64K of extended memory, where drivers can be loaded to free conventional memory.

Memory properties
for an MS-DOS–
based application

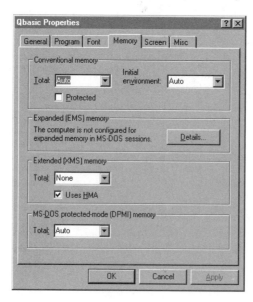

From the Screen properties, you can specify options for how the application will be displayed.

Screen properties for an MS-DOS–based application

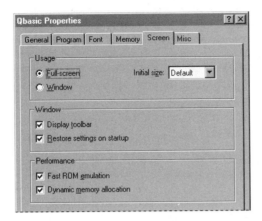

| Option | Comments |
|--------|----------|
| Usage | Specify whether the application will run in a window with an initial size you can specify, a full-screen window, or a window with a size automatically determined by the graphic mode it uses. |
| Windows | Choose whether to display a toolbar or to preserve the previous Windows 95 window settings. |
| Performance | Choose Dynamic Memory Allocation to use the Windows 95 video ROM-handling capabilities. Choose Fast ROM Emulation to enable VxD emulation of selected video ROM services and to speed up video operations, particularly text output. |

From the Misc properties, you can specify details about running your program in the foreground and in the background. You can specify whether your program must have exclusive access to the system when it is in the foreground and whether running a screen saver is allowed when the program is active. You can also specify whether the program must be suspended when it is in the background.

In addition, you can specify preferences for mouse, idle sensitivity, Windows hot keys, and other options.

Miscellaneous
properties for an
MS-DOS–based
application

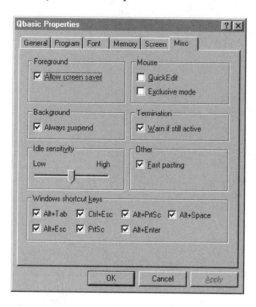

In Windows 95, the Properties dialog box replaces PIF Editor, which was used in earlier versions of Windows to optimize the settings for MS-DOS–based applications.

For information about changing the properties for executable files, see online Help. For Help on the Properties dialog box of an executable file, click the question mark button at the top of the dialog box, and then click the item you want information about.

# Setting Paths for MS-DOS–Based Applications

You can set the path for a specific MS-DOS–based application that runs in MS-DOS Mode by carrying out the following procedure.

▶ **To specify a path for MS-DOS–based applications that run in MS-DOS Mode**

1. Right-click the application's executable file, and then click Properties.

2. Click the Application tab, and then click Advanced.

3.  Make sure MS-DOS Mode is checked.

4.  In the AUTOEXEC.BAT For MS-DOS Mode area, specify the correct path.

---

**Note**  For MS-DOS–based applications that do not run in MS-DOS Mode, you can set only a working directory.

---

You can set a global path for all MS-DOS–based applications by adding a path statement to AUTOEXEC.BAT. You can also write a batch file that sets a path for an MS-DOS–based application; for example:

```
path=%path%;c:\utils;c:\norton
```

After you write the batch file, carry out the following procedure to ensure that Windows runs it before starting your MS-DOS–based application.

▶  **To run a batch file before starting an MS-DOS–based application**

1.  In the application's properties, click Program.

2.  In the Batch File area, specify the batch file's path and name.

3.  If you want the VM window in which the batch file is running to close after the batch file has finished, make sure the Close On Exit box is checked.

For more information about commands that can be used in batch files, see Appendix A, "Command-Line Commands Summary."

# Understanding the APPS.INF File

APPS.INF contains a section named [PIF95] that acts as a master list of settings for MS-DOS–based applications. Each line in this section corresponds to a subsequent entry in APPS.INF that contains information about running that specific application.

Each entry in the [PIF95] section uses the following syntax:

*app file=%title%, icon file, icon num, set working, section, other file, set pif*

| Entry | Meaning |
|-------|---------|
| *app file* | The filename, with extension, of the application's executable file. |
| *title* | The name that appears in the application's title bar. The string identifier must appear in the [Strings] section of the INF file, set to the quoted name of the application. |
| *icon file* | The file from which to extract the application's icon. |
| *icon num* | The number from the icon extraction table. The default is **0**. |
| *set working* | Allows the computer to automatically set the working directory to the one that contains the executable (**0**, the default), or prevents it from doing so (**1**). |
| *section* | The name of the corresponding section in APPS.INF that contains details about this application. |
| *other file* | The key file within a directory for this application, used when two *app file* entries are identically named. |
| *set pif* | The value allowing (**0**, the default) or preventing (**1**) creation of a PIF file for this application. |

Each section following the [PIF95] section includes entries that define any parameters, any required memory or other options, and options that can be enabled or disabled. For example:

```
[WORD.EXE]
LowMem=384
Enable=cwe
Disable=win,bgd,asp
```

The **Enabled=** and **Disabled=** entries use the following abbreviations. To separate multiple entries, use commas.

| Entry | Meaning | Entry | Meaning |
|-------|---------|-------|---------|
| aen | ALT+ENTER | eml | EMS memory locked |
| aes | ALT+ESC | ems | EMS memory |
| afp | Allow fast paste | emt | Emulate ROM |
| aps | ALT+PRINT SCREEN | exc | Exclusive mode |
| asp | ALT+SPACE | gmp | Global memory protection |
| ata | ALT+TAB | hma | Use HMA |
| awc | Automatic window conversion | lml | Low memory locked |
| bgd | Background | mse | Mouse |
| cdr | CD-ROM | net | Network |
| ces | CTRL+ESC | psc | PRINT SCREEN |
| cwe | Close on exit | rvm | Retain video memory |
| dit | Detect idle time | rwp | Run Windows applications |
| dos | Real mode | win | Run in a window |
| dsk | Disk lock | xml | XMS memory locked |

# Using OLE to Share Data Between Applications

Windows 95 includes built-in OLE functionality that enables you to share data between OLE-compliant applications. Using applications that take advantage of OLE technology, you can create OLE documents that contain multiple types of data and that allow you (or other users) to edit or display that data without running other applications.

OLE is a technology built into Windows 95 that improves on the OLE 1.0 standard. It provides services for sharing OLE objects (units of data) and the related functions needed to manipulate that data. In Windows 95, the file STORAGE.DLL manages OLE documents.

Under Windows 95, applications that use OLE technology can use new OLE objects, and new OLE applications can use OLE 1.0 objects. However, in each case, functionality is limited to OLE 1.0. For example, OLE 1.0 does not include in-place interaction, so when you double-click an object in an OLE 1.0 application, the source application starts and the object is displayed in another window.

The new OLE technology provides a way of communicating between container applications and object applications. *Container applications* maintain OLE documents, and *object applications* act as servers to provide various data objects (such as text, bitmaps, spreadsheets, spreadsheet cells, or sound clips) to be included in the OLE document. The container application does not need any information about the object application or its specific data type to communicate with it.

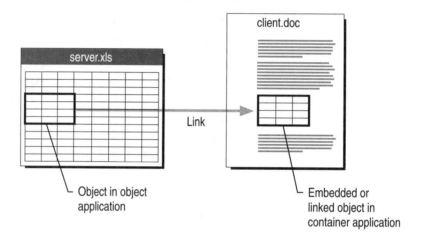

Windows 95 keeps track of OLE objects by keeping an entry for each one in the Registry. Each entry includes a unique identification tag for the object and an application identifier. The application identifier is also used as a class name when OLE objects are placed in OLE containers. For example, "Word.Document.6" is the application identifier for a Word 6.0 document.

---

**Note** With ClipBook Viewer, an OLE application that is located in the OTHER\CLIPBOOK directory on the Windows 95 compact disc, you can share OLE objects for use in documents across a network. For more information, see Help in ClipBook Viewer.

---

OLE objects can be *visually edited*, meaning that users can activate objects and edit, play, or otherwise manipulate them in the location in which they are embedded.

To enable visual editing, both the container application and the object application must be OLE-compliant and must support the OLE visual editing interface. If either the container or the object application (or both) meets only the OLE 1.0 specification, the object application will be launched in its own window for editing. For example, Corel® Draw 4.0 implements some features of OLE that do not include the visual editing interface, so when a Corel Draw 4.0 object is opened for editing, the Corel Draw 4.0 application will start in its own window.

If an embedded object has a filename extension that is not associated with any application, you may be unable to successfully activate it. You must first associate the file type with an application. For information about associating file types with applications, see online Help.

To move or copy an object, you can drag it from one container to another. When doing so, use the following key combinations.

| Mouse Action | Result |
|---|---|
| Drag and drop | Determined by target and source; usually Move |
| SHIFT+drag and drop | Move the object |
| CTRL+drag and drop | Copy the object |
| SHIFT+CTRL+drag and drop | Link the object from the source to the container |

For OLE-compliant applications, when an object is dragged between documents, it automatically becomes embedded in the destination document, unless the data type is the same for both the source and the destination application. In this case, the information is merely placed as native data.

# Technical Notes on Application Support

This section summarizes technical information about running applications under Windows 95. For information about the supporting system components, see Chapter 31, "Windows 95 Architecture."

## System Changes Affecting Application Support

The following sections describe how system changes affect 16-bit and 32-bit applications and MS-DOS–based applications.

Windows 95 changes the system configuration files, as described in Chapter 6, "Setup Technical Discussion." The following changes affect application support:

- If no **files=** line is specified in CONFIG.SYS, Windows 95 uses a setting of 60.

- Windows 95 enables file sharing by default. Therefore, it is no longer necessary to add **share.exe** to AUTOEXEC.BAT or **vshare** to SYSTEM.INI.

- Many application settings have moved from INI files to the Registry. If you install an application after Windows 95 is installed, and the setup application writes directly to the WIN.INI and SYSTEM.INI files instead of using documented functions, Windows 95 does not recognize those changes. To resolve this problem, or obtain a version of the application that is designed for Windows 95.

## Support for Win32-Based Applications

Applications that use Win32 APIs and are designed for Windows 95 can take full advantage of all Windows 95 performance enhancement features. Win32-based applications feature several benefits over Win16-based applications, including preemptive multitasking, Win32 APIs, long filename support, separate message queues, and memory protection. Each Win32-based application runs in its own fully protected, private address space, preventing it from causing the operating system or other applications to fail and preventing interference from errors generated by other applications. An added benefit is that you can manage files from the Open dialog box in Win32-based applications.

To support preemptive multitasking, the Windows 95 kernel schedules the time allotted for running applications. This results in smoother concurrent processing and prevents any one application from using all system resources without permitting other tasks to run. (An exception is when you run an MS-DOS–based application in MS-DOS Mode, which gives the application exclusive use of system resources.) Win32-based applications can implement threads to improve the level of detail at which they can take advantage of multitasking.

Under Windows 3.1, the operating system passes control to another task, allowing that task to be scheduled cooperatively, at the point when an application checks the system message queue. In this case, if an application doesn't check the message queue on a regular basis, or if the application stops and thus prevents other applications from checking the message queue, the system keeps other tasks suspended until the errant application is ended. Under Windows 95, each Win32-based application has its own message queue and thus is not affected by how other tasks access message queues.

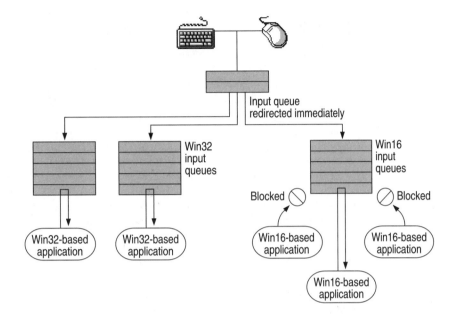

Resources allocated for each Win32-based application tracked on a per-thread basis are automatically freed when the application ends. If an application stops responding, you can press CTRL+ALT+DEL to display the Close Application dialog box, and then close the unresponsive application without affecting other running tasks.

To make the most of Windows 95, your applications should:

- Be Win32-based
- Be OLE-compliant to allow for data sharing with other applications
- Use Remote Procedure Call (RPC) for networked NetBIOS applications
- Use Windows Sockets for networked non-NetBIOS applications

Win32-based applications that run under Windows NT will run well under Windows 95 if the application does not use any Windows NT-specific APIs (such as those for security) or if it has been designed to run under both Windows 95 and Windows NT.

## Support for Win16-Based Applications

Win16-based applications designed for Windows 3.1 run under Windows 95 without modification. Windows 95 ensures that any Win16-based application runs on a 4-MB (or greater) computer as well as or better than it did under Windows 3.1. In addition, the performance of Win16-based applications is improved because it can use operating system services provided by the 32-bit system components of Windows 95, including 32-bit device driver components and 32-bit subsystems.

Windows 95 provides the same system resources to both Win32-based and Win16-based applications, but Win16-based applications cannot take advantage of preemptive multitasking. Win16-based applications share memory, a common input queue, and a common message queue, and their processes are scheduled cooperatively.

Win16-based applications benefit from preemptive multitasking of other system components, including the 32-bit print and communications subsystems and improvements made in system robustness and protection for the Windows 95 system kernel.

Because all Win16-based applications run in the same virtual machine (VM), an errant application can cause other Win16-based applications to fail, but shouldn't adversely affect Win32-based applications. However, the improvements made to overall system-wide robustness significantly increase the system's ability to recover from an errant application and improved cleanup of the system lessens the likelihood of application errors. Windows 95 tracks resources allocated by Win16-based applications and uses the information to clean up the system after an application exits or ends abnormally, thus freeing up unused resources that the rest of the system can use. If an application does fail, you can press CTRL+ALT+DEL to display the Close Application dialog box, and then close the unresponsive application without affecting other running tasks, as described in "Closing Failed Programs" earlier in this chapter.

---

**Note**  Win16-based applications cannot use long filenames. The Windows 95 file system should preserve long filenames while you use a Win16-based application to edit files. However, you will lose long filenames if you copy files from within existing Win16-based applications such as user interface replacements.

---

## Support for MS-DOS–Based Applications

Windows 95 includes many improvements over Windows 3.1 for running MS-DOS–based applications, including better printing support and improved capabilities for running hardware-intensive applications such as games.

As with Windows 3.1, each MS-DOS–based application runs in its own virtual machine (VM), which allows multiple 8086-compatible sessions to run on the CPU. This, in turn, allows existing MS-DOS–based applications to run preemptively with the rest of the system. The use of virtual device drivers (VxDs) provides common regulated access to hardware resources. Each application running in a VM appears to run on its own individual computer; this allows applications that were not designed for multitasking to run concurrently with other applications.

VMs are protected from each other, and from other running applications. This prevents errant MS-DOS–based applications from overwriting memory that is occupied or used by system components or other applications. If an MS-DOS–based application attempts to access memory outside its address space, the system notifies the user and ends the MS-DOS–based application.

One of the major difficulties MS-DOS–based applications had in the VMs in earlier versions of Windows was insufficient conventional memory space. By the time MS-DOS–based device drivers, TSR applications, and networking components were loaded with Windows, there often wasn't enough conventional memory left to allow the MS-DOS–based application to load or run. Windows 95 provides 32-bit, protected-mode driver components that replace many 16-bit, real-mode device driver and TSR counterparts, improving overall system performance and using no conventional memory. The memory savings with protected-mode components can be significant. For example, a computer using only Windows 95 protected-mode components would save more than 225K of conventional memory over the amount used by real-mode networking software, drivers for a mouse and SCSI CD-ROM drive, and SMARTDrive.

# How Windows 95 Accommodates Application Problems

Some Windows-based and MS-DOS–based applications may not run well under Windows 95 because they were written to take advantage of characteristics of older operating systems. For example, certain applications use a portion of the title bar to include items other than the title, such as a Quick Help button. Because Windows 95 title bars are not formatted in the same way as Windows 3.x title bars, some information may be overwritten when you run these old applications.

In addition, some applications use interrupts that are not automatically supported by Windows 95. Others do not handle long filenames well, or incorrectly check for the operating system's version number.

Windows 95 provides a utility to make an application that is incompatible with Windows 95 compatible. You can use this utility to troubleshoot if you have trouble printing from an application or an application stalls or has other performance problems. It provides a means to switch from EMF to RAW printer data, to increase stack memory to an application, to emulate earlier versions of Windows, and to solve other common problems that cause an application not to run with Windows 95. For more information, see online Help.

▶   **To run the Make Compatible utility**

- Click the Start button, click Run, and then type **mkcompat.exe**

---

**Notes**  Many programming tools that are not specifically designed to run under Windows 95 may run satisfactorily, but the corresponding debugging tools usually do not. Make sure that both the programming and debugging tools you use are designed for Windows 95.

Some Win16-based and MS-DOS–based disk utilities must be run with special care. In addition, some disk utilities do not perform correctly with long filenames. For more information about using Win16-based and MS-DOS–based disk utilities with Windows 95, see Chapter 20, "Disks and File Systems."

---

## Running TSRs

Some older TSRs rely on MS-DOS interrupts to monitor everything that happens on the system. However, because of its protected-mode file system, Windows 95 doesn't use MS-DOS interrupts. If Windows 95 detects that a TSR is trying to monitor these interrupts, it will accommodate the application and will send all system information through MS-DOS interrupts. This way, the TSR can monitor system events successfully. However, doing this will slow the performance of the operating system significantly.

The IOS.INI file, as described in Chapter 19, "Devices," includes a list of "safe" drivers and applications. If Windows 95 finds the application listed in IOS.INI, it will not send system events through MS-DOS interrupts, thus avoiding slowed performance.

# Fixing Version-Checking Errors

If you are using an MS-DOS–based application that was designed for an MS-DOS version other than 7.0 (which is the version that Windows 95 reports), you may receive a message that says you are not using the correct version of MS-DOS. If this is the case, you can add the application to the version table. The version table contains a list of executable files followed by the version number of MS-DOS that the applications were designed to run with.

To display the version table, type **setver** in a command prompt window. For information about the syntax, parameters, and switches you can use to add an application to the version table, type **setver /?** at the command prompt.

Windows 95 cannot report the correct MS-DOS version to applications unless the version table is loaded into memory. To load the version table, include a **device** command in CONFIG.SYS; for example:

```
device=c:\windows\setver.exe
```

If you modify the version table or CONFIG.SYS, restart the computer so the changes can take effect.

Some applications incorrectly check the version number of Windows 95. Incorrect version-checking techniques sometimes invert the two bytes that record the version number; thus, version 3.10 would be reported as 10.3. Windows 95 tries to accommodate this possible version-checking error by reporting 3.95 as the version. This way, if an application looks for a version greater than 3.10 or its inverse, 10.3, the new Windows 95 version will prove to be greater.

If the application looks for an exact match for the version number, such as Windows version 3.10, it may not run under Windows 95. To resolve this problem, add the following line to the [Compatibility] section of the WIN.INI file:

*compiled_module_name*=0x00200000

To determine the compiled module name, right-click an executable file in Windows Explorer, and then click Quick View. The Module Name line provides this information. After you have obtained the module name, the section you add to the WIN.INI file should look similar to this entry for cc:Mail™:

```
[Compatibility]
CCMAIL=0x00200000
```

Windows 95 Setup adds entries to the WIN.INI file for many applications that are known to have this problem.

---

**Note**  Do not add a permanent entry to WIN.INI for an installation application. Install your application first, and then edit the compiled module name in WIN.INI.

If a setup application incorrectly detects the version of Windows 95, you may be unable to install the application. In this case, add an entry to the [Compatibility] section of WIN.INI for the setup application (for example, SETUP=0x00200000). Install the application, and then immediately remove the section that you added to WIN.INI.

---

## Running Applications That Replace System DLLs

Some setup applications do not check the version of the system files they are installing and overwrite the newer Windows 95 versions of those DLLs. Windows 95 restores its original DLLs after every setup application runs and for the first three startups thereafter. If an application stops running or behaves erratically after you install it, you may need to obtain an updated version of the application that does not overwrite Windows 95 system files.

Earlier versions of Windows allowed applications to redistribute parts of the system with no ill effects. For example, an application might overwrite a system file with no adverse consequences.

In Windows 95, multiple system files have been consolidated to expedite the startup process. If an application tries to overwrite a system file that is no longer used, Windows allows the application to copy the file, but does not use it.

If your application must run with a replacement file, you can add that file to the Windows SYSTEM\VMM32 directory (which is initially empty after you set up Windows 95).

After you install an application, Windows 95 checks for files that are commonly overwritten by setup applications. If any are found, a dialog box appears, enabling you to restore the files from the hidden Windows SYSBCKUP directory.

# Troubleshooting Applications

### Hot keys fail to start applications.

In Windows 95, you cannot use hot keys to run applications located on the desktop. You can use hot keys to run only those applications located in the Applications folder. To start an application that is located on the desktop, double-click its icon.

### You cannot create a shortcut.

If you try to add an application to the Start menu by dragging the application's icon to the Start button, you may receive a message that says that you cannot create a shortcut. The message prompts you to place the shortcut on the desktop. This message appears if the Start Menu directory is corrupted or deleted.

▶ **To repair a corrupted or missing Start Menu directory**

1. Click the Start button, and then click Shut Down.

2. Click Restart The Computer.

   This creates a new Start Menu folder. If you continue to receive an error message when dragging items to the Start button, delete the Start Menu directory in My Computer or Windows Explorer, and then repeat this procedure.

### .LNK extensions are never displayed.

Windows 95 never displays the .LNK extension, even if you choose Show All Files on the View tab of the Options dialog box in My Computer or Windows Explorer.

### A disk utility cannot write to a disk.

Windows 95 does not support MS-DOS–based or Windows 3.1–based utilities that perform direct disk writes. Direct disk writes using the MS-DOS read sector (INT 26h) or absolute read sector (INT 13h) interfaces will fail unless the application has locked the volume for exclusive use. For information, see Chapter 20, "Disks and File Systems."

### You can't print from an application.

If you cannot print from an application, you can bypass spooling by sending printer output to a file and then dragging that file to a printer. For information about printing to a file, see Chapter 23, "Printing and Fonts."

### The taskbar is hidden.

Whenever you maximize an application, Windows 95 resizes the window so it does not cover the taskbar. However, if an application maximizes itself by using screen metrics to resize its window to take up the entire screen, the taskbar may be obscured. Because this type of application commonly has problems with the taskbar, Windows 95 hides the taskbar when this occurs, giving the application the entire screen. To display the taskbar, manually resize the application's window or minimize the application. To display the Start menu, press CTRL+ESC.

### An application on a compressed drive lacks enough memory to run.

Applications that require maximum available conventional memory should not be run on compressed drives. You might need to run such applications in MS-DOS Mode.

### Running an MS-DOS–based application causes Windows 95 to stall during startup.

To restore Windows 95, shut down and restart the computer, and then press F8 when the Starting Windows 95 message appears. In the Windows 95 Startup menu, select the option named Previous Version of MS-DOS. (This option does not appear unless you edit MSDOS.SYS, as described in Chapter 6, "Setup Technical Discussion.") Remove the following lines in AUTOEXEC.BAT by typing REM before them:

```
rem cd c:\windows\command
rem call c:\windows\command\<game.exe>
rem c:\windows\win.com/wx
```

Remove the following line in CONFIG.SYS by typing **rem**:

```
rem dos=single
```

### Text on menus and other screen elements is truncated.

Applications that depend on the system font to be a certain size may truncate the text on menus and other screen elements if the text is larger than the default setting. This may occur if users customize their screen fonts. To resolve this problem, right-click the desktop, and then click Properties. Click the Appearance tab, and then, in the Scheme list, click Windows Standard.

### Strange colors and patterns appear on the desktop.

Some Windows 3.1 applications hook into the desktop so they can be aware of all the events that take place there. When all applications were minimized in Windows 3.1, the desktop was the background area. In Windows 95, however, the background area is always covered by the new Windows 95 shell. Applications that subclass the old desktop no longer monitor any activity. If such applications attempt to draw on the old background, images will appear on the new desktop, but they will conflict with images that the Windows 95 interface draws there. Users will be unable to interact with the images such applications draw.

This problem typically occurs with screen background/wallpaper applications and with replacement user interfaces, typically located in the StartUp folder. These types of applications may also be started by **run=** or **load=** lines in WIN.INI.

To resolve this problem, remove the application from the StartUp folder or remove its entry in the WIN.INI file. Or obtain a version of the application designed for Windows 95.

### Setup program cannot create shortcuts.

Because of cooperative multitasking in Windows 3.1, Program Manager was always guaranteed to respond within a few seconds of a DDE message. For that reason, many setup applications set the DDE timeout to a very short interval. In some cases, Windows 95 may be unable to process the DDE request in the same time period due to preemptive multitasking. Setup applications may be unable to create an application group or shortcuts for this reason. If this occurs, you can manually add folders and shortcuts to the Programs menu. For more information, see online Help.

### You need to rebuild the Programs menu.

If Windows components are inadvertently deleted from the Programs menu, you can rebuild the menu. When you do, Windows 95 searches for installed components and adds shortcuts for them to the Programs menu. To rebuild the Programs menu, first rename SETUP.OLD to SETUP.INI. Then click the Start button, click Run, and type **grpconv -s** in the Open box.

For information about manually rebuilding the Programs menu, see online Help. For more information about **grpconv**, see Chapter 6, "Setup Technical Discussion."

**You need to save a Notepad or WordPad file using an unassociated filename extension.**

If you are saving a file in Notepad or WordPad and you specify a filename extension that has not been associated with an application, Notepad or WordPad will append the default filename extension to the end of the filename. Notepad uses the extension .TXT, and WordPad uses the extension .DOC.

To save a file using a filename extension that is not in the Registry, enclose the filename in quotation marks.

C H A P T E R   2 3

# Printing and Fonts

This chapter describes the Windows 95 printing subsystem and explains how to set up printers with Windows 95. It also presents an overview of font support in Windows 95.

**In This Chapter**

Windows 95 Printing and Fonts: The Basics    755

Printing and Fonts: The Issues    756

Windows 95 Printing Support Overview    757

Installing a Printer    758

    Installing Plug and Play Printers    759

    Installing Remote Printers with Point and Print    759

    Printing Documents    761

Using Microsoft Print Services for NetWare    763

Using DEC PrintServer Software for Windows 95    766

Using the Hewlett-Packard JetAdmin Utility    766

Using the Microsoft RPC Print Provider    767

Technical Notes on Windows 95 Printing    767

    Enhanced Metafile Spooling Support    767

    Bidirectional Communication Support    769

    Printer Driver Support    770

    Extended Capabilities Port Support    772

    Improved Printing Support for MS-DOS – Based Applications    773

    Deferred Printing Support    773

    Image Color Matching Support    773

Windows 95 Fonts Overview    774

Font Matching Table    775

*(continued)*

How Fonts Are Matched in Windows 95     776
Loading Fonts in Windows 95     777
Installing Additional Fonts     778
Troubleshooting Printing Problems     779
    Correcting Problems with Printer Installation     779
    Correcting Specific Printing Problems     779
Troubleshooting Font Errors     785

# Windows 95 Printing and Fonts: The Basics

Windows 95 significantly improves the printing and font capabilities of Windows version 3.x by including the following features.

**32-bit printing subsystem with bidirectional communication.**  The Windows 95 printing subsystem is compatible with the Windows NT printing subsystem, including monitors that facilitate bidirectional communication with printers.

**Quicker "return to application" time.**  Background spooling and the use of enhanced metafile (EMF) spooling significantly decreases the time it takes to return control to the application, depending on job content.

**Better conflict resolution.**  Spooling from MS-DOS–based applications solves conflicts when multiple applications, or applications based on both MS-DOS and Windows, are trying to print at the same time.

**Point and Print support.**  Point and Print support allows users to automatically install a driver for a network printer and print to a network printer. Point and Print support is available for Windows 95, Windows NT, and Novell® NetWare® printers.

**Microsoft Print Services for NetWare.**  This feature allows you to direct print jobs from a NetWare server to printers attached to computers running Windows 95.

**Image Color Matching.**  Image Color Matching (ICM) allows applications to better match the color of images displayed on the screen with those generated by an output device.

**Deferred printing support.**  Deferred printing allows mobile and other users to generate print jobs when they are not connected to a printer. The print jobs are stored on the computer until a printer becomes available. Windows 95 detects the connection and automatically spools the print jobs as a background process.

**Extended capabilities port.**  Support for parallel extended capabilities ports (ECP) allows Windows 95 to print at high speeds and work with ECP devices. Even if you do not have an ECP device, using an ECP parallel port will improve I/O performance.

**Greater font flexibility.**  Because the fonts are stored in the Registry, you can install an unlimited number of TrueType® fonts. In addition, you can print almost 1000 fonts in any document.

**Support for raster, vector, and TrueType fonts.**  As with earlier versions of Windows, Windows 95 supports raster, vector, and TrueType fonts. For more information, see WIN95RK.HLP with the *Windows 95 Resource Kit* utilities.

**Improved font handling.** Windows 95 handles downloadable soft fonts and font substitutions, and better integrates font handling with the Windows 95 user interface, which is optimized for the 32-bit environment. Windows 95 also includes an enhanced rasterizer for more accurate rendering and generating of TrueType fonts.

# Printing and Fonts: The Issues

Before configuring printers and installing fonts in Windows 95, you should consider the issues summarized in this section.

To share a printer on either Microsoft or NetWare networks, the computer must be running a 32-bit, protected-mode client, and File and Printer Sharing services must be enabled. For information, see Chapter 11, "Logon, Browsing, and Resource Sharing."

The following are general issues for printing:

- With Point and Print, users can install printers over the network if the print server includes drivers specified in the Windows 95 INF files. You need to designate which computers are running Windows 95 and which network servers will function as print servers, and configure them to store Point and Print information.

- When purchasing new printers, consider those with support for bidirectional communication and ECP ports.

- ECP ports are not automatically configurable. If your computer includes an ECP, follow the procedure "Extended Capabilities Port Support" later in this chapter to enable ECP support.

- If your printer uses font cartridges, you will also need to install the fonts on your computer.

The following are issues for printers on NetWare networks:

- To take advantage of the Win32-based NetWare print service capability, the computer must be running Microsoft Client for NetWare Networks. However, the computer does not need to run File and Printer Sharing services.

- To use Point and Print with NetWare servers, you must decide which servers will store printer driver files. You can store pointers in the NetWare bindery to the servers that have printer driver files installed on them. For information, see "Installing Remote Printers with Point and Print" later in this chapter.

# Windows 95 Printing Support Overview

In Windows 3.1, print spooling functionality was handled by Print Manager and supported by code in several different Windows-based components. The Print Manager passed a fixed amount of information to the printer whether the printer was ready to receive it or not, causing what seemed to be jerky processing.

In Windows 95, the print spooler is implemented as a series of 32-bit virtual device drivers and DLLs, and consolidates the spooler functionality into a single architecture. The new spooler provides smooth background printing by using background thread processing. This means that the spooler passes data to the printer only when the printer is ready to receive more information.

The new spooler provides quick return-to-application time and is much more powerful and flexible. It allows you to set printer properties on a per-printer basis instead of requiring global printing properties as in Windows 3.1. For example, each printer can have a different separator page and each can specify whether jobs will be printed directly or to a queue.

The following diagram illustrates how Windows 95 prints documents.

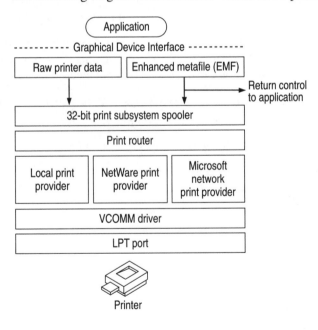

For information about enhanced metafiles, printer drivers, ECP, and other components of the printing subsystem, see "Technical Notes on Windows 95 Printing" later in this chapter. The following sections describe how to install and share printers and how to use print servers on Windows NT and NetWare networks.

# Installing a Printer

Windows 95 uses a new INF format for printer installation. Although the previous OEMSETUP.INF file format is still supported for compatibility with previous versions of Windows, the new format offers added functionality, including support for installing printing subsystem components, such as the printer driver and port monitor, and for installing Plug and Play printers. All information about an installed printer is stored in the Registry.

You can install printers in Windows 95 in the following ways:

- During or after Setup using the Add Printer wizard
- During Setup when using custom setup scripts, as described in Appendix D, "MSBATCH.INF Parameters"
- With Point and Print
- With Plug and Play

If you are upgrading from an earlier version of Windows, Windows 95 Setup automatically migrates all previously installed printers. If no printer was previously installed, Windows 95 Setup runs the Add Printer wizard to let you install a printer.

Windows 95 provides the Add Printer wizard to simplify installing printers and a central place—the Printers Folder—for running the wizard and for managing printing processes. You can open the Printers Folder in the following ways:

- From the Start menu, point to Settings, and then click Printers
- In My Computer, double-click the Printers Folder
- In Control Panel, double-click the Printers icon

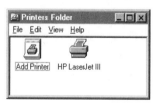

▷  **To install a printer with the Add Printer wizard**

- In the Printers folder, double-click the Add Printer icon. The Add Printer wizard leads you though the process of setting up and configuring a printer. The process is simpler than earlier versions of Windows because of Windows 95 Point and Print capability, as described in "Installing Remote Printers with Point and Print" later in this chapter.

  The only difference between installing a remote printer and a local printer with the Add Printer wizard is that you must specify the path name to the remote printer or browse to find its network location.

**Note**  You can also start the Add Printer wizard by double-clicking a printer on a print server or on a computer running Windows 95.

# Installing Plug and Play Printers

For Plug and Play-compliant printers, all you need to do is plug the printer cable into a port and start Windows 95. The printer reports its device ID to Windows 95, which searches INF files to find the ID that matches the values reported by the printer and then proceeds with installation in the following ways:

- If an exact match is found, Windows 95 automatically installs the correct printer support.

- If an exact match is not found, but a compatible driver is found, Windows 95 displays a dialog box showing the device was found and a compatible driver is available. You can then provide a disk containing a Windows 95 driver that is an exact match, ask Windows 95 to install the compatible driver it has found, or ask Windows 95 not to install a driver at all. Windows 95 automatically determines the best driver to use.

# Installing Remote Printers with Point and Print

Point and Print allows users to install a printer over a network by providing printer driver information. A user "points" to a print server, that is, opens its print queue by using Network Neighborhood, by typing its path name in the Run dialog box on the Start menu, or by starting the Add Printer wizard. Windows 95 retrieves printer-specific information from the server. The type of information retrieved depends on the type of print server to which you connect, and can include the following:

- Printer driver files

- The name of the server on which printer driver files are stored

- Printer model information, which specifies which printer driver to retrieve from the Windows directory on a local computer or on the network

**Windows 95 print server.** A computer running Windows 95 can function as a print server by providing printer drivers and settings (paper size, memory, page orientation, and so on) to another computer running Windows 95. You must share the printer, enabling File and Print Sharing services for either Microsoft networks or NetWare networks. You can apply user-level security to the shared printer. For information, see Chapter 11, "Logon, Browsing, and Resource Sharing," and Chapter 14, "Security."

**Windows NT print server.** A computer running Windows 95 can connect to a Windows NT 3.1 or 3.5 server to retrieve Point and Print information. The printer model name on the Windows NT server must have the same printer model name in the Windows 95 INF files. If the printer model names are the same, Windows 95 installs the printer driver files from the directory on the local computer or network location from which Windows 95 was installed. If the names are not the same, Windows 95 prompts you for the printer model. Printer settings are not retrievable on a Windows NT print server, so you need to adjust printer settings such as paper size on the computer running Windows 95.

Notice that a Microsoft Windows NT Client Access License is required if the computer will be connecting to servers running Windows NT Server. For information, see Chapter 8, "Windows 95 on Microsoft Networks," or contact your Microsoft reseller.

**NetWare print server.** A computer running Windows 95 can connect to an appropriately configured NetWare server to retrieve printer driver files. You can configure a NetWare print server to store printer driver files in the NetWare bindery or store references in the bindery to other servers that store the printer drivers. To configure the NetWare printer server, you must have Supervisor privileges on the server, and the client computer must be running Client for NetWare Networks.

When requested, the NetWare server automatically copies the printer drivers to the specified path on the computer running Windows 95. Notice that you should specify the driver path before you specify a model name. Because printer settings are not retrievable on a NetWare print server, you need to adjust printer settings, such as paper size, on the computer running Windows 95.

▶ **To configure the NetWare server to store Point and Print information**

1. Right-click Network Neighborhood, and then click Find Computer.

2. In the Find Computer dialog box, type the name of the print server. When it is found, double-click its icon in the name list box.

3. In the server's dialog box, double-click the icon for the printer. The print queue for that printer appears.

4. Select the print queue, click the File menu, and then click Point And Print Setup.

5. In the context menu, click Set Driver Path.

6. Type the UNC path (in the form \\*server*\*volume*\*directory*) for the driver files. For example:

   ```
   \\novsvr\sys\drivers\epson24
   ```

7. Copy the appropriate files (as specified in MSPRINT.INF) to the printer path.

8. In the context menu, click Set Printer Model.

9. In the Select dialog box, click the printer manufacturer in the Manufacturers list, and the printer in the Models list. Click OK.

▶ **To use Point and Print to connect to a NetWare printer**

1. In Network Neighborhood, double-click the NetWare server icon.

2. Drag and drop the print queue from the NetWare server window to your Printer Folders window.

3. Follow the online instructions. The Add Printer wizard prompts you to type a name for this printer.

   Windows 95 automatically copies the files for the printer driver (including .DRV, .DLL, .HLP, and other files, as needed) to the Windows SYSTEM directory.

If the print server you're using doesn't support Point and Print, you can use the Add Printer wizard to select the printer driver you want to install.

---

**Note**  Some printers take advantage of the built-in bidirectional communication ability ("Bidirectional Communication Support" later in this chapter) and initially configure device driver settings, such as available fonts and the amount of installed memory, without any user intervention.

---

# Printing Documents

In Windows 95 you can print documents in two ways.

▶ **To print a document**

- If the document is open, from the File menu, click Print.

  –Or–

  If the document is not open, drag and drop the document onto the printer icon for either a locally installed printer or a network printer. The printer icon can be in the Printers folder or on the desktop.

With the Microsoft protected-mode network clients and networks from other vendors supporting UNC paths, you no longer need a physical redirection to a network printer in order to print.

▶ **To print a document to a network printer**

1. In Network Neighborhood, double-click a network printer to open its printer queue, or click an icon for a network printer in the Printers Folder.

2. Drag and drop a document onto the printer queue or icon.

Some 16-bit applications do not work with UNC printer names. If you use a network client that does not support UNC connections, or if you need to have a redirected LPT port to support printing from a particular application, you can still make a connection to a printer by using the appropriate network commands (such as **net use lpt1:** \\*server*\*printer* or **capture lpt1:**). You can also redirect a port in the Add Printer wizard.

---

**Tip**  You can quickly locate a printer on a particular server by choosing Run from the Start button, and then typing the server name (for example, \\**myserver**). You will be logged on to the server and prompted for a password, if needed. Then a Windows Explorer window appears so you can select the printer.

---

▶ **To view documents waiting to be printed**

• Double-click the icon for the printer.

This shows the print queue and the print jobs it contains.

If you have administrative privileges for the printer, you can use the print queue dialog box to manage the printer queue and print jobs remotely. For example, you can pause and purge printer queues.

---

**Tip**  You can use WinPopup to receive a message from a printer that a print job is done. For information about how to use WinPopup, see Chapter 12, "Network Technical Discussion."

---

▶ **To change printer settings**

- Right-click the printer icon, and then in the context menu, click Properties.

  The settings you can change depend on the type of printer you have.

---

**Tip**  For easy access to a printer, use the right mouse button to drag the printer's icon from the Printers folder to the desktop, and then click Shortcut on the popup menu that appears. Then you can quickly print a document by dragging the document icon onto the printer icon.

---

# Using Microsoft Print Services for NetWare

Windows 95 includes a Win32-based utility called Microsoft Print Services for NetWare (MSPSRV.EXE), which has some of the capabilities of a NetWare PSERVER. This utility allows a NetWare server (version 2.15 or later) to direct print jobs (despool) to computers running Windows 95. The computer running Windows 95 must also be running Microsoft Client for NetWare Networks, but does not need to run File and Printer Sharing for NetWare Networks.

A NetWare PSERVER must be a dedicated computer unlike a computer running Windows 95 with Microsoft Print Services for NetWare that runs in the background using no resource except for data packet polling at a set interval. This means it won't interfere with other things the user wants to do on that computer.

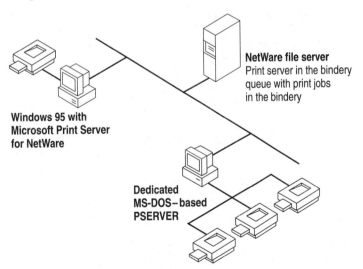

NetWare file server
Print server in the bindery
queue with print jobs
in the bindery

Windows 95 with
Microsoft Print Server
for NetWare

Dedicated
MS-DOS–based
PSERVER

Microsoft Print Services for NetWare uses the queue management services (QMS) API for queue services. It can service one queue for printing to a single printer that is locally attached to a computer running Windows 95.

When you enable the service, it logs on to the NetWare print server, attaches to the print queue, and gets a handle. Then it polls the NetWare print server and receives a header that includes information about how to complete the print job. For example, the header might include information about whether to use a banner, how many copies to print, and other information. Next, Microsoft Print Services for NetWare reads data from the job in the queue and uses Win32 calls to print to the printer. When the job is printed, it returns a call to the NetWare print server.

Microsoft Print Services for NetWare is provided on the Windows 95 compact disc in the ADMIN\NETTOOLS\PRTAGENT directory.

▶ **To install Microsoft Print Services for NetWare**

1. In the Network option in Control Panel, click Add.

2. In the Select Network Component Type dialog box, click Service, and then click Add.

3. In the Select Network Service dialog box, click Have Disk, and then type the path to the ADMIN\NETTOOLS\PRTAGENT directory.

▶ **To enable the Microsoft Print Server for NetWare**

1. Before you set up Microsoft Print Server for NetWare, check the NetWare print server and the computer running MS-DOS and is configured as the PSERVER to make sure they are both working correctly.

   If you see the following message, you will know that the NetWare print server is not configured correctly:

   ```
   Cannot determine print queue name.
   ```

2. In the Printers folder on the computer running Windows 95, right-click the printer to which the NetWare print queue will direct jobs, and then click Properties in the context menu.

3. In the print server properties, click Enable Microsoft Print Server For NetWare.

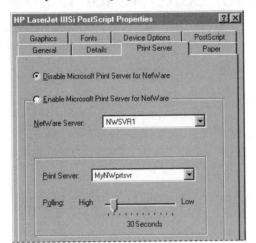

4. From the list of servers, click the NetWare server on which the queue resides.

**Note**  You must have access to this server; only those NetWare servers to which you have access are listed. Access is determined by the user account under which you logged on to the network.

When a NetWare server is selected, the available print server appears in the Print Server list.

5. Adjust the time interval for polling the print queue, and then click OK.

This setting can be adjusted as high as 15 seconds for maximum print server performance, or as low as three minutes for increased local performance. The default is 30 seconds. Click OK.

**Note**  Windows 95 supports only three ports for Microsoft Client for NetWare Networks.

# Using DEC PrintServer Software for Windows 95

DEC® PrintServer Software for Windows 95 provides support for printing directly to Digital PrintServer printers from a computer running Windows 95. This software allows extensive bidirectional communication, which allows printers to communicate both job and printer status in real time.

Also, PrintServer Software for Windows 95 lets you choose the best way to print your file. You can select the input and output trays, choose to print either duplex (double-sided) or simplex (single-sided), and print to any PrintServer printer anywhere on the network. PrintServer Software for Windows 95 provides automatic recovery in case of a printer jam so that pages are never lost.

▶ **To install PrintServer Software for Windows 95**

1. In the Network option in Control Panel, click Add.
2. In the Select Network Component Type dialog box, double-click Service.
3. In the Select Network Service dialog box, click DEC, and in the Network Services list, click DEC Print Server. Click OK.

For more information about this product, see the online Help file for PrintServer Software for Windows 95.

# Using the Hewlett-Packard JetAdmin Utility

The HP® JetAdmin utility is an administrative tool used to install and configure Hewlett-Packard® printers connected to a network using an HP JetDirect® print server (network interface). The HP JetAdmin utility operates as a Windows utility and can be used for networking when a Novell NetWare server is available or when the NetWare file (peer-to-peer) server is not available.

From the HP JetAdmin main window, you can:

- Set up a new interface and printer or change an existing configuration.
- Modify printer settings.
- Filter and sort printers that are shown in the list.

From the New or Modify window, you can:

- Configure the HP JetDirect interface and printer.
- Add or remove print queues.
- Select drivers to install and assign Windows 95 drivers to a network printer.
- Select the printer operating mode and set the printer description.

▶ **To install the HP JetAdmin Utility**

1. In the Network option in Control Panel, click Add.

2. In the Select Network Component Type dialog box, double-click Service.

3. In the Select Network Service dialog box, click Hewlett Packard in the Manufacturer's list, and click HP JetAdmin in the Network Services list. Click OK.

For more information about this product, see the online Help for the HP JetAdmin utility.

# Using the Microsoft RPC Print Provider

The Microsoft Remote Procedure Call (RPC) Print Provider enhances network printing and remote administration by providing the full set of Win32 APIs required for a Windows 95 client to administer printer queues on Windows NT servers. Using this print provider, a Windows 95 client can obtain complete accounting and job status information from the Windows NT server. The Microsoft RPC Print Provider is located on the Windows 95 compact disc in the ADMIN\NETTOOLS\RPCPP directory.

# Technical Notes on Windows 95 Printing

This section presents technical information about the following features of the Windows 95 printing subsystem:

- Enhanced metafile spooling
- Bidirectional communication support
- Printer driver support
- Extended capabilities port support
- Improved printing support for MS-DOS – based applications
- Support for deferred printing
- Image Color Matching support

# Enhanced Metafile Spooling Support

In Windows 95, all output to a non-PostScript™ printer spools as enhanced metafiles (EMFs) instead of as raw printer data as in Windows 3.1. Programs print more quickly (as much as twice as fast as Windows 3.1), so you can resume work sooner.

The following diagram shows how Windows 95 spools EMFs when printing from Windows-based applications. EMFs include instructions about how the document is to be printed. For example, if a document contains a solid black rectangle, the EMF would contain a command to draw a rectangle with the given dimensions, and then fill it in with a solid color, using the color black.

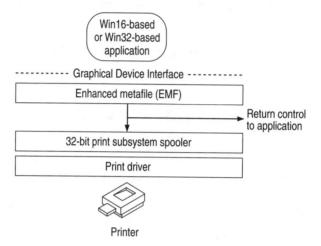

Instead of the raw printer data being generated by the printer driver, EMF information is generated by the Graphical Device Interface (GDI) before spooling. After the EMF is created, control is returned to the user, and the EMF is interpreted in the background on a 32-bit printing subsystem spooler thread and sent to the printer driver. This returns control to the user in significantly less time than waiting for the printer calls to be fully interpreted by the printer driver directly.

Some applications might be able to print only to drivers that generate raw printer data. If this is the case, you should disable EMF spooling.

▶ **To disable EMF spooling in the Printers Folder**

1. Right-click the printer icon, and then click Properties.
2. Click the Detail tab, and then click Spool Settings.

3. In the Spool Settings dialog box, select RAW in the Spool Data Format list, and then click OK.

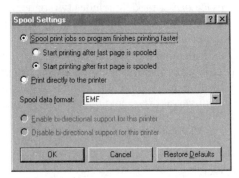

# Bidirectional Communication Support

Through bidirectional parallel communication, Windows 95 detects Plug and Play-compliant printers that return device ID values (as described in the IEEE 1284 specification). This feature allows applications to query the printer directly to find out about its physical attributes.

Bidirectional communication provides the benefit of configuring device driver settings on the server without user intervention. The printer driver can automatically determine how much memory the printer has, what device fonts are available, and so on.

Bidirectional communication also allows printers to send unsolicited messages to Windows 95 and to applications. For example, the printer might send an "out of paper" or "printer offline" message. Bidirectional communication enables much more detailed status reporting on a wider variety of information, such as low toner conditions, paper jams, maintenance needs, and so on.

To use bidirectional printing, you must have the following:

- A bidirectional printer
- An IEEE 1284-compliant cable (a cable that has "1284" printed on it)
- A correctly configured port (some parallel ports are set to AT-compatible mode by default; in this case, you need to set the port to PS/2 mode)

# Printer Driver Support

The Windows 95 device driver model includes two parts: a universal driver and a mini-driver. This device driver model makes it easier for printer manufacturers to create drivers for their printers. Windows 95 provides the universal printer driver, which communicates with other parts of the operating system and includes information pertinent to all printers. Printer manufacturers provide mini-drivers to communicate with the universal driver and with the printer itself. The following sections describe the universal driver and the PostScript mini-driver provided in Windows 95.

**Note**  Mini-drivers written for Windows 95 also work with the Windows NT 3.5 universal printer driver.

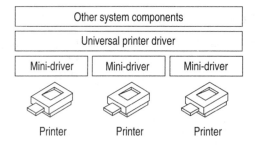

## Universal Printer Driver

The Windows 95 universal printer driver supports mainstream page description languages, including HP PCL®, Epson® ESC P/2, Canon® CaPSL, Lexmark PPDS, monochrome HP GL/2, and most of the older dot matrix technologies. Almost all non-PostScript printer drivers provided with Windows 95 are based on universal driver technology.

The universal printer driver has full support for device-resident Intellifont and TrueType scalable device fonts. It also supports downloading of TrueType outlines to PCL printers with TrueType rasterizers. Enhancements offer support for downloading unbound TrueType outlines and of character sets with more than 256 characters.

The universal printer driver includes the following:

- Full 600 dots per inch (dpi) support; changes allow future expandability to higher resolutions
- Monochrome HP GL/2 support, providing full LaserJet® 4 functionality
- Generic Text support using TTY.DRV

- Support for ESC P/2 raster graphics directly through the universal driver, rather than through mini-drivers

- Easy-to-use properties dialog boxes for configuring printer driver settings

# PostScript Mini-Driver

Microsoft worked closely with Adobe Systems to develop a PostScript mini-driver, which offers the following features:

- PostScript Level 2 support. This feature is automatically enabled for printers reporting as Level 2 from their PostScript Printer Description (.PPD) file.

- Additional support for Image Color Matching (ICM). The PostScript driver allows the server to offload ICM to the PostScript processor to improve performance. This flexibility allows you to take advantage of color raster enhancements on either the printer or the server.

- Control over output data format. The PostScript mini-driver supports CTRL+D handling, Binary Communications Protocol (BCP) and Tagged Binary Communications Protocol (TBCP), and pure binary (8-bit) channels (AppleTalk®).

- Support for version 4.2 .PPD files. These are ASCII files in driver-readable format which contain printer model information that drivers and other software retrieve in order to control a printer. These files cannot be edited. For compatibility, Windows Printer Description (.WPD) files are still supported.

- Support for Simplified Printer Description (.SPD) files. When a printer is installed, Windows 95 reads the .PPD files for each PostScript printer and creates an .SPD file, which is a simplified version of the .PPD file containing only information used by the Windows 95 PostScript mini-driver.

---

**Important**  Windows 95 does not support editing of .PPD, .SPD, or .INF files. If you need to change these files, contact Adobe Systems.

---

- Tracking of PostScript virtual memory availability in the printer. This allows you to print more complex documents than you could with Windows 3.1. However, if the printer sends a message saying it can't print because it doesn't have enough virtual memory, you can resolve the problem by changing the PostScript options settings from Optimize For Speed to Optimize For Portability.

- Easy-to-use properties dialog boxes for configuring printer driver settings.

- Support for installable device options, as described in the .PPD file, through the user interface.

# Extended Capabilities Port Support

An ECP provides high-speed printing, and support for ECP and ECP devices is included in Windows 95. If you have an ECP, you can connect either ECP or non-ECP devices to the port. In either case, using an ECP will improve I/O performance, although ECP devices will show the greatest I/O gains.

An ECP can be configured in five different ways (defined in the port's Resources properties), as shown in the following list.

| Configuration | Description |
| --- | --- |
| Basic Configuration 0 | Standard I/O ranges for LPT ports only |
| Basic Configuration 1 | Standard I/O ranges for LPT ports and any IRQ |
| Basic Configuration 2 | Standard I/O ranges for LPT ports, IRQ, and any DMA setting |
| Basic Configuration 3 | Any I/O ranges for LPT ports only |
| Basic Configuration 4 | Any I/O ranges for LPT ports and any IRQ setting |

▶ **To enable ECP support in Windows 95**

1. Consult your computer (or add-in card) manual to determine the IRQ and DMA settings selected for each of the ECP ports you want to use. You'll need this information to enable ECP support.

2. In the System option in Control Panel, click the Device Manager tab.

3. Click Ports (COM & LPT), and then select the ECP device. (Notice that you will see this device only if an Extended Capabilities port was detected on your computer. If you have multiple ECP ports, repeat steps 6 through 10 to configure each port's DMA and IRQ values.)

4. Click Properties, and then click the Resources tab. This dialog box shows an I/O range that has been detected automatically.

5. In the Settings Based On field, select Basic Configuration 2. (See the previous table for a description of possible settings for this field.)

6. In the Resource Settings list, click Interrupt Request, and then click Change Settings.

7. In the Edit Interrupt Request dialog box, type the IRQ value you noted in step 1, and then click OK.

8. In the Resources properties, click Direct Memory Access.

9. In the Edit Direct Memory Access dialog box, type the DMA value you noted in step 1, and then click OK.

10. Shut down and restart the computer so the changes can take effect. After restarting, you can take advantage of fast I/O capabilities offered by the ECP.

# Improved Printing Support for MS-DOS – Based Applications

With Windows 3.1, users printing from MS-DOS–based applications could not take advantage of the Windows-based spooling functionality offered by Print Manager, and encountered device contention issues when trying to print from MS-DOS–based applications and Windows-based applications at the same time.

Windows 95 addresses the printing limitations of Windows 3.1 by incorporating the functionality for an MS-DOS–based application to spool directly to the 32-bit Windows 95 print spooler. This support is integrated into a print spooler virtual device, which takes the output destined for a printer port and first places it in the Windows 95 print spooler before sending the data to the printer. This functionality works with all existing MS-DOS–based applications, and results in quicker return-to-application time through the use of the spooling mechanism.

Although MS-DOS–based applications do not benefit from EMF spooling (which is supported only for printing from Windows-based applications), users won't encounter device contention issues, and will instead experience smoother background printing and improved printing performance in Windows 95. The print spooling support for use with MS-DOS–based applications is automatically installed and configured, requiring no user intervention.

# Deferred Printing Support

The Windows 95 printing subsystem features support for deferred printing. This capability allows users not connected to a printer to generate print jobs, which are stored on their local computers for later printing. This feature is available only if a computer is on a network or is a portable computer that has been removed from its docking station. It is useful when working at a remote site, or when a network printer connection is temporarily lost because of network or printer problems. Deferred printing works with print jobs created in Win16-based, Win32-based, or MS-DOS–based applications.

▶ **To prepare for deferred print jobs**

1. In Control Panel, double-click the Printers folder, and then click a printer.
2. On the File menu in the Printers dialog box, click Work Offline. The printer will be dimmed in the Printers folder.

# Image Color Matching Support

Windows 95 includes Image Color Matching (ICM) support, enabling applications to offer better consistency between the color of images displayed on the screen and the color of images generated by an output device. The technology supporting ICM is licensed from Eastman Kodak.

ICM provides consistent, predictable color rendering from input, through monitor preview, to output. Applications that use ICM functionality enable portability of color information across applications, manipulating the graphic information; across users, providing consistent use of colors; and across platforms, allowing color information to easily be moved to different systems where the ICM technology has been implemented.

The key to ICM support is the use of a profile, which represents the color properties of a monitor, printer, or scanner device. The ICM profile, provided by its vendor as part of the software for the particular monitor, printer, or scanner, resides in the Windows SYSTEM\COLOR directory. The profile used by the ICM support in Windows 95 is the result of an industry consortium called InterColor 3.0, made up of many industry hardware vendors (including Kodak, Microsoft, Apple Computer, Sun Microsystems, and Silicon Graphics, among others) and industry standard-setting bodies. The InterColor group has established a consistent cross-platform color standardization process, including industry-wide standards for defining ICM properties of output and display devices.

Because Windows 95 includes ICM support as part of the operating system, application vendors can integrate ICM functionality into their applications, and thus take advantage of this new system service. To provide support for device-independent color matching, colors used in applications are tied to international (CIE-based) colorimetric standards, rather than in device-dependent form to specific hardware devices. The operating system then performs the appropriate color transformations to map the device-independent color representations to the colors supported by the physical device.

# Windows 95 Fonts Overview

Fonts are used to print text, display text on screen, and send text to other output devices. Windows 95 provides a set of Win32-based functions that developers can use to install, select, and query different fonts.

Windows 95 provides three basic kinds of fonts, which are categorized according to how the fonts are rendered for screen or print output:

- TrueType fonts are stored as mathematical models that define the outline of each character. They are much easier to work with than vector fonts because they appear the same on the screen as they do on the printed page. TrueType fonts can be scaled and rotated.

- Raster fonts are stored in files as bitmaps and are rendered as an array of dots for displaying on the screen and printing on paper. Raster fonts cannot be cleanly scaled or rotated.

- Vector fonts are rendered from a mathematical model, in which each character is defined as a set of lines drawn between points. Vector fonts can be scaled to any size or aspect ratio, but are much more limited than TrueType fonts. Windows 95 provides one vector font (MODERN.FON) to ensure backward compatibility with plotter devices. It is installed in the Windows SYSTEM\COLOR subdirectory.

Raster and vector font files have .FON filename extensions. TrueType font files have .TTF filename extensions.

---

**Note**  In Windows 95, information in the Registry points to a single .TTF file for TrueType fonts as described in "Loading Fonts in Windows 95" later in this chapter. In addition, Windows 95 includes a hidden file named TTFCACHE that contains FOT type data for TrueType fonts to ensure backward compatibility with Windows 3.1. For TrueType fonts in Windows 3.1, there are two files for each font: the .FOT file contains a relatively short header with pointer information, and the .TTF file contains the actual font data.

---

For more information about fonts provided with Windows 95, see WIN95RK.HLP with the *Windows 95 Resource Kit* utilities.

# Font Matching Table

When Windows 95 uses the font mapping table to match screen fonts to printer fonts, the characteristics used to find the closest match are, in descending order of importance: the character set, the pitch (variable versus fixed), family, typeface name, height, width, weight, slant, underline, and strikethrough. The Windows 95 search algorithm for finding fonts is the same as the one in Windows 3.1. If the necessary size and bitmap are available, the algorithm proceeds in the following sequence:

1. Use the font found in the printer's ROM.
2. Use the font found in the printer's cartridge slot.
3. Use the downloadable soft font.
4. Use the TrueType font.

Windows 95 also includes PANOSE (panose.bin), a font matching system created by ElseWare, Inc., that is based on a numeric classification of fonts according to visual characteristics. PANOSE classifies fonts by the following:

- Serif
- Proportion
- Contrast
- Stroke Variation and Arm Type
- Letterform
- Midline
- X-height

Applications use PANOSE to substitute the most appropriate available font in publications. The application searches the PANOSE database of the font numbers for the font that most closely matches the requested font.

# How Fonts Are Matched in Windows 95

When an application requests characters to print or display, Windows 95 must find the appropriate font to use from among the fonts installed on your computer. Finding the font can be complex. For example, a document might contain fonts that aren't available on the current printer, or there may be more than one font with the same name installed on the computer.

Windows 95 uses the following basic rules for matching a font:

- If the font is a TrueType font, then TrueType renders the character, and the result is sent to the display or to the printer.
- If the font is not a TrueType font, then Windows 95 uses the font mapping table to determine the most appropriate device font to use.

For information about the font mapping table, see WIN95RK.HLP with the *Windows 95 Resource Kit* utilities.

You can also choose from among fonts by comparing similar ones in the Fonts folder.

▶ **To manually match fonts**

1. In Control Panel, double-click the Fonts folder.
2. In the Fonts folder, click the View menu, and then click List Fonts By Similarity.

   In general, if you choose a TrueType font, Windows 95 sorts the list of fonts in descending order with the least similar font listed last.

The following table shows the types of Windows 95 fonts that can be printed on different kinds of printers.

| Printer type | Device fonts | Raster fonts | Vector fonts | TrueType fonts |
|---|---|---|---|---|
| Dot matrix | X | X | – | X |
| HP PCL | X | – | X | X |
| PostScript | X | – | X | X |
| Plotter | X | – | X | – |

# Loading Fonts in Windows 95

Windows 95 no longer checks the [fonts] section in WIN.INI to load fonts. The locations for all fonts are stored only in the Registry and are automatically moved when an application created for an earlier version of Windows installs a new font in the [fonts] section of WIN.INI.

When Windows 95 starts, it loads both the raster fonts and the TrueType fonts listed in the Registry.

- The raster fonts are resolution-dependent and are listed in the Registry key named Hkey_Current_Config\Display\Fonts. (This supports multiple docking scenarios for portable computers in which there can be a different resolution on the LCD screen from the one on the docking station.) The master list of all possible resolutions for raster fonts is stored in the Registry under the following key:

```
Hkey_Local_Machine\Software\Microsoft\Windows\CurrentVersion
    \Fontsize
```

- The TrueType fonts are loaded from the location specified in the key:

```
Hkey_Local_Machine\Software\Microsoft\Windows\CurrentVersion\Fonts
```

Printer drivers, which are loaded later in the startup process, look in WIN.INI to load any available soft fonts. These fonts appear within an application's list of available fonts.

---

**Notes**  Because fonts are stored in the Registry, there is no limit to the number of TrueType fonts that can be installed. In addition, almost 1000 fonts can be used simultaneously, and the same number can be printed in the same document.

In Windows 95, the Enable TrueType Fonts option is no longer available, because the user interface depends heavily upon TrueType. Also, there is no longer a separate Font Installer. You install new fonts by adding them to the Fonts Folder.

---

# Installing Additional Fonts

In Windows 95, fonts can be installed in your computer in several ways:

- Windows 95 automatically installs TrueType and its screen fonts during Setup. When you specify a printer and other options in the Printer Setup dialog box, Windows 95 includes information about font cartridges and built-in fonts for your printer.

- Install more TrueType fonts from disks. After you install TrueType fonts, you do not need to use the Fonts option in Control Panel to install them again.

- Install soft fonts from other vendors on your hard disk by using the utility supplied by the manufacturer. Then use the Fonts option in Control Panel to install the fonts for Windows 95.

- Install a new font cartridge in your printer.

For more information about adding fonts, see online Help.

---

**Note**  If a TrueType font becomes corrupted, Windows 95 detects this and marks that font as unavailable during the remainder of that Windows session and prevents it from being rendered any longer. You can choose to uninstall the font at that point.

---

▶  **To install cartridge fonts available to Windows-based applications**

- Use the installation program that came with the cartridge.

  –Or–

1. If you are using an HP LaserJet or DeskJet® PCL printer, right-click the printer's icon, and in the context menu, click Properties.

2. From the printer's Fonts properties, click the Install Printer Fonts button.

3. In the HP Font Installer dialog box, select the cartridge fonts you want to install, and then click Exit. Click OK.

If you use the Install Printer Fonts button to install fonts, they appear in the Cartridge list in the printer's Fonts properties. If you use another installation program, the fonts will not appear in this list, but are still available for use with Windows-based applications.

▶  **To make installed cartridge fonts available to Windows-based applications**

1. Make sure that the font cartridge is inserted properly in the printer.

2. Right-click the printer's icon, and in the context menu, click Properties.

3. From the printer's Fonts properties, select the cartridge fonts you want to use.

# Troubleshooting Printing Problems

This section describes how to identify and resolve printing problems.

Windows 95 provides print troubleshooting guidelines in online Help, which you should use first to resolve printing problems. If you cannot resolve the problem by using the print topics in Help, check the procedures in this section.

## Correcting Problems with Printer Installation

This section describes conditions that may interfere with installing a printer, and explains how to fix them.

### No printers are listed in the Print dialog box.

If you cannot select a specific model because no list appears, verify that the printer INF file exists. The PRTUPD.INF file in the Windows INF directory stores the information displayed in the Manufacturer and Model lists.

### Setup is unable to find printer driver files.

If the Add Printer wizard cannot find or access the needed printer driver files, it checks the installation drive and directory. If it cannot locate needed files, a dialog box prompts you to specify the path to the required printer driver files. You can either type the location of the printer driver files (installation source directory) or click Browse to search for the drive and directory location.

### File-copy error occurs during printer installation.

If an error occurs with a file copying operation during the installation process, the Add Printer wizard displays the specific error information, including the source and destination paths and filenames it was trying to copy when the error occurred. To continue, verify the location of the specified files, and then retry the installation.

## Correcting Specific Printing Problems

This section describes problems or errors that might occur when printing, and explains how to fix them.

### You cannot print to a local or network printer.

- Clear the print buffer. Turn the printer's power off, wait about five seconds, then turn the printer on, and try printing again.

- Try printing a test page.

- Verify that there is paper in the printer, that the printer is not jammed, and that there are no problems with the printer cartridge or toner.

- Trying printing to a file.

- If you can print to a file, try copying the file to the printer port (for local printers).

▶ **To copy a file to a printer port**

- At the MS-DOS prompt, type

  `copy /b` *filename* `lpt1:`

  The switch **/b** directs the system to print a binary file.

If copying the file to the printer port prints the document correctly, the problem is in the communication between Windows 95 and the printer. Check the following (and consult your printer's documentation as needed for further information):

- Check the printer, making sure it is plugged in, turned on, and online.

- Check the printer's self-test program.

- Check the printer connection and printer cable.

- Check the printer configuration.

**You cannot print because of a network-specific printing problem.**

- Make sure other network resources are available.

- Try connecting over the network to the print server.

- Try removing and adding network protocols.

If you still cannot print, the printer driver might not be working correctly.

**You cannot print because of a printer driver.**

▶ **To check the printer driver in the Printers Folder**

1. Right-click the printer's icon, click Properties, and then click Details.

2. In the Details properties, verify that the driver name is correct.

3. Click the Paper tab, and then click the About button. Verify that the driver version is the same as the one listed in the manual from the printer manufacturer.

   - Try printing using another printer driver. For example, use the Generic/Text Only or Generic Laser Printer driver. If this works, check the driver version, and either reinstall or upgrade the driver.

   - Try printing from the MS-DOS command prompt to determine whether the description for the printer driver in the Registry is invalid.

▶ **To fix the Registry description for the printer driver**

- Remove the current printer driver and reinstall it.

If you still cannot print, an application might be conflicting with the printer driver.

### You cannot print because of an application conflict.

- Try printing from a different application.

- If successful, check the failing application's configuration, and reinstall the application if needed.

If you still cannot print, determine whether you have a spooling problem.

### You cannot print because of spooler problems.

To determine whether you have a spooling problem, print directly to the port.

▶ **To disable all spooling and print directly to the port**

1. In the Printers Folder, right-click the printer's icon, click Properties, and then click Details.

2. In the Details properties, click Spool Settings.

3. In the Spool Settings dialog box, click Print Directly To The Printer.

If you can print, there is a spooling problem; do the following to correct it:

- Use **scandisk** to check disk integrity and disk space.

- Disable EMF spooling and enable RAW spooling, as described in "Enhanced Metafile Spooling Support" earlier in this chapter, and then retry printing. EMF spooling is enabled by default for all non-PostScript printers.

### You cannot print to a printer shared using a server from a network vendor other than Microsoft.

Redirect LPT1 to the shared printer, and then run the Add Printer wizard to set up the printer on LPT1. For example, if a network printer is connected to LPT1, type the following at the MS-DOS prompt:

```
net use lpt1: \\servername\sharename
```

This command depends on the network you are using; consult network documentation to find out how to redirect an LPT port, and then use the Add Printer wizard in Control Panel to set up the printer on the LPT port.

**You cannot access remote NetWare servers when making a dial-up connection.**

This problem occurs when the computer making the remote connection is also running File and Print Sharing for NetWare Networks. In this case, the File and Printer Sharing service automatically becomes the default server, but it cannot receive the information needed to find the remote servers. To avoid this problem, disable File and Printer Sharing for NetWare Networks before you make the dial-up connection.

**You cannot print because of a bidirectional printer problem.**

▶ **To disable bidirectional printing support in the Printers folder**

1. Double-click a printer's icon, click Properties, and then click Details.

2. In the Details properties, click Spool Settings.

3. In the Spool Settings dialog box, click Disable Bi-Directional Support For This Printer.

If you can now print successfully, make sure you have a 1284-compliant printer cable.

**Graphic images don't print correctly or output is garbled.**

- Start the computer in Safe Mode, and then retry printing.

- Disable Enhanced Metafile spooling ("Enhanced Metafile Spooling Support" earlier in this chapter).

- Print with a PostScript driver, if supported by the printer. If this prints, then the problem is a UNIDRV.DLL error.

- If PostScript fails, there's either a problem with the GDI or with the application. To verify that it is an application problem try printing another file or try printing from another application.

- Try printing shorter jobs or fewer jobs at a time. If you are printing a long document or several documents, the spooler may be printing one page over another.

- If the graphic is in PostScript (EPS) format, try copying the PostScript file to the printer.

- For a PostScript printer, try changing from vector-graphics to raster-graphics mode. Raster-graphics mode uses less memory.

### The printer partially prints pages.

- If the printed page is missing part of a graphic image, this may mean that the printer has insufficient memory. To check for insufficient printer memory, try reducing print resolution.

- Try printing the same graphic image from a different document and application.

- Check the printable region by running a print test from the printer.

- If the printed page is missing a section of text, check the font that is used, and verify that the font is valid and correctly installed (check the Fonts folder).

- Try printing from a different document with the same font.

- Try printing from the same document with a different font.

- Try enabling Print TrueType As Graphics.

- Try simplifying the page by reducing the number of objects, such as lines, or reduce the number of fonts.

### Printing is slower than normal.

- Start the computer in Safe Mode, and then retry printing.

- Verify that EMF spooling is enabled, as described in "Enhanced Metafile Spooling Support" earlier in this chapter.

You can also try the following:

- Use the Disk Defragmenter utility to check for excessive hard disk fragmentation, and defragment the hard disk drive.

- Check for available disk space for temporary files.

- Check for available system resources.

- Check the printer driver and reinstall it, if necessary.

- Disable the option to send TrueType fonts as bitmaps, as described in the following procedure.

▶  **To disable printing TrueType fonts as bitmaps**

1. Right-click the printer's icon, and then click Properties.

2. Click Fonts, and then click Send Fonts As.

3. In the Send Fonts As dialog box, click Outlines, and then click OK.

**The computer stalls while printing.**

▶ **To troubleshoot a computer that stalls while printing to a local printer**

1. Start the computer in Safe Mode, and then retry printing.
2. Check the printer driver version and reinstall the printer driver if needed.
3. Check the video driver, and reinstall the video driver if needed.
4. Check for adequate free disk space on the TEMP drive.
5. Delete residual spool files, and then retry printing. (See the procedure named "To Clear Residual Spool Files" later in this section.)

▶ **To troubleshoot a computer that stalls while printing to a network printer**

1. Start the computer in Safe Mode with network support.
2. Try all but the first task in the preceding procedure.

**You send a document to the printer, but nothing is printed.**

- Check that the system has enough free hard disk space.
- You may need to disable Enhanced Metafile spooling, as described in "Enhanced Metafile Spooling Support" earlier in this chapter.
- Check that the spooler has cleared the unprinted spool file.

▶ **To clear residual spool files**

1. Delete spool jobs by deleting .SPL files in the Windows SYSTEM\SPOOL\PRINTERS directory.

   For RAW print jobs, .SPL files contain the actual printer data. For EMF print jobs, the .SPL files contain a list of EMFs that reside in the TEMP directory.

2. Check the TEMP directory and delete all .TMP files. All EMFs have filenames similar to EMF*xxxxx*.TMP.

3. Shut down and restart the computer, and then try printing again. Windows 95 cleans up corrupted .SPL files and their corresponding EMFs when you restart the computer.

---

**Note** An error message may appear, although it may be hidden behind other windows, when you print from a Win32-based application in Windows 95. Press ALT+TAB to bring this message box to the foreground of your desktop.

---

# Troubleshooting Font Errors

This section describes problems with fonts that may occur and explains how to fix them.

**Fonts do not print correctly.**

▶ **To ensure that fonts are installed correctly**

1. Double-click the Fonts icon in Control Panel, and make sure the fonts are installed.
2. Double-click the font's icon, and then click Print.

You can also try the following:

- Print using a different font.
- Print a different document using the same font.
- Print with a different application using the same font.
- Print to a different printer using the same font.
- Verify the printer driver version, size, and date.
- Try using a printer-resident font.
- Print to a file, and then copy the file to a port to see if the driver or the spooler is causing the problem. For example:

  `copy` *filename.prn* `/b lpt1:`

- If the printer supports PostScript and PCL, try printing in each format.
- If it is a TrueType font, enable Print TrueType As Graphics.
- Print with a different mini-driver, such as the Generic/TTY.

### When printed, fonts appear distorted or unreadable.

- In the application, change to Print Preview mode to see if the fonts appear correct on-screen.

- Change the font size to see if the problem recurs with a larger or smaller font.

- Use a different font to see if the original font is corrupted.

- Check printer resolution. Most non-TrueType fonts are optimized for 300 dpi or greater.

- Cut and paste the formatted text into another application and print it. If the font errors still occur, the problem may be related to the specific font.

- Load a PostScript driver and select Download As TrueType. If the job prints correctly, the problem was with the printer driver or UNIDRV.DLL. Otherwise, the problem is probably in the GDI.

- Check printer memory. If the image is large, you may need more memory.

- For a laser printer, enable the option named Send Font As to print TrueType fonts as bitmaps.

### When printed, fonts overlap.

- Try different resolutions, using the same printer. If a higher or lower print resolution works, the printer driver is probably at fault. Try using another printer driver.

**Note**  If the problem persists with more than one printer driver, the problem is likely to be at the GDI level.

- For a laser printer, enable the option named Send Font As to print TrueType fonts as bitmaps, as described earlier.

- Try printing the same information with a different font.

### Fonts do not print properly when underlined or strikethrough text is selected.

- Try a different application with the same font.

- Print in a different orientation (that is, if portrait, change to landscape).

- For a laser printer, enable the option named Send Font As to print TrueType fonts as bitmaps, as described earlier.

### You cannot convert Type1 fonts to TrueType fonts in the Fonts folder.

Windows 95 does not support this capability. Type1 fonts will work with Windows 95, but you need to install ATM ™ to manage them on the screen and install them for a printer.

### Fonts are clipped when printed.

- Recheck the printable region by running a print test from the printer. (Usually, there is a test button on the printer; press this to run a test.) Adjust the paper orientation if you can.

- For a laser printer, enable the option named Send Font As to print TrueType fonts as bitmaps, as described earlier.

- Check the printer memory settings for the driver and printer. If you are printing large images, the printer memory may be insufficient; try printing small images.

### Some parts of a TrueType font are rotated, but other parts are not.

- If this occurs because the printer can only print 180-degree and 90-degree rotation (not odd-degree rotations), redefine the degrees of rotation for the image.

- For a laser printer, enable the option named Send Font As to print TrueType fonts as bitmaps, as described earlier.

- If the problem is font-related, try using another character set, or download TrueType fonts to the printer, and then try again.

### TrueType fonts do not display in an MS-DOS window.

Sometimes changing the displayed font to a TrueType font in an MS-DOS window does not change the font on the screen. TrueType fonts cannot be displayed in an MS-DOS window if the MS-DOS–based application is running in graphics mode. To work around this problem, run the MS-DOS–based application in text mode and use bitmap fonts in the MS-DOS window.

▶ **To change the font used in an MS-DOS window**

1. In the MS-DOS window, click the MS-DOS icon in the upper-left corner of the window (or press ALT + SPACEBAR).

2. Click Properties, and then click the Font tab.

3. Under Available types, click Both Font Types.

4. Click the Font size you want to display, and then click OK.

You can distinguish TrueType fonts by the "TT" designation; fonts without this designation are bitmap fonts.

---

**Tip**  If you print a document to a file, you can copy the print file to print to a printer. At the command prompt, type **copy** *filename.ext* **/b prn**

---

PART 6

# Communications

This part of the *Windows 95 Resource Kit* contains the following chapters which describe the communications capabilities of Windows 95.

### Chapter 24 Introduction to Windows 95 Communications

Describes how changes to the communications subsystem in Windows 95 have resulted in improved communications capabilities. It also briefly presents the new communications features that will be explained in other chapters in this section, and provides an overview of mobile computing features in Windows 95.

### Chapter 25 Modems and Communications Tools

Describes how to install and use modems with Windows 95, and how to configure HyperTerminal and Phone Dialer, two communications applications that come with Windows 95.

### Chapter 26 Electronic Mail and Microsoft Exchange

Describes how to use Microsoft Exchange which provides a central place for sending and receiving messages back and forth among users in a workgroup and among other messaging services such as electronic mail, faxes, and online services. Also describes how Microsoft Exchange lets you move and store documents, messages, and addresses.

### Chapter 27 Microsoft Fax

Describes how to use Microsoft Fax software to send and receive faxes and secure mail messages from your computer.

### Chapter 28 Dial-Up Networking and Mobile Computing

Describes how to use Dial-Up Networking to remotely access a network. It also describes how other Windows 95 mobile computing tools, such as Briefcase and Direct Cable Connection, allowing mobile users to stay connected to their own computers or to the network.

### Chapter 29    The Microsoft Network

Describes how to set up and register to use The Microsoft Network and includes other instructions for providing or restricting access to the service from a network, and briefly describes the features of this new online service from Microsoft.

### Chapter 30    Internet Access

Describes how to configure Windows 95 to access the Internet, and also offers some basic tips for browsing and accessing information on the Internet.

CHAPTER 24

# Introduction to Windows 95 Communications

This chapter describes how changes to the communications subsystem in Windows 95 have resulted in improved communications capabilities over Windows 3.x. It also introduces the new communications features in Windows 95.

**In This Chapter**

Overview of Communications in Windows 95    792

Improved Communications in Windows 95    794

Communications Architecture    795

# Overview of Communications in Windows 95

The Windows 95 communications subsystem allows users to make simultaneous connections to a variety of communications services, including electronic mail, fax, and online services. With Windows 95, connecting to another communication service is as easy as connecting to your network.

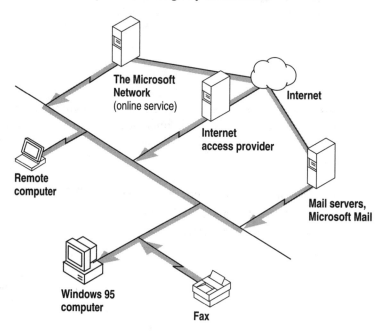

Windows 95 provides the following communications features.

**Easy modem installation and operation.**   Users need only select and configure a modem once for it to work with all applications created for Windows 95. Users can install a modem in the Modems option in Control Panel, or in an application created for Windows 95 the first time the application is run. Two other communications tools facilitate modem calling: HyperTerminal (an upgrade of Windows 3.1 Terminal) connects two computers over a modem and transfers files between them, and Phone Dialer dials voice telephone calls. For information, see Chapter 25, "Modems and Communications Tools."

**Electronic mail and the Microsoft Exchange client.**  Microsoft Exchange is a universal information client that can read and send electronic mail from any message application that supports messaging application programming interface (MAPI) services. These applications include LAN-based mail systems such as Microsoft Mail, or online-based mail systems such as CompuServe® and The Microsoft Network. The Microsoft Exchange client can also send and receive faxes and other remote messages. For information, see Chapter 26, "Electronic Mail and Microsoft Exchange."

**Microsoft Fax.**  Microsoft Fax provides a computer running Windows 95 with all the capabilities of a fax machine. With Microsoft Fax and a modem, users can exchange faxes and files as easily as printing a document or sending electronic mail. For information, see Chapter 27, "Microsoft Fax."

**Dial-Up Networking and mobile computing.**  Dial-Up Networking provides remote users with complete network capabilities, including downloading and browsing electronic mail, accessing shared files, and running a client-server application. Other mobile computing features include Briefcase, which keeps documents up-to-date on two computers; Direct Cable Connection, which connects two computers for sharing resources; deferred printing capability, which lets users generate print jobs from a remote site and print them when they return to the office; and remote mail using the Microsoft Mail client that comes with Windows 95. For information, see Chapter 28, "Dial-Up Networking and Mobile Computing," and Chapter 26, "Electronic Mail and Microsoft Exchange."

**The Microsoft Network.**  With a local phone call, this new online service offers affordable and easy access to electronic mail, bulletin boards, chat rooms, file libraries, and Internet news groups. It is the single best place to get information and support for Microsoft products. For information, see Chapter 29, "The Microsoft Network."

**Internet access.**  Windows 95 provides all the basic protocols and utilities users need to connect a computer to a server that has access to the Internet, and the software users need to browse and download information from the Internet. For information, see Chapter 30, "Internet Access."

# Improved Communications in Windows 95

The new Windows 95 communications subsystem allows applications to transmit data quickly and reliably and to cooperatively share communications devices. The new kernel and communications architecture in Windows 95 provide the following benefits.

**Improvements over Windows 3.1.**  Windows 95 replaces the monolithic communications driver architecture of Windows 3.1 with a modular driver model that allows other software and communications device manufacturers to easily plug in new communications device drivers.

**High-speed reliability.**  Windows 95 supports reliable, high-speed communications. It avoids loss of characters by keeping up with data coming in from the communications port. To quicken communications, the amount of code in the kernel that can be used by only one process at a time (critical sections) has been reduced. In addition, the network architecture and the 32-bit, protected-mode file system of the communications subsystem reduce required mode transitions and interrupt latency. The data-transmission speed in Windows 95 is limited only by the hardware characteristics of the computer, such as the processor speed and the type of communications port. Windows 95 supports communications devices with higher transmission speeds than base RS-232 devices. For example, it supports Integrated Services Digital Network (ISDN), which can communicate at speeds of 64 or 128 kilobits per second, if an ISDN vendor provides a driver.

**Higher data throughput.**  The 32-bit communications subsystem takes advantage of the preemptive multitasking architecture of Windows 95 to provide better responsiveness to communications applications, thus supporting higher data throughput. Consequently, communications transfers in Win32 applications are not as affected by other tasks running in the system as were Win16-based applications under Windows 3.1.

**Support for Plug and Play and legacy communications devices.**  Plug and Play support and device installation wizards simplify installation and configuration of Plug and Play and legacy modems and communications devices.

**Device sharing among communications applications.**  The telephony application programming interface (TAPI) arbitrates among applications that want to share the same communications ports and devices. For example, while Dial-Up Networking waits for an incoming call, Microsoft Fax can send an outgoing fax without the user having to close Dial-Up Networking.

# Communications Architecture

Windows 3.1 used a monolithic communications driver, COMM.DRV, that provided an API for Windows-based applications to interact with communications devices and the code that served as the communications port driver. This approach made it necessary to completely replace the Windows communications driver if new functionality was required by a hardware device.

Windows 95 provides a more flexible communications architecture by separating communications operations into three primary areas: Win32 communications APIs and TAPI, the universal modem driver, and communications port drivers.

VCOMM is a new communications device driver that provides the protected-mode services that allow Windows-based applications and drivers to use ports and modems. To conserve system resources, communications drivers are loaded into memory only when in use by applications. Also, VCOMM uses the new Plug and Play services in Windows 95 to assist with configuration and installation of communications devices.

The following figure shows the relationship between the VCOMM communications driver and the port drivers that communicate with hardware devices.

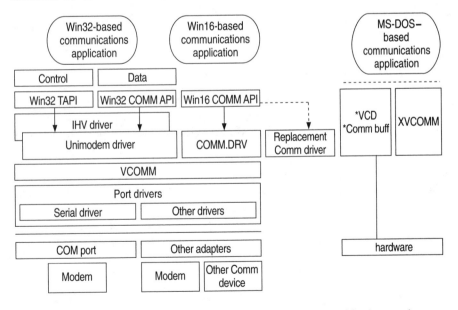

The flow path for a Win16-based application is also illustrated in the previous figure to show how compatibility is maintained when hardware or software vendors replace the Windows 3.1 COMM.DRV driver. The vendor-specific communications driver, however, communicates directly with the I/O port, rather than through VCOMM.

The following list describes the primary areas that make up the architecture.

**Win32 communications APIs and TAPI.**  The Win32 communications APIs in Windows 95 provide an interface for using modems and communications devices in a device-independent fashion. Applications call the Win32 communications APIs to configure modems and perform data I/O through them. Through TAPI, applications can control modems or other telephony devices.

**Universal modem driver.**  The universal modem driver (Unimodem) is a layer that provides services for data and fax modems and voice so that users and application developers will not have to learn or maintain difficult modem AT commands to dial, answer, and configure modems. Rather, Unimodem does these tasks automatically by using mini-drivers written by modem hardware vendors.

Unimodem is both a VCOMM device driver and a TAPI service provider. Other service providers (for example, those supporting other devices, such as an ISDN adapter, a telephone on a PBX system, or an AT-command modem) can also be used with TAPI.

**Port drivers.**  Port drivers are specifically responsible for communicating with I/O ports, which are accessed through the VCOMM driver. Port drivers provide a layered approach to device communications. For example, Windows 95 provides a port driver to communicate with serial communications and parallel ports, and other vendors can provide port drivers to communicate with their own hardware adapters, such as multiport communications adapters. With the port driver model in Windows 95, it is not necessary for vendors to replace the communications subsystem as they did in Windows 3.1.

**Windows telephony API.**  TAPI-aware communications applications no longer need to provide their own modem support list because interaction with a modem is now centralized by Windows 95. All communications services provided with Windows 95 use these services.

TAPI provides a standard way for communications applications to control telephony functions for data, fax, and voice calls. TAPI manages all signaling between a computer and a telephone network, including basic functions such as dialing, answering, and hanging up a call. It also includes supplementary functions, such as hold, transfer, conference, and call park found in PBX, ISDN, and other phone systems. TAPI also provides access to features specific to certain service providers, with built-in extensibility to accommodate future telephony features and networks as they become available.

TAPI services arbitrate requests from communications applications to share communications ports and devices in a cooperative manner. Win32-based applications can use TAPI functionality to make outgoing calls while others are waiting for incoming calls. Of course, only one call can be performed at a time, but users no longer have to close applications that are using the same communications port.

TAPI consists of two interfaces: an API that developers use to write applications and the service provider interface (SPI) that applications use to establish the connection to the specific telephone network. This model resembles the computer industry model for printers in that printer manufacturers provide printer drivers for Windows-based applications. The following figure shows the relationship between the front-end TAPI and the back-end SPI.

| Telephony-enabled applications | | | | | |
|---|---|---|---|---|---|
| Address book | Call control | Conferencing | Mail | Agent desktop | Fax or Dial-Up Networking |

-------------------------------- Telephony API --------------------------------

| Windows Telephony DLL |
|---|

-------------------------------- Service provider interface --------------------------------

| Telephony network interface | | | | |
|---|---|---|---|---|
| PBX | Cellular | ISDN | PCS | POTS |

C H A P T E R   2 5

# Modems and Communications Tools

This chapter describes how to install and use modems with Windows 95, and the other communications tools in Windows 95, including HyperTerminal, Phone Dialer, and Microsoft File Transfer.

**In This Chapter**

Modems and Communications Tools: The Basics    800

Modems and Communications Tools: The Issues    801

Setting Up a Modem    801

    Defining Your Location    803

    Setting Modem Properties    804

    Dialing Manually    808

    Displaying the Terminal Window    809

Modem Registry Keys    810

    Init Key    810

    Responses Key    811

    Settings Key    812

Using HyperTerminal    813

    File Transfer Protocols    814

    Terminal Emulation Types    815

Using Phone Dialer    815

Using Dialing Properties    817

    Defining Calling Locations    818

    Defining Calling Card Rules    819

Using Microsoft File Transfer    821

Telephony Drivers from Other Vendors    822

Troubleshooting Communications Problems    822

    Correcting Problems with Modem Installation    823

    Correcting Connection Problems    825

    Correcting Modem Access Problems with Applications    829

# Modems and Communications Tools: The Basics

Windows 95 simplifies using modems by allowing you to install and configure a modem once to work for all communications applications, just as you do for a printer. This provides the following benefits:

- Centralized modem and COM port configuration through the Modems option in Control Panel for all communications applications created for Windows 95

- Support for hundreds of brand-name modems, including automatically detecting them

- Modem connections and configuration using point-and-click instead of AT commands

---

**Note**  For applications created for Windows 3.1 or MS-DOS, you still need to define the serial port, modem type, and other modem settings within each application.

---

Windows 95 includes three tools for expanding communications capabilities:

- HyperTerminal allows you to connect two computers through a modem and telephony application programming interface (TAPI) for transferring files, and it also automatically detects data bits, stop bits, and parity.

- Phone Dialer allows you to use a computer to dial phone numbers for voice telephone calls. It includes a telephone dial pad, user-programmable speed dials, and a call log.

- Microsoft File Transfer allows you to send and receive files while talking on the phone.

With Windows 95, you can do the following:

- Set up a modem in the Modems option in Control Panel, or in a communications application created for Windows 95 (such as HyperTerminal) when you run it for the first time. Windows 95 provides an Install New Modem wizard that automatically detects the modem type and sets its default settings.

- Send and receive faxes over a modem using Microsoft Fax. For more information, see Chapter 27, "Microsoft Fax."

- Configure HyperTerminal to predefine computers to which your computer can connect.

- Configure Phone Dialer to make voice telephone calls.

- Define the location you are calling from just once in Dialing Properties. All communications tools and applications created for Windows 95 reference that location when dialing out.

- Manually dial a phone call or display a terminal window before or after dialing. For information, see "Setting Modem Properties" later in this chapter.

- Connect to a remote computer by using Dial-Up Networking. For information, see Chapter 28, "Dial-Up Networking and Mobile Computing."

# Modems and Communications Tools: The Issues

Before you install and configure a modem for use with Windows 95, you should decide the following:

- How many users need modems installed on their computers and what are the locations to which and from which they will be calling.

- What kind of security restrictions you want to apply to modems installed on individual computers, as described in Chapter 14, "Security."

- What properties you need to set for making connections, as described in "Setting Modem Properties" later in this chapter.

---

**Note**  In Windows 95, you cannot share a modem installed on another computer on the network. You can, however, share a fax modem over the network. For information, see Chapter 27, "Microsoft Fax."

---

# Setting Up a Modem

You can install a new modem in one of three ways:

- Using the Modems option in Control Panel

- Running a communications application, which causes Windows 95 to prompt you to install a modem

- Adding a modem through the Add New Hardware option in Control Panel

In all cases, the Install New Modem wizard appears, and asks if you want Windows 95 to automatically detect the modem or if you want to manually select a modem from the list of known manufacturers and modem models. If you choose the detection option, the wizard detects and then queries the modem to configure it. If it cannot detect the modem, it prompts you to select one.

When the modem has been selected, you can, if necessary, adjust its properties, such as the volume for the modem speaker, the time to wait for the remote computer to answer the call, and the maximum speed to use.

Depending on the type of modem you have, installing and configuring it might vary slightly as follows:

- If you install an internal legacy (non-Plug and Play) modem adapter, its built-in COM port must be configured by using the Add New Hardware wizard before it is installed by using the Modems option in Control Panel. In most cases, the Install New Modem wizard does this automatically for you. However, on some computers, you might also need to run the Add New Hardware wizard.

- If you are using Windows 95 PCMCIA drivers, then Windows 95 will detect and configure PCMCIA modem cards automatically when they are first inserted. Otherwise, you might need to run the Add New Hardware wizard in Control Panel to configure the card's built-in COM port. Then, you should install the PCMCIA modem card by using the Modems option in Control Panel. For more information, see Chapter 19, "Devices."

---

**Note**  Before you install a modem, check the Modems section in the Windows 95 README.TXT for possible information.

---

▶ **To install a modem by using the Modems option in Control Panel**

1. In Control Panel, double-click the Modems icon.

2. If no modem is currently installed on your computer, the Install New Modem wizard starts automatically to lead you through the steps for installing a modem. Follow the online instructions.

   –Or–

   If you are installing a second modem, click Add to start the Install New Modem wizard.

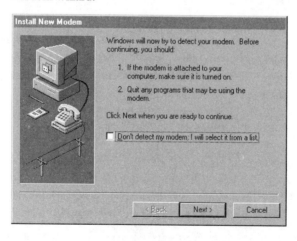

In most cases, it's best to let the Install New Modem wizard detect the modem for you. If it cannot detect the exact manufacturer and model, the wizard picks a standard configuration that is usually compatible. Your modem will still function at its maximum speed and according to factory default settings. A few advanced features might be disabled, such as enabling and disabling compression, error control, and flow control.

For information about installing a modem if your modem is not detected or listed, or about finding a better match than the standard modem, see "Troubleshooting Communications Problems" later in this chapter.

Windows 95 automatically assigns COM names to communications ports, internal modem adapters, and PCMCIA modem cards according to their base I/O port addresses as described in Chapter 19, "Devices."

# Defining Your Location

The first time you set up a modem, the Install New Modem wizard prompts you for information about the location you will usually be calling from (the Default Location), including your area code and country code. This information is stored in Dialing Properties, a communications utility that is accessible from all communications applications created for Windows 95 and in the Modems option in Control Panel.

▶ **To set dialing location information**

- Run the Install New Modem wizard, and then type the area code and country code information in the Location Information dialog box.

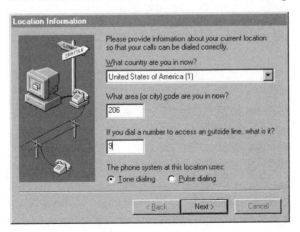

After you install the modem, more specific location information, such as calling card numbers or the number you must dial to access an outside line, can be entered into the My Locations dialog box in Dialing Properties. For information, see "Using Dialing Properties" later in this chapter.

# Setting Modem Properties

In the Modems option in Control Panel, you can globally change default modem settings for all communications applications and tools created for Windows 95. For example, if you do not want to listen to the modem speaker, you can turn it off for all tools and applications that use that modem. Alternatively, you can adjust these settings within each application.

---

**Note**  For Windows 3.1–based or MS-DOS–based applications, you need to configure the modem settings within each application.

---

▶ **To view general properties for a modem**

1. In the Modems option in Control Panel, click a modem, and then click the Properties button.

2. In General properties, view the default settings for the modem that will be used by all applications created for Windows 95.

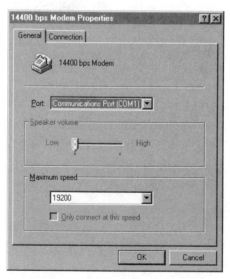

| Option | Description |
|---|---|
| Port | A port is either a COM or LPT port to which an external modem is attached, or a COM port name which identifies an internal or PCMCIA modem. Windows 95 automatically assigns a port name (COM1, COM2, COM3, or COM4) to any device it detects. Usually, the name is adjusted only if you move an external modem from one COM port to another. For PCMCIA modem cards, the port cannot be changed. |
| Speaker volume | Sets the volume for the telephone speaker, which broadcasts the dial tone, modem connection, and voices, if applicable, on the other end. To change the volume, move the slider bar to the right or left. |
| Maximum speed | This is the speed at which Windows 95 communicates with the modem. It is limited by the CPU speed of the computer and the speed supported by the communications port. Windows 95 selects a conservative default speed so that slower computers do not lose data during transfers.

Set the speed lower if the faster rate causes data errors. Set it higher for faster performance if you are using a computer with an 80486 or a Pentium™ processor. For example, 57600 might work better than the Windows 95 default setting of 38400 for v.32bis (14400 bps) modems on fast computers. If applications report data errors, then set a lower speed (for example, change it from 38400 to 19200 for v.32bis modems). |

**Tip**  If you have a slower, older computer and an external modem, you can purchase and install a 16550A UART-based COM port adapter to increase speeds. Some internal modems have an integrated 16550A UART adapter.

▶ **To change or view the connection properties**

- In General properties, click the Connection tab to display the connection options for your modem.

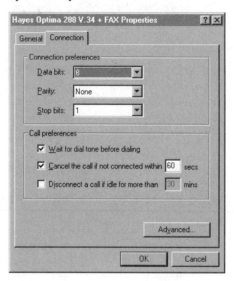

| Option | Description |
|--------|-------------|
| Connection preferences | Connection settings usually correspond to what the computer on the other end is using. Therefore, do not change connection settings by using the Modems option in Control Panel. Rather, use a specific tool or application, such as HyperTerminal, to change these settings on a connection-by-connection basis. |
| Wait for dial... | Clear this option if you are making calls from a country other than where your modem was purchased and your modem fails to properly detect the dial tone. |
| Cancel the call... | Change the number of seconds listed in this field if, for some reason, it takes a long time to make a connection; for example, this might occur when you are making an international call and there are long delays before the call is connected. |
| Disconnect a call... | Change the number of minutes listed in this option if, for some reason, there is no activity on the line; for example, increase the number if you want to stay connected to a computer bulletin board even though there is no activity. |

You can also specify settings for data bits, parity, and stop bits in the Connection properties. For information about these values, see online Help.

▶ **To view or change advanced connection properties**

- Click the Advanced button in the Connection properties to display the Advanced Connection Settings dialog box. In this box you can set error control, flow control, and modulation, and audit the modem operations.

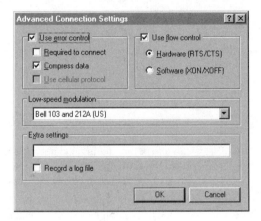

| Option | Description |
|--------|-------------|
| Use error control | Check this option to boost file transfer speeds by eliminating errors caused by noise on the telephone line. This feature is available on most newer modems. When this feature is enabled, modems sometimes have trouble connecting. If this occurs, clear the check box and try again. |
| Required to connect | Check this option if you want your modem to connect with another modem only if error control is enabled on a call. This is useful in areas with very noisy phone lines. In these cases, connecting at a slower speed can improve data throughput. |
| Compress data | Check this option to boost transmission speeds by compressing data between the modems. This feature is available on most modems. When this feature is enabled, modems sometimes have trouble connecting. If this occurs, clear the check box and try again. Using modem compression can sometimes reduce performance if the data being sent is already compressed by the application. |
| Use cellular protocol | Check this option when you want your modem to use special protocols designed to reduce errors over cellular connections. You might want to clear this when making a call on a normal noncellular telephone line. |

| Option | Description |
|--------|-------------|
| Use flow control | Check this option for all external modems to avoid loss of data. If your modem cable has RTS and CTS wires connected, you can use hardware flow control; otherwise, use software flow control. |
| Low-speed modulation | Check this option if you are having problems making an international call. Depending on the type of modem, Windows 95 provides three possible settings: Bell 103 and 212A, A (for calls in the United States), ITU-TV V.21 and V.22 (for international calls), and ITU-TV V.23 (for French Minitel calls). |
| Extra settings | Check this field to type modem commands that Windows 95 will include in the initialization sequence that it sends to the modem before dialing. Do not include the "AT" prefix in this box. The Extra Settings option is intended only for debugging purposes, and should be used only by experienced modem users. |
| Record a log file | Check this option to record commands and responses to and from the modem in the MODEMLOG.TXT file in the Windows directory. Reading this file along with a modem manual can help you solve problems. After you identify the problem, you can adjust the appropriate modem keys in the Registry. Only advanced users should use this feature. |

# Dialing Manually

Windows 95 allows you to manually dial your modem if you are having difficulty making an international call or other connection. To manually dial your modem, you need a separate telephone headset and keypad. You can request manual dialing, using slightly different procedures from within any Windows 95-based communications applications, such as HyperTerminal, Dial-Up Networking, or Microsoft Fax. The following procedure describes how to manually dial your modem by using Dial-Up Networking.

▶ **To manually control modem dialing**

1. In Dial-Up Networking, right-click a connection icon, and then click Properties.

2. Click the Configure button, and then click the Options tab.

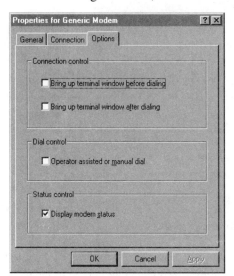

3. Click the Operator Assisted or Manual Dial option, and then click OK.

4. Double-click the connection icon in Dial-Up Networking, and then click Connect.

5. When instructed, pick up the phone and dial the number.

6. When you hear the other computer answer, click Connect and hang up.

# Displaying the Terminal Window

Before or after dialing, you can display a terminal window to type AT modem commands if a connection requires them. A terminal window can be used to log on for security purposes, to establish connections with servers that require a specific logon procedure, and for other reasons. The following procedure describes this process for Dial-Up Networking.

▶ **To display a terminal window before or after dialing**

1. In Dial-Up Networking, right-click a connection icon, and then click Properties.

2. Click the Configure button, and then click the Options tab.

3. Click the Bring Up Terminal Window Before Dialing option, or the Bring Up Terminal Window After Dialing option, and then click OK.

# Modem Registry Keys

The following section describes information stored in specific modem Registry keys that might help advanced users correct problems with the commands that Windows 95 uses to control a modem. To identify modem problems, you can enable Windows 95 to create a MODEMLOG.TXT file (as described in "Setting Modem Properties" earlier in this chapter), which contains responses to and from a modem when a connection was made. The MODEMLOG.TXT file might indicate when Windows 95 is sending an incorrect command string to a modem, or when a response code is not being correctly interpreted. After consulting the documentation for the modem, you might be able to adjust the modem's Registry keys to restore proper operation.

Modem Registry keys are stored under the following key:

`Hkey_Local_Machine\System\CurrentControlSet\Services\Class\`*Modem*

For each installed modem, Windows 95 creates one Registry key (starting with \0000); additional subkeys, which contain AT commands that Windows 95 uses to initialize, dial, and answer the modem; plus other entries that communications and modem drivers use.

Some of the more important entries that you can use to correct or optimize modem operation are described in the following sections. The full set of modem Registry keys and the INF file format are documented in the *Windows 95 Device Development Kit.*

## Init Key

The multiple, modem-command string entries in the Init key initialize the modem before Windows 95 uses it. The name of each entry is its sequence number, starting with the number **1**, and its data is the command that is sent to the modem. Usually, the Init key entry **1** is **AT<cr>**, which is sent to the modem to start it. Init entry **2** usually contains **&F** or a similar command to restore the modem to its default settings. Subsequent Init key entries contain miscellaneous commands to configure the modem so it is compatible with Windows 95.

# Responses Key

The Responses key contains strings that the modem might report to Windows 95 in response to a command or during the connection process. The name of each subkey is the text of a single modem response, and its data is a 10-byte binary value specifying the meaning of the response to Windows in a coded format. The first two characters (byte 0) specify the meaning of the response code, using one of the following values.

| Value | Type | Description |
| --- | --- | --- |
| 00 | OK | The modem accepted the previous command. |
| 01 | Negotiation Progress | Status information about a new connection is being reported. |
| 02 | Connect | A call is connected; the modem is in data mode. |
| 03 | Error | The modem rejected the previous command. |
| 04 | No Carrier | The call was disconnected. |
| 05 | No Dial Tone | No dial tone is present. |
| 06 | Busy | The dialed modem is busy. |
| 07 | No Answer | The dialed modem did not answer. |
| 08 | Ring | There is an incoming call. |

The second two characters (byte 1) specify information about a connection that is being made. It is used only for response codes of type Negotiation Progress or Connect, and is one of the following values.

| Value | Error control negotiated | Compression negotiated | Cellular protocol negotiated |
| --- | --- | --- | --- |
| 00 | – | – | – |
| 01 | – | X | – |
| 02 | X | – | – |
| 03 | X | X | – |
| 08 | – | – | X |
| 09 | – | X | X |
| 0A | X | – | X |
| 0B | X | X | X |

The next eight characters (bytes 2–5) specify the modem-to-modem line speed negotiated in bits per second (bps). The characters represent a 32-bit integer, doubleword format (byte and word reversed). Common examples for this value include the following.

| Bits per second | String |
| --- | --- |
| 2400 | 60 09 00 00 |
| 9600 | 80 25 00 00 |
| 14400 | 40 38 00 00 |
| 19200 | 00 4b 00 00 |
| 28800 | 80 70 00 00 |

The last eight characters (bytes 6–9) indicate that the modem is changing to a different port or Data Terminal Equipment (DTE) speed. Usually, this field is not used, because modems make connections at a "locked" port speed, regardless of the modem-to-modem or Data Communications Equipment (DCE) speed. However, for modems that support only "direct" modes, you can lower the DTE speed by specifying a negotiated DTE speed for a response code, using the same format as the DCE speed described in the preceding table.

# Settings Key

The Settings key contains commands for configuring various modem settings. After the Init key commands are sent, Windows 95 builds a dynamic configuration command string by concatenating various entries shown in the following table. The command string depends on the settings selected in the modem's properties.

| Subkey | Description | Example |
| --- | --- | --- |
| Prefix | Configuration command prefix | AT |
| Terminator | Configuration command suffix | <cr> |
| DialPrefix | Dial command prefix | D |
| Dial_Pulse | Use pulse dialing | P |
| Dial_Tone | Use tone dialing | T |
| Blind_Off | Detect dial tone before dialing | X4 |
| Blind_On | Do not detect dial tone before dialing | X3 |
| CallSetupFailTimeout | Specify call setup time-out | S7=<#> |
| InactivityTimeout | Specify inactivity time-out | S30=<#> |
| SpeakerVolume_Low | Low speaker volume | L1 |
| SpeakerVolume_Med | Medium speaker volume | L2 |
| SpeakerVolume_High | High speaker volume | L3 |

| Subkey | Description | Example |
|---|---|---|
| SpeakerMode_Off | Speaker always off | M0 |
| SpeakerMode_Dial | Speaker on during dial and negotiation | M1 |
| SpeakerMode_On | Speaker always on | M2 |
| SpeakerMode_Setup | Speaker on only during negotiation | M3 |
| FlowControl_Off | No flow control | &K0 |
| FlowControl_Hard | Hardware flow control | &K1 |
| FlowControl_Soft | Software flow control | &K2 |
| ErrorControl_Off | Error control disabled (normal mode, not direct) | +Q6S36=3S48=128 |
| ErrorControl_On | Error control enabled (auto reliable) | +Q5S36=7S48=7 |
| ErrorControl_Forced | Error control required to connect (reliable) | +Q5S36=4S48=7 |
| ErrorControl_Cellular | Cellular protocol enabled | \N3-K1)M1-Q1*H1 |
| Compression_On | Compression enabled | S46=138 |
| Compression_Off | Compression disabled | S46=136 |
| Modulation_CCITT | Use CCITT modulations for 300 and 1200 bps | B0 |
| Modulation_Bell | Use Bell modulations for 300 and 1200 bps | B1 |
| SpeedNegotiation_Off | Connect only at default modem speed; do not fall back | N0 |
| SpeedNegotiation_On | Use lower DCE speed to connect, if necessary | N1 |

# Using HyperTerminal

You can use HyperTerminal with a modem to connect two computers so you can send and receive files or connect to computer bulletin boards and other information programs. For example, you can use HyperTerminal to connect to an online service and to download files from a bulletin board on the online service. You can also use HyperTerminal to connect a computer directly to another computer, such as a debugging terminal.

The easiest way to install HyperTerminal is to choose Custom setup type during Windows 95 installation and then select HyperTerminal when selecting components to install.

▶ **To install HyperTerminal after Windows 95 Setup**

1. In the Add/Remove Programs option in Control Panel, click the Windows Setup tab.

2. In the Windows Setup Components list box, click Communications, and then click the Details button.

3. In the Communications dialog box, click HyperTerminal, and then click OK.

For more information, see the online Help in HyperTerminal.

# File Transfer Protocols

HyperTerminal supports the following file transfer protocols.

| Protocol | Description |
|---|---|
| Xmodem | The most common error-correcting data communications protocol. Most communications packages support (and some only support) Xmodem. This protocol is also supported by most online services. Xmodem is slower than other protocols (for example, Zmodem). |
| 1K Xmodem | A variant of traditional Xmodem, which sends data in 1K (1024-byte) blocks instead of 128-byte blocks. On some bulletin boards, this protocol is called Ymodem. |
| Ymodem | A faster version of Xmodem, transferring data in 1K blocks. |
| Ymodem-G | A variant of Ymodem designed for use with modems that support hardware error control. If you cannot transfer files by using Ymodem-G, your modem might not support error control. Use Ymodem instead. |
| Zmodem | The fastest data transfer protocol, and the primary choice of most bulletin board users. Zmodem dynamically changes its block size based on line conditions, and it is extremely reliable. |
| Kermit | An extremely flexible protocol, found most often on DEC™ VAX™ computers, IBM® mainframes, and other minicomputers. However, Kermit is quite slow and should not be used if faster options are available on the other computer. |

**Note** You can choose a file transfer protocol to use when you send or receive a file by using the Send or Receive File options in the Transfer menu, as described in online Help.

# Terminal Emulation Types

HyperTerminal supports the following terminal emulation types.

| | |
|---|---|
| ANSI | Viewdata (for the United Kingdom) |
| Minitel (for France) | DEC VT 100™ |
| Auto Detect | VT 52 |
| TTY | |

▶ **To choose a terminal emulation type**

1. Right-click a connection icon, and then click Properties.

2. In the connection's properties, click the Settings tab, and then select the emulation type.

---

**Note**  Some modems might not be able to connect to French Minitel in HyperTerminal using the Windows 95 default settings. To correct this, you need to add an extra command in the Extra Settings field in the Advanced Settings dialog box in the modem's properties. Check the modem manual for the command that enables the modem to connect in V.23 modulation to Minitel, and then add this to the Extra Settings field.

---

# Using Phone Dialer

The Phone Dialer application that comes with Windows 95 allows you to use a computer to make voice telephone calls using the calling card and location information defined in Dialing Properties. It also stores frequently dialed numbers, dials stored phone numbers, and logs telephone calls.

The easiest way to install Phone Dialer is to choose Custom Setup during Windows 95 installation and then follow the following procedure. You can also install it after Windows 95 installation in the Add/Remove Programs option in Control Panel.

▶ **To install Phone Dialer after Window 95 installation**

1. In the Add/Remove Programs option in Control Panel, click the Windows Setup tab.

2. In the Windows Setup Components list box, click Communications, and then click the Details button.

3. In the Communications dialog box, click Phone Dialer, and then click OK.

▶ **To start Phone Dialer and make a call**

1. From the Start button, point to Programs, then point to Accessories, and then click Phone Dialer.

2. In the Phone Dialer dialog box, type a phone number either from your keyboard or use the Phone Dialer numeric keypad. Click Dial.

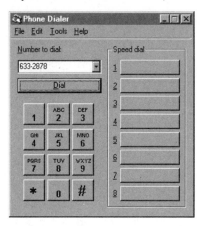

When you dial a number with Phone Dialer, the number is automatically stored in a list of your most recently used telephone numbers. All local, domestic long-distance, or international telephone numbers are stored when you type all the digits needed to dial in the Number To Dial text box. You can also store phone numbers as speed-dial numbers.

---

**Important** The Number To Dial text box can hold as many as 40 digits. Therefore, you can type a local, domestic long-distance, or international long-distance phone number in this text box. The same is true when you create speed-dial numbers.

---

If you type the area code and local telephone number, Phone Dialer automatically precedes the dialed number with a "1" if you have typed this information in the My Locations properties in the Dialing Properties dialog box. Dialing Properties is a separate communications tool described in "Using Dialing Properties" later in this chapter.

If you type nonnumeric characters (such as a hyphen or a parenthesis) in a phone number, Phone Dialer ignores them except when you type a plus sign (+) at the beginning of your number, which is international format. If you type a number in international format, you must put parentheses around the area code, for example, +1 (206) 882-8080.

For more information, see the online Help in Phone Dialer.

According to the North America Dialing Plan (a standard set of procedures that telephone companies in North America use), you must dial a "1," followed by a three-digit area code, followed by a seven-digit local phone number to make a long-distance call. There are a few cases where local phone companies have not followed this rule by allowing you to omit the initial "1" for certain numbers in adjacent area codes. Thus, the number you dial is 10 digits, not 11.

▶ **To dial long-distance calls without a "1" prefix**

1. From the Tools menu in Phone Dialer, click Dialing Properties. (For more information about this tool, see "Using Dialing Properties" later in this chapter.)

2. Verify that the area code listed here is correct for your location. (Change it if necessary.) Click OK.

3. Using any method you prefer for storing phone numbers, type the phone number as a 10-digit number, omitting the "1" prefix.

   The Windows 95 telephony number translation function sees the local area code in both the location and in the destination number, and assumes it should dial only the local number. For example, suppose you are dialing from area code 905 and can dial phone numbers with area code 416 without the "1" prefix. You would store those numbers as +1 (905) 416*xxxxxxx* where *xxxxxxx* is the local phone number.

# Using Dialing Properties

Dialing Properties is a utility that has been integrated with Phone Dialer, HyperTerminal, Dial-Up Networking, and other communications applications created for Windows 95.

The options you set with Dialing Properties are stored in the TELEPHON.INI file (instead of the Registry) to ensure backward compatibility with older 16-bit Windows telephony-enabled applications.

With Dialing Properties, you can do the following:

- Define Calling Locations, including specifying area code, country code, and in-house dialing rules
- Define calling card rules

In Windows 95, you can access Dialing Properties from the Tools menu in Phone Dialer, or by clicking the Dialing Properties button when you make a new connection in HyperTerminal. For purposes of discussion, procedures in this section describe accessing Dialing Properties from Phone Dialer.

# Defining Calling Locations

A *location* is information that Dialing Properties uses to analyze telephone numbers in international format, and to determine the correct sequence of numbers to be dialed. It need not correspond to a particular geographic location, but it usually does. For example, a location could specify the procedures needed to dial calls from your office, or from a room in a hotel. You can name locations anything you choose to help you remember and select them later. Dialing Properties allows you to add new locations, edit existing locations, and remove locations you no longer need.

▶ **To define a location in Dialing Properties**

1. Run Phone Dialer, click the Tools menu, and then click Dialing Properties.

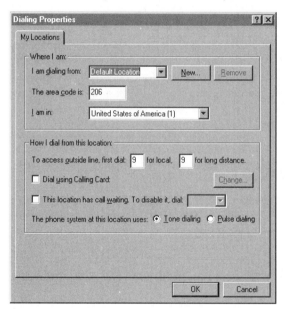

2. In the My Locations properties, type information about where you are calling from, including the following:

   - Name of your location (for example, home or office)
   - Area code
   - Name of country
   - Access number required to make a local or long-distance call
   - Whether your phone has call waiting and whether it should be disabled
   - Whether your phone uses pulse or tone dialing
   - Whether you use a calling card to make calls

3. If you want to change calling card information, click the Change button. For more information about calling cards, see "Defining Calling Card Rules" later in this chapter.

# Defining Calling Card Rules

A *calling card* is information that Dialing Properties uses to create the sequence of numbers to be dialed on a particular call. The calling card can include a calling card number that can be dialed at a specified time during call placement. However, the calling card does not have to specify a card number (in other words, calling cards can also be used to define alternative procedures for direct dialing without a calling card number). To help you remember them, you can name calling cards anything you choose.

Dialing Properties includes predefined settings for several popular calling cards, including AT&T®, Sprint, MCI, British Telecom, France Telecom Mercury, Telecom New Zealand, and others. You can modify and use these directly or copy them to create your own calling cards. Dialing Properties allows you to add new calling cards, edit existing calling cards, and remove calling cards you do not need.

The information stored in a calling card includes the name, card number, and the dialing rules for local, long-distance, and international calls.

▶ **To specify that you are using a calling card in Dialing Properties**

1. In the My Locations properties, click the Dial Using Calling Card check box.

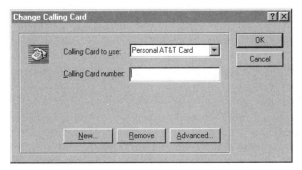

2. In the Change Calling Card dialog box, click your calling card type in the list (for example, AT&T), and then type your calling card number. Click OK.

You can also customize dialing rules by clicking the Advanced button in the Change Calling Card dialog box. The following two examples illustrate how you might use dialing rules.

If you are making a calling-card phone call from outside the United States and do not want Windows telephony applications to automatically add a "0" prefix to the number you are calling, precede the phone number with another numeric code, such as "144" in the following example.

▶ **To redefine numbers that automatically precede the phone number**

1. In the Change Calling Card dialog box, click the New button, select the name of the calling card and type the card number, and then click the Advanced button.

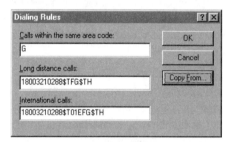

2. In the Dialing Rules dialog box, complete the dialing rule fields. Insert a comma to include a fixed two-second pause; use multiple commas to increase the time. Use the following codes as appropriate.

| Code | Description |
| --- | --- |
| E | Country code |
| F | Area code |
| G | Destination local number |
| H | Calling card number |
| W | Wait for a second dial tone |
| @ | Wait for a ringing tone followed by five seconds of silence |
| $ | Wait for a calling card prompt tone (if your modem supports it) |
| ? | Display an on-screen prompt to the user to continue dialing |

For example, if you are using a British Telecom card, you need to precede the number you dial with **144** and complete the fields as follows.

| Option | Type |
| --- | --- |
| Calls within the same area | 144,H,G |
| Long-distance calls | 144,H,0FG |
| International calls | 144,H,00EFG |

3. Click OK, and then click OK again. In the My Locations properties, remove the leading zero from your area code (for example, "71" or "81" in London). Click OK.

4. Using Phone Dialer or HyperTerminal (or another tool), store your destination number in international format with only the country code (44), area code (without the leading 0), and local number (+44(71)5551212).

   When you choose the Dial option from Phone Dialer or HyperTerminal, the tool you are using automatically expands this number to include "144" and the card number, plus the pause codes.

In another scenario, suppose your organization in the United States uses a PBX system and you need to omit the "1" prefix before the area code. Create a calling card as in the following example.

▶ **To omit the "1" prefix with a PBX system**

1. In the Change Calling Card dialog box, click New.

2. In the Create New Calling Card dialog box, type a name for your calling card, such as "Direct Dial Through PBX." Click OK.

3. In the Change Calling Card dialog box, click Advanced.

4. In the Dialing Rules dialog box, complete the text boxes and then click OK.

| Option | Type |
|--------|------|
| Calls within the same area | G |
| Long-distance calls | FG |
| International calls | 011EFG |

# Using Microsoft File Transfer

Microsoft File Transfer allows you to send or receive a file while talking on the phone. When you send or receive a file, Microsoft File Transfer switches the phone line to data mode and temporarily suspends voice mode. Microsoft File Transfer switches the phone line back to voice mode when it has finished sending or receiving.

Microsoft File Transfer is automatically installed when you install a modem that supports its file transfer capabilities. For more information, see the online Help for Microsoft File Transfer.

# Telephony Drivers from Other Vendors

There are several ways to add telephony drivers from other vendors, if necessary. Some telephony drivers work over the network and consist of software only. If this is the case, the software can be installed through the Add/Remove Programs option in Control Panel.

Hardware drivers can be installed through the Add New Hardware option in Control Panel, unless the hardware requires its own class installer. In this case, the hardware should come with a standard Setup program to install it.

You can also use the Telephony Control Panel, available in the *Win32 Software Development Kit for Windows 95 and Windows NT*, to install telephony drivers from other vendors.

---

**Note**  If you previously installed the Telephony Control Panel on your Windows 3.1 system, and you upgrade to Windows 95, the Windows 95 Telephony Control Panel will be installed automatically.

---

# Troubleshooting Communications Problems

This section describes how to solve problems with installing modems, making connections, and using applications to access the modem. Windows 95 provides a troubleshooting aid for modems in online Help. Try using online Help for troubleshooting before trying the steps included in this section. In addition, a general modem diagnostic tool is located in the Modems option in Control Panel. It provides information about each modem and COM port that have been configured on the computer.

▶ **To use the Modems Diagnostics Tool**

1. In the Modems option in Control Panel, click the Diagnostics tab.

2. In Diagnostics properties, click the Driver button to find out which communications driver is installed for Win16-based communications APIs. For these applications, the driver should be COMM.DRV. If a different driver is listed and you are having problems with using Win16-based applications, the driver is probably the cause.

3. In Diagnostics properties, click the More Info button to make sure Windows 95 can communicate with the modem. Clicking this button causes Windows 95 to send commands to and read responses from the modem, and then to display information about the modem and its COM port.

The Port Information box displays the following information:

- The IRQ and I/O address of the modem's COM port. These should match the physical configuration of the port or modem adapter.

- The UART type of the COM port, for example, 8250 or 16550A. Notice that 16550A UART ports can sustain faster connection speeds with fewer errors.

- The highest port speed supported by the modem. Never set the modem's speed higher than the speed listed here.

The Modem Information box displays the modem's responses to various AT commands that Windows 95 previously sent to it. Some modems return a response that indicates what make and model it is. This can help you select the correct modem if the Install New Modem wizard did not detect it correctly. Notice that many modems return "ERROR" for some AT commands. This means that the modem does not support that particular AT command.

The Record a Log File option in the Modems option also helps you identify modem problems by recording modem commands and responses in a MODEMLOG.TXT file, as described in "Setting Modem Properties" earlier in this chapter.

# Correcting Problems with Modem Installation

This section describes situations that can interfere with installation of a modem, and how to fix them.

### The Install New Modem wizard detected the modem as a standard modem.

This does not indicate a problem. Rather, it means that Windows 95 was unable to detect the exact make and model of a modem. Most communications applications work correctly with the Standard Modem option, that is, connections can be made successfully using the modem's factory default settings. However, advanced control of some features, such as speaker volume, error control (for example, V.42 protocol), and compression (for example, V.42bis protocol) will be disabled in the modem's properties.

If you do not want to use the Standard Modem option, you can run the Install New Modem wizard to select a specific type of modem that is similar to the modem you are using. If you specify another, similarly named model from the same manufacturer—for example, if you configure the modem as a Practical Peripherals PM9600HC when a Practical Peripherals PM9600FX modem is actually installed—Windows 95 usually treats the models as being identical and the specified configuration will probably work well.

To determine whether other modem models are compatible with the one you are using, check the modem manual. Many modems are compatible with Hayes®, Microcom®, Rockwell, or U.S. Robotics models.

**The Install New Modem wizard did not detect any new modems.**

- Make sure the modem does not already appear in the list of installed modems. Windows 95 will not redetect modems that are already installed.

- Make sure no other programs are running that might be using the modem or its COM port.

- If the modem is external, check the connection between it and your computer, and reset it by turning it off and on again.

- If the modem is internal, make sure that its built-in COM port has been configured properly in Device Manager in the System option in Control Panel. If it does not appear, run the Add New Hardware wizard to allow Windows 95 to detect and configure it.

- Make sure the modem's COM port is active and has a correct IRQ by checking its Resources configurations in Device Manager in the System option in Control Panel. Make sure the IRQ does not conflict with one in use by another device. For details, see Chapter 19, "Devices."

If the Install New Modem wizard still does not detect a modem, then there is probably a problem with the port, the cable, or the modem itself. Try the modem with an MS-DOS–based communications program, or with another computer, if possible.

**The Install New Modem wizard does not detect a PCMCIA modem.**

If the Windows 95 PCMCIA drivers are loaded, then Windows 95 should automatically detect and configure a PCMCIA modem when it is installed. Use the PCMCIA option in Control Panel to check the configuration of a PCMCIA socket driver.

If the Windows 95 PCMCIA drivers are *not* being used, then the modem card must be configured as a COM port before the Install New Modem wizard can detect and configure it as a modem.

▶ **To detect and configure a PCMCIA modem when Windows 95 PCMCIA drivers are not used**

1. Configure the modem according to the instructions that came with your original PCMCIA driver software.

2. Run the Add New Hardware wizard to detect and configure the card as a COM port.

3. Run the Install New Modem wizard to detect and configure the card as a modem.

For more information about PCMCIA devices, see Chapter 19, "Devices."

# Correcting Connection Problems

This section describes basic steps for troubleshooting communications and explains specific communications errors or problems and how to correct them.

### Modem will not dial or will not answer.

If your modem is not set up correctly, communications features might not function properly. The following procedures list steps in verifying the correct operation of your modem and the Windows 95 communications subsystem.

Because some communications programs designed for Windows 3.1 install incompatible driver files, which can cause COM ports and modems to stop working, start by verifying that the correct Windows 95 files are being loaded.

▶ **To verify that the required communications files are present**

1. Verify file sizes and dates of COMM.DRV and SERIAL.VXD in the SYSTEM directory against the original versions from the Windows 95 floppy disks or compact disc.

2. Confirm that the following lines are present in SYSTEM.INI:

```
[boot]
comm.drv=comm.drv
[386enh]
device=*vcd
```

3. To revert to the default communications drivers for Windows 95, delete communications port entries in Device Manager.

4. Run the Add New Hardware wizard in Control Panel to detect and install the Windows 95 drivers.

---

**Note**  Windows 95 does not load the SERIAL.VXD driver in SYSTEM.INI. Rather, Windows 95 loads it on demand by using the Registry. Also, there is no corresponding file for the *vcd entry in SYSTEM.INI. This is an internal file built into VMM32.VXD.

---

▶ **To verify the modem configuration by using the Modems option in Control Panel**

1. In General properties, verify that the manufacturer and model for your modem are correct. If not, you might have changed the modem and failed to reconfigure it. In this case, run the Install New Modem wizard to detect the modem and confirm it with the current Registry configuration.

2. If your modem does not appear in the list of installed modems, click Add, and then select the appropriate modem.

3. If the manufacturer and model are not correct and are not available from the list, try the Hayes-compatible option or the Generic Modem driver option, set to the maximum speed supported by the modem. Click OK.

4. Try removing any other modem entries in the list to eliminate any conflicts.

▶ **To verify that the modem is enabled by using the System option in Control Panel**

1. Click the Device Manager tab, click a modem from the list, and then click Properties.

2. Click the option named The Device Is Present, Please Use It, if this is not already selected.

▶ **To verify that the port is correct by using the Modems option in Control Panel**

1. In General properties, click a modem, and then click the Properties button.

2. In General properties for that modem, verify that the listed port is correct. If not, select the correct port. Click OK.

▶ **To determine if a serial port's I/O address and IRQ settings are properly defined by using the System option in Control Panel**

1. Click the Device Manager tab, click Ports, and then click a specific port (such as COM2).

2. Click the Properties button, and then click the Resources tab to display the current resource settings (IRQ, I/O) for that port. To find the correct settings, consult the modem manual.

3. In the Resources properties, check the Conflicting Devices List to see if the modem is using resources in conflict with other devices.

4. If the modem is in conflict with other devices, click the Change Setting button, and then click a Basic Configuration that does not cause resource conflicts.

---

**Note**  Do not try to use a modem on COM3 if there is a serial mouse or other device on COM1. Usually, COM1 and COM3 ports use the same IRQ, meaning that they cannot be used simultaneously on most computers. The COM2 and COM4 ports have the same problem. If possible, change the COM3 or COM4 port to an IRQ setting that is not in conflict.

Also, some display adapters (especially S3, 8514A and ATI mach8) have an address conflict with COM4 ports. You can work around this by using another COM port or replacing your display adapter.

---

▶ **To check the port settings by using the Modems option in Control Panel**

1. Click a modem in the list box, and then click Properties.

2. Click the Connection tab to check the current port settings, such as bits per second (speed), data bits, stop bits, and parity.

3. Click the Advanced button to check error control and flow control. If you are using Win16-based applications, turn off these advanced features.

4. Verify the UART type.

Data transmission problems can occur if a speed greater than 9600 is selected on a slower 80386-based computer not equipped with a 16550 UART, or when performing other tasks during a file download. If problems or errors occur during transmission, try lowering the speed. Attempting to use speed greater than 9600 on computers equipped with 8250 or 16450 UARTs will probably result in dropped characters.

▶ **To check the modem speed by using the Modems option in Control Panel**

1. Click a modem in the list box, and click the Properties button.

2. In General properties, check the speed to make sure it isn't set too high for either the modem or computer. Lower speeds might work, especially when using an older, slower computer.

3. Click the option named Only Connect At This Speed if it is not already selected.

---

**Tip**   To optimize communications performance, you can set the speed higher if your computer has an 80486 or a Pentium processor.

---

▶ **To disable hardware flow control if your modem cable doesn't support it**

1. In the Modems option in Control Panel, click a modem in the list box, and then click the Properties button.

2. Click the Connection tab, and then click the Advanced button.

3. If a check appears in the Use Flow Control check box, click the box to clear it.

▶ **To remove VxDs from other vendors that might be interfering with modem operation**

- Search for and comment out (type a semicolon as the first character of the line) any related entries in the SYSTEM.INI file. When commenting out a line in SYSTEM.INI, it is useful to add a comment line noting this.

### The initialization (dialing) string is improper for the modem.

If the modem will not pick up the line and dial, it might be due to an improper initialization string. Typically, the manufacturer's recommended dial command string is loaded from the corresponding modem INF file; however, if your modem driver was not available and you selected a compatible modem, the dial command string might not work correctly. Try using the modem types, and retest the modem dialing the selected number.

### The modem repeatedly drops the connection.

- Check for a bad or loose serial cable to the modem. If all connections are tight, test for a faulty cable by replacing it with a working cable, and retest the modem communications.

- Check the connection between the RJ-11 phone outlet and the modem. Verify that the connection is firmly plugged in and well connected.

- Try using a different phone line. If you have ruled out other factors, consistent modem errors might be due to problems in the telephone line used for communication.

- Disable call waiting, if it is in use. The call waiting feature can interfere with remote connections and file transfers. If you use this feature regularly, disable it only temporarily (during the time the modem is in use).

- Check communications with the host computer. The communications problems might be due to the host computer not connecting or repeatedly dropping the line.

- Try using a lower speed in the modem properties in the Modems option in Control Panel.

### The COM ports remain in Device Manager after the modem is removed.

After installing an internal modem and assigning it to a COM port that does not physically exist on your computer, the port appears in the Device Manager. After removing this adapter, you might also need to manually remove the port in Device Manager as described in Chapter 19, "Devices."

### You are unable to dial international calls.

Windows 95 allows you to set specific modem properties that assist you when making international calls over your modem. You set these properties in Dial-Up Networking, Dialing Properties, and in the modem properties.

▶ **To check location and calling card settings**

1. In Phone Dialer, click Tools, and click Dialing Properties.

2. In the My Locations properties, verify that your calling location and calling card settings are correct.

▶ **To disable dial-tone detection if your modem fails to detect a dial tone**

- In the Modems option in Control Panel, click the Connection tab, and click to clear the check box next to the Use Dial Tone option.

▶ **To increase the time between dialing if connections are taking a long time**

- In the Modems in Control Panel, click the Connection tab, and then increase the number of seconds in the Cancel the Call If Not Connected Within option.

To manually control modem dialing, see "Dialing Manually" earlier in this chapter. To display a terminal window to type AT commands before or after dialing, see "Displaying the Terminal Window" earlier in this chapter.

# Correcting Modem Access Problems with Applications

**You cannot send or receive binary files by using HyperTerminal.**

- Make sure that both computers are using the same file transfer protocol (that is, Xmodem, 1K Xmodem, Ymodem, Ymodem-G, Zmodem, or Kermit).

- If you are using the Ymodem-G file transfer protocol, ensure that your modem supports hardware error control. If it doesn't, try using Ymodem instead.

- If you are trying to use an alternative protocol (such as Kermit) and you encounter transmission errors, try Xmodem instead. Most communications packages, bulletin boards, and online services support Xmodem.

**You cannot dial with Phone Dialer.**

- In the Dialing Properties dialog box, make sure your area code and country code are correct.

- For each access number you want to use for calling out, specify, at a minimum, the country code, area code, and telephone number.

- Verify basic modem and port configurations.

**Win16-based applications cannot access the modem, but MS-DOS–based or Windows 95-based applications can.**

Make sure the communications driver for Windows 3.1-based applications is COMM.DRV in the SYSTEM.INI file. Some applications replace this driver for various reasons.

**MS-DOS–based applications cannot access the modem (especially PCMCIA modems), but all Windows-based applications can.**

- If possible, adjust the IRQ setting in the MS-DOS–based application according to the application's documentation.

- If the MS-DOS–based application's IRQ settings cannot be adjusted, adjust the IRQ settings for the modem COM port as described earlier in this section.

**MS-DOS–based and Windows 3.1-based applications cannot access the modem, but applications created for Windows 95 can.**

Make sure that Microsoft Exchange Remote Mail, Microsoft Fax, and Dial-Up Networking are not waiting for incoming calls. If they are, older applications cannot access the modem.

**Errors occur during MS-DOS–based applications communications sessions, especially file transfers.**

Increase the **COMxBuffer** setting in [386Enh] section of SYSTEM.INI. The default value is 128 bytes.

C H A P T E R   2 6

# Electronic Mail and Microsoft Exchange

This chapter describes the electronic mail and messaging features of Windows 95, including the Microsoft Exchange client. Microsoft Exchange provides a central place for sending and receiving messages within a workgroup and to and from other messaging services, such as electronic mail, faxes, and online services.

**In This Chapter**

Microsoft Exchange: The Basics   832
Microsoft Exchange: The Issues   832
Overview of Microsoft Exchange and Windows 95 Messaging   834
Setting Up the Microsoft Exchange Client   836
Using the Microsoft Exchange Client   838
    Using the Personal Address Book   839
    Configuring Addresses and Delivery Options   842
    Personal Folder Files   843
    Sorting and Viewing Messages   845
    Using Message Finders   845
Working with Documents   845
Using Multiple Microsoft Exchange Profiles   846
Using the Microsoft Exchange Client with Microsoft Mail   848
    Upgrading from Windows For Workgroups   848
    Setting Up a Microsoft Mail Workgroup Postoffice   849
    Postoffice Directory Structure   852
    Setting Up Microsoft Mail on Other Network Servers   853
Accessing a Microsoft Mail Workgroup Postoffice Remotely   853
    Configuring Microsoft Mail for Remote Access   854
    Defining Scheduled Sessions   857
    Selecting Messages to Download   857
Technical Notes on the Microsoft Exchange Client and MAPI   858
Upgrading to Microsoft Mail Server   860
Upgrading to Microsoft Exchange Server   861
Microsoft Mail Gateways   862

# Microsoft Exchange: The Basics

Windows 95 includes the Microsoft Exchange client, an advanced messaging application that retrieves messages into one inbox from many kinds of messaging service providers, including Microsoft Mail, The Microsoft Network, and Microsoft Fax. Its integration with Microsoft Fax software allows you to send rich-text documents as faxes or mail messages. Setting up Microsoft Exchange to communicate with service providers is as easy as connecting to different printers in a network environment.

With Microsoft Exchange client, you can do the following:

- Send or receive electronic mail in a Windows 95 workgroup
- Include files and objects created in other applications as part of messages
- Use multiple fonts, font sizes and colors, and text alignments in messages
- Create a Personal Address Book or use address books from multiple service providers
- Create folders for storing related messages, files, and other items
- Organize and sort messages in a variety of ways
- Send and receive messages to and from the following service providers:
  - Microsoft Mail
  - The Microsoft Network (online service)
  - Microsoft Fax
  - Other messaging services that use messaging application programming interface (MAPI) service providers

# Microsoft Exchange: The Issues

Before installing and configuring electronic mail on a network, you should decide the following issues:

- What electronic mail system will you use? Do you want to communicate with others in a workgroup, or with people on the Internet or other online services? For communicating within one workgroup, Windows 95 provides a complete Microsoft Mail workgroup postoffice and a wizard for setting it up. For communicating among workgroups, you will need to upgrade to Microsoft Mail Server, as described in "Upgrading to Microsoft Mail Server" later in this chapter.

- If you use the built-in Microsoft Mail workgroup postoffice, where will it be located, and who will administer it? The postoffice can reside on any computer in the workgroup. For best results, that computer should have ample hard disk space to contain message files, be accessible to users at all times, and have at least 8 MB of memory (RAM).

  To begin with you should allow approximately 2 MB of storage on the mail server. As the number of users and the size of stored mail messages increases, you will need to increase storage for the postoffice. When you have more than 20 users, consider using a dedicated computer for the workgroup postoffice.

  Be sure to determine the location of the postoffice before you configure Microsoft Exchange. If you choose Microsoft Mail during Setup, Windows 95 runs the Inbox Setup wizard at the end of Setup, but you cannot fully configure Microsoft Exchange if you have not created a postoffice. After Windows 95 Setup, you can configure the Microsoft Mail workgroup postoffice by running the Microsoft Workgroup Postoffice Admin wizard in Control Panel. For information, see "Using the Microsoft Exchange Client with Microsoft Mail" later in this chapter.

- Which service providers, such as Microsoft Fax, do users need to connect to? Requirements for connecting to service providers vary depending on the type of service. For example, connecting to The Microsoft Network requires that the user has a modem, Dial-Up Networking, a phone line, and an account from The Microsoft Network. You choose the service providers you want during Setup or afterward in the Mail And Fax option in Control Panel or from within Microsoft Exchange. For details, see "Setting Up the Microsoft Exchange Client" later in this chapter.

- Do you want users to connect to service providers from their individual computers or from the network? For security purposes, a network administrator might want to restrict users from communicating with other service providers from their computers. If you want users to connect to service providers through a gateway on a network server, you must purchase a gateway and an electronic mail system that allows you to connect to a gateway. For example, if you are running Microsoft Exchange with Microsoft Mail workgroup postoffice, you must upgrade the workgroup postoffice to Microsoft Mail Server and purchase a gateway. For information, see "Upgrading to Microsoft Mail Server" and "Microsoft Mail Gateways" later in this chapter.

- Will users connect to the postoffice from a remote site? If so and you are using the Microsoft Mail workgroup postoffice, you need to create a Dial-Up Networking connection to the postoffice and configure a remote access server for dial-up clients. For information, see Chapter 28, "Dial-Up Networking and Mobile Computing."

---

**Note**  If you install the Microsoft Exchange client and Microsoft Schedule+ 1.0, you will lose group scheduling capabilities.

---

# Overview of Microsoft Exchange and Windows 95 Messaging

The Microsoft Exchange client can communicate with any electronic mail system or messaging application that has a *MAPI service provider*, which is similar to a personal gateway. It specifies all the connection and addressing settings needed to communicate with a mail server on one end and with the Microsoft Exchange client on the other end.

MAPI is a set of API functions and OLE interface that allows messaging clients, such as Microsoft Exchange, to interact with various message service providers, such as Microsoft Mail and Microsoft Fax. MAPI helps Microsoft Exchange manage stored messages and define the purpose and content of messages. For more information about MAPI, see "Technical Notes on the Microsoft Exchange Client and MAPI" later in this chapter.

The Microsoft Exchange client includes an OLE-compatible rich-text editor used for reading and composing messages; it supports the use of bullets, multiple font sizes and colors, and text alignments in messages.

If you install the Microsoft Exchange client, Windows 95 provides several MAPI service providers. To install the Microsoft Mail workgroup postoffice to work with Microsoft Exchange, you must select it as a separate component under Microsoft Exchange during Windows 95 Setup or afterward by using the Add/Remove Programs option in Control Panel.

**Microsoft Mail workgroup postoffice.**  This postoffice is a workgroup edition of the Microsoft Mail Server, allowing one computer to host the postoffice and allowing other users to access that postoffice to send and receive mail. The workgroup postoffice provides the same features as the full Microsoft Mail Server, with the following exceptions:

- No mail exchange with users of other postoffices
- No access to Microsoft Mail gateways
- Simplified administration tools

**Personal Address Book MAPI service provider.**  This common address book can store electronic mail addresses and other personal messaging information such as names, phone and fax numbers, and mailing addresses from multiple messaging service providers. A Personal Address Book is accessible from applications that use MAPI.

**Personal Folder (.PST) MAPI service provider.**  The Personal Folder stores messages, forms, documents, and other information in a series of hierarchical folders. A Personal Folder acts as a universal inbox and outbox where users can send and receive messages from multiple service providers.

**Microsoft Mail Services MAPI service provider.**  This service provider connects the Microsoft Exchange client to either the Microsoft Mail workgroup postoffice or a Microsoft Mail Server (acquired separately) postoffice. To connect a computer running Windows 95 to the Microsoft Mail Server postoffices, the postoffices must reside on a network file server (such as Windows NT 3.5 or Novell®NetWare®) that supports the MS-DOS driver redirector.

See "Using the Microsoft Exchange Client with Microsoft Mail" later in this chapter for information about configuring and using the Microsoft Exchange client with a Microsoft Mail workgroup postoffice.

**Microsoft Fax MAPI service provider.**  This service provider allows the Microsoft Exchange client to send and receive faxes in the same way as electronic mail. You can receive faxes in the same universal inbox as your mail, and use the same Personal Address Book for both mail and fax recipients. For more information, see Chapter 27, "Microsoft Fax."

**The Microsoft Network MAPI service provider.**  This service provider allows the Microsoft Exchange client to send and receive mail on The Microsoft Network, an online service accessible from the Windows 95 desktop. For details, see Chapter 29, "The Microsoft Network."

**Internet Mail MAPI service provider.**  This service provider allows the Microsoft Exchange client to send and receive mail directly on the Internet or other networks using the Simple Mail Transport Protocol (SMTP) and the Post Office Protocol 3 (POP3) over TCP/IP. This product is available as part of Microsoft Plus! for Windows 95. For information, contact your Microsoft sales representative.

**CompuServe Mail MAPI service provider.**  This service provider allows the Microsoft Exchange client to send and receive mail using the CompuServe Mail Services. To use this service provider, you must have an account with CompuServe. For more information, contact CompuServe.

**Microsoft Exchange Server MAPI service provider.**  This service provider will allow the Microsoft Exchange client to connect to the Microsoft Exchange server, which is a client-server messaging system that runs on Windows NT Server. This Microsoft product will be available after the release of Windows 95.

Installing the Microsoft Exchange server will provide the Microsoft Exchange client with specific functionality, including the following:

- Inbox Assistant, a set of server-based rules for filtering, forwarding, replying to, and deleting messages

- Out of Office Assistant, a set of server-based rules for automatically forwarding and replying to mail when users are working away from the office

# Setting Up the Microsoft Exchange Client

Installing and configuring the Microsoft Exchange client consists of the following steps:

- Install the Microsoft Exchange client either during Windows 95 Setup or afterward in the Add/Remove Programs option in Control Panel or by double-clicking the Inbox on the Windows 95 desktop. The Microsoft Exchange client is installed automatically if you choose to install Microsoft Fax, The Microsoft Network, or Microsoft Mail in the Get Connected dialog box during Setup. For information, see Chapter 3, "Introduction to Windows 95 Setup." You can also install the Microsoft Exchange client after Windows 95 Setup in the Add/Remove Programs option in Control Panel.

- Choose the electronic mail system to which you will connect the Microsoft Exchange client.

- Set up a mail postoffice. If you choose the built-in Microsoft Mail workgroup postoffice and you are upgrading from previous Windows for Workgroups Mail or Microsoft Mail 3.2 postoffices, you will not need to set up a new Microsoft Mail workgroup postoffice.

- Set up the Microsoft Exchange client by running the Inbox Setup wizard either during Windows 95 Setup or afterward in the Mail And Fax option in Control Panel.

- Choose the service providers you want during setup of the Microsoft Exchange client, or afterward in the Mail And Fax option in Control Panel or in the Microsoft Exchange client.

---

**Important**   If a Microsoft Mail workgroup postoffice or another postoffice has not yet been set up when a user runs the Inbox Setup wizard, the Microsoft Exchange client can be only partially configured. After setup, the postoffice administrator can configure the Microsoft Mail workgroup postoffice for all users in the workgroup in the Microsoft Mail option in Control Panel. When those users run the Microsoft Exchange client for the first time, the postoffice location automatically appears in the postoffice location box.

---

▶ **To install the Microsoft Exchange client after Setup**

1. In the Add/Remove Programs option in Control Panel, double-click the Windows Setup tab.

2. In the Components list, click Microsoft Exchange, and then click OK.

   –Or–

   Double-click the Inbox on the Windows 95 desktop.

   The Inbox Setup wizard guides you through the configuration steps. If you choose to add Microsoft Mail Services to Microsoft Exchange, the wizard prompts you for the postoffice location (path name), user name, and password.

   If you have already created a postoffice, added users to it, and shared it with all users on the network, the postoffice name and location automatically appear in the dialog box without requiring the user to type them. In this way, setting up the Microsoft Exchange client with the Microsoft Mail workgroup postoffice is seamless for all users in the workgroup except the postoffice administrator. For information about setting up a Microsoft Mail workgroup postoffice, see "Using the Microsoft Exchange Client with Microsoft Mail" later in this chapter.

3. After the wizard has finished, shut down and restart Windows 95 for the changes to take effect.

▶ **To add a service provider**

- Double-click the Mail And Fax option in Control Panel, and then click Add.

  –Or–

1. From the Tools menu in Microsoft Exchange, click Options.

2. In the Options properties, click the Services tab, and then click Add.

3. In the Add Services To Profile dialog box, click the service providers you want, and then click Add. For information about Microsoft Exchange profiles, see "Using Multiple Microsoft Exchange Profiles" later in this chapter.

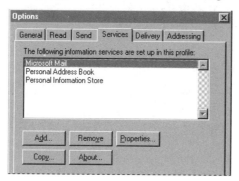

The services you select determine which specific DLLs are enabled when the Microsoft Exchange client is started. For example, if the Microsoft Mail service is added, the MSFS32.DLL file in the Windows SYSTEM directory is loaded. (To find out which DLLs are loaded for a service, click the name of that service in the Microsoft Exchange properties, then click the About button.)

The service providers each provide a setup wizard that prompts you for any required configuration information. For information about Microsoft Mail, see "Using the Microsoft Exchange Client with Microsoft Mail" later in this chapter.

---

**Tip** When you're troubleshooting Windows 95 mail issues, first remove additional service providers (except Personal Address Book and Personal Folder), and then add back each service provider, one at a time.

---

# Using the Microsoft Exchange Client

This section describes how to use the Microsoft Exchange client, including discussions about Personal Address Book, Personal Folder, and sorting and viewing messages.

▶ **To start the Microsoft Exchange client**

- On the Windows 95 desktop, double-click the Inbox.

  –Or–

  On the Programs menu, click Microsoft Exchange.

---

**Note**   The Microsoft Exchange client opens in single-pane view if you start it by double-clicking the Inbox on the Windows 95 desktop. In single-pane view, folders and messages appear in one window. Clicking the Show/Hide Folder List button on the toolbar in Microsoft Exchange switches to double-pane view. In double-pane view, you can drag and drop messages into folders.

---

The Microsoft Exchange client automatically downloads mail from all service providers when you first open your Inbox. Consequently, if you have added multiple service providers to the Microsoft Exchange client, it might take several minutes to connect to and download mail from each of them.

After you open the Microsoft Exchange client, you can choose to download mail from service providers one at a time or from all of them at once. You can also set time intervals for downloading mail from each service provider in the properties for each of them.

▶ **To download mail after you open the Microsoft Exchange client**

- On the Tools menu, click Deliver Now Using, and then point to each service provider from which you want to download mail. If you installed only one service provider, the option on the Tools menu is named Deliver Now.

## Using the Personal Address Book

The Microsoft Exchange client creates a Personal Address Book for each user when the Inbox Setup wizard is run for the first time. The Personal Address Book contains the names and addresses of people to whom users commonly send electronic mail and fax messages. Users can add names and addresses to the Personal Address Book from other electronic address books, such as the Postoffice Address List that comes with the Microsoft Mail workgroup postoffice. Users can also modify the Personal Address Book (they cannot modify address books from other service providers, such as The Microsoft Network).

With the Personal Address Book, you can do the following:

- Find and select names within different address books.
- Modify names and addresses.
- Copy addresses from other address books into the Personal Address Book.
- Add custom addresses to send messages to other messaging services, such as The Microsoft Network.
- Define groups of recipients (distribution lists) to which you want to send the same message.

---

**Tip**  You can address a mail message to selected recipients from within the Personal Address Book dialog box by selecting a name, and then clicking New Message on the File menu.

---

▶ **To find and select names within a Personal Address Book**

1. In Microsoft Exchange, click the Tool menu, and then click Address Book.

2. In the Address Book dialog box, click Personal Address Book in the Show Names From box. The names in the Personal Address Book are displayed in the list box to the left.

3. To find a name, type it in the blank box above the list. The cursor automatically moves to that name in the list.

4. If you can't find a name, click the Edit menu, and then click the Find button. In the Find dialog box, type letters that are part of the name you want to search for, and then click OK.

▶ **To modify names and addresses in the Personal Address Book**

1. In the Address Book dialog box, click the Personal Address Book in the Show Names From box, and then double-click a name in the list.

2. In the properties for that name, change the address, phone, business, and other information, and then click OK.

▶ **To add names and addresses to a Personal Address Book from another address book**

1. In the Address Book dialog box, click a different address book in the Show Names From box.

2. In that address book's list of names, click a name, click the File menu, and then click Add To Personal Address Book.

▶ **To add a custom name and address to the Personal Address Book**

1. In the Personal Address Book, click New Entry on the File menu.

2. In the New Entry dialog box, click the type of address you want to add to the Personal Address Book.

   For example, if the person is a member of The Microsoft Network, select The Microsoft Network. In the Microsoft Network address dialog box, type the Member ID and Name.

   Each messaging service has a different address dialog box. For example, if you select Internet, you must enter the SMTP and Alias of the recipient.

   All messaging services include dialog boxes named Notes, Business, and Phone in which you can store additional information about the recipient.

▶ **To create a personal distribution list**

1. In Microsoft Exchange, click the Tools menu, and then click Address Book.

2. In the Address Book dialog box, click File, and then click New Entry.

3. In the New Entry dialog box, double-click Personal Distribution List.

4. In the Distribution List dialog box, type a name for the personal distribution list, and then click the Add/Remove Members button.

5. In the Edit Personal Distribution List Members box, type a name or select it from the displayed address book, and then click Members to add it to the personal distribution list. You can add as many names as you want. When you are finished, click OK.

6. In the Distribution List dialog box, click OK to add the personal distribution list to the Personal Address Book.

▶ **To address a message to a personal distribution list**

1. In Microsoft Exchange, click the Tools menu, and then click Address Book.

2. In the Address Book, click Personal Address Book in the Show Names From box.

3. In the Personal Address Book's list of names, select the name of the personal distribution list, click the File menu, and then click New Message.

   A message form appears with the name of the personal distribution list in the To: box.

▶ **To select names when composing a message**

1. In Microsoft Exchange, click the Compose menu, and then click New Message.

2. In the new message form, click the Select Names button on the toolbar.

3. In the Select Names dialog box, click a name, and then click OK to address the message.

# Configuring Addresses and Delivery Options

You can control how a message is addressed and delivered by specifying the following address and delivery options:

- The address book to be displayed first when selecting mail recipients
- The address book to search first when looking for names that have been added manually
- The address book in which to store personal names
- The Personal Folder to which messages are delivered
- The order in which service providers should send outgoing messages

▶ **To configure address options in the Microsoft Exchange client**

1. In Control Panel, double-click the Mail And Fax option, and then click the Addressing tab.

   –Or–

   From the Tools menu in Microsoft Exchange, click Options, and then click the Addressing tab.

2. In Addressing properties, click an address book in the option named Show This Address List First.

3. Click an address book in the option named Keep Personal Addresses In.

4. To specify the search order of address books, click an address book in the option named When Sending Items, and then click the up or down arrows to the right of the list box to set the order by which the Microsoft client searches address books.

▶ **To configure delivery options in the Microsoft Exchange client**

1. In Control Panel, double-click the Mail And Fax option, and then click the Delivery tab.

   –Or–

   From the Tools menu in Microsoft Exchange, click Options, and then click the Delivery tab.

2. In Delivery properties, choose a Personal Folder File in the option named Deliver New Items To The Following Location.

3. To specify a second delivery location in case a network connection to a file server is temporarily lost, type the name of a secondary Personal Folder File in the Secondary Location box.

4. To specify an order in which service providers send messages, click a service provider in the option named Recipient Addresses Are Processed By, and then click the up or down arrows to the right of the list box to set the order in which service providers send messages.

# Personal Folder Files

A Personal Folder File, located on a local computer, stores mail messages, forms, and other information in a series of hierarchical folders. The Personal Folder functions as your universal inbox and outbox for sending messages to and receiving messages from service providers.

When you upgrade to Windows 95 from Windows for Workgroups Mail or Microsoft Mail 3.2, Windows 95 runs a Migration wizard to convert the primary message files (.MMF) to a Personal Folder File (PST format, as described in WIN95RK.HLP with the *Windows 95 Resource Kit* utilities). During Setup, Windows 95 looks first in the Windows subdirectory and then in the MSMAIL subdirectory for an .MMF file. It considers the first .MMF file it finds as the primary .MMF file and converts it. After Setup, you can convert additional .MMF files to Personal Folder format by using the Import Mail Data option in the Microsoft Exchange client. You can also use this option to convert previous Personal Address Books (.PAB files).

▶ **To convert .MMF or .PAB files in the Microsoft Exchange client**

1. In the File menu, click Import.

2. In the Specify File To Import dialog box, type the path to the .MMF or .PAB file you want to import, and then click Open.

3. In the Import Mail File dialog box, verify that the .MMF or .PAB is the one you want to import, and then click OK.

The wizard leaves your original .MMF and .PAB files intact and copies the messages into the current Personal Folder or Personal Address Book.

---

**Important**  The Microsoft Exchange client, unlike the Microsoft Exchange Server, does not support shared or replicated sets of folders to let large groups of people share documents and messages, and create rich views on them. If you have previous shared folders, they cannot be converted in the Microsoft Exchange client. You will lose the mail in these shared folders when you upgrade to Windows 95 unless you import the shared folders to another .MMF file.

---

You can add as many Personal Folder Files as you need. For example, you might want to create one Personal Folder File for archived messages and one for current messages. Or you could choose to have one Personal Folder File for messages from a specific service provider. However, no matter how many service providers you add to the Microsoft Exchange client, you need only one Personal Folder File.

▶ **To add a Personal Folder File in the Microsoft Exchange client**

1. In the Tools menu, click Options.

2. In the Options dialog box, click the Services tab, and then click Add.

3. In the Add Service To Profile dialog box, click Personal Folder, and click OK.

4. In the Create/Open Personal Folder dialog box, type a filename for the Personal Folder File, and then click Open.

5. In the Create Microsoft Personal Folders dialog box, type a name for the Personal Folder File. This name will appear in the Microsoft Exchange client Inbox. Click the type of encryption you want, and then type a password. Click OK.

   Notice that Compressible Encryption is selected by default. The Personal Folder also supports password protection to maintain the privacy of your electronic mail.

To help you manage the size of a Personal Folder, Windows 95 provides a Personal Folder compression feature. Choosing to compress a Personal Folder eliminates the empty spaces created when you delete messages.

▶ **To compress a Personal Folder in the Microsoft Exchange client**

1. From the Tools menu, click Services, and then click a Personal Folder File.

2. In the Personal Folders dialog box, click Compact Now.

---

**Note**  Because a Personal Folder is a file in the Exchange subdirectory, it can be backed up in the same way as other files in Windows 95.

---

# Sorting and Viewing Messages

The Microsoft Exchange client provides a number of ways for you to organize and manage electronic mail messages and other information. When you first use Microsoft Exchange, messages are arranged according to the date and time they were received, the sender's name, their subject, and size. You can reorganize how messages are arranged in a single folder or all folders in the following ways:

- Create a series of folders to keep groups of messages in each.
- Sort messages within a folder by category, such as the message subject title, the sender's name, and so on.

For information about performing these tasks, see the online Help for the Microsoft Exchange client.

# Using Message Finders

A message finder is a separate window that works in the same way as a filter to find messages that meet a particular set of criteria. When set up, a finder can run continuously, alerting you when matching messages arrive. The selection criteria for finding messages are the same as for filtering messages.

▶ **To view a message finder window in the Microsoft Exchange client**

1. From the Tools menu, click Find.
2. Specify the criteria you want to use to find messages. Click Advanced to find messages according to its size, date, importance, or sensitivity.

---

**Note**   You can add OLE fields to the columns you want to view, or you can sort, filter, and search on these fields (in addition to the normal messaging properties). For more information about OLE in Windows 95, see Chapter 22, "Application Support."

---

# Working with Documents

You can attach files, messages, or objects to a mail message in Microsoft Exchange. You can also drag and drop files into Microsoft Exchange, or drag and drop files attached to messages to other drives, folders, or documents on a local or networked computer. To use this OLE functionality, you must be in double-pane view. A button is provided on the Microsoft Exchange client toolbar to switch between single and double-pane view.

▶ **To attach files, messages, or objects to messages in the Microsoft Exchange client**

- In a Microsoft Exchange message, click the Insert menu, and then click File, Message, or Object.

▶ **To drag and drop files attached to messages**

- In the Microsoft Exchange Inbox, double-click the file and drag it to another folder in the Microsoft Exchange client or to a drive or folder in My Computer or Network Neighborhood. Windows 95 saves the file as an .MSG file.

---

**Note** To drag and drop files to another folder, the Microsoft Exchange client must be in double-pane view.

---

▶ **To drag and drop files into a message in the Microsoft Exchange client**

- In My Computer or Network Neighborhood, double-click a file and drag it into an open Microsoft Exchange message or folder.

---

**Tip** You can use Microsoft Exchange folders as an alternate way to store and sort files. Consider creating a hierarchy of folders to store and categorize files, creating a personalized document library. You can create more elaborate and customized views in the Microsoft Exchange client than is possible in the Windows 95 file system.

---

# Using Multiple Microsoft Exchange Profiles

The Microsoft Exchange client maintains one or more separate profiles for each user. A profile contains default settings for how messages are delivered to and from a mailbox. Individual users create a profile when they run the Inbox Setup wizard for the first time. Other profiles can be added after running the wizard. The process of creating a profile is invisible to all but advanced users or network administrators.

With Microsoft Exchange profiles, several users, each with an individual set of preferences, can share the same computer to send and receive mail. A single user can also switch between profiles, for example, between one for the office and one for a remote site. If a user is connected to multiple service providers, a profile securely stores any required passwords, allowing the user to log on to multiple mail systems with one password.

The following illustration shows four profiles for three people sharing the same computer. One person has two profiles—one for use on the road and one for the office.

| Ann (Work) | Ann (Road) | Mary | Bob |
|---|---|---|---|
| **Microsoft Mail**<br>Mailbox=Ann<br>Password=x<br>Server=\\y\data<br>Conn=LAN | **Microsoft Mail**<br>Mailbox=Ann<br>Password=x<br>Server=\\y\data<br>Conn=RAS<br>MSFAX<br>Port=COM1:<br>Modem=USR | **Microsoft Mail**<br>Mailbox=Mary<br>Password=y<br>Server=\\s\data<br>Conn=LAN | **Exchange**<br>Mailbox=Bob<br>Password=z<br>Server=\\s |

▶ **To add a profile in the Microsoft Exchange client**

1. In Control Panel, click the Mail And Fax icon, and then click Show Profiles.

2. In the Microsoft Exchange Profiles dialog box, click Add. This starts the Inbox Setup wizard, which leads you through the steps for creating a profile.

Users who share a computer, or who have multiple profiles, can select the profile to use when starting Windows 95.

▶ **To choose which profile to use at startup**

1. From the Tools menu in the Microsoft Exchange client, click Options.

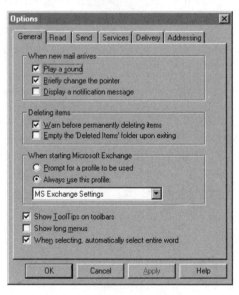

2. In General properties, click the option named Prompt For A Profile To Be Used if you want to choose a profile each time you start Microsoft Exchange.

3. Click the option named Always Use This Profile if you want to specify a default profile.

**Note**  To switch between profiles when running Microsoft Exchange, you must quit Microsoft Exchange and then choose a new profile when restarting.

# Using the Microsoft Exchange Client with Microsoft Mail

This section describes how to set up a Microsoft Mail workgroup postoffice to run with the Microsoft Exchange client. The first time you start Microsoft Exchange, you must specify the location of your postoffice. If you have not yet set up a postoffice, you cannot fully configure the Microsoft Exchange client. Consequently, you should set up a Microsoft Mail workgroup postoffice before you run the Microsoft Exchange client.

## Upgrading from Windows For Workgroups

If you install Windows 95 in the directory formerly used by Windows or Windows for Workgroups, the Microsoft Exchange client automatically upgrades the Windows for Workgroups Mail or the Microsoft Mail 3.2 Windows client to the Windows 95 Microsoft Mail workgroup postoffice. Microsoft Exchange reads any existing MSMAIL.INI file to determine where to locate the Personal Folder (.PST) and the Personal Address Book (.PAB) files. In addition, the Microsoft Exchange client automatically converts the primary .MMF file to .PST format, so that the Microsoft Mail workgroup postoffice can read it. To convert any additional .MMF files, use the Import Mail Data option in the File menu.

If you upgraded from Windows for Workgroups to Windows 95, the Microsoft Exchange client retains your workgroup postoffice for use with Windows 95. The mail postoffices for Windows for Workgroups and for Windows 95 are identical, so any users using Windows for Workgroups can still share the postoffice. The Windows 95 Microsoft Mail workgroup postoffice cannot exchange messages with other Microsoft Mail workgroup postoffices. To do this, you must upgrade the postoffice to a Microsoft Mail Server postoffice.

# Setting Up a Microsoft Mail Workgroup Postoffice

Setting up a Microsoft Mail workgroup postoffice consists of the following tasks:

- Deciding the location for the postoffice
- Deciding who will administer the postoffice
- Adding users and user information, such as office locations and passwords
- Sharing the postoffice with all users in the workgroup

▶ **To set up a Microsoft Mail Workgroup Postoffice**

1. In Control Panel, click the Microsoft Mail Postoffice icon.
2. In the Microsoft Workgroup Postoffice Admin dialog box, click Create A New Workgroup Postoffice, and then click Next.
3. Specify where you want the workgroup postoffice to be located, and then click Next.
4. In the Administrator Account Details dialog box, type information about the postoffice administrator, including name and mailbox name, and a password to restrict administration of the postoffice to the administrator. Click Next to finish creating the postoffice.

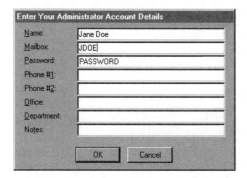

**Important**  Create only one postoffice for your workgroup, or your users will not be able to send mail to each other.

The Microsoft Workgroup Postoffice Admin wizard also allows you to manage the postoffice in the following ways:

- Add users to the postoffice
- Change user information, including replacing forgotten passwords

The workgroup postoffice manager library, WGPOADMN.DLL, is the software component that supports administrative functions such as adding or deleting users and changing passwords.

▶ **To administer a postoffice**

1. In Control Panel, click the Microsoft Mail Postoffice icon, and then click Administer An Existing Workgroup Postoffice.

2. In the space provided, type the password assigned to the administrator during setup of the postoffice, and then click Next.

3. To add users to your postoffice, click Add User. To change user information, such as a telephone number or a password, select a name from the list box, and then click Details.

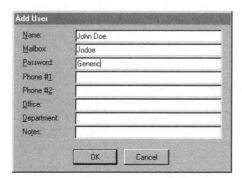

To allow users within a workgroup to access the Microsoft Mail workgroup postoffice, you must share the directory where the postoffice resides. You can share the directory through Windows Explorer in the same way you share other resources.

▶ **To share a Microsoft Mail workgroup postoffice**

1. In Windows Explorer, right-click the folder for your workgroup postoffice.

2. From the File menu, click Properties, and then click the Sharing tab.

3. In the Sharing folder, click Shared As and verify the name of the postoffice in the Share Name field. You can also add a comment in the Comment field. Other people will see the comment when they look at a list of computers on the network.

4. Under Access Type in the Sharing folder, be sure to click Full Access if you want all users in your workgroup to access the postoffice.

   –Or–

   To restrict access to the postoffice by requiring a password, click Depends On Password, and then type a password in the Full-Access Password field.

For information about user-level security, see Chapter 14, "Security."

When you configure Microsoft Mail using the Inbox Setup wizard, the wizard prompts you for a password. You can then specify whether the Microsoft Exchange client should save the password and automatically enter it when you start mail. This means that someone else using your computer can access your mail. You can change your mailbox password and require that Microsoft Mail ask for your password each time you log on to Windows 95.

▶ **To change your mailbox password in the Microsoft Exchange client**

1. From the Tools menu, point to Microsoft Mail Tools, and then click Change Mailbox Password.

2. In the Change Mailbox Password dialog box, type the old and new passwords, and then verify the new password. Then click OK.

---

**Note**  The preceding procedure is for users to change their mailbox passwords on the built-in Microsoft Mail workgroup postoffice. If you are using the Microsoft Exchange client with another electronic mail system, the exact procedure will vary.

---

▶ **To require that Microsoft Mail prompt you for a password**

1. In Control Panel, double-click the Mail And Fax icon.

2. In Services properties, double-click Microsoft Mail.

3. In Microsoft Mail properties, click the Logon tab.

4. In the Logon dialog box, make sure the option named When Logging On, Automatically Enter Password is cleared.

# Postoffice Directory Structure

A Microsoft Mail workgroup postoffice temporarily stores a message until a user retrieves it. It stores only one copy of each mail message, even when a message is addressed to multiple recipients. When sent to multiple recipients, a message has a reference count in it, which is decremented each time a recipient retrieves the message. The message itself is removed when the reference count drops to 0.

All subdirectories within the Microsoft Mail database must be present for it to function correctly. The following table lists the subdirectories and describes their purpose.

| WGPO Subdirectory | Description |
| --- | --- |
| ATT | Encrypted file attachments. |
| CAL | Microsoft Schedule+ calendar files. |
| FOLDERS | Public and private folders (with a filename extension of .FLD) for use by MS-DOS workstations. (Folders on Windows for Workgroups workstations are located in their .MMF files on the workstations.) Notice that public folders are created in this subdirectory, but the Microsoft Exchange client cannot view their contents. |
| GLB | Global system files for Microsoft Mail. These files contain local user logon information and control files to generate mail files. |
| HLP | Help files. |
| INF<br>TPL | Postoffice-defined templates. INF contains information files and TPL contains templates. ADMIN.INF and ADMIN.TPL contain template information for local postoffice users. |
| KEY | Index files that contain pointers to header records in the mailbag (.MBG) files. |
| MAI | Mail messages stored in encrypted form until the recipients' workstations retrieve them. |
| MBG | Mail headers that point to the mail (.MAI) files. For each file in this directory, there is a matching index (.KEY) file. |
| MEM | A list of the workgroup postoffice's members. |
| MMF | Mail message files. |
| NME | Pointer files for the name alias address lists. ADMIN.NME and ADMINSHD.NME list members of the postoffice address list. |
| P1 | Temporary storage for external programs. |
| GRP<br>LOG<br>USR<br>XTN | Settings for multiple postoffice configurations. These subdirectories are useful only if you upgrade to the Microsoft Mail Server. In that case, USR is used to list user names and group names for the other network, and XTN is used to list other external information. LOG contains output log files. GRP contains public and private group pointer files. |

# Setting Up Microsoft Mail on Other Network Servers

You can connect computers running Windows 95 and Microsoft Exchange to a Microsoft Mail workgroup postoffice located on a Windows NT 3.5 server, Novell NetWare server, or any other independent network file server. Setting up a Microsoft Mail workgroup postoffice on a Windows NT or Novell NetWare server is identical to setting up such a postoffice to work with Windows for Workgroups. If you want to create the WGPO on a Windows NT network server, see *Microsoft Windows NT Server 3.5 System Guide*.

# Accessing a Microsoft Mail Workgroup Postoffice Remotely

With the Microsoft Exchange client and Microsoft Mail workgroup postoffice, you can send and receive mail while working away from the office. While offline, you can compose or reply to mail, and then using a modem, telephone line, and Dial-Up Networking, you can establish a remote connection to your organization's network or to your computer, and send and receive mail.

**Remote preview of mail.**   After you dial in to the network, you can use Microsoft Mail to preview just the headers of new mail messages. That is, you can see who has sent you a message, the subject of the message, the size of the message, and the estimated time it will take to download it. This saves you time and disk space by allowing you not to download unnecessary files. You can also use remote mail when connected to Microsoft Mail on the LAN.

**Selective download.**   After you retrieve headers, you can mark messages to download or to delete. You can stay on the line after retrieving headers, or call later to download selected messages.

**Dial-Up Networking.**   The Microsoft Exchange client relies on Dial-Up Networking to connect remotely to postoffices. Because Windows 95 supports the TCP/IP, IPX/SPX, and NetBEUI protocols, you can use Dial-Up Networking to dial into many types of remote access servers to access your postoffice. For information, see Chapter 28, "Dial-Up Networking and Mobile Computing."

**Offline use.**   You can compose and address mail offline, that is, while disconnected from a network. Messages are queued up in the Microsoft Exchange outbox until the next time you connect. You can also download a copy of the Microsoft Mail Post Office Address List onto a portable computer for addressing messages when working at a remote site.

**Scheduled connections.**   You can dial in as needed to retrieve mail remotely, or you can set up scheduled connections to dial in at a specific time or at regular intervals.

**Modem sharing through TAPI.** Microsoft Exchange uses the Windows 95 telephony applications programming interface (TAPI) to dial and retrieve mail remotely. TAPI allows applications to share a modem by arbitrating modem requests among applications. For example, configuring a modem to receive incoming faxes does not prevent you making a call to download mail. Microsoft Exchange also uses the TAPI Dialing Properties tool to handle multiple locations, hotel dialing prefixes, and credit card calls. For more information, see Chapter 25, "Modems and Communications Tools."

# Configuring Microsoft Mail for Remote Access

This section describes how to configure the Microsoft Mail workgroup postoffice for remotely accessing the network. Other mail applications might also allow remote access; however, the configuration procedures will differ.

Before you configure Microsoft Mail for remote access, you need to do following:

- Install Dial-Up Networking.
- Install a modem.
- Configure the server on which the postoffice resides for remote access.

To configure Microsoft Mail for remote access, you need to do the following:

- Define a Dial-Up Networking connection to that postoffice. The Dial-Up Networking New Connection wizard is launched when you define a new connection.

You can set the following remote access features in Microsoft Mail properties:

- Whether you want remote preview of mail messages
- When you want to initiate and terminate a remote session
- Whether you want to schedule an automatic connection time
- Whether you want to remotely connect to a postoffice with a modem on startup

▶ **To configure Microsoft Mail for remote access**

1. In Control Panel, double-click the Mail And Fax icon, click Microsoft Mail, and then click Properties.

   –Or–

   From the Tools menu in Microsoft Exchange, click Services. In the Services dialog box, click Microsoft Mail, and then click Properties.

2. In Microsoft Mail properties, click the Dial-Up Networking tab and specify a Dial-Up Networking connection for a remote access session. To define a new connection, click Add Entry. The Dial-Up Networking New Connection wizard prompts you for the necessary information.

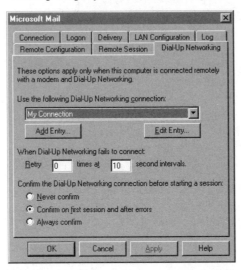

3. In Microsoft Mail properties, click Connection, and then click the option named Remote Using A Modem And Dial-Up Networking.

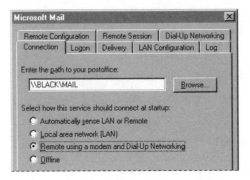

If you click the option named Automatically Sense LAN or Remote, Microsoft Mail queries the system to determine whether it should connect by using LAN or Dial-Up Networking.

If you want to work offline to compose or read mail messages before or after making a remote connecting, click Offline. This step should usually be done after logging on to Windows 95.

4. In Microsoft Mail properties, click the Remote Configuration tab. The option named Use Remote Mail option is selected by default. If you clear this option, Microsoft Mail automatically downloads mail after you have connected.

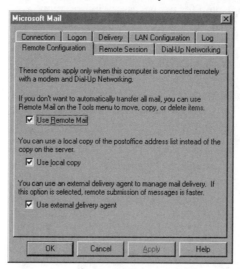

5. In Microsoft Mail properties, click the Remote Session tab and specify whether you want a remote session to start and end when you open and close Microsoft Mail, or to do so under other conditions.

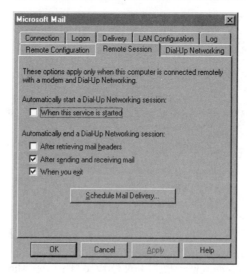

# Defining Scheduled Sessions

You can schedule a remote session with Microsoft Mail by specifying a time and connection method. The scheduled sessions are stored in the Microsoft Exchange profile. You can specify up to 16 scheduled sessions, including the following:

- Sessions at a specific date and time
- Sessions at prescribed intervals
- Sessions at specific times on specific days of the week

▶ **To define a scheduled session**

1. In Microsoft Mail properties, click the Remote Session tab, and then click the Schedule Item Delivery button.

   –Or–

   In the Tools menu in Microsoft Exchange, click Microsoft Mail, and then click Schedule Remote Mail Delivery.

2. In the Remote Scheduled Sessions dialog box, click Add.

3. In the Add Scheduled Session dialog box, click the Dial-Up Networking connection you want to use to establish the remote connection, and then specify the time for a scheduled session. If you choose Every, then you must specify a prescribed time interval.

   Notice that if you click Weekly On, the dialog box contents change so you can specify a date and time.

# Selecting Messages to Download

After you review headers for mail messages in remote mail, you can mark messages for selective downloading.

▶ **To mark messages in the Microsoft Exchange client**

1. In the Tools menu, click Remote Mail, and then click Microsoft Mail. You can also click other service providers if you have added them to Microsoft Exchange.

2. In the Remote Mail For Microsoft Mail dialog box, click the messages you want to preview.

3. Click the Edit menu, and then click Mark To Retrieve.

# Technical Notes on the Microsoft Exchange Client and MAPI

The Windows 95 messaging subsystem architecture provides power and flexibility. The core of the subsystem is MAPI, an industry standard that enables applications in Windows 95 to interact with many different messaging systems using a single interface. The MAPI architecture defines messaging clients, such as Microsoft Exchange, that interact with various messaging service providers, such as Microsoft Mail and Microsoft Fax, through MAPI, as shown in the following diagram:

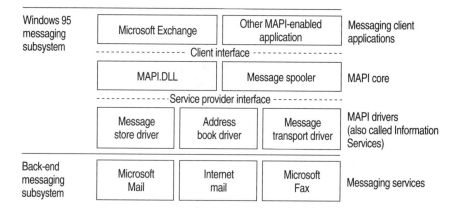

MAPI divides messaging applications into four components: MAPI subsystem, messaging clients, messaging service providers, and messaging systems.

**MAPI subsystem.**   Messaging client applications communicate with service providers through the MAPI subsystem. The client interface interacts with the MAPI subsystem to access MAPI-compliant service providers.

The client interface is one of two major functional interfaces in MAPI; the other is the service provider interface. Messaging applications that require messaging services call functions in the client interface. For example, client applications can call MAPI functions to send, receive, save, and read messages. These functions are sent to the MAPI subsystem, which calls corresponding functions within the provider interface. Service providers then implement service-provider functions to perform the indicated actions for the client. The message spooler queues outgoing messages and routes incoming messages to the proper message store folder.

**Messaging clients.**   Messaging client applications communicate with MAPI service providers through MAPI interfaces. Messaging client applications can be divided into three general categories:

- Messaging-aware applications include messaging functions as an added but not required feature, supporting the application's main purpose. An example of a messaging-aware application is Microsoft Word, which can add messaging functions by adding a Send Message command to its File menu.

- Messaging-enabled applications require some form of messaging functionality in order to meet the application's main purpose. Examples of messaging-enabled applications are the Microsoft Exchange client, Microsoft Mail, and cc:Mail™.

- Messaging-based workgroup applications go beyond basic electronic mail. They require full access to all the messaging services, including the message store providers, address book providers, and transport providers. Examples of this type of application are Microsoft Schedule+ and the public folders on a Microsoft Exchange Server.

For information about creating a messaging client, see the *Win32 Software Development Kit for Windows 95 and Windows NT* and the *MAPI 1.0 Developer's Guide*.

**Messaging service providers.**   A messaging service provider can include multiple message stores, address books, and messaging transport providers.

- Message store providers supply message storage, organization, and retrieval facilities for a messaging system.

- Address book providers supply message addressing and distribution list facilities to the messaging client.

- Messaging transport providers move messages between messaging clients or messaging stores.

MAPI selects between message store and messaging transport providers, as necessary, and merges the address books presented to it, so the client application sees one combined address book interface. Other vendors can add or replace messaging service providers to enable the Microsoft Exchange client to work with their mail systems.

# Upgrading to Microsoft Mail Server

You can upgrade your Windows 95 postoffice to a full Microsoft Mail Server postoffice by using the Microsoft Mail Post Office Upgrade product, which includes software, documentation, and licensing to extend the connectivity of your workgroup. The Microsoft Mail Server postoffice provides the following additional features:

- Executable and Help files that are not available in the Windows 95 Microsoft Mail workgroup postoffice

- Postoffice support for connections to external postoffices or gateways

- An ADMIN account not created in Windows 95 mail

- Default ADMIN.TPL and ADMIN.INF files created in Microsoft Mail Server for adding the predefined extended user information in the workgroup postoffice structure

- An administration utility (ADMIN.EXE) used to manage and configure the postoffice from any workstation on the network

- Support files for external postoffice mail transfer through a network or modem

- A routing program, EXTERNAL.EXE, that routes mail between multiple postoffices and gateways

- Client software for Windows 3.1, MS-DOS, and Apple® Macintosh® operating systems

The *Microsoft Mail Post Office Upgrade* product includes the following components:

- Software to upgrade a workgroup postoffice to a full Microsoft Mail Server postoffice

- Advanced administration tools, including tools for routing, directory synchronization, network group names, user access privileges, and mail log files, and for deleting old mail and old Mail accounts

- The EXTERNAL.EXE component, which provides the process for connecting postoffices (by means of a physical or asynchronous link) with the platform for remote access

- Client software for Windows 3.1, MS-DOS, Macintosh, and IBM® OS/2® Mail.

If you want to set up a Windows 95 Microsoft Mail workgroup postoffice to route mail between two or more postoffices, you need to do the following:

- Purchase the Microsoft Mail Post Office Upgrade for each workgroup postoffice being connected, and then follow the directions provided in the product.

- Set up a dedicated MS-DOS–based computer to act as the router. It will be running the EXTERNAL.EXE program included in the Post Office Upgrade. Notice that this MS-DOS–based computer needs networking software to connect to your postoffice servers. If the postoffices are stored on computers running Windows 95, then this computer needs a copy of Microsoft Workgroup Add-on for MS-DOS. If your postoffices are on Novell NetWare servers, then the computer running MS-DOS needs Novell client software for MS-DOS.

- If the postoffices are not on the same LAN, you need a dedicated MS-DOS–based computer to run EXTERNAL.EXE at each site, plus a modem for communicating with the other sites. Notice that Microsoft also offers versions of EXTERNAL.EXE that run on IBM OS/2 or Windows NT servers.

# Upgrading to Microsoft Exchange Server

A next-generation client-server messaging system known as Microsoft Exchange Server will be available from Microsoft after the release of Windows 95. Microsoft Exchange Server provides advanced electronic mail, scheduling, groupware applications, and custom application development. Microsoft Exchange Server includes MAPI drivers that extend the capabilities of the Windows 95 Microsoft Exchange client. For example, when Microsoft Exchange is connected to an Exchange Server, you can access a replicated "public folder," create custom forms and shared documents, schedule meetings with others, manage time and tasks, and create custom electronic forms for use in business.

Microsoft Exchange Server will require a computer running Windows NT Server version 3.5 or higher. It also includes a built-in X.400 gateway, plus support for SMTP and for Microsoft Mail for Intel® and Apple Macintosh computers. For more information about Microsoft Exchange Server, contact your Microsoft sales representative.

# Microsoft Mail Gateways

Many large organizations have multiple electronic messaging systems. In your organization, you might need to communicate with workgroups or organizations using electronic mail systems other than Windows 95 mail, such as cc:Mail, HP® Openmail, or IBM PROFS®. Microsoft offers a complete line of advanced gateways that provide reliable and sophisticated connectivity between Microsoft Mail Server and virtually any other electronic mail system within your organization.

Gateways ensure that messages always get across to their intended recipients. Addressing messages remains an easy process because people using other mail systems will be listed in your Microsoft Mail global address list—all you need to know is the name of the person you need to communicate with.

Microsoft offers gateways for the following:

| | | |
|---|---|---|
| X.400 | IBM PROFS | SNADS |
| SMTP | MHS | AT&T Easylink™ |
| MCI MAIL | Fax | |

**Note**  Microsoft Exchange Server will provide built-in support for X.400 and Internet Mail (SMTP). Users who upgrade to Microsoft Exchange Server will not need to purchase gateways for X.400 or SMTP.

Microsoft gateways support key features such as messaging backboning and message encapsulation.

- Messaging backboning lets organizations leverage their existing messaging resources by using these systems as high-performance bridges—or messaging backbones—between multiple Microsoft Mail sites.

- Message encapsulation makes it possible for users to place graphics, charts, sound, and video objects directly in mail messages for richer communication. Moreover, these complex messages can be sent across messaging backbones between distant sites without any loss of data integrity.

To connect a workgroup postoffice to another workgroup postoffice, you must purchase Microsoft Mail Postoffice Upgrade for each postoffice. To connect to another message system, such as X.400 or SMTP, you'll need to install both Microsoft Mail Postoffice Upgrade plus the appropriate gateway software.

**Note**  You will need at least one dedicated computer to act as the mail router, or the EXTERNAL.EXE program. Some gateways might require additional dedicated computers to connect to host systems. Before proceeding, you should determine your requirements by obtaining gateway datasheets.

Each message system can connect to the workgroup postoffice by using one or more specific gateways. The following table is a partial list of the Microsoft gateways needed for various message systems. If you use one of the message systems listed in this table, you need to purchase the appropriate gateway.

**Microsoft Mail Gateways for Message Systems**

| Message system | Microsoft Mail gateway |
| --- | --- |
| ARCOM 400 Swiss PTT | X.400 |
| AT&T® Easylink Services | X.400 |
| AT&T Mail | X.400 or AT&T Gateway |
| Atlas 400 | X.400 (NF mark from Afnor) |
| Banyan® Mail | MHS or X.400 |
| Beyond Mail | MHS |
| cc:Mail | X.400, MHS, SMTP, or Office Vision |
| CompuServe | SMTP or MHS |
| Computer Sciences Infonet® | X.400 |
| The Coordinator | MHS |
| Data General® CEO | X.400 |
| DaVinci Systems™ | MHS |
| DEC™ All-In-1™ | X.400, PROFS, SNADS, or SMTP |
| DEC VMS™ Mail | X.400 or SNADS |
| Dutch PTT | X.400 |
| Envoy 100/Gemdes | X.400 |
| Fax | Fax |
| Fischer International EMC2 | X.400 or SNADS |
| Gold 400 UK | X.400 |
| Higgins | MHS |

**Microsoft Mail Gateways for Message Systems** (*continued*)

| Message system | Microsoft Mail gateway |
| --- | --- |
| IBM AS/400® Office | SNADS[1] |
| IBM System/36™ | PROFS/OV |
| IBM CMS NOTES | PROFS |
| IBM DISOSS | SNADS |
| IBM OfficeVision/MVS™ | SNADS[1] |
| IBM PROFS | PROFS |
| Internet | SMTP |
| Lotus® Notes® | MHS[2] |
| Microsoft Mail for AppleTalk® | Microsoft Mail connection |
| NCR® Corporation | X.400[3] |
| Novell NetWare | MHS |
| Retix® | X.400 |
| Soft-Switch Central | SNADS |
| Sprint TeleMail | X.400 |
| Telebox 400 German PTT | X.400 |
| Touch | X.400 |
| Unisys® | X.400 |
| UNIX® SMTP | SMTP[4] |
| UUCP | SMTP[5] |
| Verimation Memo | SNADS |
| WANG® Office | MHS, X.400, or PROFS |

[1] Or through PROFS Distribution Manager if you have a VM host.

[2] Or the MS Mail-Notes Gateway by Corporate Software.

[3] Or in some cases, the AT&T Gateway

[4] SMTP is a part of TCP/IP, not UNIX. You can also have SMTP origination to a VAX or IBM host.

[5] Requires connectivity to an SMTP host that acts as a router to UUCP.

For more information about the features and benefits of Microsoft gateway products, see WIN95RK.HLP with the *Windows 95 Resource Kit* utilities.

CHAPTER 27

# Microsoft Fax

This chapter describes how to use Microsoft Fax software to send and receive faxes and editable files (files that can be changed) from your computer.

**In This Chapter**

Microsoft Fax: The Basics    866

Microsoft Fax: The Issues    868

Overview of Microsoft Fax    869

Setting Up Microsoft Fax for the User    870

Sending Faxes    872

Retrieving Faxes    874

Network Fax Service    874

Security for Microsoft Fax    877

    Establishing Security and Exchanging Keys    878

    Sending Secured Faxes    879

Technical Notes for Microsoft Fax    880

# Microsoft Fax: The Basics

With Microsoft Fax, users with modems can exchange faxes and editable files as easily as printing a document or sending an electronic mail message. Microsoft Fax is compatible with the millions of traditional Group 3 fax machines worldwide, yet it provides advanced security and binary file transfer (BFT) features that make sharing information by means of a fax easier and more powerful.

To use Microsoft Fax, you must install Microsoft Exchange. Microsoft Fax has been integrated into Microsoft Exchange as a messaging application programming interface (MAPI) service provider. All faxes sent to Microsoft Fax are received in the Microsoft Exchange universal inbox. You can send a fax by composing a Microsoft Exchange message, or by using the Send option on the File menu of a MAPI-compatible application (such as Microsoft Excel or Microsoft Word). In addition, Microsoft Fax includes a fax printer driver so that users can "print to fax" from within any Windows-based application.

Microsoft Fax provides the following key features.

**Fax at your fingertips.**  With Microsoft Fax, sending traditional faxes to Group 3 fax machines is as easy as printing a document. Additionally, Microsoft Fax uses the highest transmission speed and image compression supported by the recipient fax machine. Faxes sent in this way cannot be edited by the recipient.

**Delivery by address type.**  The MAPI service provider architecture allows you to mix different types of recipients in the *same* message. For example, it is possible to send a message simultaneously to Microsoft Mail, CompuServe®, Internet, and Microsoft Fax users as long as profiles for these destinations have been defined within Microsoft Exchange. A recipient's fax address can be selected from the Microsoft Exchange Personal Address Book, or the fax can be addressed by using an address that you use just once such as [fax: *555-1212*].

**Binary file transfer (BFT).**  Microsoft Fax supports Microsoft At Work BFT, which makes it possible to attach an editable document to a Microsoft Exchange mail message. These editable documents can be sent to users of Windows 95, Windows for Workgroups 3.11, and other Microsoft At Work™-enabled platforms.

**Security.**  Microsoft Fax lets you securely exchange confidential documents by using public key encryption or digital signatures. Any security specified by the user is applied before the message is passed to the modem or connected fax device.

**Network fax service.**  You can install a fax device in one computer and share it with other users within a workgroup. Individual computers can have their own fax devices installed and still use the shared fax device.

**Microsoft Fax Viewer.** The Microsoft Fax Viewer displays outgoing fax messages that have been queued to a local fax modem or to a Microsoft Fax network fax service. The Fax Viewer provides information about the current set of messages that are queued for transmission. You can also browse multipage faxes in thumbnail or full-page views.

**"Best available" fax format.** When you make a fax connection in Windows 95, Microsoft Fax queries and exchanges its fax capabilities with the recipient. This exchange of capabilities determines whether the recipient is a traditional Group 3 fax machine, which can only receive rendered faxes, or if the recipient has Microsoft Fax capabilities, and can receive editable files. Windows 95, Windows for Workgroups 3.11, and Microsoft At Work fax platforms are all capable of receiving binary files and traditional faxes.

- If the receiving fax device supports Microsoft Fax capabilities and an editable document is attached to a Microsoft Exchange message, then the file is transferred in its native format, in the same way as electronic mail.

- If the receiving fax device is a traditional Group 3 fax machine, then Microsoft Fax converts the document to the most compressed type of fax supported by the machine (MH, MR or MMR compression type) and transmits the image by using the best available communications protocol supported by the mutual connection (that is, V.17, V.29 or V.27).

- If Microsoft Fax sends a noneditable fax to another Microsoft Fax user, then the fax is transmitted by using the Microsoft At Work rendered fax format. This special format is much more compressed, on average, than Group 3 MMR. Therefore, the exchange of noneditable faxes between Microsoft Fax users is always faster than between Group 3 fax machines.

**Compatibility with popular fax modems.** Microsoft Fax is compatible with Class 1 and Class 2 fax modems, and provides support for high-speed fax communications (V.17, V.29, and V.27).

**Custom fax cover pages.** With Microsoft Fax, you can create new fax cover pages with a cover page designer that lets you incorporate graphics and text, or you can customize one of the predefined cover pages included with Microsoft Fax.

**Connecting to fax information services.** Microsoft Fax easily connects to fax-on-demand systems by using a built-in, poll-retrieve feature that allows you to retrieve rendered faxes or editable documents from a fax information service.

# Microsoft Fax: The Issues

Before you install and configure Microsoft Fax on the network, you will need to decide the following:

- Which users need Microsoft Fax. For every user who needs Microsoft Fax, you must also install Microsoft Exchange. All faxes sent to that user are received in the Microsoft Exchange inbox.

- Whether to install fax modems on individual computers or to designate a computer running Windows 95 to host a Microsoft Fax network fax service for other members of a workgroup.

- Which computer within a workgroup will host the Microsoft Fax network fax service. If the computer will also be used as a workstation, then a 80486-based computer with at least 12 MB of RAM is recommended. If the computer will be a dedicated fax server, then at least 8 MB of RAM is recommended. A high-speed (14.4 kbps) fax modem is strongly recommended. Depending on fax volumes, a shared fax service with this configuration could support up to 25 network fax users.

---

**Note**  When the computer hosting the shared fax modem receives faxes, Microsoft Fax does not automatically route them to individual inboxes. The workgroup administrator must use Microsoft Exchange to send a received fax to the recipient's Microsoft Exchange inbox.

---

- Whether you want to control or restrict access to the shared fax service. You can control access by defining a shared fax password, as described in "Network Fax Service" later in this chapter.

- Whether your workgroup's fax needs might be better served by a LAN fax server or commercial fax service. This depends on whether your organization has high fax volumes and inbound routing requests and as a result needs more detailed cost tracking and management. Microsoft is working with vendors of high-performance fax server platforms to ensure that their products are well-integrated with Windows 95 and Microsoft Fax.

- Whether your fax modems and fax machines are compatible with Microsoft Fax. To ensure connections with the widest variety of fax applications, fax machines, and fax modems, Microsoft Fax supports the following international standards for fax communications:

  - ITU (International Telecommunications Union, formerly the CCITT) T.30 standard for Group 3 fax machines. Microsoft At Work capabilities such as BFT are implemented as T.30 NSF (nonstandard facilities), thereby maintaining compatibility with the installed base of Group 3 fax machines.

  - ITU V.17, V.29 and V.27 standards for high-speed fax communications (up to 14.4 kbps).

  - Class 1 and Class 2 fax modems. A Class 1 fax modem is required for Microsoft At Work BFT and security. Fax rendering to traditional Group 3 fax devices is available on both Class 1 and 2 modems. Microsoft is working directly with fax modem manufacturers to ensure excellent compatibility.

  - MH, MR, and MMR compression for Group 3 fax communications.

  - Microsoft At Work fax platforms.

# Overview of Microsoft Fax

Users can easily exchange faxes and binary files in Microsoft Fax because it is accessible from the Windows 95 desktop, from within applications, or through the Microsoft Exchange inbox. As a 32-bit application, Microsoft Fax works smoothly with other applications created for Windows 95 through its support for MAPI, telephony API (TAPI), and OLE. The Send option in the File menu within any MAPI-enabled application (for example, Microsoft Excel or Word) will activate the Microsoft Exchange Send dialog box. The document appears as an icon attached to the electronic mail message.

To configure Microsoft Fax, do the following:

- Install and configure a modem for sending and receiving faxes. For more information, see Chapter 25, "Modems and Communications Tools."

- Install Microsoft Exchange and Microsoft Fax. The Microsoft Exchange Setup wizard will guide you through the installation procedure.

- Add Microsoft Fax to Microsoft Exchange.

After Microsoft Fax is configured, users can easily exchange rendered faxes and binary files. Because Microsoft Fax is provided with Windows 95 as a basic service, it is always available from within applications created for Windows 95 or through the Microsoft Exchange inbox. Faxes are always received in a user's Microsoft Exchange inbox.

# Setting Up Microsoft Fax for the User

The easiest way to install Microsoft Fax is to choose it in the Get Connected dialog box during Windows 95 Setup. You can also install it after you install Windows 95 by using the Add/Remove Programs option in Control Panel.

▶ **To install Microsoft Fax after Windows 95 installation**

1. In the Add/Remove Programs option in Control Panel, click the Windows Setup tab.

2. In the Components list box, click Microsoft Fax. If you have not previously installed Microsoft Exchange, Windows 95 automatically selects and installs it at this time. Click OK.

▶ **To configure Microsoft Fax**

1. In Control Panel, double-click the Mail And Fax icon, and then click Add.

   –Or–

   From the Tools menu in Microsoft Exchange, click Options, click the Services tab, and then click Add.

2. In the Add Services to Profile dialog box, click Microsoft Fax.

3. A Microsoft Fax warning message asks if you want to type your name, fax number, and fax device modem. Click OK.

4. In Microsoft Fax Properties, click the Message, Dialing, Modem, and User tabs, and type the appropriate information.

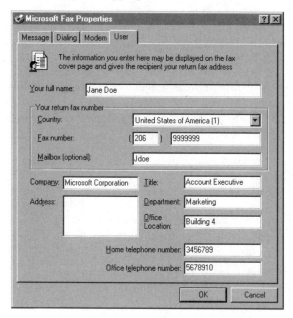

If you have installed a modem, Windows 95 automatically enters that information in the Modem properties. If you have not installed a modem, or if you want to select a different modem for sending faxes, click the Add button in the Modem properties to run the Install New Modem wizard.

**Note**  The information you type in User properties automatically appears on the cover page of faxes you send in Microsoft Fax.

After you have configured Microsoft Fax, you can change its properties by clicking the Setup option in the Fax menu in Microsoft Exchange. If you have problems setting up Microsoft Fax, see the troubleshooting information for Microsoft Fax in online Help.

# Sending Faxes

You can use Microsoft Fax to send and receive faxes by using a fax modem attached to your computer or on a network. Faxes are mail messages that are sent over the phone lines. Microsoft Fax shares the Personal Address Book with Microsoft Exchange and other MAPI providers.

The only difference between a mail message and a fax, from a Microsoft Exchange user's perspective, is the format of the recipient's address. Each Microsoft Exchange service provider, such as the Microsoft Network or Microsoft Fax, has its own format for a recipient's address.

You can send faxes from within Windows 95 in the following ways:

- Use Microsoft Exchange to create an electronic mail message and fax its contents to a recipient as described in the following procedures. If the message recipient is also using Windows 95, the message can include binary files and editable documents. Otherwise, the message will be rendered and sent as a fax.

- Print a document to the fax printer driver. If you select Microsoft Fax as the target printer for the document, and then click the Print option in the File menu, the Compose New Fax wizard will run.

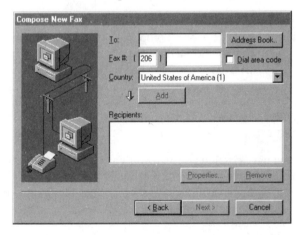

- Run the Compose New Fax wizard by double-clicking the Fax icon in the Accessories menu.

- Use Windows Explorer to drag and drop a document onto a Microsoft Fax printer icon on the Windows 95 desktop.

- Right-click a document icon in My Computer to display the context menu. In the context menu, select the Send To option, and then select the Fax Recipient option to run the Compose New Fax wizard. The application that created the original document starts so that the document can be rendered (printed). After it is rendered, the application closes.

- Use the Send option in the File menu of a MAPI mail-enabled application such as Microsoft Word or Microsoft Excel to activate Microsoft Exchange.

**Note** You can create a shortcut to the Microsoft Fax printer by right-clicking the Microsoft Fax printer icon and then dragging it to the Windows 95 desktop.

▶ **To send a fax from Microsoft Exchange**

1. In the Compose menu, click New Fax to run the Compose New Fax wizard.

2. In the Compose New Fax Wizard dialog box, select the fax recipient's name and number from your Microsoft Exchange Personal Address Book, or create a new name, and then click Next.

3. Click Yes to include a fax cover page with your message, and then click a type of predefined cover page, or click Options to define a message format and a time to send the fax.

4. In the Next dialog boxes, compose your message and insert any binary files or objects you want to include in the fax.

▶ **To send a fax from the Windows 95 Start button**

- Point to Programs, and then point to Accessories, point to Fax, and then click Compose New Fax.

With Microsoft Fax, you can attach a cover page to a fax by selecting from four predefined cover pages, or by creating a custom cover page for each recipient. The predefined cover pages are named Urgent!, Confidential!, For Your Information, and General Purpose (default). You can also customize predefined cover pages as described in the following procedure.

With the Microsoft Fax Cover Page Editor, you can also design a unique cover page for each recipient. The Cover Page Editor allows you to incorporate rich text, graphics, logos, and information from the Microsoft Exchange Personal Address Book into a cover page.

**Note** All cover pages contain recipient information that you first entered in the Microsoft Exchange Personal Address Book. Microsoft Fax inserts this information each time you send a fax.

See the following online Help topics for information about creating cover pages in Microsoft Fax:

- Attaching a predefined cover page to a fax message
- Customizing predefined cover pages
- Creating a custom cover page

# Retrieving Faxes

With the Request a Fax option, you can retrieve faxes from fax machines, fax-on-demand systems, and other fax information services that support Group 3 poll-retrieve capability. Some Group 3 fax machines allow you to retrieve editable files, software updates, and fax images by using the Microsoft At Work BFT protocol.

To retrieve faxes, you start the Request A Fax wizard in the Accessories menu or in Microsoft Exchange. The wizard allows you to download a specific document or a default document that includes the names of other available documents on the service.

▶ **To retrieve faxes using Request a Fax in Microsoft Exchange**

- Click the Tools menu, point to Microsoft Fax Tools, and then click Request A Fax.

The Request a Fax wizard guides you through the steps required to connect to a fax service and download faxes to your computer.

# Network Fax Service

With Microsoft Fax, users in the same workgroup can share a fax modem installed on one of the computers in the workgroup. After the fax modem has been shared, all other users within the workgroup can send and receive faxes through it. The computer that contains the shared fax modem is called the fax server.

The Microsoft Exchange inbox of the fax server receives all of the faxes for the workgroup. The administrator for the server uses Microsoft Exchange to route the faxes to their intended recipients in the workgroup. Received faxes appear in the Microsoft Exchange inbox and each one is identified as a fax by a special icon. If the icon represents a rendered fax, double-clicking it runs the Microsoft Fax Viewer application. Otherwise, Microsoft Exchange opens the fax as if it were an electronic mail message. You can forward and reply to faxes in the same way you would a Microsoft Exchange mail message.

Before you configure a computer running Windows 95 as a fax server, make sure it has enough memory and that it has a compatible modem. For memory requirements, see "Microsoft Fax: The Issues" earlier in this chapter.

▶ **To configure a computer as a fax server in Microsoft Exchange**

1. Click the Tools menu, click Microsoft Fax Tools, and then click Options.

2. In the Microsoft Fax Properties dialog box, click the Modem tab.

3. In Modem properties, make sure the option named Let Other People On The Network Use My Modem To Send Faxes is checked.

4. To change the Share Name for the shared fax modem, click the Properties button, and then type a new name. By default, Microsoft Fax displays the name of the Network Fax shared directory.

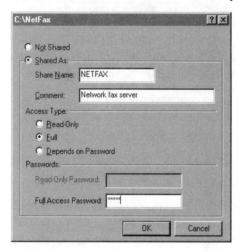

You can also define security in the shared directory's properties. If you have user-level security enabled, you can define which users can have access to the network fax service, and define their access rights. If you have share-level security enabled, you can define whether a password is required to connect to the network fax service. For more information, see Chapter 14, "Security."

If you choose Full access (the default), all users within the Windows 95 workgroup can send faxes by using the shared fax service.

5. Click OK to enable the Microsoft Fax shared fax server.

---

**Note**  Other users in the Windows 95 workgroup must know the fax server's full network name to access it. The name is formed by joining the server's computer name (defined in the Network option in Control Panel) with the shared directory name, for example, \\JOELLEN\NETFAX.

---

▶  **To configure a computer as a client to the fax server in Microsoft Exchange**

1. Click the Tools menu, click Microsoft Fax Tool, and then click Options.

2. In the Microsoft Fax Properties dialog box, click the Modem tab.

3. In Modem properties, click Add.

4. In the Add a Fax Modem dialog box, click Network Fax Server, and then click OK.

5. In the Connect to Network Fax Server dialog box, type the network name of the fax server and then click OK.

6. In the Microsoft Fax Properties dialog box, click the server name, and then click the Set as Active Fax Device button.

# Security for Microsoft Fax

Microsoft Fax protects valuable and confidential documents through encryption and digital signatures. An encrypted fax can be read only by the intended recipient, who has a set of keys to unlock it or a password. A digitally signed fax allows a recipient to verify that the purported sender of the fax is the actual sender. You can use a digital signature on its own or add a digital signature to a fax protected with password or key encryption.

**Password and key encryption.**   You can encrypt a fax or binary file by using either a simple password or a public or private key pair. Password encryption, which is the simplest security method, scrambles a fax based on a specific password. The fax recipients can only unscramble the fax if they know the password. Password encryption does not require the exchange of public keys with your recipients, but you will need to tell them the password that you used to secure the fax.

When you use key encryption, Microsoft Fax assigns you two security keys, a private key and a public key. You can exchange public keys with anyone you choose. When you send a key-encrypted message, Microsoft Fax uses the recipient's public key and your private key to encrypt the message. When the message is received, Microsoft Fax uses your public key and the recipient's private key to decrypt it. Using your own private key ensures that the message could have been sent only by you. Using the recipient's public key ensures that only the recipient can unlock the message. You can store and maintain the public keys you receive from other users in your Microsoft Exchange Personal Address Book.

**Note**   Microsoft Fax applies security only to those faxes that have been sent as editable files. Rendered faxes cannot be secured.

**Digital signatures.**   Using a digital signature to secure a fax is similar to notarizing a document; it verifies for the recipient that the person who signed the document is the person who sent it. Digital signatures prevent anyone but the sender from modifying the document while it is being sent.

Digital signatures can only be used with binary file documents, that is, those that have been attached to mail messages (not rendered). Before you can use digital signatures, you must establish security and exchange public keys with a recipient.

# Establishing Security and Exchanging Keys

The first step in using key encryption or digital signatures is establishing security.

▶ **To establish security in Microsoft Exchange**

1. Click the Tools menu, point to Microsoft Fax Tools, and then click Advanced Security.

2. In the Advanced Fax Security dialog box, click the New Key Set button.

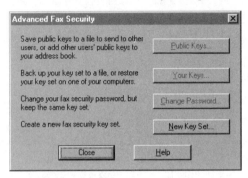

3. In the Fax Security - New Key Set dialog box, type a password, and then click OK. This password will be used for sending and receiving both key-encrypted and digitally signed faxes.

   Microsoft Fax automatically creates a public and private set of keys for you, and then it displays the Advanced Fax Security dialog box.

4. Click the Change Password button to change your fax security password but keep the same key set, or click New Key Set to create a new key set.

To use the key set to send and receive secured faxes, you must exchange public keys. To exchange public keys, you must save your public keys to a file that you can send to other users, or add other users' public keys to your address book.

▶ **To exchange a public key with another user in Microsoft Exchange**

1. Click the Tools menu, point to Microsoft Fax Tools, and then click Advanced Security.

2. In the Advanced Security dialog box, click the Public Keys button.

3. In the Managing Public Keys dialog box, click Save.

4. In the Save Public Keys dialog box, click the public keys that you want in the listbox, and then click the To: button to identify the folder where you want to save these keys. Type a name for the public keys with the file extension .AWP, and then click OK.

If you receive a public key from another user, you will need to import the .AWP key file into Microsoft Fax. After you and your recipient have exchanged public keys, you will be able to exchange secured faxes. The easiest way to exchange public keys is through electronic mail. Compose a message in Microsoft Exchange and insert your .AWP file into the message. The recipient must save the .AWP file to a directory and import the public keys into Microsoft Fax.

▶ **To import the .AWP file in Microsoft Exchange**

1. Click the Tools menu, points to Microsoft Fax Tools, and then click Advanced Security.

2. In the Advanced Security dialog box, click Public Keys.

3. In the Public Keys dialog box, click Add, and then specify the path to the .AWP file.

# Sending Secured Faxes

Microsoft Fax allows you to secure a fax on a per-message basis.

▶ **To send a secured fax**

1. In the Compose New Fax wizard, click the Options button, and then click the Security button.

2. In the Message Security Options dialog box, choose from the following methods of securing a fax:

- Click the Key-Encrypted option to encrypt your fax by using RSA public key encryption.

- Click the Password Protected option to assign a password to the fax.

- Click the option named Digitally Sign All Attachments to apply a digital signature to a document that you have attached to a mail message. You can add a digital signature to a key-encrypted or password-encrypted fax.

# Technical Notes for Microsoft Fax

This section describes technical information about Microsoft Fax architecture and Registry entries.

You can send faxes either by using the mail client or the Microsoft Fax printer driver. In each case, the message is sent to the Microsoft Fax service provider by using MAPI. If you sent the message from a mail client, it might contain text, embedded OLE formats, and attachments. If you sent it by using the Microsoft Fax printer driver, the mail message will contain a rendered format of the file as an attachment to the mail message.

MAPI allows messages to be preprocessed based on the transport protocol used to send them. The transport protocol chooses the correct modem connection, uses TAPI to create a dial string, and sends the message to that recipient. The preprocessor determines whether to render the message into a fax form to be printed by a fax machine. The rendered format is attached to the original message as a message property and is deleted either when the message is sent or when the transport protocol tries to send the message but determines it cannot.

If the message does not have to be rendered, the message is converted from its original binary format to a line image (also called a linearized form), and then it is compressed.

After the message is submitted, the transport protocol determines what type of recipient the message is intended for as follows:

- If it is a traditional fax recipient and the user has selected printed form or "best available," Microsoft Fax will render the document into the standard Group 3 image format. This can be used by standard fax machines and software. If the user selects editable form, an error message is returned.

- If the recipient is a Microsoft At Work-enabled recipient and the user has selected printed form, then it will render the document into the Microsoft Fax rendered format. This format provides high-quality images of smaller size than standard Group 3 and it is used between Microsoft At Work devices, including fax machines and printers.

- If the recipient is a Microsoft Fax recipient and the user has selected editable form, no rendering is required.

- If there is a mix of recipients, and the user has selected "best available," then Group 3 and editable versions of the document are packaged in the message.

- If the capabilities of the recipient are unknown, Microsoft Fax creates multiple formats to be sure that the proper format is available upon connect.

Fax-form messages sent to Microsoft At Work devices will be sent by using BFT with the resource-based rendering of the message sent as an attachment.

The Registry keys for a fax modem are found in:

`Hkey_Local_Machines\Software\Microsoft\At Work Fax\`*Local Modems*

For each local modem that has been installed by Windows 95, information is stored in the key named TAPI*nnnnnnnn* where *nnnnnnnn* is an arbitrary number assigned by TAPI. The TAPI key contains subkey values. Values that are important to the system administrator are described in the following tables.

The following table lists the modem command strings used to reset the modem whenever Microsoft Fax acquires it from TAPI:

| Subkey | Description |
| --- | --- |
| ResetCommand | This "AT" command string includes:<br><br>- Load factory defaults: &F<br>- Disable auto-answer: S0=0<br>- Echo OFF: E0<br>- Verbose ON: V1<br>- Quiet OFF: Q0<br><br>The default depends on fax modem. Typically, **AT&FS0=0E0V1Q0**. |

The following table lists the setup modem command string used to set up the modem before dialing or answering:

| Subkey | Description |
|---|---|
| SetupCommand | This "AT" command string includes:<br>• Max dial-tone timeout: S7=255<br>• Tie DTR drop to reset: &D3<br>• XON/XOFF flow control: Varies<br>The default depends on fax modem. Typically, **ATS7=255&D3&K4**. |
| ExitCommand | This command string is issued to the modem after hang-up, and just before releasing the port. The default is empty. |
| FixSerialSpeed | This command string specifics the port speed. The default is **19200**. |
| PreAnswerCommand | This modem command string is issued to the modem just before issuing the ATA (answer) command. Microsoft Fax will have already issued the Setup command, and the command to go to the appropriate Fax Class (Class 1 or 2). The default is empty. |
| PreDialCommand | This modem command string is issued just before issuing an ATA (dial) command. Microsoft Fax will have already issued the Setup command, and the command to go to the appropriate Fax class (class 1 or 2). The default is empty. |
| HighestSendSpeed | This modem command string specifies the highest speed to try sending a fax, in bits per second. A value of 0 forces the highest available speed. The default is **0**. |
| LowestSendSpeed | This modem command string specifies the lowest speed to try sending a fax, in bits per second. A value of 0 forces the lowest available speed. The default is **0**. |
| EnableV17Send | If 0, this command string disables use of V.17 (14.4 kbps, short train) for sending. The default is **1**. |
| EnableV17Recv | If 0, this command string disables use of V.17 (14.4 kbps, short train) for receiving. The default is **1**. |

CHAPTER 28

# Dial-Up Networking and Mobile Computing

This chapter describes how to use Dial-Up Networking to access a network from a remote location. It also describes how other Windows 95 mobile computing tools, such as Briefcase and Direct Cable Connection, can be used to connect to desktop computers or the network.

**Important** The dial-up server capabilities discussed in this chapter are only available if you purchase Microsoft Plus! for Windows 95. For more information contact your Microsoft sales representative.

**In This Chapter**

Dial-Up Networking and Mobile Computing: The Basics   885
Dial-Up Networking and Mobile Computing: The Issues   886
Overview of Dial-Up Networking   888
   Dial-Up Clients and Servers   889
   Connection Protocols   890
   Local Area Network Protocols   891
Installing Dial-Up Networking   892
Configuring Dial-Up Networking Clients and Servers   893
   Installing Protocols   894
   Defining a Dial-Up Networking Connection   894
   Configuring a Windows 95 Dial-Up Client   896
   Making a Dial-Up Networking Connection   898
   Configuring a Windows 95 Dial-Up Server   899
   Disabling Dial-Up Server Support   901
   Using Security with Dial-Up Networking   902
   Using Software and Hardware Compression to Transfer Data   903
   Connecting to a Windows NT Remote Access Server   904
   Configuring a Windows NT Server for Windows 95 Dial-Up Clients   905

*(continued)*

Connecting to a Novell NetWare Connect Server    907
Connecting to Shiva Remote Access Servers    908
    PPP Dial-Up Sequence    913
    PPP Log File    914
Overview of Windows 95 Mobile Computing Features    915
Direct Cable Connection    916
    Installing and Configuring Direct Cable Connection    917
    Cables Compatible with Direct Cable Connection    917
Using Briefcase for File Synchronization    918
    Creating and Configuring a Briefcase    918
    Updating Files with Briefcase    919
Troubleshooting Dial-Up Networking    920

# Dial-Up Networking and Mobile Computing: The Basics

Dial-Up Networking allows mobile users to work as if they are connected directly to the network. Establishing a network connection by using Dial-Up Networking works the same as establishing a network connection in the office—you just double-click a network resource.

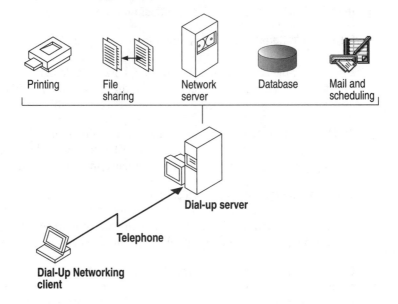

The Windows 95 Dial-Up Networking subsystem allows mobile users to designate a computer running Windows 95 as a dial-up client or server. From a remote site, you can use Dial-Up Networking to connect the dial-up client to a Windows 95 dial-up server or other remote access servers, such as Shiva® NetModem or LanRover, Novell® NetWare® Connect, and Windows NT version 3.1 or 3.5 Remote Access Service (RAS). If the client and server are running the same network protocols, the dial-up client can connect to the network to access its resources.

Notice that a Microsoft Windows NT Client Access License is required if the computer will be connecting to servers running Windows NT Server. For information, see Chapter 8, "Windows 95 on Microsoft Networks," or contact your Microsoft reseller.

Windows 95 provides the following tools to help users stay as functional as possible with the limited resources of a mobile site.

**Remote mail.**  With the Microsoft Exchange client and a Microsoft Mail workgroup postoffice, mobile users can dial in to the network to send and receive electronic mail, without requiring any additional client software or a special gateway server. To send and receive mail, mobile users make a Dial-Up Networking connection to another computer running Windows 95 to another remote access server connected to their workgroup postoffice. After connecting, they use Microsoft Exchange to send and receive their mail.

**Direct Cable Connection.**  This tool allows you to quickly and easily establish a connection between two computers by using a parallel cable or null-modem serial cable. After the connection is established, Direct Cable Connection facilitates the transfer of files from the host computer to the guest computer. The host can act as a gateway to an IPX/SPX or NetBEUI network for the guest.

**Windows 95 Briefcase.**  This file synchronization tool minimizes the task of keeping track of the relationships between files on a portable computer and on a desktop computer. With Briefcase, a user can simultaneously update related files.

**Deferred printing.**  Windows 95 supports deferred printing, which allows mobile users to generate print jobs when they are not connected to a printer. The print jobs are stored until a printer becomes available. Windows 95 detects the printer connection and automatically spools the print jobs in the background.

**Dial-Up tools from other vendors.**  This chapter describes how to use Dial-Up Networking with Windows NT, Shiva, and NetWare remote access servers. For information about using Windows 95 Dial-Up Networking to dial in to other remote access servers, or using other remote access software to dial in to Windows 95, contact your network vendor or software supplier.

# Dial-Up Networking and Mobile Computing: The Issues

To run Dial-Up Networking, the computer must have a protected-mode client, that is, one that can use the Windows 95 protected-mode transports, or others that use NDIS and provide appropriate PPP drivers. This means that you cannot use a Novell real-mode client over Dial-Up Networking, but you can use Microsoft Client for NetWare Networks.

To use Dial-Up Networking to connect to the network, you need the following hardware:

- One or more compatible modems, as described in Chapter 25, "Modems and Communications Tools."

- Enough available hard disk space to install Dial-Up Networking. Currently, about 2 to 3 MB of free disk space is required to install the client and server portions of Dial-Up Networking.

To use Dial-Up Networking to connect to the network, you will need to decide the following:

- Which computers on the network will function as Windows 95 dial-up servers. (Dial-up server capabilities are only available if you purchase Microsoft Plus! for Windows 95.)

- What kind of remote access server, other than a Windows 95 dial-up server, remote users will connect to. For example, a Windows 95 dial-up server allows only one remote connection at a time, whereas a Windows NT 3.5 remote access server allows 256 connections. Depending on the size and needs of your network, you might configure a Windows 95 dial-up client to connect to a Windows NT 3.5 server or other remote access server. For a list of the types of remote access servers that a Windows 95 dial-up client can be configured to connect to, see "Dial-Up Clients and Servers" later in this chapter.

- What type of connection protocol your dial-up client will use to connect to the remote access server. Windows 95 provides support for Point-to-Point protocol (PPP), RAS for Windows for Workgroups 3.11 and Windows NT 3.1, NetWare Connect, and Serial Line Internet Protocol (SLIP). The dial-up client and the remote access server must both be running the same connection protocol. For a complete list of protocol types, see "Connection Protocols" later in this chapter.

- What kind of local area network protocol to install on the dial-up client and server to connect the client to the network. Windows 95 supports IPX/SPX, Microsoft TCP/IP, and Microsoft NetBEUI protocols. For more information about network protocols and Dial-Up Networking, see "Local Area Network Protocols" later in this chapter.

- Whether you want to share the resources of a Windows 95 dial-up server. To enable a dial-up client to access files and printing capabilities of a dial-up server, you must install File and Printer Sharing services in the Network option in Control Panel, and also enable Allow Caller Access when configuring either user-level or share-level security on the dial-up server. For more information, see "Configuring a Windows 95 Dial-Up Server" and "Using Security with Dial-Up Networking" later in this chapter.

- What level of security you need for dial-up servers. You can enable either user-level or share-level security on a Windows 95 dial-up server. Both types of security provide password protection for the dial-up process, but do not support callback authentication. A Windows 95 dial-up client does support callback authentication when connected to other types of remote access servers, such as Windows NT Server, that supports callback authentication. For more information, see "Using Security with Dial-Up Networking" later in this chapter.

- Whether you need additional security. Windows 95 supports hardware security tools from other vendors for dial-up access, plus authentication protocols such as CHAP and SPAP.

# Overview of Dial-Up Networking

With Dial-Up Networking, you can connect from a remote site to a computer that has been configured as a remote access server, or connect to a network through the remote access server. For example, if you connect to a Windows 95 dial-up server, you can share its resources (if the Microsoft File and Printer Sharing service has been enabled), or you can use it as a gateway to a network that is running IPX/SPX and NetBEUI network protocols. As shown in the following figure a Windows 95 dial-up client can connect to a wide variety of networks because support is included for a variety of connection and network protocols.

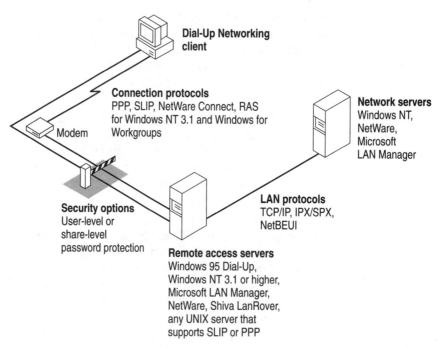

Different remote access servers provide different security systems to protect access to a network. The Windows 95 dial-up server uses pass-through user-level or share-level security as described in "Using Security with Dial-Up Networking" later in this chapter.

You can use system policies and other methods to disable dial-in access so users cannot dial in to a particular desktop computer. For information, see "Disabling Dial-Up Server Support" later in this chapter. If the user chooses to dial in to a host system such as Windows NT, Shiva NetModem or LanRover, or NetWare Connect, Windows 95 offers full connectivity.

Dial-Up Networking uses the Windows 95 communications architecture to communicate through a modem to a network. It initializes the modem, determines device status, and dials the phone number by using TAPI and the Unimodem driver. For more information, see Chapter 24, "Introduction to Windows 95 Communications." For more information about how Dial-Up Networking works, plus information about scripting for connections, see WIN95RK.HLP in the *Windows 95 Resource Kit* utilities.

A Windows 95 Dial-Up Networking configuration includes these components, as described in the following sections:

- Dial-Up clients and servers
- Connection Protocols
- Network (LAN) protocols and network servers
- Security options

# Dial-Up Clients and Servers

With Dial-Up Networking, you can configure a remote computer running Windows 95 as a dial-up client to dial in to a Windows 95 dial-up server or other remote access servers. A dial-up client, running the appropriate connection protocol, can connect to many types of remote access servers, including the following:

- Windows 95 dial-up server
- Windows NT Workstation
- Windows NT 3.1 or later
- Windows for Workgroups 3.11
- NetWare Connect
- Shiva LanRover and other dial-up routers
- Any UNIX® server that runs SLIP or PPP

# Connection Protocols

Connection protocols control the transmission of data over the wide-area network (WAN). A Windows 95 dial-up client can use the following connection protocols to connect to a remote access server:

- Point-to-Point Protocol (PPP)
- Novell NetWare Connect
- Windows NT 3.1 or Windows for Workgroups RAS (Asynchronous NetBEUI)
- Serial Line Internet Protocol (SLIP)

The type of connection protocol you choose depends on the server you are connecting to. Some connection protocols support a subset of the common network protocols. For example, PPP allows you to connect to a network server or a computer running Windows 95 with TCP/IP, IPX/SPX-compatible, or NetBEUI network protocols.

The following is a summary of connection protocols.

**Point-to-Point Protocol (PPP).**  PPP has become the standard for remote access. Microsoft recommends that you use PPP because of its flexibility and its role as an industry standard, and for future flexibility with client and server hardware and software. If a dial-up client is running PPP, it can connect to a network running IPX, TCP/IP, or NetBEUI protocols. PPP is the default protocol for the Microsoft Dial-Up adapter. For more information, see WIN95RK.HLP with the *Windows 95 Resource Kit* utilities.

**Novell NetWare Connect.**  NetWare Connect is a proprietary connection protocol. It allows a computer running Windows 95 to directly connect to a NetWare Connect server and, if running a NetWare-compatible network client, connect to NetWare servers. Windows 95 can only act as a client for connecting to a NetWare Connect server. NetWare Connect clients themselves cannot connect to a Windows 95 dial-up server directly through dial-up.

**RAS for Windows NT 3.1 and Windows for Workgroups 3.11.**  This protocol (asynchronous NetBEUI) is used to connect computers running Windows 95 to remote access servers running Windows NT 3.1 or Windows for Workgroups 3.11, or to connect computers running Windows for Workgroups 3.11 or Windows NT 3.1 to a Windows 95 dial-up server. The remote access server must be running NetBEUI.

**Serial Line Internet Protocol (SLIP).**  SLIP is an older remote access standard that is typically used by UNIX remote access servers. Use SLIP only if your site has a UNIX system configured as a SLIP server for Internet connections. The remote access server must be running TCP/IP.

Windows 95 does not provide SLIP server capabilities; SLIP is for dial-out only. Support for SLIP can be found on the Windows 95 compact disc.

# Local Area Network Protocols

Windows 95 makes it easy to configure dial-up clients and servers to access a network. When you install Dial-Up Networking, any protocols already installed on the computer are automatically enabled for Dial-Up Networking. Windows 95 includes support for TCP/IP, IPX/SPX, and NetBEUI network protocols. To configure the Windows 95 dial-up server to act as a gateway to a network, you must ensure that it and the dial-up client are running the same network (LAN) protocol as your existing network.

The following table presents the combinations of protocols you can use to run either Windows Sockets or NetBIOS applications on a network.

| Connection protocols | Network protocols (APIs) |
| --- | --- |
| NetWare Connect | IPX/SPX (Windows Sockets/NetBIOS) |
| PPP | TCP/IP (Windows Sockets/NetBIOS) IPX/SPX (Windows Sockets/NetBIOS) NetBEUI (NetBIOS) |
| RAS for Windows NT 3.1 or Windows for Workgroups 3.11 | NetBEUI (NetBIOS) |
| SLIP | TCP/IP (Windows Sockets/NetBIOS) |

**Note**  You do not need to install any network protocols when you install Dial-Up Networking; NetBEUI and the IPX/SPX-compatible protocol are automatically installed and bound to the Microsoft Dial-Up adapter. You can add protocols by using the Network option in Control Panel.

A Windows 95 dial-up server cannot act as a gateway to SLIP or IPX (over NetWare Connect) networks, as shown in the following graphic.

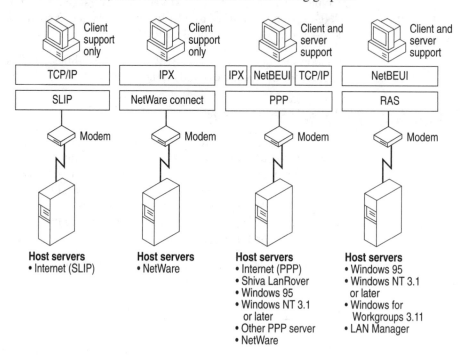

## Installing Dial-Up Networking

When you install Dial-Up Networking, you are installing all the components you need to connect to a network. For example, installing Dial-Up Networking also installs the Microsoft Dial-Up adapter, and connection and network protocols.

Before you dial up a remote connection using a modem and Dial-Up Networking, you need to make sure all the appropriate network protocols are bound to the Microsoft Dial-Up adapter or a network adapter. The easiest way to install Dial-Up Networking is during installation of Windows 95. If you didn't choose it during Setup, you can install it afterward.

---

**Note**  If you are currently using Windows for Workgroups 3.11 with RAS, Dial-Up Networking will automatically be installed when you upgrade to Windows 95.

---

▶  **To install Dial-Up Networking after you run Setup**

1. In the Add/Remove Programs Option in Control Panel, click the Windows Setup tab.

2. In the Components list, click Communications, and then click the Details button.

3. In the Communications dialog box, click Dial-Up Networking, and then click OK.

After it is installed a folder for Dial-Up Networking appears in My Computer. To run Dial-Up Networking, double-click the folder.

# Configuring Dial-Up Networking Clients and Servers

Configuring computers as Dial-Up Networking clients or servers consists of four tasks:

- Installing the appropriate network protocols and making sure they are bound to the Microsoft Dial-Up adapter. All network protocols installed before you install Dial-Up Networking are automatically bound to the Microsoft Dial-Up adapter when you install Dial-Up Networking.

- Running the Make New Connection wizard in Dial-Up Networking to set up a connection to a remote access server for the dial-up client. If you have not yet installed a modem, the wizard guides you through installing one.

- Configuring the dial-up client in Dial-Up Networking by selecting the remote access server type it will connect to, and by choosing whether to log on to the network after connecting to the remote access server. Selecting the server type automatically enables the correct connection protocol, such as PPP or SLIP.

- Optionally, installing dial-up server capabilities and configuring a computer running Windows 95 as a dial-up server in the Dial-Up Server menu in Dial-Up Networking.

# Installing Protocols

Windows 95 automatically binds the default network protocols to the Microsoft Dial-Up adapter when you install Dial-Up Networking. For most networks, these typically are the IPX/SPX-compatible and NetBEUI protocols. You can install other network protocols, such as TCP/IP, by using the Networks option in Control Panel. For information about adding protocols, see Chapter 12, "Network Technical Discussion."

▶ **To make sure the correct protocols are bound to the Microsoft Dial Up adapter or other network adapter**

- In the Network option in Control Panel, each protocol (in the Components list box) that is bound to the Microsoft Dial-Up adapter will show an arrow pointing to the adapter.

# Defining a Dial-Up Networking Connection

Windows 95 guides you through making a new remote connection when you first run Dial-Up Networking. Before creating a new Dial-Up Networking connection, you should install a modem. The Make New Connection wizard prompts you to do so, or you can install it separately by using the Install New Modem wizard in the Modems option in Control Panel. For information, see Chapter 25, "Modems and Communications Tools."

▶ **To create a Dial-Up Networking connection using the Make New Connection wizard**

1. From My Computer, double-click the Dial-Up Networking folder.

2. In the Dial-Up Networking window, double-click the Make New Connection icon.

3. The Make New Connection wizard prompts you for the information needed to define a connection, including a name for the computer you are dialing, modem type, area code, telephone number, and country code.

   The new icon for your connection appears in the Dial-Up Networking window. You need to provide this information only once for each connection you define.

---

**Note**  You can adjust the dialing string in Dialing Properties, which is accessible from the Connect To dialog box that appears when you double-click a connection icon.

---

When a user connects to a remote server, a terminal window can be displayed to support an interactive logon session with the server. After a connection is established, remote network access becomes transparent to the user.

▶ **To make sure a network connection has been established**

- Double-click Network Neighborhood, click Map Network Drive, and then type a path name to a network server.

▶ **To display a terminal window before or after dialing**

1. Click a connection icon, click the File menu, and then click Properties.

2. In General properties, click the Configure button, and then click the Options tab.

3. In the Options dialog box, click the option named Bring Up Terminal Window Before Dialing or the option named Bring Up Terminal Window After Dialing.

---

### Tip for Using Dialing Properties to Change Location Information

Dial-Up Networking is a TAPI-enabled application. This means that Dial-Up Networking can offload the work of matching the correct phone dialing string from the location to the TAPI components designed for that role. When you attempt a Dial-Up Networking connection, you can choose to edit your calling location by using Dialing Properties.

With Dialing Properties, you can specify area code, special numbers needed to reach an outside line, and calling card information you may need for the connection number. The Windows 95 TAPI services will then automatically adjust the dial string it sends to your modem.

---

The configurations you set up for each connection are stored in the Registry under

`Hkey_Current_User\RemoteAccess\Addresses\`*My Connection*

You can predefine Dial-Up Networking connections for users by including them as part of system policies. If you enable user profiles, different users sharing the same computer can use separate dialing configurations. For more information, see Chapter 15, "User Profiles and System Policies."

# Configuring a Windows 95 Dial-Up Client

You configure the Windows 95 dial-up client for each dial-in connection you define in Dial-Up Networking. Configuration consists of selecting the remote access server type to connect to and choosing whether to access the network after connecting to the remote access server. In addition, you can require an encrypted password to connect to a remote access server and check to see if the correct network protocols are installed on the dial-up client. Windows 95 automatically selects the appropriate connection protocol when you select the remote access server type for each Dial-Up Networking connection.

Windows 95 supports SLIP only as a client. The SLIP client software is provided on the Windows 95 compact disc.

▶ **To install SLIP**

1. In Add/Remove Programs in Control Panel, click the Windows Setup tab, and then click the Have Disk button.

2. In the Install From Disk dialog box, click the Browse button, and then type the path name to ADMIN\APPTOOLS\DSCRIPT\RNAPLUS.INF.

3. In the Have Disk dialog box, click UNIX Connection For Dial-Up Networking, and then click Install.

▶ **To configure the Windows 95 dial-up client**

1. In Dial-Up Networking, right-click a connection icon, and then click Properties.

2. In General properties, click the Server Type button.

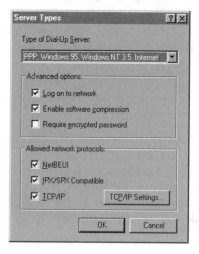

3.  In the Server Types dialog box, select the correct remote access server type.

| This server type | Connects to |
| --- | --- |
| PPP: Windows 95, Windows NT 3.5, Internet | This is the default; selecting this allows Windows 95 to automatically detect and connect to other remote access servers that are running TCP/IP, NetBEUI, or IPX/SPX over PPP |
| NRN: NetWare Connect | Novell NetWare Connect running IPX/SPX over NetWare Connect |
| Windows for Workgroups and Windows NT 3.1 | Windows 95 dial-up server; Windows NT version 3.1 or 3.5; Windows for Workgroups version 3.11 running NetBEUI over RAS |
| SLIP: UNIX Connection | Any SLIP server over TCP/IP |
| CSLIP: UNIX Connection with IP Header Compression | Any SLIP server over TCP/IP that supports IP header compression |

4.  Optionally, click the option named Log On To Network to allow access to the network after connecting to the remote access server. Notice that this option is selected by default.

    If you choose this option, Dial-Up Networking attempts to log you on to the network using the user name and password you typed when you logged on to Windows 95. The logon prompt differs depending on whether the computer is running Client for Microsoft Networks or Client for NetWare Networks, and whether your password for the network is the same as your Windows 95 password. For information, see Chapter 11, "Logon, Browsing, and Resource Sharing."

5.  Optionally, click the option named Enable Software Compression to compress information before sending it.

6.  Optionally, click the option named Require Encrypted Password to require the user to type in an encrypted password before accessing the dial-up server. For information, see "Using Security with Dial-Up Networking" later in this chapter.

---

**Tip**  If users are having trouble making remote access connections, check to see if a specific server type was selected. When a specific connection type is selected, Windows 95 will not attempt to connect using any other server type.

---

7.  Optionally, click TCP/IP settings if you are configuring a connection to the Internet. For information, see Chapter 30, "Internet Access."

# Making a Dial-Up Networking Connection

After you have defined a remote connection by using the Make New Connection wizard, you can make a connection in two ways:

- Double-click a connection icon in Dial-Up Networking.

- Connect to a remote network resource when you are working in an application other than Dial-Up Networking. If you cannot find the resource on the current network, Windows 95 responds by automatically activating Dial-Up Networking.

After you establish or end a connection, you do not need to restart the computer or restart Windows 95. When you attempt to perform the following tasks, Windows 95 starts Dial-Up Networking:

- When you try to access a network resource and your computer is not connected to any network

- When your application specifies a UNC name (which uses the form \\*servername*\*sharename*) that can't be accessed by using the local area network

- When you double-click a link that points to a remote network object; for example:

  - When an application attempts to connect to a file on a network server

  - When you reconnect to a remote OLE object

When you choose a remote connection, Windows 95 retrieves the server information from the addresses stored in the Registry. If the information is not available, you are asked to select a server from the connection icons in Dial-Up Networking, or to type a new server name.

If Dial-Up Networking cannot find the network resource, it displays a net error message. If the connection is successful, Windows 95 remembers the connection for future use.

You can disable the prompt that asks if you want to use Dial-Up Networking when you are attempting to connect to a network resource.

▶ **To disable the Dial-Up Networking prompt**

1. In Dial-Up Networking, click the Connection menu, and then click Settings.

2. Click the option named Don't Prompt To Use Dial-Up Networking.

# Configuring a Windows 95 Dial-Up Server

With Dial-Up Networking, you can configure a computer running Windows 95 to be a remote access server for dial-up clients running Windows 95, Windows for Workgroups, or Windows 3.1. The Windows 95 dial-up server can act as a gateway to a network, or as a server to the client, sharing its file and printing resources with one dial-up client at a time.

---

**Note**   Dial-up server capabilities are only available if you purchase the Microsoft Plus! for Windows 95. For information, contact your Microsoft sales representative.

---

A Windows 95 dial-up server differs from the Windows NT 3.5 dial-up server in the following ways:

- Windows 95 must have special Registry settings to act as an IP router.
- Windows NT 3.5 supports 256 remote connections, whereas Windows 95 provides one remote connection.

The Windows 95 dial-up server supports the following remote access clients:

- Windows 95 dial-up client
- Windows for Workgroups
- Windows 3.1 RAS client
- Clients running PPP

A Windows 95 dial-up server with the appropriate network protocols installed
can act as a NetBIOS gateway, as shown in the following illustration.

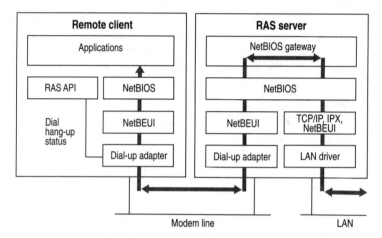

For more information about connectivity options for a Windows 95 dial-up
server, see "Overview of Dial-Up Networking" earlier in this chapter.

Configuring a computer running Windows 95 to be a dial-up server consists
of the following steps:

- Enabling File and Printer Sharing services for either Microsoft or NetWare
  networks on the dial-up server.

- Enabling user-level or share-level security on the dial-up server. For
  information, see "Using Security with Dial-Up Networking" later in this
  chapter.

- Configuring dial-up server capabilities in Dial-Up Networking, as described
  in the following procedure.

▶ **To configure a computer as a dial-up server**

1. From the Connections menu in the Dial-Up Networking, click Dial-Up Server.

2. In the Dial-Up Server dialog box, click Allow Caller Access. This dialog box
   will look different depending on whether you have enabled user-level or share-
   level security for the computer.

3. Optionally, click Change Password to define a call-in password for Dial-Up
   Networking clients, and then click OK.

   –Or–

   If you are using user-level security for peer resource sharing, select the users
   who have access to this dial-up server. Then click OK.

4.  Click the Server Type button and then select the server type.

    If you select the Default server type, the dial-up server will automatically start in PPP mode for incoming calls and switch to RAS for Windows NT 3.1 and Windows for Workgroups mode if the PPP negotiation fails. For information on PPP negotiation, WIN95RK.HLP with the *Windows 95 Resource Kit* utilities.

5.  Click OK, and the dial-up server will be ready to answer incoming calls.

Notice that changes to the server type do not apply to a connection that is currently open. Changes will apply to any future connections made to this computer.

▶ **To disconnect any users who are currently connected to this computer through Dial-Up Networking**

-   In the Dial-Up Server dialog box, click the Disconnect User button.

---

**Note**  The Microsoft Plus! Dial-Up Server for Windows 95 can use only one modem at a time. You can enable caller access on multiple modems at any one time, but only one modem can be connected.

---

# Disabling Dial-Up Server Support

You can prevent users from remotely accessing computers even if a remote connection has been previously established. You can restrict access by making direct changes to a computer's dial-up support capabilities or by using System Policy Editor to create a policy file.

▶ **To disable the dial-up server on a single computer**

1.  From the Connections menu in the Dial-Up Networking window, click Dial-Up Server.

2.  In the Dial-Up Server dialog box, click the option named No Caller Access.

You can disable dial-up support on each computer or on a system-wide basis by using System Policy Editor to change a single computer's Registry or to define policies that can be shared by multiple computers.

To disable dial-up support by using System Policy Editor, enable the option named Disable Dial-in. The Dial-Up Server menu option still appears on the Connections menu after dial-up support has been disabled, but no dialog box for setting up the dial-up server will appear. For more information, see Chapter 15, "User Profiles and System Policies."

# Using Security with Dial-Up Networking

Dial-Up Networking gives you the option of requiring a password to connect to the remote access server, depending on whether the Windows 95 dial-up server is protected with share-level or user-level security.

- Share-level security assigns a password to the Windows 95 dial-up server. When users dial in, they must provide the password before they can gain access to the server. After the connection is established, users can browse the resources on the dial-up server, subject to whatever level of security has been applied to them. Users can also log on to the network after connecting to the dial-up server if logging on to the network is enabled on the dial-up client. Because users can distribute passwords, this method is less secure than user-level security.

- User-level security restricts access to a network resource until a security provider, such as a Windows NT domain controller or a NetWare server, authenticates the request. You can require that a user's logon password to a remote access server be the same as the network and Windows 95 logon passwords.

  With user-level security, when the user accesses shared resources on the dial-up server, Windows 95 controls what rights a user has to the shared resources, such as whether the user has read-only access or full access to files. Access rights are specified in the sharing properties for each resource protected by user-level security. For more information, see Chapter 14, "Security," and Chapter 11, "Logon, Browsing, and Resource Sharing."

▶ **To configure the dial-up server to use user-level security**

1. In the Network option in Control Panel, enable File and Printer Sharing services for Microsoft or NetWare networks and enable user-level security in Access Control properties.

2. In Dial-Up Networking, click the Connections menu, and then click Dial-Up Server.

3. In the Dial-Up Server properties, click the option named Allow Caller Access, and then click Add.

4. In the Add Users dialog box, specify the users who will have permission to access the dial-up server, and then click OK.

5. In the Dial-Up Server properties, click the Server Type button, and make sure Require Encrypted Password is checked if your Dial-Up client supports encrypted passwords.

   Clicking the Require Encrypted Password option requires the client to send an encrypted as opposed to a text password. Some clients support only text passwords; however, encrypted passwords are preferred. Clearing this option doesn't disable password protection.

▶  **To configure the dial-up server to use share-level security**

1. Disable user-level security, if it is enabled, by clicking the Access Control tab in the Network option in Control Panel, or by using System Policy Editor to edit the Registry.

2. In the Network option in Control Panel, enable File and Printer Sharing services for Microsoft Networks and enable share-level security by clicking the Access Control tab. Notice that share-level security is not available on NetWare networks.

3. From the Connections menu in Dial-Up Networking, click Dial-Up Server.

4. In the Dial-Up Server dialog box, click Allow Caller Access, and then click Change Password to provide password protection for the Dial-Up server.

5. Optionally, to require password encryption, click the Server Type button. In the Server Types dialog box, make sure Require Encrypted Password is checked, and then click OK.

# Using Software and Hardware Compression to Transfer Data

To improve the throughput and transfer times when you use Dial-Up Networking, Windows 95 supports dynamic compression of information when you are connected to another computer that also understands compression—for example, a computer running Windows 95 or Windows NT.

You can choose to use either software compression (specified through the Dial-Up Server dialog box) or hardware compression. *Software compression* is performed by the remote access software; *hardware compression* is performed by the modem.

Choosing software compression specifies that your computer will try to compress information before sending it. Compression will occur only if the computer you are connecting to is using a compatible compression program.

---

**Note**  Software compression is supported only in PPP mode, not in RAS, NetWare Connect, or SLIP modes. Software compression is enabled by default in PPP mode and is preferred over hardware compression because it reduces the amount of information that needs to be transmitted to the modem.

---

▶ **To choose software compression**

1. From the Dial-Up Networking Connections menu, click Dial-Up Server.

2. In the Dial-Up Server dialog box, click the Server Type button.

3. In the Server Types dialog box, make sure the Enable Software Compression is checked.

---

**Note**  The software compression option is not available when you are connecting to a Windows NT 3.1 or Windows for Workgroups 3.1 remote access server.

---

Hardware compression is available on most newer modems at higher connection speeds. For example, V.42bis is an industry standard that allows modems to do data compression on all the data sent through them.

▶ **To choose hardware compression**

1. In the Modems option in Control Panel, click the Properties button, and then click the Connection tab.

2. In the Connection dialog box, click the Advanced button and then click use Error Control, and Compress Data.

You should leave both software and hardware compression enabled unless you are certain that the server supports software compression. When you use either type of compression on data that is already compressed, you won't see any transfer time improvement. If the computer you are connecting to doesn't support compression, these settings are ignored and data is sent uncompressed over the wire.

# Connecting to a Windows NT Remote Access Server

Connecting to a Windows NT remote access server is the same as connecting to a Windows 95 Dial-Up Networking server. All you need is the phone number of the Windows NT server when creating a connection. Dial-Up Networking negotiates the proper protocols and server connection type. You don't need to specify a default server type.

Windows NT 3.5 Server supports PPP, RAS, and SLIP clients. PPP is the recommended protocol. Windows NT 3.5 supports IPX/SPX, NetBEUI, and TCP/IP network protocols and can function as a NetBIOS gateway, IPX router, and IP router simultaneously. Windows NT 3.5 is not a SLIP server.

---

**Note**   Windows NT 3.1 supports only the RAS protocol, which is a proprietary protocol that supports only NetBEUI. It is a fast connection type, but does not allow for multiple protocols over the connection. RAS in Windows NT 3.1 cannot support the IPX/SPX or TCP/IP protocols.

Microsoft recommends that you upgrade from Windows NT Remote Access Service to Windows NT Server 3.5, which provides many additional benefits, including PPP support.

---

A Windows NT 3.1 or 3.5 remote access server provides several features that a Dial-Up Networking server does not. For an explanation of these differences, see "Configuring a Windows 95 Dial-Up Server" earlier in this chapter.

For more information about configuring a Windows NT 3.5 Server for Windows 95 Dial-Up client, see WIN95RK.HLP with the *Windows 95 Resource Kit* utilities. See also the *Windows NT Server Remote Access Service Guide*.

# Configuring a Windows NT Server for Windows 95 Dial-Up Clients

To configure a Windows NT 3.5 Server so that Windows 95 dial-up clients can remotely access it, you need to install and configure RAS.

You must be logged on as a member of the Administrators group to install and configure RAS. It can be installed during Custom Setup of Windows NT or afterward. During Express Setup, if there is not a network adapter in a computer, the user is given the option to install RAS.

RAS installation varies slightly depending on which network protocols are installed. If you use TCP/IP or IPX/SPX protocol with RAS, you should install the protocol before you install RAS, although selecting a protocol that is not installed causes that protocol to be installed at the conclusion of RAS Setup. For information about installing either protocol, see the *Windows NT Installation Guide*.

▶ **To install RAS on a computer running Windows NT 3.5 Server**

1. In the Network option in Control Panel in Windows NT 3.5, click the Network Settings dialog box, and then click Add Software.

2. In the Network Software drop-down list, click Remote Access Service, and then click the Continue button.

3. Type the path name to the distribution files, and click OK.

   RAS files are copied to the computer.

4. In the Add Port dialog box, click the port you intend to use for remote access, and then click OK.

   If you have successfully installed a multiport adapter, ISDN card, X.25 card, or other device, it should appear in this list.

5. In the RAS Auto Detection dialog box, click OK to allow RAS to automatically detect the modem connected to the port, or click Cancel to manually select a modem.

   Occasionally, when attempting to detect a modem, a dialog box appears, prompting you to select a modem from a short list. This occurs only when RAS Setup cannot distinguish between two or more modems.

6. In the Configure Port dialog box, click a modem if RAS did not detect one, and then click OK. Only supported modems are listed.

   If you are adding a port after initial RAS installation, you can use the Detect button to automatically detect the modem connected to the new port.

7. In the Port Usage box, you define whether the port will be for dial-out or dial-in use. Clicking the Dial Out Only option configures the computer as a RAS client. Clicking the Receive Calls Only option configures the computer as a RAS server. Clicking both options allows the computer to be a dial-out client and dial-out server; however, the computer cannot be both at the same time.

8. To configure settings specific to the device attached to the port, click the device, and then click the Settings button. The default settings are usually ideal. Click OK.

9. In the Remote Access Setup dialog box, configure RAS network settings by clicking the Network button. You can also reconfigure the port, if necessary, by clicking it, and then clicking buttons at the bottom of the port dialog box.

Before users can use RAS to remotely connect to Windows NT, you must grant them remote access permissions.

▶ **To grant Remote Access permission to users**

1. Double-click the Remote Access Admin icon to start the Administrators utility.

2. Set the focus on the server or domain on which you want to set permissions. To set the focus, see the Remote Access Admin online Help.

3. From the Users menu, click Permissions.

4. In the Remote Access Permissions dialog box, click the Help button for further instructions.

---

**Note**  Microsoft does not recommend granting guest accounts dial-in permission. If you do, be sure to assign a password to the guest account.

---

# Connecting to a Novell NetWare Connect Server

Windows 95 Dial-Up Networking supports connecting to Novell NetWare resources in two ways:

- Connecting directly to a Novell NetWare Connect server

- Using a computer running Windows 95 or Windows NT 3.5 as a gateway into a local area network, where NetWare servers are connected

NetWare Connect allows a Windows 95 client to dial in to a NetWare server running NetWare Connect 1.0.

---

**Note**  Windows 95 can act only as a client for connecting to a NetWare Connect server. NetWare Connect clients themselves cannot dial up a Windows 95 dial-up server.

---

The NetWare Connect connection type allows a Windows 95 client to connect directly to a NetWare Connect server and to connect to NetWare servers on the connected local area network.

To use Dial-Up Networking to connect to a NetWare Connect server, you must specify NetWare Connect as the server type in the properties for a Dial-Up Networking connection. You also need to use the Network option in Control Panel to make sure the following are enabled on a Windows 95 dial-up client or server:

- Microsoft Client for NetWare Networks

- IPX/SPX-compatible protocol bound to the Microsoft Dial-Up adapter driver

If you use Dial-Up Networking to access NetWare Connect servers, you can access data remotely, but you cannot control a computer remotely as you can with the NetWare Connect client software supplied by Novell.

# Connecting to Shiva Remote Access Servers

You can connect a dial-up client to the Shiva LanRover or NetModem/E families of remote access servers without specially configuring Dial-Up Networking.

With a Windows 95 dial-up client, you can dial in to a Shiva remote access server and connect to IPX, NetBEUI, and TCP/IP services on a network. A dial-up client connected to a Shiva server can access any network resources that a computer on the local area network can, including all other computers running Windows 95, NetWare servers, electronic mail, client-server applications, and the Internet.

In addition to supporting all the capabilities of the Windows 95 dial-up client, Shiva remote access servers offer the following capabilities:

- Data compression
- Dial back
- Dynamic Host Configuration Protocol (DHCP) support for IP address assignments during TCP/IP dial-in
- Support for Security Dynamics ACE/Server and TACACS centralized authentication
- Integrated ISDN support
- NetWare bindery information

## Configuring a Shiva Server for Windows 95 Dial-Up Clients

If you have a Shiva remote access server running on your network, you do not need to make any configuration changes to enable dial-up clients. Shiva remote access servers running release 3.5 and above are fully compatible with Windows 95 dial-up clients.

If you are installing a new Shiva remote access server, there are a few steps to configure it to support dial-up clients. You can configure all dial-up parameters for a Shiva remote access server with the Shiva Net Manager for a Windows-based application on a computer running Windows, Windows for Workgroups, or Windows 95, or with the Shiva Net Manager for Macintosh application. Shiva Net Manager for Windows 95 will be available shortly after the release of Windows 95.

Before configuring the Shiva remote access server for Windows 95 dial-up clients, you need to do the following:

- Ensure that you have properly installed the Shiva remote access server and connected it to an Ethernet or token-ring network.

- Connect your modem to the serial port of your LanRover and to the telephone line, or connect the telephone line directly to the LanRover/PLUS or NetModem/E with integrated modem.

- Install Shiva Net Manager for Windows on a computer that is attached to the Ethernet or token-ring network. Shiva Net Manager for Windows requires either IPX or TCP/IP on the personal computer.

- Make sure that dial-in access for a particular protocol or protocols is enabled.

▶ **To configure the Shiva remote access server with Shiva Net Manager for Windows 95**

1. Run Shiva Net Manager by double-clicking the SNM icon, and then double-click the name of the Shiva remote access server you want to configure in the Shiva Net Manager Device List dialog box.

2. In the Shiva remote access server Configuration dialog box, click the General configuration page from the Configure menu.

3. Check the Dial-In function to enable it, and then check the protocols that you want to enable for Windows 95 Dial-Up Networking: IP, NetBEUI, or IPX.

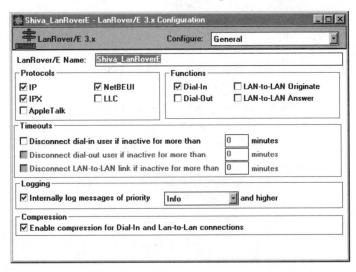

4. In the Configuration dialog box, click the Ports configuration page, and then check that all ports with modems are enabled and properly configured with modem strings.

5. If you are enabling TCP/IP dial-in, click the IP configuration page from the Configure menu, and then type the IP address of the Shiva remote access server.

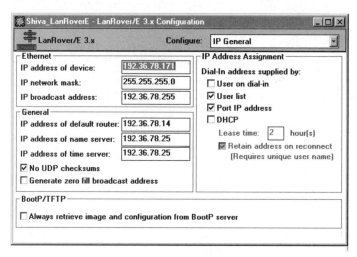

6. If you are enabling NetBEUI dial-in on a token-ring network, click the Bridging configuration page from the Configure menu, and then type the ring numbers required for source routing.

7. To save your configuration, select the Set Configuration command from the Actions menu.

You will need to create a user name and password for each dial-up user.

▶ **To store user names and password using the internal user list of the Shiva remote access server**

1. In the Shiva Net Manager Device List dialog box, click the name of the Shiva remote access server for which you want to create a dial-up user list.

2. In the Security menu, click the Get User List command.

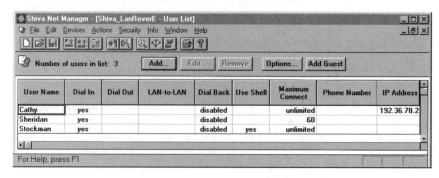

3. In the User List dialog box, click the Add button.

4. Type a user name and password for each dial-up user. Make sure that dial-up access is enabled for the user, and click OK.

5. Save the user list for the Shiva remote access server from the Security menu's Set User List command.

## Assigning TCP/IP Address to Dial-Up Clients with Shiva Remote Access

To connect a dial-up client to TCP/IP network services, the client must have an IP address. Shiva remote access servers provide different ways to assign IP addresses to dial-up clients:

- You can assign a unique IP address to each Shiva remote access server port. Every time a user dials in to a Shiva remote access server port, the dial-up client determines the IP address of the port by using the Reverse Address Resolution Protocol (RARP).

- You can assign an IP address to every dial-up client. When a user dials in, the Shiva remote access server assigns the IP address based on the user name.

- A centralized Windows NT Dynamic Host Configuration Protocol (DHCP) server can tell the Shiva remote access server which IP address to assign to the dial-up client.

- You can assign an IP address to every dial-up client. When a user dials in, the Shiva remote access server assigns the IP address based on the user name.

- The remote user can tell the Shiva remote access server which IP address to use for the dial-up client. If a user tries to obtain an illegal IP address, the Shiva remote access server allows it, but the connection fails.

If you want the Shiva remote access server to assign IP addresses to dial-up clients, see the documentation for the server.

## Security Options with Shiva Remote Access Servers

Shiva remote access servers provide several security options that prevent unauthorized access to your corporate network. You can choose the method, or combination of methods, that works best for your organization—from passwords to security devices from other vendors. Here are some of the methods that Shiva uses to provide a high level of security:

- User lists. Shiva remote access servers can store user names and passwords for controlling dial-up access to the remote access server. When you add users to the Shiva remote access server user list, they can dial in to the network, but they still need the appropriate access privileges to access any server or host on that network.

- NetWare bindery. If your organization uses NetWare bindery security features from Novell, you may not want to maintain an additional user list for a remote access server. You can use the NetWare bindery account database to provide centralized authentication services for dial-up access.

- Security devices from other vendors. You may use additional security devices to protect sensitive data on your corporate networks. Shiva remote access servers are compatible with most popular security devices, so you can evaluate and choose the security method that is appropriate for your organization.

- Security Dynamics ACE/Server. This security solution uses a UNIX server to maintain the centralized database of dial-up user privileges. Shiva remote access servers support ACE/Server authentication.

- TACACS. This is a centralized security solution that uses a UNIX server to maintain the centralized database of user privileges. Shiva remote access servers support authentication of dial-in users using TACACS.

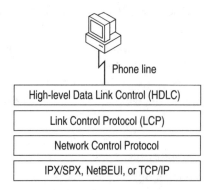

PPP is designed to work with a variety of hardware, including any asynchronous or synchronous, dedicated or dial-up, full-duplex bit-serial circuit. It can employ any common serial communications protocol, including EIA-232-E (formerly, RS-232-C), EIA-422, EIA423, EIA-530, and CCITT V.24 and V. 35. PPP does not place any particular restriction on the type of signaling, type of transmission speed, or use of modem control signals.

# PPP Dial-Up Sequence

When a user dials in to a PPP-compatible server, three things happen:

1. The Data Link Control Layer (HDLC) defines how data is encapsulated before transmission on the WAN. By providing a standard framing format, PPP ensures that various vendors' remote access solutions can communicate and distinguish data packets from each other. PPP uses HDLC framing for serial, ISDN, and X.25 data transfer.

   The PPP Data Link Control layer is a slightly modified version of the HDLC layer. The HDLC format, extensively used by IBM and others for synchronous data transfer, was modified by adding a 16-bit protocol field that allows PPP to multiplex traffic for several Network Control Protocol layers. This encapsulation frame has a 16-bit checksum, but the size of this field can be negotiated.

2. Link Control Protocol (LCP) establishes, configures, and tests the integrity of the data-link connection. LCP also negotiates authentication and determines whether compression is enabled and which IP addresses will be used. When LCP negotiates authentication of protocols, it determines what level of security validation the remote access server can perform and what the server requires.

   LCP can negotiate with any of these authentication protocols:

   - Password Authentication Protocol (PAP) uses a two-way handshake for the peer to establish its identity. This handshake occurs only when the link is initially established. Using PAP, passwords are sent over the circuit in text format, which offers no protection from playback.

   - Shiva Password Authentication Protocol (SPAP) offers encryption of PAP passwords and Novell NetWare bindery access for user account information. When Windows 95 is set up for user-level security using a NetWare server account list, this is the security type used for remote access clients.

   - Challenge-Handshake Authentication Protocol (CHAP) periodically verifies the identity of the peer, using a three-way handshake. The authenticator sends a challenge message to the peer, which responds with a value using a one-way encryption. The authenticator then checks this response and, if the values match, the authentication is acknowledged; otherwise, the connection is ended. CHAP provides protection against playback attack, because the challenge value changes in every message. Because the password is never sent over the link, it is virtually impossible to learn it. CHAP allows different types of encryption algorithms to be used, such as DES (MS-CHAP) and MD5 (MD5-CHAP). Windows 95 doesn't support ongoing challenges with CHAP, but does implement MS-CHAP, as does Windows NT.

3.  Network Control Protocols establish and configure different network protocol parameters. The type of Network Control Protocol that PPP selects depends on which protocol (NetBEUI, TCP/IP, or IPX) is being used to establish the Dial-Up Networking connection. Windows 95 supports the following:

    ■ NetBIOS Frames Control Protocol (NBF CP) is used to configure, enable, and disable the NetBEUI protocol modules on both ends of the link. NBF CP is a Microsoft-proposed protocol for NetBEUI configuration. NBF CP is currently in "draft" status with the Internet Engineering Task Force (IETF). Windows 95 provides implementations for the current draft of NBF CP (as of March 1994).

    ■ Internet Protocol Control Protocol (IPCP), defined in RFC 1332, is used to configure, enable, and disable IP Protocol modules at both ends of the link.

    ■ Internet Packet eXchange Control Protocol (IPXCP), defined in RFC 1552, is used to configure, enable, and disable IPX protocol modules on both ends of the link. IPXCP is widely implemented by PPP vendors.

# PPP Log File

You can record how the PPP layers process a call by enabling the PPPLOG file. This file contains some of the basic layers and points of any Dial-Up Networking session, and is especially useful for monitoring PPP sessions. It is recorded and stored in the Windows directory.

▶  **To enable PPP logging**

1.  In the Network option in Control Panel, double-click Microsoft Dial-Up Adapter in the list of installed network components.

2.  Click the Advanced tab. In the Property list, click the option named Record A Log File, and in the Value list, click Yes. Then click OK.

3.  Shut down and restart a computer for this option to take effect.

The following is sample content of a PPPLOG.TXT file:

```
09-01-1994 18:14:22 - Remote access driver log opened.
09-01-1994 18:14:22 - Server type is PPP (Point to Point Protocol).
09-01-1994 18:14:22 - CCP : Layer initialized.
09-01-1994 18:14:22 - NBFCP : Layer initialized.
09-01-1994 18:14:22 - IPXCP : Layer initialized.
09-01-1994 18:14:22 - FSA : Encrypted Password required.
09-01-1994 18:14:22 - LCP : Layer initialized.
09-01-1994 18:14:22 - LCP : Will try to negotiate callback.
09-01-1994 18:14:22 - LCP : Layer started.
09-01-1994 18:14:22 - LCP : Received and accepted ACCM of 0.
```

# Overview of Windows 95 Mobile Computing Features

Windows 95 eliminates many of the hardware and software configuration steps previously required when switching to or from a portable computer. Windows 95 uses hardware profiles to determine which drivers to load if the system hardware changes when you move to a new site. For more information, see Chapter 19, "Devices."

Users can be productive away from the office by using the following Windows 95 mobile computing tools:

- Briefcase allows users to update documents on a portable computer with source documents on a desktop computer or network.

- Direct Cable Connection allows users to connect a portable computer to a desktop computer to synchronize files and share other resources.

- Microsoft Exchange provides remote access to electronic mail. For information, see Chapter 26, "Electronic Mail and Microsoft Exchange."

- Microsoft Fax allows users to remotely send and receive faxes. For more information, see Chapter 27, "Microsoft Fax."

- Deferred printing allows users to generate print jobs when a physical printer is not available. For more information, see Chapter 23, "Printing and Fonts."

Other mobile computing tools, such as the following, help users manage a portable computer's limited battery power and disk space:

- With Advanced Power Management, users can use the battery indicator on the taskbar and a Suspend command on the Start menu to save power without turning off computer. For more information, see Chapter 19, "Devices."

- With DriveSpace, users can free space on their portable computer's hard disk drive and floppy disks by compressing them. For more information, see Chapter 20, "Disks and File Systems."

- With Microsoft Exchange, users can view the headers of mail messages before deciding whether to download, preventing unnecessary messages from taking up disk space.

- With Quick View, users can view the contents of a file in Windows Explorer by right-clicking a file icon. For information, see Chapter 22, "Application Support."

# Direct Cable Connection

With Direct Cable Connection, you can establish a direct serial or parallel cable connection between two computers in order to share the resources of the computer designated as the host. If the host is connected to a network, the guest computer can also access the network. For example, if you have a portable computer, you can use a cable to connect it to your work computer and network. To establish a local connection between two computers, you need a compatible serial or null-modem parallel cable.

Before you can transfer files from the host to the guest computer, the files must be in a shared directory, and File and Printer Sharing services for either Microsoft or NetWare networks must be enabled in the Network option in Control Panel. You can also apply share-level security to the shared files. For information, see Chapter 11, "Logon, Browsing, and Resource Sharing," and Chapter 14, "Security."

---

**Note**  This capability is similar to that available with Interlink for MS-DOS 6.x, which allowed users to transfer data through the serial port between two personal computers.

---

Before you install and configure Direct Cable Connection, you need to decide:

- What remote access and network protocols do you need to install on the guest and host computers? They must both be running at least one common network protocol in order to connect. The host computer can act as a gateway to an IPX/SPX or NetBEUI network, but not to a TCP/IP network.

- What kind of cable do you need? Direct Cable Connection works with serial and parallel cables. For information, see "Direct Cable Connection" earlier in this chapter.

- Do you want to assign a password to the host computer? If you assign a password on the host, all users connecting from the guest computer will be prompted for it. After connecting, the guest can access resources on the host computer according to the type of security applied to it, that is, user-level or share-level security.

---

**Note**  After the host connects to the network, it can access shared resources on the guest computer.

---

# Installing and Configuring Direct Cable Connection

To install Direct Cable Connection during Windows 95 Setup, you must choose Custom or Portable as the setup type. You can also install it after installing Windows 95.

▶ **To install Direct Cable Connection after Windows 95 installation**

1. In the Add/Remove Programs icon in Control Panel, click the Windows Setup tab.

2. In the Components list, click Communications, and then click the Details button.

3. In the Communications dialog box, click Direct Cable Connection, and then click OK.

Windows 95 provides a Direct Cable Connection wizard for establishing the connection between two computers. The wizard runs when you open Direct Cable Connection for the first time. It allows you to designate one computer as the guest and the other as a host. Before you run the wizard, you need to install Direct Cable Connection on each computer and connect them with a null-modem serial or parallel cable.

For more information about setting up Direct Cable Connection, see online Help.

# Cables Compatible with Direct Cable Connection

Windows 95 supports a serial null-modem standard (RS-232) cable and the following parallel cables:

- Standard or Basic 4-bit cable, including LapLink and InterLink cables available before 1992.

- Extended Capabilities Port (ECP) cable. This type of cable works on a computer with ECP-enabled parallel ports, which must be enabled in BIOS. This kind of parallel cable allows data to be transferred more quickly than a standard cable.

- Universal Cable Module (UCM) cable. This cable supports connecting different types of parallel ports. Using this cable between two ECP-enabled ports allows the fastest possible data transfer between two computers.

Parallel cables transmit data simultaneously over multiple lines, making it the faster of the two connection methods. Serial cables transmit data sequentially over one pair of wires, and are slower than parallel cables. Use a serial cable only if a parallel port is unavailable.

# Using Briefcase for File Synchronization

If you can use a portable computer and a desktop computer, or you are connected to a network, you must constantly work to keep the files synchronized. Windows 95 Briefcase minimizes this task by keeping track of the relationships between files on two or more computers.

With Briefcase, you can do the following:

- Create a Briefcase folder
- Add files to Briefcase
- Check the status of files in Briefcase and their related files
- Update related files, either individually or all at once
- Split related files to maintain them separately

Windows 95 provides a set of OLE interfaces that allow applications to bind reconciliation handlers to it, track the contents of Briefcase, and define the outcome of any reconciliation on a class-by-class basis. For example, when both the file in Briefcase and its synchronized copy outside have changed, Windows 95 calls the appropriate reconciliation handler to merge the two files. This could be handy when several users are simultaneously updating one large document.

## Creating and Configuring a Briefcase

Windows 95 automatically configures Briefcase and installs it on your Windows 95 desktop if you choose it during Custom Setup of Windows 95, or if you choose the Portable setup type. If you do not choose either of these Setup options, you can install Briefcase afterward in the Add/Remove Programs option in Control Panel.

▶ **To install Briefcase after Windows 95 installation**

1. In Control Panel, double-click the Add/Remove Programs icon.
2. Click the Windows Setup tab, and in the Components list click Accessories, and then click the Details button.
3. In the Accessories dialog box, click Briefcase, and then click OK.

If you install Briefcase, it appears as an icon on your Windows 95 desktop. To run Briefcase, double-click its icon.

---

**Tip**  You can use Briefcase to synchronize files between a portable computer running Windows 95 and a desktop computer running Windows NT 3.5.

---

# Updating Files with Briefcase

When you update files by using Briefcase, Windows 95 automatically replaces unmodified files with modified files. If both files have changed, Windows 95 calls the appropriate application (if available) to merge the disparate files. Before you leave the office, you can copy files from your desktop to Briefcase, and then load Briefcase onto your portable computer. When you return, Briefcase will automatically update files when you dock your portable computer if you are using a Plug and Play BIOS docking station.

For information about updating files using Briefcase and a floppy disk, see Windows 95 online Help.

---

**Tip**  For faster editing, you can move Briefcase files to a hard disk on a second computer; to do this, drag the files from the floppy disk to the second computer's hard disk. When you have finished editing the files on the desktop computer, choose Update All from Briefcase on the floppy disk. When you return to the original computer, choose Update again to replace the unmodified files on this first computer.

---

Instead of using a floppy disk with Briefcase, you can use Direct Cable Connection to connect two computers running Windows 95, and then use Briefcase to synchronize their files. For example, you can connect your portable computer to your home or office computer with Direct Cable Connection, and then update the desktop computer files to match the portable files.

For more information about Direct Cable Connection, see "Direct Cable Connection" earlier in this chapter.

▶ **To update files using Briefcase and two connected computers**

1. Copy to Briefcase any files or folders you want to work on.

2. Make changes to the files either in their original location or in Briefcase.

3. Connect the computers by using Direct Cable Connection, and then double-click My Briefcase.

4. Click the files you want to update.

5. On the Briefcase menu, click Update All or Update Selection.

---

**Note**  You can also use Briefcase to synchronize files between a portable computer and a network if the portable computer has a network connection.

---

When you open the Briefcase folder, you can check the status of any file in Briefcase to find out if it has been synchronized with its original. You can also split files from their originals if you decide to maintain them separately. For more information on these topics, see online Help.

---

**Tip** To find the copy of a file that is outside Briefcase, click Find Original in the Update Status dialog box.

---

# Troubleshooting Dial-Up Networking

This section describes problems which you may encounter in using Dial-Up Networking and how to resolve them. Windows 95 provides a troubleshooting aid for Dial-Up Networking in online Help. Try using the online Help before trying the troubleshooting steps included in this section.

You can monitor any Dial-Up Networking session for possible problems by enabling the Record a Log File option. This produces a PPPLOG.TXT file in the Windows directory, which you can reference to find out the cause of a problem. For more information, see WIN95RK.HLP in the *Windows 95 Resource Kit* utilities.

**You cannot access the Dial-Up Networking server because a user name is not valid.**
In the properties for the dial-up server, verify that the user name is in the list of users that are allowed access.

▶  **To set Dial-Up Networking Server to allow caller access options**

1. In Dial-Up Networking, click the Connections menu, and then click Dial Up Server.

2. In the the Dial-Up Server properties, click Allow Caller Access, if this is not already selected, and then view the User name list to ensure the user's name appears.

   The User name list appears only if you have chosen user-level security for the dial-up server. The type of security is selected in the Network option in Control Panel.

If the dial-up client is also running File and Printer Services for NetWare Networks, the File and Printer Sharing service automatically becomes the default server, but it cannot receive the information needed to find the remote servers.

**You cannot access remote NetWare servers when making a dial-up connection.**

Disable File and Printer Sharing Service for NetWare Networks when you make the dial-up connection.

**Software compression does not work.**

Check the settings for the dial-up server type and software compression.

▶ **To verify dial-up server and compression options in Dial Up Networking**

1. In the Connections menu, click Dial-Up Server.

2. Click the Server Type button and verify that the correct type of dial-up server is selected.

3. Check that Enable Software Compression is selected. Compression will occur only if the dial-up client and server have enabled it.

**The modem is dialing but not connecting.**

- Check the modem configuration; change the configuration if necessary.

- Verify all parameters, such as access codes, area code, and country code.

- Try choosing the driver for Generic Modem Drivers.

- If you are using an external modem, check the cable and verify that it is connected correctly.

- Check the COM port configuration in Device Manager.

For more information, see the troubleshooting section in Chapter 25, "Modems and Communications Tools."

**Dial-Up Networking Server is not answering incoming calls.**

- Disable Allow Caller Access and shut down the computer. Turn off the computer to reset the COM port. If the modem is external, turn off the modem. Turn the computer back on and reconfigure the Dial-Up Networking server, and then try again.

- If these steps fail, disable Allow Caller Access and see if any modem software can manually answer the incoming call.

- If you are using an external modem, check the cable and verify that it is connected correctly.

- If you are using an internal modem with a nonstandard IRQ selection, use Device Manager to check the IRQ setting for the COM port and change it if necessary.

- Try choosing the Generic Modem Drivers on the dial-up server.

The password for the Dial-Up Networking server is stored in the RNA.PWL file. However, simply deleting this file or removing and reinstalling Dial-Up Networking may not remove the password. If you set the Dial-Up Networking server to monitor for calls, then delete the RNA.PWL file, the password is not removed because it is stored in memory. If you shut down Windows 95 at this point, the RNA.PWL file is recreated with the password in memory.

▶ **To replace a forgotten password in a Dial-Up Networking Server**

1. Disable Allow Caller Access, and then shut down and restart Windows 95.

2. Delete the RNA.PWL file, and then restart the Dial-Up Networking.

---

**Note**  When you first connect to the Dial-Up Networking server, an error message states that the password file is missing or corrupt for every modem device you have installed. If you have any null modem devices installed (for example, when you run Direct Cable Connection it installs a modem device for every COM and LPT port you have), this error message also appears.

---

CHAPTER 29

# The Microsoft Network

This chapter describes how to install and sign up for an account with The Microsoft Network. This chapter also briefly describes the features of this new online service from Microsoft.

**In This Chapter**

The Microsoft Network: The Basics   924

The Microsoft Network: The Issues   926

Becoming a Member of The Microsoft Network   927

Security for The Microsoft Network   927

Navigating The Microsoft Network   928

    MSN Central   929

    Windows Explorer and The Microsoft Network   930

    Go Commands   931

Using Bulletin Boards   931

    Bulletin Board File Libraries   932

    Chat Rooms   934

Using Microsoft Exchange with The Microsoft Network   935

Billing   937

Becoming an Independent Content Provider (ICP)   937

# The Microsoft Network: The Basics

For anyone with a modem and phone line, The Microsoft Network offers access at any time to the rapidly expanding world of electronic information and communication. With The Microsoft Network, users can conduct business transactions, communicate with individuals and organizations around the world, and find out information on subjects they're interested in—all from the Windows 95 desktop.

The following are benefits of signing up and using The Microsoft Network.

**Minimal setup requirements.**  A connection to The Microsoft Network is built into Windows 95. If users already have a modem and phone line, all they have to do is install The Microsoft Network during or after Setup, and click The icon on the desktop to connect to The Microsoft Network and become a member. After setting up an account, users can connect to The Microsoft Network by clicking its icon.

**Familiar user interface.**  With a user interface consistent with Windows 95 and a navigational tool similar to the Windows Explorer, users will find it easy to navigate services in The Microsoft Network. Users can create Windows 95 shortcuts to specific areas within The Microsoft Network and store those shortcuts on the desktop or any other folder in My Computer. Actions such as downloading files are as simple as using drag and drop to copy the files. And users can open Microsoft Exchange within The Microsoft Network to send and receive mail.

**Multitasking.**  The Microsoft Network takes advantage of the multitasking and multithreaded design in Windows 95 so that several different tasks in The Microsoft Network can run at the same time. For example, while a file is downloading, users can browse, read electronic mail, participate in a chat room, or do anything else on The Microsoft Network.

**Worldwide access.**  Local dial-up access is available to The Microsoft Network in over 40 countries, and The Microsoft Network application will be available in many different languages. In the United States, nearly 100 percent of users can access a network Point of Presence (POP) server; outside of the United States, between 60 percent and 100 percent of users will have access by a local phone call, depending on the country.

In the release with Windows 95, The Microsoft Network offers the following features.

**Electronic mail.**  With Microsoft Exchange, users can send and receive electronic mail to and from other members of The Microsoft Network, or anyone with an electronic mailbox on the Internet.

**Bulletin boards.**  The Microsoft Network provides bulletin boards where users can join in-depth discussions on a variety of topics, including hardware or software from computer companies.

**Chat rooms.**  By participating in chat sessions, users can converse in real time with other members of The Microsoft Network by sending and receiving messages. After users find a chat room with a discussion that interests them, they can observe the conversation or send a comment for other members to see immediately.

**File libraries.**  The Microsoft Network allows users to easily connect to file libraries to download graphics, software, product support information, and articles.

**The Internet.**  With Microsoft Exchange, users can send mail to other people on the Internet, and post and reply to messages in Internet newsgroups in the same way as users would on other bulletin boards.

Users can also obtain an Internet account by using the Microsoft Plus! Internet Signup wizard, which guides Windows 95 users through the process of obtaining an Internet account. This provides the following Internet features:

- Internet Shortcuts, which allow users to create a shortcut in Windows 95 to an Internet resource.
- Internet Explorer, which allows users to browse the World Wide Web, FTP, and Gopher sites. Its full support for OLE allows users to drag and drop World Wide Web pages and links between the Internet Explorer, the Windows 95 desktop, and any other OLE-enabled application.

**Microsoft product information.**  The Microsoft Network provides users with the latest technical and support information in the following forums:

- Frequently Asked Questions provides quick answers to common technical questions.
- Microsoft Knowledge Base contains more than 50,000 detailed articles with technical information about Microsoft products, bug and fix lists, documentation errors, and answers to commonly asked technical support questions.
- Microsoft Software Library contains hundreds of free software add-ons, bug fixes, peripheral drivers, software updates, and programming aids for easy downloading at the user's convenience.
- Microsoft-Facilitated Member-to-Member Bulletin Boards provide advice and answers fast from other software users.

**Information services.**  Information services that provide news, sports, stock and weather reports, product and product support information, and special-interest group information are accessible from The Microsoft Network.

**Independent content providers (ICP).**  By becoming an ICP on The Microsoft Network, a company can sell products and services in a worldwide electronic marketplace that is accessible from the Windows 95 desktop.

# The Microsoft Network: The Issues

Before installing The Microsoft Network, consider the following issues:

- When users double-click The Microsoft Network icon to sign up for an account, The Microsoft Network automatically dials a toll-free number to download price and billing information. After users fill out the billing information, The Microsoft Network automatically dials a second local number to provide access to services on The Microsoft Network.

- If users have problems connecting, first try to resolve them by using the signup troubleshooting information in online Help. One troubleshooting topic tells you how to change the access number for a location.

  If problems persist with signup, contact The Microsoft Network product support using the telephone numbers in online Help in The Microsoft Network or in **msn.hlp** in the Windows directory. If problems persist with using The Microsoft Network, post a message in the bulletin board in Member Assistance in The Microsoft Network.

- Certain types of PBXs restrict users from accessing an outside telephone line or from dialing toll-free numbers, both of which are required to sign up for The Microsoft Network. If the user tries to sign up from such a PBX, the user might see the error message "No carrier detected," or might hear a busy signal or operator message. To correct this problem, you must configure the PBX to allow users to dial toll-free numbers and access an outside line.

- If you need to create more than one account with The Microsoft Network on a single computer, you must run Signup for each account. Click Start, click Run, and then type **signup.exe** to run the Signup utility.

- Members should invent secure passwords to protect access to their accounts. They can use the same passwords as their network logon passwords or create a different one. It is not possible to pass through an electronic mail name and password from the Windows 95 Registry. Members who want to can invent a nickname that protects their identities on The Microsoft Network.

- If your company decides to become an ICP on The Microsoft Network, you will need to provide a forum manager for your service area. Microsoft provides information about the responsibilities of a forum manager with other information about becoming an ICP. For more information, see "Becoming an Independent Content Provider (ICP)" later in this chapter.

# Becoming a Member of The Microsoft Network

Becoming a member of The Microsoft Network requires two easy steps:

- Installing The Microsoft Network during or after Windows 95 Setup
- Clicking The Microsoft Network icon on the Windows 95 desktop to start signup

The easiest way to install The Microsoft Network is to choose it in the Get Connected dialog box during Windows 95 Setup. Users can install it after Setup by using the Control Panel.

▶ **To install The Microsoft Network after Window 95 Setup**

1. In Control Panel, double-click the Add/Remove Programs icon.
2. Click the Windows Setup tab, and in the Components list click The Microsoft Network, and then click OK.

▶ **To become a member of The Microsoft Network**

1. Double-click The Microsoft Network icon on the Windows 95 desktop.
2. In The Microsoft Network dialog box, click OK.
3. The next signup box displays the three steps for signing up with The Microsoft Network. Click each button and type the appropriate information.
4. In the user information signup box, type your name, address, and phone number.
5. In the billing information signup box, type your payment method (credit card name), credit card number, and expiration date.

After users connect for the first time, they should click Member Assistance on MSN Central to read about the rules for participating in The Microsoft Network.

# Security for The Microsoft Network

The Microsoft Network security service authenticates and validates multiple members simultaneously logging on and off. The security service grants or denies members, requests to log on and to use different areas of the service based on the rights assigned by The Microsoft Network database.

In addition, The Microsoft Network establishes and manages policies that govern what actions members can perform. This ensures the confidentiality of data and the value of transactions in The Microsoft Network.

The member ID users choose when they sign up must be unique to The Microsoft Network. After a membership is terminated, The Microsoft Network does not reissue that member's member ID for 12 months to prevent confusion.

The Microsoft Network maintains a Client Negation record, which is a list of members who have been denied access for reasons of bad credit, repeated violations of The Microsoft Network rules, and so on. Members can also be excluded from individual forums for violations of rules. When users sign up, The Microsoft Network accounts database verifies that they are not on this list before approving their member IDs and passwords.

# Navigating The Microsoft Network

Viewing information on The Microsoft Network is as easy as browsing through a local area network in Windows 95, because users use the same navigational tools. To move from service to service within The Microsoft Network, users double-click icons or use Windows Explorer.

Users can navigate to any of the services offered in a forum in many different ways, including the following:

- Double-clicking an icon for the service users want.
- Right-clicking an icon to open the Windows Explorer menu (context menu), and clicking Open.
- Double-clicking a shortcut in a Windows 95 directory, in an electronic mail message, or in a bulletin board in The Microsoft Network. For more information, see "Shortcuts" later in this chapter.
- Using the Go command. For more information, see "Go Commands " later in this chapter.
- Double-clicking an icon in Favorite Places. For more information, see "Favorite Places" later in this chapter.

The Microsoft Network structures the large body of information it presents to users into a content tree. The content tree is organized so that broad categories of information are stored at the highest level, with folders at successive levels containing progressively more detailed information. The top folder in the content tree is called the Categories folder, and the contents of this folder will rarely, if ever, change.

The content tree enables users to quickly find services within The Microsoft Network and, based on a user's membership privileges, to view, subscribe, or access specific information, applications, and services.

All the services and content provided by The Microsoft Network are stored in distributed SQL databases in a Microsoft-owned data center. Initially, The Microsoft Network will have a single data center near Seattle, Washington, but Microsoft plans to provide several more data centers around the world.

# MSN Central

The primary way to enter The Microsoft Network is through MSN Central, which is the highest level of the content tree. MSN Central appears when users click the icon for The Microsoft Network. From MSN Central, users can choose the following services or tools.

| Home Page Icon | Description |
| --- | --- |
| MSN Today | Tells users what new information has been added to the service or what special events are occurring on The Microsoft Network specifically for that day. Users can click on the corresponding icons to go directly to the services. |
| Electronic Mail | Starts Microsoft Exchange, allowing users to send mail to and receive mail from members of The Microsoft Network, other users of a Microsoft Mail workgroup postoffice, and people on the Internet. |
| Favorite Places | Opens a Favorite Places folder where users can store shortcuts to their favorite bulletin boards and chat rooms. |
| Member Assistance | Contains a folder with rules and behavior guidelines, membership agreement, information about The Microsoft Network for new members, practice chats and bulletin boards, The Microsoft Network customer support, and other information. |
| Categories | Contains all the icons for the different forums offered by The Microsoft Network, such as Arts and Entertainment, Sports, and so on. A forum is a collection of services that include bulletin boards, chat rooms, and others. Clicking a forum icon opens a folder where icons for all services within the forum are displayed, including: |

- Bulletin boards to read and post messages

- Chats to carry on live conversations

- Kiosks to locate the subject matter of a forum and identify the forum manager

- File libraries to download files

# Windows Explorer and The Microsoft Network

Windows Explorer is a powerful way to navigate The Microsoft Network content tree. A Windows Explorer window in The Microsoft Network contains folders and works the same as any Windows Explorer window in Windows 95 except in the following ways:

- The files are read-only. Users can't create, edit, or drag and drop files in Windows Explorer in The Microsoft Network.

- Windows Explorer by default does not open a new window for each folder that a user opens because MSN users typically open numerous folders while exploring MSN, which can reduce available system resources. You can change this option to open a separate window for each folder in Folder properties, which can be opened from the Options item in the View menu in Windows Explorer.

▶ **To use Windows Explorer in The Microsoft Network**

- Right-click a folder or icon, and then click Explore.

In Windows Explorer, users can find out the properties of a forum or folder, including the Name, Category, Rating, Go words, and price. A forum manager for The Microsoft Network can decide which properties can function as *key words*. Key words are a means of tagging content so that users can search for information within the service.

▶ **To view the properties for each forum**

- Right-click the icon for a forum or folder in it, and then click Properties.

## Shortcuts

Shortcuts immediately take users to specific areas within The Microsoft Network. Users can drag and drop the shortcut to any Windows 95 folder, a word processing file, a bulletin board message, or any other OLE-compatible application. Double-clicking the shortcut will launch The Microsoft Network, log users on, and take users to the service that their shortcut referred to.

For information on creating shortcuts in Windows 95, see online Help.

## Favorite Places

Favorite Places are similar to shortcuts in Windows 95, but are a special feature of The Microsoft Network. Users can use Windows Explorer to add a Favorite Places icon for a folder or forum to the Favorite Places folder in MSN Central. Unlike shortcuts, users can use Favorite Places icons only for services in The Microsoft Network, and can place them only in the Favorite Places folder.

▶  **To add a service to the Favorite Places folder**

- From The Microsoft Network toolbar, click an icon, and then click the Add to Favorite Places button.

  –Or–

  Right-click an icon, and click Add To Favorite Places.

# Go Commands

Users can quickly navigate to a specific service if users know its *Go* word, a unique identifier of a service in The Microsoft Network. Go words are defined in two places: in a Kiosk or in the properties dialog box for a service.

▶  **To determine a service's Go word**

1. Right-click an icon for a specific service, and in the Windows Explorer menu, click Properties.

2. In Properties for that service, click the General tab. The Go word appears at the top of the General properties dialog box.

▶  **To navigate to a service using a Go command**

1. From the Edit menu in the window for any service, point to the Go To option, and then click Other Location.

2. In the Go To Service dialog box, type the Go word, and then click OK.

---

**Note**  If users don't know the exact name of a service or subject that users are looking for, users can use the Find option from the Start menu in Windows 95, or in the File menu in Windows Explorer in The Microsoft Network. With the Find Command, users can specify search criteria such as a specific name or topic for a particular service. For more information, see online Help.

---

# Using Bulletin Boards

A bulletin board provides a place to exchange messages. Most bulletin boards are public, which means any member of The Microsoft Network can read them. Each bulletin board has a topic, such as scuba diving, computer graphics, or current events. Users post messages about the topics to do the following:

- Ask or answer questions
- Offer opinions, ideas, or suggestions
- Share facts and exchange information
- Distribute files for other people to copy to their computers

A thread is a collection of messages users can organize chronologically or hierarchically to reflect the flow of the discussion. Messages appear in a bulletin board in three possible default views:

- List View lists all messages in the order they were sent to the bulletin board.

- Conversation View lists all original messages and their replies and is organized according to a conversation thread. To read replies, click the + icon; to read individual messages, double-click a message.

- Attached Files View lists only those messages with attached files. This is an effective way of seeing information that pertains to files rather than messages.

Message views can be further sorted in each bulletin board according to their subject, author, size, or date.

▶ **To navigate through The Microsoft Network content tree to a bulletin board**

1. In MSN Central, click Categories.

2. In the Categories window, choose a topic by double-clicking its icon.

3. Continue to double-click icons to select subcategories until you are in the forum containing the bulletin board that interests you.

4. In the forum window, double-click the bulletin board folder to see current messages.

▶ **To change the view of messages**

- In the bulletin board, click the View menu, and then click List, Conversation, or Attached Files.

▶ **To sort messages within a bulletin board**

- In the bulletin board, click the Subject, Author, Size, or Date button beneath the toolbar to sort accordingly.

# Bulletin Board File Libraries

File libraries are read-only bulletin boards. This means that only an ICP who owns the bulletin board can post messages and files there. You can read and download files in file libraries and files attached to messages in file libraries in the same way you would in a standard bulletin board. File attachments can be graphics, software, articles, product support information, and so on.

Before users download a file, they can view its size, its price, and the length of time it will take to download. When users download it, they specify the file's destination on the hard disk in the File Transfer Status dialog box.

File Transfer Status is a utility that mediates file movement between the server and the client. It allows users to view and control how the file downloads. File Transfer Status is active whenever a file is placed in the transfer queue by an application such as a bulletin board. File Transfer Status can transfer files in the background while users continue to browse through The Microsoft Network.

▶ **To download an attached file**

1. Open a message with an attachment, right-click the attachment's icon, point to File Object, and then click Properties.

2. In Properties for that message, examine the file's size, download time, price, and whether the forum manager has approved the file for downloading, and then click OK.

3. In the message, click the File menu, and then click Save As.

4. In the Save As dialog box, click the folder on the hard disk where you want the file to be saved, and then click Open. This adds the file to the queue of files to be downloaded or starts the downloading process if it is the first file to be selected for downloading.

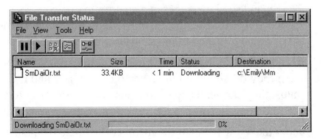

When files are queued, File Transfer Status checks for error conditions, such as insufficient space on the hard disk or invalid destination, and provides a corresponding error message. File Transfer Status then provides an opportunity to fix an error before the file is transferred. In the File Transfer Status window, the percentage of file downloaded, the time remaining, and the file's destination are displayed.

If users are downloading files that were attached using a file-compression program, File Transfer Status detects this and automatically decompresses them if the option named Automatically Decompress Files is checked in the File Transfer Options dialog box. This dialog box can be opened by clicking the Options item in the Tool menu in File Transfer Status.

# Chat Rooms

A chat room allows users to carry on a live conversation (a chat) with other members of The Microsoft Network. A chat session on The Microsoft Network is similar to a conference call. However, instead of speaking words, users type them and they are displayed on-screen by The Microsoft Network for other people to read. To participate in a chat session, users should know the following:

- Each member in the chat session is either a participant or spectator according to how the host defines the participation rules. A chat session might have one or more hosts. To become a host, you have to be a designated owner of the chat.

- A host can control the participation rights of members in a conversation. The host uses the Host Control dialog box to change the status of a member from a participant to a spectator and vice versa.

- There are several types of conversations, from one-on-one conversations to large "talk shows" in which there are a few participants and numerous spectators, to general purpose, multiple-member conversations.

- To join and send messages in a chat room, the conversation must not have exceeded its capacity, that is, the maximum number of members allowed in the conversation, and users must have the necessary security privileges.

- Before users contribute to the conversation, they can observe it for a while to see if they'd like to join in. When they're ready and if they have participant status, they can send a question, answer, or comment to the other members.

- Users can view information about a member in the Member Properties option under the View menu, if the member completed a member profile in Microsoft Exchange. For more information, see "Using Microsoft Exchange with The Microsoft Network" later in this chapter.

- Users can download a conversation history, which is a record of all messages sent to the conversation from the time a participant joined it.

▶ **To join a chat room**

1. In a forum's window, double-click the Chat icon.

   The Microsoft Network informs other participants that you have joined the conversation.

2. Type a message in the lower box and then click Send.

   Pressing ENTER also sends text and, therefore, cannot be used within a message. However, you can press CTRL+ENTER to insert a carriage return in your message.

3. To exit, click the File menu, and then click Exit.

# Using Microsoft Exchange with The Microsoft Network

The Microsoft Network has been integrated with the Microsoft Exchange client that is provided with Windows 95. All electronic mail messages sent to or from other members of The Microsoft Network appear in the same mailbox as messages from other electronic mail (such as LAN mail), or information services such as CompuServe® or the Internet.

All features of Microsoft Exchange are available to users when users run The Microsoft Network. Because both Microsoft Exchange and The Microsoft Network support binary file transfers and OLE, users can attach spreadsheets, graphics files, word processing documents, or almost any other kind of electronic file to a mail message.

Before users send and receive mail in The Microsoft Network, they must complete the following steps:

- Install and configure Microsoft Exchange, as described in Chapter 26, "Electronic Mail and Microsoft Exchange"
- Connect to The Microsoft Network

▶ **To send or receive mail within The Microsoft Network**

- In MSN Central, click E-mail to open Microsoft Exchange.

---

**Note**  When users sign up for The Microsoft Network, their primary Microsoft Exchange profile will be updated so that The Microsoft Network is included as both an information service and an address book provider. Users can send and receive mail over The Microsoft Network without further configuring Microsoft Exchange or The Microsoft Network.

---

▶ **To send mail on the Internet**

1. In MSN Central, click E-mail.
2. Click Compose, and then click New Message.
3. In the To box, specify an Internet address.

An Internet address consists of a user name and a DNS domain name, separated by the @ character. In the following example, **jim256** is the user name and **msn.com** is the domain:

```
jim256@msn.com
```

In the next example, **rks** is the user name and **seas.ucla.edu** is the domain:

```
rks@seas.ucla.edu
```

For more information about DNS domain names, see Chapter 30, "Internet Access."

Mail from other users on the Internet appears in the Microsoft Exchange Inbox along with other messages.

▶ **To download mail from The Microsoft Network at startup of Microsoft Exchange**

1. In Control Panel, double-click the Mail And Fax option.

2. In the Microsoft Exchange Settings Properties, click The Microsoft Network Online Service, and then click Properties.

3. In Transport properties, click the option named Download Mail When E-Mail Starts Up From MSN.

As a result of this procedure, The Microsoft Network connection box will be displayed every time users run The Microsoft Network. Users can cancel the connection and choose to download their mail from The Microsoft Network at a later time from within Windows 95 or from within The Microsoft Network.

▶ **To download mail from The Microsoft Network after Microsoft Exchange startup**

• In Microsoft Exchange, click the Tools menu, and point to Connect To, and then click The Microsoft Network.

The Microsoft Network maintains an address book on The Microsoft Network servers that includes the name and electronic mail address of each member of The Microsoft Network. Users can access the address book in Microsoft Exchange, or in the Member Assistance section of The Microsoft Network. The Microsoft Network address book is available only when users are connected to The Microsoft Network because it is too large to copy to a local computer.

The Microsoft Network provides separate address books for each major region in the United States, Europe, Australia, and other countries. All members can access all of these address books. All address books appear in the list of address books in the Microsoft Exchange Address Book window. For more information about using address books, see Chapter 26, "Electronic Mail and Microsoft Exchange."

▶ **To display member information**

1. In Microsoft Exchange, open The Microsoft Network address book, and then double-click a member's name.

2. In the User Information dialog box, view information about the member, such as city, birth date, comments, and so on.

# Billing

The Microsoft Network automatically charges users a monthly fee for using its services and a monthly base fee for additional blocks of time for the subscription services that users choose. If users spend time connected to a service beyond the allotted number of minutes they purchase with a subscription, The Microsoft Network assesses them a usage charge.

For example, a subscription to Forum XYZ might give users up to 20 minutes of connect time per month. Users will be charged an additional fee for the time they spend online in excess of 20 minutes.

Before users download a file, the Microsoft Network gives users information about whether there is a fee for copying it. If users download a file that has a fee, they will see the filename and the charge for downloading it.

All charges appear in a billing statement, which shows a user's current balance and all charges to the account by date. Payments and credits are shown as negative values. If there is a tax on any charge, it is figured automatically and included in the total. Users will be billed monthly; the billing date corresponds to the date they signed up for The Microsoft Network.

For more information about billing, see online Help in The Microsoft Network.

# Becoming an Independent Content Provider (ICP)

By becoming an ICP, companies can sell products and services in a worldwide electronic marketplace that is accessible from the Windows 95 desktop.

ICPs conduct business on The Microsoft Network on a transaction basis and retain the majority of the revenues from these transactions. ICPs aren't limited in the ways in which they realize revenues for their services. Variable revenue and pricing models such as subscriptions, online transactions, advertising subsidies, and ticketed events are available at the provider's discretion. Providers Transactions can be of the following types:

- Electronic files that can be downloaded
- Chat rooms with cover charges
- Forums with cover charges
- Monthly subscription fees for certain areas of a forum
- Sales of advertising and sponsorships

To obtain information about becoming an ICP, in the United States call (800) 4MSNFAX or (800) 467-6329. From outside the U.S., call (908) 885-6439. You will receive by fax a summary of The Microsoft Network, a guide to formatting your business proposal, and a nondisclosure agreement. To receive this information by mail, please write:

The Microsoft Network
Department MSN19
One Microsoft Way
Redmond, WA  98052-6399

C H A P T E R   3 0

# Internet Access

This chapter describes how to configure Windows 95 to access the Internet and offers some basic tips for browsing and accessing information on the Internet.

**In This Chapter**

Internet Access: The Basics    940
Connecting to the Internet    944
    Installing and Configuring a Modem    944
    Obtaining an Internet Account    945
    Installing TCP/IP    946
    Setting the Domain Name System Server and IP Addresses    947
    Making a Dial-Up Networking Connection    950
Navigating the Internet    955
    Using Microsoft TCP/IP Utilities    955
    Using FTP to Browse and Download Files    956
    Downloading Files with FTP    957
    Using Windows 95 Telnet    958
    Browsing the Internet with Public Domain Tools    959
Troubleshooting Internet Connections    961

# Internet Access: The Basics

The Internet is a worldwide collection of networks and gateways linked, in most cases, with the TCP/IP suite of protocols. The Internet allows a broad spectrum of business people, academics, government users, and others to exchange ideas and information in a new way. Windows 95 offers you three ways to connect to the Internet:

- You can join The Microsoft Network online service from the Windows 95 desktop to send and receive mail on the Internet and access Internet newsgroups. For more information, see Chapter 29, "The Microsoft Network."

- You can install TCP/IP and Dial-Up Networking—both of which are provided with Windows 95—to connect to Internet access providers. You connect to an access provider by using Dial-Up Networking to dial in to their PPP or SLIP servers, which are directly connected to the Internet.

- You can install TCP/IP and a network adapter so that you can connect to a company's network server that is directly connected to the Internet.

Windows 95 supports all the protocols you need to connect to an Internet access provider, including a 32-bit implementation of TCP/IP, plus PPP or SLIP. In addition, Windows 95 provides FTP and Telnet clients, which can be used to browse the Internet and download files from Internet servers.

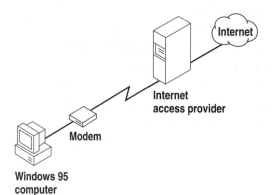

**Connecting to the Internet.**   To connect a computer running Windows 95 to an Internet access provider, you need to do the following:

- Obtain an Internet account with an Internet access provider. This is provided automatically if your company has a direct connection to the Internet.

- Install TCP/IP and Dial-Up Networking, and make sure TCP/IP is bound to the Microsoft Dial-Up adapter or a network adapter.

- Install a modem (if you dial in to the Internet) or a network adapter (if you have a direct network connection to the Internet).

- Define a Dial-Up Networking connection to an Internet access provider and define IP address information for each connection, or for your network adapter, if required.

For more information about how to do these tasks, see "Connecting to the Internet" later in this chapter.

Before you connect to the Internet, you need to decide what kinds of information you want to provide or exchange. The most common tools for finding and exchanging information and the most common sources of information are described briefly in the following list and in more detail in "Navigating the Internet" later in this chapter.

**Sending and receiving mail.**   You can send and receive mail to other individuals on the Internet or join an Internet mailing list. There are servers around the world that maintain and manage Internet mailing list communities. To send and receive mail on the Internet, you need to run an electronic mail application, a Simple Mail Transport Protocol (SMTP) client, and connect to a SMTP server. You should ask your Internet access provider if they provide this support. After you have an electronic mail account, you can join a mailing list by sending an electronic mail message to a particular mailing list server.

**USENET newsgroups.**   Newsgroup servers, supporting Net News Transport Protocol (NNTP), share information and commentary on defined topics. Each newsgroup is a bulletin board where members post and reply to messages. To connect to a newsgroup, you need the following:

- Access to an NNTP server

- A newsgroup account provided by an Internet access provider

- An NNTP reader (an application that allows you to view newsgroup information), which is available commercially or as shareware from many Internet sites

**Searching the Internet.** A variety of tools are available to help you find the information you need on the Internet. Many Internet access providers offer some of these tools, which include the following:

- Web browsers are multifaceted tools that allow you to dynamically view the World Wide Web (WWW), a network of servers that uses hypertext links to find and access files. A browser allows you to view documents on servers around the world without having to manually type each location. Most currently available browsers include versions of FTP, Telnet, Gopher, Mail and WAIS, giving you wide-ranging capabilities to search, connect, and download information on the Internet.

- File transfer protocol (FTP) is a file-sharing protocol for finding and connecting to servers, and then transferring text and binary files between a host computer and a computer. Archie is a database and a system for locating files on FTP servers. FTP sites are indexed by title and keyword, and Archie searches these indexes for the file you want. An FTP utility is provided in Windows 95.

- Telnet is a connectivity tool that allows you to start a terminal session with a telnet server. A Telnet utility is provided in Windows 95.

- Gopher is a search tool that presents information in a hierarchical menu system similar to a table of contents. Veronica is a tool that searches for text in Gopher menus.

- WAIS (Wide-Area Information Service) indexes large text files, documents, and periodicals. You can search WAIS indexes for a wide variety of information.

- Finger commands allow you to view the status of a remote site or user.

- Mail readers allow you to use electronic mail on the Internet if your Internet access provider provides you with an account.

- Search engines are sites on the Internet that allow you to enter a search command and receive a list of sites containing the specified information. Search engines generally require a Web browser, such as Mosaic.

- Helper applications are add-on tools to Internet browsers that allow you to incorporate multimedia features into files. Many Internet sites provide locations where you can find and download helper applications.

---

**Note** Windows 95 provides Telnet and FTP clients for searching and browsing the Internet as described in "Navigating the Internet" later in this chapter.

---

**Downloading information.** After you locate information, you can download it to a computer using FTP, which allows you to copy files from a host to a remote server.

**Useful publications.**  For more information about accessing and using the Internet, the following books are recommended:

Baczewski, P., and Bang, S.; Barnett, J. *The Internet Unleashed.* Indianapolis, IN: Sams Publishing, 1994.

Braun, E. *The Internet Directory.* New York: Fawcett Columbine, 1994.

Dougherty, D., and Koman, R. *The Mosaic Handbook for Microsoft Windows.* Sebastapol, CA: O'Reilly, 1994.

Falk, B. *The Internet Roadmap.* Alameda, CA: SYBEC Inc., 1994.

Gilster, P. *The Internet Navigator.* New York, NY: Wiley, 1994.

Hahn, H., and Stout, R. *The Internet Complete Reference.* Berkeley, CA: Osborne McGraw-Hill, 1994.

Hahn, H., and Stout, R. *The Internet Yellow Pages.* Berkeley, CA: Osborne McGraw-Hill, 1994.

Kehoe, B. *Zen and the Art of the Internet: A Beginner's Guide.* Englewood Cliffs, NJ: PTR Prentice Hall, 1994.

Lynch, D., and Rose, M. *Internet System Handbook.* Reading, MA: Addison-Wesley, 1993.

Maxwell, C., and Jan, G.C. *New Riders Official Internet Yellow Pages.* New Riders Publishing, 1994.

Notes, G. *Internet Access Providers: an International Resource Directory.* Westport, CT: Mecklermedia, 1994.

Randall, N. *The World Wide Web Unleashed.* Indianapolis, IN: Sams Publishing, 1994.

Smith, R., and Gibbs, M. *Navigating the Internet.* Carmel, IN: Sams Publishing, 1993.

Tennant, R., Ober, J., and Lipow, A. *Crossing the Internet Threshold: An Instructional Handbook.* Berkeley, CA: Library Solutions Press, 1993.

Tolhurst, W., Pike, M., and Blanton, K. *Using the Internet.* Indianapolis, IN: Que, 1994.

# Connecting to the Internet

Connecting a computer running Windows 95 to the Internet consists of the following steps:

- Obtaining an Internet PPP or SLIP account from an access provider (unless you are connecting through an Internet server on your network). PPP is a newer standard and offers more automatic authentication, security, and many other advantages.

- Obtaining account information (such as the user name and password) from the access provider; this is needed to connect to their server.

- Installing and configuring a modem.

- Installing Microsoft TCP/IP by using the Network option in Control Panel.

- Installing Dial-Up Networking and defining a Dial-Up Networking connection to the Internet. If your Internet access provider does not dynamically assign you DNS and IP addresses, you can set these in Dial-Up Networking for each connection you create to the Internet.

  –Or–

  Installing a network adapter and defining an IP address in the network adapter's TCP/IP properties dialog boxes.

- Connecting to the Internet.

- Browsing the Internet by using FTP or Telnet provided with Windows 95, or by using Gopher, Archie, WAIS, and other Web browsers, which are available commercially or as shareware from Internet servers.

## Installing and Configuring a Modem

Windows 95 supports a variety of modems for dial-in access. You do not need to configure a modem differently to connect to the Internet than you would for any other Dial-Up Networking connection. For information about installing and configuring modems, see Chapter 25, "Modems and Communications Tools." For information about configuring communications ports, see Chapter 19, "Devices."

# Obtaining an Internet Account

Most users connect to the Internet by dialing in to an Internet access provider's server that is directly connected to the Internet. An Internet access provider is a company or institution that provides access to the Internet for a fee. According to the Internet Network Information Center (InterNIC), there are more than 160 commercial Internet access providers around the country. Access providers offer a range of services and charge for them in a variety of ways.

---

**Tip**  Using an Internet access provider by way of remote access is a fairly inexpensive way to reach the Internet, but its effectiveness is limited by the speed of the connection and the modem. For a good modem and a normal phone line, this speed tends to be roughly between 14.4 and 28.8 kilobytes per second (kbps). For better performance, you can use one or more integrated service digital network (ISDN) lines to achieve 64 kbps or 128 kbps.

---

You can find an access provider by purchasing books or magazines that list them, some of which are included in the preceding section, or by accessing lists through an online service such as America Online® or CompuServe®. Online lists of access providers include:

- PDIAL list, access by sending electronic mail to info_deli_server@netcom.com.
- America Online or CompuServe PCWorld forums.

In deciding which access provider to use, you should consider the following:

- Does the access provider offer full Internet access?
- Does the access provider support PPP?
- Does the access provider offer technical support?
- What kind of connection speeds does the access provider support?
- What kind of search tools are provided?
- Does the access provider have an adequate number of phone lines and a large enough pipe to the Internet in order to provide good response time?
- What range of services, such as mail, does the access provider offer, and at what charge?

After you have chosen an access provider, obtain the following information from the access provider when you establish a PPP or a SLIP account. You need this information in order to configure Windows 95 to access the Internet:

- Access phone number, preferably local
- Logon name
- Logon password
- Your host and domain name, if electronic mail is part of your connection services; your host name can include a POP3 host name and a SMTP host name, which are protocols used to send and receive messages on the Internet, respectively
- The NNTP server name, if Internet newsgroups are part of your connection service
- The Domain Name System (DNS) server and IP address

All SLIP accounts require you to manually configure an IP address on your computer when you connect. Access providers who support PPP usually assign IP address automatically each time you dial in to the access provider. However, some PPP access providers might require manual configuration of an IP address as described in "Setting the Domain Name System Server and IP Addresses" later in this chapter. You also need, in most cases, to configure the IP address of the access provider's DNS server.

More information is provided about these settings in the following sections and in Chapter 12, "Network Technical Discussion."

# Installing TCP/IP

Connecting the millions of computer networks on the Internet would not be possible without a standard set of protocols. Each Internet standard is described in a document called a request for comment (RFC). TCP/IP is the standard on the Internet because it combines a number of different protocols that make it possible to communicate across interconnected networks that have diverse hardware and operating systems.

To connect to the Internet, you must install TCP/IP. Windows 95 will automatically allow (bind) TCP/IP to work with a network adapter or with the Microsoft Dial-Up adapter. You can install TCP/IP when you install Windows 95, or you can install it after Setup by using the Network option in Control Panel.

▶ **To install TCP/IP**

1. In the Network option in Control Panel, click the Add button.

2. In the Select Network Component Type dialog box, double-click Protocol.

3. In the Select Network Protocol dialog box, in the Manufacturers list, click Microsoft and then in the Network Protocols list, click Microsoft TCP/IP. Click OK.

▶ **To verify that TCP/IP is bound to the Microsoft Dial-Up adapter or a network adapter**

- In the Network option in Control Panel, scroll through the list of network components to see if an arrow to the right of TCP/IP points to the Dial-Up adapter or another network adapter.

When you install Dial-Up Networking or another network adapter, Windows 95 automatically binds TCP/IP to the adapters if TCP/IP has been previously installed. If your computer has multiple network adapters, an entry for TCP/IP is displayed for each one. You must configure each adapter with its own TCP/IP settings.

# Setting the Domain Name System Server and IP Addresses

The Internet uses the Domain Name System (DNS) to translate computer and domain names into IP addresses. A DNS server maintains a database that maps domain names to IP addresses as specified by network administrators. The DNS organizes the names of hosts in a hierarchical fashion, similar to a file system.

Before you can use TCP/IP to connect to the Internet, you need to configure a computer to recognize DNS information. Some Internet access providers dynamically assign IP addresses for DNS servers, but most do not. Most PPP Internet access providers do dynamically assign IP addresses. If an access provider does not dynamically assign either a DNS IP address or your IP address, you should set these in the TCP/IP Settings dialog box in Dial-Up Networking for each connection you create.

If, however, you have a static, direct LAN connection to the Internet or other TCP/IP network, then you should set the DNS IP address and your IP address in TCP/IP properties in the Network option in Control Panel. You do not need to set this information if your LAN's Internet access server dynamically assigns these to you; for example, if you are using a server with Dynamic Host Configure Protocol (DHCP) capabilities, such as a DHCP server on a Windows NT Server network, it will assign IP address information dynamically.

---

**Note** The following procedures assume that your computer has Microsoft TCP/IP installed as a network protocol. If your site uses another vendor's version of TCP/IP, you must configure the protocol as recommended by the protocol vendor.

---

▶ **To set the DNS IP address for a direct LAN connection to the Internet**

1. In the Network option in Control Panel, double-click the TCP/IP entry for the network adapter in the network component list.

2. In the TCP/IP Properties dialog box, click the DNS Configuration tab.

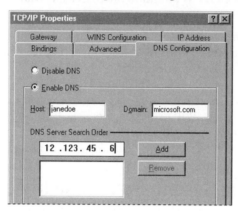

3. Click Enable DNS, and then, in the Host and Domain boxes, type your host name and domain name, respectively. These names identify you on the Internet.

4. In the DNS Server Search Order box, type the address of your LAN's DNS server in the DNS Server Search Order box.

   If your network has more than one DNS server, type each DNS server and then click Add. DNS settings are currently global across all instances of TCP/IP. This allows you to rely on a secondary DNS server if the primary DNS server is down. The first server listed is the first one searched.

▶ **To set the DNS IP address for each connection in Dial-Up Networking**

1. In Dial-Up Networking, right-click the connection you defined for the Internet, and then click Properties.

2. In the connection's properties, click Server Type, and then click TCP/IP
   Settings.

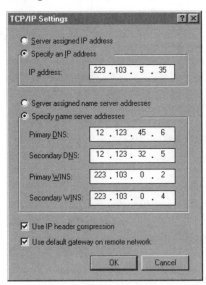

3. In the TCP/IP Settings dialog box, click the option named Specify An
   IP Address, and type your IP address.

4. Click the option named Specify Name Server Address, and then type the
   IP address of the DNS server in the Primary DNS box.

---

**Important**  Because IP addresses identify nodes on an interconnected network,
each host on the internetwork must be assigned a unique IP address, valid for
its particular network.

---

▶ **To define the IP address for a direct LAN connection to the Internet**

1. In the Network option in Control Panel, double-click TCP/IP for the network adapter.

2. In the TCP/IP Properties dialog box, click the IP Address tab, and then click the Specify An IP Address option.

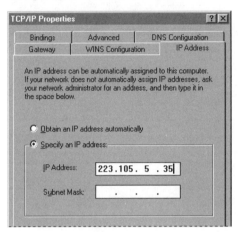

3. In the IP Address box, type your IP address. After you type the address, the subnet mask will be provided automatically. Click OK.

▶ **To define an IP address if the access provider does not dynamically assign one**

• In the TCP/IP IP Address dialog box, click the option named Specify An IP Address, and then type your IP address.

For more information about assigning DNS and IP addresses, see "Technical Notes for IP Addresses on TCP/IP Networks" in the WIN95RK.HLP with the *Windows 95 Resource Kit* utilities.

# Making a Dial-Up Networking Connection

After you install and configure TCP/IP, you need to configure a Dial-Up Networking connection to an Internet access provider. The way you configure the connection settings depends on the type of Internet server you are using.

To connect to a PPP server that supports the Password Authentication Protocol (PAP) or the Challenge-Handshake Authentication Protocol (CHAP), all you have to do is click the Dial-Up Networking connection you defined, and then type your user name and password in the Connect To dialog box. These types of servers include Windows NT 3.5, Shiva NetModem and LanRover, or any UNIX® server that supports PAP and CHAP.

To connect to PPP servers that does not support PAP or CHAP, or to connect to SLIP servers, you need to change settings in Dial-Up Networking for each Internet connection you define, as described in the following procedures.

For more information about defining a Dial-Up Networking connection, and about PAP and CHAP, see Chapter 28, "Dial-Up Networking and Mobile Computing."

## Connecting to a PPP Server

A PPP server that does not support PAP or CHAP might require that you use a terminal window to log on. In this case, you need to specify in Dial-Up Networking that a terminal window be displayed after dialing. To provide security when there is no support for PAP or CHAP, you can require that an encrypted password be used. You can also increase the connection speed by disabling network protocols other than TCP/IP.

▶ **To display a terminal window after dialing**

1. In Dial-Up Networking, right-click the connection icon you created for the Internet, and then click Properties.

2. In the Properties dialog box, click the Configure button, and then click the Options tab.

3. In the Options dialog box, click the option named Bring Up Terminal Window After Dialing so it is checked, and then click OK.

▶ **To increase connection speed and require encrypted passwords**

1. In Dial-Up Networking, right-click the connection icon for Internet, and then click Properties.

2. In the Properties dialog box, click the Server Types button.

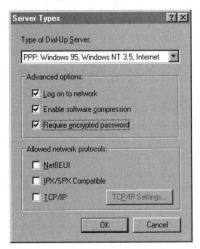

3. In the Server Types dialog box, you can increase the speed with which you connect to an Internet access provider by making sure the following options are not checked.

   - Log On To Network
   - NetBEUI
   - IPX/SPX Compatible

4. If you need to use an encrypted password, make sure the option named Require Encrypted Password is checked.

You are now ready to connect to an Internet access provider.

▶ **To connect to a PPP server that does not support PAP or CHAP**

1. In Dial-Up Networking, double-click the connection icon you created for the Internet.

2. In the Connect To dialog box, click Connect.

3. In the Terminal Window dialog box, type your user name and password and any other information that your access provider requires.

4. After you have been successfully logged on, click F7 to continue.

---

**Note**  Windows 95 does not allow you to write a script to automate the terminal window logon process.

---

## Connecting to a SLIP Server

Windows 95 Dial-Up Networking clients support SLIP and can connect to any remote access server using the SLIP standard. However, SLIP is available only on the Windows 95 compact disc.

▶ **To install SLIP**

1. In the Add/Remove Programs option in Control Panel, click the Windows Setup tab, and then click the Have Disk button.

2. In the Install From Disk dialog box, type the path name to the ADMIN\APPTOOLS\SLIP directory on the compact disc, and then click OK.

3. In the Select Network Service dialog box, click UNIX Connection For Dial-Up Networking, and then click Install.

   Both CSLIP and SLIP will appear in the Server Types dialog box in Dial-Up Networking

There are two types of SLIP accounts—uncompressed SLIP and compressed SLIP (CSLIP). You set what type of SLIP account you have for each connection you create in Dial-Up Networking.

▶ **To select the type of SLIP account for a connection in Dial-Up Networking**

1. Right-click a connection icon, and then click Properties.

2. In the connection's properties, click Server Type.

3. In the Server Type dialog box, click the option named Slip: UNIX Connection or CSLIP Connection With IP Header Compression in the Type of Server box.

---

**Note**  If you are having trouble running TCP/IP applications after connection, you might need to change the server type from CSLIP to SLIP, or vice versa.

---

SLIP servers do not have the capability to negotiate your TCP/IP address. Therefore, you must set Dial-Up Networking to display a terminal window after you dial the Internet server. After you type your user name and password, IP address information will be displayed in the terminal window as described in the following procedure.

▶ **To connect to a SLIP server**

1. In Dial-Up Networking, right-click the connection icon you created for the Internet, and then click Properties to specify that a terminal window be displayed. Click OK.

2. In General properties, click the Server Types button.

3. In the Server Types dialog box, click the option named SLIP UNIX Connection or the option named CSLIP UNIX Connection With IP Header Compression, and then click OK.

   You can also make sure the Log On To Network check box is cleared because SLIP servers allow you to log on only in a terminal window. Notice that the only protocol allowed is TCP/IP.

4. In Dial-Up Networking, double-click the icon for the connection.

5. In the Connect To dialog box, click Connect.

6. After the modem establishes a connection, the Post Dial Terminal Screen dialog box appears for you to log on to the SLIP server and receive your IP address.

   You must follow the provider's guidelines for logging on to its server. Most Internet access providers require only that you type a user name and password. However, other access providers require additional information.

   In most cases, after you type your user name and password, the access provider will display two IP addresses, a host IP address and your IP address. (If the access provider does not display the IP addresses, you should find them out from them.) The second address displayed is usually your IP address, which you should write down, and then click F7.

7. In the SLIP Connection IP Address dialog box, type your IP address, and then click OK.

8. If your Internet access provider assigns you the same IP address each time you connect then, after you finish an Internet session, type your IP address in the TCP/IP Settings dialog box for that connection in Dial-Up Networking. The next time you connect to the Internet SLIP server using this connection, you will not have to type your IP address.

---

**Note**  You can use the **ping** command at the command prompt to differentiate the local from the host IP address. At the command prompt, type **ping** and the local IP address (for example, **123.45.6.7**), and then try **ping** with another server on the Internet. If the local address works, and the server address does not, contact the access provider.

---

After you connect to an Internet access provider, Windows 95 displays a dialog box named Connected To Internet (or whatever name you gave the Dial-Up Networking connection to the Internet). You can minimize this dialog box and begin your Internet session by running FTP, Telnet, or other Internet browsing applications.

### Using WINIPCFG to Verify Internet Connections

The IP Configuration utility (WINIPCFG) is a troubleshooting utility that displays all current TCP/IP network configuration values for any computer running Microsoft TCP/IP. Network configuration values include the current IP address allocated to the computer and other useful data about the TCP/IP allocation. This utility is of particular use on networks using DHCP, allowing users to determine which TCP/IP configuration values have been configured by DHCP.

The IP Configuration utility does not, however, dynamically update information. If you make any changes, such as disconnecting, you must exit the IP Configuration utility and restart it again.

To run WINIPCFG, click the Start button, click Run, and type **winipcfg**.

For more information about IP addresses on TCP/IP networks, see the WIN95RK.HLP with the *Windows 95 Resource Kit* utilities.

# Navigating the Internet

This section provides some tips to help you find and access information on the Internet after you have connected.

## Using Microsoft TCP/IP Utilities

Windows 95 provides several TCP/IP utilities for copying files, initiating host sessions with other servers, and checking the status of your IP configuration. For more information about these tools, see Appendix A, "Command-Line Commands Summary." For more information about steps for using TCP/IP utilities such as **ping** to verify your connection, see the troubleshooting section of Chapter 12, "Network Technical Discussion."

FTP is a file-transfer protocol that allows the transfer of text and binary files between a host computer and a computer. FTP requires you to log on to the remote host for user authentication, but logging on as "anonymous" can be used to acquire free software and documents through the Internet. Some FTP servers have a limit to the number of anonymous users they can handle at any one time, so you might have to attempt to connect more than once to get a connection.

You can use FTP to access the Microsoft FTP server to get troubleshooting help and other information. This support service uses anonymous FTP to provide documentation, utilities, updated drivers, and other information for many Microsoft systems products.

▶ **To get support from Microsoft by using the Internet**

1. Make sure you are connected to your Internet provider.

2. To start FTP, click the Start menu, click Run, type **ftp**, and then click OK.

3. At the command prompt, type **open ftp.microsoft.com**

4. When you are prompted to specify a user name, type **anonymous**

5. Type your Internet account name (your electronic mail name) as your password, using the format *userid@hostname.domain*.

   As you type your Internet account name, characters might not appear on the screen. This is a security measure to protect your password.

   You are now connected to the root directory of the Microsoft FTP site.

For information about navigating and downloading files, see the following section.

# Using FTP to Browse and Download Files

This section describes how to see a listing of directories and files at an FTP site, and how to change directories and download files. Most FTP servers contain text files that describe the layout of their entire directory structure to help you find what you need. For example, the text file on DIRMAP.TXT describes that server's directory structure.

▶ **To list the directories and folders at an FTP site**

- At the ftp> prompt, type **ls**

▶ **To view more details about the current directory**

- At the ftp> prompt, type **ls -l**

This command provides a detailed listing similar to the following:

```
dr-    1   owner    group    0       Aug 23    16:23    advsys
dr-    1   owner    group    0       Aug 24    5:37     deskapps
dr-    1   owner    group    0       Aug 24    10:52    developer
-r-    1   owner    group    4161    Sep 19    7:43     dirmap.txt
-r-    1   owner    group    712     Aug 25    15:07    disclaimer.txt
-r-    1   owner    group    860     Sep 1     8:40     index.txt
```

In this listing:

- The left column indicates whether the item is a file (r) or a directory (dr).
- The fifth column indicates the byte size of each file.
- The last column describes the name of the file, directory, or link.

  A link to a file or directory somewhere else on the FTP site (similar to a shortcut to a folder or file in Windows 95).

▶ **To change directories**

- At the ftp> prompt, type **cd** *directory_name*

  For example, to get more information about desktop applications, type **cd deskapps**

▶ **To go back to the previous directory**

- At the ftp> prompt, type **cd**

  If you have navigated through many directories and want to go back to the beginning, instead of typing **cd ..** again and again, you can type **cd /** to return to the root directory of this host.

---

**Tip**  Notice that the forward slash "/" is used (as opposed to the backslash "\" that MS-DOS and Windows users are accustomed to) On most UNIX computers, the way to change directories is with the forward slash. Currently, most FTP servers you access only understand that particular command, so the forward slash will always work. However, if you dial into a computer running Windows NT, such as ftp.microsoft.com, it understands both the forward slash and the backslash.

---

# Downloading Files with FTP

To download files from the Internet, you must indicate whether the file is an ASCII or a binary file. By default, when you begin using FTP, you are working in ASCII mode. To transfer text files, it is not necessary to change modes; however, you cannot transfer a binary file while you are in ASCII mode.

---

**Tip**  Most text-based FTP clients are case-sensitive, so make sure you use the correct case when you attempt to transfer resources from these FTP sites.

---

▶ **To switch from ASCII to binary transfer mode**

- At the ftp> prompt, type **binary**

  The following message appears to confirm the change to binary transfer mode:

  ```
  200 Type set to I
  ```

▶ **To switch from binary transfer mode to ASCII**

- At the ftp> prompt, type **ascii**

  The following message appears to confirm the change to ASCII:

  ```
  200 Type set to A
  ```

▶ **To transfer a file to your computer**

- At the ftp> prompt, type **get** *filename*

  For example, to get the directory map on the Microsoft FTP server, type **get dirmap.txt**

  To place the file on a computer with a name other than the one it had on the server, type **get** *filename newname*

If you get an error, remember that you are using software that is case-sensitive, so make sure you typed the word **dirmap.txt** exactly.

When you see the ftp> prompt again, look in Windows Explorer for the DIRMAP.TXT file and open it by using a text processor such as WordPad.

▶ **To disconnect from your host**

- At the ftp> prompt, type **disconnect**

▶ **To stop using FTP**

- At the ftp> prompt, type **quit**

# Using Windows 95 Telnet

Much of the information on the Internet is still available only if you use Telnet. Windows 95 provides a version of Telnet that you can run from the Start menu.

▶ **To run Telnet from the Start menu**

1. Click the Start menu, click Run and, then type **telnet**
2. In Telnet, click the Connect menu, and then click Remote Session.
3. In the Connect dialog box, type the host name of the Telnet site to which you want to connect to.
4. In the Term Type box select a terminal mode. The default is VT-100.
5. In the Port box, select a port. The default is Telnet.
6. To start the Telnet session, click the Connect button.
7. To capture data to a file, type **terminal/start logging**

For more information about using Telnet, see online Help.

# Browsing the Internet with Public Domain Tools

In addition to FTP and Telnet, there are a variety of applications available on the Internet to navigate it, including Mosaic, Gopher, Archie, and WAIS. These applications allow you to easily access the Internet, and they offer greater searching and browsing capabilities than FTP and Telnet. The following sections provide information about several of these applications. You should contact your Internet access provider to find out locations for these programs.

---

**Note**  There are many TCP/IP applications from other vendors that offer Internet browsing, viewing, and connection capabilities. Many of these applications are 16-bit and do not currently work with the 32-bit version of TCP/IP provided with Windows 95.

---

To download these public domain and shareware applications, you need to use FTP as described in Appendix A, "Command-Line Commands Summary."

---

Caution  Windows 95 provides a 32-bit Windows Sockets interface (WINSOCK.DLL). Any attempt to override the Windows 95 interface could cause TCP/IP applications to not work correctly or could cause the computer to stop responding.

---

## Using Mosaic

NCSA Mosaic is a graphical network navigational tool that provides users with access to networked information on the Internet and the World Wide Web (WWW) distributed information system. NCSA Mosaic enables the user to retrieve and display a wide variety of data types, including text, image, video, and audio. It uses a hypertext user interface similar to Windows Help files, so you can click on a word or image of interest, and Mosaic connects you to the appropriate resource. There are now numerous versions of Mosaic available.

▶ **To access Mosaic**

1. Connect to ftp.ncsa.uiuc.edu.

2. At the ftp> prompt, type **cd /web**

3. Read the FAQ.TXT file in this directory and follow the instructions for installing Mosaic.

4. To connect to the Microsoft Word Wide Web server, click in the Document URL box, and then type **http://www.microsoft.com**

5. Click the highlighted words to navigate around the Web site.

## Using Gopher

Gopher is a tool that offers menu-based access to Internet information. Gopher hides the intricacies of FTP from the user and bypasses complicated TCP/IP addresses and connections. Users can choose information from a list of menus, and Gopher makes the connections that are necessary to retrieve the files. Gopher is most helpful when you need to find specific pieces of information on the Internet.

## Using Archie

Archie is a server that supports a database of anonymous FTP sites and their contents. It was created by the Archive Group at McGill University in Montreal, Canada, where Archie is maintained. Archie stores the contents, descriptions, and filenames about a great number of FTP sites. Archie applications are available from many major Internet sites.

## Using Wide-Area Information Server (WAIS)

With WAIS, you can browse the hundreds of databases and library catalogs on the Internet in an organized way. WAIS searches the contents of documents based on words as opposed to titles, which is what as other search tools use. After a search, WAIS displays a list of documents. This list, however, can be extremely large, so WAIS sorts the documents based on how many times a key word was found in each one. If the list is too large, you can narrow the search by specifying categories.

### Tips for Adding a Gateway Server

A dedicated connection to the Internet provides many advantages over connecting by using a modem with a telephone line to an Internet access provider. Having a gateway server can improve performance and reduce costs. You'll need to set up hardware and obtain a domain name so others can send information to your gateway.

If you set up a dedicated computer to act as a router or gateway server to the Internet, it should use a high-speed connection, such as T1 or 56KB lines, instead of a slower telephone line. The T1 line connects to the computer using a special network adapter.

Networks that connect to the Internet must obtain an official network ID from the InterNIC to guarantee unique IP network IDs. Contact the InterNIC by sending electronic mail to info@internic.net (in the U. S., call (800) 444–4345, or for Canada and overseas, call (619) 455–4600).

Internet registration requests can be sent to hostmaster@internic.net. You can also use FTP to connect to is.internic.net, then log on as anonymous and change to the /INFOSOURCE/FAQ directory. After receiving a network ID, the local network administrator must assign unique host IDs for computers within the local network.

# Troubleshooting Internet Connections

### Your modem does not dial.

Use the troubleshooting aid for modems in online Help. See also the modem troubleshooting section in Chapter 25, "Modems and Communications Tools."

### You cannot connect to the Internet access provider.

- Check the Server Types dialog box in Dial-Up Networking to make sure your server type is correct.

  - If you have a PPP account, make sure the server type is not SLIP or CSLIP.

  - If you have a SLIP account, make sure you have the correct type selected, either CSLIP or SLIP. Also, make sure you typed the correct IP address in the SLIP Connection IP Address dialog box.

- Check the Network option in Control Panel to make sure TCP/IP is bound to the Dial-Up or network adapter.

### You connect to the Internet access provider but cannot obtain information from other Internet sites.

Try using the **ping** command to connect to other Internet sites.

▶ **To test a connection is working by using the ping command**

1. At the command prompt, type

   **ping 198.105.232.1** (for the Microsoft FTP server)

   –Or–

   **ping 198.105.232.6** (for the Microsoft WWW server)

   If this works, then TCP/IP is working over your connection.

2. At the command prompt, type **ftp.microsoft.com**

   –Or–

   Run FTP or Telnet.

   If this works, then your DNS settings are correct and working.

If there is no response, check to make sure the DNS IP addresses are correct by running the IP Configuration utility (WINIPCFG).

### You cannot view or download hypertext documents.

To view or download hypertext documents, such as World Wide Web home pages, you must use an Internet browser. The Telnet and FTP utilities that are provided with Windows 95 only support basic navigation on the Internet.

# PART 7

# Windows 95 Reference

This part of the *Windows 95 Resource Kit* contains the following chapters, which provide reference information for using Windows 95.

### Chapter 31　Windows 95 Architecture

Provides a brief review of the Windows 95 architecture to assist you in understanding how the various key operating system components operate.

### Chapter 32　Windows 95 Network Architecture

Presents specific information about the architecture for the networking components in Windows 95.

### Chapter 33　Windows 95 Registry

Describes the Windows 95 Registry and presents background information about the structure and contents of the Registry.

### Chapter 34　International Windows 95

Summarizes information about local editions for Windows 95, and provides technical details about defining regional settings in setup scripts and using the multilingual support in Windows 95.

### Chapter 35　General Troubleshooting

Provides background information for troubleshooting Windows 95.

C H A P T E R   3 1

# Windows 95 Architecture

This chapter provides a brief review of the Windows 95 architecture to assist you in understanding how the key operating system components function and interrelate.

**In This Chapter**

Windows 95 Architecture Components   966

Windows 95 Registry   967

Device Drivers   969

Configuration Manager   970

Virtual Machine Manager   973

   Process Scheduling and Multitasking   974

   Memory Paging   975

   Support for MS-DOS Mode   977

Installable File Systems   977

   Installable File System Manager   978

   File System Drivers   979

   Block I/O Subsystem   981

Core System Components   984

   User   985

   Kernel   986

   Graphical Device Interface   987

User Interface   990

Application Support   990

# Windows 95 Architecture Components

Windows 95 features a new device driver model, a new file system, a new 32-bit graphics engine, and new 32-bit print, communications, and multimedia subsystems. Windows 95 is a 32-bit operating system with built-in connectivity support. It provides high performance, robustness, and complete backward compatibility.

All of these features are supported by the modular design shown in the following diagram.

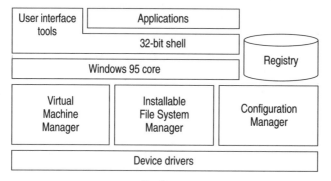

Although its architectural design is based on Windows version 3.1, Windows 95 includes several improvements over the earlier operating system:

- A fully integrated 32-bit, protected-mode operating system, which eliminates the need for a separate copy of MS-DOS.

- Preemptive multitasking and multithreading support, which improves system responsiveness and offers smooth background processing.

- 32-bit installable file systems including VFAT, CDFS, and network redirectors. These support better performance, use of long filenames, and an open architecture to support future growth.

- 32-bit device drivers, available throughout the system, which deliver improved performance and intelligent memory use.

- A complete 32-bit kernel, including memory management and process scheduling and management.

- Improved system-wide robustness and cleanup after an application ends or fails. This delivers a more stable and reliable operating environment.

- More dynamic environment configuration, which reduces the need for users to adjust their systems.

- Improved system capacity, which allows multiple applications and system tasks to run well concurrently.

This chapter describes the key components that make up the Windows 95 architecture beginning with its central information store, the Registry, and proceeding from bottom to top.

# Windows 95 Registry

The central information database for Windows 95 is called the Registry. This hierarchical database both simplifies the operating system and makes it more adaptable. The Registry simplifies the operating system by eliminating the need for AUTOEXEC.BAT, CONFIG.SYS, and INI files (except when legacy applications require them). It makes the operating system more adaptable by storing user-specific and configuration-specific information so you can share one computer among multiple users and you can have more than one configuration (such as in-the-office and on-the-road configurations) for each computer.

A primary role of the Registry in Windows 95 is to serve as a central repository for hardware-specific information for use by the hardware detection and Plug and Play system components. Windows 95 maintains information about hardware components and devices that have been identified through an enumeration process in the hierarchical structure of the Registry, as described in "Configuration Manager" later in this chapter. When new devices are installed, the system checks the existing configuration in the Registry to determine the hardware resources (for example, IRQs, I/O addresses, DMA channels, and so on) that are not being used, so the new device can be properly configured without conflicting with a device already installed in the system.

Windows 3.1 used initialization (INI) files to store system-specific or application-specific information on the state or configuration of the system. For example, the WIN.INI file stored information about the appearance of the Windows environment, the SYSTEM.INI file stored system-specific information on the hardware and device driver configuration of the system, and various INI files (such as MSMAIL.INI and WINWORD6.INI) stored application-specific information.

The Registry remedies this situation by providing a single location for a computer's configuration information. The following table shows other difficulties or limitations caused by using INI files that are overcome by using the Registry.

| Problems using INI files | Solutions using the Registry |
| --- | --- |
| INI files are text-based, and are limited to 64K in total size. | The Registry has no size restriction and can include binary and text values. |
| Information stored in INI files is non-hierarchical and supports only two levels of information (specifically, section headings with a list of key names under each). | The Registry is hierarchically arranged. |

| Problems using INI files | Solutions using the Registry |
|---|---|
| Many INI files contain a myriad of switches and entries that are complicated to configure or are used only by operating system components. | The Registry contains more standardized values. |
| INI files provide no mechanism for storing user-specific information, thus making it difficult for multiple users to share a single computer or for users who move around on the network to have access to their user-specific settings. | The Hkey_Users key stores user-specific information. |
| Configuration information in INI files is local to each system, and no API mechanisms are available for remotely managing configuration, thus making it difficult to manage multiple computers. | The Registry can be remotely administered and system policies (which are stored as Registry values) can be downloaded from a central server each time a new user logs on. For more information, see Chapter 15, "User Profiles and System Policies," and Chapter 16, "Remote Administration." |

When you upgrade from Windows 3.1 to Windows 95, system-specific information such as the static reference to loading virtual device drivers is moved, as appropriate, from the SYSTEM.INI file to the Registry.

For backward compatibility, Windows 95 does not ignore AUTOEXEC.BAT, CONFIG.SYS, and INI files, because many Win16-based applications still use them. For example, Windows 95 allows Win16-based applications to use INI files for the parameters, device drivers, and so on, that the applications need to run. In addition, Windows 95 continues to examine the [386Enh] section of SYSTEM.INI at startup to check for virtual device drivers.

One advantage of the Registry for Win32-based applications is that many of the Win32-based Registry APIs can be used remotely through the remote procedure call (RPC) mechanism in Windows 95 to provide access to Registry information across a network. This means that network administrators can use system management tools to access the contents of the Registry for any computer on the network. (Of course, the remote computer must be configured to allow remote administration, and must have user-level security.)

With Windows 95 remote administration, industry management mechanisms such as Simple Network Management Protocol (SNMP) can easily be integrated into Windows 95, simplifying the management and support burden of the network administrator. For more information, see Chapter 16, "Remote Administration."

# Device Drivers

Windows 95 provides improved support for hardware devices and peripherals including disk devices, display adapters, mice and other pointing devices, modems, fax machines, and printers.

In Windows 3.1, device drivers were, for the most part, monolithic and complex to develop. Windows 95 uses a universal driver/mini-driver architecture that makes it easier for hardware vendors to provide device-specific code for their hardware.

A *universal driver* includes most of the code necessary for devices in a particular class of devices (such as printers or modems) to communicate with the appropriate operating system components (such as the printing or communications subsystems). A mini-driver is the relatively small and simple driver that contains any additional instructions needed by a specific device. In many cases, however, the universal driver for a particular category of devices also includes the code needed to operate devices designed to the most common standard for that category. (For example, the Unimodem driver works with all modems supporting AT commands.)

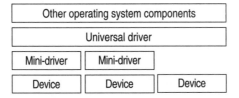

A *virtual device driver* (VxD) is a 32-bit, protected-mode driver that manages a system resource, such as a hardware device or installed software, so that more than one application can use the resource at the same time. VxD refers to a general virtual device driver—the x represents the type of device driver. For example, a virtual device driver for a display device is known as a VDD, a virtual device driver for a timer device is a VTD, a virtual device driver for a printer device is a VPD, and so forth.

With Windows 3.1, VxDs were statically loaded and took up a lot of memory space. However, Windows 95 dynamically loads VxDs—only those that are needed at any given time are loaded into memory. In addition, the new VxDs don't require all of their memory to be page-locked, thereby further increasing the available memory in the system.

VxDs support all hardware devices for a typical computer, including disk controllers, serial and parallel ports, keyboard and display devices, and so on. If the state of the hardware device can be disrupted by switching between multiple applications, the device must have a corresponding virtual device and VxD. The virtual device keeps track of the state of the device for each application and ensures that the device is in the correct state whenever an application continues.

Although most virtual devices manage hardware, some manage only installed software, such as an MS-DOS device driver or a TSR program. Such virtual devices contain code to emulate the software or ensure that the software uses data that applies only to the currently running application. Also, VxDs are often used to improve software performance.

Windows 95 virtual device driver files have a filename extension of .VXD; Windows 3.1 drivers used the .386 filename extension.

# Configuration Manager

To support Plug and Play functionality, Windows 95 architecture includes a new component called Configuration Manager, which orchestrates the configuration process. This process might involve many bus and device architectures coexisting on a single system, with more than one device type using the same bus architecture, yet with each device having a separate set of configuration requirements.. (A *bus* is the mechanism that allows information to be transferred between the computer and the device.) For example, a mouse and a keyboard can both use the same keyboard controller bus; a CD-ROM drive and a hard disk drive might both use the same SCSI bus.

As shown in the following illustration, Configuration Manager works with a number of subcomponents to identify each bus and each device on the system, and to identify the configuration settings for each device. Configuration Manager ensures that each device on the computer can use an IRQ, I/O port addresses, and other resources without conflict with other devices.

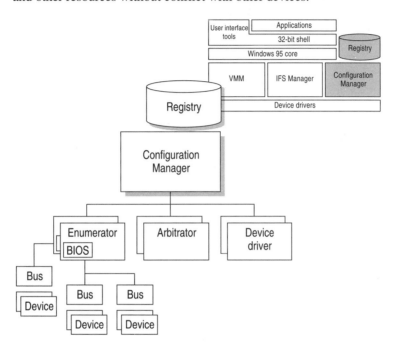

Configuration Manager also helps monitor the computer for changes in the number and type of devices present and manages the reconfiguration of the devices, as needed, when changes take place. As these events occur, Configuration Manager communicates the information to applications.

To perform its role, Configuration Manager (implemented as part of the Virtual Memory Manager, VMM32) calls on the bus enumerators to identify all the devices on their specific buses and their respective resource requirements.

*Bus enumerators* are new drivers that are responsible for creating the Windows 95 hardware tree. A *hardware tree* is the hierarchical representation of all the buses and devices on a computer. Each bus and each device is represented as a *node.* The following is a graphical representation of a hardware tree.

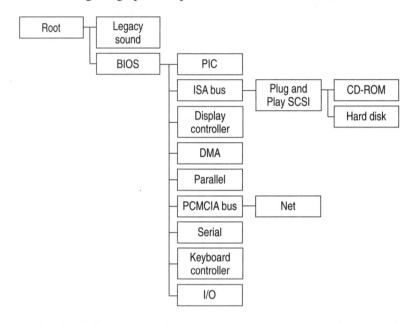

During the device enumeration process, the bus enumerator locates and gathers information from either the device drivers or the BIOS services for that particular device type. For example, the SCSI bus enumerator calls the SCSI drivers to gather information. (Some bus enumerators may instead check the hardware directly.)

For each device, a driver is loaded. When loaded, the driver waits for Configuration Manager to assign specific resources (such as IRQs) to the device. Configuration Manager calls on *resource arbitrators* to allocate resources for each device.

Resource arbitrators resolve conflicts among devices that request identical resource assignments. Windows 95 provides arbitrators for the standard I/O, memory, hardware interrupt, and DMA channel resources. (The arbitrators are separate components, rather than a part of Configuration Manager, to ensure extensibility to new types of resources, such as power allocation or automatic SCSI IDs.)

To complete the configuration process, Configuration Manager informs the device drivers about the device configuration. This process is repeated when the BIOS or one of the other bus enumerators informs Configuration Manager about an event that requires a change to the system configuration, such as the removal or insertion of a Plug and Play-compliant PCMCIA card. For more information about Plug and Play, see Chapter 18, "Introduction to System Configuration."

# Virtual Machine Manager

Just as Configuration Manager provides for all resources needed by each device on the computer, another component, Virtual Machine Manager, provides for resources needed for each application and system process running on the computer. Virtual Machine Manager creates and maintains the virtual machine environments in which applications and system processes run.

A *virtual machine* (VM) is an environment in memory that, from the application's perspective, looks as if it is a separate computer, complete with all of the resources available on the physical computer that an application needs to run. The Virtual Machine Manager provides each application with the system resources it needs. Virtual Machine Manager replaces WIN386.EXE in Windows 3.1.

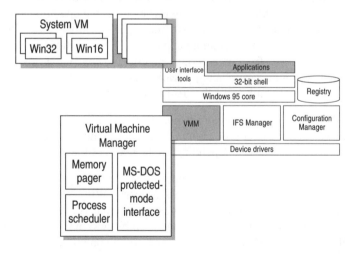

Windows 95 has a single VM called the System VM, in which all system processes run. In addition, all Win32-based and Win16-based applications run in this VM. Each MS-DOS–based application runs in its own VM. (For information on VMs, see "Core System Components" later in this chapter.)

The Virtual Machine Manager is responsible for three key areas of services:

- Process scheduling
- Memory paging
- MS-DOS Mode support for MS-DOS–based applications that must have exclusive access to system resources

The following sections discuss these three areas of service.

# Process Scheduling and Multitasking

The Process Scheduler is the component responsible for providing system resources to the applications and other processes you run, and for scheduling processes to allow multiple applications to run concurrently.

The Process Scheduler also schedules processes in a way that allows multiple applications and other processes to run concurrently. Windows 95 uses two methods for concurrent process scheduling—cooperative multitasking and preemptive multitasking.

With Windows 3.1, applications ran concurrently through a method known as *cooperative multitasking*. Using this method, the operating system required an application to check the message queue periodically and to relinquish control of the system to other running applications. Applications that did not check the message queue frequently would effectively "hog" CPU time and prevent the user from switching to another application. For compatibility reasons, Windows 95 cooperatively multitasks Win16-based applications.

Windows 95 uses *preemptive multitasking* for Win32-based applications. This means that the operating system takes control away from or gives control to another running task, depending on the needs of the system.

Unlike Win16-based applications, Win32-based applications do not need to yield to other running tasks to multitask properly. Win32-based applications can take advantage of *multithreading*, a mechanism that Windows 95 provides to facilitate the ability to run applications concurrently. A Win32-based application running in the system is called a *process* in terms of the operating system. Each process consists of at least a single thread of execution that identifies the code path flow as it is run by the operating system. A *thread* is a unit of code that can get a time slice from the operating system to run concurrently with other units of code, and must be associated with a process. However, a Win32-based application can initiate multiple threads for a given process to enhance the application for the user by improving throughput, enhancing responsiveness, and aiding background processing. Because of the preemptive multitasking nature of Windows 95, threads of execution allow code to be smoothly processed in the background.

A good illustration of this is the Windows 95 shell itself. Although the shell is a Win32-based process, each folder window that opens is a separate thread of execution. As a result, when you initiate a copy operation between two shell folder windows, the operation is performed on the thread of the target window. You can still use the other windows in the shell without interruption, or you can start a different copy in another window.

In another example, a word processing application (a process) can implement multiple threads to enhance operation and simplify interaction with the user. The application can have a separate thread that responds to keys typed on the keyboard by the user to place characters in a document, while another thread performs back-ground operations such as spelling checking or paginating, and while a third thread spools a document to the printer in the background.

---

**Note**   Some Win16-based applications may have provided functionality similar to this; however, because Windows 3.1 didn't provide a mechanism for supporting multithreaded applications, it was up to application vendors to implement their own threading schemes. The use of threads in Windows 95 makes it easy for application vendors to add asynchronous processing of information to their applications.

---

# Memory Paging

Windows 95, similar to Windows NT, uses a demand-paged virtual memory system. This system is based on a flat, linear address space accessed using 32-bit addresses.

Each process is allocated a unique virtual address space of 2 GB. The upper 2 GB is shared, while the lower 2 GB is private to the application. This virtual address space is divided into equal blocks, or *pages*.

*Demand paging* refers to a method by which code and data are moved in pages from physical memory to a temporary paging file on disk. As the information is needed by a process, it is paged back into physical memory.

The Memory Pager maps virtual addresses from the process's address space to physical pages in the computer's memory. In doing so, it hides the physical organization of memory from the process's threads. This ensures that the thread can access its process's memory as needed, but not the memory of other processes. Therefore, as shown in the following illustration, a thread's view of its process's virtual memory (as depicted on the left) is much simpler than the real arrangement of pages in physical memory.

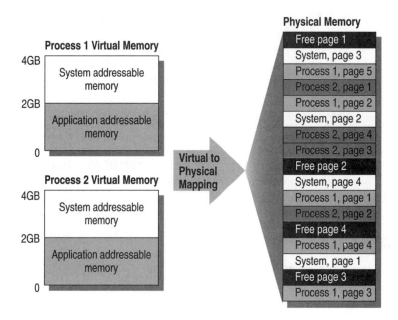

To support a 16-bit operating environment including Windows 3.1 and MS-DOS, the Intel® processor architecture uses a mechanism called a *segment*. Segments reference memory by using a 16-bit segment address, and a 16-bit offset address within the segment. A segment is 64K in size, and both applications and the operating system suffer a performance penalty for accessing information across segments.

Windows 95 addresses this issue by using the 32-bit capabilities of the 80386 (and above) processor architecture to support a flat, linear memory model for 32-bit operating system functionality and Win32-based applications. A *linear addressing model* simplifies the development process for application vendors, and removes the performance penalties imposed by the segmented memory architecture.

With this addressing model, Windows 95 allows full use of the 4 GB of addressable memory space for all 32-bit operating system components and applications. Each 32-bit application can access up to 2 GB of addressable memory space, which is large enough to support even the largest desktop application.

## Support for MS-DOS Mode

While most MS-DOS–based applications run well in Windows 95 and can run concurrently with other Win32-based and Win16-based applications, a small number of MS-DOS–based applications require exclusive access to system resources to run. In this case, it is the Virtual Memory Manager that creates this exclusive operating environment for the application called *MS-DOS Mode*. When an MS-DOS–based application runs in MS-DOS Mode, no other applications or processes are allowed to compete for system resources—all resources are at the exclusive access of the MS-DOS–based application. For related information, see Chapter 22, "Application Support."

## Installable File Systems

Windows 95 features a layered file system architecture that supports multiple file systems, including VFAT and CDFS.

The new file system architecture makes the computer easier to use and improves file and disk I/O performance. Features of the new file system architecture include long filename support and a dynamic system cache for file and network I/O.

Long filename support improves ease of use because users no longer need to reference files by the MS-DOS 8.3 filename structure. Instead, users can specify up to 255 characters to identify their documents. In addition, filenames seem less cryptic and thus easier to read because Windows 95 hides the filename extensions from users.

Windows 95 I/O performance is dramatically improved over Windows 3.1. This is because Windows 95 features 32-bit protected-mode code for reading information from and writing information to the file system, and for reading information from and writing information to the disk device. It also includes 32-bit dynamically sizable caching mechanisms, and a full, 32-bit code path is available from the file system to the disk device.

Windows 95 includes an open file system architecture for future system support. It also provides disk device driver compatibility with Windows NT.

The following figure shows the file system architecture used by Windows 95.

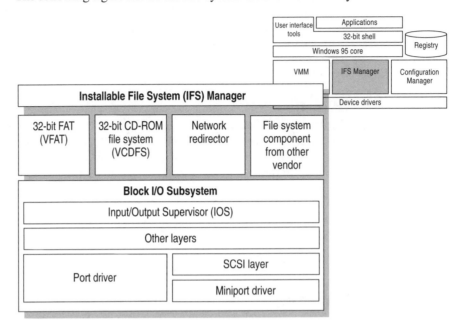

The Windows 95 file system architecture is made up of the following components:

- Installable File System (IFS) Manager. The IFS Manager is responsible for arbitrating access to different file system components.

- File system drivers. The file system driver layer includes access to FAT-based disk devices, CD-ROM file systems, and redirected network device support.

- Block I/O subsystem. The block I/O subsystem is responsible for interacting with the physical disk device.

The following sections describe these components.

# Installable File System Manager

In Windows 95, the key to access of disk and redirected devices is the Installable File System (IFS) Manager. The IFS Manager arbitrates access to file system devices, and other file system device components.

Under MS-DOS and Windows 3.1, INT 21 provided access to the file system to manipulate file information on a disk device. To support redirected disk devices (for example, a network drive or a CD-ROM drive), other system components such as the network redirector would hook the INT 21 function so that it could examine the file system request to determine whether it should handle the file I/O request or let the base file system handle it. Although this mechanism provided the ability to add more device drivers, some add-on components ran improperly and interfered with other installed drivers.

Another problem with the MS-DOS–based file system was the difficulty in loading multiple network redirectors to provide concurrent access to different network types. Windows for Workgroups provided support for running the Microsoft Windows Network redirector at the same time as an additional network redirector such as Novell® NetWare® or Banyan® VINES®; however, support for running more than two network redirectors at the same time was not supported. In Windows 95, the network redirectors are implemented as file systems under IFS Manager, so an unlimited number of 32-bit redirectors can be used.

# File System Drivers

With Windows 3.1, file system drivers were supported by MS-DOS. With Windows 95, file system drivers are Ring 0 components of the operating system. Windows 95 includes support for all of the following file systems (others can be added by other vendors):

- 32-bit FAT (VFAT) driver

- 32-bit CD-ROM file system (CDFS) driver

- 32-bit network redirector for connectivity to Microsoft network servers such as Windows NT Server, along with a 32-bit network redirector to connect to Novell NetWare servers

For information about network redirectors, see Chapter 32, "Windows 95 Network Architecture."

## VFAT File System

The 32-bit VFAT driver provides a protected-mode code path for manipulating the file system stored on a disk. Because it is reentrant and multithreaded, it provides smoother multitasking performance.

The 32-bit VFAT driver interacts with the block I/O subsystem to provide disk access to more device types than are supported by Windows 3.1. Windows 95 also supports mapping to any real-mode disk drivers that might be installed. The combination of 32-bit file access and 32-bit disk access drivers results in significantly improved disk and file I/O performance.

Benefits of the 32-bit file access driver over MS-DOS–based driver solutions include the following:

- Dramatically improved performance and real-mode disk caching software
- No conventional memory used (real-mode SMARTDrive has been replaced)
- Better multitasking when accessing information on disk
- Dynamic cache support

Both MS-DOS and Windows 3.1 used 16-bit real-mode code to manipulate the file allocation table (FAT) and to read to and write from the disk. Being able to manipulate the disk file system from protected mode removes or reduces the need to switch to real mode to write information to the disk through MS-DOS, thus resulting in a performance gain for file I/O access.

The 32-bit VFAT works with a 32-bit, protected-mode cache driver (VCACHE). This driver replaces the 16-bit, real-mode SMARTDrive disk cache software provided with MS-DOS and Windows 3.1. The VCACHE driver features better caching algorithms than SMARTDrive, to cache information read from or written to a disk drive. The VCACHE driver also manages the cache pool for the CD-ROM File System (CDFS) and the 32-bit network redirectors provided with Windows 95.

Another big improvement in VCACHE over SMARTDrive is that the memory pool used for the cache is dynamic and is based on the amount of available free system memory. Users no longer need to allocate a block of memory as a disk cache. The system automatically allocates or deallocates memory used for the cache based on system use.

For example, as you perform a large number of activities on the network, Windows 95 increases the size of the cache. As network activity decreases and more applications are started, Windows 95 decreases the cache size.

## CD-ROM File System

The 32-bit, protected-mode CDFS implemented in Windows 95 provides improved CD-ROM access and performance over the real-mode MSCDEX driver in Windows 3.1. (CDFS conforms to the ISO 9660 standard.) The CDFS driver cache is also dynamic, requiring no configuration or static allocation on the part of the user. For information about the CD-ROM cache, see Chapter 17, "Performance Tuning."

Benefits of the new 32-bit CDFS driver include the following:

- No conventional memory used (real-mode MSCDEX has been replaced)
- Improved performance over MS-DOS – based MSCDEX and real-mode cache
- Better multitasking when accessing CD-ROM information
- Dynamic cache support to provide a better balance between providing memory to run applications versus providing memory to serve as a disk cache

MSCDEX is no longer necessary under Windows 95, and is automatically removed from memory and from AUTOEXEC.BAT by Setup, and the 32-bit CDFS driver is used instead.

# Block I/O Subsystem

The block I/O subsystem in Windows 95 improves upon the 32-bit disk access "FastDisk" device architecture used in Windows 3.1 to enhance performance for the entire file system and provides a broader array of device support.

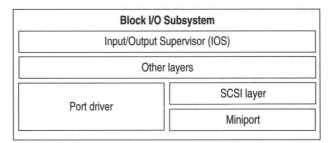

As shown in the preceding diagram, the block I/O subsystem includes the following components.

**Input/Output Supervisor (IOS).**   This component provides services to file systems and drivers. The IOS is responsible for the queuing of file service requests and for routing the requests to the appropriate file system driver. The I/O Supervisor also provides asynchronous notification of file system events to drivers. This component is described further in the following section.

**Port driver.**   This is a monolithic, 32-bit, protected-mode driver that communicates with a specific disk device such as a hard disk controller. This driver is Windows 95-specific and resembles the 32-bit disk access driver used in Windows 3.1 (for example, WDCTRL for Western Digital™-compatible hard disk controllers). In Windows 95, the driver that communicates with IDE or ESDI hard disk controllers and floppy disk controllers is implemented as a port driver. A port driver provides the same functionality as the combination of the SCSI manager and the miniport driver.

**SCSI layer.** This component applies a 32-bit, protected-mode, universal driver model architecture for communicating with SCSI devices. The SCSI layer provides all the high-level functionality common to SCSI and similar devices, and then uses a miniport driver to handle device-specific I/O calls. The SCSI Manager is also part of this system and provides the compatibility support for using Windows NT miniport drivers.

**Miniport driver.** The Windows 95 miniport driver model makes it easier for a hardware disk device vendor to write a device driver. Because the SCSI stub provides the high-level functionality for communicating with SCSI devices, the hardware disk device vendor only needs to create a miniport driver tailored to the vendor's own disk device. The Windows 95 miniport driver is 32-bit protected-mode code, and is binary-compatible with Windows NT miniport drivers. However, older miniport drivers written for Windows NT do not include Plug and Play information and, therefore, will not perform well on Windows 95.

In addition to these other layers, the Block I/O subsystem provides a real-mode mapping layer. This layer provides compatibility with real-mode, MS-DOS–based device drivers for which a protected-mode counterpart does not exist. This layer allows the protected-mode file system to communicate with a real-mode driver as if it were a protected-mode component.

The layers above the Block I/O and the real-mode mapper are protected-mode code, and the real-mode mapper translates file I/O requests from protected mode to real mode, such that the MS-DOS–based device driver can perform the appropriate operation to write or read information to or from the disk device. For example, the real-mode mapper is used when real-mode disk compression software is running and a protected-mode disk compression driver is not available.

---

**Note** Using MS-DOS–based device drivers can be a potential bottleneck because all I/O must be serialized. Also, because all of these VxDs must be page-locked, this increases the working set used by the operating system.

---

## I/O Supervisor and Driver Loading

The I/O Supervisor is a required system VxD that carries out all control and management tasks for the protected-mode file system and block device drivers in Windows 95. The I/O Supervisor loads and initializes protected-mode device drivers and provides services needed for I/O operations.

The I/O Supervisor receives requests from VFAT and CDFS file systems and loads the drivers for accessing local disk devices and drives, including SCSI and IDE. It supports WD1003-compatible drivers, takes control of real-mode drivers, and provides a mapper for real-mode drivers.

The real-mode mapper in the I/O Supervisor provides compatibility with real-mode MS-DOS device drivers for which protected-mode counterparts do not exist. For example, the real-mode mapper goes to work when real-mode disk compression software is running and a protected-mode disk compression driver is not available. This component ensures binary compatibility with existing MS-DOS–based disk device drivers in Windows 95.

The I/O Supervisor was first implemented in Windows 3.x as *BLOCKDEV, and in Windows 95 it also provides *BLOCKDEV services for older 32-bit disk access drivers. New responsibilities for the I/O Supervisor include:

- Registering drivers
- Routing and queuing I/O requests, and sending asynchronous notifications to drivers as needed
- Providing services that drivers can use to allocate memory and complete I/O requests

Windows 95 loads and initializes the I/O Supervisor as specified in a **device=** entry in SYSTEM.INI. The I/O Supervisor is initialized before clients and virtual device drivers such as APIX and *INT13, so clients and virtual device drivers can call services in the I/O Supervisor to register and carry out tasks.

To load and initialize port drivers, miniport drivers, and value-added drivers, the I/O Supervisor requires the files for these drivers to be stored in the SYSTEM\IOSUBSYS directory with the following filename extensions.

| Filename extension | Description |
|---|---|
| PDR | Port drivers, such as SCSIPORT, ESDI_506, and NEC |
| MPD | Miniport drivers |
| 386 or VXD | Value-added drivers, such as the volume tracker and vendor-supplied drivers |

The SYSTEM\IOSUBSYS directory is reserved for device drivers specifically designed to be used with the I/O Supervisor. Other clients or virtual device drivers should be stored in other directories and explicitly loaded using **device=** entries in SYSTEM.INI.

The I/O Supervisor initializes device drivers (as described in the following sections) from the bottom layer upwards, so port drivers are initialized before vendor-supplied drivers, vendor-supplied drivers before type-specific drivers, and so on. Value-added drivers are initialized in groups, layer by layer, with all drivers in one layer initialized before drivers in the next layer. The initialization order within a layer is not defined, so you cannot depend on the drivers in a group being initialized in a specific order or even that the order remains between startup operations.

For Plug and Play detection, the I/O Supervisor loads a specific port or miniport driver only if Configuration Manager requests that the driver be loaded after hardware detection locates an adapter.

# Core System Components

Similar to Windows version 3.1 and Windows for Workgroups version 3.1, Windows 95 includes a core composed of three components—User, Kernel, and graphical device interface (GDI).

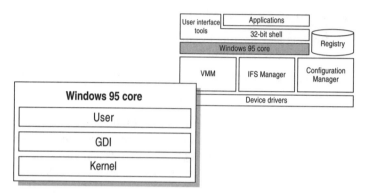

Each of these components includes a pair of DLLs—one 32-bit and one 16-bit—which provide services for the applications you run. Windows 95 is designed to use 32-bit code wherever it significantly improves performance without sacrificing application compatibility. Windows 95 retains existing 16-bit code where it is required to maintain compatibility or where 32-bit code would increase memory requirements without significantly improving performance. All the Windows 95 I/O subsystems (such as networking and file systems) and device drivers are 32-bit, as are all the memory management and scheduling components, including the Kernel and Virtual Memory Manager.

As shown in the following illustration, the lowest-level services provided by the Windows 95 Kernel are implemented as 32-bit code to ensure a high-performance core. Most of the remaining 16-bit code consists of hand-tuned assembly language, delivering performance that rivals some 32-bit code used by other operating systems.

**32-bit** **16-bit**

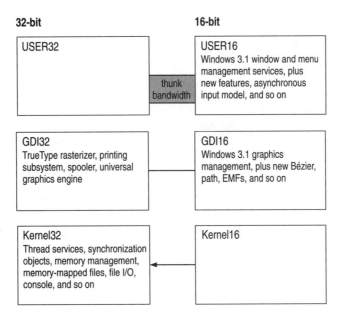

Many functions provided by the GDI—which are mostly complex, CPU-intensive functions—are now rewritten as 32-bit code to improve performance. Much of the window management code in the User components—which are small, fast functions—remains 16-bit, thus retaining application compatibility.

Windows 95 also improves on the MS-DOS and Windows 3.1 environments by implementing many device drivers as 32-bit, protected-mode code. Virtual device drivers in Windows 95 assume the functionality provided by many real-mode MS-DOS–based device drivers, eliminating the need to load them in MS-DOS. This results in a minimal conventional memory footprint, improved performance, and improved reliability and stability of the system over real-mode device drivers.

The following sections describe the services provided by these core components.

# User

The User component manages input from the keyboard, mouse, and other input devices and output to the user interface (windows, icons, menus, and so on). It also manages interaction with the sound driver, timer, and communications ports.

Windows 95 uses an asynchronous input model for all input to the system and applications. As the various input devices generate interrupts, the interrupt handler converts these interrupts to messages and sends the messages to a raw input thread area, which in turn passes each message to the appropriate message queue. Although each Win32-based thread can have its own message queue, all Win16-based applications share a common message queue.

# Kernel

The Kernel provides base operating system functionality including file I/O services, virtual memory management, and task scheduling. When a user wants to start an application, the Kernel loads the EXE and DLL files for the application.

Exception handling is another service of the Kernel. *Exceptions* are events that occur as a program runs and that require software outside of the normal flow of control to be run. For example, if an application generates an exception, the Kernel is able to communicate that exception to the application to perform the necessary functions to resolve the problem.

The Kernel also allocates virtual memory, resolves import references, and supports demand paging for the application. As the application runs, the Kernel schedules and runs threads of each process owned by an application.

The Kernel provides services to both 16-bit and 32-bit applications by using a translation process called *thunking* to map between 16-bit and 32-bit formats. Thunking converts a 16-bit value to its 32-bit equivalent.

## Virtual Memory Management

*Virtual memory* is a term that refers to the fact that the operating system can actually allocate more memory than the computer physically contains. Each process is allocated a unique virtual address space, which is a set of addresses available for the process's threads to use. This virtual address space appears to be 4 GB in size—2 GB reserved for program storage and 2 GB reserved for system storage.

The following diagram illustrates where Windows 95 system components and applications reside in virtual memory.

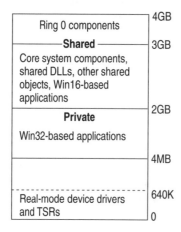

From top to bottom, here's where system and application components reside in virtual memory:

- All Ring 0 components reside in the address space above 3 GB.

- The Windows 95 core components and shared DLLs reside in the shared address space between 2 GB and 3 GB. This makes them available to all applications.

- Win32-based applications reside between 4 MB and 2 GB. Each Win32-based application has its own address space, which means that other programs cannot corrupt or otherwise hinder the application, or vice versa.

## Windows 95 Swap File

The Windows 95 virtual memory swap file implementation addresses the problems and limitations imposed in Windows 3.1.

Under Windows 3.1, users had to decide whether to use a temporary swap file or a permanent swap file, how much memory to allocate to the swap file, and whether to use 32-bit disk access to access the swap file. Users benefited from a temporary swap file in that the swap file did not need to be contiguous; Windows allocated space on the hard disk when the user started Windows, and freed up the space when the user exited Windows. A permanent swap file provided better performance; however, it required a contiguous block of space on a physical hard disk, and was static, so it did not free up space when the user exited Windows.

The swap file implementation in Windows 95 simplifies the configuration task for the user and combines the best of temporary and permanent swap files, due to improved virtual memory algorithms and access methods. The swap file in Windows 95 is dynamic; it can shrink or grow, based on the operations that are performed on the system. The swap file can also occupy a fragmented region of the hard disk with no substantial performance penalty. The swap file can also reside on a compressed volume.

You can still adjust the parameters used for defining the swap file in Windows 95; however, the need to do this is reduced by using system defaults. For information about swap file configuration options, see Chapter 17, "Performance Tuning."

# Graphical Device Interface

The Graphical Device Interface (GDI) is the graphical system that manages what appears on the screen. It also provides graphics support for printers and other output devices. It draws graphic primitives, manipulates bitmaps, and interacts with device-independent graphics drivers, including those for display and printer output device drivers.

## Graphics Subsystem

The graphics subsystem provides graphics support for input and output devices.

To gain reliability and better performance, Microsoft developed a new 32-bit graphics engine (also known as the Device Independent Bitmaps, or DIB, engine). This engine directly controls graphics output to the screen, which results in more reliable system performance. It also provides a set of optimized generic drawing functions for monochrome, 16-color, 16-bit high color, 256-color, and 24-bit true color graphic devices, and supports Bézier curves and paths.

The graphics subsystem supports Image Color Matching for better color-matching between display and color output devices. With Image Color Matching in Windows 95, users can see a better match between the colors displayed on the screen and the colors printed on a color printing device. Image Color Matching is implemented as a service within Windows 95. Applications can use the corresponding APIs and DLL to take advantage of Image Color Matching features.

As with other parts of the operating system, the Windows 95 graphics subsystem includes a universal driver/mini-driver model. As illustrated in the following, display drivers for Windows 3.1 included hardware-specific instructions, in addition to general instructions for the operating system. Now, all instructions about drawing to the screen or output device are included in the universal display driver. Mini-drivers for Windows 95 define only hardware-specific instructions. Mini-drivers are available for most leading Super VGA adapters and graphics accelerators, including S3, ATI, Tseng, Paradise, Western Digital, and Cirrus Logic.

**Old-style monolithic 16-bit driver**

Instructions for screen drawing and graphics functions

Hardware specifics

**Windows 95 universal display driver**

Instructions for screen drawing and graphics functions

**32-bit mini-driver**

Hardware specifics

**Tip**  Problems can result when Windows 95 assumes that a display adapter can support certain functionality that, in fact, it cannot. If this occurs, the side effects might be anything from small display irregularities to system lockup.

To determine whether any performance problems might be related to the display adapter, you can progressively disable enhanced display functionality using the System option in Control Panel. For information, see Chapter 17, "Performance Tuning."

## Printing Subsystem

The 32-bit Windows 95 printing subsystem improves performance through smoother background printing and faster return-to-application time. The Windows 95 spooler passes data to the printer as the printer is ready to receive more information, by using background thread processing.

Windows 95 spools enhanced metafile (EMF) format files, rather than raw printer data, to ensure quick return-to-application time (as much as two times faster than with Windows 3.1). When spooled, the EMF information is interpreted in the background, and the output is sent to the printer.

The printing subsystem supports Point and Print. When users browse the network to choose the printers they want to use, Windows 95 automatically installs the appropriate printer driver from the Windows 95 or Windows NT server.

Another feature of the Windows 95 printing subsystem is deferred printing. If no printing device is available, the user can still "print" the job. Windows 95 generates the print job, then saves it for output to the print device when one is available. Then, when the user docks the portable computer after returning to the office, the print job that was "printed" begins generating pages at the print device.

The printing subsystem also provides system-level support of bidirectional communication protocols for printers adhering to the Extended Communication Port (ECP) printer communication standard, developed by Microsoft and Hewlett-Packard. This capability allows printers to send unsolicited messages to Windows 95 and to applications. For example, the printer might send an "out of paper" or "printer offline" message. Bidirectional communication enables much more detailed status reporting on a wider variety of information, such as information about a low toner condition, details about a paper jam, instructions related to maintenance needs, and so on.

# User Interface

Windows 95 features a 32-bit user interface shell, based on Windows Explorer. This shell contains several desktop tools, including Network Neighborhood. As shown in the following figure, these tools run at the same level as other Win32-based, Win16-based, and MS-DOS–based applications.

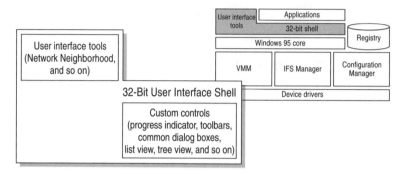

All applications and tools can take advantage of the common controls offered by the shell, such as common dialog boxes, tree views, and list views.

# Application Support

Windows 95 supports Win32-based, Win16-based, and MS-DOS–based applications.

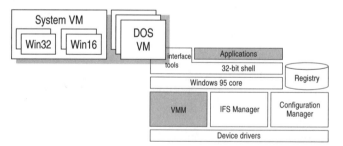

As illustrated here, Win32-based and Win16-based applications run in the System VM. Win32-based applications each run in a separate address space, while Win16-based applications run together in a shared address space. Each MS-DOS–based application runs in its own VM.

For details about using Win32-based, Win16-based, and MS-DOS–based applications in Windows 95, see Chapter 22, "Application Support." For more information about VMs, see "Virtual Machine Manager" earlier in this chapter.

CHAPTER 32

# Windows 95 Network Architecture

This chapter presents information about the architecture for the networking components in Windows 95.

**In This Chapter**

Windows 95 Network Architecture Overview    992
    OSI Reference Model and Windows 95 Architecture    992
    Redirectors and IFS Manager    994
Multiple Network Support    995
    Win32 WinNet Interface for Applications    996
    Multiple Provider Router and Service Provider Interface    997
    Network Providers    997
    WinNet16 Interface    1001
    Multiple Network Example    1001
NDIS Overview    1002
    Support for NDIS 2 Protocols    1003
    Support for NDIS Network Adapters    1003
Architecture for Network Protocols    1004
    Architecture for IPX/SPX-Compatible Protocol    1004
    Architecture for NetBEUI Protocol    1005
    Architecture for Microsoft TCP/IP Protocol    1005
Architecture for Clients, Peer Servers, and IPC    1006
    Client for Microsoft Networks Architecture    1006
    Client for NetWare Networks Architecture    1008
    Architecture for Peer Resource Sharing    1008
    IPC and Windows 95    1010

# Windows 95 Network Architecture Overview

Windows 95 provides multiple, simultaneous connections to a variety of networks (Windows NT, Novell® NetWare®, and others) and a variety of resources (files, programs, printers, host systems, and mail systems) over most popular media (Ethernet, token ring, X.25, ISDN) from almost any location.

Windows 95 networking capabilities are implemented using a high-performance, reliable, and open architecture based on the Windows Open Services Architecture (WOSA) specification. This approach provides users with a consistent interface to different services on the front end, while giving system administrators the flexibility to mix and match multiple services on the back end.

# OSI Reference Model and Windows 95 Architecture

The modular networking architecture of Windows 95 is based on two industry standard models for a layered networking architecture, namely the International Organization for Standardization (ISO) model for computer networking, called the Open Systems Interconnect (OSI) Reference Model, and the Institute of Electrical and Electronic Engineers (IEEE) 802 model. Windows NT and Windows for Workgroups are also designed according to these standard models. The ISO OSI and IEEE 802 models define a modular approach to networking, with each layer responsible for some discrete aspect of the networking process.

The OSI model describes the flow of data in a network, from the lowest layer (the physical connections) up to the layer containing the user's applications. Data going to and from the network is passed layer to layer. Each layer is able to communicate with the layer immediately above it and the layer immediately below it. This way, each layer is written as an efficient, streamlined software component. When a layer receives a packet of information, it checks the destination address, and if its own address is not there, it passes the packet to the next layer.

When two computers communicate on a network, the software at each layer on one computer assumes it is communicating with the same layer on the other computer. For example, the Transport layer of one computer communicates with the Transport layer on the other computer. The Transport layer on the first computer has no regard for how the communication actually passes through the lower layers of the first computer, across the physical media, and then up through the lower layers of the second computer.

The OSI Reference Model includes seven layers:

| 7. Application |
| 6. Presentation |
| 5. Session |
| 4. Transport |
| 3. Network |
| 2. Data Link |
| 1. Physical |

- The *Application layer* represents the level at which applications access network services. This layer represents the services that directly support applications such as software for file transfers, database access, and electronic mail.

- The *Presentation layer* translates data from the Application layer into an intermediary format. This layer also manages security issues by providing services such as data encryption, and compresses data so that fewer bits need to be transferred on the network.

- The *Session layer* allows two applications on different computers to establish, use, and end a session. This layer establishes dialog control between the two computers in a session, regulating which side transmits, plus when and how long it transmits.

- The *Transport layer* handles error recognition and recovery. It also repackages long messages when necessary into small packets for transmission and, at the receiving end, rebuilds packets into the original message. The receiving Transport layer also sends receipt acknowledgments.

- The *Network layer* addresses messages and translates logical addresses and names into physical addresses. It also determines the route from the source to the destination computer and manages traffic problems, such as switching, routing, and controlling the congestion of data packets.

- The *Data Link layer* packages raw bits from the Physical layer into frames (logical, structured packets for data). This layer is responsible for transferring frames from one computer to another, without errors. After sending a frame, it waits for an acknowledgment from the receiving computer.

- The *Physical layer* transmits bits from one computer to another and regulates the transmission of a stream of bits over a physical medium. This layer defines how the cable is attached to the network adapter and what transmission technique is used to send data over the cable.

The following diagram shows the layered components that make up the Windows 95 networking model.

Layers in the
Windows 95
networking model

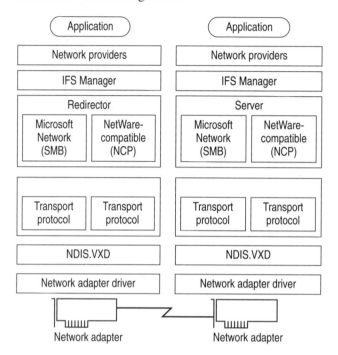

The following sections describe these elements of the Windows 95 network architecture, beginning with redirectors. Network providers are described in "Multiple Network Support" later in this chapter.

# Redirectors and IFS Manager

A network redirector provides mechanisms to locate, open, read, write, and delete files and submit print jobs. It also makes available application services such as named pipes and mailslots. When an application needs to send or receive data from a remote device, it sends a call to the redirector. The redirector provides the functionality of the Application and Presentation layers of the OSI model.

The redirectors are included in the Windows 95 network client software as the following file system drivers:

- In Client for Microsoft Networks (VREDIR.VXD), the redirector supports all networks based on Microsoft networking, which use the Server Message Block (SMB) file sharing protocol.

- In Microsoft Client for NetWare Networks (NWREDIR.VXD), the redirector supports NetWare networking products, which use the NetWare Core Protocol (NCP) file sharing protocol.

Windows 95 also supports network redirectors from other network vendors.

Because each protected-mode redirector is implemented in Windows 95 as a file system driver, the redirector is managed by Installable File System (IFS) Manager. The redirector works with IFS Manager to map local names into network devices and decides whether the application needs access to a local or remote device. IFS Manager controls file I/O transfers for all the installable file systems in Windows 95. For more information about IFS Manager, see Chapter 31, "Windows 95 Architecture."

Client for Microsoft Networks (the redirector for Microsoft networks) formats an application's request into data packet SMBs and submits the packet to the protocol. Microsoft Client for NetWare Networks (the NetWare redirector) formats requests into NCP packets. The data packet is passed by the protocol to the adapter driver.

The Windows 95 server side at this layer of the networking model supports peer resource sharing. Windows 95 provides two server services for peer networking:

- File and Printer Sharing for Microsoft Networks (the Windows 95 SMB-based server, VSERVER.VXD), which supports resource sharing among all computers on the network that use the SMB file sharing protocol.

- File and Printer Sharing for NetWare Networks (the Windows 95 NCP-based server, NWSERVER.VXD), which supports resource sharing among all computers on the network that use the NCP file sharing protocol.

# Multiple Network Support

The Windows 95 modular network provider interface, as described in this section, supports concurrent communication with several different networks. For example, a computer can have connections to computers running Windows 95 peer resource-sharing services, to servers for Windows NT and NetWare networks, and to the Internet, all at the same time.

In addition to the Windows 95 network client and peer sharing components, Windows 95 includes built-in support for the following network clients from other vendors:

- Artisoft® LANtastic® version 5.0 and later
- Banyan® VINES® version 5.52 and later
- DEC™ PATHWORKS™ (installed as a protocol)
- Novell® NetWare® version 3.11 and later
- SunSoft™ PC-NFS® version 5.0 and later

Most of these network clients can be installed along with protected-mode Windows 95 networking components. Windows 95 does not include the supporting files for these networks; you must obtain them from the network vendor. For information about these network clients, see Chapter 10, "Windows 95 on Other Networks."

Multiple network support in Windows 95 consists of these components, as described in the following sections:

- Win32 WinNet API

- Multiple provider router and service provider interface

- Network providers (including the WinNet16 interface)

Components of multiple network support in Windows 95

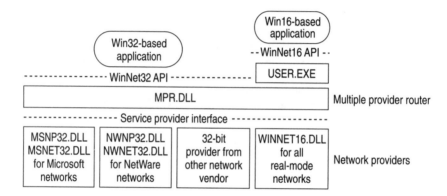

# Win32 WinNet Interface for Applications

The Win32 WinNet interface in Windows 95 provides an API that software developers can use to create single versions of applications that run unmodified on different networks. The Win32 WinNet interface is the successor to the WinNet16 interface introduced in Windows 3.0 and enhanced in Windows 3.1.

The expanded WinNet API set includes the following:

- Support for the Win32 WinNet APIs as defined in Windows NT. This set of functions and the other Win32 APIs provide all the commonly used capabilities required by applications.

- Support for the Win32 WinNet APIs for browsing network resources (directories, printers, and other resources). This includes consistent handling of authentication requirements across multiple networks and support for the NetWare server security model.

- Backward compatibility with Windows for Workgroups 3.11 and support for networks that use a WinNet16 network driver.

# Multiple Provider Router and Service Provider Interface

The multiple provider router in Windows 95 exports the Win32 WinNet APIs to applications. It provides seamless access to network services and resources, and it supports a way to access a single WinNet16 network driver. It routes incoming network requests to the appropriate network provider, using the same interface whether one or more network providers are installed.

Features common to all networks are implemented once in the multiple provider router, which reduces the code base for each network provider and ensures common behavior among networks. For example, network providers do not implement persistent connections—this feature is implemented in the multiple provider router and is entirely transparent to a network provider.

Windows 95 uses an open, modular service provider interface (SPI) to allow multiple 32-bit network providers to be installed in Windows 95 simultaneously. The service provider interface is a single, well-defined set of functions used by Windows 95 to request network services to browse servers, connect to and disconnect from servers, and so on. The multiple provider router communicates with the network providers using the service provider interface.

The service provider interface provides the needed network services to honor a Windows 95 request for network-specific services. This model is similar to the Windows 95 design for various device driver interfaces: a well-defined set of interfaces used by the operating system, with services provided by a device driver (often written by another vendor) to honor requests. These requests are then passed to the network providers.

The service provider interface enables Microsoft or other network providers to integrate varied network services seamlessly into Windows 95. The service provider interface ensures that all supported networks are identically accessed and managed through Network Neighborhood and other user interface components.

# Network Providers

Windows 95 uses an open, modular network provider interface to allow multiple network support simultaneously. Key benefits of the network provider interface architecture are the following:

- An open interface allowing any network vendor to supply tightly integrated support for Windows 95.
- Identical access to and management of network resources and components through the Windows 95 user interface, including Network Neighborhood and the Network option in Control Panel.

The network provider API calls are used by applications to request network services. Windows 95 passes a network provider call to the appropriate network provider, which then supplies the requested network service.

The network provider is a network-specific driver that implements the service provider interface call from the multiple provider router. The functions provided include authenticating users when they access a network server, managing passwords, adding or removing server connections, and browsing network resources.

Windows 95 includes the following network providers:

- MSNP32.DLL for Microsoft networks
- NWNP32.DLL for NetWare networks
- WINNET16.DLL to support a single 16-bit network provider that uses WinNet16 APIs

Windows 95 also supports any number of other 32-bit network providers. Such network providers must be supplied by other network vendors.

The Windows 95 system logon is an example of a network service provided by the network provider interface. Each network provider can provide a unique logon dialog box to suit the needs of its network server security model. After the logon is validated by the requested server, this is passed back to Windows 95, which can then use this password to unlock any network resource linked to the logon validation. In this way, Windows 95 can accommodate the various ways that network servers provide their services, yet still offer a consistent user interface.

The following summarizes the internal processes when, for example, a user double-clicks the Entire Network icon in Network Neighborhood:

1. The Windows 95 user interface generates a Win32-based network API call to enumerate servers and resources on the network.

2. The multiple provider router receives the API call and submits a service provider interface call to all the available network providers.

3. Each network provider browses its individual networks and returns the list to Windows 95, which displays all the networks and their hierarchies in the Entire Network window.

Because of the network provider support in Windows 95, users can specify server name strings in a drive connection dialog box using the syntax to which they are accustomed. A network provider knows how to correctly interpret the syntax of its own server name strings. The server name string is the syntax used by a particular network operating system to specify a shared disk resource. Microsoft network-compatible networks use the UNC format (\\*server_name*\*share_name*).

However, because the network provider knows how to interpret server name strings, users who are accustomed to using the NetWare server syntax (*server_name/volume_name:directory_name*) can type such server names wherever required in Windows 95 to access NetWare server resources. The Windows 95 user interface and the **net** command also support UNC names for connecting to NetWare resources.

## Network Provider for NetWare Networks

The network provider that supports NetWare networks (NWNP32.DLL and its support library, NWNET32.DLL) provides access to NCP-based NetWare network resources using Windows Explorer, Network Neighborhood, and Control Panel, and other Windows-based applications.

Basic architecture for network provider for the NetWare networks

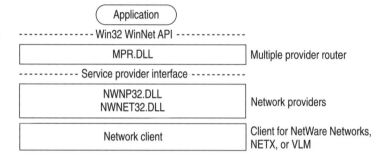

The network provider supports these functions on NetWare networks:

- Browsing NetWare networks. Bindery-based NetWare networks (versions 2.15 and above, 3.x, and 4.x with bindery emulation) use a Server-Volume-Directory hierarchy.

- Logging on to and off from a NetWare network, providing dialog boxes for network logon, and performing attachments to bindery-based servers.

- Adding and removing connections, allowing remote drive and printer connections using the NetWare format (*server/volume*:) and the UNC connections to NCP-based network resources (mapped drive or printer port, and \\*server\share*).

## Network Provider for Microsoft Networks

The network provider that supports Microsoft networks (MSNP32.DLL) provides access to SMB-based Microsoft network resources using the Windows 95 user interface, such as Windows Explorer, Network Neighborhood, and Control Panel, and other Windows-based applications.

MSNP32.DLL provides the Microsoft network-specific dialog boxes (such as the Windows NT domain logon dialog box) and code to resolve a service provider interface call from the multiple provider router to a call to Client for Microsoft Networks.

Windows 95 architecture for the network provider for Microsoft networks

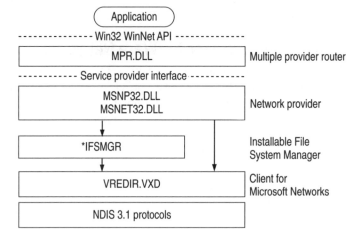

Notice that there are two arrows, one going through IFS Manager and one going directly to Client for Microsoft Networks.

- When a network request is for a generic function such as adding a connection, the call is submitted to the IFS Interface.

- When a network request is specific to a redirector, such as logging on or browsing a server, the call is sent to Client for Microsoft Networks.

The network provider supports these functions for Microsoft networking:

- Browsing Microsoft networks.

- Logging on to and off from a Windows NT or LAN Manager domain. The Microsoft network provider provides authentication services for validation by a domain controller, plus the ability to change the domain password using the Passwords option in the Windows 95 Control Panel.

- Adding or removing connections. The Microsoft network provider allows mapped drive and printer connections plus UNC connections to SMB-based network resources.

# WinNet16 Interface

The WinNet16 interface is the earlier set of network-independent APIs introduced with Windows 3.0 and enhanced in Windows 3.1. WinNet16 provides simple functionality such as connecting to a drive letter or redirecting a printer port to a network printer. Windows 95 provides support for using a single WinNet16 driver.

If a network vendor provides a WinNet16 network driver developed for Windows 3.1 and has not written a 32-bit network provider and file system driver for Windows 95, using the WinNet16 interface and WINNET16.DLL is the only way to support that network in Windows 95. The WinNet16 driver that currently works with Windows 3.1 can be used without modification under Windows 95, using the WINNET16.DLL.

If Windows 95 Setup detects a Windows 3.x installation that uses a WinNet16 network driver and there is no 32-bit network provider available, Windows 95 Setup keeps the 16-bit network driver in place and provides network functionality with the 16-bit network driver installed as the primary network.

# Multiple Network Example

In the following example, the user has installed two Windows 95 network clients (Client for Microsoft Networks and Client for NetWare Networks) and also has installed Banyan VINES support using a WinNet16 driver.

Banyan VINES uses the StreetTalk™ syntax (*file service@group@organization*) to specify server names. In trying to resolve the request to connect to Docs@Marketing@Corp from a network drive connection dialog box in Windows 95, the multiple provider router submits the request to all installed network providers. WINNET16.DLL receives the call and passes it on to VINES.DRV, which submits the drive connection request to the Banyan real-mode networking software through VVINESD.386.

This example shows a network drive connection request with multiple networks installed.

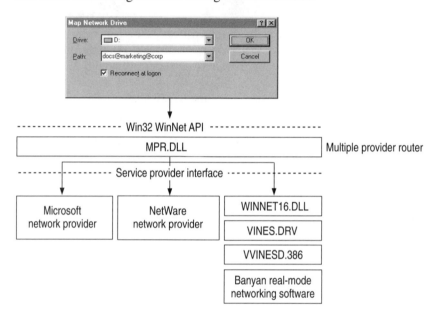

## NDIS Overview

Windows 95 supports the Network Device Interface Specification (NDIS) 2.x and NDIS 3.1 protocol drivers. This section provides some technical background information about NDIS support in Windows 95.

# Support for NDIS 2 Protocols

An NDIS 2.x protocol driver must use an NDIS 2.x network adapter driver. Both protocol drivers and network adapter drivers must load and bind in real mode before launching Windows 95.

Windows 95 architecture for NDIS 2 protocols

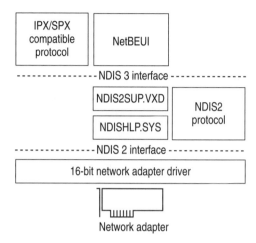

# Support for NDIS Network Adapters

For NDIS 3.1 adapter mini-drivers, the mini-driver divides the existing NDIS media access control (MAC) layer into two halves and implements only the half specific to the network adapter. These include specific details such as establishing communications with the adapter, turning on and off electrical isolation for Plug and Play, providing media detection, and enabling any value-added features the adapter may contain. The mini-driver wrapper implements the other half of the MAC functionality that remains common to all NDIS drivers. In earlier releases of NDIS, each adapter driver carried all this redundant code, so mini-drivers are faster and are roughly 40 percent smaller than existing NDIS 3.x network adapter drivers.

Windows 95 architecture for NDIS 3.1 protocols

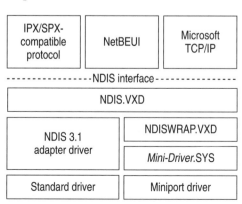

# Architecture for Network Protocols

Windows 95 includes support for IPX/SPX-compatible protocols and NetBEUI and TCP/IP. The following sections describe how support for each type of protocol is implemented in Windows 95.

## Architecture for IPX/SPX-Compatible Protocol

The Microsoft IPX/SPX-compatible protocol uses the NWNBLINK.VXD module to support NetBIOS over IPX and to support the NetBIOS programming interface.

Windows 95 architecture for IPX/SPX-compatible protocol

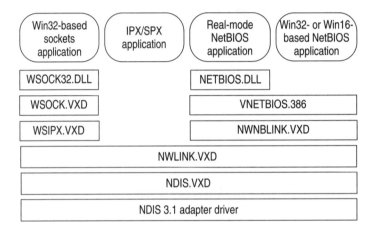

The Microsoft IPX/SPX-compatible protocol is NDIS 3.1-compliant, allowing computers running Windows 95 to communicate over a routable IPX-compatible protocol. This protocol can use Novell NetWare servers configured as routers (and other IPX routers) to transfer its packets across LANs to access resources on other computers running Windows 95.

# Architecture for NetBEUI Protocol

The NetBEUI module, NETBEUI.VXD, implements the NetBIOS framing protocol.

Windows 95
architecture for
NetBEUI protocol

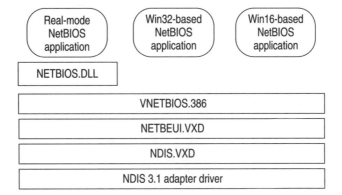

# Architecture for Microsoft TCP/IP Protocol

TCP/IP is a popular routable protocol for wide-area networks. The TCP/IP module, VTCP.VXD, is accessible through the Windows Sockets interface or through the NetBIOS interface. For information about Windows Sockets and interprocess communication mechanisms, see "NetBIOS" later in this chapter.

Windows 95
architecture for
Microsoft TCP/IP

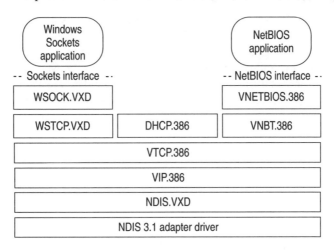

# Architecture for Clients, Peer Servers, and IPC

You can install either or both of the 32-bit, protected-mode networking clients, Client for NetWare Networks and Client for Microsoft Networks. The following sections describe the architecture for these two clients and the related peer servers, plus information about the support for interprocess communications.

Architecture for Client
for NetWare Networks
with Client for
Microsoft Networks

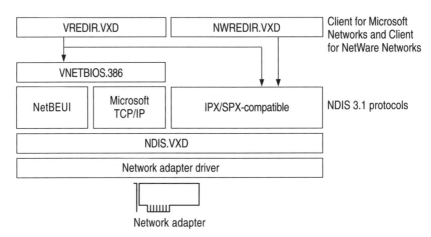

# Client for Microsoft Networks Architecture

Windows 95 provides a 32-bit protected mode file system driver to support all Microsoft networking products that use the SMB file sharing protocol. This includes LAN Manager, Windows NT, Windows for Workgroups 3.x, Workgroup Add-on for MS-DOS, and Windows 95. Network products from other vendors using the Microsoft network standard are also supported, such as LAN Manager, IBM® LAN Server, and 3Com® 3+Open®.

Windows 95
architecture for
Microsoft networking

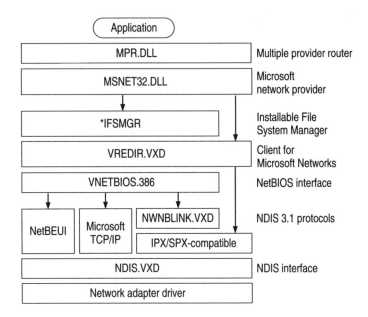

Client for Microsoft Networks supports connectivity over any NDIS protocol
that supports a NetBIOS interface and is accessible through VNETBIOS.386.
The protected-mode protocols provided with Windows 95 that support a NetBIOS
interface are the following:

- NetBEUI using NETBEUI.VXD

- NetBIOS over TCP/IP using VNBT.VXD and the TCP/IP components,
  VTCP.VXD and VIP.VXD

- NetBIOS over IPX/SPX using NWNBLINK.VXD and NWLINK3.VXD

Client for Microsoft Networks also supports connectivity over IPX/SPX using
NWLINK.VXD without the NetBIOS interface.

# Client for NetWare Networks Architecture

You can use Client for NetWare Networks in an environment where all that is needed is a 32-bit client to connect to existing NetWare servers (for example, if there is no need for SMB-based peer resource sharing services).

Architecture for Client
for NetWare Networks
as the sole client

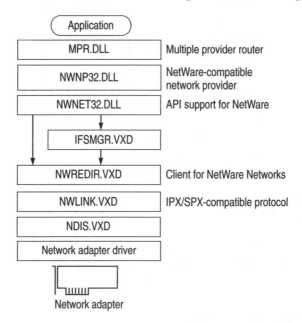

For details about the architecture for Windows 95 with Novell-supplied network clients, see Chapter 9, "Windows 95 on NetWare Networks."

# Architecture for Peer Resource Sharing

Windows 95 includes components to support file and printer sharing on Microsoft networks and NetWare networks.

When File and Printer Sharing for Microsoft Networks is installed, the Windows 95 SMB server (VSERVER.VXD) is added to the computer's configuration. This component supports all Microsoft networking products that use the SMB file-sharing protocol. The following illustration shows the basic supporting files for File and Printer Sharing for Microsoft Networks in the Windows 95 networking architecture.

Architecture for File
and Printer Sharing
for Microsoft Networks

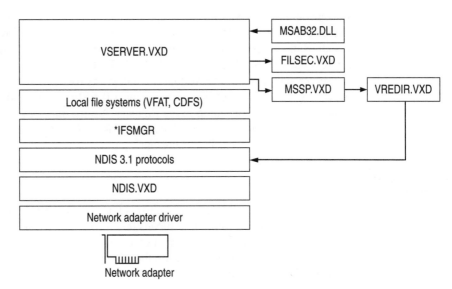

When File and Printer Sharing for NetWare Networks is installed, the
Windows 95 NCP server (NWSERVER.VXD) is added to the computer's
configuration. Client for NetWare Networks is used to get NetWare server
connection information and to enable user-level security based on a NetWare
server's user accounts. The following illustration shows the supporting files for
File and Printer Sharing for NetWare Networks in the Windows 95 networking
architecture.

Architecture for File
and Printer Sharing
for NetWare Networks

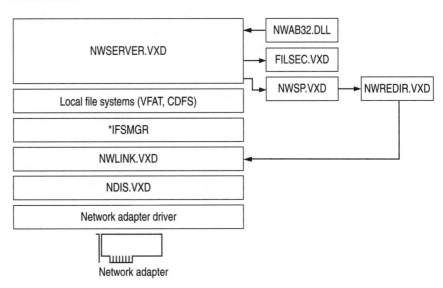

For File and Printer Sharing services with user-level security, the security provider (MSSP.VXD or NWSP.VXD) assists in validating user access when sharing a resource and in retrieving a user list when administrating the server. The network address book (MSAB32.DLL or NWAB32.DLL) translates the account lists from the server and provides the Add Users dialog box for selecting which users get access rights. The file security component (FILESEC.VXD) provides access control based on information in the Registry. Notice that these same security components support features such as remote Registry access even when File and Printer Sharing services are not present.

# IPC and Windows 95

Windows 95 includes several mechanisms that support distributed computing. Typically, distributed computing means that a computing task is divided into two parts. The first part runs on the client computer and requires minimal resources. The other part of the process runs on the server and requires large amounts of data, number crunching, or specialized hardware.

Another type of distributed computing spreads the work among multiple computers. For example, one computer can work on a complex math problem that would take a month to solve. But with distributed computing, 50 computers could work on the same math problem simultaneously and solve it in less than a day.

In both cases, a connection between computers at a process-to-process level allows data to flow in both directions. Windows 95 includes the following interprocess communication (IPC) mechanisms to support distributed computing: Windows Sockets, Remote Procedure Calls (RPC), NetBIOS, named pipes, and mailslots. The following sections provide details about these IPC implementations in Windows 95.

## Windows Sockets

Windows Sockets is a Windows implementation of the widely used U.C. Berkeley Sockets API, the *de facto* standard for accessing datagram and session services over TCP/IP. Non-NetBIOS applications must be written to the Sockets interface to access Microsoft TCP/IP protocols. Applications written to the Sockets interface include FTP and SNMP. In Windows 95, sockets support is also extended to IPX/SPX.

Windows Sockets in Windows 95 is a protocol-independent networking API tailored for use by programmers using the Windows family of products. Windows Sockets is a public specification that aims to do the following:

- Provide a familiar networking API to programmers using Windows or UNIX
- Offer binary compatibility between heterogeneous Windows-based TCP/IP stack and utility vendors
- Support both connection-oriented and connectionless protocols

Sockets provide reduced overhead when compared with a NetBIOS protocol. Non-NetBIOS built-in protocols such as TCP/IP and IPX/SPX require a NetBIOS interface and mapping layer. This extra NetBIOS software adds processing time and also adds a header to the data frame sent on the wire. For example, when the NetBIOS interface is used over TCP/IP, a NetBIOS header is added to the frame before the TCP and IP headers. Workstations running only TCP/IP cannot see this frame. However, when sockets are used, the frame is sent using TCP/IP without the addition of a NetBIOS header.

In TCP/IP, the internetwork address is the IP address of the workstation and the software process address is the port number. Source and destination IP address and port numbers are fields in the TCP/IP packet structure. In IPX/SPX, the internetwork address is the combination of the IPX network ID and the media access control (MAC) address of the network adapter, and the software process address is the IPX Socket number. Source network, destination network, node, and socket numbers are fields in the IPX/SPX packet structure.

**Note**  IPX Sockets are not the same as Windows Sockets.

For a bidirectional path, a Windows Sockets application specifies the following, depending on the protocol.

| Protocol | Source and destination socket identifiers |
|---|---|
| TCP/IP bidirectional path | IP address and port number of the source |
| IPX/SPX bidirectional path | Network ID, MAC address of the network adapter, IPX socket number |

The following table describes the supporting files for 16-bit and 32-bit Windows Sockets over TCP/IP and 32-bit Windows Sockets over IPX/SPX.

**Windows Sockets Supporting Files**

| File | Description | Comments |
| --- | --- | --- |
| winsock.dll | 16-bit Windows Sockets | Provides backward compatibility with existing 16-bit TCP/IP Windows Sockets applications such as **ping** |
| wsock.vxd | Virtualized Windows Sockets | Supports 16-bit Windows Sockets and 32-bit TCP/IP and IPX/SPX Windows Sockets |
| wstcp.vxd | Windows Sockets over TCP/IP[1] | Supports 16-bit Windows Sockets and 32-bit TCP/IP Windows Sockets |
| wsock32.dll | 32-bit Windows Socket | Supports 32-bit TCP/IP Windows Socket applications, such as **telnet**, and 32-bit IPX/SPX Windows Socket applications |
| wsipx.vxd | Windows Sockets over IPX/SPX[2] | Supports 32-bit IPX/SPX Windows Sockets |

[1]  Windows Sockets over TCP/IP are STREAMS-based over TCP and datagram-based over UDP.

[2]  Windows Sockets over IPX/SPX are STREAMS-based over SPX and datagram-based over IPX.

Popular programs such as **ftp** or **telnet** use Windows Sockets. If you are interested in developing a Windows Sockets 1.1 application, specifications for Windows Sockets are available on the Internet from ftp.microsoft.com, on CompuServe® in the MSL library, and in the *Microsoft Win32 Software Development Kit for Windows 95 and Windows NT*.

# RPC

The Microsoft RPC facility is compatible with the Open Software Foundation (OSF) Data Communication Exchange (DCE) specification for remote procedure calls and is completely interoperable with other DCE-based RPC systems such as those for HP and IBM AIX® systems. (The RPC facility is compatible but not *compliant* with the OSF specification—that is, it doesn't start with the OSF source code and build on it.)

RPC uses other IPC mechanisms, such as named pipes, NetBIOS, or Windows Sockets, to establish communications between the client and the server. With the RPC facility, essential program logic and related procedure code can exist on different computers, which is important for distributed applications.

As shown in the following diagram, Windows 95 provides RPC client support over the NetBIOS, named pipes, and Windows Sockets interfaces.

RPC client support in
Windows 95

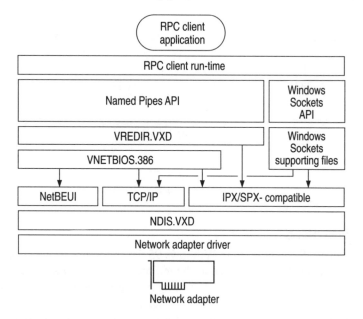

The following diagram shows how Windows 95 provides RPC server support over NetBIOS and Windows Sockets. There is no server support for RPC over named pipes. With a named-pipes RPC application, the named-pipes client can be run on the computer running Windows 95 but the named-pipes server must be set up on a LAN Manager server or Windows NT computer.

RPC server support in
Windows 95

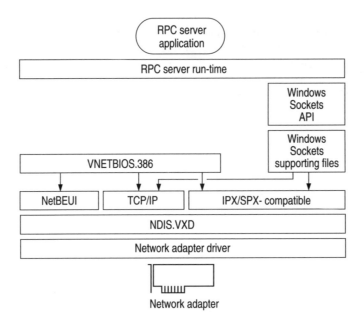

Network adapter

## NetBIOS

NetBIOS can be used in Windows 95 for communication between protocols and
upper-level software such as the redirector and server service. NetBIOS provides
backward compatibility for existing NetBIOS applications. NetBIOS provides a
protocol-independent way of creating sessions and datagrams, and supporting
name resolution over multiple protocols. NetBIOS is supported by the Microsoft
TCP/IP, NetBEUI, and IPX/SPX-compatible protocols in Windows 95. The
additional NetBIOS driver and DLL enable Windows 95 to be compatible with
NetBIOS applications and to run software that specifically requires NetBIOS. The
NetBIOS software is used only for these situations.

NetBIOS defines the interface between the redirector and the protocol layers. The
NetBIOS interface is a set of function calls that allow an application (such as the
redirector in the Windows 95 protected-mode network client) to use the services
of a Transport-layer service provider such as the NetBEUI protocol driver.

Many network applications use NetBIOS to send commands to the protocol
driver. As long as a protocol driver recognizes NetBIOS commands issued by an
application, that protocol driver can be used with any NetBIOS application. The
NetBIOS interface in Windows 95 (NETBIOS.DLL and VNETBIOS.386) is
supported by all three protocols provided with Windows 95.

The architecture for NetBIOS over the various protocols is described with the
respective protocols earlier in this chapter.

## Client-Side Named Pipes

Named pipes provides backward compatibility with existing LAN Manager installations and applications. Windows 95 supports client-side named pipes for Microsoft networks. Server-side named pipes are not supported.

Client for Microsoft Networks makes the Named Pipes API available for applications that use named pipes for IPC. However, Client for Microsoft Networks does not provide named pipes support for other networks such as Novell NetWare and Banyan VINES. A user who needs Novell NetWare or Banyan VINES named-pipes support must use the real-mode TSRs and network components provided by Novell or Banyan.

Named pipes provide an easy-to-access conduit for a one-to-one, reliable, connection-oriented data transfer between two processes. These two processes are normally differentiated as a client process and a server process. The term "server" as applied to the server process in a named-pipe application does not refer to the "server service" that is a component of the network operating system, although the server service may be (but is not necessarily) involved in making the pipe available to other workstations.

- The named-pipe server process creates the pipe and manages access to it. The resources that make up the pipe are owned by the server process and physically exist on the workstation where the server process is running.

- The named-pipe client process uses the services of the underlying network protocols to access the remote pipe resources.

Although named pipes are usually used bidirectionally, the pipe can be configured to allow communication in only one direction, such as from server to client.

A common use for named pipes is in client-server applications based on SQL. The SQL client application can be run on a computer running Client for Microsoft Networks. The Microsoft SQL Server application, however, must be set up on a LAN Manager, Windows NT, or other named-pipes server.

## Mailslots

Mailslots provide backward compatibility with existing LAN Manager installations and applications. Mailslot APIs in Windows 95 and Windows NT are a subset of the APIs in Microsoft OS/2 LAN Manager. Client for Microsoft Networks makes the Mailslots API available for applications that use mailslots for interprocess communication.

Mailslots can be used for one-to-one or one-to-many communication. A mailslot can be created on any network workstation. When a message is sent to a mailslot, the sending application specifies in the mailslot message structure whether the message is to be sent using first-class or second-class delivery.

First-class delivery is a session-oriented, guaranteed data transfer for one-to-one or one-to-many communication. Messages designated as first-class delivery can only be sent to a mailslot that was created on a server. (Notice that Windows 95 does not use first-class messaging.)

Second-class delivery is a datagram-based, unguaranteed data transfer for one-to-one and many-to-one communication. Messages designated as second-class delivery can be sent to a mailslot that was created on any workstation, or even on multiple workstations, if the message size is 400 bytes or less.

Windows 95 and Windows NT implement only second-class mailslots, which are most useful for identifying other computers or services on a network and for wide-scale identification of a service. Windows 95 uses second-class mailslots for WinPopup messages and browsing.

C H A P T E R   3 3

# Windows 95 Registry

This chapter presents background information about the structure of the Registry, and how values from Windows 3.x INI files are stored in the Registry. Notice, however, that no descriptions of individual Registry entries are provided, because such details are beyond the scope of the *Windows 95 Resource Kit*.

Caution   Wherever possible, use Control Panel or System Policy Editor to ensure values are stored properly in the Registry when changing the configuration. If you use Registry Editor to change values, you will not be warned if any entry is incorrect.

**In This Chapter**

Windows 95 Registry Overview   1018
Getting Started with Registry Editor   1019
How Windows 95 Components Use the Registry   1020
Registry Structure   1021
   Registry Hierarchy   1021
   Value Entries in the Registry Keys   1023
   Registry Files   1024
   Recovering Registry Data   1024
   Saving and Restoring the Registry   1025
Hkey_Local_Machine   1026
   Config Subtree in Hkey_Local_Machine   1026
   Enum Subtree in Hkey_Local_Machine   1027
   Software Subtree in Hkey_Local_Machine   1027
   System Subtree in Hkey_Local_Machine   1030
Hkey_Current_User and Hkey_Users   1032
Hkey_Current_Config and Hkey_Dyn_Data   1033
Initialization Files and the Registry   1034
   WIN.INI Settings in the Registry   1034
   SYSTEM.INI Settings in the Registry   1036

# Windows 95 Registry Overview

The Windows 95 Registry provides a unified database for storing system and application configuration data in a hierarchical form. Because the Registry contains all settings required to configure memory, hardware peripherals, and Windows 95-supplied network components, you may find that it is no longer necessary to configure settings in startup configuration and initialization files. Also, because settings are stored in a central location, you can provide both local and remote support for system configuration using Windows 95 tools.

The Registry is roughly analogous to the INI files used under Windows 3.x, with each key in the Registry similar to a bracketed heading in an INI file and with Registry values similar to entries under the INI headings. However, Registry keys can contain subkeys, while INI files do not support nested headings. Registry values can also consist of binary data, rather than the simple strings used in INI files.

Although Microsoft discourages using INI files in favor of Registry entries, some applications (particularly 16-bit Windows-based applications) still use INI files. Windows 95 supports INI files solely for compatibility with those applications and related tools (such as setup programs). The AUTOEXEC.BAT and CONFIG.SYS files also still exist for compatibility with real-mode system components and to allow users to change certain default system settings such as the PATH environment variable. New Win32-based applications can store their initialization information in the Registry.

The Registry provides the following benefits in Windows 95:

- A single source provides data for enumerating and configuring the hardware, applications, device drivers, and operating system control parameters. The configuration information can be recovered easily in the event of system failure.

- Users and administrators can configure computer options by using standard Control Panel tools and other administrative tools, reducing the likelihood of syntactic errors in configuration information.

- A set of network-independent functions can be used to set and query configuration information, allowing system administrators to examine configuration data on remote networked computers.

- The operating system automatically backs up the last good configuration used to start the computer.

Because user-specific Registry information can be maintained on a central network server when user profiles are enabled, users can have access to personal desktop and network access preferences when logging on to any computer, and settings for multiple users can be maintained on a single computer. Also, system policies can be used to enforce certain Registry settings for individuals, workgroups, or all users. For more information, see Chapter 15, "User Profiles and System Policies."

# Getting Started with Registry Editor

To get the most out of the material in this chapter, you will want to run Registry Editor while you are reading so that you can see the contents of the Registry on your computer. By default, Registry Editor does not appear in any menu or on the desktop. Notice, also, that Registry Editor (REGEDIT.EXE) is copied to the Windows directory automatically when Windows 95 is installed from a compact disc. Registry Editor is not available with the Windows 95 floppy disks.

---

**Tip**   You can add the Registry Editor icon to your desktop by using the right mouse button to drag REGEDIT.EXE from Windows Explorer to the desktop.

---

▶ **To run Registry Editor**

- From the Start menu, click Run and type **regedit**

▶ **To find specific data in the Registry**

- In the Registry Editor window, double-click any folder icon for a Registry key to display the contents of that key.

    –Or–

    From the Edit menu, click Find. Then type all or part of the text string you want to find, and click options to specify whether you want to find a key name, an entry name, or data.

    After Registry Editor finds the first instance of the text string, you can press F3 to search for the next instance.

Registry Editor can be used to view or modify a Registry on a local computer or on another computer over a network. Both the administrator's computer and the remote computer require the Microsoft Remote Registry service to allow remote Registry access. For more information about installing and taking advantage of the Microsoft Remote Registry service, see Chapter 16, "Remote Administration."

**Tip for Disabling Direct Editing of the Registry**

The network administrator can restrict users from being able to use Registry Editor to modify the Registry by setting a system policy named Disable Registry Editing Tools. Notice, however, that this policy does not prevent the administrator or another user from modifying the Registry by using System Policy Editor. For more information about this restriction and about using System Policy Editor to modify the Registry on individual or multiple computers, see Chapter 15, "User Profiles and System Policies."

# How Windows 95 Components Use the Registry

With Windows 95, the operating system stores and checks the configuration information in the Registry for most configuration settings during system startup. The following figure provides an overview of how various Windows 95 components and applications use the Registry.

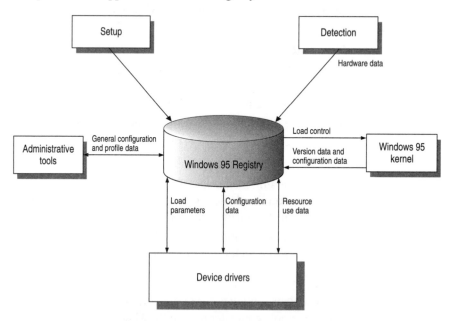

- Whenever you run Windows 95 Setup, use the Add New Hardware option in Control Panel, or run other setup programs for hardware, the Windows 95 Configuration Manager places hardware configuration data in the Registry. This information includes a list of hardware detected in the computer.

- When you install Windows 95 in the same directory as an earlier version of Windows, your previous desktop settings are moved from INI files to the Registry. When you make changes to the desktop configuration, the settings are added to the Registry.

- Each time you add or remove a Plug and Play-compliant device on a computer running Windows 95, configuration data is added to the Registry. For example, new information is added when you install a PCMCIA modem.

- Device drivers send and receive load parameters and configuration data from the Registry. This data is similar to settings defined under MS-DOS by **device=** lines in CONFIG.SYS.

- System policies, user profiles, and administrative tools such as the Windows 95 Control Panel can be used to add or modify configuration data. Registry Editor can be used to view and occasionally change the system configuration.

A set of Registry APIs can make information available through remote procedure calls (RPC) to Windows 95 management tools from other vendors. This permits administrators to view and modify configuration information remotely for hardware and software components that store information in the Registry. Notice that the Registry APIs are accessible remotely using named pipes (client-side only), NetBIOS over NetBEUI, Windows Sockets on IPX, and Windows Sockets on IP.

# Registry Structure

Registry Editor displays the contents of the Registry database in six subtrees. The hierarchical structure that appears in Registry Editor is similar to how Windows Explorer displays hierarchical directory structures.

This section describes the hierarchical organization of the Registry and defines the overall structure of keys and value entries. The actual contents or location of a specific Registry subkey may differ from what is described here, depending on the services and software are installed. However, this description of the general organization will help you understand how to navigate the Registry.

# Registry Hierarchy

The Windows 95 Registry structure represents database information specific to the computer and to individual users. The computer-specific information includes setting for hardware and software installed on the computer. The user-specific information includes settings in user profiles, such as desktop settings, preferences for certain software, and personal printer and network settings.

In the Registry, each individual key can contain data items called value entries and can also contain additional subkeys, with keys roughly analogous to directories, and value entries analogous to files. Each of the root key names begins with "Hkey_" to indicate to software developers that the key is a unique identifier, called a handle, that can be used by a program to access resources.

The following briefly describes the Registry subtrees. More details are provided in this chapter.

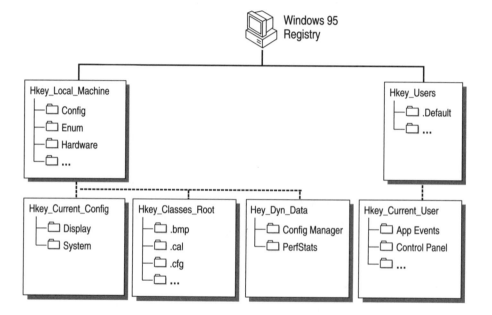

**Hkey_Local_Machine.**  This key contains computer-specific information about the type of hardware installed, software settings, and other information. This information is used for all users who log on to this computer.

**Hkey_Current_Config.**  This key points to a branch of Hkey_Local_Machine\Config that contains information about the current configuration of hardware attached to the computer.

**Hkey_Dyn_Data.**  This key points to a branch of Hkey_Local_Machine that contains the dynamic status information for various devices as part of the Plug and Play information. This information may change as devices are added to or removed from the computer. The information for each device includes the related hardware key and the device's current status, including problems.

**Hkey_Classes_Root.** This key points to a branch of Hkey_Local_Machine that describes certain software settings. This key displays the same data as it did in Windows 3.1—essential information about OLE and association mappings to support drag-and-drop operations, Windows 95 shortcuts (which are, in fact, OLE links), and core aspects of the Windows 95 user interface.

**Hkey_Users.** This key contains information about all the users who log on to the computer, including both generic and user-specific information. The generic settings are available to all users who log on to the computer. The information is made up of default settings for applications, desktop configurations, and so on. This key contains subkeys for each user that logs on to this computer.

**Hkey_Current_User.** This key points to a branch of Hkey_Users for the user who is currently logged on.

# Value Entries in the Registry Keys

Registry Editor displays data in two panes. The value entries in the right pane are associated with the selected key in the left pane.

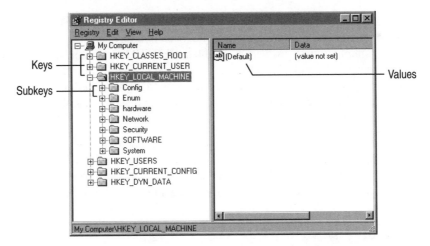

A value entry has three parts: the data type of the value (which appears as an icon), the name of the value, and the value itself. A value entry cannot be larger than about 64K. The limit to total Registry size depends on available hard disk space.

The following table lists the data types currently used by the system.

| Data type | Description |
| --- | --- |
| 🔲 | Binary data. Most hardware component information is stored as binary data, and can be displayed in Registry Editor in binary or hexadecimal format. For example, Int 13: 01. |
| 🔲 | A sequence of characters representing human-readable text. For example, BitsPerPixel: "8". |

# Registry Files

The Registry is logically one data store, but physically it consists of two different files to allow maximum flexibility for network configurations:

- User-specific information is contained in USER.DAT. The information in this file is reflected in user profiles.

- Hardware-specific and computer-specific settings are contained in SYSTEM.DAT. This information is reflected in hardware profiles and in the settings displayed in Device Manager.

By default, USER.DAT and SYSTEM.DAT are stored in the Windows SYSTEM subdirectory, but these two files can be located in physically different locations. For example, if user profiles are enabled, SYSTEM.DAT can be stored on the local hard disk and USER.DAT stored in each user's logon directory on the network, allowing "roving" users to maintain the same desktop preferences wherever they log on to the network. For shared installations, these files are stored in the machine directory.

For information about how Windows 95 chooses between local and network versions of USER.DAT when loading a user profile, and how system policies can override settings in .DAT files to enforce user-specific and computer-specific information, see Chapter 15, "User Profiles and System Policies."

# Recovering Registry Data

In Windows 95, data is written to the Registry only when a *flush* occurs—that is, when something happens after changed data has aged more than a few seconds or when an application intentionally flushes the data to the hard disk.

Each time Windows 95 successfully starts, the operating system backs up the Registry by copying the current SYSTEM.DAT and USER.DAT files to SYSTEM.DA0 and USER.DA0, respectively. If Windows 95 fails to start, the backed-up Registry from the last successful startup can be copied over the current Registry. This method recovers the last successful settings after a system failure.

# Saving and Restoring the Registry

The Registry can be exported, imported, or recreated using either the Windows-based version of Registry Editor or the real-mode version on the Windows 95 emergency startup disk. By using the export capabilities of Registry Editor, a specific branch or the entire Registry can be saved in text format as a .REG file. A branch of or the entire Registry can be restored by importing a .REG file that was created by exporting the Registry.

If you are exporting or importing Registry files using the Windows-based version of Registry Editor, use the Export and Import commands from the Registry menu. The information in online Help can guide you through this process.

In rare circumstances when the Registry is badly corrupted, you can start the computer using the Windows 95 startup disk. Then you can use the real-mode REGEDIT.EXE utility on the startup disk to import a .REG file. In this case, the following command syntax can be used at the command prompt.

**regedit** [**/L:***system*] [**/R:***user*] *file1.reg, file1a.reg...*
**regedit** [**/L:***system*] [**/R:***user*] **/e** *file3.reg* [*regkey*]
**regedit** [**/L:***system*] [**/R:***user*] **/c** *file2.reg*

| Parameter | Description |
| --- | --- |
| **/L:***system* | Specifies the location of SYSTEM.DAT. |
| **/R:***user* | Specifies the location of USER.DAT. |
| *file1.reg* | Specifies one or more .REG files to import into the Registry. |
| **/e** *file3.reg* | Specifies the filename to which the Registry should be exported. |
| *regkey* | Optionally, specifies the starting Registry key from which to export a portion of the Registry. If no value is specified, **regedit /e** exports the entire Registry. |
| **/c** *file2.reg* | Specifies the .REG file to use to replace the entire contents of the Registry. |

Caution    Use the **regedit /c** option with extreme care, and only when you are sure that the specified .REG file contains a complete image of the Registry.

Also, the *Windows 95 Resource Kit* does not provide sufficient information to guide you through the process of editing an .REG file, so it is recommended that you undertake editing an .REG file only under the guidance of your product support representative.

# Hkey_Local_Machine

Hkey_Local_Machine contains the configuration data for the local computer. The information in this database is used by applications, device drivers, and Windows 95 to determine configuration data for the local computer, regardless of which user is logged on and what software is in use.

Hardware devices can place information in the Registry automatically using the Plug and Play interface. Software for installing device drivers can place information in the Registry by writing to standard APIs. Users can place information about hardware in the Registry by using the Add New Hardware option and other options in Control Panel, or by using Device Manager, as described in Chapter 19, "Devices."

Hkey_Local_Machine contains several subkeys, as listed briefly in the following table. The rest of this section provides details about some of these keys.

| Subkey name | Contents |
| --- | --- |
| Config | A collection of configurations for the local computer |
| Enum | Information about hardware devices on the system |
| Hardware | Information about serial ports and modems used with the HyperTerminal program |
| Network | Network information created when a user logs on to a networked computer, including the user name, primary network provider, whether the logon was validated by a server, and information about the system policies processor |
| Security | Information about the network security provider and remote administration capabilities |
| Software | The computer-specific information about software installed on the local computer, along with miscellaneous configuration data |
| System | The database that controls system startup, device driver loading, Windows 95 services, and operating system behavior |

## Config Subtree in Hkey_Local_Machine

The Hkey_Local_Machine\Config subtree contains information about alternate hardware configurations for the computer. For example, it can contain information about multiple configurations to be used when the computer is connected to a network, when it is undocked from a docking station, and so on. Each alternate configuration is assigned a unique identifier, and this configuration ID has a subkey under the Config key. Each configuration appears in the list of hardware profiles in the System option in Control Panel.

When Windows 95 checks the hardware configuration at system startup, one of three things occurs:

- In most situations, the configuration ID is mapped to a unique configuration and Windows 95 selects the appropriate one automatically, and the settings for the related Config subkey are used for system configuration.

- If the user is starting the computer for the first time with new hardware components, Windows 95 creates a new configuration for the new configuration ID, and a new Config subkey is added to the Registry.

- If the configuration ID is mapped to more than one configuration (for example, because Windows 95 cannot distinguish between two configurations), the user is prompted to choose which configuration to use.

# Enum Subtree in Hkey_Local_Machine

Windows 95 bus enumerators are responsible for building the hardware tree. This includes assigning an identification code to each device on its bus and retrieving the device's configuration information, either directly from the device or from the Registry. For more information about the hardware tree and bus enumerators, see Chapter 18, "Introduction to System Configuration," and Chapter 31, "Windows 95 Architecture."

Bus enumeration information is stored in the Hkey_Local_Machine\Enum subtree. For all types of devices, subkeys contain information such as device type, assigned drive letter, hardware ID, and device manufacturer, plus driver-related information for network components.

The following table shows which devices are enumerated in typical subkeys.

| Subkey | Device enumeration |
|--------|--------------------|
| ESDI | Fixed disk devices |
| FLOP | Floppy disk devices |
| ISAPNP | Plug and Play devices on an ISA bus |
| Monitor | Monitor devices |
| Network | Network protocol, server, and bindings |
| Root | Legacy devices |

# Software Subtree in Hkey_Local_Machine

The Hkey_Local_Machine\Software subtree contains configuration information about all installed software that can write information in the Registry. The entries in this key apply for anyone using this particular computer, and include definitions for file associations and OLE information.

The software subkey contains, for example, the information you add when registering an application to use a specific filename extension and information added during installation of Windows-based applications.

The Hkey_Local_Machine\Software subtree contains several subkeys, including the Classes subkey, plus *description* subkeys for all installed software that can write to the Registry, as described in the following sections.

## Classes Subkey

The Hkey_Local_Machine\Software\Classes subkey defines types of documents and provides information about OLE and filename-extension associations that can be used by applications. Hkey_Classes_Root is an alias for this subkey.

Hkey_Classes_Root merely points to Hkey_Local_Machine\Software\Classes. The sole purpose for Hkey_Classes_Root is to provide compatibility with the Windows 3.x registration database.

The Classes subkey contains two types of subkeys:

- Filename-extension subkeys, which specify the class-definition associated with files that have the selected extension.

- Class-definition keys, which specify the shell and OLE properties of a class (or type) of document. If an application supports Dynamic Data Exchange (DDE), the Shell subkey can contain Open and Print subkeys that define DDE commands for opening and printing files, similar to the OLE and DDE information stored in the Registry under earlier versions of Windows. In the following illustration, **c:\windows\notepad.exe %1** is the open command, and the **%1** parameter stands for the selected filename in Windows Explorer when the command is carried out.

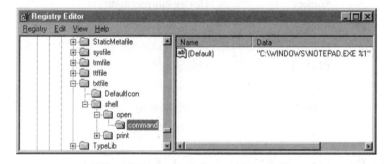

# Description Subkeys

The various Hkey_Local_Machine\Software\*Description* subkeys contain the names and version numbers of the software installed on the local computer (if that software writes information to the Registry as part of its installation process). User-specific information about the configuration of an application is stored at the same relative path under Hkey_Current_User.

---

**Important** The information in each subkey is added by the related application. Do not edit entries in these subkeys unless directed to do so by your application vendor.

---

During installation, applications record this information in the following form:

```
Hkey_Local_Machine\Software\CompanyName\ProductName\Version
```

The key named Hkey_Local_Machine\Software\Microsoft and its subkey named Windows\CurrentVersion are of particular interest. These subkeys contain information about software that supports services built into Windows 95.

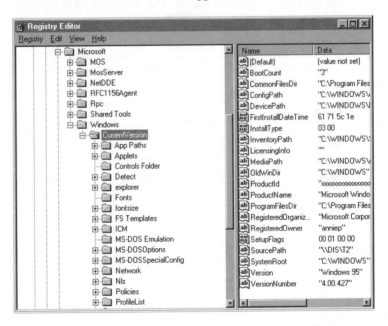

The Setup subkey under Hkey_Local_Machine\Software\Microsoft\Windows \CurrentVersion is used internally by Windows 95 for its Setup program.

# System Subtree in Hkey_Local_Machine

The data in Hkey_Local_Machine\System is organized into control sets that contain a complete set of parameters for device drivers and services that can be loaded with Windows 95.

All data that controls startup is described in the CurrentControlSet subtree under Hkey_Local_Machine\System. This control set has two parts:

- The Control key contains information used to control system startup, including the computer's network name and the subsystems to start.
- The Services key contains information to control the loading and configuration of drivers, file systems, and so on. The data in the Services key also controls how these services call each other.

## Control Subkey

The Control subkey contains startup parameters for the system, including settings for startup and shutdown, file system performance, keyboard layouts and language support, and so on. The following table describes some typical subkeys.

| Subkey | Contents |
|--------|----------|
| ComputerName | The computer name, which should be set using the Network option in Control Panel |
| FileSystem | The type and settings of the file system |
| IDConfigDB | The identification for the current configuration |
| Keyboard layouts | A list of the DLLs for the keyboard language, which should be set using the Keyboard option in Control Panel |
| Resources | Descriptions and driver information for multimedia components |
| NetworkProvider | Descriptions of the network providers |

| Subkey | Contents |
|---|---|
| Nls | Information on national language support, including language and locale preferences, which should be set using the Keyboard option in Control Panel |
| PerfStats | Statistics gathered from system components that can be viewed using System Monitor |
| Print | Information about the current printers and printing e nvironment, contained in several subkeys:<br><br>▪ Environments, which contains subkeys defining drivers and print processors for operating system environments<br><br>▪ Monitors, which can contain subkeys with data for specific network printing monitors<br><br>▪ Printers, which can contain subkeys describing printer parameters for each installed printer<br><br>▪ Providers, which can contain subkeys describing DLLs for network print services |
| Session Manager | Global variables that are maintained by the operating system, plus subkeys that list applications that do not run well under Windows 95, DLLs whose version numbers should be checked, and directories and filenames for all the Session Manager DLLs |
| TimeZoneInformation | Values for time zone settings, which should be set using the Date/Time option in Control Panel |
| Update | Value indicating whether Windows 95 was installed over an earlier version of Windows |
| VMM32 | The filenames of VxD files combined into the VMM32.VXD virtual device driver |

### Services Subkey for CurrentControlSet

The Services subkey in CurrentControlSet lists the Kernel device drivers, file system drivers, and Windows 95 service drivers that can be loaded at startup. The Services subkey also contains subkeys with static descriptions of hardware to which drivers can be attached. The following table shows some typical Services subkeys.

| Subkey | Contents |
| --- | --- |
| *Agent_name* | Subkeys for each installed system agent, such as Microsoft Network Monitor, SNMP, or network backup agents |
| Arbitrators | Subkeys for arbitrators required to manage resources between competing devices, usually including address, DMA, I/O, and IRQ arbitrators |
| Class | Subkeys for all classes of devices the operating system supports, such as disk drives, keyboard, display, mouse, and so on |
| MSNP32, NWNP32 | Subkeys for 32-bit, protected-mode network providers, including logon and security provider information |
| VxD | Subkeys for all virtual device drivers, including disk drivers, network components, disk caches, and so on |

Caution  Do not change these value entries using Registry Editor. These settings should be maintained only by the system. Settings for drivers that appear under the Services subkeys can be changed by using Control Panel or system policies.

# Hkey_Current_User and Hkey_Users

Hkey_Users contains the .Default subkey plus all previously loaded user profiles for users who have logged on. The information in the .Default subkey is used to create the user profile for a user who logs on without a personal user profile. The .Default subkey contains keys for AppEvents, Control Panel, Keyboard layouts, Network, RunMRU, and Software, among others.

Hkey_Current_User contains the database with the user profile of the user who is currently logged on. A user profile ensures that the user interface and operation of Windows 95 will be the same on any computer where that user logs on, if that person's profile is available at that computer.

Hkey_Current_User contains all the information necessary to set up a particular user environment on the computer, such as application preferences, screen colors, and security access permissions. Many of these settings are the same kind of information that was stored in WIN.INI under Windows 3.x. Hkey_Current_User includes several subkeys, some of which are described in the following table.

| Subkey | Contents |
| --- | --- |
| AppEvents | Subkeys containing the path and filename of the system sound file that plays when specific system events occur |
| Control Panel | Subkeys containing Control Panel settings, including information stored in WIN.INI and CONTROL.INI under Windows 3.x |
| Keyboard layouts | A value entry defining the current active keyboard layout, which should be set by using the Keyboard option in Control Panel |
| Network | Subkeys describing persistent and recent network connections |
| RunMRU | Subkeys listing the most recently used applications |
| Software | Subkeys describing the current user's software settings, using the same structure as Hkey_Local_Machine\Software and containing application-specific information stored in WIN.INI or private initialization files under Windows 3.x |
| StreamMRU | Subkeys for the most recently used documents |

Whenever similar data exists in Hkey_Local_Machine and Hkey_Current_User, the data in Hkey_Current_User takes precedence. For example, settings for applications and the desktop defined by the current user take precedence over default settings.

# Hkey_Current_Config and Hkey_Dyn_Data

The Hkey_Current_Config key points to the current system configuration in the collection of configurations stored in Hkey_Local_Machine\Config.

Some information in Windows 95 must be stored in RAM because it requires fast modification and retrieval that cannot wait for the Registry to flush to the hard disk. All this data can be found under Hkey_Dyn_Data.

The Hkey_Dyn_Data\Configuration Manager subkey, sometimes referred to as the hardware tree, is a record in RAM of the current system configuration. The information is drawn from the devices currently installed and loaded, or that failed loading. The hardware tree is created every time the system starts and updates whenever a change occurs to the system configuration. The information that appears in Registry Editor is provided when this key is displayed, so it is never out of date.

Hkey_Dyn_Data also contains statistics gathered for various network components in the system. These reside under Hkey_Dyn_Data\PerfStats.

VxDs from other vendors can provide dynamic data to this area too. For more information, see the *Win32 Software Development Kit for Windows 95 and Windows NT*.

# Initialization Files and the Registry

Although the Registry replaces the basic function of the initialization files used in earlier versions of Windows, the SYSTEM.INI, WIN.INI, and WINFILE.INI files still appear in the Windows directory. These files continue to be used for compatibility with earlier Windows-based applications and device drivers. For example, entries in WIN.INI and SYSTEM.INI created by Win16-based applications are not updated in the Registry, because such applications do not know how to access the Windows 95 Registry.

If you install Windows 95 as an upgrade over Windows 3.1, some INI file settings are copied into the Registry, including settings from CONTROL.INI, PROGMAN.INI, SYSTEM.INI, and WIN.INI.

Some INI file entries are not moved to the Registry, but remain in the INI file for compatibility with Win16-based applications. Most of these entries can be changed without editing the INI files by using the graphical tools provided with Windows 95. However, some INI entries cannot be set using the Windows 95 user interface. These entries are required for some applications to function properly, but shouldn't need direct modification by users.

## WIN.INI Settings in the Registry

Windows 95 migrates settings from configuration files into the Registry during Setup. The following table shows where WIN.INI entries migrated to the Registry. For information about specific WIN.INI entries moved during Windows 95 installation, see Chapter 6, "Setup Technical Discussion."

**Registry Paths for Migrated WIN.INI Sections**

| WIN.INI section | Subkey in Hkey_Current_User |
|---|---|
| [desktop] | \Control Panel\Desktop |
| [Windows] | \Control Panel\Desktop |
| [sounds] | \AppEvents\Schemes\Apps\*event*\current |

The following tables list entries retained in WIN.INI for compatibility with applications written for earlier versions of Windows. These values can be set using Control Panel and other tools in the Windows 95 interface.

**Entries in WIN.INI Retained and Supported in the User Interface**

**[Windows]:**

| | | |
|---|---|---|
| CursorBlinkRate | DoubleClickSpeed | MouseSpeed |
| Device | KeyboardDelay | MouseTrails |
| DoubleClickHeight | KeyboardSpeed | SwapMouseButtons |
| DoubleClickWidth | | |

**[Intl]:**

| | | |
|---|---|---|
| iCountry | iNegCurr | sLanguage |
| iCurrDigits | iTime | sDecimal |
| iCurrency | iTLZero | sList |
| iDate | s1159 | sShortDate |
| iDigits | s2359 | sLongDate |
| iLZero | sCountry | sThousand |
| iMeasure | sCurrency | sTime |

**[fonts]:** *font-name*

**[ports]:** *portname*

**[PrinterPorts]:** *device*

**Entries in WIN.INI Retained but Not Supported in the User Interface**

**[embedding]:** *object*

**[FontSubstitute]:** *font-name=font-name*

**[Mail]:** MAPI

**[mci extensions]:** *extension*

**[Windows]:** Load and Run

# SYSTEM.INI Settings in the Registry

The following table lists SYSTEM.INI entries that are migrated to the Registry when Windows 95 is installed in the same directory as a previous version of Windows 3.x. For information about specific SYSTEM.INI entries related to loading VxDs and configuring network components, see Chapter 6, "Setup Technical Discussion."

**Registry Paths for Migrated SYSTEM.INI Entries**

| SYSTEM.INI entry | Subkey in Hkey_Local_Machine |
|---|---|
| **[386Enh]:** | |
| Network | System\CurrentControlSet\Services\VxD\Vnetsetup |
| Transport | Software\CurrentControlSet\Services\VxD\*transport entry* |
| **[network]:** | |
| Comment | System\CurrentControlSet\Services\VxD\Vnetsetup |
| ComputerName | System\CurrentControlSet\Control\ComputerName |
| EnableSharing | System\CurrentControlSet\Services\VxD\Vnetsetup |
| LMAnnounce | System\CurrentControlSet\Services\VxD\Vnetsetup |
| LogonDomain | Network |
| LogonValidated | Network |
| MaintainServerList | System\CurrentControlSet\Services\VxD\Vnetsetup |
| Reshare | System\CurrentControlSet\Network\LanMan\*sharename*[1] |
| Username | Network\Logon |
| WorkGroup | System\CurrentControlSet\Services\VxD\Vnetsetup |

[1] The equivalent of the Reconnect settings is stored in Hkey_Current_User\Persistent.

The following tables list entries that are retained in SYSTEM.INI for compatibility with applications written for earlier versions of Windows.

### SYSTEM.INI Entries Retained and Supported in the User Interface

**[386Enh]:**

| | | |
|---|---|---|
| AllEMSLocked | Keyboard | MaxPagingFileSize |
| AllXMSLocked | KeyPasteCRSkipCount | MinUserDiskSpace |
| AltKeyDelay | KeyPasteKeyDelay | Mouse |
| AltPasteDelay | PasteSkipCount | Paging |
| DMABufferSize | KeyPasteTimeout | PagingDrive |
| Display | MaxDMAPGAddress | ScrollFrequency |
| DOSPromptExitInstructions | | |

**[boot]:**

| | | |
|---|---|---|
| display.drv | mouse.drv | sound.drv |
| keyboard.drv | network.drv | |

**[NonWindowsApps]:**

CommandEnvSize

### Entries in SYSTEM.INI Retained but Not Supported in the User Interface

**[386Enh]:**

| | | |
|---|---|---|
| Device=*filename* | Local Reboot | NetAsyncTimeout |
| KeybdPasswd | MessageBackColor | NetAsynchFallback |
| Local | MessageTextColor | NetDMASize |

**[boot]:**

| | | |
|---|---|---|
| 386grabber=*filename* | fonts.fon=*filename* | shell=*filename* |
| comm.drv=*filename* | language.dll=*library-name* | system.drv=*filename* |
| drivers=*filename* | oemfonts.font=*filename* | TaskMan.Exe=*filename* |
| fixedfon.fon=*filename* | | |

**[drivers]:**

alias=*driver-filname*

**[mci]:**

*Entries written by applications*

C H A P T E R   3 4

# International Windows 95

This chapter summarizes information about local editions and multilanguage support for Windows 95, and it provides technical details about defining regional settings in setup scripts.

**In This Chapter**

Overview of Windows 95 Local Editions    1040
Overview of International Language Support    1041
Specifying International Settings    1042
    Changing Regional Settings in Windows 95    1043
    Defining International Settings in Custom Setup Scripts    1044
    Changing the Code Page    1047
Using Multiple Languages in Windows 95    1048
    Using Multilingual Fonts with Win32-Based Applications    1051
    Using Alternate Keyboards    1052
    Using Windows 95 Support for Local Conventions    1055

# Overview of Windows 95 Local Editions

Windows 95 is being made available in the following local versions, among others:

| | | | | | |
|---|---|---|---|---|---|
| Arabic | Czech | French | Hungarian | Norwegian | Spanish |
| Basque | Danish | German | Italian | Polish | Swedish |
| Catalan | Dutch | Greek | Japanese | Portuguese | Turkish |
| Chinese | Finnish | Hebrew | Korean | Russian | Thai |

Windows 95 does not provide support for multiple Windows code pages. Just as with earlier versions of Windows, all international versions of Windows 95 are based on a single Windows code page of 256 code points. The following international versions of Windows 95 are available.

**United States.** This version of Windows 95 is based on the American National Standards Institute (ANSI) Windows code page (1252). This is the code page used for most of the single-byte language versions in North America, South America, Western Europe, Scandinavia, South Pacific, Africa, and Asia. This version will be available in English, German, Italian, Norwegian, Swedish, Dutch, French, Spanish, Portuguese, Danish, Finnish, language editions. This version also forms the base for all other versions.

**Far East.** This version of Windows 95 is available in Japanese (932), Simplified Chinese (936), Traditional (Taiwan) Chinese (950), and Korean (949). These are the only versions of Windows 95 that support the large character sets and input methods these languages require. They also support a vast array of the unique hardware used in the Far East.

**PanEuropean.** This version of Windows 95 allows the user to select the correct Windows code page for their particular language during Setup. After it is installed, the Windows code page cannot be changed. Choices include Cyrillic (1251), Central Europe (1250), Turkish (1254), Greek (1253), and Baltic (1257). This version will be available in Russian, Polish, Hungarian, Greek, Turkish, and other languages.

**Middle East.** This version of Windows 95 is available in Arabic (1256) and Hebrew (1255). These are the only versions of Windows 95 that support mixed right-to-left and left-to-right text processing. The Arabic version also includes support for Farsi (Persian).

**Thai.** This version of Windows 95 is based on the Thai code page (876).

For information about ordering a local edition of Windows 95, contact your software vendor or your local Microsoft office.

The *Win32 Software Development Kit for Windows 95 and Windows NT* and
the Microsoft Developer Network provide complete information about the
architecture, APIs, and other needs for developers who are creating or modifying
applications to run on local editions of Windows 95. For information about joining
the Microsoft Developer Network, see Appendix J, "Windows 95 Resource
Directory."

The *Windows 95 Resource Kit* is being made available in at least the following
local versions: Bahasa, Simplified and Traditional Chinese, Croatian, French,
German, Italian, Japanese, Korean, Portuguese, Slovenian, Spanish, Swedish,
and Thai. For information about ordering a local edition of *Windows 95 Resource
Kit*, contact your local bookseller or your local Microsoft office.

*Developing International Software for Windows 95 and Windows NT*, a Microsoft
Press® book by Nadine Kano, provides details about using the Windows 95
National Language Support (NLS) API and other information about developing
software for use in multiple locales. To order this publication (ISBN 1-55615-840-
8), contact your local bookseller. You can also order it directly in the United States
by calling (800) 677-7377 or through CompuServe® (**go msp**).

# Overview of International Language Support

Windows 95 offers international language support to provide solutions to
problems created when using software and exchanging documents among
different locales and languages. Windows 95 offers this support at the operating
system level for users, and at the API level for software developers. This section
summarizes this built-in international language support for using Windows 95 on
a worldwide basis, and the features that Windows 95 provides for enhancing
existing or new applications for use in different parts of the world.

**Easy-to-use multilanguage fonts and keyboard layouts.**  With Windows 95, users
can easily switch between all available languages and corresponding keyboard
layouts configured on the system. This makes it easy for users to integrate
information into a multilingual document. By using the Keyboard option in Control
Panel, users can easily add and remove keyboard layouts and languages. By using
the common Choose Font dialog box in applications created for Windows 95,
they can choose character-set scripts (such as "Greek") supported by a particular
font. For more information, see "Using Multilingual Fonts with Win32-Based
Applications" and "Using Alternate Keyboards" later in this chapter.

**Substitution for unavailable fonts when switching languages.**  When switching
between languages in a document, Windows 95 substitutes matching fonts for
the new language if the original font is not available. Users can read and use the
text for a similar character set, even if they don't have the font in which the
information was originally created.

**Preservation of language-specific attributes on the Clipboard.** Windows 95 provides additional services for application vendors to easily exchange information between internationally-aware applications, while preserving all language formatting characteristics.

**Easy addition of multilanguage support for software developers.** Developers can use the Win32 NLS API for loading, selecting, and querying keyboard layouts and languages. NLS services ensure that information is handled properly for the given culture or locale by supporting formats for date, time, calendar, number, and currency, and for sorting, character typing, and character mapping. The correct national format for information such as date format or sorting sequence is supplied automatically, based on the settings specified in the Regional Settings option in Control Panel. Win32-based applications can use Windows 95 services to automatically switch between the proper fonts and keyboard layouts as users navigate through a multilingual document. For more information, see "Using Multiple Languages in Windows 95" later in this chapter.

**Proper sorting and formatting rules for the current locale.** Different locales and cultures have different rules for interpreting information, such as algorithms for sorting or searching, and formats for time and dates. Software developers can use the Win32 NLS API to check and use the user's default locale settings or to use a specific locale setting, without using proprietary sorting methods or parsing WIN.INI or the Registry, and without locale-specific coding. This allows users to easily exchange information on a global basis, while preserving the integrity of the information. For example, the multilingual support in Windows 95 can be used in applications to account for these kinds of differences among language rules:

- In French, diacritics are sorted from right to left instead of from left to right as in English.

- In Norwegian, some extended characters follow the Z character because they are considered unique characters rather than characters with diacritics.

- In Spanish, CH is a unique character between C and D, and Ñ is a unique character between N and O.

# Specifying International Settings

During Windows 95 Setup, the operating system is configured for a default locale, either based on settings that Setup detects from the previous operating system or based on options that the user chooses. Windows 95 Setup also copies most international information for all other supported locales onto the user's hard disk drive, where applications can access them. You can specify international settings during Windows 95 Setup or change the default settings afterward in Control Panel.

During Setup, you can specify the following settings in the Computer Settings screen:

- Regional settings, for specifying the local language and, in turn, the local conventions for other settings such as date, time, and currency formats. This also sets the MS-DOS code page and MS-DOS country settings.

- Keyboard layout, for specifying the default keyboard layout to be used with Windows 95, based on local requirements. This also sets the MS-DOS keyboard layout.

- Language support, for selecting one of the following combination of languages:
  - English/Western European
  - English/Western European and Greek
  - English/Western European and Cyrillic
  - English/Western European and Central European

  Windows 95 selects the English/Western European option by default.

After Setup, you can change the following settings in Control Panel:

- Add languages and corresponding keyboard layouts using the Keyboard option, as described in "Using Alternate Keyboards" later in this chapter.

- Modify the local language default for settings such as date, time, and currency using the Regional Settings option.

- Add or remove language support (Greek, Cyrillic, or Central European) in the Add/Remove Programs option.

You can configure each of these settings by defining options in custom setup scripts, as described in the following sections. If user profiles are enabled (as described in Chapter 15, "User Profiles and System Policies"), the international settings preferences in Windows 95 can be saved in each user's profile. In this case, if a single computer is used by multiple users, each user can select a different default locale.

# Changing Regional Settings in Windows 95

To change locale conventions after Windows 95 is installed, use the Regional Settings option in Control Panel. This option sets the default system formats for country, language, date, time, currency, and numbers. You can also customize these formats.

▶ **To change regional settings in Windows 95**

- In the Regional Settings option in Control Panel, click a tab to define settings for that property, as summarized in the following list. When settings are as you want them, click OK.

| Properties tab | Description |
|---|---|
| Regional Settings | Specifies the regional settings you want, to automatically define how dates, times, currency, and numbers are displayed and sorted. |
| Number | Specifies how numbers are displayed (including the decimal character used), how digits are grouped, and how negative numbers are shown; also specifies the measurement system used. |
| Currency | Specifies how currency is displayed (including the decimal character used), how digits are grouped, and how negative values are shown. |
| Time | Specifies how time is displayed, including the hour and minute separator; also specifies how morning and afternoon times are designated. |
| Date | Specifies the calendar type, and how short and long dates are displayed; also specifies the character used as the separator between the day, the month, and the year. |

# Defining International Settings in Custom Setup Scripts

You can specify values in the [System] section of a custom setup script (such as MSBATCH.INF) to define regional, keyboard layout, and multilanguage settings other than the defaults.

To specify the regional setting in MSBATCH.INF, set **locale=** in [System] to a value listed in the [LocaleList] section of LOCALE.INF. The following table shows some of the values for regional settings that are available in the United States edition of Windows 95. For local editions of Windows 95, check LOCALE.INF entries for Eastern European, Far Eastern, Middle Eastern, and Thai values.

| Regional setting | Value | Regional setting | Value |
|---|---|---|---|
| Afrikaans | L0436 | French (Luxembourg) | L140C |
| Basque | L042D | German (Standard) | L0407 |
| Catalan | L0403 | German (Swiss) | L0807 |
| Danish | L0406 | German (Austrian) | L0C07 |
| Dutch (Standard) | L0413 | German (Luxembourg) | L1007 |
| Dutch (Belgian) | L0813 | German (Liechtenstein) | L1407 |
| English (United States) | L0409 | Icelandic | L040F |
| English (British) | L0809 | Indonesian | L0421 |
| English (Australian) | L0C09 | Italian (Standard) | L0410 |
| English (Canadian) | L1009 | Italian (Swiss) | L0810 |
| English (New Zealand) | L1409 | Norwegian (Bokmål) | L0414 |
| English (Ireland) | L1809 | Norwegian (Nynorsk) | L0814 |
| English (South Africa) | L1C09 | Portuguese (Brazilian) | L0416 |
| Finnish | L040B | Portuguese (Standard) | L0816 |
| French (Standard) | L040C | Spanish (Traditional Sort) | L040A |
| French (Belgian) | L080C | Spanish (Latin American) | L080A |
| French (Canadian) | L0C0C | Spanish (Modern Sort) | L0C0A |
| French (Swiss) | L100C | Swedish | L041D |

Values listed in the [KeyboardList] section of MULTILNG.INF specify the particular keyboard. Use one of the following strings to define the **selectedKeyboard=***value* in the [System] section of MSBATCH.INF (or a similar file).

| Keyboard layout | Keyboard value in MULTLNG.INF |
|---|---|
| Belgian | KEYBOARD_0000080C |
| Brazilian | KEYBOARD_00000416 |
| British | KEYBOARD_00000809 |
| Canadian Multilingual | KEYBOARD_00030C0C |
| Danish | KEYBOARD_00000406 |
| Dutch | KEYBOARD_00000413 |
| Finnish | KEYBOARD_0000040B |
| French | KEYBOARD_0000040C |
| French Canadian | KEYBOARD_00000C0C |
| German | KEYBOARD_00000407 |
| Icelandic | KEYBOARD_0000040F |
| Italian | KEYBOARD_00000410 |
| Latin American | KEYBOARD_0000080A |
| Norwegian | KEYBOARD_00000414 |
| Portuguese | KEYBOARD_00000816 |
| Spanish | KEYBOARD_00000C0A |
| Swedish | KEYBOARD_0000041D |
| Swiss French | KEYBOARD_0000100C |
| Swiss German | KEYBOARD_00000807 |
| United States | KEYBOARD_00000409 |
| United States-Dvorak | KEYBOARD_00020409 |
| United States-International | KEYBOARD_00010409 |

Values listed in the [OptionalComponents] section of MULLANG.INF specify the three optional languages you can add to Windows 95: Greek, Cyrillic, and Central European. Use one of the following strings to define the **multilanguage=***value* in the [System] section of MSBATCH.INF (or a similar file).

| Language | Multilanguage value in MULLANG.INF |
|---|---|
| English | English |
| Greek | English and Greek |
| Cyrillic | English and Cyrillic |
| Central European | English and CE |

For more information about creating custom setup scripts, see Chapter 5, "Custom, Automated, and Push Installations."

# Changing the Code Page

The code page is an internal table that the operating system uses to relate the keys on the keyboard to the characters displayed on the screen. Different code pages provide support for the character sets and keyboard layouts used in different countries.

When you install Windows 95, Setup checks the current system configuration to determine the regional settings:

- For Typical Setup, Windows 95 Setup automatically chooses the regional settings for the current system configuration, and then automatically installs the related code pages for Windows and MS-DOS based on the current configuration.

- For Custom Setup, you can choose to specify alternate regional settings. Windows 95 Setup automatically installs the standard Windows and MS-DOS code pages for the regional settings selected.

You can use the Regional Settings option in Control Panel to change the locale. This will affect the display in Windows-based applications. However, for MS-DOS–based applications and for the MS-DOS prompt, the code page installed during Setup is always used. Windows 95 does not include any feature that allows you to change the code page used by MS-DOS.

However, you can use CHANGECP.EXE to change the code page used for console displays (MS-DOS–based applications and the MS-DOS prompt). This application makes all the changes for fonts and other system elements in the Registry and other configuration files. CHANGECP is provided with the *Windows 95 Resource Kit* utilities.

This application is useful to you if your site uses an alternate character set other than the default code page the Windows 95 Setup uses. You know that you need an alternate code page if, after installing Windows 95, your MS-DOS–based applications do not display properly—specifically, if the wrong fonts appear or the wrong characters appear as you type.

For example, the default code page installed for French Canadian under Windows 95 is 850, but your site might use code page 863 as a standard. As another example, the United States default is 437, but some companies choose to use code page 850. In these cases, use CHANGECP to install the alternate code page.

▶ **To change the code page used for MS-DOS–based applications**

1. Copy CHANGECP.EXE and any other files in the CHANGECP directory with the *Windows 95 Resource Kit* utilities to your local Windows directory.

2. At the command prompt, type **changecp**

3. Select the code page you want from the list that appears.

   Alternately, you can type **changecp** *code_page_number* if you know the code page that you want.

CHANGECP automatically makes all related system changes. The next time you start Windows 95, the new code page will be used for all MS-DOS sessions.

---

**Important**  The CHANGECP utility is not designed to be used for changing code pages on a regular basis. Also, frequently switching the MS-DOS code page will confuse users of MS-DOS–based applications.

---

# Using Multiple Languages in Windows 95

Windows 95 provides the keyboard layouts and fonts required to type, edit, view and print documents containing many different languages. For information about creating a document that contains multilingual text, see "Using Alternate Keyboards" later in this chapter. By default, the version of Windows 95 sold in North America, South America, Western Europe, Scandinavia, Africa, and Australia includes the following keyboard languages and layouts.

**Windows 95 Languages**

| Keyboard indicator | Language | Keyboard indicator | Language |
|---|---|---|---|
| Af | Afrikaans | Is | Icelandic |
| Eu | Basque | Ba | Indonesian |
| Ca | Catalan | It | Italian (Standard) |
| Da | Danish | It | Italian (Swiss) |
| Nl | Dutch (Belgian) | No | Norwegian (Bokmål) |
| Nl | Dutch (Standard) | No | Norwegian (Nynorsk) |
| En | English (Australian) | Pt | Portuguese (Brazilian) |
| En | English (British) | Pt | Portuguese (Standard) |
| En | English (Canadian) | Es | Spanish (Argentina) |
| En | English (Caribbean) | Es | Spanish (Chile) |
| En | English (Ireland) | Es | Spanish (Colombia) |
| En | English (Jamaica) | Es | Spanish (Costa Rica) |
| En | English (New Zealand) | Es | Spanish (Dominican Republic) |
| En | English (SouthAfrica) | Es | Spanish (Ecuador) |
| En | English (United States) | Es | Spanish (Guatemala) |
| Fi | Finnish | Es | Spanish (Mexican) |
| Fr | French (Belgian) | Es | Spanish (Modern Sort) |
| Fr | French (Canadian) | Es | Spanish (Panama) |
| Fr | French (Luxembourg) | Es | Spanish (Paraguay) |
| Fr | French (Standard) | Es | Spanish (Peru) |
| De | German (Austrian) | Es | Spanish (Traditional Sort) |
| De | German (Liechtenstein) | Es | Spanish (Uruguay) |
| De | German (Luxembourg) | Es | Spanish (Venezuela) |
| De | German (Standard) | Sv | Swedish |
| De | German (Swiss) | | |

**Windows 95 Keyboard Layouts**

| | |
|---|---|
| Belgian (French) | Italian |
| British | Norwegian |
| Canadian Multilingual | Portuguese (Brazilian) |
| Danish | Portuguese (Standard) |
| Dutch | Spanish |
| Finnish | Swedish |
| French | Swiss French |
| French Canadian | Swiss German |
| German | United States |
| Icelandic | United States-Dvorak |
| Irish | United States-International |
| Italian | |

For information about adding or removing any of the languages in the preceding list, see Windows 95 online Help. To add Central European, Cyrillic, and Greek-based languages, you need to install multilanguage support, as described in the following procedure.

▶ **To install multilingual support**

1. In the Add/Remove Programs option in Control Panel, click the Windows Setup tab.

2. In the Components list, click Language Support, and then click the Details button.

3. Click the languages you want, and then click OK.

When two or more languages are installed, an icon on the taskbar indicates which keyboard is currently active. Users can switch between installed languages by clicking the keyboard icon, or by using a hot-key combination specified in the Keyboard option in Control Panel, as described in "Using Alternate Keyboards" later in this chapter.

The Windows 95 compact disc includes TrueType® fonts that contain characters for all the Western European and Eastern European languages. After you install multilingual TrueType font support, you can access the complete set of 652 characters in applications that support these fonts, such as WordPad. This allows for proper presentation of fonts for a given language.

An application that uses the common Choose Font dialog box can allow users to select from all the character sets and fonts configured in the system. The Script box in this common dialog box allows the user to choose the characteristics related to the language of the text being formatted. For example, depending on the character set and the locales available on a particular computer, the Script box could allow the user to choose from Western, Greek, Cyrillic, or Turkish characteristics for the selected typeface. Of course, the user must choose the appropriate keyboard for using related text characters.

▶ **To access multilingual TrueType fonts in WordPad**

1. Click the Format menu, and then click Font.

2. In the Font dialog box, select a font characteristic for the language in the Script box, and then click OK.

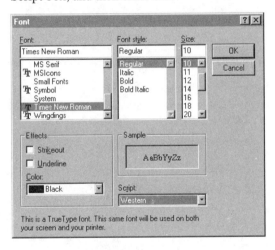

## Using Multilingual Fonts with Win32-Based Applications

For users who create or edit multilingual content in their documents, a Win32-based application that uses the international services in Windows 95 can automatically activate the correct fonts and corresponding keyboard layouts for editing specific text within a document.

Win32-based applications can indicate the language used in text in a document by tagging the text with a locale identifier. For example, such applications can automatically use spell checking, thesaurus, hyphenation engine, and grammar checking applications associated with the language of the text it is checking, if they are available. They can also format dates according to the language of the text. Applications that use locale identifiers can determine date, time, currency, and number formats, and sorting behavior, and they can use these identifiers to determine which keyboard layout and fonts to use for typing and displaying text in a particular language.

To take advantage of the multilingual font capabilities in Windows 95:

- Make sure your application uses the Win32 NLS API. For information, check the documentation that comes with the application or contact the software manufacturer.
- Install multilingual support under Windows 95, as described in this section.
- Use the application's dialog boxes for selecting language-related font attributes and for specifying the language attributes of selected information.

# Using Alternate Keyboards

If you are using an application that supports tagging text for alternate locales or languages, you can use alternate keyboards to easily create documents that contain more than one language.

▶ **To select the alternate keyboards you want to use in Windows 95**

1. In the Keyboard option in Control Panel, click the Language tab.
2. To add another keyboard, click the Add button.
3. In the Add Language dialog box, select the alternate keyboard that you want to install, and then click OK.

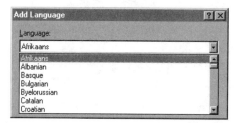

4. If you want to change the default keyboard, select the one you want in the Language list, and then click the Set As Default button.

5. If you want to specify a key combination to use to switch between keyboards, click a key combination in the Switch Languages area.

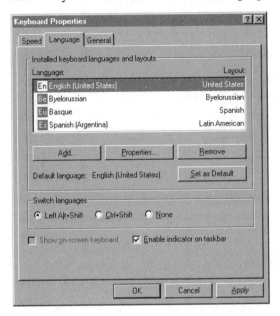

When you want to switch keyboards while working in an application such as WordPad that can take advantage of multilingual support, use the key combination you specified or use the Windows 95 taskbar.

▶  **To switch to another keyboard using the Windows 95 taskbar**

1. Click the keyboard icon on the taskbar.

2. In the menu that appears, click the language you want to use.

The icon for switching keyboard layouts appears at the right end of the taskbar.

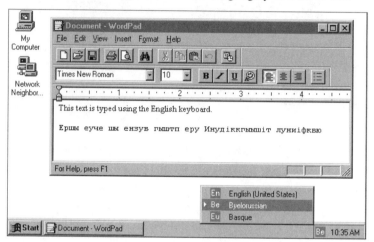

If your application uses the NLS API, you might be able to specify that rules for sorting, searching, spelling, and other actions be used for the portion of text typed using that language. Applications that use the NLS API can distinguish between the default locale the user has set for Windows 95 and the language of text in a document. For example, Microsoft Word for Windows version 6.0 makes language a text property. Just as users can format selected text as bold, italic, or double-spaced, they can format selected text as being in a specific language, as shown in the following illustration.

The Language dialog box in Microsoft Word 6.0 for Windows

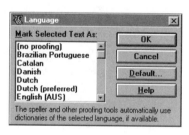

# Using Windows 95 Support for Local Conventions

A great deal of linguistic research went into creating the collection of locale information in the Windows 95 Registry and the algorithms and tables used by the Win32 NLS API, which includes support for local formats for date, time, calendars, currency, and numbers. The Windows 95 Registry contains more than 90 locale-related strings; in addition, the Win32 NLS API allows each application to request information for any locale.

The Windows 95 default date or time formats are the most commonly used formats for each locale, but applications can provide support for other local conventions. Such conventions are ways of formatting information specific to a language, local dialect, or geographic location. Currency symbols, date formats, calendars, numerical separators, and sorting orders can all be affected by these conventions.

Therefore, reformatting a number based on the locale involves more than changing the currency symbol or the decimal separator. A currency symbol can come before the numerical quantity or it can come after. It might or might not be separated from the number by spaces. The currency symbol can be one, two, or more characters. In addition, if a currency amount is negative, Windows 95 can format it in one of 16 different ways.

As another example of locale differences, some languages such as Finnish, German, Polish, and Russian have several forms for each noun. Windows 95 carries both the nominative and genitive forms of Polish and Russian month names; the form changes depending on the month name's position in the string relative to the day name. For all other languages, Windows 95 carries only one form of each month or day name.

Most locales use the Gregorian calendar, but some editions of Windows 95 also support Hijri (Middle East), Japanese, Korean, Taiwanese, and Thai calendars. (Windows 95 will add support for more calendars in the future as necessary.) Although calendars in the United States list Sunday as the first day of the week, calendars in other countries, such as Germany, list Monday as the first day of the week. Similarly, not all cultures assume that the week containing January 1 is the first week of the year. The calendar type that Windows 95 assigns to each locale accommodates such cultural preferences.

CHAPTER 35

# General Troubleshooting

This chapter provides a general approach to troubleshooting, describes built-in Windows 95 features for correcting problems, and includes procedures for identifying and correcting problems.

**Note** This is a general guide to troubleshooting. For more information, see the troubleshooting sections in other chapters of the *Windows 95 Resource Kit.*

**In This Chapter**

Troubleshooting Strategy    1059
   Analyzing Symptoms    1059
   Checking for Common Issues    1059
   Isolating and Testing the Error Condition    1060
   Checking Technical Support Resources    1061
Windows 95 Troubleshooting Aids for Startup    1061
   Using Safe Recovery with Windows 95 Setup    1062
   Verifying Installed Components with Windows 95 Setup    1063
   Using a Startup Disk    1063
   Using Windows 95 Startup Menu Options    1063
   Using WIN.COM Switches    1069

*(continued)*

Troubleshooting Procedures    1069
  Checking Specific Driver Problems    1070
  Checking for Correct File Versions    1071
  Checking for Missing System Files    1071
  Removing Unnecessary Drivers    1073
  Checking Whether a Required Driver Is Missing    1073
  Checking Entries in Startup Files    1074
  Checking for Conflicts at System Startup    1075
  Checking Device Configuration    1075
  Checking for Free Disk Space    1076
  Isolating File System Errors    1077
  Checking for Disk Corruption    1077

# Troubleshooting Strategy

To troubleshoot problems with Windows 95, follow these basic steps:

- Analyze symptoms and factors
- Check to see if the problem is a common issue
- Isolate the error conditions
- Consult technical support resources

## Analyzing Symptoms

Start troubleshooting by analyzing symptoms to determine a strategy for resolving the problem. Under what conditions does the problem occur? Which aspects of the operating system control those conditions? Is the problem specific to a subsystem (networks, video, and so on)?

Consider the following:

- Has the system or configuration ever worked? If so, what changed?
- Is the error condition reproducible or random?
- Is the error specific to a particular system, configuration, or application?
- What specific hardware and firmware is involved?
- Are any non-Windows 95 device drivers or TSRs loaded?
- Does the order by which drivers or applications start up make a difference?
- Does the error still occur with Safe Mode, or Safe Mode with Network Support? (These startup options are "Using Windows 95 Startup Menu Options" later in this chapter.)

## Checking for Common Issues

Check to see if the problem is a common issue by reviewing online Help and any .TXT files included on the Windows 95 distribution disks. For example, check SETUP.TXT and README.TXT.

For general information about the problems listed in the following table, see the related chapter in the *Windows 95 Resource Kit.*

| Problem | Related chapter reference |
|---|---|
| Cannot install Windows 95 | Chapter 6, "Setup Technical Discussion" |
| Computer won't start or Windows 95 won't run | Chapter 6, "Setup Technical Discussion" |
| Network connectivity problem | Chapter 7, "Introduction to Windows 95 Networking" |
| Local or network printing problem | Chapter 23, "Printing and Fonts" |
| Application error or general protection fault | Chapter 22, "Application Support" |

The Windows 95 online Help includes troubleshooting aids for solving specific problems with the following components of a computer:

- Printing
- Running out of memory
- Freeing disk space
- Hardware conflicts
- Running MS-DOS programs
- Using the network
- Using your modem
- Using Dial-Up Networking
- Using Direct Cable Connection
- Using a portable computer card (PCMCIA)
- Starting Windows 95

▶ **To get troubleshooting assistance from Windows 95 Help**

1. From the Start button, click Help.

2. At the Contents tab, click Troubleshooting, and then pick a topic from the list.

# Isolating and Testing the Error Condition

Eliminating variables helps determine a problem's cause. You can isolate specific causes by removing unnecessary lines in CONFIG.SYS and AUTOEXEC.BAT. Do not remove lines that are necessary to access the hard disk or to run Windows 95 Setup.

You can also isolate the cause by changing a specific value, and then testing to see if the problem has been corrected or altered. For instance, if you suspect a damaged Registry, you could restore the Registry files (SYSTEM.DAT and USER.DAT) from backup files, and then retest.

If a component fails after upgrading to a new driver, replace it with the original driver and retest. If Windows 95 startup fails while loading a real-mode device driver, or if any device driver is suspect in causing an error condition, you can test the effect of not loading a device driver. To bypass individual, real-mode device drivers, press F8 when the Starting Windows message appears and then select the Step-By-Step Confirmation option. (This process is described in detail in "Safe Mode" later in this chapter.) Removing protected-mode drivers can be done in Device Manager in the System option in Control Panel.

Test each modification individually to see if it solved the problem. Make note of all modifications and their effect on symptoms. This provides you with the information you need to contact product support personnel, if necessary, and provides an excellent reference for future troubleshooting.

## Checking Technical Support Resources

When possible, post persistent problems on the appropriate online forum. Other users may have already discovered, reported, and found workarounds for your problem. Suggestions from others may save you time in tracking down the source of the problem and might give you ideas that can help.

For information about Microsoft TechNet and how to get help from product support using online resources such as The Microsoft Network, see Appendix J, "Windows 95 Resource Directory."

# Windows 95 Troubleshooting Aids for Startup

Windows 95 contains log files and includes utilities that can assist you in correcting problems that occur during the setup or startup processes. In this section, the following built-in troubleshooting aids are described:

- Safe Recovery with Windows 95 Setup
- Installed components verification
- Startup disk
- Startup Menu options
- WIN.COM switches

# Using Safe Recovery with Windows 95 Setup

Setup uses Safe Recovery to determine what caused an installation to fail. Safe Recovery uses the information available in DETCRASH.LOG, for example, to avoid performing detection on the same device that caused Setup to fail before.

▶ **To use Safe Recovery if Setup fails**

1. Run Setup again.

2. When the Safe Recovery screen appears, click Safe Recovery.

You can also use the SETUPLOG.TXT, DETLOG.TXT, and BOOTLOG.TXT files in the root directory of the boot drive to determine why Setup failed. These text files contain, respectively, the Safe Recovery and hardware detection information in a readable form, plus a log of system startup actions. SETUPLOG.TXT, for example, will show the point at which Setup failed.

To automatically scan these log files for installation or detection errors, you can use the following commands in a setup script. Create a batch file containing the following text and run it from the root directory of the boot drive (C:\) after an unsuccessful Setup attempt.

```
@echo off
echo "Entries found in Setuplog.txt" > log.txt
find /i /n "installtype" setuplog.txt >> log.txt
find /i /n "installdir" setuplog.txt >> log.txt
find /i /n "detection" setuplog.txt >> log.txt
find /i /n "runningapp" setuplog.txt >> log.txt
find /i /n "rootfilesrenamed" setuplog.txt >> log.txt
find /i /n "error" setuplog.txt >> log.txt
find /i /n "failed" setuplog.txt >> log.txt
echo "Entries found in Bootlog.txt" >> log.txt
find /i /n "fail" bootlog.txt >> log.txt
find /i /n "error" bootlog.txt >> log.txt
find /i /n "dynamic load success" bootlog.txt >> log.txt
find /i /n "initcomplete success" bootlog.txt >> log.txt
echo "Entries found in Detlog.txt" >> log.txt
find /i /n "avoidmem" detlog.txt >> log.txt
find /i /n "detected" detlog.txt >> log.txt
find /i /n "error" detlog.txt >> log.txt
cls
type log.txt |more
```

For more information about how Safe Recovery and hardware detection work, and about the contents of the log files, see Chapter 6, "Setup Technical Discussion."

# Verifying Installed Components with Windows 95 Setup

Windows 95 provides an option for verifying installed components when Setup detects an existing Windows 95 installation. When you use the Verify option, Setup reads SETUPLOG.TXT for the installed components and reruns the Setup process to verify all system components. If Verify fails as a result of a missing or damaged file, Setup reinstalls the file. As part of this verification, Setup rebuilds VMM32.VXD and recopies any required files.

Windows 95 also provides a way in the user interface to check whether the version of DLL or support file is current. For information, see "Checking for Correct File Versions" later in this chapter.

# Using a Startup Disk

You can use a Windows 95 startup disk to load the operating system and display an MS-DOS command prompt. The startup disk also contains utilities for troubleshooting a malfunctioning operating system. You can create a startup disk during Windows 95 Setup or afterward in Control Panel.

> Caution   It is strongly recommended that you create a startup disk as part of Windows 95 Setup, and that you maintain an updated copy of the startup disk each time you change the system configuration after installing Windows 95.

If you did not create a startup disk during Setup, you can create one using a single floppy disk.

▶ **To create a startup disk after Windows 95 is installed**

- In the Add/Remove Programs option in Control Panel, click the Startup Disk tab. Then click the Create Disk button, and follow the instructions on-screen.

# Using Windows 95 Startup Menu Options

If the system fails to start, Windows 95 displays a Startup menu that contains troubleshooting options. You can also manually prompt Windows 95 to display the Startup menu.

▶ **To display the Windows 95 Startup menu**

- Restart the computer. When the Starting Windows 95 message appears, press F8.

The following table describes Startup menu options. The contents of this menu can vary, depending on the options specified in the MSDOS.SYS, and the configuration of the computer.

| Startup menu option | Description |
| --- | --- |
| Normal | Starts Windows, loading all normal startup files and Registry values. |
| Logged (BOOTLOG.TXT) | Runs system startup creating a startup log file. For information about using BOOTLOG.TXT, see Chapter 6, "Setup Technical Discussion." |
| Safe Mode | Starts Windows, bypassing startup files and using only basic system drivers. You can also start this option by pressing F5 or typing **win /d:m** at the command prompt. |
| Safe Mode with Network Support | Starts Windows, bypassing startup files and using only basic system drivers, including basic networking. You can also start this option by pressing F6 or typing **win /d:n** at the command prompt. |
| Step-By-Step Confirmation | Starts Windows, confirming startup files line by line. You can also start this option by pressing F8 when the Startup menu is displayed. For more information, see "Step-By-Step Confirmation" later in this chapter. |
| Command Prompt Only[1] | Starts the operating system with startup files and Registry, displaying only the command prompt. |
| Safe Mode Command Prompt Only[1] | Starts the operating system in Safe Mode and displays only the command prompt, bypassing startup files. Same as pressing SHIFT+F5. |
| Previous version of MS-DOS | Starts the version of MS-DOS previously installed on this computer. You can also start this option by pressing F4. This option is only available if **BootMulti=1** in MSDOS.SYS.[2] |

[1] When you start the computer at the command prompt, you can use switches with the **win** command to control Windows 95 startup for troubleshooting purposes, as described in "Using WIN.COM Switches" later in this chapter.

[2] For information about the options in MSDOS.SYS, see Chapter 6, "Setup Technical Discussion."

The following sections describe when to use these Startup menu options to troubleshoot system problems.

**Tip** Windows 95 uses entries in the MSDOS.SYS file to control Startup menu options, automatic loading of certain drivers, and path statements for system files. If Windows 95 does not start as expected, check the entries in MSDOS.SYS.

# Safe Mode

If Windows 95 fails to start normally, select Safe Mode from the Startup menu to begin troubleshooting. Windows 95 automatically initiates Safe Mode if it detects that system startup failed (for example, if a WNBOOTNG.STS signature file still exists in the Windows directory), or if the Registry is corrupted (for example, if an important key such as SYSTEM is missing), or if an application requests Safe Mode.

Safe Mode bypasses startup files, including the Registry, CONFIG.SYS, AUTOEXEC.BAT, and the [Boot] and [386Enh] sections of SYSTEM.INI, and provides you with access to the Windows 95 configuration files. You can make any necessary configuration changes, and then restart Windows 95 normally.

Use Safe Mode for system startup in situations such as the following:

- If Windows 95 fails to start after the Starting Windows 95 message appears
- If Windows 95 seems to stall for an extended period
- If Windows 95 doesn't work correctly or has unexpected results
- If you cannot print to a local printer after attempting other troubleshooting steps
- If your video display doesn't work correctly
- If your computer stalls repeatedly
- If your computer suddenly slows down
- If you need to test an intermittent error condition

When starting Windows 95 in Safe Mode, only the mouse, keyboard, and standard VGA device drivers are loaded. This makes Safe Mode useful for isolating and resolving error conditions caused by both real-mode and Windows drivers. This option is identical to typing **win /d:m** at the command line, as described in "Using WIN.COM Switches" later in this chapter.

The Startup menu can include three to four Safe Mode options, depending on whether the computer is compressed, or part of a network. Each Safe Mode option disables a different portion of the startup process, as shown in the following table.

| Action | Safe Mode | Safe Mode, Network Support | Command Prompt Only[1] |
|---|---|---|---|
| Process CONFIG.SYS and AUTOEXEC.BAT | – | – | – |
| Load HIMEM.SYS and IFSHLP.SYS | X | X | – |
| Process Registry information | – | X | – |
| Load COMMAND.COM | – | X | X |
| Load DoubleSpace or DriveSpace if present | X | X | –[1] |
| Run Windows 95 WIN.COM | X | X | – |
| Load all Windows drivers | – | – | – |
| Load network drivers | – | X | – |
| Run NETSTART.BAT | – | X | – |

[1] The Safe Mode Command Prompt Only option also loads DoubleSpace or DriveSpace if present.

## Safe Mode Command Prompt Only

Safe Mode Command Prompt Only loads the COMMAND.COM and DoubleSpace or DriveSpace (if present) files. It does not load HIMEM.SYS, IFSHLP.SYS, or Windows 95.

The following are examples of when to use Safe Mode Command Prompt Only:

- If Windows 95 fails to start, even with the Safe Mode option
- If you want to use command-line switches (such as **win /d:x**)
- If you want to use command line tools (such as editing CONFIG.SYS)
- If you want to avoid loading HIMEM.SYS or IFSHLP.SYS

## Safe Mode Without Compression

This option appears on the Startup menu only if the computer has a compressed drive. This option loads COMMAND.COM, and does not load any compression drivers. The computer starts at the real-mode command prompt.

The following are examples of when to use Safe Mode Without Compression:

- If the computer stops responding when accessing a compressed drive
- If a Corrupt CVF error occurs during system startup
- If Windows 95 fails to start, and both Safe Mode (F5) and Safe Mode Command Prompt Only (SHIFT+F5) are unsuccessful
- If you want to bypass compression drivers

## Safe Mode with Network Support

You can use the Safe Mode With Network Support option in networking environments where users might require network connectivity to recover from a system problem. If the operating system starts with Safe Mode but not with Safe Mode with Networking, the network configuration probably requires further adjustment.

The following are examples of when to use Safe Mode with Network Support:

- When Startup stalls and Safe Mode is unsuccessful
- If the computer stops responding when accessing a remote network
- If you cannot print to a network printer
- If the computer is running shared Windows 95 installation

This option loads the following files and drivers:

- HIMEM.SYS and IFSHLP.SYS (irrespective of CONFIG.SYS settings)
- DoubleSpace or DriveSpace drivers (if present)
- Windows 95
- Basic network drivers

It also processes Registry information and runs NETSTART.BAT (if required for real-mode networking from another vendor).

This option does not process CONFIG.SYS and AUTOEXEC.BAT, but does load COMMAND.COM. It only processes AUTOEXEC.BAT if no Windows 95 version of MSDOS.SYS is present, or if the [Paths] section in MSDOS.SYS is invalid and no valid **WinDir=** entry is present.

If the [Paths] section and the **WinDir=** variable are not defined in MSDOS.SYS when you use this option, NETSTART.BAT does not run; only AUTOEXEC.BAT runs, and Windows 95 fails to load.

You cannot use Safe Mode with Network Support when the Registry is corrupted.

Most existing real-mode networks run from the startup files, and all Safe Mode options bypass these files. The NETSTART.BAT file in the Windows directory contains commands for starting Microsoft or NetWare networks. NETSTART.BAT allows Windows 95 to start most real-mode networks on individual computers without running AUTOEXEC.BAT and CONFIG.SYS.

▶ **To troubleshoot a system problem if NETSTART.BAT doesn't start the network**

1. When the Starting Windows 95 message appears, press F8, and then select the Step-By-Step Confirmation option. (For more information, see the following section.)

2. Answer Yes when prompted to process startup device drivers (CONFIG.SYS) and the startup command file (AUTOEXEC.BAT).

3. Answer Yes to process all network driver lines.

## Step-By-Step Confirmation

Step-By-Step Confirmation allows you to specify which commands and drivers the system should process by confirming each line of the startup files.

The following are examples of when to use Step-By-Step Confirmation:

- If the startup process fails during loading of the startup files
- If any real-mode drivers must be loaded to run Windows 95 successfully
- If you need to check for Registry failure messages
- If you need to verify that the expected drivers are being loaded
- If you need to temporarily disable a specific driver or set of drivers
- If you need to check for errors in startup files

For information about which drivers are required for system startup, see "Checking Whether a Required Driver Is Missing" later in this chapter.

When you choose to confirm system startup line by line, the following prompts appear. You can press ENTER to confirm or ESC to skip that part of system startup.

- Load DoubleSpace (or DriveSpace) driver?
- Process the system Registry?
- Create a startup log file (BOOTLOG.TXT)?
- Process your startup device drivers (CONFIG.SYS)?

  Each line from CONFIG.SYS is displayed with the [Enter=Y,Esc=N] prompt. You can press TAB when the first CONFIG.SYS prompt appears to accept all options automatically.

- Process your startup command file (AUTOEXEC.BAT)?

  Each line from AUTOEXEC.BAT is displayed with the [Enter=Y,Esc=N] prompt. You can press TAB when the first AUTOEXEC.BAT prompt appears to accept all options automatically.

- Run WIN.COM to start Windows 95?
- Load all Windows drivers?

If you press ENTER to answer Yes to each prompt, the result is the same as starting Windows 95 normally except that the logo does not appear. Answering No to "Load All Windows Drivers?" runs Windows 95 in Safe Mode.

## Using WIN.COM Switches

The following switches are available to start Windows 95 from the command prompt when you need to isolate an error condition:

**win** [**/d:**[**f**] [**m**] [**n**] [**s**] [**v**] [**x**]]

The **/d:** switch is used for troubleshooting when Windows 95 does not start correctly. The switches in the following table can be used with the **/d:** switch.

| Switch | Description |
| --- | --- |
| f | Turn off 32-bit disk access. Try this if the computer appears to have disk problems, or if Windows 95 stalls. This is equivalent to **32BitDiskAccess=FALSE** in SYSTEM.INI. |
| m | Starts Windows 95 in Safe Mode. |
| n | Starts Windows 95 in Safe Mode with Networking. |
| s | Specifies that Windows 95 not use ROM address space between F000:0000 and 1 MB for a break point. Try this if Windows 95 stalls during system startup. This is equivalent to **SystemROMBreakPoint=FALSE** in SYSTEM.INI. |
| v | Specifies that the ROM routine should handle interrupts from the hard disk controller. Try this if Windows 95 stalls during system startup or disk operations. This is equivalent to **VirtualHDIRQ=FALSE** in SYSTEM.INI. |
| x | Excludes all of the adapter area from the memory that Windows 95 scans to find unused space. This is equivalent to **EMMExclude=A000-FFFF** in SYSTEM.INI. |

# Troubleshooting Procedures

This section provides basic instructions for troubleshooting problems that may occur when running Windows 95.

---

**Important**  Create and keep a startup disk, and verify that it works before you need it. Always make backup copies of configuration files (especially SYSTEM.DAT and USER.DAT).

A particularly good time for backing up files and updating the startup disk is after you install new devices and applications, when you have a good working configuration.

---

If you try to copy configuration or Registry files from within Windows 95, an error message might appear. In this case, you must remove the system and hidden attributes of the files and copy the files while running in Safe Mode Command Prompt Only to prevent the Registry from being loaded.

# Checking Specific Driver Problems

Loading a specific driver in CONFIG.SYS, AUTOEXEC.BAT, or Windows 95 Registry may cause a computer to stall. This could be due to a hardware or software (device driver or TSR) conflict.

To determine whether hardware or software is stalling the computer, try the following:

- Press F8 at the Starting Windows 95 message, and select Safe Mode Command Prompt Only. If this option prevents the computer from stalling on startup, a device driver or TSR is a likely cause of the problem.

  Restart the computer, and press F8 again, and then select the Step-By-Step Confirmation option to check for TSRs that are loading and may be causing the problem.

- If you use disk compression and the computer still stalls after using Safe Mode Command Prompt Only to start the computer, restart the computer in Safe Mode Without Compression by pressing CTRL+F5 when the Starting Windows 95 message appears.

- Check the CMOS settings in the computer's BIOS configuration menus, making sure the settings match your installed hardware.

- Check the hardware installation and the manufacturer's documentation to verify that all devices are correctly installed.

- Check resource settings in Device Manager for specific installed hardware to make sure no conflicts exist in the IRQ, I/O address, DMA channels, and memory addresses used. Compare your actual installation with your hardware documentation for inconsistencies in the settings used. For information, see Chapter 19, "Devices."

▶ **To check whether a specific driver is stalling the computer**

- Restart the computer. Press F8 when the Starting Windows 95 message appears, and then select the Logged (BOOTLOG.TXT) option. Search the BOOTLOG.TXT file for errors. For information about this file, see Chapter 6, "Setup Technical Discussion."

# Checking for Correct File Versions

In Windows 95, you can view a file's properties to determine its version number and other information such as when it was created. You can use this information to determine whether a DLL or other supporting file is out of date. Notice, however, that not all DLL files display this information.

▶ **To view information about a system file**

1. In Windows Explorer, right-click the filename, and then click Properties in the context menu.

2. For a supporting or executable file, click the Version tab. Use the Other Version Information list to see details about the file.

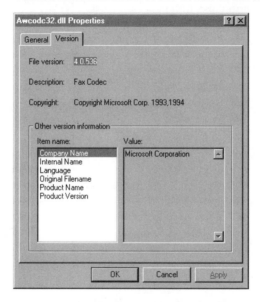

# Checking for Missing System Files

A missing operating system file prevents the startup process from continuing. If you are missing only the COMMAND.COM file, you can fix this problem from the Startup menu as described in "Safe Mode Command Prompt Only" earlier in this chapter, or from a Windows 95 startup disk as described in this section.

This section also describes how to check and restore the IO.SYS and MSDOS.SYS system files. Windows 95 uses the same names for the real-mode operating system files as MS-DOS does (IO.SYS, MSDOS.SYS, and COMMAND.COM). However, to support dual-boot, the MS-DOS versions of these files are renamed with a .DOS extension when you install or start Windows 95 after having started the computer with the previous operating system.

▶ **To replace or reinstall the real-mode operating system files on drive C**

1. Start the computer using the Windows 95 startup disk.

2. At the command prompt for the startup drive, type **sys c:** to copy IO.SYS, MSDOS.SYS, DRVSPACE.BIN, and COMMAND.COM to drive C. This rewrites the boot sector.

3. Remove the floppy disk, and then restart the computer.

If COMMAND.COM is missing, a message indicates this and prompts you to type the path for the file.

▶ **To restore COMMAND.COM using command-line commands**

1. Insert the startup disk into the floppy disk drive.

2. At the command prompt, type the following:

```
attrib -r -s -h c:\command.com
copy a:command.com c:\
```

If the Windows 95 MSDOS.SYS file is missing, a blue screen presents a message: "Invalid Vxd dynamic link call from IFSMGR (03)." This is followed by an error initializing IFSMGR, and startup fails.

Errors that appear during system startup related to the Registry, XMS, and IFSMGR, are all caused by invalid syntax in the specification of the [Paths] section of MSDOS.SYS or the **WinDir=** entry. Setting the **WinDir=** value causes IO.SYS to use that value to set the following environment variables:

```
tmp=WinDir
temp=WinDir
path=WinDir; WinDir\command
comspec=WinDir\command.com
```

If no valid **WinDir=** entry is found in MSDOS.SYS, the path defaults to C:\WINDOWS, and COMSPEC defaults to C:\COMMAND.COM.

If IO.SYS is missing, the computer stalls before the Starting Windows 95 message appears and displays a message. The message says that the system disk is invalid and prompts you to replace it. You must use a bootable Windows 95 disk (such as the startup disk) to start the computer. You will then need to reinstall the real-mode operating system files on drive C as described in the preceding procedure.

You can also restore the COMMAND.COM in Windows 95.

▶ **To restore COMMAND.COM using Windows Explorer**

1. Restart the computer, press F8 at the Starting Windows 95 message, and then select the Safe Mode option.

2. Insert the startup disk into the startup drive.

3. Using My Computer or Windows Explorer, find COMMAND.COM on the floppy disk drive, and then drag the file from the floppy disk to the root directory of the boot drive.

# Removing Unnecessary Drivers

To determine which drivers should be removed so that they will not be loaded, first try to start the computer without these drivers before removing them from CONFIG.SYS and AUTOEXEC.BAT (and .BAT files called from the AUTOEXEC.BAT).

▶ **To determine which drivers can be removed**

- Restart the computer, press F8 at the Starting Windows 95 message, and then select the Step-By-Step Confirmation option. Temporarily remove specific drivers or prevent TSRs from loading to determine whether the computer can run successfully without them.

# Checking Whether a Required Driver Is Missing

Some computers contain devices that require a specific driver in CONFIG.SYS to correctly complete the startup process, such as drivers used for partitioning, compression, video, hard disks, and so forth.

▶ **To check for missing drivers**

1. Press F8 when the Starting Windows 95 message appears, and select the Step-By-Step Confirmation option.

2. Respond Yes to all prompts. For any error messages that appear, make note of the driver involved, its location, and the specific wording of the error message. Verify that the specified driver exists in the specified location.

Do not remove any hard disk drivers, disk partitioning drivers, or disk compression drivers when starting Windows 95 using the Step-By-Step Confirmation option or while editing startup files. The following is a partial list of drivers that should not be removed.

**Drivers that Should Not Be Removed**

**Hard disk drivers:**

| | | | |
|---|---|---|---|
| ah1544.sys | ilm386.sys | scsiha.sys | sstbio.sys |
| aspi4dos.sys | nonstd.sys | skydrvi.sys | sstdrive.sys |
| atdosxl.sys | scsidsk.exe | sqy55.sys | |

**Partitioning drivers:**

| | | | |
|---|---|---|---|
| dmdrvr.bin | evdr.sys | ldrive.sys | sstor.sys |
| enhdisk.sys | fixt_drv.sys | hardrive.sys | |

**Compression drivers:**

| | | |
|---|---|---|
| dblspace.bin | drvspace.bin | sswap.com |
| devswap.com | sstor.exe | stacker.com |

To find out about other system drivers, see the documentation for the hardware or software installed on the system.

# Checking Entries in Startup Files

The CONFIG.SYS and AUTOEXEC.BAT files contain system startup drivers, settings, and paths, and you may need to verify the accuracy of these entries. To determine which drivers to load, press F8 at the Starting Windows 95 message and select Step-By-Step Confirmation.

To check entries in CONFIG.SYS, perform the following tasks:

- Verify that only necessary drivers are loading.
- Check for invalid syntax.

To check entries in AUTOEXEC.BAT, perform the following tasks:

- To display environment variables including COMSPEC, type **set** at the command prompt.
- Verify that paths are valid.

# Checking for Conflicts at System Startup

If a computer fails to start Windows 95, try the following tasks:

- Check for upper memory area conflicts. If you suspect an upper memory conflict, use **win /d:x** to start Windows 95.

- Check whether Safe Mode resolves the problem. To verify whether loading minimal drivers will resolve the problem, use F5 or **win /d:m** to start Windows 95.

- Check for conflict with 32-bit disk access. If you don't want to load 32-bit disk access, use **win /d:f** to start Windows 95.

- Check for hard disk I/O conflicts. If you want to force **VirtualHDIRQ=Off**, use **win /d:v** to start Windows 95. For more information, see "Using WIN.COM Switches" earlier in this chapter.

- Check for and remove unnecessary drivers and TSRs, and retry.

- Check for device conflicts by using Device Manager in the System option in Control Panel.

- Check for an outdated or damaged VxD by examining the BOOTLOG.TXT and then do the following:

  - If it is in the Windows SYSTEM\IOSUBSYS directory, rename it.

  - If it has a .386 filename extension, examine the [386Enh] section of SYSTEM.INI and remark out its lines. When renaming VxDs, be sure to change the .VXD extension. Windows 95 loads all files in the IOSUBSYS subdirectory that have a .VXD extension.

  - If it is in VMM32.VXD, check the Windows SYSTEM\VMM32 directory for a VMM32 file, and rename or move it.

# Checking Device Configuration

Errors are sometimes caused by conflicts between devices trying to use the same system resources. Device Manager provides a central place where you can verify that devices are configured correctly and do conflict with other devices.

▶ **To check for resource conflicts among devices**

1. In the System option in Control Panel, click the Device Manager tab.

2. Click the + (plus) symbol to the left of the device class, and then double-click a specific device to display its Properties dialog box.

3. Click the Resources tab, and check the Conflicting Device List for conflicts with another device.

---

**Note**  For network adapters, resource information is provided in the Network option in Control Panel, not in Device Manager.

Also, if you use multiple configurations, you need to first select the appropriate configuration using the list in the device's Resource properties.

---

# Checking for Free Disk Space

Running out of space on the disk drive used for TEMP and swap files can cause a variety of operational and installation errors. If you need more disk space, see the troubleshooting aid for disk space problems in online Help.

To check for free space at the command prompt, try the following:

- Use the **chkdsk** *drive* command at the command prompt to display the available disk space in the Bytes Available on Disk line.

- Use the **dir** *drive* command at the command prompt to view the bytes free at the end of the DIR display.

You might want to check the swap file settings.

For more information about troubleshooting memory problems, see Chapter 17, "Performance Tuning." See also online Help.

▶ **To check the swap file settings**

- In the System option in Control Panel, click the Performance tab, and then click the Virtual Memory button.

---

**Important**  By default, Windows 95 manages the virtual memory settings. Changing these settings can adversely affect system performance. The recommended setting in this dialog box is to let Windows manage virtual memory settings.

---

▶ **To check for lost allocation units from a command line**

1. Press F8 when the Starting Windows 95 message appears and select the Safe Mode Command Prompt Only option.

2. Run ScanDisk from the Windows COMMAND directory.

   ScanDisk detects lost allocation units, and prompts you to recover them.

For information about running ScanDisk in Windows 95, see Chapter 20, "Disks and File Systems."

▶ **To check the TEMP variable**

1. At the command prompt, type **set** to display the TEMP variable.

2. Verify that the TEMP variable points to a valid drive and directory.

   Check for free disk space on the drive that contains the TEMP directory. If you are printing multiple copies of a large document, or printing large PostScript documents, increase the minimum available free disk space.

# Isolating File System Errors

To determine what is causing file system errors, you generally need to isolate the specific subsystem or component involved. One place to start troubleshooting file system error conditions is through the System option in Control Panel. For information about troubleshooting the file system, see Chapter 17, "Performance Tuning."

# Checking for Disk Corruption

Key operating system data structures prevent system startup if they are damaged. These structures include the master boot record, the boot sector, the file allocation table, and the core operating system files.

Caution  Back up key data files before performing any disk repair operations.

Do not run any disk utilities that are not specifically designed for Windows 95. Earlier versions of disk repair utilities may not work properly. To prevent possible data loss, use a disk utility such as ScanDisk which is specifically designed for Windows 95. For details, see Chapter 20, "Disks and File Systems."

▶ **To check for disk corruption with Safe Mode Command Prompt Only**

1. Restart the computer, press F8 when the Starting Windows 95 message appears, and then select the Safe Mode Command Prompt Only option.

2. Change to the Windows COMMAND directory, and then type **scandisk**.

   This method will also check and repair the file allocation table.

If corruption is detected, you may need to replace system files and structures.

# PART 8

# Appendixes

8

This part of the *Windows 95 Resource Kit* contains supplemental technical information for administrators and users of Windows 95.

### Glossary

Defines the technical terms used in the *Resource Kit*.

### Appendix A    Command-Line Commands Summary

Lists and describes commands that can be used at the command prompt or in batch scripts in Windows 95. This includes MS-DOS and networking commands, EMM386, commands for ScanDisk, Defrag, and DiskSpace, and TCP/IP commands.

### Appendix B    Windows 95 System Files

Provides information about the system files supplied with Windows 95, the directory structure, and the standard files installed for various Windows 95 configurations.

### Appendix C    Windows 95 INF Files

Describes the format of device information (INF) files and provides detailed information on the purpose of each section in the file.

### Appendix D    MSBATCH.INF Parameters

Defines the setup script parameters and provides setup script examples.

### Appendix E    Microsoft Systems Management Server

Provides information about Microsoft Systems Management Server and how it can be used to install and maintain Windows 95 on networked computers.

### Appendix F    Macintosh and Windows 95

Describes how Microsoft Windows NT Server Services for Macintosh makes it possible for computers running Windows 95, MS-DOS, Windows, Windows for Workgroups, Windows NT, and Apple Macintosh to share files and printers.

### Appendix G    HOSTS and LMHOSTS Files for Windows 95

Describes how to modify HOSTS and LMHOSTS files to support address-to-name resolution on networks that use TCP/IP.

### Appendix H    Shortcuts for Windows 95

Summarizes the shortcuts built into Windows 95 for using the keyboard and mouse to quickly accomplish common actions. This includes a summary of some accessibility shortcuts.

### Appendix I    Accessibility

Describes new features in Windows 95 that make Windows 95 more accessible for people with disabilities.

### Appendix J    Windows 95 Resource Directory

Provides information on obtaining additional support and information for Windows 95 and getting the most out of using Microsoft products.

# Glossary

## A

**ACK**  An acknowledgment signal.

**active window**  The window in which the user is currently working. An active window is typically at the top of the window order and is distinguished by the color of its title bar.

**agent**  Software that runs on a client computer for use by administrative software running on a server. Agents are typically used to support administrative actions, such as detecting system information or running services.

**application programming interface (API)**  A set of routines that an application program uses to request and carry out lower-level services performed by the operating system.

**ASCII file**  *See* text file.

**associate**  To identify a filename extension as "belonging" to a certain program, so that when you open any file with that extension, the program starts automatically.

## B

**batch program**  An ASCII file (unformatted text file) that contains one or more commands. A batch program's filename has a BAT or CMD extension. When you type the filename at the command prompt, the commands are processed sequentially.

**binding**  A process that establishes the communication channel between a protocol driver and a network adapter driver.

**BIOS enumerator**  Responsible, in a Plug and Play system, for identifying all hardware devices on the motherboard of the computer. The BIOS supports an API that allows all Plug and Play computers to be queried in a common manner.

**branch**  A segment of the directory tree, representing a directory and any subdirectories it contains.

**browse**  To look through lists of directories, files, user accounts, groups, domains, or computers.

**buffer**  A reserved portion of memory in which data is temporarily held, pending an opportunity to complete its transfer to or from a storage device or another location in memory.

**buffering**  The process of using buffers to hold data that is being transferred, particularly to or from I/O devices such as disk drives and serial ports.

**bus enumerator**  A new type of driver required for each specific bus type, responsible for building ("enumerating") the hardware tree on a Plug and Play system.

## C

**Card Services**  A system component that is a protected-mode VxD, linked with the PCMCIA bus driver. Card Services passes the event notification from socket services to the PCMCIA bus driver, provides information from the computer's cards to the PCMCIA bus driver, and sets up the configuration for cards in the adapter sockets.

**cascading menu**  A menu that is a submenu of a menu item. Also known as a hierarchical menu.

**CDFS**  Compact disc file system, which controls access to the contents of CD-ROM drives.

**character mode**  A mode of operation in which all information is displayed as text characters. This is the mode in which MS-DOS–based applications are displayed in windows in Windows 95. Also called alphanumeric mode or text mode.

**class**  1. For OLE, the definition of a data structure and functions that manipulate that data. Objects are instances of a class; that is, an object must be a member of a given class. 2. For hardware, the manner in which devices and buses are grouped for purposes of installing and managing device drivers and allocating resources. The hardware tree is organized by device class, and Windows 95 uses class installers to install drivers for all hardware classes.

**client**  A computer that accesses shared network resources provided by another computer (called a server). *See also* server.

**codec**  Compression/decompression technology for digital video and stereo audio.

**computer name**  A unique name of up to 15 characters that identifies a computer to the network. The name cannot be the same as any other computer or domain name in the network, and it cannot contain spaces.

**Configuration Manager**  The central component of a Plug and Play system that drives the process of locating devices, setting up their nodes in the hardware tree, and running the resource allocation process. Each of the three phases of configuration management—boot time (BIOS), real mode, and protected mode—has its own configuration manager.

**context menu**  A menu that is displayed at the location of a selected object (sometimes called a context menu or shortcut menu). The menu contains commands that are contextual to the selection.

**Control menu**  *See* context menu.

**controller**  *See* domain controller.

# D

**data frame**  Logical, structured packets in which data can be placed. The Data Link layer packages raw bits from the Physical layer into data frames. The exact format of the frame used by the network depends on the topology.

**datagram**  A packet of data and other delivery information that is routed through a packet-switched network or transmitted on a local area network.

**DDE**  *See* dynamic data exchange.

**default**  An operation or value that the system assumes, unless the user makes an explicit choice.

**device**  A generic term for a computer component, such as a printer, serial port, or disk drive. A device frequently requires its own controlling software called a device driver.

**device contention**  The way Windows 95 allocates access to peripheral devices, such as a modem or a printer, when more than one application is trying to use the same device.

**device driver**  A program that enables a specific piece of hardware (device) to communicate with Windows 95. Although a device may be installed on your computer, Windows 95 cannot recognize the device until you have installed and configured the appropriate driver.

**device ID**  A unique ASCII string created by enumerators to identify a hardware device and used to cross-reference data about the device stored in the Registry.

**device node**  The basic data structure for a given device, built by Configuration Manager; sometimes called devnode. Device nodes are built into memory at system startup for each device and enumerator with information about the device, such as currently assigned resources. The complete representation of all device nodes is referred to as the hardware tree.

**DHCP**  *See* Dynamic Host Configuration Protocol.

**Dial-Up Networking**  A service that provides remote networking for telecommuters, mobile workers, and system administrators who monitor and manage servers at multiple branch offices. Users with Dial-Up Networking on a computer running Windows 95 can dial in for remote access to their networks for services such as file and printer sharing, electronic mail, scheduling, and SQL database access.

**directory tree**  The directories and subdirectories branching out from the root directory in the FAT file system.

**disk caching**  A method used by a file system to improve performance. Instead of reading and writing directly to the disk, frequently used files are temporarily stored in a cache in memory, and reads and writes to those files are performed in memory. Reading and writing to memory is much faster than reading and writing to disk.

**DLL**  *See* dynamic-link library.

**DMA channel**  A channel for direct memory access that does not involve the microprocessor, providing data transfer directly between memory and a disk drive.

**DNS**  *See* Domain Name System.

**dock**  To insert a portable computer into a base unit. Cold docking means the computer must begin from a power-off state and restart before docking. Hot docking means the computer can be docked while running at full power.

**docking station**  The base computer unit into which a user can insert a portable computer, to expand it to a desktop equivalent. A typical dock provides drive bays, expansion slots, all the ports on the desktop computer, and AC power.

**domain**  For Microsoft networking, a collection of computers that share a common domain database and security policy that is stored on a Windows NT Server domain controller. Each domain has a unique name. *See also* workgroup.

**domain controller**  The Windows NT Server computer that authenticates domain logons and maintains the security policy and the master database for a domain.

**Domain Name System (DNS)**  Sometimes referred to as the BIND service in BSD UNIX; a static, hierarchical name service for TCP/IP hosts. A DNS server maintains a database for resolving host names and IP addresses, allowing users of computers configured to query the DNS to specify remote computers by host names rather than IP addresses. DNS domains should not be confused with Windows NT networking domains.

**dynamic data exchange (DDE)**  A form of interprocess communication (IPC) implemented in the Microsoft Windows family of operating systems. Two or more programs that support dynamic data exchange (DDE) can exchange information and commands. Most DDE functions have been superseded in later versions of OLE.

**Dynamic Host Configuration Protocol (DHCP)**  A protocol for automatic TCP/IP configuration that provides static and dynamic address allocation and management.

**dynamic-link library (DLL)**  An application programming interface (API) routine that user-mode applications access through ordinary procedure calls. The code for the API routine is not included in the user's executable image. Instead, the operating system automatically modifies the executable image to point to DLL procedures at run time.

# E

**EISA**  Enhanced Industry Standard Architecture, a bus design specified by an industry consortium for x86-based computers. An EISA device uses cards that are upwardly compatible from ISA.

**encapsulated PostScript (EPS) file**  A file that prints at the highest possible resolution for your printer. An EPS file may print faster than other graphical representations.

**enumerator**  A Plug and Play device driver that detects devices below its own device node, creates unique device IDs, and reports to Configuration Manager during startup. For example, a SCSI adapter provides a SCSI enumerator that detects devices on the SCSI bus.

**environment variable**  A string consisting of environment information, such as a drive, path, or filename, associated with a symbolic name that can be used by Windows 95. You use the System option in Control Panel or the **set** command from the command prompt to define environment variables.

**event**  1. An action or occurrence to which an application might respond. Examples of events are clicks, key presses, and mouse movements. 2. Any significant occurrence in the system or in a program that requires users to be notified, or an entry to be added to a log.

# F

**FAT file system**  A file system based on a file allocation table, maintained by the operating system, to keep track of the status of various segments of disk space used for file storage. The 32-bit implementation in Windows 95 is called the Virtual File Allocation Table (VFAT).

**file allocation table (FAT)**  *See* FAT file system.

**file sharing**  The ability of a Microsoft network computer to share parts (or all) of its local file systems with remote computers. You can share resources if File and Printer Sharing services are enabled on the computer.

**file system**  In an operating system, the overall structure in which files are named, stored, and organized.

**File Transfer Protocol (FTP)**  A service that supports file transfers between local and remote computers. FTP supports several commands that allow bidirectional transfer of binary and ASCII files between computers. The FTP client is installed with the TCP/IP connectivity utilities.

**focus**  The area of a dialog box which receives input. To find the focus, look for highlighted text (for example, in a list box) or a button enclosed in dotted lines.

**folder**  A type of container of objects (typically files).

**font**  A set of attributes for characters.

**frame**  *See* data frame.

**free space**  An unused and unformatted portion of a hard disk that can be partitioned or subpartitioned. Free space within an extended partition is available for the creation of logical drives. Free space that is not within an extended partition is available for the creation of a partition, with a maximum of four partitions allowed.

**friendly name** A name, typically identifying a network user or a device, intended to be familiar, meaningful, and easily identifiable. A friendly name for a printer might indicate the printer's physical location (for example, "Sales Department Printer").

**FTP** *See* File Transfer Protocol.

## G

**gateway** A computer connected to multiple physical networks, capable of routing or delivering packets between them.

**graphics engine** The print component that provides WYSIWYG support across devices.

## H

**handle** 1. In the user interface, an interface added to an object that facilitates moving, sizing, reshaping, or other functions pertaining to an object. 2. In programming, a pointer to a pointer—that is, a token that lets a program access a resource identified in another variable. *See also* object handle.

**hardware branch** The hardware archive root key in the Registry, which is a superset of the memory-resident hardware tree. The name of this key is Hkey_Local_Machine\Hardware.

**hardware tree** A record in RAM of the current system configuration, based on the configuration information for all devices in the hardware branch of the Registry. The hardware tree is created each time the computer is started or whenever a dynamic change occurs to the system configuration.

**hierarchical menus** *See* cascading menu.

**Hkey_Classes_Root** A predefined Registry handle that contains OLE and file-class association data. This key is a symbolic link to a subkey of Hkey_Local_Machine\Software.

**Hkey_Current_User** A predefined Registry handle that defines the current user's preferences, including environment variables, personal program groups, desktop settings, network connections, printers, and application preferences. This key maps to a subkey of Hkey_Users.

**Hkey_Local_Machine** A predefined Registry handle that defines the hardware and operating system characteristics such as bus type, system memory, installed device drives, and boot control data.

**Hkey_Users** A predefined Registry handle that defines the default user configuration for users on the local computer and configuration data from user profiles stored on the local computer.

**home directory** A directory that is accessible to the user and contains files and programs for that user. A home directory can be assigned to an individual user or can be shared by many users. *See also* machine directory.

**host** Any device that is attached to the internetwork and uses TCP/IP.

**host table** The HOSTS or LMHOST file that contains lists of known IP addresses mapped to host names or NetBIOS computer names.

**HPFS** File system primarily used with the OS/2 operating system version 1.2 or later. It supports long filenames but does not provide security.

## I

**IETF** *See* Internet Engineering Task Force.

**INF file**  A file that provides Windows 95 Setup with the information required to set up a device, such as a list of valid logical configurations for the device, the names of driver files associated with the device, and so on. An INF file is typically provided by the device manufacturer on a disk.

**INI files**  Initialization files used by Windows-based applications to store per-user information that controls application startup. In Windows 95, such information is stored in the Registry, and INI files are supported for backward compatibility.

**internal command**  Commands that are stored in the CMD.EXE file and that reside in memory at all times.

**International Organization for Standardization (ISO).**  An international association of member countries, each represented by its leading standard-setting organization—for example, ANSI (American National Standards Institute) for the United States. The ISO works to establish global standards for communications and information exchange.

**Internet Engineering Task Force (IETF)**  A consortium that introduces procedures for new technology on the Internet. IETF specifications are released in documents called Requests for Comments (RFCs).

**internet group name**  In Microsoft networking, a name registered by the domain controller that contains a list of the specific addresses of computers that have registered the name. The name has a 16th character ending in 0x1C.

**interrupt**  An asynchronous operating condition that disrupts normal execution and transfers control to an interrupt handler. Interrupts are usually initiated by I/O devices requiring service from the processor.

**interrupt request lines (IRQ)**  Hardware lines over which devices can send signals to get the attention of the processor when the device is ready to accept or send information. Typically, each device connected to the computer uses a separate IRQ.

**I/O device**  An input/output device, which is a piece of hardware used for providing information to and receiving information from the computer—for example, a disk drive, which transfers information in one of two directions, depending on the situation. Some input devices, such as keyboards, can be used only for input; some output devices (such as a printer or a monitor) can be used only for output. Most of these devices require installation of device drivers.

**I/O request packet (IRP)**  Data structures that drivers use to communicate with each other.

**IP address**  Used to identify a node on a network and to specify routing information on an internetwork. Each node on the internetwork must be assigned a unique IP address, which is made up of the network ID, plus a unique host ID assigned by the network administrator. In Windows 95, the IP address can be configured statically on the computer or configured dynamically through DHCP.

**IP router**  A computer connected to multiple physical TCP/IP networks that can route or deliver IP packets between the networks. *See also* gateway.

**IPX/SPX**  Transport protocols used in Novell® NetWare® and other networks. For Windows 95, the NWLINK.VXD module is used to implement the IPX/SPX-compatible protocol.

**IRP**  *See* I/O request packet.

**IRQ**  *See* interrupt request lines.

**ISA** Industry Standard Architecture bus design of the IBM® PC/AT®.

**ISO** *See* International Organization for Standardization.

# K

**Kernel** The portion of Windows 95 that manages the processor.

**kernel driver** A driver that accesses hardware.

# L

**legacy** Hardware and device cards that don't conform to the Plug and Play standard.

**link** (v.) To form a connection between two objects. (n.) 1. For OLE, a reference to an object that is linked to another object. 2. For networking, a connection at the LLC layer that is uniquely defined by the adapter's address and the destination service access point (DSAP). 3. Also refers to shortcuts.

**list box** In a dialog box, a box that lists available choices—for example, a list of all files in a directory. If all the choices do not fit in the list box, there is a scroll bar.

**LLC** Logical link control, in the Data Link layer of the networking model.

**LMHOSTS file** A local text file that maps IP addresses to the NetBIOS computer names of Microsoft networking computers outside the local subnet. In Windows 95, this file is stored in the Windows directory.

**local printer** A printer that is directly connected to one of the ports on your computer.

**localization** The process of adapting software for different countries, languages, or cultures.

**logical drive** A subpartition of an extended partition on a hard disk.

**login script** A batch file that runs automatically every time the user logs on. It can be used to configure a user's working environment at every logon, and it allows an administrator to control a user's environment without managing all aspects of it.

# M

**MAC** Media access control. A layer in the network architecture.

**MAC address** The address for a device as it is identified at the Media Access Control layer in the network architecture.

**machine directory** For shared installations, the directory that contains the required configuration files for a particular computer. The machine directory contains WIN.COM, the Registry, and startup configuration files.

**management information base (MIB)** A set of objects that represent various types of information about a device, used by SNMP to manage devices. Because different network-management services are used for different types of devices or protocols, each service has its own set of objects. The entire set of objects that any service or protocol uses is referred to as its MIB.

**map** To translate one value into another.

**MAPI** *See* messaging application program interface.

**messaging application program interface (MAPI)** A set of calls used to add mail-enabled features to other Windows-based applications.

**MIB** *See* management information base.

**miniport driver**  A 32-bit installable driver that allows easy additions. Windows NT was the first operating system to use miniport drivers.

**MS-DOS–based application**  A program that is designed to run with MS-DOS, and, therefore, may not be able to take full advantage of all Windows 95 features.

# N

**name registration**  The method by which a computer registers its unique name with a name server on the network. In a Microsoft network, a WINS server can provide name registration services.

**name resolution**  The process used on the network for resolving a computer address as a computer name, to support the process of finding and connecting to other computers on the network.

**named pipe**  An interprocess communication (IPC) mechanism that allows one process to communicate with another local or remote process.

**NDIS**  *See* Network Device Interface Specification.

**NetBEUI transport**  NetBIOS (Network Basic Input/Output System) Extended User Interface. A local area network transport protocol provided with Windows 95. *See also* NetBIOS interface.

**NetBIOS interface**  A programming interface that allows I/O requests to be sent to and received from a remote computer. It hides networking hardware from applications.

**NetBIOS over TCP/IP**  The networking module that provides the functionality to support NetBIOS name registration and resolution.

**network basic input/output system (NetBIOS)**  A software interface for network communication.

**network adapter driver**  Software that coordinates communication between the network adapter and the computer's hardware and other software, controlling the physical function of the network adapters.

**network directory**  *See* shared directory.

**Network Device Interface Specification (NDIS)**  In Windows networking, the interface for network adapter drivers. All transport drivers call the NDIS interface to access network adapters.

**network provider**  The component that allows a computer running Windows 95 to communicate with the network. Windows 95 includes providers for Microsoft networking and for Novell NetWare networks; other providers' DLLs are supplied by the respective networks' vendors.

**NTFS**  Windows NT file system.

# O

**object**  1. An entity or component, identifiable by the user, that may be distinguished by its properties, operations, and relationships. 2. Any piece of information, created by using a Windows-based application with OLE capabilities, that can be linked or embedded into another document.

**object handle**  Code that includes access control information and a pointer to the object itself.

**OLE**  The name that describes the technology and interface for object interaction. A way to transfer and share information between programs.

**OLE object**  A discrete unit of data that has been supplied by an OLE application—for example, a worksheet, module, chart, cell, or range of cells.

# P

**package** An icon that represents an embedded or linked object. When you choose the package, the program used to create the object either plays the object (for example, a sound file) or opens and displays the object.

**packet** A transmission unit of fixed maximum size that consists of binary information representing both data and a header containing an ID number, source and destination addresses, and error-control data.

**page** In memory, a fixed-size block.

**paging file** *See* swap file.

**partition** A portion of a physical disk that functions as though it were a physically separate unit. *See also* system partition.

**password** A unique string of characters that must be provided before logon or access to a resource or service is authorized.

**path** Specifies the location of a file within the directory tree.

**PCI** The Peripheral Component Interconnect local bus being promoted as the successor to VL. This type of device is used in most Pentium™ computers and in the Apple® PowerPC™ Macintosh®.

**PCMCIA** The Personal Computer Memory Card International Association standard for the credit card-sized interface cards in portables and other small computers.

**permission** A rule associated with an object (usually a directory, file, or printer) in order to regulate which users can have access to the object and in their manner of access.

**Plug and Play BIOS** A BIOS with responsibility for configuring Plug and Play cards and system board devices during system power-up; provides run-time configuration services for system board devices after startup.

**Point-to-Point Protocol (PPP)** An industry standard that is part of Windows 95 Dial-Up Networking to ensure interoperability with remote access software from other vendors.

**popup menu** *See* context menu.

**port** A connection or socket used to connect a device, such as a printer, monitor, or modem, to your computer. Information is sent from your computer to the device through a cable.

**port replicators** Low-cost docking station substitutes that provide one-step connection to multiple desktop devices.

**postoffice** A temporary message store, holding the message until the recipient's workstation retrieves it. The postoffice exists as a directory structure on a server and has no programmatic components.

**PPP** *See* Point-to-Point Protocol.

**preemptive multitasking** An operating system scheduling technique that allows the operating system to take control of the processor at any instant, regardless of the state of the currently running application. Preemption guarantees better response to the user and higher data throughput.

**primary partition** A portion of a physical disk that can be marked for use by an operating system. There can be up to four primary partitions (or up to three, if there is an extended partition) per physical disk. A primary partition cannot be subpartitioned.

**print device** Refers to the actual hardware device that produces printed output. *See also* printer.

**print monitor**  The component that receives information from the printer driver by way of the spooler and sends it onto the printer or destination file. The print monitor tracks physical devices so the spooler doesn't have to.

**print provider**  A software component that allows the client to print to the print server's device.

**printer**  Refers to the software interface between the application and the print device. *See also* print device.

**printer driver**  A program that controls how your computer and printer interact.

**printer sharing**  The ability for a computer running Windows 95 to share a locally attached printer for use on the network.

**program file**  A file that starts a program. A program file has an EXE, PIF, COM, or BAT filename extension.

**properties**  Attributes or characteristics of an object used to define its state, appearance, or value.

**properties dialog box**  A secondary window that displays the properties of an object.

**protocol**  A set of rules and conventions by which two computers pass messages across a network. Networking software usually implements multiple levels of protocols layered one on top of another. Windows 95 includes NetBEUI, TCP/IP, and IPX/SPX-compatible protocols.

# R

**redirector**  Networking software that accepts I/O requests for remote files, named pipes, or mailslots and then sends (redirects) them to a network service on another computer. Redirectors (also called network clients) are implemented as file system drivers in Windows 95.

**Registry**  The database repository for information about a computer's configuration. The Registry supersedes use of separate INI files for all system components and applications that know how to store values in the Registry.

**Registry Editor**  An application, provided with Windows 95, that is used to view and edit entries in the Registry.

**remote administration**  Administration of one computer by an administrator located at another computer and connected to the first computer across the network.

**remote procedure call (RPC)**  A message-passing facility that allows a distributed program to call services available on various computers in a network. Used during remote administration of computers, RPC provides a procedural view, rather than a transport-centered view, of networked operations.

**Request for Comments (RFC)**  An official document of the Internet Engineering Task Force (IETF) that specifies the details for protocols included in the TCP/IP family.

**resource**  Any part of a computer or a network, such as a disk drive, printer, or memory, that can be allotted to a program or a process while it is running.

**RFC**  *See* Request for Comments.

**root directory**  *See* directory tree.

**router**  1. The printing model component that locates the requested printer and sends information from the workstation spooler to the print server's spooler. 2. In network gateways, computers with two or more network adapters that are running some type of routing software, with each adapter connected to a different physical network.

**routing** The process of forwarding packets to other gateways until the packet is eventually delivered to a gateway connected to the specified destination.

**RPC** *See* remote procedure call.

# S

**screen buffer** The size reserved in memory for the MS-DOS Prompt display.

**SCSI** Small computer standard interface. This is a multidevice, chained interface used in many devices such as hard disk drives and CD-ROM drives.

**Serial Line IP (SLIP)** An industry standard that can be used with Windows 95 Dial-Up Networking to ensure interoperability with remote access software from other vendors.

**server** For a LAN, a computer running administrative software that controls access to all or part of the network and its resources. A computer acting as a server makes resources available to computers acting as workstations on the network. *See also* client.

**server message block (SMB)** The protocol developed by Microsoft, Intel, and IBM that defines a series of commands used to pass information between network computers. The redirector packages SMB requests into a network control block (NCB) structure that can be sent over the network to a remote device. The network provider listens for SMB messages destined for it and removes the data portion of the SMB request so that it can be processed by a local device.

**service** A process that performs a specific system function and often provides an application programming interface (API) for other processes to call. If services are RPC-enabled, their API routines can be called from remote computers.

**session** A connection that two applications on different computers establish, use, and end. The Session layer performs name recognition and the functions needed to allow two applications to communicate over the network.

**share** To make resources, such as directories and printers, available to network users.

**share name** The name of a shared resource.

**shared directory** A directory that network users can connect to.

**shared resource** Any device, data, or program that is used by more than one other device or program. For Windows 95, refers to any resource that is made available to network users, such as directories, files, printers, and named pipes.

**shell** A generic term used to refer to the interface supplied by the operating system.

**Simple Network Management Protocol (SNMP)** A protocol used by SNMP consoles and agents to communicate.

**SLIP** *See* Serial Line IP.

**SMB** *See* server message block.

**SNMP** *See* Simple Network Management Protocol.

**socket** A bidirectional pipe for incoming and outgoing data between networked computers. The Windows Sockets API is a networking API used by programmers creating TCP/IP-based sockets programs.

**socket services** A protected-mode VxD that manages the PCMCIA adapter hardware. It provides a protected-mode PCMCIA Socket Services 2.x interface for use by Card Services. A socket services driver must be implemented for each separate PCMCIA controller that is used.

**source directory**  The directory that contains the file or files you intend to copy or move.

**spooler**  A scheduler for the printing process. It coordinates activity among other components of the print model and schedules all print jobs arriving at the print server.

**static VxD**  A VxD that is loaded statically during system startup. A static VxD can be loaded in Simple Network Management Protocol (SNMP) a number of different ways, including a line in SYSTEM.INI, a response to an INT 2F call, or by way of device enumeration by the Plug and Play static device enumerator.

**status bar**  A line of information related to the program in the window. Usually located at the bottom of a window. Not all windows have a status bar.

**string**  A data structure composed of a sequence of characters, usually representing human-readable text.

**stubs**  Nonexecutable placeholders used by calls from the server environment.

**subnet**  On the Internet, refers to any lower network that is part of the logical network identified by the network ID.

**subnet mask**  A 32-bit value that allows the recipient of IP packets to distinguish the network ID portion of the IP address from the host ID.

**swap file**  A special file on your hard disk. With virtual memory under Windows 95, some of the program code and other information is kept in RAM while other information is temporarily swapped to virtual memory. When that information is required again, Windows 95 pulls it back into RAM and, if necessary, swaps other information to virtual memory. Also called a paging file.

**syntax**  The order in which you must type a command and the elements that follow the command.

**system partition**  The volume that contains the hardware-specific files needed to load Windows 95. *See also* partition.

# T

**TAPI**  *See* telephony application program interface.

**TCP/IP**  Transmission Control Protocol/Internet Protocol. The primary wide area network (WAN) transport protocol used in Windows 95 to communicate with computers on TCP/IP networks and to participate in UNIX-based bulletin boards and electronic mail services.

**telephony application program interface (TAPI)**  A set of calls that allows applications to control modems and telephones, by routing application function calls to the appropriate "service provider" DLL for a modem.

**Telnet service**  The service that provides basic terminal emulation to remote computers supporting the Telnet protocol over TCP/IP.

**text file**  A file containing only letters, numbers, and symbols. A text file contains no formatting information, except possibly linefeeds and carriage returns. A text file is an ASCII file.

**thread**  An executable entity that belongs to a single process, comprising a program counter, a user-mode stack, a kernel-mode stack, and a set of register values. All threads in a process have equal access to the processor's address space, object handles, and other resources. In Windows 95, threads are implemented as objects. 2. A collection of electronic mail messages organized chronologically and hierarchically to reflect the flow of the discussion.

**thunking**   The transformation between 16-bit and 32-bit formats, which is carried out by a separate layer in the VM.

**time-out**   If a device is not performing a task, the amount of time the computer should wait before detecting it as an error.

**toolbar**   A standard control that provides a frame for a series of shortcut buttons providing quick access to commands. Usually located directly below the menu bar. Not all windows have a toolbar.

**transport protocol**   Defines how data should be presented to the next receiving layer in the networking model and packages the data accordingly. It passes data to the network adapter driver through the NDIS interface.

## U

**UNC**   Universal naming convention. *See also* UNC names.

**UNC names**   Filenames or other resource names that begin with the string \\, indicating that they exist on a remote computer.

**Unimodem**   Name used to refer to the universal modem driver. It is a driver-level component that uses modem description files to control its interaction with the communications driver, VCOMM.

**user account**   Refers to all the information that defines a user to Windows 95. This includes such things as the user name and password required for the user to log on, the groups in which the user account has membership, and the rights and permissions the user has for using the computer and accessing its resources.

**user name**   A unique name identifying a user account to Windows 95. An account's user name cannot be identical to any other group name or user name of its own domain or workgroup. *See also* user account.

## V

**value entry**   A parameter under a key or subkey in the Registry. A value entry appears as a string with three components: name, type, and value.

**VM**   *See* virtual machine.

**virtual machine (VM)**   A complete MS-DOS environment and a console in which to run an MS-DOS–based application or Windows 16-bit applications. A VM establishes a complete virtual x86 (that is, 80386 or higher) computer running MS-DOS. Any number of VMs can run simultaneously. Also known as a virtual DOS machine.

**virtual printer memory**   In a PostScript™ printer, a part of memory that stores font information. The memory in PostScript printers is divided into banded memory and virtual memory. The banded memory contains graphics and page-layout information needed to print your documents. The virtual memory contains any font information that is sent to your printer either when you print a document or when you download fonts.

**visual editing**   The ability to edit an embedded object in place, without opening it into its own window.

**VL**   The Video Electronic Standards Association (VESA). Local bus standard for a bus that allows high-speed connections to peripherals.

**volume**   A partition or collection of partitions that have been formatted for use by a file system.

**VxD**  Virtual device driver. The *x* represents the type of device — for example, a virtual device driver for a display is a VDD and a virtual device driver for a printer is a VPD.

# W

**wildcard**  A character that represents one or more characters. The question mark (?) wildcard can be used to represent any single character, and the asterisk (*) wildcard can be used to represent any character or group of characters that might match that position in other filenames.

**Win32 API**  A 32-bit application programming interface for both Windows 95 and Windows NT. It updates earlier versions of the Windows API with sophisticated operating system capabilities, security, and API routines for displaying text-based applications in a window.

**Windows Internet Name Service (WINS)**  A name resolution service that resolves Windows networking computer names to IP addresses in a routed environment. A WINS server, which is a Windows NT Server computer, handles name registrations, queries, and releases.

**Windows NT**  The portable, secure, 32-bit, preemptive-multitasking member of the Microsoft Windows operating system family. Windows NT Server provides centralized management and security, advanced fault tolerance, and additional connectivity. Windows NT Workstation provides operating system and networking functionality for computers without centralized management.

**Windows NT file system (NTFS)**  An advanced file system designed for use specifically with the Windows NT operating system. NTFS supports file system recovery and extremely large storage media, in addition to other advantages. It also supports object-oriented applications by treating all files as objects with user-defined and system-defined attributes.

**WINS**  *See* Windows Internet Name Service.

**workgroup**  A collection of computers that are grouped for viewing purposes. Each workgroup is identified by a unique name. *See also* domain.

**workstation**  In general, a powerful computer having considerable calculating and graphics capability. *See also* domain controller, server.

APPENDIX A

# Command-Line Commands Summary

Windows 95 retains and enhances most of the functionality of MS-DOS and LAN Manager. This appendix lists and briefly describes all the command-line commands available in Windows 95. The list includes commands you can use to modify CONFIG.SYS files, write batch programs, and change international settings.

For information about a specific command, use command-line help, which provides syntax, notes about how the command works, and examples of how to use it.

▶ **To get information about a command by using command-line help**

- At the command prompt, type the command name followed by a space and **/?**

  For example, for information about the **dir** command, type **dir /?** at the command prompt.

**In This Appendix**

Command Syntax   1097
Using the Command Prompt   1099
   Editing Commands with Doskey and Editing Keys   1099
   Pausing or Canceling a Command   1100
   Transferring Information to or from a Command-Prompt Window   1100
Native Windows 95 Commands   1102
   Network Commands   1106
   Commands Used in CONFIG.SYS Files   1107
   Commands Used in Batch Programs   1109
   Commands Used to Change International Settings   1110
   Commands Not Included in Windows 95   1111

(*continued*)

Command-Line Switches for Specific Commands    1111
    EMM386 Command-Line Switches    1111
    Windows Explorer Command-Line Switches    1118
    Xcopy and Xcopy32 Command-Line Switches    1118
Command-Line Switches for Disk Utilities    1123
    Defrag    1123
    DrvSpace    1124
    ScanDisk    1134
TCP/IP Utilities    1136
    Arp    1137
    Ftp    1137
    Nbtstat    1140
    Netstat    1142
    Ping    1143
    Route    1145
    Telnet    1146
    Tracert    1146

# Command Syntax

*Syntax* is the order in which you must type a command and the elements that follow the command. Commands have up to four elements: *command name*, *parameters*, *switches*, and *values*. In the following illustration, the first example lists all hidden files in the C:\LETTERS directory. The second example allows up to 10 users to connect to the C:\USERS\PUBLIC directory.

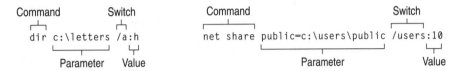

Besides these four elements, command symbols can be used to direct the output. Each element is explained below.

**Command Name.**   States the action you want Windows 95 to carry out. Some commands (such as the **cls** command, which clears the screen) consist only of a command name. Most commands require more than a name. For all network commands, type **net** followed by a space and the command name, as in the following:

**net config**

**Parameter.**   Defines or creates the object you want Windows 95 to act on. Windows 95 sometimes requires additional information, which you specify in one or more parameters after the command name. For example, the **del** command requires a parameter that is the name of the file you want to delete. Some commands require more than one parameter. For example, to rename a file by using the **rename** (**ren**) command, you must include the original name of the file in addition to the new name. The following command renames LETTER.TXT to MEMO.TXT:

**ren letter.txt memo.txt**

---

Caution   Some commands accept semicolons to separate parameters. For example, if you wanted to delete all files on drive A and typed **del a;\\*.\*** by mistake, Windows 95 would erase the file A in the current directory and all files in the root directory of the current drive.

---

Position in the syntax line determines how a command works and whether a parameter is a *source* (first) or a *destination* (second). In the example above, the source, LETTER.TXT, specifies the location of data to be transferred or used as input to a command. The destination, MEMO.TXT, specifies a location to which the data specified by source is to be transferred.

**Switches.** Modify how a command performs a task. A switch is a forward slash (/) or a hyphen (-), usually followed by words, letters, or numbers. Some commands do not have switches, whereas others have several. If a command has more than one switch, you type them one after the other, separated with a space. Switches can be in any position or order after the command name. Some commands accept more than one switch after a forward slash. Other commands, such as TCP/IP utilities, accept a hyphen (-) instead of the forward slash.

---

**Tip**  The terms "parameter" and "switch" are often interchanged, since both elements follow the command name. The only meaningful difference between a switch and parameter is the presence of a forward slash or hyphen to indicate a switch and the parameter position in the syntax line to indicate whether the parameter is a source or a destination. The term "argument" is also used to refer to parameters or switches.

---

With some network commands for real-mode networking, a prompt appears that requires a user response before a task can be completed. To force a Yes or No answer for all responses, append the **/yes** (**/y**) or **/no** (**/n**) switch to a command. For example, stopping the workstation service when working in Command Prompt Only mode causes Windows 95 to stop dependent services; Windows 95 prompts you before stopping each dependent service unless the **/yes** switch is included, as in the following:

**net stop workstation /y**

**Value.** Determines how a switch works. A value is a colon (:) or an equal sign (=), followed by a word, letter, or number and must immediately follow the switch it modifies without a space. The following example of the **format** command contains two values—the file system to use (VFAT in the following example) and a volume label (Backup2):

**format d:  /f:1.2 /v:backup2**

Check the syntax for the specific command in online Help to determine whether the command you want to use requires an equal sign or a colon.

**Command symbols.**  Direct the input or output of a command and permit conditional execution of a command. Used with commands and filter commands, the command symbols are powerful tools.

| Symbol | Purpose |
| --- | --- |
| > | Redirects output. |
| >> | Appends redirected output to existing data. |
| < | Redirects input. |
| \| | Pipes output. |

**Sort**, **more**, and **find** are the built-in filter commands that work in the same way as command symbols, to allow you to sort input and output, cause output to the screen to be displayed one screen at a time, and search for specified text in a file.

# Using the Command Prompt

This section explains how to:

- Simplify entry of repetitive commands.
- Pause or cancel execution of a command.
- Cut and paste information to or from a command-prompt window.

# Editing Commands with Doskey and Editing Keys

Windows 95 provides Doskey to give you quick access to your most recent commands and enable you to assign frequently used commands to a single keystroke. Doskey is also available for character-based programs that accept buffered input. Doskey allows you to assign multiple commands to a single key or a typed alias. In addition to Doskey, several editing keys allow you to use and edit the last command you typed, as described in the following table.

**Keys for Editing at the Command Prompt**

| Key | Description |
| --- | --- |
| **Doskey:** | |
| UP ARROW or DOWN ARROW | Cycles through commands previously entered. |
| F7 | Displays all of the previous commands in a list. Press F9 and then choose a number from the list, and press ENTER (or press ESCAPE to cancel). |

**Keys for Editing at the Command Prompt** (*continued*)

| Key | Description |
| --- | --- |
| **Other editing keys:** | |
| F1 | Displays the last command one character at a time. |
| F3 | Displays the entire command. |
| BACKSPACE or LEFT ARROW | Moves the cursor in a command. |
| INS | Toggles between insert and overtype mode. |

# Pausing or Canceling a Command

You can pause or stop the output of a command.

▶ **To pause the output of a command**

- Press CTRL+S or PAUSE.

  Press any key except PAUSE to restart the output of the command. You can stop and restart the output of a command as many times as you want.

▶ **To stop Windows 95 from completing a command**

- Press CTRL+BREAK or CTRL+C.

---

**Important**   Any action Windows 95 carried out before you pressed CTRL+BREAK or CTRL+C cannot be undone.

---

# Transferring Information to or from a Command-Prompt Window

You can transfer information to or from the command prompt. The following topics describe how to do this using the Edit buttons in a window or using QuickEdit mode in a window or in full-screen mode.

In full-screen mode, you can also use the Edit menu commands to copy and paste information in any window, not just command-prompt windows. The data is transferred as text or as a bitmap to the Clipboard depending on how it was copied.

---

**Tip**   To quickly switch a command prompt or MS-DOS–based application between a full screen and a window, press ALT+ENTER.

---

## Copying and Pasting Information Using Edit Buttons

When running MS-DOS Prompt or an MS-DOS–based application in a window, you can use the Edit buttons to copy and paste text at the command prompt.

▶ **To select and copy text at the command prompt**

1. Click the Mark button, and then select the text you want to copy, using either the mouse or the arrow keys.

2. Click the Copy button.

    This places the selected text on the Clipboard, so you can paste it anywhere, not just at the command line.

▶ **To paste text at the command prompt**

1. Make sure the text you want is on the Clipboard.

    This text can come from any source, not just from the command line.

2. Place the insertion point where you want to paste it, and then click the Paste button.

## Copying and Pasting Information Using QuickEdit Mode

QuickEdit mode allows you to copy and paste text in command-prompt windows using only the mouse, bypassing the Edit commands. QuickEdit mode copies data only when the command prompt is running as a window; however, you can paste text either in a window or a full screen.

---

**Note**  When QuickEdit mode is on, the mouse works as usual in MS-DOS–based applications that are running in a full screen; the mouse does not work when such applications run in a window if QuickEdit mode is on. Use the **start** command to retain use of the mouse when starting a program from a command-prompt window with QuickEdit mode enabled.

---

▶ **To copy and paste text at the command prompt using QuickEdit mode**

1. If necessary, turn on QuickEdit mode in the window properties.

2. Position the pointer at the beginning of the text you want to copy. Press the left mouse button. Keeping the left mouse button depressed, drag the cursor to the last character of the section you want to copy and release the left mouse button. The portion of the screen you want to copy is highlighted.

3. Right-click to copy the highlighted area to the Clipboard. The highlight will disappear.

4. Right-click to copy the contents of the Clipboard to the command-prompt cursor. If you copy more than one line, a carriage return (CR) is added at the end of each line.

You must still use the Paste command from the Edit menu to paste the contents of the Clipboard into Windows-based applications.

# Native Windows 95 Commands

A *native* command takes advantage of the 32-bit operating system. Most commands familiar to MS-DOS users are now native Windows 95 system commands.

Some commands, such as **dir** and **chdir**, are *internal*, meaning the command resides in memory at all times. Internal commands can be run at the command prompt and in batch files.

Other commands, such as **drvspace** and **xcopy**, are *external*, meaning the command is stored in its own file and loads from disk when you use the command. External commands can be run at the command prompt, from Windows Explorer, from the Run command, or from the Start menu, and can also be run in batch files. Batch commands are for use in batch programs only.

The following tables summarize the commands included with Windows 95. Unless otherwise specified, you can type these commands at the command prompt.

**Internal[1] and External[2] Commands**

| Command | Purpose |
| --- | --- |
| **attrib**[2] | Displays or changes file attributes. |
| **break**[1] | Sets or clears extended CTRL+C checking. |
| **cd**[1] | Displays the name of the current directory or changes the current directory. |
| **chcp**[1] | Displays the number of the active character set (code page). You can also use this command to change the active character set for all devices that support character-set switching. |
| **chdir**[1] | See the **cd** command. |
| **chkdsk**[2] | Checks the status of a disk and displays a status report. Can also fix disk errors. However, Windows ScanDisk (**scandskw**) is the recommended command for repairing disks. |
| **cls**[1] | Clears the screen. |
| **command**[2] | Starts a new instance of the command interpreter. |
| **copy**[1] | Copies one or more files to the location you specify. |
| **ctty**[1] | Changes the terminal device used to control the computer. |

**Internal[1] and External[2] Commands** (*continued*)

| Command | Purpose |
|---|---|
| **date**[1] | Displays the date and prompts you to change the date, if necessary. |
| **drvspace**[2] | Compresses hard disk drives or floppy disks, and configures drives that were compressed by using DriveSpace or DoubleSpace. This is a Windows-based utility; for information, see the syntax description. |
| **debug**[2] | Starts the Debug program, which you can use to test and debug executable files. |
| **defrag**[2] | Reorganizes the files on a disk to optimize disk performance. This is a Windows-based utility; for information, see the syntax description. |
| **del (erase)**[1] | Deletes the files you specify. |
| **deltree**[2] | Deletes a directory and all the files and subdirectories that are in it. |
| **dir**[1] | Displays a list of the files and subdirectories that are in the current or specified directory. |
| **diskcopy**[2] | Copies the entire contents of one floppy disk to another floppy disk. |
| **doskey**[2] | Loads the Doskey program into memory. The Doskey program recalls command-line commands, and it enables you to edit command lines and create and run macros. Doskey loads by default. |
| **edit**[2] | Starts a text editor you can use to create and edit ASCII text files. |
| **emm386**[2] | Enables or disables EMM386 expanded-memory support. Also provides support for loading real-mode device drivers in the upper memory area (UMA) if both EMM386.EXE and HIMEM.SYS are loaded with **device=** commands in CONFIG.SYS. |
| **erase**[1] | See the **del** command. |
| **exit**[1] | Quits the command interpreter (COMMAND.COM) and returns to the program that started the command interpreter, if one exists. |
| **expand**[2] | Decompresses a compressed file. |
| **fc**[2] | Compares two files and displays the differences between them. |
| **fdisk**[2] | Starts the Fdisk program, which configures a hard disk for use with Windows 95. Although you can run this command at the command prompt, you cannot use it while running Windows 95 on the drive that contains the Windows system files. |
| **find**[2] | Searches for a specific string of text in a file or files. |
| **for**[2] | Runs a specified command for each file in a set of files. |
| **format**[2] | Formats a disk for use with Windows 95 or MS-DOS. You can use the right-click a drive icon in Windows Explorer to use a Windows-based version of this command. |
| **keyb**[2] | Starts the Keyb program, which configures a keyboard for a specific language. |

**Internal[1] and External[2] Commands** (*continued*)

| Command | Purpose |
| --- | --- |
| **label**[2] | Creates, changes, or deletes the volume label (name) of a disk. |
| **lh**[1] | See the **loadhigh** command. |
| **loadfix**[2] | Ensures that a program is loaded above the first 64K of conventional memory. |
| **loadhigh (lh)**[1] | Loads a program into upper memory. |
| **md**[1] | Creates a directory or subdirectory. |
| **mem**[2] | Displays the amount of used and free memory on the computer. |
| **mkdir**[1] | See the **md** command. |
| **mode**[2] | Configures a printer, serial port, or display adapter; sets the typematic rate; redirects printer output from a parallel port to a serial port; prepares, selects, refreshes, or displays the numbers of the character sets (code pages) for parallel printers or the keyboard and screen; displays the status of all the devices installed on the computer. |
| **more**[1] | Displays one screen of output at a time. |
| **move**[2] | Moves one or more files to the location you specify. Can also be used to rename files and directories. |
| **nlsfunc**[2] | Starts the Nlsfunc program, which loads country-specific information for national language support (NLS). |
| **path**[1] | Indicates which directories the operating system should search for executable files (programs). |
| **prompt**[1] | Changes the appearance of the command prompt. |
| **rd**[1] | Deletes (removes) a directory. |
| **ren**[1] | Changes the name of the file or files you specify. |
| **rename**[1] | See the **ren** command. |
| **rmdir**[1] | See the **rd** command. |
| **scandisk**[2] | Checks disks and the file system for damage, and repairs them, if needed. Windows ScanDisk (**scandskw**) is the recommended command for repairing disks. |

**Internal**[1] **and External**[2] **Commands** (*continued*)

| Command | Purpose |
|---------|---------|
| **set**[1] | Displays, sets, or removes environment variables. |
| **setver**[2] | Displays the version table. Reports a version number to programs or device drivers designed for earlier versions of MS-DOS. |
| **smartdrv**[2] | Starts or configures SMARTDrive, which creates a disk cache in extended memory.<br><br>**Important**  Under Windows 95, do not place the **smartdrv** command in AUTOEXEC.BAT. Windows 95 uses another method of disk caching. |
| **sort**[2] | Reads input, sorts data, and writes the results to the screen, a file, or another device. |
| **start /W**[2] | Allows you to run a Windows-based program from the command line and wait for it. For information about other switches that can be used with **start**, see the online Help for the command. |
| **subst**[2] | Associates a path with a drive letter. |
| **sys**[2] | Creates a startup disk by copying hidden Windows 95 system files and the command interpreter (COMMAND.COM) to the disk. |
| **time**[1] | Displays the system time or sets the computer's internal clock. |
| **type**[1] | Displays the contents of a text file. |
| **ver**[1] | Displays the operating system version number. |
| **verify**[1] | Directs the operating system to verify that files are written correctly to a disk, and displays the status of verification. |
| **vol**[1] | Displays the volume label and serial number for a disk, if the disk has them. |
| **xcopy**[2] | Copies directories, their subdirectories, and files (except hidden and system files). For information, see the syntax description. |

[1] Internal commands can be used in batch files and at the command prompt.

[2] External commands can be run from the command prompt or in batch files, or can be run from Windows Explorer, the Run command, or other parts of the Windows 95 user interface.

# Network Commands

The following networking commands can be used at the command prompt, in batch files, and in configuration files such as AUTOEXEC.BAT. Some commands are applicable only in real mode, such as before Windows 95 starts, or if your computer uses only real-mode networking.

| Command | Purpose |
| --- | --- |
| **net config** | Displays the controllable services that are running. |
| **net diag** | Runs the Microsoft Network Diagnostic program to display diagnostic information about your network. |
| **net help** or **net /?** | Provides a list of network commands and topics you can get help with, or provides help with a specific command or topic. |
| **net init**[1] | Loads protocol and network adapter drivers without binding them. This may be necessary for network adapter drivers from other vendors. You can bind them using **net start bind**. |
| **net logoff**[1,2] | Breaks the connection between your computer and the network resources to which it is connected. |
| **net logon**[1,2] | Identifies you as a member of a workgroup. |
| **net password**[2,3] | Changes your logon password. |
| **net print**[2] | Displays or controls print jobs. |
| **net start**[1] | Starts a service or displays a list of started services. |
| **net stop**[1] | Stops a network service. |
| **net time** | Synchronizes the computer's clock with that of a server or domain, or displays the time for a server or domain. |
| **net use** | Connects a computer to or disconnects it from a shared resource, or displays information about computer connections. |
| **net ver** | Displays the type and version number of the network redirector you are using. |
| **net view** | Displays a list of servers or displays resources being shared by a server. |

[1] This command is available only in real mode, and cannot be used in a VM window.

[2] This command is not supported for NetWare NCP servers.

[3] The form **net password /domain:***name* or **net password** \\*server* can be used in a VM window. However, the standard form of **net password** is available only in real mode, and cannot be used in a VM window.

# Commands Used in CONFIG.SYS Files

You can use the commands listed in the following table in CONFIG.SYS files.

| Command | Purpose |
| --- | --- |
| **break** | Sets or clears extended CTRL+C checking. You can use this command at the command prompt or in a batch file. |
| **buffers** and **buffershigh**[1] | Allocates memory for a specified number of disk buffers when the computer starts. The **buffershigh** form causes reserved memory to be taken out of the UMA. You can use these commands only in CONFIG.SYS. |
| **country** | Enables the operating system to use country-specific conventions for displaying dates, times, and currency; for determining the order by which characters are sorted; and for determining which characters can be used in filenames. You can use this command only in CONFIG.SYS. |
| **device** | Loads the device driver you specify into memory. You can use this command only in CONFIG.SYS. |
| **devicehigh** | Loads the device driver you specify into upper memory. You can use this command only in CONFIG.SYS. |
| **dos** | Specifies that the operating system should maintain a link to the UMA, load part of itself into the high memory area (HMA), or both. You can use this command only in CONFIG.SYS. |
| **drivparm** | Defines parameters for devices such as disk and tape drives when you start the operating system. You can use this command only in CONFIG.SYS. |
| **fcbs** or **fcbshigh**[1] | Specifies the number of file control blocks (FCBs) that the operating system can have open at the same time. The **fcbshigh** form causes reserved memory to be taken out of the UMA. You can use these commands only in CONFIG.SYS. |
| **files** or **fileshigh**[1] | Specifies the number of files that the operating system can access at one time. The **fileshigh** form causes reserved memory to be taken out of the UMA. You can use these commands only in CONFIG.SYS. |
| **include** | Includes the contents of one configuration block within another. You can use this command only in CONFIG.SYS. |
| **install** | Loads a memory-resident program into memory. You can use this command only in CONFIG.SYS. |

| Command | Purpose |
|---|---|
| **lastdrive** or **lastdrivehigh**[1] | Specifies the maximum number of drives you can access. The **lastdrivehigh** form causes reserved memory to be taken out of the UMA. You can use these commands only in CONFIG.SYS. |
| **menucolor** | Sets the text and background colors for the startup menu. You can use this command only within a menu block in CONFIG.SYS. |
| **menudefault** | Specifies the default menu item on the startup menu and sets a time-out value, if desired. You can use this command only within a menu block in CONFIG.SYS. |
| **menuitem** | Defines up to nine items on the startup menu. You can use this command only within a menu block in CONFIG.SYS. |
| **numlock** | Specifies whether the NUMLOCK setting on the numeric keypad is set to ON or OFF. You can use this command only within a menu block in CONFIG.SYS. |
| **rem** | Enables you to include comments (remarks) or prevent commands in a batch program or CONFIG.SYS from running. |
| **shell** | Specifies the name and location of the command interpreter you want Windows 95 to use. You can use this command only in CONFIG.SYS. |
| **stacks** or **stackshigh**[1] | Supports the dynamic use of data stacks to handle hardware interrupts. The **stackshigh** form causes reserved memory to be taken out of the UMA. You can use these commands only in CONFIG.SYS. |
| **submenu** | Defines an item on a startup menu that, when selected, displays another set of choices. You can use this command only within a menu block in CONFIG.SYS. |
| **switches** | Specifies special options. Used only in CONFIG.SYS. |

[1] Windows 95 automatically reserves memory in the UMA unless CONFIG.SYS contains the entry **dos=noauto** or if HIMEM.SYS and EMM386 are not loaded.

The following device drivers can be loaded in CONFIG.SYS using a
**device=** statement.

| Device driver | Description |
|---|---|
| **display.sys** | Enables you to display international character sets on EGA, VGA, and LCD monitors. This device driver must be loaded by a **device** or **devicehigh** command in CONFIG.SYS. |
| **driver.sys** | Creates a logical drive that you can use to refer to a physical floppy disk drive. This device driver must be loaded by a **device** or **devicehigh** command in CONFIG.SYS. |
| **emm386.exe** | Provides support for loading real-mode device drivers in the UMA if both EMM386.EXE and HIMEM.SYS are loaded with **device=** commands in CONFIG.SYS. |
| **himem.sys** | Himem is an extended-memory manager—a program that coordinates the use of your computer's extended memory, including the HMA, so that no two applications or device drivers use the same memory at the same time. This device driver must be loaded by a **device** command in CONFIG.SYS, and the command line must come before any commands that start applications or device drivers that use extended memory. |
| **keyboard.sys** | Enables the operating system to use a keyboard other than the standard U.S. QWERTY keyboard layout. You can use this command only in CONFIG.SYS. |
| **mscdex.exe** | Provides access to CD-ROM drives. |

# Commands Used in Batch Programs

Batch programs (also called batch files) allow you to simplify routine or
repetitive tasks. A *batch program* is an unformatted text file that contains one
or more commands and has a .BAT or .CMD filename extension. When the
filename is typed at the command prompt, the commands in the file are run
sequentially.

Any command can be included in a batch file. In addition, several commands allow conditional processing of the commands in the batch file. For example, the **if** command carries out a command based on the results of a condition. Other commands allow you to control input and output and to call other batch programs. You can use the following commands in batch programs.

**Commands for Use in Batch Files**

| Command | Purpose |
| --- | --- |
| call | Calls one batch program from another without causing the first batch program to stop. |
| choice | Prompts the user to make a choice in a batch program. Displays a specified prompt and pauses for the user to choose from among a specified set of keys. |
| echo | Displays or hides the text in batch programs when the program is running. Also indicates whether command-echoing is on or off. |
| for | Runs a specified command for each file in a set of files. You can use this command in batch programs or at the command prompt. |
| goto | Directs the operating system to a line in a batch program that is marked by a label you specify. You can use this command only in batch programs. |
| if | Performs conditional processing in batch programs. You can use this command only in batch programs. |
| pause | Suspends processing of a batch program and displays a message that prompts you to press any key to continue. You can use this command only in batch programs. |
| rem | Enables you to include comments (remarks) or prevent commands in a batch program or CONFIG.SYS from running. |
| shift | Changes the position of replaceable parameters in a batch program. You can use this command only in batch programs. |

# Commands Used to Change International Settings

You can use the following commands to change international settings such as country codes, keyboard layouts, and character sets (code pages):

| | | |
| --- | --- | --- |
| chcp | keyb | nlsfunc |
| country | mode | |

# Commands Not Included in Windows 95

The following commands are not included with the basic Windows 95 files:

| | | | |
|---|---|---|---|
| **append**[1] | **graftabl** | **monoumb.386**[1] | **romdrive.sys** |
| **assign** | **graphics**[1] | **msav** | **share** |
| **backup**[1] | **help** | **msbackup**[1] | **sizer**[1] |
| **chkstate.sys**[1] | **instsupp.bat**[1] | **power** | **smartmon** |
| **comp** | **interlnk**[1] | **print**[1] | **tree**[1] |
| **dosshell** | **intersvr**[1] | **printer.sys** | **undelete**[1] |
| **edlin**[1] | **join** | **qbasic**[1] | **unformat** |
| **ega.sys** | **loadfix**[1] | **ramdrive.sys** | **vsafe** |
| **expand**[1] | **memcard** | **recover** | |
| **fasthelp** | **memmaker**[1] | **replace**[1] | |
| **fastopen** | **mirror** | **restore**[1] | |

[1] This command is available in the OTHER\OLDDOS directory on the Windows 95 compact disc.

# Command-Line Switches for Specific Commands

This section describes command-line switches for certain commands or executable files that are of particular interest in Windows 95. These include the following:

- **emm386**
- **explorer** (Windows Explorer)
- **xcopy**

## EMM386 Command-Line Switches

This section provides correct syntax and other details for using EMM386 command-line switches.

### EMM386

Enables or disables EMM386 expanded-memory support.

The EMM386 device driver, EMM386.EXE, provides expanded-memory support and also provides access to the upper memory area. For information about EMM386.EXE, see its entry later in this section.

**Syntax**   **emm386 [on|off|auto] [w=on|w=off]**

To display the current status of EMM386 expanded-memory support, type **emm386** at the command prompt:

**Parameters**          **on|off|auto**

Activates the EMM386 device driver (if set to **on**), or suspends the EMM386 device driver (if set to **off**), or places the EMM386 device driver in auto mode (if set to **auto**). Auto mode enables expanded-memory support only when a program calls for it. The default value is **on**.

**w=on|w=off**

Enables (if set to **w=on**) or disables (if set to **w=off**) Weitek coprocessor support. The default value is **w=off**.

**Notes on EMM386**     **Installing the EMM386.EXE device driver.** To use the **emm386** command, you must also install the EMM386.EXE device driver by using the **device** command in CONFIG.SYS.

**Reactivating EMM386 expanded-memory support.** If EMM386 was loaded when the VM was started but is not currently in use, the **on** parameter reactivates expanded-memory support.

**Suspending EMM386 expanded-memory support.** If EMM386 expanded-memory support is currently active, handle 0 is the only handle allocated, and EMM386 is not providing access to the upper memory area. The **off** parameter suspends EMM386 expanded-memory support. When EMM386 expanded-memory support is off, the EMM386.EXE device-driver header is changed so that programs cannot use expanded memory. This enables you to run programs that do not comply with the Virtual Control Program Interface (VCPI).

## EMM386.EXE

**Caution**  Use EMM386.EXE parameters carefully. You can make the computer inoperable if you use them incorrectly.

Provides access to the upper memory area and uses extended memory to simulate expanded memory. This is for MS-DOS–based applications that need expanded memory. The EMM386.EXE device driver must be loaded by a **device** command in CONFIG.SYS. EMM386 uses extended memory to simulate expanded memory for programs that can use expanded memory. EMM386 also makes it possible to load programs and device drivers into upper memory blocks (UMBs).

**Note**  The EMM386.EXE device driver is different from the EMM386 command used to enable expanded-memory support.

| | |
|---|---|
| **Syntax** | **device=**[*drive***:**][*path*]**emm386.exe** [**on**\|**off**\|**auto**] [*memory*] [**min=***size*]<br>[**m***x*\|**frame=***address*\|**p***mmmm*] [**p***n***=***address*] [**x=***mmmm-nnnn*]<br>[**i=***mmmm-nnnn*] [**b=***address*] [**L=***minXMS*] [**a=***altregs*] [**h=***handles*]<br>[**d=***nnn*] [**ram=***mmmm-nnnn*] [**noems**] [**novcpi**] [**highscan**] [**verbose**]<br>[**win=***mmmm-nnnn*] [**nohi**] [**rom=***mmmm-nnnn*] [**nomovexbda**] [**altboot**] |

**Parameters**

[*drive***:***path*]
    Specifies the location of the EMM386.EXE file.

**on**\|**off**\|**auto**
    Activates the EMM386 device driver (if set to **on**), or suspends the EMM386
    device driver (if set to **off**), or places the EMM386 device driver in auto mode
    (if set to **auto**). Auto mode enables expanded-memory support and upper
    memory block support only when a program calls for it. The default value
    is **on**. Use the **emm386** command to change this value after EMM386 has
    started.

*memory*
    Specifies the maximum amount of extended memory (in kilobytes) that you
    want EMM386 to provide as expanded/Virtual Control Program Interface
    (EMS/VCPI) memory. This amount is in addition to the memory used for
    UMBs and EMM386 itself. Values for *memory* are in the range 64 through
    the lesser of either 32768 or the amount of extended memory available when
    EMM386 is loaded. The default value is the amount of free extended memory.
    If you specify the **noems** switch, the default value is 0. EMM386 rounds the
    value down to the nearest multiple of 16.

**Switches**

**min=***size*
    Specifies the minimum amount of EMS/VCPI memory (in kilobytes) that
    EMM386 will provide, if that amount of memory is available. EMM386
    reserves this amount of extended memory for use as EMS/VCPI memory
    when EMM386 is loaded by **device=emm386.exe** in CONFIG.SYS. EMM386
    may be able to provide additional EMS/VCPI memory (up to the amount
    specified by the *memory* parameter) if sufficient XMS memory is available
    when a program requests EMS/VCPI memory. Values are in the range 0
    through the value specified by the *memory* parameter. The default value is 256.
    If you specify the **noems** switch, the default value is 0. If the value of **min** is
    greater than the value of *memory*, EMM386 uses the value specified by **min**.

**m***x*
    Specifies the address of the page frame. Valid values for *x* are in the range 1
    through 14. The following list shows each value and its associated base
    address in hexadecimal format:

| | | | |
|---|---|---|---|
| 1 => C000h | 5 => D000h | 9 => E000h | 12 => 8800h |
| 2 => C400h | 6 => D400h | 10 => 8000h | 13 => 8C00h |
| 3 => C800h | 7 => D800h | 11 => 8400h | 14 => 9000h |
| 4 => CC00h | 8 => DC00h | | |

**frame=***address*

Specifies the page-frame segment base directly. To specify a specific segment-base address for the page frame, use the **frame** switch and specify the address you want. Valid values for *address* are in the ranges 8000h through 9000h and C000h through E000h, in increments of 400h. To provide expanded memory and disable the page frame, you can specify **frame=none**; however, this may cause some programs that require expanded memory to work improperly.

**/p***mmmm*

Specifies the address of the page frame. Valid values for *mmmm* are in the ranges 8000h through 9000h and C000h through E000h, in increments of 400h.

**p***n***=***address*

Specifies the segment address of a specific page, where *n* is the number of the page you are specifying and *address* is the segment address you want. Valid values for *n* are in the range 0 through 255. Valid values for *address* are in the ranges 8000h through 9C00h and C000h through EC00h, in increments of 400h. The addresses for pages 0 through 3 must be contiguous in order to maintain compatibility with version 3.2 of the Lotus/Intel/Microsoft Expanded Memory Specification (LIM EMS). If you use the **m***x* switch, the **frame** switch, or the **/p***mmmm* switch, you cannot specify the addresses for pages 0 through 3 for the **/p***mmmm* switch.

**x=***mmmm-nnnn*

Prevents EMM386 from using a particular range of segment addresses for an EMS page or for UMBs. Valid values for *mmmm* and *nnnn* are in the range A000h through FFFFh and are rounded down to the nearest 4-kilobyte boundary. The **x** switch takes precedence over the **i** switch if the two ranges overlap.

**i=***mmmm-nnnn*

Specifies a range of segment addresses to be used (included) for an EMS page or for UMBs. Valid values for *mmmm* and *nnnn* are in the range A000h through FFFFh and are rounded down to the nearest 4-kilobyte boundary. The **x** switch takes precedence over the **i** switch if the two ranges overlap.

**b=***address*

Specifies the lowest segment address available for EMS "banking" (swapping of 16-kilobyte pages). Valid values are in the range 1000h through 4000h. The default value is 4000h.

**L=***minXMS*

Ensures that the specified amount (in kilobytes) of extended memory will still be available after EMM386 is loaded. The default value is 0.

**a=***altregs*

Specifies how many fast alternate register sets (used for multitasking) you want to allocate to EMM386. Valid values are in the range 0 through 254. The default value is 7. Every alternate register set adds about 200 bytes to the size in memory of EMM386.

**h=**_handles_

Specifies how many handles EMM386 can use. Valid values are in the range 2 through 255. The default value is 64.

**d=**_nnn_

Specifies how many kilobytes of memory should be reserved for buffered DMA. Discounting floppy-disk DMA, this value should reflect the largest DMA transfer that will occur while EMM386 is active. Valid values for _nnn_ are in the range 16 through 256. The default value is 16.

**ram=**_mmmm-nnnn_

Specifies a range of segment addresses to be used for UMBs and also enables EMS support. If you do not specify a range, EMM386 uses all available adapter space to create UMBs and a page frame for EMS.

**noems**

Provides access to the upper memory area but prevents access to expanded memory.

**novcpi**

Disables support for VCPI applications. This switch must be used with the **noems** switch. If you specify the **novcpi** switch without specifying the **noems** switch, EMM386 does not disable VCPI support. If you specify both switches, EMM386 disregards the _memory_ parameter and the **min** switch. Disabling support for VCPI applications reduces the amount of extended memory allocated.

**highscan**

Specifies that EMM386 use an additional check to determine the availability of upper memory for use as UMBs or EMS windows. On some computers, specifying this switch may have no effect or cause EMM386 to identify upper memory areas as available when they are not. As a result, the computer might stop responding.

**verbose**

Directs EMM386 to display status and error messages while loading. By default, EMM386 displays messages only if it encounters an error condition. You can abbreviate **verbose** as **V**. (To display status messages without adding the **verbose** switch, press and hold ALT while EMM386 starts and loads.)

**win=**_mmmm-nnnn_

Reserves a specified range of segment addresses for Windows instead of for EMM386. Valid values for _mmmm_ and _nnnn_ are in the range A000h through FFFFh and are rounded down to the nearest 4-kilobyte boundary. The **x** switch takes precedence over the **win** switch if the two ranges overlap. The **win** switch takes precedence over the **ram**, **rom**, and **i** switches if their ranges overlap.

**nohi**

Prevents EMM386 from loading into the upper memory area. Normally, a portion of EMM386 is loaded into upper memory. Specifying this switch decreases available conventional memory and increases the upper memory area available for UMBs.

**rom=***mmmm-nnnn*

Specifies a range of segment addresses that EMM386 uses for shadow RAM—random-access memory used for read-only memory (ROM). Valid values for *mmmm* and *nnnn* are in the range A000h through FFFFh and are rounded down to the nearest 4-kilobyte boundary. Specifying this switch may speed up the system if it does not already have shadow RAM.

**nomovexbda**

Prevents EMM386 from moving the extended BIOS data from conventional memory to upper memory.

**altboot**

Specifies that EMM386 use an alternate handler to restart the computer when you press CTRL+ALT+DEL. Use this switch only if the computer stops responding or exhibits other unusual behavior when EMM386 is loaded and you press CTRL+ALT+DEL.

**Notes on EMM386.EXE**

**Must install HIMEM.SYS before EMM386.EXE.**  You must include a **device** command for the HIMEM.SYS device driver in CONFIG.SYS before the **device** command for EMM386.EXE.

**Using EMM386 memory switches.**  Unless you want to use EMM386 to provide access to the upper memory area, you need not specify memory switches on the **device** command line. EMM386 usually runs properly with the default values. In some cases, however, you might want to control how EMM386 uses memory. For example, you can control where EMM386 puts the EMS page frame or which segments it uses for EMS pages. You can use as many of these memory switches as you want, in any order you want.

**Using EMM386 to provide access to the upper memory area.**  In addition to providing access to expanded memory, EMM386 provides access to the upper memory area, which you can use to load certain programs and device drivers. You must use either the **ram** or **noems** switch to provide access to the upper memory area.

To give the operating system access to the upper memory area but not to expanded memory, use the **noems** switch. To give the operating system access to both the upper memory area and expanded memory, use the **ram** switch. The **ram** switch provides access to less of the upper memory area for running device drivers and programs than does the **noems** switch. In either case, you must include the **dos=umb** command in CONFIG.SYS. The **device** command for EMM386.EXE must precede any **devicehigh** commands.

**EMM386.EXE
Examples**

To start EMM386 as an expanded-memory emulator, using the default values, add the following lines to CONFIG.SYS:

```
device=himem.sys
device=emm386.exe
```

Because no location is specified, MS-DOS searches for the EMM386.EXE file in the root directory of the startup drive.

To specify that EMM386 allocate a maximum of 4096K of memory and a guaranteed 256K of memory (the default value), and to specify that the EMM386.EXE file is located in the DOS directory on drive C, add the following line to CONFIG.SYS:

```
device=c:\dos\emm386.exe 4096
```

To emulate expanded memory, specify the segment-base address D000h for the EMS page frame, and allocate 512K of memory to EMM386, use one of the following commands:

```
device=emm386.exe 512 frame=d000
```

```
device=emm386.exe 512 p0=d000 p1=d400 p2=d800 p3=dc00
```

Suppose that, in addition to specifying the conditions set in the preceding commands, you want to prevent EMM386 from using the segment addresses E000h through EC00h. To do this and to specify that EMM386 can use 127 handles, add the following line to CONFIG.SYS:

```
device=emm386.exe 512 frame=d000 x=e000-ec00 h=127
```

To provide access to the upper memory area but not provide EMS/VCPI memory, add the following line to CONFIG.SYS:

```
device=emm386.exe noems novcpi
```

To provide access to the upper memory area and provide EMS/VCPI memory, add the following line to CONFIG.SYS:

```
device=emm386.exe ram
```

# Windows Explorer Command-Line Switches

You can use the command-line switches for Windows Explorer in shortcut links or batch files, for example, to run Windows Explorer with a specified file selected.

**Syntax**

**explorer** [/**n**] [/**e**][,/**root**,*object*][[,/**select**],*subobject*]

**Parameters**

**/n**

Always open a new window (even if the specified folder is already open).

**/e**

Use Windows Explorer view. The default is Open view.

**/root,***object*

Specify the object in the normal namespace that will be used as the root of this Windows Explorer Folder. The default is to just use the normal namespace root (the desktop).

*subobject*

Specify the folder to receive the initial focus unless **/select** is used. The default is the root.

**/select**

Specifies that the parent folder is opened and the specified object is selected.

**Windows Explorer Examples**

To open a window rooted at \\myserver so you can easily browse the whole server, but nothing else:

```
explorer /e,/root,\\myserver
```

To open a folder window on C:\WINDOWS (or make an open window active) and select CALC.EXE, use:

```
explorer /select,c:\windows\calc.exe
```

# Xcopy and Xcopy32 Command-Line Switches

This command is used to copy files and directories, including subdirectories. Use the **xcopy32** form to preserve long filenames.

**Syntax**

**xcopy32** *source* [*destination*] [/**w**] [/**p**] [/**c**] [/**v**] [/**q**] [/**f**] [/**l**] [/**d**[:*date*]] [/**u**]
[/**i**][/**s** [/**e**]] [/**t**] [/**k**] [/**r**] [/**h**] [/**a**l/**m**] [/**n**] [/**exclude**:*filename*]

**Parameters**

*source*

Specifies the location and names of the files you want to copy. *Source* must include either a drive or a path.

*destination*

Specifies the destination of the files you want to copy. *Destination* can include a drive letter and colon, a directory name, a filename, or a combination.

**/w**

Displays a message asking you to press a key to begin copying files, and waits for your response before starting to copy files.

**/p**

Prompts you to confirm whether you want to create each destination file.

**/c**

Ignores errors.

**/v**

Verifies each file as it is written to the destination file to make sure that the destination files are identical to the source files. This switch is ignored because the functionality is inherent to the Windows 95 operating system. The switch is accepted only for compatibility with previous versions of MS-DOS.

**/q**

Suppresses display of **xcopy** messages.

**/f**

Displays source and destination filenames while copying.

**/l**

Does not copy files, only displays (lists) files that would be copied.

**/d**[**:***date*]

Copies only source files changed on or after the specified date. If the *date* value is missing, **xcopy** copies all *source* files that are newer than the time of existing *destination* files. This option allows you to update only files that have changed. Notice that dates in the twenty-first century must be specified using four digits (for example, /D:1-1-2001 if *m-d-y* is the date format). That is, /D:1-1-01 is interpreted as 1 January 1901 rather than 1 January 2001.

**/u**

Copies (updates) only files from *source* that exist on *destination*.

**/i**

If *source* is a directory or contains wildcards, and *destination* does not exist, **xcopy** assumes *destination* specifies a directory name and creates a new directory and then copies all specified files into the new directory. By default, **xcopy** prompts you to specify whether *destination* is a file or directory.

**/s**

Copies directories and subdirectories, unless they are empty. If you omit this switch, **xcopy** works within a single directory.

**/e**

Copies all subdirectories, even if they are empty. Used with the **/s** and **/t** switches.

**/t**

Copies only subdirectory structure (tree), not files. To copy empty directories, you must include the **/e** switch.

**/k**

Copies files and retains the read-only attribute on destination files if present on the source files. By default, the read-only attribute is removed.

**/r**

Copies over read-only files.

**/h**

Copies files with the hidden and system file attributes. **Xcopy** will not copy hidden or system files by default.

**/a**

Copies only source files that have their archive file attributes set. This switch does not modify the archive file attribute of the source file. For information about how to set the archive file attribute, see the online Help for the **attrib** command.

**/m**

Copies source files that have their archive file attributes set. Unlike the **/a** switch, the **/m** switch turns off archive file attributes in the files specified in source. For information about how to set the archive file attributes, see the online Help for the **attrib** command.

**/n**

Copies using aliases (short file or directory names). This switch is required when copying files or directories from a VFAT volume to a FAT volume or when the 8.3 file naming convention is required on the destination volume.

**/exclude:***filename*

Excludes the files listed in the specified file from the copy operation. The exclusion file can have a list of exclusion patterns (one per line, no wild card characters are supported). If any exclusion pattern in the file matches any part of the path of a subject file, that file is not copied.

**Notes on Xcopy**

**Default value for destination.**  If you omit *destination*, the **xcopy** command copies the files to the current directory.

**Specifying whether the destination is a file or a directory.**  If *destination* does not contain an existing directory and does not end with a backslash (\), **xcopy** prompts you with a message in the following format:

```
Does destination specify a file name
or directory name on the target
(F = file, D = directory)?
```

You can avoid this prompt by using the **/i** switch, in which case **xcopy** assumes the destination is a directory if the source is more than one file or a directory.

**Xcopy sets an archive attribute for destination files.**  **Xcopy** creates files with the archive attribute set, whether or not this attribute was set in the source file. For information, see the online Help for **atttrib** command.

**Xcopy vs. diskcopy.**  If you have a disk that contains files in subdirectories and you want to copy it to a disk that has a different format, you should use the **xcopy** command instead of **diskcopy**. The **diskcopy** command copies disks track by track; it requires that your source and destination disks have the same format. **Xcopy** has no such requirement. In general, use **xcopy** unless you need a complete disk image copy.

**Xcopy exit codes.**  The following list shows each exit code and a brief description of its meaning:

| | |
|---|---|
| 0 | Files were copied without error. |
| 1 | No files were found to copy. |
| 2 | The user pressed CTRL+C to terminate **xcopy**. |
| 4 | Initialization error occurred. There is not enough memory or disk space, or you entered an invalid drive name or invalid syntax on the command line. |
| 5 | Disk write error occurred. |

You can use the **errorlevel** parameter on the **if** command line in a batch program to process exit codes returned by **xcopy**.

**Xcopy Examples**

To copy all the files and subdirectories (including any empty subdirectories) from the disk in drive A to the disk in drive B, type:

```
xcopy a: b: /s /e
```

To include any system or hidden files in the previous example, add the **/h** switch when typing:

```
xcopy a: b: /s /e /h
```

To update files in the REPORTS directory with the files in the directory RAWDATA that have changed since December 29, 1993, type:

```
xcopy \rawdata \reports /d:12/29/93
```

To update all the files that exist on \REPORTS in the previous example, regardless of date, type:

```
xcopy \rawdata \reports /u
```

To obtain only a list of the files that would be copied for the previous command, without copying the files, type:

```
xcopy \rawdata \reports /d:12/29/93 /l > xcopy.out
```

The file XCOPY.OUT lists every file that would be copied.

To copy the \CUSTOMER directory and all subdirectories, including empty directories, to the directory \PUBLIC\ADDRESS on network drive H and retain the read-only attribute, while being prompted when a new file is being created on H, type the following:

```
xcopy \customer h:\public\address /s /e /k /p
```

To issue the previous command and ensure **xcopy** creates, without prompting, the directory \ADDRESS if it does not exist, add the **/i** switch:

```
xcopy \customer h:\public\address /s /e /k /p /i
```

You can create a batch program to perform **xcopy** operations and use the batch **if** command to process the exit code in case an error occurs. For example, the following batch program uses replaceable parameters for the **xcopy** *source* and *destination* parameters:

```
@echo off
rem COPYIT.BAT transfers all files in all subdirectories of
rem the source drive or directory (%1) to the destination
rem drive or directory (%2)
xcopy %1 %2 /s /e
if errorlevel 4 goto lowmemory
if errorlevel 2 goto abort
if errorlevel 0 goto exit
:lowmemory
echo Insufficient memory to copy files or
echo invalid drive or command-line syntax.
goto exit
:abort
echo You pressed CTRL+C to end the copy operation.
goto exit
:exit
```

To use this batch program to copy all files in the C:\PRGMCODE directory and its subdirectories to drive B, type the following command:

```
copyit c:\prgmcode b:
```

The command interpreter substitutes C:\PRGMCODE for **%1** and B: for **%2**, then uses **xcopy** with the **/e** and **/s** switches. If **xcopy** encounters an error, the batch program reads the exit code and goes to the label indicated in the appropriate **if errorlevel** statement. Windows 95 displays the appropriate message and exits from the batch program.

# Command-Line Switches for Disk Utilities

This section describes the commands that can be used from the command line to run the Windows-based versions of the ScanDisk, DriveSpace, and Disk Defragmenter disk utilities. These commands are provided to allow these disk utilities to be run from batch files.

---

**Note**  To provide compatibility with existing batch files, Windows 95 provides a **start** command to allow synchronous use of Windows-based programs from the command-line. To run a Windows-based program from the command-line and wait for it, use this syntax:

**start /W** "*program_name arguments*"

---

## Defrag

This command controls Windows 95 Disk Defragmenter. For more information about this utility, see Chapter 20, "Disks and File Systems."

**Syntax**

**defrag** [*drive:* | **/all**] [**/F** | **/U** | **/Q**] [**/noprompt**] [**/concise** | **/detailed**]

**Parameters**

*drive:*
Drive letter of the disk to be optimized.

**/all**
Defragment all local, nonremovable drives.

**/F**
Defragment files and free space.

**/U**
Defragment files only.

**/Q**
Defragment free space only.

**/concise**
Display the Hide Details view (default).

**/detailed**
Display the Show Details view.

**/noprompt**
Unattended mode; do not stop and display confirmation messages.

# DrvSpace

This command controls Windows DriveSpace at the command line, and can be used with either DblSpace or DrvSpace drives. These command switches are maintained for use in batch files and for compatibility with the compression utilities provided in MS-DOS version 6 and higher. Each switch performs the indicated operation, without asking for any additional input before beginning.

Additionally, the **/interactive** switch can be added to any command line to have DriveSpace ask for any missing parameters, and the **/noprompt** switch can be added to any syntax except the **/info** and **/settings** command-lines. The **/noprompt** switch prevents any confirmation dialog boxes from appearing (except for error messages). Notice that there is no way to prevent error messages from being displayed.

When you run DriveSpace without command-line arguments, the DriveSpace Manager appears, with menu commands for selecting the operations to perform. For more information about this utility, see Chapter 20, "Disks and File Systems."

**Syntax**

**drvspace /compress** *d:* [**/size**=*n*| **/reserve**=*n*] [**/new**=*e:*]
**drvspace /create** *d:* [**/size**=*n* | **/reserve**=*n*] [**/new**=*e:*] [**/cvf**=*nnn*]
**drvspace /delete** *d:*\**d??space.**nnn*
**drvspace /format** *d:*\**d??space.**nnn*
**drvspace /host**=*e: d:*
**drvspace** [**/info**] *d:*
**drvspace /mount** {[=*nnn*] *d:* | *d:*\**d??space.**nnn*} [**/new**=*e:*]
**drvspace /move** *d:* **/new**=*e:*
**drvspace /ratio**[=*n*] *d:*
**drvspace /settings**
**drvspace /size**[=*n*| **/reserve**=*n*] *d:*
**drvspace /uncompress** *d:*
**drvspace /unmount** *d:*

**Parameters**

**d??space.***nnn*
The filename of the hidden compressed volume file on the host drive, which can be either DRVSPACE.*nnn* or DBLSPACE.*nnn*, where *nnn* represents the actual filename extension.

The following sections provide details for these parameters.

If you add switches or parameters to the **drvspace** command, the operating system carries out the requested task without starting the DriveSpace program. The command syntax differs from task to task, as summarized in the following list.

| Action | Command |
| --- | --- |
| Compress a hard disk drive or floppy disk. | **drvspace /compress** |
| Create a new compressed drive in the free space on an existing drive. | **drvspace /create** |
| Delete a compressed drive. | **drvspace /delete** |
| Format a compressed drive. | **drvspace /format** |
| Display information about a compressed drive. | **drvspace /info** |
| Mount a compressed volume file (CVF). When DriveSpace mounts a CVF, it assigns it a drive letter; you can then use the files that CVF contains. | **drvspace /mount** |
| Change estimated compression ratio of a compressed drive. | **drvspace /ratio** |
| Change the size of a compressed drive. | **drvspace /size** |
| Uncompress a compressed drive. | **drvspace /uncompress** |
| Unmount a compressed drive. | **drvspace /unmount** |

**Notes on Drvspace**

**Fixing problems with drives compressed using DriveSpace.**   DriveSpace no longer provides a Chkdsk command as in earlier versions. Instead, Windows 95 includes the new ScanDisk program, a full-featured disk analysis and repair utility. ScanDisk can check and repair both uncompressed drives and DriveSpace or DoubleSpace drives. It can even check and repair unmounted DriveSpace or DoubleSpace compressed volume files. For more information, see "ScanDisk" later in this appendix.

**DBLSPACE.BIN, DRVSPACE.BIN, and DRVSPACE.SYS.**   DBLSPACE.BIN or DRVSPACE.BIN is the part of the system that provides access to the compressed drives. When you start the computer, the operating system loads D??SPACE.BIN along with other operating system functions, before carrying out the commands in CONFIG.SYS and AUTOEXEC.BAT. D??SPACE.BIN initially loads in conventional memory, since it loads before device drivers that provide access to upper memory. Normally, if the hard disk drive has been compressed using DriveSpace, D??SPACE.BIN is loaded even if you press F8 and choose an alternate startup option.

DRVSPACX.VXD is the protected-mode driver for DriveSpace. This driver takes over from the real-mode D??SPACE.BIN driver when Windows 95 switches to protected mode. The real-mode driver is required for starting the computer, but after the system switches to protected mode, DRVSPACX ensures that you have 32-bit, protected-mode performance, and the memory used by the real-mode driver is reclaimed.

The DBLSPACE.SYS device driver does not provide access to compressed drives; instead it determines the final location of D??SPACE.BIN in memory. When loaded with a **device** command, the DBLSPACE.SYS device driver moves D??SPACE.BIN from the top to the bottom of conventional memory. When loaded with a **devicehigh** command, DBLSPACE.SYS moves D??SPACE.BIN from conventional to upper memory, if available. Whenever possible, DBLSPACE.SYS moves a portion of D??SPACE.BIN into the HMA.

**How DriveSpace assigns drive letters.**  When you compress a drive using DriveSpace, it creates a new drive and assigns a drive letter to that drive. DriveSpace skips the first four available drive letters and assigns the next available drive letter to the new drive. For example, if the computer has only drives A, B, and C, DriveSpace skips letters D, E, F, and G, and assigns drive letter H to the new drive.

When assigning letters to additional drives (for example, if you compress another drive), DriveSpace works backwards from the first drive letter it assigned. In the example above, DriveSpace would next assign the letter G.

DriveSpace attempts to avoid drive-letter conflicts with drives created by **fdisk**, RAMDrive, networks, or other installable device drivers that assign drive letters. However, if a drive-letter conflict does occur, DriveSpace resolves the conflict by reassigning its drive letters.

## Drvspace /Compress

Compresses the files and free space on an existing hard disk drive, floppy disk, or other removable media. Compressing an existing drive makes more space available on that drive.

---

**Note**  DriveSpace cannot compress a drive that's completely full. To compress the startup hard disk drive, the drive must contain at least 2 MB of free space. Other hard disk drives and floppy disks must contain at least 768K of free space. (DriveSpace cannot compress 360K floppy disks.)

---

**Syntax**

**drvspace /compress** *drive1*: [**/new**=*drive2*:] [**/reserve**=*size*]

**Parameters**

*drive1*:
>    Specifies the existing drive you want to compress.

**Switches**

**/compress**
>    Compresses the hard disk drive or floppy disk specified by the drive parameter. This switch can be abbreviated to **/com**.

/**new**=*drive2*:
> Specifies the drive letter for the uncompressed (host) drive. After DriveSpace compresses an existing drive, the system will include both the existing drive (now compressed) and a new uncompressed drive. If you omit the /**new** switch, DriveSpace assigns the next available drive letter to the new drive.

/**reserve**=*size*
> Specifies how many megabytes of space to leave uncompressed. Because some files do not work properly when stored on a compressed drive, you may want to reserve some uncompressed space. The uncompressed space will be located on the new uncompressed drive. This switch can be abbreviated to /**reser**.

**Drvspace /Compress Examples**

To compress drive D, type the following command:

```
drvspace /compress d:
```

On drives larger than 256 MB, more space will be left on the host (because D??Space drives cannot be larger than 512 MB). Because this command does not specify how much space to leave uncompressed, DriveSpace leaves 2 MB of uncompressed space (the default). Because the command does not specify a drive letter for the uncompressed drive, DriveSpace assigns the next available drive letter to the new uncompressed drive (the host drive).

To direct DriveSpace to compress drive E, assign the drive letter F to the new uncompressed drive (the host drive), and leave 4 MB of uncompressed space on drive F, type the following command:

```
drvspace /compress e: /new=f: /reserve=4
```

## Drvspace /Create

Creates a new compressed drive by using free space on an uncompressed drive. The new compressed drive will provide more storage capacity than the amount of space it uses.

**Syntax**

**drvspace /create** *drive1*: [/**new**=*drive2*:] [/**size**=*size* | /**reserve**=*size*] [/**cvf**=*nnn*]

**Parameters**

*drive1*:
> Specifies the uncompressed drive that contains the space you want to use to create the new drive.

**Switches**

/**create**
> Creates a new compressed drive by using free space on the uncompressed drive specified by *drive1*. This switch can be abbreviated to /**cr**.

/**new**=*drive2*:
> Specifies the drive letter for the new compressed drive. The /**new** switch is optional; if you omit it, DriveSpace assigns the next available drive letter to the new drive.

**/reserve=**_size_

Specifies how many megabytes of free space DriveSpace should leave on the uncompressed drive. To make the compressed drive as large as possible, specify a size of 0.

You can include either the **/reserve** switch or the **/size** switch, but not both. If you omit both switches, DriveSpace uses all but 2 MB of free space. The **/reserve** switch can be abbreviated as **/reser**.

**/size=**_size_

Specifies the total size, in megabytes, of the compressed volume file. (This is the amount of space on the uncompressed drive that you want to allocate to the compressed drive.) You can include either the **/reserve** switch or the **/size** switch, but not both.

**/cvf=**_nnn_

Reports extension of the CVF file.

**Drvspace /Create Examples**

To create a new compressed drive that uses all available space on uncompressed drive E, type the following command:

```
drvspace /create e: /reserve=0
```

To create a new compressed drive by using 10 MB of space on uncompressed drive E, type the following command:

```
drvspace /create e: /size=10
```

To create a new compressed drive by using space on uncompressed drive D, and to direct DriveSpace to leave 2.75 MB of free space on drive D, type the following command:

```
drvspace /create d: /reserve=2.75
```

The following command creates a new compressed drive by using all but 2 MB of the space on drive D:

```
drvspace /create d:
```

Because the command includes neither the **/reserve** switch nor the **/size** switch, DriveSpace uses the default value for the **/reserve** switch and leaves 2 MB of space on drive D.

## Drvspace /Delete

Deletes the selected compressed drive and erases the associated compressed volume file.

<hr>

Caution   Deleting a compressed drive erases the entire drive and all the files it contains.

<hr>

**Syntax**

**drvspace /delete** *d*:**\d??space.###**

**Parameters**

*d*:**\d??space.###**
> Specifies the drive you want to delete. (DriveSpace will not allow you to delete any drive containing open files, including the drive containing Windows 95.)

**Switch**

**/delete**
> Deletes the specified drive. This switch can be abbreviated as **/del**.

**Drvspace /Delete Example**

The following command directs DriveSpace to delete the compressed volume for drive C:

```
drvspace /delete h:\dblspace.###
```

DriveSpace then deletes the compressed volume file for drive C. This completely erases the compressed drive and all the files it contains.

## Drvspace /Format

Formats the selected compressed drive.

<hr>

Caution   Formatting a compressed drive deletes all the files it contains. You cannot unformat a drive that has been formatted by using **drvspace /format**.

<hr>

**Syntax**

**drvspace /format** *d*:**\d??space.###**

**Parameters**

*d*:**\d??space.###**
> Specifies the drive you want to format. (DriveSpace will not allow you to format any drive containing open files, including the drive containing Windows 95.)

**Switch**

**/format**
> Directs DriveSpace to format the specified compressed drive. This switch can be abbreviated as **/f**.

| | |
|---|---|
| **Drvspace /Format Example** | The following command directs DriveSpace to format compressed drive E: |

```
drvspace /format h:\dblspace.###
```

DriveSpace then formats compressed drive E, which completely erases all the files on it.

## Drvspace /Info

Displays information about the selected drive's free and used space, the name of its compressed volume file, and its actual and estimated compression ratios. You can use this command while Windows is running.

| | |
|---|---|
| **Syntax** | **drvspace** [**/info**] I [*drive*:] |
| **Parameters** | *drive*:<br>Specifies the compressed drive about which you want information. If you don't specify a drive letter, DriveSpace displays information about the current drive. |
| **Switch** | **/info**<br>Directs DriveSpace to display information about the selected drive. This switch is optional and can be omitted as long as you specify a drive letter. |
| **Drvspace /Info Examples** | The following command displays information about the current drive: |

```
drvspace /info
```

The following command displays information about drive C:

```
drvspace /info c:
```

The following command displays information about drive E:

```
drvspace e:
```

## Drvspace /Mount

Establishes a connection between a compressed volume file (CVF) and a drive letter so that you can use the files the CVF contains. DriveSpace usually mounts CVFs automatically. You need to mount a CVF only if you previously unmounted it.

| | |
|---|---|
| **Syntax** | **drvspace /mount**[=*nnn*] *drive1*: [**/new**=*drive2*:]<br>**drvspace /mount** *d*:**\d??space.###** [**/new**=*drive2*:] |
| **Parameters** | *drive1*:<br>Specifies the drive that contains the compressed volume file you want to mount. You must specify a drive letter. |

**Switches**

**/mount**=*nnn*

    Directs DriveSpace to mount the compressed volume file with the filename extension specified by the *nnn* parameter. For example, to mount a CVF named DBLSPACE.001, you would specify **/mount**=001. If you omit the *nnn* parameter, DriveSpace attempts to mount the compressed volume file named DBLSPACE.000.

**/new**=*drive2*:

    Specifies the drive letter to assign to the new drive. This switch is optional; if you don't specify a drive letter, DriveSpace assigns the new drive the next available drive letter.

**Drvspace /Mount Examples**

To mount a compressed floppy disk in drive A, type the following:

```
drvspace /mount a:
```

To mount the compressed volume file DBLSPACE.001 located on uncompressed drive D, type the following:

```
drvspace /mount=001 d:
```

# Drvspace /Ratio

Changes the estimated compression ratio of the selected drive. DriveSpace uses this ratio to estimate how much free space the drive contains. You might want to change the estimated compression ratio if you plan to store new files with a compression ratio that differs greatly from the current ratio.

**Syntax**

**drvspace /ratio**[=*r.r*] [*drive*:]

**Parameters**

*drive*:

    Specifies the drive for which you want to change the estimated compression ratio. If you do not specify a drive, DriveSpace changes the estimated compression ratio for the current drive.

**Switch**

**/ratio**=*r.r*

    Changes the estimated compression ratio of the specified drive. To change the ratio to a specific number, specify the ratio you want. You can specify a ratio from 1.0 to 16.0. However, not all drives can accept values in this entire range. If you don't specify a ratio, DriveSpace sets the drive's estimated compression ratio to the average actual compression ratio for all the files currently on the drive. This switch can be abbreviated as **/ra**.

**Drvspace /Ratio Examples**

To change the estimated compression ratio of the current drive to match that drive's actual compression ratio, type the following command:

```
drvspace /ratio
```

To change the estimated compression ratio for drive D so that it is 3.2 to 1, type the following:

```
drvspace /ratio=3.2 d:
```

To change the estimated compression ratio of the current drive to 6 to 1, type the following:

```
drvspace /ratio=6
```

# Drvspace /Size

Enlarges or reduces the size of a compressed drive. You might want to enlarge a compressed drive if its host drive contains plenty of free space. You might want to reduce its size if you need more free space on the host drive.

| | |
|---|---|
| **Syntax** | **drvspace /size**[*=size1* | **/reserve**=*size2*] *drive***:** |
| **Parameters** | *drive***:** |
| | Specifies the drive you want to resize. |
| **Switches** | **/size**=*size1* |

**/size**=*size1*

Changes the size of the specified drive. You can specify the new size of the drive by using the *size1* parameter. The size of the drive is the number of megabytes of space that the drive's compressed volume file uses on the uncompressed (host) drive.

You can specify the drive's new size by using either the *size1* parameter or the **/reserve** switch, but not both. If you include neither the *size1* parameter nor the **/reserve** switch, DriveSpace makes the drive as small as possible.

**/reserve**=*size2*

Specifies how many megabytes of free space you want the uncompressed (host) drive to contain after DriveSpace resizes the drive. The **/reserve** switch can be abbreviated as **/reser**.

You can specify the drive's new size by using either the **/reserve** switch or the *size1* parameter of the **/size** switch, but not both. If you include neither the **/reserve** switch nor the *size1* parameter, DriveSpace makes the drive as small as possible.

**Drvspace /Size Examples**

To change the size of drive C so that its compressed volume file uses 60.5 MB of space on drive D, type the following command:

```
drvspace /size=60.5 c:
```

To change the size of drive E so that its host drive, drive D, contains 20 MB of free uncompressed space, type the following command:

```
drvspace /size /reserve=20 e:
```

To change the size of drive C so that it is as large as possible, type the following command:

```
drvspace /size /reserve=0 c:
```

# Drvspace /Uncompress

Uncompresses a drive that was compressed by using DriveSpace.

**Syntax**

**drvspace /uncompress** *drive*:

**Parameter**

*drive*:
    Specifies the drive you want to uncompress.

**Switch**

**/uncompress**
    Uncompresses the specified drive.

**Notes on Drvspace /Uncompress**

**Backing up before uncompressing.**   Before uncompressing the drive, you should back up the files it contains. If you include the **/interactive** switch, DriveSpace will prompt for this.

**Invalid pathnames after uncompressing.**   When you uncompress a drive, DriveSpace either changes that drive's letter or the letter of its host drive (depending on how the compressed drive was originally created). DriveSpace shows how the drive letters will change when it uncompresses the drive. Some programs have settings that include explicit pathnames and drive letters. If a program's settings specify a drive that is no longer valid after uncompressing, the program will probably display an error message or be unable to find one of its components or data files. In that case, you need to correct the drive letter specified by that setting.

**Disk space.**   You can uncompress a drive only if the data it contains will fit on the host drive. If you use the **drvspace /uncompress** command, and DriveSpace indicates the drive will not have enough free disk space, delete unnecessary files or move them to another drive.

**Duplicate filenames on compressed and host drives.**   If the root directories of the compressed and host drives contain files or directories with identical names, DriveSpace cannot uncompress the compressed drive. If this happens, DriveSpace displays an error message. Remove or rename one copy of each file, and then try uncompressing the drive again.

**Uninstalling DriveSpace.**   When you uncompress the last mounted compressed drive, DriveSpace first uncompresses the drive, and then prompts you to remove the DrvSpace driver from memory.

**Drvspace /Uncompress Example**

To uncompress drive E, type the following command:

```
drvspace /uncompress e:
```

### Drvspace /Unmount

Breaks the connection between the selected drive's compressed volume file and its drive letter. Unmounting a drive makes it temporarily unavailable.

You cannot unmount a drive containing open files, including the drive containing Windows 95.

**Syntax**            **drvspace /unmount** [*drive:*]

**Parameters**        *drive:*
                      Specifies the drive you want to unmount. This parameter is optional; if you omit it, DriveSpace unmounts the current drive.

**Switch**            **/unmount**
                      Unmounts the specified compressed drive.

**Drvspace**          To unmount compressed drive E, type the following command:
**/Unmount**
**Example**           ```
                      drvspace /unmount e:
                      ```

# ScanDisk

This command syntax controls Windows ScanDisk. For more information about this utility, see Chapter 20, "Disks and File Systems."

---

**Note**  At the command prompt (for example, when you use F8 to start only the command prompt), you can use **scandisk** with the same switches to run the MS-DOS–based equivalent for this command. At the command prompt, type **scandisk /?** for more information.

---

**Syntax**            **scandskw** [*drive:*] [**/A**] [**/N**] [**/P**]
                      **scandisk** *drive:***\dblspace.***nnn*
                      **scandisk** *drive:***\drvspace.***nnn*

**Parameters**        *drive:*
                      Specifies one or more drives to be checked.

                      **/A** or **/All**
                      Checks all local, nonremovable hard disk drives.

                      **/N** or **/NonInteractive**
                      Starts and closes ScanDisk automatically. However, this switch does not prevent ScanDisk from stopping to report errors found on the drive.
                      ```

**/p** or **/Preview**

Runs ScanDisk in Preview mode, where it reports and seems to correct errors that it finds, but it does not actually write changes to the disk.

---

**Important**   When running **scandskw** in Preview mode, it appears as though ScanDisk is fixing errors, but it is not. Also, notice that unlike other settings in ScanDisk, the **/Preview** switch is not saved in the Registry, so the next time you run ScanDisk, it is no longer in Preview mode.

To determine whether ScanDisk is running in Preview mode, look for the tag "(Preview)" in the caption of the main ScanDisk window.

---

**dblspace.***nnn* or **drvspace.***nnn*

Checks the specified unmounted DoubleSpace or DriveSpace compressed volume file, where *nnn* is the filename extension for the hidden host file.

The following table describes the codes provided when ScanDisk finished running.

| Exit code | Description |
|-----------|-------------|
| 0x00 | Drive checked, no errors found |
| 0x01 | Errors found, all fixed |
| 0xFA | Check could not start—cannot load or find DSKMAINT.DLL |
| 0xFB | Check could not start—insufficient memory |
| 0xFC | Errors found, but at least some were not fixed |
| 0xFD | At least one drive could not be checked |
| 0xFE | Check was canceled |
| 0xFF | Check was terminated because of an error |

You can capture the exit code in a batch file to define an action to take in the event of particular exit code. For example:

```
start /w scandksw c: d: /n
if errorlevel exitcode goto command
...
```

In this sample, **start /w** forces the batch file to stop and wait for **scandskw** to finish (otherwise, because it is a Windows-based program, the batch file would continue as soon as **scandskw** had been launched). Also in this example, if the actual exit code is greater than or equal to the exit code specified by *exitcode*, the batch file runs the specified *command*; otherwise, it continues to the next line in the batch file. The **goto** *command* entry could specify any command you want.

# TCP/IP Utilities

The TCP/IP utilities offer network connections to non-Microsoft hosts such as UNIX® system computers. You must have the TCP/IP network protocol installed to use the TCP/IP utilities. These tools are installed automatically when you install Microsoft TCP/IP.

| Command | Purpose |
| --- | --- |
| **arp** | Displays and modifies the IP-to-Ethernet address translation tables. |
| **ftp** | Transfers files to and from a node running **ftp** service; similar to **tftp**. |
| **nbtstat** | Displays protocol statistics and current TCP/IP connections using NetBIOS over TCP/IP. |
| **netstat** | Displays protocol statistics and current TCP/IP connections. |
| **ping** | Verifies connections to a remote host or hosts. |
| **route** | Manually controls network routing tables. |
| **tracert** | Determines the route taken to a destination. |

**Note**  Switches used in the syntax for all TCP/IP utilities are case-sensitive. For example, for the **nbtstat** command, the switch **-R** has a different effect from the **-r** switch.

▷  **To get help on TCP/IP utilities**

- At the command prompt, type **-?** followed by a space and the command name. For example, type **ping -?** to get help on the **ping** command.

**Important**  The FTP and Telnet utilities rely on password authentication by the remote computer. Passwords are not encrypted before being sent over the network. This allows another user equipped with a network analyzer on the same network to steal a user's remote account password. For this reason, it is strongly recommended that users of these utilities choose different passwords for their workgroup, computer, or domain from the passwords used when connecting to computers that are not on Microsoft networks.

The following presents a complete reference for the TCP/IP commands included with Windows 95.

# Arp

This diagnostic command displays and modifies the IP-to-Ethernet or IP-to-token ring address translation tables used by the address resolution protocol (ARP).

**Syntax**

**arp -a** [*inet_addr*] [**-N** [*if_addr*]]
**arp -d** *inet_addr* [*if_addr*]
**arp -s** *inet_addr ether_addr* [*if_addr*]

**Parameters**

**-a**

Displays current ARP entries by querying TCP/IP. If *inet_addr* is specified, only the IP and physical addresses for the specified computer are displayed.

**-d**

Deletes the entry from the ARP cache table that is specified by *inet_addr*.

**-s**

Adds an entry in the ARP cache to associate the IP address *inet_addr* with the physical address *ether_addr*. The physical address is given as 6 hexadecimal bytes separated by hyphens. The IP address is specified using dotted decimal notation. The entry is permanent, that is, it will not be automatically removed from the cache after the timeout expires.

**-N** [*if_addr*]
Displays the ARP entries for the network interface specified by *if_addr*.

*ether_addr*
Specifies a physical address.

*if_addr*
Specifies, if present, the IP address of the interface for which the address translation table should be modified. If not present, the first applicable interface will be used.

*inet_addr*
Specifies an IP address in dotted decimal notation.

# Ftp

This connectivity command transfers files to and from a computer running an FTP service. The **ftp** command can be used interactively or by processing ASCII text files.

**Syntax**

**ftp** [**-v**] [**-n**] [**-i**] [**-d**] [**-g**] [*host*] [**-s:** *filename*]

**Parameters**

**-v**

Suppresses display of remote server responses.

**-n**

Suppresses autologon upon initial connection.

**-i**

Turns off interactive prompting during multiple file transfers.

**-d**

Enables debugging, displaying all FTP commands passed between the client and server.

**-g**

Disables filename globbing, which permits the use of wildcard characters in local file and path names. (See the FTP **glob** command.)

*host*

Specifies the host name or IP address of the remote host to connect to.

**-s:** *filename*

Specifies a text file containing FTP commands; the commands will automatically run after **ftp** starts. Use this switch instead of redirection (>).

▶ **To use the ftp command**

- At the command prompt, type **ftp** plus any desired switches and press ENTER.

  For example, you might type **ftp -s:myfile.scr**

The following table shows the FTP commands available when Microsoft TCP/IP is installed on a computer.

**FTP Commands in Microsoft TCP/IP**

| Command | Purpose |
|---------|---------|
| ! | Runs the specified command on the local computer. |
| ? | Displays descriptions for **ftp** commands. Identical to **help**. |
| **append** | Appends a local file to a file on the remote computer, using the current file type setting. |
| **ascii** | Sets the file transfer type to ASCII, the default. |
| **bell** | Toggles a bell to ring after each file transfer command is completed. By default, the bell is off. |
| **binary** | Sets the file transfer type to binary. |
| **bye** | Ends the FTP session with the remote computer and exits **ftp**. |
| **cd** | Changes the working directory on the remote computer. |
| **close** | Ends the FTP session with the remote server and returns to the command interpreter. |
| **debug** | Toggles debugging. When debugging is on, each command sent to the remote computer is printed, preceded by the string --->. By default, debugging is off. |

**FTP Commands in Microsoft TCP/IP** (*continued*)

| Command | Purpose |
|---------|---------|
| **delete** | Deletes files on remote computers. |
| **dir** | Displays a list of a remote directory's files and subdirectories. |
| **disconnect** | Disconnects from the remote computer, retaining the **ftp** prompt. |
| **get** | Copies a remote file to the local computer, using the current file transfer type. |
| **glob** | Toggles filename globbing. Globbing permits use of wildcard characters in local file or path names. By default, globbing is on. |
| **hash** | Toggles hash-mark (#) printing for each 2048 bytes data block transferred. By default, hash-mark printing is off. |
| **help** | Displays descriptions for FTP commands. |
| **lcd** | Changes the working directory on the local computer. By default, the current directory on the local computer is used. |
| **literal** | Sends arguments, verbatim, to the remote FTP server. A single FTP reply code is expected in return. |
| **ls** | Displays an abbreviated list of a remote directory's files and subdirectories. |
| **mdelete** | Deletes multiple files on remote computers. |
| **mdir** | Displays a list of a remote directory's files and subdirectories. Allows you to specify multiple files. |
| **mget** | Copies multiple remote files to the local computer using the current file transfer type. |
| **mkdir** | Creates a remote directory. |
| **mls** | Displays an abbreviated list of a remote directory's files and subdirectories. |
| **mput** | Copies multiple local files to the remote computer, using the current file transfer type. |
| **open** | Connects to the specified FTP server. |
| **prompt** | Toggles prompting. During multiple file transfers, **ftp** provides prompts to allow you to selectively retrieve or store files; **mget** and **mput** transfer all files if prompting is turned off. By default, prompting is on. |
| **put** | Copies a local file to the remote computer, using the current file transfer type. |
| **pwd** | Prints the current directory on the remote computer. |
| **quit** | Ends the FTP session with the remote computer and exits **ftp**. |
| **quote** | Sends arguments, verbatim, to the remote FTP server. A single FTP reply code is expected in return. Identical to **literal**. |

**FTP Commands in Microsoft TCP/IP** (*continued*)

| Command | Purpose |
| --- | --- |
| **recv** | Copies a remote file to the local computer, using the current file transfer type. Identical to **get**. |
| **remotehelp** | Displays help for remote commands. |
| **rename** | Renames remote files. |
| **rmdir** | Deletes a remote directory. |
| **send** | Copies a local file to the remote computer, using the current file transfer type. Identical to **put**. |
| **status** | Displays the current status of FTP connections and toggles. |
| **trace** | Toggles packet tracing; displays the route of each packet when running an FTP command. |
| **type** | Sets or displays the file transfer type. |
| **user** | Specifies a user to the remote computer. |
| **verbose** | Toggles verbose mode. If on, all FTP responses are displayed; when a file transfer completes, statistics regarding the efficiency of the transfer are also displayed. By default, verbose is on. |

# Nbtstat

This diagnostic command displays protocol statistics and current TCP/IP connections using NetBIOS over TCP/IP.

**Syntax**

**nbtstat** [**-a** *RemoteName*] [**-A** *IP_address*] [**-c**] [**-n**] [**-R**] [**-r**] [**-S**] [**-s**] [*interval*]

**Parameters**

**-a**

Lists the remote computer's name table given its host name.

**-A**

Lists the remote computer's name table given its IP address specified in dotted decimal notation.

**-c**

Lists the contents of the NetBIOS name cache, with the IP address of each name.

**-n**

Lists local NetBIOS names. In this listing, "Registered" indicates that the name has been registered on this network node, either by b-node broadcast or by a WINS server.

**-R**

Reloads the LMHOSTS file after purging all names from the NetBIOS name cache.

**-r**

Lists name resolution statistics for Windows networking. On a computer configured to use WINS, this option returns the number of names resolved and registered broadcast or WINS.

**-S**

Displays both workstation and server sessions, listing the remote hosts by IP address only.

**-s**

Displays both workstation and server sessions. It attempts to convert the remote host IP address to a name using the HOSTS file.

*interval*

Redisplays selected statistics, pausing *interval* seconds between each display. Press CTRL+C to stop redisplaying statistics. If this parameter is omitted, **nbtstat** prints the current configuration information once.

**Notes on Nbtstat**

The column headings generated by the **nbtstat** utility have the following meanings.

Input
Number of bytes received.

Output
Number of bytes sent.

In/Out
Whether the connection is from the computer (outbound) or from another system to the local computer (inbound).

Life
The remaining time that a name table cache entry will live before it is purged.

Local Name
The local NetBIOS name associated with the connection.

Remote Host
The name or IP address associated with the remote host.

Type
This refers to the type of name. A name can either be a unique name or a group name.

*<03>*
Each NetBIOS name is 16 characters long. The last byte often has special significance, because the same name can be present several times on a computer. This notation is the last byte converted to hexadecimal. For example, <20> is a space in ASCII.

State

The state of NetBIOS connections as shown in the following list:

| State | Meaning |
|-------|---------|
| Accepting | An inbound session is currently being accepted and will be connected shortly. |
| Associated | A connection endpoint has been created and associated with an IP address. |
| Connected | The session has been established. |
| Connecting | The session is in the connecting phase where the name-to-IP address mapping of the destination is being resolved. |
| Disconnected | The local computer has issued a disconnect, and it is waiting for confirmation from the remote computer. |
| Disconnecting | A session is in the process of disconnecting. |
| Idle | This endpoint has been opened but cannot receive connections. |
| Inbound | An inbound session is in the connecting phase. |
| Listening | This endpoint is available for an inbound connection. |
| Outbound | A session is in the connecting phase where the TCP connection is currently being created. |
| Reconnecting | A session is trying to reconnect if it failed to connect on the first attempt. |

# Netstat

This diagnostic command displays protocol statistics and current TCP/IP network connections.

**Syntax**

**netstat** [-**a**] [-**ens**] [-**p** *protocol*] [-**r**] [*interval*]

**Parameters**

**-a**

Displays all connections; server connections are usually not shown.

**-e**

Displays Ethernet statistics. This may be combined with the -**s** option.

**-n**

Displays addresses and port numbers in numerical form (rather than attempting name look-ups).

**-s**

Displays per-protocol statistics. By default, statistics are shown for TCP, UDP, ICMP, and IP; the -**p** option may be used to specify a subset of the default.

-p *protocol*

Shows connections for the protocol specified by *protocol*; *protocol* may be **tcp** or **udp**. If used with the **-s** option to display per-protocol statistics, *protocol* may be **tcp**, **udp**, **icmp**,or **ip**.

-r

Displays the contents of the routing table.

*interval*

Redisplays selected statistics, pausing *interval* seconds between each display. Press CTRL+C to stop redisplaying statistics. If this parameter is omitted, **netstat** prints the current configuration information once.

**Notes on Netstat**

The **netstat** utility provides statistics on the following network components.

| Statistic | Purpose |
|---|---|
| Foreign Address | The IP address and port number of the remote computer to which the socket is connected. The name corresponding to the IP address is shown instead of the number if the HOSTS file contains an entry for the IP address. In cases where the port is not yet established, the port number is shown as an asterisk (*). |
| Local Address | The IP address of the local computer, and the port number the connection is using. The name corresponding to the IP address is shown instead of the number if the HOSTS file contains an entry for the IP address. In cases where the port is not yet established, the port number is shown as an asterisk (*). |
| Proto | The name of the protocol used by the connection. |
| (state) | Indicates the state of TCP connections only. The possible states are the following: |

| | | |
|---|---|---|
| close_wait | fin_wait_1 | syn_received |
| closed | fin_wait_2 | syn_send |
| established | listen | timed_waitlast_ack |

# Ping

This diagnostic command verifies connections to one or more remote hosts.

**Syntax**

**ping** [-t] [-a] [-n *count*] [-l *length*] [-f] [-i *ttl*] [-v *tos*] [-r *count*] [-s *count*] [[-j *host-list*] | [-k *host-list*]] [-w *timeout*] *destination-list*

**Parameters**

-t

Pings the specified host until interrupted.

-a

Specifies not to resolve addresses to host names.

**-n** *count*

Sends the number of echo packets specified by *count*. The default is 4.

**-l** *length*

Sends echo packets containing the amount of data specified by *length*. The default is 64 bytes; the maximum is 8192.

**-f**

Sends a Do Not Fragment flag in the packet. The packet will not be fragmented by gateways on the route.

**-i** *ttl*

Sets the Time To Live field to the value specified by *ttl*.

**-v** *tos*

Sets the Type Of Service field to the value specified by *tos*.

**-r** *count*

Records the route of the outgoing packet and the returning packet in the Record Route field. A minimum of 1 to a maximum of 9 hosts must be specified by *count*.

**-s** *count*

Specifies the time stamp for the number of hops specified by *count*.

**-j** *host-list*

Routes packets by means of the list of hosts specified by *host-list*. Consecutive hosts may be separated by intermediate gateways (loose source routed). The maximum number allowed by IP is 9.

**-k** *host-list*

Routes packets by means of the list of hosts specified by *host-list*. Consecutive hosts may not be separated by intermediate gateways (strict source routed). The maximum number allowed by IP is 9.

**-w** *timeout*

Specifies a time-out interval in milliseconds.

*destination-list*

Specifies the remote hosts to ping.

**Note on Ping**

The **ping** command verifies connections to remote host or hosts, by sending Internet Control Message Protocol (ICMP) echo packets to the host and listening for echo reply packets. The **ping** command waits for up to 1 second for each packet sent and prints the number of packets transmitted and received. Each received packet is validated against the transmitted message. By default, four echo packets containing 64 bytes of data (a periodic uppercase sequence of alphabetic characters) are transmitted.

You can use the **ping** utility to test both the host name and the IP address of the host. If the IP address is verified but the host name is not, you may have a name resolution problem. In this case, be sure that the host name you are querying is in either the local HOSTS file or in the DNS database.

The following shows sample output for **ping**:

```
C:\>ping ds.internic.net

Pinging ds.internic.net [192.20.239.132] with 32 bytes of data:

Reply from 192.20.239.132: bytes=32 time=101ms TTL=243
Reply from 192.20.239.132: bytes=32 time=100ms TTL=243
Reply from 192.20.239.132: bytes=32 time=120ms TTL=243
Reply from 192.20.239.132: bytes=32 time=120ms TTL=243
```

# Route

This diagnostic command manipulates network routing tables.

**Syntax**

**route** [**-f**] [*command* [*destination*] [**MASK** *netmask*] [*gateway*]]

**Parameters**

**-f**

Clears the routing tables of all gateway entries. If this parameter is used in conjunction with one of the commands, the tables are cleared prior to running the command.

*command*

Specifies one of four commands.

| Command | Purpose |
|---------|---------|
| **print** | Prints a route |
| **add** | Adds a route |
| **delete** | Deletes a route |
| **change** | Modifies an existing route |

*destination*

Specifies the host-to-send *command*.

**MASK**

Specifies, if present, that the next parameter be interpreted as the *netmask* parameter.

*netmask*

Specifies, if present, the subnet mask value to be associated with this route entry. If not present, this parameter defaults to 255.255.255.255.

*gateway*

Specifies the gateway.

# Telnet

This connectivity command starts terminal emulation with a remote system running a Telnet service. Telnet provides DEC™ VT 100™, DEC VT 52, or TTY emulation, using connection-based services of TCP.

To provide terminal emulation from a Windows 95 computer, the foreign host must be configured with the TCP/IP program, the Telnet server program or daemon, and a user account for the computer running Windows 95.

The Telnet application is found in the Accessories program group if you install the TCP/IP connectivity utilities. Telnet is a Windows Sockets-based application that simplifies TCP/IP terminal emulation with Windows 95.

---

**Note**  Microsoft does not provide the Telnet server daemon (**telnetd**).

---

**Syntax**        **telnet** [*host* [*port*]]

**Parameters**    *host*

Specifies the host name or IP address of the remote system you want to connect to, providing compatibility with applications such as Gopher and Mosaic.

*port*

Specifies the remote port you want to connect to, providing compatibility with applications such as Gopher and Mosaic. The default value is specified by the **telnet** entry in the SERVICES file. If no entry exists in the SERVICES file, the default connection port value is decimal 23.

# Tracert

This diagnostic utility determines the route taken to a destination by sending Internet Control Message Protocol (ICMP) echo packets with varying Time-To-Live (TTL) values to the destination. Each router along the path is required to decrement the TTL on a packet by at least 1 before forwarding it, so the TTL is effectively a hop count. When the TTL on a packet reaches 0, the router is supposed to send back an ICMP Time Exceeded message to the source system. The **tracert** command determines the route by sending the first echo packet with a TTL of 1 and incrementing the TTL by 1 on each subsequent transmission until the target responds or the maximum TTL is reached. The route is determined by examining the ICMP Time Exceeded messages sent back by intermediate routers. Notice that some routers silently drop packets with expired TTLs and are invisible to **tracert**.

| | |
|---|---|
| **Syntax** | **tracert [-d] [-h** *maximum_hops*] **[-j** *host-list*] **[-w** *timeout*] *target_name* |
| **Parameters** | **-d** |

    Specifies not to resolve addresses to host names.

**-h** *maximum_hops*
    Specifies maximum number of hops to search for target.

**-j** *host-list*
    Specifies loose source route along *host-list*.

**-w** *timeout*
    Waits the number of milliseconds specified by *timeout* for each reply.

*target_name*
    Specifies the host name of the destination computer.

**Notes on Tracert**    The following shows sample output for **tracert**. The first column is the hop number, which is the Time To Live (TTL) value set in the packet. Each of the next three columns contains the round-trip times in milliseconds for an attempt to reach the destination with that TTL value. An asterisk (*) means that the attempt timed out. The fourth column is the host name (if it was resolved) and IP address of the responding system.

```
C:\>tracert ds.internic.net

Tracing route to ds.internic.net [198.49.45.10]
over a maximum of 30 hops:

1   <10 ms <10 ms    *     [131.107.1.100]
2    10 ms <10 ms   10 ms seattle1-gw.nwnet.net [192.80.12.82]
3     *     10 ms   10 ms enss143-enet.nwnet.net [192.35.180.2]
4    20 ms    *     10 ms t3-3.seattle-cnss8.t3.ans.net [140.222.88.4]
5    30 ms   30 ms   20 ms t3-0.los-angeles-cnss8.t3.ans.net [140.222.8.1
6    70 ms   70 ms   80 ms t3-0.new-york-cnss24.t3.ans.net [140.222.24.1]
7    80 ms   81 ms   80 ms t3-0.denver-cnss40.t3.ans.net [140.222.40.1]
8   100 ms   91 ms   90 ms t3-1.new-york-cnss32.t3.ans.net [140.222.32.2]
9    90 ms   90 ms   91 ms mf-0.new-york-cnss36.t3.ans.net [140.222.32.196]
10  100 ms   90 ms   91 ms t1-0.enss222.t3.ans.net [140.222.222.1]
11  140 ms  191 ms  100 ms ds.internic.net [198.49.45.10]

Trace complete.
```

APPENDIX B

# Windows 95 System Files

This appendix provides an overview of information about the system files supplied with Windows 95.

**In This Appendix**

Windows 95 Distribution Disk Storage Overview    1150
Using the Extract Program to Extract Files    1150
Setup Files Overview    1152
Directory File Structure and File Locations    1153
    Location of Key System Files    1154
    Location of System Files on Compressed Disks    1156

# Windows 95 Distribution Disk Storage Overview

Windows 95 is stored on the distribution disks as cabinet files (*.CAB). When the Windows 95 disks are created, files are compressed into folders. The Windows 95 files are read in and written as one, continuous byte-stream, which compresses the entire stream and divides it into folders as appropriate. Folders can fill one or more cabinets. The following defines the terms used to describe the distribution files.

**Cabinet.**  A normal file that contains pieces of one or more files, usually compressed.

**Folder.**  A decompression boundary. Large folders enable higher compression, because the compressor can refer back to more data in finding patterns. However, to retrieve a file at the end of a folder, the entire folder must be decompressed.

The Windows 95 distribution disks use distribution media format (DMF), which is a special read-only format for 3.5-inch floppy disks that permits storage of 1.7 MB of data.

# Using the Extract Program to Extract Files

The Extract program supports command-line extraction of files from the cabinet (*.CAB) storage format on disk. Extract does not support any other compression system (that is, it is not backward-compatible with any previous Microsoft disk utilities).

The Extract program (EXTRACT.EXE) can be found in the Windows COMMAND directory, or on the Windows 95 disks.

---

**Important**  The information in this section is provided for use if your product support representative indicates that you should use the Extract program to extract a compressed file from the Windows 95 cabinet files.

In general, you should use the Add/Remove Programs or Network options in Control Panel to install applications and supporting software from the Windows 95 disks.

If system files are missing or damaged, run Windows 95 Setup from the Windows 95 disks (or network distribution source), and choose the option to validate and restore files.

---

**Syntax**

**extract** [/y] *compressed_file* [*destination_file*]

–Or–

**extract** [/y] [/A] [/D | /E] [/L *location*] *cabinet_file* [*file_specification* ...]

**Parameters**

**/A**

Process all files in a cabinet set, starting with the *cabinet_file*.

**/D**

Provide only a directory listing (do not extract).

**/E**

Force extraction.

**/L** *location*

Use the directory specified by *location*, instead of the current directory, as the default location to place extracted files.

**/Y**

Overwrite files in the destination without prompting. The default is to prompt the user if the destination file already exists, and allow one of the following:

- Overwrite the file

- Skip the file

- Overwrite this file and all subsequent files that may already exist

- Exit

*compressed_file*

This is a cabinet file that contains a single file (for example, FILE1.EX_, which contains FILE1.EXE). If *destination_file* is not specified, then the file is extracted and given its original name in the current directory.

*destination_file*

This can be either a relative path (.:, .., C:FILE1, and so on) or a fully qualified path. This can specify either a file (or files, if wildcards are included) or a directory. If a directory is specified, then the filename stored in the cabinet is used. Otherwise, *destination_file* is used as the complete filename for the extracted file.

*cabinet_file*

This is a cabinet file that contains two or more files. If no *file_specification* parameter is specified, then a list is displayed of the files in the cabinet. If one or more *file_specification* parameters are specified, then these are used to select the files to be extracted from the cabinet. Wildcards are allowed to specify multiple cabinets.

*file_specification*

This specifies files to be extracted from the cabinets. This can contain the **?** and **\*** wildcards. Multiple *file_specification* values can be supplied.

The following table provides some examples.

| Command | Behavior |
| --- | --- |
| **extract** *filename.ex_* | Assuming *filename.ex_* contains just the single file FILENAME.EXE, then *filename.exe* is extracted and placed in the current directory. |
| **extract** *filename.ex_* *file2*.exe | Assuming *filename.ex_* contains just the single file *filename.exe*, then *filename.exe* is extracted and placed in the current directory in the file *file2.exe*. |
| **extract** *cabinet.1* | Assuming *cabinet.1* contains multiple files, then a list of the files stored in that cabinet is displayed. |
| **extract** *cabinet.1* **.exe* | Extracts all .EXE files from *cabinet.1* and places them in the current directory. |

# Setup Files Overview

The following table describes the key files used for Windows 95 Setup.

| Filename | Description |
| --- | --- |
| setup.exe | The real-mode Setup component that initializes Windows 95 Setup. If this file is started from MS-DOS, it calls the real-mode stub. If started from within Windows, it is a 16-bit Windows stub. |
| suwin.exe | The protected-mode Setup components responsible for calling all other DLLs used in Setup. |
| setupx.dll | The primary DLL used during the Copy Files phase to perform most of the installation procedures. It is responsible for reading INF files, handling disks, and copying files. |
| netdi.dll | The module called early in the Setup process to install networking services. |

Also, the WININSTx.400 directory is created at the beginning of the Windows 95 Setup process. This directory contains a minimal set of files used during setup and requires about 6 to 7 MB of free disk space. This directory is removed upon successful completion of Windows 95 installation.

# Directory File Structure and File Locations

The following shows the typical default directory structure created for Windows 95.

```
\Windows
    Command
    Config
    Cursors
    Desktop
    Fonts
    Help
    Inf
    Media
    Pif
    Recent
    Sendto
    Spool
        Printers
    Start Menu
        Programs
            Accessories
            Games
            Multimedia
            System
            StartUp
    Sysbckup
    System
        Color
        Iosubsys
        Viewers
        Vmm32
    Temp
```

# Location of Key System Files

The following table lists the directories where various types of Windows 95 system files and supporting files are stored.

**Key Paths to Windows 95 Files**

| File type | Directory[1] |
|---|---|
| Core Windows 95 files | Windows |
| Shortcuts to applications | Windows PROGRAMS |
| MS-DOS commands | Windows COMMAND |
| Printer drivers | Windows SPOOL\PRINTERS |
| Help files | Windows HELP |
| Font files | Windows FONTS |
| Setup and device installation files | Windows INF |
| PIF files | Windows PIF |
| Drivers | Windows SYSTEM |
| VxDs | Windows SYSTEM |
| I/O Subsystem | Windows SYSTEM\IOSUBSYS |
| Viewers | Windows SYSTEM\VIEWERS |
| VxDs added after installation | Windows SYSTEM\VMM32 |

[1] "Windows" refers to the directory that is specified during the installation process to contain the Windows 95 files.

The following table shows where key Windows 95 files are stored when Windows 95 is installed on the local hard disk of a computer. For information about installing Windows 95 on a server for a network client computer to run a shared copy, see Chapter 4, "Server-Based Setup for Windows 95."

**Location of Key Windows 95 Files**

| Description | Filename | Location |
|---|---|---|
| Real-mode operating system and system detection | IO.SYS | Root directory of startup drive |
| Command-line processor | COMMAND.COM | Root directory of startup drive |
| Real-mode stub to start Windows 95 | WIN.COM | Windows |
| Protected-mode Virtual Machine Manager (VMM) | VMM32.VXD | Windows SYSTEM |
| Registry | SYSTEM.DAT | Windows |
| Registry current backup | SYSTEM.DA0 | Windows |
| Registry when first created by Setup | SYSTEM.NEW | Windows |
| User Registry | USER.DAT | Windows |
| User Registry first created by Setup | USER.NEW | Windows |
| Log of the Setup process | SETUPLOG.TXT | Root directory of startup drive |
| Hardware detection log | DETLOG.TXT | Root directory of startup drive |
| Log of Windows 95 startup process | BOOTLOG.TXT | Root directory of startup drive |
| Real-mode network configuration | PROTOCOL.INI | Windows |

# Location of System Files on Compressed Disks

If you install Windows 95 on a compressed drive, Windows 95 Setup will place the following files on the boot drive.

**Windows 95 Files on the Boot Drive**

| | | |
|---|---|---|
| AUTOEXEC.BAT | DBLSPACE.BIN[1] | MSDOS.SYS[1] |
| AUTOEXEC.DOS | DETLOG.TXT[1] | NETLOG.TXT |
| BOOTLOG.PRV[1] | DRVSPACE.BIN[1] | SETUPLOG.TXT[1] |
| BOOTLOG.TXT[1] | DRVSPACE.INI[1] | SUHDLOG.DAT[1] |
| COMMAND.COM | IO.DOS[1] | SYSTEM.1ST[1] |
| COMMAND.DOS | IO.SYS[1] | WINA20.386 |
| CONFIG.DOS | MSDOS.---[1] | |
| CONFIG.SYS | MSDOS.DOS[1] | |

[1] Indicates a hidden file.

The WIN386.SWP file is added to the host drive by Windows 95 Setup. Although the host drive is usually the same as the boot drive, it doesn't have to be. For example, if part of drive D is used to create the compressed drive H, then D is the host for H, but C is the host drive. Therefore, WIN386.SWP will be placed in the root of D if Windows is installed on drive H. The remaining Windows 95 files are placed on the compressed drive in the specified Windows directory.

Windows 95 Setup adds the same files as listed earlier in this section to the boot drive when installing Windows 95 on an uncompressed drive that is not the boot drive. The only difference is that WIN386.SWP will be placed on the same drive as the Windows directory. For example, if you have drives C and D, and if you install Windows 95 on D:\WINDOWS, then WIN386.SWP will be on the root of D. Otherwise, it will be placed as described earlier for compressed drives.

APPENDIX C

# Windows 95 INF Files

This appendix describes the structure for the information files (INF) used to configure devices and networking components in Windows 95.

This information is of particular use if you are creating custom setup scripts. This description of the INF file format will help you read the information in the Windows 95 INF files to find the values to be provided in MSBATCH.INF. The general format is also used for statements in the [Install] section of MSBATCH.INF.

**In This Appendix**

Windows 95 Device Information Files Overview   1158

General INF File Format   1158

[Version] Section   1159

[Manufacturer] Section   1160

[Manufacturer Name] Section   1160

[Install] Section   1161

    [Logical Configuration] Sections   1162

    [Update AutoExec] Section   1163

    [Update Config] Section   1164

    [Update INI] Section   1164

    [Update IniFields] Section   1165

    [Add Registry] Section   1165

    [Delete Registry] Section   1166

    [Ini to Registry] Section   1166

    [DestinationDirs] Section   1166

    [File-List] Section   1168

    [SourceDisksFiles] Section   1169

    [SourceDisksNames] Section   1170

[ClassInstall] Section   1170

[Strings] Section   1171

Sample INF File   1172

# Windows 95 Device Information Files Overview

Device information (INF) files provide information used by Windows 95 to install software that supports a given hardware device. When hardware manufactures introduce new products, they must create INF files to explicitly define the resources and files required for each class of device.

The format of the INF files is based on Windows 3.x INF files:

- Section names are enclosed in brackets ([ ]) and must be unique within an INF file.

- Keys within a section do not have to be unique, but the order of keys within a section is significant.

- Private sections in an INF file are not evaluated by Windows 95.

The operating system detects the unique ID of each device installed. For the device identified, a specific section of the INF file provides information on that class of device; the following describes the information contained in a typical INF file section.

# General INF File Format

An INF file is organized in several sections which define information that Setup and the hardware detection process use to determine the resource needs of the hardware device and to install software for that device. An INF file is organized by hardware, with each class of device described in its own section. Within each device section, the following general organization applies.

[Version] section
Contains a simple header that identifies the INF and the class of device this INF supports.

[Manufacturer] and [*Manufacturer Name*] sections
Lists all the individual manufacturers of the devices identified in this file and lists all the devices built by that manufacturer. These entries are displayed directly to the user and used to generate the appropriate Registry entries. There must always be at least one manufacturer section.

[*Install*] section
Describes the device driver and physical attributes of the hardware device. It also identifies the names of all the [*Install*] sections that contain information and instructions for installing this device.

[ClassInstall] section
Defines a new class for this device. Optional.

Miscellaneous control section
    Specifies how a device is handled by the Windows 95 user interface.

[Strings] section
    Defines all localizable strings used in the INF file.

Each section contains one or more entries. The typical entry consists of a key and a value separated by an equal sign. Keys within a section do not have to be unique, but the order of keys may be significant depending on the purpose of the section. An INF file can include comments—any string of text, up to the end of the line, that starts with a semicolon. A comment can start anywhere on a line. For example:

```
Key=value    ; comment
```

For complete details about the syntax and use of statements in Windows 95 INF files, see the *Win32 Software Development Kit for Windows 95 and Windows NT*.

# [Version] Section

Syntax

**[Version]**
**Signature="$Chicago$"**
**Class=***class-name*
**Provider** =*INF_creator*
**LayoutFile=***filename.inf*

The [Version] section defines the standard header for all Windows 95 INF files.

*class-name*
    Defines the class in the Registry for any device installed from this INF. The following are some examples of class names:

| | | | |
|---|---|---|---|
| Adapter | Hdc | Monitor | PCMCIA |
| Cdrom | Keyboard | Mouse | Ports |
| Display | MCADevices | MTD | Printer |
| EISADevices | Media | NetNetService | SCSIAdapter |
| Fdc | Modem | Nodriver | System |

*filename.inf*
    Names the INF file that contains the layout information (source disks and files) required for installing this driver software. Typically, for Windows 95 components, this is LAYOUT.INF. This line is optional. If not given, the [SourceDisksNames] and [SourceDisksFiles] sections must be given in this INF.

This example shows a typical [Version] section:

```
[Version]
Signature="$Chicago$"
Provider=%MSFT%
Class=Adapter
LayoutFile=LAYOUT.INF
```

# [Manufacturer] Section

**Syntax**      **[Manufacturer]**
*manufacturer-name* | *%strings-key%=manufacturer-name-section*

The [Manufacturer] section identifies the manufacturer of the device and specifies the name of the [*Manufacturer Name*] section that contains additional information about the device driver.

*manufacturer-name*
   Name of the manufacturer. This name can be any combination of printable characters, but must uniquely identify the manufacturer and must be enclosed in double quotation marks.

*strings-key*
   Name of a string as defined in a [Strings] section.

*manufacturer-name-section*
   Name of the [*Manufacturer Name*] section. This name can be any combination of printable characters, but must uniquely identify the manufacturer name.

The following example shows a typical [Manufacturer] section in which a string key, %M1%, is used to identify the manufacturer. In this example, the [*Manufacturer Name*] section is APEXD.

```
[Manufacturer]
%M1%=APEXD      ; Strings key for this manufacturer
```

# [*Manufacturer Name*] Section

**Syntax**      [*manufacturer-name*]
*device-description=install-section-name, device-id[,compatible-device-id]...*

The [*Manufacturer Name*] section gives the device description and identifies the [*Install*] section for this device. The *manufacturer-name-section* name must be defined in the [Manufacturer] section.

*device-description*
> Description of the device to install. This can be any combination of printable characters or a strings key.

*install-section-name*
> Name of the [*Install*] section for this device.

*device-id*
> Identifier for this device.

*compatible-device-id*
> Identifier of a compatible device. More than one compatible-device identifier can be given, but each must be preceded by a comma.

The following example shows a typical [*Manufacturer Name*] section. The name of the [*Install*] section for this device is SuperSCSI. This device-id is *PNPA000 and its compatible device identifier is *PnPA001.

```
[APEXD]
%DevDesc1% = SuperSCSI, *PNPA000, *PnPA001
```

For each driver installed using this INF file, Setup uses the information in these [*Manufacturer Name*] sections to generate Driver Description, Manufacturer Name, DeviceID, and Compatibility list entries in the Registry.

# [*Install*] Section

**Syntax**

[*install-section-name*]
**LogConfig** = *log-config-section-name*[,*log-config-section-name*]...
**Copyfiles**=*file-list-section*[,*file-list-section*]...
**Renfiles**=*file-list-section*[,*file-list-section*]...
**Delfiles**=*file-list-section*[,*file-list-section*]...
**UpdateInis**=*update-ini-section*[,*update-ini-section*]...
**UpdateIniFields**=*update-inifields-section*[,*update-inifields-section*]...
**AddReg**=*add-registry-section*[,*add-registry-section*]...
**DelReg**=*del-registry-section*[,*del-registry-section*]...
**Ini2Reg**=*ini-to-registry-section*[,*ini-to-registry-section*]...
**UpdateCfgSys**=*update-config-section*
**UpdateAutoBat**=*update-autoexec-section*
**Reboot | Restart**

The [*Install*] section identifies the additional sections in the INF file that contain descriptions of the device and instructions for installing files and information needed by the device drivers. The *install-section-name* must be defined in a [*Manufacturer Name*] section and consist of printable characters.

Not all entries in this section are needed or required. If an entry is given, it must specify the name of a section. (An exception to this is the **CopyFiles** entry.) More than one name can be given for each entry, but each additional name must be preceded by a comma. The exact format and meaning of the corresponding entry depends on the entry type and is described in later *sections*. Each [*Install*] section should include the creation date of the driver set.

The **Reboot** or **Restart** entries can be added to the [*Install*] section to force the system to either restart or to reboot the machine after performing the commands in the [*Install*] section.

This example shows a typical [*Install*] section. It contains a **LogConfig** entry that identifies two logical configuration sections for this device. It also contains **Copyfiles** and **AddReg** entries that identify the sections containing information about which files to install.

```
[SuperSCSI]
; Apex Drivers Model 01 - SuperSCSI+
Log_Config = With_Dma, WithoutDMA
Copyfiles=MoveMiniPort, @SRSutil.exe
AddReg=MOD1
```

The **CopyFiles** entry provides a special notation that allows a single file to be copied directly from the copy line. An individual file can be copied by prefixing the file name with an @ symbol. The destination for any file copied using this notation will be the **DefaultDestDir** as defined in the [DestinationDirs] section. The following example shows how to copy individual files:

```
CopyFiles=FileSection1,@myfile.txt,@anotherfile.txt,LastSectionName
```

# [*Logical Configuration*] Sections

**Syntax**

[*log-config-section-name*]
**ConfigPriority** = *priority-value*
**MemConfig** = *mem-range-list*
**I/OConfig** = *io-range-list*
**IRQConfig** = *irq-list*
**DMAConfig** = *dma-list*

A [*Logical Configuration*] section defines configuration details, such as IRQs, memory ranges, I/O ports, and DMA channels. An INF file can contain any number of [*Logical Configuration*] sections, as many as are needed to describe the device dependencies. However, each section must contain complete details for installing a device. The *log-config-section-name* must be defined by the **LogConfig** entry in the [*Install*] section.

Not all entries are needed or required. If an entry is given, it must be given appropriate values as described in the subsequent *sections*.

Each entry can specify more than one resource. However, during installation only one resource from an entry is used. If a device needs multiple resources of the same type, multiple entries must be given. For example, to ensure two IRQs for a device, two **IRQConfig** entries must be given. If a device does not require an IRQ, no **IRQConfig** entry should be given. For each entry, Setup builds binary logical configuration records and adds these to the driver section of the Registry.

# [*Update AutoExec*] Section

**Syntax**

[*update-autoexec-section*]
**CmdDelete**=*command-name*
**CmdAdd**=*command-name*[*,command-parameters*]
**UnSet**=*env-var-name*
**PreFixPath**=*ldid*[*,ldid*]
**RemOldPath**=*ldid*[*,ldid*]
**TmpDir**=*ldid*[*,subdir*]

The [*Update AutoExec*] section provides commands to manipulate lines in the AUTOEXEC.BAT file. The *update-autoexec-section* name must appear in an **UpdateAutoBat** entry in the [*Install*] section.

Not all entries are needed or required. The section can contain as many **CmdAdd**, **CmdDelete**, and **UnSet** entries as needed, but only one entry for **PreFixPath**, **RemOldPath**, and **TmpDir** can be used per file.

Setup processes all **CmdDelete** entries before any **CmdAdd** entries.

For information about LDID values, see "[Update INI] Section" later in this appendix.

# [*Update Config*] Section

**Syntax**

[*update-config-section*]
**DevRename**=*current-dev-name,new-dev-name*
**DevDelete**=*device-driver-name*
**DevAddDev**=*driver-name,configkeyword*[*,flag*][*,param-string*]
**Stacks**=*dos-stacks-values*
**Buffers**=*legal-dos-buffer-value*
**Files**=*legal-dos-files-value*
**LastDrive**=*legal-dos-lastdrive-value*

The [*Update Config*] section provides commands to add, delete, or rename commands in CONFIG.SYS. The *update-config-section* name must appear in an **UpdateCfgSys** entry in the [*Install*] section.

Not all entries are needed or required. This section may contain as many **DevRename**, **DevDelete**, and **DevAddDev** entries as needed, but the other commands may only be used once per section. When processing this section, Setup processes all **DevRenames** entries first, all **DevDelete** commands second, and all **DevAddDev** commands last.

# [*Update INI*] Section

**Syntax**

[*update-ini-section*]
*ini-file, ini-section,* [*old-ini-entry*], [*new-ini-entry*], [*flags*]

.
.
.

Replaces, deletes, or adds entries in the given INI file. This is similar to the INF support in Windows 3.1. The *update-ini-section* name must appear in an **UpdateInis** entry in the [*Install*] section. The optional action *flags* can be one of these values:

0    Default. Matches Value of *old-ini-entry* Key, ignores its value. If Key is present, replaces with *new-ini-entry*. If *old-ini-entry* is NULL, the *new-ini-entry* is added unconditionally. If *new-ini-entry* is NULL, the *old-ini-entry* is deleted.

1    Matches both Key and Value of *old-ini-entry*. Update is done only if both Key and Value match.

2    Conditional and matches only the Key of *old-ini-entry*. If Key in *old-ini-entry* already exists, do not replace with *new-ini-entry*.

3    Conditional and matches both Key and Value of *old-ini-entry*. If the *Key=Value* of *old-ini-entry* exists, do not replace with *new-ini-entry*.

The wildcard character (*) can be used in specifying the Key and Value, and they will be interpreted correctly.

The *ini-file* name can be a string or a strings key. A strings key has the form *%strkey%* where *strkey* is defined in the [Strings] section in the INF file. In either case, the name must be a valid filename.

The name should include the name of the directory containing the file, but the directory name should be given as a logical directory identifier (LDID) rather than an actual name. Setup replaces an LDID with an actual name during installation.

An LDID has the form *%ldid%* where *ldid* is one of the predefined identifiers or an identifier defined in the [DestinationDirs] section. For LDID_BOOT and LDID_BOOTHOST, the backslash is included in the LDID, so %30%boot.ini is the correct way to reference BOOT.INI in the root of the boot drive.

The following examples illustrate entries in this section:

```
%11%\sample.ini, Section1,, Value1=2   ; adds new entry
%11%\sample.ini, Section2, Value3=*,   ; deletes old entry
%11%\sample.ini, Section4, Value5=1, Value5=4   ; replaces old entry
```

# [*Update IniFields*] Section

**Syntax**

[*update-inifields-section*]
*ini-file*, *ini-section*, *profile-name*, [*old-field*], [*new-field*]

Replaces, adds, and deletes fields in the value of a given INI entry. Unlike the [*Update INI*] section, this section replaces, adds, or deletes portions of a value in an entry rather than the whole value. The *update-inifields-section* name must appear in an **UpdateIniFields** entry in the [*Install*] section.

Any previous comments in the line are removed because they might not be applicable after changes. When looking in the INI file for fields in the line, spaces, tabs, and commas are used as field delimiters. However, a space is used as the separator when the new field is appended to the line.

# [*Add Registry*] Section

**Syntax**

[*add-registry-section*]
*reg-root-string*, [*subkey*], [*value-name*], [*Flag*], [*value*]
.
.
.

Adds subkeys or value names to the Registry, optionally setting the value. The *add-registry-section* name must appear in an **AddReg** entry in the [*Install*] section.

# [*Delete Registry*] Section

**Syntax**         [*del-registry-section*]
                   *reg-root-string*, *subkey*, [*value-name*]
                   .
                   .
                   .

Deletes a subkey or value name from the Registry. The *del-registry-section* name
must appear in an **DelReg** entry in the [*Install*] section. This section can contain
any number of entries. Each entry deletes one subkey or value name from the
Registry.

# [*Ini to Registry*] Section

**Syntax**         [*ini-to-registry-section*]
                   *ini-file*, *ini-section*, [*ini-key*], *reg-root-string*, *subkey*, *flags*
                   .
                   .
                   .

Moves lines or sections from an INI file to the Registry, creating or replacing an
entry under the given key in the Registry. The *ini-to-registry-section* name must
appear in an **Ini2Reg** entry in the [*Install*] section.

# [DestinationDirs] Section

**Syntax**         **[DestinationDirs]**
                   *file-list-section=ldid*[*,subdir* ]
                   .
                   .
                   .

                   **DefaultDestDir=***ldid*[*,subdir* ]

The [DestinationDirs] section defines the destination directories for the given
[*File-List*] sections and optionally defines the default directory for any [*File-List*]
sections that are not explicitly named.

*file-list-section*
    Name of a [*File-List*] section. This name must have been defined in a
    **Copyfiles**, **RenFiles**, or **DelFiles** entry in the [*Install*] section.

*ldid*

A logical disk identifier (LDID). Can be one of these values:

00      Null LDID; this LDID can be used to create a new LDID

01      Source drive:\pathname

02      Temporary Setup directory; this is valid only during Windows 95 Setup

03      Uninstall directory

04      Backup directory

10      Windows directory

11      SYSTEM directory

12      IOSUBSYS directory

13      COMMAND directory

14      Control Panel directory

15      Printers directory

16      Workgroup directory

17      INF directory

18      Help directory

19      Administration

20      Fonts

21      Viewers

22      VMN32

23      Color directory

25      Shared directory

26      Winboot

27      Machine specific

28      Host Winboot

30      Root directory of the boot drive

31      Root directory for host drive of a virtual boot drive

32      Old Windows directory if it exists

33      Old MS-DOS directory if it exists

*subdir*

Name of the directory, within the directory named by *ldid*, to be the destination directory.

The optional **DefaultDestDir** entry provides a default destination for any **Copyfile** entries that use the direct copy notation (@filename) or any [*File-List*] section not specified in the [DestinationDirs] section. If **DefaultDestDir** is not given, the default directory is set to LDID_WIN.

This example sets the destination directory for the MoveMiniPort section to the Windows IOSUBSYS directory, and sets the default directory for other sections to be the BIN directory on the boot drive:

```
[DestinationDirs]
MoveMiniPort=12
; Destination for MoveMiniPort Section is windows\iosubsys
DefaultDestDirs=30,bin  ; Direct copies go to Boot:\bin
```

# [*File-List*] Section

A [*File-List*] section lists the names of files to be copied, renamed, or deleted. Entries in this section have three forms, depending on the type of entry in the [*Install*] section that defines the section name.

A [*File-List*] section for a **CopyFiles** entry has this form:

[*file-list-section*]
*destination-file-name*,[*source-file-name*],[*temporary-file-name*]

The *file-list-section* name must appear in the **CopyFiles** entry.

*destination-file-name*
   Name of the destination file. If no source filename is given, this is also the name of the source file.

*source-file-name*
   Name of the source file. Required only if the source and destination names are not the same.

*temporary-file-name*
   Name of the temporary file for the copy. Setup copies the source file but gives it the temporary filename. The next time Windows 95 starts, it renames the temporary file to the destination filename. This is useful for copying files to a destination that is currently open or in use by Windows.

The following example copies three files:

```
[CopyTheseFilesSec]
file11                 ; copies file11
file21, file22, file23 ; copies file22, temporarily naming it file23
file31,file32          ; copies file32 to file31
```

A [*File-List*] section for a **RenFiles** entry has this form:

[*file-list-section*]
*new-file-name,old-file-name*

.
.
.

The *file-list-section* name must appear in the **RenFiles** entry.

This example renames the files FILE42, FILE52, and FILE62 to FILE41, FILE51, and FILE61, respectively:

```
[RenameOldFilesSec]
file41,file42
file51,file52
file61,file62
```

A [*File-List*] section for a **DelFiles** entry has this form:

[*file-list-section*]
*filename*

.
.
.

The *file-list-section* name must appear in the **DelFiles** entry.

This example deletes three files:

```
[DeleteOldFilesSec]
file1
file2
file3
```

In the preceding examples, the given filenames are assumed to have been defined in the [SourceDisksFiles] section and the logical disk numbers that appear in this section have been defined in the [SourceDisksNames] section.

# [SourceDisksFiles] Section

**Syntax**            [**SourceDisksFiles**]
*filename=disk-number*

.
.
.

Names the source files used during installation and identifies the source disks that contain the files. The ordinal of the source disk defined in *disk-number* must be defined in the [SourceDiskNames] section.

This example identifies a single source file, SRS01.386, on the disk having ordinal 1:

```
[SourceDisksFiles]
SRS01.386 = 1
```

# [SourceDisksNames] Section

**Syntax**    **[SourceDisksNames]**
*disk-ordinal="disk-description",disk-label,disk-serial-number*

Identifies and names the disks used for installation of the given device drivers.

This example identifies one source disk and assigns it ordinal 1. The disk description is given as a strings key:

```
[SourceDisksNames]
1 = %ID1%, Instd1, 0000-0000
```

# [ClassInstall] Section

**Syntax**    **[ClassInstall]**
**Copyfiles**=*file-list-section[,file-list-section]...*
**AddReg**=*add-registry-section[,add-registry-section]...*
**Renfiles**=*file-list-section[,file-list-section]...*
**Delfiles**=*file-list-section[,file-list-section]...*
**UpdateInis**=*update-ini-section[,update-ini-section]...*
**UpdateIniFields**=*update-inifields-section[,update-inifield-section]...*
**AddReg**=*add-registry-section[,add-registry-section]...*
**DelReg**=*del-registry-section[,del-registry-section]...*

The [ClassInstall] section installs a new class for a device in the [Class] section of the Registry. Every device installed in Windows 95 has a class associated with it (even if the class is "UNKNOWN"), and every class has a class installer associated with it. Setup processes this section if one of the devices defined in this INF file is about to be installed and the class is not already defined. Not all entries are needed or required.

The following example specifies the class entry for Setup to create in the Registry (AddReg=SampleClassReg), and specifies a normal [*Install*] section in [SampleClassReg]. In this example, the Class description is required, and the relative key (HKR) denotes the class section. This example creates the class Sample and registers the description, installer, and icon for the class:

```
[ClassInstall]
Addreg=SampleClassReg
CopyFiles=@Sample.cpl

[SampleClassReg]
HKR,,,,%SampleClassDesc%
HKR,,Installer,,Sample.cpl
HKR,,Icon,HEX,00,00
```

# [Strings] Section

**Syntax**          **[Strings]**
          *strings-key=value*

          .

          .

          .

The [Strings] section defines one or more strings keys. A strings key is a name that represents a string of printable characters. Although the [Strings] section is generally the last section in the INF files, a strings key defined in this section may be used anywhere in the INF file that the corresponding string would be used. Setup expands the strings key to the given string and uses it for further processing. Using a strings key requires that it be enclosed in percent signs (%). The [Strings] section makes localization easier by placing all localizable text in the INF file in a single section. Strings keys should be used whenever possible.

*strings-key*
    A unique name consisting of letters and digits.

*value*
    A string consisting of letters, digits, or other printable characters. It should be enclosed in double quotation marks if the corresponding strings key is used in an entry that requires double quotation marks.

The following example shows the [Strings] section for a sample INF file.

```
[Strings]
MSFT="Microsoft"
M1="APEX DRIVERS"
DevDesc1=APEX DRIVERS SCSI II Host Adapter
ID1="APEX DRIVERS SuperSCSI Installation disk"
```

# Sample INF File

This example assumes a fictitious piece of hardware, a SCSI II Host Adapter
built by a company named Apex Drivers. The board requires four I/O ports that
can be based at 180H, 190H, 1A0h, or 1B0h. The board requires one exclusive
IRQ chosen from 4,5,9,10, or 11. The board can use a DMA channel if one is
assigned.

```
;SCSI.INF
;
; Standard comment

[Version]
Signature="$WINDOWS 95$"
Provider=%MSFT%
HardwareClass=SCSIAdapter

[Manufacturer]
%M1%=APEXD   ; Strings key for this manufacturer

[APEXD]
%DevDesc1% = SuperSCSI, *PNPA000, *PnPA001

[SuperSCSI]
; Apex Drivers Model 01 - SuperSCSI+
Log_Config = With_Dma, WithoutDMA
Copyfiles=MoveMiniPort, @SRSutil.exe
AddReg=MOD1

[With_DMA]
; Primary Logical Configuration
ConfigPriority = NORMAL
I/OConfig = 4@180-1B3%fff0(3:0:)
; Allocate 4 ports at base 180,190,1A0 or 1B0, device decodes
; 10bits of I/O address and uses no Aliases.
IRQConfig = 4,5,9,10,11  ; Allocate Exclusive IRQ 4, 5, 9, 10 or 11
DMAConfig = 0,1,2,3  ; Allocate DMA Channel 0, 1 ,2 or 3

[Without_DMA]
; Secondary Logical Configuration
ConfigPriority = SUBOPTIMAL
I/OConfig = 4@180-1B3%fff0(3:0:)
IRQConfig = 4,5,9,10,11

[MOD1]
HKR,,DevLoader,,I/OS
HKR,,Miniport,,SRSmini.386
```

```
[DestinationDirs]
MoveMiniPort=12
; Destination for MoveMiniPort Section is windows\iosubsys
DefaultDestDirs=30,bin   ; Direct copies go to Boot:\bin

[SourceDiskSFiles]
SRS01.386 = 1

[SourceDisksNames]
1 = %ID1%, Instd1, 0000-0000

[MoveMiniPort]
SRS01.386

[Strings]
MSFT="Microsoft"
M1="APEX DRIVERS"
DevDesc1=Apex Drivers SCSI II Host Adapter
ID1="Apex Drivers SuperSCSI Installation disk"
```

A P P E N D I X   D

# MSBATCH.INF Parameters

Windows 95 Setup can be run with setup scripts to automate installation when you have defined the options and parameters to be installed on users' computers.

Customization actions that required editing Windows 3.x INF files are all accomplished by means of statements in setup scripts that use MSBATCH.INF format. For information about the procedures for creating and using setup scripts, see Chapter 5, "Custom, Automated, and Push Installations."

**In This Appendix**

Setup Script Parameters   1176
    [Setup]   1177
    [System]   1180
    [NameAndOrg]   1182
    [InstallLocationsMRU]   1182
    [OptionalComponents]   1183
    [Network]   1184
    [netcard_ID]   1191
    [MSTCP]   1193
    [NWLink]   1196
    [NWRedir]   1196
    [NWServer]   1197
    [VRedir]   1198
    [VServer]   1198
    [Printers]   1199
    [Strings]   1200
    [Install]   1200
MSBATCH.INF Sample File   1204
Windows 95 Network Adapter INF Summary   1207

# Setup Script Parameters

This section summarizes the parameters that can be used in setup scripts.

**Setup-Related Parameters**

**[Setup] parameters:**

| | | |
|---|---|---|
| Devicepath | InstallType | TimeZone |
| EBD | PenWinWarning | Uninstall (with BackupDir) |
| Express | ProductID | Verify |
| InstallDir | SaveSUBoot | VRC |

**[System] parameters:**

| | | |
|---|---|---|
| Display | Machine | PenWindows |
| DisplChar | Monitor | Power |
| Keyboard | Mouse | Tablet |
| Locale | Multilanguage | |

**[NameAndOrg] parameters:**

| | | |
|---|---|---|
| Name | Org | Display |

**[InstallLocationsMRU] parameters:** List of paths

**[OptionalComponents] parameters:** List of descriptions

**[Printers] parameters:** Printers to install

**Network-Related Parameters**

**[Network] parameters:**

| | | |
|---|---|---|
| Clients | HDBoot | RPLSetup |
| ComputerName | IgnoreDetectedNetcards | Services |
| Description | NetCards | Security |
| DefaultProtocol | PassThroughAgent | ValidateNetcardResources |
| Display | Protocols | Workgroup |
| DisplayWorkstationSetup | RemoveBinding | WorkstationSetup |

**[*netcard*_ID] parameters:**    Values from the INF file for the network adapter

**[MSTCP] parameters:**

| | | |
|---|---|---|
| DHCP | Gateways | PrimaryWINS |
| DNS | Hostname | ScopeID |
| DNSServers | IPAddress | SecondaryWINS |
| Domain | IPMask | WINS |
| DomainOrder | LMHostPath | |

| | | |
|---|---|---|
| **[NWLink] parameters:** | Frame_Type | NetBIOS |
| **[NWRedir] parameters:** | FirstNetDrive | ProcessLoginScript |
| | PreferredServer | SearchMode |
| **[NWServer] parameters:** | BrowseMaster | Use_SAP |
| **[VRedir] parameters:** | LogonDomain | ValidatedLogon |
| **[VServer] parameters:** | LMAnnounce | MaintainServerList |

The setup script parameters are not case-sensitive. They are also not required; if they don't appear in a setup script, Windows 95 Setup just uses default values.

Display of most Setup dialog boxes can be disabled in the setup script so that users cannot change any setting. If the dialog boxes are not disabled, sources of information for parameters are given the following priority:

- Information specified in the setup script
- User input
- Detection information

In this section, the descriptions for an option can contain any of six possible entries, as described in the following table. For an example of the resulting file, see "MSBATCH.INF Sample File" later in this appendix.

| Entry | Description |
|---|---|
| Parameter | The name of the parameter as it appears in a setup script |
| Values | The values that can be assigned to the parameter and what they mean |
| System policy | The name of the corresponding parameter for this entry in System Policy Editor; if no entry appears, there is no system policy |
| Default | The built-in value that is used if no other value is provided |

# [Setup]

This section sets parameters for control of the Setup process.

**Device Path**

This parameter specifies whether Windows 95 should check a source installation path to find INF files, rather than looking only in the Windows INF directory when installing devices. If this parameter is set to 1, network administrators can later add INF files to a single source location to ensure that up-to-date drivers are installed any time a new device is installed on computers running Windows 95. However, set this value to 1 only if the installation source files are in a network directory (not floppy disks or CD).

Notice also that **Devicepath=1** causes the entire INF database to be rebuilt each time a user changes a network component or changes drivers for any device.

| | |
|---|---|
| Parameter | Devicepath |
| Values | 0 = Do not add a source directory path for INFs<br>1 = Add the installation source directory to the path for finding INFs |
| Default | 0 |

**Emergency
Startup Disk**

This parameter specifies whether to create the emergency Startup Disk during Setup (the command-line override for this is **/ie**). For a setup script intended for hands-free installation, you might want to specify **ebd=0** so that the user isn't prompted to insert or remove the floppy disk. If you need to specify **ebd=1**, you can also add a **reboot=0** entry, so that Setup will not attempt to restart the computer while the floppy disk is in the drive.

| Parameter | EBD |
|---|---|
| Values | 0 = Do not create an emergency Startup Disk<br>1 = Create an emergency Startup Disk |
| Default | 1 |

**Express**

This parameter specifies whether the user can provide input during Setup. If **express=1**, then Windows 95 Setup uses only the settings specified in MSBATCH.INF or built-in defaults and does not ask the user to confirm or enter input. This setting disables most of the user interface for Setup.

| Parameter | Express |
|---|---|
| Values | 0 = Allow user input<br>1 = Run Setup using only values in MSBATCH.INF |
| Default | 0 |

**Install Type**

This parameter specifies the type of installation for Windows 95 Setup.

| Parameter | InstallType |
|---|---|
| Values | 0 = Compact<br>1 = Typical<br>2 = Portable<br>3 = Custom |
| Default | 1 |

**Installation
Directory**

This parameter specifies the directory where Windows 95 is to be installed or, for shared installations, the machine directory.

| Parameter | InstallDir |
|---|---|
| Values | Directory name |
| Default | Windows directory, if present |

**Pen Windows
Warning**

This parameter specifies whether to display a warning if an unknown version of Pen Windows is installed.

| Parameter | PenWinWarning |
|---|---|
| Values | 0 = Do not display the warning<br>1 = Display the warning |
| Default | 1 |

**Product ID**

This parameter specifies the product ID for your site, which is printed on the Windows 95 compact disc or your Certification of Authenticity.

| Parameter | ProductID |
|-----------|-----------|
| Values | string |
| Default | none |

**Save SUBOOT Directory**

This parameter specifies whether to save the SUBOOT directory for Server-based Setup.

| Parameter | SaveSuBoot |
|-----------|-----------|
| Values | 0 = Delete SUBoot directory<br>1 = Save directory |
| Default | 0 |

**Time Zone**

This parameter specifies the time zone to set on the computer.

| Parameter | TimeZone |
|-----------|-----------|
| Values | String enclosed in quotation marks, as described in the following list |
| Default | The time zone currently set on the computer |

**Time zone strings**

| | | | |
|---|---|---|---|
| Afghanistan | Czech | Israel | Samoa |
| Alaskan | Dateline | Lisbon Warsaw | Saudi Arabia |
| Arabian | E. Europe | Mexico | South Africa |
| Atlantic | E. South America | Mid-Atlantic | Sydney |
| AUS Central | Eastern | Mountain | Taipei |
| Azores | Egypt | New Zealand | Tasmania |
| Bangkok | Fiji | Newfoundland | Tokyo |
| Canada Central | GFT | Pacific | US Eastern |
| Cen. Australia | GMT | Romance | US Mountain |
| Central | Greenwich | Russian | W. Europe |
| Central Asia | Hawaiian | SA Eastern | West Asia |
| Central Pacific | India | SA Pacific | West Pacific |
| China | Iran | SA Western | |

**Uninstall**

This parameter is used to specify whether Setup should create a compressed backup version of the existing Windows and MS-DOS directories to be used for automatically uninstalling Windows 95. If you specify **Uninstall=5**, you also must add a value for **BackupDir=***path* that specifies the directory where Setup should place the compressed backup files.

| Parameter | Uninstall |
|---|---|
| Values | 0 = Do not allow user to specify Uninstall options, and do not create backup files for uninstalling Windows 95 |
| | 1 = Show Uninstall options for user to choose |
| | 5 = Do not show Uninstall options, but automatically create backup files for uninstalling Windows 95 |
| Default | 1 |

**Verify**

This parameter, provided principally for use by OEMs, specifies whether to run Setup in Verify mode. Most users should not include this entry in a setup scripts. Setting **Verify=1** will prevent Uninstall in all cases.

| Parameter | Verify |
|---|---|
| Values | 0 = Do a full installation |
| | 1 = Run in Verify mode (not the same as MS-DOS **verify**) |
| Default | 0 |

**Version Checking**

This parameter defines whether Windows 95 Setup will overwrite existing files automatically, even if the date of the local copy is later than the date for the file in the distribution source.

| Parameter | VRC |
|---|---|
| Values | 0 = Prompt user to confirm before overwriting more recent files |
| | 1 = Overwrite all without prompting for confirmation |
| Default | 0 |

# [System]

This section sets parameters for modifying the system settings.

---

**Tip**  The correct entries for MSBATCH.INF can be copied from similarly named entries in SETUPLOG.TXT for a computer on which Windows 95 has been installed with devices identical to those that you want to install from a setup script.

---

The following entries are based on INF section names:

- **Locale=**_INF_section_name_ in LOCALE.INF (see also Chapter 34, "International Windows 95")
- **Machine=**_INF_section_name_ in MACHINE.INF
- **PenWindows=**_INF_section_name_ in PENWIN.INF
- **Power=**_INF_section_name_ in MACHINE.INF or similar file (for advanced power management support)
- **Tablet=**_INF_section_name_ in PENDRV.INF or similar file

The following entries use INF descriptions. The choice must be in the list of compatible devices for that class.

- **Display=**_INF_description_ in MSDISP.INF or a similar file

  For example, from the description **%SuperVGA.DriverDesc%=SVGA** for Super VGA, the entry in MSBATCH.INF would be **display=svga**.
- **Keyboard=**_INF_description_ in KEYBOARD.INF
- **Monitor=**_INF_section_name_ in MONITOR.INF
- **Mouse=**_INF_section_name_ in MSMOUSE.INF or a similar INF file
- **SelectedKeyboard=**_INF_section_name_ in MULTILNG.INF (specifies the keyboard layout)

**Display Characteristics**

This parameter sets the initial display characteristics.

| Parameter | DisplChar |
|---|---|
| Values | _ColorDepth, x, y_ where:<br>$ColorDepth$=bits per pixel<br>$x$ = horizontal resolution<br>$y$ = vertical resolution |
| Default | 4,640,480 |

**MultiLanguage**

This parameter sets the type of multilanguage support installed for Windows 95.

| Parameter | MultiLanguage |
|---|---|
| Values | English = Installs support for English and Western European languages<br>Greek = Adds additional support for Greek<br>Cyrillic = Adds additional support for Cyrillic<br>CE = Adds additional support for Eastern European languages |
| Default | English |

> **Caution**  If **Express=1**, you cannot add parameters to override safe detection for network adapters, SCSI controllers, or sound cards—which in some cases requires installing support after Setup is complete. If you need to force installation of certain hardware when **Express=1**, add specific entries in the [System] section.

# [NameAndOrg]

This section defines the name and organization for Windows 95 Setup, and specifies whether the user is to be shown the Name and Organization dialog box.

**Name**

This parameter specifies the full user name for this installation.

| | |
|---|---|
| Parameter | Name |
| Values | String |
| Default | None |

**Organization**

This parameter specifies the registered organization for this installation.

| | |
|---|---|
| Parameter | Org |
| Values | String |
| Default | None |

**Display**

This parameter specifies whether the Name and Organization dialog box appears during Windows 95 Setup.

| | |
|---|---|
| Parameter | Display |
| Values | 0 = Do not display name and organization<br>1 = Display name and organization |
| Default | 1 |

# [InstallLocationsMRU]

This section specifies the paths to add to the list of directories that the user can choose when Windows 95 Setup prompts for a path. For example, this section could appear as follows to specify local and network file locations:

```
[InstallLocationsMRU]
mru1=a:\
mru2=c:\
mru3=\\winserver\source
```

To force the path for files from which to copy, use **CopyFile=** and related statements in an [Install] section and specify the complete path for the component files.

# [OptionalComponents]

This section contains the descriptions that appear in the Optional Components dialog box in Windows 95 Setup.

To create entries for this section, type the description enclosed in quotation marks. Each description is followed by 1 (install) or 0 (do not install). The strings that specify the optional components to install are defined in INF files.

Another way to define entries for this section is to copy the [OptionalComponents] section in SETUPLOG.TXT from a computer that already has all the optional components installed that you want defined in the setup script. For an example, the entries to install Briefcase and Net Watcher are as follows:

```
[OptionalComponents]
"Briefcase"=1
"Net Watcher"=1
```

The following lists show the strings for the optional components defined in the Windows 95 standard INF files. Additional strings can be defined by other application developers.

**Optional Component Strings**

| | | |
|---|---|---|
| Accessibility Options | Document Templates | Online User's Guide |
| Accessories | Flying Through Space | Paint |
| Audio Compression | Games | Phone Dialer |
| Backup | HyperTerminal | Quick View |
| Blank Screen | Jungle Sound Scheme | Robotz Sound Scheme |
| Briefcase | Media Player | Sample Sounds |
| Calculator | Microsoft Exchange | Screen Savers |
| CD Player | Microsoft Fax | Scrolling Marquee |
| Character Map | Microsoft Fax Services | Sound Recorder |
| Clipboard Viewer | Microsoft Fax Viewer | System Monitor |
| Communications | Microsoft Mail Services | System Resource Meter |
| Curves and Colors | Mouse Pointers | The Microsoft Network |
| Defrag | Multimedia | Utopia Sound Scheme |
| Desktop Wallpaper | Musica Sound Scheme | Video Compression |
| Dial-Up Networking | Mystify Your Mind | Volume Control |
| Direct Cable Connection | Net Watcher | Windows 95 Tour |
| Disk compression tools | Object Packager | WordPad |
| Disk Tools | | |

# [Network]

This section specifies the parameters and options for installing networking components. The categories for these parameters include the following:

- Installation parameters
- Computer identification parameters
- Shared installation parameters
- Security parameters
- User interface options

## Installation Parameters in [Network]

**Clients**

This parameter specifies the network clients to be installed. It is a list of the device IDs used in the INF files. These IDs are not limited to those in the Windows 95 INF files (NETCLI.INF and NETCLI3.INF). A site that has an INF file from another vendor can use any device IDs listed in it. However, if you are installing a client other than those listed in the INF files provided with Windows 95, you need to obtain an updated Windows 95 INF file from your vendor.

If you are installing multiple clients, the first client in this list will start first whenever the computer is started.

Specify multiple networks in a comma-separated list. If the list contains two network clients, or lists multiple networks with a primary-only network (such as IBM® OS/2® LAN Server), Windows 95 Setup presents an error message and displays the Network Configuration properties for changing the selection. The verification process that occurs in Setup still takes place.

| | |
|---|---|
| Parameter | Clients |
| Values | Comma-separated list of client device IDs (see the following table) |
| Default | Defaults in NETDEF.INF |

The following table shows the valid device IDs for network clients as specified in NETCLI.INF and NETCLI3.INF (which are Windows 95 INF files).

| Device ID | Network |
|---|---|
| lant5 | Artisoft® LANtastic® version 5.x and 6.x |
| netware3 | Novell® NetWare® version 3.x |
| netware4 | Novell NetWare version 4.x |
| nwredir | Microsoft Client for NetWare Networks |
| pcnfs50 | SunSoft® PC-NFS® version 5.x and greater |
| vines552 | Banyan® VINES® version 5.52 and greater |
| vredir | Client for Microsoft Networks |

**Network Card Drivers**

This parameter specifies the drivers to be installed for network adapters as a list of the device IDs used in the INF files. These IDs are not limited to those included in the Windows 95 INF files. A site that has an INF file from another vendor can use any device IDs listed in that file.

---

**Important**   In general, it is recommended that you rely on detection in Windows 95 Setup to install the correct driver and define the correct configuration settings.

---

When a network adapter is listed, the usual verification takes place. Windows 95 Setup chooses an NDIS 3.1 driver, if available; otherwise, it uses an NDIS 2.x driver.

| Parameter | NetCards |
|---|---|
| Values | Comma-separated list of network adapter device IDs |
| Default | Results of detection |

For example, the following entries would install drivers for Intel® EtherExpress™ 16 or 16TP plus 3Com EtherLink II or IITP:

```
netcards=*PNP812D,*PNP80F3
```

**Ignore Detected NetCards**

This parameter specifies whether Setup will use the detected information to configure network adapters or use values specified by the **netcards=** parameter in the setup script.

| Parameter | IgnoreDetectedNetCards |
|---|---|
| Values | 0 = Do not ignore detected adapters<br>1 = Ignore the detected network adapters and use the values specified for **NetCards=***deviceID* |
| Default | 0 |

**Protocols**

This parameter specifies the protocols to be installed as a list of the device IDs used in the INF files. These IDs are not limited to those in the Windows 95 INF files. A site that has an INF file from another vendor can use any device IDs listed in that file.

---

**Note** If you are installing a protocol other than those listed in the INF files provided with Windows 95, you need to get an updated Windows 95 INF file from your vendor.

---

Setup verifies these settings, so it is possible to specify only the network clients and let Windows 95 Setup choose the protocols. For example, if you specify **Clients=pcnfs50**, then Windows 95 Setup adds NFSLINK.

| | |
|---|---|
| Parameter | Protocols |
| Values | Comma-separated list of protocol device IDs, as described in the following table |
| Default | Defaults in NETDEF.INF |

The valid device IDs for protocols in the Windows 95 INF file (NETTRANS.INF) are the following.

| Device ID | Protocol |
|---|---|
| dec40 | DECnet™ version 4.1 Ethernet protocol |
| dec40t | DECnet version 4.1 token ring protocol |
| dec50 | DECnet version 5.0a Ethernet protocol |
| dec50t | DECnet version 5.0a token ring protocol |
| ipxodi | Novell-supplied IPXODI protocol |
| msdlc | Microsoft DLC (real mode) |
| mstcp | Microsoft TCP/IP |
| ndisban | Banyan VINES NDIS Ethernet protocol |
| ndtokban | Banyan VINES NDIS token-ring protocol |
| netbeui | Microsoft NetBEUI |
| nfslink | Sun PC-NFS protocol |
| nwlink | IPX/SPX-compatible protocol |
| nwnblink | NetBIOS support for IPX/SPX-compatible protocol |

**Default Protocol**     This parameter sets the default protocol (which is assigned LANA 0), which is the specified protocol bound to the specified network adapter (if the computer has more than one network adapter). If no adapter is specified, the default is the first instance of the specified protocol. Set this value if, for example, the computer will run software that requires a protocol to be bound to LAN adapter (LANA) 0, which can only be defined by setting that protocol as the default protocol. For more information about LAN adapter numbers, see Chapter 12, "Network Technical Discussion."

If **netbios=1,** you must set **defaultprotocol=nwnblink** if you want to specify IPX/SPX-compatible protocol as the default.

| | |
|---|---|
| Parameter | DefaultProtocol |
| Values | A protocol device ID as defined in **protocol=** and, optionally, a network adapter device ID, as defined in **netcards=**. |
| Default | 0 |

The folowing example sets the default protocol as an instance of NetBEUI bound to a particular adapter:

```
DefaultProtocol=netbeui,*pnp812d
```

**Remove Binding**     This parameter removes the binding between the two devices. This parameter is used to tune bindings in a setup script.

| | |
|---|---|
| Parameter | RemoveBinding |
| Values | Comma-separated list of device IDs |
| Default | None |

**Services**     This parameter specifies the network services to be installed as a list of the device IDs used in the INF files. These IDs are not limited to those in the Windows 95 INF files. A site that has an INF file from another vendor can use any device IDs listed in that file. When a service is listed in a setup script, the usual verification still takes place.

The only service installed by default is VSERVER (File and Printer Sharing for Microsoft Networks) if peer sharing services were enabled for Windows for Workgroups.

| | |
|---|---|
| Parameter | Services |
| Values | Comma-separated list of service device IDs, as described in the following table |
| Default | Windows 95 Setup defaults, depending on the value of **InstallType** |

The following shows the valid device IDs defined in several different INF files.

| Device ID | Service | INF file |
|-----------|---------|----------|
| bkupagnt | Arcada® Backup Exec agent | BKUPAGNT.INF |
| cheyagnt | Cheyenne® ARCserve agent | CHEYENNE.INF |
| jadm | HP® Network Printer service for Microsoft | HPNETPRN.INF |
| janw | HP Network Printer service for NetWare | HPNETPRN.INF |
| nmagent | Microsoft Network Monitor agent[1] | NMAGENT.INF |
| nwserver | File and Printer Sharing for NetWare Networks | NETSRVR.INF |
| pserver | Microsoft Print Service for NetWare Networks[1] | MSPSRV.INF |
| remotereg | Microsoft Remote Registry service[1] | REGSRV.INF |
| snmp | Microsoft SNMP agent[1] | SNMP.INF |
| vserver | File and Printer Sharing for Microsoft Networks | NETSRVR.INF |

[1] Available in the ADMIN directory of the Windows 95 compact disc.

For information about using the INFINST utility to set up files from the ADMIN directory on the Windows 95 compact disc for installation from a network directory, see Chapter 5, "Custom, Automated, and Push Installations."

# Computer Identification Parameters in [Network]

**Computer Name**

This parameter sets the computer's network name.

| | |
|---|---|
| Parameter | ComputerName |
| Values | String of up to 15 alphanumeric characters and no blank spaces. The name must be unique on the network and can contain the following special characters: |
| | ! @ # $ % ^ & ( ) - _ ' { } . ~ |
| Default | Generated from the first eight characters of the user name |

**Description**

This parameter is the description for the computer (mainly used by peer servers such as File and Printer Sharing for Microsoft Networks).

| | |
|---|---|
| Parameter | Description |
| Values | 48 characters long, containing no commas |
| Default | User name from licensing information |

**Workgroup**    This parameter sets the workgroup for the computer.

| | |
|---|---|
| Parameter | Workgroup |
| Values | String of up to 15 alphanumeric characters and no blank spaces. The name must be unique on the network and can contain the following special characters: |
| | ! @ # $ % ^ & ( ) - _ ' { } . ~ |
| System policy | Workgroup settings (under policies for Microsoft Client for Windows Networks) |
| Default | Workgroup previously specified; otherwise, a new name is generated from user licensing information by taking the first 15 characters of the organization name. For example, an organization name of "Microsoft Corporation" results in "MicrosoftCorpo" as the default workgroup. |

# Shared Installation Parameters in [Network]

**Hard Disk Boot**    This parameter specifies whether, for a client computer running a shared copy of Windows 95 from a server, Setup should configure Windows 95 so that it starts from the hard disk but runs from a shared network copy.

| | |
|---|---|
| Parameter | HDBoot |
| Values | 0 = Start from the server or floppy disk if **WorkstationSetup=1** |
| | 1 = Start from the hard disk and run from the network |
| Default | 0 |

The following table shows the settings for this parameter and the RPLSetup parameter, depending on how the computer runs Windows 95.

| Windows 95 location | HDBoot | RPLSetup |
|---|---|---|
| Hard-disk boot, Windows 95 on a server | 1 | 0 |
| Floppy-disk boot, Windows 95 on a server | 0 | 0 |
| Remote boot, Windows 95 on a server | 0 | 1 |

**Remote-Boot (RPL) Setup**    This parameter specifies that Setup should create a disk image on the network server for a remote-boot workstation during Workstation Setup. This parameter is ignored if a corresponding Workstation Setup value is not defined. (Therefore, setting **RPLSetup=1** does not automatically set **WorkstationSetup=1**.)

| | |
|---|---|
| Parameter | RPLSetup |
| Values | 0 = Don't do a remote-boot setup |
| | 1 = Do a remote-boot setup if **WorkstationSetup=1** |
| Default | 0 |

**Workstation Setup**  This parameter specifies whether Setup configures a client computer to run Windows 95 locally or as a shared copy from a server. If this parameter is set to No (0), Windows 95 Setup runs normally. If this parameter is set to Allow (1) and if Setup is running from a server, Setup asks if the user wants to install Windows 95 as a shared copy or on the local hard disk. For more information, see Chapter 4, "Server-Based Setup for Windows 95." See also the table for the **HDBoot** parameter earlier in this section.

| | |
|---|---|
| Parameter | WorkstationSetup |
| Values | 0 = Allow a standard setup (local files) |
| | 1 = Allow a shared workstation setup (run from a server) |
| Default | 0 |

**Display Workstation Setup**  This parameter specifies whether the Setup user interface appears during installation of Windows 95 on a workstation that will run a shared copy of Windows 95. Setting this value to 0 forces the value defined for **WorkstationSetup** in the script.

| | |
|---|---|
| Parameter | DisplayWorkstationSetup |
| Values | 0 = Do not display user interface |
| | 1 = Display user interface |
| Default | 0 |

# Security Parameters in [Network]

**User Security**  This parameter specifies the security model to be used and, for user-level security, the type of pass-through agent (that is, server or domain). A client with a security provider must be installed for these values to have an effect.

| | |
|---|---|
| Parameter | Security |
| Values | share = share-level security |
| | nwserver = user-level security, validated by a NetWare server |
| | domain = user-level security, validated by a Windows NT domain |
| | msserver = user-level security, validated by a computer running Windows NT Workstation |
| System policy | User-level Access Control settings (under policies for Access Control) |
| Default | share |

**Pass-Through Agent**

This parameter specifies the pass-through agent for user-level security. This value is ignored in share-level security.

| | |
|---|---|
| Parameter | PassThroughAgent |
| Values | Server or domain name |
| System policy | User-level Access Control settings (under policies for Access Control) |
| Default | No value, or the value of **Workgroup** if **Security=domain**, **Preferred Server** if **Security=nwserver**, or none. The default is the value of **PreferredServer** if **Security=nwserver**; otherwise, there is no default. |

## User Interface Options for [Network] Parameters

**Display**

This parameter controls whether any of the Network Configuration dialog boxes appear in Custom Setup.

| | |
|---|---|
| Parameter | Display |
| Values | 0 = Do not display<br>1 = Display |
| Default | 1 |

**Validate NetCard Resources**

This parameter specifies whether to display a dialog box to resolve resource conflicts if a partial configuration is detected or if there is an IRQ conflict for a network adapter.

| | |
|---|---|
| Parameter | ValidateNetCardResources |
| Values | 0 = Do not display a wizard page<br>1 = Display a wizard page to resolve resource conflicts |
| Default | 1 |

# [netcard_ID]

The actual name for this section is the identifier for the network adapter, as defined in the related INF file. This section sets parameters for a specific network adapter, as defined in the [netcard.NDI] sections of the network device INF files provided with Windows 95.

---

**Important**   In general, it is recommended that you rely on detection in Windows 95 Setup to install the correct driver and define the correct configuration settings.

---

All entries for a [netcard_ID] section depend on the specific adapter. The actual parameters and settings for a specific network adapter can be found in that adapter's INF file in the Windows INF directory.

To locate settings for a network adapter, check NET.INF for entries such as the following:

```
CardBrand=brand of network adapter
INFFile=file where these settings can be found
```

In the related INF file for the specific network adapter, search for the adapter's name. For example, you might find the following entry for an Intel EtherExpress 16 network adapter:

```
;*******************************************************************
; *PNP812D  Intel Etherexpress 16 or 16TP
;*******************************************************************
```

The information in the *netcard*.INF file is followed by the specific settings, using this format:

```
;netcard model name
[<adapter>.NDI]
actual settings for adapter
```

For example, for the adapter in the previous example, the following entry appears in the NETEE16.INF file:

```
[*PNP812D.ndi]
AddReg=*pnp812d.ndi.reg,EXP16.ndi.reg
```

Based on the **AddReg=** entry in this statement, you need to search for the [*pnp812d.ndi.reg] or [EXP16.ndi.reg] sections in the INF file to find the parameters required for a particular adapter. For example, for the related Intel EtherExpress adapter, the following sections appear in NETEE16.INF:

```
[*PNP812D.ndi.reg]
.

.

.

HKR,NDI\params\Interrupt,resc,1,04,00,00,00
HKR,NDI\params\IOAddress,resc,1,02,00,00,0
HKR,NDI\params\DMAChannel,ParamDesc,,"DMA Channel"
```

These entries describe the parameters that can be specified for the adapter in a setup script. Further, in this same part of the *netcard*.INF file, the statements also indicate the kinds and ranges of values that can be specified for a particular parameter. For example, in NETEE16.INF, the following statements indicate that for **DMAChannel=** you must specify an integer in the range of 1–3, where the default value is 1:

```
HKR,NDI\params\DMAChannel,type,,int
HKR,NDI\params\DMAChannel,default,,1
HKR,NDI\params\DMAChannel,min,,1
HKR,NDI\params\DMAChannel,max,,3
```

The following entry in NETEE16.INF indicates that for **Transceiver=** you can specify the values **external** or **onboard** (based on the first string that appears after the **enum** item):

```
HKR,NDI\params\Transceiver,default,,onboard
HKR,NDI\params\Transceiver,type,,enum
HKR,NDI\params\Transceiver,enum,external,,external
HKR,NDI\params\Transceiver,enum,onboard,,onboard
```

Based on the previous examples, the following shows an example of the [*netcard*] section you would add to MSBATCH.INF to set parameters for an Intel EtherExpress 16 or 16TP network adapter:

```
[*PNP812D]
Interrupt=
IOAddress=
DMAChannel=2
Transceiver=external
```

Notice that you only need to set values for the parameters where you do not want to use the defaults. For a list of possible parameters for some common network adapters, see "Windows 95 Network Adapter INF Summary" later in this appendix.

# [MSTCP]

This section sets parameters for Microsoft TCP/IP. For more information about TCP/IP, see Chapter 12, "Network Technical Discussion."

**DHCP**

This parameter specifies whether TCP/IP is configured to use DHCP for dynamic TCP/IP configuration.

| | |
|---|---|
| Parameter | DHCP |
| Values | 0 = Don't enable DHCP |
| | 1 = Enable DHCP |
| Default | 1 |

**DNS**
This parameter enables DNS name resolution. You must also set **DNS=1** if you plan to use LMHOSTS for name resolution.

| | |
|---|---|
| Parameter | DNS |
| Values | 0 = Disable DNS<br>1 = Enable DNS |
| Default | 0 |

**DNS Servers**
This parameter is a list of the DNS servers to use in the order to try them.

| | |
|---|---|
| Parameter | DNSServers |
| Values | Comma-separated list of DNS server names |
| Default | None |

**Domain**
This parameter sets the DNS domain that this computer is in.

| | |
|---|---|
| Parameter | Domain |
| Values | String |
| Default | None |

**Domain Order**
This parameter sets a list of DNS domains for host name resolution in the order to try them.

| | |
|---|---|
| Parameter | DomainOrder |
| Values | Comma-separated list of DNS domains |
| Default | None |

**Gateways**
This parameter lists the IP gateways (sometimes called IP routers) in the order they are to be used.

| | |
|---|---|
| Parameter | Gateways |
| Values | Comma-separated list of IP addresses |
| Default | None |

**Hostname**
This parameter sets the DNS hostname for this computer (usually the same value as **ComputerName**).

| | |
|---|---|
| Parameter | Hostname |
| Values | String |
| Default | None |

**IP Address**

This parameter sets the computer's IP address if DHCP is not enabled.

| | |
|---|---|
| Parameter | IPAddress |
| Values | Internetwork Protocol (IP) address (###.###.###.###) |
| Default | None |

**LMHOST File Path**

This parameter sets the path and filename of the LMHOST file.

| | |
|---|---|
| Parameter | LMHOSTPath |
| Values | Path |
| Default | None |

**Primary WINS Server**

This parameter sets the primary WINS name server.

| | |
|---|---|
| Parameter | PrimaryWINS |
| Values | IP address (###.###.###.###) |
| Default | None |

**Secondary WINS Server**

This parameter sets the secondary WINS name server.

| | |
|---|---|
| Parameter | SecondaryWINS |
| Values | IP address (###.###.###.###) |
| Default | None |

**Scope ID**

This parameter sets the scope ID.

| | |
|---|---|
| Parameter | ScopeID |
| Values | String |
| Default | None |

**Subnet Mask**

This parameter sets the IP subnet mask for TCP/IP if DHCP is not enabled.

| | |
|---|---|
| Parameter | IPMask |
| Values | IP address (###.###.###.###) |
| Default | None |

**WINS**

This parameter enables WINS for NetBIOS computer name resolution.

| | |
|---|---|
| Parameter | WINS |
| Values | 0 = Disable WINS<br>1 = Enable WINS resolution<br>DHCP = Enable WINS but get parameters from DHCP server |
| Default | 1 |

# [NWLink]

The parameters in this section specify settings for the IPX/SPX-compatible protocol and are valid only if **protocols=nwlink** is also specified in the setup script. For more information about these parameters as defined using the Network option in Control Panel, see Chapter 12, "Network Technical Discussion."

**Frame Type**

This parameter specifies the default frame type for IPX.

| Parameter | Frame_Type | |
|-----------|------------|---|
| Values | 0 = 802.3 | 4=Auto |
| | 1 = 802.2 | 5=Token ring |
| | 2 = Ethernet II | 6=Token ring SNAP |
| Default | 4 | |

**NetBIOS**

This parameter specifies whether NetBIOS support for IPX/SPX should be installed.

| Parameter | NetBIOS |
|-----------|---------|
| Values | 0 = Don't install NWNBLINK |
| | 1 = Install NWNBLINK |
| Default | 0 |

# [NWRedir]

For more information about these values for Client for NetWare Networks as specified using the Network option in Control Panel, see Chapter 9, "Windows 95 on NetWare Networks."

**First Network Drive**

This parameter specifies the first network drive to which to attach in login scripts for Client for NetWare Networks. This parameter overrides the equivalent setting in NET.CFG.

| Parameter | FirstNetDrive |
|-----------|---------------|
| Values | Drive letter ("A" or "A:" are equivalent) |
| Default | F: |

**Preferred Server**

This parameter specifies the NetWare preferred server. This parameter does not override the equivalent setting in NET.CFG.

| Parameter | PreferredServer |
|-----------|-----------------|
| Values | String |
| System policy | Preferred Server settings (under policies for Microsoft Client for NetWare Networks) |
| Default | None |

**Process Login Script**

This parameter specifies whether login script processing is enabled when running Microsoft Client for NetWare Networks.

| | |
|---|---|
| Parameter | ProcessLoginScript |
| Values | 0 = Disable login script processing |
| | 1 = Enable login script processing |
| Default | 1 |

**Search Mode**

This parameter specifies the NetWare search mode. The values correspond exactly to the values specified in NET.CFG for Novell NetWare.

| | |
|---|---|
| Parameter | SearchMode |
| Values | 0–7 |
| System policy | Search Mode settings (under policies for Microsoft Client for NetWare Networks) |
| Default | 0 |

# [NWServer]

For more information about these values for File and Printer Sharing for NetWare Networks as specified using the Network option in Control Panel, see Chapter 11, "Logon, Browsing, and Resource Sharing."

**Browse Master**

This parameter specifies whether a computer configured with File and Printer Sharing for NetWare Networks can be elected browse master.

| | |
|---|---|
| Parameter | BrowseMaster |
| Values | 0 = This computer cannot be a browse master |
| | 1 = This computer can be a browse master |
| | 2 = This computer is the preferred browse master |
| Default | 1 |

**SAP Browsing**

This parameter specifies whether a computer configured with File and Printer Sharing for NetWare Networks uses Server Advertising Protocol (SAP) browsing. Enabling SAP browsing allows a computer with File and Printer Sharing for NetWare Networks to be seen by any NetWare client, but the computer does not appear in a workgroup in Network Neighborhood.

| | |
|---|---|
| Parameter | Use_SAP |
| Values | 0 = Disable SAP browsing (use workgroup style browsing) |
| | 1 = Use SAP style browsing |
| Default | 0 |

# [VRedir]

For more information about these values for Client for Microsoft Networks as specified using the Network option in Control Panel, see Chapter 8, "Windows 95 on Microsoft Networks."

**Validated Logon**

This parameter specifies whether logons are validated on a Windows NT domain. If you set this value to 1, be sure to specify a value for **LogonDomain**.

| | |
|---|---|
| Parameter | ValidatedLogon |
| Values | 0 = Don't validate logons |
| | 1 = Validate logon |
| Default | 0 |

**Logon Domain**

This parameter specifies the Windows NT domain to use for logon validation. It can be set even if **ValidatedLogon=0**. If **ValidatedLogon=1**, you must set a correct value for **LogonDomain** to ensure that Windows 95 Setup has access to any required files on a protected network resource, and to ensure that the user can log on successfully when installation is completed.

| | |
|---|---|
| Parameter | LogonDomain |
| Values | String |
| System policy | Log on to Windows NT settings (under policies for Microsoft Client for Windows Networks) |
| Default | Value of **Workgroup** in [Network] |

# [VServer]

For more information about these values for File and Printer Sharing for Microsoft Networks as specified using the Network option in Control Panel, see Chapter 11, "Logon, Browsing, and Resource Sharing."

**Announce**

This parameter specifies whether the computer configured with File and Printer Sharing for Microsoft Networks announces its presence to LAN Manager computers on the network. Setting this value to 1 increases network traffic but makes browsing faster.

| | |
|---|---|
| Parameter | LMAnnounce |
| Values | 0 = Don't announce VSERVER to the network |
| | 1 = Announce VSERVER to network |
| Default | 1 |

**Browse Master**

This parameter specifies how the computer configured with File and Printer Sharing for Microsoft Networks behaves in a browse master election.

| | |
|---|---|
| Parameter | MaintainServerList |
| Values | 0 = Disabled (this computer cannot be a browse master) |
| | 1 = Enabled (this computer is the browse master) |
| | 2 = Auto (the computer can be a browse master if required) |
| Default | 2 |

# [Printers]

This section is used to install one or more printers during Setup by specifying a user-defined name for identifying the printer, the model name, and the printer port. Each printer to be installed has a separate entry in this section using the following syntax:

*PrinterName=DriverModel,Port*

The following restrictions apply:

- The length of the friendly name for the printer name cannot exceed 32 bytes (31 characters plus a NULL character). If the name specified in the custom setup script is too long, Setup will truncate it to fit the requirement.

- The model name must be recognized by Windows 95. You can see the list of supported printer models in the Add Printers wizard or in the printer INF files.

- No commas or quotation marks can be used in any string.

---

**Note**  If the setup script contains a [Printers] section with no entries, the user will not be asked to select a printer the first time that Windows 95 runs.

---

**Friendly Name**

This parameter specifies the friendly name, model, and port for a printer to be installed. The printer's friendly name is the name that appears in the Printers folder. The model name must be the exact name of a printer driver that is supported under Windows 95; otherwise, Setup skips this entire section.

| | |
|---|---|
| Parameter | *PrinterName*= any string that does not contain these characters: |
| | \   ,   ;   = |
| Values | *DriverModel* = The exact driver name for any printer model supported under Windows 95 |
| | *Port* = The port that this printer is attached to (such as LPT1) or a UNC path name to a network print queue |
| Default | None |

The following example installs a local printer and a network printer:

```
[Printers]
"My BJC600"="Canon Bubble-Jet BJC-600",LPT1
"IIIsi Next Door"="HP Laserjet IIIsi",\\Server_1\PrtShr_1
```

# [Strings]

The [Strings] section defines one or more string keys that Setup expands to the defined string and uses it for further processing. In other sections, a strings key can be used by enclosing it in percent signs (%).

| Parameter | *String_Key = Value* |
|---|---|
| Values | *String_Key* = A unique name made up of letters and digits. |
|  | *Value* = Letters, digits, or other printable characters. It should be enclosed in quotation marks if the corresponding string key is used in an entry that requires double quotation marks. |

The following shows three examples of strings keys:

```
[Strings]
MSFT="Microsoft"
M1="APEX DRIVERS"
DevDesc1=APEX DRIVERS SCSI II Host Adapter
```

# [Install]

The [Install] section sets parameters for copying additional files as part of Windows 95 installation. The format for this section is identical to the format for the [Install] section in general INF files, as defined in Appendix C, "Windows 95 INF Files."

The following sections provide these examples for using the [Install] section for custom installations:

- Installing custom bitmaps and shortcuts
- Enabling user profiles and remote administration
- Replacing configuration entries

## [Install] Example: Copying Custom Files

This section describes MSBATCH.INF entries for copying custom files while installing Windows 95. In the following example, custom files are copied for a bitmap file containing a corporate logo plus a shortcut to be placed in Network Neighborhood. These custom files must be created by the administrator and placed with the Windows 95 source files on the network.

```
[install]
CopyFiles=newfiles.Copy

[NEWFILES.Copy]
my_corp.bmp      ; bitmap file
my_link.lnk      ; file that contains the shortcut

[DestinationDirs]
newfiles.copy=25   ; shared Windows directory
```

The statement in [DestinationDirs] specifies where files are to be copied. Common values include the following for shared installations:

- 10 = machine directory
- 11 = Windows SYSTEM directory
- 25 = Windows directory

Notice that the most flexible means of providing custom links for multiple users is to use system policies. For information about using system policies to create a custom Network Neighborhood or a custom desktop, see Chapter 15, "User Profiles and System Policies."

## [Install] Example: Enabling User Profiles and Remote Administration

If you plan to take advantage of user profiles and to allow administration of remote computers, you can enable these capabilities using setup scripts. The following entries are required in MSBATCH.INF to enable these features.

```
[Install]
AddReg=User.Profiles,Remote.Admin

[User.Profiles]
HKLM,"Network\Logon","UserProfiles",1,1

[Remote.Admin]
HKLM,"Security\Access\Admin\Remote",%Server_Domain_Username%,1,ff,00
```

```
[Network]
Security=<domain_or_server>  ;enables user-level security
PassThroughAgent=<provider_name>
services=remotereg    ;installs the Microsoft Remote Registry agent

[strings]
; specifies the server containing the group or individual account
; to be allowed remote administration capabilities
Server_Domain_Username = "<server_or_domain\account>"
```

▶ **To define the custom values required for enabling remote administration**

1.  To enable user-level security, set the appropriate values in the [Network] section for **Security=** and **PassThroughAgent=**.

    For example, on a NetWare network, if the security provider is a server named NWSVR1:

    ```
    Security=server
    PassThroughAgent=NWSVR1
    ```

    On a Windows NT network, if the security provider is a domain named NTDOM1:

    ```
    Security=Domain
    PassThroughAgent=NTDOM1
    ```

2.  In the [Strings] key, define the value for **%server_domain_username%** to specify the location for the list of user accounts, plus the names of accounts for users who will be allowed remote administration capabilities for this particular computer.

    For example, for a NetWare network, the following specifies the server containing the group or individual account, plus the account name to be given remote administration capabilities:

    ```
    Server_Domain_Username = "NWSVR\HELPDESK"
    ```

    For a Windows NT network, the following specifies the domain containing the account, plus the account name to be given remote administration capabilities:

    ```
    Server_Domain_Username = "NTDOM1\ADMIN"
    ```

---

**Important**  You must also make sure that the related files supporting Microsoft Remote Registry services are installed with the Windows 95 source files. To do this, use INF Installer, as described in Chapter 5, "Custom, Automated, and Push Installations."

---

When you enable remote administration in this way, Setup automatically adds the appropriate Administrators account (including Supervisor and Domain Administrators under Windows NT) to the list of persons or groups allowed to administer the computer remotely, and sets the permissions required for remote administration.

Enabling user profiles in a setup script is equivalent to selecting the items in the Passwords option in Control Panel named Users Can Customize Their Preferences And Desktop Settings and Include Desktop Icons And Network Neighborhood Settings.

### ▶ To enable group policies

- If you want to enable group policies for both the Client for Microsoft Networks and Client for NetWare networks, add the following entries to MSBATCH.INF:

```
[Install]
Addreg=User.Profiles.Reg, Group.Policies.Reg
Copyfiles=Group.Policies.Copy

[User.Profiles.Reg]
HKLM,Network\Logon,UserProfiles,1,1

[Group.Policies.Reg]
HKLM,Network\Logon,PolicyHandler,,"GROUPPOL.DLL,ProcessPolicies"
HKLM,System\CurrentControlSet\Services\MSNP32\NetworkProvider,
    GroupFcn,,"GROUPPOL.DLL,NTGetUserGroups"
HKLM,System\CurrentControlSet\Services\NWNP32\NetworkProvider,
    GroupFcn,,"GROUPPOL.DLL,NWGetUserGroups"

[Group.Policies.Copy]
grouppol.dll

[DestinationDirs]
Group.Policies.Copy = 11
```

For information about user profiles and group policies, see Chapter 15, "User Profiles and System Policies." For information about remote administration of a computer's Registry, see Chapter 16, "Remote Administration."

### [Install] Example: Replacing Configuration Entries

This section presents some sample entries for replacing entries in configuration files as part of Windows 95 Setup.

Depending on the common network configuration at your site, you may determine that you need to remove a line from one or more configuration files as a global procedure before starting Windows 95 Setup. For example, you may want to use a protected-mode protocol such as Microsoft TCP/IP instead of the real-mode version of TCP/IP currently being using on the target computers. The following kinds of entries can be used to make these changes during the installation process.

---

**Note**  If you want to remove TSRs when installing Windows 95 on a NetWare network, you should modify the NETDET.INI file rather than making modifications using MSBATCH.INF. For information, see Chapter 9, "Windows 95 on NetWare Networks."

---

```
[Install]
UpdateInis=update_prot.Ini
UpdateCfgSys=Update_config.sys
UpdateAutoBat=Update_autoexec.bat

[Update_prot.Ini]
system.ini,386enh,"device=mytcp.386"

[Update_config.sys]

[Update_autoexec.bat]
```

# MSBATCH.INF Sample File

This section shows a sample setup script.

```
[Setup]
Express=0          ; allows user input
InstallType=1      ; Typical Setup
EBD=1              ; create startup disk
InstallDir=C:\WINDOWS
Verify=0
PenWinWarning=1
ProductID=999999999
```

```
[NameAndOrg]
Name="User One"
Org="Your Company Name"
Display=1        ; User Information dialog box is displayed

[OptionalComponents]
"Accessories"=1
"Communications"=1
"Disk Tools"=1
"Multimedia"=1
"Screen Savers"=0
"Disk compression tools"=1
"Paint"=1
"HyperTerminal"=1
"Defrag"=1
"Blank Screen"=1
"Scrolling Marquee"=1
"Calculator"=1
"Object Packager"=1
"Backup"=0
"Phone Dialer"=1
"Clipboard Viewer"=0
"Microsoft Fax"=0
"Microsoft Fax Services"=0
"Microsoft Fax Viewer"=0
"Accessibility Options"=0
"The Microsoft Network"=0
"Audio Compression"=0
"Video Compression"=1
"Sound Recorder"=0
"Volume Control"=0
"Media Player"=1
"Microsoft Exchange"=0
"Microsoft Mail Services"=0
"Briefcase"=0
"Document Templates"=1
"WordPad"=1
"Dial-Up Networking"=0
"Direct Cable Connection"=0
"Mouse Pointers"=0
"Windows 95 Tour"=0
"Online User's Guide"=0
"Desktop Wallpaper"=0
"System Monitor"=0
"Net Watcher"=0
"Character Map"=0
"Curves and Colors"=0
"Mystify Your Mind"=0
"Flying Through Space"=0
```

```
"Games"=0
"Quick View"=0
"Sample Sounds"=0
"Musica Sound Scheme"=0
"Jungle Sound Scheme"=0
"Robotz Sound Scheme"=0
"Utopia Sound Scheme"=0
"CD Player"=0

[System]
"Display"="Tseng Lans ET4000"
"Keyboard"="Standard 101/102-Key or Microsoft Natural Keyboard"
"Machine"="MS_CHICAGO"
"Monitor"="NEC MultiSync 2A"
"Mouse"="Standard Serial Mouse"
"Power"="No APM"
"Locale"="L0409"
"UI Choice"="Win95UI"
"Multilanguage"="English"

[InstallLocationsMRU]
MRU1=C:\WINDOWS
MRU2=C:\User
MRU3=\\win_svr\source files\home_dir

[Network]
Display=0                ; Network Options do not appear in Setup
ComputerName=W95_1
Workgroup=test_group
Description="This is a lab test computer"
Clients=vredir,nwredir
Security=Domain
PassThroughAgent=Test_domain
WorkstationSetup=0    ; not a shared installation of Windows 95
HDBoot=1

[VREDIR]
ValidatedLogon= 1
LogonDomain=test_domain
```

# Windows 95 Network Adapter INF Summary

This section presents details about the settings for common network adapters, as defined in the [*netcard*.NDI] sections of the INF files provided with Windows 95. Other adapters are also listed; their settings can be found in the appropriate file in the Windows INF directory. The NET.INF file contains the master information for detecting and configuring network adapters. The specific INF files for network adapters include the following:

| | | | |
|---|---|---|---|
| net3com.inf | netcpq.inf | netnice.inf | netsmc.inf |
| netamd.inf | netgen.inf | netnovel.inf | netsmctr.inf |
| netflex.inf | nethp.inf | netoli.inf | nettcc.inf |
| netcable.inf | netibm.inf | netppp.inf | nettulip.inf |
| netdec.inf | netmadge.inf | netprot.inf | netub.inf |
| netee16.inf | netncr.inf | netracal.inf | netxir.inf |

For information about how to find entries for a particular network adapter in an INF file, see "[netcard_ID]" earlier in this appendix.

**3COM**

**Cardbrand**=3COM
**INFFile**=NET3COM.INF

```
[*PNP80F3]
Interrupt=
IOAddress=
DMAChannel=
MaxTransmits=
DataTransfer=
XmitBufs=
Transceiver=
```

The following adapters also have settings in the file NEC3COM.INF:

3Com EtherLink Plus®
3Com EtherLink III®
NCR Token-Ring 4 Mbs ISA
NCR Token-Ring 16/4 Mbs ISA

NCR StarCard
NCR® WaveLAN AT
TokenLink

**Digital Equipment Corporation**

**Cardbrand**=Digital Equipment Corp.
**INFFile**= NETDEC.INF

```
;DEC DE201 Etherworks Turbo TP
[*PNP80EB]
Interrupt=
IOAddress=
RamAddress=
MaxMulticasts=
Maxtransmits=
AdapterName=
```

The following adapters also have settings in the file NETDEC.INF:

DEC (DE211) Etherworks® MC/TP
DEC (DE212) Etherworks MC/TP_BNC
DEC (DE100) Etherworks LC
DEC (DE200) Etherworks Turbo
DEC (DE101) Etherworks LC/TP
DEC (DE202) Etherworks Turbo/TP_BNC

DEC (DE102) Etherworks LC/TP_BNC
DEC EE101 (Built-In)
DECpc 433 WS (Built-In)
DEC Ethernet (All Types)
DEC (DE210) Etherworks MC

**IBM**

**Cardbrand**=IBM
**INFFile**= NETIBM.INF

```
;IBM Token Ring
[*PNP80C9]
MaxTransmits=
Primary
Alternate=
RecvBufs=
XmitBufs=
MaxPacketSize=
ProductID=
NetworkAddress=
Iobase=
RecvBufSize=
XmitBufSize=
```

The following adapters also have settings in the file NETIBM.INF:

IBM Token Ring 4/16Mbs
IBM Token Ring II/Short
IBM Token Ring (All Types)

**Intel**

**Cardbrand**=Intel
**INFFile=** NETEE16.INF

```
;Intel Etherexpress 16 or 16TP
[*PNP812]
IOBaseAddress=
IRQ=
IOAddress=
Transceiver=
IOChrdy=
IOChannelReady=
```

The following adapters also have settings in the file NETEE16.INF:

Intel EtherExpress PRO
Generic 595
Intel EtherExpress 16 (MCA)

**MADGE**

**Cardbrand**=MADGE
**INFFile=** NETMADGE.INF

```
;Madge Networks Smart 16/4 PC Ringnode
[*PNP81D7]
RxTxSlots=
NetworkAddress=
MaxFrameSize=
RxBufferSize=
TxBufferSize=
MaxTransmits=
Watchdog=
CopyAllData=
AutoOpen=
OpenOptions=
NoMmio=
PromiscuousModeX=

[MadgeISA]
IrqNumber=
IOAddress=
MemBase=
DMAChannel=
```

The following adapters also have settings in the file NETMADGE.INF:

Madge Networks Smart 16/4 Ringnode (All ISA Types)
Madge Networks Smart 16/4 AT/P Ringnode
Madge Networks Smart 16/4 AT Ringnode
Madge Networks Smart 16/4 ISA Client Plus Ringnode
Madge Networks Smart 16 Ringnode

**Novell**

**Cardbrand**=Novell
**INFFile**= NETNOVEL.INF

```
[ne2000]
InterruptNumber=
IOBaseAddress=
Interrupt=
IOBase=
```

The following adapters also have settings in the file NETNOVELL.INF:

| | |
|---|---|
| Artisoft AE-1 | National Semiconductor AT/LANTIC |
| Artisoft AE-2 or AE-3 | NE1000 Compatible |
| Ethernode 16-AT3 | Novell Ne2000 Plus |
| National Semiconductor Ethernode *16AT | Zenith Data Systems NE2000 Compatible |

**Proteon**

**Cardbrand**=Proteon
**INFFile**=NETPROT.INF

```
;Proteon Token Ring (P1392)
[*pnp81eb]
IntLevel=
IOBase=
DMAChannel=
LinkSpeed=
CardSpeed=
Media=
CableType=
DMAClock=
SAEN=
MaxTransmits=
NetworkAddress=
```

The following adapters also have settings in the file NETPROT.INF:

| | |
|---|---|
| Proteon ISA Token Ring (1340) | Proteon ISA Token Ring (1347) |
| Proteon ISA Token Ring (1342) | Proteon Token Ring (P1392+) |
| Proteon ISA Token Ring (1346) | Proteon Token Ring (P1390) |

**Racal**

**Cardbrand=**Racal
**INFFile=** NETRACAL.INF

```
; Racal NI6510
[*pnp8113]
IOBase=
MaxReceives=
MaxTransmits=
MaxMulticasts=
```

The Racal NI5210/8 or NI5210/16 adapter also has settings in the file NETRACAL.INF.

**SMC**

**Cardbrand=**SMC
**INFFile=** NETSMC.INF

```
;SMC9000
[*Smc9000]
Interrupt=
Port_Num=
Xt_Type=
Micro_Channel=
```

The following adapters also have settings in the file NETSMC.INF:

| | |
|---|---|
| ArcNet Compatible | SMC EtherCard™ adapters |
| Pure Data PDI508+ (ArcNet) | SMC EtherElite adapters |
| Pure Data PDI516+ (ArcNet) | SMC StarCard PLUS adapters |
| SMC® ArcNet adapters | SMC TokenCard Elite |

**Thomas-Conrad**

**Cardbrand=**Thomas-Conrad
**INFFile=** NETTCC

```
;Thomas-Conrad (All Arcnet Types)
[*pnp8326]
Interrupt=
IOBase=
MemoryBase=
PacketSize=
```

The following adapters also have settings in the file NETTCC.INF:

| | |
|---|---|
| TC6045 | Thomas-Conrad TC6142 |
| TC6145 | Thomas-Conrad TC6242 |
| TC6245 | Thomas-Conrad TC4035 |
| Thomas-Conrad TC6042 | Thomas-Conrad TC4045 |

APPENDIX E

# Microsoft Systems Management Server

This appendix provides information about Microsoft Systems Management Server, which can be used to install and maintain Windows 95 on networked computers.

For more information about Microsoft Systems Management Server, contact your Microsoft sales representative or see the documentation provided with Systems Management Server. For information online, type **go msnet** at any CompuServe® command prompt and choose Section 16; or connect to the Microsoft World Wide Web site at **http://www.microsoft.com** and select BackOffice Information and White Papers.

**In This Appendix**     Microsoft Systems Management Server Overview    1214
Systems Management Server Requirements    1215
Systems Management Server Services    1217
Using Systems Management Server to Deploy Windows 95    1219

# Microsoft Systems Management Server Overview

In a corporate environment where you might have hundreds, or even thousands, of computers, the process of upgrading to Windows 95 can become complex — especially if you want to deploy Windows 95 on all computers at the same time. This appendix discusses how you can use Microsoft Systems Management Server to automate the large-scale deployment of Windows 95, making the upgrade process faster, easier, and less expensive for your organization. It also describes the services offered by Systems Management Server for centralized management of computers in an enterprise network, including inventory, software distribution and installation, management of shared applications, remote management and troubleshooting, and network protocol analysis.

Systems Management Server organizes computers into a hierarchy of sites. A site is a group of servers and client computers typically located in a single geographical area. A site can consist of one or more domains (that is, a set of servers and clients that are managed as a group) existing on the same LAN.

Systems Management Server uses the terms central, primary, and secondary to identify the capabilities of sites in the hierarchy. A central site is a primary site at the top of the hierarchy, from which all sites and computers in the hierarchy can be administered.

A primary site has its own Microsoft SQL Server™ database, which contains all of the hardware and software inventory information for the site and its subsites (sites attached below it in the hierarchy). The primary site can run the Systems Management Server Administrator tool for local administration of the site server and all subsites. A primary site must be running Windows NT Server.

A secondary site is a site that does not have a SQL Server database or the Systems Management Server Administrator tool. This site is administered from any site above it in the hierarchy and has no subsites. A secondary site must be running Windows NT Server.

A primary site can have either secondary sites or other primary sites beneath it in the hierarchy. A secondary site must have a primary site above it and can have no sites below it.

The following figure illustrates a sample Systems Management Server hierarchy. The hierarchical site structure is depicted on the administration console, so that you can easily identify a computer based on its location.

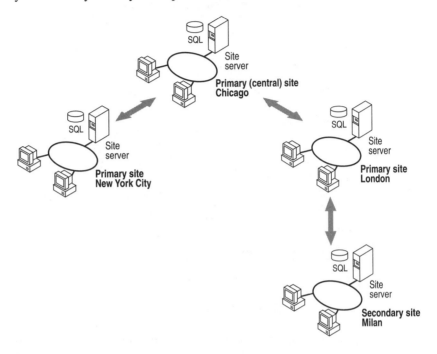

# Systems Management Server Requirements

The following lists the basic requirements for using Microsoft Systems Management Server:

- Windows NT Server version 3.5 or later
- Microsoft SQL Server version 4.21 or later
- A 486/66 or better processor
- 32 MB of memory (recommended)
- A hard disk with at least 100 MB available
- A network-accessible CD-ROM drive
- A network adapter
- A Microsoft Mouse or compatible pointing device (a mouse is recommended but optional)

Microsoft Systems Management Server supports the following connection protocols, networking options, and clients.

**Supported Protocols, Clients, and Networks**

**Connection protocols:**

| | |
|---|---|
| Asynchronous | Remote Access Service (RAS) |
| IPX/SPX | SNA |
| ISDN | TCP/IP |
| NetBEUI | X.25 |

**Clients:**

| | |
|---|---|
| Apple® Macintosh® System 7™ | MS-DOS 5.0 or later |
| DEC Ultrix™ | Sun® Solaris |
| DEC VMS™ | Windows 3.1 or later |
| HP-UX® | Windows NT 3.1 or later |
| IBM AIX® | Windows for Workgroups 3.11 or later |
| IBM OS/2® version 1.x or 2.x | Windows 95 |

**Networks:**

| | |
|---|---|
| DEC™ PATHWORKS™ | Novell® NetWare® 3.x or 4.x |
| IBM® LAN Server 3.x | (in 3.x compatibility mode) |
| LAN Manager 2.1 or later | Windows NT Server |

The following table lists the typical requirements for sites in a Systems Management Server hierarchy, based on an installation of up to 1000 computers. These requirements are grouped according to how each server is used. Notice that all of the servers must be running Windows NT Server. Systems Management Server requires a Windows NT file system (NTFS) partition.

**Systems Management Server Servers**

| Processor and server type | RAM | Disk space | Recommendations |
|---|---|---|---|
| **Central site server:** | | | |
| Intel® 486/66<br>Intel Pentium<br>DEC Alpha<br>MIPS® R4000™ | 32–96 MB | 1 GB | A high-performance computer is recommended due to the heavy load placed on the central-site computer by Microsoft Systems Management Server and SQL Server. |
| **Primary or secondary site:** | | | |
| Intel 486/66<br>Intel Pentium<br>DEC Alpha<br>MIPS R4000 | 24 MB | 100 MB<br>40 MB | 28 MB of RAM is required if SQL Server is on the same computer as the primary-site server. |

**Systems Management Server Servers** (*continued*)

| Processor and server type | RAM | Disk space | Recommendations |
|---|---|---|---|
| **SQL Server:** | | | |
| Intel 486/66 Intel Pentium DEC Alpha MIPS R4000 | 20 MB | | 28 MB of RAM is required if SQL Server is on the same computer as the primary-site server. Storage requirements depend on the size of the installation. |

**Systems Management Server Clients**

| Processor and operating system | RAM | Disk space | Recommendations |
|---|---|---|---|
| Intel x86<br><br>Windows 3.x, Windows for Workgroups, MS-DOS 5.x or greater | 4 MB | 100 MB | Client components require 4.5 MB of storage and 7 KB of conventional memory. |
| 68040 PowerPC™<br><br>Macintosh System 7.x | 16 MB | 80 MB | Client components require 3 MB of storage. |

# Systems Management Server Services

This section describes the services provided by Systems Management Server to make it easier to manage computers on the network.

**Hardware and software inventory.**  Systems Management Server automatically retrieves detailed information about both the hardware and software for every computer within your enterprise and stores the information in a standard SQL Server database. The inventory properties of the computer can include the microprocessor, the various drives, the network adapter, the memory, the IRQ table, and a number of other hardware-related components.

Two types of software inventory information are available. The detailed identification inventory looks for a particular set of files (for example, EXE and DLL files) to verify that all of the required files are present and are valid versions. The comprehensive audit inventory checks the files on the computer's disk against a predefined list of applications. Systems Management Server can also collect copies of the computer's configuration files and add them to an archive. These inventory features are useful for tracking maintenance and planning upgrades.

**Software distribution and installation.**  Systems Management Server makes it easy to automatically distribute commercial or internally developed applications, upgrades or fixes, or virus-checking software to selected personal computers on the local network and at remote sites. Systems Management Server distributes and installs software in package form. Packages can be used to install software on client computers; packages can also install and share software on a network server, or identify existing software on target computers and collect specified files.

**Management of shared applications.**  Systems Management Server can control access to shared applications to balance loads and provide fault tolerance and metering. When sharing applications, you can also automatically view a program group tailored to a specific user, no matter which computer the user uses to log on to the network. You determine which network users (or user groups) need access to specific server applications. The server applications database is replicated on all of the logon servers at a site.

**Remote control and troubleshooting.**  Systems Management Server provides two remote management features: Help Desk and Diagnostics. Help Desk provides direct access to a client (including the ability to carry out commands, transfer files, and restart the computer), allowing you to troubleshoot and support individual remote computers. The Diagnostics utilities allow you to view the current hardware and software configuration of a workstation.

**Network protocol analysis.**  The Network Monitor component of Systems Management Server is a diagnostic tool that allows you to look at the details of network packets, perform remote captures on a packet anywhere on the network, and gather network statistics about a group of personal computers. It enables you to capture and analyze network traffic and detect connection problems or potential network bottlenecks.

For more information about Systems Management Server, see WIN95RK.HLP with the *Windows 95 Resource Kit* utilities.

The following publications also provide more information:

- *Microsoft Systems Management Server Administrator's Guide*
- *Microsoft Systems Management Server Resource Kit*
- *Microsoft Systems Management Server Evaluation Guide*
- *Microsoft Systems Management Server Deployment Guide*
- *Microsoft Windows NT Resource Kit*
- *Microsoft SQL Server Resource Kit*

# Using Systems Management Server to Deploy Windows 95

Whether you are upgrading ten or ten thousand clients to Windows 95, Systems Management Server allows you to perform an automatic upgrade with no intervention from you or the user.

For an overall deployment plan, see the general and detailed discussions provided in Chapter 1, "Deployment Planning Basics," and Chapter 2, "Deployment Strategy and Details." This section provides specific information about how Systems Management Server tools help you in planning for and automating the Windows 95 rollout to your company.

The first step in the upgrade process is to determine which of your computers are appropriate for upgrading to Windows 95. Using Systems Management Server, query the SQL Server database to locate all computers that match the upgrade specifications. A predefined query included in Systems Management Server examines the CPU, the operating system, the available hard disk space, the installed RAM, and so on. You can use this query as is or modify it to include additional criteria important to your installation.

After identifying the target computers, you are ready to roll out Windows 95 to target computers. The following is an overview of the steps involved in deploying Windows 95 with Systems Management Server.

- Create and share a package source directory for the Windows 95 files. This directory can be on any server that can be shared with the network.

- Copy the appropriate files from the Windows 95 compact disc to the new package source directory.

  If you are copying from the compact disc, you can use the Server-based Setup (**netsetup**) to copy all files to the source directory. For information, see Chapter 4, "Server-Based Setup for Windows 95." If you are copying from a server that already contains an installation created using Server-based Setup, you can use **xcopy** to copy the files and the directory structure.

- From the Systems Management Server 1.1 compact disc, copy the following files to the package source directory:

  - WIN95.INF file from SMS\LOGON.SRV\MSTEST

  - DOS2W95.EXE file from SMS\LOGON.SRV\MSTEST (if you are setting up clients that run MS-DOS)

- Review the INF file for your configuration, and make appropriate changes (such as changing the time zone).
- Create a package containing the Windows 95 source directory.
- To install Windows 95 on one or more clients, create a mandatory job to distribute the package to the clients.
- Send the job to the target computer.

A P P E N D I X   F

# Macintosh and Windows 95

This appendix describes how you can integrate Apple® Macintosh® computers and computers running Windows 95 on the same network using the Windows NT Server Services for Macintosh, and offers tips for users who are switching from Apple Macintosh to Windows 95.

**In This Appendix**     Windows NT Services for Macintosh   1222
Exchanging Mail Between Windows 95 and Macintosh   1222
Switching from Macintosh to Windows 95   1223

# Windows NT Services for Macintosh

Microsoft Windows NT Server Services for Macintosh is a thoroughly integrated component of Microsoft Windows NT Server, making it possible for computers running Windows 95, MS-DOS, Windows, Windows for Workgroups, Windows NT, and Apple Macintosh to share files and printers. After Services for Macintosh is set up, that computer can function as an AppleTalk® router. Routing capability is supported for AppleTalk Phase 2.

With Services for Macintosh, Macintosh computers need only the Macintosh operating system software to function as workstations; no additional software is required. You can, however, set up the optional user authentication module, which provides a secure logon to the computer running Windows NT Server.

When you set up Services for Macintosh on a computer running Windows NT Server, the AppleTalk Protocol, File Server for Macintosh, and the Print Server for Macintosh are started, or enabled. An explanation for each of these follows:

- The AppleTalk Protocol is the layer of AppleTalk Phase 2 protocols that delivers data to its network destination. The AppleTalk Protocol can be configured through the Network icon in the Windows NT Server Control Panel.

- File Server for Macintosh, also called MacFile, allows you to designate a directory as a Macintosh-accessible volume, ensures that Macintosh filenames are valid Windows NT file system (NTFS) names, and handles permissions. When set up, File Server for Macintosh commands appear in the Windows NT Server File Manager and Server Manager under the MacFile menu.

- Print Server for Macintosh, also called MacPrint, allows all network users to send print jobs to a spooler on the computer running Windows NT Server and continue to work, rather than wait for their print jobs to complete. Windows-based users can also review the print jobs in Print Manager.

Setting up Services for Macintosh creates an icon in Control Panel on the Windows NT Server computer, which gives you the same server administration capabilities as the MacFile menu, excluding volume management. For complete information, see the *Windows NT Server Services for Macintosh* documentation.

# Exchanging Mail Between Windows 95 and Macintosh

Upgrading a Windows 95 postoffice to a full Microsoft Mail Server postoffice with the *Microsoft Mail Post Office Upgrade* product allows clients running MS-DOS, Windows, Windows for Workgroups, Windows 95, Windows NT, Macintosh, and OS/2 to exchange mail.

However, before Macintosh clients can use the Microsoft Mail Server, you need a file server capable of sharing files for both Intel-compatible computers and Macintosh computers. Windows 95 File and Print Sharing services do not work with Macintosh computers. Therefore, you need to install the Microsoft Mail Server on a Windows NT or a Novell® NetWare® server.

# Switching from Macintosh to Windows 95

The following section offers tips to Apple Macintosh users who are new to Windows 95.

**How different is the Windows 95 desktop?**  Your drives are not on the desktop but are easily accessible by double-clicking My Computer. Then double-click the drive with contents you want to view.

You can put shortcuts to programs and documents directly on the desktop for easy access. Shortcuts are similar to aliases on the Macintosh. You can remove a shortcut from the desktop by deleting its icons. To create a shortcut, right-click a folder or file, and then choose the Shortcut option.

Deleted files are temporarily moved to the Recycle Bin. You can double-click the Recycle Bin icon to see its contents (and restore any contents). To permanently delete a file or program, open the File menu, and then click Empty Recycle Bin.

**Why does the mouse have two buttons?**  Use the left button—the main button— for most tasks unless the right button is specified in a Help procedure. If you click an item using the right button, a menu is displayed containing commands specific to the item.

**How do I find documents?**  Documents are stored in folders. To view the folders on your computer, double-click My Computer, and then double-click a drive. Double-click a folder to see its contents.

**How do I start a program?**  All programs are on the Start menu. Click the Start button, point to Programs, point to the program folder, and then click the program name.

**How can I switch between programs?**  A program button is added to the taskbar at the bottom of the desktop each time you open a program. The taskbar works in a manner similar to the Apple Macintosh Application menu, but instead of opening a menu, you click the button on the taskbar to switch between programs. You can drag the taskbar to the top or to either side of the desktop.

**How do I save a document?**  You can save a document by using the Save command on the File menu. You can save it to any folder on any drive, and change which folder you save it to in the Save dialog box. Here are a few things you need to know when saving documents.

- In Windows 95, the hard disk drive and floppy disk drives are identified by a letter. Most hard disk drives are assigned the letter C. Usually, the floppy disk drives are A and B.

- A path tells you where the document is located. It contains the drive letter and folder names in which the file is stored. For example, a path could be: C:\JUNE\WORK\SCHEDULE. This tells you that the SCHEDULE document is located on the C drive in a folder named WORK that is in the JUNE folder.

**How do I open a menu?**  Click once to open the menu, and then click your selection. You no longer need to press and hold the mouse button to keep the menu open.

**How do filenames differ between systems?**  In Windows 95, you can now use long filenames (up to 256 characters). Each file has a three-character filename extension (*filename.ext*) to identify the file type (sometimes it also identifies the program that created the file). Filename extensions are not included when documents are listed on the Start menu or displayed in My Computer.

**What are the three icons in the upper right corner?**  The three icons in the upper right corner of the desktop window are used as follows:

| | |
|---|---|
| ▣ | Use this icon to reduce the window to a button on the taskbar. Click the taskbar button to open the window again. |
| ▣ | Use this icon to enlarge the window so that it covers the entire desktop (except for the taskbar). |
| ☒ | Use this icon to close the window. |

**Where do I find the items from the Macintosh menu?**  The following procedures are used to find programs and documents in Windows 95:

- Click the Start menu to see most menu items.
- Customize system settings by pointing to Settings.
- Point to Documents to see a list of the documents you recently opened.
- Use Shut Down to exit Windows 95.

**How can I use the Windows online Help to learn more?**  To view a list of Help topics or search for a topic using the Help index, open Help from the Start menu.

For help on specific items in a window, click the question mark in the upper right corner of the dialog box, and then click the item to find out about it.

APPENDIX G

# HOSTS and LMHOSTS Files for Windows 95

This appendix describes how to modify HOSTS and LMHOSTS files to support address-to-name resolution in Windows 95 networking.

- The HOSTS file is used as a local Domain Name System (DNS) equivalent to resolve host names to IP addresses.
- The LMHOSTS file is used for name resolution when a Windows Internetwork Name Service (WINS) server is not available to resolve NetBIOS computer names to IP addresses.

Each of these files is also known as a *host table*. Sample versions of LMHOSTS (called LMHOSTS.SAM) and HOSTS files are added to the Windows directory when you install Windows 95 with TCP/IP support. These files can be edited using any ASCII editor, such as WordPad or Edit.

---

**Important**  To use LMHOSTS or HOSTS files for name resolution, the Enable DNS option must be selected. To do this, use the DNS Configuration tab in TCP/IP properties in the Network option in Control Panel.

---

**In This Appendix**     Setting Up HOSTS Files    1226
Setting Up LMHOSTS Files    1227

# Setting Up HOSTS Files

Microsoft TCP/IP can be configured to search the local host table file, HOSTS, for mappings of remote host names to IP addresses. The HOSTS file format is the same as the format for host tables in the Version 4.3 Berkeley Software Distribution (BSD) UNIX */etc/hosts* file. For example, the entry for a computer with an address of 192.102.73.6 and a host name of TREY.RESEARCH.COM looks similar to this:

```
192.102.73.6    trey.research.com
```

Edit the sample HOSTS file that is created when you install TCP/IP to include remote host names and their IP addresses for each computer with which you will communicate. This sample file also explains the syntax of the HOSTS file.

Host names are used in virtually all TCP/IP environments. A host name always corresponds to an IP address that is stored in a HOSTS file or on a DNS server and is assigned by an administrator to identify a TCP/IP host or default gateway. A host name can be used in place of an IP address when using **ping** or other TCP/IP utilities.

Host names are not used in the Windows 95 network user interface, such as Network Neighborhood or NET.EXE. The only time a host name is used to access a Windows–based computer is when **ping** or **ftp** or another TCP/IP utility is used. In this case, the host name and corresponding IP address must be stored in a HOSTS file.

The HOSTS file is a static file used to map host names to IP addresses. This file provides compatibility with the UNIX HOSTS file. The following describes HOSTS file entries:

- A single entry consists of an IP address corresponding to one or more host names.

- Entries are case-sensitive. Therefore, it is a good idea to assign multiple host names with different cases.

For example, to connect to the UNIX host ARCHIVE.RESEARCH.COM at the IP address 144.3.56.200, make two entries in the HOSTS file:

```
144.3.56.200 ARCHIVE.RESEARCH.COM
144.3.56.200 archive.research.com
```

This way, a user can connect to ARCHIVE using a utility, whether or not the CAPS LOCK is enabled.

A HOSTS file must reside on each system. By default, the host name **localhost** is an entry in the HOSTS file with the loopback address 127.0.0.1.

The HOSTS file is parsed whenever a host name is referenced. Names are read in a linear fashion. The most commonly used names should be near the beginning of the file. HOST file entries do not replace or interact with Windows-based NetBIOS computer names in any way.

The following shows the default HOSTS file provided with Windows 95.

```
# Copyright (c) 1994 Microsoft Corp.
#
# This is a sample HOSTS file used by Microsoft TCP/IP for Windows 95
#
# This file contains the mappings of IP addresses to host names. Each
# entry should be kept on an individual line. The IP address should
# be placed in the first column followed by the corresponding host name.
# The IP address and the host name should be separated by at least one
# space.
#
# Additionally, comments (such as these) may be inserted on individual
# lines or following the computer name denoted by a '#' symbol.
#
# For example:
#
#      102.54.94.97     rhino.acme.com          # source server
#      38.25.63.10      x.acme.com              # x client host
127.0.0.1     localhost
```

# Setting Up LMHOSTS Files

When you use Microsoft TCP/IP on a local network with any combination of computers running Windows 95, Windows NT, LAN Manager, or Windows for Workgroups, server names are automatically matched to their corresponding IP addresses. However, to match server names across remote networks connected by routers (or gateways), you can use the LMHOSTS file if WINS servers are not available on the network. The LMHOSTS file is commonly used to locate remote computers for Microsoft networking file, printer, and remote access services, and for domain services such as logon, browsing, replication, and so on.

The LMHOSTS file used by Windows 95 contains mappings of IP addresses to Microsoft networking computer names (which are NetBIOS names). Microsoft LAN Manager 2.x TCP/IP LMHOSTS files are compatible with Microsoft TCP/IP.

Microsoft TCP/IP loads the LMHOSTS file into memory when the computer is started. The LMHOSTS file is a text file in the Windows directory that lists the IP addresses and computer names of remote Windows networking servers that you want to communicate with. The LMHOSTS file should list all the names and IP addresses of the servers you regularly access.

For example, the LMHOSTS table file entry for a computer with an address of 192.45.36.5 and a NetBIOS computer name of Finance1 looks like this:

```
192.45.36.5     finance1
```

The format for the LMHOSTS file is the same as the format for host tables in 4.2 MSD UNIX systems. The computer name is optionally enclosed in quotation marks (this is necessary for computer names that contain spaces).

▶ **To create an LMHOSTS file**

1. Use a text editor to create a file named LMHOSTS, or edit the default file named LMHOSTS.SAM in the Windows directory and then save this file as LMHOSTS.

2. In the LMHOSTS file, type the IP address and the host name of each computer that you want to communicate with. Separate the items with at least one space.

Entries in the LMHOSTS file are not case-sensitive.

You will want to use LMHOSTS for smaller networks or to find hosts on remote networks that are not part of the WINS database (because name query requests are not broadcast beyond the local subnetwork). If WINS servers are in place on an internetwork, users do not have to rely on broadcast queries for name resolution, because WINS is the preferred method for name resolution. Therefore, with WINS servers in place, LMHOSTS may not be necessary.

However, the LMHOSTS file is read when WINS or broadcast name resolution fails, and resolved entries are stored in a system cache for later access. When the computer uses the replicator service and does not use WINS, LMHOSTS entries are required on import and export servers for any computers on different subnetworks participating in the replication.

You can use Notepad or any other text editor to edit the sample LMHOSTS.SAM file that is automatically installed in the Windows directory. The following rules apply for entries in LMHOSTS:

- Each entry should be placed on a separate line.

- The IP address should begin in the first column, followed by the corresponding computer name.

- The address and the computer name should be separated by at least one space or tab.

- The # character is usually used to mark the start of a comment. However, it can also designate special keywords, as described in this section.

The keywords listed in the following table can be used in LMHOSTS using Microsoft TCP/IP. Notice, however, that LAN Manager 2.x treats these keywords as comments.

| Keyword | Meaning |
|---|---|
| #PRE | Added after an entry to cause that entry to be preloaded into the name cache. By default, entries are not preloaded into the name cache but are parsed only after WINS and name query broadcasts fail to resolve a name. #PRE must be appended for entries that also appear in #INCLUDE statements; otherwise, the entry in #INCLUDE is ignored. |
| #DOM:*domain* | Added after an entry to associate that entry with the domain specified by *domain*. This keyword affects how the Browser and Logon services behave in routed TCP/IP environments. To preload a #DOM entry, you must also add the #PRE keyword to the line. |
| #INCLUDE *filename* | Forces the system to seek the specified *filename* and parse it as if it were local. Specifying a Universal Naming Convention (UNC) *filename* allows you to use a centralized LMHOSTS file on a server. You must add a mapping for the server before its entry in the #INCLUDE section and also append #PRE to ensure that it is preloaded (otherwise, the #INCLUDE will be ignored). |
| #BEGIN_ALTERNATE | Used to group multiple #INCLUDE statements. Any single successful #INCLUDE statement causes the group to succeed. |
| #END_ALTERNATE | Used to mark the end of an #INCLUDE grouping. |
| \0x*nn* | Support for nonprinting characters in NetBIOS names. Enclose the NetBIOS name in double quotation marks and use \0x*nn* hexadecimal notation to specify a hexadecimal value for the character. This allows custom applications that use special names to function properly in routed topologies. However, LAN Manager TCP/IP does not recognize the hexadecimal format, so you surrender backward compatibility if you use this feature.<br><br>Notice that the hexadecimal notation applies only to one character in the name. The name should be padded with blanks so the special character is last in the string (character 16). |

The following example shows how all of these keywords are used:

```
102.54.94.98    localsrv #PRE
102.54.94.97    trey     #PRE #DOM:networking #net group's PDC
102.54.94.102   "appname        \0x14"  #special app server
102.54.94.123   popular  #PRE #source server
#BEGIN_ALTERNATE
#INCLUDE \\localsrv\public\lmhosts    #adds LMHOSTS from this server
#INCLUDE \\trey\public\lmhosts        #adds LMHOSTS from this server
#END_ALTERNATE
```

In the preceding example:

- The servers named **localsrv** and **trey** are preloaded so they can be used later in an #INCLUDE statement in a centrally maintained LMHOSTS file.

- The server named **"appname        \0x14"** contains a special character after the 15 characters in its name (including blanks), so its name is enclosed in double quotation marks.

- The server named **popular** is preloaded, based on the #PRE keyword.

### Guidelines for LMHOSTS

When you use a host table file, be sure to keep it up to date and organized. Follow these guidelines:

- Update the LMHOSTS file whenever a computer is changed or removed from the network.

- Use #PRE statements to preload popular entries into the local computer's name cache and to preload servers that are included with #INCLUDE statements.

- Because LMHOSTS files are searched one line at a time from the beginning, you can increase the speed of searches for the entries used most often by placing frequently used servers near the top of the file. Follow these with less frequently used servers, and then remote #INCLUDE statements. The #PRE entries should be at the end of the file, because these are preloaded into the cache at system startup time and are not accessed later. Comment lines add to the parsing time, because each line is processed individually.

APPENDIX H

# Shortcuts for Windows 95

This appendix summarizes the shortcuts that are built into Windows 95 for using the keyboard and mouse to quickly accomplish common actions.

**In This Appendix**    Shortcuts for Objects, Folders, and Windows Explorer    1232
General Keyboard-Only Commands    1234
Accessibility Shortcuts    1234
Microsoft Natural Keyboard Keys    1235

# Shortcuts for Objects, Folders, and Windows Explorer

The following brief procedures and tables summarize the standard shortcuts for working with objects in the Windows 95 user interface, including folders on the desktop and Windows Explorer.

▶ **To copy a file**

- Press CTRL while you drag the file to a folder.

▶ **To create a shortcut**

- Press CTRL+SHIFT while you drag the file to the desktop or a folder.

▶ **To close the current folder and all its parent folders**

- Press SHIFT and click the Close button on the folder.

▶ **To tab through pages in a properties dialog box**

- Press CTRL+TAB or CTRL+SHIFT+TAB.

▶ **To switch between opening a new window and closing an existing window**

- Press CTRL and double-click a folder.

    If you have more than one window open, this operation closes the active window. If you have only one window open, this operation opens a new window.

▶ **To bypass Auto-Run when inserting a compact disc**

- Press SHIFT while inserting the compact disc.

**Shortcuts for a Selected Object**

| Shortcut | Action |
| --- | --- |
| F2 | Rename |
| F3 | Find |
| CTRL+X | Cut |
| CTRL+C | Copy |
| CTRL+V | Paste |
| DEL key | Delete |
| SHIFT+DEL | Delete file immediately without putting it in Recycle Bin |
| ALT+ENTER | Display properties |
| ALT+double-click | Display properties |

**Shortcuts for a Selected Object** (*continued*)

| Shortcut | Action |
|---|---|
| CTRL+click the right mouse button | Place alternative commands on the context menu (Open With) |
| SHIFT+double-click | Explore an object; if the object does not have an Explore command, this starts the default action (usually the Open command) |

**Shortcuts for Managing Folders and Windows Explorer**

| Shortcut | Action |
|---|---|
| F4 | In Windows Explorer, display the combo box and move the input focus to the list |
| F5 | Refresh display |
| F6 | In Windows Explorer, move the focus between panes |
| CTRL+G | In Windows Explorer, choose the Go To command |
| CTRL+Z | Undo |
| CTRL+A | Select All |
| BACKSPACE | Go to the parent folder |

**Shortcuts in the Windows Explorer Tree**

| Shortcut | Action |
|---|---|
| * on numeric keypad | Expand everything under the selection |
| + on numeric keypad | Expand the selection |
| – on numeric keypad | Collapse the selection |
| RIGHT ARROW | Expand the current selection if it is not expanded; otherwise, go to the first child |
| LEFT ARROW | Collapse current selection if it is expanded; otherwise, go to the parent |
| CTRL+arrow key | Scroll without moving the selection |

**Shortcuts in the Common Open and Save dialog boxes**

| Shortcut | Action |
|---|---|
| F4 | Display the Look In list |
| F5 | Refresh the view |
| BACKSPACE | Go to the parent folder if the focus is on the View window |

# General Keyboard-Only Commands

The following table shows commands for completing actions from the keyboard.

**General Keyboard-Only Commands**

| Shortcut | Action |
| --- | --- |
| F1 | Start Help |
| F10 | Go to menu mode |
| SHIFT+F10 | Display context menu for selected item |
| CTRL+ESC | Display Start menu and move the focus to the taskbar |
| CTRL+ESC, ESC | Move the focus on the taskbar so you can use TAB and then SHIFT+F10 for context menu, or use TAB and arrow key to change tasks, or use TAB to go to the desktop |
| ALT+TAB | Switch to the next running application |
| ALT+M | When the focus is on the taskbar or desktop, minimize all windows and move the focus to the desktop |
| ALT+S | When no windows are open and no items are selected on the desktop, display the Start menu; then use arrow keys to select menu commands |

# Accessibility Shortcuts

The following table summarizes the Windows 95 shortcuts for Accessibility features. For information about these features, see Appendix I, "Accessibility."

**Accessibility Shortcuts**

| Shortcut | Action |
| --- | --- |
| Press SHIFT 5 times | Toggle StickyKeys on and off |
| Press RIGHT SHIFT for 8 seconds | Toggle FilterKeys on and off |
| Press NUMLOCK for 5 seconds | Toggle ToggleKeys on and off |
| Press LEFT ALT+LEFT SHIFT+NUMLOCK | Toggle MouseKeys on and off |
| Press LEFT ALT+LEFT SHIFT+ PRINTSCREEN | Toggle HighContrast on and off |

# Microsoft Natural Keyboard Keys

The following table summarizes the shortcut keys available on the Microsoft
Natural Keyboard™.

**Microsoft Natural Keyboard Keys**

| Shortcut | Action |
| --- | --- |
| WIN+R | Display Run dialog box |
| WIN+M | Minimize All |
| SHIFT+WIN+M | Undo Minimize All |
| WIN+F1 | Start Help |
| WIN+E | Start Windows Explorer |
| WIN+F | Find files or folders |
| CTRL+WIN+F | Find computer |
| WIN+TAB | Cycle through taskbar buttons |
| WIN+BREAK | Hot key to display System properties dialog box |

APPENDIX I

# Accessibility

This appendix describes the new features in Windows 95 that support enhanced accessibility. This appendix also provides information about other Microsoft products and services that make Windows 95 more accessible for people with disabilities.

For information about creating custom setup support to accommodate accessibility needs, see Chapter 5, "Custom, Automated, and Push Installations."

**In This Appendix**

Accessibility in Windows 95: Overview    1238
Windows 95 Accessibility Features    1239
    General Accessibility Enhancement Features    1239
    Features for Users with Low Vision    1242
    Features for Making Keyboard and Mouse Input Easier    1244
    Features for Users Who Are Deaf or Hard-of-Hearing    1246
    Features Supporting Alternative Input Devices    1249
    Features for Software Developers    1249
    Using Accessibility Features in Windows 95    1250
Microsoft Services for People Who Are Deaf or Hard-of-Hearing    1251
Keyboard Layouts for Single-Handed Users    1251
Microsoft Documentation on Audio Cassettes and Floppy Disks    1252
Accessibility-Enhancing Utilities from Other Vendors    1252
Getting More Information on Accessibility    1253

# Accessibility in Windows 95: Overview

Microsoft is committed to making computers easier to use for everyone, including individuals with disabilities. In recent years Microsoft has established close relationships with users who have disabilities, organizations representing disabled individuals, workers in the rehabilitation field, and software developers who create products for this market. Based on their combined input, Microsoft has defined specific design goals for Windows 95:

- Integrate and improve the features from the accessibility product Access Pack for Microsoft Windows that compensate for difficulties some individuals have using the keyboard or the mouse

- Make the visual user interface easier to customize for people with limited vision

- Provide additional visual feedback for users who are deaf or hard-of-hearing

- Provide new API and "hooks" for ISVs developing accessibility aids, including those that allow blind individuals to use Windows

- Make information on accessibility solutions more widely available and increase public awareness of these issues

Windows 95 offers several enhancements designed to meet these accessibility goals. The primary improvements in accessibility for Windows 95 are:

- Scalable user interface elements

- Features that compensate for difficulties in using the keyboard

- Keyboard emulation of the mouse

- Support for alternative input devices that emulate the keyboard and mouse

- Visual cues to tell the user when the application is making sounds

- Notification to other applications when the user has limited vision, needs additional keyboard support due to difficulty using a mouse, or wants visual captions to be displayed for speech or other sounds

- Notification to other applications when they should modify behavior to be compatible with accessibility software utilities running in the system

- Optimized keyboard layouts for users who type with a single hand, a single finger, or a mouthstick

- Audible prompts during Setup for users who have low vision

- Color schemes that are optimized for users with low vision

- Documentation that includes accessibility information

Windows 95 Setup installs Accessibility Options automatically. To use a computer that does not have Accessibility Options installed, perform the following procedure.

▶ **To install accessibility features under Windows 95**

1. In the Add/Remove Programs option in Control Panel, click the Windows Setup tab.

2. In the list of components, click Accessibility Options and then click OK.

# Windows 95 Accessibility Features

Windows 95 accessibility features fall into the following categories:

- General accessibility features
- Features for users with limited vision
- Features for users who have difficulty using a keyboard or mouse
- Features for users who are deaf or hard-of-hearing
- Features supporting the use of alternate input devices
- Features supporting the development of accessible software

# General Accessibility Enhancement Features

This section describes general enhancements to the operating system that support accessibility. These include:

- Online Help
- Control Panel support for accessibility features
- Emergency hot keys
- Accessibility time-out
- Accessibility status indicator

## Online Help

An Accessibility section in the Windows 95 Help contents and index provides a quick reference and pointer to topics that can help adjust the behavior of the system for people with disabilities.

## Control Panel Support for Accessibility Features

The Accessibility Options icon in Control Panel controls most of the accessibility features in Windows 95. With Accessibilities properties, users can turn the accessibility features on or off, customizing keyboard, sound, display, and mouse operation for their own particular needs.

Accessibility
properties dialog box
in Control Panel

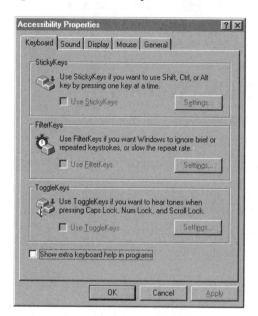

## Emergency Hot Keys

The emergency hot keys provide an alternate method of activating accessibility features, for persons who could not use the computer without first having accessibility features in effect. Also known as shortcuts, the emergency hot keys allow the user to temporarily turn on the specific needed feature. Then, after a feature has been turned on, the user can navigate to Control Panel and adjust the feature to the user's own preferences, or turn the feature on permanently. The same hot key temporarily turns off the feature, if it gets in the way, or if another person wants to use the computer without this feature.

Hot keys are designed to be unique key combinations that should not conflict with keys used by applications. If such a conflict does arise, the hot keys can be disabled, and the user can still use the feature or not, as needed.

As a precaution against accidental use, pressing an emergency hot key causes special tones to sound (a rising siren tone for on, and a falling siren tone for off), and causes a confirmation dialog box to appear, briefly explaining the feature and how it was activated. If the user pressed the hot key unintentionally, the user can cancel the feature's activation at this time. The confirming dialog box also provides a quick path to more detailed help and to the Control Panel settings for the hot-key feature, in case the user wants to disable the hot key permanently.

The following table shows how the hot keys work.

| To turn on | Press the following keys |
| --- | --- |
| StickyKeys | SHIFT five times |
| MouseKeys | Left ALT + left SHIFT + NUM LOCK |
| FilterKeys, with default settings active | Right SHIFT and hold it down for eight seconds |
| FilterKeys with SlowKeys and RepeatKeys set to the most conservative values | Right SHIFT and hold it down for 12 seconds |
| FilterKeys with BounceKeys and RepeatKeys set to the most conservative values | Right SHIFT and hold it down for 16 seconds |
| ToggleKeys | NUM LOCK and hold it down for five seconds |
| High-contrast Key | Left ALT, left SHIFT, and PRINT SCREEN keys simultaneously |

## Accessibility Time-out

The time-out feature of the Accessibilities properties dialog box turns off accessibility functionality after the computer has been idle for a certain period of time. It returns the operating system to its default configuration. This feature is useful on computers shared by multiple users.

## Accessibility Status Indicator

While an accessibility feature is in use, Windows 95 can display an optional visual indicator that tells the user which accessibility features are turned on. This helps users unfamiliar with the accessibility features to identify which ones are in effect. The indicator also provides feedback on the keys and mouse buttons currently being "held down" by the StickyKeys and MouseKeys features. The status indicator can appear on the system taskbar, or as a free-floating window; users can choose the displayed size from a range of different sizes.

Accessibility Status
Indicator Window

In the preceding illustration, the three rectangles represent the left SHIFT, CTRL, and ALT keys. As each modifier key is held down by the StickyKeys feature, the corresponding rectangle appears filled.

The mouse in the Accessibility status indicator window may show either the left or the right button shaded, depending on which is selected. Pressing 5, +, or INS is equivalent to using that button. If you have selected working with both buttons (equivalent to using the middle button on a three-button mouse), both buttons are shaded. If you lock down one or more mouse buttons using the INS key, the status indicator shows those buttons as being filled, rather than shaded. (To release them, press DEL.)

The stop watch indicates that the keyboard response is being affected by SlowKeys, BounceKeys, or RepeatKeys features.

# Features for Users with Low Vision

This section describes the specific accessibility features that Windows 95 provides to users with limited vision, including:

- Scalable user interface elements
- Customizable display for mouse pointer
- High-contrast mode

## Scalable User Interface Elements

Users who have limited vision or who suffer eyestrain during normal use of a video display can now adjust the sizes of window titles, scroll bars, borders, menu text, and other standard screen elements. These sizes are completely customizable using Appearance properties in the Display option of Control Panel. Users can also choose between two sizes for the built-in system font.

## Customizable Display for Mouse Pointer

Users who have difficulty seeing or following the mouse pointer can now set the following characteristics, to improve visibility of the mouse pointer:

- Pointer size
- Pointer color
- Speed of the pointer
- Visible trails of pointer movement
- Animation of the pointer

Customizable mouse pointer display schemes are loaded automatically when you install Windows 95 from the compact disc, using Typical setup. If another setup type is used, install the schemes after Setup is run, using the Add/Remove Programs icon in Control Panel. After installation, the user can select, through the Mouse option in Control Panel, a small, medium, or large mouse pointer scheme on a monochrome display.

In addition, with the Windows 95 compact disc, the user can install color schemes and select from red, gray, yellow, green, or violet 16-color schemes for the mouse pointer. Settings for pointer speed and for showing pointer trails (of user-specified lengths) are also available.

**Note**  Not all displays support mouse pointer color schemes.

Windows 95 features an animated hourglass pointer for better viewing.

## High-Contrast Color Schemes

Windows 95 color schemes allow users to choose from several well designed sets of screen-color options, designed both to match users' individual tastes and to meet their visual needs. The new color schemes in Windows 95 include high-contrast colors, such as white text on a black background, or black text on a white background. These high-contrast color schemes optimize the visibility of screen objects, making it easier for users with visual impairments.

## High-Contrast Mode

Many users with low vision require a high degree of contrast between foreground and background objects, in order to distinguish the objects. For example, some users may not be able to easily read black text on a gray background, or text drawn over a picture. By setting a global flag, users can now instruct Windows 95 and applications to display information with a high degree of contrast. Activating high-contrast mode automatically selects the user's preferred color scheme.

Users can activate high-contrast mode using Accessibility Options in Control Panel, or using an emergency hot key sequence (pressing left ALT, left SHIFT, and PRINT SCREEN keys simultaneously).

# Features for Making Keyboard and Mouse Input Easier

This section describes accessibility features that assist users who may have difficulty using the keyboard or the mouse.

Notice that even without installing accessibility features you can use the TAB key in dialog boxes to move the focus (that is, the outline that indicates where you are currently working in the dialog box), and use the arrow keys to select items in a list. In property sheets that have multiple tabs, you can press CTRL+TAB to select each property sheet in order from left to right. Or press the TAB key until the focus is in the tab for the current property sheet, and then press an arrow key to select the next sheet.

## StickyKeys

Many software programs require the user to press two or three keys at one time. For people who type with a single finger or a mouthstick, that isn't possible. StickyKeys allows users to press one key at a time and instructs Windows to respond as if they had been pressed simultaneously.

When StickyKeys is on, pressing any modifier key (that is, CTRL, ALT, or SHIFT) latches that key down until the user releases the mouse button or presses a key that is not a modifier key. Pressing a modifier key twice in a row locks the key down until it is tapped a third time.

Users can adjust StickyKeys functionality in Control Panel, or turn the feature on or off using an emergency hot key (pressing the SHIFT key five consecutive times).

## FilterKeys

The sensitivity of the keyboard can be a significant problem for some individuals, for example, if they often press keys accidentally because of a tremor, or because they cannot remove their fingers from keys quickly. Windows 95 includes a series of features designed to work either individually or in combination to compensate for problems in keyboard usage. These features are called SlowKeys, RepeatKeys, and BounceKeys.

SlowKeys instructs Windows 95 to disregard keystrokes that are not held down for a minimum period of time. This allows a user to brush against keys without any effect, and when the user gets a finger on the proper key, the user can hold the key down until the character appears on the screen.

RepeatKeys lets users adjust the repeat rate or disable the key-repeat function on their keyboards. Most keyboards allow users to repeat a key just by holding it down. Although this feature can be convenient for some users, it poses a problem for individuals who can't lift their fingers off the keyboard quickly.

BounceKeys is useful for persons with tremors whose fingers tend to bounce on the keys when pressed or released. When BounceKeys is turned on, this feature instructs your computer to ignore unintended keystrokes.

Users can adjust FilterKeys functionality using the Accessibility Options icon in Control Panel, or turn on or off the specific FilterKeys feature using an emergency hot key. Holding down the right SHIFT key for eight seconds causes a single sound to play and activates this group of features with the user's default settings. If those settings are not appropriate, holding down the key for 12 seconds causes two quick beeps to sound, and turns on the BounceKeys and RepeatKeys features, with their most conservative settings. Holding down the key for 16 seconds causes three quick beeps to sound, and turns on the SlowKeys and RepeatKeys features with their most conservative settings.

## MouseKeys

This feature lets individuals control the mouse pointer using the keyboard. Although Windows 95 is designed to allow the user to perform all actions without a mouse, some applications may still require one, and a mouse may be more convenient for some tasks. MouseKeys is also useful for graphic artists and others who need to position the pointer with great accuracy. Users do not need to have a mouse to use this feature.

When MouseKeys is on, use the following keys to navigate the pointer on the screen:

- Press one of the numbered keys (also called the arrow keys) on the numeric keypad—except 5—to move the pointer in the direction indicated in the following figure.

Keys on the numeric keypad that control the mouse pointer

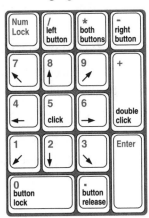

- Use the 5 key for a single mouse-button click and the PLUS SIGN (+) key for a double-click.

- To drag and release an object, place the pointer on the object and press INS to begin dragging. Move the object to its new location and press DEL to release it.

- Select the left, right, or both mouse buttons for clicking by pressing the forward slash (/) key, the minus sign (-) key, or the asterisk (*) key, respectively.

- Hold down the CTRL key while using the arrow keys (numeric keys, except for 5) to cause the pointer to "jump" across large sections of the screen.

- Hold down the SHIFT key while using the arrow keys to move the mouse a single pixel at a time for greater accuracy.

Users can adjust MouseKeys in Control Panel, or turn the feature on or off using an emergency hot key (pressing the left ALT, left SHIFT, and NUM LOCK keys simultaneously).

---

**Note** If the MouseKeys feature is on but NUM LOCK is off, the MouseKeys icon in the taskbar shows that MouseKeys is disabled.

---

## ToggleKeys

ToggleKeys provides audio cues—high and low beeps—to tell the user whether a toggle key is active or inactive. It applies to the CAPS LOCK, NUM LOCK, and SCROLL LOCK keys.

Users can adjust ToggleKeys in Control Panel, or turn the feature on or off using an emergency hot key (holding down the NUM LOCK key for eight seconds).

# Features for Users Who Are Deaf or Hard-of-Hearing

ShowSounds and SoundSentry provide visible feedback in place of audible signals or speech, to users who have hearing disabilities or who work in extremely noisy conditions.

## ShowSounds

This is a global flag that instructs applications to provide visible feedback—in effect asking the applications to be "closed-captioned."

## SoundSentry

SoundSentry tells Windows to send a visual cue, such as a blinking title bar or a screen flash whenever there is a system beep. This allows users to see the message that may not have been heard.

# WinChat

You can use the WinChat utility to have an electronic conversation with up to seven other people who are using Windows 95. Unlike an electronic mail message that you compose, save, and then send to another person, a WinChat message is visible to others as you type it. The WinChat utility is provided in the OTHER\CHAT directory on the Windows 95 compact disc.

This utility is appropriate to install on all computers running Windows 95 in an environment that includes users who are deaf or hard-of-hearing. WinChat is the best alternative form of communication when an interpreter or a text telephone (called a "TT" or "TDD") is not available.

If Windows 95 users previously ran WinChat under Windows for Workgroups, and upgraded to Windows 95 in their previous Windows directory, WinChat is still available on their computers.

If Windows 95 is installed on a computer that did not previously have Windows for Workgroups installed, you can install WinChat from the Windows 95 compact disc.

▶ **To install WinChat on a computer running Windows 95**

1. In the Add/Remove Programs option in Control Panel, click the Windows Setup tab.

2. Click the Have Disk button. In the Install From Disk dialog box, supply the path to the OTHER\CHAT directory on the Windows 95 compact disc.

3. In the Have Disk box, click the WinChat entry in the Components list, and click the Install button.

▶ **To make a call or add a person to a call**

1. On the toolbar in WinChat, click the Dial button. Or choose Dial in the Conversation menu.

2. In the Select Computer dialog box, type the computer name of the person you want to chat with, and then choose the OK button.

   The message in the status bar informs you if the person answers.

You can type your message in the WinChat window before calling someone. The top window displays what you type. The bottom window displays what the other person is typing. Each time you add a person to your conversation, a new window opens. If there are six people in a conversation, there are six windows open.

Only the person who initiates the call can add another person to the conversation or end the conversation.

When a person is added, that person can view the typed conversation that has already taken place. The names of the people in the conversation appear in the title bar and the status bar.

To move between the windows, click the window you're moving to, or press F6. When you finish your conversation, hang up.

When someone calls you, you answer the call to begin your conversation. If WinChat is running, a sound is emitted, and a message appears in the status bar. If WinChat is not running, it starts as an icon on your desktop.

▶  **To answer a call**

- If the WinChat window is open, click the Answer button on the toolbar. Or choose Answer from the Conversation menu.

  If WinChat is running as an icon, double-click the icon, or select it and then press ENTER.

After you answer the call, you can start typing your message.

When you finish your conversation, hang up to disconnect from other participants' computers.

▶  **To hang up**

- On the toolbar, click the Hang Up button. Or choose Hang Up in the Conversation menu. Or quit WinChat; it will hang up for you.

You can choose to have your computer ignore incoming calls unless WinChat is running.

▶  **To prevent incoming calls**

1. From the Options menu, choose Preferences.
2. Clear the Autostart Chat When Called check box, and then click OK.

Use the commands on the Options menu to control preferences for window styles, background color, and fonts, and to control the display of the tool bar and status bar. You can also use the Options menu to control whether WinChat rings when there is a call.

▶  **To turn the sound on or off**

- From the Options menu in WinChat, choose Sound.

  A check mark next to the Sound command indicates that sound is on.

If you have a sound card, you can change the sound of the incoming or outgoing ring by using the Sound option in Control Panel.

# Features Supporting Alternative Input Devices

This section describes Windows 95 support for the use of alternative input devices.

## SerialKeys

This feature, in conjunction with a communications aid interface device, allows the user to control the computer using an alternative input device. Such a device needs only to send coded command strings through the computer's serial port to specify keystrokes and mouse events, which are then treated as if they were normal keyboard or mouse input.

## Support for Multiple Pointing Devices

The new Plug and Play architecture in Windows 95 inherently supports multiple pointing devices working in combination. This allows seamless addition of alternative pointing devices, such as head-pointers or eye-gaze systems without the need to replace or disable the normal mouse.

# Features for Software Developers

This section describes how the design of Windows 95 makes it easier for software developers to make their products accessible to individuals with disabilities.

## Accessibility Guidelines for Software Developers

Windows 95 contains many built-in accessibility features. To make a computer running Windows 95 truly accessible, application developers must provide access to their applications' features, taking care to avoid incompatibilities with accessibility aids.

As part of the *Win32 Software Development Kit for Windows 95 and Windows NT* and *The Windows Interface Guidelines for Software Design*, Microsoft has provided developers with documentation which not only outlines these important concepts, but provides technical and design tips to help ISVs produce more accessible applications. Most of these tips will mean very little additional work to the designer, as long as the application designer is aware of the issues and incorporates accessibility into the application design at an early stage. By providing this information to application developers, Microsoft hopes to increase the general level of accessibility of all software running on the Windows platform.

## Methods for Simulating Input

Windows 95 now allows developers of voice-input systems and other alternative input systems to easily simulate keyboard and mouse input using fully documented and supported procedures.

## New Common Controls

Many accessibility aids have difficulty working with applications that implement nonstandard controls. Windows 95 introduces a whole new set of controls available for mainstream software developers, and these standardized implementations are designed to cooperate with accessibility aids.

# Using Accessibility Features in Windows 95

To see how the accessibility features in Windows 95 make it easy to customize the appearance and behavior of the computer, try them out, using the following procedures.

▶ **To perform mouse actions from the keyboard**

- Press the left ALT, the left SHIFT, and the NUM LOCK keys simultaneously. You'll be able to drag and drop, and click or double-click both the primary and secondary mouse buttons by using your keyboard's numeric keypad.

  For more information, see "MouseKeys" earlier in this appendix.

▶ **To perform an ALT+TAB action with a pencil**

1. Press a SHIFT key five consecutive times to start StickyKeys. When StickyKeys is activated, press the ALT key and see what happens. Press TAB and you'll have just typed two keys at once with a single finger.

2. Press the ALT key twice, then press TAB a few times to see the ALT + TAB window and cycle through all the tasks you have running. When you're satisfied, press ALT one more time to release it.

3. When you're ready to move on, turn off this feature by pressing two keys at the same time. Don't forget to watch the status indicator on the system taskbar.

   This feature is helpful to users who type with only one finger or who use a mouthstick.

▶  **To get accessibility support for MS-DOS–based applications**

- Start an MS-DOS–based application and try StickyKeys or MouseKeys. These features are available whenever you need them, regardless of what you may be doing, even when you're running MS-DOS–based applications.

▶  **To improve on-screen readability**

- Press left ALT + left SHIFT + PRINT SCREEN and try to find a screen appearance that's better suited to your needs.

  This feature is useful for individuals who can't read black text on a gray background because all the lines blur together.

# Microsoft Services for People Who Are Deaf or Hard-of-Hearing

Through a text telephone (TT/TDD) service, Microsoft provides people who are deaf or hard-of-hearing with complete access to Microsoft product and customer services.

You can contact Microsoft Sales and Service on a text telephone by dialing (800) 892-5234 between 6:30 A.M. and 5:30 P.M. Pacific time. For technical assistance you can contact Microsoft Product Support Services on a text telephone at (206) 635-4948 between 6:00 A.M. and 6:00 P.M. Pacific time. Microsoft support services are subject to Microsoft prices, terms, and conditions in place at the time the service is used.

# Keyboard Layouts for Single-Handed Users

Microsoft distributes Dvorak keyboard layouts that make the most frequently typed characters on a keyboard more accessible to people who have difficulty using the standard "QWERTY" layout. There are three Dvorak layouts: one for two-handed users, one for people who type with the left hand only, and one for people who type with the right hand only. The left-handed or right-handed keyboard layouts can also be used by people who type with a single finger or a wand. You do not need to purchase any special equipment in order to use these features.

Microsoft Windows already supports the two-handed Dvorak layout, which can be helpful in preventing or relieving some repetitive-motion injuries associated with typing. To get this layout, choose the International icon from Control Panel. The two layouts for people who type with one hand are distributed as Microsoft Application Note GA0650. It is also contained in file GA0650.ZIP on most network services or GA0650.EXE on the Microsoft Download Service. For instructions on using Microsoft Download Service to obtain this application note, see Appendix J, "Windows 95 Resource Directory."

# Microsoft Documentation on Audio Cassettes and Floppy Disks

People who have difficulty reading or handling printed documentation can obtain most Microsoft publications from Recording for the Blind, Inc. Recording for the Blind distributes these documents to registered members of their distribution service either on audiocassettes or on floppy disks. The Recording for the Blind collection contains more than 80,000 titles, including Microsoft product documentation and books from Microsoft Press. You can contact Recording for the Blind at the following address or phone numbers:

| Recording for the Blind, Inc. | Phone: | (800) 221-4792 |
| 20 Roszel Road | Fax: | (609) 987-8116 |
| Princeton, NJ 08540 | Phone outside U.S.: | (609) 452-0606 |

Windows 95 documentation is available online in the CD-ROM version of Windows 95. This is also available from Recording for the Blind, Inc.

# Accessibility-Enhancing Utilities from Other Vendors

A wide variety of hardware and software products designed to help people with disabilities use personal computers is currently available from other vendors. Among the different types of products available for the MS-DOS, Microsoft Windows, and Microsoft Windows NT operating systems are:

- Programs that enlarge or alter the color of information on the screen for people with visual impairments
- Programs that describe information on the screen in braille or in synthesized speech for people who are blind or have difficulty reading
- Hardware and software utilities that modify the behavior of the mouse and keyboard
- Programs that enable users to "type" using a mouse or their voice

- Word or phrase prediction software that allows one to type more quickly and with fewer keystrokes
- Alternate input devices, such as single switch or puff-and-sip devices, for those who cannot use a mouse or a keyboard

For more information on these types of products, see the following section.

# Getting More Information on Accessibility

For more information on Microsoft products and services for people with disabilities, contact Microsoft Sales Information Center at the following address:

| | | |
|---|---|---|
| Microsoft Sales Information Center | Voice telephone: | (800) 426-9400 |
| One Microsoft Way | Text telephone: | (800) 892-5234 |
| Redmond, WA 98052-6393 | Fax: | (206) 635-6100 |

The Trace R&D Center at the University of Wisconsin–Madison produces a book and a compact disc that describe products that help people with disabilities use computers. The *Trace Resource Book* provides descriptions and photographs of about 2,000 products. The compact disc, titled *CO-NET CD*, provides a database of more than 18,000 products and other information for people with disabilities. It is issued twice a year.

You can contact the Trace R&D Center at the following address or telephone numbers:

| | | |
|---|---|---|
| Trace R&D Center | Voice telephone: | (608) 263-2309 |
| S-151 Waisman Center | Text telephone: | (608) 263-5408 |
| 1500 Highland Avenue | Fax: | (608) 262-8848 |
| Madison, WI 53705-2280 | | |

For general information and recommendations on how computers can help specific people, consult a trained evaluator who can best match your needs with the available solutions. An assistive technology program in your area will provide referrals to programs and services that are available to you. To locate the assistive technology program nearest you, contact:

| | | |
|---|---|---|
| National Information System Center | Fax: | (803) 777-6058 |
| for Developmental Disabilities | Voice/text phone | |
| Benson Building | in the U.S.: | (803) 777-4434 |
| University of South Carolina | Voice/text phone | |
| Columbia, SC 29208 | outside the U.S.: | (803) 777-6222 |

APPENDIX J

# Windows 95 Resource Directory

This appendix provides information on obtaining additional support and information for Windows 95. This appendix also discusses the different Microsoft sources for support and assistance.

**In This Appendix**

Online Information About Windows 95     1256

Getting Answers to Your Technical Questions     1256

Hardware Compatibility Information     1258

Windows 95 SDK Information     1258

Microsoft TechNet     1258

Microsoft Developer Network     1258

Microsoft Solution Providers     1259

Microsoft Technical Education     1259

Microsoft Consulting Services     1259

Microsoft Knowledge Base     1260

Microsoft Software Library     1260

Microsoft Download Service     1260

Microsoft CompuServe Forums     1261

Obtaining Drivers Electronically     1261

Resources for ICM     1262

# Online Information About Windows 95

For Windows 95 information, see the WinNews areas on most major online services and networks.

| Online service | WinNews access procedures |
| --- | --- |
| The Microsoft Network | From the Windows 95 desktop, click the Microsoft Network icon. Then click Microsoft and, in the Microsoft menu, select Windows 95. Click WinNews. |
| America Online® | Use the keyword **winnews** |
| CompuServe® | Type **go winnews** |
| FTP on the Internet | Type **ftp://ftp.microsoft.com /PerOpSys/Win_News** |
| GEnie™ | Download files from the WinNews area under the Windows 95 RTC. |
| Prodigy™ | Type **jump winnews** |
| World Wide Web on the Internet | Type **http://www.microsoft.com** |

As an alternative to these online sources, the biweekly *WinNews Electronic Newsletter* is available. Subscribers receive this newsletter by mail, eliminating the need for regularly checking the WinNews areas for updates. To subscribe, type an Internet mail message addressed to **enews@microsoft.nwnet.com** with the words **subscribe winnews** as the only text in your message.

# Getting Answers to Your Technical Questions

For answers to your questions and help with technical problems regarding Windows 95:

- First, check online Help (press the F1 key), the printed documentation set, and the information in the following files.

  | | |
  | --- | --- |
  | display.txt | network.txt |
  | general.txt | printers.txt |
  | internet.txt | readme.txt |
  | mouse.txt | setup.txt |
  | msn.txt | support.txt |

- For fast answers to common questions and a library of technical notes delivered by recording or fax, call Microsoft FastTips for Windows 95 at (800) 936-4200, available seven days a week, 24 hours a day, including holidays. Microsoft FastTips is an automated system, accessible by touch-tone phone.

- Use The Microsoft Network or CompuServe to interact with other users and Microsoft Product Support Services (PSS) engineers, or to access the Microsoft Knowledge Base for product information. For CompuServe members, type **go winnews** to access the forum for Windows 95, or type **go mskb** to access the Microsoft Knowledge Base at any ! prompt.

  For an introductory CompuServe membership kit, call (800) 848-8199 and ask for operator 463. For information about Microsoft forums on CompuServe, see "Microsoft CompuServe Forums" later in this appendix; for information about Knowledge Base, see "Microsoft Knowledge Base" later in this appendix.

- Use the Microsoft Download Service (MSDL) to access the latest technical notes on common support issues for Windows 95 and to access the Windows Driver Library by modem. The MSDL is available by modem at (206) 936-6735, seven days a week, 24 hours a day, including holidays. For more information, see "Microsoft Download Service" and "Obtaining Drivers Electronically" later in this appendix.

- Contact a Microsoft Solution Provider for installation services and follow-up product support. These companies have individuals who have been qualified as Microsoft Certified Professionals on Windows 95. For a referral to a Microsoft Solution Provider in your area, please call Microsoft at (800) SOLPROV (or (800) 765-7768). For more information, see "Microsoft Solution Providers" later in this appendix.

- Get technical support from a Microsoft engineer. Support is available for no charge from a Microsoft PSS engineer, by means of a toll line, for the first 90 days of using Windows 95. The 90-day period begins the day of your first call. Call (206) 637-7098 between 6:00 A.M. and 6:00 P.M. Pacific time, Monday through Friday, excluding national holidays. For support outside the United States, contact your local Microsoft subsidiary.

  After the initial 90-day free period has expired, support is available from a Microsoft PSS engineer and charged by the length of time used or by the occurrence. Call (900) 555-2000 ($2 per minute, $25 cap) or (800) 936-5700 ($25 per incident). For support outside the United States, contact your local Microsoft subsidiary.

  Support for Microsoft TCP/IP for Windows 95 is not available from the standard Windows 95 PSS phone lines. To request TCP/IP support for Windows 95, please contact a Microsoft Solution Provider or enroll in one of the Microsoft fee-based support plans. For further information, call Microsoft Inside Sales at (800) 227-4679.

  Microsoft Text Telephone (TT/TDD) services are available for people who are deaf or hard-of-hearing. Using a special TT/TDD modem, dial (206) 635-4948, between 6:00 A.M. and 6:00 P.M. Pacific time, Monday through Friday. For more information about the accessibility of Microsoft products and services to the deaf or hard-of-hearing, see Appendix I, "Accessibility."

# Hardware Compatibility Information

Microsoft makes available a list of hardware which has been demonstrated to be compatible with Windows 95. For peripherals listed, manufacturers have submitted models for testing by Microsoft Compatibility Labs (MCL); for computers listed, manufacturers have submitted system compatibility testing results to MCL. The hardware compatibility list does not constitute a complete list of computers which currently run Windows 95.

For a current hardware compatibility list, see the WinNews area on CompuServe or The Microsoft Network.

# Windows 95 SDK Information

Developers who are writing applications to run under Windows 95 should obtain the *Win32 Software Development Kit for Windows 95 and Windows NT* (SDK). The SDK is available with a Level-2 subscription to the Microsoft Developer Network. For more information, see "Microsoft Developer Network" later in this appendix.

# Microsoft TechNet

Microsoft TechNet is the comprehensive worldwide information service designed for those who support or educate users, administer networks or databases, create automated solutions, and recommend or evaluate information-technology solutions. For an annual TechNet subscription fee, subscribers receive two compact discs (CDs) per month containing Microsoft Knowledge Base, Resource Kits, up-to-date drivers, and other information. TechNet also maintains a CompuServe forum (**go technet**) for up-to-the-minute news. To subscribe in the United States and Canada, using your credit card, call (800) 344-2121, weekdays, between 6:30 A.M. and 5:30 P.M. Pacific time. For international orders, call (303) 684-0914 (in the United States) for contacts in your area.

# Microsoft Developer Network

Microsoft Developer Network is an annual, two-tiered membership program for developers of applications for the family of Microsoft Windows operating systems. Level-1 members receive four quarterly updates to the Development Library, a source of sample applications and development tools and utilities; six bimonthly issues of the *Developer Network News*; a dedicated CompuServe forum (**go msdn**); and other benefits. Level-2 membership adds four quarterly updates to the Development Platform, offering the latest released versions of Microsoft software and device development kits and operating systems, plus support.

To join the Developer Network in the United States and Canada, call (800) 759-5474, 6:30 A.M. to 5:30 P.M. For local contacts outside North America, call (303) 684-0914.

# Microsoft Solution Providers

Microsoft Solution Providers are independent organizations that provide consulting, integration, development, training, technical support, or other services with Microsoft products. Microsoft equips Solution Providers with information, business development assistance, and tools that help create additional value with Microsoft-based software technology. To locate a Microsoft Solution Provider in your area, or for more information on the Microsoft Solution Provider program in the United States, call Microsoft at (800) SOLPROV (or (800) 765-7768). In Canada, call (800) 563-9048.

# Microsoft Technical Education

Microsoft Authorized Technical Education Centers provide computer professionals with the knowledge required to expertly install and support Microsoft solutions and help prepare individuals for Microsoft Certified Professional exams. Under the Microsoft Certified Professional program, individuals can authoritatively establish that they possess the skills and knowledge to implement and support solutions with Microsoft products.

For more information on the Microsoft Certified Professional program, call Microsoft at (800) 636-7544 in the United States and Canada. For full course descriptions and referral to a Microsoft Authorized Technical Education Center, call (800) SOLPROV (or (800) 765-7768) in the United States and Canada. In other countries, contact the local Microsoft subsidiary.

For the Microsoft Education and Certification Roadmap, see E&CMAP.ZIP from Library 5 of the Solution Provider forum on CompuServe (**go msedcert**).

# Microsoft Consulting Services

Microsoft Consulting Services (MCS) provides services that enable corporations, governments, and other institutions worldwide to design and build client-server applications using Microsoft technology. MCS consultants are experienced in designing custom solutions for order entry, payroll, and a variety of other business functions. For more information, call (800) 426-9400 or the Microsoft Consulting Services office nearest you. For Microsoft Solutions Framework, a reference guide from MCS describing how to build and deploy distributed enterprise systems based on Microsoft tools and technologies, call (206) 703-4MSF (or (206) 703-4673) in the United States, or call the Microsoft Canada Customer Support Centre at (905) 712-0333, extension 7291.

# Microsoft Knowledge Base

Microsoft Knowledge Base (KB) is a primary source of product information for Microsoft support engineers and customers, containing detailed how-to articles, plus answers to technical support questions, bug lists, fix lists, and documentation corrections. Knowledge Base articles are available on CD with a membership in the Microsoft Developer Network or a subscription to Microsoft TechNet, and available online from CompuServe (**go mskb**, or **go mdkb** for the developer Knowledge Base), the Internet, and Microsoft Download Service.

# Microsoft Software Library

The Microsoft Software Library (MSL) is a collection of files pertaining to all Microsoft products, including drivers, utilities, Help files, and Application Notes. Microsoft Software Library files are available online from The Microsoft Network, CompuServe, the Internet, and Microsoft Download Service. You can also get the Microsoft Software Library on CD by becoming a member of the Microsoft Developer Network (MSDN) or by subscribing to Microsoft TechNet.

# Microsoft Download Service

Microsoft Download Service (MSDL) operates in the same manner as any MS-DOS–based computer bulletin board system (BBS). MSDL contains Application Notes, driver files, and other types of support files you might want to download.

To use MSDL, you must have a modem and a terminal package such as Microsoft Works, Windows Terminal, Procomm, or Crosstalk™. If you experience difficulty while you are working with the MSDL, try calling a local BBS so you can avoid paying long-distance charges while trying to determine the cause of the problem. Technical support is not available on the MSDL.

MSDL supports 1200, 2400, 9600, and 14,400 baud rates (V.32 and V.42), with 8 data bits, 1 stop bit, and no parity. After you have chosen these settings, you can begin the session as follows.

▶ **To connect to Microsoft Download Service**

1. Call MSDL at (206) 936-6735.
2. Type your full name and the location you are calling from.
3. At the MSDL Main Menu, type the number of the option you want.

From this menu you can download files, search the file index, view instructions on using MSDL, obtain a Windows driver library update, and obtain other information.

# Microsoft CompuServe Forums

In addition to forums offered for Microsoft TechNet and Microsoft Knowledge Base, Microsoft sponsors a variety of other forums on CompuServe; these forums are known collectively as the Microsoft Connection. Topics for some of these forums include information on Microsoft Corporation, Microsoft services, desktop and development applications, personal and advanced operating systems, shareware, and vendors. For access to the Microsoft Connection, type **go microsoft** at any CompuServe command prompt.

# Obtaining Drivers Electronically

The Windows Driver Library (WDL) is a collection of new and updated printer, display, sound, and network drivers for use with Microsoft Windows. Network drivers on the WDL include NDIS 2 and NDIS 3 drivers for network adapters not included in the Windows 95 retail product. As new and updated files become available, they are added to the WDL.

If you have a modem, the drivers are available electronically for downloading at no charge on services such as Microsoft Download Service (using the File index option in the main menu), CompuServe (using **go msl**), and GEnie (using Software Libraries in the IBM PC/Tandy roundtables menu). However, notice that standard connect-time fees and long-distance telephone charges, if any, apply when you download files. When you connect to any of these services, please read the WDL.TXT for a complete list of the devices the WDL supports.

If you do not have access to a modem, you can obtain an individual driver from the WDL on a disk by calling Microsoft Product Support Services at (206) 637-7098.

When searching for a WDL driver (or a WNTDL driver for Windows NT), you can use any of these keywords:

| | | |
|---|---|---|
| **audio** | **misc** | **S#** |
| **display** | **netcard** | **storage** |
| *manufacturer name* | **printer** | **x86** |
| **mips** | **Q#** | |

▶ **To download a file from the Windows Driver Library**

1. Locate the device in the WDL.TXT file. Make note of the name of the file listed next to the device. You need to download this file from your download service.

2. If you are downloading to a floppy disk, you need to have a formatted blank disk. If you are downloading to your hard disk, create a new subdirectory in which you will place the files.

---

**Important** Do not download files directly into your Windows directory. Doing so could overwrite files essential to the proper operation of your system.

---

3. Follow the downloading procedure used by your downloading service. The file you download is the executable (.EXE) file that you identified in step 1. This file contains all the files you need to support your device.

   Download the .EXE file to your floppy disk or to the new subdirectory you created on your hard disk.

4. Change to the floppy disk drive (or the subdirectory on your hard disk) that contains the .EXE file. At the MS-DOS prompt, type the filename and then press ENTER.

When the .EXE file finishes running, all the files you need to support your device, such as a .DRV (Windows Driver Library) file and the OEMSETUP.INF file, are set up. You also have a .TXT file that contains instructions for installing the device drivers (or other software) and a licensing agreement.

If you have problems extracting files, try downloading the files again.

# Resources for ICM

Eastman Kodak, the supplier of the default color-matching method for ICM in Windows 95, has a wide array of advanced color management technology and products including device profiles which can be used to optimize your system. To get more information, call (800) 752-6567. You can also write to Eastman Kodak, Color Management Group, 164 Lexington Road, Billerica, MA 01821.

# Index

!, FTP command 1138
# (pound sign)
    Device Manager symbol 613
    LMHOSTS file 1228
$ (dollar sign), hiding resources from browsing 401, 406
* (asterisk)
    Device Manager symbol 613
    Windows Explorer shortcut 1233
+ (plus sign)
    storing phone numbers with Phone Dialer 816
    Windows Explorer shortcut 1233
- (minus sign)
    command-line syntax 1098
    Windows Explorer shortcut 1233
-?, getting help on TCP/IP command-line utilities 1136
/ (forward slash)
    command-line syntax 1098
    navigating the Internet with FTP 957
/?, getting help on command-line commands 1095
; (semicolon)
    command-line usage 1097
    including comments in MSBATCH.INF 154, 1159
: (colon), command-line syntax 1098
= (equal sign)
    command-line syntax 1098
    editing MSBATCH.INF 154
\\ (backslashes), UNC path names 407
>, >>, < (redirection symbols), command-line syntax 1098
?, FTP command 1138
| (pipe symbol), command-line syntax 1098
16-bit
    DLLs, core system components 984
    network clients, disadvantages 335
    network provider 998
    processors, troubleshooting Setup B1 error message 238
    WinNet16 interface 335, 1001
24-bit display monitors, multimedia computers 706
32-bit
    address space 976
    cache used by protected-mode redirector 251, 286
    DLLs, core system components 984
    drivers for network protocols and adapters 250
    kernel, performance tuning 554
    network clients, advantages 335
    processors, troubleshooting Setup B1 error message 238
    Win32 SDK information 1258
    Win32 WinNet interface 252, 335, 996
3270 emulators, Client for NetWare Networks support 286
386MAX software utility, troubleshooting Setup 239

3Com network adapters
    File and Printer Sharing 398
    INF file settings 1207

## A

Abbreviations used in Resource Kit xviii
Access
    directory access rights 468
    Internet *See* Internet
    local access control list 469
    NetWare networks
        controlling 406
        Network Neighborhood 381
        Show Dots and file access limits 318
        synchronizing credentials 330
    remote network connections *See* Dial-Up Networking
    restricting *See* Restricting access
    system policies, User-Level Access Control 507, 514
    to File and Printer Sharing, restricting 275, 400, 1198
    to network drives, troubleshooting 696
    to servers, troubleshooting 237
Accessibility features
    customizing Setup with BATCH.EXE 82, 155–157
    general enhancements
        Control Panel support 1240
        emergency hot keys 1240–1241
        online help 1239
        status indicators 1241–1242
        time-out, turns off accessibility functionality 1241
    getting more information 1253
    hard-of-hearing or deaf users
        ShowSounds 1246
        SoundSentry 1246
        WinChat 1247–1248
    low-vision users
        high-contrast color schemes 1234, 1243
        high-contrast mode 1234, 1243
        mouse pointer, customizable display 1242–1243
        recorded documentation 1252
        scalable user interface elements 1242
    making keyboard and mouse input easier
        BounceKeys 1245
        FilterKeys 1234, 1244–1245
        MouseKeys 1234, 1245–1246
        RepeatKeys 1244
        SlowKeys 1244
        StickyKeys 1234, 1244, 1250
        ToggleKeys 1234, 1246

Accessibility features *(continued)*
    MS-DOS–based applications  1251
    overview  1238
    shortcuts  1234
    software development features and guidelines  1249–1250
    supporting alternative input devices
        multiple pointing devices support  1249
        SerialKeys  1249
Accounts
    Internet  945–946
    The Microsoft Network  924, 927
    user *See* User accounts
Acronyms used in Resource Kit  xviii
Adapters
    bus adapter types supported by Windows 95  690
    CD-ROM, safe detection for proprietary adapters  187
    dial-up, network protocol bindings  891, 893, 894, 947
    display *See* Display adapters
    increasing modem speed with UART-based COM port
        adapter  805
    installing legacy modems  802
    network *See* Network adapters
    ROMs *See* ROMs
    SCSI, troubleshooting  637
Add New Hardware wizard
    adding other vendors' telephony drivers  822
    description  600
    enabling PCMCIA cards  615–617
    installing legacy devices  607
    installing legacy modem adapters  802
    lists of supported hardware  603
    recovering from faulty installation of Windows 3.x
        drivers  603
Add Printer wizard
    connecting to NetWare printers  761
    installing printers  758–759
    troubleshooting printer installation  779
Add/Remove Programs option *See* Control Panel
Address books
    customizing fax cover pages  873
    messaging service providers  858
    Microsoft Exchange *See* Microsoft Exchange
    Microsoft Fax  866, 877
    Personal Address Book
        MAPI service provider  835
        overview  839–841
        PAB files, converting  843
    The Microsoft Network  936
Addresses
    address space
        32-bit  976
        virtual memory management  986–987
    Dial-Up Networking  898
    DMA *See* DMA addresses

Addresses *(continued)*
    electronic mail *See* Microsoft Exchange
    I/O *See* I/O, addresses
    IP *See* IP addresses
    linear addressing model  976
    localhost loopback address, HOSTS files  1226
    network adapters included in MACHINES.INI,
        determining for shared installations  140
ADM files, policy templates  518–524
ADMIN$, shared resource for remote administration  532
ADMIN.ADM, default system policy file  518
Administration
    corporate deployment of Windows 95 *See* Deploying
        Windows 95
    managing large networks *See* Microsoft Systems
        Management Server
    remote *See* Remote administration
    system policies *See* System policies
    user profiles *See* User profiles; USER.DAT
Administrative Setup *See* Server-based Setup utility
Advanced Power Management (APM)  99, 640
Advanced SCSI Programming Interface (ASPI)
    APIs  693
    safe drivers  631
Advertising options, browsing on NetWare
    networks  403–405, 409, 411–412
Agents
    backup
        Arcada  541
        Cheyenne ARCserve  542–543
        device IDs for use in setup scripts  1188
        included with Windows 95  540
        NetWare login scripts  366, 377
    Compression Agent  670, 673
    network
        benefits of using protected-mode networking
            components  253
        device IDs for use in setup scripts  1188
        Network Monitor agent  458, 544–546, 1188
    Remote Registry agent
        removing  551
        setting network logon options  374
    SNMP *See* SNMP, agent
    System Agent
        description  670
        running ScanDisk  661
        scheduling tasks  671
    system management
        installing  458
        overview  457
ALT key
    accessibility status indicator  1242
    bringing running applications to the foreground  720

ALT key *(continued)*
  forcing MS-DOS–based applications to run in full-screen
    windows  729
  shortcuts
    accessibility  1234
    for selected objects  1232
    keyboard  1234
  StickyKeys feature  1244, 1250
  switching between command-prompt window and full-
    screen modes  1100
America Online
  finding Internet access providers  945
  obtaining information about Windows 95  1256
  obtaining Windows 95 Reviewer's Guide  39
"Analyzing Your Computer" message  146
Analog video
  *See also* Digital video; Multimedia; Video
  MCI device types  701
Animation
  *See also* Multimedia
  MCI device types  701
APIs
  Advanced SCSI Programming Interface  693
  client-side named pipes  1015
  communication, logical ports supported  602
  defined by Novell, Windows 95 support  285, 304–305
  Image Color Matching  *See* Image Color Matching (ICM)
  locking volumes while running disk utilities  654
  mailslots  1015–1016
  Master Password, password cache overview  470–471
  Messaging application programming interface  *See* MAPI
  National Language Support  1042, 1052, 1054–1055
  Open Datalink Interface (ODI)  309–310
  other vendors' network clients  334
  QMS used by Print Services for NetWare  763
  Registry system administration using RPCs  1021
  Telephony application programming interface  *See* TAPI
  Win16
    communications applications  795, 822
    network provider  998
    WinNet16 interface  1001
  Win32
    remote administration, Windows 95 architecture  968
    running applications  *See* Applications, Win32-based
    WinNet interface  252, 335, 996
  Win32-based communications architecture  795–797
  Windows Sockets IPC implementation  1010–1012
  WinNet16 thunk and translation  339
append, FTP command  1138
Apple Macintosh
  AppleTalk Protocol  908, 1222
  exchanging mail with Windows 95  1222
  File Server for Macintosh  1222
  switching to Windows 95, tips  1223–1224

Apple Macintosh *(continued)*
  Windows NT Services for Macintosh  1222
Applications
  *See also* Programs; Software; Utilities
  adding or removing
    using Control Panel  717
    using Setup  77
  adding or sorting on Start or Programs menus  722, 749
  APPS.INF  *See* APPS.INF file
  "Cannot open file *.INF" error message  239
  caution about changing directory during Setup  86
  closing failed programs  725, 743
  communications  *See* Communications, applications
  container applications (OLE)  740
  customizing settings
    default policy definitions  492
    troubleshooting  527
    with system policy templates  518
    with user profiles  482
  demand paging  556
  developing international versions, documentation  1041
  fixing version-checking errors  747–748
  hardware profiles  617–618
  information contained in machine directories  122
  installing
    APPS.INI file  719
    decisions  716
    INF Installer  157
    sharing across networks  718–719
    with Add/Remove Programs option  717
    with custom setup scripts  157–159
  legacy, loading fonts  777
  Make Compatible utility  746
  memory-resident  *See* TSRs
  Messaging application programming interface  *See* MAPI
  Microsoft Software Library  1260
  migrating settings during Setup  72, 220, 1034–1037
  MS-DOS–based
    accessibility support  1251
    APPS.INF file  726–729, 737–739
    changing code pages  1047–1048
    changing fonts  733
    communications hardware support  602
    configuring memory settings  727–728
    configuring PIF files  718, 726–727, 729–736
    default policy definitions  492
    deferred printing  773
    defining memory allocation  734
    display fonts  785–788
    games  729
    installing with Add/Remove Programs option  718
    modem communications  800, 804, 829–830
    mouse drivers  627
    MS-DOS Mode  *See* MS-DOS Mode

Applications, MS-DOS–based *(continued)*
overview 714–716
preemptive multitasking 745
printing support 773
removing 720
restricting access 513
retaining use of mouse in QuickEdit mode 1101
running in real-mode from shared installations 142
setting paths 736–737
setting properties 729–736
specifying hot keys 731
specifying working directories 731
switching between window and full-screen 1100
system resource capacity 558, 559, 714
technical notes 745
transferring information 1101–1102
troubleshooting 750
TSRs 746
Virtual Machine Manager 973–977
virtual machines (VMs) 745, 973, 990
Windows 95 support 990
NetBIOS *See* NetBIOS programming interface
network Plug and Play support 259
new, updating startup disk 1069
object applications (OLE) 740
opening 720
password cache overview 470–471
removing with Add/Remove Programs option 720
restricting access 513, 527
running *See* Running applications
shortcuts, location of key files 1154
starting *See* Running applications
switching between 1223
system
changes 741
management tools 456
resource capacity 554, 558–560, 714
Systems Management Server software distribution and installation 1218
TAPI-aware 796
that replace system DLLs 748
troubleshooting *See* Troubleshooting, applications
UNC path names *See* UNC names
Win16-based
communications APIs 795, 822, 829
communications hardware support 602
cooperative multitasking 974
deferred printing 773
INI files 968, 1034
mouse drivers 627
overview 715–716
preemptive multitasking 744
removing 720
system resource capacity 558, 559, 714

Applications, Win16-based *(continued)*
technical notes 744
Windows 95 support 990
Win32-based
communications hardware support 602
deferred printing 773
locale IDs 1051
mouse drivers 627
National Language Support (NLS) API 1042
overview 714–716
preemptive multitasking 742, 974
technical notes 742–743
troubleshooting printing 784
using multilingual fonts 1051
Win32 SDK information 1258
Windows 95 support 990
Win32 WinNet interface 252, 335, 996
Windows 95 architecture 990
Windows Sockets *See* Windows Sockets
working directories 719, 731
APPS.INF file
entries 737–739
installing MS-DOS–based applications 718
running MS-DOS–based applications 726, 729
syntax 738
APPS.INI file 719
Arcada backup agent
configuring 541
contacting Conner Peripherals 541
device ID for use in setup scripts 1188
installing 458, 541
required components 541
running 541
Archie
Internet access overview 942
navigating the Internet 960
Architecture, Windows 95
application support 990
communications 795–797
components 966–967
Configuration Manager 970–973
core system components
GDI 987–989
Kernel 986–987
overview 984–985
swap file 987
User 985
user interface 990
virtual memory management 986–987
device drivers 969–970
installable file systems
file system drivers 979
Installable File System Manager 979
overview 977–978

Architecture, Windows 95 *(continued)*
    messaging subsystem  857–858
    multimedia  700
    network *See* Network architecture
    Registry  967–968
    Virtual Machine Manager
        memory paging  975–977
        MS-DOS Mode support  977
        overview  973–974
        process scheduling and multitasking  974–975
Archive attribute
    MS-DOS–based applications  730
    xcopy command-line switches  1120
ArcNet networks
    NDIS drivers, overview  414
    network adapters  314, 1211
    required NetWare-supplied support files  327
Arguments, command-line syntax  1098
arp, TCP/IP utility
    command-line switches  1137
    troubleshooting TCP/IP connections  449–451
ARROW keys
    selecting menu commands  1234
    Windows Explorer shortcuts  1233
Artisoft LANtastic
    copying Windows 95 files to a server  114
    network adapters, INF file settings  1210
    network client device ID  1185
    servers, connecting to  340
    setting up for Windows 95 networking  339–340
    sole network client  337
AS/400, terminal emulation connections  359
ascii, FTP command  1138
ASCII files, transferring with FTP  957–958
Associating file types with applications  721–722, 741, 752
AT modem commands  809, 810–813, 822, 881–882
AT&T StarLAN
    Client for Microsoft Networks, overview  264–265
    File and Printer Sharing  398
ATTACH, NetWare command  391
Attachmate gateway, mainframe connectivity  358
Attributes
    attrib command  221, 1102, 1072
    MS-DOS–based applications  730
    xcopy command-line switches  1120
Audio
    *See also* Digital audio; Multimedia; Sound
    line routing, description  704
    MCI device types  701
    MIDI support  703–704
    mixer controls  704
    purchasing multimedia computers  706–708
    recording, editing, and playing  703–704
    viewing MCI drivers  712

Audio *(continued)*
    Volume Control tool  704
    Windows 95 multimedia architecture  700
Auto-Run, bypassing when inserting CDs  1232
AUTOEXEC.BAT
    backing up before running Setup  78
    changes for Windows 95  210–213
    checking entries  1074
    Client for NetWare Networks settings  299
    configuring computers for shared installations  126–132
    deleting when removing Windows 95  229
    disabling TSRs, drivers, and batch files before running
        Setup  77, 179, 1204
    editing tip  211
    entries now found in IO.SYS  210
    location on compressed disks  1156
    net commands  1106–1107
    NETX settings  317
    optimizing conventional memory  575
    optimizing performance of MS-DOS–based
        applications  729, 732
    processing at startup  197, 205, 209–213
    real-mode DLC protocol
        with IBM LanSupport  356
        with ODI network adapter drivers  354
    removing old mouse driver entries  627
    replacing configuration entries using custom setup
        scripts  1204
    Safe Mode system startup  142
    Safe Recovery option entries  184
    setting up dual boot capabilities with Windows 95 and
        MS-DOS  221
    SNAPSHOT.EXE  127
    startup process for shared installations  139
    troubleshooting strategies  1060
    [Update AutoExec] INF file section  1163
    VLM settings  324
    Windows 3.x settings removed from Windows 95  564
AUTOMATE.INF, customizing Setup for
    accessibility  155–157
Automating Windows 95 installation *See* MSBATCH.INF;
    Push installations; Setup scripts; Microsoft Systems
    Management Server
Automounting, disabling when compressing floppy disks  668
AVI files, description  702
AWP files, public security keys  879

**B**

B-node name resolution  436, 438
B1 error message, troubleshooting Setup  238
Backing up
    Microsoft Exchange Personal folders  844
    Registry backed up on system startup  1024

Backing up *(continued)*
  system configuration files  78, 1069
BACKSPACE key
  editing command line  1099
  going to parent folders, shortcut  1233
Backup
  agents  *See* Agents, backup
  Microsoft Backup overview  656
  minimum backup interval  646
  peer-to-peer networks  267
  system management tools  456, 653
"Bad or missing file" error message  241
Banyan VINES
  copying Windows 95 files to a server  114
  multiple network example  1001
  network client device ID  1185
  networks supported by Windows 95  334
  protocol device IDs  1186
  servers, connecting to  343
  setting up for Windows 95 networking  341–343
BATCH.EXE
  creating custom setup scripts  146
  customizing Setup for accessibility  82, 155–157
  overview  153–154
Batch files
  AUTOEXEC.BAT  *See* AUTOEXEC.BAT
  automating Windows 95 installation  *See* MSBATCH.INF;
    Setup scripts
  Batch Setup
    creating custom setup scripts  146
    customizing Setup for accessibility  82, 155–157
    overview  153–154
  capturing ScanDisk exit codes  1135
  command-line commands  1109–1110
  disabling TSRs and batch files before running
    Setup  77, 179, 1204
  net commands  1106–1107
  NETSTART.BAT  *See* NETSTART.BAT
  running  677, 727, 737
  setup scripts  *See* MSBATCH.INF; Setup scripts
  specifying for MS-DOS–based applications  731, 733
  troubleshooting Setup installation or detection errors  1062
  Windows 95 commands  1102
  Windows Explorer command-line switches  1118
  xcopy command-line switches  1122
Baud rate
  *See also* Speed
  choosing Internet access providers  945
  communications hardware support  602
  configuring modems  805, 812
  international standards for fax communications  869
  Microsoft Download Service (MSDL)  1260
  Microsoft Fax Registry entries  881–882
  network fax service requirements  868

BBSs  *See* Bulletin boards
bell, FTP command  1138
Bernoulli drives
  requirements for installing Windows 95  71
  Windows 95 support  693–694
Billing information, The Microsoft Network  926, 937
binary, FTP command  1138
Binary file transfer
  *See also* Downloading, files; Transferring data
  Dial-Up Networking software and hardware
    compression  903–904
  Direct Cable Connection  886, 916–917
  File Transfer Status utility  932–933
  FTP protocol  955–958
  Microsoft Fax
    digital signatures  877–880
    overview  866–870
    security  877
  Microsoft File Transfer  800, 821
  The Microsoft Network electronic mail  935
  troubleshooting  829, 830
bind rpl, NetWare command  138
Bindery emulation for pass-through security on NetWare
  networks  408, 462, 469–470, 911
Bindings
  binding network adapter drivers to protocols  421
  changing for IPX/SPX-compatible protocol  429
  configuring NetBEUI  445
  Dial-Up Networking  891, 893, 894, 947
  LANA numbers  426
  Novell RIPL.NLM  138
  protocol drivers and network adapters, description  414
  RemoveBinding, MSBATCH.INF parameter  1187
  troubleshooting  448
  updating VxDs bound into monolithic VMM32.VXD  197
BIOS
  booting Plug and Play-compliant devices  196
  display configuration programs  625
  Energy Star Monitor support  625
  hot docking support  591
  incompatible setting, troubleshooting startup  242
  non-Plug and Play, installing legacy devices  604
  Plug and Play
    bootstrapping  196
    hardware profiles  618
    installing legacy devices  604, 607
    loading protected-mode VxDs at startup  199
    requirements  604
    specification  196
  ROM BIOS virus checking, troubleshooting Setup  238
  VESA BIOS Extensions for Power Management  625
Block devices
  I/O Supervisor (IOS)  982–984
  overview  690

Block devices *(continued)*
    safe drivers  631
Block I/O subsystem
    elements provided in Windows 95  690
    overview  981–984
    VFAT driver interaction  979
Boot disks
    *See also* Startup disk
    MS-DOS  227
    remote-boot computers *See* Remote-boot workstations,
        remote-boot disk images
Boot Manager, OS/2
    restoring after Windows 95 installation, tip  227
    troubleshooting Windows 95 installation  240
BOOTCONF.SYS
    creating remote-boot disk images  136
    format of records  138
    parameters  138–139
BootDelay=, MSDOS.SYS entry  204
BootFailSafe=, MSDOS.SYS entry  204
BootGUI=, MSDOS.SYS entry  204
Booting
    *See also* Startup; Startup disk
    boot devices, real-mode drivers  632
    boot drives
        boot sector modified by Setup  183
        modifying after Setup  184
        shared installations  127, 1189
    boot partitions, troubleshooting  239
    dual booting *See* Dual-boot operating systems
    from floppy disks
        configuring AUTOEXEC.BAT  131
        configuring computers for shared installations with
            protected-mode clients  130–131
        configuring computers for shared installations with
            real-mode clients  134
        disk space required for shared installations  111
        files copied to startup disk  131
        installing Windows 95 with setup scripts  124–125
        machine directories  108–109, 122–124
        memory required for shared installations  112
        NDIS 2.x protocol drivers  415
        overview of Server-based Setup  106–107
        startup disk, networking support for shared
            installations  128, 131
        swap file requirements for shared installations  112
    legacy devices  196
    Plug and Play-compliant devices  196
    rebooting computer with CTRL+ALT+DEL  234
    reinstalling real-mode operating system files  1071
    remote-boot *See* Remote-boot workstations
    starting Windows 95 *See* Startup; Startup folder
BootKeys=, MSDOS.SYS entry  204

BOOTLOG.TXT
    description  216
    hard disk location  1155
    location on compressed disks  1156
    sections for determining errors  216–217
    startup information  218
    Startup menu Logged option  1064, 1070
    troubleshooting
        strategies  1062
        VxDs loaded at startup  1075
BootMenu=, MSDOS.SYS entry  204
BootMenuDefault=, MSDOS.SYS entry  204
BootMenuDelay=, MSDOS.SYS entry  204
BootMulti=, MSDOS.SYS entry  204, 221, 225, 243, 1064
Bootstrapping in the BIOS phase  196
BootWarn=, MSDOS.SYS entry  205
BootWin=, MSDOS.SYS entry  205
BounceKeys, accessibility feature  1245
break command  1105, 1107
Briefcase
    Dial-Up Networking overview  886
    installing  73, 918
    synchronizing files  793, 918–920
Broadcast name resolution  436
Broadcasting
    *See also* SAP Advertising
    messages with WinPopup  445–447, 762
Browse Master elections
    designating master browse servers  385
    running Windows 95 *See* Browsing, running Windows 95
Browse servers
    browse list  386–387, 1199
    BrowseMaster, MSBATCH.INF parameter  1197
    for Microsoft networks  384
    MaintainServerList, MSBATCH.INF parameter  1199
    troubleshooting  385, 409
BrowseMaster, MSBATCH.INF parameter  1197
Browsing
    browse servers *See* Browse servers
    file systems on remote computers  532
    network resources
        browse list  386–387, 1199
        Client for NetWare Networks  391–394
        connecting to drive and printer resources  383
        creating desktop shortcut  381
        description  380
        designating browse master  384
        dial-up server security  902
        GetNearestServer broadcasts  412
        hiding resources from browsing  401, 406
        in common dialog boxes  382–383
        managing SAP browsing for NetWare
            networks  403–405, 411–412

Browsing, network resources *(continued)*
net view command 384–385
Net Watcher requirements 532
Network Neighborhood 364, 388–391
on Microsoft networks 384–387
on NetWare networks 388–395
on TCP/IP subnetworks 387, 438
overview 364
role of workgroups in Windows 95 380
Show Dots and file access limits, NetWare
servers 318
troubleshooting 408–411
using other vendors' network clients 334
WANs 366
Windows NT 394–395
Workgroup Advertising 403, 409
workgroup configuration 366
running Windows 95
with Windows for Workgroups 276
with Windows NT 272
with Workgroup Add-on for MS-DOS 277, 386
the Internet
Archie 960
FTP protocol 956–958
Gopher 960
Mosaic 959
overview 940
public domain tools 942, 959–960
Telnet 958
WAIS 960
Web browsers 942
The Microsoft Network 928–934
buffers command 1107
buffers=, IO.SYS entry 203
buffershigh command 1107
Bulletin boards
Internet access overview 941
The Microsoft Network 924, 931–933
Burst-mode
NCPs, Client for NetWare Networks support 286
packets, IPX/SPX protocol 415
turning off support for packet-burst protocol 302
Bus
adapter types supported by Windows 95 690
description 970
device classes 591–592
EISA 594
enumeration
Enum subtree in Hkey_Local_Machine key 1027
illustrated 971
Plug and Play-compliant devices 972
ISA 594
local-bus video, purchasing multimedia computers 706
PCI 596, 706

Bus *(continued)*
SCSI 637, 595
speed, performance tuning 556
VL 596
Buttons
mouse
accessibility status indicator 1242
configuring mouse behavior 628
navigating in Windows 95 Setup 82
taskbar, cycling through, shortcut 1235
used for command-prompt windows 1101
bye, FTP command 1138

**C**

CAB files 1150
Cabinets, Windows 95 distribution disks 1150
Cables
Direct Cable Connection 886, 916–917
thinnet or twisted pair, peer-to-peer networks 266
Caching
CD-ROM cache
*See also* CDFS file system
CDFS supplemental cache 569, 695–696
description 567
optimizing 569–570
client-side caching of network data 251, 286
disks, optimizing file system performance 564
NameCache Registry setting 566
passwords *See* Passwords, caching
PathCache Registry setting 566
SMARTDrive installed during Setup 179
VCACHE
description 695
performance tuning 554
VFAT file system 679, 980
Windows 95 architecture, overview 977–978
Calling cards, phones *See* Dialing Properties
Canceling command-line commands 1100
"Cannot open file *.INF" error message 239
CAPTURE, NetWare command 392, 393, 402
Castoff all, NetWare utility 289
cd command 1105, 1138
CD Key identification number 120
CD Player 703
CD-ROM
bypassing Auto-Run, shortcut 1232
cache
*See also* CDFS file system
CDFS supplemental cache 569, 695–696
description 567
optimizing 569
VCACHE driver 980
CDFS *See* CDFS file system

CD-ROM *(continued)*
    changing computer settings in Custom Setup 99–100
    copying Windows 95 files 181–182
    device detection and configuration 66, 88–91, 184–188
    drives
        IDE 691
        purchasing multimedia computers 706–708
        response failure during Setup, troubleshooting 238
        Setup requests new source path, troubleshooting 239
        sharing with NETX or VLM clients *See* SAP
          Advertising
        troubleshooting 637–640, 711
        Windows 95 support 693–694
    hardware required for running Windows 95 69
    loaded at system startup from CONFIG.SYS 630
    multimedia files 702
    peer resource sharing services 97
    running Server-based Setup 115
    safe detection for proprietary adapters 187
    SCSI translator drivers 692
    sharing drives 365, 402
    starting Windows 95 Setup
        from MS-DOS 80
        from Windows 3.x or Windows for Workgroups 79
    startup disk limitations 181
    system management tools 456
CDFS file system
    description 678
    IOS.INI entry 633
    multimedia overview 702
    optimizing CD-ROM cache 567–568
    overview 980
    supplemental cache 569, 695–696
    troubleshooting display adapters 640
    VCACHE driver 980
Certificate of Authenticity, product ID number 88
Certified Professional program 1259
Challenge-Handshake Authentication Protocol 913, 950
CHANGECP.EXE 1047–1048
Characters
    *See also* Fonts
    case sensitivity
        HOSTS files 1226
        TCP/IP command-line switches 1136
    character sets
        changing code pages 1047–1048
        changing language 1051
        Choose Font dialog box 1051
        command-line commands 1110
        Windows 95 multilingual support 1048–1051
    computer names 98
    configuring desktop display settings 624
    conventions used in this manual xvii
    DNS domain names 443

Characters *(continued)*
    global command-line character limit 687
    host names 443
    navigating the Internet with FTP 957
    permitted in long filenames or aliases 680
    printing *See* Fonts
    storing phone numbers with Phone Dialer 816
    workgroup names 98
Charting performance, System Monitor 576–577
Chat rooms, The Microsoft Network 934, 924
chcp command 1102
chdir command 1102
Checkboxes, checking, clearing, or filling Registry options
    with System Policy Editor 496–498
"Checking Your Hard Disk" message 146
Cheyenne ARCserve backup agent
    configuring 543
    contacting Cheyenne 542
    device ID for use in setup scripts 1188
    included with Windows 95 252, 283
    installing 458, 542
    required components 542
    running 543
chkdsk command 1076, 1102
Choose Font dialog box 1051
Classes, devices *See* Devices, classes
Clicking, shortcuts for selected objects 1232
Client access licenses for Windows NT Server 274–275
Client computers
    *See also* Workstations
    configuring
        as clients to fax servers 876
        WinPopup 446
    deciding on the preferred client configuration *See*
        Deploying Windows 95
    description 23
    installing Windows 95 *See* Setup scripts; Server-based
        Setup utility; Shared installations
    migrating from Windows 3.x, example 167–169
    remote *See* Dial-Up Networking; Remote computers
    requirements for user profiles 145
    shared installations
        computers starting from floppy disks, configuring
          network clients 130–131, 134
        computers starting from hard disks, configuring
          network clients 128–130, 134
        MACHINES.INI 140–142
        network adapter addresses 140
        remote-boot workstations 131, 133, 135
        requirements 112
        setmdir command 140–142
Client for Microsoft Networks
    32-bit cache used by protected-mode redirector 251
    accessing resources using Network Neighborhood 381

Client for Microsoft Networks *(continued)*
    as Primary Network Logon client  265, 269, 370
    configuring
        logon validation for Windows NT domains  94
        network logon  370–371
        procedure  268–271
        shared installations for computers starting from hard
          disks  128
    description  250
    enabling logon validation  260
    File and Printer Sharing  *See* File and Printer Sharing
    installing
        File and Printer Sharing  396
        procedure  268
        with other networks  337
    introduction  95
    long filename support  681, 682
    low-memory computers  557
    MSBATCH.INF parameters
        network client device IDs  1185
        [VRedir] section  1198
    multiple network example  1001
    necessary for implementing user profiles on networks  480
    network adapter drivers required for networking support
      for shared installations  111
    network protocols  418
    overview  264–265
    peer-to-peer networks  266–267
    PROTOCOL.INI  277–279
    requirements for user profiles on client computers  145
    restricting access
        policy example  507
        system policy settings  515
    running
        login scripts  374–375
        Windows 95 in a mixed network
          environment  271–277
    setting network logon options with system policies  374
    System Monitor categories and settings  582
    using with NETX network client  308, 314–316
    using with VLM network client  308, 322
    VREDIR.VXD  994
    Windows 95 network architecture  1006
Client for NetWare Networks
    32-bit cache used by protected-mode redirector  251, 286
    as Primary Network Logon client  371–372
    browsing network resources  391–394
    configuring
        maximum packet size, LIP protocol  302
        network logon  371–373
        notes  302
        properties  372
        protected-mode network adapter drivers  297

Client for NetWare Networks, configuring *(continued)*
        setting options  371–372
        setting shell version for OVL files  303
        settings  302–303
        shared installations on computers starting from hard
          disks  129
        shared installations on remote-boot
          workstations  131–133
        turning off packet-burst protocol  302
        with ODI network adapter drivers  298
    description  250
    ensuring user logon capabilities in setup scripts  153
    File and Printer Sharing  *See* File and Printer Sharing
    installing
        after Setup  296
        File and Printer Sharing  396
        protected-mode networking support  253, 294–295
    loading TSRs  377
    logon validation  260, 363
    long filename support  681, 682
    low-memory computers  557
    MSBATCH.INF parameters
        network client device IDs  1185
        [NWRedir] section  1196–1197
    multiple network example  1001
    necessary for implementing user profiles on networks  480
    NetWare API support  304–305
    network adapter drivers required for networking support
      for shared installations  111
    network protocols  418
    optimizing network performance  573
    overview  284–286
    printing to NetWare print queues  283
    reasons to choose or not to choose  287–288
    redirector  295
    required support files  300–301
    requirements for user profiles on client computers  145
    restricting access with system policies  507, 514
    running
        login scripts  376–378
        NetWare utilities  305
    setting
        NetWare search mode  328
        network logon options with system policies  373
    specifying browsing preference  403
    storing Point and Print information on NetWare
      servers  760–761
    summary of settings  299
    support for shared installations  139–140
    System Monitor categories and settings  582
    troubleshooting  329–330
    using Print Services for NetWare  756
    Windows 95 network architecture  1008

Clients
DHCP
Dial-Up Networking connections to Shiva
servers 908, 911
TCP/IP protocol, description 416, 432–433
dial-up *See* Dial-Up Networking
Internet access *See* File Transfer Protocol (FTP); Telnet
messaging 858
Microsoft Exchange
*See also* Microsoft Exchange
changing view 839
configuring during Setup 104
installing 837
overview 832–836
setting up 836–837
starting 838
Windows 95 communications overview 792
network *See* Network clients
peer-to-peer networks 266–267
protected-mode, configuring computers for shared
installations 126–133
real-mode, configuring computers for shared
installations 134–135
Systems Management Server requirements 1216–1217
WINS 416, 432
Clipboard, international language support 1042
Clipbook Viewer, sharing OLE objects 740
close, FTP command 1138
Closed-captioned, accessibility feature 1246
Closing
desktop windows 1224
failed programs 725, 743
folders, shortcut 1232
System Agent 672
windows, shortcut 1232
cls command 1102
Coax cabling, Thinnet 266
Coaxial adapters, connecting to hosts 360
Code pages
changing 1047–1048
command-line commands 1110
country command 1107
local editions of Windows 95 1040–1041
used by MS-DOS 1047–1048
Colors
bits per pixel-to-colors conversion 620
customizing
with system policies 492, 511
with user profiles 482
display
configuring desktop 624
high-contrast color schemes 1234, 1243
resolution and color modes 623–624
SVGA, purchasing multimedia computers 706–708

Colors *(continued)*
editing performance charts 577
Image Color Matching *See* Image Color Matching (ICM)
troubleshooting applications 750
COM ports
*See also* Ports, communications; Ports, serial
configuring 628–630
description 629
I/O addresses assigned to communications devices 629
installing modems
configuring options 805
configuring ports 803
increasing external modem speed with UART-based
COM port adapter 805
legacy modem adapters 802
troubleshooting 822, 826–827
listed in Device Manager 629
Plug and Play-compliant 629
COMM.DRV, Win16-based communications
driver 795, 822, 829
comm.drv=, SYSTEM.INI entry 214
"command" command 1102
COMMAND.COM
deleting when removing Windows 95 230
hard disk location 1155
location on compressed disks 1156
modifying boot drive after Setup 184
program properties dialog box 206
reinstalling real-mode operating system files 1071
restoring 1072–1073
setting up dual boot capabilities with Windows 95 and
MS-DOS 221
startup process for shared installations 139
Command-line commands
*See also specific command names*
batch file commands 1109–1110
built-in Windows 95 commands 1102–1105
canceling 1100
checking
free disk space 1076
TEMP variable 1077
command symbols 1098
CONFIG.SYS files 1107–1109
conventions used in this manual xvii
editing 1099
extracting Windows 95 installation files 1150–1152
getting help 1095
increasing keyboard buffer character limit 687
international settings 1110
location of key files 1154
net commands
listed 1106–1107
switches 1098
troubleshooting network installation 262

Command-line commands, net commands *(continued)*
    used in NetWare login scripts 392–394
  not included in Windows 95 1111
  pausing 1100
  reinstalling real-mode operating system files 1071
  restoring COMMAND.COM 1072
  scheduling programs with System Agent 677
  switches 1098
  syntax 1097–1099
  troubleshooting Setup installation or detection errors 1062
Command prompt
  browsing network resources 384–385
  changing passwords on NetWare servers 474
  checking
    memory 236
    removal of real-mode mouse drivers 627
  commands *See* Command-line commands
  copying configuration files to startup disk 1069
  defragmenting disks 658
  external Windows 95 commands 1102
  formatting hard disks 651
  full-screen mode 1100
  getting help on command-line commands 1095
  internal Windows 95 commands 1102
  keyboard buffer character limit 687
  removing Windows 95 227–233
  running
    LFNBK utility 687
    ScanDisk 661
    Server-based Setup 115
    Setup with setup scripts 125
  Setup command-line switches 80
  Startup menu options 1064, 1066
  troubleshooting network installation 262
  viewing NetWare servers 392
  windows, transferring information 1100–1102
Command shells, loading from CONFIG.SYS 206
Commands
  alternative, placing on context menus, shortcut 1232
  AT modem commands 809–813, 822, 881–882
  batch files 1109–1110
  built-in Windows 95 commands 1102–1105
  CONFIG.SYS files 1107–1109
  keyboard, shortcuts 1234
  context commands for NetWare servers 390
  managing NetWare server connections 391–394
  MCI commands 701
  MS-DOS *See* Command-line commands
  NetWare *See specific command names*
  The Microsoft Network Go commands 931
  used at command prompt *See* Command-line commands
Comments
  including in MSBATCH.INF 154
  INF files 1159

Comments *(continued)*
  rem command 1108
Common Access Method (CAM)
  safe drivers 631
  SCSI devices 693
Common dialog boxes *See* Dialog boxes
Communications
  applications
    configuring ports 628–630
    Dialing Properties 803
    installing modems 792, 801
    setting modem properties 804–808
    Win16-based APIs 795, 822
    Windows 95 hardware support 602
  architecture 795–797
  connection properties 806–808, 815
  devices
    COMM.DRV, Win16-based
      applications 795, 822, 829
    I/O addresses assigned 629
    resources, description 628
    universal modem driver 796
    VCOMM device driver 795–796
    Windows 95 driver model 794
    Windows 95 support 589–591, 602
  Dialing Properties *See* Dialing Properties
  fax *See* Fax; Microsoft Fax
  hardware
    required for running Windows 95 69
    Windows 95 support 602
  IP addresses *See* IP addresses
  IPC
    channel provided for remote administration 532
    Windows 95 network architecture 1010–1016
  MAPI *See* MAPI
  Microsoft Exchange *See* Microsoft Exchange
  modems *See* Modems
  ports *See* Ports, communications
  resources 628
  TAPI 794, 796–797, 800
  terminal emulation applications 359–360
  The Microsoft Network *See* The Microsoft Network
  tools
    Direct Cable Connection 886, 916–917
    HyperTerminal *See* HyperTerminal
    other vendors' dial-up tools 886
    overview 800–801
    Phone Dialer *See* Phone Dialer
    updating files 919
  troubleshooting *See* Troubleshooting, communications
  Windows 95 subsystem 792–794
Communities, SNMP, adding 551
Compact Setup 73

Compose New Fax wizard
   customizing cover pages  873
   running  872
Compressed volume files (CVFs)
   DrvSpace /mount command-line switch  1130
   DrvSpace /unmount command-line switch  1134
   mounting, troubleshooting  697
   overview  662
   running ScanDisk  660
Compression
   data, modem transfer
      configuring  811, 812
      enabling for Dial-Up Networking  897, 903–904, 921
      modem transfer  807
      The Microsoft Network  933
      troubleshooting  823
   disks *See* Disk compression
   IP Header Compression  952
   Microsoft Exchange Personal Folders  844
   SLIP accounts, Internet access  952
Compression Agent data compression application  670, 673
CompuServe
   CompuServe Mail MAPI service provider  836
   finding Internet access providers  945
   Microsoft Certified Professional program  1259
   Microsoft Developer Network (MSDN)  1258
   Microsoft Fax overview  866
   Microsoft forums  1261
   Microsoft Knowledge Base  1260
   Microsoft Software Library  1260
   Microsoft TechNet  1258
   obtaining
      current Novell-supplied files  305, 325–327
      drivers from the Windows Driver Library  1261
      hardware compatibility information  1258
      information about Systems Management Server  1213
      information about Windows 95  1256
      LFNBK utility  685
      patch for sharing or lock violations on NetWare
        servers  291
      RIPL software from Novell  135
      Windows 95 Reviewer's Guide  39
      Windows Sockets specifications  1012
   ordering publications from Microsoft Press  39, 1041
   the Microsoft Connection  1261
   Windows 95 communications overview  792
   Windows 95 technical support  1256
ComputerName, MSBATCH.INF parameter  1188
Computers
   *See also* Workstations
   analyzing during Setup  88–91
   boot drive *See* Boot drive
   changing settings in Custom Setup  99–100
   client *See* Client computers

Computers *(continued)*
   default system policies  493
   device detection and configuration during
      Setup  66, 88–91, 180–181, 184–187
   hardware
      compatibility information  1258
      required for running Windows 95  69
   installing Windows 95 *See* Setup
   laptops *See* Portable computers
   legacy *See* Legacy computers
   local *See* Local, computers
   low-memory
      paging  564
      performance tuning  557
   managing *See* System, management
   Microsoft Compatibility Labs (MCL)  1258
   multimedia, purchase guidelines  706–708
   names
      ComputerName, MSBATCH.INF parameter  1188
      fully qualified domain name (FQDN)  443, 444
      name resolution *See* Name resolution
      naming conventions  98
      required for Windows 95 Setup  68, 98
      setting when installing networking support  257
   non-Plug and Play *See* Legacy computers
   notebooks *See* Portable computers
   number of network connections allowed  251
   peer-to-peer networks  266–267
   Plug and Play-compliant *See* Plug and Play
   remote *See* Dial-Up Networking; Remote computers
   security *See* Security; User-level security
   servers *See* Servers
   shared installations *See* Server-based Setup utility; Shared
      installations
   user profiles *See* User profiles
comspec=, AUTOEXEC.BAT entry  210, 1072
CONFIG.POL system policy file
   *See also* System policies
   automatic downloading  498, 525–526
   description  490
   setting priority levels for groups  503
   troubleshooting  525–526
   vs. SYSTEM.DAT and USER.DAT  479
CONFIG.SYS
   backing up before running Setup  78
   changes for Windows 95  206–209
   checking entries  1074
   commands  1107–1109
   defining expanded memory  203, 734
   deleting when removing Windows 95  230
   device class detection  185
   device= entry *See* device=
   disabling drivers and TSRs before running
      Setup  77, 179, 1204

CONFIG.SYS *(continued)*
   editing tip  207
   entries now found in IO.SYS  202–203
   files= entry  318, 741
   general guidelines for device entries  630
   increasing global command-line character limit  687
   installing new devices  606
   loading EMM386.EXE  1112
   loading hardware profiles and real-mode drivers at
      startup  197
   location on compressed disks  1156
   NETX settings  317
   optimizing conventional memory  575
   optimizing performance of MS-DOS–based
      applications  729, 732
   overriding default values in IO.SYS  203
   processing at startup  197, 206–209
   RAM configuration for Windows 95  235
   real-mode DLC protocol with IBM LanSupport  356
   removing old mouse driver entries  627
   replacing configuration entries using custom setup
      scripts  1204
   safe detection  187
   Safe Mode system startup  142
   setting up dual boot capabilities with Windows 95 and
      MS-DOS  221
   startup disk limitations  181
   system startup with MS-DOS multiple configurations  224
   troubleshooting
      "Bad or missing file" error message  241
      hard disk device drivers  698
      "Standard Mode: Fault in MS-DOS Extender"  239
      strategies  1060
   [Update Config] INF file section  1164
   VLM settings  324
   Windows 3.x settings removed from Windows 95  564
Configuration information
   *See also* System, startup files
   backing up configuration files  1069
   final system configuration phase in Setup  183
   needed for system startup  630
   NET.CFG, NetWare configuration file  311
   networking settings in Control Panel  250, 254
   Plug and Play-compliant devices  180–181
   real-mode network clients  253
   Registry *See* Registry
   replacing configuration entries using custom setup
      scripts  1204
   safe detection  185–186
   setting for shared installations
      protected-mode clients  126–132
      real-mode clients  134–135
   upgrading existing Windows configuration  220, 1021
   Windows 3.x settings removed from Windows 95  564

Configuration Manager
   loading protected-mode VxDs at startup  199
   overview  970–973
Configuring the system  *See* System, configuration
Connections
   automatic reconnection for lost server connections
      Client for Microsoft Networks  270, 370
      Client for NetWare Networks  285
      Windows 95 networking feature  251
   checking connections to network resources  260
   coaxial adapters  360
   connecting to
      Artisoft LANtastic servers  340
      Banyan VINES servers  343
      DEC PATHWORKS printers  344
      IBM OS/2 LAN Server servers  347
      NetWare drives  389
      NetWare printers  761
      NetWare servers with Client for NetWare
         Networks  391
      network printers  759–761
      remote computers  535–539
      remote printers  759–761
      servers using other vendors' network clients  334
      SunSoft PC-NFS servers  347
   Dial-Up Networking  *See* Dial-Up Networking
   Direct Cable Connection  *See* Direct Cable Connection
   host connectivity and Windows 95  349–360
   Internet  *See* Internet, connections
   managing NetWare server connections
      troubleshooting  408–411
      using commands  391–394
      using Windows NT  394–395
   Microsoft Exchange  *See* Microsoft Exchange
   modems  800, 806–813
   NetBIOS, nbtstat utility  1140–1142
   network connection failure during Setup  237
   number of network connections allowed  251
   persistent
      Client for Microsoft Networks  270, 370
      Client for NetWare Networks  305, 391
      connecting to drive and printer resources  383
      connecting to NetWare servers  391
      customizing with user profiles  482
      drive letters  383
      Hkey_Current_User Registry key  1033
   remote  *See* Dial-Up Networking; Remote computers
   server connections, customizing with user profiles  482
   The Microsoft Connection, CompuServe  1261
   The Microsoft Network  *See* The Microsoft Network
   troubleshooting  *See* Troubleshooting, connections
   UNC path names, syntax  407
   Windows 95 communications subsystem  792–794

Console displays
*See also* Applications, MS-DOS–based; MS-DOS
changing code pages 1047–1048
Consulting Services 1259
Container applications (OLE) 740
Control Panel
accessibility features 1240
accessing Printers folder 758
Add/Remove Programs option
adding other vendors' telephony drivers 822
creating a startup disk 1063
installing applications 717
installing mouse pointer schemes 1243
removing applications 720
customizing settings
with system policies 490, 492
with user profiles 482
Display option
changing display drivers 621–622
changing to VGA display driver 636
choosing desktop wallpaper 497
configuring desktop appearance 625–626
configuring display resolution 623–624
customizing user interface elements 1242
overview 619
Keyboard option, selecting alternates 1052–1053
Mail And Fax option
adding Microsoft Exchange profiles 847
adding service providers to Microsoft Exchange
client 838
configuring Microsoft Exchange addressing and
delivery options 842
configuring Microsoft Mail for remote access 853
Modems option
choosing hardware compression 904
installing modems 792, 802
ports listed in Device Manager 629
viewing modem properties 804
Mouse option, configuring mouse behavior 628
Multimedia option, viewing audio MCI drivers and sound
card properties 712
Network option
checking network components 261–262
configuring DNS name resolution 442
configuring network adapters 420–425
configuring network components 250, 254
disabling network adapters 574
displaying, shortcut 254
installing drivers and protocols 419
installing networking components 255
network adapter resource information 1076
setting computer and workgroup names 257, 380
Passwords option
changing passwords 471, 473

Control Panel, Passwords option *(continued)*
disabling user profiles 486
enabling remote administration manually 533
enabling user profiles 485
synchronizing logon passwords 472
Regional Settings option 1043–1044
related options in WRKGRP.INI files 164
restricting access 506, 509–510
restricting user actions *See* System policies; User profiles
Sound option 703
SYSDETMG.DLL, hardware detection modules 190
System option
adjusting virtual memory swap files 563
changing graphics performance settings 570
checking device configuration 1075
checking virtual memory allocation 1076
creating hardware profiles 618
determining whether drivers are running in real mode
or protected mode 630
displaying Device Manager 592
enabling ECP support 772
file system troubleshooting options 569–570
optimizing hard disk performance 565
performance tuning 555
removing protected-mode drivers 1061
reserving drive letters for removable media 652
setting supplemental cache size for CDFS 696
Troubleshooting dialog box 696
troubleshooting display adapters 989
troubleshooting file system errors 1077
tools
checking devices in Device Manager 244
hardware device management 600
system configuration 588–589
updating startup disk after installing Windows 95 181
Controllers
floppy disk 693–694
IDE
Plug and Play functionality 597
Windows 95 support 691–692
SCSI 693
Windows 95 port driver 981
Conventional memory
checking from command prompt 235
optimizing 575
required by Windows 95 234
running MS-DOS–based applications 734, 745
Conventions used in this manual xvii
Converting
filenames of Program Manager groups 183, 245–246
mail message MMF or PAB files to PST format 843
thunking, Windows 95 Kernel 986
Cooperative multitasking 974
copy command 697, 1102

Copying
     configuration files to startup disk 1069
     custom files during Windows 95 installation 1201
     files, shortcut 1232
     information
          command-prompt windows 1101
          xcopy command-line switches 1118–1122
     minimal installation of Windows 3.x DLLs used by
          Windows 95 Setup 81
     objects, shortcut 1232
     Windows 95 files
          technical discussion 181–182
          to a server for shared installations 114–121
Core files damaged or missing, troubleshooting startup 242
country command 1107
Country settings
     *See also* Code pages; International Windows 95
     changing code pages 1047–1048
     changing in Control Panel 1043–1044
     command-line commands 1110
     defining in custom setup scripts 1044–1047
     specifying during Setup 1042–1043
Cover Page Editor, customizing fax cover pages 873
CTRL key
     accessibility status indicator 1242
     canceling command-line commands 1100
     closing failed programs 725, 743
     cycling through pages in properties dialog box 1232
     keyboard shortcuts 1234
     moving focus in properties dialog box 1244
     opening and closing windows 1232
     pausing command-line commands 1100
     rebooting computer 234
     Safe Mode Without Compression startup option 1070
     shortcuts 1232–1233
     StickyKeys feature 1244
ctty command 1102
Currency
     specifying regional settings 1044
     Windows 95 support for local conventions 1055
Current hardware profile *See* Hardware, profiles
Cursors
     configuring mouse behavior 628
     correcting mouse pointer display problems 571
     customizing mouse pointer display 1242–1243
Custom access, specifying directory access rights 468
Custom installations
     Batch Setup
          creating custom setup scripts 146
          customizing Setup for accessibility 82, 155–157
          overview 153–154
     copying custom files, example 1201
     custom setup scripts
          configuring Windows NT logon 370

Custom installations, custom setup scripts *(continued)*
          creating 147–153
          defining Run-Once options 158–159
          examples 1201–1206
          INF Installer 158
          installing applications 157–159
          migrating from Windows 3.x, example 167–169
          parameters *See* MSBATCH.INF, parameters
          running 162–163
          Server-based Setup options 148–153
          specifying regional settings 1044–1047
     customizing detection for NetWare networks 159
     device detection and configuration during Setup 66
     editing MSBATCH.INF 154–155
     enabling user profiles and remote administration,
          example 1201–1203
     installing other software 157–159
     introduced 144
     issues 145
     Make Script button 147
     migrating from Windows 3.x, example 167–169
     replacing configuration entries, example 1204
     setup script methods 146
     user profiles and policy files 166
     WRKGRP.INI files 164–166
Custom Setup
     Advanced Options dialog box 145
     batch installation *See* BATCH.EXE; Custom installations;
          MSBATCH.INF; Setup scripts
     changing computer settings 99–100
     disk space required 69, 87
     installing
          Client for Microsoft Networks 337
          File and Printer Sharing 396
          Novell-supplied client support 306–308, 320–321
          protected-mode networking support 253
     introduced 73
     retaining Windows 3.x Program Manager 724
     selecting
          network components 93–97
          Setup type 87
     skipping detection of certain hardware 89, 186, 191
Custom setup scripts *See* Custom installations
Customizing
     applications
          with system policy templates 518
          with user profiles 482
     desktop *See* Desktop, customizing
     detection for NetWare networks 159
     fax cover pages 873
     Network Neighborhood with system policies 382
     Setup for accessibility requirements 82, 155–157
     user interface elements 1242

Customizing *(continued)*
  Windows 95
    *See also* Custom installations
    components that cannot be skipped or
      customized  145
    device detection and configuration during Setup  66
    setup scripts  *See* MSBATCH.INF; Setup scripts
    user profiles and policy files  166
    WRKGRP.INI files  163–165
Cutting objects, shortcut  1232
CVFs  *See* Compressed volume files (CVFs)

**D**

DAT files
  backing up before running Setup  78
  SYSTEM.DAT  *See* System policies; SYSTEM.DAT
  USER.DAT  *See* User profiles; USER.DAT
Data
  backing up  *See* Backup
  compression  807
    *See also* Disk compression
    modem transfer  811, 812, 823
  sharing using OLE  739–740
  specifying regional settings  1044
  transferring
    *See also* Binary file transfer; Microsoft File Transfer
    binary files  *See* Binary file transfer
    Dial-Up Networking software and hardware
      compression  903–904
    Direct Cable Connection  886, 916–917
    File Transfer Status utility  932–933
    FTP protocol  955–958
    HyperTerminal  *See* HyperTerminal
    protocols supported by HyperTerminal  814, 829
    setting modem properties  804–808
    TAPI  *See* TAPI
    troubleshooting communications  822–830
    Windows 95 communications overview  794
  types, Registry value entries  1024
  Windows 95 support for local conventions  1055
Data Link Control  *See* DLC protocol
date command  1103
DblSpace  *See* DoubleSpace disk compression software
DblSpace=, MSDOS.SYS entry  205
DCI  *See* Display Control Interface (DCI)
Deaf or hard-of-hearing users  *See* Accessibility features, hard-
  of-hearing or deaf users
debug command  1103, 1138
DEC network adapters, .INF file settings  1208
DEC PATHWORKS
  accessing servers and resources from Windows 95  276
  Client for Microsoft Networks, overview  264–265
  copying Windows 95 files to a server  114

DEC PATHWORKS *(continued)*
  DECnet protocol  345
  File and Printer Sharing  398
  networks supported by Windows 95  334
  printers, connecting to  344
  setting up for Windows 95 networking  344–346
  versions supported by Windows 95  94
DEC PrintServer Software  766
DECnet protocol
  alternatives  345
  device IDs for use in setup scripts  1186
Default
  computer policies  493
  device classes  605
  gateway
    configuring TCP/IP  435
    HOSTS file  1226–1227
    mapping remote host names to IP
      addresses  1226–1227
  IO.SYS values, overriding  203
  language, changing  1052
  MSDOS.SYS values  206
  setup script  *See* MSBATCH.INF; Setup scripts
  user policies
    default policy definitions  492–493
    editing  501–503
DefaultProtocol, MSBATCH.INF parameter  1187
Deferred printing  *See* Printing, deferred
defrag command  1103, 1123
Defragmenting disks
  before running Setup  78
  command-line switches  1123
  ContigFileAllocSize Registry setting  567
  Disk Defragmenter  *See* Disk Defragmenter
  locking volumes while running disk utilities  654
  procedure  657–658
  troubleshooting printing  783
del command  1103
DEL key, deleting objects  1232
delete, FTP command  1139
Deleting
  compressed drives, DrvSpace command-line
    switches  1129
  files and directories
    Recycle Bin  655, 1223
    when removing Windows 95  229, 232
  hardware profiles  618
  logical drives  649
  NetWare drive and print connections  393
  objects, shortcuts  1232
  partitions  649
deltree command  1103
DELTREE.EXE, removing Windows 95  229–232

Deploying Windows 95
    checklists  20
    conducting the pilot rollout  32–33, 56–57
    deciding on the preferred client configuration  23–29, 44
    finalizing rollout plans  34, 58
    ideal configuration, key features  44–45
    installing Windows 95 using Systems Management
      Server  *See* Microsoft Systems Management Server
    other optional features  48–49
    overview  19–20
    performing lab tests and evaluations  29–31, 49–52
    planning the pilot rollout  31–32, 52–56
    recommended features for network clients  45–48
    reviewing Windows 95 features  21, 39
    rolling out Windows 95  35
    teams  20–23, 41–43
Description, MSBATCH.INF parameter  1188
Desktop
    configuring appearance  624–626
    customizing
        hiding all items  508, 513
        installing applications  716
        Microsoft Plus! enhancements  671
        with system policies  490, 492, 504, 507, 511, 526
        with user profiles  482, 486
    Energy Star Monitor screen savers  625
    enforcing mandatory configuration  166
    information contained in machine directories  122
    shortcuts  *See* Shortcuts, desktop
    troubleshooting applications  750
    Windows 95 vs. Apple Macintosh  1223
Desktop folder  483–484
Destination path, setting in Server-based Setup  117–118
DETCRASH.LOG
    creation  191
    running Setup Safe Recovery option  1062
    using  187
Detecting hardware
    Auto-Detect option  190, 588
    customizing detection for NetWare networks  159
    DETCRASH.LOG  187, 1062
    DETLOG.TXT  187, 190–194, 1062, 1155
    during Setup  66, 88–91, 180–181, 184–187
    enabling PCMCIA cards  614–617
    hardware profiles  617–618
    modems
        Install New Modem wizard  801
        troubleshooting  823–824
        Windows 95 features  800
    MSDET.INF, detection modules  190
    NETLOG.TXT  194–195
    Plug and Play-compliant and legacy devices  185
    Registry role  967
    safe detection  *See* Safe detection

Detecting hardware *(continued)*
    system configuration overview  588–589
    system devices, DETLOG.TXT entries  192
    troubleshooting  190–194, 238, 698, 1062
DETLOG.TXT
    description  190–191
    detecting network adapters  192
    detecting system devices  192
    entries  191–193
    hard disk location  1155
    I/O addresses checked  193
    location on compressed disks  1156
    Plug and Play-compliant devices  194
    skipping detection of certain device classes  191
    troubleshooting strategies  1062
    using  187
Device drivers  *See* Drivers
Device Independent Bitmaps (DIBs)  988
Device Manager
    changing
        device drivers  610–612
        display drivers  621
        mouse drivers  627
        PCMCIA memory window  616
        resource settings  608–613
    checking
        device configuration  1075
        devices  244
        display drivers  635
    communications ports  629
    configuring devices manually  604
    description  590, 600
    device symbols  613
    enabling hardware profiles  618
    enhanced PCMCIA support  616–617
    MSDET.INF, detection modules  190
    recovering from faulty installation of Windows 3.x
      drivers  603
    removing protected-mode drivers  1061
    running  609
    troubleshooting resource conflicts  609, 1075
    viewing hardware tree  592
    Windows 95 device classes  591–592
device=
    CONFIG.SYS entry
        commands used for loading drivers  1109
        compared to Registry interaction  1021
        description  1107
        determining partition types  647
        loading EMM386.EXE  1112
        troubleshooting startup  241, 243
    SYSTEM.INI entry
        caution for port drivers  694
        entries added  214

device=, SYSTEM.INI entry *(continued)*
 initializing I/O Supervisor 983
devicehigh command 1107
DevicePath, MSBATCH.INF parameter 1177
Devices
 Advanced Power Management (APM) support 99, 640
 block devices
  I/O Supervisor (IOS) 982–984
  overview 690
  safe drivers 631
 boot devices, real-mode drivers 632
 CD-ROM *See* CD-ROM
 changing computer settings in Custom Setup 99–100
 changing resource settings
  Plug and Play-compliant devices 608
  with Device Manager 608–613
  with Registry Editor 614
 checking in Device Manager 244
 classes
  configuring 605
  examples 591–592
  fax modems, international standards 869
  general INF file format 1158–1159
  INF file sections 1159–1171
  skipping detection 186, 191
  System subtree in Hkey_Local_Machine 1030–1032
 communications *See* Communications, devices
 configuring manually with Device Manager 604
 configuring network adapter resource settings 421–424
 detection and configuration during
  Setup 66, 88–91, 180–181, 184–187
 device not recognized, troubleshooting startup 244
 Devicepath, MSBATCH.INF parameter 1177
 disk devices
  troubleshooting 698
  Windows 95 support 589–591, 690–691
 docking, Windows 95 support 600–602, 693–694
 drivers *See* Drivers
 Enum subtree in Hkey_Local_Machine key 1027
 hardware profiles 617–618
 ID values
  installing devices 606, 1158
  network components, MSBATCH.INF
   parameters 1184–1188
  Nibble mode 597
  PCMCIA devices 596
  Plug and Play-compliant devices 595
  SCSI devices 594
 identifying performance problems with System
  Monitor 578–583
 INF files *See* INF files
 installing 606–607
 ISA 197, 594
 LastDrive=, NETX 318

Devices *(continued)*
 LastDrive=, VLM 324
 legacy
  Add New Hardware wizard 607
  changing resource settings 608–613
  computers *See* Legacy computers
  installing on computers with non-Plug and Play
   BIOS 604
  installing with Add New Hardware wizard 607
  ISA cards 594
  jumpers and switches 613
  mouse drivers 627
  Registry role 590
  safe detection 185
  starting 196
  Windows 95 communications subsystem 794
 management tools 600
 MIDI, configuring 104
 multimedia
  detection and configuration during
   Setup 66, 88–91, 184–187
  device classes 605
  MCI device types 701
  Media Control Interface (MCI) 701
  troubleshooting 710–712
  Windows 95 support 703
 overview 604–606
 PCI 596
 PCMCIA
  *See also* PCMCIA cards
  enabling 614–617
  Hkey_Dyn_Data Registry key 1022, 1033
  installing 591
  overview 595–596
  Registry information 1021
 Plug and Play-compliant *See* Plug and Play
 pointing devices *See* Mouse; Pointing devices
 removable media devices *See* Removable media drives
 SCSI
  Advanced SCSI Programming Interface 693
  block device drivers 690
  bus adapter types supported by Windows 95 690
  Common Access Method 693
  loading dynamic drivers at startup 198–199
  overview 595
  safe detection 186
  troubleshooting 637–639
  Windows 95 support 692–693
 support in Windows 95 589–591
 troubleshooting *See* Troubleshooting, device configuration
 VL 596
DHCP
 clients, TCP/IP protocol 416, 432–433
 Dial-Up connections to Shiva servers 908, 911

DHCP *(continued)*
  MSBATCH.INF parameter 1193
Diagnostics
  diagnostic servers, establishing 262
  Modem Diagnostics tool 822–823
Dial-Up Networking
  accessing
    Internet *See* Internet
    network resources 898
    remote OLE objects 898
  configuring dial-up adapter bindings 894, 947
  connection protocols
    *See also specific protocol names*
    installing 894
    supported by Windows 95 887, 890–892
  connections
    defining 894–895
    enabling software and hardware
      compression 897, 903–904, 921
    logging on 897
    managing 898
    NetWare Connect servers 907–908
    password encryption 896–897, 902–903, 951
    PPP servers 951–952
    Registry key 895
    Shiva servers 908–912
    shortcuts in Custom Network Neighborhood 382
    SLIP servers 952–954
    troubleshooting 921
    Windows NT remote access servers 904–905
  decisions 887
  deploying Windows 95 49
  description 885
  dial-up clients
    assigning IP addresses for Shiva connections 911
    configuring 893, 896–897, 905–907
    types supported by Windows 95 889, 899
  dial-up servers
    configuring 893, 899–901
    connection limits 887
    disabling support 901
    disconnecting users 901
    Internet access *See* Internet
    sharing resources 887
    troubleshooting 921
    types supported by Windows 95 889
  dialing modems manually 808
  Dialing Properties *See* Dialing Properties
  disabling prompt 898
  displaying terminal window 809, 895
  hardware requirements 69, 886
  installing 892
  Internet access
    making connections 950–954

Dial-Up Networking, Internet access *(continued)*
    overview 940–942
    PPP servers 951–952
    SLIP servers 952–954
  Make New Connection wizard
    configuring dial-up servers and clients 893
    configuring Microsoft Mail for remote
      access 853–855
    creating connections 894
  overview 885–892
  Point-to-Point protocol *See* Point-to-Point protocol (PPP)
  remote access servers *See* Remote access servers
  restricting access 506, 515
  security
    configuring dial-up servers 900
    options 902
    share-level 903
    Shiva remote access servers 911
    user-level 900, 902–903
  troubleshooting 920–922
  Windows 95 communications overview 793
  Windows 95 mobile computing features 915
Dialing Properties
  *See also* Communications; Modems; Phone systems
  defining calling card rules 819–821
  defining calling locations 818
  description 817
  setting location information 803, 895
  TELEPHON.INI file 817
Dialing, phones *See* Phone Dialer
Dialog boxes
  Choose Font dialog box 1051
  common
    browsing 382–383
    creating folders 382
    shortcuts 1233
  logon, displayed at system startup 379
  moving focus 1244
  running applications 720
dibeng.drv=, SYSTEM.INI entry 214
Digital audio
  *See also* Audio; Multimedia
  MCI device types 701
  MIDI support 703–704
Digital signatures, Microsoft Fax security 877–880
Digital video
  *See also* Multimedia; Video
  AVI files 702
  determining format of clips 705
  Display Control Interface (DCI) 702
  MCI device types 701
  playing and recording 705
  Windows 95 multimedia device support 703

dir command
    checking free disk space  1076
    compressed drives  662
    description  1103
    FTP command  1139
    troubleshooting SCSI devices  639
Direct Cable Connection
    compatible cables  917
    description  916
    installing  917
    introduced  886
    updating files  919
    Windows 95 communications overview  793
    wizard  917
Direct memory access (DMA)  *See* DMA addresses
Directories
    browsing FTP sites, Internet access  956
    choosing Windows directory during Setup  85–86, 1178
    deleting
        Recycle Bin  655, 1223
        when removing Windows 95  228, 231
    [DestinationDirs] INF file section  1166–1168
    dir command
        description  1103
        troubleshooting SCSI devices  639
    directory structure created by Setup  121, 1153
    home directories  *See* Home directories
    machine directories  *See* Machine directories
    Microsoft Mail postoffice structure  851
    missing or corrupted Start Menu directory  749
    NetWare user accounts  487
    root directory, long filenames  685, 697–698
    shared
        connecting to network resources  383
        File and Printer Sharing configuration  400, 406
        share-level security  466
    sharing  *See* Sharing resources
    Show Dots and file access limits, NetWare servers  318
    specifying directory access rights  468
    TEMP files  *See* TEMP files
    working directories
        *See also* Machine directories
        creating shortcuts  719
        specifying for MS-DOS–based applications  731
    xcopy command-line switches  1118–1122
Disable SAP Advertising policy  411
Disabling
    automatic NetWare login  474, 514
    automounting when compressing floppy disks  668
    Dial-Up Networking  515
    Dial-Up Networking prompt  898
    dial-up server support  901
    drivers
        before running Setup  77, 179, 1204

Disabling, drivers *(continued)*
        Step-By-Step Confirmation startup
            option  1068–1069
    emergency hot keys  1241
    Enhanced Metafile Format (EMF)  768
    File and Printer Sharing  516
    Find command  513
    MS-DOS Mode warning  732
    MS-DOS prompt  513
    NetWare messages during Server-based Setup  289
    network adapters, optimizing network performance  574
    password caching  471, 515
    protected-mode drivers, optimizing file system
        performance  568
    Registry editing tools  513, 1020
    roving user profiles  487
    Run command  508, 513
    Shut Down command  513
    spooling  781
    TSRs
        before running Setup  77, 179, 1204
        troubleshooting strategies  1073
    user profiles  486
disconnect, FTP command  1139
Disconnecting
    from Internet hosts  958
    users from dial-up servers  901
Disk compression
    *See also specific utility names*
    caution  646
    changing free space and estimated compression
        ratio  669–670, 1131
    command-line switches  *See* Command-line commands;
        DoubleSpace disk compression software
    compressed volume files (CVFs)  660, 662, 697
    Compression Agent  670, 673
    defragmenting disks  78, 657
    drivers
        changing drive size  667
        requirements for installing Windows 95  71
        required for system startup  1074
        unsafe  631
    DriveSpace 3 compression manager  675–677
    extracting Windows 95 installation files  1150–1152
    guidelines for fine-tuning compression  674
    host drives  662
    Microsoft Plus! enhancements  670, 672
    removing Windows 95  230, 232
    Safe Mode Without Compression startup  1066, 1070
    setting up dual boot capabilities with Windows 95 and
        MS-DOS  221
    swap files  562, 664
    troubleshooting  239, 697
    uncompressed size of drives displayed by Fdisk  649

Disk compression *(continued)*
    using DriveSpace 663–670
    Windows 95 distribution disks 1150
    Windows 95 utilities 645
Disk Defragmenter
    command-line switches 1123
    compressed drives 657, 670
    defragmenting disks 657–658
    description 645
    locking volumes while running disk utilities 654
    optimizing disk I/O 646
    performance tuning tool 555
    scheduling with System Agent 676
    troubleshooting printing 783
Disk space
    compressing data *See* Disk compression; DriveSpace disk
        compression software
    defragmenting compressed hard disks before running
        Setup 78
    disk management tools
        command-line switches 1123–1135
        overview 653
    freeing by using Recycle Bin 655
    insufficient
        "Not Enough Disk Space" message 146
        troubleshooting printing 783
        troubleshooting Setup 240
        troubleshooting startup 1076–1077
    limited, Compact Setup 73
    omitting minimum disk space check during Setup 81, 87
    required for installing
        Dial-Up Networking 886
        Microsoft Mail workgroup postoffice 833
        Windows 95 69, 87, 92
    requirements for shared installations 111
    troubleshooting access problems to network drives 696
diskcopy command 1103
Disks
    caching
        CDFS supplemental cache 569, 695–696
        optimizing file system performance 564
        SMARTDrive installed during Setup 179
        VCACHE 554, 679, 695, 980
    checking and defragmenting before running Setup 78
    chkdsk command 1102
    compression *See* Disk compression
    defragmenting *See* Defragmenting disks; Disk
        Defragmenter
    disk devices
        device classes 605
        troubleshooting 698
        Windows 95 support 589–591, 690–691
    drive response failure during Setup, troubleshooting 239
    file systems *See* File systems

Disks *(continued)*
    floppy, drives booting from *See* Floppy disks
    hardware required for running Windows 95 69
    management utilities
        command-line switches 1123–1135
        Microsoft Backup 656
        Microsoft Plus! 670–671
        overview 653
        provided with Windows 95 645
        Recycle Bin 655
        Registry APIs 1021
        troubleshooting 696
        volume locking 654
        Windows 95 volume tracker 652
    mirroring, unsafe drivers 631
    MS-DOS boot disks 227
    PCMCIA drivers 596
    remote-boot disk images 132, 135–137
    scanning for errors *See* ScanDisk
    space *See* Disk space
    startup disk *See* Startup disk
    troubleshooting
        *See also* Defragmenting disks; Disk Defragmenter
        checking for disk corruption 1077
    Windows 95 distribution disks 1150
    Windows 95 volume tracker 652
Display
    adapters *See* Display adapters
    changing computer settings in Custom Setup 99–100
    correcting mouse pointer display problems 571
    desktop appearance, configuring 619, 625–626
    device detection and configuration 66, 88–91, 184–187
    drivers *See* Display adapters, drivers
    hardware required for running Windows 95 69
    high-contrast color schemes 1234, 1243
    MSBATCH.INF parameters 1181, 1182, 1190, 1191
    processor and bus speed, performance tuning 556
    refreshing in Windows Explorer, shortcut 1233
    resolution
        bits per pixel-to-colors conversion 620
        configuring 623–624
        purchasing multimedia computers 706–708
        troubleshooting 634
    setting graphics compatibility options 570–571
    specifying MS-DOS–based application properties 735
    troubleshooting
        applications 750
        display resolution 634
        Safe Mode startup option 1065–1066
    utilities, running 625
    VESA Display Power Management Signaling 626
Display adapters
    adapter invalid when upgrading to Windows 95 100
    changing refresh rate 625

Display adapters *(continued)*
  changing type 625
  device classes 605
  drivers
    changing 621–623
    changing graphics performance settings 571
    checking with Device Manager 635
    Display Control Interface (DCI) 702
    Energy Star Monitor support 625
    installing and configuring using Setup 77
    installing Windows 3.x versions 622–623, 636
    miniport, performance tuning 556
    overview 619–620
    performance tuning 556
    troubleshooting 634, 635
    Windows 95 support 600–601
  Energy Star Monitor support 626
  graphics performance 571, 783
  purchasing multimedia computers 706–708
  resolution and color modes 623–624
  setting graphics compatibility options 570–571
  troubleshooting 635, 640, 989
  VESA Display Power Management Signaling 626
  Windows 95 support 589–591, 600–601
Display Control Interface (DCI) 702
Display option *See* Control Panel
DISPLAY.SYS, loading in CONFIG.SYS 1109
DisplayWorkstationSetup, MSBATCH.INF parameter 1190
DisplChar, MSBATCH.INF parameter 1181
Distributed computing *See* Interprocess communications
DLC protocol
  connectivity to network printers 350
  device IDs for use in setup scripts 1186
  HDLC, Dial-Up Networking 913
  installing 351
  mainframe connectivity 349–353
  obtaining software 351
  real-mode
    IBM LanSupport 355–357
    with NDIS network adapter drivers 351
    with ODI network adapter drivers 354
  troubleshooting connection problems 360
DLLs
  caution about changing Windows directory during
    Setup 86
  checking file versions 1071
  core system components 984
  device class installers, hardware detection 190
  enabled when starting Microsoft Exchange client 838
  GROUPPOL.DLL, group policies 491, 502
  Image Color Matching *See* Image Color Matching (ICM)
  installing with custom setup scripts 157–159
  keyboard layout, Registry subkey 1030
  NetWare API support 304–305

DLLs *(continued)*
  network providers included with Windows 95 998–1000
  running applications that replace system DLLs 748
  WGPOADMN.DLL 849
  Windows 3.x DLLs used by Windows 95 Setup 81
  Windows Sockets supporting files 1012
  WinNet16 interface 1001
DMA addresses
  assigned to Plug and Play ISA cards 196
  Configuration Manager 971–973
  configuring
    legacy devices 613
    network adapter resource settings 421–424
  device detection and configuration during Setup 180–181
  extended capabilities ports (ECPs) 772
  information included in PROTOCOL.INI 278
  NetWare configuration file *See* NET.CFG
  used by mutiple devices 185
DNS *See* Domain Name System (DNS)
DNSServers, MSBATCH.INF parameter 1194
Docking
  *See also* Portable computers
  cold docking 694
  description 694
  devices, Windows 95 support 591, 693–694
  hardware profiles 617–618
  hot docking
    description 591, 694
    device support in Windows 95 591
    PCMCIA cards 596
    Plug and Play network adapters 142, 251, 259
  loading raster fonts 777
  stations
    description 694
    device support in Windows 95 591
    display driver support 601
    port replicators used as substitutes 694
  warm docking
    description 694
    for Plug and Play network adapters 251, 259
    PCMCIA cards 596
Documentation
  available on audiocassettes and floppy disks 1252
  conventions used in this manual xvii
  foreign language versions of Resource Kit 1041
  ordering publications from Microsoft Press 39, 1041
  overview of this manual xv
  Windows 95 Reviewer's Guide 39
Documents
  attaching to electronic mail messages 845–846
  editing, Windows 95 multilingual support 1048–1051
  faxing *See* Fax; Microsoft Fax
  hypertext, troubleshooting downloading from Internet 962

Documents *(continued)*
  OLE
    audio clips 703
    drag and drop 741
    sharing data between applications 740
  printing
    changing printer settings 763
    fonts 775–777
    Microsoft Fax 793
    procedure 761
    to network printers 762
    troubleshooting 779–784
    viewing waiting documents 762
  saving
    creating folders from within common dialog
      boxes 382
    Windows 95 vs. Apple Macintosh 1224
  synchronizing files with Briefcase 918–920
  Windows 95 vs. Apple Macintosh 1223
Domain Name System (DNS)
  domain name resolution 437, 440–444
  HOSTS file 1226–1227
  Internet connections 946–950
  mapping remote host names to IP addresses 1226–1227
  MSBATCH.INF parameters 1194
  server search order 443
Domains
  checking connections to network resources 260
  DNS *See* Domain Name System (DNS)
  logon
    enabling logon validation 260
    ensuring user logon capabilities in setup scripts 153
    mapping workgroups 164–166
    troubleshooting network installation 260
  MSBATCH.INF parameters 1194
  NetWare 287
  running Windows 95 in a mixed network
    environment 271–277
  suffix search order 444
dos command 1107
DOS *See* DR DOS; MS-DOS
DOS interrupts, running TSRs under Windows 95 746
DOS partitions, deleting 649
dos=, IO.SYS entry 202
doskey command 1103
Doskey, editing command-line commands 1099
DoubleBuffer=, MSDOS.SYS entry 205
DoubleSpace disk compression software
  *See also* Disk compression
  caution 697
  compressing floppy disks 667–668
  description 645
  DrvSpace command-line switches 1124–1134
  removing Windows 95 230, 232

DoubleSpace disk compression software *(continued)*
  requirements for installing Windows 95 71
  swap files 662
DOWN ARROW key, Doskey use 1099
Downloading
  drivers from the Windows Driver Library 1261–1262
  faxes 874
  files
    File Transfer Status utility 932–933
    from the Internet 940, 942, 956–958
    from The Microsoft Network 924, 929, 932–933
  hypertext documents from Internet, troubleshooting 962
  mail
    from service providers in Microsoft Exchange 839
    from The Microsoft Network 935–936
    remote access 852–856
  Microsoft Download Service (MSDL) 1257, 1260–1261
DPMS *See* VESA Display Power Management Signaling
DR DOS
  dual-booting functionality, troubleshooting startup 243
  upgrading to Windows 95 226
Drag and drop
  in Microsoft Exchange
    attaching files or objects to messages 845–846
    switching view 839
  OLE 741
  printing to Microsoft Fax 872
  The Microsoft Network
    downloading files 924
    shortcuts 930
Drive letters
  assigning for removable media 652–653
  host drives
    compressed volumes 662
    compressing floppy disks 667
  NetWare networks 393
  persistent connections 383
  Windows 95 vs. Apple Macintosh 1224
driveparm command 237, 1107
DRIVER.SYS, loading in CONFIG.SYS 1109
Drivers
  adding using Setup 77, 244
  backing up critical real-mode drivers before running
    Setup 78
  block devices
    I/O Supervisor (IOS) 982–984
    overview 690
    safe drivers 631
  CD-ROM
    CDFS file system 569, 678, 695–696
    safe detection for proprietary adapters 187
  changing with Device Manager 610–612
  checking README and SETUP.TXT files for supported
    hardware 77

Drivers *(continued)*
communications devices
COMM.DRV, Win16-based
applications 795, 822, 829
communications architecture 795–797
other vendors' telephony drivers 822
universal modem driver 796
VCOMM 795–796
Windows 95 driver model 794
CONFIG.SYS commands 1109
device classes 591–592
device detection and configuration during
Setup 66, 88–91, 180–181, 184–187
Device Manager list 190, 610
disabling
before running Setup 77, 179, 1204
Step-By-Step Confirmation startup option 1068–1069
disk compression, requirements for installing
Windows 95 71
disk devices
troubleshooting 698
Windows 95 support 690–691
display *See* Display adapters, drivers
DLC protocol driver, printer connectivity 350
dynamically loaded, startup 197–198
file systems
CDFS 980
file system drivers 979
overview 979
VFAT 979–980
from other vendors
installing with custom setup scripts 157–159
troubleshooting startup 244
hardware profiles 617–618
high-speed floppy disk 693
IBM, real-mode DLC 355–357
loaded by
IO.SYS 200
SYSTEM.INI 968
location of key files 1154
MCI, troubleshooting 710–712
Microsoft Software Library 1260
migrating from Windows 3.x, caution 603
mini-driver architecture 589, 969–970 , 988
miniport
*See also* SCSI; Windows NT, miniport drivers
block device drivers 690
MPD extension required 983
performance tuning 556
troubleshooting hard disk device drivers 698
Windows 95 block I/O subsystem 690
Windows 95 subsystem architecture 982
Windows 95 support 692–693
mouse 626–627

Drivers *(continued)*
NDIS *See* NDIS network drivers
network adapters *See* Network adapters, drivers
Network Monitor agent 544–545
network protocol drivers *See* Network protocols, drivers
non-SCSI port drivers 694
obtaining electronically 1261–1262
ODI *See* ODI network adapter drivers
PCMCIA cards
*See also* PCMCIA cards
overview 595–596
pointing devices
overview 626–627
Windows 95 support 602
printers *See* Printer drivers
protected-mode *See* Protected-mode, drivers
real-mode *See* Real-mode, drivers
Registry interaction 1021
required for system startup 1074
safe driver list 631–633
SCSI
Advanced SCSI Programming Interface 693
block device drivers 690
Common Access Method 693
loading dynamic device drivers at startup 198
safe detection 186
Windows 95 support 692–693
sound cards, safe detection 187
static *See* VxDs
system management tools 456
System subtree in Hkey_Local_Machine key 1032
troubleshooting 1061, 1070, 1073
universal driver
description 969
graphics subsystem 988
modems 796
printers 770
unnecessary, removing 1073
unsafe 631
VCACHE 695
virtual device drivers *See* VxDs
Windows 95 port driver 981
Windows Driver Library 1261–1262
Drives
*See also* Disks; Hard disks
Bernoulli
requirements for installing Windows 95 71
Windows 95 support 693–694
boot drives
*See also* Booting, boot drives
modifying after Setup 184
booting from floppy disks *See* Booting, from floppy disks
CD-ROM *See* CD-ROM
checking and defragmenting before running Setup 78

Drives *(continued)*
>   choosing Windows directory during Setup 85–86, 1178
>   lastdrive command 1108
>   compressed *See* Disk compression
>   connecting to *See* Connections
>   defragmenting *See* Defragmenting disks; Disk
>       Defragmenter
>   device classes 605
>   floppy disk drives, troubleshooting 696
>   formatting 650–651
>   hardware required for running Windows 95 69
>   host drives *See* Host drives
>   IDE 691–692, 694
>   LastDrive parameter, NETX 318
>   LastDrive parameter, VLM 324
>   letters *See* Drive letters
>   locking volumes while running disk utilities 654
>   logical
>       creating DOS partitions 650
>       deleting 649
>       IDE drives 691
>   network, mapping *See* Mapping, network drives
>   network, troubleshooting access 696
>   partitioning 647–649
>   PCMCIA drivers 596
>   remote, long filename support 682
>   removable media *See* Removable media drives
>   response failure during Setup, troubleshooting 238
>   size of drives displayed by Fdisk 649
>   startup disk limitations 181
>   system management tools 456
>   Windows 95 volume tracker 652
DriveSpace disk compression software
>   *See also* Disk compression
>   caution 646, 697
>   changing free space and estimated compression
>       ratio 669–670, 1131
>   changing size of compressed drives 1132
>   command-line switches 1124–1134
>   compressing drives 664–666, 1126–1127
>   deleting compressed drives 1129
>   description 645
>   DriveSpace 3 compression manager 671–672
>   formatting compressed drives 1129
>   guidelines for fine-tuning compression 674
>   Microsoft Plus! enhancements 670, 676
>   overview 663–664
>   performance tuning tool 555
>   recommended driver 555
>   removing Windows 95 230, 232
>   requirements for installing Windows 95 71
>   running on drives containing open files 666
>   swap files 562, 664
>   uncompressing drives 667, 1133

DriveSpace disk compression software *(continued)*
>   using with floppy disks 667–668
drvspace command 1103, 1124–1131
DrvSpace *See* DriveSpace disk compression software
DRVSPACE.BIN, reinstalling real-mode operating system
>   files 1071
DrvSpace=, MSDOS.SYS entry 205
Dual-boot operating systems
>   installing Windows 95
>       minimum version required 68
>       running Setup 72
>       with MS-DOS 219, 221
>       with Windows 3.x 219, 221
>       with Windows for Workgroups 219, 221
>       with Windows NT 219, 225
>   removing Windows 95 230, 233
>   troubleshooting startup 243
Dvorak keyboard layouts 1251–1252
Dynamic Host Configuration Protocol *See* DHCP
Dynamically loaded drivers, startup 198

**E**

E-mail *See* Electronic mail
Eastman Kodak, contacting 1262
EBD, MSBATCH.INF parameter 1178
edit command 1103
Editing
>   AUTOEXEC.BAT, tip 211
>   calling cards 819
>   command-line commands 1099
>   CONFIG.SYS, tip 207
>   default system policies 501–503
>   documents, multilingual support 1048–1051
>   HOSTS and LMHOSTS file samples 1225, 1228
>   MSBATCH.INF 154–155
>   OLE objects visually 740
>   performance charts 577
>   Registry *See* Registry, editing
>   remote registries 535–614
>   system policy templates 519
>   USER.DAT 483
Eicon gateway, mainframe connectivity 358
EISA devices 594, 690
Electronic mail
>   *See also* Microsoft Mail
>   address books *See* Address books
>   contacting InterNIC 961
>   Internet access 935, 941, 946
>   Message File Conversion wizard 843
>   messages
>       addressing *See* Microsoft Exchange
>       attaching files or objects 845–846
>       delivering *See* Microsoft Exchange

Electronic mail, messages *(continued)*
 downloading from service providers  839
 encapsulation  861
 exchanging with Apple Macintosh systems  1222
 managing  845
 Personal Folders *See* Microsoft Exchange, Personal
  Folders
 messaging backboning  861
 Microsoft Exchange *See* Microsoft Exchange
 Microsoft Fax *See* Fax; Microsoft Fax
 performing push installations  167
 remote mail *See* Remote mail
 The Microsoft Network
  choosing services  929
  description  924
  downloading  935–936
  using with Microsoft Exchange  935–936
 troubleshooting, tip  838
 Windows 95 communications subsystem  792–794
 Windows 95 messaging subsystem architecture  857–858
Embedded objects *See* OLE
Emergency Startup disk *See* Startup disk
emm386 command  1103, 1111–1117
EMM386.EXE device driver
 allocating memory to MS-DOS–based applications  734
 command-line switches  1111–1117
 defining expanded memory in CONFIG.SYS  203
 loading in CONFIG.SYS  1109, 1112
Emptying Recycle Bin  655
Encryption
 data, unsafe drivers  631
 key, Microsoft Fax  866, 877–880
 passwords
  Dial-Up Networking connections  896–897, 902–903
  Internet connections  951
  Microsoft Fax  866, 877–880
ENDCAP, NetWare command  394
Ending tasks  725, 743
Energy Star Monitor support  625–626
Enhanced Metafile Format (EMF)
 disabling  768
 new features in Windows 95  755
 optimizing printing performance  572
 overview  767–769
 troubleshooting  781
 Windows 95 printing subsystem  989
Environment variables  209, 210
erase command  1103
Errors
 *See also* BOOTLOG.TXT; Troubleshooting
 advantages of Win32-based applications  742
 checking with ScanDisk  659–661
 chkdsk command  1102
 correcting display driver problems  571

Errors *(continued)*
 fixing application version-checking errors  747–748
 messages *See* Messages
 modem error control  807, 811, 812, 823
 ScanDisk exit codes  1135
 Setup, troubleshooting  233–240
 sharing or lock violations on NetWare servers  291
 startup, troubleshooting  241–244, 1072
 technical support  1256–1257
 troubleshooting printing from Win32-based
  applications  784
Estimated compression ratio  669–670, 1131
Ethernet networks
 Dial-Up Networking connections to Shiva servers  908
 network adapters
  configuring  425
  INF files settings  1207–1211
  NDIS drivers, overview  414
  requiring special consideration  423
 network protocol device IDs  1186
 Thinnet cabling  266
Exchange *See* Microsoft Exchange
Exclusive Mode *See* MS-DOS Mode
Executing *See* Running
exit command  1103
expand command  1103
Expanded memory
 checking from command prompt  235
 defining in CONFIG.SYS  203
 EMM386 command-line switches  1111–1117
 required by Windows 95  236
 running MS-DOS–based applications  734
Exploring objects, shortcut  1232
Express, MSBATCH.INF parameter  1178
Extended capabilities ports (ECPs)
 benefits  756
 bidirectional communication  989
 enabling  772
 limitations  756
 optimizing printing performance  557
 parallel modems  602
 Plug and Play  597
 possible configurations  772
Extended DOS partitions  649, 650
Extended memory
 EMM386.EXE command-line switches  1112–1117
 running MS-DOS–based applications  734
 XMS provider installed during Setup  179
Extract program, extracting installation files  1150–1152

**F**

F1 key
 editing command line  1099

F1 key *(continued)*
  starting Help 1234
F2 key, renaming objects 1232
F3 key
  editing command line 1099
  finding information in Registry Editor 1019
  finding objects 1232
  restarting Setup after failure 234
F4 key
  displaying Look In list in common dialogs 1233
  starting previous version of MS-DOS 1064
  Windows Explorer shortcut 1233
F5 key
  refreshing view 1233
  Safe Mode startup option 1064
F6 key
  moving focus in Windows Explorer 1233
  Safe Mode with Network Support startup option 1064
F8 key
  correcting loading of all specified drivers 244
  creating boot log 216
  displaying Startup menu 1063
  removing Windows 95 227–233
  Safe Mode system startup *See* Safe Mode system startup
  Step-By-Step Confirmation 1061, 1064, 1068–1069
  verifying loading of HIMEM.SYS 235
F10 key, going to menu mode 1234
Failure *See* Troubleshooting
FastTips, Windows 95 technical support 1256
FAT partitions
  installing Windows 95 over OS/2 226
  long filename support 683
  requirements for installing Windows 95 71
  Windows 95 file system 645
Fax
  *See also* Microsoft Fax
  Compose New Fax wizard 872, 873
  cover pages 871, 873
  Microsoft Exchange, communications overview 792
  modems
    international standards for fax communications 869
    Registry entries 881
  network fax service
    memory requirements 868
    passwords 868
    restricting access 868
    sharing fax modems 874–877
  Request A Fax wizard 874
  servers
    configuring client computers 876
    evaluating need for 868
    memory requirements 868
    sharing fax modems 874–877
  TAPI *See* TAPI

Fax *(continued)*
  Windows 95 communications subsystem 792–794
  Windows 95 technical support 1256
fc command 1103
fcbs command 1107
fcbs=, IO.SYS entry 203
fcbshigh command 1107
fdisk command 1103
Fdisk partitions
  marking partitions as active 240
  requirements for installing Windows 95 71
Fdisk utility
  creating DOS partitions 650
  deleting partitions or logical drives 649
  description 645
  partitioning hard disks 647–649
File and Printer Sharing
  administering computers remotely 390, 530, 538
  Browse Master parameter 385
  browsing network resources 380
  Client for Microsoft Networks as Primary Network Logon client 265
  considerations 367
  default policy definitions 492
  displaying browse list with net view command 386
  ensuring LAN Manager workstation access 400, 1198
  hard disk speed, performance tuning 556
  installing 396
  Large Internetwork Packet (LIP) protocol, Client for NetWare Networks support 285, 302
  long filename support 682
  Microsoft networks
    configuring browse masters 399–400
    device ID for use in setup scripts 1188
    MSBATCH.INF [VServer] section 1198
    overview 398
    sharing directories 400
    troubleshooting 411
  NetWare networks
    bindery emulation 408, 462, 469–470, 911
    compared with Windows for Workgroups 401
    considerations 367
    device ID for use in setup scripts 1188
    installing 396
    long filename support 682
    MSBATCH.INF [NWServer] section 1197
    Net Watcher constraints 538
    notes on Novell-supplied commands 391–394
    overview 365
    pass-through security 292
    requirements 401
    SAP Advertising 411
    security 397–398
    share names vs. NetWare volume names 407

File and Printer Sharing, NetWare networks *(continued)*
    sharing directories  406
    troubleshooting Dial-Up Networking  920–922
    user-level vs. share-level security  460, 462–464
    Windows 95 network architecture  1009
  network clients  335
  networking support  251
  optimizing network performance  574
  overview  364–365, 396
  peer-to-peer networks  267
  restricting access  506, 511, 516
  restricting user actions *See* System policies; User profiles
  running Windows 95
    with Windows for Workgroups  276
    with Windows NT  272
    with Workgroup Add-on for MS-DOS  277, 386
  security
    bindery emulation  408
    decisions  461–462
    overview  397–398
    share-level  466
    user-level vs. share-level  460, 462–464
  sending messages with WinPopup  447
  services  97
  sharing resources on dial-up servers  887
  System Monitor categories and settings  583
  troubleshooting
    connections  408–411
    network installation  261
  Windows 95 network architecture  1008–1010
"File not found", sharing or lock violations on NetWare
  servers  291
File Server for Macintosh  1222
File systems
  block I/O subsystem  690, 981–984
  CDFS  569, 678, 695–696, 980
  enabling Windows 3.1 file system  689
  FAT *See* FAT partitions
  file system drivers  979
  HPFS *See* HPFS partitions
  included with Windows 95  678–679
  Installable File System Manager
    determining file system drivers  679
    overview  979
    passing short filenames  680
    tunneling to preserve long filenames  569, 681
    Windows 95 network architecture  994–995
  NTFS *See* NTFS partitions
  optimizing performance
    disk performance profiles  565–567
    overview  564–565
    System Monitor categories and settings  580
    troubleshooting options  569–570
  overview  645, 977–978

File systems *(continued)*
  provided by other vendors  679
  remote administration browsing  532
  System subtree in Hkey_Local_Machine key  1030
  troubleshooting strategies  1077
  turning off extended file system features  689
  VFAT  566–567, 678, 695, 979–980
  Windows 95 architecture  977–984
File Transfer Protocol (FTP)
  connecting to hosts  449
  downloading files from the Internet  956–958
  FTP commands  1138
  Internet access  940, 942, 955–958
  Microsoft FTP server, getting help  955
  password authentication, caution  1136
  stopping FTP  958
File Transfer Status utility  932–933
FILER, NetWare command  402
Files
  aliases
    description  680
    LFNBK utility  687
    naming policy  684
    other file systems  682
    troubleshooting  698
    turning off numeric tails  688
    valid characters  680
    viewing  681
  ASCII, transferring over the Internet with FTP  957–958
  associating file types with applications  721–722, 741, 752
  attaching to electronic mail messages  845–846, 935
  backing up *See* Backup
  browsing FTP sites, Internet access  956
  checking for correct versions  1071
  checking for errors with ScanDisk  659–661
  copying, shortcut  1232
  copying Windows 95 files
    technical discussion  181–182
    to a server for shared installations  114–121
  deleting
    Recycle Bin  655, 1223
    shortcuts  1232
    when removing Windows 95  228, 231
  disk management tools  653, 1123–1135
  downloading
    File Transfer Status utility  932–933
    from the Internet  940, 942, 956–958
    from The Microsoft Network  924, 929, 932–933
  File and Printer Sharing *See* File and Printer Sharing
  "File not found", sharing or lock violations on NetWare
    servers  291
  files command  1107
  hidden, attrib command  221
  initialization files *See* INI files

Files *(continued)*
    log files *See* Log files
    migrating settings when upgrading to Windows 95  220
    MS-DOS files deleted when upgrading to
        Windows 95  223–224
    multimedia  702
    names
        converting Program Manager groups during
            Setup  183, 245–246
        long *See* Long filenames
    organizing for shared installations  109
    policies *See* Policies
    printing to printers  763
    read-only, attrib command  221
    recently used
        customizing settings with user profiles  482
        Registry settings, tuning performance  566
    Registry data files *See* DAT files
    saving, creating folders from within common dialog
        boxes  382
    Setup
        directory structure created  121, 1153
        extracting with Extract program  1150–1152
        location of key files  1154
        overview  1152
        Windows 95 distribution disks  1150
    shared, connecting to network resources  383
    Show Dots and file access limits, NetWare servers  318
    synchronizing with Briefcase  73, 793, 918–920
    system
        *See also* System, startup files
        attrib command  221
        location of key files  1154–1155
        location on Windows 95 distribution disks  1156
        missing, troubleshooting  241–242, 1071–1072
    text, transferring with FTP  957–958
    The Microsoft Network file libraries  924, 932–933
    transferring *See* Binary file transfer; Transferring, files;
        Microsoft File Transfer
    xcopy command-line switches  1118–1122
files command  1107
files= entry
    CONFIG.SYS
        file access limit for NetWare servers  318
        system changes affecting application support  741
    IO.SYS  202
fileshigh command  1107
FilterKeys, accessibility feature  1234, 1244–1245
find, command-line command  1062, 1103
Find command, disabling  513
Finding
    messages in Microsoft Exchange  845
    objects  1232, 1235
FirstNetDrive, MSBATCH.INF parameter  1196

Floppy disks
    compressing data *See* Disk compression; DriveSpace disk
        compression utility
    controllers  693–694, 981
    creating a startup disk  1063
    disabling automounting  668
    drives booting from *See* Booting, from floppy disks
    high-speed, driver  693
    mounting
        description  668
        DrvSpace /mount command-line switch  1130
        DrvSpace /unmount command-line switch  1134
    non-SCSI port drivers  694
    removable media drives  693–694
    running Setup, troubleshooting  238–240
    software-based media ejection  694
    updating files with Briefcase  919
    Windows 95 distribution disks  1150
    Windows 95 startup disk *See* Startup disk
    Windows 95 volume tracker  652
Flow control, configuring modems  807, 812, 827
Folders
    *See also specific folder names*
    Briefcase  918–920
    checking for errors with ScanDisk  659–661
    converting Program Manager groups during
        Setup  72, 183, 220, 245–246
    creating from within common dialog boxes  382
    customizing  504, 507, 512
    Personal, Microsoft Exchange *See* Personal Folders
    share names vs. NetWare volume names  407
    shortcuts  1232–1233
    The Microsoft Network content tree  928, 929
    Windows 95 distribution disks  1150
    Windows 95 vs. Apple Macintosh  1224
    Windows Explorer command-line switches  1118
FON files  775
Fonts
    cartridges, installing  756, 778
    configuring display settings  624–625
    customizing with user profiles  482
    filename extensions  775
    loading  777
    location of key files  1154
    matching  775–777
    MS-DOS–based applications  733, 785–788, 1047–1048
    multilingual support
        changing code pages  1047–1048
        changing language  1051
        Choose Font dialog box  1051
        languages and keyboard layouts listed  1048–1050
        locale IDs  1051
        MS-DOS–based applications  1047–1048
        TrueType fonts  1050

Fonts, multilingual support *(continued)*
    Win32-based applications 1051
  new features in Windows 95 755–756
  number used simultaneously 777
  overview 774
  printer fonts 775
  raster fonts 774, 777
  regional settings *See* Code pages; International
    Windows 95
  screen fonts 775
  troubleshooting 783, 785–788
  TrueType fonts 755–788, 1050
  vector fonts 774, 777
for command 1103
Foreign languages *See* International Windows 95; Languages
format command 1103
Format utility 645, 650–651
Formatting
  compressed drives 1129
  documents, multilingual support 1048–1051, 1055
  format command 1103
  hard disks 650–651
  locale IDs, Win32-based applications 1051
  Windows 95 multilingual support 1042
FOT files 775
Frame type
  Client for NetWare Networks 299, 330
  Frame_Type, MSBATCH.INF parameter 1196
  NET.CFG 311
  NetWare network clients 331
Free disk space *See* Disk space
Frequently-used commands, Doskey editing 1099
Friendly names, printers, MSBATCH.INF parameter 1199
FTP *See* File Transfer Protocol (FTP)
ftp, TCP/IP utility
  command-line switches 1137–1138
  HOSTS file 1226
Fully qualified domain name (FQDN) 443, 444

**G**

Games
  Display Control Interface (DCI) 702
  local-bus video, purchasing multimedia computers 706
  MS-DOS–based 729
Gateway Service for NetWare, Windows NT 395
Gateways
  Attachmate 358
  configuring TCP/IP 435
  dedicated Internet connections 961
  Dial-Up Networking
    configuring dial-up servers 899
    NetWare Connect servers 907–908
    network protocols 891

Gateways, Dial-Up Networking *(continued)*
    overview 888
    Shiva servers 908–912
    troubleshooting 920–922
    Windows NT remote access servers 904–905
  Eicon 358
  HOSTS and LMHOSTS files 1225–1230
  mainframe connectivity 358–360
  Microsoft Exchange
    connecting to service providers 833
    Exchange Server 860
  Microsoft Mail 861–863
  MSBATCH.INF parameter 1194
  NetWare for SAA 358, 359
  WallData RUMBA 358
gdi.exe=, SYSTEM.INI entry 214
GDI system component
  32-bit vs. 16-bit 984
  GDI.EXE and GDI32 200
  overview 987
  Windows 95 graphics subsystem 988
  Windows 95 printing subsystem 989
GEnie
  obtaining information about Windows 95 1256
  obtaining Windows 95 Reviewer's Guide 39
get, FTP command 1139
Getting help *See* Help
glob, FTP command 1139
Go commands, The Microsoft Network 931
Go To command, Windows Explorer shortcut 1233
Gopher
  Internet access overview 942
  navigating the Internet 960
  Telnet command-line switches 1146
Graphical Device Interface *See* GDI system component
Graphics
  accelerators, drivers included in Windows 95 601
  device-independent bitmaps (DIBs) 988
  Graphical Device Interface *See* GDI system component
  Image Color Matching *See* Image Color Matching (ICM)
  scanners, MCI device types 701
  setting compatibility options 570–571
  troubleshooting
    display adapters 989
    printing 781
  Windows 95 display drivers 620
  Windows 95 graphics subsystem 988
Group 3 fax machines 866–870, 874
Group policies *See* System policies
GROUPPOL.DLL 491, 502
Groups
  Program Manager
    backing up before running Setup 78
    converting to folders 72, 183, 220, 245–246

Groups, Program Manager *(continued)*
    security *See* Security; User-level security
    Startup *See* Startup folder
GRP files
    backing up before running Setup  78
    migrating group settings during Setup  86
    STARTUP.GRP *See* STARTUP.GRP

# H

Hard disks
    changing location of virtual memory swap files  563
    checking and defragmenting before running Setup  78
    "Checking Your Hard Disk" message  146
    compressing data *See* Disk compression; DriveSpace disk
        compression software
    creating DOS partitions  650
    defragmenting *See* Defragmenting disks; Disk
        Defragmenter
    deleting partitions  649
    disk devices
        device classes  605
        PCMCIA drivers  596
        troubleshooting  239, 698
        Windows 95 support  690–691
    drivers required for system startup  1074
    file systems *See* File systems
    formatting  650–651
    hardware required for running Windows 95  69
    local, for shared installations
        configuring AUTOEXEC.BAT  128
        configuring for protected-mode clients  128–130
        configuring for real-mode clients  134
        disk space requirements for shared installations  111
        files copied to startup disk  129, 182
    management utilities
        command-line switches  1123–1135
        Microsoft Plus!  670–671
        overview  653
        provided with Windows 95  645
        troubleshooting  696
        Windows 95 volume tracker  652
    optimizing performance
        disk performance profiles  565–567
        file system  569–570
        speed  556
    partitioning  647–649
    purchasing multimedia computers  706–708
    removable media devices *See* Removable media drives
    scanning for errors *See* ScanDisk
    size of drives displayed by Fdisk  649
    system management tools  456
    Windows 95 volume tracker  652

Hard-of-hearing or deaf users *See* Accessibility features,
    hard-of-hearing or deaf users
Hardware
    *See also* Devices
    adding using Setup  77
    changing computer settings in Custom Setup  99–100
    checking README and SETUP.TXT files before running
        Setup  77
    communications device support  602
    compatibility information  1258
    compression, Dial-Up Networking  897, 903–904
    configuring network adapter resource settings  421–424
    detecting *See* Detecting hardware
    device classes  591–592
    Hardware Conflict troubleshooting aid  634
    Hkey_Current_Config Registry key  1022, 1033
    loading at startup  197
    multimedia *See* Multimedia, devices
    network cards *See* Network adapters
    new *See* Add New Hardware wizard; New hardware
    optimizing performance  556–557
    Plug and Play-compliant devices *See* Plug and Play
    profiles  197, 617–618
    removable media devices *See* Removable media drives
    requirements
        for Dial-Up Networking  886
        for installing Windows 95  69–70
        Systems Management Server  1215
    settings, default computer policies  493
    support in Windows 95  589–591
    system configuration overview  588–589
    Systems Management Server inventory  1217
    system management tools  456
    tree  592, 972, 1033
Hardware Conflict troubleshooting aid  634
hash, FTP command  1139
HDBoot, MSBATCH.INF parameter  1189
HDLC, Dial-Up Networking  913
Headphones, troubleshooting multimedia problems  712
Help
    accessibility features  1239
    F1 key  1234
    files, location  1154
    getting for command-line commands  1095
    Microsoft Software Library  1260
    obtaining from Microsoft
        on the Internet  955
        on The Microsoft Network  924
    opening  1224
    Setup command-line switches  81
    starting, shortcut  1235
    technical support  1256–1257
    troubleshooting  1060
help, FTP command  1139

Hewlett-Packard JetAdmin
    description 766–767
    device IDs for use in setup scripts 1188
    installing 767
Hidden attribute
    attrib command 221
    MS-DOS–based applications 730
    xcopy command-line switches 1120
Hiding desktop items 508, 513
High memory area (HMA), allocating memory to
    MS-DOS–based applications 734
High-speed floppy disk driver 693
HIMEM.SYS
    loading in CONFIG.SYS 1109
    Safe Mode Command Prompt Only startup option 1066
    verifying loading using F4 235
himem.sys, IO.SYS entry 202
Hkey_Classes_Root Registry key 1023, 1028
Hkey_Current_Config Registry key 1022, 1033
Hkey_Current_User Registry key 1023, 1032–1033
Hkey_Dyn_Data Registry key 1022, 1033
Hkey_Local_Machine Registry key 1022, 1026–1029
Hkey_Users Registry key 1023, 1032–1033
HMA See High memory area (HMA)
Home directories
    See also Machine directories; Mail directory
    necessary for implementing user profiles on networks 480
    Windows NT 375
Host drives
    compressed volume files (CVFs)
        description 662
        DrvSpace /mount command-line switch 1130
        DrvSpace /unmount command-line switch 1134
        mounting, troubleshooting 697
        running ScanDisk 660
    compressing drives 664–666, 1126–1127
    compressing floppy disks 667
    increasing free space available on compressed drives 669
    overview 662
    uncompressing drives with DriveSpace 667, 1133
    unhiding 665
Host tables See HOSTS file; LMHOSTS file
Hostname, MSBATCH.INF parameter 1194
Hosts
    DNS host names 441–443
    host drives See Disk compression; Host drives
    Internet See Internet
    name resolution See HOSTS file; LMHOSTS file; Name
        resolution
    Windows 95 connectivity
        See also Mainframe connectivity
        mainframe connectivity 350–358
        overview 349
        terminal emulation applications 359–360

HOSTS file
    See also LMHOSTS file; Name resolution
    case sensitivity 1226
    DNS host names 441–443
    localhost loopback address 1226
    name resolution 436
    sample version included with Windows 95 1225
    setting up 1226–1227
HostWinBootDrv=, MSDOS.SYS entry 204
Hot docking See Docking; Plug and Play
Hot keys
    displaying System properties dialog 1235
    emergency hot keys, accessibility 1240–1241
    shortcuts See Keys, shortcuts; specific key names
    specifying for MS-DOS–based applications 731
    switching between installed languages 1050, 1052–1053
    troubleshooting application startup 749
HP Open View for Windows 547
HPFS partitions
    long filename support 682–684
    requirements for installing Windows 95 71
HyperTerminal
    configuring modem connection properties 806, 815
    description 800, 813
    dialing modems manually 808
    Dialing Properties See Dialing Properties
    file transfer protocols 814, 829
    installing 813
    terminal emulation types 815
    troubleshooting binary file transfer 829
    Windows 95 communications overview 792

I

IBM LAN NetView, remote administration tools 547
IBM LanSupport with real-mode DLC protocol 355–357
IBM OS/2 LAN Server
    browsing network resources 387
    Client for Microsoft Networks, overview 264–265
    copying Windows 95 files to a server 114
    File and Printer Sharing 398
    networks supported by Windows 95 334
    running with Windows 95 275–276
    servers, connecting to 347
    setting up for Windows 95 networking 346–347
    versions supported by Windows 95 346
IBM PC Support, connecting to AS/400 systems 359
IBM token-ring network adapters, .INF file settings 1208
Icons
    adding applications to Start or Programs menus 722, 749
    assigning to Program Manager items 724
    Control Panel tools for system configuration 588–589
    desktop
        customizing with system policies 504, 507

Icons, desktop *(continued)*
  installing Registry Editor on desktop 1019
  restricting access 512
installing MS-DOS–based applications 718
Microsoft Exchange fax icons 875
Net Watcher 537
printing
  to Microsoft Fax 872
  to network printers 762
Registry value entry data types 1024
running applications 720, 749
shortcuts *See* Shortcuts, desktop
taskbar
  description 1224
  switching between installed languages 1050
  switching to other keyboards 1053
The Microsoft Network Favorite Places 929, 930
upper right corner of desktop window 1224
ICPs *See* Independent content providers (ICPs)
IDE controllers
  Plug and Play functionality 597
  Windows 95 port driver 981
  Windows 95 support 691–692
IDE drives
  non-SCSI port drivers 694
  Windows 95 support 691–692
Identification
  CD Key identification number 120
  setting computer and workgroup names when installing
    networking support 257
  specifying computer during Setup 98
IFS Manager *See* Installable File System Manager
ifshlp.sys, IO.SYS entry 202
IgnoreDetectedNetCards, MSBATCH.INF parameter 1185
Image Color Matching (ICM)
  contacting Eastman Kodak 1262
  description 988
  device-independent color usage 601
  introduced 755
  overview 773–774
  PostScript mini-driver 771
  profiles 774
Implementing Windows 95 in corporate environments *See*
  Deploying Windows 95
Inbox Assistant, Microsoft Exchange 836
Inbox Setup wizard
  creating Microsoft Exchange profiles 846
  decisions 832–834
  installing Microsoft Exchange client 104, 837
¬clude command 1107
  ¬orrect MS-DOS version" error message 239
    ¬ndent content providers (ICPs), The Microsoft Network
      ¬iption 926
        ¬ 937–938

Independent content providers (ICPs), The Microsoft Network
  *(continued)*
  sign-up requirements 926
INF files
  APPS.INF *See* APPS.INF file
  "Cannot open file *.INF" error message 239
  custom setup scripts *See* MSBATCH.INF
  device class detection 185
  device IDs 1185–1188
  example 1172, 1204–1206
  general file format 1158–1159
  INF Installer 157
  installing
    new devices 606
    other software 157–159
    software without Windows 95 INF files 159
  LOCALE.INF, regional settings list 1044
  MSDET.INF, hardware detection modules 190
  MULTILING.INF keyboard strings 1046
  overview 1158
  sections 1158–1204
  settings for common network adapters 1207–1211
  strings keys 1171, 1200
  technical notes on network adapters 427
INF Installer 157
Information providers, The Microsoft Network *See*
  Independent content providers (ICPs)
INI files
  backing up before running Setup 78
  information contained in machine directories 122
  migrating system settings during Setup 86, 1021
  Registry
    *See also* Registry
    comparison 967
    overview 1018–1019
    Win16-based applications 1034
  replacing configuration entries using custom setup
    scripts 1204
  searching PROTOCOL.INI during safe detection for
    network adapters 186, 192–193
Init, modem Registry key 810
Initialization files *See* INI files
INS key, editing command line 1099
install command 1107
Install New Modem wizard
  automatic modem detection 801
  configuring Dialing Properties 803
  installing new modems 802
  troubleshooting modem installation 823–824
Installable File System Manager (IFS)
  determining file system drivers 679
  overview 979
  passing short filenames 680
  tunneling to preserve long filenames 681
  Windows 95 network architecture 994–995

Installation policy
    customizing Windows 95  166
    setting in Server-based Setup  117–118, 148–153
InstallDir, MSBATCH.INF parameter  1178
Installing
    applications  *See* Applications, installing
    drivers, device detection and configuration during
        Setup  66, 88–91, 180–181, 184–187
    fonts  778
    legacy devices  607
    modems  *See* Modems
    multilingual support  1050–1051
    network clients  *See specific client names*
    network components
        after Windows 95 is installed  255
        drivers and protocols  419
        NETLOG.TXT  194–195
        recommended method  254
        troubleshooting  259–262
        using Control Panel  255
        using Setup  254
    new devices  606–607
    other vendors' networking support  336–337
    printers  *See* Printers
    real-mode drivers  603
    system management tools  457–458
    utilities  *See specific utility names*
    Windows 3.x device drivers, caution  603
    Windows 95  *See* Server-based Setup utility; Setup;
        Shared installations
InstallType, MSBATCH.INF parameter  1178
Insufficient disk space, troubleshooting Setup  240
INT 13, safe drivers  631
Intel LANDesk, remote administration tools  547
Intel network adapters, .INF file settings  1209
International Windows 95
    command-line commands  1110
    country command  1107
    keyboards
        MULTILING.INF strings  1046
        using alternate keyboards  1052–1054
        Windows 95 multilingual support  1041, 1048–1051
    local editions  1040–1041
    multilingual support
        *See also* Languages
        fonts  *See* Fonts, multilingual support
        installing  99, 1050–1051
        languages and keyboard layouts listed  1048–1050
        local conventions  1055
        locale IDs  1051
        MultiLanguage, MSBATCH.INF parameter  1181
        overview  1041–1042
        using alternate keyboards  1052–1054
        Win32-based applications  1051

International Windows 95  *(continued)*
    National Language Support API  1042, 1052, 1054–1055
    specifying regional settings
        changing code pages  1047–1048
        changing in Control Panel  1043–1044
        during Setup  99, 1042–1043
        in custom setup scripts  1044–1047
        listed in LOCALE.INF  1044
        TimeZone, MSBATCH.INF parameter  1179
        using alternate keyboards  1052–1054
    System subtree in Hkey_Local_Machine key  1030
Internet
    access
        FTP protocol  955–958
        IP router required  899
        overview  940–943
        providers  945–946, 961–962
        tools  942
        Windows 95 communications overview  793
        Windows Sockets providers  959
        World Wide Web (WWW)  942
    accounts  945–946
    bulletin boards  941
    compatibility provided by TCP/IP protocol  416, 431
    connections
        access providers  945–946
        Dial-Up Networking  950–954
        DNS server addresses  947–950
        increasing speed  951
        IP addresses  947–950
        overview  944
        password encryption security  951
        PPP servers  951–952
        requirements  941
        SLIP servers  952–954
        subnet masks  947–950
        troubleshooting  961–962
        verifying with WINIPCFG  954
    contacting InterNIC  961
    dedicated gateway servers  961
    Dial-Up Networking connections to Shiva servers  908
    distributing host information  441
    electronic mail
        provider information required  946
        sending  941
        The Microsoft Network  924, 929, 935–936
    getting help and information from Microsoft  955
    Internet Mail MAPI service provider  836
    Mail Service, installing  93
    Microsoft Fax overview  866
    Microsoft Software Library  1260
    navigating  955–960
    obtaining
        information about Systems Management Server  1213

Internet, obtaining *(continued)*
  information about Windows 95  1256
  official network ID  961
  Windows 95 Reviewer's Guide  39
  Windows Sockets specifications  10!2
  SLIP protocol *See* Serial Line Internet Protocol (SLIP)
  The Microsoft Network features  924–926
  useful publications  943
  USNET newsgroups  941, 946
Interprocess communications (IPC)
  channel provided for remote administration  532
  client-side named pipes  1015
  mailslots  1015–1016
  Microsoft RPC facility  1012–1013
  NetBIOS programming interface  1014
  Windows 95 network architecture  1010–1016
  Windows Sockets implementation  1010–1012
Interrupts
  # (pound sign), tested device configuration symbol  613
  * (asterisk), device conflict symbol  613
  booting Plug and Play-compliant devices  196
  checking
    PCMCIA sockets  616
    settings in Control Panel  261
  configuring
    legacy devices  613
    network adapter resource settings  421–424
    with Configuration Manager  971–973
  device detection and configuration during Setup  180–181
  DOS, running TSRs under Windows 95  746
  ECP parallel ports  772
  I/O addresses assigned to communications devices  629
  information included in PROTOCOL.INI  278
  NetWare configuration file *See* NET.CFG
  optimizing file system performance  570
  Registry hardware tree  592
  troubleshooting
    modem installation  822, 826–827, 829–830
    network installation  261
  used by mutiple devices  185
  ValidateNetCardResources, MSBATCH.INF
    parameter  1191
I/O
  addresses
    assigned to Plug and Play ISA cards  196
    checking settings in Control Panel  261
    communications devices  629
    Configuration Manager  971–973
    configuring legacy devices  613
    configuring network adapter resource
      settings  421–424
    DETLOG.TXT entries  193
    device detection and configuration  180–181

I/O, addresses *(continued)*
    disabling ISA enumerator, troubleshooting
      startup  241
    information included in PROTOCOL.INI  278
    NetWare configuration file *See* NET.CFG
    troubleshooting modem installation  822, 826–827
    troubleshooting network installation  261
    used by mutiple devices  185
  block I/O subsystem
    elements provided in Windows 95  690
    overview  981–984
    VFAT driver interaction  979
  optimizing by running Disk Defragmenter  646
  ports *See* Ports, I/O
  subsystem, location of key files  1154
I/O Supervisor (IOS)
  block device drivers  690
  description  981
  file system drivers  679
  loading drivers
    overview  982–984
    port drivers  695
  media change detection  653
  troubleshooting hard disk device drivers  698
IO.SYS
  boot sector of boot drive modified by Setup  183
  hard disk location  1155
  location on compressed disks  1156
  missing, troubleshooting  1072
  modifying boot drive after Setup  184
  old AUTOEXEC.BAT entries  210
  old CONFIG.SYS entries  202–203
  overriding default values  203
  reinstalling real-mode operating system files  1071
  renamed to WINBOOT.SYS  201
  Safe Mode system startup  142
  setting up dual boot capabilities with Windows 95 and
    MS-DOS  221
  starting real-mode operating system  201–203
  startup process for shared installations  139
IOS.INI
  information included  631
  running TSRs under Windows 95  746
  safe driver list  631–633
  syntax  632
IOS.LOG
  real-mode drivers  565
  troubleshooting protected-mode drivers  633
IP addresses
  checking with ping, Internet access  954
  configuring TCP/IP
    manually  433–435
    with DHCP  432–433
  Dial-Up connections to Shiva servers  908, 911

IP addresses *(continued)*
    host tables 1225–1230
    Internet accounts 946–950
    MSBATCH.INF parameter 1195
    name resolution
        DNS 437, 440–444
        HOSTS file 1226–1227
        LMHOSTS file 1227–1230
        WINS 437–439
    SLIP accounts, Internet access 952
    troubleshooting TCP/IP
        connections 449–451, 954, 1137–1147
    verifying configuration with WINIPCFG 954
IP Header Compression 952
IP routers
    HOSTS and LMHOSTS files 1225–1230
    required for Internet Dial-Up Networking access 899
IPAddress, MSBATCH.INF parameter 1195
IPC *See* Interprocess communications (IPC)
IPC$, shared resource created when enabling remote
    administration 532
IPL workstations, remote *See* Remote-boot workstations
IPMask, MSBATCH.INF parameter 1195
IPX/SPX protocol
    *See also* IPX/SPX-compatible protocol
    monolithic IPX 312–313, 327
    Open Datalink Interface (ODI) 310
    required NetWare-supplied support files 326
    using NetBIOS over IPX 430
IPX/SPX-compatible protocol
    *See also* IPX/SPX protocol
    advantages 418
    changing bindings 429
    configuring 428–429
    configuring Client for NetWare Networks 300
    description 415–416
    Dial-Up Networking 891
    frame type 300, 330, 332, 429, 448
    installed during Setup 96
    loading TSRs with Client for NetWare Networks 377
    mainframe connectivity 349
    MSBATCH.INF parameters
        [NWLINK] section 1196
        protocol device IDs 1186
    NDIS 2.x protocol drivers 415
    necessary for remote administration 531
    overview 427
    peer-to-peer networks 267
    running Remote Registry service 535
    support for shared installations 139
    System Monitor categories and settings 580
    technical notes 431
    troubleshooting 448

IPX/SPX-compatible protocol *(continued)*
    using
        on NetWare networks 288
        with NetWare network clients 286
    Windows 95 network architecture 1004
    Windows Sockets IPC implementation 1011
IRQs *See* Interrupts
ISA
    bus adapters 594, 690
    cards
        description 594
        determining I/O and DMA to be assigned 196
        disabling ISA enumerator 241
    devices 594

## J

JetAdmin for NetWare *See* Hewlett-Packard JetAdmin
Jumpers, configuring legacy devices 613

## K

Kermit protocol 814, 829
Kernel system component
    32-bit vs. 16-bit 984
    KRNL386.EXE 200
    overview 986–987
    performance tuning 554
    System Monitor categories and settings 580
    Windows 95 communications overview 794
Key encryption, Microsoft Fax 866, 877–880
keyb command 1103
Keyboard
    accessibility features 1244–1246, 1250
    buffer, command line character limit 687
    changing computer settings in Custom Setup 99–100
    command-line commands 1110
    device classes 605
    device detection and configuration 66, 88–91, 184–187
    Hkey_Current_User Registry key 1033
    keyb command 1103
    keys *See* Keys
    layouts
        Dvorak 1251–1252
        for single-handed users 1251–1252
        System subtree in Hkey_Local_Machine key 1030
    MSBATCH.INF parameters 1181
    numlock command 1108
    selecting information in command-prompt windows 1101
    system management tools 456
    troubleshooting input devices 640
Keys
    *See also specific key names*

Keys *(continued)*
    accessibility features *See* Accessibility features, making
      keyboard and mouse input easier
    CD Key identification number  120
    command-line editing keys  1099–1100
    hot keys *See* Hot keys
    INF files  1159
    international language support  1041
    layouts
      changing code pages  1047–1048
      locale IDs  1051
      MULTILING.INF strings  1046
      specifying during Setup  1043
      using alternate keyboards  1052–1054
      Windows 95 multilingual support  1048–1051
    Microsoft Natural Keyboard  1235
    numlock command  1108
    Registry *See* Registry
    shortcuts
      accessibility  1234
      bypassing Auto-Run when inserting CDs  1232
      closing folders  1232
      copying files  1232
      creating  1232
      cycling through pages in properties dialog box  1232
      for selected objects  1232
      keyboard commands  1234
      Microsoft Natural Keyboard  1235
      opening and closing windows  1232
      Windows Explorer  1233
    strings  1171, 1200
    switching between installed languages  1050, 1052–1053
Knowledge Base  1260

**L**

label command  1104
LAN Manager
    browsing network resources  387
    Client for Microsoft Networks, overview  264–265
    client-side named pipes  1015
    copying Windows 95 files to a server  114
    File and Printer Sharing  398–401
    long filenames  682–683
    mailslots  1015–1016
    NetBEUI protocol, description  416, 417, 419, 444–445
    networks supported by Windows 95  250
    preparing for push installations  172
    running with Windows 95  275–276
LAN Server (IBM OS/2) *See* IBM OS/2 LAN Server
LANA numbers
    description  426
    designating browse master in Registry  387
    setting for network adapters  426

LANA numbers *(continued)*
    troubleshooting NetBIOS application failure  448
lanabase=, SYSTEM.INI entry  214
Languages
    *See also* International Windows 95
    Choose Font dialog box  1051
    MultiLanguage, MSBATCH.INF parameter  1181
    switching between installed languages  1050, 1052–1053
    using alternate keyboards  1052–1054
    Windows 95 multilingual support  1048–1055
LANs
    Dial-Up Networking connection protocols  891
    troubleshooting with Network Monitor agent  544
LANtastic *See* Artisoft LANtastic
Laptop computers *See* Portable computers
Large Internetwork Packet (LIP) protocol, Client for NetWare
   Networks support  285, 302
Laser discs, Windows 95 support  703
lastdrive command  202, 318, 324, 1108
lastdrivehigh command  1108
lcd, FTP command  1139
LEFT ARROW key, editing command line  1099
Legacy
    applications, loading fonts  777
    computers
      booting devices  196
      bootstrapping in the BIOS phase  196
      Plug and Play-compliant devices  590, 593
      Setup hardware detection phase  180
    devices *See* Devices, legacy
    modem adapters, installing  802
    network adapters, configuring  423
LFNBK utility
    command-line syntax  687
    installing  686
    preparing to enable Windows 3.1 file system  689
    removing and restoring long filenames  646, 684
    using for temporary filename compatibility  685–687
lh command  1104
Licenses, Windows NT Server  274–275
Linear addressing model  976
Link Control Protocol (LCP)  913
Linked objects *See* OLE
literal, FTP command  1139
LM Announce property
    ensuring LAN Manager access to File and Printer
      Sharing  275, 400
    LMAnnounce, MSBATCH.INF parameter  1198
    optimizing network performance  574
    troubleshooting File and Printer Sharing  411
LMHOSTPath, MSBATCH.INF parameter  1195
LMHOSTS file
    *See also* HOSTS file; Name resolution
    browsing resources on TCP/IP subnetworks  387, 438

LMHOSTS file *(continued)*
   creating 1228
   keywords 1229–1230
   LMHOSTPath, MSBATCH.INF parameter 1195
   name resolution 436
   sample version included with Windows 95 1225
   setting up 1227–1230
   troubleshooting TCP/IP connections 449–451
Load balancing, enabling on Windows NT networks 501
load rpl, NetWare command 138
loadfix command 1104
loadhigh command 1104
LoadTop=, MSDOS.SYS entry 205
Local
   access control list, managing 469
   bus video, purchasing multimedia computers 706
   computers
      connecting together *See* Direct Cable Connection
      definition 65
      disabling dial-up server support 901
      disabling user profiles 486
      Hkey_Local_Machine Registry key 1022, 1026–1029
      manual downloading of system policies 500
      running Windows 95 Setup 75
   editions of Windows 95 *See* International Windows 95
   hard disks, for shared installations
      configuring AUTOEXEC.BAT 128
      configuring for protected-mode clients 128–130
      configuring for real-mode clients 134
      disk space requirements for shared installations 111
      files copied to startup disk 129, 182
   printers 779
Locales
   *See also* International Windows 95
   changing code pages 1047–1048
   changing in Control Panel 1043–1044
   defining in custom setup scripts 1044–1047
   listed in LOCALE.INF 1044
   MSBATCH.INF parameter 1181
   specifying during Setup 1042–1043
   using IDs to determine language 1051
   Windows 95 support for local conventions 1055
localhost loopback address, HOSTS files 1226
Locking volumes while running disk utilities 654
Log files
   *See also* BOOTLOG.TXT; DETCRASH.LOG;
      DETLOG.TXT; IOS.LOG; NETLOG.TXT;
      SETUPLOG.TXT
   modem communications 808, 810, 822
   PPP, Dial-Up Networking 914, 920
   Setup Safe Recovery 187–190, 1062
Logging on
   as a different user, shared installations 142
   disabling automatic NetWare login 474, 514

Logging on *(continued)*
   ensuring user logon capabilities in setup scripts 153
   Hkey_Users Registry key 1023, 1032–1033
   login scripts *See* Login scripts
   modems, displaying terminal window 809
   other vendors' network clients 334
   passwords *See* Passwords
   Quick Logon 271
   restricting access *See* Restricting access
   system policies *See* System policies
   to Dial-Up Networking connections *See* Dial-Up
      Networking
   to NetWare servers *See* Netware servers, logging on
   to networks
      configuring 369–373
      considerations 366
      dialog box displayed 379
      NetWare networks 363, 369
      other networks 251
      overview 363, 367–369
      troubleshooting login scripts 408
      using system policies 373–374
   to The Microsoft Network 926, 927
   to Windows 95 200
   to Windows NT networks
      configuring Client for Microsoft Networks during
         Setup 94
      logon validation 368
      system policy settings 515
      Windows 95 logon password 472–473
   unified logon prompt 460
   user authentication *See* Logon validation
   user profiles *See* User profiles
Logical drives
   creating DOS partitions 650
   deleting 649
   IDE drives 691
Login scripts
   backing up before running Setup 78
   Client for Microsoft Networks as Primary Network Logon
      client 269
   Microsoft networks
      advantages 374
      assigning to users 375
      description 374
      parameters 375
      troubleshooting 408
   migrating from Windows 3.x, example 167–169
   NetWare networks
      Client for NetWare Networks support 286
      configuring network logon 370
      enabling 371
      FirstNetDrive, MSBATCH.INF parameter 1196
      installing Windows 95 on NetWare networks 290

Login scripts, NetWare networks *(continued)*
    net commands 392–394
    network logon considerations 366
    overview 363, 375–379
    preparing for push installations 174
    ProcessLoginScript, MSBATCH.INF parameter 1196
    troubleshooting 330, 408
  path statements, caution 126
  push installations 76, 125, 169–176
  running custom setup scripts 163
  server requirements for shared installations 111
  troubleshooting 408
  Windows NT servers, preparing for push installations 172
LOGIN, NetWare command 391, 405
LOGIN.EXE stub, connecting to NetWare servers 412
Logo=, MSDOS.SYS entry 205
Logon Banner 507, 514
Logon domains
  logon validation
    configuring Client for Microsoft Networks 94
    enabling 260
    MSBATCH.INF parameters 1198
    overview 363
  mapping workgroups 164–166
  network logon considerations 366
  troubleshooting network installation 260
Logon validation
  configuring 369–373
  connecting to NetWare drives 389, 474
  description 269
  ensuring user logon capabilities in setup scripts 153
  File and Printer Sharing security 397–398
  logging on to other networks 251
  login scripts 374–375, 408
  master system policy files 166, 292
  MSBATCH.INF parameters 1198
  overview 363, 367–369
  Primary Network Logon client *See* Primary Network
    Logon client
  restricting access *See* Restricting access
  role of workgroups in Windows 95 380
  synchronizing credentials to access NetWare servers 330
  system management overview 456
  The Microsoft Network 927
  troubleshooting network installation 260
  unified logon prompt 460
  using system policies 373–374
  Windows 95 logon password 472–473
  Windows NT, configuring Client for Microsoft
    Networks 94, 269–270, 370
LogonDomain= entry, setup scripts 153, 1198
Long filenames
  administrative considerations 684–685
  aliases

Long filenames, aliases *(continued)*
    description 680
    LFNBK utility 687
    naming policy 684
    other file systems 682
    troubleshooting 698
    turning off numeric tails 688
    valid characters 680
    viewing 681
  creating at MS-DOS prompt 687–688
  disk compression utilities, caution 646
  establishing file naming policy for mixed network
    environments 646, 684
  LAN Manager with HPFS and HPFS/386 volumes 683
  LFNBK utility
    enabling Windows 3.1 file system 689
    removing and restoring long filenames 646, 684
    using for temporary compatibility 685–687
  network clients 335
  network compatibility 681–684
  network resources 252
  not supported by old MS-DOS commands 222
  number of characters 680, 687
  other vendors' command shells 206
  overview 679–681
  root directory 685, 697–698
  running ScanDisk when removing Windows 95 228, 231
  support necessary for implementing user profiles on
    networks 480
  technical notes 688–689
  troubleshooting 697–698, 1077
  tunneling 569, 681
  turning off numeric tails for filename aliases 688
  using on NetWare servers 285, 290–291
  utility incompatibility 684, 685, 697–698
  Windows 95 protected-mode clients 682
  Windows 95 vs. Apple Macintosh 1224
  Windows NT with HPFS or NTFS volumes 683–684
Lotus Notes
  configuring LANA number 426
  using NetBIOS over IPX 430
Low vision users *See* Accessibility features, low vision users
LPT ports
  *See also* Ports, parallel
  description 629
  installing modems 805
ls, FTP command 1139

**M**

MAC layer *See* Media Access Control (MAC) layer
Machine directories
  creating, for shared installations 108–109, 122
  description 108–109

Machine directories *(continued)*
  DestinationDirs value 1201
  file organization 109
  information, for shared installations 109, 122, 129
  introduced 106
  mandatory user profiles 166
  NETSETUP.POL 117
  NetWare networks 166, 480
  Safe Mode system startup 142
  server requirements for shared installations 111
  setmdir command 128, 140–142
  specifying in login scripts 375
  swap file requirements for shared installations 112
  TEMP directory for diskless workstations 210
MACHINES.INI
  computers starting from floppy disks 130
  startup process for shared installations 139
  technical notes 140–142
Macintosh *See* Apple Macintosh
MADGE network adapters, .INF file settings 1209
Mail *See* Electronic mail; Microsoft Mail; Remote mail
Mail directory, NetWare networks 487
Mail servers *See* Microsoft Mail, workgroup postoffice
Mailslots 1015–1016
Mainframe connectivity
  coaxial adapters 360
  DLC protocol 349–353
  gateways 358–360
  IPX/SPX-compatible protocol 349
  NetBEUI protocol 349
  SNA Server 358, 359
  TCP/IP protocol 358
  terminal emulation applications 359–360
MaintainServerList, MSBATCH.INF parameter 1199
Maintenance Setup 76
Make Compatible utility 746
Make New Connection wizard
  configuring dial-up servers and clients 893
  configuring Microsoft Mail for remote access 853–855
  creating connections 894
Mandatory user profiles
  advantages 479
  customizing Windows 95 166
  defining 489
  system management overview 456
  vs. system policies 480
MAP, NetWare command 391, 393, 402
MAP DEL, NetWare command 393
MAP ROOT, NetWare command 394
MAPI
  messaging clients 858
  Microsoft Exchange *See* Microsoft Exchange
  Microsoft Fax overview 866–870, 880–882
  service providers

MAPI, service providers *(continued)*
  adding to Microsoft Exchange client 838
  CompuServe Mail MAPI service provider 836
  configuring delivery options 842
  description 834, 857–858
  downloading messages 839
  Internet Mail MAPI service provider 835
  Microsoft Exchange profiles 846–848
  Microsoft Fax MAPI service provider 835
  Personal Address Book MAPI service provider 835
  Personal Folder (.PST) MAPI service provider 835
  The Microsoft Network MAPI service provider 835
Mapping
  computer names and IP addresses *See* Name resolution
  fonts 775–777
  network drives
    AUTOEXEC.BAT entries, shared installations 128
    connecting to drive and printer resources 383
    connecting to NetWare drives 389
    WinNet16 interface 339
  protected-mode to real-mode drivers 630–633, 982–984
  workgroups to logon domains 164–166
Mark button, selecting information at command-prompt 1101
Master
  browse servers
    browse list 386–387
    BrowseMaster, MSBATCH.INF parameter 1197
    for Microsoft networks 384
    troubleshooting 385, 409
  system policy files 166, 292
MAXIMUM.POL, system profile example 506, 508
MaxRemovableDrivePartition, Registry entry 653
MCA bus adapters 690
MCI *See* Media Control Interface (MCI)
md command 1104
mdelete, FTP command 1139
mdir, FTP command 1139
Media Access Control (MAC) layer
  NDIS 3.1 adapter mini-drivers 1003
  Plug and Play enhancements, NDIS drivers 414
Media Control Interface (MCI)
  device types 701
  troubleshooting drivers 710–712
Media Player 705, 712
mem command
  checking memory 235
  checking removal of real-mode mouse drivers 627
  description 1104
Memory
  32-bit address space 976
  changing PCMCIA memory window 616
  conventional
    checking from command prompt 235
    optimizing 575

Memory, conventional *(continued)*
    required by Windows 95 234
    running MS-DOS–based applications 734, 745
DMA addresses *See* DMA addresses
expanded
    checking from command prompt 235
    defining in CONFIG.SYS 202
    EMM386 command-line switches 1111–1117
    required by Windows 95 234
    running MS-DOS–based applications 734
extended
    EMM386.EXE command-line switches 1112–1117
    running MS-DOS–based applications 734
    XMS provider installed during Setup 179
heaps 558, 559
HMA, allocating memory to MS-DOS–based
    applications 734
linear addressing model 976
mem command *See* mem command
other vendors' memory managers, loading from
    CONFIG.SYS 206
paging
    *See also* Swap files
    demand paging 556, 975
    dirty memory pages 564
    disk space required for running Windows 95 69
    optimizing file system performance 564
    planning configuration of swap and TEMP files in
      Server-based Setup 112
    Windows 95 architecture 975–977
performance tuning
    disk performance profiles 565–567
    low-memory computers 557, 564
    network 573–574
    overview 557
    RAM 562–563
    System Monitor categories and settings 581
RAM
    accessed by Plug and Play BIOS 196
    configuration for Windows 95 235
    Hkey_Dyn_Data Registry key 1033
    Microsoft Fax network fax service requirements 868
    performance tuning 562–563
    required for Microsoft Mail workgroup postoffice 833
    required for running Windows 95 69
required by Setup
    general requirements 69
    STARTUP.GRP file 170
running MS-DOS–based applications 575, 727, 729, 977
swap files *See* Swap files
system resource capacity 558–560, 714
troubleshooting
    checking virtual memory allocation 1076
    printing 783

Memory, troubleshooting *(continued)*
    Setup failure to start 234–235
    upper memory area conflicts 1075
UMBs
    allocating memory to MS-DOS–based
      applications 734
    EMM386.EXE command-line switches 1112–1117
virtual
    *See also* Swap files
    caution 563
    checking allocation 1076
    swap files 562–563, 987
    Windows 95 management 986–987
    Windows 3.x vs. Windows 95 558, 559
    workstation requirements for shared installations 112
Memory Manager, System Monitor categories and
    settings 581
Memory Pager 975
Memory-resident programs *See* TSRs
menucolor command 1108
menudefault command 1108
menuitem command 1108
Menus
    adding applications 722
    CONFIG.SYS commands 1108
    context menu shortcuts 1232, 1234
    customizing settings with user profiles 482
    displaying Startup menu 1063
    going to menu mode, shortcut 1234
    troubleshooting applications 750
    Windows 95 vs. Apple Macintosh 1224
Message File Conversion wizard 843
Messages
    "Analyzing Your Computer" 146
    B1 Setup error message 238
    "Bad or missing file" 241
    broadcasting with WinPopup 445–447, 762
    "Checking Your Hard Disk" 146
    correcting display driver problems 571
    Dial-Up Networking
      disabling prompt 898
      overview 885
      troubleshooting passwords 922
    electronic mail *See* Electronic mail
    "Incorrect MS-DOS version" 239
    "Invalid VxD dynamic link call from IFSMGR" 1072
    Microsoft Fax overview 866–870, 880–882
    "MS-DOS Uninstall" 145
    NetWare, disabling during Server-based Setup 289
    "Not Enough Disk Space" 146
    "OS/2 Detected" 145
    "Preparing Directory" 146
    "Previous MS-DOS files not found" 243
    "Quit All Windows programs" 145

Messages *(continued)*
   sharing or lock violations on NetWare servers  291
   The Microsoft Network bulletin boards  931–932
   "Unable to connect to servers"  450
   WinChat  1247–1248
Messaging application programming interface *See* MAPI
mget, FTP command  1139
Microsoft Backup overview  656
Microsoft Certified Professional program  1259
Microsoft Client for NetWare Networks *See* Client for
  NetWare Networks
Microsoft Compatibility Labs (MCL)  1258
Microsoft CompuServe forums  1261
Microsoft Consulting Services  1259
Microsoft Developer Network (MSDN)  1258
Microsoft DoubleSpace *See* DoubleSpace disk compression
  software
Microsoft Download Service (MSDL)  1257, 1260–1261
Microsoft DriveSpace *See* DriveSpace disk compression
  software
Microsoft Exchange
   *See also* Microsoft Fax; Microsoft Mail
   address books
     customizing fax cover pages  873
     Microsoft Fax key encryption  877
     Microsoft Fax overview  866
     Personal Address Book  839–841
     Personal Address Book MAPI service provider  835
     The Microsoft Network  936
   addressing messages  840–842
   attaching files or objects to messages  845–846
   client  836–837, 839
   configuring during Setup  104
   delivering messages, configuring options  842
   deploying Windows 95  48
   Dial-Up Networking *See* Dial-Up Networking
   Exchange Server  860
   inbox
     fax icons  875
     faxes received  866
     Inbox Assistant  836
   Inbox Setup wizard
     creating Microsoft Exchange profiles  846
     decisions  832–834
     installing Microsoft Exchange client  104, 837
   installing  93
   managing messages, overview  845
   MAPI *See* MAPI
   message finders  845
   messaging clients  858
   Out of Office Assistant  836
   overview  832–836
   Personal Folders *See* Personal Folders
   profiles  843, 846–848

Microsoft Exchange *(continued)*
   service providers
     adding to Microsoft Exchange client  838
     configuring delivery options  842
     description  834, 857–858
     downloading messages  839
     listed  834–836
     Microsoft Exchange profiles  846–848
   sorting and viewing messages  845
   using with The Microsoft Network  935–936
   Windows 95 communications overview  792
Microsoft Fax
   *See also* Fax
   architecture  880–882
   Compose New Fax wizard  872, 873
   cover pages  871, 873
   deploying Windows 95  49
   digital signatures  877–880
   installing  870–871
   MAPI service provider  835
   Microsoft Exchange *See* Microsoft Exchange
   overview  866–870
   printing from Windows Explorer  872
   Registry entries  881–882
   retrieving faxes  874
   security
     digital signatures  877–880
     key and password encryption  877–880
     overview  866
   sending faxes  872–873
   sharing fax modems  874–877
   Windows 95 communications overview  793
   Windows 95 messaging subsystem architecture  857–858
Microsoft File Transfer  800, 821
Microsoft Knowledge Base  1260
Microsoft Mail
   *See also* Electronic mail
   configuring for remote access  853–855
   converting MMF or PAB files to PST format  843
   gateways  861–863
   Microsoft Exchange
     *See also* Microsoft Exchange
     adding to  837
     setting up on other servers  852
   Postoffice Admin wizard  848
   Server postoffices  859–860, 1222
   Windows 95 messaging subsystem architecture  857–858
   workgroup postoffices
     accessing remotely  852–856
     administering  849
     changing mailbox password  850
     decisions  833
     description  834
     Dial-Up Networking overview  885

Microsoft Mail, workgroup postoffices *(continued)*
    directory structure 851
    memory requirements 833
    Microsoft Exchange limitations 848
    setting up 848
    sharing 849
Microsoft Natural Keyboard keys 1235
Microsoft Network *See* The Microsoft Network
Microsoft Network Client *See* Client for Microsoft Networks
Microsoft Network Monitor agent *See* Network Monitor agent
Microsoft Network Server *See* File and Printer Sharing
Microsoft Plus! utilities 661, 670
Microsoft Press, ordering publications 39, 1041
Microsoft product and customer services, access to by hard-of-hearing or deaf users 1251
Microsoft RPC facility 1012–1013
Microsoft RPC Print Provider 767
Microsoft RPLIMAGE utility 136–137
Microsoft Software Library 926, 1260
Microsoft Solution Providers 1257, 1259
Microsoft SQL Server, Systems Management Server overview 1214
Microsoft Systems Management Server
    clients supported 1216–1217
    deploying Windows 95 1219–1220
    installing software without INF files 159
    Network Monitor component 1218
    obtaining additional information 1213
    overview 1214–1215
    performing push installations 47, 53, 76, 167
    remote administration tools 547
    requirements 1215–1217
    services 1217–1218
    sites, terminology 1214
    SQL Server database 1214, 1219
Microsoft TechNet 1258
Microsoft Technical Education 1259
Microsoft Text Telephone (TT/TDD) services, technical support 1257
MIDI
    MID files 702
    purchasing multimedia computers 706–708
    sequencers 701, 711
    troubleshooting 710–711
    Windows 95 support 703–704
Migrating from Windows 3.x
    application settings and files 72, 219, 1034–1037
    GRP and .INI information 86
    printer information 758
    push installation example 167–169
Minimize All, shortcut 1235
Miniport drivers *See* Drivers, miniport; SCSI; Windows NT
Mirroring disks, unsafe drivers 631

mkdir command
    description 1104
    FTP command 1139
    long filenames 685
mls, FTP command 1139
MMF files 843
Mobile computing *See* Dial-Up Networking; Remote computers
mode command 1104
Modems
    AT modem commands 809, 810–813, 822, 881–882
    baud rate 805, 812
    cellular protocol 807, 811
    communications ports
        configuring 803, 805
        installing legacy modem adapters 802
        listed in Device Manager 629
    data compression 807, 811, 812, 823
    device classes 605
    Dial-Up Networking *See* Dial-Up Networking
    dialing 808, 825–828
    Dialing Properties *See* Dialing Properties
    Direct Cable Connection 886, 916–917
    displaying terminal window 809
    emulation types supported by HyperTerminal 815
    error control 807, 811, 812, 823
    external, increasing speed with UART-based COM port adapter 805
    fax *See* Fax; Microsoft Fax
    flow control 807, 812, 827
    hardware
        compression 903–904
        required for running Windows 95 69
    installing
        decisions 801
        Install New Modem wizard 801–803, 823–824
        legacy modem adapters 802
        methods 801
        troubleshooting 822–824
        using Control Panel 792, 802
        using Setup 77
    Internet access 944
    log files 808, 810, 822
    Microsoft Download Service (MSDL) 1257, 1260–1261
    obtaining drivers from the Windows Driver Library 1261–1262
    overview 800–801
    parallel, Windows 95 support 602
    PCMCIA *See* PCMCIA cards, modems
    properties 804–808
    Registry keys 810–813
    RS-232 ports *See* COM ports
    speaker volume 805, 812, 823
    speed 805, 812

Modems *(continued)*
  support in Windows 95  589–591
  tone dialing  806
  transferring files  *See* Binary file transfer; Transferring,
    files; Microsoft File Transfer
  troubleshooting  *See* Troubleshooting, modems
  universal modem driver  796
  Windows 95 communications subsystem  792–794
Monitors
  *See also* Display
  24-bit display, purchasing multimedia computers  706
  advantages of Plug and Play  593
  changing display types and drivers  621–623
  Energy Star Monitor support  626
  hardware required for running Windows 95  69
  MSBATCH.INF parameter  1181
  print
    DEC PrintServer Software  766
    Hewlett-Packard JetAdmin  766–767, 1188
    System subtree in Hkey_Local_Machine key  1031
  running display utilities  625
  system management tools  456
  VESA Display Power Management Signaling
    (DPMS)  626
  Windows 95 support  600–601
Monolithic IPX
  configuring Windows 95  312–313, 316
  required NetWare-supplied support files  327
Monolithic protocols, NDIS drivers  1003
Monolithic VMM32.VXD  197
more command  1104
Mosaic
  Internet access overview  942
  navigating the Internet  959
  Telnet command-line switches  1146
  useful publications  943
Mounting
  compressed volume files (CVFs)
    DrvSpace /mount command-line switch  1130
    DrvSpace /unmount command-line switch  1134
    troubleshooting  697
  floppy disks, data compression  668
Mouse
  accessibility features
    facilitating input  1244–1246, 1250
    MouseKeys  1234, 1245–1246
    status indicators  1242
  changing computer settings in Custom Setup  99–100
  configuring behavior  628
  device classes  605
  device detection and configuration  66, 88–91, 184–187
  drivers  602, 626–627
  hardware required for running Windows 95  69

Mouse *(continued)*
  making mouse input easier  *See* Accessibility features,
    making keyboard and mouse input easier
  MSBATCH.INF parameter  1181
  MS-DOS–based drivers  627
  OLE drag and drop  741
  Plug and Play  627
  pointer display
    correcting problems  571
    customizing  1242–1243
  transferring information in command-prompt
    windows  1101–1102
  troubleshooting input devices  640
  Windows 95 vs. Apple Macintosh  1223
MouseKeys, accessibility feature  1234, 1245–1246
move command  1104
MPD files  693, 983
mput, FTP command  1139
MS-DOS
  APIs defined by Novell, Windows 95 support  285,
    304–305
  applications  *See* Applications, MS-DOS–based
  boot disks  227
  commands  *See* Command-line commands; *specific
    command names*
  components in Windows 95, technical notes  560–561
  customizing Windows 95 Setup for
    accessibility  82, 155–157
  "Incorrect MS-DOS version" error message  239
  installing Windows 95
    dual-booting  219, 221
    fdisk partition requirements  71
    files deleted  223–224
    final system configuration phase  183
    minimum version required  68
    push installations  172
    running Windows 95 Setup  72, 179
    Setup unable to find valid boot partition,
      troubleshooting  239
    starting Windows 95 Setup  80
    upgrading  219, 223–224
    with VLM network client  320–321
    XMS provider installed  179
  mouse drivers  627
  "MS-DOS Uninstall" message  145
  "Previous MS-DOS files not found" error message  243
  prompt
    changing code pages  1047–1048
    creating long filenames  687–688
    disabling  513
  running after installation of Windows 95, tip  222
  "Standard Mode: Fault in MS-DOS Extender"  239
  starting previous version  205, 1064
  system startup with MS-DOS multiple configurations  224

MS-DOS *(continued)*
    utilities, configuring computers for shared
        installations 126
    virtual machines *See* Virtual machines (VMs)
    Workgroup Add-on *See* Workgroup Add-on for MS-DOS
MS-DOS Mode, running MS-DOS–based applications
    AUTOEXEC.BAT 732
    CONFIG.SYS 732
    description 727
    disabling warning 732
    optimizing performance of games 729
    performance tuning 575
    real-mode drivers 632
    setting paths 736–737
    specifying 732
    troubleshooting 750
    Virtual Machine Manager role 977
MSBATCH.INF
    automated installation failure, troubleshooting Setup 240
    configuring Windows NT logon 370
    creating
        custom setup scripts 76, 147–153
        default setup script 119–120
        startup disk 101
    defining Run-Once options 158–159
    editing 154–155
    ensuring user logon capabilities 153
    examples
        copying custom files 1201
        enabling user profiles and remote
            administration 1201–1203
        replacing configuration entries 1204
    file format 1158–1159
    including comments 154
    INF Installer 157
    installation policy options recorded 118
    installing
        applications 157–159
        new devices 606
        other software 157–159
        Windows 95 124–125, 146
    location specified as command-line parameter 125
    parameters 1176–1211
    push installations
        ensuring replacement of STARTUP.GRP 171
        NetWare servers 175
        using login scripts 169
        Windows NT servers 174
    running 80, 162–163
    sample file 1172, 1204–1206
    sections *See* INF files, sections
    Server-based Setup options for custom scripts 148–153
    setting
        display 99

MSBATCH.INF, setting *(continued)*
    installation directory 85
    installation type 87
    name and company name 88
    network components 94–96
    software components to be installed 92
    Setup command-line switches 81
    SETUPLOG.TXT entries 189
    specifying
        computer and workgroup names 98, 257
        regional settings 1044–1047
    syntax 154
MSDET.INF, hardware detection modules 190
MSDN, Microsoft Developer Network 1258
MSDOS.SYS
    boot sector of boot drive modified by Setup 183
    default values 203–205
    "Invalid VxD dynamic link call from IFSMGR" 1072
    location on compressed disks 1156
    modifying boot drive after Setup 184
    reinstalling real-mode operating system files 1071
    setting up dual boot capabilities with Windows 95 and
        MS-DOS 221
    special startup values 203–205
    starting real-mode operating system 201–203
    troubleshooting startup 1064
MSG files, attaching to electronic mail messages 845–846
MSN Central, The Microsoft Network 929
Multiconfig
    *See also* Hardware, profiles
    running menu options by means of hardware profiles 618
MultiLanguage, MSBATCH.INF parameter 1181
MULTILING.INF, keyboard strings 1046
Multimedia
    audio overview 703–704
    CDFS supplemental cache 570, 695–696
    changing computer settings in Custom Setup 99–100
    computer purchase guidelines 706–708
    data streams 702, 705
    devices
        classes 605
        detection and configuration during
            Setup 66, 88–91, 184–187
        Display Control Interface (DCI) 702
        MCI device types 701
        System subtree in Hkey_Local_Machine key 1030
        troubleshooting 710–712
        Windows 95 support 703
    digital video overview 700–703, 705
    features 700
    files 702
    hardware required for running Windows 95 69
    local-bus video 706
    Media Player 705, 712

Multimedia *(continued)*
    troubleshooting problems 709–712
Multiple Link Interface Driver (MLID) *See* ODI network
    adapter drivers
Multitasking
    cooperative 974
    MS-DOS–based applications 745
    preemptive
        overview 974
        performance tuning 554
        Windows 95 communications subsystem 794
    Win16-based applications 744
    Win32-based applications 742
Multithreading 974
Musical Instrument Digital Interface *See* MIDI

# N

Name, MSBATCH.INF parameter 1182
Name resolution
    broadcast name resolution 436
    description 436
    Dial-Up Networking connections to Shiva servers 911
    DNS
        description 437
        Internet connections 946–950
        overview 440–444
    HOSTS and LMHOSTS files 436, 1225–1230
    troubleshooting TCP/IP
        connections 449–451, 1143–1145
    WINS 437–439
Named pipes 1015
Names
    characters permitted in computer names 98
    computer names *See* Computers, names
    device classes 591–592
    DNS domain names 443
    Domain Name System *See* DNS
    establishing file naming policy for mixed network
        environments 646, 684
    F2 key, renaming objects 1232
    fully qualified domain name (FQDN) 443, 444
    host names
        *See also* LMHOSTS file; Name resolution
        description 443
    information required for Windows 95 Setup 68, 98
    Internet accounts 946
    label command 1104
    long filenames *See* Long filenames
    multiple network example 1001
    Name, MSBATCH.INF parameter 1182
    NetBIOS, nbtstat utility 1140–1142
    printers, MSBATCH.INF parameter 1199
    ren command 1104

Names *(continued)*
    resolving *See* Name resolution
    setting computer and workgroup names during network
        installation 257
    share names 407
    UNC names 407
    user name
        specifying in login scripts 375
        used for logging on to Windows 95 201
    viewing file aliases 681
    workgroup names 98
National Language Support API 1042, 1052, 1054–1055
Natural Keyboard keys 1235
Navigating in Windows 95 Setup 82
nbtstat, TCP/IP utility
    command-line switches 1140–1142
    troubleshooting TCP/IP connections 449–451
NCR network adapters, .INF file settings 1207
NCSA Mosaic *See* Mosaic
NDIS network drivers
    choosing 418
    DEC PATHWORKS networks 344
    mini-driver model 415, 1003
    NDIS 2 protocols 1003
    NDIS 2.x protocol drivers 415
    NDIS 3.1 adapter mini-drivers 1003
    obtaining electronically 1261–1262
    optimizing network performance 574
    overview 414–415, 1002
    PCMCIA network adapters 596
    peer-to-peer networks 267
    real-mode DLC protocol 351
    technical notes 427
    Windows Driver Library 1261–1262
NET.CFG
    file format 309
    IPX/SPX technical notes 431
    setting network adapter options 311–312
    setting shell version for OVL files 303
    Show Dots and file access limits 318
    troubleshooting NetWare network clients 331
Net commands
    AUTOEXEC.BAT entries, shared installations 128
    changing passwords on NetWare servers 474
    configuring computers for shared installations 126
    determining network adapter addresses 140
    listed 1106–1107
    net start full 172
    switches 1098
    troubleshooting network communications 262
    troubleshooting TCP/IP connections 449
    used in NetWare login scripts 392–394
NET.INF, network cards 1207
net view command, browsing network resources

net view command, browsing network resources *(continued)*
    at MS-DOS prompt  384
    description  1106
    displaying browse list  386
    NetWare networks  392
    on LAN Manager-compatible networks  387
    troubleshooting tool  385
Net Watcher tool
    constraints  538
    monitoring remote shared resources  537–539
    remote administration tool  530
    remote computer requirements  532
    running from Network Neighborhood  539
    SAP Advertising  412
NetBEUI protocol
    advantages  417, 419
    asynchronous *See* Remote Access Service (RAS)
    configuring manually  445
    DEC PATHWORKS networks  345
    description  416
    device IDs for use in setup scripts  1186
    Dial-Up Networking
        connecting to Shiva servers  908
        network protocols required  891
    installed during Setup  96
    mainframe connectivity  349
    NDIS 2.x protocol drivers  415
    necessary for remote administration  531
    overview  444
    peer-to-peer networks  267
    running Remote Registry service  535
    support for shared installations  139
    troubleshooting  447
    Windows 95 network architecture  1005
NetBIOS programming interface
    Dial-Up Networking
        gateway  899
        network protocols required  891
    IPC implementation  1014
    IPX/SPX protocol, description  415, 418
    LANA numbers  426
    Microsoft RPC facility  1012–1013
    MSBATCH.INF parameter  1196
    NetBEUI protocol  416, 417, 419, 444–445
    NetBIOS over IPX  430, 1004
    NetBIOS over TCP/IP
        description  416, 419
        nbtstat utility  1140–1142
    NetWare configuration file *See* NET.CFG
    network protocol device IDs  1186
    troubleshooting application failure  448
    Windows 95 network architecture  1004
NetCards, MSBATCH.INF parameter  1185

NETDET.INI file, customizing detection for NetWare
    networks  159
NETLOG.TXT  194–195
NETSETUP.EXE *See* Server-based Setup utility
NETSETUP.POL  117
NETSTART.BAT
    Safe Mode system startup  142, 1067–1068
    startup process for shared installations  139
netstat, TCP/IP utility
    command-line switches  1142–1143
    troubleshooting TCP/IP connections  449–451
NetWare
    configuration file *See* NET.CFG
    diskless workstations *See* Remote-boot workstations
    Microsoft Client for NetWare Networks *See* Client for
        NetWare Networks
    ODI drivers *See* ODI network adapter drivers
    Print Services *See* Print Services for NetWare
    real-mode network clients *See* NetWare networks, NETX;
        NetWare networks, VLM
NetWare Connect, Dial-Up Networking
    *See also* Dial-Up Networking
    connecting to remote access servers  890–892
    connecting to servers  907–908
    dial-up servers supported by Windows 95  889
    overview  887
NetWare for SAA gateway  358, 359
NetWare Naming Service (NNS)  287
NetWare networks
    ARCNet network adapters  314, 327
    backing up data  541–543
    browsing network resources
        controlling access  406
        description  380
        troubleshooting  408–411
        using Client for NetWare Networks  391–394
        using Network Neighborhood  388–391
        using Windows NT  394–395
    commands *See specific command names*
    configuring
        logon  371–373
        ODI drivers  309–310
        remote-boot workstations  131–133
    context commands for NetWare servers  390
    copying Windows 95 files to a server  114
    determining network adapter addresses for shared
        installations  140
    Dial-Up Networking
        NetWare Connect  907–908
        overview  885–892
        troubleshooting  920–922
    disabling automatic login  474, 514
    drive letters, tip  393

NetWare networks *(continued)*
    File and Printer Sharing *See* File and Printer Sharing,
      NetWare networks
    Gateway Service for NetWare, Windows NT 395
    installing
      JetAdmin for NetWare 767
      protected-mode networking support 253, 294–295
    installing Windows 95
      automated installation 290
      customizing detection 159
      overview 293–295
      preparation 293–295
      source files 289
    IP protocol 286, 287
    IPX/SPX protocol 288, 415, 427, 431
    load rpl command 138
    logging on to Windows 95 369
    login scripts *See* Login scripts, NetWare networks
    long filenames 252, 681
    machine directories 166, 480
    managing connections
      LOGIN.EXE stub 412
      troubleshooting 408–411
      using commands 391–394
      using Windows NT 394–395
      with Client for NetWare Networks 391
    monolithic IPX 312–313, 316, 327
    network clients
      *See also herein* NETX; VLM
      device IDs for use in setup scripts 1185
      multiple network support 995
      using other vendors' network clients 334
    network provider 998–999
    networks supported by Windows 95 334
    NETX network client
      accessing resources using Network
        Neighborhood 381
      configuring computers for shared
        installations 134–135
      enabling SAP browsing 403–405
      File and Printer Sharing 396, 398, 401
      installing correct adapter type 308
      installing Windows 95 306–308
      installing with Client for Microsoft Networks 308
      introduced 283
      LastDrive parameter 318
      long filenames not supported 682
      managing SAP browsing 411–412
      manual downloading of system policies 500–501, 526
      NET.CFG, NetWare configuration file 311
      NetWare API support 304–305
      overview 286–288
      processing login scripts 376
      reasons to choose or not to choose 287–288

NetWare networks, NETX network client *(continued)*
    required NetWare-supplied support files 325–327
    requirements for starting Windows 95 306
    running login scripts 379
    SearchMode, MSBATCH.INF parameter 1197
    setting in custom setup script 307
    sharing resources 403–407
    Show Dots and file access limits 318
    switching to from Client for Microsoft Networks 308
    troubleshooting 331–332
    troubleshooting system policies 526
    unified logon unavailable 373
    using as sole client 316
    using search mode with Windows 95 328
    using with Client for Microsoft Networks 314–316
Novell-supplied software *See* Novell, software
parameters for BOOTCONF.SYS 138–139
preparing for push installations 172
printing
    connecting to printers 760, 761
    notes on commands 392–394
    Point and Print 283, 755, 760–761
    print servers 572, 760–761
    Print Services for NetWare 755, 756, 763–765
    share names vs. NetWare volume names 407
    specifying shared printer resources 407
    Windows NT Gateway Service for NetWare 395
routing mail between postoffices, requirements 860
running
    NetWare utilities with Client for NetWare
      Networks 305
    Windows 95, overview 283–284
search mode
    system policy settings 514
    using with Windows 95 327–329
setting up user profiles 487, 489
supported by Windows 95 250
system policies
    automatic downloading 498–499, 526
    logon process 492
    manual downloading 499–501
    troubleshooting 526
TCP/IP protocol 288
UNC path names, syntax 407
user accounts
    Mail directory 487
    user-level vs. share-level security 460, 462–464
user-level security 460, 464, 533
using Microsoft Exchange with Microsoft Mail 852
versions supported by Windows 95 94
VLM network client
    accessing resources using Network
      Neighborhood 381

NetWare networks, VLM network client *(continued)*
 configuring computers for shared
  installations  134–135
 description  319
 enabling SAP browsing  403–405
 File and Printer Sharing  396, 398, 401
 installing  320–321
 installing with Client for Microsoft Networks  308
 introduced  283
 LastDrive parameter  324
 long filenames not supported  682
 managing SAP browsing  411–412
 manual downloading of system policies  500–501, 526
 NetWare API support  304–305
 overview  286–288
 processing login scripts  376
 reasons to choose or not to choose  287–288, 319
 required NetWare-supplied support files  325–327
 requirements for starting Windows 95  306
 running login scripts  379
 setting in custom setup script  307
 sharing resources  403–407
 troubleshooting  331–332
 troubleshooting system policies  526
 unified logon unavailable  373
 using as sole client  323–324
 using search mode with Windows 95  328
 using with Client for Microsoft Networks  322
 volume names vs. share names  407
 Windows 95 password cache  470–471
 workstation shell
  accessing resources on NetWare servers  293
  Show Dots and file access limits  318
  troubleshooting NetWare networks  331–332
NetWare servers
 bindery emulation  408, 462, 469–470, 911
 browsing network resources
  connecting to drives in Network
   Neighborhood  388–389
  context commands  390
  description  380
  LOGIN.EXE stub  412
 configuring
  network logon  371–373
  to support Windows 95  289–292
 connecting to  *See* NetWare networks, managing
  connections
 context commands  390
 interoperation with Client for NetWare Networks  285
 logging on
  before starting Windows 95  306
  considerations  366
  enabling logon validation  260
  LOGIN.EXE stub  412

NetWare servers, logging on *(continued)*
  overview  363
  passwords  330
  synchronizing credentials  330
  to Windows 95  369
 long filenames  290–291, 681
 mapping workgroups  164–166
 net commands  392–394
 NNS Add-on  287
 passwords  373, 474
 persistent connections  391
 preferred
  logging on to Windows 95  369, 371–373
  PreferredServer, MSBATCH.INF parameter  1196
  specifying  371–372
 preparing for push installations  174, 175
 print servers  572, 760–761
 routing mail between postoffices, requirements  860
 setting installation path in Server-based Setup  116
 sharing or lock violations, error messages  291
 Show Dots and file access limits  318
 troubleshooting  330, 331
 user profiles  292
 using Microsoft Exchange with Microsoft Mail  852
 viewing from command prompt  392
 Windows 95 password cache  470–471
 workstation shell  293
Network adapters
 addresses included in MACHINES.INI, determining for
  shared installations  140
 ARCNet  314, 327
 bind rpl, NetWare command  138
 checking
  for live network connections  260
  resource information  1076
  settings, drivers, and bindings in Control Panel  261
 configuring
  in Control Panel  254
  properties  420–425
  resource settings  421–424
  TCP/IP  *See* TCP/IP protocol
  with real-mode networking  278
 device classes  605
 device IDs for use in setup scripts  1185
 disabling  574
 drivers
  binding to protocols  421
  choosing  417–418
  configuring Client for NetWare Networks  297–299
  configuring properties  420–425
  correct adapter type for NetWare clients  308
  description  414
  detecting, DETLOG.TXT entries  192
  installing after Setup  419

Network adapters, drivers *(continued)*
    NDIS *See* NDIS network drivers
    obtaining electronically 1261–1262
    Open Datalink Interface (ODI) *See* ODI network
      adapter drivers
    required for networking support for shared
      installations 111
    safe detection 186, 192
    selecting and configuring in Custom Setup 93–94, 96
    system management tools 456
    SYSTEM.INI changes 214
    Windows Driver Library 1261–1262
  frame type
    Client for NetWare Networks 330
    Frame_Type, MSBATCH.INF parameter 1196
    NET.CFG, NetWare configuration file 311
    NetWare network clients 331
    network settings for Client for NetWare
      Networks 299
  hardware required for running Windows 95 69
  INF files
    format 427, 1185
    settings for common adapters 1207–1211
  information included in PROTOCOL.INI 278
  installing
    after Windows 95 is installed 255
    correct adapter type for NetWare clients 308
    protected-mode networking support 253
    using Control Panel 255
  LAN adapter numbers *See* LANA numbers
  monolithic IPX 312–313
  MSBATCH.INF parameters 1185–1193, 1207–1211
  NET.CFG, NetWare configuration file 311–312
  ODI *See* ODI network adapter drivers
  optimizing network performance 574
  PCMCIA cards *See* PCMCIA cards; Plug and Play
  Plug and Play-compliant *See* Plug and Play
  requiring special consideration under Windows 95 423
  setting LANA numbers 426
  troubleshooting network installation 261
Network architecture
  client-side named pipes 1015
  File and Printer Sharing 1008–1010
  Installable File System Manager 979, 994–995
  interprocess communications (IPC) 1010–1016
  mailslots 1015–1016
  Microsoft RPC facility 1012–1013
  multiple
    network example 1001
    network providers, overview 334
    network support 995–996
    provider router 997
  NDIS overview 1002–1003
  NetBIOS programming interface 1014

Network architecture *(continued)*
  network clients 1006–1008
  network protocols 1004–1005
  network providers 997–1000
  OSI reference model 992–994
  redirectors 994–995
  service provider interface 997
  support built into Windows 95 250–252, 264–265
  Win32 WinNet interface 996
  WinNet16 interface 1001
Network-based Setup *See* Server-based Setup utility
Network clients
  *See also* Client for Microsoft Networks; Client for
    NetWare Networks
  Artisoft LANtastic 337
  configuring in Control Panel 254
  configuring TCP/IP 434
  deploying Windows 95 45–48
  DHCP, TCP/IP protocol 416, 432–433
  installing 255
  logon validation 260, 363
  low-memory computers 557
  MSBATCH.INF parameters 1184, 1185, 1196–1197
  multiple network providers, overview 334
  multiple network support 334, 995–996
  NetWare *See* NetWare networks, NETX; NetWare
    networks, VLM
  network protocols 418
  optimizing network performance 573
  other vendors'
    installing 336–337
    listed 995
    tip for using 334
  planning for shared installations 110–111
  Primary Network Logon client *See* Primary Network
    Logon client
  protected-mode *See* Protected-mode, network clients
  provided with Windows 95 250
  real-mode *See* Real-mode, network clients
  selecting during Setup 93–95
  software and versions supported by Windows 95 94
  Windows 95 network architecture 1006–1008
  WINS, TCP/IP protocol 416, 432
Network drivers *See* Network adapters, drivers; NDIS
  network drivers
Network interface cards *See* Network adapters
Network Monitor agent
  benefits of using protected-mode network
    components 253
  configuring driver 546
  description 544
  device ID for use in setup scripts 1188
  installing 458, 544–545
  running 545–546

Network Neighborhood
  browsing network resources
    *See also* Browsing, network resources
    description 380
    hiding resources 401, 406
    in common dialog boxes 382–383
    on NetWare networks 388–391
    on other networks 251
    overview 364, 380–382
    troubleshooting 410
    using other vendors' network clients 334
    WANs 366
    workgroup configuration 366
  connecting to NetWare printers 761
  creating
    desktop shortcut to network resources 381
    folders 382
  customizing
    restricting access 512–513
    with system policies 382, 504, 507
  displaying Control Panel Network option, shortcut 254
  installing and sharing applications 718–719
  Point and Print, installing remote printers 759–761
  remote administration
    managing computers remotely 539
    NetWare computers 390
  restricting user actions *See* System policies; User profiles
  running applications 720
  running Server-based Setup 115
  troubleshooting network installation 260
  Windows 95 network provider support illustrated 998
  Windows 95 user interface 990
Network option *See* Control Panel
Network Performance Monitor, System Monitor categories and settings 583
Network printers
  configuring Client for Microsoft Networks 94
  connecting to 759–761
  printing to 762
  troubleshooting 784, 1067–1068
Network protocols
  *See also specific protocol names*
  AppleTalk 1222
  binding with network adapter drivers 421
  burst-mode NCPs 286
  choosing 418–419
  configuring in Control Panel 254
  DECnet 345
  DefaultProtocol, MSBATCH.INF parameter 1187
  Dial-Up Networking 891, 908
  drivers
    choosing 417–418
    description 414
    installing after Setup 419

Network protocols, drivers *(continued)*
    NDIS 418, 1003
    installing 255
    low-memory computers 557
    mainframe connectivity 349, 358
    NetBEUI 349, 1005
    NetBIOS over IPX 430, 1004
    netstat utility 449–451, 458, 1142–1143
    network architecture 1004–1005
    overview 415–417
    peer-to-peer networks 267
    Plug and Play-enabled 258
    protocol device IDs for use in setup scripts 1186
    Protocols, MSBATCH.INF parameter 1186
    remote access *See* Dial-Up Networking, connection protocols
    selecting and configuring in Custom Setup 93–94, 96
    Systems Management Server
      *See also* Systems Management Server
      Network Monitor component 1218
      WAN options 1216
    troubleshooting 447–451
    turning off support for packet-burst protocol 302
Network providers
  16-bit 998
  mapping workgroups to logon domains 164–166
  Microsoft networks 998–1000
  multiple, Windows 95 architecture 334, 997
  NetWare networks 998–999
  overview 997–1000
  System subtree in Hkey_Local_Machine key 1030
Network redirectors *See* Network clients; Redirectors
Network resources
  accessing, Dial-Up Networking 898
  browsing *See* Browsing, network resources
  changing passwords 473
  checking connections to 260
  creating desktop shortcut to 381
  creating folders 382
  printer connectivity, DLC protocol 350
Network services
  configuring in Control Panel 254
  installing after Windows 95 is installed 255
  low-memory computers 557
  selecting and configuring in Custom Setup 93–94, 97
  Services, MSBATCH.INF parameter 1187
  System subtree in Hkey_Local_Machine key 1032
Network=, MSDOS.SYS entry 205
Networking
  installing components 254–257
  issues 253
  logon validation *See* Logon validation
  mainframe connectivity 350–360

Networking *(continued)*
   migrating settings to Windows 95 during
      Setup 72, 1034–1037
   multiple network providers, overview 334
   name resolution *See* Name resolution
   network clients *See* Network clients
   Plug and Play *See* Plug and Play
   restricting user actions *See* System policies; User profiles
   running Windows 95 in a mixed Microsoft network
      environment 271–277
   shared copies of Windows 95 *See* Server-based Setup
      utility; Shared installations
   support
      *See also* Protected-mode, networking support; Real-
        mode, networking support
      built into Windows 95 250–252, 264–265
      for shared installations 139–140
      installing, recommended method 253
      other vendors' network clients 336–337
      setting computer and workgroup names 257
      troubleshooting 259–262
Networks
   Artisoft LANtastic *See* Artisoft LANtastic
   Banyan VINES *See* Banyan VINES
   cabling 266
   configuring components using Setup 77, 253, 254
   DEC PATHWORKS *See* DEC PATHWORKS
   File and Printer Sharing services *See* File and Printer
      Sharing
   hardware required for running Windows 95 69
   IBM OS/2 LAN Server *See* IBM OS/2 LAN Server
   information required for Windows 95 Setup 68
   installing and sharing applications 718–719
   installing components
      after Setup 255
      NETLOG.TXT 194–195
      recommended method 254
      using Control Panel 255
      using Setup 77, 253, 254
   long filename support 681–684
   Microsoft Fax overview 868–870
   number of connections allowed 251
   optimizing performance 573–574
   peer resource sharing *See* File and Printer Sharing
   peer-to-peer 266–267
   protected-mode components *See* Protected-mode, network
      components
   restricting access *See* Restricting access
   Safe Mode with Network Support startup 1067–1068
   selecting components in Custom Setup 93–97
   service providers *See* MAPI, service providers; Microsoft
      Exchange, service providers
   starting at system startup 258
   starting Windows 95 Setup 80

Networks *(continued)*
   startup disk limitations 181
   system policies *See* System policies
   The Microsoft Network *See* The Microsoft Network
   using user profiles *See* User profiles, using on networks
   Win32 WinNet interface 252, 335, 996
NETX *See* NetWare networks, NETX network client
New Fax wizard 873
New hardware
   Add New Hardware wizard *See* Add New Hardware
      wizard
   installing and configuring drivers using Setup 77, 244
   installing new devices 606–607
   modems *See* Modems
   printers *See* Printers, installing
   Run-Once Registry key 183
   updating startup disk 1069
NICs *See* Network adapters
NLIST SERVER, NetWare command 392
nlsfunc command 1104
"Not Enough Disk Space" message 145
Notational conventions used in this manual xvii
Notebook computers *See* Portable computers
Novell
   *See also* NetWare
   commands, notes 391–394
   DR DOS
      dual-booting functionality, troubleshooting
        startup 243
      upgrading to Windows 95 226
   MS-DOS APIs, Windows 95 support 285, 304–305
   NCPs, packet signatures 286, 287
   NetWare Naming Service (NNS) 287
   network adapters, INF file settings 1210
   NMS, remote administration tools 547
   Open Datalink Interface (ODI) *See* ODI network adapter
      drivers
   real-mode network clients *See* NetWare networks, NETX;
      NetWare networks, VLM
   software
      ensuring that it is running 306
      obtaining current files 305, 325–327
      Open Datalink Interface (ODI) 309–310
      patch for sharing or lock violations on NetWare
        servers 291
      RIPL, obtaining from CompuServe 135
NTFS partitions
   long filename support 682–684
   not available locally from within Windows 95 272
   requirements for installing Windows 95 71
Numbers
   LANA *See* LANA numbers
   Microsoft Fax addresses *See* Addresses, Microsoft
      Exchange address book

Numbers *(continued)*
   phone *See* Phone Dialer
   specifying regional settings 1044
   Windows 95 support for local conventions 1055
numlock command 1108
NUMLOCK key, accessibility shortcuts 1234
NWLINK protocol
   *See also* IPX/SPX-compatible protocol
   loading TSRs with Client for NetWare Networks 377
   MSBATCH.INF parameters 1186, 1196
   overview 427
NWREDIR.VXD 994

# O

Object applications (OLE) 740
Objects
   attaching to electronic mail messages 845–846
   monitoring system performance *See* System Monitor
   OLE *See* OLE
   shortcuts 1232–1233
ODI network adapter drivers
   ARCNet network adapters 314, 327
   choosing 418
   configuring Client for NetWare Networks 298
   configuring Windows 95 309–310
   determining correct adapter type for NetWare clients 308
   loading TSRs with Client for NetWare Networks 377
   NET.CFG, NetWare configuration file 311
   real-mode DLC protocol 354
   required NetWare-supplied support files 326
   switching to NETX from Client for Microsoft
      Networks 308
   technical notes 427
   tips for installing Windows 95 310
OEM character set, rules for long filenames 680
OLE
   attaching files or objects to mail messages 845–846
   audio clips 703
   Briefcase 918–920
   container applications 740
   drag and drop 741
   editing objects visually 740
   Hkey_Classes_Root Registry key 1023, 1028
   MAPI service providers 834, 857–858
   Microsoft Fax overview 866–870, 880–882
   object applications 740
   remote objects, Dial-Up Networking 898
   sharing data between applications 739–740
   The Microsoft Network 930, 935
   Windows 95 support 714
Online Help *See* Help
open, FTP command 1139

Open Datalink Interface (ODI) *See* ODI network adapter
   drivers
Open dialog box, shortcuts 1233
Opening
   applications 720
   Help 1224
   menus, Windows 95 vs. Apple Macintosh 1224
   new windows, shortcut 1232
Operating systems
   advantages of Win32-based applications 742
   demand paging 556
   dual-booting *See* Dual-boot operating systems
   installing Windows 95 over other operating
      systems 219–227
   protected-mode *See* Protected-mode
   real-mode
      *See also* COMMAND.COM; IO.SYS; MSDOS.SYS;
         Real-mode
      reinstalling system files 1071
   specifying in login scripts 375
   starting Windows 95 *See* Startup
   startup disk *See* Startup disk
   system management tools 456
   Windows 95 installation requirements 67–68
   Windows 95 networking support 250–252, 264–265
   Windows NT Server 273–274
Optimizers *See* Defragmenting disks; Disk Defragmenter
Optimizing performance
   *See also* Tuning performance
   conventional memory 575
   disk I/O, running Disk Defragmenter 646
   file system
      CDFS 569
      disk performance profiles 565–567
      overview 564–565
      troubleshooting options 569–570
   hard disks 565–567
   MS-DOS–based applications
      *See also* Applications, MS-DOS–based
      defining memory allocation 734
      speeding up video operations 735
   networks 573–574
   printing 572–573
   swap files 562–563
   tracking performance data with System Monitor 576–583
Option ROMs *See* ROMs
Optional components, MSBATCH.INF strings 1183
Org, MSBATCH.INF parameter 1182
OS/2
   dual-booting functionality, troubleshooting startup 243
   long filename support 683–684
   "OS/2 Detected" message 145
   requirements for installing Windows 95 68, 71

OS/2 *(continued)*
    restoring Boot Manager after Windows 95
       installation 227
    routing mail between postoffices, requirements 860
    running Windows 95 Setup 72
    troubleshooting Windows 95 installation 240
    upgrading to Windows 95 226–227
    Windows 95 Setup components that cannot be skipped or
       customized 145
OS/2 LAN Server *See* IBM OS/2 LAN Server
OSI reference model 992–994
Other vendors
    command shells 206
    contact information
       Cheyenne 542
       Conner Peripherals (Arcada) 541
    dial-up tools 886
    disk compression utilities
       size of drives displayed by Fdisk 649
       troubleshooting 697
    disk management utilities
       caution 645
       Registry APIs 1021
       Windows 95 volume tracker 652
    disk partitioning software, requirements for installing
      Windows 95 71
    drivers
       installing with custom setup scripts 157–159
       troubleshooting startup 244
    file systems 679
    memory managers, loading from CONFIG.SYS 206
    network clients
       installing network support 336–337
       listed 995
       tip for using 334
    PCMCIA cards 595, 615
    remote administration tools 547
    software, installing with custom setup scripts 157–159
    system administration agents 457
    system management software, using to automatically
      install Windows 95 76, 167
    telephony drivers 822
    utilities
       accessibility-enhancing 1252–1253
       long filename incompatibility 684, 685, 697–698
Out of Office Assistant, Microsoft Exchange 836
Overlay video 701, 703
Overriding
    default values in IO.SYS 203
    VxDs in VMM32.VXD 243
OVL files, setting shell version 303

**P**

P-node name resolution 437
PAB files 843
Packets
    burst-mode
       IPX/SPX protocol 415
       NCPs 286
       turning off support for packet-burst protocol 302
    LIP support for NetWare networks 285, 302
    NCP packet signatures 286, 287
    verifying transmission 1143–1147
    Windows 95 network architecture 995
Paging *See* Memory, paging; Swap files
pagingfile= entry, SYSTEM.INI
    computers starting from floppy disks 130
    computers starting from hard disks 130
    remote-boot workstations 133
PAP *See* Password Authentication Protocol (PAP)
Parallel modems, Windows 95 support 602
Parallel ports *See* Ports, parallel
Parameters vs. switches, command-line syntax 1098
Partitioning hard disks 647–649
Partitions
    caution when creating 647
    deleting 649
    determining type, CONFIG.SYS device= entry 647
    drivers required for system startup 1074
    extended 649, 650
    FAT
       installing Windows 95 over OS/2 226
       long filename support 683
       requirements for installing Windows 95 71
    fdisk
       deleting 649
       marking as active 240
       partitioning hard disks 647–649
       requirements for installing Windows 95 71
    HPFS
       long filename support 682–684
       requirements for installing Windows 95 71
    IDE drives 691
    NTFS
       long filename support 682–684
       not available locally from within Windows 95 272
       requirements for installing Windows 95 71
    primary 649, 650
    removable media devices *See* Removable media drives
    requirements for installing Windows 95 71
    Setup unable to find valid boot partition 239
Pass-through authentication
    bindery emulation, NetWare networks 408, 462, 464
    user-level vs. share-level security 460, 462–464

Pass-through security for peer resource sharing on NetWare networks 292
Password Authentication Protocol (PAP) 913, 950
Password List Editor 458, 460, 471–472
PassThroughAgent, MSBATCH.INF parameter 1191, 1202
Passwords
    backing up PWL files before running Setup 78
    caching
        description 460
        disabling 471, 515
        NetWare passwords 474
        network logon 460
        overview 470–471
        setting Windows NT network logon options with system policies 374, 515
        system management overview 456
        Windows 95 logon password 472–473
    changing 471, 473
    decisions for implementing network security model 461–462
    default policy definitions 492
    Dial-Up Networking
        configuring clients 896–897
        configuring servers 902–903
        troubleshooting 921
    encryption
        Dial-Up Networking connections 896–897, 902–903
        Internet connections 951
        Microsoft Fax 866, 877–880
    FTP and Telnet authentication, caution 1136
    guidelines 476
    Internet accounts 946
    logging on to
        NetWare servers 330
        other networks 251
        The Microsoft Network 926
        Windows 95 200
    logon validation, overview 363, 367–369
    Microsoft Exchange
        changing mailbox password 850
        profiles 846–848
        sharing Microsoft Mail workgroup postoffices 849
    needed for running Net Watcher 538
    NetWare servers
        changing 474
        tips 373
        using with Windows 95 474
    network fax passwords, restricting access to fax service 868
    Password List Editor 458, 460, 471–472
    peer-to-peer networks 267
    setting password policy 476
    sharing directories or printers, share-level security 466
    system policy settings 460, 475, 515

Passwords *(continued)*
    unified logon prompt 460
    user-level vs. share-level security 460, 462–464
    Windows 95 logon password 472–473
Passwords option *See* Control Panel
Pasting
    information in command-prompt windows 1101
    objects, shortcut 1232
Path
    connecting to NetWare drives 389
    destination, setting in Server-based Setup 117–118
    Devicepath, MSBATCH.INF parameter 1177
    path command 1104
    path statements in login scripts, caution 126
    PathCache Registry setting 566
    rules for long filenames 680
    setting for MS-DOS–based applications 736–737
    setting server installation path in Server-based Setup 116
    Setup requests new source path, troubleshooting 239
    specifying for MS-DOS–based applications 733
    UNC path names, syntax 407, 719
    Windows 95 vs. Apple Macintosh 1224
path command 1104
path=, AUTOEXEC.BAT entry 210
pause, MCI command 701
Pausing, command-line commands 1100
PC Support, connecting to AS/400 systems 359
PCI devices 596, 690
PCMCIA cards
    *See also* Plug and Play
    advantages of Plug and Play 593
    device classes 605
    device support in Windows 95 590
    enabling 614–617
    enhanced PCMCIA support 616–617
    installing devices 591
    modems
        configuring options 805
        enabling 614–617
        installing 802
        ports listed in Device Manager 629
        troubleshooting 824
    NDIS drivers, overview 414
    networking overview 258–259, 595–596
    not listed in Add New Hardware wizard 615
    supported by Windows 95 690
    troubleshooting 615–617
    wizard 614–617
PCONSOLE, NetWare command 402
PDR files 983
Pen Windows, MSBATCH.INF parameters 1178, 1181
Peer resource sharing *See* File and Printer Sharing
Peer-to-peer networks 266–267
Performance

Performance *(continued)*
    charts, configuring with System Monitor  576–577
    optimizing  *See* Optimizing performance; Tuning
        performance
    tracking data with System Monitor  537
Permissions
    granting Remote Access permission for Dial-Up
        Networking  907
    user-level security  467–468
Persistent connections  *See* Connections, persistent
Personal Address Book  835, 839–841, 843
Personal Folders, Microsoft Exchange
    adding  844
    backing up  844
    compressing  844
    converting MMF or PAB files to PST format  843
    description  843
    Personal Folder (.PST) MAPI service provider  835
Personal settings  *See* User profiles; USER.DAT
Phone Dialer
    description  800, 815
    dialing methods  816
    Dialing Properties  *See* Dialing Properties
    installing  815
    long-distance calls without "1" prefix  817
    starting  816
    storing phone numbers  816–817
    troubleshooting  829
    Windows 95 communications overview  792
Phone systems
    *See also* Communications; Fax; Modems
    dialing numbers  *See* Phone Dialer
    Dialing Properties  *See* Dialing Properties
    Direct Cable Connection  886, 916–917
    Microsoft Fax overview  866–870
    Microsoft Text Telephone (TT/TDD) services, technical
        support  1257
    modems  *See* Modems
    TAPI  796
    The Microsoft Network  *See* The Microsoft Network
PIF files
    command-line switches  1143–1145
    HOSTS file  1226
    location of key files  1154
    PIF Editor substitute  718
    running MS-DOS–based applications  726–736
    settings defined in APPS.INF  737–739
ping, TCP/IP utility
    checking IP addresses, Internet access  954
    troubleshooting TCP/IP connections  449–451, 954, 962
play, MCI command  701
Playing
    CDs  703, 711
    digital video  705

Playing *(continued)*
    WAV files, troubleshooting  709–710
Plug and Play
    booting devices  196
    computers, Setup hardware detection phase  180–181
    Configuration Manager  971–973
    DETLOG.TXT, hardware detection  194
    devices
        changing resource settings  608–613
        EISA  594
        extended capabilities ports (ECPs)  597
        Hkey_Dyn_Data Registry key  1022, 1033
        installing  593, 606
        ISA  196, 594
        loading protected-mode VxDs at startup  199
        mouse and pointing device drivers  627
        PCI  596
        PCMCIA  595–596, 614–617
        Registry information  1021
        safe detection  185
        SCSI  595
        types  594–597
        VL  596
        Windows 95 communications subsystem  794
    docking  *See* Docking
    drawbacks of using ODI drivers with Client for NetWare
        Networks  298
    drivers loaded by I/O Supervisor  984
    dynamic configuration  590
    enabled protocols  258
    IDE drives  691
    LANA numbers  426
    MPD files included with Windows 95  693
    NDIS drivers, overview  414
    network clients  335
    network protocols  417
    networking overview  251, 258–259, 592–593
    non-Plug and Play-compliant computers  *See* Legacy
        computers
    ports, configuring  628–630
    printers  759, 769, 989
    Registry interaction  967
    requirements  604
    serial ports  629
    Windows 95 block I/O subsystem  690
Plus! utilities  *See* Microsoft Plus! utilities
Point and Print
    connecting to remote printers  759–761
    installing remote printers  759–761
    NetWare print queues  283
    NetWare print servers  760–761
    specifying shared printer resources  383, 407
    Windows 95 printing subsystem  989
    Windows NT print servers  760

Point-to-Point protocol (PPP)
  Dial-Up Networking
    *See also* Dial-Up Networking
    connecting to remote access servers 890–892
    dial-up sequence 913–914
    log file 914, 920
    overview 887
    software and hardware compression 903–904
  Internet access to PPP servers 940, 951–952
Pointers, mouse *See* Cursors
Pointing devices
  *See also* Mouse
  accessibility features *See* Mouse
  changing computer settings in Custom Setup 99–100
  configuring behavior 628
  device classes 605
  device detection and configuration 66, 88–91, 184–187
  drivers
    changing 627
    overview 626–627
    Windows 95 support 602
  MSBATCH.INF parameters 1181
  Plug and Play-compliant 627
  support for multiple devices 1249
  support in Windows 95 589–591
  system management tools 456
  troubleshooting input devices 640
POL files 479
Policies
  file naming, mixed network environments 646, 684
  group policies *See* System policies
  installation policy
    customizing Windows 95 166
    setting in Server-based Setup 117–118, 148–153
  passwords, enforcing security 475–476
  policy files
    ADM files 518–524
    CONFIG.POL 490
    editing *See* System Policy Editor
    logon process 492
    master system policy files 166, 292
    POLICY.DAT, location 1155
  system *See* System policies
POLICY.DAT, location 1155
Portable computers
  Advanced Power Management support 99, 640
  disabling time-out intervals before running Setup 78
  display driver support 601
  docking, description 694
  hardware profiles 617–618
  loading raster fonts 777
  mobile computing

Portable computers, mobile computing *(continued)*
    *See also* Dial-Up Networking; Direct Cable
      Connection; Remote computers
    Briefcase 918–920
    deferred printing 989
    Windows 95 features 915
  optimizing performance 566
  PCMCIA cards *See* PCMCIA cards
  Plug and Play-compliant
    network protocols 417
    networking overview 258–259
  pointing devices 602
  port replicators used as docking station substitutes 694
Portable Setup 73
Ports
  COM *See herein* communications; serial
  communications
    communications architecture 795–797
    configuring 628–630
    description 629
    I/O addresses assigned to devices 629
    installing modems 802, 803, 805, 822, 826–827
    listed in Device Manager 629
    Plug and Play-compliant 629
  device classes 605
  Direct Cable Connection tool *See* Direct Cable
    Connection
  disabling ISA enumerator, troubleshooting startup 241
  I/O
    addresses included in DETLOG.TXT 190
    I/O Supervisor 983
    PDR extension required 983
    port drivers 983
    safe detection for devices 185–187
    troubleshooting hard disk device drivers 698
    Windows 95 port driver 981
  LPT *See herein* parallel
  MIDI, purchasing multimedia computers 707
  network adapters *See* Network adapters
  non-SCSI port drivers 694
  parallel
    description 629
    Direct Cable Connection *See* Direct Cable
      Connection
    extended capabilities ports (ECPs) 772
    number supported 602
    Plug and Play functionality 597
    possible configurations 772
    printing to network printers 762
  Plug and Play-compliant, configuring 628–630
  printers, configuring 628–630
  printing
    extended capabilities ports *See* Extended capabilities
      ports (ECPs)

Ports, printing *(continued)*
    troubleshooting 781
  replicators used as docking station substitutes 694
  serial
    communications hardware support 602
    communications ports 628–630
    connecting mice or pointing devices 627
    I/O addresses assigned to communications
      devices 629
    listed in Device Manager 629
    number supported 602
    Plug and Play-compliant 629
    pointing devices 602
  sound cards, troubleshooting 639
Postoffices *See* Microsoft Mail
PostScript
  ATMWorkaround= entry added to WIN.INI 215
  matching fonts 777
  mini-driver 770, 771
  troubleshooting 781, 1076
PPP *See* Point-to-Point protocol (PPP)
PPPLOG.TXT 914, 920
Preemptive multitasking *See* Multitasking, preemptive
Preferred NetWare servers *See* NetWare servers, preferred
PreferredServer= entry, setup scripts 153, 1196
"Preparing Directory" message 145
"Previous MS-DOS files not found" error message 243
Primary DOS partitions 649
Primary Network Logon client
  Artisoft LANtastic 339
  Client for Microsoft Networks 265, 269, 370
  Client for NetWare Networks 371–372
  installing File and Printer Sharing 397
  logon process 379
  unified logon prompt 460
  Windows 95 logon password 472–473
PrimaryWINS, MSBATCH.INF parameter 1195
Print jobs
  background print rendering 555
  Dial-Up Networking overview 886
  generating from remote sites *See* Printing, deferred
Print Services for NetWare
  device ID for use in setup scripts 1188
  installing 764
  introduced 755
  Microsoft Client for NetWare Networks 756
  overview 763–765
Printer drivers
  bidirectional communication support 989, 769
  installing remote printers with Point and Print 759–761
  location of key files 1154
  Microsoft Fax overview 880–882
  obtaining electronically 1261–1262
  overview 770

Printer drivers *(continued)*
  Plug and Play-compliant printers 759
  PostScript mini-driver 770, 771
  troubleshooting 779–784
  universal printer driver 770
  Windows Driver Library 1261–1262
Printer Installation wizard
  *See also* Add Printer wizard
  installing printers during Setup 103
Printers
  changing settings 763
  connecting to
    customizing connections with user profiles 482
    DEC PATHWORKS printers 344
    network drive and printer resources 383
    remote printers 759–761
    Windows NT printers 760
  DEC PrintServer Software 766
  device classes 605
  drivers *See* Printer drivers
  File and Printer Sharing *See* File and Printer Sharing
  installing
    Add Printer wizard 758–759
    and configuring during Setup 77, 103, 183
    font cartridges 756, 778
    methods 758
    or changing after Setup 104
    Plug and Play-compliant 759
    remote, with Point and Print 759–761
    troubleshooting 779
    upgrading to Windows 95 758
  Microsoft RPC Print Provider 767
  MSBATCH.INF parameters 1199
  network *See* Network printers
  performance tuning 557
  Plug and Play-compliant 759, 769, 989
  ports
    configuring 628–630
    extended capabilities ports *See* Extended capabilities
      ports (ECPs)
  Printer Installation wizard 103, 183
  remote 759–761
  sharing
    *See also* File and Printer Sharing
    protected-mode client necessary 756
    using share-level security 466
  support in Windows 95 589–591
  System subtree in Hkey_Local_Machine key 1031
  troubleshooting 779–784
  Windows NT
    ensuring logon validation 94
    retrieving Point and Print information 760
Printers folder
  accessing 758

Printers folder *(continued)*
    DLC protocol device driver, network connectivity  350
    installing or changing printers after Setup  104, 758–759
Printing
    background print rendering  555
    bidirectional communication support  769, 989
    DEC PrintServer Software  766
    deferred
        Dial-Up Networking overview  886
        introduced  755
        overview  773
        Windows 95 communications overview  793
        Windows 95 printing subsystem  989
    defining spool settings  572
    documents  *See* Documents, printing
    Enhanced Metafile Format (EMF)  572, 767–769, 989
    Hewlett-Packard JetAdmin utility  766–767
    Image Color Matching  *See* Image Color Matching (ICM)
    in Windows 95, overview  757
    Microsoft Fax overview  880–882
    Microsoft RPC Print Provider  767
    MS-DOS–based applications  773
    NetWare networks  *See* NetWare networks, printing
    optimizing performance  572–573
    Point and Print  *See* Point and Print
    PostScript files  *See* PostScript
    print monitors  *See* Monitors, print
    printer fonts  775
    troubleshooting  749, 779–784
    TrueType fonts  755, 770, 783, 785–788
    Windows 95 multilingual support  1048–1051
    Windows 95 printing subsystem  989
    Windows NT print servers  760
PRINTSCREEN key, accessibility shortcuts  1234
Process Scheduler  974
Processes, technical notes on MS-DOS components  560–561
ProcessLoginScript, MSBATCH.INF parameter  1196
Processors
    486 vs. 386  556
    B1 error message, troubleshooting Setup  238
    hardware required for running Windows 95  69
    performance tuning  556
    specifying in login scripts  375
    speed  556
    Symmetric Multiple Processor not supported by
       Windows 95  69
Prodigy
    obtaining information about Windows 95  1256
    obtaining Windows 95 Reviewer's Guide  39
Product ID number  88, 120, 1179
Profiles
    disk performance  565–567
    hardware  *See* Hardware, profiles
    Image Color Matching  *See* Image Color Matching (ICM)

Profiles *(continued)*
    Microsoft Exchange  *See* Microsoft Exchange, profiles
    roving  *See* User profiles
    user  *See* User profiles
Program Manager
    assigning icons to items  724
    groups
        backing up before running Setup  78
        converting to folders  72, 183, 220, 245–246
    retaining when upgrading from Windows 3.x  723–724
    limitations in Windows 95  723
    running applications  720, 723–724
Programs
    *See also* Applications
    adding or removing using Setup  77
    associating file types  721–722, 741, 752
    batch programs  *See* Batch files
    developing international versions, documentation  1041
    failed, closing  725, 743
    installing with custom setup scripts  157–159
    long filename incompatibility  684, 685, 697–698
    memory-resident  *See* TSRs
    MS-DOS Mode  *See* MS-DOS Mode
    scheduling tasks with System Agent  672–673
    switching between  1223
    Systems Management Server software distribution and
       installation  1218
    Windows 95 vs. Apple Macintosh  1223
Programs folder
    customizing  504, 507, 512
    description  484
    restricting user actions  *See* System policies; User profiles
    running applications  749
    user profile components  483
Programs menu  722, 751
prompt command  1104, 1139
prompt=, AUTOEXEC.BAT entry  210
Properties
    checking for correct file versions  1071
    Dialing  *See* Dialing Properties
    dialog box, shortcuts  1232, 1244
    displaying, shortcuts  254, 1232
    Microsoft Network option  930
    MS-DOS–based applications
       configuring  718, 729–736
       PIF files  726–727
Protected-mode
    cache, VFAT file system  679, 980
    drivers
       configuring Client for NetWare Networks  297, 299
       determining  630
       disabling, optimizing file system performance  568
       DriveSpace  555
       mapping to real-mode drivers  630–633, 982–984

Protected-mode, drivers *(continued)*
    removing 1061
    troubleshooting 633
IPX/SPX protocol *See* IPX/SPX-compatible protocol
loading operating system at startup 199
network clients
    *See also* Client for Microsoft Networks; Client for
      NetWare networks; Network clients
    client-side caching of network data 251, 286
    configuring computers for shared
      installations 126–133
    File and Printer Sharing 251, 261
    installing networking support 253
    long filename support 682
    multiple network providers, overview 334
    necessary for implementing user profiles 480
    necessary for sharing printers 756
    planning for shared installations 110
    preparing STARTUP.GRP file 170
    requirements for user profiles 145
    tip for using other vendors' clients 334
networking support
    components 250
    installing 253, 294–295
    new features in Windows 95 95
    startup process for shared installations 139
    support for shared installations 139–140
network components
    advantages 253
    protocols 415–419, 444
redirectors *See herein* network clients
VxDs, loading at startup 199
Proteon network adapters, .INF file settings 1210
PROTOCOL.INI
    hard disk location 1155
    migrating settings to Windows 95 during Setup 72, 220
    real-mode network initialization, overview 277–279
    safe detection for network adapters 186, 192
    starting networks at system startup 258
    troubleshooting
      connection problems with DLC protocol 360
      network installation 262
Protocol Manager, Plug and Play enhancements 414
Protocols
    *See also* Network protocols; *specific protocol names*
    burst-mode NCPs 286
    Dial-Up Networking connections to Shiva servers 908
    Link Control Protocol (LCP) 913
    LIP support for NetWare networks 285, 302
    modem data transfer
      cellular protocol option 807, 811
      supported by HyperTerminal 814, 829
    monolithic, NDIS drivers 1003
    MSBATCH.INF parameter 1186

Protocols *(continued)*
    NetWare Connect 887, 890–892, 907–908
    Reverse Address Resolution Protocol (RARP) 911
    Service Advertising Protocol (SAP) *See* SAP Advertising
PSERVER *See* Print Services for NetWare networks
PST files 843
Public keys, Microsoft Fax security 877–879
Pure Data network adapters, .INF file settings 1211
Push installations
    deploying Windows 95 47
    methods of performing 167
    migrating from Windows 3.x, push installation
      example 167–169
    net start full command 172
    NetWare servers 174, 175
    options 76
    overview 167
    performing with Systems Management Server 47, 53
    providing memory required by Setup 170
    running login scripts 176
    STARTUP.GRP 170–171
    upgrading earlier versions of Windows 170
    using login scripts to run setup scripts 125, 169–176
    Windows NT servers 172, 174–175
put, FTP command 1139
pwd, FTP command 1139
PWL files
    logon validation 367
    password caching 460, 470–471
PWLEDIT tool *See* Password List Editor

## Q

Quick Logon 270
QuickEdit mode 1101
quit, FTP command 1139
"Quit All Windows programs" message 145
Quitting
    System Agent 672
    Windows 95 513, 724
quote, FTP command 1139

## R

Racal network adapters, .INF file settings 1211
RAM *See* Memory, RAM
RARP *See* Reverse Address Resolution Protocol (RARP)
RAS *See* Remote Access Service (RAS)
Raster fonts 774, 777
rd command 1104
Read-only
    attribute
      attrib command 221

Read-only, attribute *(continued)*
    MS-DOS–based applications  730
    xcopy command-line switches  1120
  sharing directories or printers with share-level
    security  466
  specifying directory access rights  468
Real-mode
  drivers
    backing up before running Setup  78
    boot devices  632
    BOOTLOG.TXT  216
    installing  603
    IOS.INI file  631–633
    IOS.LOG  565
    loading at startup  197
    mapping protected-mode drivers  630–633, 982–984
    missing or damaged, troubleshooting startup  244
    MS-DOS components, technical notes  560–561
    MS-DOS Mode applications  632
    NDIS 2.x protocol drivers  415
    overview  630–632
    removing old mouse drivers  627
    safe driver list  631–633
    Stacker disk compression software  565
    startup disk limitations  181
    troubleshooting  639
    vs. protected-mode drivers  632
    WinNet16 interface  335, 338–339
  network clients
    configuration settings  253
    configuring computers for shared
      installations  134–135
    disadvantages  335
    Novell NetWare 3.x  *See* NetWare networks, NETX
    Novell NetWare 4.x  *See* NetWare networks, VLM
    preparing for push installations  172
  network components, troubleshooting  262
  network protocol  444
  networking support
    configuring adapters  278
    installing  253
    MS-DOS Mode applications running from shared
      installations  142
    network initialization file  *See* PROTOCOL.INI
    startup disk, networking support for shared
      installations  128
    startup process for shared installations  139
  operating system
    *See also* COMMAND.COM; IO.SYS; MSDOS.SYS
    reinstalling system files  1071
    starting  201–203
Recent folder  483, 484
Recently used
  applications, Hkey_Current_User Registry key  1033

Recently used *(continued)*
  command-line commands, recalling  1099
  files
    customizing settings with user profiles  482
    Hkey_Current_User Registry key  1033
    Registry settings, tuning performance  566
  installation paths, MSBATCH.INF parameter  1182
  phone numbers, Phone Dialer  816–817
Recording
  digital video  705
  for the Blind, Microsoft product documentation  1252
  sound  703, 704
Recovering Registry data  1024–1025
recv, FTP command  1140
Recycle Bin
  deleting objects, shortcut  1232
  overview  655
  Windows 95 vs. Apple Macintosh  1223
Redirectors
  *See also* Network clients
  Installable File System Manager  979, 994–995
  NWREDIR.VXD provided by Client for NetWare
    Networks  994
  VCACHE driver  980
  VREDIR.VXD provided by Client for Microsoft
    Networks  268
  Windows 95 network architecture  994–995
Reformatting hard disks  650–651
Refreshing display in Windows Explorer, shortcut  1233
REG files  1025
Regional editions  *See* International Windows 95
Registry
  adding SNMP communities  551
  APIs  1021
  associating file types with programs  721–722
  benefits  1018
  DAT files  *See* SYSTEM.DAT; USER.DAT
  description  967–968
  designating browse master  387
  device detection and configuration during
    Setup  66, 88–91, 180–181, 184–187
  Dial-Up Networking connections key  895
  editing
    caution  1017
    checking, clearing, or filling options  496–498
    default policy definitions  492
    restricting access  506, 513, 1020
    with Registry Editor  531, 536, 614, 1019–1020
    with System Policy Editor  495, 531, 535, 1020
  enabling Windows 3.1 file system  689
  finding specific information  1019
  flushes, description  1024
  font storage  755
  hardware tree  592, 972, 1033

Registry *(continued)*
    hierarchy 967–968, 1021–1023
    Hkey_Classes_Root Registry key 1023, 1028
    Hkey_Current_Config 1022, 1033
    Hkey_Current_User Registry key 1023, 1032–1033
    Hkey_Dyn_Data Registry key 1022, 1033
    Hkey_Local_Machine key 1022, 1026–1029
    Hkey_Users Registry key 1032–1033
    INF file sections 1165
    installing
        applications 717
        new devices 606
    loading fonts 777
    long filename support for NetWare servers 291
    Microsoft Fax entries 881–882
    migrating system settings during
        Setup 72, 1021, 1034–1037
    modem keys 810–813
    NameCache setting 566
    OLE objects 740
    overview 967–968, 1018–1019
    PathCache setting 566
    Plug and Play usage 967
    recovering data 1024–1025
    remote administration *See* Remote computers, managing
        remote registries
    Remote Registry service *See* Remote Registry service
    removing remote agents 551
    resource management 590
    restoring data 1025
    Run-Once key 183
    saving data 1025
    structure 967–968, 1021–1024
    system policy entries 490
    SYSTEM.INI settings 1036
    troubleshooting
        modem commands 810
        restoring DAT files 1061
        system Registry file missing 242
        wrong applications run at Windows 95 startup 244
    turning off numeric tails for long filename aliases 688
    use by Windows 95 operating system 1019–1021
    value entries 1022–1024
    WIN.INI settings 1034
    Win16-based applications' use of INI files 1034
    Windows 95 system management 457
Registry Editor
    changing device resource settings 614
    managing remote registries 536
    overview 1019–1020
    remote administration tool 530
    remote computer requirements 532
    restoring Registry data 1025
    restricting access to 1020

Registry Editor *(continued)*
    running 614, 1019
    testing changes made 614
    vs. System Policy Editor 531
    vs. Windows 3.x INI files 967
rem command 1108
Remote access servers
    *See also* Dial-Up Networking, dial-up servers
    connection protocols 890–892
    disabling dial-up server support 901
    installing RAS 906
    Microsoft Mail postoffices 852–856
    NetWare Connect servers 907–908
    security options 902–903
    Shiva servers 908–912
    troubleshooting 920–922
    types supported by Windows 95 889
    Windows 95 dial-up servers 887, 899–901
    Windows NT 887, 904–907
Remote Access Service (RAS)
    Dial-Up Networking *See* Dial-Up Networking; Remote
        access servers
        configuring Windows NT servers for Windows 95
            dial-up clients 905–907
        connecting to remote access servers 890–892
        overview 885, 887
    granting Remote Access permission 907
    installing 906
    troubleshooting with Network Monitor agent 544
Remote administration
    backup agents *See* Agents, backup
    deploying Windows 95 46
    enabling
        automatically 533, 1201–1203
        manually 533
        on NetWare networks 533
        shared resources created 532
    general requirements 532
    granting privilege 532
    Net Watcher *See* Net Watcher tool
    Network Monitor agent 544
    Network Neighborhood
        managing computers remotely 539
        NetWare computers 390
    other vendors' tools 547
    overview 530
    Registry Editor *See* Registry Editor
    Remote Registry service *See* Remote Registry service
    setting up after Setup 532
    system management overview 456
    System Monitor *See* System Monitor
    System Policy Editor *See* System Policy Editor
    Systems Management Server tools 1218
    Win32-based APIs 968

Remote-boot workstations
  configuring
    AUTOEXEC.BAT  132
    for Client for NetWare Networks  131–133
    for real-mode networking  135
  disk space required for shared installations  111
  installing Windows 95 with setup scripts  124–125, 1189
  loading RPL on a NetWare server  138
  machine directories  108–109, 122–124
  memory required for shared installations  112
  overview of Server-based Setup  106–107
  parameters for BOOTCONF.SYS  138–139
  remote-boot disk images
    creating  135–137
    description  132
    networking support for shared installations  1189
  RPLSetup, MSBATCH.INF parameter  1189
  startup disk
    files copied  132, 133
    networking support for shared installations  128
  swap file requirements for shared installations  112
  TEMP and TMP environment variables  210
  Windows 95 Setup for shared installations  75
Remote computers
  administering  *See* Remote administration
  browsing file systems  532
  connecting to
    troubleshooting  *See* Troubleshooting, connections
    with Net Watcher  538
    with Registry Editor  536
    with System Monitor  537, 539
    with System Policy Editor  535
  FTP and Telnet password authentication, caution  1136
  generating print jobs from remote sites  *See* Deferred
    printing
  HOSTS file  1226–1227
  managing remote registries
    Win32-based APIs  968
    with Registry Editor  532, 536, 614
    with System Policy Editor  532, 535
  monitoring shared resources with Net
    Watcher  532, 537–539
  network access  *See* Dial-Up Networking
  Network Monitor agent  544
  remote host names, mapping to IP addresses  1226–1227
  synchronizing files with Briefcase  918–920
  troubleshooting, Systems Management Server tools  1218
  viewing with System Monitor  537
  Windows 95 mobile computing features  915
Remote drives, long filename support  682
Remote mail
  Dial-Up Networking overview  885
  Internet access  941, 946
  Microsoft Exchange

Remote mail, Microsoft Exchange  *(continued)*
    overview  792, 834
    profiles  846–848
  Microsoft Mail postoffices  852–856
  scheduling sessions  856
  Windows 95 communications overview  793
Remote printers, connecting to  759–761
Remote Procedure Calls (RPCs)
  Microsoft RPC facility  1012–1013
  system administration via Registry APIs  1021
Remote Program Load  *See* RIPL
Remote Registry service
  benefits of using protected-mode network
    components  253
  device ID for use in setup scripts  1188
  installing  458, 534
  Registry overview  1019
  removing  551
  setting network logon options  374
  technical notes  535
  user-level security  460
Remote Update system policy  499–501, 525
remotehelp, FTP command  1140
Removable media drives
  assigning drive letters  652–653
  block device drivers  690
  compressing data  *See* Disk compression; DriveSpace disk
    compression utility
  identifying volumes  652
  MaxRemovableDrivePartition entry  653
  requirements for installing Windows 95  71
  software-based media ejection  694
  tracking  652
  troubleshooting SCSI devices  637
  Windows 95 support  693–694
RemoveBinding, MSBATCH.INF parameter  1187
Removing
  applications with Add/Remove Programs option  720
  calling cards  819
  Find command from Start Menu  513
  long filenames  *See* LFNBK utility
  protected-mode drivers  1061
  remote agents  551
  Run command from Start Menu  508, 513, 535
  unnecessary drivers  1073
  users from the local access control list  469
  Windows 95
    components using Setup  77
    description  227
    from a Windows NT computer  233
    from the command line  227–230
    using previous operating system  230–233
ren command  1104

rename command
    description 1104
    FTP command 1140
    long filenames 697
Renaming objects, shortcut 1232
Repair Setup 76
Repairing disks *See* ScanDisk
RepeatKeys, accessibility feature 1244
Request A Fax wizard 874
Reserving drive letters for removable media 652
Resolution, display *See* Display, resolution
Resource Kit
    *See also OVERVIEW.HLP on Resource Kit disks*
    foreign language versions 1041
    overview xv
    setup scripts included 146
    standard abbreviations and acronyms xviii
    system policy files included 506
    utilities included xvii
Resources
    communications resources, description 628
    customizing connections with user profiles 482
    device settings *See* Devices
    long filenames *See* Long filenames
    network *See* Network resources
    peer resource sharing *See* File and Printer Sharing
    resource arbitrators 972
    shared *See* Shared resources
    system
        assessing performance 560
        capacity 558–560, 714
        scheduling with Process Scheduler 974
        troubleshooting printing 783
        Virtual Machine Manager 973–977
        Windows 95 improvement 554
Responses, modem Registry key 811–812
Restarting Setup after failure 234
Restoring
    COMMAND.COM 1072–1073
    long filenames *See* LFNBK utility
    OS/2 Boot Manager after Windows 95 installation 227
    persistent connections
        Client for Microsoft Networks 270, 370
        Client for NetWare Networks 305, 391
    REGEDIT.EXE command-line switches 1025
    Registry data 1025
Restricting access
    *See also* System policies; User profiles
    to network fax service 868
    to Registry editing tools 1020
    using local access control lists 469
    with system policies
        customizing desktop 507
        decisions 481

Restricting access, with system policies *(continued)*
        defining desktop settings 511
        description 479
        examples 506–508, 535
        system management overview 456
        to computer-specific settings 514–517
        to Control Panel 506, 509–510
        to File and Printer Sharing 511
        to security options 465
        to shell settings 512
        to system settings 513
Retrieving faxes 874
Retrieving mail messages *See* Downloading, mail
Reverse Address Resolution Protocol (RARP) 911
Rights
    The Microsoft Network chat rooms 934
    user-level security 467–468
RIGHTS, NetWare command 402
RIPL
    creating remote-boot disk images 135–137
    loading on NetWare servers 138
    Microsoft RPLIMAGE utility 136–137
    workstations *See* Remote-boot workstations
RLL bus adapters 690
rmdir command 1104, 1140
ROMs
    booting legacy devices 196
    incompatible BIOS setting, troubleshooting startup 242
    interactions with Plug and Play BIOS 196
    ROM BIOS virus checking, troubleshooting Setup 238
    specifying MS-DOS–based application properties 735
Root directory, long filenames 685, 697–698
route, TCP/IP utility 1145
Routing
    audio lines, description 704
    configuring TCP/IP 435
    IP routers
        HOSTS and LMHOSTS files 1225–1230
        required for Internet Dial-Up Networking access 899
    IPX/SPX protocol, description 415
    mail between postoffices, requirements 860
    multiple provider router 997
    network routing tables, route utility 1145
    setting up dedicated Internet connections 961
    Windows NT Services for Macintosh 1222
Roving profiles 487–488
RPC Print Provider 767
RPCs *See* Remote Procedure Calls (RPCs)
RPLSetup, MSBATCH.INF parameter 1189
RS-232 ports *See* COM ports; Ports, communications
Run command
    disabling 508, 513, 535
    external Windows 95 commands 1102
    Windows Explorer command-line switches 1118

Run-Once options, Setup *See* Setup, Run-Once options
Running
   *See also* Starting
   applications *See* Running applications
   batch files
      before starting MS-DOS–based applications  737
      using command prompt settings  727
      with System Agent  677
   CONFIG.SYS and AUTOEXEC.BAT  197, 205–213
   MS-DOS after installing Windows 95, tip  223
   services at startup, system policy settings  517
   Setup *See* Setup, running
   utilities *See specific utility names*
   Windows 95
      with DEC PATHWORKS  276
      with IBM OS/2 LAN Server  275–276
      with LAN Manager  275–276
      with Windows for Workgroups  276
      with Windows NT  271–274
      with Workgroup Add-on for
        MS-DOS  277, 386, 444–445
Running applications
   adding applications to Start or Programs menus  722, 749
   APPS.INF *See* APPS.INF file
   associating file types with applications  721–722, 741, 752
   at startup, system policy settings  517
   bringing to foreground  720
   closing failed programs  725, 743
   fixing version-checking errors  747–748
   methods for opening  720
   MS-DOS–based *See* Applications, MS-DOS–based;
     MS-DOS Mode, running MS-DOS–based applications
   scheduling system resources with Process Scheduler  974
   sharing data using OLE  739–740
   that replace system DLLs  748
   troubleshooting
      desktop shortcut hot keys  749
      NetBIOS application failure  448
      unassociated filename extensions  752
   TSRs *See* TSRs
   using Windows 3.x Program Manager  723–724
   Win16-based  744
   Win32-based  742–743
   Windows 95 support, overview  714–716
   Windows 95 vs. Apple Macintosh  1223

## S

Safe detection
   network adapters  186, 192
   overview  184–186
   proprietary adapters for CD-ROM  187
   SCSI controllers  186
   skipping detection of certain device classes  186, 191

Safe detection *(continued)*
   sound cards  187
Safe Mode system startup
   changing graphics performance settings  571
   changing to VGA display driver  636
   options  1064
   overview  1065–1066
   recovering from faulty installation of Windows 3.x device
     drivers  603
   Safe Mode options  1065–1070
   security considerations  462
   shared installations  142
   testing changes made in Registry Editor  614
   troubleshooting display  634
   troubleshooting graphics printing  783
   win command, switches  1069, 1075
Safe Recovery *See* Setup, Safe Recovery option
SAP Advertising
   description  403
   Disable SAP Advertising policy  411
   GetNearestServer broadcasts  412
   managing SAP browsing for NetWare
     networks  403–405, 409, 411–412
   Use_SAP, MSBATCH.INF parameter  1197
Save dialog box, shortcuts  1233
SaveSUBoot, MSBATCH.INF parameter  1179
Saving
   documents  382, 1224
   public keys, Microsoft Fax  879
   Registry data  1025
ScanDisk
   checking for disk corruption and lost memory allocation
     units  1077
   command-line switches  1134–1135
   exit codes  1135
   locking volumes while running disk utilities  654
   overview  658–659
   putting in Startup group  646, 653
   running
      automatically with Setup  78
      before enabling Windows 3.1 file system  689
      on unmounted CVFs  660, 697
      procedure  659–661
      when removing Windows 95  228, 231
   scheduling with System Agent  672
   skipping  78, 81
   technical note for Windows 95 Setup  84
scandisk command  1104, 1134–1135
Scanners, MCI device types  701
Scanning disks for errors *See* Defragmenting disks; Disk
  Defragmenter; ScanDisk
Scheduling
   Process Scheduler  974
   remote mail sessions  856

Scheduling *(continued)*
    tasks with System Agent  675
Scope IDs
    configuring WINS name resolution  439
    ScopeID, MSBATCH.INF parameter  1195
    troubleshooting TCP/IP connections  449
Screen
    *See also* Display; Monitors
    cls command  1102
    fonts  775
    properties, configuring MS-DOS–based applications  735
    troubleshooting applications  750
Screen savers
    changing passwords  473
    energy-saving  625–626
Scripts
    login *See* Login scripts
    setup *See* Setup scripts
SCSI
    adapters and buses
        troubleshooting  637
        types supported by Windows 95  690
    controllers
        safe detection  186
        Windows 95 port driver  981
        Windows 95 support  693
    devices *See* Devices, SCSI
SCSI Manager  981
SDK information  1258
Search mode, NetWare networks
    restricting access, system policy settings  514
    SearchMode, MSBATCH.INF parameter  1197
    using with Windows 95  327–329
SecondaryWINS, MSBATCH.INF parameter  1195
Security
    decisions  461–462
    Dial-Up Networking *See* Dial-Up Networking, security
    File and Printer Sharing *See* File and Printer Sharing
    Internet connections, PPP servers  951
    master system policy files  166, 292
    Microsoft Fax  866, 877–880
    MSBATCH.INF parameters  1190, 1202
    passwords
        *See also* Passwords
        enforcing with system policies  475
        guidelines  476
        NetWare passwords  474
        password cache  470–471
        Windows 95 logon password  472–473
    restricting access *See* Restricting access
    role of workgroups in Windows 95  380
    setting up for shared resources  464–465
    share-level *See* Share-level security
    system management overview  456

Security *(continued)*
    The Microsoft Network  927
    user-level *See* User-level security
    Windows 95, overview  460–464
    WRKGRP.INI files  76
Segments, description  976
Select All command, Windows Explorer shortcut  1233
Selecting
    information in command-prompt windows  1101
    items in dialog boxes  1244
send, FTP command  1140
Sending
    faxes
        methods  872–873
        Microsoft Fax overview  866–870
        Microsoft Fax Registry entries  881–882
    files *See* Binary file transfer; Transferring, files;
       Microsoft File Transfer
    mail
        Dial-Up Networking overview  885
        Internet access  941, 946
Serial Line Internet Protocol (SLIP)
    compressed and uncompressed accounts  952
    Dial-Up Networking  890–892
    installing  896, 952
    Internet access to SLIP servers  940, 952–954
Serial ports *See* Ports, serial
SerialKeys, accessibility feature  1249
Server-based Setup utility
    *See also* Shared installations
    CD Key identification number  120
    client computer requirements  112
    copying Windows 95 files to a server  114–121
    creating
        default setup script  119–120
        machine directories  108–109, 122–124
    custom installations *See* Custom installations
    directory structure created  121
    installing Windows 95 source files on NetWare
       networks  289
    main tasks  113–114
    NETSETUP.POL  117
    network path, system policy settings  517
    overview  106–107
    push installations *See* Push installations
    running  115
    SaveSUBoot, MSBATCH.INF parameter  1179
    server requirements  111
    setting
        destination path  117–118
        installation policy  117–118
        server installation path  116
    troubleshooting  240

Servers
    access impossible during Setup, troubleshooting  237
    automatic reconnection for lost server connections
        Client for Microsoft Networks  270, 370
        Client for NetWare Networks  285
        Windows 95 networking feature  251
    browse servers  *See* Browse servers
    checking connections to network resources  260
    connecting to
        Artisoft LANtastic servers  340
        Banyan VINES servers  343
        customizing with user profiles  482
        DEC PATHWORKS servers  344
        IBM OS/2 LAN Server servers  347
        SunSoft PC-NFS servers  347
    copying Windows 95 files to a server  114–121
    dial-up  *See* Dial-Up Networking
    ensuring user logon capabilities in setup scripts  153
    establishing diagnostic servers  262
    fax servers  868–877
    File Server for Macintosh  1222
    LAN Manager, ensuring visibility to Windows 95
        computers  275
    mail  *See* Microsoft Mail, workgroup postoffice
    NetWare  *See* NetWare servers
    peer servers  *See* File and Printer Sharing
    peer-to-peer networks  266–267
    PPP  *See* Dial-Up Networking; Internet; Point-to-Point
        protocol (PPP)
    preferred  *See* NetWare servers, preferred
    push installations  *See* Push installations
    remote access  *See* Remote access servers
    shared installations  *See* Server-based Setup utility; Shared
        installations
    Shiva  *See* Shiva servers
    Systems Management Server  *See* Microsoft Systems
        Management Server
    troubleshooting TCP/IP connections  450
    viewing machine directories  123
    Windows NT  *See* Windows NT, Server
    WINS  *See* WINS
Service Advertising Protocol (SAP)  *See* SAP Advertising
Services
    communications, Windows 95 subsystem  792–794
    Microsoft Consulting Services  1259
    Microsoft Download Service (MSDL)  1257, 1260–1261
    NetWare Naming Service (NNS)  287
    network  *See* Network services
    peer resource sharing  *See* File and Printer Sharing
    running at startup, system policy settings  517
    Windows 95 service provider interface  997
    Windows Internet Naming Service  *See* WINS
    Windows NT Services for Macintosh  1222
Services, MSBATCH.INF parameter  1187

set command  1077, 1105
setmdir command, machine directories for shared
    installations  128, 140–142
SETPASS, NetWare command  474
Setup
    adding, removing, and configuring Windows 95
        components  77
    administrative  *See* Server-based Setup utility
    analyzing the computer  88–91
    basic tasks  65–66
    Batch Setup
        creating custom setup scripts  146
        customizing Setup for accessibility  82, 155–157
        overview  153–154
    command-line switches  80
    components that cannot be skipped or customized  145
    configuring Microsoft Exchange  104
    continuing after stall  91
    copying Windows 95 files  181–182
    creating a startup disk  101, 102, 181–182, 1063
    custom installations  *See* Custom installations
    Custom Setup  *See* Custom Setup
    customizing for accessibility  82, 155–157
    device detection and
        configuration  66, 88–91, 180–181, 184–187
    disabling TSRs  77, 179, 1204
    failure  *See* Safe Recovery option, Setup
    files
        directory structure created  121, 1153
        extracting with Extract program  1150–1152
        location of key files  1154
        overview  1152
        Windows 95 distribution disks  1150
    final system configuration phase  183
    gathering information
        checking disk space required  87
        choosing Windows directory  85–86
        selecting Setup type  87
        technical discussion  179–180
    help  81
    initializing the system  183
    installation requirements
        hardware  69–70
        memory  68
        NetWare networks  293–295
        operating system  67–68
        partitions  71
    installation types  73–78, 1178
    installing networking support
        after Windows 95 is installed  255
        NetWare networks  293–295
        Novell-supplied NetWare client support  306–308
        other vendors  336–337
        recommended method  253, 254

Setup, installing networking support *(continued)*
    troubleshooting 259–262
    using Control Panel 255
    with ODI drivers, tips 310
  installing Windows 95 over other operating systems
    DR DOS 226
    dual-booting with MS-DOS 219, 221
    dual-booting with Windows 3.x 219, 221
    dual-booting with Windows for Workgroups 219, 221
    dual-booting with Windows NT 219, 225
    MS-DOS 222–224
    OS/2 226
    overview 219
    Windows 3.x 219–220, 1021
    Windows for Workgroups 219–220, 1021
  local installation 75
  log files
    DETCRASH.LOG 187, 1155
    DETLOG.TXT 187, 190–194, 1062
    SETUPLOG.TXT 187–190, 1155
  maintenance 76
  memory, STARTUP.GRP file 170
  messages *See* Messages
  migrating .GRP and .INI information from
    Windows 3.x 86
  navigating 82
  new features 66–67
  omitting minimum disk-space check 81, 87
  overview 65–67
  Product ID number 88, 120, 1179
  providing user information 88
  push installations *See* Push installations
  quick start 65–66
  repair 76
  retaining Windows 3.x Program Manager 724
  Run-Once options
    configuring MIDI devices 104
    defining in setup scripts 158–159
    defining in system policies 517
    description 102
    initializing the system after Setup 183
    installing and configuring printers 103
    setting local time zone 103
  running
    Batch Setup 153
    for shared installations 75
    from a network computer 80
    from custom setup scripts 162–163
    from MS-DOS 80
    from MS-DOS or Windows 72, 179
    from Windows 3.x or Windows for Workgroups 79
    on local computers 75
    on Windows NT computers 272
    Server-based Setup 115

Setup *(continued)*
  safe detection *See* Safe detection
  Safe Recovery option
    choosing 83
    DETCRASH.LOG 1062
    introduced 76
    lines placed in AUTOEXEC.BAT during
      installation 184
    log files 187–195, 1155
    skipping detection of certain hardware 89, 186, 191
    troubleshooting strategies 1062
    using after Setup failure 91
  ScanDisk, technical note 84
  scripts *See* Setup scripts; Shared installations
  selecting network components 93–97
  selecting software components 91–93
  server-based *See* Server-based Setup utility; Shared
    installations
  setting local time zone 103, 1179
  shared installations *See* Shared installations
  skipping
    detection of certain hardware 89, 186, 191
    ScanDisk check 78, 81
  specifying
    computer identification 98
    regional settings 1042–1043
  system files to back up first 78
  troubleshooting *See* Troubleshooting, Setup
  verifying installed components 1063
SETUP.EXE 1152
Setup scripts
  *See also* MSBATCH.INF
  automated installation failure, troubleshooting 240
  batch installation 67, 76
  custom *See* Custom installations
  default, creating 119–120
  deploying Windows 95 47
  ensuring user logon capabilities 153
  examples 1201–1204
  included with Windows 95 Resource Kit 146
  information required 68
  machine directories 124
  parameters *See* MSBATCH.INF, parameters
  push installations *See* Push installations
  running from a network computer 80
  sample file 1204–1206
  SETUPLOG.TXT entries 189–190
  shared installations *See* Shared installations
  skipping creation 119
  troubleshooting Setup installation or detection errors 1062
SETUPLOG.TXT
  categories 189
  copying entries to MSBATCH.INF 1180, 1183
  description 188

SETUPLOG.TXT *(continued)*
    entries 189–190
    hard disk location 1155
    location on compressed disks 1156
    troubleshooting strategies 1062
    using 187
setver command 1105
setver.exe, IO.SYS entry 202
Share-level security
    description 460, 462–464
    Dial-Up Networking 900, 902, 903
    password needed for running Net Watcher 538
    peer-to-peer networks 267
    Security, MSBATCH.INF parameter 1190, 1202
    setting up for shared resources 464–465
    using 466
Shared directories
    *See also* Shared resources
    connecting to network resources 383
    File and Printer Sharing configuration 400, 406
    share-level security 466
Shared files *See* Shared resources
Shared installations
    *See also* Server-based Setup utility
    benefits 108
    client computers
        *See also* Client computers, shared installations
        determining network adapter addresses 140
        requirements 112
    copying
        custom files during Windows 95 installation 1201
        Windows 95 files to a server 114–121
    creating
        default setup script 119–120
        machine directories 108–109, 122–124
    default directory structure 121
    definition 65
    description 75
    file organization 109
    installation directory 109
    installing Windows 95 with setup scripts 124–125, 1201
    logging off, then logging on as a different user 142
    machine directories *See* Home directories; Machine
      directories; Mail directory
    MACHINES.INI 140–142
    methods for creating 106
    migrating from Windows 3.x, example 167–169
    MS-DOS Mode applications 142
    MSBATCH.INF parameters 1189–1190
    NDIS 2.x protocol drivers 415
    network adapter drivers required 111
    networking support 139–140
    overview of Server-based Setup 106–107
    planning

Shared installations, planning *(continued)*
        custom installations 145
        for network clients 110–111
    remote-boot workstations
        configuring for Client for NetWare
          Networks 131–133
        configuring for real-mode networking 135
        RPLSetup, MSBATCH.INF parameter 1189
    Safe Mode system startup 142, 1067–1068
    server requirements 111
    setmdir command 140–142
    setting configuration information
        computers starting from floppy disks 130–131, 134
        computers starting from hard disks 128–130, 134
        protected-mode clients 126–133
        real-mode clients 134–135
        remote-boot workstations 131, 133, 135
    specifying boot drive 1189
    startup process 139
    swap files 133
    typical use 107
    WorkstationSetup, MSBATCH.INF parameter 1190
Shared resources
    browsing, net view command 384, 385
    created when enabling remote administration 532
    creating with Net Watcher, example 538
    dial-up servers 887
    Direct Cable Connection *See* Direct Cable Connection
    File and Printer Sharing *See* File and Printer Sharing
    network fax service 868–877
    optimizing file system performance 569–570
    password cache overview 470–471
    peer resource sharing *See* File and Printer Sharing
    remote, monitoring with Net Watcher 537–539
    setting up security 464–465
    share names vs. NetWare volume names 407
    share-level security 466
    user-level security 467
    Windows NT Gateway Service for NetWare 395
Sharing
    *See also* Shared resources
    applications across networks 718–719
    CD-ROM drives 365, 402
    fax modems 874–877
    files *See* File and Printer Sharing
    Microsoft Mail workgroup postoffices 849
    printers
        *See also* File and Printer Sharing
        protected-mode client necessary 756
        using share-level security 466
shell command 1108
shell=, IO.SYS entry 203
Shells
    command shells 206

Shells *(continued)*
    Novell workstation shell *See* NetWare, workstation shell
    setting shell version for OVL files, Client for NetWare
      Networks  303
    Windows 95 user interface  990
SHIFT key
    accessibility shortcuts  1234
    accessibility status indicator  1242
    avoiding moving items to Recycle Bin  655
    bypassing Auto-Run when inserting CDs  1232
    closing folders, shortcut  1232
    copying configuration files to startup disk  1069
    displaying context menus  1234
    Safe Mode Command Prompt Only startup option  1064
    shortcuts for selected objects  1232
    StickyKeys feature  1244
Shiva servers, Dial-Up Networking connections  908–912
Shortcut keys *See* Hot keys; Keys; *specific key names*
Shortcuts
    accessibility  1234
    bypassing Auto-Run when inserting CDs  1232
    closing folders  1232
    copying custom files during Windows 95
      installation  1201
    creating  1232
    customizing desktop icons
      restricting access  512
      with system policies  504, 507
      with user profiles  482, 486
    cycling through pages in properties dialog box  1232
    desktop
      adding applications to Start or Programs
        menus  722, 749
      creating to network resources  381
      Hkey_Classes_Root Registry key  1023, 1028
      path for MS-DOS–based applications  733
      running applications  720
      troubleshooting applications  749–752
      Windows 95 vs. Apple Macintosh  1223
    displaying Control Panel Network option  254
    emergency hot keys, accessibility  1240–1241
    keyboard commands  1234
    managing folders and Windows Explorer  1233
    Microsoft Natural Keyboard keys  1235
    opening and closing windows  1232
    printing to network printers  762
    setting display options  619
    Setup unable to create, troubleshooting  751
    specifying working directories for Win16 applications  719
    switching between window and full-screen mode  1100
    The Microsoft Network  930
    to applications, location of key files  1154
    Windows Explorer command-line switches  1118
Show Dots feature  318

ShowSounds, accessibility feature  1246
Shut Down command, disabling  513
Simple Mail Transport Protocol (SMTP), Internet access
    overview  941
Simple Network Management Protocol *See* SNMP
Siren tones, rising and falling  1241
Sites, Systems Management Server terminology  1214
Skipping
    creation of default setup script in Server-based Setup  119
    detection of certain hardware during Setup  89, 186, 191
    ScanDisk check during Setup  78, 81
    Setup components that cannot be skipped or
      customized  145
SLIP *See* Serial Line Internet Protocol
SLIST, NetWare command  392, 402
SlowKeys, accessibility feature  1244
Small networks  266–267
SMARTDrive
    "Cannot open file *.INF" error message  239
    configuration information removed from Windows 95  564
    disk caching installed during Setup  179
    VCACHE driver working with VFAT file system  695, 980
smartdrv command  1105
SMC network adapters, .INF file settings  1211
SMS *See* Microsoft Systems Management Server
SNA Server  358, 359
SNAPSHOT.EXE  127
SNMP
    agent
      adding communities  549–550
      configuring  548
      device ID for use in setup scripts  1188
      installing  458, 548
      remote administration tools  547
      removing  551
    restricting access, system policy settings  516
    support  252, 283
    Windows 95 architecture overview  968
Sockets, Windows *See* Windows Sockets
Software
    *See also* Applications; Programs
    Arcada, contact information  541
    Cheyenne, contact information  542
    compression, Dial-Up Networking  897, 903–904, 921
    development
      accessibility guidelines  1249
      international versions, documentation  1041
      Win32 SDK information  1258
    installing
      *See also* INF files; MSBATCH.INF
      INF Installer  157
      with custom setup scripts  157–159
    Microsoft Software Library  926, 1260
    network drivers *See* Network adapters, drivers

Software *(continued)*
  new, updating startup disk  1069
  Novell-supplied  *See* Novell, software
  selecting components during Windows 95 Setup  91–93
  Software subtree in Hkey_Local_Machine  1027–1029
  system management tools  456
  Systems Management Server  *See* Microsoft Systems
    Management Server
  utilities included with Windows 95  xvii
Solution Providers  1257, 1259
sort command  1105
Sorting
  applications on Start or Programs menus  722
  numbers, specifying regional settings  1044
  messages in Microsoft Exchange  845
  The Microsoft Network bulletin board messages  932
  Windows 95 language support  1042, 1054–1055
Sound
  *See also* Audio; Digital audio; Multimedia
  accessibility features
    emergency hot keys  1240–1241
    ShowSounds  1246
    SoundSentry  1246
    ToggleKeys  1234, 1246
    WinChat  1247–1248
  assigning clips to events  703
  cards
    hardware required for running Windows 95  69
    purchasing multimedia computers  706–708
    safe detection  187
    troubleshooting  639, 709–712
    viewing properties  712
  Hkey_Current_User Registry key  1033
  Media Control Interface (MCI)  701
  MIDI support  703–704
  mixer controls  704
  playing CDs  703, 711
  recording  703, 704
  Volume Control tool  704
  Windows 95 multimedia architecture  700
sound.drv=, SYSTEM.INI entry  214
Sound Recorder  703, 704, 709
SoundSentry, accessibility feature  1246
Source
  INF file sections  1169
  Setup requests new source path, troubleshooting  239
Space, disks  *See* Disk space
Speaker volume
  configuring modem options  805, 812
  troubleshooting  823
Speed
  CD-ROM drives, purchasing multimedia
    computers  706–708
  choosing Internet access providers  945

Speed *(continued)*
  communications
    baud rate  602
    high-speed reliability  794
  configuring modems  801, 805, 812, 822, 827
  customizing mouse pointer display  1242
  high-speed floppy disk driver  693
  international standards for fax communications  869
  MS-DOS–based video operations  735
  optimizing hard disks  556
  optimizing Internet connections  951
Spooling
  defining spool settings for print performance  572
  disabling  781
  Enhanced Metafile Format (EMF)  767–769, 781
  new features in Windows 95  755
  overview  757
  printing support for MS-DOS–based applications  773
  spool directory for printing, information contained in
    machine directories  122
  troubleshooting printing  783
SQL Server, Systems Management Server overview  1214
Stacker disk compression software
  *See also* Disk compression
  caution  646
  real-mode disk driver without protected-mode
    replacement  565
  removing Windows 95  229, 232
  requirements for installing Windows 95  71
  troubleshooting  697
stacks command  1108
stacks=, IO.SYS entry  202
stackshigh command  1108
"Standard Mode: Fault in MS-DOS Extender"  239
STANDARD.POL, system profile example  506–507
start command
  retaining use of mouse in command-prompt
    windows  1101
  start /W  673, 1105
Start menu
  adding applications  722, 749
  external Windows 95 commands  1102
  missing or corrupted directory, troubleshooting  749
  running applications  720
  Shut Down command  513
  sorting applications  722
  Windows Explorer command-line switches  1118
Start Menu folder
  customizing
    restricting access  512
    with system policies  504, 507, 508, 535
    with user profiles  482
  troubleshooting
    missing or corrupted directory  749

Start Menu folder, troubleshooting *(continued)*
    wrong applications run at Windows 95 startup 244
Starting
    *See also* Running; *specific utility names*
    applications *See* Running applications
    earlier version of MS-DOS 205, 1064
    Help, shortcut 1235
    networks at system startup 258
    restarting Setup after failure 234
    Setup *See* Setup, running
    Windows 95 *See* Startup
    Windows Explorer, shortcut 1235
STARTNET.BAT, logging on to NetWare servers before
    starting Windows 95 306
Startup
    *See also* Startup menu
    automatic reconnection for lost server connections
        Client for Microsoft Networks 270, 370
        Client for NetWare Networks 305, 391
    bootstrapping in the BIOS phase 196
    configuration information needed 630
    creating boot log 216
    disk *See* Startup disk
    displaying Startup menu 1063
    errors *See* BOOTLOG.TXT
    files executed *See* System, startup files
    folder *See* Startup folder
    initializing static VxDs 197–199
    loading
        dynamic device drivers 198
        hardware profiles and real-mode drivers 197
        protected-mode operating system 199
    logging on to NetWare servers using
        AUTOEXEC.BAT 306
    power-on self-test (POST) 196
    process for shared installations 139
    processing CONFIG.SYS and
        AUTOEXEC.BAT 197, 206–213
    Quick Logon 271
    running applications and services, system policy
        settings 517
    Safe Mode system startup *See* Safe Mode system startup
    starting networks 258
    system startup files *See* System, startup files
    troubleshooting *See* Troubleshooting, startup
    verifying loading of HIMEM.SYS 235
    Windows 95 startup process 195–218, 1066
Startup disk
    backing up configuration files 1069
    creating 101, 102, 181–182, 1063
    EBD, MSBATCH.INF parameter 1178
    files copied
        computers starting from floppy disks 131
        computers starting from hard disks 129

Startup disk, files copied *(continued)*
        remote-boot workstations 132, 133
        required files 182
    formatting hard disks 651
    limitations 181
    reinstalling real-mode operating system files 1071
    remote-boot workstations
        files copied 132
        networking support for shared installations 128
    restoring Registry data 1025
    shared installations
        computers starting from floppy disks 131
        computers starting from hard disks 129
        file location 109
        networking support 128
        remote-boot workstations 132, 133
    troubleshooting strategies 1063
    updating
        after installing new devices or applications 1069
        after installing Windows 95 181
Startup folder, customizing 504, 507, 508, 512
STARTUP.GRP file 170–171
Startup menu
    displaying 1063, 1234
    options 1064–1070
    troubleshooting strategies 1063–1069
Static VxDs *See* VxDs
status, FTP command 1140
StickyKeys 1234, 1244, 1250
Status indicator, accessibility feature 1241–1242
Step-By-Step Confirmation startup 1061, 1064, 1068–1069
stop, MCI command 701
Storage space *See* Disk space
Strings, INF file keys 1171, 1200
submenu command 1108
Subnet masks
    configuring TCP/IP 434
    Internet access 947–950
    IPMask, MSBATCH.INF parameter 1195
subst command 1105
Sun NetManager, remote administration tools 547
SunSoft PC-NFS
    copying Windows 95 files to a server 114
    network protocol device IDs 1186
    network client device ID 1185
    networks supported by Windows 95 250, 334, 995
    servers, connecting to 347
    setting up for Windows 95 networking 347–349
    versions supported by Windows 95 94
SuperStor disk compression software 71
SVGA display, purchasing multimedia computers 706–708
Swap files
    *See also* Memory, paging
    changing size 1076

Swap files *(continued)*
    compressed drives  664
    configuring shared installations
        computers starting from floppy disks  130
        computers starting from hard disks  130
        remote-boot workstations  133
        requirements  112
    demand paging  556
    disk space
        required for running Windows 95  69
        troubleshooting  1076–1077
    optimizing  562–563
    overview  987
    planning configuration in Server-based Setup  112
    Windows 95 vs. Windows 3.x  987
Switches
    command-line commands *See specific command names*
    configuring legacy devices  613
    creating boot log during system startup  216
    REGEDIT.EXE, restoring Registry data  1025
switches command  1108
Switching
    between installed languages  1050, 1052–1053
    between programs  1223
    from Apple Macintosh to Windows 95  1223–1224
    to other keyboard layouts  1053
Symmetric Multiple Processor not supported by
  Windows 95  69
Synchronizing
    credentials to access NetWare servers  330
    files with Briefcase  73, 793, 918–920
    logon passwords  472
sys command  1071, 1105
SYSCON, NetWare command
    determining user ID  487
    editing login scripts  375
    peer servers using SAP advertising  402
    running with Client for NetWare Networks  305
    user-level security providers  405
System
    *See also* Operating systems
    attribute
        MS-DOS–based applications  730
        xcopy command-line switches  1120
    configuration
        *See also* Registry
        changing device resource settings  608–613
        Configuration Manager  970–973
        device classes  591–592, 605
        Device Manager  590
        device support in Windows 95  589–591
        display  619–626
        hardware profiles  617–618
        hardware tree  592, 972, 1033

System, configuration *(continued)*
        mouse  626–628
        overview  588–589
        Plug and Play overview  592–593
        Registry overview  1018–1019
    core components
        GDI  987–989
        Kernel  986–987
        overview  984
        swap file  987
        User  985
        user interface  990
        virtual memory management  986–987
    files *See herein* startup files
    initializing after Setup  183
    management
        information stored in Registry  457
        installing tools  457–458
        overview  456–457
        user profiles  456
    resources *See* Resources, system
    Safe Mode startup *See* Safe Mode system startup
    startup disk *See* Startup disk
    startup files
        AUTOEXEC.BAT  205, 209–213
        backing up before running Setup  78
        BOOTLOG.TXT  216–218, 1062, 1075
        checking entries  1074
        COMMAND.COM  1071–1072
        CONFIG.SYS  205–209
        IO.SYS  201–203, 1071–1072
        location of key files  1154–1155
        location on compressed disks  1156
        missing, troubleshooting  1071–1072
        MSDOS.SYS  203–205, 1071–1072
        overview  200
        Registry file missing  242
        reinstalling real-mode operating system files  1071
        replacing configuration entries using custom setup
          scripts  1204
        required drivers  1074
        Step-By-Step Confirmation startup
          option  1068–1069
        SYSTEM.INI  213–215
        WIN.INI  213, 215
    troubleshooting *See* Troubleshooting
    tuning performance *See* Tuning performance
System Agent
    description  670
    quitting  676
    running ScanDisk  661
    scheduling tasks  675–678
SYSTEM.DAT
    backing up  1024, 1069

SYSTEM.DAT *(continued)*
  description 1024
  hard disk location 1155
  information contained in machine directories 122
  initializing the system after Setup 183
  logon and network access settings 490
  REGEDIT.EXE command-line switches 1025
  Registry file missing, troubleshooting startup 242
  restricting access to computer-specific settings 514–517
  startup process for shared installations 139
  system policies 492
  troubleshooting strategies 1061
  vs. CONFIG.POL 479
SYSTEM.INI
  changes for Windows 95 214–215
  correcting display errors 571
  device= entry 214, 694, 983
  installing new devices 606
  loading static VxDs at startup 197–198, 968
  migrating settings during Setup 72, 220, 1036
  pagingfile= entry
    computers starting from floppy disks 130
    computers starting from hard disks 130
    remote-boot workstations 133
  preparing push installations 172
  processing at startup 213–215
  recovering from faulty installation of Windows 3.x
    drivers 603
  Registry
    settings 1036
    vs. initialization files 1034
  safe detection for sound cards 187
  troubleshooting
    startup failure due to other vendors' drivers 244
    VxDs loaded at system startup 1075
  Windows 95 version of display drivers 622
System Monitor
  built-in categories and settings 580–583
  configuring performance charts 576–577
  identifying performance problems 578–583
  performance-tuning tool 555
  remote administration tool 530
  remote computer requirements 532
  running from Network Neighborhood 539
  System subtree in Hkey_Local_Machine key 1030
  tracking performance data 576–577
  viewing remote computers 537
System option *See* Control Panel
System policies
  *See also* User profiles
  adding SNMP communities 550
  advantages 479
  CONFIG.POL
    automatic downloading 498, 525–526

System policies, CONFIG.POL *(continued)*
  description 490
  setting priority levels for groups 503
  troubleshooting 525–526
  creating 501–503
  customizing desktop 504, 507
  Default Computer 493, 501–503
  Default User
    default policy definitions 492–493
    editing 501–503
    logon process 492
  deploying Windows 95 45
  description 479
  Disable SAP Advertising policy 411
  disabling
    dial-up server support 901
    password caching 471
    Registry editing tools 1020
  downloading 498–501
  enforcing password security 475
  examples 506–508, 535, 1203
  files required 491
  group policies
    creating 502–503
    enabling in custom setup scripts 1203
    files required 491
    installing 494
    introduced 479
    logon process 492
    setting priority levels for groups 503
    troubleshooting 527
  implementing
    decisions 481
    necessary steps 482
    overview 498–501
  logon process 492
  migrating from Windows 3.x, example 167–169
  NetWare networks 492, 526
  overview 490–493
  password controls 460, 475
  Remote Update policy 499–501, 525
  restricting access *See* Restricting access
  restricting user actions 479, 506–517
  setting
    long filename policy for NetWare servers 291
    Registry option states 496–498
  settings 508–517
  system management overview 456
  System Policy Editor *See* System Policy Editor
  templates
    editing 519
    key words, syntax, and symbols 520–524
    overview 518–519
  troubleshooting 525–528

System policies *(continued)*
   update options 517
   vs. mandatory user profiles 480
   Windows NT networks
      logon process 492
      troubleshooting 525
System Policy Editor
   changing Registry settings 479, 1020
   configuring SNMP agent 548
   creating
      custom Network Neighborhood 382
      group policies 502
      setup scripts 120
   default policy definitions 492–493
   disabling
      dial-up server support 901
      password caching 471
   editing default system policies 501
   enabling load balancing on Windows NT networks 501
   installing 458, 482, 494–495
   managing remote registries 535
   manual downloading of policies 500
   overview 493
   Policy File mode 495–498
   Registry mode 495, 535
   remote administration tool 530
   remote computer requirements 532
   setting network logon options 374
   system policy
      entries in Registry 490
      settings 508–517
      templates 518–524
   troubleshooting system policies 525–528
   using 495–498
   vs. Registry Editor 531
System startup *See* Startup; Startup disk; Startup menu
Systems Management Server *See* Microsoft Systems
   Management Server


**T**

TAB key, moving focus in dialog boxes 1244
Tape drives
   backup agents included with Windows 95 540
   system management tools 456
TAPI
   description 794
   HyperTerminal 800
   Microsoft Exchange and remote mail access 853
   Microsoft Fax overview 796–797, 866–870, 880–882
Taskbar
   bringing running applications to the foreground 720
   cycling through buttons, shortcut 1235
   hidden, troubleshooting 749

Taskbar *(continued)*
   icons 1224
   switching
      between installed languages 1050
      between programs 1223
      to other keyboards 1053
Tasks
   ending 725, 743
   multitasking *See* Multitasking
   scheduling with System Agent 676
TCP/IP protocol
   advantages 419
   configuring 432–435
   DEC PATHWORKS networks 345
   description 416
   device IDs for use in setup scripts 1186
   Dial-Up Networking
      binding dial-up adapter 947
      connecting to Shiva servers 908–912
      network protocols required 891
   installed during Setup 96
   installing 946
   Internet access 940, 946
   mainframe connectivity 349, 358
   mapping host names to IP addresses *See* HOSTS file
   MSBATCH.INF parameters 1193–1195
   necessary for remote administration 531
   overview 431–432
   running Remote Registry service 535
   support for shared installations 139
   troubleshooting 449–451, 954
   using on NetWare networks 288
   utilities 432, 1136–1147
   Windows 95 network architecture 1005
   WINIPCFG utility 433, 449, 954
TCP/IP subnetworks, browsing resources 387, 438
TDI network adapters 417
Technet 1258
Technical support 1256–1257
TELEPHON.INI file 817
Telephone systems *See* Phone systems
Telephony application programming interface *See* TAPI
Telephony drivers, other vendors' 822
Telnet
   command-line switches 1146
   connecting to hosts 449
   Internet access 940, 942, 958
   password authentication, caution 1136
   running 958
   using TCP/IP for host connectivity 358
TEMP files
   AUTOEXEC.BAT entries 209
   checking TEMP variable 1077
   configuring shared installations

TEMP files, configuring shared installations *(continued)*
    computers starting from floppy disks  130
    computers starting from hard disks  130
    remote-boot workstations  133
  free space recommended on TEMP drive  1076
  planning configuration in Server-based Setup  112
  troubleshooting free disk space  1076–1077
Terminal
  communications program *See* HyperTerminal
  emulation
    applications for host connectivity  359–360
    Telnet utility  1146
    types supported by HyperTerminal  815
  window, displaying  809, 895
Testing disks with ScanDisk  659–661
Text files, transferring with FTP  957–958, 1137–1138
Text Telephone (TT/TDD) services, technical support  1257
The Microsoft Connection, CompuServe  1261
The Microsoft Network
  accounts  924, 926–927, 937
  benefits  924
  billing information  926, 937
  bulletin boards  931–933
  chat rooms  934
  content tree  928–930
  deploying Windows 95  49
  description  924
  Favorite Places  929, 930
  features  924–926
  getting help and information from Microsoft  924
  independent content providers (ICPs)  926–938
  installing  927
  keywords  930
  MAPI service provider  835
  Microsoft Exchange
    *See also* Microsoft Exchange
    using together  935–936
    Windows 95 communications overview  792
  MSN Central  929
  navigating  928–931
  obtaining
    hardware compatibility information  1258
    information about Windows 95  1256
    Windows 95 Reviewer's Guide  39
  passwords  926
  Properties option  930
  rules and etiquette  927
  security  927
  shortcuts  930
  troubleshooting  926
  Windows 95 communications overview  793
Thinnet cabling  266
Third parties *See* Other vendors
Thomas-Conrad network adapters, .INF file settings  1211

Threads
  description  974
  MS-DOS components, technical notes  560–561
  multithreading  974
  The Microsoft Network bulletin boards  932
Thunking
  Windows 95 Kernel  986
  WinNet16 thunk and translation  339
Time
  locale IDs, Win32-based applications  1051
  specifying regional settings  1044
  Windows 95 support for local conventions  1055
time command  1105
Time-outs, accessibility feature  1241
Time zone
  MSBATCH.INF parameter  1179
  setting  103
  System subtree in Hkey_Local_Machine key  1031
ToggleKeys, accessibility feature  1234, 1246
Token-ring networks
  device IDs for specifying network protocols in setup
    scripts  1186
  Dial-Up Networking connections to Shiva servers  908
  IPX/SPX technical notes  431
  network adapters
    configuring  425
    INF file settings  1207–1211
    NDIS drivers, overview  414
    requiring special consideration  423
Toolbars  482
Tools
  *See also specific utility names*
  checking and repairing disks *See* Defragmenting disks;
    Disk Defragmenter
  communications
    *See also* Direct Cable Connection; HyperTerminal;
     Phone Dialer
    other vendors' dial-up tools  886
    updating files  919
  default policy definitions  492
  diagnostics
    net diag command  262
    TCP/IP utilities  432
  disk management
    command-line switches  1123–1135
    Microsoft Plus!  670–671
    overview  653
    provided with Windows 95  645
    Registry APIs  1021
    troubleshooting  696
    volume locking  654
  DriveSpace, performance tuning  555
  hardware device management  600
  Internet access  942

Tools *(continued)*
   mobile computing 915
   Password List Editor 460, 471
   Registry-editing *See* Registry Editor; System Policy Editor
   remote administration
      *See also* Net Watcher; Network Monitor agent;
         Registry Editor; System Monitor; System Policy
         Editor; Systems Management Server
      from other vendors 547
   restricting access to 513
   system configuration 588–589
   system management 456–458
   Volume Control 704
trace, FTP command 1140
tracert, TCP/IP utility 449–451, 1146–1147
Tracking
   performance data with System Monitor 537, 576–583
   removable media drives 652
Transferring
   data
      binary files *See* Binary file transfer
      Dial-Up Networking software and hardware
         compression 903–904
      Direct Cable Connection 886, 916–917
      file transfer protocols supported by
         HyperTerminal 814, 829
      File Transfer Status utility 932–933
      FTP protocol 955–958
      HyperTerminal *See* HyperTerminal
      setting modem properties 804–808
      TAPI *See* TAPI
      troubleshooting communications 822–830
      Windows 95 communications overview 794
   files
      *See also* Binary file transfer; Microsoft File Transfer
      ftp command-line switches 1137–1138
      Microsoft File Transfer 800, 821
      troubleshooting 830
   information
      Clipboard international language support 1042
      command-prompt windows 1100–1102
Transport protocols *See* Network protocols; Protocols
Troubleshooting
   Advanced Power Management (APM) support 640
   applications
      cannot create shortcut 749
      checking file versions 1071
      correcting display driver problems 571
      desktop shortcut hot keys 749
      fixing version-checking errors 747–748
      hidden taskbar 749
      LNK extensions not displayed 749
      MS-DOS–based 750
      printing 749, 779–784

Troubleshooting, applications *(continued)*
      Programs menu 751
      screen elements truncated 750
      Setup unable to create shortcuts 751
      that replace system DLLs 748
      unassociated filename extensions 752
      wrong applications run at Windows 95 startup 244
   CD-ROM drives 637–640, 711
   checking virtual memory allocation 1076
   Client for NetWare Networks 329–330
   communications
      modems 810–813, 822–830, 961–962
      WINIPCFG utility 954
   connections
      DLC protocol 360
      File and Printer Sharing 408–411
      Internet connections 961–962
      IPX/SPX-compatible protocol 448
      login scripts 408
      NetWare networks 408–411
      shared resources 410
      TCP/IP protocol 449–451, 954
   device configuration
      checking for missing drivers 1073
      display problems 634–635
      hard disk device drivers 698
      Hardware Conflict troubleshooting aid 634
      PCMCIA cards 615–617
      protected-mode drivers 633
      resource conflicts 609, 1075
      SCSI devices 637–639
      troubleshooting strategies 1061
   Dial-Up Networking 920–922
   disks
      *See also* Defragmenting disks; Disk Defragmenter
      checking for disk corruption 1077
   display *See* Display, troubleshooting; Display adapters,
     troubleshooting
   downloading hypertext documents from Internet 962
   electronic mail 838
   File and Printer Sharing 261, 408–411
   file systems
      optimizing performance 569–570
      strategies 1077
   floppy disk drives 696
   fonts 785–788
   hardware detection 190–194, 237, 698
   Internet connections 961–962
   LANs or WANs with Network Monitor agent 544
   login scripts 408
   long filenames 697–698, 1077
   low-memory computers 557
   name resolution 1143–1145
   MCI drivers 710–712

Troubleshooting *(continued)*
   Microsoft Exchange, tip  838
   mounting CVFs  697
   multimedia problems  709–712
   name resolution  449–451
   network drive access  696
   network installation  259–262
   network protocols  447–451
   network resource browsing  385, 408–411
   NETX network client  331–332
   printing
      applications  749
      correcting problems  779–784
      network printers  1067–1068
   Setup
      automated installation failure  240
      B1 error message  238
      "Cannot open file *.INF" error message  239
      communication with devices impossible  238
      Copy File phase  238
      DETLOG.TXT, hardware detection  190–194
      errors reported during installation process  236
      "Incorrect MS-DOS version" error message  239
      insufficient disk space  240
      login scripts  408
      NETLOG.TXT  194–195
      network connection failure  237
      OS/2  240
      restarting Setup after failure  234
      running Setup from floppy disks  236–237
      server access impossible  237
      Safe Recovery option  1062
      Setup failure to start  234
      Setup requests new source path  239
      Setup stops during hardware detection  237
      Setup unable to find valid boot partition  239
      SETUPLOG.TXT  188–190, 1062
      "Standard Mode: Fault in MS-DOS Extender"  239
      unable to create shortcuts  751
      verifying installed components  1063
      virus checking software  238
   Stacker disk compression software  697
   startup
      *See also* Startup disk
      "Bad or missing file" error message  241
      checking file versions  1071
      checking for conflicts  1075
      damaged or missing core files  241
      device not recognized  244
      dual-booting, previous operating system doesn't
        work  243
      failure from installing other vendors' drivers  244
      hard disk device drivers  698
      incompatible BIOS setting  242

Troubleshooting, startup *(continued)*
      insufficient disk space  1076–1077
      "Invalid VxD dynamic link call from IFSMGR"  1072
      missing system files  1071–1072
      MSDOS.SYS file  1064
      "Previous MS-DOS files not found"  243
      real-mode drivers missing or damaged  244
      Startup menu options  1063–1069
      system Registry file missing  242
      VxD error returns to command prompt  243
      win command, switches  1069, 1075
      Windows 95 stalls during first restart after
        installation  241
      wrong applications run  244
   strategies  1059–1077
   system policies  525–528
   Systems Management Server tools  1218
   technical support  1256–1257
   The Microsoft Network connections  926
   TrueType fonts  785–788
   viewing remote computers with System Monitor  537
   VLM network client  331–332
TrueType fonts  755, 774–778, 785–788, 1050
TSRs
   disabling
      before running Setup  77, 179, 1204
      troubleshooting strategies  1073
   install command  1107
   IOS.INI file  631–633
   NetWare
      Client for NetWare Networks support  286, 294–295
      customizing detection during Setup  159
      network logon considerations  366, 377
   running under Windows 95, DOS interrupts  746
   troubleshooting
      strategies  1070
      Windows 95 conventional memory  234
   using TCP/IP for host connectivity  358
TTF files  775
TT/TDD services, technical support  1257
Tuning performance
   *See also* Optimizing performance
   built-in performance tuning tools  555
   computer hardware issues  556–557
   conventional memory  575
   demand paging  556
   display adapters  556
   file systems
      CDFS  569
      disk performance profiles  565–567
      overview  564–565
      troubleshooting options  569–570
   hard disks
      disk performance profiles  565–567

Tuning performance, hard disks *(continued)*
    speed 556
  improvements provided by Windows 95 554
  low-memory computers 557, 564
  miniport drivers 556
  networks 573–574
  optimizing swap files 562–563
  overview 558
  printers 557
  printing 572–573
  processor and bus speed 556
  setting graphics compatibility options 570–571
  system resource capacity 558–560, 714
  tracking performance data with System Monitor 576–583
  Windows 95 self-tuning features 554–555
Tunneling to preserve long filenames 569, 681
Twisted pair cabling 266
type command 1105, 1140
Typical Setup
  description 73
  ensuring user logon capabilities in setup scripts 153
  skipping detection of certain hardware 89
Typographic conventions used in this manual xvii

# U

UMBs *See* Upper memory blocks (UMBs)
UNC names
  path names, syntax 407, 719
Undo command, Windows Explorer shortcut 1233
Undo Minimize All, shortcut 1235
Undocking
  *See also* Docking; Portable computers
  hardware profiles 617–618
Unified logon prompt 460
Unimodem, universal modem driver 796
Uninstalling
  applications 720
  Windows 95 227–233, 1180
Universal driver
  description 969
  graphics subsystem 988
  modems 796
  printers 770
Universal Naming Convention *See* UNC names
UP ARROW key, Doskey use 1099
Updating
  startup disk
    after installing new devices or applications 1069
    after installing Windows 95 181
  VxDs bound into monolithic VMM32.VXD 197
Upgrading to Windows 95
  display adapter invalid 100
  files to back up before running Setup 78

Upgrading to Windows 95 *(continued)*
  from other operating systems 219–227
  retaining Program Manager 723–724
  installation requirements 67–71
  installed application settings 717
  installing printers 758
  migrating settings during Setup 1034–1037
  preparing STARTUP.GRP file 170
  push installation example 166–169
  removing Windows 95 231
  running Windows 95 Setup 72, 179
  Upgrade user account, running custom setup scripts 162
Upper memory blocks (UMBs)
  allocating memory to MS-DOS–based applications 734
  EMM386.EXE command-line switches 1112–1117
Use_SAP, MSBATCH.INF parameter 1197
user, FTP command 1140
User accounts
  enabling logon validation 260
  NetWare networks Mail directory 487
  security *See* Security; User-level security
  system management overview 456
  Upgrade, running custom setup scripts 162
USER.DAT
  backing up 1024, 1069
  description 1024
  desktop settings 490
  editing 483
  hard disk location 1155
  REGEDIT.EXE command-line switches 1025
  system policies 492
  troubleshooting strategies 1061
  user profile components 483
  vs. CONFIG.POL 479
user.exe=, SYSTEM.INI entry 214
User-Level Access Control 507, 514
User-level security
  deploying Windows 95 48
  description 460, 462–464
  Dial-Up Networking 900, 902–903
  enabling remote administration 533, 1202
  managing user lists 469
  necessary for remote administration 531
  NetWare networks 533
  pass-through security for peer resource sharing on
    NetWare networks 292
  rights and permissions 467–468
  setting up for shared resources 464–465
  specifying directory access rights 468
  using 467
  Windows NT networks 533
USER.MAN profile 166, 489
User name
  logging on to Windows 95 200

User name *(continued)*
　specifying in login scripts  375
User profiles
　*See also* System policies
　advantages  479, 1019
　client computer requirements  145
　Client for Microsoft Networks as Primary Network Logon
　　client  265
　creating  485
　defining Dial-Up Networking connections  895
　deploying Windows 95  46
　description  479
　disabling  486
　enabling  485–486, 507, 517, 1201–1203
　Hkey_Current_User Registry key  1032–1033
　implementing  480
　logon dialog box displayed  379
　machine directories  *See* Home directories; Machine
　　directories; Mail directory
　mandatory
　　advantages  479
　　customizing Windows 95  166
　　defining  489
　　system management overview  456
　　vs. system policies  480
　migrating from Windows 3.x, example  167–169
　NetWare servers  292
　overview  482–484
　roving profiles  487–488
　specifying regional settings  1043
　system management overview  456
　using on networks
　　defining mandatory user profiles  489
　　NetWare networks  487, 489
　　Windows NT  486, 489
User system component
　32-bit vs. 16-bit  984
　overview  985
　USER.EXE and USER32  200
Users
　controlling choices with WRKGRP.INI files  76
　disconnecting from dial-up servers  901
　ensuring user logon capabilities in setup scripts  153
　Hkey_Users Registry key  1023, 1032–1033
　name required for Windows 95 setup  68
　profiles  *See* User profiles
　restricting actions  *See* System policies; User profiles
　security  *See* Security; User-level security
Utilities
　*See also specific utility names*
　accessibility-enhancing  1252–1253
　default policy definitions  492
　disk management
　　command-line switches  1123–1135

Utilities, disk management *(continued)*
　　Microsoft Plus!  670–671
　　overview  653
　　provided with Windows 95  645
　　Registry APIs  1021
　　troubleshooting  696
　　volume locking  654
　display, running  625
　included with Windows 95  xvii
　installing with custom setup scripts  157–159
　long filename incompatibility  684, 685, 697–698
　Microsoft Plus!  661, 670
　Microsoft Software Library  1260
　MS-DOS–based, configuring computers for shared
　　installations  126
　NetWare, running with Client for NetWare Networks  305
　restricting access  513

**V**

ValidatedLogon= entry, setup scripts  153. 1198
ValidateNetCardResources, MSBATCH.INF parameter  1191
VCACHE
　description  695
　performance tuning  554
　VFAT file system  679, 980
VCOMM, communications driver  795–796
VCRs, Windows 95 support  703
Vector fonts  774, 777
ver command  1105
verbose, FTP command  1138
verify command  1105
Verify, MSBATCH.INF parameter  1180
Version
　checking, MSBATCH.INF parameter  1180
　checking system file versions  1071
　INF file section  1159
　fixing application version-checking errors  747–748
　setting shell version for OVL files, Client for NetWare
　　Networks  303
　setver command  1105
　ver command  1105
VESA Display Power Management Signaling (DPMS)  626
VFAT file system  566–567, 678, 695, 979–980
VGA display adapter, troubleshooting  635
Video
　*See also* Digital video; Multimedia
　cards  *See* Display adapters
　clips  *See* Digital video
　display  *See* Display
　display adapters  *See* Display adapters
　local-bus  706
　Media Control Interface (MCI)  701
　Windows 95 multimedia architecture  700

Videodisc players, MCI device types  701
Virtual device drivers  *See* VxDs
Virtual Machine Manager
    loading VxDs at startup  197–199
    memory paging  975–977
    MS-DOS Mode support  977
    overview  973–974
    process scheduling and multitasking  974–975
Virtual machines (VMs)
    description  973
    running Fdisk utility  647
    running MS-DOS–based applications  745
Virtual memory  *See* Memory, virtual; Swap files
Virus checking software
    incompatible BIOS setting, troubleshooting startup  242
    long filename incompatibility  684, 685, 697–698
    Systems Management Server software distribution and
        installation  1218
    troubleshooting
        non-removal of virus  698
        protected-mode drivers  633
        Setup  238
VL devices  596, 690
VLM  *See* NetWare networks, VLM network client
VMM32.VXD
    Configuration Manager overview  971
    hard disk location  1155
    initializing static VxDs  197–199
    MS-DOS components, technical notes  560–561
    overriding VxDs  243
    System Monitor categories and settings  581
    System subtree in Hkey_Local_Machine key  1031
    troubleshooting VxDs loaded at startup  1075
    verifying installed components with Setup  1063
vol command  1105
VOLINFO, NetWare command  402, 405
Volume Control tool  704
Volumes
    compressed  *See* Disk compression
    HPFS  *See* HPFS partitions
    identifying on removable media drives  652
    locking while running disk utilities  654
    NTFS  *See* NTFS partitions
    Windows 95 volume tracker  652
VRC, MSBATCH.INF parameter  1180
VREDIR.VXD
    *See also* Client for Microsoft Networks
    description  994
    installing  268
VTP cabling  266
VxDs
    block device drivers  690
    description  969
    device support in Windows 95  590

VxDs  *(continued)*
    I/O Supervisor requirements at startup  983
    initializing the system after Setup  183
    initializing, BOOTLOG.TXT  216
    "Invalid VxD dynamic link call from IFSMGR"  1072
    loading, BOOTLOG.TXT  216
    location of key files  1154
    mouse drivers  627
    NDIS mini-driver model  415, 1003
    overriding in VMM32.VXD  243
    overview  969
    protected-mode, loading at startup  199
    static, initializing at startup  197–199
    System subtree in Hkey_Local_Machine key  1031–1032
    SYSTEM.INI files  968
    technical notes  969
    troubleshooting
        BOOTLOG.TXT  1075
        VxD error returns to command prompt  243
    updating drivers bound into monolithic
        VMM32.VXD  197
    VCOMM, communications driver  628
    Virtual Machine Manager  197–199
    Windows 3.x drivers, caution  603
    Windows Sockets supporting files  1012
    WinNet16 interface  339

# W

WAIS  *See* Wide-Area Information Service (WAIS)
WallData RUMBA gateway, mainframe connectivity  358
Wallpaper, customizing  482, 492, 511, 526
WANs
    browsing network resources  366
    choosing network protocols  419
    connection protocols  890–891
    troubleshooting with Network Monitor agent  544
Warm docking  *See* Docking
Wave audio
    MCI device types  701
    troubleshooting  709–710
    WAV files  702, 709–710
Waveform audio
    *See also* Audio; Digital audio; Multimedia; Sound
    mixer controls  704
    Volume Control tool  704
Wide-Area Information Service (WAIS)
    Internet access overview  942
    navigating the Internet  960
win command  1069, 1075
WIN.COM, hard disk location  1155
WIN.INI
    changes for Windows 95  215
    fixing application version-checking errors  747–748

WIN.INI *(continued)*
    information contained in machine directories  122
    installing new devices  606
    loading final system components at startup  200
    loading fonts  777
    migrating settings during Setup  72, 220, 1034
    processing at startup  213, 215
    Registry settings  1034
Win16-based applications  *See* Applications, Win16-based
Win32 SDK information  1258
Win32 WinNet interface
    mulltiple provider router  997
    Windows 95 network architecture  996
    Windows 95 support  252, 335
Win32-based applications  *See* Applications, Win32-based
WIN386.SWP, performance tuning  562–563
WINBOOT.SYS  201
WinBootDir=, MSDOS.SYS entry  204
WinChat, accessibility feature  1247–1248
WinDir=, MSDOS.SYS entry  204, 242, 1072
Windows 3.x
    administrative setup  *See* Server-based Setup utility
    applications  *See* Applications, Win16-based
    configuration information
        migrating settings to Windows 95  1034–1037
        removed from Windows 95  564
    device drivers
        caution  603
        display adapter invalid when upgrading  100
    display drivers, installing  622–623, 636
    enabling Windows 3.1 file system  689
    installing Windows 95
        *See also* Setup
        caution about changing Windows directory  86
        copying minimal installation of DLLs used by
          Setup  81
        dual-booting  219, 221
        memory required for running Setup  69
        migrating .GRP and .INI information  86
        minimum version required  68
        preparing for push installations  172
        push installation example  167–169
        retaining Program Manager  723–724
        running Setup  72, 79, 179
        upgrading  219, 1021
    Windows 95 improvements  966
Windows 95
    accessibility  *See* Accessibility features
    architecture  *See* Architecture, Windows 95
    built-in commands  1102–1105
    conventional memory required  234
    corporate implementation  *See* Deploying Windows 95
    directory structure created by Setup  121, 1153
    distribution disks  1150

Windows 95 *(continued)*
    dual booting with other operating systems  *See* Dual-boot
        operating systems
    extracting installation files  1150–1152
    hardware compatibility information  1258
    improvements over Windows 3.x  966
    installing  *See* Setup
    local editions  *See* International Windows 95
    logging on  *See* Logging on; Startup
    mainframe connectivity  350–360
    MS-DOS components, technical notes  560–561
    networking  *See* Network architecture; Networking
    obtaining online information  1256
    optional components, MSBATCH.INF strings  1183
    Product ID number  88, 120, 1179
    quitting  513, 724
    Registry  *See* Registry
    removing
        description  227
        from a Windows NT computer  233
        from the command prompt  227–230
        using previous operating system  230–233
    Resource Kit  *See* Resource Kit
    running in a mixed Microsoft network
        environment  271–277
    security overview  460–464
    self-tuning features  554–555
    Setup  *See* Setup
    shared copies  *See* Shared installations
    starting  *See* Logging on; Startup
    startup disk  *See* Startup disk
    startup process  195–218
    technical support  1256–1257
    version, fixing version-checking errors  747–748
    Win32 Software Development Kit (SDK)
        information  1258
    WinNews subscription  1256
Windows 95 Setup  *See* Setup
Windows Driver Library, obtaining drivers  1261–1262
Windows Explorer
    accessing Printers folder  758
    checking for correct file versions  1071
    command-line switches  1118
    displaying graphical form of Format utility  645
    external Windows 95 commands  1102
    installing or changing printers after Setup  104
    LNK extensions not displayed  749
    restoring COMMAND.COM  1073
    running
        applications  720
        Registry Editor  1019
        Server-based Setup  115
    sending faxes  872
    sharing directories

Windows Explorer, sharing directories *(continued)*
    Microsoft networks  400
    NetWare networks  406
    with share-level security  466
  sharing Microsoft Mail workgroup postoffices  849
  sharing printers with share-level security  466
  shortcuts  1232–1233
  starting, shortcut  1235
  The Microsoft Network content tree  928, 930
  troubleshooting TCP/IP connections  449
  viewing
    file aliases  681
    property settings for MS-DOS–based
      applications  729
  Windows 95 user interface  990
Windows for Workgroups
  administrative setup  *See* Server-based Setup utility
  browsing network resources  384–387
  determining network adapter addresses for shared
    installations  140
  dial-up servers supported by Windows 95  889
  File and Printer Sharing  398–401, 411
  installing Windows 95  *See* Setup
  long filenames not supported  682
  Mail, converting MMF or PAB files to PST format  843
  NetBEUI protocol, description  416, 417, 419, 444–445
  networks supported by Windows 95  250
  running with Windows 95  276
  STARTUP.GRP file  170–171
Windows Internet Naming Service  *See* WINS
Windows NT
  browsing network resources  384–387, 394–395, 408–411
  domains
    configuring Client for Microsoft Networks  94, 269,
      270, 370
    File and Printer Sharing security  397–398
    logging on to Windows 95  368
    MSBATCH.INF parameters  1198
    network logon considerations  366
    specifying in login scripts  375
    system policy settings  515
  enabling load balancing  501
  File and Printer Sharing
    configuring the browse master  399–400
    overview  398
    security  397–398
    sharing directories  400
    user-level vs. share-level security  460, 462–464
  Gateway Service for NetWare  395
  home directories  375, 480
  installing Windows 95
    copying Windows 95 files to a server  114
    dual booting  219, 225
    minimum version required  68

Windows NT, installing Windows 95 *(continued)*
    NTFS partitions  71
    preparing servers for push installations  172, 174–175
    running Setup  72
  IPX/SPX protocol, description  415
  logging on, system policy settings  515
  login scripts  172, 374–375, 408
  logon validation
    *See also* Client for Microsoft Networks; Logging on,
      to networks
    configuring Client for Microsoft
      Networks  94, 269, 270, 370
    configuring in custom setup scripts  370
    description  368
    MSBATCH.INF parameters  1198
    setting options with system policies  374
  managing NetWare server connections  394–395
  miniport drivers
    block device drivers  690
    MPD extension required  983
    troubleshooting hard disk device drivers  698
    Windows 95 block I/O subsystem  690
    Windows 95 subsystem architecture  982
    Windows 95 support  692–693
  NetBEUI protocol, description  416, 417, 419, 444–445
  networks
    browsing resources with Network Neighborhood  *See*
      Network Neighborhood
    logging on to Windows 95  368
    long filenames  252, 683–684
    supported by Windows 95  250
  printers
    configuring Client for Microsoft Networks  94
    optimizing performance  572
    retrieving Point and Print information  760
  remote access servers
    configuring for Windows 95 dial-up clients  905–907
    connecting to  904–905
    connection limits  887
    supported by Windows 95  889
  removing Windows 95  233
  routing mail between postoffices, requirements  860
  running with Windows 95  271–274
  Server
    client access licenses  274–275
    installing RAS  906
    Microsoft Exchange Server  860
    overview  273–274
    remote access servers  904–905
    remote administration tools  547
  Services for Macintosh  1222
  setting up
    security for shared resources  464–465
    user profiles  486, 489

Windows NT *(continued)*
  system policies
    automatic downloading  498–499, 525
    logon process  492
    manual downloading  499–501
    troubleshooting  525
  using Microsoft Exchange with Microsoft Mail  852
  Windows 95 password cache  470–471
Windows Sockets
  Internet access provider caution  959
  IPC implementation  1010–1012
  IPX/SPX protocol, description  415, 418, 427
  Microsoft RPC facility  1012–1013
  name resolution *See* Name resolution
  network protocols required for Dial-Up Networking  891
  obtaining specifications  1012
  overview  1010–1012
  supporting files  1012
  TCP/IP protocol, description  416, 419, 432, 1005, 1011
WINFILE.INI  1034
WINIPCFG utility
  description  433, 449
  verifying TCP/IP configuration  954
WinNet16 interface
  16-bit network provider  998
  introduced  335
  multiple network example  1001
  overview  1001
  using 16-bit network drivers  338–339
WinNews subscription  1256
WinPopup
  broadcasting messages  445–447, 762
  configuring on client computers  446
  installing  446
  use of mailslots  1016
WINS
  clients, TCP/IP protocol  416, 432
  MSBATCH.INF parameters  1195
  name resolution  437–439, 1227–1230
  scope IDs  439, 449
  troubleshooting  449–451
  vs. DNS  440
Wizards
  *See also specific wizard names*
  configuring MIDI devices  104
  configuring peripheral devices during Setup  183
  hardware device management  600
  installing and configuring hardware using Setup  77
  setup process  66
  system configuration  588–589
WordPad
  accessing multilingual TrueType fonts  1051
  switching to another keyboard layout  1053
Workgroup Add-on for MS-DOS

Workgroup Add-on for MS-DOS *(continued)*
  determining network adapter addresses for shared installations  140
  long filenames not supported  682
  routing mail between postoffices, requirements  860
  running with Windows 95  277, 386, 444–445
Workgroup, MSBATCH.INF parameter  1189
Workgroups
  *See also* WRKGRP.INI files
  browsing shared resources
    browse list  386–387
    configuring for effective network browsing  366
    net view command  384, 385
    role in Windows 95  380
  checking connections to network resources  260
  checking, clearing, or filling Registry options with System Policy Editor  497–498
  mapping to logon domains  164–166
  Microsoft Fax overview  868–870
  Microsoft Mail workgroup postoffice *See* Microsoft Mail
  name required for Windows 95 setup  68, 98
  naming conventions  98
  restricting user choices  164–166
  role in Windows 95  380
  running Windows 95 in a mixed network environment  271–277
  setting name when installing networking support  257
  sharing fax modems  874–877
  system policy settings  515
  Workgroup, MSBATCH.INF parameter  1189
Working directories
  creating shortcuts  719
  specifying for MS-DOS–based applications  731
Workstations
  *See also* Client computers; Computers
  changing computer settings in Custom Setup  99–100
  checking connections to network resources  260
  client computers *See* Client computers
  device detection and configuration during Setup  66, 88–91, 180–181, 184–187
  diskless *See* Remote-boot workstations
  information required for Windows 95 setup  68
  installing Windows 95 *See* Installing, Windows 95; Setup
  LAN Manager, ensuring access to File and Printer Sharing  275, 400, 1198
  MSBATCH.INF parameters  1190
  number of network connections allowed  251
  remote-boot *See* Remote-boot workstations
  requirements for shared installations  112
  setting name when installing networking support  257
WorkstationSetup, MSBATCH.INF parameter  1190
World Wide Web (WWW)
  downloading hypertext documents from Internet, troubleshooting  962

World Wide Web (WWW) *(continued)*
    Internet access overview  942
    obtaining
        information about Systems Management Server  1213
        information about Windows 95  1256
        Windows 95 Reviewer's Guide  39
    useful publications  943
    using Mosaic  959
WRKGRP.INI files
    Control Panel-related options  164
    defining to control users' choices  76
    settings  164–165
    storage directory  145
    uses  164
    workgroup names  98

# X

xcopy command
    command-line switches  1118–1122
    description  1102
    installing Windows 95 from floppy disks using Systems
      Management Server  1219
Xmodem protocol  814, 829

# Y

Ymodem protocol  814, 829

# Z

Zmodem protocol  814, 829

*continued from page ii*

Eastman Kodak is the supplier of the default color matching method, known as Image Color Matching (ICM), in Windows 95. (For more information about Eastman Kodak products, see Appendix J, "Windows 95 Resource Directory.")

Jointly developed by Microsoft and Systems Compatibility Corporation (SCC), Quick Viewers for popular file formats are included in Windows 95. (SCC offers additional viewers and features in its Outside In for Windows product.)

U.S. Patent No. 4955066

# 3.5-INCH FLOPPY DISK ORDER FORM

The technical guide to planning for, installing, configuring, and supporting Windows 95 in your organization

The core set of utilities for the *Microsoft® Windows® 95 Resource Kit* CD are also available on a set of 3.5-inch floppy disks—for only **$4.95** (including shipping and handling—in the U.S. only).

To order, please fill out this form and enclose it in an envelope along with your check for $4.95 (U.S. funds only) and send to:

**Microsoft Press**
**Attn: Windows 95 Resource Kit Disks**
**P.O. Box 3011**
**Bothell, WA   98041-3011**

Name

Address

City                              State                ZIP

**Outside the U.S., credit card orders only.** Your credit card will be charged $4.50 (U.S. funds), plus shipping, for each set of disks ordered. To order, please phone 206-936-8661 or mail this form to:

**International Sales Information Center**
**Attn: Windows 95 Resource Kit Disks**
**One Microsoft Way**
**Redmond, WA   98052-6393**

Credit Card #                                         Expiration Date

Signature

Please allow 2-3 weeks for delivery.

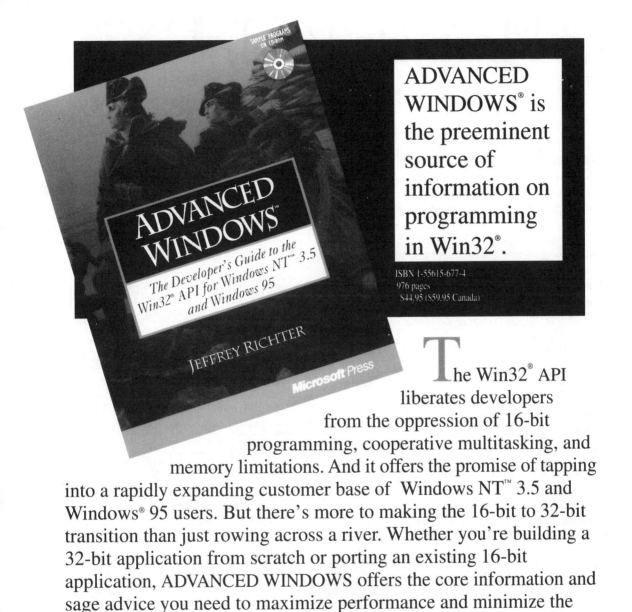

# Moving to Windows™ 95?

## *The Windows™ 95 Transition Report™ will take you there . . . and beyond!*

If your company is making the move to Windows 95—or considering it—let the *Windows 95 Transition Report* be your guide.

This monthly newsletter will help your company or department develop a solid transition plan by helping you answer such questions as:

- ▲ How much time and money will we need?
- ▲ What resources, hardware, and software are necessary?
- ▲ What do users and developers need to learn?
- ▲ What's the impact on mission-critical apps?
- ▲ What are the effects of 32-bit architecture?

**12 issues only $199**

Then, as you successfully progress with your migration, *Windows 95 Transition Report* helps you:

- ▲ Set up networks with Windows 95
- ▲ Work with mixed-platform networks
- ▲ Optimize Windows 95 telephony capabilities
- ▲ Use the Microsoft Network, and more

Whether you're an MIS manager, a network administrator, a consultant, or a Solution Provider, the *Windows 95 Transition Report* will guide you through a smooth transition—and beyond!

*100% guaranteed—see next page.*

## To order, call toll-free 800/788-1900

Mention order code "DNB" (or fill out the order form on next page)

---

### PINNACLE
Pinnacle Publishing, Inc.

18000 72nd Avenue South, Suite 217 ▲ Kent, WA 98032 ▲ 206/251-1900 ▲ Fax 206/251-5057
In Europe, contact Tomalin Associates ▲ +44 (0) 1371 811299 ▲ Fax +44 (0) 1371 811283

# MICROSOFT LICENSE AGREEMENT
### (Book Companion Disks/CD-ROM)